THE Pacific Islands

A publication produced by Asia Pacific Press and supported by funding from the Australian Agency for International Development (AusAID).

Editors

Editorial Advisory Board

THE Pacific Islands

an encyclopedia

Edited by

Brij V Lal and

Kate Fortune

University of Hawai'i Press
Honolulu

The views expressed in this publication are those of the authors and not necessarily those of the Government of Australia or the Australian Agency for International Development (AusAID).

Printed in China
05 04 03 02 01 00 5 4 3 2 1

Library of Congress Cataloging-in-Publication Data

The Pacific Islands: An Encyclopedia / edited by Brij V. Lal and Kate Fortune.

p. cm.

Includes bibliographical references (p.) and index.

ISBN 0-8248-2265-X

1. Oceania. I. Lal, Brij V. II. Fortune, Kate.

DU17.E53 1999

995-DC21 99-34571

CIP

Cover images

"Face paint": Huli (Highlands) woman at a *singsing* at Mount Hagen, Papua New Guinea, Carol Taylor (Canberra)

Typical atoll, Ha'apai Islands, Tonga, Peter Hendrie (Pacific Journeys Melbourne)

Vaiusu Catholic Church, Upolu, Peter Hendrie (Pacific Journeys Melbourne

Tivaevae: quilts of the Cook Islands (detail), Kate Fortune

Market produce, AusAID

Tuna fishing in New Caledonia, AusAID

The yellow hydrocoral *Distichopora* sp has stinging nematocysts in its tentacles which allow it to kill and eat plankton (detail). Neville Coleman (Australian Marine Photographic Index, Springwood, Queensland)

Ni-Vanuatu children on Tanna, against a woven wall, Peter Hendrie (Pacific Journeys Melbourne)

New Caledonia Easter Service, Julie Mackenzie, Ministry of Foreign Affairs and Trade, Wellington

University of Hawai'i Press books are printed on acid-free paper and meet the guidelines for permanence and durability of the Council on Library Resources.

Designed by Asia Pacific Press.
Printed by the Everbest Printing Company.

CONTENTS

Contents

ILLUSTRATIONS

Figures

Maps

Tables

PREFACE

The Pacific is an ocean of islands, fragments of time and space which lie haphazardly across its vast expanse. Of varying sizes and shapes, with complex histories of geological and natural evolution, unique mysteries of settlement over thousands of years, a diversity of cultures, and long and varied encounters with the outside world, the islands have been imagined and represented in narratives, songs, chants, rituals and ceremonies for as long as humans have lived there. This volume is the latest, and assuredly not the last, attempt to understand the remarkable world of the Pacific islands in all its variety and complexity through a range of perspectives contributed by scholars across the world. It brings together discrete or scattered information on the major aspects of Pacific island life, including the physical environment, peoples, history, politics, economy, society and culture.

Editing an encyclopedia of the Pacific islands has been a daunting task. First, there is the sheer geographical scope of the area, which may have discouraged similar attempts in the past. Second, the very notion of an encyclopedia—a comprehensive compendium of hard, factual information on a particular branch of knowledge—seems hopelessly old fashioned in the current intellectual climate. The selection of contributors and entries produced its own particular difficulties. Then there was the logistical nightmare of coordinating contributions from 200 scholars scattered around the globe over the half decade that this work has been in the making.

The difficulties, though considerable, did not deter us. We drew on the expertise of our Editorial Board consisting of distinguished representatives from all the major disciplines and located in several countries. It advised the Editors on the selection of entries and contributors. Its input was invaluable. We adopted flexibility and inclusiveness as our operational principles in commissioning contributions. Our focus was on the island Pacific in the three traditional culture regions of Melanesia, Polynesia and Micronesia. These terms are abstractions, and we treat them as such. There are important differences among the island groups but there are underlying commonalities of culture, social structure, and historical experience as well. And it is these commonalities that Pacific island peoples are increas-ingly exploring through institutional cooperation and creative expression.

We have been similarly flexible in our treatment of Maori and Aboriginal entries. Before the advent of formal colonialism, New Zealand was regarded as part of the insular Pacific, and it is considered here as such. Aboriginal links to the islands were more tenuous. In more recent times, cultural developments in these two (and other similarly situated) communities have found resonance in the islands. This is reflected in our selection of entries. How the Maori and the Aboriginal people use music, art and literature to establish ancient links or articulate their particular concerns is viewed with close interest, and sometimes emulated, in the islands. The connections are clear in the contexts in which they appear. But Australia and New Zealand are not profiled here separately.

We have attempted to be balanced in our coverage of the different island regions, but we acknowledge the constraints. Some areas and subjects are simply better known than others, and this unevenness is reflected in contemporary scholarship upon which our work draws. The expertise and experience of our contributors also shaped the nature and scope of our project. It would have been impossible to include a word here about every important topic in every island group in the Pacific. We see the entries here on prehistoric cultivation, for example, or on systems of social classification, or material culture, as examples and illustrations, indicators of trends and not as exhaustive, final statements. We have done our best to ensure the accuracy of the information, and we crave the readers' indulgence for the few errors that may have escaped our editorial eye. We have attempted to present the material in the accessible, intelligent language of ordinary discourse, but the variety of subjects covered from a wide range of perspectives has led to the retention of some technical vocabulary, especially in the earlier sections dealing with the physical and natural environment.

A conventional encyclopedia does not countenance opinions, just objective, verifiable, uncontroversial facts arranged alphabetically and authoritatively. Its underlying principle is consensus about, not contestation over, established truths. Ours obviously is not a conventional encyclopedia. It reflects the mood and temper of our times. We live in a time of bewildering change and abrupt discontinuities, continually readjusting our moral and intellectual compass to comprehend the meaning of the world around us. Unlike our predecessors, we accept the tentativeness and inescapable subjectivity of knowledge and the rapid displacement of dualities and dogmas by a quest in favour of shaded meanings. We acknowledge the complex dialectics between the past and the present, and the politics of representing other people and cultures. Our project reflects these new intellectual developments, especially in the longer essays. We celebrate diversity. There will be debate about emphases and interpretations and differences of opinion, sometimes about similar topics, but this is a strength, not a weakness. We are comfortable with the knowledge that scholarship is partial, fluid and changing.

A word about the issue of visual representation is necessary. Wherever possible, we have sought to illustrate the text with appropriate photographs. Images have the capacity to enrich a reader's appreciation of the subject or open a window to the past that, truly, is worth a thousand words. Nonetheless, the visual representation of the West's others is problematic. Like other indigenous peoples, Pacific islanders have been subject to invasive missionary and anthropological scrutiny which has included taking photographic and filmic evidence of their differences from Western observers. This is particularly so with the clothing and decorating of the body, especially the female body. We have taken great care to select images which do not dehumanize or exoticize Pacific island peoples. Still, it is important for readers to remember that images, like other cultural products, do not reflect 'reality' but rather construct it from historical, cultural and political perspectives. Images may provide as much information about the photographer as the photographed.

Spelling and pronunciation

The text attempts to conform to the spelling and use of diacritical marks adopted by various island countries, with the exception of French place-names which have been anglicized. The macron (line above a letter) indicates a lengthening of the vowel sound. The 'okina' mark (reverse apostrophe) indicates a glottal stop between syllables. In Fijian words, 'b' is pronounced 'mb', 'd' is pronounced 'nd', 'g' is pronounced 'ng', 'q' is pronunced 'ngg', and 'c' is pronounced 'th'. In the Samoan language, 'g' is pronounced 'ng', and 't' may be pronounced 'k'. In Kiribati, 'ti' is pronounced 's'.

Measurement

Weights and measures in the text mostly use the metric system.

Length: 1 inch = 25.4 mm; 1 foot = 30.4 cm; 1 yard = 0.91 m; 1 mile = 1.61 km.

Area: 1 acre = 0.405 hectares; 1 sq km = 100 hectares; 1 sq mile = 2.59 sq km.

Mass: 1 ounce = 28.35 grams; 1 pound = 0.454 kg; 1 ton = 1.02 tonnes.

How to use this volume

Unlike most encyclopedias, *The Pacific Islands: An Encyclopedia* is organized according to broad subject areas. In organizing it this way, we hoped to avoid the fragmentation that arises from the alphabetical arrangement of articles and to provide readers with more richly contextualized information. We have provided the following tools to assist them in finding their way around this volume.

■ ***Expanded table of contents.*** The table of contents includes the title of all entries in the encyclopedia. It should give readers an excellent and detailed overview of the encyclopedia.

■ ***Cross-references and related sections.*** Within each article are the titles of other relevant sections in SMALL CAPS. Readers can locate sections either through the table of contents or the section index.

■ ***Index.*** The encyclopedia has a comprehensive and extensive subject index. We have made a particular effort to index all Pacific persons and Pacific organizations, no matter how fleeting the reference to them in the text might be.

■ ***Other research tools.*** In addition to entries and cross-reference aids, the encyclopedia contains a ***glossary*** and ***list of abbreviations*** at the front of the volume.

CD-ROM

The Pacific Islands: An Encyclopedia includes a CD-ROM version to enable readers to exploit the search and navigation potentials of this medium. Please note that the electronic version is intended to complement rather than be a substitute for printed text. It includes an electronic ***help guide***.

The electronic version comprises portable document format (PDF) files which are fully ***text searchable*** and have ***hyperlinks*** connecting contents and indexes to the text. In addition, the CD-ROM contains a ***map library*** in Adobe Illustrator format. We encourage readers to modify the maps for their own purposes, and request that the Cartography Unit, Research School of Pacific and Asian Studies, The Australian National University, be acknowledged as the author. Finally, some of the images reproduced in the encyclopedia are not subject to copyright restriction. These we have included in a Pacific ***photo library*** so that readers may use them for their own purposes. They have been scanned at a low resolution (72 dpi) and are suitable for use in electronic publications. Those interested in high resolution reproduction may contact Asia Pacific Press.

ACKNOWLEDGMENTS

This project has taken nearly a decade, and we are grateful to the institutions and individuals who have supported us over that period. The Division of Pacific and Asian History in the Research School of Pacific and Asian Studies at The Australian National University served as its home. One of its former convenors, Professor Mark Elvin, provided the initial blessing, which his successors continued to bestow on us. Dorothy Macintosh, Jude Shanahan and Julie Gordon helped us with cheerful advice and administrative support. AusAID, Australia's principal international aid agency, gave us generous financial assistance which enabled us to complete the project in a timely fashion. We were honored that the Australian Department of Foreign Affairs and Trade chose the encyclopedia as Australia's gift to the South Pacific Commission, now named the Pacific Community, to mark its 50th anniversary. We express our grateful thanks to Foreign Minister Alexander Downer for his personal support and interest.

We also acknowledge the support and warm encouragement of friends and colleagues worldwide who urged us on when we were plagued with doubt or faced seemingly insurmountable difficulties. Max Quanchi of the Queensland University of Technology was involved with the project in its early stages, and we continued to benefit from his infectious enthusiasm and helpful advice. Members of the Editorial Board, chaired by Professor Donald Denoon, reviewed submissions, suggested names of contributors and topics of contributions, and generally oversaw the project. We are grateful, in particular, to those based in the Coombs Building at The Australian National University: they did not mind—at any rate, did not give the impression of minding—what time of day we knocked on their door for a chat about "that encyclopedia thing again." But our greatest debt is, of course, to our contributors, most of whom we know but some of whom we have not yet met, who put aside their own work to prepare entries for us. As months and then years passed, they understandably began to wonder whether the project would ever be completed. We hope that they will be pleased with the final product. We thank you for your patience.

Tikka Wilson and Tracey Hansen of Asia Pacific Press at the National Centre for Development Studies, The Australian National University saw the manuscript through the final stages of production with exemplary care and professionalism. Their advice on technical matters has greatly improved the accessibility of the text. Sue Whigham produced an exquisite and sensitive design. Maree Tait, of Asia Pacific Press, provided moral support when we needed it most. Pamela Kelley, our editor at the University of Hawai'i Press, was equally enthusiastic, and we are indebted to her for her advice. To all our friends across the world who shared our dream and helped us realize it, to our families who put up with our obsessive work habits and tolerated the disruptions which they caused on the domestic front, *Kia Ora, Vinaka Vakalevu, Dhanyabad*.

Our own exhilarating and enriching journey of exploration and discovery has now sadly come to an end. We have enjoyed every moment of it. We now offer the fruit of our endeavour to our readers, wherever they are, in the hope that this volume will launch their own private journeys of exploration and reflection on the rich and beautiful world of the Pacific islands with all its triumphs and tragedies, accomplishments and setbacks, as it stands on the threshold of the new millennium.

Brij V. Lal
Kate Fortune

CONTRIBUTORS

DAVID **AKIN** (DA)
Independent Scholar, formerly University of California, San Diego

BRYANT J **ALLEN** (BJA)
Senior Fellow, Department of Human Geography, Research School of Pacific and Asian Studies, The Australian National University, Canberra

RODERIC **ALLEY** (RA)
Senior Fellow, Department of Politics, Victoria University of Wellington, Wellington

MICHAEL **ALPERS** (MA)
Director, Institute of Medical Research, Goroka, Papua New Guinea

ATHOLL **ANDERSON** (AA)
Professor, Department of Archaeology and Natural History, The Australian National University, Canberra

FRÉDÉRIC **ANGLEVIEL** (FA)
Department of History, L'Université Française du Pacifique, Noumea

CHARLES W **ARNADE** (CWA)
Professor of International Studies and History, University of South Florida, Florida

DIRK ANTHONY **BALLENDORF** (DAB)
Professor of History & Micronesian Studies, Micronesian Area Research Center, University of Guam, Guam

JOHN **BARKER** (JB)
Associate Professor, Anthropology and Sociology, University of British Columbia, Vancouver

RICHARD **BEDFORD** (RDB)
Professor of Geography, University of Waikato, Hamilton

JOSHUA A **BELL** (JAB)
Department of Ethnology & Museum Ethnography, Hertford College, Oxford

PETER **BELLWOOD** (PB)
Archaeology and Anthropology, The Australian National University, Canberra

GEOFF **BERTRAM** (GB)
Economics Department, Victoria University of Wellington, Wellington

NIKO **BESNIER** (NB)
Professor, Department of Anthropology, Victoria University of Wellington, Wellington

TERRY G **BIRTLES** (TGB)
Associate Professor in Applied Geography, University of Canberra, Canberra

FILIPE N **BOLE** (FNB)
Educator and former Senator, Government of the Republic of the Fiji Islands, Suva

LISSANT **BOLTON** (LB)
Fellow, Centre for Cross-Cultural Research, The Australian National University, Canberra

HEATHER **BOOTH** (HB)
Demography Program, Research School of Social Sciences, The Australian National University, Canberra

R MICHAEL **BOURKE** (RMB)
Department of Human Geography, Research School of Pacific and Asian Studies, The Australian National University, Canberra

DAVID L **CALLIES** (DLC)
Benjamin A Kudo Professor of Law, William S Richardson School of Law, University of Hawai'i, Honolulu

KEITH LUJAN **CAMACHO** (KLC)
University of Hawai'i–Mānoa, Honolulu

IAN C **CAMPBELL** (ICC)
Department of History, University of Canterbury, Christchurch
RAJESH **CHANDRA** (RC)
Professor and Deputy Vice-Chancellor, University of the South Pacific, Suva
LINLEY **CHAPMAN** (LC)
Manuscript Editor, Center for Pacific Islands Studies, University of Hawai'i–Mānoa, Honolulu
DAVID A **CHAPPELL** (DAC)
Associate Professor, Department of History, University of Hawai'i, Honolulu
WILLIAM C **CLARKE** (WCC)
Institute of Pacific Studies, University of the South Pacific, Suva
SUSAN **COCHRANE** (SC)
Responsable, Département des Arts Contemporains Kanak et Océanien, Noumea
MARIA SYLVIA **CODECASA** (MSC)
Independent scholar, Italy and Australia
NEVILLE **COLEMAN** (NC)
Curator, Australasian Marine Photographic Index, Springwood, Queensland
CHRIS **CORNE** (CC)
Department of Linguistics, University of Auckland, Auckland
ALISTAIR **COUPER** (ADC)
Professor, Seafarers International Research Centre, Department of Maritime Studies and International Transport, University of Wales, Cardiff
MARJORIE TUAINEKORE **CROCOMBE** (MTC)
Former Director of Extension Services, University of the South Pacific, Suva; former Director of the Centre for Pacific Studies, University of Auckland, Auckland
RON **CROCOMBE** (RGC)
Professor Emeritus, University of the South Pacific, Suva
PAUL **D'ARCY** (PD'A)
Lecturer in History, Victoria University of Wellington, Wellington
PETER **DAUVERGNE** (PD)
Formerly Department of International Relations, Research School of Pacific and Asian Studies, The Australian National University, Canberra
GREG **DENING** (GD1)
Emeritus Professor of History, University of Melbourne, Melbourne
DONALD **DENOON** (DD)
Professor of History, Division of Pacific and Asian History, The Australian National University, Canberra
MARION **DIAMOND** (MD)
Reader in History, Department of History, University of Queensland, Brisbane
SINCLAIR **DINNEN** (SD)
Fellow, State, Society & Governance in Melanesia Project, The Australian National University, Canberra
BRONWEN **DOUGLAS** (BD)
Fellow, State, Society & Governance in Melanesia Project, The Australian National University, Canberra
NGAIRE **DOUGLAS** (ND1)
Lecturer, Centre for Tourism, Southern Cross University, Lismore, New South Wales
NORMAN **DOUGLAS** (ND2)
Researcher & Publisher, Alstonville, New South Wales
GARY **DOWSE** (GD2)
Medical Epidemiologist, Communicable Disease Control Branch, Health Department of Western Australia, Perth
JOHN **DUNMORE** (JD)
Emeritus Professor of History, Massey University, Palmerston North

Contributors

TOM **DUTTON** (TD)
Retired Senior Fellow in Linguistics, The Australian National University, Canberra

LEIATAUA KILIFOTI **ETEUATI** (KE)
High Commissioner for Samoa in Australia, Canberra

BEN **FINNEY** (BF)
Professor of Anthropology, University of Hawai'i–Mānoa, Honolulu

STEWART **FIRTH** (SF)
Professor of Politics, University of the South Pacific, Suva

KATE **FORTUNE** (KRF)
Editor and Research Associate, Division of Pacific and Asian History, Research School of Pacific and Asian Studies, The Australian National University, Canberra

SHARLENE **FUROTO** (SBCLF)
Social Work Department, Brigham Young University Hawai'i–Laie, Hawai'i

BILL **GAMMAGE** (BG)
Professor, Humanities Research Centre,
The Australian National University, Canberra

JOHN **GARRETT** (JG1)
Retired Lecturer at Pacific Theological College, Suva,
and former Communications Director of the World Council of Churches

PAUL **GERAGHTY** (PG)
Director, Institute of Fijian Language and Culture, Suva

MICHAEL **GODDARD** (MG)
Department of Sociology and Anthropology,
University of Newcastle—Central Coast Campus, New South Wales

NICHOLAS J **GOETZFRIDT** (NJG)
Associate Professor and Librarian, RFK Library, Learning Resources,
University of Guam, Guam

DAVID **GOLDSWORTHY** (DG1)
University of New England, Armidale, New South Wales

JACK **GOLSON** (JG2)
Emeritus Professor, Department of Archaeology and Natural History,
The Australian National University, Canberra

CHRIS A **GREGORY** (CAG)
Reader in Anthropology, Faculty of Arts,
The Australian National University, Canberra

NIEL **GUNSON** (WNG)
Retired Senior Fellow, Division of Pacific and Asian History,
The Australian National University, Canberra

DESH **GUPTA** (DG2)
Department of Economics, University of Canberra, Canberra

EMMA **GYURIS** (EG)
Postgraduate Coordinator, Tropical Environment Studies and Geography,
James Cook University, Townsville

JOHN R **HAGLELGAM** (JRH)
Regents Professor, College of Micronesia–FSM, Palikir;
and former President of Federated States of Micronesia, Pohnpei

RICHARD **HAMASAKI** (RH)
University of Hawai'i–Mānoa, Honolulu

DAVID **HANLON** (DH)
Professor, Department of History, University of Hawai'i–Mānoa, Honolulu

CHRISTY **HARRINGTON** (CH)
Department of Anthropology, University of Otago, Dunedin

GRAHAM **HASSALL** (GH1)
Research Fellow, Asia-Pacific Program, Centre for Comparative Constitutional Studies, University of Melbourne, Melbourne

PHILIP **HAYWARD** (PH)
Editor, *Pacific Beat,* and Head, Department of Media & Communication Studies, Macquarie University, Sydney

'I FUTA **HELU** ('IFH)
Professor, 'Atenisi University, Tonga

PETER **HEMPENSTALL** (PJH)
Professor and Head, Department of History, University of Canterbury, Christchurch

PHYLLIS S **HERDA** (PSH)
Senior Lecturer in Women's Studies, University of Auckland, Auckland

VILSONI **HERENIKO** (VH)
Associate Professor, Center for Pacific Islands Studies, University of Hawai'i–Mānoa, Honolulu

RICHARD A **HERR** (RAH1)
Reader in Politics, School of Government, University of Tasmania, Hobart

COLIN E **HINDSON** (CEH)
Associate Professor (Adjunct), Griffith University, Queensland

GEOFFREY **HOPE** (GH2)
Professor, Department of Archaeology and Natural History, Research School of Pacific and Asian Studies, The Australian National University, Canberra

ANTONY A **HOOPER** (AAH)
Emeritus Professor of Social Anthropology, University of Auckland, Auckland

ROBERT A **HOOPER** (RAH2)
Executive Producer, Television Programming and Production, KPBS-TV, San Diego

BRUCE **HORSFIELD** (BH)
Associate Professor of Mass Communication, University of Southern Queensland, Toowoomba, Queensland

ALAN **HOWARD** (AH)
Professor, Department of Anthropology, University of Hawai'i–Mānoa, Honolulu

KERRY **HOWE** (KRH)
Professor of History, Massey University, Auckland Campus, Albany

KERRY **JAMES** (KEJ)
Honorary Associate, Macquarie University and University of New South Wales, Sydney

FELIX Y ATTAH **JOHNSON** (FYAJ)
Associate Professor of Psychiatry, University of Papua New Guinea, Port Moresby

GIFF **JOHNSON** (GJ)
Editor, *Marshall Islands Journal*; correspondent, *Pacific Magazine, Pacific Islands Monthly*, Majuro Atoll

IAN **JOHNSTON** (IJ)
Director, South Pacific Bureau for Educational Assessment, Suva

MARGARET **JOLLY** (MJ)
Convenor—Gender Relations Project, The Australian National University, Canberra

CHRISTINE **JOURDAN** (CJ)
Associate Professor, Department of Sociology and Anthropology, Concordia University, Montreal

ADRIENNE L **KAEPPLER** (ALK)
Curator of Oceanic Ethnology, Smithsonian Institution, Washington DC

TIMOTI **KARETU** (TK)
Professor; former Director, Maori Language Commission, Wellington

SUE **KEAYS** (SK)
Formerly University of Queensland, Brisbane

PETER **KIELY** (PK)
Partner, Kiely Thompson Caisley; and
New Zealand Director–Pacific Forum Line, Auckland

CHRIS **KISSLING** (CK)
Professor of Transport Studies, Division of Environmental Management and Design, Lincoln University, Canterbury

ROBERT C **KISTE** (RCK)
Director, Center for Pacific Islands Studies, University of Hawai'i–Mānoa, Honolulu

RODERIC **LACEY** (RL1)
Associate Professor, University Fellow, Australian Catholic University, Ballarat

BRIJ V **LAL** (BVL)
Professor and Director, Centre for the Contemporary Pacific,
The Australian National University, Canberra

PADMA **LAL** (PL)
Program Coordinator in Agricultural & Resource Economics,
Australian Centre for International Agricultural Research, Canberra

KURT **LAMBECK** (KL)
Research School of Earth Sciences, The Australian National University, Canberra

ROBERT **LANGDON** (RL2)
Visitor, Division of Pacific and Asian History,
The Australian National University, Canberra

HUGH **LARACY** (HL)
Associate Professor of History, University of Auckland, Auckland

HELEN REEVES **LAWRENCE** (HRL)
Former Convenor, Graduate Program (Music), School of Music,
The Australian National University; now Faculty of Creative Arts, University of Papua New Guinea, Port Moresby

STEPHANIE **LAWSON** (SL1)
Professor of International Relations, University of East Anglia, Norwich

SUZANNA **LAYTON** (SL2)
Lecturer in Print Journalism, School of Film, Media and Culture Studies,
Griffith University, Nathan, Queensland

JACQUELINE **LECKIE** (JL1)
Senior Lecturer in Social Anthropology, Department of Anthropology,
University of Otago, Dunedin

ANTONY D **LEWIS** (ADL)
Oceanic Fisheries Coordinator, Secretariat of the Pacific Community, Noumea

JOHN **LIDSTONE** (JL2)
Professional Studies, Queensland University of Technology, Queensland

JEANETTE **LITTLE** (JL3)
Librarian, Pacific Theological College, Suva

LAMONT **LINDSTROM** (LL)
Professor and Head, Department of Anthropology, University of Tulsa

VICTORIA **LUKERE** (VL)
Former Lecturer, Department of History, Victoria University of Wellington, Wellington

BARRIE **MACDONALD** (BM)
Professor of History, Pro-Vice Chancellor, Massey University, Palmerston North

CLUNY **MACPHERSON** (CM1)
Senior Lecturer, Department of Sociology, University of Auckland, Auckland

GRANT **McCALL** (GMcC)
Associate Professor, School of Sociology,
University of New South Wales, Kensington

PHILIP **McDERMOTT** (PMcD)
Professor of Resource and Environmental Planning, Massey University, Palmerston North

ROGER F **McLEAN** (RFMcL)
Professor and Head of School of Geography and Oceanography, University College, Australian Defence Force Academy, Canberra

SAMUEL F **McPHETRES** (SMcP)
Teacher of history, Northern Marianas College, Saipan

JULIAN **MAKA'A** (JM)
Solomon Islands Broadcasting Corporation, Honiara

EWAN **MAIDMENT** (EM)
Executive Officer, Pacific Manuscripts Bureau, The Australian National University, Canberra

HELENE **MARSH** (HM)
Professor and Head, School of Tropical Environment Studies and Geography, James Cook University, Townsville

MAC **MARSHALL** (MM)
Professor, Department of Anthropology, University of Iowa, Iowa

HONOR C **MAUDE** (HCM)
Independent Scholar, Canberra

RON **MAY** (RJM)
Senior Fellow, Research School of Pacific and Asian Studies, The Australian National University, Canberra

LARRY W **MAYO** (LWM)
Associate Professor & Director, Anthropology Program, DePaul University, Chicago

MICHAEL A **MEL** (MAM)
Head of Department of Expressive Arts and Religious Education, University of Papua New Guinea, Goroka

ISABELLE **MERLE** (IM)
Chargée de recherche, Conseil National de la Recherche Scientifique, Marseille

CLIVE **MOORE** (CM2)
Associate Professor of History, University of Queensland, Brisbane

JANE FREEMAN **MOULIN** (JFM)
Associate Professor of Ethnomusicology, Music Department, College of Arts and Humanities, University of Hawai'i–Mānoa, Honolulu

RICHARD **MOYLE** (RM)
Senior Lecturer in Ethnomusicology and Director, Archive of Maori and Pacific Music, University of Auckland, Auckland

STEVE **MULLINS** (SM)
Senior Lecturer in Humanities, Central Queensland University, Rockhampton

DOUG **MUNRO** (DM)
Reader in History, School of Social and Economic Development, University of the South Pacific, Suva

HIROSHI **NAKAJIMA** (HN1)
Professor; Executive Director, The Pacific Society, Tokyo

SIRUS **NARAQI** (SN)
Professor, Faculty of Medicine, University of Papua New Guinea, Port Moresby

HANK **NELSON** (HN2)
Professor of History, Research School of Pacific and Asian Studies, The Australian National University, Canberra

KARL **NEUENFELDT** (KN)
Lecturer, Communication and Media Studies, Central Queensland University, Rockhampton

ROBERT **NICOLE** (RN)
Department of History/Politics, University of the South Pacific, Suva
YOSHIHARU **NISHIOKA** (YN)
Senior Researcher, The Pacific Society, Tokyo
PATRICK D **NUNN** (PDN)
Professor and Head, Department of Geography,
University of the South Pacific, Suva
EUGENE **OGAN** (EO)
Professor Emeritus of Anthropology, University of Minnesota, Minneapolis
MICHAEL R **OGDEN** (MRO)
Department of Communication, University of Hawai'i–Mānoa, Honolulu
JONATHAN KAMAKAWIWO'OLE **OSORIO** (JKO)
Assistant Professor, Center for Hawaiian Studies,
University of Hawai'i–Mānoa, Honolulu
MIDORI **OSUMI** (MO)
College of Culture and Communication,
Tokyo Women's Christian University, Tokyo
JOHN **OVERTON** (JO)
Professor of Development Studies, Institute of Development Studies,
Massey University, Palmerston North
THOMAS C **PANHOLZER** (TCP)
Department of Languages and Literature, College of Micronesia–FSM, Pohnpei
ALISON **PASCIUTO** (AP)
Department of Anthropology, Washington State University, Pullman
MEGAN **PASSEY** (MP1)
University of Papua New Guinea, Port Moresby
MARK R **PEATTIE** (MRP)
Senior Research Fellow, Hoover Institution on War, Revolution and Peace,
Stanford University, California
MALCOLM **PHILPOTT** (MP2)
Department of Mass Communication, Faculty of Arts,
University of Southern Queensland, Toowoomba, Queensland
JOHN A **PIPER** (JAP)
Former career diplomat with Australian Department of Foreign Affairs and Trade,
Visiting Fellow, The Australian National University, Canberra
PETER **PIRIE** (PP)
Former Head of Population Program, Secretariat of the Pacific Community
NANCY J **POLLOCK** (NJP)
Department of Anthropology, Victoria University of Wellington, Wellington
GUY **POWLES** (CGP)
Associate Professor, Law Faculty, Monash University, Melbourne
COLLEEN **PRITCHARD** (CP)
National Archives of Australia, Canberra
MAX **QUANCHI** (MQ)
Senior Lecturer, School of Humanities,
Queensland University of Technology, Brisbane
FRED **RADEWAGEN** (FR)
Director, Pacific Islands Washington Office & Publisher,
The Washington Pacific Report
CAROLINE **RALSTON** (CR)
Retired Associate Professor of History, Macquarie University, Sydney
ASESELA **RAVUVU** (AR1)
Professor and Director, Institute of Pacific Studies,
University of the South Pacific, Suva

ANTHONY J **REGAN** (AJR)
Fellow in Political and Social Change, The Australian National University, Canberra

PHILIP F **REHBOCK** (PFR)
Professor, Department of History, University of Hawai'i, Honolulu

JAN **RENSEL** (JR)
Adjunct Assistant Professor in Department of Anthropology, University of Hawai'i–Mānoa, and a freelance manuscript editor, Honolulu

DALE **ROBERTSON** (DR)
Institute for Polynesian Studies, Brigham Young University–Hawai'i, Laie

FLORENTINO **RODAO GARCIA** (FRG)
Spanish Association for Pacific Studies, Instituto Complutense de Asia, Universidad Complutense de Madrid, Madrid

DONALD H **RUBINSTEIN** (DHR)
Professor, Micronesian Area Research Center, University of Guam, Mangilao

ALAN **RUMSEY** (AR2)
Fellow, Department of Anthropology, The Australian National University, Canberra

PETER **SACK** (PS1)
Senior Fellow, Division of Law, Research School of Social Sciences, The Australian National University, Canberra

RICHARD **SCAGLION** (RS1)
Professor, Department of Anthropology, University of Pittsburgh, Pittsburgh

DERYCK **SCARR** (DAS)
Independent Scholar, formerly Division of Pacific and Asian History, The Australian National University, Canberra

PENELOPE **SCHOEFFEL** (PS2)
Acting Director–Development Studies, University of Auckland, Auckland

HEINZ **SCHÜTTE** (HS)
Independent Scholar, Paris

PAUL **SHARRAD** (PS3)
Associate Professor of English, University of Wollongong, New South Wales

DOROTHY **SHINEBERG** (DS1)
Visitor, Research School of Pacific and Asian Studies, The Australian National University, Canberra

JEFF **SIEGEL** (JS)
Associate Professor, School of Languages, Cultures and Linguistics, University of New England, Armidale

MICHAEL T **SKULLY** (MTS)
Professor, Department of Accounting and Finance, Monash University, Melbourne

LARRY E **SMITH** (LES)
Dean, Program on Education & Training, East–West Center, Hawai'i

ROSALEEN **SMYTH** (RS2)
Associate Professor, Communication Studies, Deakin University, Victoria

MATTHEW **SPRIGGS** (MS)
Professor, Department of Archaeology and Anthropology, The Australian National University, Canberra

RUTH SAOVANA **SPRIGGS** (RSS)
Research Scholar, The Australian National University, Canberra

KAREN **STEVENSON** (KS)
Lecturer in Fine Arts, University of Canterbury, Christchurch

AMY KU'ULEIALOHA **STILLMAN** (AKS)
Ethnomusicology, University of Hawai'i–Mānoa, Honolulu

DONOVAN **STOREY** (DS2)
Lecturer in Development Studies, Massey University, Palmerston North

SANDRA **TARTE** (ST)
Lecturer in Politics, School of Social and Economic Development, University of the South Pacific, Suva

PAUL W **TAYLOR** (PWT)
Australian Volcanological Investigations, Sydney

ALLAN **THOMAS** (AT1)
Director, Stout Research Centre, Victoria University of Wellington, Wellington

NICHOLAS **THOMAS** (NT)
Professor and Director, Centre for Cross-Cultural Research, The Australian National University, Canberra

ANDREW **THORNLEY** (AT2)
Lecturer in Church History, Pacific Theological College, Suva

ANNA **TIRAA** (AT3)
Fisheries & Environmental Resource Consultants, Rarotonga, Cook Islands

GARRY W **TROMPF** (GWT)
Professor in the History of Ideas, School of Studies in Religion, University of Sydney, Sydney

DARRELL **TRYON** (DT)
Senior Fellow in Linguistics, Research School of Pacific and Asian Studies, The Australian National University, Canberra

EMMA KRUSE **VAAI** (EKV)
Lecturer in English, National University of Samoa, Apia

JON **VAN DYKE** (JVD)
Richardson School of Law, University of Hawai'i, Honolulu

HOWARD **VAN TREASE** (HVT)
Director, Extension Services, University of the South Pacific, Suva

JOSEPH **VERAMU** (JV)
Lecturer, Institute of Education, University of the South Pacific, Suva

JOHN D **VINCE** (JDV)
Professor of Paediatrics, University of Papua New Guinea, Port Moresby

ERIC **WADDELL** (EW)
Professor and Head, School of Geosciences, University of Sydney, Sydney

A CROSBIE **WALSH** (ACW)
Professor and Director of Centre for Development Studies, University of the South Pacific, Suva

ALAN **WARD** (AW1)
Emeritus Professor, University of Newcastle, New South Wales

R GERARD **WARD** (RGW)
Emeritus Professor of Human Geography, The Australian National University, Canberra

MARION W **WARD** (MWW)
Independent Scholar, Canberra

DICK **WATLING** (DW)
Principal, Environmental Consultants Fiji, Suva

DAVID A K **WATTERS** (DAKW)
Professor of Surgery, University of Papua New Guinea, Goroka

ALBERT **WENDT** (AW2)
Professor, Department of English, University of Auckland, Auckland

REINA **WHAITIRI** (RW)
Senior Tutor in English, Course Coordinator, English Department, University of Auckland, Auckland

GEOFFREY M **WHITE** (GMW)
Senior Fellow, East–West Center, University of Hawai'i, Honolulu

PETER G **WILLIAMS** (PGW)
Fisheries Database Manager, Oceanic Fisheries Program, Secretariat of the Pacific Community, Noumea

ELIZABETH **WOOD-ELLEM** (EW-E)
Research Associate, University of Melbourne, Melbourne

CHARLES **YALA** (CY)
Research Fellow, Economic Studies Division, National Research Institute, Port Moresby

MICHAEL W **YOUNG** (MWY)
Retired Senior Fellow, Department of Anthropology, The Australian National University, Canberra

TERRY KANALU **YOUNG** (TKY)
Assistant Professor, Center for Hawaiian Studies, University of Hawai'i–Mānoa, Honolulu

ABBREVIATIONS

A

AAP	Australian Associated Press
ABC	Australian Broadcasting Corporation
ABCFM	American Board of Commissioners for Foreign Missions
ADRAF	Rural Land Management and Development Agency (French)
AFL–CIO	American Federation of Labor Congress of Industrial Organizations
AIATSIS	Australian Institute of Aboriginal and Torres Strait Islander Studies
AIDS	auto-immune deficiency syndrome
ALTA	Agricultural Landlords and Tenants Act
ANGAU	Australian New Guinea Administrative Unit
ANU	Australian National University
AOSIS	Alliance of Small Island States
AP	Associated Press
ASEAN	Association of South East Asian Nations
ATSIC	Aboriginal and Torres Strait Islander Commission
AusAID	Australian Agency for International Development

B

BCL	Bougainville Copper Ltd
BHP	Broken Hill Proprietary
BIG	Bougainville Interim Government
BKATM	Botakin Karikirakean Aroia Tan Makuri
BOAC	British Overseas Airways Corporation
BPC	British Phosphate Commission
BRA	Bougainville Revolutionary Army
BTG	Bougainville Transitional Government
BYU-H	Brigham Young University-Hawai'i

C

CDC	Curriculum Development Centre
CEP	Centre d'Expérimentation du Pacifique
CEPAC	Episcopal Conference of the Pacific
CFP	French Pacific franc
CICC	Cook Islands Christian Church
CINAT	Cook Islands National Arts Theatre
CIRAD	Agriculture Research and Development Centre
CJD	Creutzfeldt-Jakob disease
CMS	Church Missionary Society
CPIS	Center for Pacific Islands Studies
CRA	Conzinc Riotinto of Australia
CRIA	Committee on Regional Institutional Arrangements
CSR	Colonial Sugar Refinery

D

DAC	Development Assistance Committee
DHPG	Deutsch Handelsund Plantagen-Gesellschaft
DHPG	Deutsche Handels-und Plantagen Gesellschaft

E

EEZ	exclusive economic zone
EEZ	export processing zone

EFO	Établissements Français d'Océanie
ENSO	El Niño Southern Oscillation
EU	European Union

F

FBC	Fiji Broadcasting Commission
FCAATSI	Federal Council for the Advancement of Aborigines and Torres Strait Islanders
FFA	Forum Fisheries Agency
FINTEL	Fiji International Telecommunications Ltd
FLNKS	Front de la Libération Nationale Kanak et Socialiste
FLP	Fiji Labour Party
FLP	Front de Libération de la Polynésie
FLP	Polynesian Liberation Front
fob	free-on-board
ForSec	Forum Secretariat
FSC	Fiji Sugar Corporation
FTUC	Fiji Trade Union Congress
FWA	Federation of Workers' Associations (PNG)

G

GDP	gross domestic product
GNP	gross national product
GRDP	gross regional domestic product
GSP	Generalized System of Preferences

H

HART	Housing Authority Relief Trust
HF	high frequency (radio)
HIV	human immuno-deficiency virus
HRPP	Human Rights Protection Party (SAM)

I

ICFTU	International Confederation of Free Trade Unions
IFREMER	French Institute for Marine Research
ILUW	International Longshoremen's and Warehousemen's Union
IMF	International Monetary Fund
INTELSAT	International Telecommunications Satellite Organization
IOC	Intergovernmental Oceanographic Commission of UNESCO
IPS	Institute for Polynesian Studies
IPS	Institute of Pacific Studies
IUD	intrauterine device

K

KTTC	Komiti Talafakafonua Tonga Traditions Committee
KS/BE	Kamehameha Schools/Bishop Estate
KTUC	Kiribati Trade Union Congress

L

LKS	Libération Kanak Socialiste
LMS	London Missionary Society

Abbreviations

M

MA	Mataungan Association
MARC	Micronesian Area Research Center
MF	Mobile Force (VAN)
MFO	Sinai Multinational Force and Observers
MIRAB	MIgration, Remittances, Aid and Bureaucracy
MSC	Missionaries of the Sacred Heart

N

NADEPA	National Democratic Party
NBHC	New Broken Hill Consolidated
NBK	Nan'yô Kôhatsu
NCD	National Capital District (PNG)
NDL	Nord Deutscher-Lloyd
NEI	Netherlands East Indies
NEMS	National Environmental Management Strategies
NFIP	Nuclear Free and Independent Pacific
NFP	National Federation Party (FIJI)
NGDC	New Guinea Development Company
NGK	Neu Guinea Kompagnie
NGO	non-government organization
NLTB	Native Land Trust Board
NPAP	National People's Action Party
NPF	National Provident Fund
NRSF	National Reconnaissance and Surveillance Force
NUP	National United Pati
NZFOL	New Zealand Federation of Labour

O

ODA	Official Development Aid
OECD	Organization of Economic Cooperation and Development
OPM	Organisasi Papua Merdeka (Free Papua Movement)
ORSTOM	French Institute of Scientific Research for Development through Cooperation

P

PACT	Pacific Area Cooperative Telecommunications
PACTEL	Pacific Regional Television Survey Project
PALIKA	Parti de Libération Kanak
PAMBU	Pacific Manuscripts Bureau
PATA	Pacific Area Travel Association
PATCRA	Papua New Guinea/Australia Trade and Commercial Relations Agreement
PCC	Pacific Council of Churches
PCC	Polynesian Cultural Centre
PCRC	Pacific Concerns Resource Centre
PFL	Pacific Forum Line
PIANGO	Pacific Islands Association of Non-Government Organizations
PIB	Papuan Infantry Battalion
PIBA	Pacific Islands Broadcasting Association
PILOM	Pacific Islands Law Officers Meeting
PIM	Pacific Islands Monthly
PINA	Pacific Islands News Association
PIP	Pacific Islands Studies Program
PJA	Pacific Journalists Association

PLA	Panguna Landowners' Association
PNGDF	Papua New Guinea Defence Force
PTC	Pacific Theological College
PTP	Pacific Telecommunications Project
PTUC	Pacific Trade Union Community

R

RA	Radio Australia
RC	Rassemblement Calédonien
RDPT	Rassemblement Démocratique des Populations Tahitiennes
RFMF	Republic of the Fiji Islands Military Forces
RPCR	Rassemblement Pour la Calédonie dans la République
RSPAS	Research School of Pacific and Asian Studies, ANU

S

SDA	Seventh-Day Adventists
SFNH	Société Française des Nouvelles Hébrides
SICHE	Solomon Islands College of Higher Education
SIDF	Solomon Islands Defence Force
SINTA	Solomon Islands National Teachers Association
SINUW	Solomon Islands National Union of Workers
SIPEU	Solomon Islands Public Employees Union
SLN	Société le Nickel
SOI	southern oscillation index
SOPAC	South Pacific Applied Geoscience Commission
SPARTECA	South Pacific Regional Trade and Economic Cooperation Agreement
SPBEA	South Pacific Bureau for Educational Assessment
SPC	South Pacific Commission
SPCAS	South Pacific Creative Arts Society
SPEC	South Pacific Bureau for Economic Cooperation
SPOCC	South Pacific Organizations Coordinating Committee
SPOCTU	South Pacific and Oceanic Council of Trade Unions
SPREP	South Pacific Regional Environment Programme
SPSM	South Pacific Sugar Mills Limited
SPTC	South Pacific Tourism Council
STD	sexually transmitted disease
STL	Solomon Taiyo Limited
SVD	Society of the Divine Word
SVT	Soqosoqo ni Vakavulewa ni Taukei

T

TB	tuberculosis
TCSP	Tourism Council of the South Pacific
TEAL	Tasman Empire Airways Limited
TEAL	Tasman Empire Airways Ltd
TFF	tax free factory
TFF/TFZ	Free Factories/Tax Free Zone Scheme (FIJI)
TOM	Territoires d'Outre-Mer
TOSU	Overseas Seamen's Union
TSIMA	Torres Strait Islanders Media Association
TTPI	US Trust Territory of the Pacific Islands
TUP	Torres United Party
TVNZ	Television New Zealand

U

UC	Union Calédonienne
UCNH	Union des Communautés des Nouvelles Hebrides
UFP	French University of the Pacific
UMP	Union of Moderate Parties
UNCED	United Nations Conference on Environment and Development
UNCEN	Universitas Cenderawasih
UNCLOS	United Nations Convention on the Law of the Sea
UNIFIL	United Nations Interim Force in Lebanon
UNIKOM	Iraq-Kuwait Observation Mission
UNSW	University of New South Wales
UNTEA	United Nations Temporary Executive Authority
UPNG	University of Papua New Guinea
UPNH	Union de la Population des Nouvelles Hébrides
USP	University of the South Pacific
USQ	University of Southern Queensland
USTKE	Union of Kanak and Exploited Workers
UTC	Universal Time Coordinated

V

VCR	video cassette recorder
VOC	Vereenigde Oostindische Compaigne

W

WFTU	World Federation of Trade Unions
WMMS	Wesleyan Methodist Missionary Society
WRWGU	Wholesale and Retail Workers' General Union
WSNUW	Western Samoa National Union of Workers
WSPSA	Western Samoa Public Service Association
WWW	World Wide Web

GLOSSARY

A

ahu, ʻahu	stone temple platform (Polynesia)
ʻaiga	family, kin group (SAM)
alii, aliʻi	chief, of chiefly descent (SAM, HI); ariʻi (FRPOL)
aliʻi-kapu	paramount chief (HI)
ANZUS Pact	mutual security treaty signed between Australia, New Zealand and United States of America in 1951; New Zealand was suspended after it introduced a nuclear-free policy in the 1980s
ariki	paramount chief (CI)
atoll	coral reef, typically ring-shaped, enclosing a lagoon
atua	deity (Polynesia)

B

bagnes	French convict prisons
bai	men's club house, community ceremonial house (PAL)
barrier reef	offshore coral reef
bata	village house (KIR)
Beretitenti	paramount leader, president (KIR)
betelnut	kernel of nut chewed for pleasure and relaxation
bilas	body decoration, personal adornment, finery (PNG)
bilum	string bag used as a carry-all (PNG)
Bose Levu Vakaturaga	Fijian Great Council of Chiefs
bure	village house (FIJI)

C

caldera	wide crater formed after volcanic collapse or explosion
Caldoche	white rural settler in New Caledonia
cantonnement	colonial policy of confining Maohi to reserves (FRPOL)
coastwatcher	Allied intelligence agent working behind Japanese lines in Pacific War
copra	dried kernel of coconut

D

dalo	taro (FIJI)
Demi	lit. 'half': of mixed (French and Maohi or Chinese) descent (FRPOL)
deputé	deputy, member of parliament (French Territories)

E

EEZ	Exclusive Economic Zone, offshore strip extending 200 nautical miles, giving a country control of resource rights
endemic	native to a particular area, and existing only there

F

faʻa Samoa	Samoan way of life, customary etiquette
faʻafine	man who acts and dresses as a woman (SAM); also called mahu (FRPOL, HI); fakaleiti or fakafine (TON); binabinaaine (KIR)
fagogo	fables, family story-telling form (SAM)
faipule	village or wider district; also its elected representative (SAM, TOK)
fale	village house (SAM); also called fare (FRPOL)
fono	formal meeting, especially legislature (SAM, TOK)
Forum countries	members of the South Pacific Forum
fringing reef	coral reef along island shore

G

gendarmerie	French police station
guano	droppings of seabirds, used as fertilizer
guyot	submerged island, where rising water levels outpaced coral growth

H

haka	warlike dance and chant (NZ)
haole	European (HI)
haus tambaran	ancestral spirit house, men's ceremonial house (PNG)
heiau	ancient stone temple (HI)
hiri	trading voyage (PNG)
hula	traditional dance (HI)
hupahupa	drum dance (CI)

I

i-Kiribati	indigenous inhabitant of New Caledonia
Iroij	paramount chief (RMI)

K

Kanak	indigenous inhabitant of New Caledonia
kanaka	person of Polynesian or Melanesian descent; formerly colonial term for villager (PNG); and for South Sea islander indentured labourer
Kanaka Maoli	Native Hawaiians (the True People)
Kaneka	of contemporary culture of New Caledonia
kapu	see tabu
kastom	customary tradition (VAN)
kava	traditional ceremonial drink, a mild narcotic made from root of pepper shrub; also called yaqona (FIJI)
kiap	colonial patrol officer, district officer (PNG)
kohanga reo	Maori language immersion pre-school centre (NZ)
kuhina nui	regent, co-ruler (HI)
kumara	sweet potato (Polynesia); also called kaukau (PNG)

L

lakatoi	outrigger canoe with crab-claw sails (PNG)
lanai	covered porch (HI)
laplap	loincloth or sarong (PNG); also called lavalava (SAM); pareu (FRPOL); sulu (FIJI); vala (TON)
Lavelua	paramount chief (WF)
leeward	point or side sheltered from wind
lei	garland (of flowers, shells, etc) worn around neck, also called ei (CI)
Line	equator, as in crossing the Line, and also Line Islands
lingua franca	language serving as medium of communication
lotu	Christian church, congregation; also called lotu toga, rotu (FIJI)
luluai	village headman appointed by colonial government (PNG)

M

mamaia	religious movement in 19th-century Tahiti
mana	authority, spiritual power; also called mina
Maohi	indigenous inhabitant of French Polynesia
Maori	indigenous inhabitant of New Zealand and of Cook Islands

marae	stone temple platform (Polynesia); tribal meeting place (NZ); also called malae (SAM); rara (FIJI)
matai	titled person, of chiefly descent (SAM)
mataqali	descent group, landowning community (FIJI)
matrilineal	relating to descent through mother or female line
mau	protest movement (SAM)
meke	traditional song and dance performance (FIJI)
metropolitan	of the chief city, or relating to the colonial power
moai	ancestral stone statue of Rapanui
Mother Hubbard	loose-fitting 'missionary dress', also called muumuu
motu	low-lying islet

N

nahnken	chief (FSM)
Nahnmwarki	paramount chief (FSM)
national	term of reference used officially for indigenous Papua New Guineans
ni-Vanuatu	indigenous inhabitant of Vanuatu

P

pa	fortified village (NZ)
Pacific Rim	continents and countries bordering on Pacific Ocean
pa'langi, palagi	European (SAM); also called papalagi, papa'a
pakeha	European (NZ)
patrilineal	relating to descent through father or male line
polymath	very learned person
prau, proa	Malay outrigger canoe, typically with triangular sail

R

rangitira	leader, chief (Polynesia); also ra'atira (FRPOL)
raskol	lit. 'rascal': juvenile street criminal (PNG)
ratu	title for Fijian chiefs, used as a prefix to their name
ra'ui, rahui	ban, temporary closure (Polynesia)

S

singsing	festival involving dance, singing and usually feasting (PNG)
Spanish Lake	Pacific Ocean, referring to the dominance of Spanish explorers in the region in the 15th and 16th centuries
subduction	the action of one tectonic plate wedging under another

T

tama'aiga	highest chiefly family (SAM)
tāmūrē	fast-tempo dance (FRPOL)
tapa	barkcloth; also kapa (HI); saipo (SAM); masi (FIJI); ahu (FRPOL)
tapu	taboo; sacred, sacrosanct; also kapu (HI)
tatau	tattoo (FRPOL)
taukei	common people, indigenous people (FIJI)
te reo	Maori language (NZ)
tiare	gardenia (FRPOL)
tiki	ornamental image of semi-human form, endowed with magical properties (NZ)
tivaevae	quilt (CI); also tifaifai (FRPOL)
tohunga	pre-European priest, healer, wise man; also called kahuna (HI); tahua (FRPOL)
trade wind	regularly occuring wind blowing towards equator from either northeast or southeast

trepang	bêche-de-mer, sea slug
Tu'i	paramount chief, ruler (Polynesia)

U

umu	earth oven (NZ, CI); also called imu (HI); lovo (FIJI)

V

va'a	canoe (FRPOL); also called va'aalo (SAM)
vaka vanua	customary behaviour, 'way of the land' (FIJI)
vanua	land (FIJI); also called whenua (NZ); fenua (FRPOL)

W

waiata	Maori song
wantok	lit. 'one talk': person speaking the same language, from the same district, a neighbour or compatriot (PNG)
windward	point or side exposed to wind

one

physical environment

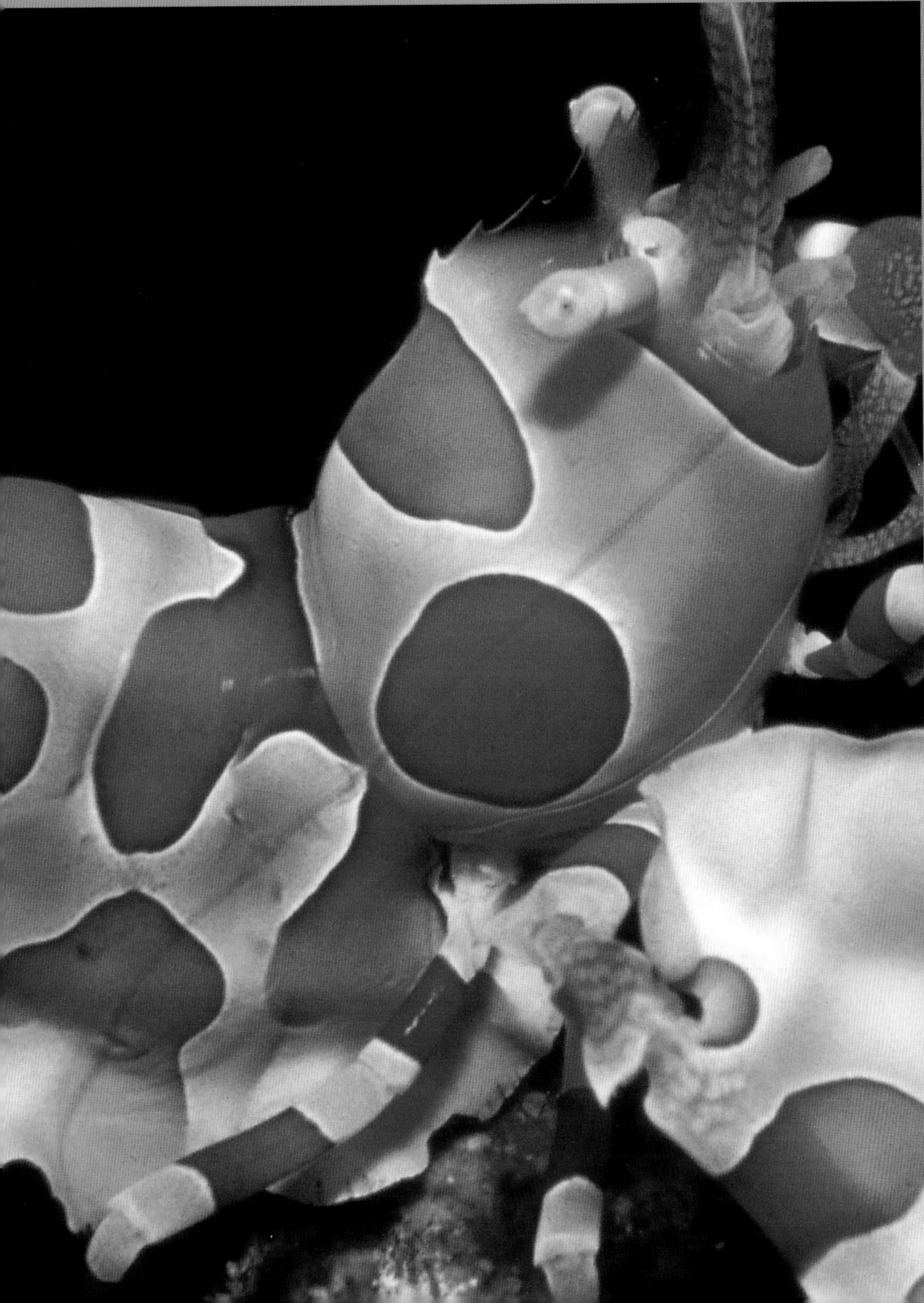

Contributors

Article contributors

AA	Atholl Anderson
ADL	Antony D Lewis
BJA	Bryant J Allen
DW	Dick Watling
EG	Emma Gyuris
GH2	Geoffrey Hope
HM	Helene Marsh
ICC	Ian C Campbell
JL2	John Lidstone
KL	Kurt Lambeck
KRF	Kate Fortune
MQ	Max Quanchi
MS	Matthew Spriggs
NC	Neville Coleman
PD'A	Paul D'arcy
PDN	Patrick D Nunn
PGW	Peter G Williams
PL	Padma Lal
PWT	Paul W Taylor
RFMcL	Roger F McLean
RGW	R Gerard Ward
RL2	Robert Langdon
RMB	R Michael Bourke
WCC	William C Clarke

Photo contributors

Bourke, Michael (The Australian National University, Canberra): 32, 33, 34, 35, 44

Coleman, Neville (Australasian Marine Photographic Index, Springwood, Queensland): 1 (detail), 4, 6, 7, 9, 10, 11, 12, 13, 21 (left), 29 (bottom)

Great Barrier Reef Marine Park Authority (Queensland): 15

Gyuris, Emma (James Cook University, Townsville): 16

Hendrie, Peter (Pacific Journeys, Melbourne): 3, 5, 12, 24, 31, 48

Hope, Geoffrey (The Australian National University, Canberra): 22, 28, 29 (top, middle), 30

Marshall Islands Visitors Authority (Majuro, Republic of the Marshall Islands): 21 (right), 37 (top, middle)

Nelson, Hank (The Australian National University, Canberra): 26, 36 (bottom), 47, 48 (bottom)

New Caledonia Tourism (Sydney): 37 (top right)

Nunn, Patrick D (University of the South Pacific, Suva): 40, 41

Panholzer, Thomas C (College of Micronesia–FSM, Pohnpei): 36 (left)

Royal New Zealand Air Force Photography: 49

Maps

ANU Cartography: 17, 19, 20, 24, 25, 26

Secretariat of the Pacific Community (Noumea), courtesy of Peter G Williams: 45

ONE THE SEA

Oceanic environment

The Pacific Ocean is a vast body of water, covering an area greater than all the world's land mass combined. It is also the deepest ocean, and larger than all other oceans combined. Bering Strait in the north is separated from Antarctica in the south by 14 800 km. The Pacific Ocean is 16 700 km wide at the equator, and over 19 000 km at its widest point, from Singapore to Panama. In places, no land breaks its surface for thousands of kilometres.

The earth's surface has not always had its present configuration. Its crust consists of a thick layer of rock divided into large plates that float upon a relatively plastic underlying mantle. Throughout geological history these plates have been constantly in motion. The fossil record and other geological evidence suggests that 200 million years ago all of the world's land mass was joined in one supercontinent, *Pangaea* (one earth), and surrounded by an all encompassing sea, *Panthalassa* (one sea), which included much of the present-day Pacific Ocean. In contrast, the other great oceans, the Atlantic, Indian and Arctic, only came into being as *Pangaea* began to drift apart. The Pacific alone has always been an ocean. To colonize the islands away from its western margins, all forms of life have had to come to terms with sea passages of varying sizes.

During the *Pleistocene* era, beginning 2 or 3 million years ago, a series of wide swings in global temperature occurred. In the cooler phases sea levels were lowered by as much as 145 m as vast quantities of water were impounded in huge ice caps until warmer phases began to melt them. At the sea's lowest level most of island Southeast Asia was joined to the mainland of Asia in a land mass named *Sunda* by scientists. Present-day New Guinea, Australia and Tasmania were joined as *Sahul*, with only 57 km separating it from *Sunda* at its closest point. Lowered sea levels also increased the size of Pacific islands, thus reducing distances between them. The large-scale temperature fluctuations that occurred throughout the *Pleistocene* stabilized in the *Holocene* era which began about 10 000 years ago, but fluctuations in average temperature still occurred. The period 1350 to 700 BP (before the present) was generally one of mild, warmer conditions known as the Little Climatic Optimum. It was followed by cooler average conditions in the so-called Little Ice Age that continued until last century. Neither period was severe enough to alter sea levels dramatically, but the temperature variations were enough to influence the distribution of some flora and fauna.

The Pacific Ocean in recent geological times can be envisaged as two distinct zones. One is a zone of islands, the other largely devoid of islands. Their features are shaped by the movement of the various tectonic plates that constitute the earth's crust in this part of the globe. Where lighter oceanic plates collide with the heavier continental plates of the Pacific Rim the earth's crust is ruptured by great fractures and the molten magma underneath this crust extrudes violently through these fractures in volcanic activity. Sometimes the earth's crust is thrust upward as the continental plates ride over the lighter oceanic ones. The result is a host of volcanic cones rising from the ocean floor along these zones of plate interaction and the resulting fracture lines. Through time some cones rise above the ocean's surface. They may continue to grow above the surface,

Muri Lagoon, Rarotonga, Cook Islands

but in time begin to subside under their own weight or are eroded by wind, rain and sea. When conditions are favourable, atolls form from the coral remains of living organisms that establish themselves in shallow, warm waters atop subsided volcanoes. Coral may also form in the shallow coastal waters off islands where their preferred mix of warm, saline and clear, sunlit water occurs. About 80 per cent of the world's islands lie within the area bounded by Tokyo, Jakarta and Rapanui (Easter Island). Outside this area the plates of the Pacific's seabed tend to drift apart rather than collide, so that the underlying magma oozes through the crust under much less pressure. Gentle sea floor basins and ridges that do not break the ocean's surface are the result, creating a huge area of 'empty' ocean in the northern and eastern Pacific.

Most Pacific islands are grouped in clusters or arcs, with few islands existing in total isolation. Geologically they are divided into two groups by the

Andesite line which runs to the east of New Zealand, Tonga and Fiji, then west to an area north of Solomon Islands and New Guinea before turning north again and running east of Yap and the Mariana Islands. To the west of this line islands are made up of a variety of ancient continental rocks, and include many large islands with a greater abundance of resources than tends to be the case east of the Andesite line. Here, the generally smaller oceanic islands are made up primarily of volcanic basaltic rocks. While high oceanic islands can attract high rainfall on their windward aspects, their leeward coasts can be prone to drought. The coral-capped, low-lying atolls of the region are also prone to drought, and to the ever-present threat of damage to vegetation and ground water supplies posed by storm and typhoon waves.

Most terrestrial flora and fauna came originally from the western margins of the Pacific. There is a marked diminution of flora and fauna species as one moves eastward. For example there are over 550 species of land birds in New Guinea, 127 in Solomon Islands, 54 in Fiji, 17 in Society Islands and only 4 on Henderson Island in the southeast corner of Oceania. This west–east gradient is not only a function of distance from Asia, but also of the vectors for diffusion. Terrestrial flora and fauna colonize new islands by means of flotsam drifting on ocean currents, or blown by the winds or attached to birds. On the new island, survival depends on the suitability of the new environment to the species' needs. High islands generally offer more favourable conditions.

Mangrove forests act as a buffer against huge seas, and also provide protective cover to schools of juvenile fish and shrimps. Many fish species sleep amongst the mangroves

There is also a less marked diminution of Pacific marine species from west to east. Few marine species have the ability to move across the oceans without restriction. The nature of marine ecosystems means that most marine species inhabit the benthic (ocean floor) or neritic (near shore) zones rather than the pelagic (open ocean) zone of the ocean. Their movement is restricted by their tolerance limits to temperature, salinity and viscosity, as well as the availability of food sources. The reef and mangrove ecosystems of island coastlines are amongst the most productive ecosystems in the world. Mangrove forests protect the island foreshores while supporting large numbers of inter-tidal organisms. The open ocean of the tropical Pacific is a relatively poor environment by comparison, except where upwelling enriches upper layers with nutrients in the form of the remains of dead organisms that have descended from the euphotic (sunlit) zone. Near-shore species colonize other coastal locations by drifting as larvae on ocean currents. Colonization succeeds when the currents encounter islands, and the sea passage is not too extensive or devoid of nutrition to enable sufficient number of larvae to form a viable population.

The atmospheric and oceanic circulation systems that help species colonize the Pacific also influence its weather and climate patterns. A number of wind systems operate in the Pacific. In the more open eastern two-thirds a series of zones cross the ocean from east to west, each with its own distinct pattern of surface winds. In the higher latitudes of both hemispheres strong westerlies blow for most of the year. Between them are two belts of trade winds. In the northern hemisphere these blow from the northeast, while in the south they blow from the southeast. Their strength diminishes in the western third of the Pacific Ocean. The trade winds are not continuous, but generally blow for at least part of every month of the year. They are most consistent between May and September. For the remainder of the year winds blow from both east and west. The equatorial area between the trade wind belts is known as the doldrums, and is characterized by light variable winds and calms as well as squalls, heavy showers and thunderstorms.

The western Pacific is dominated by monsoon and typhoon weather patterns arising from annual heating and cooling of the Asian land mass. Monsoon winds blow from the northwest away from Asia in the Northern Hemisphere winter, and from the southeast towards Asia in the summer. Typhoons or hurricanes occur in much of the western part of the tropical Pacific. Associated high winds and torrential rains cause much devastation to the islands in their path.

Rainfall patterns vary widely. Generally areas near the equator in the western Pacific experience high rainfall with limited seasonal variation. An area of low rainfall extends along the equatorial belt in the east and central Pacific. Further north and south annual rainfall diminishes, and marked seasonal variation occurs. Monsoonal weather patterns also tend to produce marked seasonality in rainfall. At a localized level, high island mountain barriers force moisture-laden oceanic winds upwards, resulting in high rainfall on the windward slopes. With most of their moisture released, the winds descend on the leeward slopes as hot, dry winds that draw moisture from the land.

The same winds create waves upon the malleable surface of the ocean. When the winds subside, or the wave train advances beyond the wind systems that initiated them, they continue as swells. Swells may run in the same direction for hundreds or even thousands of miles unless they are subdued by contrary winds or disrupted by land barriers. The Pacific also displays a wide range of tidal oscillations across its entire surface. Tidal range, the difference between low and high tide, tends to be greater on the margins of the Pacific than in mid ocean. Much of the daily and seasonal behaviour of nearshore marine biota is oriented to tidal patterns.

Winds also influence surface-layer circulation patterns in the ocean. Two vast loops of ocean currents, or gyres, dominate the Pacific Ocean. The one north of the equator flows clockwise, while the other in the south flows anti-clockwise. The currents on the western side of these gyres increase in intensity as they flow away from the equator. These currents are deflected in places by islands, particularly the southern westward-moving flow. Between these two gyres is the Equatorial Countercurrent which flows eastward from the Caroline Islands across to Panama. Other, separate circulation systems operate towards the polar extremities. Circulation systems also exist at greater depths under the influence of differences in ocean water density.

Ocean–atmosphere interaction goes further than the influence of winds on surface water circulation. Much of the world's climate is determined by the exchange of heat and moisture between ocean and atmosphere. As the planet's largest body of water, the Pacific has a crucial role in this process, demonstrated by recent advances in our understanding of the so-called ENSO (EL NIÑO Southern Oscillation) phenomenon. El Niño involves the periodic disruption of the upwelling of nutrient-rich cool waters into the relatively shallow surface layer off the coast of Peru. If deprived of this rich infusion, the coastal fishery has been estimated to diminish by as much as 90 per cent. Until recently explanations of this phenomenon focused on weakening of the southeast trade winds, which, when strong, allowed upwelling by driving surface water westward away from the coast. But now explanations emphasize atmospheric pressure differences across the Pacific, for which ENSO is a measure. When pressure gradients lead to stronger than usual westerly winds in the western Pacific, these winds disrupt the ocean surface layer across the whole of the equatorial region by blowing surface water eastward. Off Peru this leads to a deepened warm surface layer that is far less productive than the upwelling mix under other conditions. Instead of being abnormal, El Niño is the extreme warm-surface phase of an 18–24 month cycle that also exhibits an extreme cool-surface phase known as La Niña. These cycles are irregular, but they seem to occur every 3–7 years. Much of the globe is affected. For example, in an El Niño phase unusually heavy rain occurs in subtropical

Typical atoll, Ha'apai, Tonga

Chile and the equatorial Pacific, while drier than usual conditions plague Australia and Indonesia, and lower than average monsoon rains are experienced around the Indian Ocean region. In a La Niña phase the opposite conditions apply.

Climatic conditions and weather patterns can vary dramatically from year to year in some locations. Onotoa atoll in Kiribati had 216 cm of rain in 1946, but only 17 cm of rain in 1950. Natural hazards can suddenly devastate areas. If modern monitoring equipment is unavailable, little warning of the destruction may be received. The main unheralded threats are typhoons, TSUNAMI and VOLCANIC ACTIVITY. Typhoons tend to be concentrated in 4-month periods every year, but they have occurred during every month. Their high winds carve a path of destruction, while the accompanying storm waves are particularly devastating to low-lying coastal areas and atolls. Tsunami are sea waves generated by seismic disturbances on the sea floor. They move across the ocean surface at astonishing speeds, until they encounter shallow coastal waters where they are slowed down so that water begins to pile up to form crests up to 30 m in height. Such waves hit the shore with awesome destructive force just minutes after the tell-tale rapid recession of the shoreline. Where seismic activity occurs on land, the main threat to humans is from the lava, gases and debris emitted from volcanic eruptions. Although scientific research is improving our knowledge of the Pacific environment, and allowing us to anticipate its dangers better, there is still much to be learnt. The Pacific will continue to provide both sustenance and challenges to human societies in the foreseeable future.—PD'A

The underwater world

The underwater world, steeped in mythology, is to many people a mysterious place fraught with danger. Through fear, sedentary ways of life, lack of money or opportunity, few people (apart from the holders of traditional knowledge on the ocean) know much about its inhabitants, even though they may know the cycles of the seasons and what lives where, from a hunter-gatherer's point of view.

Terrestrial land forms have been defined by various geological factors (generally referred to as regions), and the land flora and fauna zones are based on assemblages of vegetation. In the ocean environment, the defined areas distinguishing one zone from another are not always clear-cut, nor are they predictable in regard to where one specific type of sea weed or animal be found. This is especially so in the sub-littoral zone where mobile animals such as fish may visit a number of different habitats within this zone during the day, on a full tide, yet at night may sleep in another. Depending on environmental influences, depth, rough (exposed reef front), or calm conditions (protected lagoon), the same animal (sponges and shells for example) may appear structurally different, or exhibit a different colour or pattern.

In the Pacific Ocean, the major life form zones begin just above the high tide level (often referred to as the splash zone), which is also called the supra-littoral zone. The seashore (between the tides) is known as the littoral zone. From below low-tide level from 60 m down to 400 m is the outer sub-littoral zone; from 400 m to beyond, is the Continental Shelf zone. The vertical water column from surface to sea floor is generally referred to as the open ocean zone, and the abyssal zone refers to the vast areas of

The tiny (8 cm) Ludwig's basket star, *Conocladus ludwigi*

Nodose sea star, *Protoreaster nodosus*, a large (20 cm) varicoloured species

Necklace sea star, *Fromia monilis*, (around 10 cm) may be seen at depths of 2–30 m

abyssal (seabed) plain where there are several deep narrow OCEAN TRENCHES.

Within these zones, 100 000 or more species of marine creatures may live; from microscopic organisms to giant blue whales. The area is so vast that estimating species is difficult, though scientists believe there are more than 4500 species of fish, 500 species of CORALS, 6000 sponges, 20 000

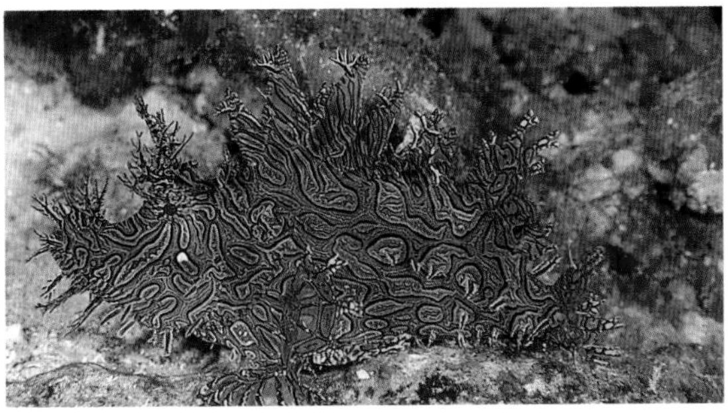

The lacy scorpionfish, *Rhinopias aphanes*, has venomous dorsal spines concealed in its fronded appearance. Growing to around 23 cm, it may be pink, greenish, yellow or black

Violet soldierfish, *Myripristis violacea*

Angelfish, *Pomacanthus navarchus*, found off the northern Great Barrier Reef, Papua New Guinea and Solomon Islands

White-lined rock cod, *Anyperodon leucogrammicus*, with a still-breathing soldierfish (spines extended) stuck tail-first in the rock cod's throat and gills

MOLLUSCS and up to 30 000 CRUSTACEANS. Thousands remain undescribed, with new species being discovered regularly.

The waters adjacent to continents or surrounding larger islands support a greater species diversity and abundance of marine life than waters farther offshore. This is due to the immense volume of run-off waters and rivers disgorging nutrients and minerals washed down from the larger land masses during the wet seasons creating vast algal blooms which in turn feed huge numbers of zooplankton, up the food chain. Due to this phenomenon, inshore waters are often cloudy and discoloured around larger land masses (in season) when compared to the crystal-clear waters of the outer Pacific areas.

Many species of fish and marine invertebrates range across the entire temperate or tropical regions. However, due to isolation, many different island land masses possess species endemic to their particular waters, and also very limited in range. Few Pacific countries have had the capacity to record and study their entire range of marine flora and fauna, so few baseline marine surveys are available at a national level. However, a great deal of work has been, and is still being done by scientists and field naturalists, especially in areas where research stations exist.

Australia, Hawai'i, the Americas, New Zealand and New Caledonia have all produced a number of popular field guides based on their marine flora and fauna, and the combined knowledge contained within their universities, museums and public aquariums allows identification of most of the larger and more common species. Other Pacific islands maintain marine research stations, some public aquariums or tourist operations based on marine activities, especially snorkelling, scuba diving and reef walking. Some have, to a smaller extent, produced marine educational materials in conjunction with these adventure-based activities.

In many areas marine resources have been heavily harvested by more established, highly mechanized predatory nations which have fished beyond the sustainable yield, causing some fisheries to collapse. Global warming, particularly over the last decade, has caused huge declines in coral reef populations due to sea surface temperatures remaining at high levels for long periods, causing corals to bleach and die (see CLIMATE CHANGE). Mining and logging companies have contributed to huge losses of sea creatures due to dumping of toxic wastes and mud slides caused by road building through virgin rainforests around mountainsides. Mangrove forests, sea grass meadows and fringing CORAL reefs are particularly vulnerable to human interference, pollution and disturbance.—NC

Pelagic fish

Pelagic fish are those which inhabit the surface layers of coastal and oceanic waters, in contrast to demersal (bottom) and CORAL reef-associated fishes. They are common, highly visible and economically very important to Pacific islands—not surprising in a region which is less than 2 per cent land, and largely open ocean. They range in size from small (less than 10 cm) ANCHOVIES and sardines, important forage and baitfish, through the coastal mackerels, trevallies, barracudas and bonitos, spectacular flying fish and *mahi mahi*, to large oceanic marlin and TUNA which may exceed 500 kg in weight. They are typically predatory fishes, streamlined and capable of rapid movement and extensive migration in their domain. The *Wahoo Acanthocybium solandri*, an oceanic mackerel, has been timed at speeds of over 80 km per hour in short bursts, whilst some tuna, well adapted for cruising the vast oceanic expanses, regularly cross the Pacific Ocean. Other pelagic fish, such as the large sunfish *Mola mola*, drift passively in ocean currents yet grow to 500 kg or more. Many pelagic fish occur in schools of hundreds of tonnes or more, whereas others may be solitary.

The most important pelagic fish group economically are the tuna—the waters surrounding the Pacific islands support the world's largest tuna fishery, with annual catches of over one million tonnes, and tuna represent a vital source of economic opportunity to many countries. The open ocean is not especially productive, however, and tuna tend to concentrate in areas of abundant food—along current boundaries, near islands and seamounts, and also, curiously, under various floating objects. Tuna are captured by a variety of fishing gear—large purse-seine nets which encircle whole surface schools, baited longlines tens of kilometers in length, and pole-and-line vessels. The latter attract fish by broadcasting live bait—other small pelagic fish such as anchovies—to enable tuna to be captured by poles and lures. There is a long history of traditional fishing for tuna in the islands, especially in Polynesia where limited land and lagoon areas encourage reliance on the ocean and pelagic fish as a primary food source. Many pelagic fish, notably the marlins, are also important gamefish much sought after by anglers throughout the Pacific islands.

Pelagic fish numbers tend to vary more on local scales than is the case for most species, influenced by oceanic events such as EL NIÑO, changes in migration patterns, variations in food sources and fluctuations in survival of young fish. At the end of the 20th century the Pacific islands face a challenge in the development of a regime for the sustainable management of the globally significant resources of pelagic fish in their waters, to the ultimate benefit of all parties.—ADL

Skipjack tuna

Skipjack tuna (*Katsuwonus pelamis*) is the most abundant tuna in the Pacific islands region, found all year round in tropical waters, where the main biomass is concentrated, and seasonally in subtropical and temperate waters. One million tonnes of skipjack is harvested annually in the region, and possibly several times more could be taken on a sustainable basis. This remarkable species is one of the smallest tuna, typically attaining only 10 kg in weight, compared to the 200 kg maximum size of the other tropical tuna, yellowfin (*Thunnus albacares*) and bigeye (*Thunnus obesus*), with which it often swims.

Skipjack is thus probably the single most valuable living marine resource available to the Pacific islands, and achieves this heroic status in one of the least productive parts of the world's oceans, the western Pacific warm pool. Two things contribute to this success. First, the species has a series of adaptations which enable it to search widely and locate its scarce food (small fish and crustaceans) in the vast oceanic realm. It has warm bloodedness (unusual for a fish), a very high metabolic rate, and the capacity for continuous rapid swimming. Second, production in the warm pool benefits from plankton redistributed westwards by currents from the more productive central and eastern Pacific; this production also shifts in accordance with EL NIÑO events, and skipjack and fisheries for them follow these shifts in food distribution (see Figure 1.12, page 45).

Skipjack are also very resilient to exploitation: growth is rapid, reproduction is frequent, and individuals of the population turn over rapidly, being continually replaced.— ADL

Ocean anchovy

The Pacific islands, because of their small size and the absence of large productive ocean current upwellings in the region, lack the large fisheries for small pelagic fish species seen in other ocean areas, such as the anchoveta of Peru, the sardines of Japan and California and the pilchards of South Africa. Such fisheries contribute nearly half of the world's fisheries production in some years. The sheltered lagoons of some high islands in the region do support small-scale baitfisheries for SKIPJACK TUNA pole-and-line fishing, but otherwise small pelagic fish contribute little to food supplies in the region.

Recent work has shown, however, that there may be a little-known, unsung exception to this—the ocean anchovy (*Encrasicholina punctifer*). This small silvery species, which grows to around 6 cm in length and rarely lives beyond six months, is an inhabitant of the clear open ocean waters, often many hundreds of miles from land. It appears to be increasingly abundant in patches throughout the surface ocean layers of the western Pacific. Although seldom seen by coastal dwellers, it is encountered by tuna fishermen in large schools driven to the surface by tuna. The tuna, distracted by their frenzied feeding on the anchovies, are then much more vulnerable to capture by purse-seine nets. Other studies show that ocean anchovy are very important food items for a range of ocean species, but especially tuna, and it is becoming clear that this species may be the crucial link in transforming plankton carried into the western Pacific from elsewhere into food for tuna, and thus helping to support the world's largest tuna fishery.—ADL

Sharks

Sharks are large predatory fish, which inhabit several distinct areas of the Pacific islands region: surface layers of the coastal and oceanic waters, fringing/barrier reefs, lagoons and estuaries, and deep offshore oceanic waters. Sharks are often misrepresented as aggressive, fearsome creatures, but very few species that inhabit the waters of the islands are known to be of any danger to humans. Of more concern in recent times has been the effect of humans on shark populations, given that their biological characteristics (slow-growth, late maturity, low fecundity and productivity, and long life) make them much more vulnerable than most other commercially exploited fish species. In many islands, sharks form an important part of culture and customs. Sharks' teeth were made into blades for carving tools, and for sharp-edged clubs in warfare.

The most common species in surface waters are the blue shark (*Prionace glauca*), the silky shark (*Carcharhinus falciformis*), and the oceanic white-tip (*Carcharhinus longimanus*). These species are voracious feeders, and prey on various PELAGIC FISH, such as TUNA and squid. The oceanic shark species are frequently caught by commercial tuna fishing vessels operating throughout the islands. The fins are valued and are carefully processed on board the vessel before transportation to the lucrative Asian shark fin markets.

Common species found around barrier and fringing coral reefs include the grey reef shark (*Carcharhinus amblyrhychos*), the black-tip reef shark (*Carcharhinus melanopterus*), and the white-tip reef shark (*Triaenodon obesus*). The grey reef shark appears to be the most active of the reef sharks and is believed to exhibit aggressive gestures, such as arching their back while swimming in broad sweeps, as a reaction to potential threats in 'protecting' their territory. The Galapagos shark, *Carcharhinus galapagensis* (pictured), is common across the entire region. A size of 3 m has been recorded, but most of those encountered by divers in the western Pacific range from 1.5–2 m. Although curious by nature it is not regarded as highly dangerous. These sharks typically feed on the variety of reef fishes that abound in these environs.

The deep-water sharks of the region are typically found at depths of more than 500 m. The great white shark, *Carcharodon carcharias*, is found throughout

Galapagos shark, *Carcharhinus galapagensis*

the Pacific. It grows to 12 m long, and can weigh more than 3000 kg. It ranges in colour from brown to dull grey-blue, usually darker on the top of its body, shading to a paler grey underbelly. The whale shark, *Rhincodon typus*, the world's biggest, grows to 15 m long. The most common deep-water shark is probably the gulper (*Centrophorus* spp). A small commercial fishery targets certain deep-water sharks for the shark-liver oil market.—PGW & NC

Rays

The ray (of the order Hypotremata) is a large sea fish allied to the SHARK, both having a skeleton made of cartilage, and five pairs of gills. Rays can be identified by the ventral location of their gills, and the distinctive large pectoral fins on the sides of their head. The manta ray, *Manta birostris*, which can extend to 3 m across the width of its fins, lives in offshore waters where it feeds on plankton. The blue-spotted fantail ray, *Taeniura lymna* (pictured), is a shallow-water species, which lives in lagoons and sheltered

Blue-spotted fantail ray, *Taeniura lymna*

Bright red spiky soft corals, *Dendronephthya* sp, together with yellow and red gorgonian sea fan, *Melithaea ocracea*—both octocorals, with eight fringed tentacles

Faulkner's coral, *Tubastrea faulkneri*

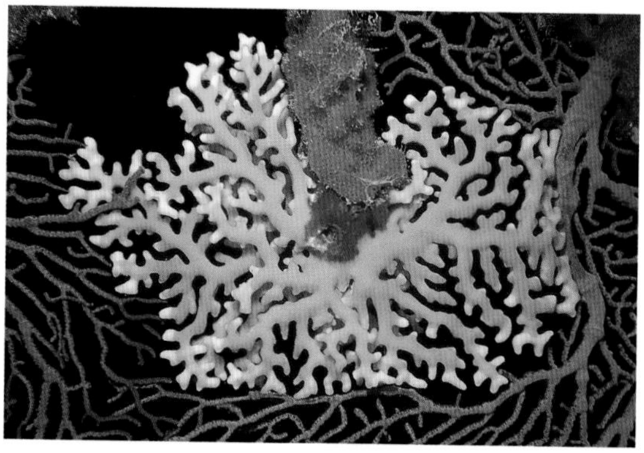

The yellow hydrocoral, *Distichopora* sp, has stinging nematocysts in its tentacles which allow it to kill and eat plankton

waters, hiding during the day beneath low ledges and under the sand. Similar to most sting-rays (the popular name for the family Dasyatidae), it has one or two highly venomous serrated barbs on its long tapering tail and can inflict painful injuries. Rays living on the sea floor usually feed on MOLLUSCS, CRUSTACEANS and other small organisms living in the sand or mud.—NC

Corals

Corals are tiny coelenterata which attach themselves to the reef, producing a knobby 'bud' that becomes a new coral, identical to its parent, continuing to divide into a colony of thousands as they mature. The coral secretes a skeleton of calcium carbonate that forms the reef structure, while the living coral animals remain as a thin surface covering, growing towards the sun, forming remarkable shapes and colours. Beneath the living veneer, the reef platform becomes a solid limestone structure that may be hundreds of metres thick. The reefs of the Pacific islands today have developed over several thousand years, growing at an average rate of about 1 m every 1000 years. Their diversity comes from a wide variety of plant and animal life, emerging from the structure created by hard reef-building corals that flourish in warm, clear tropical waters with maximum sunlight.

Hard corals have smooth tentacles with knobs at the tip, each polyp having six tentacles (or a multiple of six). Soft corals have limestone crystals in their tissues so they remain flexible, and they have eight tentacles with feathery fringes. Gorgonians are flexible, growing into long thin whiplike strands or flat, lacy fans. Mushroom corals occur singly on the sea floor, shaped like a mushroom cap, and using their tentacles to 'sail' in the currents.

Because algae grows on the surface of the reef and within the cells of coral and other invertebrates (sponges, sea anemones, MOLLUSCS and sea squirts), coral reefs produce their own nutritional requirements and are well able to sustain themselves. Sea anemones, closely related to coral, also occur singly, and grow up to 60 cm in width.—NC & KRF

Further reading

Allen, G, 1996. *Marine Life of the Pacific and Indian Oceans*, Periplus Editions.

Molluscs

The Mollusc family of sea animals are soft-bodied and usually hard-shelled. They include limpets, snails, clams, cuttlefish, octopus, oysters, mussels, and squid. Throughout the Pacific islands they are an important form of food, and their shells are valued as decorations (see BILAS), and as trade objects, especially if they are good quality collectors' items. A popular shell in tourist markets is the pearly nautilus, *Nautilus pompilius.* Mostly a deep-water dweller, it lives at depths exceeding 200 m during daylight hours, and at night it moves up the reef walls into relatively shallow water, where it preys on sleeping fish and crustaceans.

In traditional societies, many shells were used as a form of money, such as cowry shells and green sea snails (*Turbo marmorata*). The giant clam *Tridacna gigas* is the world's largest bivalve, with an adult growing to over 1 m long. Heavily poached throughout the Pacific by clam boats during the 1960s, 1970s and early 1980s, they are now sometimes farmed by islanders.—NC & KRF

Crustaceans

Crustaceans are a large class of mainly aquatic arthropods with hard shells, including crabs, crayfish, lobsters, and shrimps or prawns. Many varieties are found throughout the Pacific islands, in rivers and lakes as well as in the sea, forming an important source of food and sometimes, a significant export item. The Harlequin shrimp, *Hymenocera picta* (pictured, right), is widespread throughout the Pacific, but due to its secretive nature is seldom seen in its natural sea habitat. Normally living in pairs, the larger female and the male hunt small sea stars together.

Many kinds of crabs inhabit the coastal and swamp areas of the islands. The large robber crab climbs trees and eats COCONUTS, pandanus and galip nuts. Mud crabs, eaten by islanders, are found among mangroves and in swamps. One of the marine species that lives in a commensal relationship with large sea anemones, Oshima's porcellanid crab, *Neopetrolisthes oshimai* (pictured, bottom right), can crawl upon the venomous surface of its host sea anemone with impunity. Towards dusk, or at night when the current is running, the crab moves up to the edge of the sea anemone and sieves plankton with hairy arm-like appendages flung out in rhythmic alternation from the 'mouth'.—NC & KRF

Whales, dolphins and porpoises

Whales, dolphins and porpoises are marine mammals known as cetaceans. Baleen whales are *Mysticeti*, with plates in the roof of the mouth instead of teeth. They feed by 'sifting' plankton or fish through the bristle-like sides of these triangular plates. Their other distinguishing characteristic is that they have

Giant clam, *Tridacna gigas*

Pearly nautilus, *Nautilus pompilius*

Harlequin shrimp, *Hymenocera picta*

Oshima's porcellanid crab, *Neopetrolisthes oshimai*

two blow-holes, although the effect when they blow is usually of a single spout. The 'toothed' whales, together with dolphins and porpoises, belong to the *Odontoceti* order of sea mammals. The size, number and visibility of their teeth is related to their feeding habits—a sperm whale has 18–25 distinct thick teeth only in its lower jaw; common dolphins have two rows of 40–55 small, sharply pointed teeth; and other squid-eating species have few or no visible teeth. Toothed whales have a single external blow-hole, which may produce only a puff of vapour.

Baleen whales found in the Pacific region include the blue whale (*Balaenoptera musculus*), which is the largest living animal in the world. Found in all oceans, it roams the North Pacific, and has been recorded at more than 30 m in length. Southern right whales (*Eubalaena australis*) are found around the coasts of New Zealand, off Western Australia and around Campbell Island. Northern right whales (*Eubalaena glacialis*) are found in the northern Pacific

Bottlenose dolphin, *Tursiops truncatus*

but rarely south of Ogasawara (Bonin Islands) and grow to about 17 m. Fin whales (*Balaenoptera physalus*), around 26 m in length, are found mostly in temperate waters or nearer the poles in the warmer seasons. They roam along Japan's Pacific coast, and in parts of the southwestern Pacific. The minke whale (*Balaenoptera acutorostrata*) grows to about 10–11 m. Found throughout the world, it has been hunted in the North Pacific. The humpback whale (*Megaptera novaeangliae*) is found in the North Pacific—around the Mariana, Ogasawara and Ryukyu islands; in the Hawaiian islands; and along the Californian coast. In the South Pacific, it is found from New Zealand to Tonga and in the Coral Sea. Protected since 1964, humpbacks have been slow to recover from drastic depletion due to whaling. Growing to a length of 15–16 m, they have distinctive long pale flippers and a long thin head. Gray whales (*Eschrichtius robustus*) are found in the eastern Pacific and especially off the Californian coast. With a distinctive gray mottled body and short fins, gray whales grow to about 14 m in length.

Whale watching off Maui, Hawai'i

Toothed whales commonly seen in the Pacific Ocean include sperm whales (*Physeter macrocephalus*). Although their numbers have been reduced by former whaling, sperm whales occur around the Hawaiian Islands, in the west around the Galapagos, along the equatorial belt and near New Guinea, and throughout Polynesia. With a huge head, blunt snout, dark body and distinct dorsal hump, a sperm whale grows to 12 m (females) and 18 m (males). The pygmy sperm whale (*Kogia breviceps*) is found in temperate and tropical waters, and is often reported in strandings in the Tasman Sea and on the east coast of New Zealand as well as on the west coast of North America. Growing to a length of about 3 m, it has a sharklike, shortish head, with crescent markings behind each eye that look like gills, and flippers below them.

A number of different beaked whales are found in the Pacific. Baird's beaked whale (*Berardius bairdii*) is found in the northern seas and grows to 11–12 m. Inhabiting waters deeper than 1000 m, they live on deep-sea fish, octopus and squid and are able to submerge for up to 20 minutes at a time. They have an elongated body and a distinct curved forehead with a dolphin-like snout. Cuvier's beaked whale (*Ziphius cavirostris*) reaches an adult length of about 7 m, and has a small head with a sloping forehead ending in a short beak. The Tasman beaked whale (*Tasmacetus shepherdi*) has been seen across the South Pacific. Reaching a length of 6–7 m, it has the beaked whale's rounded forehead and dolphin-like snout. The strap-toothed whale (*Mesoplodon layardii*) reaches more than 6 m and has a dark upper body with a white underbelly. Named for the strap-shaped pair of teeth that extend upwards and curl over the upper jaw, it is found throughout the southern temperate and tropical oceans. Gray's beaked whale (*Mesoplodon grayi*) occurs in southern temperate latitudes and has been frequently reported in New Zealand waters. Growing to about 6 m in length, it has a small head with a long narrow beak. Hector's beaked whale (*Mesoplodon hectori*) occurs in both the North and South Pacific. Growing to about 4 m, it has a lighter-coloured underbelly and a pair of mandibular teeth located near the tip of the lower jaw.

In the group known as oceanic dolphins are the melon-headed whales (*Peponocephala electra*) which grow to about 2.7 m in length and have a rounded (melon-shaped) head, white lips, long pointed flippers and a high dorsal fin. Found in tropical and subtropical oceans, usually in herds of more than 150, the species has been sighted in the central Pacific and around Hawai'i. Similar in size and shape to melon-headed whales, the pygmy killer whales (*Feresa attenuata*) are found in the central and eastern Pacific and around Hawai'i. They also have white lips but they are distinguished by their colouring—a dark brownish cape on their backs and a white patch on the underbelly—as well as by rounded tips on their flippers. Killer whales (*Orcinus orca*) grow to about 7 m (females) and 9.5 m (males). They have a very prominent triangular dorsal fin, and distinctive black and white markings including white patches above and behind the eyes and white lines curving across the flanks. Living in pods of up to 30, killer whales occur throughout the Pacific Ocean at all times of the year.

■ *Dolphins* Dolphins found in the Pacific Ocean include the rough-toothed dolphin (*Steno bredanensis*), which is frequently observed in herds of about 50 animals, occasionally in proximity to bottlenose dolphins, or yellowfin TUNA. Found in deep water in tropical and warm temperate seas, rough-toothed dolphins are distinguished by their sloping forehead, long slender beak and slim body with relatively long flippers and wide flukes. Growing to about 2.75 m, the body is often covered with whitish blotches, and the lips and tip of snout are white. Dusky dolphins (*Lagenorhynchus obscurus*) occur in warm and cold temperate waters of the southern Pacific Ocean, especially off Argentina and in New Zealand waters. Lacking a prominent beak, it is distinguished by its back-sloping two-toned dorsal fin and horizontal dark pointed streaks along its back. Growing to a maximum length of about 2 m, dusky dolphins—in herds of up to 50—perform spectacular leaps and somersaults and have been known to dive about 150 m. Pacific white-sided dolphins (*Lagenorhynchus obliquidens*) occur in very large herds (up to 1000 or more) in the northern Pacific Ocean, especially along the coast of Japan. Growing to at least 2.3 m, Pacific white-sided dolphins have a short thick beak, a noticeably hooked dorsal fin that is white towards the tail, and very marked horizontal dark stripes along its back, above its white sides. An acrobatic species, a herd often leaps and churns up the sea.

As their name suggests, common dolphins (*Delphinus delphis*) occur widely throughout the world's oceans in tropical and warm temperate seas. A gregarious species found in large herds (several hundred to more than 1000 animals), they have been known to accompany both vessels and whales for long distances. Growing to a length of about 2.4 m, common dolphins are slender, streamlined animals with a long dark beak, black lips, and distinctive body colouration: a whitish chest and belly and a dark cape curving below the prominent dorsal fin. Bottlenose dolphins (*Tursiops truncatus*) also occur widely across the Pacific from northern Japan and southern California to Australia and Chile, in coastal areas as well as offshore. Usually seen in small groups (10–25 animals), the species is adaptable and apparently happy to come into close contact with human activities. Often found in aquariums and

Spinner dolphin, *Stenella longirostris*

marine parks, bottlenose dolphins are noted for their long-term frequenting of particular locations where people have been able to befriend them. They live for about 35 years. Growing to a length of 3.5–4 m, they have a short blunt beak and a rounded head, with a distinct crease at the top of the snout. The fullish body (chunkier in front of the tall dorsal fin) is dark brown with a gradual fading into the light-coloured belly.

Among the species found in tropical and warm temperate seas, often in deep water, are Fraser's dolphins (*Lagenodelphis hosei*), usually in large groups of 100 up to 1000 animals. Fraser's dolphins have a stocky build about 2.5 m long, with a short beak, relatively small flippers and dorsal fin, and a distinctive wide black horizontal marking above the white belly. Risso's dolphin (*Grampus griseus*) is usually seen in herds of 25 or more (up to a few hundred animals), and grows to a length of nearly 4 m. Light grey with a darker dorsal fin and flippers, adult animals are often marked by extensive scarring and they have rounded heads with a blunt snout and no beak. The variety of spotted dolphin (*Stenella* spp) found in the Pacific Ocean reaches a length of about 2.3 m. Sometimes occurring in herds of more than 1000, spotted dolphins are often seen in the eastern tropical Pacific in much smaller groups of 50 or fewer. They are quite acrobatic animals, frequently schooling with other species including spinner dolphins, and their size and colouration varies according to geography. Those found in coastal regions tend to be larger and sturdier; in the central and western Pacific (around Hawai'i and Japan), their spots are indistinct, but those found off the North American coasts have noticeable spotting, which increases with age. They have a long beak, a slightly sloping forehead and often have white lips. Spinner dolphins—long-snouted (*Stenella longirostris*) and short-snouted (*Stenella clymene*)—are often found among spotted dolphins as well as with herds of smaller whales. Occurring in herds of about 200 animals up to more than 1000, they are a playful, agile species. Feeding on fish and squid, they dive to depths of more than 60 m. Growing to a length of a little over 2 m, spinner dolphins have long slim beaks and sleek bodies. In the Hawaiian and short-snouted varieties, their colouration—dark grey back, lighter brown-grey sides and paler, whitish belly—is well defined.

■ *Porpoises* Among porpoises found in the Pacific Ocean are the harbour porpoise (*Phocoena phocoena*) which occurs in temperate and sub-arctic waters of the northern hemisphere. In the northern Pacific, this species has been observed along North American and Japanese coastal areas and especially off Alaska. The harbour porpoise grows to about 2 m in length and has a stocky body, no forehead or snout, and a small, sloping dorsal fin. Its dark grey or brown back fades to a lighter greyish-brown on its sides and a whitish belly. It is mostly found in small groups of 5–10 animals. Burmeister's porpoise (*Phocoena spinipinnis*) occurs in the southern hemisphere only and has been observed in the Pacific in the temperate coastal waters from Chile to Peru. Growing to a length of about 1.8 m, Burmeister's porpoise has a stocky body with a very low-set dorsal fin that slopes back into a blunt end. It is dark grey all over apart from a lighter grey belly. The spectacled porpoise (*Phocoena dioptrica*) occurs only in cold temperate and sub-antarctic waters of the southern hemisphere. In the Pacific it has been sighted off the coasts of Uruguay and Tierra del Fuego, and in sub-antarctic regions near New Zealand. Similar in shape to the harbour porpoise, the spectacled porpoise is longer (up to 2.2 m) and has more sharply defined colouration: a black back, with white sides, belly and flippers, and the white marking including a line over each eye. Dall's porpoise (*Phocoenides dalli*) is found only in the northern North Pacific. Growing to a length of 2.2 m, it has a small head and thick, chunky body and is mostly black with very distinct white patches on its dorsal fin and central sides and belly region. It has small pointed flippers and comparatively wide tail flukes. The finless porpoise (*Neophocaena phocaenides*) is found only in warm temperate waters of the northern coastal regions, and has been observed near Japan, sometimes in herds of up to 50 animals. Pale greyish in colour, it is slender-bodied with a rounded head, no beak and no dorsal fin. Growing to about 1.9 m in length, the finless porpoise is a coastal and riverine species.—KRF

Source/further reading

Leatherwood, S and Reeves, R R, 1987. *The Sierra Club Handbook of Whales and Dolphins*, Sierra Club Books.

Sea lion

Hooker sea lions (*Phocarctos hookeri*) once roamed the coasts of the Pacific Ocean. They were plentiful around the shores of New Zealand, off California, and around the coasts of Peru and Chile. By the 19th century they were being systematically pursued by British and American sealers and the species was in danger of extinction. Fur seals (*Arctocephalus forsteri*) and an endemic species of sea lion (*wollebacki*) survive in the GALAPAGOS ISLANDS.

Sizeable Hooker sea lion colonies still exist in the CHATHAM ISLANDS and the remote sub-Antarctic Auckland Islands, about 400 km south of New Zealand. Protected over the last 150 years, their isolation has allowed their population to reach 11–15 000. In early 1998 a mysterious disease appeared to be responsible for killing thousands of pups. It appeared unlikely that the cause was a virus (although a distemper-like virus has been responsible for thousands of deaths of seals in the North Sea, the Mediterranean and on African coasts) because viruses tend to affect only one species, and in the Auckland Islands, fur seals have also been found dead. The remaining possibilities are a bacterial infection or a biotoxin, since poisonous neurotoxins can be emitted by some marine algae, and during EL NIÑO periods the algae can multiply rapidly.—KRF

Dugong

The dugong (*Dugonidae*) is a large sea cow, the only member of the order Sirenia to be found in the Pacific islands. It ranges from the Ryukyu Islands in the north, through the Philippines and Palau, south to Papua New Guinea and Torres Strait and east to Solomon Islands, New Caledonia and Vanuatu. Adult dugong grow to a length of about 2.5–3 m and may live about 75 years. Fairly slow-moving, the dugong lives in the shallow waters surrounding many island groups in this region, feeding at night on the seagrasses which grow in the tropical Indo–Pacific waters. It is probable that dugongs originally occurred in this region broadly coincident with the distribution of their seagrass food, and that present-day dugongs in the islands are relict populations. The evidence for this is largely anecdotal and it is likely that densities were always low in the waters of islands surrounded by only a narrow band of shallow water.

The western islands of Torres Strait, however, surrounded by a vast underwater plain which includes more than 16 000 sq km of seagrass-supporting habitat, may be the most important dugong habitat in the world. Based an aerial survey in 1996, the Torres Strait region is estimated to support a population of some 28 000 dugongs. This may even underestimate the number actually present, because the correction for animals which are unseen due to water turbidity is conservative; and not all the available habitat can be surveyed for logistical reasons. Not surprisingly, the cultural and dietary value of dugongs is also most developed in the Torres Strait region where it is estimated that close to 1000 dugongs per year are hunted in the most culturally important indigenous fishery in the region.

The various causes of dugong mortality are poorly documented in most other areas of the Pacific islands. However, there are persistent reports from many countries of accidental drownings in fishers' gill nets and traps. Subsistence hunting is widespread although the dugong is now legally protected in most Pacific island countries. Solitary dugongs have become a tourist attraction in two locations in Vanuatu, and the dugong has become an icon of the conservation movement in Okinawa (Ryukyus).—HM

Dugong

Further reading

Bryden, M M, Marsh, H and Shaughnessy, P, 1998. *Dugongs, Whales, Dolphins and Seals: a guide to the sea mammals of Australasia*, Allen and Unwin.

Marsh, H and Lefebvre, L W, 1994. 'Sirenian status and conservation efforts', *Aquatic Mammals*.

Turtles

Turtles are REPTILES of the order Chelonia, also called the Testudines or Testudinata. Their evolutionary history has been traced back to the age of dinosaurs and they may be considered living fossils. There are approximately 250 species of turtles found worldwide from the tropics to temperate regions, in terrestrial, freshwater, and marine habitats. Most of these are found in North America and Southeast Asia, with only a few species in the Pacific islands region. Papua New Guinea supports 9 or 10 freshwater species, however, and the Galapagos Islands have 11 subspecies of the giant land tortoise, including the well-known *Geochelone nigra*.

Of the world's seven species of sea turtle, however, five are widespread throughout Oceania. The green turtle (*Chelonia mydas*) is a herbivore found in shallow water reefal habitats where abundant seagrass and algae provide forage. Together with the spongivorous hawksbill turtle (*Eretmochelys imbricata*), it is the most commonly encountered species both at feeding grounds and on nesting beaches in the tropical Pacific. Loggerhead turtles (*Catetta caretta*) are carnivores, feeding on MOLLUSCS and other invertebrates. The leatherback turtle (*Dermochelys coriacea*) is the largest of all turtles. It is a pelagic animal feeding on jellyfish and other soft-bodied animals.

Both loggerhead and leatherback turtles are known to the residents of many islands but are rarely observed nesting. The small olive Ridley (*Lepidochelys olivacea*) is rarely sighted within the islands region and its nesting is limited to Papua New Guinea.

Most turtles, including all the marine species, grow slowly and live for a long time. In addition, marine turtles migrate long distances between feeding and breeding areas, often crossing international boundaries. They take several decades to reach maturity. Adults breed once every 2–7 years and the

Green turtle, *Chelonia mydas*, nesting

Young hawksbill turtle, *Eretmochelys imbricata*

Leatherback turtle, *Dermochelys coriacea*, (largest of all turtles) nesting

Loggerhead turtle, *Caretta caretta*, nesting

proportion of mature turtles breeding in any year is influenced by a number of environmental parameters related to food availability. These characteristics, and the fact that most of their lives are spent at sea, makes monitoring, management and conservation of populations difficult.

Sea turtles feature prominently in the myths and legends of the indigenous people of Oceania, and turtles have provided food, tools and ornaments. Many rules, rituals and traditional ownership patterns have developed to govern and regulate the hunting and consumption of turtles and to ensure their sustainable use. In recent decades, however, persistent over-harvesting of eggs, and of both immature and mature turtles, especially nesting females, has caused a significant decline in numbers of sea turtles in the region. The number of hawksbill turtles especially has diminished over the last few decades and that species is now rapidly approaching extinction. Effective conservation will require a change in perceptions and behaviour toward the harvesting of sea turtles. In addition to mortality directly caused by humans, increasing numbers of sea turtles throughout their range suffer from the poorly understood but debilitating and most often fatal fibropapilloma disease. The cause of the disease is not known, but appears to be associated with terrestrial runoff from areas of intense agriculture and urbanization. No measures are within reach for the prevention and treatment of this disease.—EG

Further reading

Hirth, H F, 1993. 'Marine turtles', in A Wright and L Hill (eds), *Nearshore Marine Resources of the South Pacific*, Forum Fisheries Agency and ICOD.

Limpus, C J, 1995. 'Global overview of the status of marine turtles: a 1995 viewpoint', in K A Bjorndal (ed.), *Biology and Conservation of Sea Turtles*, Smithsonian Institution Press.

Ocean trenches

A major geological feature of the Pacific Ocean is that the sea floor has nearly linear ocean deeps around much of its periphery (Figure 1.1). The typical ocean depth is about 5 km, but in these trenches the sea floor plunges down to twice this depth, falling away nearly 11 km below sea level in the Mariana Trench, south of Guam and east of the Philippines. The Kermadec Trench, east of Norfolk Island, is another. Their lengths are of the order of thousands of kilometres, whereas their width is only about 100 km. The Peru-Chile Trench is about 4500 km long and the Tonga Trench is deeper than 9 km over a distance of about 700 km. Profiles of

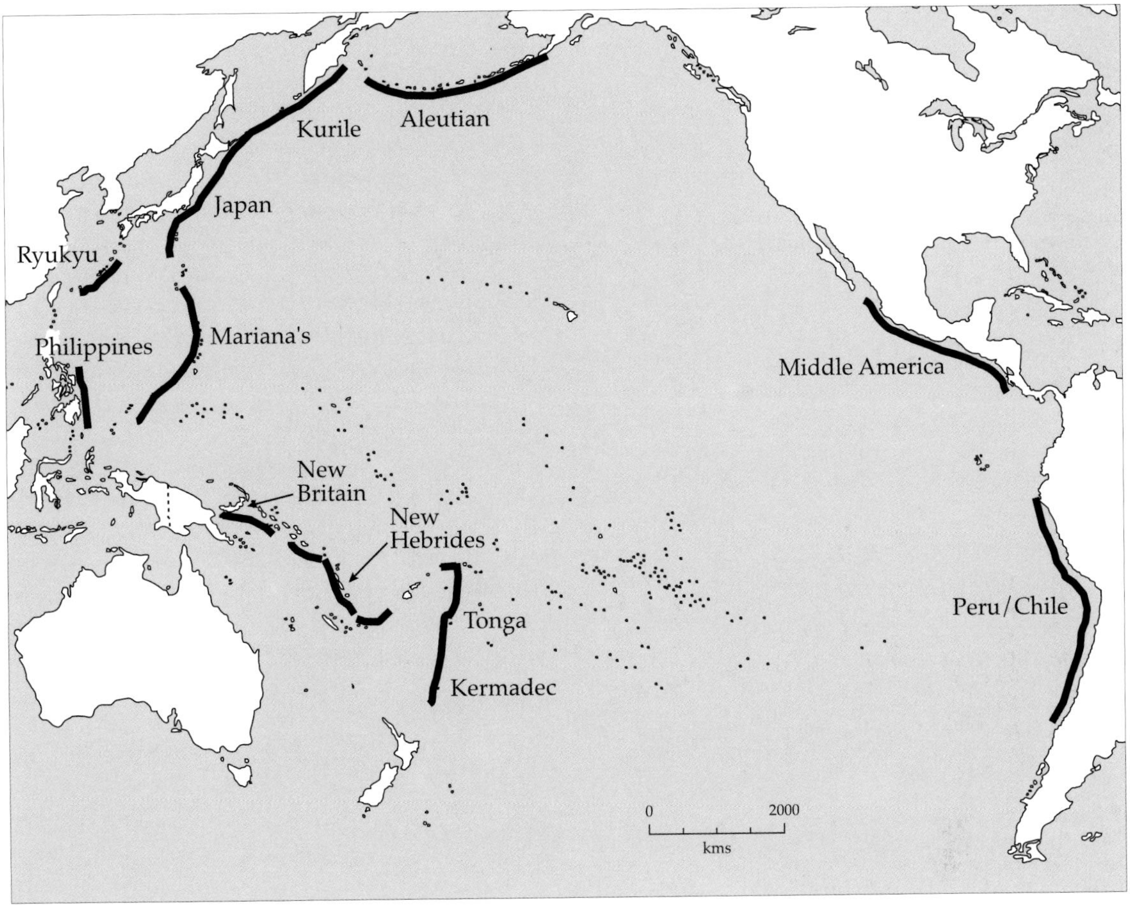

Figure 1.1 The 5, 8 and 10 km bathymetric contours of the Pacific Basin illustrating the locations of the major trench systems

bathymetry across the trenches have a characteristic asymmetrical V-shaped pattern (Figure 1.3) and exhibit a considerable uniformity from one trench to the next.

The trenches are the surface expression of that part of the plate tectonics process known as subduction. Here the oceanic crust and lithosphere (the upper 50–70 km of the Earth that behaves approximately as a strong elastic layer) sinks into the mantle (Figure 1.2). This subduction is the response to buoyancy forces and to compressive forces acting within the lithosphere that are driven by mantle convection. The gentler sloping wall of the trench marks the down-thrusting lithosphere and the steeper wall marks the overriding plate. Sediments collect in the trench but do not accumulate in great quantity, being transported into the mantle along with the lithospheric plate. The trenches, therefore, play an important role in recycling crustal rocks and fluids back into the mantle.

As the plate is subducted into the warmer mantle it is subjected to changes in its stress and in its temperature. If the associated bending and thermal stresses exceed the strength of the lithosphere, fracturing occurs. Much of the world's earthquake activity occurs along the trench systems, in response to these alterations and to the compressive forces. Because of the relatively steep gradients of the

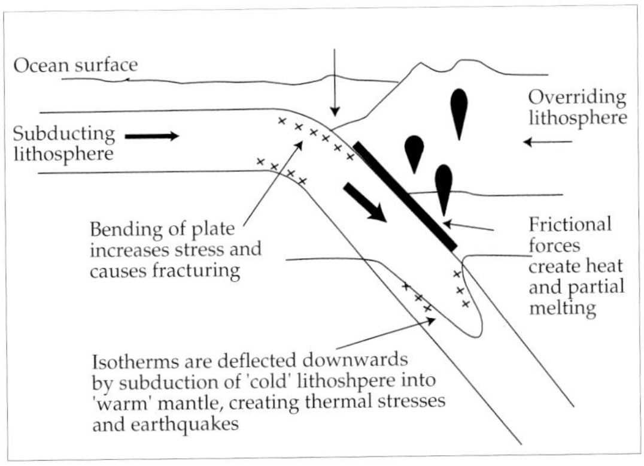

Figure 1.2 A schematic illustration of the upper mantle structure beneath the trench, showing the subducting and overriding lithospheric plates and the location of earthquake and volcano occurrences (not to scale)

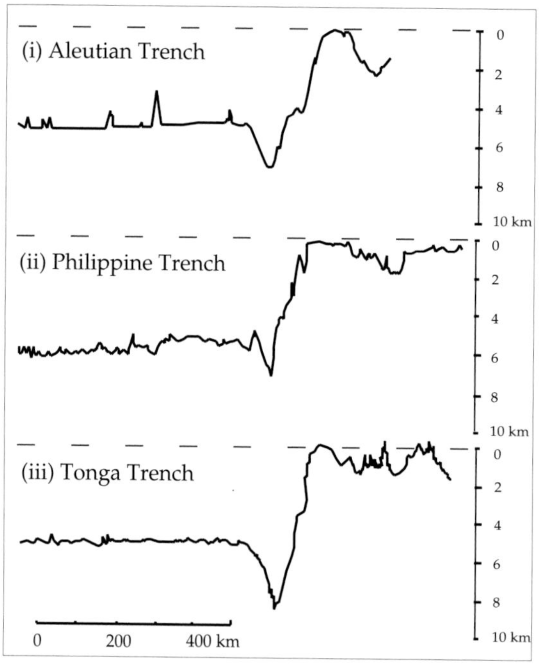

Figure 1.3 Three bathymetric profiles across ocean trenches: (i) Aleutian Trench, (ii) Philippines Trench, (iii) Tonga Trench. In all three, the ocean basin is on the left-hand side and the island groups behind the trench are on the right-hand side. It is the lithosphere on the ocean side that is being subducted. The small short wavelength variations on the ocean sites are small submarine volcanoes, one of which is about to disappear into the Philippine Trench

trench walls and the earthquake activity below the trenches, submarine landslides can occur. These can be large enough to displace large volumes of water and create TSUNAMI. Frictional forces between the subducting and overriding pieces of lithosphere generate heat which, when combined with the fluids being subducted along with the sediments, results in some melting of the deeper rocks and in subsequent volcanism. As a consequence, much of the major volcanism occurs in the overriding part of the plate at a distance of up to a few hundred kilometres from the trench (Figure 1.2).—KL

Minerva Reefs

The Minerva Reefs, two large reefs 402 km southwest of Tongatapu, were originally beyond the western international boundary of Tonga as defined by King George TUPOU I in 1887. They were known and occasionally visited by Tongan fishermen, however, possibly for generations before European contact. Formerly called Nicholson's Shoal, they were renamed after the wreck there of an Australian whaling vessel, *Minerva*, in 1829.

In 1962 a Tongan-owned and crewed boat, *Tuaikaepau*, on its way to Auckland was wrecked on one of the outcrops of the Minerva Reefs. After being stranded for 102 days, the emaciated survivors (most of the crew) were found by the Royal New Zealand Air Force and brought to Nukuʻalofa, where they were warmly welcomed as they were taken from the wharf to be received by Queen SĀLOTE. After this incident, the Tongan government later erected a platform and placed beacons as a guide for shipping in the area, and in 1972, attempted to clarify the issue of the reefs' legal status by official 'annexation', basing the claim on traditions of ancient Tongan exploitation of the reefs. The nations of the SOUTH PACIFIC FORUM subsequently recognized the Tongan annexation, and the reefs were renamed Teleki-tonga and Teleki-tokelau. Later, in the wake of the Law of the Sea agreements (INTERNATIONAL LAW AND THE PACIFIC OCEAN), Fiji challenged the Tongan annexation because of the implications for extending the Tongan Exclusive Economic Zone (EEZ) into what otherwise might have been Fijian EEZ.—KRF & ICC

Further reading

Campbell, I C, 1992. *Island Kingdom: Tonga ancient and modern,* Canterbury University Press.

TWO THE LAND

Geological history of the Pacific

The Pacific is the world's largest ocean, representing about 30 per cent of the Earth's surface area. The Pacific Basin is a geologically young feature, the age of the sea floor rarely exceeding 100 million years, compared with ages greater than 1000 million years for parts of the bordering continents and with about 4500 million years for the age of the Earth. The margins of the basin are characterized by OCEAN TRENCHES with their associated earthquakes and volcanoes. In the interior of the basin lies a submarine mountain range rising from the average sea floor depth of about 5 km to within about 2 km of the surface. This ridge system runs from near Macquarie Island south of New Zealand, to Easter Island and on to the Gulf of California with bifurcations to the Galapagos Islands and to Central America and Ecuador. In some instances this ridge extends to the surface of the oceans as isolated volcanic islands or groups of islands, for example Easter Island. The ocean basin floor also contains broad topographic 'swells' which stand up to 2 km above the surrounding sea floor and are accentuated by volcanic structures, many of which rise above sea level. The Hawaiian swell and islands is one example of this; another is the Tuamotu swell. The ocean basin con-

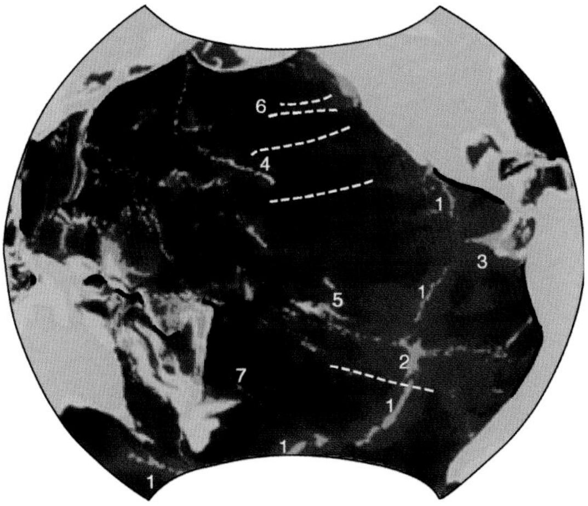

Figure 1.4 Bathymetry of the Pacific Basin. Water depth deepens from pale to dark shades. Major features are the ocean ridges (1); the ocean swells (4=Hawaiian swell), (5=Tuamotu swell); submerged volcanic island chains (7=Liouville chain); and ocean trenches, the dark narrow features (see also Figure 1.1, OCEAN TRENCHES). Some of the major fracture zones are shown by the dashed lines including the Mendocino and Pioneer fracture zones at 6. Easter Island (2) is at the intersection of the ridge system with the Easter fracture zone to the east and the Tuamotu swell to the west. The Galapagos Islands are at 3

tains many other volcanic structures, most of which do not reach the ocean surface. Other characteristic features of the Pacific Basin are long linear fracture zones, orthogonal to the ridge system and trending parallel to some of the chains of volcanic islands. These zones ordinarily separate regions of sea floor with different depths. Figures 1.4 and 1.5 illustrate the various features: Figure 1.4 their locations and Figure 1.5 some characteristic bathymetric profiles across them.

These geological features of the Pacific are the surface expressions of mantle convection and plate tectonics and are witness to a turbulent Earth. The ridges are giant cracks in the ocean lithosphere (the cold, relatively rigid outer layer of the Earth) where mantle magma descends to the sea floor and, upon cooling, forms new lithosphere pushing the older material apart. The cracks re-form and new magma rises, continuing the process. Over time, the lithosphere on the two sides of the magma-injection line moves apart and its age, measured since the time of solidification of the magma, increases with its growing distance from the ridge axis. This is the process of sea floor spreading, the rates of which can be measured by precise geodetic positioning methods. Observed values are typically of the order of a few centimetres per year. The East Pacific Ridge spreading rate, exceeding 10 cm per year, is one of the fastest recorded. The molten material is lighter than the surrounding cooler material and it is forced up to heights above the 'normal' sea floor depth. As the lithosphere moves away from the ridge crest, the newly injected magma slowly cools and contracts, leaving the characteristic ridge profile illustrated in Figure 1.5(i). Any volcanic peaks formed on the ridge or its flanks also subside with time.

As the sea floor expands at the ridge axis, so it is subducted at the ocean trenches. This latter process occurs where the newly created lithosphere has cooled sufficiently for it to lose much of its buoyancy when pushed along by the spreading process. It tends to sink back into the underlying mantle. The rates of convergence at the trenches can be measured, reaching rates of 10 cm per year. The large fracture zones, whose characteristic bathymetric signal across them is illustrated in Figure 1.5(iii), are mainly a geometrical by-product of the combination of sea floor spreading and subduction of irregular shaped plates on a spherical planet. Figure 1.4 illustrates the locations of only some of these fractures.

Ocean swells are created by heating of the lithosphere from underneath by rising mantle convection currents, or plumes. The associated thermal expansion causes a swelling of the sea floor and, where

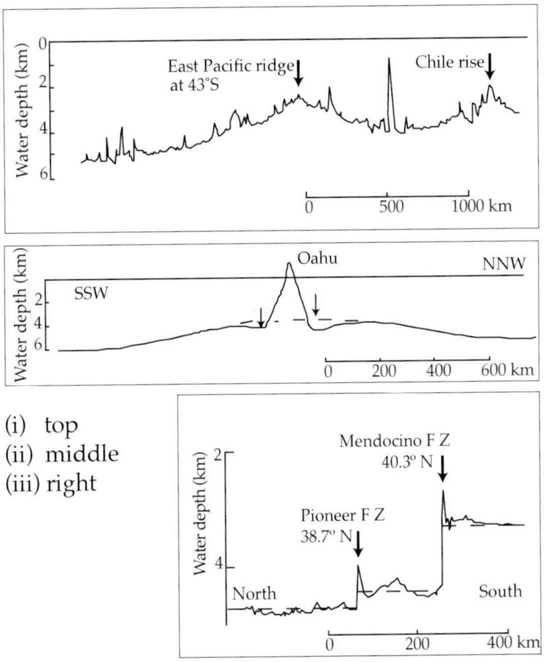

Figure 1.5 Characteristic bathymetric signals across (i) submerged ocean ridges, (ii) ocean swells, and (iii) fracture zones. In (i) the main ridge system is the East Pacific Rise but the section crosses a second spreading axis to the west of Chile. In (ii) the small arrows identify the moat superimposed on the broader sea floor swell that is created by the flexure of the lithosphere. In (iii) the bathymetric profile runs north–south across two fracture zones (FZ). Note the different scales used for the three profiles

cracks in the lithosphere develop, large volcanic complexes form. The mantle plumes are relatively stable, but because of the sea floor spreading, the lithosphere moves over them, cooling when removed from the source of heat, and volcanism ceases until a new crack forms over the stationary plume. This leaves behind a characteristic swell or wake of the plume as a gradually deepening sea floor and subsiding islands. The Hawaiian ridge forms a classic example. Figure 1.4(ii) illustrates the bathymetric cross-section across the swell at the island of O'ahu. The swell is the broad feature, about 1500 km across and up to 2 km high. Under the weight of the volcanic island of O'ahu, the crust is locally depressed forming moats around the base .

The Pacific islands, mostly formed by volcanic activity that reached the surface, record many of these plate tectonic processes. An island formed and then eroded to sea level will subside along with the sea floor as the underlying lithosphere cools. This results in the characteristic guyot, the wave-eroded volcano whose surface is now below sea level. In warmer waters coral growth may be sufficiently rapid for reef complexes to form and keep the island at sea level despite sea floor subsidence. This produces the characteristic ATOLLS of the Pacific. If the lithosphere supporting the island moves over a mantle plume, it will be uplifted, only to sink again later once it moves 'downstream' from the heat source. At some of the subduction zones the lithosphere tends to flex upwards. Islands riding towards the trench will first experience an uplift before being destroyed in the subduction processes. The rates of these movements, fortunately, are small.

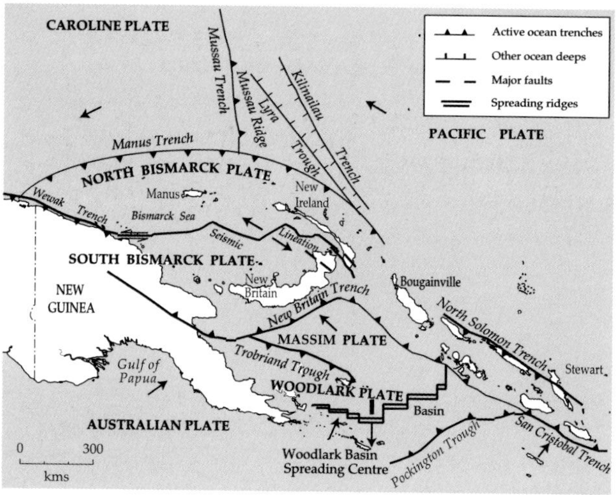

Figure 1.6 Papua New Guinea plates

In some parts of the Pacific Basin the interaction of the Pacific Plate with its adjacent tectonic blocks or plates becomes quite complex. An example of this occurs in the Papua New Guinea region where the Pacific and Australian plates converge (Figure 1.6). Here the deformation occurs over a broad zone, extending from east of New Ireland into the Papuan Highlands, with small pieces of lithosphere jostling each other as they are squeezed between the Pacific and Australian Plates. Within this area, the subduction of the Solomon Sea lithosphere beneath New Britain and Solomon Islands and Bougainville has associated with it major earthquake and seismic activity. Sea floor spreading occurs in the southern part of the Solomon Sea (the Woodlark Spreading Centre) and along short segments in the Bismarck Sea. Major faults extend into the Papuan mainland. Measurements indicate that horizontal movements occur at rates of up to 10 cm per year and the region as a whole is a microcosm of the tectonics that occur on a Pacific scale.—KL

■ *Atolls* Atolls consist of a narrow annular rim of coral reef surrounding a central lagoon which commonly reaches depths of 30–50 m. On the atoll rim there may be reef islands, either sandy cays or shingle motu (islets) that rarely reach more than 2–3 m above sea level and form the 'garlands in the sea' which are so obvious when flying over in an aircraft, but were described in those terms by Charles Darwin from the deck of the *Beagle* over 150 years ago.

The origin of atolls and reef islands has fascinated explorers, naturalists and scientists for more than 200 years, for both are made up exclusively of coralline materials. Therein lies a paradox. CORALS only grow to depths of around 30 m and yet coral atolls rise from the floors of the deepest ocean basins from depths of 3000–4000 m below sea level. How then have they formed? Some 19th century theorists thought the atoll perimeter represented the rim of an ancient volcano and that the lagoon represented the volcano crater. In this view, at a depth of about 30 m a geological unconformity between the overlying coralline limestone and underlying basaltic volcanic rock would be expected. Darwin thought otherwise. After seeing fossil marine shells at high altitude in the Andes mountains of South America and having crossed the Pacific Ocean with its variety of island types, Darwin argued that to counterbalance continental uplift, the ocean basins would need to subside. Atolls therefore resulted from coral growth flourishing on a continually subsiding volcanic foundation, first as fringing reefs, then as barrier reefs, and ultimately as atolls.

Typical small island vegetation: Milne Bay area, Papua New Guinea

Scientific tests of this hypothesis were initially carried out on Funafuti Atoll, Tuvalu, just over 100 years ago by three Anglo–Australian expeditions from 1896 to 1898. When coring ceased at a depth of 340 m, the drill was still in coralline limestone and not in the volcanic rocks expected. Ultimate confirmation of Darwin's 'coral reef theory' came through the post-World War II drilling into the Pacific atolls of BIKINI in 1947 and Enewetak in 1951 in the Marshall Islands where volcanics beneath limestone were reached at depths of from 410–780 m and 1283–1405 m respectively. Comparable thicknesses of limestone over basalt were found at Midway, Moruroa and Fangataufa atolls.

Of the 425 atolls in the world, most are in the Pacific though the word is Maldivian. Some Pacific countries and territories are made up entirely or predominantly of sea level atolls such as the Marshall Islands, Tuvalu, Kiribati and Tokelau, while the Tuamotus in French Polynesia has the largest concentration of atolls in the world. Some states such as Nauru or islands such as Banaba (Ocean Island) are raised atolls whose isolation and 'on the line' (equator) location provide a sought-after haven for sea birds who nest among the *Pisonia* woodlands where their droppings interact with rainwater and coral to form the rock PHOSPHATE deposits (GUANO) which are mined for superphosphate fertilizer.

Atolls have often been of strategic importance. During World War II, the Battle of Tarawa became a turning point in the Pacific conflict as the Allied forces used the atolls of the Marshall and Caroline Islands as stepping stones pushing towards the Philippines and ultimately Japan. Centuries before, if not two to three millenia ago, the recently emergent atoll islands of the central Pacific served as stepping stones in a reverse direction for the migrations of the Micronesians and Polynesians including the establishment of the first peoples on Fiji, Tonga and Samoa.

Because they are small and isolated, and perhaps because they were distant from the metropolitan powers, Pacific atolls became the focii for British, American and French atmospheric and then underground nuclear bomb testing which was carried out on the atolls of Kiritimati (Christmas Island) in Kiribati, Enewetak and Bikini in the Marshall Islands and Moruroa and Fangataufa in French Polynesia from the late 1940s to mid 1990s. In the case of the atmospheric tests in the Marshall Islands downwind atolls received doses of radiation that required the removal of people from the islands.

Atoll islands are small, young and fragile. They have a limited resource base, being made up exclusively of reef-derived materials with poor soils, low biodiversity and a groundwater table small in quantity and poor in quality. Some atolls are subject to tropical CYCLONES; others suffer from DROUGHT. While there are many present-day problems including increasing urbanization in atoll capitals such as Funafuti, SOUTH TARAWA and MAJURO, all atoll populations are concerned about their future vulnerability to CLIMATE CHANGE and sea-level rise consequent upon global warming. Erosion of islands, inundation and sea water intrusion into groundwater lenses are just some of the potential impacts which may ultimately render the islands uninhabitable.—RMcL

Typical lagoon, Marshall Islands

High tropical mountains

The tropical Pacific lands are largely the result of crustal plate collisions that are going on to the present day, so the terrains are often extremely young and mountainous, with volcanoes in some areas. The highest mountains are formed in the Indonesian arc due to the northward movement of the Indo-Australian plate over the Pacific plate. These retain the only remnant glaciers on two mountains, Mandala (4600 m) and Carstensz (Jaya)—the highest peak on any island on Earth at 4884 m. Three other peaks over 4600 m in Irian Jaya Province had ice-caps in historical times, but the ice has retreated rapidly in the last century. On the island of New Guinea, about 2200 sq km of terrain was glaciated 18,000 years ago, with glaciers reaching down to 3050 m from the higher mountains. The only other tropical islands with clear evidence of glaciation are Kinabalu (4101 m), in Sarawak, and the giant shield volcanoes of the island of Hawai'i, such as Mauna Kea (4205 m). Other notable mountains include the high volcanoes of Sumatra, Java and Lombok (Rinjani 3726 m) and fold mountains on Sulawesi (Rantekombolo 3455 m) and Taiwan (Yu Shan 3997 m).

Tropical mountains on the true oceanic islands are less than 2000 m with the exception of some peaks on the islands of New Britain (Sinewa 2438 m), Bougainville (Balgi 2743 m) and Guadalcanal (Mt Popmanas 2447 m). The most spectacular of all is the dissected shield volcano of Tahiti (Mt Orohena 2241 m, on an island with a diameter of only 30 km). On the much larger islands of Vanuatu (Tabwensava 1879 m), Samoa (Silisili 1858 m), New Caledonia (Panie 1628 m), and Fiji (Tomanivi 1323 m), the mountain peaks are lower, possibly because they are older and have been eroded.

Mt Carstensz (Jaya) in Irian Jaya, from the north

The tropical mountains are mostly very wet, with maximum precipitation often reaching 12 000 mm per year on the windward side between 600 m and 2500 m altitude. Rainfall may reduce gradually above this, but even the summits in New Guinea receive over 2500 mm. Strong daily uplift forms clouds by mid-morning so that evaporation is low. Soils vary, but at temperatures below about 10°C, organic matter breaks down slowly and peaty soils form. These changes lead to characteristic zonation in the vegetation cover, from liane and palm-rich lowland broad-leaved forest to montane forests with reducing leaf size and stature, few lianes but increasing loads of epiphytes such as moss and ORCHIDS. Around 3000 m altitude, subalpine forests (often with conifers and abundant tree ferns, and leaf lengths averaging 1–2 cm) replace the montane forests, reaching irregular tree lines as high as 4000 m on limestone soils. Above this there is a

Mt Wilhelm, highest mountain in Papua New Guinea, with snow

shrub-rich subalpine zone of grasses and shrubs which is replaced by true alpine tundra-like herbfields and grasslands on the summits. The zonations are variable, and isolated mountains close to the sea often display zonation boundaries at much lower altitudes, being topped by a low shrubland on exposed summits.

Compared with African and Andean tropical mountains, the Pacific mountains are much more humid and equable. Strangely, this humidity has restricted tuber growing to a zone below 2500 m and mostly below 2200 m, because of insufficient sunlight. Very intense agriculture is found in intermontane basins in New Guinea, where local cloud formation creates sunny valley centres. These areas, at an altitude of around 1500 m, support over 1 million inhabitants. Other highland areas are utilized as hunting grounds, and extensive grasslands have built up during the last 10 000 years due to fire.—GH2

Volcanic activity

The Pacific region has the highest density of volcanoes on earth, and most islands owe their existence to a long history of volcanic activity. Within the region, more than 250 volcanoes have experienced activity since the first visits by Europeans (Table 1.1). Eruptions have varied from small-magnitude events causing little or no concern, such as Yasur, Vanuatu, to large-magnitude, CATACLYSMIC ERUPTIONS that have resulted in the loss of many lives, such as Mt Lamington, Papua New Guinea, in 1951. Because of the large number of volcanoes and the frequency of eruptions, evaluation and management of volcanic hazards and their effects is of major concern.

Although many islands within the central Pacific have not experienced eruptions in the recent past, geological studies indicate that the majority of the islands have been formed during extended prehistoric periods of volcanic activity. Many coralline ATOLLS are remnants of large volcanic complexes with all signs of activity long since eroded. Several volcanoes (such as Macdonald, French Polynesia) have erupted in recent times.

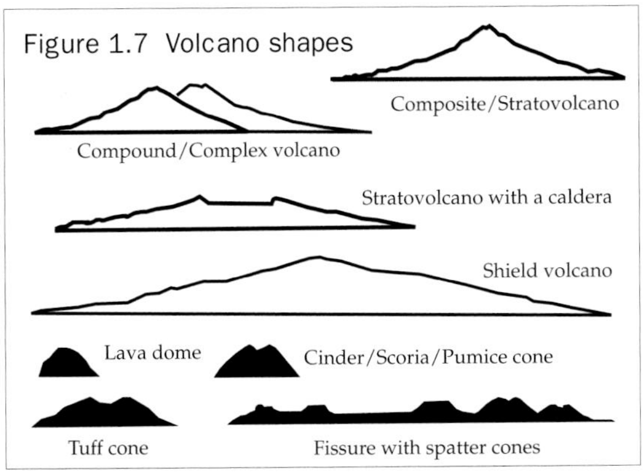

Figure 1.7 Volcano shapes

Because of the diverse geologic environments in the region, volcanoes take many forms. Figure 1.7 shows a number of known volcanic structures. Perhaps the most common structures in the countries that rim the Pacific are the composite/strato, compound/complex and volcanoes with a caldera. Late (Tonga) and Lopevi (Vanuatu) are typical composite/stratovolcanoes that are composed of interbedded lava flows and tephra layers. Langila (Papua New Guinea) and Soretimeat (Vanuatu) are typical of compound/complex volcanoes, composed of a number of stratovolcanoes that have coalesced. Calderas, sometimes filled with lakes, are also common features on many volcanoes. They have been formed during the partial collapse of the central part of the volcano during large magnitude eruptions. Pago and Dakataua (Papua New Guinea), *East Epi* (Vanuatu), and Tofua (Tonga) are typical of volcanoes with calderas. Shield volcanoes, on the other hand, dominate the volcanic structures in the central Pacific. Fernandina and Volcan Wolf (Galapagos), Mauna Loa and Kīlauea (Hawai'i), and Savai'i (Samoa) are typical shield volcanoes. Other structures may be formed during an individual eruption of a volcano (Figure 1.7). Lava domes have been formed at Metis Shoal (1995, Tonga) and at Mt Lamington (1951, Papua New Guinea). Fissure vents and rows of smaller craters have formed during effusive eruptions of Kīlauea (1983–present, on Hawai'i), Niuafo'ou (1929, Tonga) and during the Matavanu eruption (1905–11, on Savai'i). Pyroclastic (cinder, scoria, pumice or tuff) cones have been formed during the eruption of Vulcan (Rabaul, Papua New Guinea, 1937), Waiowa (Papua New Guinea) and Niuafo'ou (1886, Tonga).

Volcanoes may exist as subaerial structures, commonly forming the island chains typical of Solomon Islands, Vanuatu and Tonga or of the central Pacific islands, including Hawai'i, Galapagos and Samoa. They may also occur as submarine volcanoes that erupt below the sea, occasionally building a structure that may appear above the surface, such as Kavachi (Solomon Islands) and Metis Shoal and Falcon Island (Tonga). Frequently, these structures are quickly eroded by the waves. During some submarine eruptions, large pumice rafts are formed, such as Curacoa (1973, Tonga).

The products of erupting volcanoes are also quite diverse, with the most common being lava and tephra. Two types of lava flows produced during effusive eruptions are known. 'Aa' flows are commonly thick and blocky, moving only a short distance from the vent. This type has been reported during eruptions at Bagana (Papua New Guinea) and during explosive phases of the 1946 eruption of Niuafo'ou (Tonga). The second type of lava flow is 'pahoehoe', meaning ropy, typified by the voluminous flows during the eruption of Kīlauea (Hawai'i). Tephra (fragmental or pulverised volcanic material), is produced during explosive eruptions. Tephra may occur as columns that are ejected vertically, sometimes to heights of 10–15 km above the vent. The tephra is then dispersed radially away from the volcano under the effect of prevailing winds, depositing regionally extensive tephra deposits, such as the tephra column produced during the 1994 eruption of Vulcan (Papua New Guinea), which reached 20 km above the earth's surface, with thick deposits of tephra being deposited to the north and west of Rabaul. Tephra is also ejected horizontally as pyroclastic flows which are concentrated mixtures of volcanic gases and tephra, and are perhaps the most destructive volcanic phenomena. Disastrous pyroclastic flows were produced during the 1567–68 eruptions at Savo, Solomon Islands, the 1951–56 eruptions, of Mt Lamington, and the 1991 eruption of Mt Pinatubo (Philippines). Ballistic ejecta, or blocks of solid volcanic material ejected during explosive eruptions, have also been reported. Such

Table 1.1 Volcanoes and volcanic eruptions

	Number of volcanoes	Number of recorded eruptions
Galapagos	15	61
Hawai'i	10	114
Samoa	7	5
Tonga	11	59
Vanuatu	19	140
Solomon Islands	9	43
Papua New Guinea	56	88
Philippines	55	59
Mariana Islands	14	53
Ryukyu/Bonin Islands	30	251

Note: Recorded eruptions refers to periods of activity since European contact.
Source: Simkin and Seibert, 1994.

blocks were ejected to a distance of 1.5 km from the vent during the 1994 eruption of Tavurvur (Rabaul, Papua New Guinea). Other phenomena that occur during eruptions include the release of volcanic gasses, earthquakes, ground subsidence and volcanically generated TSUNAMI, as in the collapse of Ritter Island (Papua New Guinea). Volcanic activity and its associated phenomena are mentioned in the oral traditions of many Pacific cultures.—PWT

Further reading

Blong, R J, 1982. *The Time of Darkness: local legends and volcanic reality in Papua New Guinea*, Australian National University Press.

Simkin, T and Siebert, L, 1994. *Volcanoes of the World: a regional directory, gazetteer, and chronology of volcanism during the last 10 000 years*, Geoscience Press.

Taylor, P W, 1995. 'Myths, legends and volcanic activity: an example from northern Tonga', *The Journal of the Polynesian Society*, 104(3).

—— (ed.), forthcoming. *Volcanic Hazards and Emergency Management in the Southwest Pacific*, SOPAC Technical Bulletin.

■ *Volcanoes of Hawai'i* The best known and most active Pacific volcanoes are found in the Hawaiian islands, especially on Hawai'i. Although geological studies indicate that the entire island chain, from Hawai'i to Kure, 2400 km to the northwest (Figure 1.8), is of volcanic origin, only the islands of Hawai'i and Maui have experienced eruptions in historic times. At least 10 volcanoes have been active since the islands were sighted by Captain James COOK in 1778. Of these, Kīlauea and Mauna Loa, on Hawai'i, have been the most active. Manua Loa has experienced at least 39 periods of activity and Kīlauea, its close neighbour, has erupted at least 63 times. Eruptive activity at Haleakalā on Maui was reported in 1790, and recent submarine eruptions (1986 and 1996) have been reported at Lō'ihi, off the south coast of Hawai'i. Although the volcanic structures observed on the islands of Kaho'olawe, Lāna'i, Moloka'i, O'ahu, Kaua'i and Ni'ihau suggest recent activity, no records of eruptions are known.

The eruption of Kīlauea that began in January 1983 is still continuing at the vent of Pu'u 'O'o on the East Rift Zone. The dominantly effusive activity has produced extensive lava flows, adding more than 223 hectares of new land along the south coast (Figure 1.9). This eruption has destroyed more than 150 houses and large tracts of arable land in the Royal Gardens subdivision and along the Kamokuna, Waha'ula and Kalapana coast, causing more than US$100 million in damage to local communities.

Lava flow, Kīlauea

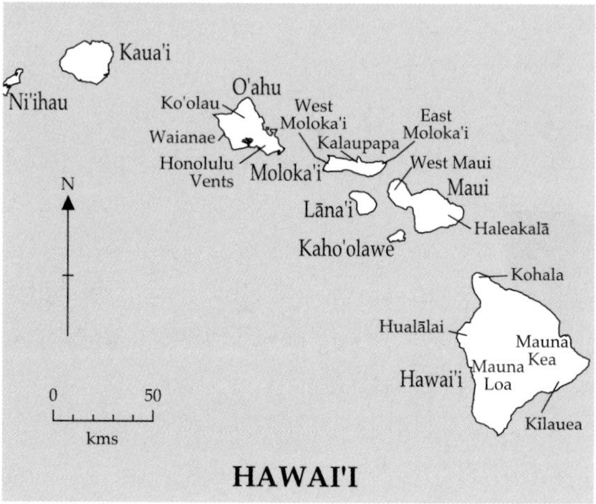

Figure 1.8 The major volcanic centres of the Hawaiian Islands. The names of the islands and volcanoes are identical for Kaho'olawe, Lāna'i, Kau'i, Ni'ihau and Kaula

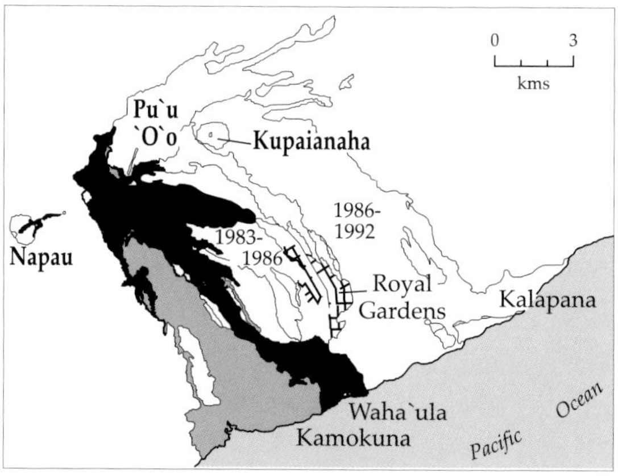

Figure 1.9 The distribution of the lava flows from the 1983–98 eruption of Kīlauea volcano. The flows that have been emplaced from January 1997 to February 1998 are black. Flows emplaced between 1983 and 1996 are stippled. Three main vents that have been active during the eruption, Pu'u 'O'o, Kupaianaha and Napau, are also shown

The volcanoes of the Hawaiian islands are predominantly lava shields built up by the voluminous outpourings of lava. The island of Hawai'i consists of the five coalescing lava shield volcanoes of Mauna Kea, Mauna Loa, Kīlauea, Hualālai and Kohala. Many of the lava shields are capped by numerous cinder/spatter cones, such as Hualālai and Mauna Kea on Hawai'i, Haleakalā on Maui and the Honolulu Vents on O'ahu, which have been formed during late-stage explosive activity. Explosive eruptions are also known to have occurred at Kīlauea during 1790 and 1924. The hot base surges that accompanied the 1790 eruption caused the deaths of an estimated 80–100 soldiers, loyal to the Hawaiian chief Keoua, who were travelling across the summit of the volcano near the vent. Few other fatalities directly linked to eruptive activity at the Hawaiian volcanoes are known. A number of fatalities are known to have occurred during earthquakes and TSUNAMI that accompanied some eruptions.

Because of the frequency of, and sometimes continuous activity at, the Hawaiian volcanoes, the United States Geological Survey maintains the Hawaiian Volcano Observatory, to study the Hawaiian volcanoes and monitor their activity. Since the observatory was founded in 1912 by Thomas A Jaggar, an extensive monitoring network has been established. Techniques and instruments that are used include visual observation, seismometers, tiltmeters, gravity meters, levelling networks, electronic distance measurements, temperature measurements and geochemical sampling.

In Hawaiian mythology, Kīlauea volcano is the home of Pele, the fire goddess, and eruptions occur when she is unhappy. These beliefs have a profound effect on many of the local communities, and many Hawaiians will warn visitors not to disturb her 'fingers'—the lava flows that have been produced. It is common to see offerings, which include full bottles of gin wrapped in ti leaves, left on the sometimes still warm lava flows, as an offering to calm her wrath.—PWT

Further reading

Decker, R W, Wright, T L and Stauffer, P H (eds), 1987. *Volcanism in Hawaii,* 2 Vols, US Geological Survey Professional Paper 1350.

Macdonald, G A, Abbott, A T and Peterson, F L, 1983. *Volcanoes of Hawaii: the geology of Hawaii,* University of Hawai'i Press.

Wood, C A and Kienle, J (eds), 1990. *Volcanoes of North America: United States and Canada,* Cambridge University Press.

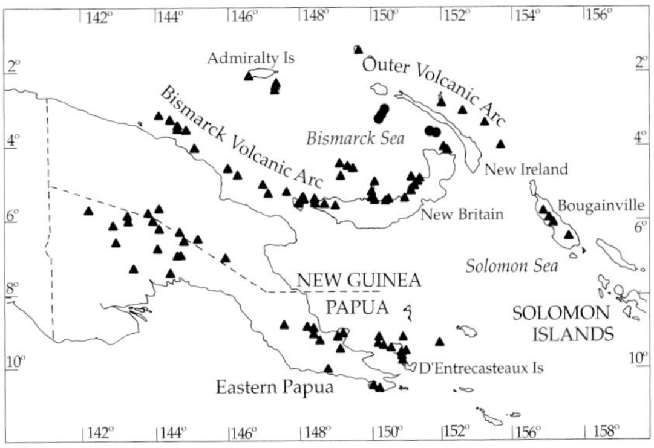

Figure 1.10 Distribution of volcanoes of Papua New Guinea. Some of the major volcanoes are shown with solid triangles, and the submarine volcanic complexes are shown with solid circles

■ *Volcanoes of Papua New Guinea* Papua New Guinea, in a geologically complex part of the southwest Pacific, comprises more than 600 islands. Volcanism has played a major role in its geological development, with at least 55 volcanic structures known to have experienced periods of activity during Holocene and historic times. Recorded activity varies from major explosive eruptions causing considerable damage and affecting large areas (such as Mt Lamington in 1951), to hot springs and mild fumarolic activity (Walo and Musa River).

There are five major volcanic regions.

- The Central Highlands comprising the large highly-dissected stratovolcanoes, such as Doma Peaks and Yelia, and the recently active volcanoes of Eastern Papua, such as Mt Lamington and Mt Victory.
- The Bismarck Volcanic Arc which comprises the volcanoes of the north coast, such as Manam, Karkar and Long Island, and the volcanoes along New Britain, such as Langila, Ulawun and Rabaul. The volcanoes of this region are by far the most frequently active with at least 165 eruptions reported during historic times from the 13 known volcanoes. Langila has been in an almost continual state of mild to moderate explosive activity since 1973. The eruptions of Manam (1996), Karkar (1979) and at Rabaul (1937 and 1994) resulted in a number of fatalities.
- The Outer Volcanic Arc comprising the volcanoes of the Admiralty Islands, such as Baluan and Tuluman, the volcanic islands along the northeast coast of New Ireland, such as Lihir and Ambittle.
- The stratovolcanoes of Bougainville island, such as Balbi and Bagana. The lava cone of Bagana has been in a state of continuous effusive to mildly explosive activity since 1972.

- The submarine volcanic complexes of the Eastern Manus Basin of the Bismarck Sea, such as Vienna Woods, Pacmanus and SuSu Knolls hydrothermal fields.

Because of the large number of active and potentially active volcanoes the government, through the Rabaul Volcanological Observatory, has established an extensive volcano monitoring network. Tremors, craters and underwater vents are monitored by 11 seismic and vulcanology observatories, using visual observation, seismometers, tiltmeters, gravity meters, levelling networks, electronic distance measurements, temperature measurements and geo chemical sampling. Data collected during the monitoring programs allow scientists to assess the current, or the potential for future, activity. Papua New Guinea has perhaps some of the richest mineral deposits in the Pacific region—the gold deposits of Ok Tedi and Porgera in the Central Highlands, and Lihir, and the extensive copper deposits at Panguna, Bougainville. (See MINING IN THE PACIFIC ISLANDS.) Most of these deposits are associated with volcanism.

Matupi (Tavurvur) at Rabaul, after an eruption in 1996

Numerous oral traditions have been recorded from the Central Highlands and the north coast of New Guinea, suggesting periods of volcanic activity many generations ago. Traditions from the Highlands have described a 'time of darkness' which may have been caused by a major volcanic event at Long Island. Other traditions from the Madang region suggest an island known as Yomba was once located off the north coast of New Guinea, but was destroyed during a large volcanic eruption.—PWT

Further reading

Johnson, R W (ed.), 1976. *Volcanism in Australasia*, Elsevier.

—— and Threlfall, N A, 1985. *Volcano Town: the 1937–43 Rabaul eruptions*, Robert Brown and Associates.

■ *Sepik River* The Sepik River is the second biggest river (1100 km) in Papua New Guinea, with a huge catchment area that begins in Sandaun (West Sepik) and Irian Jaya, and includes East Sepik, Enga, and Madang. The river's lower 900 km, to its delta on the

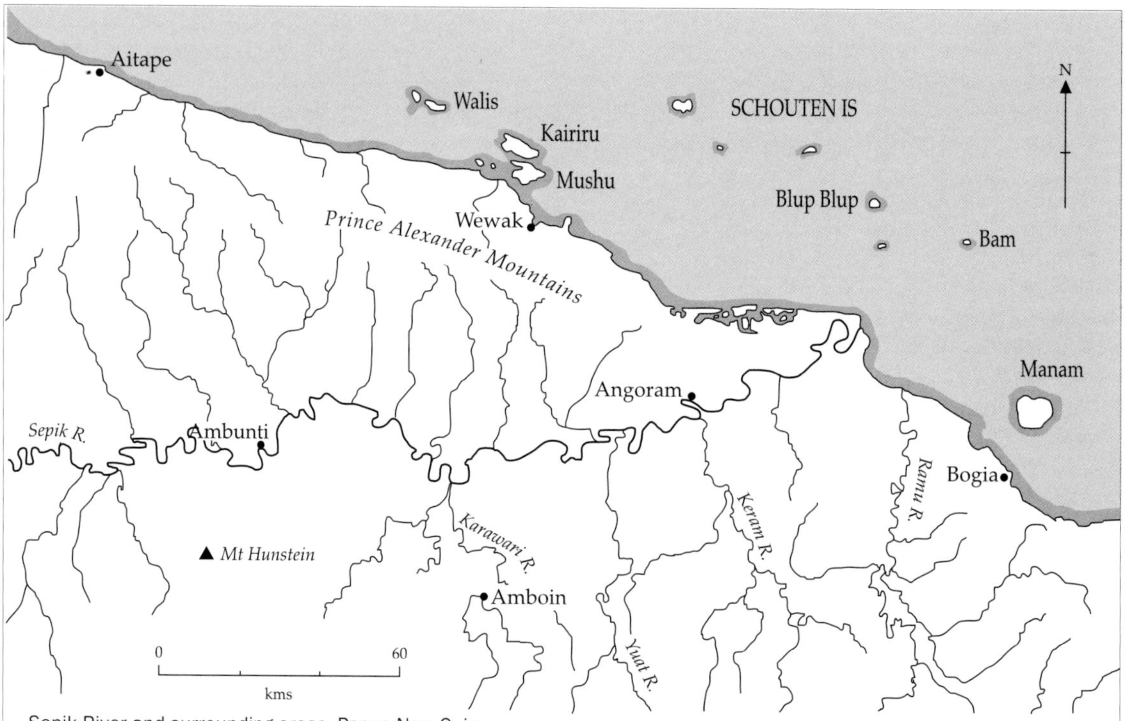

Sepik River and surrounding areas, Papua New Guinea

north coast, forms a series of twisting, serpentine loops across a broad flood plain with some 1500 small lakes, many natural and man-made canals (*barats*), and several large, permanent swamps. The Sepik basin (once a vast inland sea) is a densely populated area, and the river has offered a traditional trading route for large dugout canoes.

European exploration began in 1885, and German missions were established among the more accessible riverside settlements. From the first reports and photographs of the distinctive river villages with their towering ceremonial houses, SEPIK ART and especially the highly decorated masks and wood carvings have been in demand by the world's museums. Traders, labour recruiters, anthropologists and collectors descended on the river during the 1920s and 1930s, but the remoteness and difficult terrain of the upper reaches defied the efforts of the Australian administration until after 1946.—KRF

■ *Fly River* The Fly River in the Western Province is Papua New Guinea's longest river (1200 km), draining south from the 4000 m central cordilla and traversing 750 km before discharging into the Gulf of Papua just north of Daru in the Torres Strait. In 1893 the Dutch and British 'bent' the border between Papua and 'West New Guinea' (now Irian Jaya) for 100 km to allow for a sweep of the river across the 141st meridan. Not mapped fully until the 20th century and supporting a sparse littoral population, the river is now busy with barge traffic serving the Ok Tedi mine. Kiunga, 790 km up river, is Papua New Guinea's only major inland port. Mine wastes and pollution have affected the higher reaches and are increasing downstream. The second branch of the river, the Lagaip-Ok Om-Strickland, joins the Fly-Ok Tedi south of Lake Murray.—MQ

THREE PLANTS, BIRDS AND ANIMALS

Prehistoric plants and animals

The fowl, pig and dog are commonly said to be the only domestic creatures known to Pacific islanders. But the fowl-like megapode, which has a similar name in Sulawesi, New Guinea, Solomon Islands, Vanuatu and Niuafo'ou, Tonga, also seems likely to have been carried from place to place in early times as a source of eggs. Moreover, recent research has shown that in Polynesia alone there were three breeds of fowl, two breeds of pig, and at least two breeds of dog at the time of European contact.

The three breeds of domestic fowl were a large, heavy one ideally suited for culinary purposes; a smaller, cockfighting breed; and a tailless, rumpless breed with the capacity to lay blue-shelled eggs. The first was evidently brought to New Guinea/Melanesia from Southeast Asia many thousands of years ago and thence to Polynesia. The second was unknown in New Guinea/Melanesia and must have been carried directly from Southeast Asia to Western Polynesia. The island of Futuna seems likely to have been its point of entry and c200 BC the likely date. The blue-egg chicken was evidently carried across the Pacific from Japan to Ecuador in about 3000 BC and thence to Easter Island early in the Christian era. The first two breeds were widely dispersed in both Western and Eastern Polynesia; the blue-egg chicken only reached some Eastern Polynesian islands. Distinct vocabularies help to trace the migration paths of the three breeds.

Pigs are thought to have been introduced into New Guinea from Indonesia about 10 000 years ago. Most islands had only one breed in pre-European times, but in the western Polynesian islands of Futuna, 'Uvea, Samoa and Tonga, as well as neighbouring Rotuma, there were two. One was known as *pauka* (or a cognate term); the other was called *mo.* The first was small, long-nosed, long-legged and razor backed. It was undoubtedly the first arrival, and was carried on to eastern Polynesia. Early visitors to Tahiti described it as a Chinese breed, suggesting that it could have reached Polynesia from Taiwan where the pig is called *bauwak* in one of its disappearing Austronesia languages. The *mo* pig, which is short-nosed and squat, appears to have reached Western Polynesia (probably Futuna) from New Guinea or Melanesia where **mpoRok* and **mpoRo* are reconstructed proto-terms for pig.

Archaeologists believe that Oceanic people brought dogs to the Pacific about 4000 years ago, but they did not reach either Vanuatu or New Caledonia prehistorically, and the names for them elsewhere suggests diversity of origin and possibly diversity of breed. Early European accounts are usually vague, but most seem to have answered the description of the pariah dogs of China. They had pointed noses; small v-shaped, pricked ears; thick, straight legs; usually short-haired coats and tails; and they could not bark. In Tahiti, such dogs were bred for food. A long-haired breed, probably a spaniel, evidently reached the Tuamotu archipelago in 1526 in the Spanish caravel SAN LESMES. Tahitians used its long hair to ornament their breast plates and made voyages to the Tuamotus to trade for it. Spanish dogs also seem likely to have reached New Zealand as there are two Maori words for dog: *kuri,* a reflex of the usual Polynesian term, and *pero*, as in Spanish *perro*.

Many of the cultivated plants in prehistoric Melanesia, Micronesia and Polynesia were identical, although Melanesia had several that were unknown in the other two areas. The American botanist W Arthur Whistler has claimed that voyaging canoes brought at least 72 such plants to Polynesia after it was settled more than 3000 years ago. Seventy of these are of Southeast Asian or New Guinea/Melanesian origin, but only 26 were more or less universal in their distribution (that is present in the Tongan, Samoan, Cook, Society, Marquesan and Hawaiian groups). Ten were dispersed only to the first four; two were known only in western Polynesia and Cook Islands; 21 were common to western Polynesia only; and seven got no further than Tonga. One of the plants was the American sweet potato. Another was the bottle gourd (*Lagenaria siceraria*) which, although native to the Old World, was present in western South America prehistorically. Both the sweet potato and gourd evidently reached Easter Island from Ecuador with the blue-egg chicken during the first Christian millennium. They were later dispersed as far afield as Hawai'i and New Zealand in eastern Polynesia.

Whistler's 26 plants of pan-Polynesian distribution include more than a dozen food plants, namely giant taro (*Alocasia macrorrhiza*), breadfruit (*Artocarpus altilis*), coconut (*Cocos nucifera*), taro (*Colocasia esculenta*), the *ti* plant (*Cordyline fruticosa*), three species of yam (*Dioscorea* spp), banana (*Musa* spp), pandanus (*Pandanus tectorius*), sugarcane (*Saccharum officinarum*), Malay apple (*Syzygium malaccense*), arrowroot (*Tacca leontopetaloides*) and *Solanum viride* which has no English name. The other introduced plants comprise three timber trees: *Calophyllum inophyllum, Cordia subcordata* and *Thespesia populnea;* two dye plants: *Curcuma longa* and *Morinda citrifolia;* as well as the paper mulberry (*Broussonetia papyrifera*), a source of bark cloth; the gardenia (*Gardenia taitensis*); the kava plant (*Piper methysticum*); bamboo (*Schizostachyum glaucifolium*); wild ginger (*Zingiber zerumbet*); and *Tephrosia purpurea,* the source of a fish poison.

Six of Polynesia's introduced plants—arrowroot, banana, breadfruit, coconut, paper mulberry, sugarcane and *Tephrosia*—have different names in some parts of the region, suggesting different paths of migration. The paper mulberry, virtually unknown in Melanesia, appears to have reached western Polynesia (probably Futuna) directly from Southeast Asia. The same also seems true of the banana which is generally called *futi* in western Polynesia but *meika,* or a variant, in the east.

Montane tree-fern shrubland, at Murray Pass, Wharton Range, Papua New Guinea

The banana probably reached Polynesia from both the west and the east. It was evidently carried across the entire Pacific from the southern Philippines to Ecuador in about 200 BC and thence to Easter Island with the sweet potato, bottle gourd and blue-egg chicken. Like them, it was later dispersed from Easter Island to other parts of Eastern Polynesia. Other, strictly American plants that apparently had a similar history were the soapberry (*Sapindus saponaria*), tobacco (*Nicotiana tabacum*), pineapple (*Ananas comosus*), 26-chromosome cotton (*Gossypium barbadense*), capsicum (*Capsicum* spp), tomato (*Lycopersicon esculentum*), maize (*Zea mays*), manioc (*Manihot utillissima*) and white potato (*Solanum tuberosum*). Evidence that the last three items were present on prehistoric Easter Island is contained in a passage in a Spanish account of the island written in 1770, but unpublished in English until 1986.—RL2

Plants of the Pacific

There is a remarkable diversity of plant life in the Pacific islands, but outside Papua New Guinea, the number of species is not large. The high proportion of endemic plants—found only on one island or in one island group—is attributable to the isolation of many of the islands. Of the species found widely throughout the Pacific, including both sides of

Ant plant (*Myrmecodia brassii*, Rubiaceae family), an epiphyte on subalpine shrubs

Gentiana crutwellii, in alpine grassland at 3650 m, Papua New Guinea

Red mangrove *Rhizophora stylosa*

Torres Strait, most are adapted to dispersal by sea water, and are represented in coastal habitats including mangrove swamps.

On those islands with heavy rainfall, high temperatures and humidity, the vegetation is lush and green. Dense rainforest occurs throughout Melanesia. In areas with lower rainfall or seasonal dry periods, there are more open forests, savanna woodlands on leeward slopes, and many coastal and river-valley swamplands. On some of the larger islands extensive grasslands have developed.

On the small, low-lying coral islands of the Pacific, vegetation is sparse. The porous soil allows the ubiquitous COCONUT palm and pandanus to flourish, but many of the smaller islands are treeless. In near-drought conditions, only scattered grasses, bushes and herbaceous plants can survive. This low-growing beach scrub commonly includes *Pemphis acidula*, *Allophylus cobbe*, *Messerschmidia* (*Tournefortia*) and *Scaevolia*, as well as various herbaceous and woody creepers and climbers.

Mangroves, the characteristic vegetation of tidal coastal zones, develop in river estuaries carrying large quantities of fine sediment, and along gradually shelving coastlines protected from strong currents and wave action. In areas with low and strongly seasonal rainfall, *Avicennia marina* is the most common species.

Unlike the smaller islands, the flora of Papua New Guinea is one of the richest in the world. Among the high montane flora, a genus such as *Rhododendron* produces a great number of species. The main vegetation types of the upper montane zone (from 3000 m above sea level) are forest and grassland, with the forest rich in species from the families Myrsinaceae, Ericaceae, Myrtaceae and Rubiaceae. Above the tree line (at about 3900 m), dense shrubberies open out into low single shrubs and finally, above 4400 m, there are steep, stony slopes with rosette and cushion herbs, mosses, lichens and low ferns.

Commonly occurring species of the beach and lowland regions include sago palm (*Metroxylon sagu*), which grows in swampy woodland; nipa palm (*Nypa fruticans*), covering extensive areas of estuaries and tidal creeks; and several varieties of *Melaleuca* trees. Swamp grasses grow densely over vast areas of alluvial plains, along the larger rivers and in lake regions. Small free-floating aquatic vegetation occurs in these areas, in water less than 3 m in depth. Patches of reddish brown *Azolla imbricata*, yellowish green *Pistia stratiotes*, the white and blue-flowering waterlilies of the genera *Nymphaea* and *Nymphoides*, and the large pink-flowering lotus, *Nelumbo nucifera*, form colourful mosaic patterns across lakes and lagoons. The coarse, tall sedges *Thoracostachyum sumatranum* and *Scleria* fill swampy depressions, interspersed with the robust, fleshy, broad-leaved herb *Hanguana malayana*, and the fern *Cyclosorus*.

Swamp forest is found in upper courses of the major rivers, and in better drained sites. The lower montane areas (1000–3000 m above sea level) are mostly forested, with vast stretches of grassland in the higher regions. The most common canopy trees belong to the families Fagaceae, Lauraceae, Elaecarpacae, and Myrtaceae, with *Ilex*, *Dryadodaphne* and *Planchonella*, and, at higher levels, conifers. Forest plants can occur in several forms—the *Pittosporum* at high altitudes is found as a tree, shrub, thick woody climber and epiphyte.—KRF

Further reading

Paijmans, K (ed.), 1976. *New Guinea Vegetation*, Commonwealth Scientific and Industrial Research Organisation and Australian National University Press.

■ *Sandalwood* The sandal tree, an evergreen with the botanical name of *Santalum album*, belongs to the family Santalaceae. Today the tree grows mainly in the forests of India and in the Timor Islands of Indonesia but it was discovered in the islands of the Pacific about 1790—the first major marketable product to attract traders. (See SANDALWOOD TRADE.) As the tree grows, the essential oil develops in the roots and in the core of dark heartwood (which is covered by outer sapwood), a gradual development requiring at least 15–20 years. Full maturity is reached after 60–80 years. The distilled oil is one of the oldest known perfumes, mentioned in Indian literature more than 2000 years ago, and used both for its rare medicinal properties and as a cosmetic for centuries in Egypt, China and India. The wood is suited for intricate and delicate carving, and sandalwood oil and paste continue to be used in religious rites, funerals, and for incense.—KRF

Pandanus growing at about 2000 m, at Kosipe, Papua New Guinea

Indigenous food crops

The starchy staples and supplementary greens that make up most of the Pacific's indigenous crop plants are grown under a wide variety of cultivation systems, ranging from classic polycultural swiddens to highly intensive, monocultural plots of sweet potato, yams, *Colocasia* taro, or *Cyrtosperma* swamp taro. (See AGRICULTURE.) Commonly, the short-term crops (some biennial or a few years longer) exist within a landscape where also abounds a variety of tree crops, which supply fruits, nuts, leaves, oils, beverage, and, in places, staple foods such as sago starch or breadfruit.

The classic staple tubers of the ancient Pacific are the aroid *Colocasia* taro ('true taro') and some five or six species of yams, most importantly *Dioscorea alata* ('great yam') and *Dioscorea esculenta*. The ecological characteristics of taro and yams manifest the Pacific's archetypal contrasting environments of 'the wet and dry', wherein the two paths towards agricultural intensification are irrigation of taro and short-fallow dryland cultivation of yams (and sweet potato after its introduction)—although taro can also be grown as a dryland crop. The other particularly important arid crop is *Cyrtosperma* taro (giant swamp taro), which requires at least three years to mature and is grown widely on ATOLLS under a system that combines pits excavated to the water table and a man-made soil composted with collected leaves. *Cyrtosperma*'s large, coarse tuber provides, with coconut and breadfruit, the main source of carbohydrate in the agriculturally inhospitable atoll environment, while the crop was also the staple in the agriculturally rich environment of the Rewa delta in Fiji. There are two less important tuber-producing aroids. *Alocasia macrorrhiza*, which requires less moisture than taro, produces a large above-ground edible stem, acrid because of its high calcium oxalate content and usually considered inferior in taste to taro. The relic plant *Amorphophallus paeoniifolius*, which has a corm that requires much preparation to make it edible, is no longer used. Other food crops that have largely fallen out of use (unless as famine foods) and so serve as witnesses of agricultural change from earlier times include *Tacca leontopetaloides* (Polynesian arrowroot), *Pueraria lobata* (a tuber-bearing legume), and *Cordyline fruticosa*, the ritually and decoratively important *ti* plant, which bears a sugar-rich root, now not used for food.

The sweet potato requires special mention. Although it has been in central Polynesia for at least a thousand years, it originated in tropical America—unlike the other significant Pacific foods present at the time of European entry, all of which have an Asian or western Pacific origin. Easier to grow, quicker to mature, and often higher-yielding than taro or yams, sweet potato—whatever its routes of entry—spread widely throughout the high islands of the Pacific, flourishing especially as an intensive dryland crop in parts of the Hawaiian islands, in temperate Polynesian New Zealand, and, most significantly, across the Highlands of New Guinea.

Bananas, which are a staple in a few places and widely grown as an important supplementary food, are in fact giant perennial herbs and so function something like a tree in food gardens and continue producing after most other crops have been har-

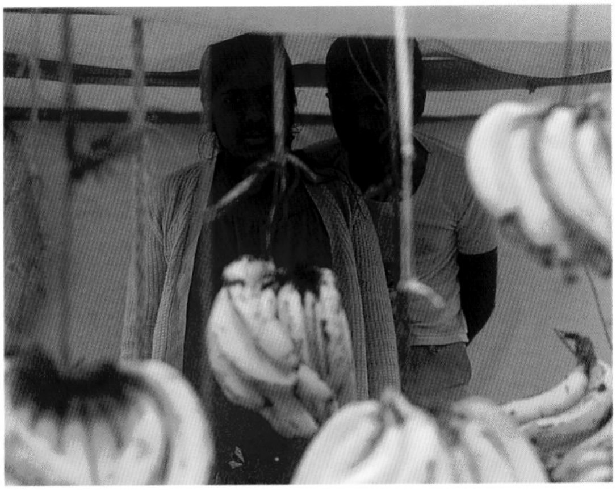

Bananas at street market, Viti Levu, Fiji

vested. Banana (*Musa* spp) taxonomy is complex, with all cultivated varieties or clones being hybrids derived from wild species and then subject to a history of human selection and mutation. Most indigenous Pacific bananas are *Eumusa* section hybrids, some of which are 'plantains', that is, fat, blunt, starchy cooking bananas, while others have a thinner, sweeter fruit that can be eaten raw. Separate from the *Eumusa* complex is *Musa troglodytarum* (the *fe'i* banana, or 'mountain plantain'), which may be a New Guinean or New Caledonian domesticate, and was introduced as far east as the Marquesas.

Sugarcane, possibly a New Guinean domesticate, was an aboriginal introduction through the rest of the Pacific, where it was grown for its sugar-laden stems, which were chewed to extract the juice. In the carbohydrate and fibre-rich indigenous diet, this supplementary food (or 'drink', as it was often classified) was one of the few sources of sucrose—in sharp contrast to the current diet, rich in refined sugar.

At the least, there are a few score other short-term supplementary food crops in the aggregate of indigenous crops in the Pacific islands, with Melanesian islands being much richer in supplementary foods than the Polynesian or Micronesian islands and, especially, atolls. Though of nutritional importance, the supplementary crops, which could mostly be classed as greens or vegetables, were not considered as real food compared with the starchy staples. They included crucifers, gourds, a melon, turmeric, a ginger, *Saccharum edule* (the lowland 'pitpit' of Papua New Guinea; *duruka* in Fiji), *Setaria palmifolia* (highland 'pitpit'), the nutritious, dark-leaved *Hibiscus manihot*, amaranths, and a few legumes, such as the yam bean *Psophocarpus tetragonolobus*, which possesses edible beans, leaves, pods, and even a tuber, which is sometimes eaten in New Guinea. Ferns and wild and cultivated trees also provide edible leaves, and the leaves of *Colocasia* taro are commonly eaten.

The Pacific's crop inventory has been enlarged by the introduction of vegetables such as onions, carrots, cabbages and new sorts of beans. And two more crops from tropical America joined the sweet potato in augmenting the staple diet. Cassava ('*manioc*') has spread widely, as it has throughout the tropical world, because of its simple cultivation requirements and high yield in poor soils. Initially it was little favoured as a human food but was fed to pigs; but increasingly it is part of the daily diet in many parts of the Pacific. The other addition to starchy staples is *Xanthosoma* taro, the American counterpart to *Colocasia* taro. Unlike *Colocasia, Xanthosoma* is always a dryland plant and will produce in relatively poor soils compared with the indigenous taro. The American grain maize has also become an important supplementary food in some parts of the Pacific; and the white potato has in the past several decades become a significant subsistence and cash crop at high elevations in Papua New Guinea, reflecting the crop's origin in the tropical highlands of the Andes in South America.—WCC

Further reading

Massal, E and Barrau, J, 1956. *Food Plants of the South Sea Islands*, South Pacific Commission Technical Paper 94.

Oliver, D, 1989. 'Foods and food getting: the islands', in *Oceania: the native cultures of Australia and the Pacific islands*, 2 Vols, University of Hawai'i Press.

Coconuts The coconut (*Cocos nucifera L*) is almost ubiquitous along the coastal fringe of most inhabited Pacific islands, and it grows on many uninhabited islands. Its importance is reflected in descriptions such as 'the tree of life' and, given its many useful products, such names are justifiable. The coconut is now thought to be indigenous to the Southeast Asia-Melanesia region and to have been domesticated there. How the coconut was spread across the islands of the Pacific and Indian Oceans provokes considerable argument. Some earlier botanists argued that coconut palms could not become established after nuts washed ashore without human help. It is now known that nuts can remain viable after floating in the sea for up to three months, and can germinate and survive without human intervention. It is possible that the original wild nuts had a more elongated shape and thicker husk than domesticated nuts and therefore might remain viable in seawater for longer periods. A COMPUTER SIMU-

LATION by Gerard Ward and Muriel Brookfield suggests that Pacific wind and current patterns make it unlikely that the coconut reached its extreme 15th century Pacific dispersal in western Panama and Colombia without human intervention. It appears that the plant did reach some parts of Melanesia and Polynesia prior to human settlement but human carriage was probably necessary for coconuts to become established in the more remote island groups such as the Marquesas and Hawai'i.

In earlier centuries coconuts provided islanders with food and drink; animal feed; fibre for string, including lashings for canoes and buildings; thatch and timber for houses; fuel wood; and, in some areas, fermented 'toddy' for alcohol. In Micronesia in the late 1800s, Truk (Chuuk) islanders extracted oil from dried coconut for use in personal adornment. On atolls, with limited land resources, coconuts were especially important in contributing a high proportion of food and other material needs. Many nuts are still used for subsistence purposes. (See also COPRA AND COCONUT OIL.)—RGW

Major starch foods

Of the 12 major starch foods grown and eaten in Pacific island communities, most are root crops.

Taro, *Colocasia esculenta,* generally known as true taro, or dalo. This was grown as both an irrigated crop or on dry land. The soil environment is said to have produced a sweeter root, and to have increased yield. Many varieties were developed over time in each of the islands, with 72 named varieties known in Hawai'i in the 1930s.

The corm was eaten as well as the young leaves. The corm had to be peeled carefully, and well cooked in order to eliminate the noxious calcium oxalate raphides found just under the skin; improperly cooked corms caused an unpleasant rash around the mouth. The corm was usually served in whole slices. The young green leaves were mixed with other foods, or just with coconut cream, baked in a leaf package in the earth oven. Taro was also eaten in fermented form in some societies. In Hawai'i one, two and three-day-old fermented taro was distinguished by its consistency and taste. This form of fermented taro has a high nutritional value as it is easily absorbed by infants and the sick because the starch granules are particularly small.

Giant swamp taro, *Cyrtosperma chamissonis,* known as *babai* in Kiribati. This plant, growing to 3–4 m when properly cared for in rich damp soil, is used mainly on atolls. Special cultivation techniques were developed in Kiribati to ensure the social status of the producer of the largest root corm. The very

Taro on display, New Ireland, Papua New Guinea

large corms weighing 1–4 kg are very fibrous. They require long cooking in an earth oven. They also contain a lot of calcium oxalate crystals. They are an important food for any social occasion.

Giant taro, *Alocasia macrorrhiza.* This is a perennial crop that is widely spread across the Pacific. It grows in areas of reasonable rainfall, whether on low or high islands, and will regenerate itself if left unattended. The stem is the starchy food part of this plant, which is particularly highly regarded in Tonga.

Coco-yam, *Xanthoso masagittifolium,* Tarotarua. A late introduction into the Pacific from the Americas where it is widespread in the Caribbean and elsewhere. The small cormels attached to the stem are the part that is eaten, and considered very tasty, especially in Tonga.

Yams, *ufi*, many varieties, *Dioscorea* spp. *D alata* and *D esculenta* are the two species most commonly eaten in the Pacific, though the species is widely known as a food plant throughout the tropics. Yams are very highly regarded in some island societies, where they are considered the *Ali'i* or King of foods. Competitions were held in Pohnpei to produce the longest yam, while there was considerable competitive spirit over the yam houses in the Trobriands. A cult centred around the yam is widespread amongst SEPIK communities. The very white flesh of the yam is part of its high prestige value. It has a delicate flavour, and is an essential offering to visitors. Captain COOK participated in the celebration of the first yam of the season in Tonga, the *inasi*.

Sweet potato, *Ipomoea batatas.* A recently introduced species originating in South America, but may have entered the Pacific via the Philippines.

This food plant was important in the Highlands of New Guinea where it has adapted to cooler temperatures; it was also used there to feed pigs. In New Zealand it was also valued, many varieties being developed by Maori. It could be stored in specially constructed storehouses. The sweet potato became a general cultivar in many of the islands with reasonably fertile soil, although it has seldom achieved the status of most preferred starchy food except in Highland New Guinea and New Zealand.

Cassava, *Manihot esculenta*. Cassava is also a recent introduction from South America. It has been included among the traditional foods, as it has become a major locally grown starch food. Its rapid popularity in the last 40 years is due to its fast growing tubers, so it is particularly suited as a food crop which can be planted at the end of the shifting cultivation cycle after other tuberous food crops have taken much of the nutrients from the soil. The quality of the starch in cassava varies between varieties, but it is becoming more generally recognized as an important contributor to diets, even though nutritionally it rates below some other root crops.

Easily grown and reasonably cheap, cassava is often served together with other starches. It is not a first preference food, nor is it suitable to be served at feasts, but is a very important fall-back food, that can be left in the ground for harvesting at short notice. The Pacific cassava is the sweet variety, but it still contains a considerable level of cyanide, so must be well cooked. It is also used as a crop suitable for feeding pigs. In Polynesian languages cassava has been named *ka ʻufi*, indicating its similar root shape to the *ʻufi* or yam, but that it is secondary to that highly regarded crop.

Polynesian arrowroot, *Tacca leontopetaloides*. Polynesian arrowroot is a seasonal plant that grows well on atolls. It consists of small white starchy bulbs which can be harvested for about a month or left in the ground to multiply for subsequent years. The starch in the bulbs is highly toxic due to the presence of hydrocyanogens, and thus must be very well leached before it is cooked. It is most commonly prepared as a flour, in which form it is mixed with other starches such as banana or pumpkin. *Poke* in the Cook Islands is a favourite dish based on arrowroot starch.

The remaining major starch foods are tree crops.

Breadfruit, *Artocarpus altilis*. This highly favoured fruiting tree is widespread across the Pacific. The fruit is produced seasonally, but some varieties may produce up to three or even four crops a year, the last two crops being small in size and in number of fruits. The green fruits when mature are about the size of a boy's head (as the explorer Dampier noted). The fruit is starchy, becoming sweeter as it ripens. Many varieties have been developed in the Pacific, with Captain BLIGH's infamous expedition (see MUTINY ON THE BOUNTY) being responsible for export of this tree crop to the Caribbean as a ready source of food for the slave population there.

Artocarpus altilis, the seedless variety, is more widespread than the seeded variety (*Artocarpus mariennensis*). The seeds are a valuable additional food source, and in parts of New Guinea only the seeds are eaten. Both the seedless and the seeded varieties must be cooked before the starch is edible. The fruits are most commonly roasted in the coals, but may be boiled, or cooked in package foods, mixed with coconut cream in the earth oven. Today breadfruit chips are a tasty new way of serving this traditional food.

Breadfruit was one of the main foods that was preserved by fermentation in pits, particularly in Polynesia. Excess ripe fruits were peeled and processed by soaking them in salt water before placing the paste in lined pits in sandy areas. After two months or more the paste was ready for eating, prepared into loaves and baked in the earth oven. The most elaborate use of fermented breadfruit together with fresh breadfruit was developed in the Marquesas.

Breadfruit ready for cooking

Bananas. Two varieties of bananas are important in the Pacific. The most widely used variety is the plantain (*Musa troglodytarum*)—the large fruit, often orange or red, or green, was a common form of starch. The fruits were boiled or roasted in the coals to yield a favoured starchy vegetable. They were commonly served with coconut cream. The smaller dessert variety that becomes yellow when ripe (*Musa paradaisica*) was used, but mainly as children's food, or for snacks. Bananas were also preserved in pits, particularly in Fiji.

Pandanus. Many varieties of this tree which produces very large fruits seasonally have been developed. The fruiting varieties must be vegetatively propagated. The fruits are used mainly on atolls as a supplementary starch when breadfruit is not available. Each large fruit consists of many drupes which may be eaten raw or cooked. Some varieties must be boiled to release the starch. The orange paste is embedded in a fibrous mass that is discarded; the base of the drupe contains seeds which may be eaten in some varieties. The paste is sweet and a highly nutritious source of Vitamin A.

Sago palm, *Metroxyolon* spp. The pith of the sago palm may be harvested all year round. It has been widely used in the western Pacific as a staple food, particularly in the lowlands of Papua New Guinea. The pith was made into sago flour by pounding and leaching. Sago may be stored damp or dried, and can be mixed with water and boiled to form a thick paste; or mixed as 'cakes'; or baked in bamboo sections.—NJP

Galip nut, Karkar Island, Papua New Guinea

Indigenous tropical fruit, *Pouteria Maclayana*

Indigenous fruit and nuts

Many fruit and nut species are used as food throughout the Pacific. Most are 'indigenous' plants which have been domesticated in the region or were domesticated elsewhere and introduced in pre-European times. Some are rich in carbohydrate, such as breadfruit and Polynesian chestnut, and can be dietary substitutes for root crops and bananas. Others are rich in oil, and valuable where the oil or fat content of diets is low. Some fruits and nuts provide useful amounts of vitamins. A variety of fruits and nuts grow in all inhabited Pacific environments from tiny atolls at sea level to over 3000 m in the New Guinea Highlands. They are most important as foods on small to medium size islands where a number of species are common. On these islands, villagers have selected superior types.

The significance of indigenous fruit and nuts in villagers' diets varies. On certain atolls where people plant few root crops, coconuts contribute more than half of dietary calories. This contrasts with evidence of a decline in importance of fruit and nuts in recent decades. On Karkar, off the north coast of Papua New Guinea, the following species were important foods until early this century: coconuts, galip nut, breadfruit, Polynesian chestnut, sea almond and the fruit of *Pouteria maclayana* and *Dracontomelon dao*. Following the introduction of steel tools, arable agriculture became more important and fruit and nuts have become less evident in Pacific islanders' diet. A similar situation occurs on Malo Island (off Santo, in Vanuatu) where villagers have names for over 100 types of breadfruit and there are many fruit and nut species. However, New World taro (*Xanthosoma*) and other recently adopted root crops have replaced breadfruit in villagers' diets in recent decades.

Some fruit and nut species are widely distributed throughout the region. Sea almond, for example, grows and is eaten in many coastal locations.

Flower of nut tree, *Barringtonia procera*

Other species have a more restricted range. Okari nut was known only from the south side of New Guinea (Irian Jaya and Papua New Guinea). Species of Canarium provide edible nuts from the Philippines and eastern Indonesia through Melanesia as far east as Fiji.

All fruit and nut species described here are sold in local markets. A number of attempts have been made since 1980 to commercialize production and sale of indigenous nuts in Papua New Guinea, Solomon Islands and Vanuatu. The most successful venture so far has been the Kava Shop in Port Vila. Locally grown *nangai* (Canarium), *navele* (Barringtonia) and *natapoa* (sea almond) nuts are processed and sold in Vila.

Two species are important sources of starchy food, especially on small-to-medium islands. These are breadfruit (*Artocarpus altilis*) and Polynesian chestnut (*Inocarpus fagifer*). Breadfruit is grown up to 1300 m in Papua New Guinea. On the New Guinea mainland, in locations broadly coinciding with those where non-Austronesian languages are spoken, only the nuts are eaten. Elsewhere, where Austronesian languages are spoken, both the flesh and nuts are used. In Polynesia, seedless forms have been selected. The seed of Polynesian chestnut is roasted and used as a source of starch. It is a minor food on many islands and important on some.

A number of nuts provide oil in diets, notably the ubiquitous COCONUT. Coconuts are most important in coastal locations across the Pacific, and even on New Guinea they are grown as high as 1000 m. Various species of the genus Canarium are significant food sources in coastal and near-coastal locations, with *Canarium indicum* probably the most important overall. As well as the edible kernel, Canarium provides edible oil and a hard shell which has a number of economic uses.

Sea almond (*Terminalia catappa*) is grown on or near the seashore throughout most of the Pacific. The kernel is commonly eaten, especially by children. On some islands, villagers have selected types with soft shells and larger kernels. Okari nut (*Terminalia kaernbachii*) was confined to inland locations on the south side of New Guinea up to an altitude of 1100 m, but it has become more widely grown. The kernel is large and is regarded by some as one of the best indigenous nuts.

A number of Pandanus species produce edible, oil-rich nuts at high altitude in Papua New Guinea. The cultivated karuka nut (*Pandanus julianettii*) is common in highland valleys at altitudes of 1800–2600 m and the 'wild' species (*P brosimos*) grows as high as 3100 m. In contrast with most other Pacific nut species, few karuka nuts remain unharvested during the season in the New Guinea Highlands. In the absence of coconut and other nuts, karuka nuts provide one of the few sources of oil in the mainly vegetable diet of highlanders.

Marita (*Pandanus conoideus*) grows in New Guinea's highland valleys up to 1700 m. It produces a long cylindrical red or yellow fruit up to 1 m long. Villagers produce a rich oily sauce from the cooked fruit, used to garnish vegetables such as sweet potato. In contrast with marita, which is found only on New Guinea, golden apple (*Spondias cytherea*) is commonly found on islands across the Pacific. It is usually a minor fruit. Ton (*Pometia pinnata*), related to lychee and rambutan, is another indigenous fruit that is widely distributed from New Guinea to Vanuatu. In season, significant quantities are eaten in some locations.

Malay apple (*Syzygium malaccense*) is commonly grown in lowland locations in many islands and is a common fruit in season. *Burckella obovata* is another minor fruit species, distributed from the smaller islands of Papua New Guinea to Solomon Islands and Vanuatu. The fruit—refreshing and somewhat tart—has perhaps the greatest potential of the indigenous fruit to be adopted in other parts of the world.—RMB

Further reading

Stevens, M L, Bourke, R M and Evans, B R (eds), 1996. *South Pacific Indigenous Nuts*, Australian Centre for International Agricultural Research.

Walter, A and Sam, C, with Bataille, Bompard, Bonnemere and Tcherkesoff, 1998. *Fruits d'Océanie: utilisation traditionnelle des arbres fruitiers du Pacifique Ouest*, ORSTOM.

Yen, D E, 1974. 'Arboriculture in the subsistence of Santa Cruz, Solomon Islands', *Economic Botany*, 28.

■ *Betelnut* The betelnut tree (a kind of palm, *Areca catechu*) was probably brought into the Pacific islands from Southeast Asia and became widely established in many parts of Melanesia. The kernel of the nut is consumed with the leaf, fruit or stem of a vine (*piper betle*), and is often chewed with lime obtained from seashells, coral or mountain lime. It is then expectorated, not swallowed, and leaves the mouth and lips red. The mixture's properties are similar to that of nicotine, producing a general feeling of wellbeing. It is also widely claimed to diminish hunger and fatigue.

Store selling betel nut in Kolonia

In contemporary Papua New Guinea, betelnut has become a major cash crop, in a flourishing trade that has had no input from government. (Household spending on betelnut is calculated as 2.7 per cent of all consumer spending for the purposes of the consumer price index.) Betelnut has recently been introduced into the Highland regions where villagers have developed a taste for it. Growing only up to altitudes of 1000 m, it is now transported from the lowlands in large quantities. It provides income to rural producers and supports many of the urban squatters and economically marginal people living in Port Moresby, Lae and Madang. In some parts of Micronesia also, it is currently grown, used and sold. (See also ALCOHOL AND DRUG ABUSE; CANCER IN PAPUA NEW GUINEA.)—KRF

Tropical flowers

■ *Orchids* Orchids grow in many parts of Papua New Guinea, in about 3000 varieties. One third of them are in two vast and varied classes (*Bulbophyllum* and *Dendrobium*) that are epiphytes, growing high in the tree canopy. Except for those growing in some high mountain forests, most orchids have inconspicuous flowers. The *Dendrobium engae* (yellow, black and white) appears on the provincial flag of Enga Province, and a research centre for mountain orchids has been established at Laiagam in Enga. In the lower montane forest areas, orchids commonly occur in tree crowns, low on the trunks, and on the ground in sunlit parts of the forest floor. There are also many ground-dwelling orchid varieties in dry savannah areas. A wide variety of orchids from different areas is displayed at the Liptzauga Botanical Sanctuary, a plant research centre in Mt Gahavisuka Park near Goroka.

Fibres from orchid stems have been traditionally used as string, while parts of some orchid plants are used in TRADITIONAL HEALING PRACTICES. Leaves of the orchids *Spathoglottis* and *Dendrobium* are often used to wrap quantities of salt.—KRF

■ *Bougainvillea* The beautiful flowering climber known as bougainvillea, which now grows widely in tropical Pacific, is an introduced genus, developed from a specimen of *Bougainvillea spectabilis* collected by Philibert Commerson in Rio de Janeiro (where Captain BOUGAINVILLE waited two months to meet up with his supply ship) and sent back to Paris in 1767. The plant pictured grows in Rabaul, Papua New Guinea.—KRF

■ *Frangipani* The sweet-smelling frangipani (*Plumeria* spp) grows widely throughout the Pacific islands. A common decoration for festive occasions and dancing, the flowers are strung into garlands (*ei*, or *lei* in Polynesia), which are worn both on the head and around the neck, and are frequently presented to welcome visitors and tourists.

■ *Florilegium* The *Florilegium* is a set of 738 botanical drawings based on the colour drawings, quick sketches and notes of the artist Sydney Parkinson during James COOK's first voyage in 1768–71. It is more commonly known as *Banks' Florilegium* after

Bougainvillea

Tropical flowers: Red flame tree, 'Flamboyant'

Hibiscus

Frangipani

Joseph BANKS, the botanist and scientist who accompanied Cook and who later spent 12 years personally funding a project to convert Parkinson's rough sketches and notes into copper-plate engravings. This included matching the drawings with the thousands of specimens from the voyage held in the Royal Botanic Gardens at Kew and in Bank's own herbarium and library. The plates include flora from Australia, Brazil, Java, Madeira, New Zealand, Society Islands and Tierra del Fuego. Banks died before the set was printed and published. As a trial run, several black ink impressions were taken from the plates before the set was lodged at the British Museum in 1827. Individual prints and short sets of some prints were later printed and can be found in repositories around the world. The full set or *Florilegium* was not published until 1980–88.—MQ

Marine birds

Marine birds are not abundant in the Pacific. Numbers do not generally compare to many temperate coastal areas where enormous colonies of a variety of species are commonly found. Seabird communities, like the foods they exploit, depend far more strongly on water conditions than general climate and in particular the nutrient status of the surrounding seas. The most nutrient-rich seas are found in areas of oceanic 'upwelling' and current 'convergences', neither of which occur in the islands to any significant extent. Nonetheless, there is an interesting diversity with about 40 species known to breed and many more which are vagrants or migrate through the tropical Pacific.

Marine birds have a long history of cultural significance for Pacific islanders, especially for traditional navigators who have long known that seabirds have differing feeding habits and relationships with the land. By identifying specific seabirds they could reliably know their general proximity to land, and by following their flight paths in the early morning or evening, the direction of land. Certain seabirds such as the crested tern *Sterna bergii* are confined to the close proximity of coastal areas and shallow waters and are rarely out of sight of land. Others such as the boobies and noddies are offshore species venturing well out of sight of land, but invariably returning each night to roost on land. The most enigmatic marine birds are the pelagic species such as the sooty tern (*Sterna fuscata*) and petrels such the collared petrel (*Pterodroma brevipes*) and the Tahiti petrel (*Pterodroma rostrata*). These birds return to land only to breed and otherwise remain exclusively out at sea.

Many seabirds make long migrations, some of them from areas across the Pacific to equivalent climatic zones in the other hemisphere. This is the case with several species of shearwater and petrel. In certain locations, the migratory paths are well defined and close to land and large numbers of migrants are seen at the same time each year.

The survival of most species of marine bird is threatened in the Pacific. Ever since the arrival of the first voyagers, seabirds have been an important part of the islanders' diet. For some species this has been a sustainable exploitation over the centuries, but many species have become lost from island groups through over-exploitation. Some, such as Abbott's booby (*Sula abbotti*), are no longer found in the Pacific.

Current threats to marine birds include continuing direct exploitation, habitat disturbance and destruction, and introduced predators.

Many Pacific islanders continue the traditional practice of annually taking the eggs or young from seabird colonies. Until recently, for instance, on Kiritimati (Christmas Island), adult and young red-tailed *Phaethon rubricauda* along with boobies and FRIGATE-BIRDS were extensively taken, while the eggs of sooty terns were taken in hundreds of thousands.

Human population increase and the now-common occurrence of motorboats is ensuring that previously uninhabitable and small, distant islands are visited, modifying or destroying their habitats. This threatens nesting marine birds which are now more reliant on a dwindling supply of undisturbed breeding sites.

Introduced mammalian predators pose a serious threat to nesting marine birds. The only naturally occurring predators in the islands are a few birds of prey which were not a significant threat to seabirds. This changed with the arrival of the Polynesian rat *Rattus exulans* which was introduced by the first voyagers. However, it was after European contact that the most serious predators of nesting seabirds were introduced. These include the Indian mongoose (*Herpestes auropunctatus*) which is confined to Fiji and Hawai'i. More widespread and serious are the black rat (*Rattus rattus*) and the feral cat, both of which are probably responsible for the precarious status of the Fiji petrel (*Pseudobulweria macgillivrayi*), one of the world's rarest birds.—DW

Further reading

Harrison, P, 1983. *Seabirds: an identification guide*, Beckenham, United Kingdom.

■ *Frigate-bird* Frigate-birds have a singular flight silhouette with long, thin wings, a tapering forked or scissor-like tail and a strong hooked bill. They are amongst the most distinctive and best-known seabirds of the tropical Pacific. Their presence over or close to land is considered by many islanders to signal bad weather or even hurricanes out to sea.

Frigate-birds walk with the greatest difficulty, cannot swim, and have the largest wingspan to body-weight ratio of any bird, and thus are amongst the most aerial of all seabirds. Characteristically they soar high above the oceans from where they plummet to harass seabirds such as boobies and terns, forcing them to drop or disgorge recently caught food. The molester then catches the falling offerings in mid air, or deftly plucks them off the ocean surface while still in flight. Seabirds carrying food back to nestlings are particularly vulnerable to the harassment of frigate-birds. This 'piratic behaviour' is termed klepto-parasitism.

Above all, frigate-birds are opportunistic feeders and so also catch their own food. Characteristically, they seek out schools of surface-feeding TUNA to snatch disturbed flying fish or other tuna-prey and then scavenge on the dead and dying or pieces of fish left after tuna-feeding frenzies. Frigate-birds will also visit seabird nesting colonies and swoop down, plucking unguarded nestlings from their nests, and occasionally turning to cannibalism as they practise this behaviour amongst their own kin.

Frigate-birds breed in small colonies, generally building nests in small bushes. They raise a single young which has a long period of juvenile dependency, such that successful breeders will only breed every two years. There are five species of frigate-bird in the world, two of which, the greater frigate-bird (*Fregata minor*) and the lesser frigate-bird (*Fregata ariel*), are found in the Pacific islands. They are difficult to distinguish at sea.—DW

Land birds

■ *Bird of paradise* The colourful bird of paradise (family Paradisaeidae) of Papua New Guinea lives in lowland rainforests and lower mountain forests. There are 12 varieties endemic to Papua New Guinea, and a total of 33 varieties are 'protected native animals'. The most spectacular courtship displays are made by a group known as kumuls, including the blue bird of paradise (*Paradisaea rudolphi*), emperor, Goldie's, and Raggiana (Count Raggi's). Their behaviour includes puffing out their chest plumage, hanging upside down during their display, dancing and shrieking. Living mostly in treetops, where they feed on fruit and insects, the birds of paradise range in length from about 16–18 cm (king, magnificent, yellow-breasted) up to 100–110 cm (brown sicklebill, black sicklebill, *Epimachus*). The bird (which is featured on the national emblem and the flag) has a prominent place in traditional culture, in several myths and dance performances, and its feathers are widely used as items of decoration (BODY DECORATION (BILAS) IN PAPUA NEW GUINEA).—KRF

■ *Kagu* (Cagou) The flightless kagu or cagou (*Rhynochetus jubatus*) is found only in New Caledonia, where it is the national bird. About the size of a domestic fowl, its body plumage is soft and grey. It has striped brown and white wings, and a crest of feathers which are raised during display or when the bird is aroused. Its cry is almost a barking sound. It is endangered by its slow movement which leaves it vulnerable to introduced predators, and is becoming rare. The kagu lives in the humid forests of the central range and the coastal districts of Grande Terre, where it eats insects, worms and snails.—KRF

Frogs and toads

Several kinds of frogs and toads are found across the Pacific islands. In the tropics they are mainly nocturnal. Ordinary frogs (family Ranidae) are found quite widely, with some unusual endemic varieties such as Günther's toothed frog, of Solomon Islands. There are about 60 kinds of tree-frogs (family Hylidae) in the islands, usually bush or tree-dwelling, and several of these occur in Papua New Guinea and Solomon Islands.

Ground toads (*Bufo*) are found in Solomon Islands, the Marianas, and Hawai'i. The South American cane toad (*Bufo marinus*) was introduced into the islands, mainly to assist the SUGAR industry, because it feeds on some kinds of agricultural pests. It has become a destroyer of native frogs and smaller reptiles, however, and is now a problem in Hawai'i, Papua New Guinea, Tonga and Vanuatu.—KRF

Reptiles

Reptiles found widely in the Pacific islands include lizards, snakes and TURTLES. (See also GALAPAGOS ISLANDS, where all reptiles apart from sea turtles are endemic.) Crocodiles are not found outside of Palau, Papua New Guinea and Solomon Islands.

Lizards are plentiful throughout the Pacific. The banded iguana (*Brachylophus fasciatus*), which is a tree-dweller, is found in Fiji and Tonga. About 150 lizard species occur in Papua New Guinea. None are poisonous, although larger animals have a painful bite. Most types of lizard and their eggs are eaten. Several kinds of monitor lizard (including a large variety that grows to almost 2 m) are found throughout the islands of Micronesia. There are several kinds in Papua New Guinea too, where the skin of the spotted goanna is used for the kundu drum. The dragon lizard (family Agamidae) grows to about 1 m in length. The small gecko lizard (family Gekkonidae) which grows up to 25 cm long, occurs widely throughout the Pacific, and is often found inside houses. Skinks are also common, mostly living in trees.

Snakes, both land varieties and sea snakes, occur widely through the Pacific islands. Blind snakes (family Typhlopidae) are small, burrowing, wormlike snakes that are found throughout the tropical regions. Palau has a rare golden burrowing snake. The Brahminy blind snake (*Typhlops braminus*) occurs in most parts of the western Pacific.

Papua New Guinea has 56 varieties of land snakes, including 23 poisonous kinds, 20 poisonous sea snakes, and 14 water snakes. The snakes most dangerous to humans are

- death adders (*Acanthophis antarcticus*)—brown, and usually less than 1 m in length
- Papuan taipans (*Oxyuranus scutellatus*)—glossy back, with a red-orange streak, and up to 3 m in length
- Papuan black snakes (*Pseudechis papuanus*)—shiny black, and up to 2 m in length
- New Guinea brown snakes (*Pseudonaja textilis*), and Papuan whip snakes (*Demansia olivacea*)—both about 1.5 m in length.

Some poisonous varieties are found in Solomon Islands. The Samoan islands have no poisonous snakes, but a few harmless varieties are found on Savai'i. Fiji has two species, the rare but poisonous *bolo loa*, and a harmless boa which grows to about 2 m. Across the islands of Micronesia, poisonous sea snakes have been found only in Palau.

Pythons and boas (family Boidae) are common among the non-poisonous snakes found in the islands, especially varieties of the Pacific boa (*Enygrus*) found from New Guinea to French Polynesia. Papua New Guinea's amethystine rock-python (*Liasis amethystinus*) grows to 7–8 m in length. The common ground boa (*Candoia asper*) is a dark brown snake about 1 m long. Another common non-poisonous snake is the green tree snake (*Dendrelaphis*), about 1.5 m long, which feeds on frogs and birds. Tree snakes (thin and fast-moving) are usually active during the day.

Sea snakes, belonging to the family Hydrophiidae, occur widely in warm coastal waters and tidal rivers. A similar group of banded sea snakes, family Elapidae, breathe air and lay their eggs on land. Usually brightly coloured, they may be recognized as sea snakes by their paddle-shaped tails. The banded small-eyed snake (*Micropechis elapoides*) is found in Solomon Islands. Water snakes live in mangrove areas and in freshwater lakes and rivers.

Crocodiles (both freshwater and saltwater) are found in Papua New Guinea, in lowland lakes, swamps and rivers. The freshwater variety occurs only in swampy areas of mainland Papua New Guinea and on Fergusson Island, Milne Bay. The larger (up to 6 m in length) saltwater crocodile is found in all island provinces and coastal areas, including the inland lakes area of the Sepik River. Crocodile eggs and meat provide food, and crocodile skin is exported, especially to Japan, with strict regulations governing the size of export skin to protect young and breeding animals. In Solomon Islands, saltwater crocodiles live in the brackish mangrove swamps of the river deltas. In Palau there are two saltwater species.—KRF

Further reading

Loveridge, A, 1946. *Reptiles of the Pacific World,* Macmillan.

FOUR CLIMATE AND NATURE

Environmental change

Although concentrated within the tropics, the Pacific islands represent every major climate division in the region. The modern environments of these islands reflect not only their present climates, but also the effects of former climates. The great erosional valleys of the Hawaiian group, for instance, clearly did not form under today's comparatively dry conditions but probably date from a time of much higher rainfall. There is also growing evidence that the grasslands of many tropical islands developed around 22 000 years ago when this part of the Pacific was much drier than it is today.

View from the highest peak on Totoya Island, southeast Fiji, from the wet forested (windward) side of the island, looking towards the dry grass-covered (leeward) side. Such grasslands formed around 17 000 years ago and have persisted in the rain shadows of high islands like Totoya

Pacific islands are relatively young parts of the earth's surface. Most formed no more than a few million years ago. The changes which took place during the late Neogene (what used to be called the Quaternary Era—the last 1.8 million years or so) involve three aspects: climate change, sea-level change, and tectonic or land-level change.

The earth's climate oscillated during the late Neogene between warm (interglacial) times such as that in which we now live, and cool (glacial) times when ice advanced across the land far beyond its present limits. Ice caps grew on a few islands; besides New Zealand and Japan, ice advanced down the flanks of Mauna Kea on Hawai'i and Mt Carstensz (Jaya) in Irian Jaya during several of the latest Neogene glacial episodes. When these ice ages ended, temperatures rose rapidly and much of this ice melted.

Lowered temperatures during these ice ages also lowered sea level and disrupted interglacial wind and ocean-current patterns. On most islands, except perhaps the Hawaiian group, this lowered precipitation levels. On Easter Island and in the Galapagos group, large lakes now exist in volcanic craters which were dry around the height of the last glacial (ice age) maximum. PHOSPHATES, which existed in mineable quantities on many mid-Pacific islands 100 years or so ago, are not forming today because these islands receive too much rain and the GUANO is washed away before it decomposes. Most of the rock phosphates on islands like Banaba (Ocean Island) and Nauru formed during ice ages when the climate of these islands was much drier, and guano was not washed off the surface.

Melting ice was the main cause of the rapid sea-level rise which marked the end of these ice ages. Conversely, the beginning of each ice age, when terrestrial ice sheets grew rapidly, was marked by a (much slower) fall in sea level. The effects of these changes on island environments have been investigated in detail only for the last great ice age, which began around 100 000 years ago and ended perhaps 10 000 years ago. Sea level fell to a minimum of - 125–130 m (relative to its present level) around the glacial maximum, some 17 000 years ago.

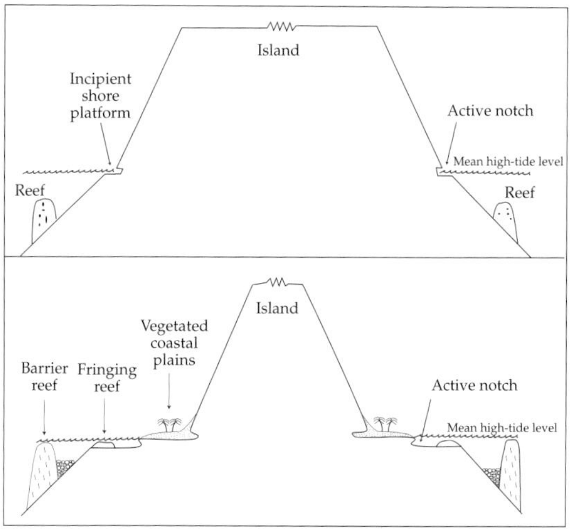

Figure 1.11 Diagram of the gradual formation of fringing reefs and coastal plains around a volcanic island. The tidal action of the sea erodes coastal cliffs and creates a platform upon which coral grows, while the volcanic rock crumbles and forms soil

Ha'atu'upai Beach, Tongatapu, Tonga: double notch cut in bedrock limestone cliff, uplifted after a large earthquake some 800 years ago. The upper notch (indicated by hammer) is thought to have been at sea level originally

The effect of sea-level changes was most marked on low islands and those surrounded by coral reef. Islands which were low during an interglacial would have been transformed into high islands during the glacial. Kwajalein Atoll—one of the largest of these low islands today—would have become a massive island, of great significance in both oceanographic and biogeographic senses, during the last ice age. The main part of Fiji would have become a much larger landmass than it is today; iguanas were among the animals at this time utilizing land connections which are now drowned. For the earliest humans in the western Pacific, the islands would have been larger and closer together than they are today, and people may have been far more mobile within the region than we yet realize. The traces of this mobility lie along the ice-age coasts, where people built their settlements: but these coasts now lie under tens of metres of ocean, overgrown by reef, and buried with sediment.

The rapid rise in sea level at the end of the last ice age may have provided the impetus for the human migration out of east Asia which led eventually to the initial colonization of islands east of Solomon Islands. The islands which the earliest settlers encountered were quite different to those which had existed at the height of the ice age. The climate was warmer and moister, with resulting vegetation change. The grassland savannas, which had taken over during the dry glacial maximum, changed in composition and were gradually replaced by rainforest, at least in the wettest parts of the islands. Increasing wetness also led to faster landscape change; weathering became more intense, and processes of erosion more effective.

Islands rapidly drowned. Many island coasts today are highly embayed—a direct consequence of drowning during postglacial sea-level rise. Many CORAL reefs in the Pacific today were not growing during the last ice age because ocean temperatures were too low. Those that did grow were comparatively impoverished. As postglacial sea level began to rise, so did ocean temperatures, and reefs began growing once more in much of the Pacific. Some reefs could not grow at the same rate as the rising sea level and eventually drowned; a large number of drowned reefs west of Savai'i in Samoa are thought to have formed in this way. Other reefs grew upwards at the same rate as sea level rose; those off the Huon Peninsula in Papua New Guinea, around New Caledonia and at Tarawa Atoll in Kiribati are examples. Most common within the Pacific are the reefs which grew upwards and eventually caught up with sea level.

Some of these 'catch-up' reefs are living today only because sea level has fallen within the last few thousand years. It is now almost certain that sea level in the Pacific during the Holocene (the last 10 000 years) peaked between 6000 and 3000 years ago, perhaps 1–2 m above its present level, since when it has fallen. These sea-level changes were driven by temperature changes. The Holocene thermal maximum was around the same time; temperatures have cooled notably since then. Vegetation responded to these temperature changes, so ecosystems were probably in a state of change on many islands when people settled them first (probably) in the late Holocene.

Many environmental changes during the late Holocene have been routinely blamed on human impact without any real evidence. Fires, for example, which could have been associated with increased incidence of lightning on more arid island environments—even those occupied by humans—are seen as clear signs of vegetation firing by humans. On some islands, the occurrence of charcoal bands in sedimentary sequences has been taken as the first sign of human presence. Such reasoning should be suspected, particularly when corroborative indicators of human presence are lacking, as they are on Mangaia in the southern Cook Islands where this debate was focused in the 1990s.

Many post-settlement Pacific environmental changes traditionally attributed to human impact have been questioned, in the light of knowledge of climate and other non-human changes. Two marked climate changes in the last c1200 years are becoming increasingly better known. During the Little Climatic Optimum (c1200–700 years ago), temperatures rose and precipitation levels fell in most of the tropical and subtropical Pacific. Water-conservatory strategies developed by people at this time led to agricultural terracing and irrigation modifications to many islands; elaborate systems on Aneityum in Vanuatu first attracted the attention of archaeologists to this island.

This period was followed by the Little Ice Age (c600–200 years ago), when temperatures, precipitation and sea level were all low. Of particular interest to the study of recent environmental change is the transition between the Little Climatic Optimum and the Little Ice Age around 650 years ago, when there was apparently a rapid fall in both temperature and sea level, and a massive, albeit short-lived, rise in precipitation. The latter devastated resource-production systems, and caused landscape changes of a scale probably unmatched during the post-settlement history of most islands. Natural vegetation—forest or grassland—adapted to the dry warm conditions of the Little Climatic Optimum, was damaged to such an extent that it has perhaps never recovered.

The sudden drop in available resources for human consumption led to societal breakdown and inter-tribal conflict. Easter Island—immortalized (albeit for the wrong reasons) in the Kevin Costner film *Rapanui*—is one of the best-known examples. But the trend is apparent elsewhere. In Fiji, the Vuda Phase begins around this time and marks the end of unfortified coastal settlements and the start of fortified hilltop ones.

A rise in temperature, precipitation and sea level over the past 200 years has heralded the end of the Little Ice Age. The result, possibly sustained or amplified in recent decades as a consequence of the human-enhanced greenhouse effect, has been continued changes in island environments, although these changes have themselves sometimes been amplified by human actions. Rising temperatures in recent decades have been cited as a cause of increased tropical cyclone incidence, a phenomenon considered as a major cause of accelerated landscape change on islands like Viti Levu in Fiji. Most island coasts have been drowned in the past century or so as a consequence of sea-level rise at a rate of perhaps 1.5 mm per year. This seemingly negligible rise can produce dramatic effects on gently-sloping island coastlines. If climate changes in the future as most models predict, then the rate of recent changes could increase sharply.

Late Neogene environmental changes on many islands, particularly in the southwest quadrant of the Pacific Ocean, have been dominated by vertical movements of the land. Such islands lie close to the ocean trench marking the place on the Earth's surface where one section of crust (a plate) is being pushed beneath another. This type of convergent plate boundary is associated with vertical movements, some down but mostly upwards. The north-facing coasts of Choiseul in Solomon Islands are dominated by a series of steps reaching over 800 m above sea level, each of which corresponds to an emerged coral reef, analogous to that growing offshore today.

The nature of these long-term island uplifts is not well understood. For much of the late Neogene, slow continuous aseismic uplift (vertical creep) has been dominant at rates ranging from 1.6–1.9 mm per year for Maré in the Loyalty Islands of New Caledonia to perhaps 10 mm per year on Middleton Island in Alaska. For more recent periods, uplift coincident with large earthquakes (coseismic uplift) has been recorded. During the 1964 Prince William Sound earthquake in the northernmost Pacific, parts of Kodiak Island subsided 2.3 m while parts of Montague Island were lifted more than 11 m, both within seconds. More typically, Guadalcanal in Solomon Islands was lifted up 1.5 m in the 1961 earthquake. Similar effects have been felt in the Fiji–Tonga region perhaps every 800–1000 years.

It is sometimes difficult to separate the environmental legacy of tectonic change from that of sea-level change. For example, most low coastal plains around most island coasts today formed as a result of the late Holocene sea-level fall. Yet some of these coastal plains are slightly higher or lower than expected, reflecting the significant role of tectonic changes also in their formation.

The character of modern island environments is determined largely by climate and geology. Rates of landform development are much greater in the humid tropics than in the dry equatorial parts of the Pacific. At Ok Ningi in the New Guinea Highlands, the land surface is being lowered by as much as 4 mm/yr. In the drier parts of the Hawaiian group, the rate is 0.04 mm/yr. Active volcanoes continue to build islands in the Pacific: Mauna Loa–Kīlauea volcano on Hawai'i is one of the best studied, and Rabaul (VOLCANOES OF PAPUA NEW GUINEA) has one of the most regularly erupting volcanoes.

The idea of environmental change is not novel in most parts of the world, although it remains so in the Pacific. Many long-term developments are planned on the assumption that, were it not for human impact, island environments would be unchanging. This view needs to be dislodged for effective planning, especially because of the threats posed to Pacific island environments by future climate change, particularly sea-level rise, predicted from models of the human-enhanced greenhouse effect. There is a tendency to believe that sea-level rise is a key issue for all Pacific islands. Undoubtedly it is for low-lying islands; but such a view has undoubtedly encouraged complacency among some decision makers when firm and far-sighted decisions should perhaps have been taken.—PDN

Further reading

Nunn, P D, 1994. *Oceanic Islands,* Blackwell.

Climate change

There is dispute among scientists whether global warming is a factor in climate change and therefore a problem for the future. The debate rests on four assumptions: that the earth's climate is warming up; that human activity is the main cause; that warming will have disastrous consequences; and that early multilateral action is required to arrest those consequences. Each of these assumptions is the cause of some argument.

What is not in dispute is that global climatic patterns are undergoing change, and that many consequences of that change are affecting countries of the Pacific. Recent observations have shown that the Northern Hemisphere is warming less than the Southern Hemisphere. One reason is that the heavily populated land masses in the north produce more atmospheric pollution, dampening the solar radiation heating capacity on earth. The situation is quite different in the Southern Hemisphere, where air pollutants' distribution and density are less, and absorption and reflection of incoming solar radiation does not occur to the same degree.

There are also geographic characteristics which cause climatic differentiation between the two hemispheres. These include the polar Antarctic continent; the Pacific, Atlantic and Indian oceans—a very large ocean mass which has a thermal moderating effect; a subcontinent—South America—separating the two largest oceans of the world, with a high vertebral mountain chain running from north to south over the entire subcontinent, and extending to the southernmost latitudes; continental Australasia (Australia and New Zealand); and the important southern portion of the African continent, located in subtropical latitudes.

This geographic framework creates special effects in the atmospheric and oceanic circulations of the southern hemisphere including the development of the polar vortex, a seasonal and regional particularity observed during each winter over the Antarctic continent. The equatorial EL NIÑO (and La Niña) cycle also plays a major part in short-term climate change affecting Pacific countries.

Changes attributed to global weather patterns include DROUGHT, excessive rainfall and flooding, increased frequency of violent hurricanes (also known as CYCLONES, or typhoons in East Asia), rising sea levels and the spread of insect-borne diseases. Many smaller islands of the Pacific, in particular those with low-lying atolls or extensive coastal settlement, have deep concerns about the potential impact of climate change, especially rising sea levels and changing weather patterns. They are vulnerable to inundation; and others could lose their freshwater sources. The survival of some island states—including Kiribati, Tuvalu and Tokelau—and the economic, social and cultural viability of many others, is seen to be threatened by global 'greenhouse gas' emissions and other human influences on the global climate.

Pacific island countries, frequently in concert with other island countries from the Indian Ocean and Caribbean through the Alliance of Small Island States (AOSIS), and through the SOUTH PACIFIC FORUM, have taken a leading role in international negotiations on climate change, including both the Earth Summit in Rio de Janeiro and the Kyoto Conference (REGIONAL COOPERATION AND INITIATIVES). Island states supported adoption of the 1997 Kyoto Protocol which, when ratified, will provide legally binding commitments by developed countries for reductions in emissions of carbon dioxide and other greenhouse gases, and also supported the establishment of rules for international implementation mechanisms to ensure attainment of the Kyoto objectives.

Broad strategic directions relating to climate change are covered in the National Environmental Management Strategies (NEMS) of many island countries, although more work is needed to develop detailed strategies for adoption. In their view, an effective global response to the practical effects of climate change requires ongoing, active cooperation and strengthened action by all countries. Vulnerable island states share a particular concern about adaptation measures necessary to counter existing and anticipated climatic change effects.—PL & KRF

Drought

Many Pacific island countries are vulnerable to drought, with its associated conditions of plant stress and diminishing quantities of fresh water. Islanders in the western Pacific especially have experienced lengthy periods (of 5–6 years, sometimes) of below-normal rainfall with some frequency. Even severe drought has occurred many times over several thousand years. In recent years, the causes and effects of CLIMATE CHANGE have become the subject of media attention as well as scientific debate. With or without severe drought, higher temperatures entail greater evaporation, and increase stresses in agriculture, and urgent conservation measures are required for both food crops and cash crops. Dramatic weather patterns—both drought and abnormally heavy rain—are attributable to the EL NIÑO phenomenon (and La Niña), which have significant consequences for agriculture.

Effects of major drought in the Pacific region, 1997

Irian Jaya and Papua New Guinea experienced probably the most prolonged and severe drought for 100 years in 1997, caused by El Niño. Shortages of food and water became critical in many rural areas, and drought-related health problems caused increased mortality rates in many isolated regions. A number of key institutions—including many hospitals, health centres, aid posts and schools—were forced to close, mainly due to lack of water. Emergency drought-relief programs were instigated, but the rugged terrain and isolation of many communities made an effective response difficult. Highlands provinces suffered from repeated frosts occurring at lower than normal altitudes that destroyed almost all vegetation and therefore affecting many more people. There were also widespread and destructive fires, with the combined impact leaving thousands of villagers dependent on famine foods such as wild yams, ferns, leaves and banana roots. With worst-affected rural areas left without food, water and electricity, there was considerable movement of people to urban centres. Primary production and related operations in the industrial sector were affected, and mines closed.

Crops devastated by drought in large areas of Papua New Guinea, 1997

In Fiji devastating effects of El Niño were experienced in 1998, with severe drought conditions occurring in many parts of the country. In particular, the drought caused a major disruption to the SUGAR INDUSTRY. Agriculture, tourism, manufacturing industries, and education were also adversely affected. In the Republic of the Marshall Islands, the absence of rain so depleted the Majuro reservoir that water had to be brought in from outside the country. In Solomon Islands, there was serious damage to subsistence food gardens, and many daily activities, including schools, were disrupted.

For the smaller atoll countries of the Pacific, supply of adequate fresh water is an ongoing problem, even when rainfall remains at average levels. In recognition of the importance of safe, reliable water supplies, the South Pacific Applied Geoscience Commission (SOPAC) established a Water Resources Unit, aiming at sustainable utilization of water resources in member countries (REGIONAL COOPERATION AND INITIATIVES).—BJA

Further reading

Allen, B J and Bourke, R M, 1997. *Report of an Assessment of the Impacts of Frost and Drought in Papua New Guinea,* Australian Agency for International Aid and Development.

Allen, B J and Brookfield, H C (eds), 1989. 'Frost and drought in the Highlands of Papua New Guinea', *Mountain Research and Development,* 9(3).

El Niño

The climate of the Pacific islands is influenced by a fluctuating pattern of atmospheric pressure imbalances occurring between the northern Australian/

Indonesian region and the central Pacific Ocean. When the air pressure is abnormally high in one region, it is usually correspondingly low in the other. Measurements of the difference in sea-level atmospheric pressure, recorded at Tahiti and Darwin, are used to create the southern oscillation index (SOI). Highly negative values of the SOI usually accompany below-normal air pressures and warmer sea surface temperatures in the central and eastern equatorial Pacific, known as an El Niño phase. This Spanish term (El Niño, 'baby boy', is a reference to the Christ child) arose because the phenomena it describes usually occur around Christmas time off the coast of Chile and Peru, when the sea surface temperature warms. Fish disappear, birds fall out of the sky (dead from starvation in the absence of fish), fishing communities suffer; and in the deserts, there is flash flooding which sweeps people out of the dry gullies. At the other end of the cycle, highly positive values produce the reverse situation, known as La Niña.

The warm water that occurs off Chile in December sometimes moves out in a tongue into the Pacific over the following six months. In the western Pacific, sea surface temperatures fall relative to those in the east. This means that the 'normal' situation is reversed, with cooler water in the western Pacific and warmer water in the eastern and central regions. The changes in sea surface temperature influence the temperature and pressure of the air above the huge mass of the Pacific Ocean. A vertical circulation of air which 'normally' rises over the western Pacific and sinks over the central and eastern ocean reverses its direction. This vertical movement of air along the equator is referred to as the 'Walker Circulation', after a British meteorologist who studied

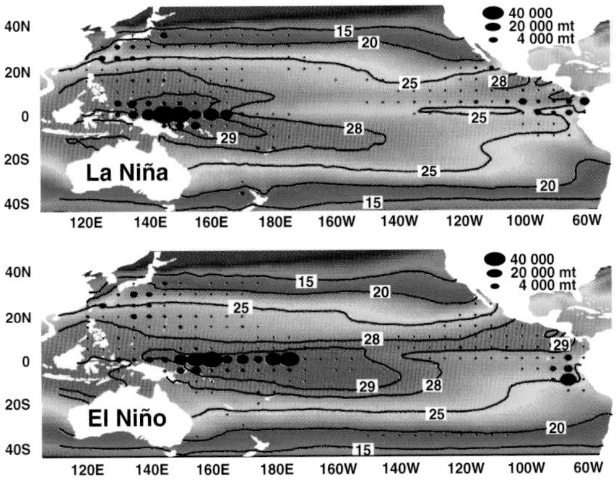

Figure 1.12 Distribution of purse seine tuna catch in metric tonnes (mt), shown in relation to fluctuating sea surface temperatures (Celsius)
Source: SPC.

Indian monsoons in the 19th century and who first hypothesized the cause of the failure of monsoons, and hence drought and famine in India. Rising, warm, moist air is unstable and results in rain and thunderstorms. Sinking, cool, dry air results in very little rain.

El Niño has a global impact and can cause great extremes in weather, although the frequency of its occurrence suggests that it could well be regarded as a normal condition. Significant El Niño episodes—lasting for 6 months or more—may create severe and widespread DROUGHT conditions, such as have been experienced by Papua New Guinea and Fiji in 1982–83, and 1997–98. They may also bring abnormally heavy rain to the central and eastern Pacific. The correlation between El Niño and drought is not predictable, and could be taken as confirmation that the trans-Pacific circulation patterns are always in an unsteady state. The period of the southern oscillation is very irregular, varying between about 2 and 10 years, with an average period of 3–4 years.—BJA

Natural disasters

The Pacific Ocean has almost all the agents with the potential of being hazardous to human life. While not all geophysical or atmospheric events are of equal severity, some are particularly powerful in their effects, but in an area as large as the Pacific, even these extreme events are not necessarily associated with disasters. Only when extreme natural events impinge on a vulnerable human community does a disastrous situation emerge. Hazardous physical events may be attributed broadly to plate movements and atmospheric movements (GEOLOGICAL HISTORY OF THE PACIFIC). The main plate in this area is the Pacific plate, with the Indo-Australian plate, the Philippines, Cocos and Nasca plates around the edge. The Pacific Rim consists almost entirely of plate boundaries which, together with the boundaries of minor platelets, create a dynamic geo-physical environment.

The Indo-Australian plate is drifting northwards, currently at about 6–10 cm per year. This oblique convergence with the Pacific plate has produced a series of island arcs and microplates north and east of the mainland of Papua New Guinea. Virtually all the islands of the southwest Pacific lie on plate boundaries. Movements of the earth's crust along these plate boundaries result in mountain building, island uplift and the many earthquakes that occur along the island chain from New Zealand through Fiji to Papua New Guinea, as well as in Japan and along the western seaboard of North America.

These movements are also responsible for most of the volcanoes which together create the Pacific rim of fire. These volcanoes account for about 80 per cent of all above-sea volcanoes on earth. Of these most (about 80 per cent) occur at convergent boundaries where rocks at the earth's surface are absorbed back into the molten layer by the process of subduction, and 15 per cent occur where the plates are diverging or spreading apart. The remaining volcanoes, such as those of the Hawaiian Islands, occur in the middle of the plates at mantle hotspots which are thought to originate where giant plumes of hot material rise from deep within the earth's mantle and impinge on the base of the earth's crust resulting in volcanoes on the plate as it passes over the hotspot.

VOLCANIC ACTIVITY and earthquakes may be severe events themselves, but they are also associated with other hazardous events such as landslides and TSUNAMI. Damage was caused in the southwest Pacific by tsunami initiated by the earthquakes in Chile in 1960 and Alaska in 1964. It has been suggested that large landslides from the flanks of volcanoes on Réunion Island in the Indian Ocean and in Hawai'i may also have caused tsunami in the Pacific. The areas with the greatest risk of landslides are the earthquake-prone mountainous areas on or near the plate boundaries. Young soft rocks forming steep-sided mountain ranges in tectonically active areas often induce orographic rainfall and are particularly susceptible to landslides. Similarly, the flanks of volcanoes such as Kelut in eastern Java and in Papua New Guinea are susceptible to volcanic mud flows when heavy rainfall is associated with earthquakes. Pacific islands are at risk because many are relatively low and easily inundated by tsunami and storm surges due to CYCLONES.

Over the region, there is a high probability of large destructive earthquakes. Prime areas are the Philippines, China, Indonesia, Papua New Guinea, Solomon Islands and New Zealand. In the eastern rim countries of Central and South America, further earthquakes are likely. There is less likelihood of large destructive earthquakes in the Pacific islands.

The main atmospheric features with the potential to be hazardous to humanity in the Pacific are cyclones and the effects of ENSO (EL NIÑO–Southern Oscillation) events. The incidence and severity of cyclones in the southwest Pacific is relatively low compared with those of the North Pacific east of the Philippines. Most tropical cyclones move towards the poles and may last from a few days to a few weeks. Cyclones may result in very heavy rainfall (over 800 mm per day near the eye has been recorded), and even after the cyclone crosses the coast and deteriorates to a rain depression, rainfall can still be high over huge areas. One estimate is that a mature cyclone can produce a total of 17 cubic km of rainfall per day. This rainfall can cause flooding over large areas, and flooding may lead to landslides in at-risk areas.

Nonetheless, even the most extreme natural events only result in a disaster if they impinge on vulnerable communities. An understanding of disasters therefore rests on an understanding of the relative vulnerability of the communities who live in the islands and around the coastal Pacific Rim. Vulnerability may be defined as the capacity of any person or group to anticipate, cope with, resist and recover from the impact of an extreme natural event. Levels of vulnerability may vary according to socio-economic status, class, caste, ethnicity, gender, disability, age or seniority, depending on the particular mores of a community. Within communities at all levels, some members are more vulnerable than others, and in this sense, vulnerability may be contrasted with security or capability to protect one's community, home and family and to re-establish one's livelihood.

In poor countries where the economic costs of disasters may exceed 3–4 per cent of the gross national product, the effects of disasters on the national economies and the individual welfare of their people may be dramatic and set back development aims for decades. However, although some very poor countries are disaster-prone, disaster death-rates are generally higher in middle income countries that are experiencing rapid economic development, war or other upheavals. Such countries include Guatemala, Nicaragua, Peru, South Korea and Papua New Guinea. Only three of the countries that possess high disaster death-rates as measured by Red Cross data are included in the World Bank's list of low-income economies. The other four are middle and upper-middle-income countries. Around the Pacific Rim lie countries with widely differing economic status, including a number of the 'tiger' economies. Even when measures of disaster other than deaths, such as economic losses, are used, the pattern of vulnerability remains complex since poor countries have proportionately less infrastructure to lose than middle-income countries. Given the recency of their URBANIZATION and infrastructure development, people in many of the countries in and around the Pacific are very vulnerable to disaster both individually and nationally.

The small islands rarely appear in global databases of disasters since they are excluded by the criteria for entry. Their low populations and population densities mean that few events kill more than 10 persons. Their relatively low levels of economic development mean that the dollar value of infrastructure loss may be regarded as insignificant at international levels and they rarely appeal for international assistance. However, the vulnerability of their societies to extreme natural events may be extreme. For example, when Cyclone Uma, a category 3–4 cyclone, passed over Port Vila in Vanuatu in 1987, it damaged nearly all buildings, power and water supplies were affected, the storm surge damaged the sea walls and reached the main street of the town, and more than 40 boats were lost in the harbour. The total cost of this cyclone has been calculated as 150 per cent of Vanuatu's GNP. Given the death toll of 55 persons—which is about the same as that of Cyclone Tracy which hit Darwin in 1974—it has been estimated that if this event were to be scaled up to the size of the population and economy of Australia, the disaster would be measured at a death toll of 5234 and economic losses of A$390 billion. In the context of Pacific countries, small disasters can have huge consequences. Given the generally higher incidence of smaller events and the number of small nations, there is a high probability of relatively frequent disasters producing devastating consequences.

Islanders must be in a position to reduce their vulnerability if they are to mitigate an impending disaster. Surviving the immediate impact may not mean ultimate survival for either individuals or communities. For example, in 1985 four cyclones crossed the 361 islands of Fiji within a period of two months. Their effect was to destroy 30 per cent of the country's agricultural production in the short term and reduce longer term output as 80 per cent of the tree crops and much of the sugarcane were damaged. An increase in the growth of crops such as SUGAR for export and a reduction in the growth of root crops which had been shown to be more resistant to storm damage, made the people more vulnerable to the storm since they were deprived of the money to pay for the imported food on which they had come to rely. The flooding of the remaining area of subsistence fields with brackish water only added to their vulnerability.

Self-sufficiency in food production and buildings of local materials (which cause little direct damage to people when struck by extreme winds) may appear to western eyes to indicate poverty, but the cash economy (of imported foods and new lifestyles) with which it is being replaced, may, at least in the short term, increase vulnerability. Examples may be found in the rapidly growing urban areas of the Philippines, other coastal areas of Asia and in central and South America.

The Pacific region may suffer from higher incidences of extreme natural events than any other area of the world, but ultimately the incidence of disaster depends on the vulnerability of the people. Much of this vulnerability rests, in turn, on global economic trends, making disaster in the Pacific region a global responsibility.—JL2

Cataclysmic eruptions

Three of the 10 largest volcanic eruptions in the world in the last 10 000 years occurred in Island Melanesia. About 3500 years ago, Mt Witori erupted on New Britain; then about 1850 years ago, Ambrym volcano on Vanuatu; and about 1300 years later, Kuwae volcano erupted and blew the island of that name apart, an event still recorded in oral traditions in the central Vanuatu area.

Burns Philp store in Rabaul, destroyed in eruption, September 1996

The huge Ambrym eruption created the present caldera in the centre of the island. Post-caldera eruptions on Ambrym have continued, although nowhere near the same scale, up to the present. In December 1913 an eruption and accompanying earthquakes caused widespread local damage to fertile land and coconut plantations. Mission stations and villages were affected in eruptions in 1929 and 1946, and another in 1950 brought about the resettlement of about 400 Ambrym residents on Efate.

The Kuwae eruption was triggered by the interaction of sea water with hot magma, possibly beginning in about 1450 but with the major explosion occurring over a day or two probably in late 1452. Kuwae would have been an island of a few kilometres in width, with two volcanic cones; now there is a submarine caldera between the islands of Epi and

Yasur volcano, Vanuatu

Tongoa, with a submerged volcano that periodically makes a brief appearance above sea level. The eruption released huge amounts of dust and acid gases into the stratosphere, producing a world-wide impact on climate for the next few years. When Captain COOK visited in 1774, he named the group of seven islands and smaller islets the Shepherd Islands.

On the island of Tanna in southern Vanuatu, Yasur volcano produced two major eruptions between 1400 and 800 years ago. The last serious eruption was in 1878 when the southeastern end of the island was uplifted, reducing the depth of the harbour at Port Resolution. The volcano has remained active but not dangerous, and the ease of visitor access to the crater's rim is now promoted.

Scene of destruction after Rabaul eruption, September 1996

In Papua New Guinea, the town of Rabaul is located inside the huge caldera of a volcano on the northern tip of the Gazelle Peninsula of New Britain. The magma chamber or epicentre, a kilometre below ground, erupted in the 6th century AD, forming a harbour after the eastern wall collapsed and the ocean flooded the crater. The oral traditions of the Tolai people of the Rabaul area explain that they moved into the Gazelle Peninsula some time after this devastating eruption either killed off or forced out whoever lived there before. Archaeological evidence indicates that the areas of the main LAPITA sites on Watom Island, just off the east end of New Britain, were used for gardening before the eruption, and then Watom may have been abandoned for about 600 years. A ring of active, dormant and extant volcanoes now surrounds Rabaul's harbour with major eruptions having occurred in 1878, 1937 and 1994. The small vent called Tavurvur (or Matupi) and an island called Vulcan in Rabaul's harbour resulted from the latest eruptions. (See also HIGH TROPICAL MOUNTAINS; VOLCANIC ACTIVITY).—MS & MQ

Further reading

Spriggs, M, 1997. *The Island Melanesians*, Blackwell.

Cyclones

Cyclones are extremely low pressure systems around which high winds blow, rotating anti-clockwise in the northern hemisphere and clockwise in the southern hemisphere. They are also called typhoons (Chinese for 'big wind') in Asia and hurricanes in the Americas, and form over oceans where sea-surface temperatures are 26–27°C. Cyclones rarely form within 5–6 degrees of latitude of the equator, and this, with the need for high surface temperatures, means that there are two belts of cyclone creation, north and south of the equator. A mature tropical cyclone may be up to 2000 km across with an 'eye' of gently sinking air of 10–15 km across. The highest wind speeds occur just outside the eye and may reach 300 km/hr. The eye of the cyclone moves forward at about 10–20 km/hr but if it stops moving, the sea-surface temperature beneath quickly cools and the cyclone may deteriorate into a rain depression. The low pressure centre of the cyclone lifts the ocean surface by up to 1 m and this, with the effects of the strong winds outside the eye, can cause storm surges especially when the cyclone crosses the coastline.

There is a bright side to the pattern of hazards across the Pacific. The sheer size and global significance of the region, and the range of economic capacity of the countries within it, mean that significant resources have been allocated to various warning systems, especially for tsunami and hurricanes. Earthquakes and volcanic eruptions are much more difficult to forecast with current knowledge.

Hurricane Warning System: Hurricane activity is very closely monitored by all the countries of Oceania and adjacent areas. Any hurricane activity is monitored and photographed continuously by satellites and transmitted to many earth stations.

The US National Oceanographic and Atmospheric Administration (NOAA) National Weather Service Hurricane Center in San Francisco covers the eastern Pacific; the weather forecasting office in Hawai'i covers the central Pacific; the Joint US Navy-Air Force Typhoon Warning System in Guam covers the western Pacific. The Japan meteorological organization in Tokyo covers also a great part of the western and central Pacific Ocean. Hurricane information for the South Pacific is provided by Fiji, New Zealand, Australia, and French Polynesia. Thus the entire Pacific is covered and warnings can be provided to any region. Warning information of potentially hazardous approaching tropical cyclones will include information on the storm type, central pressure given in millimetres, observed wind speeds within the storm, storm location, speed and direction of movement, extent of the affected area, visibility, and state of the sea as well as any other information that may be available.—JL2

Tsunami

Tsunami are sea waves generated quickly by sea floor disturbances such as earthquake activity, volcanic eruptions, or landslides occurring either under the sea or close enough to the sea to cause a wave. Tsunami waves, usually only 1–2 m in height, can travel great distances and at great speed—more than 800 km per hour. Areas most at risk are funnel-shaped bays and harbours—hence the name 'tsunami', which comes from the Japanese word for 'harbour wave'. The eruption of Krakatoa in 1883 was responsible for one of the most significant volcano-induced tsunami ever. It resulted in the Pacific Ocean resonating with wave disturbances for many weeks. Major tsunami earthquakes that have been felt in the Pacific islands have often been generated by submarine earthquakes around the Pacific Rim. The Chilean earthquake of May 1960 affected many Pacific islands as did the great Alaskan earthquake of Easter 1964.

The devastating effects of tsunami such as these drew attention to the need for an improved warning system, leading to the establishment of an International Tsunami Warning Center based in Hawai'i. In 1965 the Intergovernmental Oceanographic Com-

After-effects of the Aitape tsunami in July 1998, which struck the northern coast of Papua New Guinea

mission (IOC) of UNESCO accepted an offer by the United States to expand its Tsunami Warning Center in Honolulu to become the headquarters of an International Pacific Tsunami Warning System. The IOC also accepted the offer of other IOC member countries to integrate their existing facilities and communications into this system. The existing US Warning System was then integrated with those of Japan, the Soviet Union, Chile, and of other regional centres, and became a truly international warning system. Twenty-six nations are now members of this network, which uses numerous seismic and tidal stations and provides tsunami watches and warnings for all the Pacific. While warnings and travel times of tsunami generated by distant earthquakes or volcanic eruptions can be made with great accuracy, warnings are impossible for local tsunami.

On the evening of Friday 17 July 1998 a massive tsunami swept over the sand barrier that forms the outer margin of Sissano Lagoon in the Aitape district of West Sepik province, on the northern coast of Papua New Guinea. The wave was 7–10 m high, in places up to 15 m, and damage associated with it extended up to 2 km inland. Four villages—Arop, Malo, Sissano and Warapu—were wiped out. Over 2100 people were killed, including 250 children and teachers at the three community schools, and hundreds of people were injured. Because of its remoteness, its complex of land and water, and the scale of the disaster, the area had to be abandoned and the lagoon became a 'death lake'. Detailed surveys by scientific teams after the event found that severe damage and extreme wave heights were confined to a relatively short (30 km) stretch of coast between Aitape and Sissano villages. They also found there was no warning of the tsunami, although in places the earthquake, which resulted in substantial submarine movements and seaslides off the coast, was felt minutes before the wave arrived. In Aitape, the time interval between the generating earthquake and wave arrival was just a few minutes.

The northern side of the island of New Guinea is vulnerable to tsunami. Running parallel with the coast and just a few kilometres offshore lies the turbulent boundary between two tectonic plates which are constantly moving against each other. This movement causes land and submarine earthquakes, some of which will cause tsunami. Indeed, since records began nearly every generation in this area has suffered tsunami devastation. Recent incidents occurred in Papua New Guinea on 16 August 1996, and on 17 February 1996 in Irian Jaya, when 116 people were reported killed or missing and 10 000 homeless. Major damage occurred at Biak Island just 30–40 km southwest of the earthquake's epicentre. Immediately prior to that event and further west, a tsunami devastated the central part of Sulawesi Island in Indonesia on 1 January 1996. The magnitude of this tsunami did not reach that of 12 December 1992, when over 2000 people were killed on Flores Island after waves reaching 20 m in height devastated the coastal region. Papua New Guinea received a grant of US$600 000 (K1.3 million) from the United States to install an early warning seismic monitoring system following the Aitape tsunami in July 1998.—RFMcL & JL2

two peoples

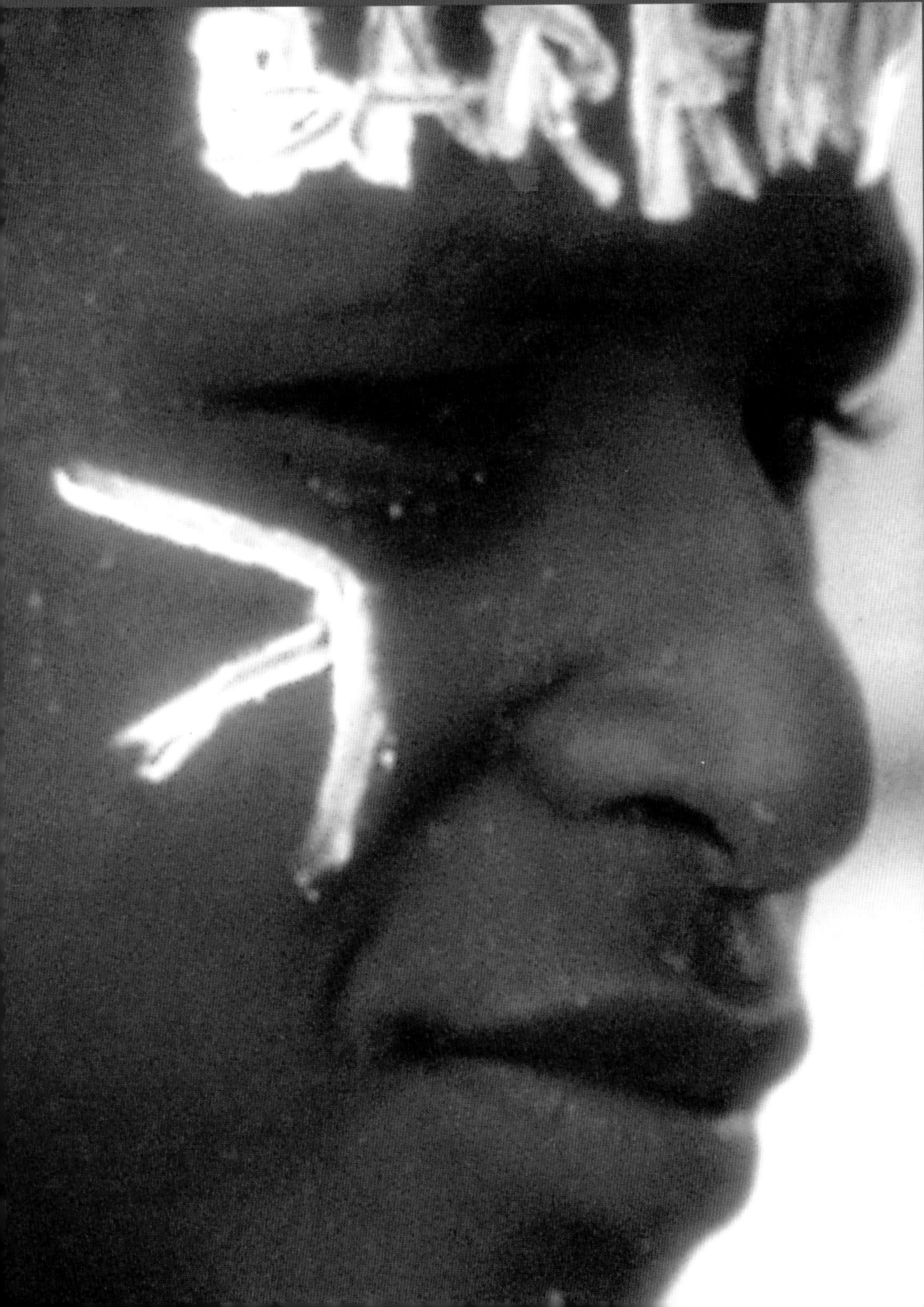

Contributors

Article contributors

AA	Atholl Anderson
BF	Ben Finney
BVL	Brij V Lal
CC	Chris Corne
CJ	Christine Jourdan
CM1	Cluny Macpherson
CM2	Clive Moore
DAB	Dirk Anthony Ballendorf
DAC	David A Chappell
DAS	Deryck Scarr
DH	David Hanlon
DS2	Donovan Storey
DT	Darrell Tryon
EO	Eugene Ogan
GJ	Giff Johnson
GMcC	Grant McCall
HVT	Howard Van Trease
JG2	Jack Golson
JS	Jeff Siegel
KEJ	Kerry James
KRF	Kate Fortune
KRH	Kerry Howe
MJ	Margaret Jolly
MO	Midori Osumi
MQ	Max Quanchi
MS	Matthew Spriggs
MTC	Marjorie Tuainekore Crocombe
PB	Peter Bellwood
PD'A	Paul D'arcy
PG	Paul Geraghty
PMcD	Philip McDermott
RB	Richard Bedford
RCK	Robert C Kiste
RGC	Ron Crocombe
RGW	R Gerard Ward
RL2	Robert Langdon
SMcP	Samuel F McPhetres
TCP	Thomas C Panholzer
TD	Tom Dutton
TK	Timoti Karetu

Photo contributors

Crawford House Publishing, Bathurst, New South Wales: reproduced from *Arts of Vanuatu* (1996)—plate 89: 59

Canberra Times, 1972; photographed by John Lamont: 112

Cunningham, Lawrence J (University of Guam, Mangilao): 94

Fortune, Kate (Wellington): 113, 115

Hendrie, Peter (Pacific Journeys, Melbourne): 92, 93 (top), 103

Kiste, Robert C (Center for Pacific Islands Studies, University of Hawai'i–Manoa, Honolulu): 74, 101, 102, 104 (left)

Lawrence, Helen Reeves (Papua New Guinea): 93 (bottom)

McCall, Grant (Centre for South Pacific Studies, University of New South Wales, Kensington): 58

McPhetres, Samuel F (Saipan, Commonwealth of the Northern Mariana Islands): 89, 104 (right)

Marshall Islands Visitors Authority (Majuro, Republic of the Marshall Islands): 62, 88, 98, 99 (left)

Ministry of Information, Republic of the Fiji Islands (Suva): 105

National Library of Australia (Canberra): 80, 95

New Caledonia Tourism (Sydney): 99 (bottom left), 100

Palau Visitors Authority (Palau): 97 (bottom)

Panholzer, Thomas C (College of Micronesia–FSM, Pohnpei): 96, 97 (top)

Waters, Sheila (Melbourne): photographs by Sarah Chinnery (1887–1970): 73, 79

Wellington Newspapers Ltd (New Zealand): photograph by John Selkirk: 75

West, Richard (Canberra): 51 (detail), 72, 90

Maps

Bellwood, Peter (The Australian National University, Canberra): 66

ONE SETTLEMENT

Footsteps from Asia: the peopling of the Pacific

The colonization of the Pacific region began more than 35 000 years ago, long before written records. Scholars may therefore disagree about every major statement presented here, but a persuasive consensus of opinion combines the majority views from within a number of disciplines. The disciplines concerned in this quest include the palaeoenvironmental sciences (which can inform about matters such as past land bridges, the nature of ancient climates and possible environmental encouragements to migration); biological anthropology, concerned with genetic and population history; comparative linguistics, concerned with the histories and relationships of languages; and archaeology, concerned with ancient lifestyles and material cultures.

The peoples of the Pacific—comprising loose geographical groupings termed Australians, Indonesians, Melanesians, Micronesians and Polynesians—are each distinct in certain respects, and interrelated in others. Genes, languages and cultures do not always correlate: people who speak closely related languages may sometimes differ physically, or people of similar physical appearance may speak unrelated languages, as in much of New Guinea and eastern Indonesia. From time to time, people have changed their language or intermarried frequently with people of a different cultural and genetic background.

Such mixing does not always occur, however, and linguistic stability might have been a very significant (but obviously not universal) factor in human prehistory, especially in the further reaches of the Pacific. The most interesting questions are not about degrees of mixtures between populations and cultures, but about varying speeds of change. Has the generation of human diversity in the Pacific proceeded gradually but at an even rate since first settlement, or with occasional rapid bursts of change interrupting long periods of relative stasis? Such questions divide the evolutionary sciences (including prehistory) profoundly. This essay favours a trajectory of the latter punctuated equilibrium type.

As far as biological origins are concerned, Aboriginal populations of Australia and New Guinea are quite closely related and both groups probably share a common origin in Indonesia over 35 000 years ago. On the other hand, the peoples of Indonesia, Micronesia and Polynesia show clear signs of a recent (post 3000 BC) Asian ancestry, especially in aspects of their DNA. The peoples of island Melanesia beyond New Guinea derive from both these major sources. Languages break down slightly differently to biology (although there is much overlap); about 270 million people throughout Indonesia, Philippines, Malaysia and the Pacific islands speak languages classified into a single language family termed Austronesian. These peoples include most of the island Melanesians, but only a few coastal peoples in New Guinea and none of the Aboriginal Australians. The languages of the Austronesian family are closely related through genetic affiliation and commonality of descent, a sure sign that they expanded relatively recently. The languages of Australia and New Guinea have diversified much more into a large number of families which retain no clear relationships with each other, reflecting much longer time spans—even tens of millennia—of differentiation.

A widely agreed classification of Pacific peoples is now listed, combining data from ethnography, linguistics and biological anthropology.

- The first group comprises the Aboriginal peoples of Australia, whose languages are not known to relate to languages spoken outside Australia, and who must descend in part from founder populations who first reached northern Australia more than 35 000 years ago. Australians are identified by a managerial forager prehistoric lifestyle (associated with vegetational burning, replanting, sporadic wetland ditching and other landscape-altering activities) and remained largely isolated from Asia. (Not entirely isolated, however—dogs, perhaps new stone tool types and Indonesian traders broke the barriers from time to time.)
- The second group comprises the peoples of the interior and parts of coastal New Guinea, who speak a variety of languages in many families loosely grouped together as 'Papuan' (or 'non-Austronesian'). Papuan-speaking New Guineans share a close genetic heritage with Australians, since Australia and New Guinea were frequently joined by dry land across Torres Strait during glacial periods. New Guineans at European contact were mainly agriculturalists, as a result of agricultural origins located possibly in the Highlands more than 6000 years ago.
- The third group comprises all the other peoples of the Pacific region—indeed the majority if we include island Southeast Asia—who can be classified as speakers of Austronesian languages, descendants in full or in part of a major episode of agricultural population expansion from the

Asian mainland which commenced around 6000 years ago in southern China and Taiwan and which reached its near-final shoreline in New Zealand about 800 years ago.

This classification reflects linguistic evidence as much as data from archaeology and genetics. (See LANGUAGES OF THE PACIFIC BASIN.) Languages mark the boundaries of most living societies more coherently than material culture or genes, and languages have more coherent and traceable patterns of transmission. Still, languages cannot tell the whole story. Their relationships cannot be traced back far enough in time with any certainty. Furthermore, preliterate language history cannot easily be dated by linguistic means because languages change at different rates. Archaeology goes to the heart of the matter by excavating the detritus of the day, even if the day was 10 000 years ago. But alas, archaeological detritus never reveals a complete cultural system in the way that a living language does: archaeologists spend much of their time arguing over questions with many plausible answers.

■ ***First colonists*** The story begins somewhere in eastern Africa where our ancestors evolved into a coherently human form between about 5 and 2 million years ago. Between 2 and 1 million years ago (the dates are hotly disputed) the first humans migrated into Asia, reaching China and Java. According to some scholars, the present native populations of eastern Asia and Australasia descend from the early *Homo erectus* ('*Pithecanthropus*') populations of China and Indonesia respectively. The latter were able to migrate to Java when the Sunda continental shelf (which links the Malay Peninsula, Sumatra, Java, Bali and Borneo) was exposed as dry land. This occurred whenever high latitude glaciers waxed under glacial conditions, leading to alterations in sea level. But—hot dispute again—perhaps a majority of modern scholars regard Asian *Homo erectus* as an extinct side branch of human evolution and favour a derivation of both Asians and Australasians from 'anatomically modern humans', inheritors of a major spurt in cranial evolution who overran the Old World and its earlier inhabitants (Neanderthals and Pithecanthropines) from an African homeland at some time between 40 000 and 200 000 years ago.

For Australia and the Pacific these debates about the deeper roots of humanity are marginal since all information so far tells us that humans only crossed the seas of eastern Indonesia between 60 000 and 35 000 years ago, at a time when everyone agrees that anatomically modern humans were doing the migrating. There are no signs that *Homo erectus* ever made the journey to Australia, although the final word might not yet have been said. (Claims have even been made for a human presence in Australia before 100 000 years ago, but again these are not universally accepted.)

What do we know about the first Australasians? Was Australia essentially settled by only one founder population, or by two or three? The skeletal and genetic evidence does not give a decisive answer, and current theories favour either a single basic origin presumably in Indonesia, or a double origin with populations coming from both Indonesia and China, or even a triple origin with separate sources for Tasmanians and New Guineans, southern Australians and northern Australians. The single-origin hypothesis is widely accepted today, and the descendants of the first settlers of Australia, as they grew in numbers and spread across the continent, would have established a continent-wide genetic configuration which would have been very hard for later arrivals to alter in any major way, unless they brought in superior technology or perhaps an epidemic to which they (but not their predecessors) had some resistance. Whatever the number of migrant waves, Australia was settled through all habitable areas from Cape York to Tasmania, coastal forests to interior semi-arid lands, by at least 35 000 years ago in radiocarbon time and at least 50 000 years ago in luminescence-dating time (scholars do not yet know how these two dating systems correlate in real years).

Until about 4500 years ago the archaeology of Australia reveals no major changes in the stone-using foraging lifestyle established by the first settlers, but after this approximate date the widespread appearance across the southern two-thirds of Australia of new tool forms (backed blades and microliths) suggests some degree of population shuffling. Linguistic history also appears to support the idea of increasing inter-group contact after this time (the languages of much of Australia show signs of close relationship, but whether due to borrowing or common descent is not clear), as may the arrival of the domestic dog (the dingo) from presumed Austronesian sources in Indonesia.

The colonizations of Australia and New Guinea involved remarkable chain-like sea crossings, perhaps the earliest evidence of anything approaching conscious intent on the part of humans. The people who reached Australia perhaps migrated from Bali, down the Lesser Sunda chain of islands, finally to reach Australia from Timor or Roti. This involved the first human crossing of the 'Wallace Line' of biogeographers, between Bali and Lombok, plus a leg from Roti or Timor to Australia which might have been at least 100 km wide, via now-submerged islands offshore from the Kimberley Plateau. Other groups could have migrated from Borneo via Sulawesi and the northern Moluccas to New Guinea. By 35 000 years ago people had reached the Bismarck Archipelago east of New Guinea, and Solomons Islands soon after. Just how far people could travel out of sight of land is unknown, but by 20 000 years ago it is apparent that they could make crossings up to 200 km wide (New Guinea to the Admiralty Islands). There is also evidence for the purposeful movement of marsupials (especially wallabies, cuscus and bandicoots) to islands both west and east of New Guinea in order to stock hunting landscapes. Obsidian from New Britain was also traded by this time in the Bismarck Archipelago, over a limited area.

As far as New Guinea is concerned, radiocarbon evidence indicates colonization of the coasts by 35 000 years ago and the highlands by at least 30 000 years ago. Soon after 10 000 years ago there occurred a transition to an agricultural mode of production, one of the few recorded in world history. Ancient agriculture in New Guinea was based on shifting cultivation and swamp cultivation using ditch drainage of taro and other fruits and tubers (no cereals), but no domestic animals were present until the pig was introduced less than 3000 years ago. Unlike the agricultural and seafaring traditions of the Austronesians, those of the New Guinea peoples were relatively non-expansive, at least in pre-Austronesian times. New Guineans intensified production at home, Austronesians essentially moved their homes, eventually more than half-way around the world.

■ ***The Austronesians*** As the most widespread linguistic population on record prior to the European colonizations of the last few centuries, the Austronesians settled more than half of the earth's circumference in tropical and warm temperate latitudes. Their dispersal, which took place mainly between 3000 BC and 1000 AD, took them from a homeland in the region of southern China and Taiwan ultimately to places as far apart as Madagascar, Hawai'i and Easter Island.

The Austronesians are defined as such because they all speak Austronesian languages. This circumstance alone is a guarantee of a high degree of shared ancestry and history, although it has already been noted that Austronesians today are not entirely a unified population in terms of biological affinity. Nevertheless, the languages of the Austronesian family share an ultimate common origin in Taiwan at least 5000 years ago. Since then they have undergone an immense amount of migration, cultural divergence and adaptation to new, strange and often highly challenging environments.

Linguistic analysis indicates a southern Chinese (Fujian coast?) origin for the pre-Austronesian roots of the family (perhaps related at this distant remove to the roots of the Tai and Austroasiatic language families), followed by colonization of Taiwan (the linguistic homeland of Proto-Austronesian), and then a dispersal southwards through the Philippines into northern Indonesia. From here, later population dispersals proceeded west to the Malay Peninsula, southern Vietnam and Madagascar, and east to Irian Jaya and Oceania.

The deep roots of Austronesian expansion were sown at least 3000 years before the Austronesians themselves began to differentiate as a linguistically distinct people. Between 10 000 and 8000 years ago, people in the region from the Yellow to the Yangtze basins in China began to cultivate and domesticate plants, especially foxtail millet and rice. The reasons for these developments are not of concern here, but the inevitable result was that an expansion of the human cultural system became imperative as agriculture took over. In a world only lightly populated by hunters and gatherers, those groups who first developed systematic agriculture had a short-lived but decisive competitive edge. Constant outwards colonization into neighbouring untilled or uninhabited lands was the reaction of many successful groups, including the early Austronesians, who also had the advantage of an early development of seafaring technology, including canoes with sails, amongst the small islands off the coast of southern China.

The Proto-Austronesian vocabulary, which correlates well with the early Neolithic archaeological cultures of Taiwan, suggests a people growing rice and millet, with domestic pigs and dogs (and perhaps chickens), canoes, and knowledge of tattooing and use of the bow and arrow. Soon after the Proto-Austronesian phase, in the Proto-Malayo-Polynesian linguistic phase perhaps located c2500 BC in the Philippines, tropical crops such as banana, coconut and breadfruit were added to the diet. In the archaeological record, agricultural societies with sedentary villages, domesticated pigs and chickens, pottery, polished stone tools and the remains of rice were present in southern China after about 7000 years ago. In Taiwan, archaeological cultures identified by such features appeared at some time between 4000 and 3000 BC.

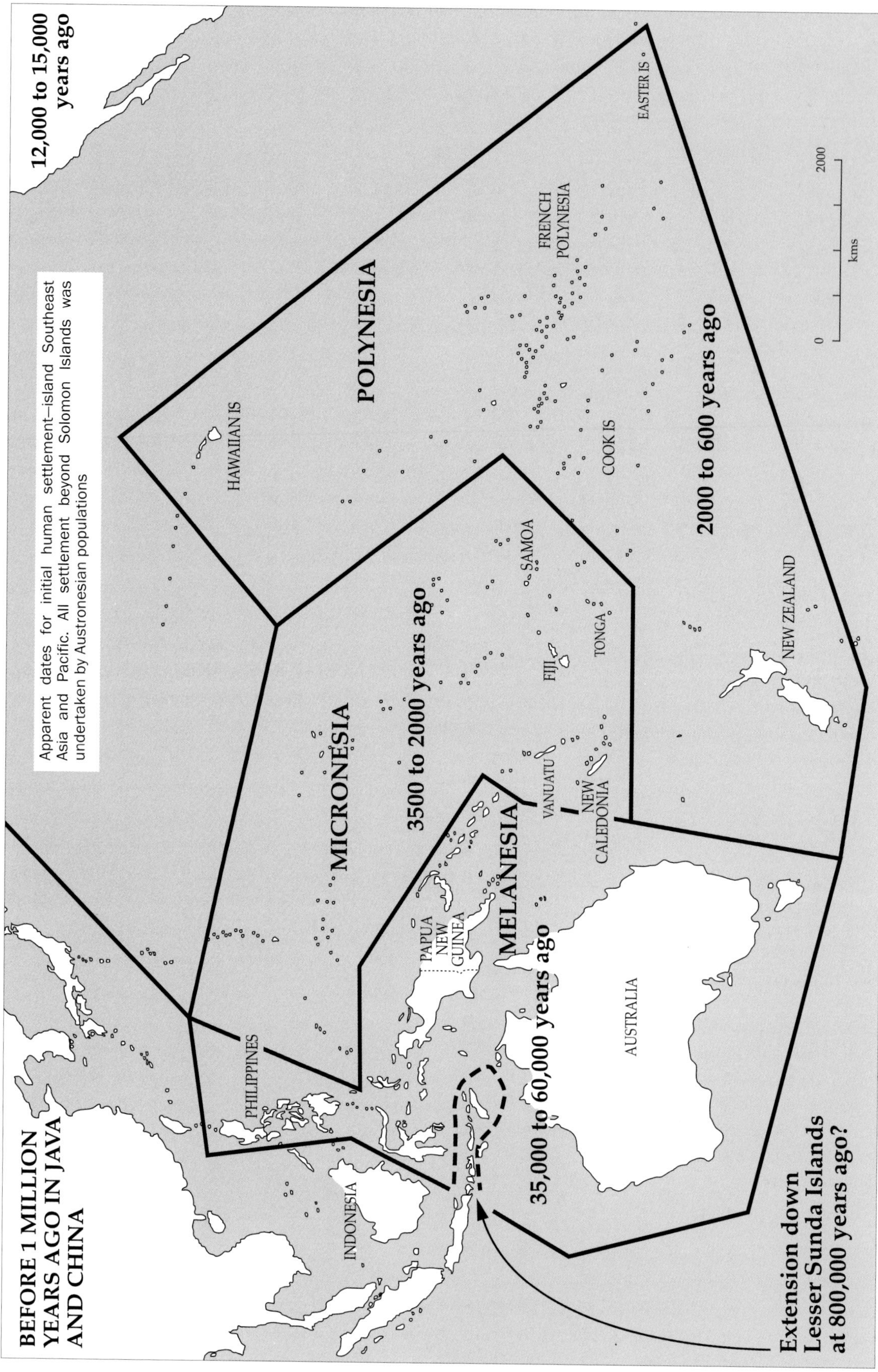

Apparent dates for initial human settlement–island Southeast Asia and Pacific. All settlement beyond Solomon Islands was undertaken by Austronesian populations

One of the next steps seems to have been a southwards and eastwards move which incorporated, perhaps between 2500 and 1500 BC, the Philippines, eastern Indonesia and northern Borneo. By 1500 BC settlers had reached the Mariana Islands of western Micronesia, by 1200 BC parts of island Melanesia (especially the Bismarcks, Solomon Islands, New Caledonia, Vanuatu, Fiji) and finally (by about 850 BC) western Polynesia (Tonga, Samoa, Wallis and Futuna). A similar movement occurred to the west—Java, Sumatra, Malaysia and eventually Madagascar—but the major southwards and eastwards move into the Pacific was undoubtedly one of the most astonishing bouts of colonization in early human history. In a period of about 1000 years Austronesians spread themselves from Taiwan, through island Southeast Asia into Melanesia and central Oceania, over about 7000 km of land and sea. To do this they had to cross ocean gaps up to 800 km wide and develop systematic strategies for exploring and colonizing far-away islands.

There are several important social reasons why such a phenomenal population dispersal occurred. One is that the process of colonization itself can increase the status of an individual and his/her descendants; Micronesian and Polynesian legends (for example the famous Maori 'Fleet' stories) are full of the exploits of founder-figures, after whom kin groups were named and whose direct descendants still form aristocratic lineages today. Some small islands might also have become overpopulated quite quickly, especially if we think of birthrates similar to those typical of recent European colonists into fertile, relatively disease-free and lightly populated landmasses such as the heavily colonized parts of Australia and North America (averaging seven children per family in White Australia in the 1840s and 1850s). The *Bounty* mutineers and their Austronesian (Tahitian) partners in Pitcairn recorded similarly spectacular growth rates. Yet overpopulation is clearly not the real reason for Austronesian expansion, and record rates of population growth may be the result rather than the cause of such large-scale population dispersals.

The main underlying reason for the Austronesian diaspora was the possession of an efficient agricultural economy combined with reliable access to meat sources, especially fish. Hunters and gatherers cannot easily colonize small isolated islands; often there is simply insufficient food to support a viable population. The Neolithic inhabitants of southern coastal China, between 5000 and 3000 BC, by developing both systematic food production and also successful methods of maritime travel, could put their tremendous potential for demographic growth to work in new and welcoming environments. Once colonization began, the only process to stop it, apart from geographical or technological barriers, would have been other populations empowered with equal demographic and cultural advantages.

The early Austronesians of course met such populations—the Austroasiatic speakers of Peninsular Malaysia, Vietnam, perhaps parts of Borneo, and the Papuan speakers of New Guinea. Such prior populations, when strongly entrenched like the Papuans, delayed colonization and, in the interior New Guinea, made it impossible before modern Indonesian transmigration. Austronesians have settled pockets of coastline around New Guinea, seemingly only within the past 2000 years according to both archaeological and linguistic evidence. Indeed, the impressive dominance of the Melanesian phenotype in the western Pacific indicates strongly that some of the Austronesian languages of Melanesia spread by processes of language shift. In other words, some coastal and island populations who had descended from the initial colonists of Melanesia abandoned their native languages to adopt the languages of the incoming Austronesians.

The early Austronesian colonization of Oceania is equated with the Proto-Oceanic stage of Austronesian linguistic history and with the LAPITA CULTURE of archaeology. The latter involved a well-documented and rapid spread of population from the Bismarck Archipelago into the previously unsettled islands east of Solomon Islands, spanning much of Melanesia and western Polynesia, at the end of the second millennium BC. Lapita sites are coastal or on small offshore islands, generally of small village size, and in some cases contain stilt houses built over lagoons. Obsidian from New Britain and Admiralty Islands was traded as far as Santa Cruz to the east and Sabah to the west, and occasional pieces also reached as far east as Fiji. Untanged stone adzes, shell adzes and a range of shell ornaments and tools also characterize Lapita sites, as does the pottery.

Although Lapita skeletons are few—and all date from rather late in the Lapita sequence—those that have been studied indicate a population with both Polynesian and Melanesian affinities. One recently discovered skeleton from Fiji is also reported to have East and Southeast Asian affinities, in accord with the suggestions about the ultimate origins of this population from archaeology and linguistics. However, we do not yet know what the earliest (that is, c1200 BC) Lapita colonists looked like, although the answer is likely to be quite close to modern Polynesians and eastern Indonesians. The present population of the islands of Melanesia, from the Bismarcks to Fiji, has certainly not descended solely from the most ancient Lapita groups of the Bismarcks at c1200 BC; very strong gene flow from the pre-Austronesian populations of the New Guinea region occurred at least as far east as Fiji, although the circumstances of this gene flow are still very hard to reconstruct. What is clear in island Melanesia is that the Lapita culture had disappeared from the archaeological record by some time between 500 BC and the time of Christ, replaced by different pottery styles emphasising incised and paddle-impressed styles of surface decoration. Although some aspects of these later cultures, widespread in all regions of Melanesia from coastal New Guinea to Fiji, may have part-Lapita origins, there is far more to modern Melanesia than just a transformation of Lapita. The term 'Melanesia' is only of loose geographical value; in human terms there is no unity and Melanesia has a very complex prehistory.

Polynesia and Micronesia, on the other hand, are relatively homogenous in terms of language, culture and human biology. The Polynesians are the direct descendants of the Lapita peoples who colonised through Melanesia in the late second millennium BC, albeit also with some degree of later gene flow from eastern Melanesia. After the demise of the Lapita culture about 2000 years ago the ancestral Polynesians in Tonga and Samoa ceased to make pottery on a large scale, but other Polynesian artifact types (for example fishhooks, shell ornaments, stone adzes) of later prehistory clearly owe much to Lapita forebears, as well as much to inevitable processes of local innovation. For instance, the eastern Polynesian stone temples (known as *marae* and cognate forms in most areas, but as *heiau* in Hawai'i and *ahu* in Easter Island and parts of the Marquesas) appear to be the results of independent architectural elaboration only paralleled very faintly in other Austronesian regions. The same applies to the famed *moai* ancestral stone statues placed on the Easter Island *ahu*, although here we enter a confused debate about American parallels which still defies easy solution.

Moai (stone figures portraying ancestors) look out from Rano Raraku, the extinct volcano site where most of the c1000 known examples were carved from basalt

The Micronesians are basically of dual origin. The Mariana Islands were colonized from Taiwan or the Philippines about 1500 BC and early archaeological sites there have a decorated form of pottery rather like Lapita (related types also occur in the Cagayan Valley in northern Luzon, dating to about 1000 BC). The other Micronesian islands—Carolines, Marshalls, Kiribati, and possibly Yap—were apparently colonized by populations from central Melanesia about 1500 years later, perhaps from the eastern Solomons or Vanuatu. A possible reason for this occurring so long after the Marianas and eastern Melanesia may be that the atolls of Micronesia were predominantly submerged until about 2000 years ago, making the finding of the very few high volcanic islands of eastern Micronesia very difficult. Since that time Micronesians have met and intermarried widely—for instance, the Yapese network of trade and tribute spanned a huge region from Yap into the Carolinean atolls. But the Mariana and Belau people still speak languages of Western Malayo-Polynesian affinity whereas the other Micronesians speak Oceanic languages. So trade and intermarriage, which occurred through all the islands of Micronesia, have not erased ancient linguistic differences.—PB

Lapita culture

Early recognition of Lapita culture was based on the elaborately decorated pottery, much of it executed by small toothed (dentate) stamps similar to tattooing chisels. Other decorative techniques included incision using a sharp-edged tool, and clay strips of various kinds applied to the pot surface. The pottery was generally coated with a red slip, and some designs were highlighted with a white infill of clay or lime.

This pottery was first reported in 1909 by Father Meyer, a Catholic missionary on the island of Watom off the northeast coast of New Britain. In 1917, more pottery was found in New Caledonia, at Lapita (which gave its name to the entire cultural complex), but it was not until similar pottery emerged on the Isle of Pines in New Caledonia in 1948 that connections between the three sites were recognized. Further excavations at Lapita by Gifford and Shutler in

Lapita pottery excavated in Malo, Vanuatu

1952, and the recognition of similarities to pottery collected in Tonga by Gifford in 1920–21, led to the definition of a Lapita style, distributed from the Bismarcks to Polynesia from about 1500 BC over a period of about 1000 to 1500 years. By the start of the Christian era it had lost its distinctive features.

Evidence for the Lapita culture stretches from Manus and the Vitiaz Strait (between New Guinea and New Britain) in the west, to Tonga and Samoa in the east. The linkage between the west-to-east spread of Lapita from Melanesia into western Polynesia and the spread of Austronesian languages is now widely accepted. (See FOOTSTEPS FROM ASIA.) It is generally believed that the foundations of Polynesian languages go back to the eastern extension of Lapita in a region previously uninhabited, and that the immediate Lapita 'homeland' is further west in the Bismarck Archipelago.

In addition to the distinctive pottery, Lapita represents the first convincing evidence for developed agriculture in the region, indicated by evidence of erosion consistent with hillside gardens and the extension of settlement to areas where non-agricultural subsistence would be unlikely or impossible. It marks the first appearance of the three Pacific domesticated animals: pigs, dogs and chickens—and therefore the beginnings of Pacific animal husbandry. The settlement pattern itself—coastal villages often consisting of stilt houses over lagoons, or on small offshore islands in the Bismarcks and the Solomons—is a new development. Lapita sites do not generally re-occupy previously used locations apart from where Lapita deposits occur in rock shelters. There is a distinctive Lapita stone adze kit not found in previously settled areas, and similarly, a distinctive range of shell ornaments including beads, rings and discs. Finally, Lapita represents a major extension in the range of New Britain and Admiralties obsidian, not found outside that island group in pre-Lapita locations. All these components amount to a Lapita cultural complex that represents initial human colonization of remote Oceania, south and east of Solomon Islands.

Lapita is primarily of Southeast Asian origin, although it may be debated whether the bearers of this culture were in large part an intrusive group moving into the Bismarcks from the west, or resident groups which adopted some southeast Asian material cultural items and with this newly acquired technology, were able to settle the region from Solomon Islands to Samoa within a few hundred years. The linguistic and genetic evidence for physical migration rather than vague diffusional processes appears to be overwhelming.

The migrants' initial success in establishing settlements in the Bismarcks and Solomons may have been due to the demographic advantages imparted by an integrated animal husbandry and agricultural economy in an area previously inhabited by low-density hunter-gatherer or low-intensity horticultural groups. The prior existence of an agricultural economy on the New Guinea mainland may explain why significant Austronesian settlement appears to have been delayed for over 1000 years after the Bismarcks were settled. It would be wrong to see the new colonists as immediately blanketing the Bismarcks and Solomons. Initial numbers must have been small; their settlements were marginal to the already inhabited larger islands; and even before the Lapita influx, there must have been some limited recruitment from local non-Austronesian groups to explain certain genetic markers found in Polynesian populations.—MS

Settlement of New Guinea

People were in mainland New Guinea by 40 000 years ago, as part of the settlement of the enlarged Australian continent of which it formed a part during the lowered sea levels of the last Pleistocene 'Ice Age' (see FOOTSTEPS FROM ASIA). The immigrants, *Homo sapiens sapiens*, arrived by sea out of the islands of eastern Indonesia. Their sea-going skills were further deployed in early colonization of the large islands of New Britain and New Ireland (by 35 000 years ago) and, subsequently and more unexpectedly, of Buka in the northern Solomon Islands, over the horizon from New Ireland (shortly after 30 000 years ago), and of the Admiralty Islands (today Manus Province), requiring many hours of sailing out of sight of land (before 14 000 years ago).

The newcomers had the ability to exploit both coast and inland. The latter was predominantly constituted by rainforest, not an easy environment for hunter-gatherers because of the dispersed nature of its resources, and even less so in the islands, where fauna and flora are impoverished. It seems that problems were overcome through resource management, including opening up the forest cover to promote the growth of useful plants. There is evidence in the valleys of the central cordillera for an exceptional development of plant management techniques, which by 6000 years ago had taken on the character of systems of cultivation. Some 10 000 years ago the present climate was attained and, with the accompanying rise in sea level, New Guinea separated from Australia around 8000 years ago.

Contemporary New Guinea agriculture is based on a variable suite of root and tree crops originating for the most part in Southeast Asia, like yam, taro and banana, but including exotic items like sweet potato. Some of the plants in question are indigenous to New Guinea itself and may have been domesticated there. Whether this is the case or not, there is no doubt that domesticated plants from southeast Asia came to enrich and transform the indigenous system, while the three domesticated animals of the New Guinea, and wider Pacific, agricultural complex—pig, dog and chicken—arrived from that same general region.

What the developments in plant-based systems owed to the settlement of new groups from overseas is uncertain. The people involved in them almost certainly spoke languages of one or more of the apparently unrelated non-Austronesian (or Papuan) families dominant in mainland New Guinea today, but none of these has any demonstrable relationship with languages outside the immediate region. The pronounced linguistic diversity suggests that the families in question have great antiquity in New Guinea, beyond even the possibility of establishing any relationship with Australian descendants of languages dating from the initial settlement.

A series of innovations in the archaeological record of the Bismarck Archipelago around 3500 years ago constitutes definitive evidence of connections with the Southeast Asian world. They include chickens and dogs definitely, and pigs and pottery possibly, though claims for the earlier presence of both of the latter items on the New Guinea mainland have their champions. The new appearances belong to LAPITA CULTURE, which went on to make the first settlement of islands beyond the Solomons chain. Linguistic and genetic evidence indicates that Lapita involved immigrants from southeast Asia speaking Austronesian languages of the Oceanic subgroup, which in the Bismarcks and Solomons replaced most of the languages of resident communities.

Classic Lapita is not a phenomenon of the mainland, however, where pottery of so-called red-slipped type, related to or descended from it, is lowland and patchy in distribution. This parallels the distribution of Oceanic-type Austronesian languages on the mainland, whose speakers seem to have arrived there from the Bismarcks, with their pottery, and spread coastally, in places as recently as 2000 years ago.

At this date and subsequently there is renewed evidence of external contacts in the variable form of pottery, metal or rock art of Southeast Asian affinity in island or mainland New Guinea. The occurrences may have fallen short of the settlement of migrant groups, but could have represented the opening of the door for the Asian 'Bronze Age' influences that art historians have long claimed to see in some styles of New Guinea ethnographic art. They may have been a byproduct of the trade in natural products that accompanied the rise of early states in mainland southeast Asia and western Indonesia and went on to involve an increasingly wider world.

The focus of this trade came to be the islands immediately west of New Guinea, with their spices, aromatic woods and barks, resins, sea slugs, shells and pearls. Before the colonial era in the 19th century the direct effects on New Guinea itself were essentially restricted to the western extremities of the island, which entered the commerce mainly as the source of BIRD OF PARADISE plumes and slaves. Some things ran well ahead of colonial rule, however. One of these was the sweet potato, a tropical American plant introduced into eastern Indonesia no earlier than the 16th century. This quickly took over as the agricultural staple throughout montane New Guinea, where it proved more productive than existing root crops and laid the basis for the populous cultures that so impressed the first outsiders to see them, some 70 years ago.—JG2

Settlement of the eastern Pacific

The eastern Pacific includes all the islands settled initially by bearers of East Polynesian culture as well as several others in the region which were probably not colonized until the advent of European shipping (Galapagos, Lord Howe, Juan Fernandez). The main archipelagoes (excluding here Hawai'i, which is described as part of the northern Pacific, although it was also settled initially by East Polynesians), are the Cooks, Societies, Australs, Tuamotus, Marquesas, and Pitcairn groups extending out to isolated Easter Island, and the southwest group of New Zealand together with the Kermadecs, Chathams and Norfolk islands.

The tropical archipelagoes lie within the south-east tradewinds and consist of about 150 islands, half of them atolls in the Tuamotus and the remainder mainly high, basaltic islands. The total land area is less than 5000 sq km, and Tahiti (1042 sq km) is by far the largest island. The temperate archipelagoes, all high islands, are dominated by the comparatively huge and diverse landmass of New Zealand at 269 000 sq km, with 1100 sq km distributed amongst the remaining islands. Norfolk and the Kermadecs are subtropical but New Zealand lies in the westerly wind belt and ranges from warm to cool temperate with marked windward-leeward variations in climate and vegetation.

Historical linguistics suggest that the immediate origin of East Polynesian languages lies in the area of Samoa to Tuvalu, and certainly East Polynesian culture is clearly descended from West Polynesian which developed out of LAPITA CULTURE after about 500 BC in Tonga and Samoa. It is possible that once settlement had occurred in East Polynesia, probably first in the Tahiti-Cooks region, the languages of Easter Island, and those of the Marquesas and Mangareva (also Hawaiian), became relatively isolated earlier than Tuamotuan, Maori and Moriori which remain closer to Tahitian and Cook Island Maori.

The period of East Polynesian colonization is not yet generally agreed. It is possible that some islands were occupied soon after the arrival of Lapita colonists in West Polynesia, about 3000 years ago. However, no Lapita ceramics, indeed very few sherds at all, have been found in East Polynesia, where the material culture is aceramic, and those potential traces of early settlement discerned in a few pollen spectra from swamp cores that extend to about 3000 years ago, or in some radiocarbon dates of up to 2000 years old on the bones of *Rattus exulans*, a human commensal, can be explained alternatively. Radiocarbon dates from archaeological sites suggest that no settlement had occurred earlier than about 500 AD, except perhaps in the northern Cooks where it might have begun several hundred years earlier, and the most recent data are pushing the age of initial colonization towards 800 AD in tropical East Polynesia and 1200 AD in the New Zealand region.

Only people of East Polynesian culture settled the eastern Pacific prehistorically, but it is possible that there was a small contribution towards the culture complex from South America. The sweet potato (*Ipomoea batatas*), found in Tahiti, is of South American origin and some architectural features on Easter Island, notably the stonework of Ahu Vinapu, may be as well. The overwhelming contribution of population and culture, nevertheless, is clearly from ancestral sources in West Polynesia.

Within each of the main archipelagoes of tropical East Polynesia, there was frequent interaction and exchange, especially of luxury goods such as fine basalt adzes, pearl shell and red feathers, and there was some contact over longer distances between all the main tropical groups, especially during the early centuries of settlement. In the temperate region however, current evidence indicates both that there was no post-colonization interaction with the tropical islands and little or no contact between New Zealand and any of the outlying groups. These differences probably reflect the relative difficulty of VOYAGING, using double CANOES rigged with Oceanic spritsail. Distances were shorter and wind and sea conditions milder and more predictable in the tropics than in the temperate region.

Distance and climate account also for variation in regional economies in prehistory. The full range of transportable cultigens and domesticates, notably taro, yam, sweet potato, banana, COCONUT, pig, dog and chicken, reached the tropical region and were developed into intensive mixed gardening systems with irrigation in heavily settled areas such as Tahiti. Only the dog and some of the root crops, notably sweet potato, flourished in New Zealand, but the South Island and CHATHAM ISLANDS were effectively beyond the range of any prehistoric horticulture. Foraging in southern New Zealand focused initially upon seals and the huge (up to 230 kg body-weight), flightless birds known as moa (*Dinornithiformes*). These soon became extinct, along with many other birds, a pattern of early over-exploitation recognized throughout the eastern Pacific. TURTLE breeding colonies, stocks of large reef fish and other resources were also heavily depleted at an early stage. To some extent associated with the exploitation of these easily-gathered food reserves, early settlement patterns were focused on nucleated villages. As populations and horticultural operations expanded in later prehistory there was a trend towards dispersed family settlements.

East Polynesian society, described in the journals of European voyagers, was essentially chiefly in varying degrees. Where high population densities occurred on the larger high islands, notably in Tahiti and Easter Island, there was marked social stratification together with craft specialization, elaboration of religion and ritual behaviour and the development of massive, monumental structures. In New Zealand, where population density remained low, and on the atolls generally, there was less social complexity and little monumental architecture. However, the developing militarism inherent in Polynesian society, especially marked in the Marquesas and Easter Island, was manifested in New Zealand and Rapa, and to a much lesser extent elsewhere, by the construction of large forts (*pa*), defended by earthworks and palisades.

East Polynesian prehistory was relatively brief. European discovery began with Mendaña, who sighted the Marquesas in 1595, and the other groups were visited over the succeeding two centuries, most notably by British expeditions under Captain COOK in the 1770s. At that time there were about 100 000 New Zealand Maori, 45 000 Society Islanders, 35 000 Marquesans and approximately 20 000 people distributed throughout the smaller islands of the region.—AA

Settlement of the northern Pacific

Most of Oceania lies south of the equator, but in Micronesia and the Hawaiian Islands, early settlement of the Pacific islands extended into the northern Pacific. These two locations provide an interesting contrast in their settlement history and in the degree to which modern academic studies have illuminated their pasts.

Micronesia consists of a nearly continuous sprinkling of islands extending east from a chain of high islands that are orientated southwest to northeast, and form the region's western boundary. Thousands of islands make up Micronesia, most of them coral atolls. The region starts about 600 km east of the Philippines, and runs east then southeast almost to Fiji. The region's 7.4 million sq km of ocean contains only 2700 sq km of land. Scarcity of land, along with the constant spectre of DROUGHT or typhoon damage, dominates much of the thoughts and actions of the region's inhabitants.

The record of Micronesia's early history is scant, because of the limited amount of archaeological fieldwork, and the problems inherent in excavating small, intensively settled atoll islets that are often ravaged by storms. The most coherent pattern for early colonization and settlement has come from linguistic evidence. The Nuclear Micronesian languages of eastern and central Micronesia are most closely related to Austronesian dialects centred on northern Vanuatu. Only the languages of Palau, Yap and the Mariana Islands in the west are not closely related to Nuclear Micronesian, nor to each other. These high islands on the western fringe seem to have been settled from the Philippines and Indonesia, by peoples who did not move on to colonize other islands further east. Rather, the atolls just to the east seem to have been settled from the east, by peoples who had come from atoll-dominated eastern Micronesia.

Sunset on Marshall Islands

There is limited evidence for the early colonization of Palau and Yap. The nearby Mariana Islands, however, appear to have been settled by at least 1500 BC. The many differences between northern Vanuatu and Marshall Islands languages suggest to linguists that at least 3000 years have elapsed since these two began to diverge from a common ancestral tongue. The atolls and a few high islands further west have given dates of 1000–2200 years ago. Local traditions and archaeological evidence suggest that the atoll dwellers remained mobile, and maintained extensive inter-island exchange networks well after colonization because of the precarious nature of atoll living.

The history of the Hawaiian archipelago on the other hand is portrayed as having occurred in relative isolation after initial colonization of its high volcanic southeastern islands. Stretching for thousands of kilometres in a northwest to southeast direction, the Hawaiian chain is one of the most isolated island groups in the world. Initial colonization has been dated to around 1700 years ago, probably from the Marquesas Islands judging from similarities in artifacts recovered by excavation. In the past decade there has been considerable debate about the dating of colonization, however, with some arguing for 2000–3000 years ago, while others have suggested that the first reliable dates only occur around 1300 years ago.

A number of substantial archaeological projects have been conducted in the Hawaiian Islands. Hawaiian history is generally interpreted by archaeologists as a process driven by increasing pressure on resources fuelled by an ever-increasing population, and the demands of status rivalry between chiefs. Migration was not an option. Traditions of the arrival of outsiders prior to sustained western contacts in the late 1700s are usually dismissed as being of limited influence or impossible to substantiate. However, some scholars have made strong cases for these traditions as references to first, Tahitian contact, and later Spanish contact with the island chain. The prehistory of the northern Pacific remains far from settled.—PD'A

Further reading

Bellwood, P, 1987. *The Polynesians,* revised ed., Thames and Hudson.

——, Fox, J J and Tryon, D (eds), 1995. *The Austronesians: historical and comparative perspectives,* Department of Anthropology, The Australian National University.

Blust, R A, 1995. 'The prehistory of the Austronesian-speaking peoples: a view from language', *Journal of World Prehistory,* 9.

Flood, J, 1995. *Archaeology of the Dreamtime,* Angus & Robertson.

Hill, A V S and Serjeantson, S (eds), 1989. *The Colonization of the Pacific: a genetic trail,* Clarendon Press.

Irwin, G J, 1992. *The Prehistoric Exploration and Colonization of the Pacific,* Cambridge University Press.

Kirch, P V, 1997. *The Lapita Peoples,* Blackwell.

Lourandos, H, 1997. *Continent of Hunter-Gatherers,* Cambridge University Press.

Spriggs, M, 1997. *The Island Melanesians,* Blackwell.

—— and Anderson, A, 1993. 'Late colonization of East Polynesia', *Antiquity,* 67(255).

Polynesia, Melanesia and Micronesia

The islands of the Pacific Ocean are often identified by their location within the three traditional cultural areas described as Polynesia, Melanesia and Micronesia. The name Polynesia comes from the Greek words *poly* (many) and *nesos* (islands), and was first used in 1756 by the French explorer Charles Brosses in reference to all Pacific islands. In 1831 DUMONT D'URVILLE proposed the three-way division which is still used today. In this loose terminology, Polynesia refers to the region of the central Pacific containing the island groups of Hawai'i and Samoa, Marquesas, Cook Islands, Tonga, Tokelau, Tuvalu and French Polynesia, and extending to New Zealand in the southwest and Rapanui (Easter Island) in the southeast.

Melanesia was named from the Greek word *melos* (black), referring to the dark skin of the inhabitants of the southwestern region of the Pacific. Melanesia usually refers to the islands from the Bismarck Archipelago, Solomon Islands, Vanuatu, New Caledonia, Fiji and the intervening islands, although Fiji on the boundary is culturally marginal. Micronesia, coming from the Greek word *micros* (small), refers to the scattered small islands of the northwestern region of the Pacific. Micronesia contains the Mariana, Caroline and Marshall groups, being the countries today known as Commonwealth of the Northern Mariana Islands, the Federated States of Micronesia, the Republic of the Marshall Islands, Kiribati, Guam and Palau.—KRF

TWO LANGUAGE

Languages of the Pacific Basin

The Pacific Ocean (including all of the islands of Melanesia, Micronesia and Polynesia, but excluding Japan and island Southeast Asia) is home to almost 20 per cent of the world's languages, making it the region with the highest ratio of distinct languages to population numbers, with 1000 indigenous languages for a total population of under 10 million. This means roughly one distinct language for every 10 000 Pacific islanders (including New Zealand). In addition, English and French are widely used as national languages and languages of education (French in New Caledonia, Wallis and Futuna, and French Polynesia, and English elsewhere). Spanish is used on Easter Island.

A number of pidgin languages are used in the islands, usually as a lingua franca, especially in Melanesia, where there is a high density of different vernacular languages. The major pidgin languages which have a largely English-based word-store are TOK PISIN (Papua New Guinea), SOLOMON ISLANDS PIJIN, and BISLAMA (Vanuatu). In Papua New Guinea there is also a pidginized variety of Motu (the language spoken around Port Moresby), known as Hiri Motu, used along the Papuan coast. In Fiji there are two pidgin varieties, namely FIJI PIDGIN ENGLISH, used between Fijians and Fiji Indians, and FIJI HINDI or Fiji Baht, used within the multilingual Indian communities.

While considerable use of a lingua franca is common throughout Melanesia, it is also noteworthy that there is extensive multilingualism in local vernacular languages throughout the region. It is not uncommon in island Melanesia, for example, for a child to grow up speaking his mother's and father's language (often different because of exogamous marriage rules), a neighbouring language, a pidgin lingua franca and a metropolitan language, usually English or French.

The languages of the Pacific islands belong to two distinct families, Austronesian and Papuan. The Papuan language family is located mainly on the

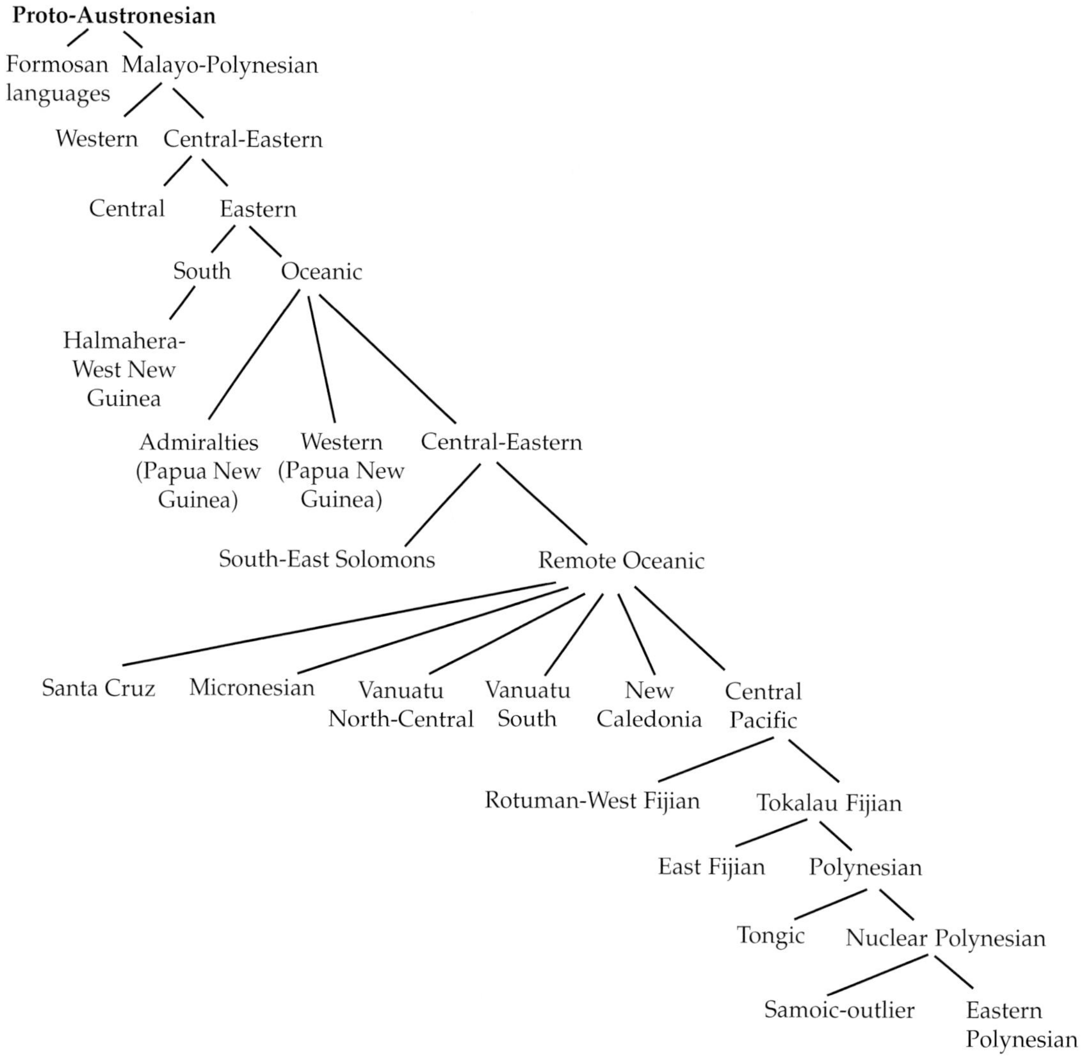

Figure 2.1 The Austronesian language family

island of New Guinea, covering both Irian Jaya and Papua New Guinea. In New Guinea, Papuan languages are spoken mainly in areas inland (while Austronesian languages are spoken mainly in coastal regions). Papuan languages are also spoken in parts of Halmahera, Timor, Alor and Pantar in eastern Indonesia. East of mainland Papua New Guinea, Papuan languages are also spoken in parts of New Britain and New Ireland, Bougainville and Solomon Islands as far southeast as the Santa Cruz group.

There are some 750 Papuan languages whose genetic relationships remain unmapped. While the Austronesian languages, below, are all known to be genetically related (descended from a common ancestral language spoken about 6000 years ago), it is currently believed that the Papuan languages are not all genetically related. Indeed, some linguists consider that they belong to at least 60 different language families, each with its common ancestral language.

As early as 1975 it was posited that a large group of Papuan languages share a common origin, called the Trans-New Guinea Phylum. This group of Papuan languages is claimed to extend over almost all of the mountainous spine of New Guinea, including most of the non-Austronesian languages to the south and many of those to the north of the central highlands, together with the non-Austronesian languages of Alor, Pantar and Timor. Over the past 20 years further research has confirmed that there is indeed a valid genetic group comprising up to 500 Papuan languages.

The core of the members of the Trans-New Guinea Phylum consists of the many small subgroups spoken in the central mountain ranges of New Guinea, beginning east of the Bird's Head, together with the Asmat-Kamoro and Awyu-Dumut groups in the south-west lowlands. Added to these are two large groups in north-east New Guinea: the Madang group (about 100 languages) and the Finisterre-Huon group (about 70). Other groups included tentatively in the Trans-New Guinea Phylum include the Eleman, Marind, Kiwai, Inanwatan and Timor-Alor-Pantar groups. Much basic research remains to be done before the genetic relationships of the Papuan languages can be determined with confidence, especially in the case of the 250 or so languages known to lie outside the Trans-New Guinea Phylum. Because of the extreme time depths involved (over 50 000 years for the Papuan languages), the task is daunting.

The remainder of the languages spoken in the Pacific islands are all known to be members of the great Austronesian language family. The major subgroups of this family are represented in Figure 2.1.

It is considered that the original Austronesian language, a multi-dialectal language, was spoken somewhere in southern China about 6000 years ago, and that some of its speakers migrated first to Taiwan. The Taiwanese Austronesian languages were originally grouped into three categories, Atayalic, Rukau-Tsouic and Paiwanic, but they are now considered almost impossible to sub-group, representing up to nine first order groups of Taiwan languages. Austronesian languages outside Taiwan are members of a single higher-order language subgroup, known as Malayo-Polynesian.

The distribution of the Austronesian languages may be seen in the map on the following page. The great Oceanic subgroup, which extends from a north–south line drawn at about 130°, just east of the Bird's Head in Irian Jaya, includes all the Austronesian languages of Oceania except Chamorro (Mariana Islands) and Palau, in Micronesia, which link more closely with languages in the Philippines and Indonesia. The Oceanic languages fall into three major subgroups. The Remote Oceanic subgroup includes all of the languages of the Pacific east of southeast Solomon Islands. The Central Pacific subgroup contains the Fijian and Polynesian languages. The coastal areas and offshore islands around Papua New Guinea are inhabited by speakers of some 220 Austronesian languages. In Solomon Islands there are 62 indigenous languages, of which 56 are Austronesian (6 Papuan). Vanuatu has 113 languages and New Caledonia 28, while Fiji has two indigenous vernaculars, Western and Eastern Fijian. There are some 30 Polynesian languages (all Austronesian), of which 16 are spoken outside Triangle Polynesia, on small islands in Melanesia and Micronesia. In the tiny islands which make up Micronesia, there are some 15 languages spoken today.

English is the predominant language of the Pacific Basin, although French is spoken in New Caledonia, Wallis and Futuna, and French Polynesia. The languages of education are mainly English and French, although local vernaculars are used, especially in Polynesia where, unlike Melanesia, there is normally only one vernacular per island state. Added to this is the very long tradition of literacy in Polynesian languages, beginning with the arrival of the first Christian missionaries. The language of education on Rapanui (Easter Island) is Spanish. After World War II, practical orthographies were devised for the Micronesian languages, nearly all of these being taught alongside English in the Micronesian states. In island Melanesia a number of vernaculars are taught in schools, with limited success and limited support from island governments.

None of the Pacific languages has a writing system or written literature predating those developed by missionaries. The exception is the *rongorongo* script of Easter Island, a system of pictograms which has defied decipherment in spite of many attempts and claims of success.

The languages of the great Oceanic subgroup of the Austronesian family are considered to have had their homeland in the New Britain–New Ireland area (east of the Papua New Guinea mainland) about 3500 years ago, their founding societies being associated with LAPITA CULTURE. They spread rapidly throughout island Melanesia about 300 years later, as did the Lapita pottery, and by 3000 years ago had spread as far east as Fiji and west Polynesia. From there they gradually extended further east as far as Easter Island.

These languages (like all Austronesian languages) are basically verb-initial or verb-second in the sentence, whereas Papuan languages are characterized by a verb-final word order. Oceanic Austronesian languages have prepositions, while Papuan languages have postpositions. As a result of contact with Papuan languages, many of the Austronesian languages in the Papua New Guinea area have become verb-final languages (subject + object + verb) instead of the expected subject + verb + object word order. Papuan languages are often highly

Distribution of Austronesian languages

agglutinative, unlike their Oceanic Austronesian counterparts. The feature which contrasts most starkly with the Austronesian languages is the distinction between dependent and independent verbs in Papuan languages. In this system, the independent verbs have a full range of inflections (suffixes indicating subject, tense and mood), while the dependent verbs are considerably reduced in their inflectional possibilities.

The Pacific Basin, with the exception of Japan and island Southeast Asia, is characterized by a vast number of languages and societies with very small populations, especially in Melanesia. This very characteristic, together with the rapidly increasing impact of European languages through the media, threatens the survival of many of them. Even Polynesian languages, Tahitian and New Zealand Maori, with relatively higher numbers of speakers, are imperilled as the impact of major world languages is severely affecting the use of Oceanic languages between parents and children.

One mitigating influence is the increasing use of Pacific vernacular languages on radio and television (to a lesser extent), and in the print media. In Polynesia, as well as in the metropolitan languages, there are radio broadcasts in Tahitian, Cook Islands Maori, Niuean, Wallisian, Samoan, Tongan, Fijian (and Hindi) and New Zealand Maori, while in Micronesia there are broadcasts in Kiribatese, Marshallese, Kosraean, Pohnpeian, Yapese, Ulithian, Woleaian, Chuukese and Palauan. In Melanesia, however, there is very limited RADIO BROADCASTING in vernaculars, with only a dozen languages represented in Papua New Guinea, and scarcely any in Solomon Islands, Vanuatu and New Caledonia. Television is almost exclusively in metropolitan languages, as are the major daily newspapers. The threat to the vernacular languages of the Pacific is obvious.—DT

Further reading

Tryon, D, (ed.), 1995. *Comparative Austronesian Dictionary*, Mouton de Gruyter.

Wurm, S, Mühlhäusler, P and Tryon, D (eds), *Atlas of Languages of Intercultural Communication in the Pacific, Asia and the Americas*, Mouton de Gruyter.

Kanak languages of New Caledonia

New Caledonia, as a French overseas territory, has French as its official language. Indigenous languages are spoken by Melanesians (Kanaks), and some Indonesian and Polynesian languages are spoken by immigrants who settled there mainly after World War II. In all, 28 indigenous languages, distinct in phonology and grammar, have been counted. They belong to the Oceanic branch of the Austronesian language family.

Kanaks had a tradition of bilingualism (or even trilingualism) which enabled them to maintain the identity of their tribe, while fulfilling the need for alliances with neighbouring tribes through exchange and intermarriage. There was no single language that enjoyed particular prestige. This situation has changed since French colonization, as the native population has often been dispersed from its traditional dwelling places. Today's lifestyle involves increased mobility, as people spend some time in villages and towns or in NICKEL MINING to earn money. Children are often separated from their parents and sent to schools in villages, where Kanak languages are suppressed in the educational system. In this situation, Kanak languages in general are not passed to the younger generation properly, except for some languages such as Lifu (Drehu), Paicî, Houaïlou (Ajië) and Hârâcùù. Some languages have completely disappeared, or are spoken by very few people. Half of the New Caledonian languages have less than 1000 speakers, and risk extinction. With growing concern about endangered indigenous culture and language, some Melanesian languages have begun to be taught at schools and made available as options for baccalauréat.

New Caledonian languages can be grouped into six: Extreme North—Yâlayu, Kumak, Caaàc and Yuanga; North—Jawé, Nemi, Fwâi, Pije, Pwapwâ, Pwaamei and dialects of Voh-Koné; Central—Cèmuhî and Paicî; South—Arhö, Arhâ, Ajië, Orowe, Neku, Nerë, Tîrî, Xârâcùù and Xârâgùré; Extreme South—Drubea and Numèè; Loyalty Islands—Faga-Uvéa, Iaai, Drehu and Nengone. The northern group includes languages which have a large number of consonants. They are distinguished from the central and southern languages by the occurrence of aspirated stops, nasals and continuants, and postnasalized stops. The number of vowels, on the contrary, is relatively small. They still have consonants such as prenasalized stops, velarized labials as well as labialized velars, and some have retroflex/dental contrast in stops, continuants and nasals. Word final consonants common in the north and in the LOYALTY ISLANDS are not found in the central and southern groups. Languages in the central and extreme south are tone languages.

Languages in the Loyalty Islands are somewhat different. They do not have the prenasalized stops commonly found in the main island languages; they lack nasal vowels but have aspirated nasals and continuants. Faga-Uvéa spoken on Ouvea is the only Polynesian language found among the Melanesian languages. Grammatical differences among New Caledonian languages are relatively minor compared to the differences in phonology. They concern word order, subject marking, case marking on pronouns, tense and aspect marking, verbal morphology, and so on.—MO

Further reading

Haudricourt, A G, 1971. 'New Caledonia and the Loyalty Islands', in T A Sebeok (ed.), *Current Trends in Linguistics, Vol 8: Linguistics in Oceania*, Mouton.

Languages of Papua New Guinea

There are more languages spoken in Papua New Guinea than in any other area of comparable size, an estimated 750 being spoken there. The languages also show great genetic diversity with a major division between Austronesian and non-Austronesian.

The Austronesian languages stretch from Madagascar in the west to Easter Island and Hawai'i in the east. This family contains an estimated 1000 languages and includes about 270 million speakers, making it the largest and most widespread language family in the world. In Papua New Guinea Austronesian languages are generally scattered around the coast of the mainland and across the neighbouring offshore islands, except near Port Moresby and Lae where they have penetrated far inland.

Austronesian languages of Papua New Guinea belong to the Oceanic subgroup of Austronesian. That is, they are all more closely related to one another than any is to any other Austronesian language. They are descended from an ancestor thought to have arrived in northwest Melanesia around 4000 years ago. All the Austronesian languages of Papua New Guinea are structurally similar. They generally have

- a relatively simple phonology that includes five vowels (a, e, i, o, u) and a set of consonants which include p, t, k, b, d, g, h, m, n, r, t, v, w, y. Of these, r and l alternate as representatives of the one phoneme in different positions, v is pronounced as a bilabial fricative (unlike English), and the voiced stops b, d, g may be prenasalized and sound like mb, nd, and ngg. There may also be a voiced velar fricative and a glottal stop. Syllables are usually open (that is, end in a vowel) and uncomplicated
- a subject-verb-object word order, except in certain areas where the order is subject-object-verb resulting, it is believed, from contact with neighbouring Papuan languages which usually have the verb last in the sentence
- a pronominal system that includes two sets of pronouns, a free set and a bound set. The latter are usually different in form and occur obligatorily with the verb where they agree with the subject and object of the sentence, such as *na* in Motu ('I') and *-mu* ('you') as in *na ita-mu* ('I see you'). Free pronouns are used in other positions. As well the sets distinguish between first person plural inclusive and first person plural exclusive. That is, there are two words for 'we', one of which indicates that the person being spoken to is included in whatever action is being contemplated or performed and the other indicates that the person being spoken to is not so included
- a core vocabulary that includes hundreds of words such as *mata* 'eye', *tama* 'father', *sina* 'mother', *lima* 'five', *rua* 'two', *manu* 'bird' found in Motu which are related to one another (by sound) across the entire Austronesian family
- a counting system based on 'five' or 'ten' which enables speakers easily to count up to very large numbers. There are also usually different sets of numbers for counting different types of objects such as coconuts, yams and spears.

Motu, Dobu, Wedau, Kuanua (or Tolai) and Jabêm are among the most familiar of these languages to linguists and others in the wider world because of their use by early missionaries as church languages. An increasing number of Austronesian languages have been and are continuing to be studied and described and literature prepared in them, however.

Austronesian languages seldom have large speech communities. Kuanua (or Tolai) with an estimated 60 000 speakers and Motu with an estimated 14 000 speakers are the largest. Magori, spoken on the southeast coast of the mainland tail of the country by an estimated 120 or so speakers, is probably the smallest, excluding Ouma, Laua and Bina nearby which were recorded in the late 1960s and early 1970s but are now probably extinct.

Non-Austronesian languages include all other indigenous languages of Papua New Guinea. They are the more numerous and occupy the rest of the mainland and some interior regions in the major islands of New Britain, New Ireland and Bougainville. One, Yele, or Yeletnje, occupies Rossel Island in the extreme east. There are estimated to be over 800 non-Austronesian languages, exactly how many depending on how 'language' is defined. On average these languages are small, although some (such as Enga in the western Highlands with over 160 000 speakers) are very large. Others, such as Bimumarien in the eastern Highlands with just over 100 speakers, are very small. The average size is estimated to be between 3500 and 4000 speakers.

For a long time these languages seemed a bewildering diversity, being unrelated to each other, except for a few small groups, or to any other languages outside Papua New Guinea. As better materials have become available since World War II, however, so too have researchers come to see that many of them are related to one another in families, and only a handful appear to be unrelated to any other language. There are about 60 such families. In 1970 two linguists at the Australian National University, McElhanon and Voorhoeve, proposed, on the basis of certain typological and lexical resemblances, that many of these families belong to one large group, the Trans-New Guinea Phylum. This hypothesis, later extended by Wurm to include other languages, was not widely accepted, however, as it had not been confirmed by careful comparative study leading to the discovery of regular sound correspondences. Recent analysis of a wider range of lexical and morphological evidence by A K Pawley supports a modified hypothesis, namely that while the position of some of the proposed member groups remains uncertain, a large core of the languages earlier assigned to the Trans-New Guinea Phylum do indeed fall into a single family. Strictly speaking, the term 'Papuan', often used interchangeably with 'non-Austronesian', can only be applied to these latter languages, the implication being that they have descended from a single ancestral language. The rest remain 'non-Austronesian' without any claim as to their genetic interrelatedness. It is a convenience to refer to them all, however, as Papuan languages. As yet, 'non-Austronesian' languages have not been shown to be related to any languages outside the Papua New Guinea area.

In their structural features Papuan languages vary considerably from family to family and isolate to isolate. There are, however, a number of features which are more or less common to Trans-New Guinea Phylum languages.

- A phonology that is usually more complicated than that in Austronesian languages, especially in the number and range of consonant and vowel sounds. Thus in any one language there may be bilabial trills, preglottalized voiced and voiceless stops, velar stops with lateral release, labio-velar stops and nasals, uvular or post velar stops, implosive stops, and complex syllable structures involving several consonants. There is also a tendency for stops and fricatives to be in allophonic variation.
- A two-valued tonal system.
- A sentence structure in which the verb invariably comes last, and there is usually just one main verb. Where a sentence contains several verbs, all except the main one are morphologically structured to indicate subordination. Whereas English has a number of conjunctions like 'when, in order to, because, after, before' there are no corresponding ones in Papuan languages. The relationships between the clauses containing these (English) conjunctions and the main clause are indicated by the verb.
- A verb structure that makes the verb the most complicated element in the sentence, often including elements that distinguish person, number, tense, aspect and mood more elaborately than in English, as well as elements that cross-refer to such other elements in the sentence as the subject, object, indirect object, and benefactor. In addition it may include elements that refer to whether an event represented by the verb was seen by the reporter or not.
- A verb system that uses a subset of the most common verbs in combination with nouns or other elements to form other verbs. The most often encountered such verbs are 'do', 'hit' and 'say', but others include 'get', 'put', 'die', 'eat', 'go' and 'come'. Kalam, spoken in the mountains inland of Madang, has only about 90 distinct verbs, the rest being formed by such combinations.
- A so-called 'medial verb' system where subordinate or non-final verbs use different sets of suffixes to indicate when the actor of the main clause is the same or different from that of the subordinate clause. For example, with Koiari, *Eke mime da momi!* ('Give me that!'), the *-me* in *mime* indicates that the actor is the same in both clauses in the sentence. Compare this with *Da manuge ahu otinu* ('I took it and he went'), where they are different.
- A counting system based on 'two' but often accompanied by a more complicated system based on parts of the body.—TD

Further reading

Foley, W A, 1986. *The Papuan Languages of New Guinea,* Cambridge University Press.

McElhannon, K A & C L Voorhoeve, 1970. *The Trans-New Guinea Phylum: explorations in deep-level genetic relationships,* Pacific Linguistics B-16.

Pawley, A, 1998. 'The Trans-New Guinea Phylum hypothesis: a reassessment', in C Baak, J Miedema and C Ode (eds), *Perspectives on the Bird's Head, Irian Jaya, Indonesia: conference proceedings,* Amsterdam.

Wurm, S, 1982. 'Papuan languages of Oceania', *Ars Linguistica, 7*, Gunter Narr.

French language in the Pacific

French is an official language in Vanuatu, New Caledonia and Dependencies, Wallis and Futuna, and French Polynesia. It shares official status with English and BISLAMA in Vanuatu, with English in a few regional organizations (like the PACIFIC COMMUNITY), and with Tahitian in French Polynesia. There are perhaps 400 000 speakers of French, including many for whom it is an imperfectly known second language. Less than 100 000 are native speakers of either New Caledonian French or Tahitian French, the two specific varieties—different from each other and from any other French. Each has its distinctive pronunciation, a few grammatical foibles, and especially its own expressions and words.

In New Caledonia, after French annexation in 1853, there were successively Tahitian troops, ni-Vanuatu (New Hebridean) workers, sugar planters from Réunion along with Indian labourers, Berber deportees, Japanese, Vietnamese, Javanese, Tahitians, Wallisians, and others. There were also small numbers of French West Indians in the 1960s and 1970s; French from Algeria and Vietnam in the 1950s, from newly independent African states in the 1960s, and from Vanuatu in the 1980s. All had some effect, but a more significant source of lexical items in New Caledonian French was the administrative link with the French-speaking world: flora vocabulary from plants taken from the West Indies to New Caledonia via Tahiti is but one of several examples. Early influences came from the penal administration (troops, convicts, administrators), and it is probable that levelling of metropolitan French regional and dialectal differences took place prior to the arrival of these individuals. Such levelling accounts in part for the New Caledonian French phonology (as well as some lexical items). Contact with Melanesian (Kanak) languages was a further influence.

The English-speaking world has had extensive lexical influence. Settlers from Australia provided a lot of the vocabulary of cattle raising, American servicemen during World War II bequeathed a number of words (such as terms for military equipment), and new sporting activities are introduced along with their English vocabulary (wind-surfing, for example). Nevertheless, the main source of New Caledonian French lexical terms which are not 'general French', is internal innovation, as settlers struggled to come to terms with a new physical and social environment.

New Caledonian French is relatively uniform. There is some regional variation in fauna, flora, and grazing vocabulary, and the language is subject to normative pressures (towards Standard French) from schooling, the media, and the presence of metropolitan French speakers. French is also the lingua franca, although the KANAK LANGUAGES OF NEW CALEDONIA, Houaïlou (Ajië) and Lifu (Drehu), have a limited, intra-Kanak/inter-tribal role in some areas. As a second language, French is subject to interference from the speaker's mother tongue. In some rural areas where Europeans and Kanak live in (close) proximity, the French of at least some of the former has patterns and features which closely resemble those of the latter. Furthermore, highly stereotyped (and often pejorative) spoken and written versions of Kanak French are used for literary, comic, satirical and political purposes. Knowledge of French is widespread among both the indigenous people and immigrant groups, but is highly variable. Reduced contact varieties are common in the far South (and one of these, Tayo, has creolized) and among some immigrant groups. Most Kanak tribes have members living and working in Noumea, and some language shift towards French has occurred and is occurring among Noumea-based Kanak.

Tayo is spoken by the people of St Louis, a village established near the capital, Noumea, in 1860. Their ancestral languages were different; an urgent need for a means of interethnic communication forced them to use the only things they had in common, French words and general Kanak grammar. The language that emerged differs from all other contact varieties of French, in New Caledonia or world-wide; it is not mutually intelligible with French.

In French Polynesia, the English of explorers, missionaries, whalers, traders, settlers, BEACHCOMBERS and others impacted lexically on Tahitian and then on the emergent local variety of French. In the 19th and early 20th centuries, English was more widely spoken in Tahiti than French. Chinese (and other) immigration had little effect. There are some survivals of French regionalisms in Tahitian French, but the main influence, in pronunciation and vocabulary, is from Tahitian. Unlike New Caledonia, French Polynesia never experienced large-scale European settlement, although the French presence has increased steadily from the 1960s. Early settlers intermarried with the local population, and this has been a continuing feature. It has given rise to a distinct group definable in social and cultural more than ethnic terms and known as the *Demis* (literally 'Halves'), generally bilingual in French and Tahitian.

While Tahitian has filled the role of lingua franca since before European contact, knowledge of French among Polynesian speakers has steadily increased from about the 1960s. This bilingualism has given Tahitian French its characteristic pronunciation, and also accounts for the lack of internal innovation in the Tahitian French lexicon: Tahitian words are borrowed instead. French in Tahiti is subject to normative pressures similar to those in New Caledonia, although perhaps less so on account of the widespread bilingualism, the fact that French is not the mother tongue of the majority of the population, and the status of Tahitian as an official language (acquired in 1980).

For Vanuatu, New Caledonian French has been the major 'external' influence on the French spoken by French settlers and planters, given the close links with their counterparts in New Caledonia. BISLAMA is the primary vehicular language, with French (and English) reserved for more 'official' roles. Perhaps up to one third of the population has some knowledge of French.

Wallis and Futuna constitute a special case. French settlement is limited to a few functionaries, teachers, and ecclesiastics. Emigration to New Caledonia began in 1943 (workers for the Allied military installations) but did not reach significant proportions until the 1970s. The French state school system was established only in 1961. Since then, knowledge of French has increased markedly, partly due to schooling but principally because of temporary and permanent emigration to New Caledonia: French is perceived as an important tool for economic advancement.—CC

Further reading

Corne, C, 1998. *From French to Creole: the development of new vernaculars in the French colonial world*, University of Westminster Press.

—— and Hollyman, J, 1996. 'French in the South Pacific', in S A Wurm, P Mühlhäusler and D Tryon (eds), *Atlas of Languages of Intercultural Communication in the Pacific, Asia, and the Americas*, Mouton de Gruyter.

Crowley, T, 1989. 'English in Vanuatu', *World Englishes*, 8(1).

Ehrhart, S, 1993. *Le créole français de St-Louis (le tayo) en Nouvelle-Caledonie*, Buske.

Trading languages in Papua New Guinea

Wherever speakers of different languages came together to trade in Papua New Guinea in days gone by, they communicated in one of four possible ways: (a) they used body language to communicate their wishes as they exchanged goods silently; (b) one party tried to learn the language of the other; (c) they used a third, completely different language which both happened to know from other contacts; (d) they developed a new, pidgin language sufficient for their trading purposes. Which one they chose depended on the social circumstances of the time and what language each spoke. All four strategies were used at different times and in different situations. Two, (b) and (d), are particularly interesting for the processes of simplification or pidginization involved. The best documented cases of the results of these processes come from southeast mainland Papua New Guinea where long-distance sea trading occurred. This area is inhabited by speakers of the Austronesian and non-Austronesian languages, scattered around the coast except in the areas immediately east and west of Port Moresby where they have penetrated inland and spread out over the lowland valleys of the large Kemp Welch and Angabunga (St Joseph's) rivers respectively. The non-Austronesian language speakers occupy the remainder. Central to this area live the Motu, a group of Austronesians who inhabit maritime villages in and around Port Moresby and for some 80 kilometres or so along the coast on either side, who are thought to have immigrated two or more millennia ago. At the time of European contact they were engaged in long-distance trade with non-Austronesian language speakers from the Gulf of Papua.

One group of these is known collectively as the Koriki and the other the Elema. The Koriki inhabit the low-lying Purari river delta while the Elema inhabit the coastal area just east of this as far east as Cape Possession. The Elema languages are only very distantly related to Koriki, if they are related at all. The most spectacular aspect of the Motu-Elema-Koriki trade were the HIRI TRADING VOYAGES to the Gulf of Papua to exchange pots and other items for sago, canoe logs and other Gulf products. On these voyages the Motu traders spent about three months in the Gulf, where they attempted to learn the languages of their trading partners.

In the Koriki case, while the Motu acquired a large part of the vocabulary of the Koriki language they were not able to understand some of the more complex elements of the language, so they used a simplified version which their trade partners then also used to communicate with them. In the Elema case, perhaps because of the number of languages involved and the differences in vocabularies between them, the Motu never learned the vocabulary of these languages to the same extent. Instead they developed, in association with their trade partners, a composite language made up of elements of their own language and that of their different trade partners. This language then became the language of trade in this area. These two languages are referred to in the literature as the Hiri Trading Language, Koriki variety, or HTL(K); and Hiri Trading Language, Elema variety, or HTL(E), although the Motu had no special name for them.

These two languages were not the only languages used by the Motu for trade. They had a simplified version of their own language which they apparently used for communicating with those who came to visit them in their own villages. This 'foreigner talk' version of their language was not related to the HTL(K) and HTL(E) trade languages used on their *hiri* and was quite separate from them. In keeping with established practice this 'language' was used to communicate with the first European missionary to settle in the area, Dr W G LAWES, who unsuspectingly learned it as the real language of the Motu and used it in early mission literature. After that this simplified Motu was extended in use by the arrival of a relatively large number of unofficial 'visitors' that came to what later became known as British New Guinea or Papua before a strong government presence was established there.

Some of these foreigners were later employed by the government as interpreters, guides, boatmen and unofficial policemen and were probably responsible for a form of this language being adopted by members of the Armed Native Constabulary, the first official police force that was established by the first Governor of British New Guinea, Governor MacGregor in 1890. Thereafter the language became strongly associated with an expanding police force, whence it derived the name Police Motu. As the unofficial language of administration and economic development it spread throughout British New Guinea/Papua until by the time of independence in 1975, it was spoken throughout most of the southern half of the country and had become the mother tongue of a small but increasing number of speakers. In 1970 its name was changed to Hiri Motu in the mistaken belief that the language was a continuation of a *hiri* trading language. This new name was subsequently adopted as the official name of the language and at independence it was recognized as one of the country's two unofficial national languages and guaranteed equal status with the other, TOK PISIN.

These pidgin languages are but a selection of those developed by Papua New Guineans for trade purposes. Wherever they have been recorded, however, they involve only Austronesians trading with Non-Austronesians (as in the cases just described) or

Dance group from the Gulf of Papua, preparing for Hiri Moale festival, Port Moresby

Non-Austronesians trading with Non-Austronesians (as in the Yimas and Arafundi areas of the East Sepik Province). There are no documented cases of such languages being developed between Austronesians trading with Austronesians in Papua New Guinea, although there are some putative cases in the literature which have been shown not to be real cases, probably because Austronesian languages in Papua New Guinea are all very similar and were therefore probably easy for Austronesian traders to learn.—TD

Further reading

Dutton, T, 1982. 'Language of wider communication (or lingua francas)', in D King and S Ranck (eds), *Papua New Guinea Atlas: a nation in transition*, Robert Brown & Assoc. with University of Papua New Guinea.

——, 1985. *Police Motu: iena sivarai* (= its story), University of Papua New Guinea Press.

Tok Pisin

Tok Pisin, Papua New Guinea's most widespread lingua franca, used to be called 'Neo-Melanesian' or 'New Guinea Pidgin'. At independence, it was spoken by about half the population, most of whom lived in the northern half of the country in the former German (and then Australian) New Guinea, where it was the lingua franca and unofficial language of administration. Since then the number of speakers has increased to an estimated two-thirds or more of the population. This number is constantly expanding as more areas are brought into closer contact with areas where the language is widely spoken, and as it spreads into areas formerly the preserve of Hiri Motu, the unofficial language of administration of Papua before independence and one of the TRADING LANGUAGES IN PAPUA NEW GUINEA. At independence, Tok Pisin and Hiri Motu were recognized as the two unofficial national languages, guaranteed equal status. A knowledge of Tok Pisin or some other indigenous language is a prerequisite for PNG citizenship. The constitution has been translated into it and it is beginning to assume a greater role in formal education.

Present-day Tok Pisin is the product of diverse social and linguistic forces. It began in the central Bismarck Archipelago area (around New Ireland, the Duke of York Islands and the Gazelle Peninsula of New Britain) when labourers were recruited to work on German-owned plantations in Samoa from the late 1870s onwards. There they learned a form of Pacific Pidgin English that had developed as a result of European and islander attempts to communicate. This was brought back by recruits returning to their villages, and it gradually merged with other varieties of jargon and pidgin English derived from other sources, to become the lingua franca as German plantations began to open. When the Second Reich formally annexed the Bismarck Archipelago, parts of Solomon Islands and the north-east New Guinea mainland in 1884, the developing Tok Pisin was cut off from English and other varieties of pidgin English. As a result it acquired much of its present-day distinctive vocabulary, from local languages such as Tolai (or Kuanua) of the Gazelle Peninsula (about 15 per cent) and German (about 5 per cent), for example. This form of the language was then spread to the New Guinea mainland as German economic activity developed there. After World War I, when Australia took over the Mandated Territory of New Guinea, Tok Pisin spread even more rapidly as labour recruiting continued and as it was used as the unofficial language of administration. Between the two world wars, written forms were developed by missions for local use. During World War II its importance grew as the medium of mass communication and propaganda, and afterwards it was increasingly used on radio and in newspapers, and for informal education. Attitudes to the language also improved. Whereas it had been regarded as a 'bastard' English and generally despised, it is now increasingly accepted as a language in its own right. Despite its historical links, Tok Pisin is not a dialect of English, and is not intelligible to English speakers. It is a Pacific language, not an English one, that was developed by islanders, and it spread without, indeed despite, European intervention. Except for those speaking Hiri Motu, it has been the major means of communication between Papua New Guineans who have no other common language. There is now also a significant and growing number of speakers for whom it is their mother tongue.

Tolai people working in colonial Rabaul in the 1920s contributed many words to Tok Pisin as it is spoken today

Tok Pisin is closely related to SOLOMON ISLANDS PIJIN and to BISLAMA spoken in Vanuatu. Tok Pisin is distinguished from these sister varieties, however, by several grammatical structures and a large number of common vocabulary items derived from German, local and other sources.—TD

Further reading

Dutton, T (with Dicks, T), 1985. *A New Course in Tok Pisin (New Guinea Pidgin)*, Pacific Linguistics, D-67.

Mühlhäusler, P, 1979. *Growth and Structure of the Lexicon of New Guinea Pidgin*, Pacific Linguistics, C-52.

Wurm, S A and Mühlhäusler, P (eds), 1985. *Handbook of Tok Pisin (New Guinea Pidgin)*, Pacific Linguistics, C-70.

Bislama

Bislama is the national language of Vanuatu, where it is the only lingua franca spoken by almost all the population. (There are 113 local vernacular languages spoken throughout the archipelago, all Austronesian. English and French are the languages of formal education. There is very little French–English bilingualism because of the separate traditions and areas of influence of the French and British CONDOMINIUM administrations.) Bislama is an English-based pidgin language, a sister dialect of TOK PISIN (Papua New Guinea) and SOLOMON ISLANDS PIJIN. These dialects, sometimes known as Melanesian Pidgin or even Neo-Melanesian, are in the main mutually intelligible, although there are some problems of communication due to different grammatical structures and vocabulary.

Bislama had its origins in Pacific and Australian maritime jargon or South Seas English, reinforced and developed on the plantations of Queensland (and to a lesser extent New Caledonia, Samoa and Fiji) where approximately 50 000 ni-Vanuatu labourers worked between 1863 and 1906. At the end of that period ni-Vanuatu were employed in the many COPRA plantations in Vanuatu, and this proximity in the workplace away from their home islands contributed further to the development and reinforcement of the grammatical and lexical features which distinguish Bislama from the other English-based pidgins of the Pacific.

Market at Port Vila

Since 1971 there have been Bible translations in Bislama, used by all denominations. However, Bislama is not greatly used as a written medium, and not as a medium of instruction in schools. It is used in political tracts and in health and agricultural literature, and is a regular part of the government newspaper, the *Vanuatu Weekly*. A Bislama-language newspaper, *Wantok*, appears irregularly, published by the *Trading Post*, a bi-weekly. There is no official spelling for Bislama. The spelling system adopted by the Vanuatu Christian Council is followed approximately in government publications. Beyond this, however, the spelling of Bislama is idiosyncratic, which has obvious negative effects for Bislama literacy.

Bislama is the language of parliament, and is used on Radio Vanuatu approximately 80 per cent of the time, and in news bulletins on TV Vanuatu. It is used between ni-Vanuatu of different mother tongues, and between many expatriates and ni-Vanuatu in day-to-day situations. While a number of regionalisms exist in vocabulary, and occasionally in syntax, Bislama has become fairly well standardized, especially since Radio Vanuatu has achieved almost nationwide coverage after independence.

With the influx of ni-Vanuatu to the urban centres, PORT VILA and Luganville, Bislama has become a creole, the mother tongue of more than 5000 young ni-Vanuatu whose parents come from different islands or have different first languages. For the rest of the population it remains an indispensable pidgin.—DT

Fiji Hindi

Fiji Hindi (sometimes called Fiji Hindustani or Fiji Baht) is the informal language of virtually all Fiji Indians. It is an 'immigrant *koine*', comprising features of several of the regional dialects of Hindi. These were spoken by the Indian indentured labourers who were brought to Fiji from 1879 to 1916. (Although Fiji Hindi is sometimes called *Bhojpuri*, this is the name of just one of the many dialects that contributed to the language.) It also has a few grammatical features of Bazaar (market) Hindustani and the pidginized Hindi previously spoken by Europeans and South Indians on Fiji's sugarcane plantations.

Most of the vocabulary of Fiji Hindi comes from the Hindustani lingua franca and the eastern Hindi dialects of India, but there are many words from Fijian, especially for names of local flora and fauna (such as *dalo* [taro] and *walu* [kingfish]). Many words from English are also found in Fiji Hindi (such as room, towel, book and reef), but some have slightly different meanings. For example, the word *book* in Fiji Hindi includes magazines and pamphlets, *motor* means car and *gate* means field or paddock.

Fiji Hindi is used in nearly all informal settings, such as in the family and among friends. The 'Standard Hindi' of India is considered appropriate for formal contexts, such as public speaking, radio broadcasting and writing. The Hindu majority write in Standard Hindi using the *Devanagari* script with many words taken from the ancient language, Sanskrit. Muslims use the Perso-Arabic script and words taken from Persian and Arabic. (This literary style is often considered a separate language, called Urdu.) Fiji Indians have to learn Standard Hindi or Urdu in school along with English, so while they all speak Fiji Hindi informally, not everyone knows the formal varieties.

Negative attitudes towards Fiji Hindi are common, especially the belief that it is just a 'broken' or 'corrupted' version of Standard Hindi, which is thought to be the 'pure' or correct language. The truth is that Fiji Hindi is a legitimate dialect with its own grammatical rules and vocabulary unique to Fiji, just as Australian English is unique to Australia.—JS

Fiji Pidgin English

The 19th century Melanesian Pidgin English that gave rise to the contemporary pidgins of New Guinea, Solomon Islands and Vanuatu was never spoken to any extent in Fiji. During the plantation era of the late 1800s, the preferred language of wider communication among non-Europeans was Fijian, usually in the form of Pidgin Fijian.

There is, however, a totally different type of English-lexified mixed language that developed in the 20th century, known locally as simply 'English', but referred to by some linguists as 'Fiji Pidgin English', while others suggest that it is not, strictly speaking, a 'pidgin'. It appears to have originated around the late 1800s when part-European children—usually the offspring of European fathers and Fijian mothers—moved from a Fijian-speaking home environment to one of the urban schools for European children where English was the norm. In the late colonial period it was reinforced by the rules enforced in many schools, and some homes too, requiring children to speak only English. Today it is probably the most common means of intercommunal communication in urban centres, and especially schools, and has become the first language of some young urban part-Europeans.

In its basilectal form, it shows many similarities to Fijian. Its intonation and phonology are almost identical (except that the voiced stops are not prenasalized), pronouns are obligatorily marked for dual and plural number (for example, *astu* for first person dual) and the copula is zero. Many words have the semantic range of their Fijian equivalent rather than the English source: thus, *blaf* (from English 'bluff') has the same range as Fijian *lasu* (to tell a lie, to give the wrong answer, to kid someone); and *wan* ('one', corresponding to *dua*) is both the number one and the indefinite article. Some features such as possession show little or no influence from Fijian.

While the vocabulary is mostly derived from English, there is a considerable borrowing from Fijian and, to a lesser extent, from FIJI HINDI. Differences may be observed between native speakers of Fijian and Hindi, but these variations have never been studied systematically.—PG

Further reading

Arms, D G, Milner, G B and Geraghty, P, 1984. *Duivosavosa—Fiji's Languages: their use and their future*, Bulletin 8, Fiji Museum.

Siegel, J, 1987. *Language Contact in a Plantation Environment: a socio-linguistic history of Fiji*, Cambridge University Press.

Languages of Polynesia

The Polynesian Triangle, as defined by anthropologists, extends from Hawai'i in the north, to Tonga and Samoa in the west, to Aotearoa/New Zealand in the south, and Rapanui (Easter Island) in the east. Other territories contained within the triangle are Cook Islands, Niue, Tokelau, Tahiti, Rurutu, Paumotu, Rotuma and the Marquesas.

Since 1990, representatives of these territories have met biennially to discuss issues of common concern with regard to language. The group that met initially in Aotearoa is called the 'Polynesian Languages Forum'. It has since met in Hawai'i, Tahiti, Aotearoa again in 1995, Tahiti again in 1998, and the next meeting is in Rapanui in January 2001.

Children at a Kohanga Reo (Maori 'language nest') in Huntly, New Zealand, 1992

In relation to language maintenance and survival, the Samoan and Tongan languages of western Polynesia are the most robust; but as increasing numbers of these islanders migrate in search of employment and higher education, the languages are threatened. Migrants tend to remain in their new countries, raising their families there, and as they become removed from a constantly reinforcing language environment, their languages become threatened. The children tend to speak the local language, using the parental language in the home, and, eventually, becoming more fluent in the local language and less in the parental tongue. When these children marry, their children often speak the local language only.

Cook Islands, Niue and Tokelau have more of their population in Aotearoa/New Zealand than at home—in many cases now third and fourth generations—and so all those languages are under a severe threat from the all-pervading influence of English.

Maori and Hawaiian have, since the late 1970s, been actively involved in language maintenance and survival. Both languages appeared to be threatened with extinction but are now comparatively healthy. The threat will continue to recede as long as speakers of both languages maintain and sustain their endeavours. Both have introduced *kohanga reo* (total immersion pre-schools), *kura kaupapa* Maori (total immersion schools from primary to secondary), and many universities that teach all their courses in particular departments through the medium of Maori.

Te Kohanga Reo is funded in New Zealand at the same rate as other chartered early childhood services. The New Zealand government declared Maori an official language of the country in 1987 and established the Maori Language Commission as part of that legislation. Its principal role is to promote the Maori language as an everyday means of communication and to provide policy advice to government.

Most languages of Polynesia continue to be threatened, but island governments continue to seek ways and means to maintain their viability.—TK

Solomon Islands Pijin

Like Bislama in Vanuatu, Solomon Islands Pijin is a lingua franca used throughout the country. An English-based pidgin, like Bislama and Papua New Guinea Tok Pisin, it is also known sometimes as Melanesian Pidgin, Neo-Melanesian or even Pidgin English. It is a necessary lingua franca in this nation of over 60 vernacular languages (each with its own dialect variations), for while English is the language of instruction in schools, it is not a language in which all Solomon Islanders communicate readily.

Pijin, as it is known in Solomon Islands, had its origins in 19th century maritime jargon or South Seas English (sometimes known also as SANDALWOOD English). This was the lingua franca used, in its varieties, on the WHALING and trading vessels which crisscrossed the Pacific between Sydney, Fiji, Tahiti, Hawai'i, Pohnpei and Canton in the first half of the 1800s. This lingua franca underwent major development between the 1860s and the end of the century, when large numbers of ni-Vanuatu, Solomon Islanders and Papua New Guineans worked together on the PLANTATIONS of Queensland, Fiji, New Caledonia and Samoa. It was general practice for speakers of different mother tongues to be assigned to work together, and in order to communicate with each other, they used the Pacific maritime jargon which had existed for over 50 years. It was this which developed into a stable code with fixed grammatical rules during the plantation period (1863–1906).

Nearly all Solomon Islanders worked in either Queensland or Fiji, sometimes both. Most of those engaged in plantation work overseas were from Malaita, the most densely populated island. At the end of the recruiting period, COPRA plantations were developed back in the Solomons, with the majority of labour again coming from Malaita. This contributed to the development of a distinctive Solomons pidgin (as opposed to Vanuatu BISLAMA and Papua New Guinea TOK PISIN), and to the belief that Solomons Pijin owes much to the grammatical structures of Malaitan languages, for all of the pidgin languages of Melanesia have a strong and identifiable grammatical structure which mirrors much of the grammar of Melanesian languages, even though most of the vocabulary derived originally from English.

As with the other Pacific pidgins, there is little Pijin literature apart from Bible translations, which began to be produced in the 1970s. The status and use of Pijin for educational purposes in Solomon Islands has been hotly debated. No official spelling has been developed, although many agencies follow the spelling developed by the Solomon Islands Christian Association. There is a long tradition of using Pijin for evangelical purposes, beginning with the establishment of the Queensland Kanaka Mission in the 19th century, continued today by the South Sea Evangelical Mission, mainly on Malaita. The use of Pijin in the churches has broadened considerably since Pijin translations of the Scriptures have been available.

Apart from its evangelical uses, Solomons Pijin is the normal means of communication between Solomon Islanders in urban areas. It is widely used on radio, in newspapers (along with English), and in the parliament. It has become the first language of increasing numbers of young Solomon Islanders, especially in urban areas, whose parents speak different Solomons languages.—DT

THREE VOYAGING

Wondering minds and wandering keels

When space turned around, the earth heated
When space turned over, the sky reversed
When the sun appeared standing in shadows
To cause light to make bright the moon,
When the Pleiades are small eyes in the night,
From the source in the slime was the earth formed
From the source in the dark was darkness formed
From the source in the night was night formed
From the depths of the darkness, darkness so deep
Darkness of day, darkness of night
Of night alone
Did night give birth
Born was Kumulipo in the night, a male
Born was Ko'ele in the night, a female.

This *Kumulipo* chant, from Hawai'i in the early 18th century, is perhaps the most developed piece of pre-European oral literature ever recorded in the island Pacific. It connects universal creation with the genealogy of a high chief, figuratively representing the human growth and political development of a particular royal child. Many of the larger maritime societies of the Pacific have GENEALOGIES which begin with the gods and often with the creation of the universe, as in *Kumulipo*. In Tongan mythology, creation begins with a separation of land and sea mediated by the spirit world, Pulotu. The world comes into being through recurrent acts of brother-sister incest among deities who then divided the cosmos among them. The goddess or god Hikule'o received Pulotu, the god Tangaloa the sky, the god Maui the underworld.

These myths have no unanimous or final answers. In another Polynesian representation, human life comes from clay blown upon by the spirit's breath—'spirit' being the equivalent of (Greek) *logos* meaning all that can be known of the essence of God. Animism is usually evident. Among the Massim people of Papua New Guinea, the giant sea eagle Manubutu scatters Nidula or Goodenough people as they emerge fully formed from the sacred hill Yauyaba into the watery Massim world. Myth serves everywhere to mediate between humankind and the creation gods of human imagination. In southeast Solomon Islands, Ngarieru, chief of the sea-spirits, covers his human form with fish and sea-birds, and is greatly feared and avoided at his home on the north coast of San Cristobal (Makira). Represented as a wooden carving, however, he becomes a familiar protective effigy on the front of canoe-houses. In northeastern Fiji, Dakuwaqa, the shark-god whose twin landed in human form on a reef to beget the Ai Sokula line of chiefs—at whose death sharks rise in adjoining waters—still remains a known figure. Ardent Christians may be on more or less familiar terms with him, as well as with their own specific Kalou Vu or ancestral spirit. Dakuwaqa may be called *Komaiawai*, 'He from the Sea', equivalent presumably to Gomewe of New Caledonia who created intelligence in human kind.

Deities apart, the island Pacific abounds in named culture heroes and demi-gods suited to peoples who live close to the natural world and may travel much by sea and live off its fruits. So the Polynesian demi-god Maui fishes islands out of the sea with his magic hook, for seafaring humankind to make landfall. Like Prometheus in Greek legend, he brings fire too, and generally works his way to humans' advantage, into the sphere of the gods that control the natural world.

In Banks Islands (Vanuatu), death among human beings results from misapplication of a form of the magic which accompanies all human activities. The natural world is to be controlled, and the adjoining spirit worlds propitiated, by rites appropriately observed. The legendary demi-god Qat danced and beat his slit-gongs before images of human beings he had carved; and thus he brought them to life. Marawa followed suit, but, by burying his images, made them rot, and by doing so brought death upon human beings.

Imagination, feeding on the immediate physical environment of ocean and islands, endowed volcano and shark with human and divine attributes. Human memory scattered the seas with place-names reminiscent of former island homelands—most notably but elusively, perhaps, that 'Avaiki' that, while it may represent an original geographical point of Southeast Asian departure, has taken on the attributes of a spirit world itself. In Cook Islands mythology, for instance, 'Avaiki' is seen as occupying the interior of the vast coconut-shell conceptualized as defining the limits of the universe. Among the Enga group in the Papua New Guinea Highlands, Sky People are at the beginning of time. Enga link themselves to these *Yalyaki* from the Sky through sacred stones placed in groves where, at the end of their own migration from the Gulf of Papua, the Enga ancestors first observed rites ensuring fertility. Fertility and movement across land and sea—these are particular themes in Pacific oral literature, along with warfare. '*O Lono, Lono, Lono-ka-eho*!' runs one poetic invitation to a man of rank to sail to Hawai'i from a foreign land that may be Tahiti.

Lono descended from the gods
Chief of the fertile land of Nana,
Here are the vessels, come aboard,
Return and dwell on green-backed Hawai'i
A land discovered in the ocean,
Risen up out of the waves,
From the very depths of the sea,
A piece of white coral left dry in the ocean,
Caught by the hook of the fisherman
The great fisherman of Kapaahu,
The great fisherman of Kapuhe'euanu'u
When the vessels land, come aboard,
Sail away and possess Hawai'i, an island
An island is Hawai'i,
An island is Hawai'i for Lonokaeho to dwell in.

The seafaring theme recurs, and often the theme of status driving the world with all its demi-gods, heroes and tricksters, shipbuilders and at times reluctant navigators too. 'Puakauooa was chief. The feast in Taaoa in his honour was a magnificent death feast,' begins a series of tales in the Marquesas Islands (French Polynesia) about a voyage across the deep sea. A double-hulled vessel went in search of valuables such as garlands of scented blossoms more durable than gardenia or hibiscus, or fruit, or red parrot feathers to fringe the loin-cloths of chiefs and women of high rank. (Red was the sacred colour.) Those who initiated the voyage are opposed by their father who knows the course and the difficulties: 'You have to go far out to sea, there is no more food and it is long before land is found.'

Yet they persist. With 'seven times 20' in their crew they sail or paddle on, island by island, identifying themselves by their names, their father's name, and the refrain 'ever from beyond the sky'. 'Like the wind we glide behind the sky, our hair darts into the air', they cry in reply to challenges from the zenith stars of each island. In this way they are proving that they can navigate by the night sky, following their father's embarkation instructions. They sail across the passages between many islands, and from the northwestern end of the Marquesas chain, 'they travelled to the middle of the ocean. Their food ran out, the water ran out, and the men died.' Only 40 men remain when they come at last to an island where, revived, they succeed in trapping unwary parrots that fly in, saying 'A good land, no people in it'. When these men arrive home at last with the feathers, however, the waiting women regard parrot feathers as a poor return for their dead men. 'Why did you die like this? Because you went to fetch red feathers for our daughters! You have died, my husband!' The parrots' comment sums up the early Polynesian attitude to voyaging and land-finding seen in another Marquesan chant. This canoe song recounts how Tiki Matohe sets sail 'with a fine chosen band' in a double-hulled vessel 'to seek a place where none dwells, and there found a new home'. 'Seeking out new land' was the established phrase, still used in common speech in 1865 and recorded by J B THURSTON in Gilbert Islands (Kiribati).

It is more common for language to require decoding. So, when Tongatapu is hauled up out of the sea on a fish-hook obtained by descendants of the demi-god Maui from Manu'a in Samoa, symbolism seems to point to political influence. Manu'a, an island of high status, is reckoned the probable origin of the father of the first TU'I TONGA, and the mythology which represents this sacred chief of Tonga as son of the sky-god Tangaloa by a Samoan woman is not incompatible with this reading.

Knowledge conveyed by word of mouth is always malleable. Oral traditions could both flow from temporal power and be used to support it. Knowledge could also be entirely pragmatic and practical, as with sailing directions down star-paths, from Tonga to Caroline Islands. Chants are more likely to record how a vessel must be built. Its construction is accompanied by incantation that must be correct in order to ensure a successful result and prosperous voyaging. The tree for the keel should be judged sound, by supernatural means, before being felled. Forest gods must be placated. Rata, a widely known Polynesian figure, is one shipbuilder or commissioner of ships whose work at first is sometimes in vain. In the Tahitian version, he is a man whose father and uncles have been lost at sea. Due propitiation of wood-sprites permits his last vessel to be built and then launched triumphantly, and he sails off to defeat the giant Tridanca clam which has been the death of his kinsmen. It was always prudent to invoke the spirit world before setting sail. As an invocation of gods in Tahiti ran

If I sail my *va'a*
Through the breaking waves
Let them pass under
Let my *va'a* pass over
O god Tane!
If I sail my *va'a*
Through the towering waves
Let them pass under

Let my *va'a* pass over
O god Tane!

Sky was equated with sea, on the smaller islands especially, and it was imagined that ships and men broke through at the horizon. The island itself might be envisioned as a human form, or as an *atua*, a deity in human form, stretched out face-downwards. In Gilbertese oral traditions, a ship actually produced people. Whole families rose out of the sawdust falling from the cutting of the planking during construction of the great *barua* or double-hulled canoe *Te Kaburoro*, and when she sailed, a woman rose through the spray out of this fast-moving vessel's wake.

Ships might enter into local cosmologies after they had been brought ashore for the last time, and social divisions on shore might then be conceptualized as vessels themselves. So it is on Tanna of Vanuatu, for instance, where the past is a dream-world, with the first humans envisaged as magical beings in a magical cosmos, and the first men on Tanna viewed as wandering around in the form of magical stones, all marking out territory for themselves. In Tannese mythology, arrival is generally given greater significance than the sea journeys to the island. Also, the land discovered and possessed is more important than the sea, a process common in the western Pacific. These origins were solely male, with women being seen as later arrivals, adding culture to nature, bringing cooked food and civilization to a primitive world of warring men. And the sea was sometimes feared as a devouring element containing strange, threatening lands, in this mythology. 'Everything comes from the sea', says a mythical Tannese sage, 'but our destiny is on land.'—DAS

Further reading

Bonnemaison, Joel, 1987. *Tanna: les hommes lieux*, Editions de l'ORSTOM.

Gill, William Wyatt, 1876. *Myths and Songs from the South Pacific*, Henry S King.

Henry, Teuira, 1928. *Ancient Tahiti*, Bishop Museum.

Von den Steinen, Karl, 1988. *Marquesan Myths*, Marta Langridge (tr.), J Terrell (ed.), Target Oceania and the Journal of Pacific History.

Canoes and rafts

Canoes have an essential role in islands life, and many different types have been recorded. All Pacific islands had some form of simple, single-hulled canoes for daily travel, fishing and transport. These were usually dug-outs, perhaps with outriggers for stability, propelled by paddles and sometimes a sail. Where local timbers were scarce or unsuitable for canoe building, islanders sometimes brought logs considerable distances or improvised with mangrove species or sago palm stems. Easter Islanders used planks bound together with sennit and caulked with fine coconut fibre and breadfruit sap. Micronesians had single outrigger canoes, which they built in carefully proportioned sections, finely hand-sewn and tightly lashed with coconut rope. In Tonga double-hull canoes and outrigger canoes had a platform built across the whole width, with a single mast, and were called *tongiaki*. Similar canoes in Tahiti, fitted with two masts, were called *pahi*. In Samoa the small outriggers called *va'aalo*, used for fishing and short trips, were owned by individuals and families, but the larger craft (long-boats called *fautasi* and double canoes called *'alia*) belonged to a village. Many coastal areas used rafts (especially in New Guinea's offshore islands and in inland riverways and lake systems). Plaited coconut, pandanus (screw pine)

Ceremonial Tubuan (spirit) figure in Dukduk costume, with a decorated Tolai canoe, near Rabaul, East New Britain, 1929

matting, or sago palm leaves were widely used as sails.

Long-distance trading voyages, and wars with other groups, required more complex double-hulled outrigger sailing canoes and multi-hulled vessels, sometimes several metres long, as well as many varieties of sail shape and construction. Canoe building often carried high status, because of the enormous skill required of the canoe specialist, and the vessels themselves could be regarded as a sign of chiefly status and village wealth. Micronesian craftsmen, whose engineering masterpieces included deep-sea vessels more than 12 metres in length, had a sophisticated understanding of hydrodynamics, using the principles of drag and lateral drift, and the need for stability in crosswinds. Builders of these ocean-going canoes used many 'modern' techniques such as double-vee-shaped hulls, planking, ribbing and caulking. The great sailing canoes of Fiji were huge craft, about 30 metres long, capable of carrying 200 warriors or a substantial cargo. The 'double canoes' (*waqa tabu*) of the seafaring Bauans had vast leg-of-mutton pandanus-matting sails, for their trading expeditions. The Hawaiians also built canoes for warfare. The famous *peleleu* fleet of KAMEHAMEHA I had up to 800 canoes (for transporting his troops in his war against Kaua'i) consisting of large double canoes, each with a sail and a platform.—KRF

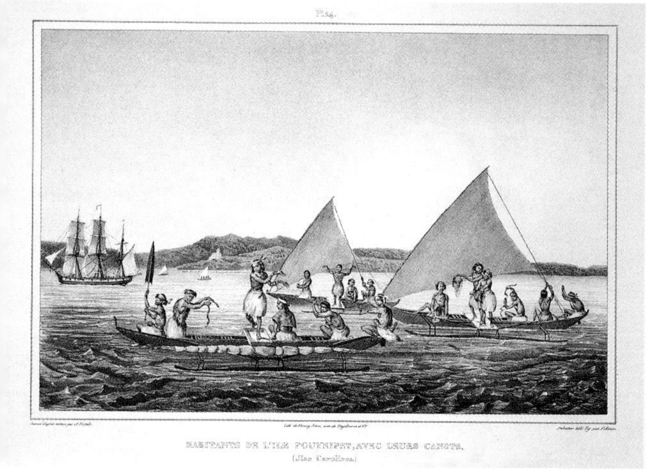

'Inhabitants of the island of Pouynipet [Pohnpei], with their canoes, 1835', lithograph by Lleon Jean Baptiste Sabatier

Hōkūle'a

Hōkūle'a, the 19 m long Polynesian double canoe reconstructed by the POLYNESIAN VOYAGING SOCIETY, made her first long voyage in 1976 sailing from Hawai'i to Tahiti and back. By 1996 she had sailed more than 60 000 nautical miles throughout Polynesia, retracing ancient sailing routes to rediscover traditional ways of sailing and navigating. The resultant findings and insights have revolutionized thinking about Polynesian voyaging and how the islands were explored and settled. *Hōkūle'a*'s many accomplishments sparked a renaissance in voyaging throughout Polynesia, as people from other islands have taken to reconstructing their own voyaging canoes, re-learning traditional wayfinding methods and testing their craft and skills over ancestral sea routes.—BF

Polynesian voyaging society

In 1973 artist Herb Kane, canoe paddler Tommy Holmes and anthropologist Ben Finney, all based in Hawai'i, founded the Polynesian Voyaging Society in order to shed light on disputed theories of Polynesian seafaring and settlement by reconstructing double-hull voyaging canoes and then testing them and traditional navigation methods over the long sea routes of prehistory. In 1975 the Society launched the double canoe HŌKŪLE'A and the following year sailed her from Hawai'i to Tahiti and back. The Society has continued sailing *Hōkūle'a* and other reconstructed canoes around Polynesia, and has extended the vessel's role to include training students in the traditional arts of canoe sailing and navigation, and in applying lessons learned from voyaging to the challenges of contemporary life.—BF

■ *Kupe* According to Maori traditions, the first human to visit Aotearoa/New Zealand was the gifted fisherman and navigator Kupe. He set out from his homeland of Hawaiki in pursuit of a giant octopus that kept stealing bait from his fishing lines. Kupe followed the octopus to Aotearoa and finally caught up with it in Raukawa (Cook Strait), where he confronted and killed it. After exploring parts of the coastline, Kupe then returned to tell his compatriots of this new uninhabited land. Hawaiki was in tropical eastern Polynesia, with Ra'iatea (Society Islands) and Rarotonga (Cook Islands) most commonly identified with it.—PD'A

■ *Tupaia* When Captain James COOK reached Tahiti in 1769 he met a remarkable man named Tupaia (c1725–70), a high-born polymath originally from Ra'iatea who was skilled in geography, meteorology, navigation and other indigenous arts. Tupaia's great geographical knowledge attracted Cook who, following the Tahitian's recital of the names of islands surrounding Tahiti and their bearings and sailing days away, drew up a chart that arguably includes the Marquesas, Tuamotus, Australs, Societies, Cooks and a number of west Polynesian islands. Tupaia also outlined for Cook the principles of indigenous navigation, and how Tahitian sailors waited for westerly wind shifts when they wanted to sail east, facts crucial to Cook's prescient sketch of how Polynesia was settled from island Southeast Asia. At the request of the chief scientist, Joseph BANKS, Cook took Tupaia on board HMS *Endeavour* for the voyage back to England. Tupaia guided the *Endeavour* over several hundred miles of ocean from Borabora to the Australs, and further impressed the English, during the long traverse across the Pacific and around New Zealand and Australia, by always being able to point back to Tahiti. Sadly, Tupaia died while the *Endeavour* was in dry-dock in Batavia (Jakarta), and the opportunity to learn more about Polynesian navigation from him was lost.—BF

■ *Nainoa Thompson* In 1980 Nainoa Thompson (1953–) became the first Hawaiian in centuries to navigate a canoe to another archipelago when he guided the reconstructed voyaging canoe HŌKŪLEʻA from Hawaiʻi to Tahiti and back by non-instrument, quasi-traditional methods. Mau PIAILUG, the master navigator from Micronesia, trained him for that voyage, and Nainoa in turn has become the master navigator and acknowledged leader of the renaissance in Polynesian voyaging. In addition to guiding *Hōkūleʻa* on subsequent voyages through Polynesia in 1985–87, 1992 and 1995, Nainoa has counselled groups from throughout the region in their own projects to reconstruct and sail voyaging canoes, and has trained a new generation of Polynesian navigators.—BF

■ *Mau Piailug* Mau Piailug (1932–) is one of the leading navigators on Satawal in the Federated States of Micronesia where traditional navigation is still vigorously practised. When he was only five or six, Mau started learning traditional wayfinding from his grandfather, and was formally initiated as a navigator (*pelu*) some 10 years later. In 1976 he navigated the reconstructed Polynesian voyaging canoe HŌKŪLEʻA on her maiden voyage to Tahiti, and subsequently trained the Hawaiian navigator Nainoa THOMPSON. He has become widely respected throughout the Pacific for his navigational skills and his willingness to share them with aspiring navigators from other islands, for which he has been awarded an honorary doctorate by the University of Hawaiʻi.—BF

Kon-Tiki expedition

This 1947 expedition sought to demonstrate that South American Indians could have reached Polynesia on a balsa-log raft in prehistoric times and settled there. A group of six Scandinavians, headed by a 32-year old Norwegian, Thor Heyerdahl, undertook the voyage, naming the raft *Kon-Tiki*, after a sun-king in South America. A replica of rafts used on the Ecuadorian and Peruvian coasts in prehistoric and early Spanish times, it was built in Callao, Lima. Because its crew did not then know how to steer it by its moveable centre-boards, or *guaras*, it was towed into the open sea to begin its voyage. The voyage ended at Raroia Atoll in the Tuamotu Archipelago of French Polynesia, after the raft had covered 6700 km of ocean in 101 days. Some sweet potatos carried from Callao were still viable.

The *Kon-Tiki*'s voyage was a major step in undermining a theory that had originated in 1778 with J R Forster, Captain COOK's erudite scientist on his second voyage. Forster had asserted that there was 'no distant or accidental similarity' between the American and Pacific languages and that the 'wretchedness and small size' of American sailing craft proved 'incontestably' that Pacific islanders had not come from America.

Forster's linguistic claim was disproved in 1847 when the term for sweet potato in Ecuadorean Quechua was found to be *cumar*, virtually the same as *kumara* in some Polynesian languages. However, because the American origin of the sweet potato was not recognized until the 1920s, Forster's belief persisted among Pacific scholars.

Heyerdahl became interested in Polynesian origins in 1937–38 during fieldwork on Fatuhiva, Marquesas Islands, as a biology student at Oslo University. The constant east-to-west trade winds suggested to him that prehistoric American Indians could have reached Polynesia much more easily than Polynesians from the west. Back in Oslo, Heyerdahl abandoned biology and went to British Columbia in late 1939 to study the culture of the Kwakiutl Indians of the Ben Coola Valley. In several articles, he argued that stone carvings in the Ben Coola Valley were identical to those in the Marquesas, and that the builders of EASTER Island's huge stone statues were pre-Inca people who had established settlements in the Marquesas, Hawaiʻi, Society Islands and Tonga. When the Germans invaded Norway in 1940, Heyerdahl joined the Free Norwegian Forces in Canada and set aside a manuscript, 'Polynesia and America: a study of prehistoric relations', until World War II ended.

In 1946 Heyerdahl tried to persuade scholars in New York to read his manuscript and support its publication. No one would believe that American Indians could have reached Polynesia by balsa raft, so Heyerdahl organized the *Kon-Tiki* expedition to try to prove otherwise. His account of it, published in Norwegian in November 1948, sold only moderately, but a Swedish edition sold 100 000 copies in its first year, and after an English edition appeared in 1950, the book was on its way to becoming one of the greatest best-sellers of all time. By 1968, more than two million copies had been sold in Great Britain alone and there were translations in more than 60 languages.

Heyerdahl's previously rejected manuscript appeared in 1952 as *American Indians in the Pacific: the theory behind the Kon-Tiki expedition*. Reviewers invariably hailed the expedition as an exciting, daring achievement, but most were unconvinced that American Indians had played any significant role in Polynesian prehistory. Most academics were also unswayed by the reports of Heyerdahl's later archaeological expeditions to the Galapagos Islands and Easter Island. However, recent research into the origin of Easter Island's cultivated plants and domestic fowls at the time of European contact has strongly indicated a prehistoric American connection, reinforcing many of Heyerdahl's ideas.—RL2

Computer simulations of ancient voyages

Many theories have been advanced to explain how people were able to make the long ocean journeys necessary to discover and settle the Pacific islands. In 1963 Andrew Sharp argued that the principal mechanism was 'accidental voyaging' resulting from vessels being blown away from a home island and drifting aimlessly until reaching, and settling, a new island. Computer simulation offered a new means of testing such hypotheses. Michael Levison, Gerard Ward and John Webb developed a simulation model of the Pacific, its islands, monthly frequencies of wind force and direction, quarterly frequencies of current strength and direction, and the chances of survival in small vessels, in order to test where drift voyages might go to from over 150 starting points. Each experiment from a particular starting point began two voyages on each day of the year. The study showed that although short accidental drift voyages might account for settlement of many islands within one archipelago, it was highly unlikely that the settlement of Hawai'i, New Zealand and Easter Island, and many other relatively isolated islands or groups, could have occurred as a result of accidental drift. On the other hand, simulation experiments showed that if navigators deliberately sought to hold a preferred course, vessels with the sailing qualities of Polynesian canoes could have made the necessary long crossings. Thus intentional navigation was a more likely hypothesis.

Geoffrey Irwin used the same basic geographical data to develop a more refined model. He successfully tested the hypothesis that navigators seeking new lands would be able to sail on upwind courses on an outward bound leg and then, using traditional navigation techniques (see PIAILUG), have good chances of a safe return home on an easier downwind course. His 1992 study provides strong support for this hypothesis of deliberate search and discovery by two-way voyaging. It supports the arguments of Finney, Lewis, and others who have tested traditional navigation techniques by long voyages (see HŌKŪLE'A) made without the use of instruments.—RGW

Further reading

Barrow, T, 1972. *Art and Life in Polynesia*, A H & A W Reed.

Heyerdahl, T, 1950. *The Kon-Tiki Expedition by Raft across the South Seas*, tr. F H Lyon, Allen & Unwin.

Irwin, G, 1992. *The Prehistoric Exploration and Colonisation of the Pacific*, Cambridge University Press.

Levison, M, Ward, R G and Webb, J W, 1973. *The Settlement of Polynesia: a computer simulation*, University of Minnesota Press and Australian National University Press.

Lewis, D, 1973. *We, the Navigators: the ancient art of landfinding in the Pacific*, Australian National University Press.

Sharp, A, 1957. *Ancient Voyagers in the Pacific*, Penguin Books.

FOUR DEMOGRAPHY

Early populations

Written records of Pacific island population sizes, growth rates, densities, structures and distributions commence with the European journeys of exploration. The journals and diaries of ships' captains, scientists, missionaries and traders contain a wealth of information on island populations, and they have been used extensively by scholars to establish characteristics of 'pre-contact' populations. Their estimates of population sizes have been accepted, often quite uncritically, as 'reliable' figures for populations at the time of protracted contact with Europeans. They have been elevated to the status of 'benchmarks' for the assessment of subsequent population change.

Norma McArthur is sceptical of the value of such estimates. After an extensive review of the available evidence, including a long period of archaeological field work in Vanuatu, McArthur concluded that 'critical evaluation of the early historical estimates of the size of a non-literate population newly contacted by literate peoples discourages the acceptance of much of the information recorded'. The main problem was exaggeration of population size which created an illusion of a more severe population decline than was warranted during the early years of sustained contact between indigenous peoples and European colonists. (See DEPOPULATION.)

A classic study of the remote atoll of Ontong Java, a Polynesian outlier in Solomon Islands, will suffice to illustrate the need for caution in using early population estimates. In the 1920s, soon after the first official 'census' of Ontong Java established that the population in 1921 was 1016, the anthropologist Ian Hogbin estimated that 'at the opening of the century there were at least 5000 people on Ontong Java'. He based this estimate on the records of the captain of HMS *Torch* which visited the island in 1900. Hogbin's assessment of massive population decline between 1900 and 1921 remained the received wisdom on Ontong Java's early 20th century demography until Tim Bayliss-Smith attempted to establish the human 'carrying capacity' of Ontong Java. His detailed assessment of the island's ecology, economy and society showed that

> It seems unlikely that food resources would have permitted the population to increase beyond 2000, and there is sufficient evidence of cultural checks on population growth to suggest that numbers may have been regulated at a level somewhere below this ceiling.

A very different perspective on the extent of depopulation is obtained if the carrying capacity estimate of 2000 is used instead of Hogbin's estimate of 5000.

There is a need to try to explain the large difference between Bayliss-Smith's assessment of the maximum population which the Ontong Java ecosystem could have supported, and several estimates by visitors around the turn of the century. Bayliss-Smith attempts this when he notes

> The very considerable size of Ontong Java, the large number of islands (approximately 125), the many different settlement sites, the problems of navigation within the lagoon all meant that it would have been difficult for visitors in the early contact period to gain a coherent impression of an entire atoll population. The people, however, were much more mobile than the visitors, and their undoubted tendency to flock to any point where a foreign ship dropped anchor may well have conveyed an erroneous impression of the populousness of the atoll.

There is no way of establishing precisely what the pre-European contact population was on Ontong Java, or indeed on any Pacific island. Contemporary demographic and archaeological evidence about hitherto isolated populations tends to suggest that previous historical and anthropological reporting was 'demonstrably inadequate' to use McArthur's words. For various reasons, then, it would seem that the extent of depopulation in Pacific island countries (including New Zealand) during the 19th and early 20th centuries was grossly exaggerated. Considerable caution needs to be exercised when using the reports of itinerant traders, missionaries and naval officers as sources of population estimates for Pacific islands in the early years of European contact.—RDB

Further reading

Bayliss-Smith, T, 1986. *Ontong Java Atoll: population, economy and society, 1970–1986*, Department of Agricultural Economics and Business Management, University of New England.

Bedford, R D, 1980. *Perceptions, Past and Present, of a Future for Melanesia*, 1979 Macmillan Brown Lectures, University of Canterbury.

Carroll, V (ed.), *1975. Pacific Atoll Populations*, Association for Social Anthropology in Oceania Monograph 3, University of Hawai'i Press.

Hogbin, H I, 1930. 'The problem of depopulation in Melanesia as applied to Ontong Java (Solomon Islands)', *Journal of the Polynesian Society*, 39(1).

McArthur, N, 1967. *Island Populations of the Pacific*, The Australian National University.

Fatal impact

The notion that western contact had devastating cultural and biological consequences for islanders is one of the most persistent themes in Pacific historiography. From the 1770s to the 1930s, as commentators evolved their stereotype categories of islanders, ranging from 'NOBLE SAVAGES' to 'ignoble savages' and 'Romantic savages', it was persistently argued that DEPOPULATION to the point of extinction seemed likely. This belief was ultimately based upon an assumption of the innate superiority of active, initiative-taking western culture compared to the passivity and helplessness of 'primitive' and 'degenerate' island societies. These ideas were increasingly promulgated throughout the 19th century and reached their peak in the early 20th century. They were underpinned by interrelated ideas about human cultures and nature. For example, Biblical interpretation highlighted the notion of degeneracy as various human societies dispersed from the formative homeland in the Middle East, some of whom found their way into the Pacific ocean. Later 'comparative science', which postulated Aryan origins for some Pacific islanders, reinforced the concept of cultural regression. There was also an ongoing environmental determinism, which argued that the tropical environment was culturally and racially debilitating. As well, biological and social Darwinism posited both an evolutionary (as well as a geographic) distance between western and Pacific cultures, along with immutable natural laws that doomed islanders' survival. Ethnographic and anthropological theory reinforced, and was reinforced by, such notions, and with early 20th century functionalism, explained how Pacific societies were static, fragile and bound to collapse and disappear in a changing world. Depopulation in Pacific islands was more a requirement of the western mind than an observed phenomenon.

By the 1930s it was apparent that island populations were not in fact doomed for extinction. Indeed there was an overall population increase, leading to some instances of apparent 'overpopulation'. Anthropologists also began to appreciate island cultures' ability to change, adapt and survive, as represented in theories of 'acculturation'. The Australian National University-based 'island-centred' school of Pacific historians that has dominated post-war Pacific historiography, rejected the assumptions of earlier Pacific historians who focused on the activities of colonial agents in their imperial context, and instead examined island events in an indigenous cultural context. This approach emphasized the adaptiveness and resilience of island communities. Without playing down the effects of epidemic diseases and cultural disruption, they argued that the blanket assumption of a Fatal Impact needed modification to take into account island communities' resilience and capacity for adaptation, adoption, and the implementation of their own cultural initiatives. They also argued that to focus solely on changes in response to modernization can overlook important continuities of islanders' values and organizations. Demographers have also shown that depopulation during the contact period, in the sense of relatively short-term decreases in population due, for example, to epidemic diseases, (as opposed to a demographic collapse to oblivion) was far from a uniform phenomenon in the Pacific islands, and was often on a lesser scale than the earlier extinctionists claimed.

However, the idea of a massive Fatal Impact remains active at a popular as opposed to a scholarly level, illustrated by the continuing success of Alan Moorehead's *The Fatal Impact* (1966). Also in more recent times the idea of a Fatal Impact has been promoted vigorously by those involved in anti-colonial discourse, and particularly by supporters of claims to indigenous sovereignty in Hawai'i. This has provoked debates about the size of some pre-European island populations, with proponents of the Fatal Impact claiming unprecedentedly huge populations in order to heighten the extent of alleged depopulation and consequent cultural dislocation.—KRH

Depopulation

There has been lengthy debate about depopulation of the indigenous peoples of the Pacific both as to numbers and causes. Earlier scholars such as Norma McArthur warned of easy acceptance of early estimates by foreign explorers and missionaries before reliable census-taking. Some modern scholarship points to the conclusion that Pacific islands were not densely populated at the time of contact. The opposing view is for a dramatic revision upwards of populations at contact and thus a more precipitous gradient of decline, particularly in those islands visited early by Europeans—Guam by the Spanish from 1521, Tahiti by the French and then the British from 1767, and later, Hawai'i by the British from 1778. Stannard suggested in 1989 that prior to foreign contact Hawaiians may have numbered at least 800 000—that is, about three times greater than most previous estimates. He noted that early estimates, such as those of King on COOK's third voyage, were of the less-populated leeward coasts, and he claimed that archaeological evidence attested both to the extraordinary fertility of irrigated taro cultivation and of very high population densities. Native Hawaiian numbers probably plummeted to a low of 40 000 in the 1890s. Stannard's thesis is influential if controversial.

In Fiji, although estimates of pre-contact population must be 'radically unstable', as Lukere (1997) has indicated, the documented decline is steady. There are estimates of 200 000–300 000 from the 1840s, the official estimate at Cession in 1874 is 150 000, the colonial census of 1881 is 114 478, and in 1921 it is 84 470. Aneityum in southern Vanuatu, studied in detail by McArthur, presents another smaller example of precipitous decline, paradoxically at variance with her own general caution about overestimating depopulation. In 1858 there were 3513 people, at the nadir in 1941 only 186. Although the population has increased since, it is still at most only 94 per cent of pre-contact figures.

The role of ENDEMIC AND INTRODUCED DISEASES needs to be acknowledged. The principal cause of all such depopulation was the introduction of a wide variety of novel bacterial and viral diseases to which islanders had not been earlier exposed, and to which they had no immunity. Several wreaked immediate and dramatic mortality—the measles epidemic of 1875 killed one in four Fijians. Influenza, tuberculosis, dysentery, whooping cough, and smallpox were all novel sicknesses with high rates of mortality and morbidity, especially among infants and young children. But as well as increased mortality, reduced fertility was significant in the demographic decline over successive generations—'barrenness' followed the obvious and terrible afflictions of venereal disease (notably gonorrhea). In islands with a tropical rainforest climate where YAWS existed, there was also considerable immunity against syphilis. MALARIA was indigenous to all of the islands west of Fiji excluding New Caledonia, and this recurring, chronic illness must have compounded the effects of new diseases, especially for children and pregnant women. The densely populated Highlands of Papua New Guinea, not in direct contact with foreigners till the 1930s, seems to have suffered less from depopulation caused by novel disease, some of which were treatable with sulphur drugs or penicillin in later years.

At the height of the demographic devastations of the 19th and early 20th century Pacific, foreign observers named many causes, not just introduced diseases. The *Decrease Report* of Fiji (1896), like innumerable reports and analyses of the period, sifted through a litany of possible causes—including introduced firearms, ALCOHOL ABUSE, the COLONIAL LABOUR TRADE, and even novel styles of clothing. Indigenous causes were also blamed—warfare with its associated fatalities and famines, the drinking of KAVA, abortion, infanticide, widow-strangling, early marriage, POLYGYNY, sexual abstinence especially post-partum, and even the deficiencies of indigenous mothering—in spite of the obvious survival of these conditions by pre-contact populations. In such discourses about the 'dying race', mothers were singled out for blame and reform, particularly in the sanitation and public health regimes of colonial Fiji.

Some early foreign observers theorized the interaction of exogenous and indigenous causes. The anthropologist RIVERS witnessed the devastation of introduced diseases in Solomon Islands, Vanuatu and Papua New Guinea, but saw this as compounded by an indigenous psychology of despair and despondency, especially for men encountering foreign power. Such speculation as to causes was not just the prerogative of outsiders. Islanders too agonized and theorized about the death and disease in their midst. Oral traditions and written histories by Hawaiians such as Kamakau and Malo lamented the devastation and sterility, implicating Cook and his crew. A Fijian *meke* on the 'wasting sickness' or dysentery lamented the arrival of foreigners, which caused men and women to wither like plantains on a dying tree. Foreign settlers and especially missionaries were often seen both as the source of suffering and of its potential cure. Indigenous explanations, like those of foreign missionaries, combined corporeal and spiritual causes. In many places the successive scourges were thought to result from the wrong-doing of the living, *tapu* violations, the abandonment of ancestors or deities, or at least their lesser force and efficacy in combat with the Christian God and foreign power. Disease and depopulation were thus intimately linked with the processes of Christian prosyletization and indigenous conversion or resistance. Arguably Christian conversion, changing patterns of conjugality, and acceptance of European notions of health and hygiene combined with the development of increasing natural immunity to reverse the course of depopulation and even, in some places, occasioned what some perceived as 'overpopulation' by the late 20th century.—MJ

Further reading

Bushnell, A F, 1993. 'The Horror' reconsidered: an evaluation of the historical evidence for population decline in Hawai'i, 1778–1803, *Pacific Studies*, 16(3).

Decrease Report, 1896. *Report of the Commission Appointed to Inquire into the Decrease of the Native Population*, Fiji Government Printer.

Denoon, D, 1995. 'Pacific island depopulation: natural or un-natural history?', in L Bryder and D A Dow (eds), *New Countries and Old Medicine: proceedings of International Conference on the History of Medicine and Health*, Pyramid Press.

Lukere, V, 1997. *Mothers of the Taukei: Fijian women and 'the decrease of the race'*, PhD dissertation, The Australian National University.

McArthur, N, 1967. *Island Populations of the Pacific*, Australian National University Press.

Stannard, D E, 1989. *Before the Horror: the population of Hawai'i on the eve of Western contact*, University of Hawai'i Press.

Voluntary migration

Local population movements within and between islands have been for the most part 'voluntary'. The movers have chosen to relocate instead of being 'forced' to move. The boundary between voluntary and forced migration is not always clear, however. Children sent to live with relatives in another village do not necessarily move 'voluntarily', any more than a young man or woman 'sent' overseas by a well-intentioned family for education or to work. Nonetheless, there is a tendency in the literature on population movement in the Pacific to regard most movements (including those associated with much of the COLONIAL LABOUR TRADE) as voluntary.

Migration within indigenous societies was commonly associated with marriage, land acquisition, trade, and warfare. Customs relating to residence of brides after marriage varied depending on whether patrilineal or matrilineal descent systems prevailed, but it was common in many places for a woman to move into her husband's community. Interaction between communities was promoted by these marriage ties. In the larger islands of Melanesia, individuals as well as families (and groups of families) moved periodically to gain access to more productive gardening land. Membership of communities changed as a result of a steady ebb and flow of people. Trade in specialized products was also widespread both within the large islands of Melanesia and between the scattered islands of the central and eastern Pacific. Inter-group warfare was a common cause of population movement. This movement, which remains important in parts of Papua New Guinea, was often forced.

The establishment of plantations, missions, administrative centres and, later, towns and industrial centres, widened the range of potential destinations for islanders, especially from the mid 19th century. Movement between rural settlements and the centres of colonial economic, political and cultural activity was generally 'voluntary'. Colonial administrations encouraged islanders to become involved in the introduced religions, to acquire money to purchase imported goods (and to pay imposed head-taxes) and, through the latter part of the 19th and early 20th centuries, to cluster in more accessible coastal locations rather than remain living inland. During the 20th century there has been a significant population redistribution in many parts of the Pacific associated with this interior-to-coast movement.

Migration from villages to the early Pacific towns was often discouraged by colonial governments. In Melanesia, regulations restricted urban settlement of islanders before World War II. Melanesian towns were alien enclaves, not indigenous settlements. In Polynesia and Micronesia, on the other hand, towns often evolved out of indigenous villages, and there were few restrictions on movement of islanders in and out. Following the war, voluntary migration to places of wage employment in rural and urban areas accelerated significantly. In Melanesia this usually took the form of CIRCULAR MOBILITY rather than permanent relocation of populations. Plantation labour forces changed continuously as villagers moved in and out of short-term (often seasonal) wage employment, while town populations contained increasing numbers of 'temporary townsfolk'.

In Polynesia and Micronesia there was an international dimension to post-war circular mobility. I-Kiribati, for example, went to work on plantations in Vanuatu in the 1950s and 1960s; Cook Islanders worked in phosphate mines on Makatea while I-Kiribati and Tuvaluans went to Nauru for similar work. Samoans, Tongans, Cook Islanders, Niueans and Tokelauans were gradually drawn into New Zealand's post-war industrial expansion as a cheap labour reserve. Much of this voluntary international migration was circular rather than permanent, although New Zealand has become 'home' to sizeable Pacific island Polynesian populations over the past 40 years. Circular mobility from urban bases in New Zealand has become the norm for most New Zealand-born Pacific islanders. (See PACIFIC ISLANDERS IN NEW ZEALAND.)

In a review of migration in the islands, R Gerard Ward writes

> Unlike most diaspora of recent times, [the movement of islanders overseas] is not caused by war, expulsion or famine; it is not forced movement; it is not the flight of dispossessed to the margins of the occupied world. And unlike those diaspora in which there was a major break from the source area, physically, socially and often emotionally, in Oceania very close ties have been maintained between source and destination areas and communities. It has resulted in an unusual, if not unique creation of transnational social and economic relationships at family levels which in some respects transcend the state as the primary socio-economic grouping for whole peoples.

Voluntary migration has accelerated in recent years throughout the region. Migration within rural areas, between villages and towns (and vice-versa) and, for Polynesians and Micronesians in particular, to countries on the Pacific Rim, is often the major determinant of population change at the level of the local community. Yet within these more mobile societies, customary forms of population circulation have endured. Externally generated changes have reinforced customary circuits of voluntary migration, and added new ones. Chapman and Prothero argue: 'Had mobility not been part of the lifestyles and thinking of indigenous peoples before western contact, then the territorial fluidity of wage labour demanded by externally defined developments would not have occurred so easily nor in ways that had mutual advantages'.

In a region where population movement has been voluntary, long traditions of local circular mobility and the flexibility of indigenous social structures have ensured that islanders would willingly take advantage of economic opportunities and social developments in other island countries or overseas. Colonial governments, more than indigenous resistance to change, restricted mobility for many years both by internal regulations designed to keep people in villages, and by imposing international borders between island groups. In the postcolonial Pacific, these borders still exist, remaining significant impediments to voluntary movement internationally. Notwithstanding the realities of the nation-state system, Hau'ofa has stressed that Pacific peoples must 'overturn all hegemonic views that aim ultimately to confine us again, physically and psychologically, in the tiny spaces which we have resisted accepting as our sole appointed place, and from which we have recently liberated ourselves'.—RDB

Further reading

Bedford, R D, 1991. 'Migration and development in the Pacific islands: reflections on recent trends and issues', in R Thakur (ed), *The South Pacific*, Macmillan.

Chapman, M C and Prothero, R M, 1985. *Circulation in Population Movement: substance and concepts from the Melanesian case*, Routledge & Kegan Paul.

Connell, J and J R Lea, 1993. *Pacific 2010: planning the future: Melanesian cities in 2010*, National Centre for Development Studies, The Australian National University.

——, 1995. *Pacific 2010: urbanisation in Polynesia*, National Centre for Development Studies, The Australian National University.

Ward, R G, 1997. 'Expanding worlds of Oceania: implications of migration', in K Sudo and S Yoshida (eds), *Contemporary Migration in Oceania: diaspora and network*, Japan Center for Area Studies Symposium Series, National Museum of Ethnology.

Forced migration

Involuntary migrations are not new to Pacific peoples. As long as humans have inhabited the islands, NATURAL DISASTERS have forced them to flee their homelands. Human agency has also been at work. Oral histories are replete with accounts of warfare in which the vanquished were expelled.

Forced migrations have been an instrument of colonial policy, and the colonial era increased the involuntary movement of peoples. Spain, the first colonial power in the Pacific, depopulated the Northern Marianas when most of its Chamorro people were forcibly relocated to Guam. In New Caledonia, France moved the indigenous population to reservations. After the Sokehs rebellion on Pohnpei, German authorities exiled the rebels to Saipan. Alienation of land for plantations caused the dislocation of many people, and BLACKBIRDERS and the indentured labour trade transplanted islanders, willingly and unwillingly, within the region and to Australia and South America. Few island groups escaped the consequences of World War II, when thousands of islanders and hundreds of communities were moved to make way for military installations, and the fields of battle were often made uninhabitable. (See EBEYE.)

Outright coercion declined after the war, and some element of negotiation has been involved in the relocation of peoples. Power relations between the colonizers and the colonized remained unequal, however. In some instances people had no real alternative but acquiescence in the wishes of the administering authority. When the United States selected their homelands as nuclear test sites, the populations of BIKINI and Enewetak atolls in Marshall Islands had to accept relocation at the hands of the Americans. Other populations have been forced to move within the Marshalls because of radiological fallout and to make way for the activities at the American missile range at Kwajalein Atoll. PHOSPHATE mining on Banaba Island made relocation inevitable for its people, and nearly caused the removal of Nauru's population.

Relocation has been used to solve other problems. Persuasion as well as incentives have been used to obtain cooperation. In response to impending overpopulation, British authorities moved people from the southern Gilberts (in pre-war times) and Tikopia. The labour needs of Europeans entered into the Tikopia case, and other motives may have been involved with the resettlement of Gilbertese. In any event, in response to the failure of their initial relocation in the Phoenix Islands, Gilbertese themselves initiated a second relocation, this time to Solomon Islands. CYCLONES, earthquakes, TSUNAMI and DROUGHT have also provided the rationale for relocations.

Governments of independent nations have initiated their own relocation schemes. As before, the degree of coercion has varied. In Papua New Guinea, peoples displaced by MINING operations have had little real voice in the matter. In Kiribati, population pressure has again caused relocation. The British experiment is being repeated, but this time, the Line Islands are receiving resettled populations.

Less than voluntary migrations will continue. Population growth, mining and logging operations, and possibly rising sea levels and the resulting environmental degradation will inevitably contribute to the movement of people in and beyond the region.—RCK

FIVE LIVING IN CITIES

Urbanization

Urban places do not often feature when development issues facing Pacific island countries are appraised, although the region is becoming increasingly urban. The only real metropolitan centre in the Pacific islands is HONOLULU, with a population of more than 870 000. Excluding Hawai'i, some 45 per cent of islanders now live in towns and cities within the region, but governments have been slow to respond to the consequences of urbanization. Policy is still largely oriented towards rural development. An apparent lack of attention to problems of urban poverty, environmental degradation, unemployment and infrastructure suggests that urban growth is seen as analogous to urban decline, which prejudices the sustainability of urban centres.

'Downtown', Majuro, Marshall Islands

Different notions of Pacific urbanization need to be highlighted at the outset. The urban areas considered here range from relatively large cities like PORT MORESBY, SUVA, NOUMEA, and PAPE'ETE (all with populations of more than 50 000), through the rapidly growing urban areas of Vanuatu and Solomon Islands, to the slowly growing Polynesian towns of APIA and NUKU'ALOFA and the small but distressed atoll towns of SOUTH TARAWA, MAJURO and Funafuti. Towns may be semi-rural and residential, with little differentiation between urban and rural villages. By contrast, larger cities may feature significant industrialization, foreign investment, and evidence of global engagement. The development issues facing urban places are also diverse. They include employment, access to potable water, difficulties of waste disposal, high rates of disease and crime, often associated with squatter settlements, access to housing and land, and conflicts with customary landowners.

Urbanization in the Pacific has been comparatively late, reflecting the colonial experience. Many urban areas have developed sizeable and permanent populations only in the last few decades. As centres of European administration and residence, early towns were physically segregated and culturally separated from indigenous populations. In Melanesia, tight curfews and harsh penalties were imposed on indigenous people in town outside established hours. In some places the legacy of separation remains, in the differentiation of towns by ethnicity, clan or language, and class. Consequently, many urban places are still 'cities apart, cities of parts', perhaps comprising several towns, each with their own narratives, experiences and built environments. Early urban growth was a product of transitory migration. Observers and governments alike anticipated that urban populations would not be permanent, although today, island towns are made up of second and third generation residents, even if 'home' is considered to be elsewhere. This was the view of 84 per cent of residents surveyed in South Tarawa (Kiribati), although 40 per cent were born in the town.

While they may have lived in town all their lives, many urban islanders maintain strong links with the family village (through remittances or visits), in order to retain the right to return in old age, or sooner. Village and ethnic associations abound in every urban area, forming tight-knit groupings generally more potent and relevant than class formations. Although these kinship links remain strong and migration is still important, especially in rapidly growing towns, there is little transient about the increasingly dominant demographic, economic and social role of urban places. Many islands are clearly facing an urban future, however different it may be from the urban experience in other regions of the world.

Pacific towns did not emerge as engines of modernization in rural societies. They developed on the back of colonial administrative designs and post-independence public sector growth. Consequently, urbanization has not been led by industrialization, nor shaped by significant structural changes in the economy. Indeed, most urban places have a very narrow economic base. Industrialization is not widespread, and contributes little to GDP, especially when compared with agriculture, tourism and remittances, despite its promotion even in smaller states, such as Tonga through the Small Industries Centre and Tuvalu in the 'mini industrial zone'. Noumea's economy is largely dependent on NICKEL MINING, although TOURISM and the service industries provide more employment than nickel.

Only in larger cities has industrialization developed to any significant level, with Fiji the most spectacular case. In the mid 1980s Fiji had a small industrial sector, based on food-processing and directed at the internal market. After the 1987 coup, however, the military administration pursued an export oriented agenda. This was based on the pursuit of foreign capital for manufacturing in the Tax Free Factory (TFF) and Export Processing Zone (EPZ). Today, manufacturing accounts for 12 per cent of GDP and employs over 24 000 workers. The principal benefactor of this shift is the garment industry, which boomed from an income of F$4 million in 1986, to over F$200 million in 1997. However, even this success has been aided by regional preferential trading agreements such as the South Pacific Regional Trade and Economic Cooperation Agreement (SPARTECA), betraying the marginal viability of small scale manufacturing remote from the world's main markets. Such foreign investment has been criticized as temporary, establishing weak local linkages, and relying on low wage and unskilled female labour.

Typically, Pacific urban centres rely on large bureaucracies, remittances and services for an economic base. In French Polynesia the NUCLEAR TESTING program offered employment prospects which brought growing numbers of islanders from the outer regions to Pape'ete. Even in cities with relatively wide production bases, such as Port Moresby, the public sector dominates. Around 40 per cent of all wage employment in the region is in the public sector. In smaller states reliance on the public sector is even higher. Government accounts for nearly 70 per cent of paid employment in Funafuti (Tuvalu), 60 per cent in Vanuatu, and between 50–60 per cent in Apia. Informal employment in activities such as domestic assistance, handicrafts, cooking, vending and small-scale manufacturing also plays a critical role, although there is little recognition of this by authorities. More generally, urban economies are characterized by a low wage formal sector dominated by government service (which no longer provides employment for school leavers), a large informal sector, and a fledgling industrial sector.

Though Pacific urban centres are small by international standards, their impact on the environment, social order and cultural norms is considerable. Much of this pressure results from urban primacy. In some instances, such as Samoa, Tuvalu, Kiribati, Cook Islands and Solomon Islands, there is only one identifiable urban centre. In others, secondary towns are very small and growing at a much slower rate than their capitals. Papua New Guinea and Fiji offer the only examples of significant secondary towns. Urban primacy is reflected in and determines the distribution of educational opportunities, health facilities, commercial ventures, access to international travel, and superior infrastructure. It reinforces an emergent division between rural and urban, especially in terms of access to formal employment opportunities and to public services.

Towns offer an outlet for those whose needs are not met in still largely subsistence rural areas. The main town is often the only place with a cash economy. In Vanuatu the ratio of urban:rural income is

Garapan (Saipan, Northern Marianas) has undergone a tourist boom since the 1970s: street scene in a hotel district

18:1. The urban economy accounts for 60 per cent of GDP in Fiji, 50 per cent in Solomon Islands, and 40 per cent in Kiribati. However, expectations of earning a cash income are often short-lived as formal employment in island towns does not match job-seekers' needs. Indeed, the benefits of the urban economy are distributed far from equally. The ratio of expatriate income to ni-Vanuatu income is 16:1. In Solomon Islands 70 per cent of total income accrues to less than 2 per cent of the population. In effect, urbanization transfers rural poverty to urban poverty.

Despite growing urban poverty (those living below the urban poverty line in Fiji increased from 12 per cent to 30 per cent between 1977 and 1991), Pacific leaders and communities are reluctant to confront poverty. The term is 'generally avoided and unwelcome'. Harsh and socially alienating lifestyles result, with particularly negative consequences for women and youth. Governments often undercount unemployment. Where available, more accurate data provide alarming evidence of the difficulties of finding urban jobs. For example, in the Marshall Islands, 57 per cent of urban teenage youth are unemployed. There are only around 370 000 wage-earning jobs for the region's 1.8 million economically active population. The difficulty of providing adequate employment for burgeoning populations will pose a challenge to both public and private sectors in the future.

Poverty is particularly evident among urban youth. For many, drawn to town for education, returning to conservative village lifestyles is an unappealing option. They are often caught betwixt or between. As expressed by one ni-Vanuatu youth

> Everything in VILA depends on money. I'd like to start a small business but I don't have the money. If I wanted to go back to my island, I'd need the money for the plane or the ship. So I just have to stay here in Vila which I'm not happy about because until I can find work, I won't be able to do anything...I'll just spear around until I get the chance to work and start something.

For girls the choice is not much better. One Solomon Islands fifth-form student despaired

> If a girl leaves school after Form 1 she can't do anything. She either goes back to the village and plants a garden or, if she stays in town, she might get a job like a waitress. But there's not much choice. Maybe she can become a housegirl.

Even the partially educated may choose to stay in town, and are often drawn into informal sector work such as shoe-shining, vending, or even begging. Others are drawn into crime or SUICIDE. Cities such as Port Moresby and, to a lesser extent, Suva are characterized by young men roaming the streets surveying homes defended by grilled windows. Traditional structures are often inadequate to deal with urban unemployment and the needs of living in a capitalist environment, placing great stress on social structures and family units. Providing a sense of place and meaning for young 'rascals' (RASKOLS) will continue to present a challenge to governments and societies alike.

Pacific urban growth also has serious consequences for the environment, particularly given the fragile coastal ecologies in which they are located. Examples of environmental degradation common to Third World cities are now evident in the Pacific,

Street scene, Port Moresby, Papua New Guinea

particularly access to water and effective waste disposal. Generally, towns lack comprehensive sewerage and sanitation systems, and environmental protection codes. Sewerage in Tarawa and HONIARA is regularly pumped out to sea in the absence of treatment facilities. The destruction of inshore fisheries by pollution is common.

Many pressing environmental problems occur in the smallest states. As elsewhere, it is also the poor who live in the most marginal and unhealthy environmental conditions. In the atolls of Majuro, Tarawa and EBEYE, lagoon pollution, a lack of potable water and available land, and high population densities (reaching 28 205 per sq km in Ebeye and 5400 per sq km in Betio, Tarawa) are signs of urban crises. Problems of access to land are common. Majuro and Ebeye house two-thirds of Marshallese on just 11 per cent of the country's land. Average household size is 9.4. Some 42 per cent of the urban population of Tuvalu of less than 4000 suffers from lack of access to land. Funafuti suffers from land and sea pollution, and waste disposal problems.

Access to housing is another challenge for urban authorities. Squatter settlements constitute a significant proportion of many urban areas. Suva has an estimated 30–50 informal settlements (URBAN SQUATTING IN FIJI), Honiara has over 30. Sizeable squatter populations are also evident in Tarawa. Where they exist, profit-oriented housing authorities have made no significant impact on the condition of the urban poor.

Bong's study of Blacksands, a large and growing informal settlement north of Port Vila on custom land, illustrates the conditions in sprawling cities. Informal settlements account for 30–40 per cent of Port Vila's rapidly growing population. In Blacksands nearly one-third of 5 to 15-year olds did not attend school, with girls disproportionately unlikely to attend. Overall unemployment ran at 55 per cent, and female unemployment at 71 per cent. Water supply was limited to wells, there was no electricity and only two VIP toilets. Despite these conditions, the population doubled between 1989 and 1997. Blacksands continues to attract migrants and escapees from the expense of the city.

Island towns overlie social and physical worlds that predate them, posing particular governance challenges. Many urban places are a collation of villages (Apia) or have been developed on customary land alienated by colonial and post-colonial governments (in the Melanesian states). They occupy a unique and occasionally precarious niche, traversing modernity and custom, rural and urban, highlighting the contested nature of Pacific urbanization and its uneasy coexistence with traditional authorities. Urban land is generally administered through complex formal and informal relationships between state, custom authorities and clans that determine the right to live in urban places. For authorities, lack of access to land compounds problems of providing infrastructure, sewerage and landfills, housing, public parks and recreation areas. For communities, it inflates prices on even marginal freehold land. Customary owners often demand that public land be returned to them to provide for their own clan's expanding population. Migrants without local kinship links inhabit the most marginal urban land and have their 'rights' to live in town constantly challenged by other groups. The key question is, how will governments and populations reconcile traditional and customary needs and rights with the new and changing needs of urban populations?

These conflicts are accentuated as the 'urban footprints' of island cities continue expanding into customary lands. Greater Apia, for example, stretches for 40 kms. Some 50 villages make up the 'official' town although dozens more can be included as the peri-urban fringe. Pape'ete's population overflows into the neighbouring Faa'a district. A majority of Port Vila's population resides outside town boundaries on land informally leased from individual chiefs. In Fiji, urban extensification has created the region's first urban corridor. The Lami–Suva–Nausori belt has grown 107 per cent over the past decade. In 2005 this agglomeration could house 264 000 people, two-thirds of the country's urban population and over one-quarter of national population. Conflicts between urban managers and customary governors are unique to the region. They provide challenges and opportunities to municipal authorities and custom leaders alike, the resolution of which will determine the nature of distinctive Pacific urban places.

Development challenges in the Pacific islands have been exacerbated by relatively ineffectual urban governance. Even in comparatively small jurisdictions, a host of national agencies are involved in urban development, although the issues may be peripheral to their roles. This fragments responsibility, authority and accountability. Even where municipal councils exist, their impact has been limited. They usually operate on meagre budgets with limited expertise. They experience regular political interference (particularly with regard to land).

The problems municipal authorities face have much to do with their contested legitimacy. They were often derived from colonial models of administration. Consequently, they bear little relevance to the form of governance necessary to accommodate the needs of custom and traditional powers. For example, efforts at revenue generation for urban services may be hindered where customary lands and leaders are predominant, or where a majority of 'residents' live outside the council's jurisdiction (Port Vila and Honiara). Such failings underlie the demise or maldevelopment of administrations modelled on western urban planning philosophies.

Island towns face 'typical' urban problems, yet experience unique challenges because of their locations, their geographies, and their customary settings. Consequently, it is difficult to define their futures through reference to other regions. Projecting urbanization in the Pacific in the 21st century and proposing measures to enhance its sustainability are fraught. Nevertheless, the challenges facing the region's towns and cities are manifest—and numerous. They include: providing shelter and infrastructure for growing populations; reducing and reversing land and sea pollution; addressing urban poverty and unemployment; coping with urban growth in the face of a shortage of available land; reducing the social anomie arising from the dislocation of individuals and communities and the breakdown of traditional social structures; and developing models of governance attuned to the distinctive physical, social and political setting.

These challenges are made more urgent by the desire, and necessity, of Pacific leaders to engage in global markets in order to sustain local income and generate foreign exchange. The pursuit of foreign investment, adding value to rural products, developing manufacturing, and attracting tourists all increase the stresses of urban living. Nevertheless, towns and cities in the Pacific will continue to attract rural migrants and retain educated youth. They will persist as the contested interface between modernity and tradition, globalization and community.

Opportunities do exist for a positive Pacific urban experience, but they may require alternative forms of governance to be fully realized. People and culture-centred urban development could see obstacles to western planning being treated as the elements of a potentially more sustainable form of Pacific city. Community structures, for example, still strong in many island states, could form the basis for service delivery. Most of all, a shift is required from a contested post-colonial model of governance towards one that integrates the customary with the progressive, that recognizes changing standards and expectations without losing sight of the distinctive environmental and social qualities and constraints of the Pacific. Innovative approaches to physical development and inclusionary governance must draw on the region's strengths to realize a sustainable future for permanent and expanding urban populations.—DS2 & PMcD

Further reading

Bong, J, 1995. Blacksands Settlement research project, (unpublished).

Chandra, R, 1998. 'Industrialisation', in R Chandra and K Mason (eds), *An Atlas of Fiji*, School of Social and Economic Development, University of the South Pacific.

Connell, J and Lea, J, 1993. *Pacific 2010: planning the future: Melanesian cities in 2010*, National Centre for Development Studies, Australian National University.

——, 1995. *Pacific 2010: urbanisation in Polynesia*, National Centre for Development Studies, Australian National University.

——, 1998. *Island Towns: managing urbanization in Micronesia*, Occasional Paper 40, Center for Pacific Studies and Research Institute for Asia and the Pacific.

■ ***Apia*** Apia, the capital of SAMOA, lies on the central northern coast of Upolu. It is the only urban centre and the sole export port, and has a population of about 36 000. The commercial core and main government area of Apia spreads along Beach Road, fringing the harbour. Many of the two-storeyed white wooden buildings with red roofs date from the German administrative era. In recent years, modern ferro-concrete buildings have been added, including

Apia Harbour, Samoa

government offices and the Central Bank, built on reclaimed land north of Beach Road, opposite the Catholic cathedral. Towards the western end of Beach Road and along the Mulinuu Peninsular, other government buildings—and parliament—are interspersed with industrial sites and housing. In the residential areas there are older parts comprising a scatter of government-owned and private wooden houses dating to the 1800s; groups of more modern single or double-storeyed houses on freehold or government land; and the irregular mix of *fale* (now mostly built of non-traditional materials) and houses of the urban villages.

In the 1830s the shore of Apia Bay had only one village, between the Vaisigano River and Mulivai Stream. Other settlements lay east or west of the bay, or further inland. The beach area of the bay was therefore left relatively open for occupation by some of the first European residents. The sheltered harbour provided haven for ships and the area became the focus for missionaries, traders and other Europeans, with intense demands for land.

In 1879 Apia was recognized as a separate entity from the rest of Samoa when a municipality was established by the WESTERN PACIFIC HIGH COMMISSION, largely under the control of the British, German and United States consuls. The municipality no longer exists as an administrative unit and its boundaries no longer match the present urban area, which includes the *faipule* districts of Vaimuga West and Faleata East. By the mid 1950s, 18.7 per cent of the country's people lived in Apia, and that percentage has increased only slightly to about 21.2 per cent. Apia's population has similarly grown slowly since 1971 when it was just over 30 000.

Because of its relatively small size, the nature of land tenure in the suburban and peri-urban area, and the area's social history, many of the residential parts of the town have a distinctly semi-rural atmosphere which is similar to that of the nearby villages whose people commute to work in the town. Nevertheless, it has an unusually wide range of functions

Police in street parade, Apia, Samoa

for its size and in many respects offers facilities (such as specialist health services) that are found elsewhere only in much larger centres. Samoa remains a rural and agricultural country; Apia is the centre of higher education, the preeminent tourist destination, and the major commercial market for food crops and fish.—RGW

■ *Avarua* Avarua (meaning 'two harbours') is built around the two small harbours of Takuvaine and Avatiu on the northern part of the island of Rarotonga, in COOK ISLANDS. Avarua lies in Te Au O Tonga district, one of three land divisions created several hundred years ago by two great chiefly ancestors, Tangiia and Karika. However, it did not become the most prominent centre of Rarotonga, let alone of the Cook group, until after missionaries of the LONDON MISSIONARY SOCIETY landed in 1823. Avarua soon became their national headquarters. Trading ships also concentrated there and Avarua evolved from the mid 1800s as the religious and commercial capital of Cook Islands. Both harbours have been used at various times but both are exposed and neither is big enough for large vessels, which must remain outside the reef while their passengers are lightered ashore. All inter-island ships

A group of drummers from Pukapuka taking part in a street parade in Avarua, Cook Islands

and smaller international vessels now use the Avatiu harbour, which is also used by yachts, small tourist ships and local fishermen.

Avarua did not become the administrative and educational centre of Cook islands until the first British resident was appointed for Cook Islands in 1890 and the Federal Parliament established thereafter. The concentration on Avarua increased steadily, and today it has a population of about 2000 although most people who work in Avarua live elsewhere on Rarotonga. Government offices, banks, travel agencies, large stores and other commercial enterprises are located in the town. Plans for the redesign and construction of Avarua (following the damage caused by Hurricane Sally in 1987) have been on hold for nearly a decade owing to financial constraints. Despite the small population, direct jet services reach Avarua from New Zealand, Australia, Fiji, Tahiti, Hawai'i and Los Angeles (the international airport, built in 1974, is situated on the outskirts of Avarua) because tourism has become the largest source of national income. However, the hotels are distributed around the coasts of Rarotonga, so Avarua does not see much tourist activity.—MTC

■ *Hagatna* (Agana) Hagatna, capital city of the island of GUAM, has a total area of one square mile, and is located about halfway down on the western side of the island. It is the political centre of the island and also has many shops, businesses and commercial establishments. Its population during the day is many thousands, but it is nearly deserted in the evenings and overnight due to the rapid commercial development over the past three decades. In 1960 the census showed 1642 residents but in 1998 it was reported that only 17 families still claimed residence there.

Hagatna, formerly known as Agana, has always been the principal settlement on Guam. Hagatna is the Chamorro word, but it was called Agana by the first Catholic missionaries who arrived in 1668, led by the Jesuit Father Diego Luis de Sanvitores, and were given land to build their church and mission. The French explorer, Crozet, arrived in 1772 and described Agana as follows

> The chief settlement, which the Spaniards call Agana, is situated four leagues to the north of [Apra] Harbor on the [western] seacoast, at the foot of some low mountains, in a beautiful country full of springs, and watered by a small, very clear, and good brook. The [Spanish governor] of the island lives there. The streets of the town are laid out in straight lines, the private houses are, for the most part built solidly of wood, raised on

> piles, about three feet [1 metre] above the ground, and most of them are roofed with shingles, or with tiles, the rest with palm leaves. There is a beautiful church highly decorated according to Spanish custom. The [governor's] house is spacious and well built.

During the seven and a half weeks that Crozet remained in Guam, he had many opportunities to observe the habits of the people and to study their way of life. Nothing was too small or insignificant to escape his attention. He estimated that the indigenous inhabitants numbered about 1500. Besides Agana, there were 21 small settlements, all on the sea coast. Such settlements were usually composed of five or six families, who made their living by fishing and by growing grain crops and vegetables.

In 1819 another French explorer, Louis de FREYCINET, visited Guam. His artist, Arago, further described the palace in Agana, the environs of the city, and the general way of life of the people

Hagatna, Guam: traffic on Marine Drive, Tamuning

> [The] palace is built of stone and wood. It is...whitewashed, and cleaned...Eight pieces of artillery defence the gate. At its side is a very neat and spacious guardhouse...At the back of the palace is a pretty large piece of ground called the garden. The square (Plaza de Espana) in front of this edifice is the only one in the city. The country round the town is not much cultivated. There are humble huts round which a few yards of rice, Indian corn, yams, and tobacco are cultivated. At Agana there is a royal college and several secondary schools. The common people are very superstitious at Agana, and more so in the country.

With the American capture of Guam from the Spanish in 1898, the palace and the city of Agana were taken over by US naval personnel. Governor G L Dyer described Agana in 1904 as a place where two-thirds of the population, or about 7000 people, lived. In the heart of the city was the great church of

Government House, residence of governor, Guam

Dulce Nombre de Maria, built on the original site given to the missionaries in 1668. Spread out from the church on all sides was the public housing of Agana.

During World War II, Agana was completely destroyed, and then rebuilt following the end of the hostilities by the US Navy. The new Hagatna was laid out differently, and all configurations of former times were changed except for the Plaza de Espana. Today, Hagatna and its environs are among the most modern in all the Pacific.—DAB

Further reading

Nelson, E G and Nelson, F J, 1992. *The Island of Guam; description and history from a 1934 perspective,* Ana Publications.

■ ***Honiara*** Honiara, the capital of SOLOMON ISLANDS, is located at Point-Cruz on the north shores of GUADALCANAL, extending along a narrow coastal strip between ridges and hills in the south and the sea in the north. This configuration has not allowed for easy urban expansion, and people have had to make the most of the terraces and gullies that comprise the natural landscape of the town. Like other capital cities of the region, Honiara began as a colonial town. It was created after World War II on the grounds of the military base built by the American Forces. Honiara is a young capital city, but active demographically as attested by the census figures: 3534 inhabitants in 1959; 11 191 in 1970; 14 942 in 1976; 21 233 in 1981; 30 413 in 1986. The 1996 population is unofficially estimated at 55 000. In 1986 (the last census), 14 000 people were under the age of 18. Solomon Islanders come to town to look for work, but also to take the pulse of the town, to increase education opportunities for their children, to visit kin and WANTOKS, to escape what some perceive as the constraints of custom, and for some, to escape the poverty associated with land shortage. The infrastructures of the town are stretched in the face of such a dramatic increase in population. The older housing estates of Vura and Mbuavale have been supplemented by the sprawling housing estate of Naha, by new suburbs at Ngosi and Mbuburu. Squatter settlements have appeared inside and outside the town boundaries, particularly in the south.

In the 1950s and 1960s, living in Honiara was predominantly a male prerogative: customary rules made it difficult for young women to leave home alone, and housing facilities in Honiara were insufficient to cater to families. As a result, the great majority of the workers were males who left their families in the village and came to town alone. On the eve of independence, and with increases in the level of education, more work opportunities became available to Solomon Islanders in Honiara. More families settled in town, and young women joined their male counterparts in search for paid work. Very soon, children were born in Honiara, creating a first generation of Solomon Islanders who identified primarily with Honiara rather than the home village of their parents. It was also the first generation to be born into a predominantly Pidgin-speaking (SOLOMON ISLANDS PIJIN) world.

Honiara is characterized by ethnic and linguistic diversity: most of the country's 64 languages are represented in Honiara. Bi-ethnic marriages are increasing. A well-travelled and educated urban élite offers cultural models of urban social relations and values complementing the more village-oriented values of many Honiarans. Yet young urban people, increasingly disconnected from the world of the village, look to popular culture, generated locally or imported from abroad, as their medium of cultural expression: rock concerts and soccer matches, videos and T-shirts, marches and banners, dress and hair fashion, new words and new body language—all contribute to the increasing cultural complexity of the town. This popular culture is not associated with any particular ethnic group.

Honiara is the international gateway of the country. It is administered by the Honiara Town Council. As capital, Honiara is the seat of the central government, and houses the national parliament, the national ministries, the high court of justice, the central bank, as well as head offices of national and international companies.—CJ

■ ***Honolulu*** Honolulu, capital of HAWAI'I, lies on the south coast of O'ahu, and is the centre of business, government and tourism for the state. With a resident population of more than 870 000, Honolulu is characterized by the high-rise urban development and high-density commercial entertainment of the city area and the adjacent beach resort of Waikīkī. To the southeast, the extinct volcanic crater of Diamond Head (named by British sailors in 1825 after the discovery of worthless calcite crystals) has become a famous landmark. To the west is PEARL HARBOR, now a naval base, which was a land-locked, shallow lagoon until 1911.

Honolulu's name ('sheltered bay') reflects its initial role as a supply centre for Pacific fur traders, the WHALING industry, and those engaged in the SANDALWOOD TRADE. It was no more than a village when the English merchant captain, William Brown, visited in 1792–93, but it grew in importance and size when King KAMEHAMEHA I established his court on the inner harbour for a time in the early 19th century, and continued to expand even when the royal residence moved to LAHAINA (on Maui) which was capital of the kingdom from 1819.

By 1850, when Honolulu was proclaimed capital city of the Hawaiian group, its population of about

The port of Honolulu, the seat of government, Sandwich Islands (Hawai'i) in July 1847

10 000 included several hundred Europeans (*haole*). As whaling declined, the town's residential areas developed and its character changed. Both the government and the business community became involved in land speculation, hoping to find prosperity in SUGAR. Racial tensions improved during the reign of Alexander Liholiho (Kamehameha IV)—a period which introduced elegance, dancing and theatre into Honolulu's social life. A British-style Episcopal Church was built, and the first hospital was opened. Within a few years, tourism emerged: the Hawaiian Hotel (built in 1871) opened a branch in Waikīkī in 1875, and this former coastal village

with its 2 km of beach began to be seen as a leisure resort. By the turn of the century, a regular tram-car service brought visitors to Waikīkī, and the first substantial Moana Hotel opened; then in 1922, a reclamation project prepared the way for today's urban development.

In the downtown area of Honolulu, there is an area of 'Old Chinatown' on the northern side, its origins dating back to the arrival of Chinese workers in Hawai'i from 1852. Beside Honolulu Harbor is the 56-metre Aloha Tower, built in 1926. The present legislative building, the State Capitol (a massive, supra-roofed structure designed to suggest the islands' volcanic and oceanic origins), replaced the former state legislature in the centre of town, 'Iolani Palace, built for the royal family in 1882, and then restored in 1978. The University of Hawai'i, a state university established in 1907, which enrols nearly 20 000 students, has its main campus at Mānoa, the eastern valley just north of Diamond Head (with another campus in West O'ahu, and a third at Hilo, on Hawai'i). The international airport is to the west of Honolulu, and the main port at Honolulu continues to serve O'ahu.—KRF

Further reading

Daws, G, 1967. 'Honolulu in the 19th Century', *Journal of Pacific History*, 2.

■ ***Kolonia*** Kolonia Town, the largest urban district in the Federated States of Micronesia, lies at the north end of Pohnpei between Commercial Harbor to the west and Dausokele Bay to the east. An independent entity run by a town council, it broke away from the Nett Municipality in May 1965. The population (about 7000, including the surrounding municipalities) fluctuates depending upon school season and summer; less than 4000 are officially resident, and most land is leased for residential and commercial use. Only four areas, Pohn Rakied, Ninseitamw, the Catholic Mission, and the Protestant Mission lands, are privately owned.

Most businesses on Pohnpei are located in Kolonia or just beyond its borders in Nett Municipality. The urban area has hotels, retail businesses, gas stations, hardware stores, tyre repair businesses, grocery stores, bars, a movie theatre, car dealers, laundromats, pharmacies, private dentists and a private physician. In the mid 1990s there were 12 churches, two private elementary schools, and one state college campus.

Kolonia was not always a cluster of commerce and residents. Formerly known as Mesenieng, meaning 'face of the wind', it was held in religious awe by the Pohnpeians before western contact, a place where several shrines were located. Politically, after the fall of the Saudeleurs between the 14th and 15th centuries, Mesenieng fell under the control of the ruler of Nett, which itself became part of Sokehs. But by the time the Spanish arrived Nett had become a separate entity. Subtle changes began when in 1865–67 missionaries from the AMERICAN BOARD OF COMMISSIONERS FOR FOREIGN MISSIONS (ABCFM) established an active mission, calling their new home Canaan. They thought they had bought the peninsula, bounded to the south by the Dewen Neu River; but their 'ownership' developed into a hot controversy when the Spanish arrived. Under the Treaty of Tordesillas, Spain claimed Pohnpei on 27 July 1886, and within a year had begun to build their colonial government.

Spanish and Pohnpeians were immediately locked in fierce intrigue often reflecting local power struggles, which themselves were cloaked in religious conflicts between Protestant and growing Catholic influence. Pohnpeian success in battle against the Spanish was temporary: the Spanish returned and built Fort Alphonse XIII, naming the area La Colonia (The Colony). However, they were soon replaced by the Germans.

The Mesenieng area's metamorphosis continued under the Germans who raised their flag on 12 October 1899, and replaced most of the Spanish fortifications. They built streets and new buildings but not a town; they had come to Micronesia only to raise revenue to feed the expanding German Empire. They called the area Die Kolonie. At first the Germans used the carrot and stick method to encourage Pohnpeians to increase COPRA production, but after the Pohnpeians in Sokehs rose in rebellion, the Germans threw away the carrot. They seized all the land in Die Kolonie for administration, except for lots in Pohn Rakied, Ninseitamw, and the Catholic and Protestant mission areas. Their rule was short, however, for world circumstances again

Kolonia Town, Federated States of Micronesia: main street looking south

Kolonia: view from Pohndolap on Sokehs Island

dictated that another ruler would make a total transformation of Mesenieng.

The Japanese came in a bloodless take-over on 7 October 1914. They built a town, now called Koronia, with more than 900 structures of wood or corrugated tin, placed neatly in well-kept neighborhoods. The main street, Namiki (today called Kaselehlie), was described as the 'Ginza of Micronesia': there were parks and places of entertainment. Among the stores were shops selling ice sticks and bakery products, more than 20 restaurants, a dairy, a slaughterhouse, a pharmacy, more than 15 dispensaries, second-hand stores, curio shops, and butcher and liquor shops.

A huge fishing fleet based itself along the town's northern shores, and pleasant residential areas were built as part of the economic growth. Large businesses developed, a telephone system was installed, a hydro-electric generating plant was built in the mountains of Nett, and a substantial agricultural station set up near the present American Embassy. Koronia prospered, though it remained an enclave of Japan, with Micronesians essentially barred from living in most of the Mesenieng area. By 1941 Koronia's Japanese population numbered about 3000, representing 50 per cent of those living in the Pohnpei Branch District which included Kosrae and outer islands.

With Japan's entry into war against America, Koronia became a military garrison, which by 1945, was laid to waste by the massive fire bombing in which American war planes dumped 118 tons of bombs and more than 600 incendiaries on Pohnpei (May–October 1944). The site of today's college baseball field reportedly exploded for a week because of the large stockpile of ammunition stored there. One priest wrote that Koronia ceased to exist at the end of the first two days of attacks. The buildings left standing were the Nambo department store, the Japanese school, the Protestant church, the Catholic Mission Bell Tower, and a single wooden house in Pohn-Rakied.

After the war, under the US Navy administration, Pohnpeians began returning to Mesenieng, now called Kolonia Town. At first Micronesians were not allowed to purchase alcohol, but in the early 1960s bars—with names such as Darling, Lovely, Seaman, Lynn's, Frank's, Smiling, and Bamboo Inn—became notorious. The main street had small shops and bars with hitching posts and swinging saloon doors, like an American Wild West show. Five movie theatres opened in Kolonia Town, and several large stores. Religious preference remained evenly divided between Protestants (ABCFM) and Roman Catholics until the 1970s when other groups began to compete. The population more than doubled from 1963 to 1970, to over 2800.—TCP

Further reading

Peattie, M, 1988. *Nan'yô: the rise and fall of the Japanese in Micronesia, 1885–1945,* University of Hawai'i Press.

Price, W, 1944. *Japan's Islands of Mystery,* William Heinemann.

Ward, M C, 1989. *Nest in the Wind: adventures in anthropology on a tropical island*, Waveland Press.

■ *Koror* Koror, the capital of PALAU, lies at the centre of three small islands, Koror, Ngerkebesand and Malakal, just off the southwest tip of the larger island of Babelthaup, and connected to it by a long suspension bridge. With an estimated population of nearly 12 000, Koror is the most densely populated urban centre in Micronesia. Its services and facilities extend on to the smaller adjacent islands, connected by causeways, and Palau's main airport (Airai) is on the southern end of Babelthaup. Koror has been rebuilt since the end of the Pacific War, but its early history reflected the successive periods of colonial occupation of the western Caroline Islands. At the

Koror, Palau

turn of the century, Germany had a small administrative outpost in the Palau Islands, but when Palau became a Japanese colony after 1914, Koror became a thriving Japanese town. In March 1922, the civil government office of Japan's South Seas Government (Nan'yô-chô) was moved from the naval headquarters on Dublon (Chuuk) to Koror. Like SAIPAN and KOLONIA (Pohnpei), Koror contained a rash of small artisan shops and service establishments, and most of the amenities of Japanese small-town life including cinemas, restaurants, beauty parlours and even geisha houses. As administrative centre of the whole territory, Koror soon had a very large bureaucracy in place and as centre of a large Japanese fishing industry, there were growing numbers of Koreans and Okinawans brought in as labour. Koror had a population of 25 000 Japanese (four times the local population) in 1935.—KRF

■ *Majuro* Majuro Atoll, the capital of the Republic of the MARSHALL ISLANDS, came into prominence at the close of World War II, as US military forces

Capital Building (government), Majuro, Marshall Islands

established their headquarters and a major air base on the atoll. The deep, sheltered lagoon provided anchorage for a vast navy fleet as the US military fought the Japanese for control of the Marshall Islands and other Micronesian islands to the west.

During the Japanese and German administrations, Jaluit Atoll had been the government headquarters. Majuro became the headquarters for the US Navy administration and later its civilian (Trust Territory) government, although it was still a largely rural atoll until the mid 1960s. At that time, significant increases in US government funding began expanding job opportunities, and Majuro's population began to rise with the influx of islanders from the remote, outer atolls. There was also a major shift in Majuro's population structure. The local population had been settled in Laura village, a rural community at the far western tip of Majuro Atoll. The Americans, however, set up operations in the eastern end of the atoll on islands that came to be known as 'downtown'. Prior to the 1970s, it required a boat to travel from Laura to the downtown area, but then the US government completed a 50 km road. Still the longest paved road in Micronesia, it involved connecting islands by causeway from downtown to Laura, increasing access to the growing urban area. Jobs, educational opportunities, a hospital, and new businesses encouraged people to move into the downtown area, although in the late 1990s, there is some population drift back to Laura and into more rural sections of Majuro as downtown reaches saturation.

In 1958, two-thirds of all Marshall Islanders lived in outer atolls, but the 1988 national census showed that two-thirds were living in the two urban centres of Majuro and Ebeye, with nearly half the population in Majuro.

Majuro has a large and active private sector, but it is primarily service-oriented. Retail and wholesale stores, handicraft shops, restaurants, night-clubs, taxi companies, and hotels have survived for years by recirculating funds provided by the United States through a Compact of Free Association that came into effect in 1986. For many years, government was the business, but the private sector now employs more workers. Since the mid 1990s, the national government has slashed its work force by 25 per cent as part of a reform process supported by the Asian Development Bank.

Majuro has excellent basic infrastructure. Since 1982, a 12 megawatt power plant has provided consistent electricity, fuelling growth in the private sector; and a new power plant planned for 1999. In the early 1990s, the Majuro-based National Telecommunications Authority installed fibre optic cable and established new satellite links, including Internet access, dramatically improving communications. Air Marshall Islands provides air service connecting Majuro with Kiribati, Tuvalu and Fiji each week, while Continental Micronesia services the islands from Hawai'i and Guam. Majuro, because of its key location in the central Pacific, has become a transshipment port for both container ship cargo and tuna caught by purse-seiners on the high seas. The primary industry in Majuro is the Tobolar Copra Processing Plant, which exports US$2–$3 million of coconut oil annually. A fleet of Chinese longline fishing vessels based in Majuro has increased the export of tuna from Majuro, but has provided little employment, as alien workers man the boats and operate the fish base. There are upwards of 1000 non-Marshallese living in Majuro (principally Americans, Chinese and Filipinos), the majority of whom are

Assumption Church, Majuro, Marshall Islands

contract workers in skilled jobs. An influx of Chinese businesses in the late 1990s has raised concerns about competition with locally owned businesses, but most of these businesses are operated by individuals who purchased Marshall Islands passports (during a now-defunct government passport program) and are, therefore, Marshall Islands citizens.

Other businesses, notably Robert Reimers Enterprises, the largest local company in the country, are promoting tourism-related activities and aquaculture development in an effort to develop a productive, rather than service, economy. A fledgling tourism industry began (1996) to bring in scuba divers and sports fishermen for tours to the outer islands. Majuro is being used as a hub (with the Outrigger Marshall Islands Resort and Hotel Robert Reimers as the two primary tourist hotels) to feed visitors to outer island destinations for diving, snorkelling and sports fishing. Best developed is a dive resort at Bikini, where a fleet of World War II ships and submarines lies on the lagoon floor. In addition, Robert Reimers Enterprises operates both clam and black-lip pearl oyster farms; its oysters, hatched in the outer islands and then grown at a facility in Majuro, are sold to the American aquarium market. The pearl industry is in its infancy.—GJ

■ *Noumea* Noumea, capital of NEW CALEDONIA, was originally called Port-de-France by Tardy de Montravel. Founded on 25 June 1854, its name was changed to Noumea in 1866 to avoid confusion with Fort-de-France in Martinique in the Caribbean. The previous year, on 24 September 1853, France had taken possession of New Caledonia to consolidate the presence of French Marist priests at Balade and Pouebo, in the north of the country, with the intention of establishing a penal colony on the island.

According to the 1996 census, the population of New Caledonia topped 200 000 for the first time. Noumea had a population of 76 000, the population of Greater Noumea (Noumea, Dumbéa, Paita and Mont-Dore) reaching approximately 100 000. Seventy per cent of the total population lives in the Southern Province, New Caledonia being divided administratively into three provinces, Southern, Northern and LOYALTY ISLANDS. Between 1854 and the 1920s Noumea grew from a few wooden houses scattered between Artillery Point and Semaphore Hill, to a small town of 10 000 inhabitants in 1927.

While Noumea is well situated on a peninsula in the far southwest of the mainland of New Caledonia, it has no local water supply, water being pumped in some distance from the Yahoué and Dumbea Rivers. The heart of Noumea is built in a checker-board pattern moving away from the main wharf to the hills behind, prominent among which is the cathedral, built by convict labour in the 19th century. Since the discovery of nickel in 1873, the economy of New Caledonia, and particularly Noumea, has been in large measure mineral based, as New Caledonia is the world's fourth largest producer of nickel ore. Apart from nickel, there are also large deposits of chrome, iron, manganese and cobalt. The Société le Nickel, founded in 1880, has a large smelter in Noumea, at Ducos. A record of 7.7 million tonnes of nickel ore was achieved in 1971, at the height of a nickel boom which brought with it dramatic development in the greater Noumea area. Although there was a significant drop in demand for nickel after this time, the Société le Nickel accounts for 80 per cent of the territory's exports.

When New Caledonia ceased being a penal colony at the beginning of the 20th century, the population grew slowly until the arrival of the Americans in 1942, at which time Noumea became an important base for both US and Allied forces during World War II. After the war, in 1947, the headquarters of the

Noumea: St Joseph's Cathedral and Moselle Bay

South Pacific Commission (known as the PACIFIC COMMUNITY since 1997) was established in Noumea at Anse Vata, occupying the site of the South West Pacific Allied Command headquarters. In 1956 New Caledonia became a French Overseas Territory (Territoire d'Outremer) and a Territorial Assembly was established. A few years later the nickel boom of the 1960s attracted large numbers of metropolitan French, and Pacific islanders, mainly from Wallis and Futuna and from the then New Hebrides (today Vanuatu). In the 1980s the population increased again, this time due to the exodus from the rural areas of New Caledonia in the face of increasing insecurity.

Since the signing of the MATIGNON ACCORDS in 1988 Noumea has been both the capital of New Caledonia and of the Southern Province. Apart from being the headquarters of the Pacific Community, Noumea also houses the offices and laboratories of a number of French higher education and research

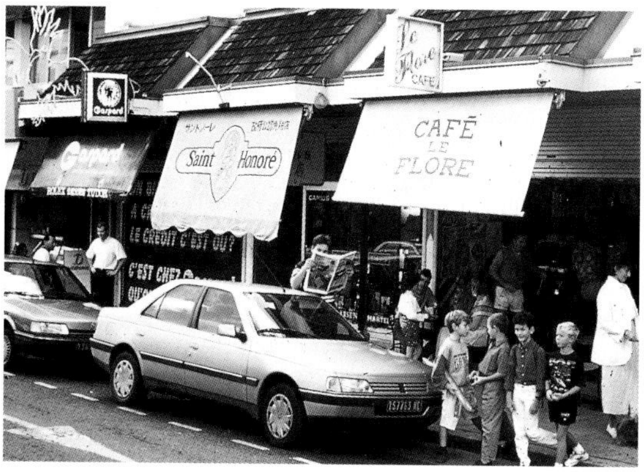

Noumea street scene, New Caledonia

institutions, including ORSTOM (French Institute of Scientific Research for Development through Cooperation), CIRAD (Agricultural Research and Development Centre), IFREMER (French Institute for Marine Research), the Institut Pasteur de Nouméa and the Centre Universitaire de Nouvelle-Calédonie (part of the French University of the Pacific (UFP)), planned to become autonomous in 1999.

A major Pacific cultural centre, the CENTRE JEAN-MARIE TJIBAOU, was opened in Noumea in May 1998, coinciding with the signing of the NOUMEA ACCORD which provides for substantial devolution of powers from France, leading to a referendum on independence for New Caledonia in 2013.—DT

■ ***Nuku'alofa*** Nuku'alofa, the capital of TONGA, stretches along the harbourside on the northern coast of Tongatapu, the largest island in the group. The census for the Nuku'alofa division enumerates the people living in the two contiguous villages of Kolomotu'a ('the old village'), and Kolofo'ou ('the new village'), which originally comprised Nuku'alofa. By the 19th century, Kolomotu'a was inhabited by important chiefs of Tongatapu's Western district. A short time later, Kolofo'ou was founded by the missionaries and the first monarch. In 1829, the Wesleyan missionaries made the 'new town' their headquarters, from which they planned to convert the whole of Tonga to their faith and denomination. They built the first school there. Other schools and colleges followed so that it became the educational centre to which people flocked. When King George TUPOU I, proclaimed king by at least some of the population in 1845, made it his capital, Nuku'alofa also became the centre of power and administration. Port facilities developed in the wide harbour and, as it was the main port of entry for goods, business firms developed shops and warehouses there.

The town at first grew slowly but by 1936 it had a population of 4000 and with the arrival of an increasing stream of migrants was beginning to expand along the waterfront west to Sopu, east to Touliki, and south to the edge of the Fanga Kakau Lagoon. By 1976 the population had grown to over 18 000. Today, the area designated as Greater Nuku'alofa includes not only the original two villages but newer areas such as Tofoa further along the lagoon side, and the area of Ma'ufanga, which lies between the harbour and the lagoon to the east of the original settlement. Once known as a sanctuary for fugitives, Ma'ufanga, which lies within the estate of the noble Fakafanua, has become a highly desirable residential area. Less desirable is the swampy area of Popua further along at the eastern point of the northern shores of Tongatapu. The government opened this area for settlement in 1982 to accommodate people, mostly from Sopu, whose homes had been flooded during Cyclone Isaac, and other landless newcomers who had nowhere else to live.

The pressure on urban land is great, now that the government has no more town land to distribute. Many of the residential blocks (*'api kolo*) in Popua were in fact leased by prosperous local speculators to await the growth in demand as the people continue to move to the capital in search of better educational and employment opportunities. In addition to the increased population accommodated in the more recent 'urban sprawl', the daytime population of Nuku'alofa swells to many more thousands as office workers, vendors, and school children travel in daily from other villages. Nearby populous villages, such as Ha'ateiho, are almost regarded now as 'dormitory' suburbs of the capital. Almost continuous conurbation stretches to other villages on all major roads leading into the town. Pangai, the major town in Ha'apai, and Neiafu in Vava'u have also attracted people because they are administrative, educational and employment centres, but not to the same degree that Nuku'alofa has.—KEJ

Further reading

James, K E, 1995. 'Right and privilege in Tongan land tenure', in R G Ward and E Kingdon (eds), *Land, Custom and Practice in the South Pacific*, Cambridge University Press.

■ *Pago Pago* Pago Pago, the capital of AMERICAN SAMOA, has one of the best natural harbours in Oceania. Facing south and located almost at the midpoint of Tutuila Island, the bay is 1 km wide at its entrance and 4 kms long. Mt Pioa, the majestic 500 m high 'Rainmaker', guards the east side of the bay and helps to capture 500 cm of precipitation annually—hence the title of Somerset Maugham's famous short story about Sadie Thompson, 'Rain'. From there a scenic volcanic rim curves westward and southward to 600 m Mt Matafao. At the head of the bay, Pago Pago village clusters around the mouth of Vaipito stream. The 1990 census classified one-third of the inhabitants of American Samoa as 'urban', almost half (8000) of whom live between the coast and foothills around Pago Pago Bay. On its south side lie the downtown area (Fagatogo), government offices, port facilities, Samoan High School, and the Rainmaker Hotel, and on its north side are two tuna canning factories. Besides container freighters, pleasure craft and the occasional cruise ship, tuna fishing boats comprise the bulk of the harbour's water traffic. The United States naval coaling station closed down in 1951.

Pago Pago is the seat of the high chiefly title Mauga (Mountain), whose status derives from a successful war of liberation in the 15th century that drove Tongan rulers from Tutuila. In the 1820s a New England beachcomber known locally as 'Salemi' converted the Mauga to Christianity, and by 1830 LONDON MISSIONARY SOCIETY missionaries and WHALING ships began to arrive in Pago Pago Bay, along with epidemics like influenza, which killed the Mauga himself in 1839. Samoans traded COCONUT products for metal tools, tobacco and firearms, and by the 1870s treaties permitted the United States to install a consul and, in principle, a naval coaling depot, while passing steamships regularly used the harbour. After Samoan civil wars and foreign interventions in the late 1800s, the islands were partitioned in 1899 between Germany and the United States. In 1900, Mauga Moi Moi signed a Deed of Cession and became a district governor under the new US naval station, but in 1920, he initiated a Mau, or protest movement, to force the US Congress to ratify the Cession treaty (in 1929). The Mau also demanded a civil administration, and in 1951 the territory was transferred to the Interior Department. Since the 1970s, American Samoans have been able to elect their own governor and representative to Washington DC. They remain US 'nationals', not citizens, to protect their chiefly and communal landholding systems, and over half have emigrated to the United States.—DAC

Maota Fono (building that houses the legislature), Pago Pago, American Samoa

■ *Pape'ete* Pape'ete, capital of FRENCH POLYNESIA, lies on the northwest coast of Tahiti. Originally situated on the shores of a bay (its name *pape ete* means 'water basket'), it has since extended eastward and inland. The main business area extends along the waterfront, and many streets are tree-lined and attractive, with modern commercial development and fashionable shopping alongside older buildings with graceful architecture and colonial charm. Pape'ete, the largest settlement in French Polynesia, has a population of about 24 000, with a similar number living in the neighbouring Faa'a district, bringing the total to more than 50 000.

The port has played a significant part in Pape'ete's development, offering a sheltered harbour all year round, while Matavai Bay—the adjacent anchorage used by most early European visitors—is disadvantaged by its northerly exposure for several months of the year. William Pascoe Crook, a missionary of the LONDON MISSIONARY SOCIETY, established a mission station at Pape'ete in 1818, and by the mid 1820s it had become the main commercial port for the island group and the seat of government. The opening of schools and a large church attracted Tahitians to the area, and before long there was a regular English service for the visiting crews of the British and American WHALING ships. By the late 1830s, 70 to 80 whalers visited it annually and several dozen foreigners made a living from the floating population of seamen, deserters and malcontents who brawled and bartered on the waterfront. Missionaries gained freehold rights to land, but other foreigners were permitted only leases. J A Moerenhout, a Belgian merchant, opened a United States consulate in 1835, and George PRITCHARD, a former missionary, became the British consul in 1837. Both men played prominent roles in the events that forced Queen POMARE to accept a French protectorate in 1842. By then the foreign population was about 70. The French made Pape'ete their administrative centre, and the colonial town acquired hotels, restaurants and tourist facilities. A total of 431 ships, representing 30 000 tons, visited Pape'ete in 1864. In 1902, its population was 3750 and in 1910, 4882.

During World War I, two German raiders bombarded the town (1914) without inflicting much damage. In World War II, Tahitians voted to support the Free French government of General de Gaulle and hundreds of islanders enlisted to fight overseas. Post-war Pape'ete was the scene of lively political events (in 1947 and 1958–59) involving the charismatic leader Marcel POUVANA'A A OOPA. (See TRADE UNIONS, and NATIONALISM IN FRENCH TERRITORIES.) The town's growth quickened with the opening of an international airport at Faa'a in 1960. In 1963, plans were announced to modernize the port to enable it to cope with an influx of troops, technicians and supplies for the proposed NUCLEAR TESTING site at Moruroa Atoll. When the work was completed three years later, 35 acres of coral reef had been reclaimed and the picturesque harbour islet of Motu Uta had been virtually obliterated. Meanwhile TOURISM had increased tenfold from 1959.

Riots occurred in Pape'ete in 1991 over proposed taxes. There was more violence in 1995 following the first underground nuclear test at Moruroa, when paratroopers, legionnaires and paramilitary gendarmes had to be flown in to secure order.—RL2

■ ***Port Moresby*** Port Moresby, capital of PAPUA NEW GUINEA, lies in a dry region on the south coast, on the site of several Motu–Koitabu villages (Hanuabada, Vabukori and Kila Kila), the eastern terminus of HIRI TRADING VOYAGES from the Gulf of Papua. Built over the low hills east of the harbour, it extends into the Waigani–Boroko–Taurama valley and the eastern plain that includes Jacksons Airport,

PNG National Museum, Port Moresby, Papua New Guinea

Waigani Swamp and Bomana. The harbour was named by Captain John Moresby in 1873, the same year that the first LONDON MISSIONARY SOCIETY teachers arrived. In 1884 Port Moresby became headquarters for the newly proclaimed British New Guinea. Traders in marine products began to operate along the coast in the 1870s and 1880s, which led to the establishment of trade stores in Port Moresby, but the settlement remained small. The town area was surveyed in the 1880s, the government purchasing land for official purposes and private sale, but economic development was slow.

Until the 1910s Port Moresby was second to Samarai as a service centre for Papua's COPRA and RUBBER plantations, and the small goldfields in the eastern islands. In 1901 the town contained only about 50 Europeans, one store owned by BURNS PHILP, and one hotel. Communications were by ship: road systems did not reach far out of town, and the first airfield was built at Kila Kila in the 1920s. The town expanded slowly, and by 1940 it contained less than 1000 Europeans and 1000 Papuans. Government policies excluded most Asians from Papua, and most Papuans were excluded from the town area after dark, the surrounding villages acting as dormitories for workers.

The Japanese attempted to capture Port Moresby in 1941, bombing raids causing serious damage. Allied forces used the town and neighbouring Sogeri plateau as a strategic war base. In 1945 Port

Moresby became the capital of the newly amalgamated Territory of Papua and New Guinea and the Australian government began substantial funding of the public sector, encouraging private investment and leading to rapid growth of Port Moresby. New suburbs developed—industrial and commercial Badili in the 1950s, residential Hohola, Gordon and Six Mile in the 1960s, residential Gerehu in the 1970s, and Waigani in the 1970s, the latter housing the parliament, university, diplomatic missions and government offices. The population was estimated at 40 000 in 1966, 100 000 in 1975, and 240 000 in 1996, but including squatters and the transient population, it is now closer to 400 000, making Port Moresby the biggest city in Melanesia. It is the centre of manufacturing and communications for the nation, but remains isolated, not linked by road to the populous Highlands or Lae, the second city.

Port Moresby had an elected City Council from 1971 to 1980, when it was suspended for mismanagement and replaced by a National Capital District (NCD) administration. The original villages are now incorporated into Port Moresby. Indigenous migrants have flocked to the city in recent decades altering its ethnic composition. The Motu–Koitabu are now less than 10 per cent of the population, 60 per cent of the residents were born outside the NCD, and 25 per cent live in squatter settlements.—CM2

Further reading

Oram, N D, 1976. *Colonial Town to Melanesian City: Port Moresby, 1884–1974*, Australian National University.

Stuart, I, 1973. *Port Moresby: yesterday and today*, Pacific Publications.

Rannells, J, 1995. 'National Capital District (NCD)', in *PNG: a fact book on modern Papua New Guinea*, 2nd ed., Oxford University Press.

■ ***Port Vila*** Port Vila, capital of the Republic of VANUATU, is situated on the island of Efate, roughly in the centre of the archipelago of 90 islands in the southwest Pacific. Greater Port Vila has a population approaching 35 000. It is the seat of government and of the Supreme Court of Vanuatu. Port Vila also houses the Emalus campus of the University of the South Pacific, an English and a French-language secondary school (Malapoa College and the Lycée Bougainville), a Teachers College and an Institute of Technology.

Port Vila is a municipality, with a mayor and town hall. Its satellite telecommunications system was set up to service the Finance Centre created in 1971, when Vanuatu was declared a tax haven. Radio Vanuatu operates both AM and FM services from Port Vila and from Luganville (Espiritu Santo), and since 1992 there has been a television service, at present limited to the Port Vila urban area. It has a wharf capable of handling vessels up to 40 000 tonnes and an airstrip able to accept medium-range jet aircraft. Port Vila is a major tourist destination, with three luxury and several budget tourist hotels.

Port Vila had its first European settlers in 1873, when a Presbyterian mission was set up on Iririki Island in Port Vila Harbour. However, it was primarily a French-speaking area in its early days, following the opening of a trade store there in 1882 by the Compagnie Calédonienne des Nouvelles-Hébrides and the establishment of French planters. In the 1930s Port Vila had a population of about 1000, consisting mainly of European settlers and administrators. It included Chinese and Japanese artisans and farmers, as well as Vietnamese plantation labourers imported from Indo-China since the early 1920s. During these years the residence of ni-Vanuatu

Port Vila, Vanuatu

(indigenous inhabitants of Vanuatu) in Port Vila was strictly limited, those not from Efate or unemployed being permitted to remain no longer than 15 days.

The real development of Port Vila began with the arrival of American troops in May 1942 during World War II. They provided much of the infrastructure of modern Port Vila, including Bauerfield airport. After the expiry of the Vietnamese labour contracts in 1947, many moved to Port Vila and Santo. Wallisian and Tahitian plantation labour was recruited in 1956, most of whom ended up either in urban jobs or working in the Forari manganese mine in east Efate. In 1963 most of the Vietnamese labour force was repatriated, the Vietnamese population falling from 1600 in 1956 to 397 in 1967. Between 1955 and 1967 the ni-Vanuatu population in Port Vila grew from 200 to 1100 as a result of increased rural–urban mobility. In the 1970s these numbers increased at a rate of 7.2 per cent per annum. At the same time expatriate numbers tripled, with 13 new overseas banks opening offices. In the late 1960s and early 1970s the town became a staging post during the nickel boom in neighbouring New Caledonia; up to 10 000 ni-Vanuatu worked in the nickel mines during this period.

Urbanization has continued unabated, with urban growth at 5.8 per cent between 1967 and 1979. In 1979 ni-Vanuatu migrants made up 46 per cent of Port Vila's population, with a female growth rate of 6.1 per cent since 1972. The majority of ni-Vanuatu migrants come from Tanna, Tongoa, Paama, Pentecost, Ambae, Ambrym and Malakula, mostly grouped together in suburban communities. The census of 1989 indicates that earlier trends have continued, with the exception that most non ni-Vanuatu labourers were repatriated about the time of independence in 1980.—DT

Street scene, Port Vila, Vanuatu

■ ***Saipan*** In 1962 Saipan was selected as the capital of what is now the Commonwealth of the NORTHERN MARIANA ISLANDS, but was then a Trust Territory—established by the United Nations in 1947, and administered by the US federal government—which encompassed all the Micronesian islands under the Japanese from 1914–44.

Among other things, the selection of Saipan resulted in greater development of certain areas of the island. Today, the area known as Capitol Hill (formerly Army Hill under the US Navy) is the seat of the executive and legislative branches of the Commonwealth government. This was because during a 10-year period the American military authorities utilized Saipan as a guerrilla training base for nationalist Chinese fighting in the Chinese civil war. During this period, typhoon-proof buildings were introduced for naval personnel. Water, power and other infrastructure was concentrated in this area (to the detriment of the indigenous civilian communities in the rest of the island). With the Trust Territory moving in, it was natural that the High Commissioner and the Congress of Micronesia take advantage of this established facility. Under the Trust Territory also, the judicial system was established in the area known as Susupe (on the west coast of Saipan), known to World War II buffs as the site of Camp Susupe where non-combatant civilians were sheltered during the battle for Saipan. When the majority of the population of the Northern Marianas voted to become a commonwealth within the American political system, and constitutional government was installed in 1978, it was simply a question of local authorities gradually moving in to the homes and offices of the former administrators.

Saipan: view of Nikko Hotel at San Roque, near Marpi, with La Fiesta Shopping Mall on right

Saipan's port has container facilities, and the international airport, in the south, is not far from the government centre. Garapan, which had been the Japanese administrative centre and primary residential and commercial area, was totally demolished during the June–July 1944 invasion. It remained a sleepy little residential village until the tourist boom started in the late 1970s. It is now the population center of Saipan, with world-class resort hotels and a rather gaudy 'Ginza' providing entertainment and shopping to the tourists.

Residential housing has revolutionized formerly tranquil rural villages throughout the island and the population is no longer concentrated in a few areas. The 65 000 residents of Saipan (including almost 40 000 contract workers primarily from Asia) are now in every part of the island. However, Capitol Hill and Susupe remain the centres of local government.—SMcP

■ ***Suva*** Suva, capital of the Republic of the FIJI Islands, is located in the southeast corner of Viti Levu, the largest island in the archipelago. It became the capital in 1882, taking over from LEVUKA, the major port of the 19th century, which could no longer accommodate the burgeoning trade and a rapidly increasing European population. The colonial government bought the land from the Melbourne-based POLYNESIA COMPANY, which had been given the site, along with 80 940 ha of land in various parts of the islands, by Ratu Seru CAKOBAU in return for the company paying his debt to the United States. By 1870 a few European settlers were trying to grow sugar on the peninsula and a sugar mill was built on the land that is today the heart of Suva's business activity, Victoria Parade. The experiment failed because of inexperience and expense. After purchasing the land, the government marked out a township one mile square from Walu Bay to the present-day Thurston (Botanical) Gardens next to Government House. The main part of Suva was designed by Colonel F E Pratt of the Royal Engineers, appointed in 1875 to act as Surveyor General and Director of Works, and his assistants W Stephens and Colonel R W Arthur.

Today the only major surviving link to the Polynesian Company in Suva is the suburb of Toorak, named after the fashionable suburb in Melbourne. The mildly sloping hilltop with an unobstructed view of Suva Harbour provided the best residential location in the new town. Other picturesque parts of the city with early roots are Cumming Street, reclaimed from a low-lying swamp and the hub of today's duty-free business; Central Suva with streets named after colonial personalities such as Pratt, Chief Justice Gorrie, and Lands Commissioner Williamson, early settlers such as Joske, Renwick and Thompson, and British figures beginning with Queen Victoria, Gladstone, Disraeli, Forster, Kimberly, Macarthur, Lord Carnarvon and Commodore Goodenough; Victoria Parade; the Triangle—the true centre of Suva just opposite the Central Post Office; the old Town Hall; the Suva City Library; Government Buildings; Albert Park; the Grand Pacific Hotel; Thurston Gardens; the Fiji Museum; and the

Street scene, Suva, c1965

Domain, until recently an exclusive European residential area.

Present-day Suva, with a peri-urban population (1999) estimated at more than 170 000, bears little resemblance to its origins. Wooden shops and shaky awnings have mostly been replaced or refurbished, and multi-storeyed buildings mark the city skyline. Residential suburbs have spread to include the Tamavua Heights, parts of Lami (technically a township in its own right), and the rapidly expanding population corridor encompassing the Laucala Beach Estate and Nasinu. Suva is the most cosmopolitan city in the South Pacific, with a multi-racial population of Fijians, Indo-Fijians, Europeans, Chinese, part-Europeans, Rotumans, and other Pacific islanders. Since 1968 it has been home to the regional UNIVERSITY OF THE SOUTH PACIFIC, established at the former New Zealand airbase at Laucala Bay, as well as the base for a number of other regional and international organizations, including the Secretariat of the SOUTH PACIFIC FORUM and various agencies of the United Nations. With its central location in the South Pacific, its sound public infrastructure and modern communication networks, Suva remains the most important capital city in the region.—BVL

Sources/further reading

Schutz, A J, (with L G Usher), 1978. *Suva: a history and guide*, Pacific Publications.

Stanley, David, 1996. *Fiji Islands Handbook*, Moon Publications.

■ *South Tarawa* (Betio/Bairiki/Bikenibeu) The only urban centre in KIRIBATI is at the southern end of the island of Tarawa. What was originally a string of islets divided by shallow tidal passages has been joined by causeways to form a single continuous ribbon of island 28 km in length, commonly referred to simply as South Tarawa. It has become the capital and main administrative, communication and commercial centre. It is divided into two separate administrative units: the Betio Town Council and the Teinainano Urban Council, each of which is represented in the Maneaba ni Maungatabu (parliament) by three representatives. According to 1999 estimates, about 28 340 people—32 per cent of the country's population—now live on South Tarawa.

The islet of Betio has a population of more than 10 000, concentrated on 1.67 sq km of land, and is the most densely populated part of Kiribati. It is the country's main port and commercial centre and home to the Ministry of Transport, Communication and Tourism, the Ministry of Public Works, the High Court, the Tarawa Technical Institute, the Marine

Training Centre and the headquarters for the Cooperative Society.

The Teinainano Urban Council extends from Bairiki to Tanaea and consists of densely populated centres interspersed with rapidly disappearing undeveloped areas planted in coconut trees. The seat of government is at Bairiki, which accommodates Parliament, the Office and Residence of the President, the Ministry of Finance, the Ministry of Home Affairs, the Ministry of Labour, the Ministry of Environment and Natural Resources Development, the main post office, a satellite transmission dish, the Bank of Kiribati and the library and archive complex. Bikenibeu, 15 km further along the island, is home to the Ministry of Education and the Ministry of Health, Family Planning and Social Welfare. Related institutions nearby include a new hospital (that also accommodates the Ministry and the Nursing School), the government-run, co-educational King George V/Elaine Bernacchi High School and the Tarawa Teachers' College. The country's international airport is at Bonriki at the extreme eastern end of South Tarawa. The churches have also established their headquarters within the Teinainano Urban Council, which has transformed a number of villages. The Catholic Church has a large resident staff and high school at Teaoraereke; the Kiribati Protestant Church is at Antebuka and its Theological College at Tangintebu; the Seventh-Day Adventists are at Korobu; the Mormon Church and large high school and the Assembly of God Church are at Eita; and the Baha'i are in Bikenibeu. The University of the South Pacific has a centre at Teaoraereke.

Urbanization has brought mixed blessings to South Tarawa. A sealed road now runs the entire length from Betio to Tenaea and electricity and telephones are available throughout. At the same time, the strain on the fragile atoll environment due to the massive increase in population is clearly evident. Water is a major problem. Families with iron roofed houses collect rainwater for drinking, while those without depend on wells and water pumped from reserves along the atoll, which can be quite brackish during periods of drought. The sewage system, installed in the urban area following a cholera epidemic in 1977, is reticulated separately using sea water. While the building of causeways along the entire length of South Tarawa has improved communication, it has increased pollution levels in the lagoon due to the closing of tidal passages. Most families on South Tarawa, even those with wage earners, still depend on the sea for at least part of their food. The pollution and over-fishing due to the high population, however, are putting pressure on resources and increasing the dependency on expensive imported substitutes. In addition, as building and house construction expands, the number of coconut and other useful trees and plants is being reduced, adversely affecting the standard of living of the population as a whole.—HVT

SIX DIASPORA

Pacific diaspora

Originally a Greek term meaning a dispersal of exiles, diaspora has been applied to a variety of migrations in history, from the spread of Christians or Jews out of the Roman Middle East to the trans-Atlantic slave trade. Diaspora is an apt term for the history of human settlement of the Pacific islands, where four stages may be distinguished. The first saw the forebears of contemporary islanders move out of Southeast Asia and into the central Pacific around 6000 years ago. The second saw them disperse to settle the farthest reaches of the eastern Pacific—the region now known as Polynesia. The third saw Europeans move into the Pacific to claim islands in the names of various states, and then to import labour for their PLANTATIONS. The final phase has seen descendants of the earliest settlers moving around within the Pacific forming new settlements. The contemporary Pacific is the consequence of all these movements.

Around 6000 years ago, a group of people moved out of southeast China or Taiwan into the Philippines, the Malay Peninsula, Indonesia and eventually into the Pacific (FOOTSTEPS FROM ASIA). These people, referred to as Austronesians, moved probably in relatively small numbers, into the islands of the western Pacific at two points. The first entered the northwestern Pacific and settled in the Marianas, Yap and possibly Nauru. The second entered south of the equator, across New Guinea, where they encountered aboriginal settlers, and moved through the Bismarck Archipelago and the islands of Vanuatu to New Caledonia. Their descendants moved out of this region in two waves. The first travelled northwest to settle the Kiribati group, Marshall Islands and eventually Caroline Islands around 4000 years ago. The second moved to Fiji around 3500 years ago and created the platform from which Polynesia would be settled.

Around 3200 years ago, voyagers left their base in western Polynesia and sailed 4000 km eastward to the Marquesas where they settled before setting out for the islands of Hawai'i in the north, Rapanui (Easter Island) in the southeast, and Tuamotu and

Society Islands to the south. From the Society Islands their descendants sailed southwest where they discovered and settled the Austral and Cook groups before making their final, and longest journey to Aotearoa/New Zealand which they reached about 1200 years ago, completing the second stage of the diaspora.

The third stage followed the emergence and expansion of capitalism in western Europe. It had long been widely believed that a great southern continent existed, *Terra Australia incognita*, richly endowed with gold, silk and spices, and offering great potential wealth to the state which 'discovered' it. The growth of demand for raw materials in Europe led to a renewed interest in the discovery of the fabled continent. European voyages into the Pacific had, however, to await improvements in navigation techniques and ship technology. European exploration and settlement in the Pacific can be conveniently divided into three periods. The 1500s were dominated by the Spanish and Portuguese searching for land for the king and souls for the church; the 1600s by the Dutch searching for resources and opportunities to trade; and the 1700s by the French and English, driven initially by the desire to advance science and prestige, and to annex lands in the process. The 1700s culminated in the systematic exploration and mapping carried out by Captain James COOK's expeditions.

The earliest phase of this exploration resulted in limited settlement mostly connected with missionary and itinerant trading activity. The 1800s saw the establishment first of small European missionary communities and then commercial enclaves and the establishment of more intensive political and commercial relations. The need for land for penal settlements and food for a burgeoning industrial population resulted in the creation of a series of 'white settler colonies' which involved a rather larger European presence. These settler enclaves were established to exploit land and marine resources and to extract minerals, to produce food and raw materials for industries of Europe and a market for their industrial production. This process frequently involved the dispossession and marginalization of the original inhabitants. Descendants of those colonists remain a significant element of contemporary Pacific populations.

With the establishment of plantations came a demand for cheap labour. In many but by no means all cases, this labour was recruited locally. This led, in some cases, to the formation of early diasporic communities, as groups moved from 'home' regions to places where employment opportunities were available, and formed distinctive enclaves in which their cultures, languages and forms of social organization were reproduced as for instance in the case of Rotumans in Fiji.

Where local people were reluctant to provide labour, as in Samoa, or were unable to provide sufficient labour, as in Hawai'i, or where they were discouraged from doing so by colonial powers, as in Fiji, indentured labour was introduced from China, India, Melanesia and the Philippines. The barrack-type accommodation in which labourers were initially housed provided opportunities for the formation and growth of new diasporic communities. Despite repatriation, and intermarriage, the descendants of these early labourers remain distinctive elements of many national Pacific populations.

The final phase of the Pacific diaspora which has led to the dispersal of the descendants of the original settlers of the islands from the isles settled by their forebears is a consequence of uneven economic development within the region. This began with the illegal and forced recruitment and transportation of Melanesians to Australia and of Polynesians to South America. It was followed by a period when islanders shipped on WHALING and trading vessels working around the Pacific, served as missionaries beyond the shores of their homes, were deported by colonial powers whose rule they opposed, and served in the armies of colonial powers. Some of these migrants settled but intermarried and left only vestiges of their cultures, languages and social organization in their new homes.

All of these, however, were numerically small compared to the diaspora that followed World War II as industrialization in the region generated large wage differentials and an escalating demand for labour. This has led to the formation of new diasporic communities as Pacific islanders, increasingly aware of these new opportunities and with access to improved transport, have left their homes for metropolitan centres.

The opportunity to move internationally varies according to the proximity of former colonial powers and the constitutional relationships which developed with them before DECOLONIZATION commenced in the 1960s. Some islanders can move relatively easily and have formed diasporic communities throughout the Pacific, while others are effectively unable to move. The citizens of Cook Islands, Niue, and Tokelau Islands have opted for constitutional arrangements that entitle them to dual citizenship, and enable them to move freely between their island homes and New Zealand. American Samoans have opted to remain an unincorporated territory of the United States with similar freedom of movement. Citizens of French Pacific territories are also entitled to live and work in France and her territories. Others have more limited opportunities to migrate. The citizens of Samoa, who opted for independence in 1962, have preferential but not unrestricted entry into New Zealand; and those of Kiribati routinely serve on German ships throughout the world and as labourers in the Nauruan PHOSPHATE industry. The citizens of former British territories such as Solomon Islands and Fiji, and protectorates such as Tonga, have rather fewer opportunities to move.

The large numbers involved in this recent diaspora may have profound social, demographic and economic consequences for Pacific island states and societies. In some cases, where migration has been unrestricted, 'overseas' communities are now larger than the home ones. (See PACIFIC ISLANDERS IN NEW ZEALAND.) Nor has this process run its course. Many island populations are experiencing limited, and sometimes negative, growth. Even when opportunities for out-migration have not been as readily available (as for instance in Samoa and Tonga), large diasporic communities have formed. The resident population of Samoa has been estimated at 166 000, while some 76 200 expatriate Samoans live abroad in American Samoa, New Zealand and the United States; and for Tonga the figures are 97 400 in the islands and 39 400 overseas. The overseas populations are even larger if the children of island-born parents are added.

The consequences are varied but profound. In extreme cases, DEPOPULATION may distort the demographic profiles and lead to negative growth rates as the young migrate and form their families in diasporic communities. The loss of their labour and most primary production may have significant consequences for the small, vulnerable economies of the nations which they leave. Furthermore, apparently higher incomes, standards of living and degrees of personal freedom in diasporic communities may generate a continuing demand for migration which may lead to the progressive loss of a nation's human capital.

A kinship ethic which underlies the culture of Pacific societies produces linkages between home and diasporic communities within which goods and people pass. Remittances, in cash and kind, from expatriate communities have a variety of social and economic effects. Raised financial and material expectations lead to pressure on governments to manage economies in ways that will meet escalating and sometimes unrealistic demands. This leads to increased dependence on external sources of finance such as migrants' remittances, overseas loans and FOREIGN AID, all of which may have an impact on national sovereignty. Furthermore, the continued availability of these resources in a continually changing global economy is by no means assured.

World views and lifestyles are invariably modified by contact with other people's new technologies and institutions in diasporic communities so that accelerated rates of social and cultural change are apparent. Where these expatriate groups are larger than the populations in communities of origin, and where ideas and people travel relatively easily and frequently between them, their impact on the definition of a home society's 'norms' may be significant. Diasporic communities may in time have profound impacts on the reshaping of the home societies' social organization and culture.—CM1

Cross-cultural contacts

Early Pacific history contains many examples of people who crossed cultural boundaries and found themselves in new environments. Some reports have remained tantalizing glimpses only, as for example, the probable first recorded contact between Japanese and Pacific islanders in 1171 (see JAPAN AND THE PACIFIC). The people who cross cultural boundaries and adapt to their new environments—sometimes called trans-culturites—may also contribute innovations to their host society, but generally in ways that do not overtly disrupt that culture. In the Pacific, the best example of trans-culturites were the so-called BEACHCOMBERS who assimilated to their host communities while also using their linguistic and technical skills to mediate with foreign ships. Because they were small in numbers, their very survival often required that they earn acceptance. There were mechanisms for this in pre-colonial Oceania: when canoe voyagers arrived on strange beaches, they might have to assimilate and work their way up in status over several generations, unless they were accorded enough prestige to make a change in the host system, as when Pa'ao modified the religion and chiefly hierarchy of Hawai'i. Later, Christian missionaries learned indigenous languages to preach to the islanders, but they also opposed INDIGENOUS RELIGIOUS SYSTEMS. Polynesian-style FEASTING was introduced into Solomon Islands and other parts of Melanesia by Tongan missionaries, and has since become 'traditional'. Islander missionaries also taught new ways of using materials familiar to local people, such as pandanus, coconut fibre and timber, which then became absorbed into local cultures. The degree of change introduced by trans-culturites may have varied. The assumption is that indigenous people made the major decisions about reforms in their own societies, but returned labourers or islanders educated overseas (having been exposed to new ideas) can act as trans-culturites.—DAC

Kanaka seamen

These Pacific islanders were kidnapped or recruited for labour aboard Euro-American ships, beginning with 11 Chamorros taken from Guam in 1526 to man the pumps of a leaky Spanish ship. By the 1790s, as the CHINA TRADE developed, more foreign vessels needed local sailors to replace crew losses caused by desertion or death. Tahitians, Maori and Hawaiians were among the earliest to explore this opportunity, sometimes at the urging of their chiefs who wanted to learn more about Euro-American technology. By the mid 19th century, thousands of Oceanians worked on foreign vessels, comprising perhaps one-fifth of the sailors in the US whaling fleet. They were often discharged on any island when their services were no longer needed and hence became BEACHCOMBERS, but others sailed to Asia, the Americas, or even to Europe. Henry Opukahaia, who inspired the first missionaries to go to his native Hawai'i, had arrived in New England as a common sailor. Such recruits often received new names and went through other initiations (like the rites of Neptune when they first crossed the equator) until they learned the terms and skills needed to be accepted. Some remained boat-handlers, while others rose to the rank of harpooner or mate and earned equal pay with Europeans. They sometimes helped ships to recruit other 'kanakas' (a Hawaiian word for person that in trade pidgin referred to natives, especially menial workers) in the PLANTATION labour trade.—DAC

Beachcombers

The term beachcombers was applied to European vagrants—often survivors of shipwrecks or deserters from whaling or trading vessels—who became some of the earliest settlers in the Pacific islands. Having aquired island wives, many took a leading role in the exploitation of SANDALWOOD and BÊCHE-DE-MER.—KRF

San Lesmes

The *San Lesmes,* a Spanish caravel of 80 tons, was the first European ship to be lost in the Pacific. It disappeared on a voyage from the Strait of Magellan to the Moluccas in June 1526. The *San Lesmes* was one of seven ships that left Spain in July 1525, bound for the Moluccas for a cargo of spices. The expedition's commander was García Jofre de Loaisa. His second-in-command was Juan Sebastian Elcano, who became the first man to circumnavigate the globe when he brought MAGELLAN's ship *Victoria* home to Spain in September 1522.

Loaisa's fleet reached the eastern entrance to the Strait of Magellan in January 1526. Elcano's ship, *Sancti Spiritus,* with about 90 men, was soon wrecked in a storm with the loss of nine lives. Another large ship disappeared, and a third turned tail and returned to Spain. The remaining four—Loaisa's flagship *Santa Maria de la Victoria,* two caravels (*San Lesmes* and *Santa Maria del Parral*) and a pinnace—later went north to the Santa Cruz River for much-needed repairs. By June 1526, heavily overcrowded with men from the *Sancti Spiritus,* they were again separated by storm. Only the flagship reached the Moluccas. The pinnace, almost without food, reached Mexico; and the *Santa Maria del Parral* was wrecked in the Philippines with the loss or enslavement of its crew. The *San Lesmes*, with about 53 men on board—Spaniards (mainly Basques and Galicians), Italians, Germans and Flemings—was never seen again.

In 1929, over four centuries later, four ancient iron cannon were found on the reef of Amanu Atoll, 800 km east of Tahiti. One was recovered, taken to Tahiti and presented to the local museum, but later lost. Two others, recovered in 1969, were identified as being of a type that had gone out of use in Europe in about 1550, leaving little doubt that they had belonged to the *San Lesmes*. The cannon became the starting point for a reconstruction of events.

It was argued that the *San Lesmes* ran aground at Amanu by night, that the crew pushed their four heavy guns overboard to lighten and refloat the vessel, and that they proceeded on a westerly course in search of a haven to make repairs. After calling at Anaa Atoll, 400 km east of Tahiti, where some men evidently left the ship, the remainder sailed on until reaching Opoa, on Ra'iatea, 200 km northwest of Tahiti. There they established a base and either repaired the caravel or built another. Many of the men, some with Polynesian wives, then tried to return to Spain by sailing southwest for the Cape of Good Hope. This course brought them to the North Island of New Zealand (then unknown to Europeans) where, for some reason, they settled. Maori traditions about the *Arawa* and *Tainui* 'canoes' appear to take up the story. They tell how one group of immigrants settled in the Bay of Plenty while another went on to Kawhia on the west coast. Those who came without women took wives from among the *tangata whenua* ('people of the land'). By COOK's time, 250 years later, people of part-European, part-Polynesian descent had spread over much of the North Island. The men of the *San Lesmes* who had settled on Anaa and Ra'iatea also thrived, and left many Hispano-Polynesian descendants in the Tuamotu Archipelago and Society Islands. A party of such people also appears to have drifted to Ra'ivavae in the Austral group, 500 km south of Tahiti, whence some of their descendants reached Easter Island towards the end of the 17th century.

Among the evidence for this reconstruction are numerous descriptions from the explorer period of light-featured, European-looking people on the islands mentioned, some having red hair and blue eyes. There are also suggestive traditions, seemingly Biblical religious beliefs and items of material culture of European origin. In the case of New Zealand, at least two Spanish words—*perro* 'dog' and *come* 'eat'—were evidently borrowed into the Maori language. As for Easter Island, 18 islanders with no known non-Easter Island ancestors were found in 1971 to be carriers of certain genes that are peculiar to Europeans and especially common among Basques.—RL2

Further reading

Langdon, R, 1975. *The Lost Caravel*, Pacific Publications.

——, 1988. *The Lost Caravel Re-explored*, Brolga Press.

Circular mobility

Circular mobility refers to population movements that involve moderately long durations of stay at a destination followed by return to the places from which the movers originated. It is also referred to as 'repeat migration', 'pendular migration' and 'floating migration'. Circular mobility is an enduring form of population movement in the Pacific islands. It was common in indigenous societies throughout the region, accelerated during the colonial era by the COLONIAL LABOUR TRADE and the development of missions and administrative centres, accentuated greatly in some places by the Second World War, and fostered in more recent years by a post-colonial emphasis on 'traditional' rural heritages and cultures amongst Pacific islanders. Circular mobility remains an essential component of human spatial movement in the Pacific, notwithstanding the rapid growth of urban populations both in the island countries and immigrant communities in cities on the Pacific Rim. Circulation between town and village, or between metropolitan centre on the rim and town or rural area in the islands, is at the heart of the complex systems of resource use, income generation, and 'world enlargement' which characterize contemporary Pacific societies.—RB

Further reading

Bedford, R D, 1973. *New Hebridean Mobility: a study of circular migration*, Department of Human Geography HG 9, The Australian National University.

Chapman, M C and Prothero, R M, 1985. *Circulation in Population Movement: substance and concepts from the Melanesian case*, Routledge & Kegan Paul.

Girmitiya

Girmitiya refers to Indian indentured immigrants who came under an 'agreement' (shortened by an illiterate people to 'girmit') to work on PLANTATIONS in Fiji. Indentured migration began in 1879, five years after Fiji became a Crown Colony. By the time emigration ended in 1916, 60 965 Indian indentured men, women and children had been transported to Fiji: 45 439 from northern India, embarking ships at Calcutta, and the remaining from southern India, leaving from the port of Madras. The indenture system itself was abolished and all existing indentures cancelled on 1 January 1920. The agreement specified the terms and conditions of employment in Fiji. Indenture would begin on the day of arrival in Fiji, with migrants expected to do work relating to cultivation or manufacture for nine hours each weekday and five hours on Saturday, Sunday being free. Adult males would receive a daily wage of one shilling for completed work and women nine pennies, while pay for work done by children would be at the discretion of the overseer. The agreement also required employers to provide free medical care and housing as well as rations for the first five months on a scale provided by the Government of Fiji. The migrants were entitled to return to India at the end of their five-year contract at their own expense, and at government expense after 10 years of 'industrial residence' in the colony. About 24 000 Indian migrants and their families returned, but the majority stayed on, encouraged by the colonial government keen to develop a dependable pool of local labour supply and by the prospect (and for many the reality) of better economic opportunities in Fiji.

Most girmitiyas recalled indenture as a harsh and demeaning experience; they labelled it 'narak', meaning hell. Institutions and practices of the old world broke down, including religious rituals and ceremonies, caste and a sense of community. A severe disparity in sex ratio rendered marital relationships vulnerable to rupture in the overcrowded living quarters on the plantation estates; labourers were punished severely for breaches of labour regulations; and diseases such as diarrhoea, dysentery and related ailments took a particularly heavy toll in the 1890s. But while witnessing much dismal destruction, indenture also spawned a distinctively new Fiji-Indian society, more open, relaxed, egalitarian, individualistic and enterprising, speaking a language cobbled together from the dialects and languages the migrants brought with them, free from the restrictive cultural protocols and practices of rural India. The origins of the social structure, world view and moral order of the Fiji-Indian community lie in the period of girmit.—BVL

Further reading

Lal, B V, 1983. *Girmitiyas: the origins of the Fiji Indians*, Journal of Pacific History monograph.

Gillion, K L, 1962. *Fiji's Indian Migrants: a history of the end of indenture in 1920,* Melbourne University Press.

Kanakas in Australia

Kanakas or 'South Sea islanders' were the Melanesian indentured labourers taken to Australia in the second half of the 19th century. Several hundred were imported as labourers on pastoral properties in 1847 (see Ben BOYD), but the majority entered the country between 1863 and 1904. In this period 62 000 three-year contracts were issued to import about 50 000 islanders, the majority being single males aged 15–35 years from LOYALTY ISLANDS, New Hebrides (Vanuatu) and Solomon Islands, and a small minority from the eastern islands of modern Papua New Guinea, Gilbert (Kiribati) and Ellice (Tuvalu) Islands. About 6 per cent of recruits were female.

When Sydney trader Captain Robert Towns sent the schooner *Don Juan* to persuade Pacific islanders to work at 10 shillings per month, he gave an assurance that they would be returned to their homes after a year, and insisted that all recruitment had to be voluntary. Not all recruiters were as scrupulous, and inevitable clashes occurred between BLACKBIRDERS and villagers who were unwilling to cooperate.

Kanakas—sometimes erroneously named Polynesians—worked mainly in the SUGAR industry between Cairns in Queensland and the Tweed River district of New South Wales, where their labour built the foundation and guaranteed the success of the industry. Most signed on two or more times, and 835 were granted 'tickets' in 1884 which exempted them from restrictions and allowed them to seek employment independently. In 1901 when new legislation was introduced—ending recruitment and ordering total deportation by 1907—as part of the sugar industry restructuring and a 'White Australia' series of Acts, there were 10 000 islanders in Australia, many having lived in the country for 10–20 years. After 7068 were repatriated between 1904 and 1908, those remaining included 1654 who had been given deportation exemptions, and up to another thousand who had already gained citizenship or who hid until the repatriations were complete. Less than 300 families remained. Most were unmarried and died in the 1920s and 1930s, although a few of the original Kanaka labourers survived until the 1960s.

After the deportation scheme ended, South Sea islanders were bound by trade union and other restrictions regarding employment, and many continued to work in the pastoral and maritime industries, started small farms and market gardens, or joined the itinerant workforce. Coastal cities such as Rockhampton, Mackay, Gladstone and Bundaberg developed sizeable islander communities, mainly living on the fringes of town. They retained substantial aspects of their largely Melanesian cultures, with regional differences gradually blurring as one community emerged, united by their colonial experience, pidgin English and Christianity. Today there are more than 15 000 descendants of the original Kanakas in Australia, many of them fifth and sixth generation. They now represent about 10 per cent of the total black community, and since the 1970s, they have re-established links with long-lost families in the islands.

In the 1980s and 1990s, after a long period as a marginalized minority with poor health, welfare, education and employment experience, and without access to government-funded programs granted to other ethnic and minority groups, a major lobbying campaign was launched, with the Pacific Islander Association being active during the deportation era. In 1974 a national lobby group formed, with branches along the coast. Two major national reports by non and semi-government bodies in the 1990s finally led to public and government recognition, and most of the log of claims listed by the islander associations has been achieved. Books by Faith BANDLER, Noel FATNOWNA and Mabel Edmunds popularised the Kanaka story. South Sea islanders are now a distinctive but dispersed and not necessarily cohesive community in multicultural Australia. (More recent Pacific migrants to Australia are generally referred to collectively as Pacific islanders.) (See also VOLUNTARY MIGRATION; COLONIAL LABOUR TRADE; KANAKA SEAMEN.)—MQ

Further reading

Corris, P, 1973. *Passage, Port and Plantation: a history of Solomon Islands labour migration, 1870–1914*, Melbourne University Press.

Edmunds, M, 1992. *No Regrets*, University of Queensland Press.

Graves, A, 1993. *Cane and Labour: the political economy of the Queensland sugar industry, 1862–1906*, Edinburgh University Press.

Mercer, P, 1995. *White Australia Defied: Pacific islander settlement in north Queensland*, James Cook University.

Moore, C, 1985. *Kanaka: a history of Melanesian Mackay*, Institute of Papua New Guinea Studies and University of Papua New Guinea.

■ ***Dr Faith Bandler*** Faith Bandler (1918–), Australian political activist and writer, was born in Tumbulgum in New South Wales, and named Ida Lessing Mussing, the second child in a family of eight. Her father, Wacvie Peter Mussing from Biap village, Ambrym, in Vanuatu, had been taken to Australia in 1883 when he was 12. (See KANAKAS IN AUSTRALIA.) Her mother was Scottish-Indian, born in Brisbane. Educated at Murwillumbah and Cleveland Street Night School in Sydney, Faith married Hans Bandler in 1952, and became involved in indigenous politics as co-founder of the Australian-Aboriginal Fellowship in 1956. One of the crucial leaders of the 1967 referendum campaign to enable the Commonwealth government to legislate on behalf of indigenous Australians and to include them in the national census, Dr Bandler was also General Secretary of the Federal Council for the Advancement of Aborigines and Torres Strait Islanders (1970–73). In 1976 she was awarded an MBE but refused to accept it.

Faith Bandler at Parliament House, Canberra, July 1972

While maintaining her interest in indigenous affairs, as Director of the Co-operative for Aborigines and Islanders in the 1970s, and in women's issues, since the mid 1970s Bandler has turned her formidable talents to obtaining recognition and special benefits for the descendants of her father's people, Australia's South Sea islanders, brought to Queensland as indentured labourers, 1863–1904. Most of the islanders were repatriated under 1901 Commonwealth White Australia legislation, but some 2000 remained, who had intermarried mainly with indigenous Australians. Instrumental in the formation of the Australian South Sea Islanders United Council in 1974, Bandler helped lobby the Australian government. In 1991 at her urging, the Evatt Foundation commissioned a survey of the islanders, which led to a wider government investigation by the Human Rights and Equal Opportunity Commission, published as *The Call for Recognition*. The final result was the 1994 announcement of a package of grants, programs and special funding for Australia's South Sea islander community. Dr Bandler has written several books about her political activities and her family, and appeared on many radio and television programs.—CM2

Further reading

Bandler, F, 1977. *Wacvie*, Rigby.

——, 1984. *Welou: my brother*, Wild and Woolley.

——, 1989. *Turning the Tide: a personal history of Federal Council for the Advancement of Aborigines and Torres Strait Islanders*, Aboriginal Studies Press.

Bandler, F and Fox, L, 1980. *Marani in Australia*, Rigby.

■ ***Noel Fatnowna*** Noel Oliver Fatnowna (1929–91), Australian ambulance officer, community leader and historian, was born at Eulberti farm outside of Mackay, Queensland, fifth of nine children surviving from 14 born to Harry Fatnowna and Grace Kwasi, second generation Australian Solomon Islanders whose parents were brought to Queensland as indentured labourers in the SUGAR industry. The Fatnownas are one of the largest and most prominent islander families in the district. His grandfather Kwailiu was an important early leader, and his father Harry was an Anglican lay-preacher who in the 1920s introduced SEVENTH-DAY ADVENTISM to the islander community. Noel's childhood was spent happily in a half-traditional and half-European lifestyle, centred on his family, school, church and expeditions to the beaches and creeks. Noel Fatnowna was educated at Eimeo State School, but perhaps more influential was his contact with the first generation of islanders, his real teachers.

At 21 Fatnowna became an ambulance officer, a position he held for the next 41 years. Locally he was involved in fundraising and public relations for the ambulance which, with his church activities and his work with the Aboriginal and islander community, plus his interest in local history, made him well known in the district. He had a long involvement with the Queensland government as an adviser on indigenous health and was Queensland Commissioner for Pacific Islanders, 1977–83. Fatnowna was awarded the British Empire Medal in 1982. A great raconteur and always fascinated by the history of his people, in the 1970s Fatnowna helped establish the re-linking process between Australian Solomon Islanders and their homeland, which later became the subject of a book.—CM2

Further reading

Fatnowna, N, 1989. *Fragments of a Lost Heritage*, ed. Roger Keesing, Angus & Robertson.

Pacific islanders in Australia

There are about 25 000 Pacific islanders resident in various part of Australia, mainly in Queensland, New South Wales and Victoria, with a small number in the Australian Capital Territory. This figure excludes an equal number of Maori from New Zealand, with whom Pacific islanders from the rest of Oceania have little association, and Torres Strait Islanders, who are citizens of Australia.

Tonga and Samoa send the most migrants, with smaller numbers from Fiji, Cook Islands and Niue. There are a few from Solomon Islands, Papua New Guinea and Vanuatu married to Australians scattered around the country, along with a few dozen Nauruans, Rapanui, I-Kiribati and Tuvaluans. With the exception of a few I-Kiribati and Nauruans, there are few people from Micronesian islands in Australia. A look at any recent census of Australia will reveal several thousand persons born in Papua New Guinea, but the vast majority of these are the offspring of Europeans who worked in that former Australian territory.

Indo-Fijians are found in small numbers in Australia, mainly in the wake of the 1987 FIJI COUPS. More usually, though, Indo-Fijians swelled existing chain migration patterns to Canada. Most distinguish themselves from other arrivals from Fiji by following their own faiths (Moslem, Sikh and Hindu) and their sub-continent ethnic origins, continuing the separation that characterized ethnic relations in their country of birth.

There are concentrations of islanders in the suburbs of Sydney, Melbourne, Brisbane, and Canberra. The focal point for these communities is their churches, separated by denomination and island country of origin (in Sydney, for example, Samoan Methodist Church and Tongan United Church of Australia, Cook Islands Christian Church in Liverpool). For many years at the Sydney Wesley Centre there has been a Sunday afternoon service in Rotuman.

Working through their church or, increasingly, community advocacy groups, Pacific islanders participate in multicultural arts festivals, promote edu-

Member of Cook Islands Christian Church Vainetini (women's group), demonstrating her embroidery work at an exhibition of quilts in Canberra, June 1998

cation for their offspring and encourage healthy lifestyles. They also organize cultural groups promoting arts and crafts and support community projects in their home countries, through remittances. Islanders may be seen frequently in the central markets in Australia's capital cities shopping for their preferred vegetables such as taro, sweet potato, cassava and yams.

Many islanders in Australia have relatives in other overseas countries, especially New Zealand, Canada and the United States. They maintain fairly frequent contact through posted audio and video tapes and by telephone, a major item of expenditure in most islander households. There is some recent (1998) research that young Tongans are enthusiastic users of special 'chat rooms' on the Internet. (See ELECTRONIC NETWORKING.)

Australian census data makes it impossible to tell how many islander migrants have come directly to Australia and how many have either been born or spent some length of time in New Zealand. Tongans and Samoans may have passed through the extensive islander communities in New Zealand whilst Cook Islanders, Niueans and Tokelauans all have New Zealand passports and have no legal difficulties settling in Australia.

There are two ways that islanders are seen as 'problems' in Australia society. First, Tongans, Samoans and Fijians have a reputation for being overstayers. Of the overall figure of 100 000 or so overstayers or illegals in Australia, islander numbers are very small, whether in absolute terms or relative to their arrival numbers, British and Lebanese origin travellers outnumbering them by several times.

Second, in the 1990s, east coast capital city welfare agencies came to see islanders as problem families, prompting the employment of a few community workers from those backgrounds. In this respect, they differ little from other recently arrived, visible populations of similar (lower) class position in Australia.

There is largely undocumented sojourning (temporary residence) by citizens of Papua New Guinea in Australia's Torres Strait Islands, some of them only a few kilometres distant from foreign soil. There is no evidence that these sporadic movements result in any further transfer to the main populated areas of Australia.

Pacific islanders migrate easily and for long periods. Most writers on and from this community remind us that this is merely a continuation of the considerable movement of that population throughout the Pacific Basin over many centuries of settlement. (See PACIFIC DIASPORA.) Arrivals today in Pacific Rim countries follow old ties to colonial metropoles.—GMcC

Further reading

McCall, G and Connell, J (eds), 1993. *A World Perspective on Pacific Islander Migration: Australia, New Zealand and the USA*, Pacific Island Monograph 6, Centre for South Pacific Studies.

Pacific islanders in New Zealand

Maori from eastern Polynesia settled Aotearoa/New Zealand at least 1200 years ago. Adapting to a very different climate and physical environment, they established settlements and nations (*iwi*). A second, small inflow occurred in the 19th century when Pacific islanders visited New Zealand as crew on sailing ships and as students at missionary training establishments. Probably no more than a few hundred settled at any given time, and did not form permanent enclaves. From 1901 Cook Islanders and Niueans were New Zealand citizens but few moved to New Zealand. Samoans were 'New Zealand Protected Persons' who did not have automatic right of entry, but many part-European Samoans settled in New Zealand in the 1930s.

The largest in-migration occurred after World War II when islanders from New Zealand's territories and former territories (Cook Islands, Niue and Samoa) moved into unskilled and semi-skilled employment. Pay was far higher than in the islands, and working conditions better. Demand for this labour continued until the mid 1980s when island migration peaked, and then fell after 1984 when the restructured economy and the dismantling of protection for New Zealand industries saw many factories close. An easy visa scheme for short-term visitors from the islands in the 1980s led to many illegal overstayers, especially from Fiji, Samoa and Tonga. Many have remained due to amnesties or evasion.

By 1996 some 202 236 people of Pacific island descent were enumerated in the New Zealand census. The islander population continues to increase rapidly, growing by 55 per cent to constitute 6 per cent of the New Zealand population between 1986 and 1996. Pacific islanders do not constitute a single 'community' but rather a series of sub-populations including the Samoans (50 per cent), Cook Islanders (22 per cent), Tongans (15 per cent), Niueans (8 per cent), Fijians (3 per cent) and Tokelauans (2 per cent).

By 1996, 58 per cent of islanders in New Zealand had been born there, fostering a different sense of identity and experiences to those who were island-born. This group, with common Pacific island ancestry and experiences, and from similar locations, is shaping a new and distinctive identity and is

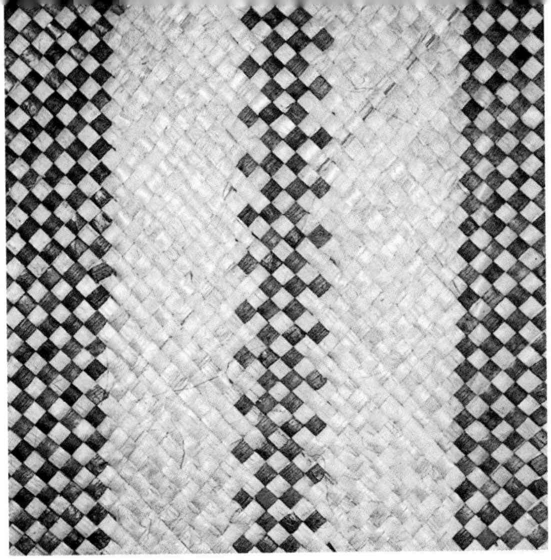

Detail of fine mat (*kie kie*) from Tokelau, presented to the Umiumiga Community Centre in Naenae, Wellington, as a gift from the people of Nukuonu in 1998

increasingly seen as a distinctive sub-population. High levels of Pacific island out-marriage have produced a large sub-population whose ethnic identity is complex and distinctive. Cultural retention seems to have been greatest among Samoans (the largest community), and Tokelauans who, though few in number, come from an isolated culture and are the most concentrated community in New Zealand.

More than 80 per cent of island migrants, despite their mainly rural background, are found in urban centres with populations of 30 000 or more: especially in Auckland (65 per cent), but also in Wellington, Christchurch, Dunedin, and some timber industry towns in central North Island. There is a continuing tendency to dispersal in smaller regional centres where work is available and housing is less expensive.

Chain migration concentrated the migrants in certain sectors of the economy, notably manufacturing (37.7 per cent), personal and community services (23.8 per cent) and wholesale, retail and hospitality (14.5 per cent), all of which were adversely affected from 1984 on by economic restructuring and later by the Asian economic crisis. This has produced historically high levels of island unemployment (16 per cent, double the national rate); a depressed median annual income of NZ$12 400, mostly from wages and salaries (55 per cent) or government benefits (32 per cent); low levels of home-ownership (50.9 per cent of islander households in rented or leased accommodation compared with a national figure of 23.1 per cent). Some 64 per cent of the Pacific island population aged 15 and over participate in the labour force (71 per cent of males and 59 per cent of females). Of these people, 66 per cent are in full-time paid work, 18 per cent in part-time work and 16 per cent are seeking employment. This situation has deteriorated with the collapse and relocation offshore of 'traditional' manufacturing industries, deregulation of the labour market and the casualization of labour.

The Pacific island population in New Zealand is relatively young, with a median age of 20.4 years, compared with 32.3 years for the total population. The New Zealand-born children have not found employment easily despite weak economic growth through the early 1990s. Many, however, have yet to enter the labour market. New Zealand-born islanders are generally better qualified than island-born parents and are likely to be more upwardly mobile. With the benefits of more cultural capital and better formal educational qualifications than their migrant parents, they may transform the islanders' sociodemographic profile in another generation as long as economic growth occurs.

The future composition of the immigrant Pacific island population will be shaped by new forces. Cook Islanders, Niueans and Tokelau Islanders remain New Zealand citizens and can thus move freely between the islands and New Zealand. However, the restructuring of the New Zealand economy and changes in immigration regulations mean that Samoan, Fijian and Tongan migration will be largely confined to young, skilled and educated people or those admitted under family reunion programs. The Pacific island population in New Zealand is growing at a faster rate than the total population. Whether islanders currently resident in New Zealand will stay is an open question. Pacific island kin groups—which have been called 'transnational kin corporations'—can and do move between various parts of these groups for a variety of reasons. This trend seems likely to continue and New Zealand will remain one of several 'off-island villages' between which people will continue to circulate.—CM1

Pacific islanders in the United States of America

The main category of Pacific island arrivals in the United States from the early 1800s to the 1860s were sailors. Hawaiian, Tahitian and other Polynesian and some Micronesian men remained in the ports of Massachusetts and later California. A Hawaiian community was established in California by 1830 and many Polynesians joined the California gold rush in the 1860s.

Religion was another incentive. Polynesian Protestant theology students first went to the United States in 1819 and still do. MORMONS believe that the promised land is within the United States and that Polynesians are from Israel, and Polynesian nations have a higher proportion of Mormons than any other country in the world, so a high proportion of Polynesian migrants are Mormon. The first colony of Hawaiian, Maori, Tahitian and Samoan Mormons was established in Utah in 1889.

Constitutional arrangements provide other avenues. US acquisition of Hawai'i, American Samoa and Guam in 1898 facilitated access to the mainland although with restrictions until after World War II. The post-war trusteeship in Micronesia gave no automatic right of entry, but many went to the United States for education or other purposes and some remained. When the trusteeship ended in 1986 for the Federated States of Micronesia, Marshall Islands and Northern Marianas, and 1994 for Palau, free entry was guaranteed and migration multiplied.

Military employment provided another channel. The US naval presence in Hawai'i from the 1850s, and in American Samoa and Guam from 1898, created work for Pacific islanders, mainly in menial tasks until after World War II, but opened thereafter and by the 1980s Guam islanders were over-represented in the US officer corps. The closing of the American Samoa naval base in 1951 and the offer of jobs in the navy in Honolulu and California initiated a major exodus. Illegal immigration has been common for Tongans and Fijians, and for people from independent Samoa moving via American Samoa. Few Melanesians from beyond Fiji have settled in the United States.

The number of Pacific islanders in the United States is an open question. Almost all knowledgeable persons consider the census figures to be gross understatements, both because those who are there illegally avoid such forms, but also because many islanders in the United States avoid filling in forms which they fear (generally inaccurately) might expose them in some undesirable way. Apart from 255 000 Hawaiians in Hawai'i and on the mainland, the largest category of Pacific islander is Samoan of whom there are at least 170 000 (including 56 000 in American Samoa, but others spread far and wide including 500 in Fairbanks, Alaska). Chamorros number about 160 000 (including 64 000 on Guam and 20 000 in the Northern Marianas). About half of the 25 000 other Micronesians in the United States live in Guam and Saipan. An estimated 35 000 Tongans, 15 000 Fijians and 5000 Tahitians reside in the United States, mainly in California and Hawai'i.

Degrees of retention of Polynesian or Micronesian culture vary. Some have integrated into mainstream United States, others maintain a considerable degree of cultural homogeneity outside the workplace. Given the tiny populations of Pacific islanders and the high rates of intermarriage with other Americans (more than half the Samoans in Hawai'i marry non-Samoans, and the rate may be higher on the mainland), cultural retention tends to be high only where there are concentrations. Carson City in California is one focus for Samoans, Agora for Guam islanders, and the state of Utah, as headquarters of the Mormon church, has attracted many Samoans and Tongans. Whereas for more than a hundred years Pacific islanders in the United States were almost exclusively men, with the exception of some island women married to Americans who had been in the Pacific, by the 1980s the numbers were becoming balanced.

Given the different languages in the islands, the generally lower standards of education, and cultural values which did not emphasise accumulation or long hours of work, most islanders remain in the lower income and skill categories. However, many have excelled in professional and amateur sports, military service, religious ministry, entertainment (and, alas, in crime), and some in the professions and business.—RGC

Ebeye

Ebeye, a small island in the southeastern corner of the greater Kwajalein Atoll complex, has served as a resettlement site for peoples displaced by American military interests and NUCLEAR TESTING in the Marshall Islands. Prior to 1946, fewer than 20 people lived on the island. The United States Army's construction of an air base on Kwajalein Island turned nearby Ebeye into a labour camp in the immediate post-war period. In 1960, the increased safety and security requirements of more sophisticated missile testing at Kwajalein resulted in the forced relocation of people from other areas of the atoll and surrounding islands. Other Marshallese came voluntarily, attracted by the presence of family, the prospects of employment and a more comfortable lifestyle. Ebeye soon had the highest number of skilled Micronesian workers, the highest per capita income, the highest retail prices, and the highest concentration of population per acre of any island or atoll environment in the United States Trust Territory of the Pacific islands.

Disaster struck in 1963. A severe polio epidemic was followed by deadly outbreaks of gastro-enteritis and influenza. By 1966, Ebeye, with more than 4500 persons crammed into an area a little more than 0.1 sq mile, was described as the most congested, sickly and socially demoralized community in Micronesia. Government efforts to reduce the population, limit future migration, and promote the social and economic development of the island all failed. Despite the problems, people kept moving to Ebeye. By 1978, the island's population exceeded 8000. Problems identified as serious in the 1960s now become critical. Educational, housing, and medical services could not begin to keep up with the demands of the population. Ebeye's physical infrastructure and public utilities proved woefully inadequate. Sanitation facilities were particularly appalling. Over-the-water outhouses meant the deposit of raw sewage directly into the waters of the lagoon, where the bacteria count at times reached levels 25 000 times higher than those identified as safe by the World Health Organization. With slightly over 50 per cent of the population under 14 years of age, reports pointed to a host of youth problems that included ALCOHOL AND DRUG ABUSE, delinquency, and a high incidence of venereal disease.

Dissatisfaction among that segment of Ebeye's population forced to migrate to the island because of American missile testing resulted in a series of sail-ins and temporary reoccupations of home islands; these began in the late 1960s and carried into the early 1980s. Operation Homecoming in June 1982 witnessed the reoccupation of islands in the complex by 1000 landowners who, by this time, had combined to form the Kwajalein Atoll Corporation. The occupation forced cancellation of at least one missile test. Despite the initially forceful response of military officials on Kwajalein, and the Marshall Islands government's support of American strategic interests, these protests won increased rental payments, a reduced lease schedule, funds for the improvement of Ebeye's infrastructure, return to their owners of six islands in the north of the atoll's restricted area, and the granting of visitation and access rights to other islands previously off-limits. The Compact of Free Association between the United States and the Republic of the Marshall Islands, declared operative in November 1986, has provided millions of dollars in capital improvement and infrastructure development funds for Ebeye.

Since 1986, a new power plant and desalination facility have been built. The hospital on Ebeye has been renovated, public utilities upgraded, recreational programs and facilities expanded, and the physical appearance of the island made more attractive. The Kwajalein Atoll Development Authority has commissioned a long-range plan for redevelopment, the centre-piece of which is a causeway linking Ebeye with islands immediately to the north. The causeway is expected to allow for resettlement of some of Ebeye's population to these islands, alleviating the tremendous overcrowding that still exists. These improvements aside, Ebeye remains a tragic example of the social and environmental costs inflicted upon Marshall Islanders by American colonialism.—DH

Multi-ethnic population of Hawai'i

The multi-ethnic population of modern Hawai'i comprises immigrants or descendants of immigrants, but each ethnic group has a distinctive history of migration and residence. First to settle the archipelago were Polynesians, almost certainly from Marquesas Islands. Other Polynesians may have come later from Society Islands. It is the descendants of these earliest settlers who today are classed as Native Hawaiians. Estimates of their numbers in 1778, when Captain James COOK put the islands on European maps, vary widely—from 200 000 to more than 800 000. Certainly contact with the western world and its diseases triggered a devastating population decline that threatened Native Hawaiians with extinction. (See DEPOPULATION.)

By 1831, when American Protestant missionaries took the first census, there were fewer than 130 000 Hawaiians, and their numbers dwindled to about 40 000 in 1920. They had also begun intermarrying with foreigners, leading in the 20th century to conflicting definitions of 'Hawaiian'. In the last 70 years, the largely mixed-ancestry group called Native Hawaiians has grown rapidly, in the mid 1990s comprising between 12.5 per cent and 18.8 per cent of the state's population. More than one-third of the Native Hawaiians listed in the 1990 US census lived in the other 49 states, mostly on the west coast. Those resident in Hawai'i have long lagged behind other ethnic groups in socioeconomic status, demonstrated in lower incomes and life expectancy but higher rates of juvenile delinquency and receipt of public assistance. However, the last 25 years have seen a remarkable increase in self-esteem and political activism among Native Hawaiians which is

Table 2.1 Total resident population of Hawai'i, 1992: 1 138 870

	Number	Percentage of total
Unmixed	717 409	
Caucasian	265 211	23.3
Japanese	224 801	19.7
Filipino	119 256	10.5
Chinese	52 612	4.6
Black	19 998	1.7
Korean	16 051	1.4
Hawaiian	9 118	0.8
Samoan	5 539	0.5
Puerto Rican	4 823	0.4
Mixed	421 461	
Part-Hawaiian	211 629	18.6
Non-Hawaiian	209 832	18.4

Source: Adapted from *The State of Hawai'i Data Book*, 1996.

beginning to produce improvements in their social welfare.

Foreigners began to migrate to the islands soon after European contact. Socially most significant were Caucasians (*haole* in Hawaiian), especially Protestant missionaries arriving from America in 1820. Though their numbers remained small until 1880, *haole* transformed the archipelago's political economy, creating SUGAR and pineapple industries. They led the overthrow of the Hawaiian monarchy in 1893, and succeeded in getting the United States to annex the islands as a territory in 1898. Though never the largest ethnic group during territorial history, a *haole* oligarchy stood at the top of the socioeconomic pyramid.

The oligarchy's need for cheap labour on sugar and pineapple plantations was crucial in creating today's multi-ethnic population. Legislation passed by the Hawaiian Kingdom in 1850 permitted recruitment of indentured labor. These workers came from many countries but the overwhelming majority were Chinese, Japanese and Filipinos arriving in that order. Chinese were mostly single males who often intermarried with Native Hawaiians. From 1881, large numbers of Japanese males were recruited; these later brought over 'picture brides' to begin families. By 1900 Japanese constituted the largest ethnic group in Hawai'i, a position they maintained for 70 years. Passage of the Organic Act in 1900 made United States laws applicable to the new territory and transformed labour recruitment. The heyday of Filipino immigration was 1906–46. Filipinos recruited for plantation work during this period neither brought wives nor intermarried extensively and persisted as a predominantly male group in the population.

1959 was a crucial year in changing Hawai'i's population structure, bringing both statehood and jet air travel. Immigration from the mainland United States increased sharply, making *haole* the largest single ethnic group though constituting less than 24 per cent of the population in 1992. Later developments, notably the United States Immigration and Nationalization Act of 1965, also affected immigration patterns. A new wave of Filipino immigration took place. Their numbers were ten times those of other non-*haole* arriving during this period; they were likely to arrive in family groups with more education than the earlier male plantation labourers. New immigrants also came from Korea, Southeast Asia, Samoa and other Pacific islands.

Perhaps the most noteworthy single fact about today's population in the island state is the high rate of intermarriage between ethnic groups. This began in the 1800s when Native Hawaiian women married foreigners, but now the pattern extends throughout the community, even to Japanese males who for decades chose wives from within their own group. Although the picture of the islands as a 'melting pot' of smooth inter-ethnic relations has been overdrawn, the facts that *haole* remain a minority, and that more than one-third of the population is classed as 'mixed'—either part-Hawaiian or non-Hawaiian—make the state unique in America.—EO

Further reading

Fuchs, L H, 1981. *Hawaii Pono: a social history,* Harcourt, Brace Jovanovich.

three

history

Contributors

Article contributors

AJR	Anthony J Regan
AT2	Andrew Thornley
AW1	Alan Ward
BM	Barrie Macdonald
BVL	Brij V Lal
CM2	Clive Moore
CP	Colleen Pritchard
CR	Caroline Ralston
CWA	Charles W Arnade
DAB	Dirk Anthony Ballendorf
DAC	David A Chappell
DAS	Deryck Scarr
DD	Donald Denoon
DH	David Hanlon
DLC	David L Callies
DM	Doug Munro
DS1	Dorothy Shineberg
EM	Ewan Maidment
EW-E	Elizabeth Wood-Ellem
FNB	Filipe N Bole
FRG	Florentino Rodao Garcia
GD1	Greg Dening
GMcC	Grant McCall
GMW	Geoffrey M White
GWT	Garry W Trompf
HL	Hugh Laracy
HN2	Hank Nelson
HS	Heinz Schütte
ICC	Ian C Campbell
IM	Isabelle Merle
JB	John Barker
JD	John Dunmore
JG1	John Garrett
JL1	Jacqueline Leckie
JL3	Jeanette Little
JRH	John Haglelgam
KE	Leiataua Kilifoti Eteuati
KEJ	Kerry James
KRF	Kate Fortune
KRH	Kerry Howe
MD	Marion Diamond
MQ	Max Quanchi
MRP	Mark R Peattie
MTC	Marjorie Tuainekore Crocombe
MWY	Michael W Young
NT	Nicholas Thomas
PB	Peter Bellwood
PFR	Philip F Rehbock
PJH	Peter Hempenstall
PS1	Peter Sack
PS3	Paul Sharrad
RC	Rajesh Chandra
RCK	Robert C Kiste
RGW	R Gerard Ward
RL1	Roderic Lacey
RL2	Robert Langdon
RSS	Ruth Saovana Spriggs
SF	Stewart Firth
SK	Sue Keays
TGB	Terry G Birtles
TKY	Terry Kanalu Young
WNG	Niel Gunson

Photo contributors

Alexander Turnbull Library (National Library of New Zealand, Wellington): Smith II Album (F-137665-1/2): 146

ANU Photography (The Australian National University, Canberra): 170; courtesy Niel Gunson: 178, 179, 207 (right); courtesy Robert Langdon: 218, 245; photographs by Akira Matsumura reproduced from *Contributions to the ethnography of Micronesia*, (University of Tokyo, 1918): 140, 236

Australian War Memorial (Canberra), reference no. 14028: 249

Bellwood, Peter (The Australian National University, Canberra): 122

Cunningham, Lawrence J (University of Guam, Mangilao): 146, 266

Greenpeace New Zealand Inc (Auckland): 259

Gunson, Niel (The Australian National University, Canberra): engraving from *Fiji and The Fijians* (1858), by Thomas Williams: 144

Hendrie, Peter (Pacific Journeys, Melbourne): 119 (detail), 123

McCall, Grant (Centre for South Pacific Studies, University of New South Wales, Kensington): 124

McPhetres, Samuel F (Saipan, Commonwealth of the Northern Mariana Islands): 244

National Library of Australia (Canberra): 143, 153, 162, 170, 207 (left top and bottom), 209, 243

New Caledonia Tourism (Sydney): 182, 226

Oxford University Press: reproduced from *Omai: Pacific envoy* (1977): 160

Panholzer, Thomas C (College of Micronesia–FSM, Pohnpei): 232, 233

Thomas, Nicholas (Centre for Cross-Cultural Research, The Australian National University, Canberra): 168, 169, 196

Waters, Sheila (Melbourne): photographs by Sarah Chinnery (1887–1970): 139, 230

West, Richard (Canberra): 262, 264

Maps

ANU Cartography: 205

ONE HISTORIES IN THE PACIFIC

Genealogies

Genealogies or oral lineage recitals formed the core of traditional narratives commemorating the past of Pacific islands cultures and indicate the individual's place in society and his or her claims to land use. In societies where a cyclical or shamanic concept of time prevailed, such as in the greater part of Melanesia, and also in some matrilineal societies, as in Micronesia, genealogies tended to be short, simply linking the generations within living memory with clan or totemic ancestors. In other societies, mostly in Polynesia, genealogies were often of great length.

Longer genealogies can be classified into four main types: narrative, index, truncated and king lists. Narrative genealogies were of several kinds: some were narrated in story form beginning with the gods and relating the adventures of a chiefly line down to a present day titleholder, others started from an apical ancestor and gave the names of all the progeny of each generation to the present, and some consisted of single names or pairs of names covering many generations.

Index genealogies are not necessarily long in themselves and often constitute the opening section of a narrative genealogy. They begin with an apical ancestor and include all the major titleholders and heads of branches in one or two generations as if they were siblings. Truncated genealogies are similar to the short genealogies of Melanesian societies. They usually consist of the ancestral god, the clan or national leader from whom ego descends, the ancestor who gave his name to the family and all the generations within living memory.

King lists are not strictly genealogies though often treated as such. They are either lists of successive titleholders often coming from different families or they show all the titleholders of an individual titleholder's family without any indication of relationship.

Great care is needed in using genealogies. Some of the longer genealogies (50, 100, 200 names) require a knowledge of key figures as the listener is expected to move backwards and forwards in time as the narrator follows alternate descents or switches from the paternal to the maternal line. Many published genealogies have lost the connectives required to make them intelligible. Some genealogies are localized and follow the descent of a subsidiary title, even though the titleholder is a famous figure better known by other titles.

To use genealogies for dating events is also fraught with pitfalls. Many high chiefly titles passed down through the first born whereas high priestly titles were likely to pass down through the last born. Thus the disparity between the generational reckoning for primogeniture and ultimogeniture could be one generation for every normal generation.

Genealogies were recited at all major rites of passage and installations. In some societies, particularly where historical knowledge was considered the intellectual property of talking chiefs or orators (Samoa) or of the senior chiefs of a village, genealogies were zealously guarded and public recitations were often truncated. In societies where personal rank took precedence over titular authority (Tonga) genealogies were usually kept by senior family members, particularly women, so that everyone knew who stood 'high' or 'low' in relation to themselves. Traditionally genealogies were taught in schools of learning or to apprentice chiefs or chosen members of the extended family who showed an aptitude for learning. Mnemonic devices were often used such as the carved pedigree sticks (Cook Islands), or the braided loincloths (Society Islands) which were lengthened for every generation. Since the introduction of writing, many families have their own genealogy books.

Genealogies have formed a major part of the land court records in most of the Pacific countries as they are regarded as essential evidence in land court disputes. Despite the rigour of cross-referencing, genealogies are more than ever exposed to manipulation due to the decline of ancient religious sanctions, the abortive demise of traditional custodians of knowledge, and the rewards of litigation.—WNG

■ *Nan Madol, Pohnpei* Nan Madol, now spectacular ruins forming one of the largest archaeological sites in the Pacific, was built in the shallow lagoon between the tiny island of Tewmen and the fringing reef on the eastern coast of Pohnpei. In the eastern Caroline Islands of Micronesia, coastal settlements existed about 2000 years ago, but in about the 10th century, construction of Nan Madol began—a complex temple city of canals, covering a total area of about 70 hectares and containing a population of perhaps 1000 people. More than 90 platforms (artificial islets separated by narrow canals) were built in coral rubble and basalt rock transported to the lagoon from quarries high in the mountains. Some of the walls of the citadels and fortresses are 6–8 m high, forming compounds of residential and ceremonial structures. Oral histories record Nan Madol as the capital of the Saudeleur dynasty, who ruled

Pohnpei as a centralized state until a number of lower-ranking chiefs rebelled, causing a breakdown of power into several smaller groups. Ceremonial use of the site had ceased by the time the first Europeans arrived in the late 1500s, and it was abandoned by the time the ruins were first reported by an American, L H Gulick, in 1835.—KRF

■ *Lelu Ruins, Kosrae* Kosrae, at the eastern end of the Caroline Islands, is a basalt island surrounded by fringing reef. Lelu, the main village, is a volcanic islet on the eastern side where a spectacular urban complex called Pol Falat was built about 1600. Like NAN MADOL (480 km away), it consisted of stone walls (up to 10 m high) surrounding residential and ceremonial compounds, extensively constructed among a network of canals. In the early 1800s the paramount chief of Kosrae and other high-ranking chiefs ruled a population estimated at about 1000–1500. In 1915 the Kosrae population was estimated at 500, with about 220 living at Lelu.—KRF

■ *Ha'amonga-a-Maui* The Ha'amonga-a-Maui, a massive trilithon (stone archway) which is one of the earliest traditional monuments on Tonga, was constructed at Heketa on the northeast coast of Tongatapu by the eleventh TU'I TONGA, Tu'itatui, probably before 1200. Sometimes said to have been built to symbolize his two sons and the bonds between them, the structure could have been associated with solar observations, as has been proposed by King Tāufa'āhau TUPOU IV, because it is oriented towards the summer solstice and has markings indicating the winter solstice. It has two upright columns of coral limestone 5 m high, estimated to weigh 30–40 tonnes each, and these supports have deep notches cut to carry the carved 6 m lintel. Oral traditions record that Tu'itatui ordered the stone to be brought from distant islands for both the Ha'amonga-a-Maui and other large coral columns nearby, and that one of these stone slabs (Maka Fakinanga) was where he stood, protecting his back, to address his chiefs. The monument is associated with a number of sites believed to have been former royal residences.—ICC & KRF

Ha'amonga-a-Maui, Tongatapu

Further reading

Bellwood, P, 1978. *Man's Conquest of the Pacific*, Collins.
Campbell, I C, 1992. *Island Kingdom: Tonga ancient and modern*, Canterbury University Press.

■ *Heiau, ancient stone temples of Hawai'i* The *heiau* temples that played a significant role in ancient Hawaiian religion ceased to be built after 1819 when the *kapu* (taboos) were overturned. Descriptions and sketches by early European visitors (including Captain COOK in 1778) provide some information, but archaeological investigations (begun in 1906 by John F G Stokes of the BISHOP MUSEUM) have provided considerable evidence to supplement oral traditions about early Hawaiian society. Walled temples hid rituals which included human sacrifice, and concealed ceremonial mysteries from view. There were dozens of these complex structures consisting of terraces, walls and platforms arranged in many variations—some similar to Tahitian structures but mostly different from the *marae* (*malae* in Samoa and Tonga) and *ahu* platforms of central Polynesia. Cook also noted the presence of numerous 'oracle' towers—tall structures covered with bark cloth, used by priests—on or close to the platforms.

Honaunau, a little to the south of Kealakekua Bay on the west coast of Hawai'i, is the site of Hale-o-Keawe, mausoleum of Hawaiian kings. Described by a researcher in 1823 as comprising a thatched house, in a fenced and paved enclosure, containing the bones of chiefs tied in bundles, together with chiefly garments, and carved images with red-feather decorations, the site was in ruins but has now been reconstructed for visitors. It is only one corner of a remarkable construction known as Pu'uhonua, 'place of refuge', believed to be more than 300 years old. Further reconstruction has restored a section of the 4 m high wall, which originally carried images along the top, and one of the three *heiau* platforms it contained.

Another great temple, Pu'ukohola, is at Kohala on Hawai'i. According to Hawaiian legend, KAMEHAMEHA I consulted a soothsayer about how to achieve sovereignty over all Hawai'i, and was advised to build a great new *heiau* for the war god Kukailimoku. The huge undertaking involved the guidance of many priests, and the participation of thousands of workers in carrying stone from far

Hale o Keawe, Heiau temple site, Hawai'i

afield for the walls and platforms, before it was completed in about 1791.—KRF

Further reading

Bellwood, P, 1978. *Man's Conquest of the Pacific*, Collins.

Stokes, J F G, 1991. *Heiau of the Island of Hawai'i*, Bishop Museum Press.

■ *Who carved the statues of Easter Island?* Following the success of the KON-TIKI expedition in 1947, Thor Heyerdahl published his major theory that South American Indians first colonized EASTER ISLAND about 800 AD, followed by Polynesians who arrived from Asia via the British Columbian coast after 1200. The Polynesians then defeated the descendants of the South Americans about 1670 and the latter disappeared leaving very few traces. But since 1952, most scholars have disagreed with Heyerdahl's theory of a primary American colonization in favour of a purely Polynesian prehistory for the island.

First, the Rapanui language belongs to the Eastern Polynesian subgroup of Austronesian, the most widespread pre-Columbian language family in the world. The speakers of Austronesian languages spread from Taiwan into the Philippines and Indonesia after about 2000 BC, then after 1300 BC into the western Pacific. By 850 BC, they had reached Tonga and Samoa. Austronesians probably reached Easter Island about 700 AD. No evidence exists for prolonged linguistic contact with American Indians, and Austronesians certainly did not enter Polynesia via British Columbia.

Second, the archaeology of Easter Island is widely claimed to be basically Polynesian in terms of its portable artifacts. The *ahu* and statues have parallels elsewhere in eastern Polynesia. Had there been a major American colonization of the island, we would expect to find more cultural traces in the form of pottery, maize and Andean domesticated animals. Yet the evidence for South American contact is not negligible. The sweet potato is an Andean crop which was introduced into Polynesia long before Spanish contact. Recent excavations at the site of Tucume in northern Peru have produced adobe friezes of birdmen just like those carved on rocks at Orongo on Easter Island. The fine stone masonry on the seaward face of Ahu Vinapu I is of Inca type. Some scholars suggest that the stone towers (*tupa*) on Easter Island are derived from the *chullpa* burial towers of the Andes. Between AD 1200 and 1500, therefore, groups of South Americans probably

Easter Island temple platform, Ahu Akivi, or 'Seven Moai'—one of the last platforms constructed, probably in the 1300s, and restored in 1960 by William Mulloy

reached Easter Island to add their knowledge to the cultural pool. But they seem to have had only a small impact on the actual Rapanui population and its language. Heyerdahl's settlement sequence has been reversed by modern research, but a high degree of mystery still remains.—PB

Rapanui archaeology

Pillage archaeology has been a feature of European engagement with Rapanui, ever since W J Thompson, an officer of the US Navy warship *Mohican*, blasted an *ahu* (temple structure) at Vinapu in 1886, and carried off considerable loot, now in the Smithsonian Institution in Washington. In 1868, a precious *moai* (ancestral stone figure) was removed by the British Navy, for display in the British Museum. The French Navy in 1870 severed the head of a figure, for display in the Musée de l'Homme. A Belgian warship removed a full figure in 1936, for display in Brussels, just a year after Chile declared the island a national park.

Serious archaeological work on Rapanui began before World War I with Katherine Scoresby Routledge, whose notes and publications have been invaluable. The Franco-Belgian expedition, responsible for carrying off another multi-tonne *moai*, included Henri Lavacherry, who made a detailed survey of the rock art. Father Sebastian Englert, Catholic priest on the island (1936–69), took a methodical amateur's interest in the island's traditions, making the first inventory of surface features. Contemporary archaeology started with the visit of the Norwegian expedition, led by Thor Heyerdahl. Its members included Carlyle Smith, Arne Skjølsvold, Edwin Ferdon and William Mulloy, with the young Chilean Gonzalo Figueroa as a kind of apprentice. Skjølsvold, Mulloy and Figueroa maintained an association with Rapanui, the latter now an important figure in the management of archaeological resources.

Rapanui Pedro Atan contemplates the damage caused by Paymaster Thompson's gunpowder blast in 1886, which broke open the wall at Ahu Vinapu

Regular air services (and the integration of Rapanui into Chile) brought other archaeologists for varying periods: Patrick McCoy and William Ayres, who were students of Mulloy; and Americans Georgia Lee, Jo Anne Van Tilburg, Christopher Stevenson and Charles Love, who have each made crucial contributions to Rapanui history. William Liller has contributed to the field of archaeo-astronomy, and Annette Bierbach and Horst Cain have proposed imaginative readings of ancient rock art. George Gill and his colleagues Scott Baker, Douglas Owsley and Patrick Chapman have discovered challenging details of the origins of the Rapanui population. Rock art has attracted the attention of Elena Charola, Ana Maria Arredonda and Heidi Esen-Bauer, with Felicia Rounds Beardsley a specialist in tool technologies, lithic and bone.

Michel and Catherine Orliac have studied the evolution of Rapanui culture. John Flenley stands alone with his detailed research on paleobotany, complementing his work in eastern Polynesia. Steadman has studied ancient food systems, especially the impact of human occupation on the bird population. Claudio Cristino and Patricia Vargas, the latter director of the Institute for Easter Island Studies at the University of Chile, have conducted research over 20 years. Sergio Rapu was the first Rapanui to be trained in archaeology, and he made the discovery of the *moai*'s inset eyes. Sonia Haoa continues that research tradition to the present day. Areas remaining to be researched include the method(s) of moving the *moai*, the energy basis required from such a small polity in order to mobilize such a quantity of public works, the origins of the Rapanui themselves, and ancient contacts between the island, other parts of the Pacific and the Americas.—GMcC

The 2.42 m Hoa Haka Nanaia ('Surf-riding friend'), removed from its cave site in 1868 by a British navy exploration ship, and now on display at the British Museum, London

Oral history in the Pacific: whose voices are heard?

Pangia, an Enga elder from the Papua New Guinea Highlands, was deeply suspicious of me when I began questioning him about his ancestral history in July 1972. In the following month, his adopted son, my research assistant, sat in the men's house with Pangia, who allowed him to tape-record their conversation. Pangia knew the names of fathers and sons from the founder of his community down to himself and his own sons; but he now recognized that his knowledge of these traditions was incomplete. For him, that was disturbing.

Despite his new sense of incompleteness, Pangia proceeded to teach his son basic elements of their genealogical history, the thread that bound him to his ground and gave him his name and identity. His teaching was embodied in what Enga call *kongali pii* (picture talk)—symbolic, poetic language. For me, as outsider, speaking another language, the information provided additional insight into Enga men's knowledge of specific strands of their oral traditions.

Vincente Diaz, a Chamorro-speaking scholar of Filipino-Pohnpeian ancestry, interprets the living voices of Chamorro oral traditions in contemporary tales of survival. Reviewing the record made by the wife of an American naval officer stationed in Guam just before the Japanese invasion, Diaz reinterprets her assessment of the way the language had changed (that it typified the demise of the purity of the Chamorro language) differently. He asserts that it provides evidence of a process of Chamorro influence on the use of Spanish and English in Guam, and argues that it signifies the durability and tenacity of Chamorro caught in colonial entanglements—representing persistence and resistance rather than demise.

Judith Binney, author of a study of Te Kooti, the Maori prophet and founder of the Ringatu church, discusses the need to ensure that the writing of Maori history gives Maori understandings and values their full weight, referring to the trend in New Zealand towards ensuring that the narration of history takes place in ways that are meaningful to Maori. For her, the act of writing history can be an encounter between the multifaceted human past and the individual who is constructing the present narrative. This act of reconstruction allows different voices to speak, revealing people in their own times and contexts. She stresses that no one owns the past; it is 'inhabited by all our ancestors'. The conflicts between historical sources, both written and oral, cannot be reconciled. The historian does not attempt to interweave a variety of sources, nor to smooth away their differences, but rather to juxtapose different ways of recording and understanding—to maintain historical integrity.

The decolonizing of history requires attentive and subtle strategies, drawing on a wide range of sources and recognizing the contexts, filters and positions from which differing voices are represented. Oral sources, which allow indigenous voices to be heard, have real value when located within their own determining contexts, and when recognized alongside other sources—not reconciled or smoothed away.

Klaus Neumann's 1992 study of Tolai history presented recorded testimonies in a deliberate way which plots his own movement through this process of construction. His odd-numbered chapters are all concerned with the colonial past, using different forms of presentation and selected episodes to highlight different themes. The even-numbered chapters establish the contexts in which this history has been constructed and in which Tolai produce their histories.

Neumann takes the issue of colonization, domination and modes of discourse further when he discusses the translation of oral texts in native tongues to written texts in the language of writer and reader. With the use of a tape recorder, the translator needs to strive for an 'authentic' rendering of the oral material. He explains that he has chosen different ways of quoting oral histories: summarizing them in his own words or translating them as accurately as possible. This indicates the tension between the desire to let the reader listen to Tolai histories and the realization that the most the reader can get is the historian's own perceptions and recreations of the histories.

The historian, as historian, constructs a work, shaping what is received from raw sources into that work. When we turn to histories of Pacific islanders, even those based largely on indigenous oral sources, whose voices are heard? How do we hear those voices in the written texts, when they are translated into the language of the reader and are mediated in the works of historians writing according to the rules of the academy?

Neumann affirms his stance as a practising oral historian who creates spaces in which Tolai voices may be heard, attesting that his work is an exercise in translation and mediation. Tolai concepts must be translated so that non-Tolai can understand them. This is the task of those who seek to accompany Pacific islanders in processes by which they and their pasts are decolonized, freed and heard, not only in their own islands and tongues, but in larger post-colonial worlds.

The historian needs to act as a bridge, too. Neumann proposes that his book needed to bridge the many different contexts in which it developed—libraries; conversations at men's secluded places on the Gazelle Peninsula; writing in the shade of an open hut; working on a word processor in an academic environment; relaxing in periods of silence; sitting with friends. The historian is a mediator, translator between cultures, and a bridge between diverse contexts, balancing and keeping alive the revelations of written and oral sources. It is through the action of the attentive and skilled oral historian that readers hear the voices of Pacific islanders.

Conscious of the implications of Pangia's teaching, at the end of my own enquiry into Enga oral tradition in 1975, I posed four questions which need to be asked of indigenous oral sources

- what kind or form of oral source is this?
- what is the context of this tradition?
- what is its territory, span or provenance?
- how was the tradition transmitted and what were the actual circumstances in which this variant was recorded?

I hoped that my brief overview could be challenged and remade by later Enga historians. That dream is now being realized. New possibilities are revealed if historians work in partnership with native speakers. After a decade of intensive enquiry by Polly Weissner, a German-speaking American anthropologist, and Akii Tumu, an Enga historian, a new work demonstrates this potential—the result of a working partnership between a 'curious European' and an Enga investigator, in intensive cooperation with Enga narrators. They see their work as both a continuation and a beginning: their hope is that Enga can look back into their past and encourage the younger generation to build on their research. By providing extensive translated passages from their Enga sources, they have sought to convey a feeling of how Enga portray their own history and to document the fieldworkers' reasoning. They hope to reflect the cultural heritage and life experience of individual Enga participants through this process, providing a sense of the person as a means to evaluate testimonies and place them in a broader context.

Here and in the other partnerships, these processes of mediation, translation and bridge-building are not exercises in colonial dominance but reciprocal, two-way encounters and conversations between tellers and listeners, questioners and respondents. The outcome of the 10-year cooperative enterprise between Weissner and Tumu is an investigation of the course of history of selected Enga tribes and clans over 200 years. Throughout this complex history, the voices of many protagonists, tellers and teachers of traditions are recorded and translated, possibly becoming a stimulus to further exploration, questioning and reshaping.

Voices are being heard that are mediated and translated; they are voices of islanders and they are speaking in Pacific contexts beyond empires and in larger spheres. They give us heart and open the lives of Pacific islanders to further conversations and more questioning.—RL1

Further reading

Binney, J, 1995. *Redemption Songs: a life of Te Kooti Arikirangi Te TurukiI*, Auckland University Press/Bridget Williams Books.

Diaz, V, 1994. 'Simply Chamorro: telling tales of demise and survival in Guam', *The Contemporary Pacific: A Journal of Island Affairs*, 6(1) Spring.

Lacey, R, 1975. Oral traditions as history: an exploration of oral sources among the Enga of the New Guinea Highlands, PhD dissertation, University of Wisconsin.

Neumann, K, 1992. *Not the Way it Really Was: constructing the Tolai past*, University of Hawai'i Press.

Wiessner, P and Akii, T, 1998. *Historical Vines: the formation of regional networks of exchange, ritual and warfare among the Enga*, Smithsonian Institute Press.

Cartography in the Pacific

Charts of the west Pacific coastline might have been used by Arab and Chinese convoys trading in ivory, incense, gold, spices and silk as they traversed the Indian Ocean via the Malacca Straits as early as the 9th century, but there is no cartographic record of those early voyages. In contrast, Polynesian and Micronesian navigators have long constructed rudimentary 'maps' from strips of cane tied together to represent wave or wind direction between islands marked by the position of sea shells. Details of star locations were also shown. Polynesians knew names for about 200 fixed stars and could determine their latitudinal position from stellar tracks and solar movements, allowing for the summer and winter solstices. Record of such astronomical knowledge can be dated from 1200 AD by a trilithon (HA'AMONGA-A-MAUI) on Tongatapu.

European contact with the Pacific Ocean dates from the 13th-century voyage by Marco Polo on a Chinese junk after his contact with 'Cathay' and 'Malayur', but more significant was the 16th-century discovery of the eastern shores of this 'Mer del Sud' by Spanish conquistadors, led across the Panama isthmus by Vasco Núñez de Balboa (1513). Only eight years later (1519–21), the first European impressions of the 'pacific' nature and vast dimensions of the ocean were established by Ferñao de Magalhães (MAGELLAN), whose voyage of circumnavigation posed an immediate challenge to European world maps based on northern hemisphere projections. The first cartographic solution was to construct three-dimensional globes to plot new information, but without adequate knowledge to determine longitude. The papal Treaty of Saragoza (5 April 1529) guaranteed Portuguese security of Indian Ocean and Moluccan trade until the merger with the crown of Spain (1580) but interpreted the bulk of the unexplored Pacific as Spanish domain to be entered only via the Strait of Magellan. After colonization and mapping of the American west coast, Spanish merchants turned their attention westwards to trade with the Orient from the ports of Callao (Peru) and Acapulco (Mexico). Spanish trading outposts in the Philippines were opened at Cebu (1565) and Manila (1571).

At the same time, searches from Callao by Alvaro de Mendaña (1567–68) and Pedro Fernández de Quirós (1606–07) for the fabled Terra Australis and King Solomon's legendary gold-bearing islands of 'Ophir' led to discovery and mapping of several 'South Sea' islands (now Tuvalu, Guadalcanal, Malaita, San Cristobal, Choiseul, New Georgia, Marquesas, Solomon Islands, Duff Islands, Vanuatu and Tuamoto archipelago). These were plotted incorrectly and out-of-scale on atlas maps prepared on the new Mercator projection by the Antwerp mapping house of Abraham Orteliu during the early years of the 17th century.

European standards of map precision were improved by the new Protestant Republic of Batavia after it commandeered the lucrative Portuguese spice trade by a succession of merchant fleets during 1598. Later coordination of such enterprise by formation of the Vereenigde Oostindische Compaigne (VOC) resulted in the design of larger sailing ships ('East Indiamen') and VOC market monopoly of all European trade with eastern Asia. Based in Amsterdam, the VOC hydrographic office compiled detailed maritime charts from the logbooks, coastal surveys and sketch maps of its navigators.

A governor general of the East Indies, Antoonij van Diemen, in 1639 sent Mattijs Quast and Abel Tasman from the port of Batavia (now Jakarta) to search for reported islands of gold and silver east of Japan. Although unsuccessful, this voyage greatly improved VOC cartography of the western Pacific. A second voyage (1642–43) by Tasman circumnavigated the continent he named 'Nova Hollandia' and mapped van Diemen's Land before additional discovery of 'Zeelandia Nova' which he claimed as better suited to future Dutch colonization. Tasman's two ships also made the first European contacts with Tonga, Fiji and New Ireland. Tasman's third voyage (1644) surveyed the northern coastline of New Holland and part of New Guinea. Cartographic knowledge assembled from VOC surveys, including the Quast and Tasman voyages, attracted international interest through an atlas (1646) released by Joan Blaeu, the VOC hydrographer, and in Blaeu's magnificent new wall map of the world which featured at the signing of the Treaty of Munster (1648). This edition delineated an imagined continuous coastline from northern New Guinea to Van Diemen's Land.

Dutch efforts to sail via the tempestuous southeast Spanish route into the Pacific ran into greater difficulty. Isaac le Maire, an Amsterdam merchant, hired Willem Corneliszoon Schouten from the Dutch port of Hoorn to open this alternative trading route to the East Indies. Sailing south of the Magellan Strait (1615), Schouten found and mapped Staten Island and a new channel (Le Mair Strait) which led them around a headland (Cape Hoorn). He then sailed northwest to the Tuamotus and the northern islands of Tonga ('Hoorn Islands') to the Moluccas. Similar use of the southeast tradewinds by Jacob Roggeveen (1722) led to the discovery and charting of Easter Island, Samoa and several atolls.

Parallel French interest in trade with the Spanish ports of Chile and Peru (1695–1720) produced high quality charts of this coast which were consulted by Roggeveen. The prospect of discovering an unknown southern continent in the South Pacific stimulated Charles de Brosses, president of the French Academy of Sciences, to examine the records of 65 European voyages as the basis of his *Histoire des Navigations aux Terres Australes* (1756). Supported by a Pacific map drawn by Didier and Charles de Vaugondy, de Brosses classified the islands of the Pacific into three groups: Magellanic, Australasie and Polynésie.

The buccaneer adventures of William Dampier, recording his contacts with Chile, Peru, the Galapagos Islands, Mexico, Guam, the Philippines and China, were published in 1697 as a best-seller. (See also WRITING ABOUT THE PACIFIC.) During 1699, Dampier discovered and surveyed the coast of New Britain. Further inter-island visits by Dampier (1703–07 and 1708) retained public interest through the rescue of Alexander Selkirk—the source of inspiration for *Robinson Crusoe* (1719) and *Gulliver's Travels* (1726). With improved navigation instruments,

Captains John Byron and Patrick Mouat (1764–66) corrected the locations of several of the Tokelau and Kiribati islands, but British imagination was fuelled by the voyage by Captain Samuel WALLIS (1767–68) who found a tropical paradise (Tahiti) which he claimed by right of conquest as 'King George III's Land', before sailing west to northern Tonga, the Wallis and Futuna group, Marshall Islands and Ladrones Islands. Lieutenant Philip CARTERET (1767–69) discovered Pitcairn Island and Moruroa, mapped the Santa Cruz and Solomon Islands and claimed New Ireland, New Britain and the Admiralty Islands as British discoveries.

At approximately the same time as the Wallis and Carteret voyages, a similar French venture led by Louis-Antoine de BOUGAINVILLE sailed in the same waters where he claimed 'Nouvelle-Cythère' (Tahiti) as a French possession. Bougainville's expedition, prepared with the assistance of de Brosses and the French Academy of Sciences, was equipped with a naturalist, astronomer and an artist and heralded a new scientific approach to European maritime exploration. Botanical and zoological specimens were examined, collected and preserved, with notes and a cartographic record of every landfall. Bougainville's voyage identified 5000 plant species (3000 previously unknown) and included 1500 drawings as well as charts. The route coincided with much of that taken by Roggeveen and Carteret, but Bougainville corrected the plotted locations of the Samoan archipelago, Quirós' Espiritu Santo and Solomon Islands. He named the Louisiade Archipelago in honour of his king. Bougainville's report, published in 1771, popularized Nouvelle-Cythère as the Garden of Eden but it was quickly eclipsed by the return of Lieutenant James COOK in the *Endeavour.*

James Cook's posting to Lord Anson's upgraded Royal Navy introduced him to military trigonometrical land surveying techniques which he adapted to coastline and harbour surveys of Newfoundland and Labrador. Here also, his careful observation of a solar eclipse attracted the notice of the Royal Society just as it negotiated with the Admiralty for a planned South Seas voyage to Tahiti for precise determination of its longitudinal meridian by observation of the transit of Venus during June 1769. No further observation would be possible until 1874, when Cook was given command. Equipped with a prefabricated portable observatory, two powerful telescopes and every modern navigational aid available, Cook proceeded to Tahiti via Le Maire Strait and Cape Horn. From Tahiti he sailed west to map and take British possession of Society Islands, New Zealand and New Wales (later renamed New South Wales). His coastline surveys marked a new level of accuracy and the expedition's botanical, zoological and ethnographic results stunned the scientific world. Cook's second voyage (1772–75), this time equipped with chronometers for precise fixing of longitude, ranked as the first to cross the Antarctic Circle in search of the elusive Terra Australis. Cook also rechecked the meridian of Tahiti and corrected the map positions of the Cook Islands, Tongan islands, Easter Island and Marquesas Islands. He found, named and charted the New Hebrides, New Caledonia and Norfolk Island.

Cook did not plan a return to the Pacific, but Royal Society anxiety to find a northwest passage resulted in his third voyage (1776–80) which included the unexpected discovery of the Hawaiian Islands, named in honour of Lord Sandwich. Cook then charted the North American west coast from Nootka Sound to the Bering Strait, before returning to Hawai'i for the winter. After his death at Kealakekua Bay, his officers continued the task of charting the North Pacific until (north of 76 degrees latitude) they reached the ice barrier within Bering Strait. The first accurate chart of the entire Pacific Ocean, published in 1784, is a memorial to Cook.

The American rebellion on 1776 distracted British maritime interest from the Pacific and replaced it with French expeditions. During 1785, La PÉROUSE took command of a venture with a larger scientific staff than any previous European voyage. La Pérouse clearly sought to emulate Cook and, with chronometers, achieved a similar high standard in charting the coast of northwest America, as well as several Pacific islands and the China Sea. At Petropavlosk he despatched copies of the new charts to Paris by courier, before following his new orders to hasten to Botany Bay. In March 1788 La Pérouse's ships sailed for Vanuatu, but vanished as a long-term mystery. Despite onset of the French Revolution (1789), friends persuaded Louis XVI to authorize a search. Although unsuccessful, a well-equipped expedition commanded by d'Entrecasteaux (1791–94) completed new charts of the Van Diemen's Land coast and adjacent islands, as well as Admiralty Islands, Tonga, Kermadec Islands, Loyalty Islands, New Caledonia, Solomon Islands, Louisiade Archipelago and New Britain, where d'Entrecasteaux died.

British reaction, with notions of penal settlement in New Albion, directed Commander George Vancouver to survey the American northwest coast (1791–95). This added considerable detail to Cook's charts and identified many inlets and islands, before Vancouver sailed west to make the first complete survey of the Hawaiian islands. Surveys by Matthew Flinders (1801–03) provided similar detailed charts of the Australian coastline, but elsewhere in the Pacific the French were more active. Louis de FREYCINET remapped the Samoan islands in detail (1817–20) and Duperry and DUMONT D'URVILLE (1822–29) completed a thorough cartographic survey of Micronesia. Dumont D'Urville also corrected several errors in Cook's charts of New Zealand, and at Vanikoro found wreckage from the La Pérouse voyage.

Subsequent 19th-century cartography of the Pacific has focused on the confirmation or correction of longitudinal location, coastline details and adjacent topography with intensified international efforts, which have included Russian and US surveys. Possibly the most useful charts have been those prepared of the Tuamotus and Fiji Islands by Thaddeus Fabian von Bellingshausen (1819–21); surveys of Pitcairn Island, the Iles Gambier and the Tuamotus by Commander Frederick William Beachey, RN (1825–28); charts of coral atolls by Captain Robert Fitzroy, RN in the *Beagle* (1831–36); and 180 charts by the US EXPLORING EXPEDITION (1838–42), commanded by Lieutenant Charles Wilkes, in a far-ranging voyage throughout the central and northwest Pacific.—TGB

Further reading

Badger, G, 1996. *The Explorers of the Pacific*, 2nd ed., Kangaroo Press.

Histories in the Pacific islands

The development of academic history writing in the Pacific has been profoundly influenced by patterns of institutional support. From the 1880s, New Zealand pakeha scholars pioneered academic research in Polynesian history as an extension of their encounters with Maori, and the Polynesian Society and its journal published their articles. That pattern was mirrored in Hawai'i, where the Bernice P BISHOP MUSEUM supported social researchers in several disciplines and published on Polynesian and Micronesian topics. (See Peter BUCK.) No such support was available for Melanesian studies, in part because the Australian public was content to leave that to ethnographers. The pioneering British scholars W H R RIVERS (*The History of Melanesian Society*, 1914) and C G SELIGMAN (*The Melanesians of British New Guinea*, 1910) drew no distinction between history and anthropology, but anthropologists from MALINOWSKI onwards explicitly wrote in structural-functional and a-historical terms. Conversely, academic historians left the Pacific islands to anthropologists. For many years Douglas Oliver's *The Pacific Islands* (1961) was the most accessible and most cited survey of historical as well as ethnographic conditions.

Until the 1960s at least, Pacific history research and writing were dominated by non-islanders. From the 1950s the Research School of Pacific Studies at the Australian National University (ANU) became the largest concentration of historians and other social scientists with Pacific interests; the *Journal of Pacific History* the leading outlet for historical articles; and ANU Press the leading publisher. Since the demise of ANU Press in the 1980s, University of Hawai'i Press has become the leading publisher in the field. Other significant journals include *The Contemporary Pacific*, published in the University of Hawai'i; *Pacific Studies*, published by Brigham Young University; and *Journal de la Société des Océanistes*, published by Musée de l'Homme in Paris. A handful of very able islander scholars studied in these institutions and publish in these journals, but their numbers have been too small for them to determine the agenda of scholarship.

Island universities enjoy fewer resources, and island-based scholars have relatively fewer opportunities. However, the INSTITUTE OF PACIFIC STUDIES at the UNIVERSITY OF THE SOUTH PACIFIC in Fiji is a prolific publisher and promoter of islanders' research, through books, monographs and articles in the *Journal of Pacific Studies*, and earlier through *Pacific Perspectives*. The UNIVERSITY OF PAPUA NEW GUINEA publishes *Yagl-Ambu* and the proceedings of the annual *Waigani Seminar*, and the MICRONESIAN AREA RESEARCH CENTER in Guam publishes *Isla*, a journal of Micronesian research.

James Davidson wrote the charter for one branch of the discipline in his 'Problems of Pacific history', and Greg Dening defined another approach in his 'Ethnohistory in Polynesia: the value of ethnohistorical evidence', both in the first issue of the *Journal of Pacific History* (1967). Both were anxious to recover islander agency, but Davidson leaned towards contemporary and political issues, while Dening's engagement with anthropology led him towards reflexive writing, focused on the late 18th century. Gananath Obeyesekere's *The Apotheosis of Captain Cook: European mythmaking in the Pacific* has revived debate about the role of foreign scholars, as well as methods of ethnohistorical analysis. Marshall Sahlins —the subject of Obeyesekere's critique—responded with *How 'Natives' Think—about Captain Cook for example*. (See DEATH OF CAPTAIN COOK.) Perversely, however, this often acrimonious debate continues to be conducted by non-indigenous scholars.

Few scholars—and almost all non-indigenous—have attempted general histories. Kerry Howe, *Where the Waves Fall* (1984), was first in the field, its value limited only by his decision to end the narrative when colonialism began. More recent is Kerry Howe, Robert Kiste and Brij Lal (eds), *Tides of History: Pacific islands in the 20th century* (1994). The most accomplished is O H K Spate's trilogy, *The Pacific Since Magellan* (1979–88)—but it is explicitly about great power strategic issues. The most useful single-volume work is Deryck Scarr, *The History of the Pacific Islands: kingdoms of the reefs* (1990); and one of the most recent is Donald Denoon, Stewart Firth, Jocelyn Linnekin, Malama Meleisa and Karen Nero (eds), *Cambridge History of the Pacific Islanders* (1997). The most seminal contribution to regional perspectives is Epeli Hau'ofa, 'Our sea of islands'. Much more common is the publishing of national histories, such as James Griffin, Hank Nelson and Stewart Firth, *Papua New Guinea: a political history* (1979); John Waiko, *A Short History of Papua New Guinea* (1993); Brij Lal, *Broken Waves: a history of the Fiji islands in the 20th century* (1992); and Malama Meleisea, *The Making of Modern Samoa: traditional authority and colonial administration in the modern history of Western Samoa* (1987), to name only a few.

Gender relations have been studied mainly by ethnographers. The most complete descriptions come from feminist scholars writing since the 1970s, who have often written in an historical mode. One of the preoccupations of this scholarship is the influence of colonial institutions and officials in re-shaping relations between women and men. This agenda has been shaped largely by Marilyn Strathern (ed.), *Dealing with Inequality* (1987); O'Brien and Tiffany, *Rethinking Women's Roles* (1984); Annette Weiner, *Women of Value, Men of Renown* (1976); and Margaret Jolly, *Women of the Place: kastom, colonialism and gender in Vanuatu* (1994). Other influential studies include Claudia Knapman, *White Women in Fiji 1835–1930: the ruin of empire?* (1986); and LILI'UOKALANI's autobiographical work, *Hawai'i's Story by Hawai'i's Queen* (1964).

Missionary activity has generated a vast literature, dominated by historians, whereas anthropologists have often sought to discount recent religious change in order to reconstruct pre-Christian belief systems. The most influential studies include W N Gunson, *Messengers of Grace: evangelical missionaries in the south seas 1797–1860* (1978); Gavan Daws, *Holy Man: Father Damien of Molokai* (1973); James Clifford, *Person and Myth: Maurice Leenhardt in the Melanesian world* (1982); John Garrett's trilogy, *To Live Among the Stars: Christian origins in Oceania* (1982), *Footsteps in the Sea: Christianity in Oceania to World War II* (1992) and *Where Nets were Cast: Christianity in Oceania since World War II* (1997); and Diane Langmore, *Missionary Lives: Papua, 1874–1914* (1989). Conversely, anthropologists rather than historians have led the field in examining 'cargo cults' and millenarian movements generally. The agenda for these studies was set out by Peter Worsley, *The Trumpet Shall Sound* (1968), which presented millenarian movements as political reactions against colonialism, and Peter Lawrence, *Road Belong Cargo* (1964), which set them in a much broader context. Although most scholars now disown the pejorative term 'cargo cult', the literature continues to grow.

Demographic and health studies are relatively recent developments. The pioneer of professional demographic studies was Norma McArthur, whose work is summarized in her *Island Populations of the Pacific* (1967). More focused studies include David Stannard, *Before the Horror* (1989); and Stephen Kunitz, *Disease and Social Diversity: the European impact on the health of non-Europeans* (1994). Gerard Ward and R G Crocombe pioneered land tenure studies (see CUSTOMARY LAND TENURE). These are brought up to date by Gerard Ward and Elizabeth Kingdon, *Land, Custom and Practice in the South Pacific* (1995).

Economic history is not well developed, but has attracted economic anthropologists (such as Richard Salisbury, *From Stone to Steel*, 1962, and T S Epstein, *Capitalism: primitive and modern*, 1968), as well as economic historians including Dorothy Shineberg, *They Came for Sandalwood* (1967), Ken Buckley and Kris Klugman, *The History of Burns Philp* (1981 and 1983), Judith Bennett, *Wealth of the Solomons* (1987), and Bruce Knapman, *Fiji's Economic History, 1874–1939* (1987).

The modern historiography of labour recruiting and the plantation experience begins with Peter Corris, *Passage, Port and Plantation: a history of Solomon Islands labour migration* (1973); and Deryck Scarr, 'Recruits and recruiters' (1967). Many episodes are described in Clive Moore, Jacqueline Leckie and Doug Munro (eds), *Labour in the South Pacific* (1990). The best modern introduction is Brij Lal, Doug Munro and Ed Beechert (eds), *Plantation Workers: resistance and accommodation* (1994).

Understandably the Pacific War looms large in the agenda of historical studies. Hank Nelson's researches are summarized in 'Taim Bilong Pait: the impact of the Second World War on Papua New Guinea' in *Southeast Asia under Japanese Occupation* (1980). A broader account is Geoffrey White and Lamont Lindstrom (eds), *The Pacific Theater* (1989).

For 30 years the PACIFIC MANUSCRIPTS BUREAU at the ANU has microfilmed 'at risk' manuscript material, and circulates copies to the major libraries specializing in Pacific studies. Another valuable resource is the many excellent DOCUMENTARY (NON-FICTION) FILMS and television programs that have been made, since the 1970s especially. Many are listed in Diane Aoki (ed.), *Moving Images of the Pacific Islands: a guide to films and videos* (1994).—DD

Further reading

URL http://sunsite.anu.edu.au/spin/RSRC/PMB/

Bennett, J, 1987. *Wealth of the Solomons: a history of a Pacific archipelago*, University of Hawai'i Press.

Buckley, K and Klugman, K, 1981 and 1983. *The History of Burns Philp*, 2 vols, Allen & Unwin.

Corris, P, 1973. *Passage, Port and Plantation: a history of Solomon Islands labour migration*, Melbourne University Press.

Denoon, D, Firth, S, Linnekin, J, Meleisa, M and Nero, K (eds), 1997. *Cambridge History of the Pacific Islanders*, Cambridge University Press.

Epstein, T S, 1968. *Capitalism: primitive and modern: some aspects of Tolai economic growth*, Australian National University Press.

Griffin, J, Nelson, H and Firth, S, 1979. *Papua New Guinea: a political history*, Heinemann Educational.

Hau'ofa, E, 1993. 'Our sea of islands', in E Waddell, V Naidu and E Hau'ofa (eds), *A New Oceania: rediscovering our sea of islands*, University of the South Pacific.

Howe, K R, 1991/1984. *Where the Waves Fall*, Allen & Unwin.

——, Kiste, R C and Lal, B V (eds), 1994. *Tides of History: Pacific islands in the 20th century*, University of Hawai'i Press.

Knapman, B, 1987. *Fiji's Economic History, 1874–1939: studies of capitalist colonial development*, Australian National University Press.

Knapman, C, 1986. *White Women in Fiji 1835–1930: the ruin of empire?*, Allen & Unwin.

Kunitz, S, 1994. *Disease and Social Diversity: the European impact on the health of non-Europeans*, Oxford University Press.

Kuykendall, R S and Grove Day, A, 1976/1948. *Hawai'i: a history: from Polynesian kingdom to American state*, Prentice-Hall.

Lal, B V, 1992. *Broken Waves: a history of the Fiji islands in the 20th century*, University of Hawai'i Press.

——, Munro, D and Beechert, E (eds), 1994. *Plantation Workers: resistance and accommodation*, University of Hawai'i Press.

Lawrence, P, 1964. *Road Belong Cargo: a study of the Cargo movement in the southern Madang district, New Guinea*, Manchester University Press.

McArthur, N, 1967. *Island Populations of the Pacific*, Australian National University Press.

McCoy, W, (ed.) 1980. *Southeast Asia under Japanese Occupation*, Yale University Press.

Meleisea, M, 1987. *The Making of Modern Samoa: traditional authority and colonial administration in the modern history of Western Samoa*, Institute of Pacific Studies, University of the South Pacific.

Moore, C, Leckie, J and Munro, D (eds), 1990. *Labour in the South Pacific*, James Cook University of Northern Queensland.

O'Brien, D and Tiffany, S W, 1984. *Rethinking Women's Roles: perspectives from the Pacific*, University of California Press.

Oliver, D, 1975/1961. *The Pacific Islands*, University of Hawai'i Press.

Rivers, W H R, 1914. *The History of Melanesian Society*, Cambridge University Press.

Salisbury, R, 1962. *From Stone to Steel: economic consequences of a technological change in New Guinea*, Melbourne University Press.

Scarr, D, 1967. 'Recruits and recruiters: a portrait of the Pacific islands labour trade', *Journal of Pacific History*, 2.

——,1990. *The History of the Pacific Islands: kingdoms of the reefs*, Macmillan.

——, (forthcoming). *Passages through tropical time.*

Seligman, C G, 1910. *The Melanesians of British New Guinea*, Cambridge University Press.

Shineberg, D, 1967. *They Came for Sandalwood: a study of the sandalwood trade in the southwest Pacific, 1830–1865*, Melbourne University Press.

Spate, O H K, 1979–1988. *The Pacific Since Magellan*, 3 vols, Australian National University Press.

Strathern, M (ed.), 1987. *Dealing with Inequality: analysing gender relations in Melanesia and beyond*, Cambridge University Press.

Waiko, J D, 1993. *A Short History of Papua New Guinea*, Oxford University Press.

Ward, R G and Kingdon, E, 1995. *Land, Custom and Practice in the South Pacific*, Cambridge University Press.

Weiner, A B, 1976. *Women of Value, Men of Renown: new perspectives in Trobrian exchange*, University of Texas Press.

White, G and Lindstrom, L (eds), 1989. *The Pacific Theater: island representations of World War II*, University of Hawai'i Press.

Worsley, P, 1968. *The Trumpet Shall Sound: a study of 'cargo' cults in Melanesia*, Schocken Books.

Pacific History Association

The Pacific History Association was set up in Australia in 1981, with the aim of encouraging the exchange of information among individuals and bodies interested in Pacific history and related studies. It promotes study, discussion, writing and publication of material on Pacific history, and produces a newsletter twice yearly. The Pacific History Association emerged from a meeting of Pacific historians in May 1980, in South Australia, and its constitution was adopted a year later.—RL2

Pacific Manuscripts Bureau (PAMBU)

The Pacific Manuscripts Bureau, popularly known as PAMBU, identifies and makes preservation copies of archives, manuscripts and rare publications relating to the Pacific islands. One of the very few long-term archival projects in the world based on international cooperation, the Bureau is funded by a consortium of seven Pacific research libraries. By 1998 it had produced more than 3000 reels of 35 mm microfilm, together with associated catalogues and indexes. The microfilms, distributed widely by subscription and direct sales, provide a valuable resource for academic research.

The Bureau was established at the RESEARCH SCHOOL OF PACIFIC AND ASIAN STUDIES, The Australian National University, in April 1968, following a report by H E Maude (commissioned by Gordon Richardson, the Mitchell Librarian) which recommended 'the location, cataloguing and copying of manuscripts relating to the Pacific by the establishment of a jointly-operated Manuscripts Clearing Centre'. Initially the Bureau was supported by the University of Hawai'i Library, Honolulu; Mitchell Library, Sydney; Alexander Turnbull Library, Wellington; the ANU University Library, and the National Library of Australia (NLA), both in Canberra. Additional participants in the consortium are the Library of the University of California, San Diego, and the University of Auckland Library.

The Bureau's first executive officer, Robert Langdon (formerly assistant editor of the PACIFIC ISLANDS MONTHLY), sought out and microfilmed personal papers (such as diaries and correspondence); church and mission archives; plantation, trading and some company archives; linguistic material; genealogies; and vernacular records. Special projects were organized to microfilm the logs of Pacific voyages of Yankee whalers, the extensive archives of the Marist Oceania Province, and manuscripts in Papua New Guinea. The Bureau's work complemented microfilming programs run by the Australian Joint Copying Project, the Central Archives of the Western Pacific, and the archives of the US Trust Territories in Micronesia.

Langdon also edited and published a number of indexes to the documents filmed by the Bureau, and supervised the compilation of a major in-house index to Pacific island manuscripts. Since its inception, the Bureau's activities have been reported in its newsletter, *Pambu*, through detailed descriptions of the material filmed.

In recent years since the appointment of Ewan Maidment as executive officer, the Bureau has developed some shifts in emphasis in its program. Reinstating its former policy of active surveying and filming trips in the islands, it has extended its acquisition range to include more contemporary material and items of interest to a wider academic audience. The aim is to microfilm more records produced by islanders themselves, for instance those relating to economic and political issues (such as the FIJI COUPS and the BOUGAINVILLE CONFLICT). In close collaboration with archival, academic and other organizations in the islands, the Bureau's current program is aimed at ensuring the preservation and accessibility of at-risk Pacific islands archives—records of political parties, businesses, trade unions, churches and other NGOs, judicial and scientific records, and the post-colonial press.—EM

TWO INDIGENOUS CHIEFLY SYSTEMS, TITLES AND TRADE

Early society and authority systems

Authority structures differed widely in the Pacific depending on topography and the occupation and ancestry of the people. Over 40 000 years ago the agricultural people who settled and planted gardens in New Guinea developed societies in which 'BIG-MEN' or successful entrepreneurs were influential in the secular sphere. Spiritual authority frequently lay in the domain of the spirits themselves who in some places were impersonated by their representatives who made annual visitations in masks (see RITUALS) to preside at initiations and pass judgements as manipulated by the gerontocracy. Sorcerers also proliferated.

At various times, especially during the second millennium BC, Austronesian-speaking pottery-making peoples from Southeast Asia moved into the island world, some along the coastal areas of New Guinea into Melanesia eventually reaching Fiji, Tonga and Samoa. In the north others moved into Micronesia. These seafaring people were great traders and formed various trading cycles in obsidian and other artifacts, the most notable being in LAPITA pottery. People from Samoa/Tonga eventually reached Society Islands and Marquesas Islands.

Secular authority in these societies was usually exercised by village headmen or elders and spiritual authority was in the hands of shamans or 'spirit anchors'. These societies would have been predominantly matrilineal. As Samoa, the Society Islands and the Marquesas (less so) shared a system by which temporal paramountcy could be attained by the accumulation of district titles, it is possible this system of authority was a legacy of the Lapita period.

Sometime before 200 AD a new wave of invaders from Southeast Asia appears to have arrived in the western Pacific. This seafaring aristocracy introduced earth ovens and well-digging which reduced the need for pottery. Over the next few hundred years they also reached the Leeward Society Islands where they introduced the cult of their sea god Tangaloa which replaced the Papa-Atea/Tane cult of the earlier settlers. Very probably the sophisticated ideas of divine kingship associated with brother-sister marriage and a philosophy of appositional polarities found in Samoa, Borabora and later in Hawai'i were introduced at this time as well as the role of the priestess sister.

In the period between the 7th and 13th centuries (AD) island traditions affirm a great deal of movement and inter-island contact. This period, paralleled by the so-called barbarian invasions in Europe, was also marked in the Pacific by EL NIÑO conditions, which enabled west-to-east voyages contrary to the norm, and volcanic eruptions. Based on traditions with some archaeological and linguistic backing, the following people movements with suitable intervals took place (or, in some instances, appear to have taken place) symptomatic of a population explosion. First, the settlement of the Hawaiian islands from the west by a people with strong Indonesian affinities (kingship, puppetry, kite flying, mythological motifs) via the Society Islands or direct from Samoa; and then the arrival of Papa-Atea/Tane cult people from the Society Islands in Manu'a and warfare with the Pulotu cult people of Samoa-Tonga. Then there was the interregnum of a Tu'i Tonga Nui on Tongatapu and the final expulsion of the Papa-Langi cult people from Tonga; followed by the first settlement in New Zealand of Papa-Rangi/Tane cult people. The next stage was the rise of the Saudeleur rulers on Pohnpei and the building of NAN MADOL; the building of Leluh (LELU RUINS, KOSRAE); and then the migratory movements of the Rongo and other clans between Samoa and the Gilbert Islands. Later came the invasion and despotism of the Tongan warlord Loimata (Roimata) in southern Vanuatu; and then the probable arrival of people of Marquesan origin in New Zealand via Rapa.

During the 14th, 15th and early 16th centuries we can assume a long period of isolated development except for regional expansion. The Tu'i TONGA, a living fertility god who traced his origins to Manu'a, was also *hau* or secular ruler, and under the five kings of the Takalaua dynasty, who resided in Manu'a, tribute was exacted from many of the islands of central Polynesia as far afield as the Ellice Islands (Tuvalu). The claim that there was a Tongan empire at this time cannot be demonstrated since there was no central bureaucracy, no sustained occupation and each new king had to establish his own right to tribute. Marriage patterns linked the Tongan spiritual monarchy with Samoa, as the mother of the Tu'i Tonga in this period was always a Samoan.

In Micronesia the so-called YAP 'TRADE EMPIRE' was really a trading cycle, and though Pohnpei and Kosrae flourished in this period they were largely self-contained. In Hawai'i each island had its own sacred king and war leader. In the Society Islands sacred kings and war leaders, favoured in Ra'iatea and Borabora, sought to control the titular paramountcy system favoured in Tahiti. Throughout the island world there was a strange dichotomy as leadership appeared to fluctuate between the sacred and the temporal, in reality between two manifestations of the sacred, the realm of the fertility god (approximating to spiritual) and the realm of the war god (approximating to temporal authority). Both gods had phallic manifestations and often reversed roles depending on whose supporters were victorious.

In Samoa where the paramountcy in the west had long been exercised by Malietoa, a new system evolved—perhaps because of the decline in political authority of both the Tui Manu'a and the Tu'i Tonga—by which the ceremonial paramount had to acquire four titles known as the *tafaifa*. Although the system was now broader based it still advantaged the Malietoa, Tui Atua and Tui Aana lineages at the expense of the sacred lineages of Savai'i. The first to hold the *tafaifa* was the highly connected female ruler Salamasina. The titular system also changed in Tonga in this period with the appointment of a younger royal sibling with hereditary status, the Tu'i Ha'a Takalaua, to govern Tonga during the absence of the Tu'i Tonga in Samoa. Until the end of the Takalaua dynasty the Tu'i Ha'a Takalaua was virtually *hau* or king of Tonga and took a highborn Samoan wife as the Tu'i Tonga had done previously.

Indigenous chiefly systems

Authority structures changed again with new people movements in the late 16th and 17th centuries, a period again affected by severe El Niño conditions, volcanic action and the advent of Europeans. The significant movements, in random order, were the arrival in Viti Levu of the superior tapa-making people and the establishment of patrilineal dynasties in Fiji from about the end of the 16th century (FIJIAN CHIEFLY STATUS); and the invasion of Tonga from Wallis and the Lau Islands, the defeat of the Takalaua dynasty, the successions of 'Uluakimata I and his dynasty and the rise of the Tu'i Kanokupolu. This was accompanied by the complete 'Fijianization' of Tonga (Fale Fisi, *fahu*, Tameha system, royal wife-strangling), a religious revolution (?female war god replaced by male Fijian war god, and male fertility god replaced by female variant), and replacement of the Samoan royal wife by the daughter of the *hau*. The *hau* system by which the war leader or temporal king could be challenged also dates from this period. There was the occupation of the southern Cook Islands (except Mangaia) by people from Samoa and the Society Islands; and then the arrival in New Zealand of Tangaroa-cult people directly from Ra'iatea, possibly with the assistance of Spanish navigators (SAN LESMES, THE LOST CARAVEL).

The arrival of Europeans in the Pacific had no direct effect on authority structures until missionaries had been in the islands for some time but there were serious indirect influences. In areas badly affected by famines such as the Marquesas and Niue, kings in their capacity as living fertility gods were rendered ineffective and were frequently killed or deposed to be replaced by regional shamans. Diseases brought by Europeans and the dearth of food resources after supplying visitors had a similar effect. Also BEACHCOMBERS had little respect for sacred kings. By the end of the 18th century the Tu'i Tonga had so declined in prestige that it was comparatively easy for the *hau* to abolish the office and assume the alternate mantle of a Christian king.

Quite early the island paramounts, sacred kings and aspiring paramounts heard about European kings and were compared to them. Exploring captains brought gifts from European kings and local potentates were not backward in seeking arms and assistance to put down rivals. Missionaries were anxious to secure stable government and unashamedly championed those chiefs most likely to secure it, irrespective of whether or not the succession was guaranteed by custom. Thus in Tahiti the missionaries supported the chief POMARE II who had accumulated a majority of district titles though he was not the only chief eligible for paramountcy. The succession of his infant son was contrary to custom though fortunately his titular widow Pomare Vahine was able to reign as regent until the monarchy was stabilized under her niece POMARE IV. In Ra'iatea the missionaries supported Tamatoa V though custom disqualified him on account of his marriage to a commoner, and the consequent war drove the missionary John WILLIAMS from his station.

Although the Tahitian monarchy survived under French protection until 1880 when Pomare V abdicated, the separate monarchies of Ra'iatea, Borabora and Huahine had remained independent until that time and the Ra'iateans even resisted by appointing a rebel king. Short-lived monarchies under the French in Nukuhiva and the Gambiers ended with the death of their incumbents.

In Samoa the missionaries regarded the kingship as belonging to the Malietoa family but had to acknowledge the rights of the Tupua family supported by the Catholic party. International interest secured the appointment of vice-kings until the short-lived monarchy was abolished at the end of the German administration. Convention, however, has ensured that the Samoan head of state belongs to one of the families previously eligible for the *tafaifa*, and two heads of state were appointed jointly in 1962. The Americans abolished the monarchy in Manu'a as being inconsistent with the US constitution. In contrast the French have allowed the kings of Wallis and Futuna to continue in a customary capacity.

Other short-lived Christian kingdoms included Niue, Loyalty Islands, Cook Islands and Fiji. Although Queen Makea of Rarotonga was only one of several high chiefs on the island, she reigned in Cook Islands from 1888 to 1901 when the protectorate passed to New Zealand. Even so, the ARIKI and other ranking chiefs often had considerable authority in the Cooks at district level and Mangaia remains a chiefly theocracy. Fiji was a short-lived white settlers' kingdom in 1871–74 with the paramount chief of Bau (CAKOBAU) as nominal sovereign until British annexation. Customary kingdoms survived in a number of small islands including the Northern Gilberts (no longer extant) and the provinces of Fiji.

The two most established island monarchies were Hawai'i and Tonga. Both had been united by a powerful high chief—Hawai'i by KAMEHAMEHA I and Tonga by Tāufa'āhau (George TUPOU I). Both sought to maintain their independence by diplomatic negotiation with the imperial powers. Unlike Hawai'i where much of the land had passed to local

American interests Tonga had a policy which sought to give land to all its citizens. The Tongan monarchs, despite their personal religious preferences, were also firmly attached to the Methodist tradition which gave the kingdom its Christian character. The later Hawaiian sovereigns, however, alienated many Americans. Kamehameha V and Queen Emma were almost ostentatious in their preference for ANGLICAN worship at the expense of the American Congregational services introduced by the missionaries, and King Kalākaua made no secret of his sympathy for the old non-Christian ways of his people by cultivating the *kahuna* or pagan experts. The indigenous monarchy was soon brought down by American interests and Hawai'i was finally incorporated as a full state of the United States.

Despite the chequered careers of the high chiefs, authority at the (district and village) level of CHIEFS and 'BIG-MEN' who owned land often remained fairly constant throughout the 19th century. Also in this period Christian pastors took on many of the functions and characteristics of the spiritual chiefs and priests, often at the expense of their secular counterparts. In Tonga the decision of Tupou I to reward his rivals and former opponents with noble status in his new kingdom has feudalized if not fossilized a traditional authority structure.—WNG

■ *Ali'i and Hawaiian chiefly status* The *ali'i* (chiefly class) of the ancient Hawaiian kingdom were believed to be descended from gods, with the highest chief, the *ali'i-kapu*, thought of as sacred. Below the *ali'i* were the priests, and the common people were known as the *maka'āinana*, those who lived on the land. The ruler of each island kingdom was called the *ali'i-aimoku*, sometimes referred to as *ke ali'i-nui* (the great chief) to distinguish him from lesser chiefs. A combination of chiefly rank (by birth) and natural ability (leadership) determined the choice of *ali'i-aimoku*, and his authority was supreme. The essentially feudal nature of his powers included rights to the land which the *ali'i* might then be granted in return for services. The *ali'i* could transfer their allegiance to another overlord, however, and commoners similarly could move into the service of another chief.—KRF

■ *Ariki* An *ariki* holds the hereditary title of high chief in the Cook Islands. They are heads of a *vaka* or tribe. The *ariki* is supported by a number of *mataiapo* or chiefs of major lineages and by *rangitira* or chiefs of minor lineages. In pre-Christian times, only men held chiefly titles, and ideally succession to titles followed the male line. It was believed that *ariki* were descended from the gods and were *tapu* or sacred. The powers of an *ariki* were wide-ranging. During the era of great mission influence from 1821 to the end of that century, the powers of *ariki* were enhanced, while those of lesser chiefs shrank. The powers of all chiefs were greatly curbed by the colonial government from 1901 onwards. From 1856 a few women on Rarotonga came to hold *ariki* titles, but not those of the lesser chiefs who were involved with day-to-day administration. No women held chiefly titles on the other islands until well into the 1900s. Today there are more women *ariki* titleholders than men, with five of the six *ariki* titles on Rarotonga held by women.

The Cook Islands Constitution provides for up to 14 holders of *ariki* titles to be appointed (by the Queen's Representative) to the House of Ariki. The House of Ariki meets once annually to discuss matters relating to tradition referred to it by parliament (a very rare occurrence in practice). It may make recommendations to parliament, but it has no law-making or executive powers.—MTC

■ *Tongan chiefly status and the Tu'i Tonga* Tonga, the last remaining Polynesian kingdom, appears to have been one of the most centralized and highly stratified societies in the Pacific. Its former chiefly system was supremely aristocratic. Religious significance was attributed to high birth rank as signifying proximity to the gods.

According to Tongan legend, one of the *Kau Tangaloa*—the gods who lived in the sky—was the father of the first Tu'i Tonga, 'Aho'eitu, who thus represented both spiritual and temporal power. The Tu'i Tonga was sole ruler of Tonga until the pressures of population growth and increased administrative responsibilities obliged him to delegate authority to some of his close relatives, sending them to different districts. Over time, the descendants of some of these chiefs began to take on powers of their own. Political instability increased, and it became apparent that the Tu'i Tonga could no longer maintain effective control of both spiritual and temporal spheres. The position of *hau* was then created for the temporal leader, and the Tu'i Tonga became the sacred chief. The *hau* was first held by the Tu'i Ha'atakalaua dynasty until the late 1400s, and from the early 1600s, it was in the hands of the Tu'i Kanokupolu dynasty. The collective name for these lines is *Kauhala'uta*, a category which includes *Falefā* chiefs, and the Tu'i Pelehake. The other noble titles are collectively known as *Kauhalalalo*. High-ranking women were valued for the god-like qualities it was believed they imparted to their children.

As the powers of the local chiefs grew, the authority of the *hau* came to be primarily ceremonial. At village level, chiefly power was absolute, and some of these chiefs aspired to much greater territorial ambitions, ready to challenge the authority of both the Tu'i Tonga and the *hau*. By the 1790s, Tuku'aho, who was then Tu'i Kanokupolu, was trying to regain supremacy over the other chiefs when he was killed. It was his grandson, Tāufa'āhau (King George TUPOU), who finally succeeded in this attempt, a process that included openly challenging the rival royal line. He broke the ancient custom of allowing the eldest daughter of the *hau* (his sister) to marry the heir to the Tu'i Tonga, Laufilitonga, and followed this with a crucial victory in battle against him in 1826. When the defeated Laufilitonga was installed as Tu'i Tonga in the following year, his subordination to Tāufa'āhau ended the political aspirations of the Tu'i Tonga. When Laufilitonga died in 1865, Tāufa'āhau terminated the title.

Traditionally there were some 200 chiefly titles, with a series of graduated statuses separating high-born aristocrats and titled chiefs from their speaking chiefs (*matāpule*), skilled artisans (*mua*) and common labourers (*tu'a*). Before the 1875 Constitution dismantled the system, chiefs commanded both territories and the people on them. They provided protection and leadership to their people in return for labour service, supplies of food, traditional wealth—the MATS and BARKCLOTH (tapa) made by women—and, importantly, men to help fight their wars with rival chiefs.—KJ & KRF

■ ***Pohnpeian chiefdoms*** By 1874, the island of Pohnpei lay divided into five distinct chiefdoms, each governed by a sacred paramount chief, the *nahnmwarki*, and a more secular and governing chief, the NAHNKEN. Each stood at the head of a line of chiefly titles. The rankings for the titles in each of these two lines varied from chiefdom to chiefdom; actual succession to the highest titles could involve personality, circumstance, rivalry and deception as well as seniority. The chiefdoms themselves often proved tenuous political entities plagued by clan struggles for power, by the defiant autonomy of certain regions, and by the persistence of loyalties to earlier political groupings or alliances.

The deeper patterns of the Pohnpeian past involve the arrival of different groups of people who, over time, established a place on the island and who both contributed to and were affected by a particular way of living that came to be called *tiahk en sapw* or the 'custom of the land'. If the land bound people together, there persisted a diversity of practices and beliefs reflective of those other lands and distant times from which the islands' different settlers had come. Over time, there did emerge a resilient, flexible, although internally divided cultural order accustomed to the selective incorporation of foreign peoples, technologies and ideas. The arrival of the first European ship off Pohnpei in the late 1500s marked not necessarily a singular occurrence but rather another happening in a larger pattern of events that took place on *keilahn aio* or 'the other side of yesterday'.

However, violent resistance to Spanish colonial rule from the chiefdom of Nett in 1887 and from northern Madolenihmw in 1890 left Spanish officials hostages in a land they purported to rule. To the end of the 19th century, Pohnpeians remained in control of their island. Intensified contact with the western world during the 1800s brought epidemic disease, foreign goods and economic practices, Christianity and colonialism. Though these developments proved deeply disturbing, even destructive, Pohnpeians persisted as an independent, culturally distinct people. In an ironic sense, the imposition of colonialism gave definition and clarity to what it meant to be Pohnpeian in an increasingly larger, more complex world.—DH

■ ***Nahnken*** *Nahnken*, which translates literally as 'Favoured One', is the most senior and powerful title for a second line of ruling chiefs in each of the five chiefdoms that now exist in Pohnpei. These two ruling lines comprise nobles and their children. From the ranks of the nobles or *soupeidi*, meaning 'those who face down', comes the paramount chief or *nahnmwarki*. The children of the *soupeidi*, called *serihso* or 'sacred children', constitute a second line of chiefs at whose head stands the *nahnken*.

Likened to a prime minister or 'talking chief' in the ethnographic literature on Pohnpei, the *nahnken* often supervised the daily administration and ceremonial etiquette within a chiefdom, and acted as an intermediary between the people and the more sacral, distant and ritually potent chief, the *nahnmwarki*. While affected by more than two centuries of contact and colonialism, the title of *nahnken* is still honoured and respected by Pohnpeians today. Theoretically, the *nahnken* is the eldest blood son of a reigning *nahnmwarki*, though in actuality, things are not always this simple. The charter for the title of *nahnken* appears to lie in the story of Nahlepenien, the son of Pohnpei's first *nahnmwarki*, Isohkelekel. Despite a string of ceremonial transgressions and inappropriate behaviours, Nahlepenien could do nothing to diminish his father's affection for him. Considered chiefly by dint of his paternal lineage, the *nahnken*'s interests and activities are expected to be more worldly.—DH

■ *Traditional leadership in Micronesia* The customary power of traditional chiefs in Micronesia varied from culture to culture. On Kosrae the power was centralized in a very powerful ruler, while on Yap it was decentralized and subjected to elaborate checks and balances built into the customary political relationship. In Palau, power was vested in the heads of two alliances of villages, which were involved in constant fighting for domination. In Chuuk, the most powerful traditional leaders were the village chiefs. In Marshall Islands, the most powerful leaders were the two paramount chiefs, one heading each of the two island chains—the Ratak and Ralik. Surprisingly, for low island chiefs, these two paramount chiefs had absolute power. The five POHNPEIAN CHIEFDOMS were headed by traditional paramount chiefs, although the exercise of their customary power was checked by the head of a chiefly parallel line. His relationship to the paramount chief is like a father-son relationship, the paramount chief being the father. In the outer islands of Chuuk and Yap, each island had its paramount chief.

In spite of the varied power of the traditional chiefs in Micronesia, almost all inherit their position through their mother. In Palau, the senior women in the chiefly clan select the paramount chief. Yap is the exception to this general rule. Both the age of the mother and her son were important determining factors for leadership positions in all Micronesian societies. Quite often a young man who had customary claim to a leadership position would be bypassed in favour of an older man. When this happened, usually the older man served in that position until death, then the rightful holder of the title could assert his right. The exercise of customary chiefly power was the domain of men. In a few cases, women would become chiefs, but the effective power would be exercised by men.

The Kosraean and Chamorro cultures have been completely destroyed by western influence and the dramatic depopulation that both places experienced in the post-contact period. For the rest of Micronesia, the legitimacy of the traditional chiefs continued in different form and degree. During the Spanish occupation, Micronesian chiefs were tolerated and often used to inform their people of Spanish policy. In general, traditional leaders continued to rule their people. When the Germans took control of Micronesia, they found it expedient to govern through the local chiefs. In Pohnpei, the Germans took away the high chief's power to give and take land from his people. This was substituted for a land tenure system that gave freehold title to the head of the family, in effect destroying the traditional matrilineal land tenure system, and creating a patrilineal system in its place. This had little impact on the customary power of the traditional chiefs in Pohnpei. Like chiefs in other parts of Micronesia, they continued to rule their people as they had before the colonial period. In fact the German settlement in KOLONIA, Pohnpei, was saved during the Sokehs Rebellion by the German governor's appeal for protection to the traditional leaders of the other four kingdoms. In the Carolines, chiefs were used as the recruiting agents for native labourers to work in the phosphate mine in Angaur, Palau. The Japanese continued this practice of rule through the traditional chiefs in the villages.—JCH

■ *Fijian chiefly status* Fiji's chiefly system is at the heart of the Fijian political and socioeconomic systems; it draws its strengths from a well-defined hierarchy of groups and sub-groups with clearly specified roles, which have their roots in history and tradition. The relationships of groups and subgroups are governed by adherence to recognized codes of protocol and custom.

Every Fijian belongs to an *i tokatoka* (extended family group), and is a member of a *mataqali* (landowning unit, or group of *i tokatoka*), which belongs to a *yavusa* (CLAN comprising a number of *mataqali*) that is part of a *vanua* (bigger social and political unit comprising a number of *yavusa*). Each subgroup is related to, or has relatives in, other subgroups. Membership of each subgroup confers status on every Fijian family unit, and identifies its role in the *i tokatoka, mataqali, yavusa* and *vanua*.

Each subgroup has a leader or chief, normally chosen by members from among themselves. In a *mataqali, yavusa*, or *vanua*, these leaders know their responsibilities with respect to members of the subgroup, as defined in custom and tradition. It is the proper performance of these responsibilities that confers mutual respect between members and their chiefs. They are interdependent, bound by traditional ties of mutual support for survival, and reinforced by kinship.

The Fijian social system, of which the chiefs are an integral part, remains today as it has been for generations. Largely impervious to new political and social influences, it provides a strong basis of self-reliance for the Fijian people. As long as leaders satisfy the criteria of modern leadership, including formal education, relevant experience, and concern for others, they are chosen without the necessity of extensive mud-slinging campaigns. There is an inherent preference for leaders who, by tradition, birth and experience, have been assigned the role of leadership. It is significant that such leaders cannot be removed from their position within the clan or tribe (except by death), but their policies can be influenced from below. Traditional land tenure also has an integral place within this system, since the *mataqali* is the land-owning unit, and it is the land which ultimately identifies and binds the group. (See also FIJI NATIVE LAND TRUST BOARD.)

The chiefly system is thus inextricably and indivisibly interwoven with the Fijian political and social system, resting on the pattern of rights and responsibilities allotted to various *mataqali* within a *yavusa*. These *mataqali* functions are headed by *na mataqali turaga* (chiefly *mataqali*). The chief of the *yavusa* is chosen from this *mataqali*, who are invariably males of the chiefly line, inheriting leadership in descending order of age. The eldest son of the chief succeeds only after the death of the chief's youngest brother. Next in ranking is *na mataqali sauturaga* (second in line to the chiefly *mataqali*), who has an administrative function, ensuring that the chief's decisions are implemented, followed by *na mataqali matanivanua* (chief's spokesman *mataqali*), who is the intermediary between chiefs and the *vanua*, and the ambassador of the *yasuva* to other *yasuva* and *vanua*. Members of this *mataqali* are respected for their skills in communication and oratory.

There are several other traditional *mataqali* functions, the warrior *mataqali* (*na mataqali bati*), carpenters and craftsmen *mataqali* (*na mataqali mataisau*), seafarers and fishers *mataqali* (*na mataqali gonedau*), and priestly *mataqali* (*na mataqali bete*), but some of the functions of these *mataqali* have completely disappeared or been modified. In spite of changes, however, the system itself remains strong and cohesive. Respect for the chief is woven into Fijian custom, with special forms of greetings to a chief, who is never addressed by his name, but is referred to as a plural entity. Formal ceremonies of welcome, when a chief visits, include promises of loyalty, and the appropriate chiefly response uses a special form of speech. The chiefly system incorporates a fundamental and mutually recognized acceptance of the social and political values of leadership, respect, dignity, cohesion and protection.—FNB

Further reading

Bole, F N, 1992. 'Fiji's chiefly system and its pattern of political self-reliance', in R Crocombe, U Neemia, A Ravuvu and W Vom Busch (eds), *Culture and Democracy in the South Pacific*, Institute of Pacific Studies, University of the South Pacific.

■ *Samoan matai titles* The *matai* system, in which chiefly titles are earned through a combination of birth and ability, has been the backbone of the *fa'a Samoa* or the Samoan way of life for more than 1000 years. Each *aiga*—family or kin group, the basic unit in the Samoan social structure, whose members are related by descent, adoption or marriage—possesses a *matai* chiefly title which they serve, and which defines their place in the community, including their relationship to others outside the *aiga*. The *matai* titleholder is chosen to hold the family *matai* title by the local family members, together with relatives who live elsewhere, from among themselves. They normally choose the person who they think will serve the family interests best. Where there is no titleholder, the family members still participate fully in village affairs through recognition of the title itself in the village hierarchy, except in the *matai* council in which only a titleholder may represent the family.

Once chosen, the new *matai* assumes control over the family assets and the activities of its members, and he represents the family in village affairs. This control is custodial in nature, as the family assets are vested in the title itself and not in the holder. For their part, the untitled family members render the *matai* their *tautua* or service and support. The relationship between the *matai* and his family is based on the recognition by each party of the indispensable value of the role and contribution of the others to the welfare of the family. Both the *matai* and family members possess powerful means of redress, should the relationship become unacceptable to any one of them.

Matai titles have their origins in honours created and bestowed by holders of paramount or prominent *matai* titles or honours won in war. The origins of paramount or prominent *matai* titles are usually traced to the ancient Samoan gods. Oral literature indicates that there was a time when all Samoa was a single family called *'Sa Tagaloa'*, and the *matai* title was awarded to deserving heads of family groups, with those below them obliged to render feudal services. Members of each family can recount the origins of their title, and the *tulafale*—the orators, keepers of Samoan traditions—can recount the origins of paramount or prominent *matai* titles.

Matai titles are of two orders, the *alii* (chiefs) and the *tulafale* (orators). *Alii*, the source of authority, are titular chiefs to whose title and person were attached a sanctity which placed them above involvement in common tasks, such as speaking on their own behalf or distributing food and wealth, tasks which were performed by the *tulafale* whose role resembled that of an administrator. *Matai* titles are strictly ranked both within the village and in the wider context of district and nation. The rank and status of each title is strictly observed in each applicable context. Failure to do so would bring serious consequences.

The village *matai* council, made up of all village *matai*, is the supreme authority in the village, as it has been for generations. It regulates village life, and it enforces its decisions. There is no local government organization except the council to control village affairs. The village (*nu'u*) is the basic and most stable unit of political organization, and it is made up of all the families in a defined locality. The village is constituted in a formal structure by the village *faalupega*, which is a fixed set of honorific greetings recognizing the *matai* titles, their origins, connections, functions, rights, and duties in the village and often beyond it. The *faalupega* defines the place and role of each person in the village and the relationships between them, in recognizing each *matai* title. The same applies to the *faalupega* of traditional Samoan districts, and the *faalupega* of Samoa as a whole.

When Samoa became independent in 1962, the two joint heads of state possessed the highest *tama'aiga* titles, and only *matai* titleholders were entitled either to vote or to be candidates in general elections. The United Nations, to whom universal suffrage was an article of faith, approved this situation after it accepted the central place and special role of *matai* in Samoan society. The system changed only after a referendum in 1990, in which every Samoan citizen aged 21 or more voted. Universal suffrage won just 51 per cent of the vote. However, only *matai* titleholders are eligible to be candidates for 47 of the 49 parliamentary seats.—KE

Hiri trading voyages

Over recent centuries, annual voyages were conducted by the Motu language speakers around Port Moresby to the Eleman language speakers around Koriki in the Gulf of Papua. The 300 km journeys in the Motuan double-hulled *lakatoi* used the prevailing winds, sailing west each October or November carrying clay pots manufactured by the Motu women, stone axes from the inland mountains, and armlets from Hula, Aroma and Mailu. The expedition returned in December or January, their *lakatoi* rebuilt with new hulls, laden with sago, tobacco, betelnut and other wetland products. Last century the annual *hiri* fleet of 20–30 *lakatoi* carried as many as 25 000 pots to the Gulf, returning laden with about 25 tons of sago. The trading served a variety of purposes, linking several distinct linguistic groups in ceremonial and economic exchanges as complex as the *kula* trade, integral to the whole exchange system of southeast New Guinea. Sago was a crucial food for the Motu in the dry season, and the pots, axes and armbands were needed in the Gulf, where there were no local resources to manufacture them. The Motu obtained their stone axes from inland villages and traded sago to them in return, also trading sago to the armband manufacturers further east. From the 1870s items of European manufacture were also observed circulating through the *hiri*.

The annual human interaction also led to the development of Hiri Motu, a simplified trading version of Motu, which was used by early Europeans as a *lingua franca*. (See TRADING LANGUAGES IN PAPUA NEW GUINEA.) On these voyages the Motu

Lakatoi vessel traditionally used on trading voyages along the Papuan coast of Papua New Guinea—photographed in 1922 by Sarah Chinnery

traders spent about three months in the Gulf while they deconstructed the canoes they arrived in and constructed larger ones for the return journey. Their partners lived in villages at the mouths of the many large rivers that flow into the sea around the Gulf. Intermarriages occurred and the trade link drew Gulf people to Port Moresby once it became a mission and administrative centre. The *hiri*, disrupted by war in 1941, was resumed after 1945 in a limited fashion until the early 1960s.—CM2

Further reading

Groves, M, 1972. 'Hiri', *Encyclopedia of Papua New Guinea*, vol. 1, Melbourne University Press and University of Papua New Guinea.

Williams, F E, 1932–33. 'Trading voyages from the Gulf of Papua', *Oceania*, 3(2).

Indigenous chiefly systems

Kula exchange system

The inter-island *kula* voyages of the Trobriand islanders of eastern Papua New Guinea, which possibly began some 500 years ago, were documented by Bronislaw MALINOWSKI in 1920. In the *kula* exchange, decorative shell armbands were traded for necklaces of gold-lipped oyster-shells and other trinkets in a complex set of rituals incorporating myths, formal ceremonies and magic and representing transactions of both political and economic value. Highly decorated Trobriand men travelled long distances—traditionally by ornately carved and painted outrigger canoe, but by the 1970s often by motorboat—from Kiriwina, to conduct the exchange among people with different, although related, languages and traditions. Men from one village or village cluster combined under a chief's leadership to sail to a distant island to meet their *kula* partners who lived there. Months later, the former hosts would make the journey to visit those who had been their guests. The necklaces moved in a clockwise direction, passed from partner to partner, while the armshells moved in the opposite direction. Usually only men who had been involved in *kula* for many years managed to become renowned experts. They competed to acquire specific partners, gaining fame as their names were circulated in relation to the largest and most valuable shells that each had obtained. Knowledge, high status and sorcery could help some *kula* players to claim success and earn fame. After a man died, his trading partners might decide to transfer his shells on to a different 'path' if they lacked confidence in his son, who was yet to gain *kula* experience. In more recent society, the inter-island *kula* exchange might assist a young Trobriander to build up his business contacts or enhance his political career.—KRF

Further reading

Malinowski, B K, 1920. 'Kula: the circulating exchanges of valuables in the archipelagoes of Eastern New Guinea', *Man*, 51.

Weiner, A B, 1988. *The Trobrianders of Papua New Guinea*, Holt, Rinehart and Winston.

Yap 'trade empire' and stone money

Archaeological and linguistic evidence suggests that the Caroline Islands may have been settled in two separate waves: Yap from the Philippines and Palau from the Sulawesi region. Prehistoric settlement in the Caroline Islands included coastal communities and inland villages, with Yap as the centre of what has been called an empire. Status was determined by birth rather than by personality or achievements. Yap's political system was complex: people were segregated into nine classes with authority pyramiding down from a few leaders whose influence and power extended to quite distant tributary islands. The chiefs exacted 'tribute' from surrounding peoples up to 1100 km away. Every two or three years, a fleet of large canoes set out from the distant eastern atolls, joined by additional canoes on the way until about 20 arrived at Yap. Each canoe represented a single community and each carried official gifts—presented as tribute to the heads of the Yapese clans that claimed figurative ownership of the donors' home islands—as well as goods for trade. On Yap, there was an élite of landowners who lived on the coast, dominating the remaining population who lived inland, and were obliged to supply them with food and labour.

From about the 17th century, Yap islanders used to sail to Palau (about 380 km to the southwest) to quarry and carry home the stone money (*raay*, large discs or wheels of pale yellow limestone—not found on Yap—which they valued as money). The value of each piece depended mainly on its size but also the fineness of the stone, its colour, and the regularity of its shape. A hole was formed in the centre so that a cord made of bark (or a stick or pole for larger pieces) could be passed through to allow it to be car-

Yap stone money, photographed by Matsumura in 1915

ried. From the 19th century, when larger vessels were available to transport them, larger discs—some more than a metre in diameter (see picture), and weighing about 100 kg—were mined. Smaller discs were kept indoors while the larger wheels were laid against walls or trees, and substantial quantities were owned by chiefs and rich men, with up to 100 in the compounds of village clubhouses.

The difficulty of the voyage by canoe or raft, and the labour involved in extracting and cutting the wheels, made the money precious. As well as currency, the stone money served as ornament and an outward symbol of the prosperity of the chief or village owning the stockpile of discs. Once outsiders began to intervene in the process—there were Japanese reports that two Americans were making the discs in Palau in 1890, and transporting them to Yap—the currency's value diminished and the discs were less highly prized. Trading was a feature of Micronesian life, and two kinds of shell money were also used in Yap for general trade purposes.—KRF

Traditional authority and distribution of food

Whereas in Melanesia the greater variety of spirit-imaging in traditional religions mirrors diversity in leadership structures, both Polynesian and Micronesian 'vertical' cosmologies suggest strong chieftainships and nobilities. Melanesia had its chiefs, yet it is more discussed for its 'BIG-MEN'—leaders who jostle for prominence in war leadership and economic exchanges within a more egalitarian atmosphere. Priests are known in Melanesia, but they are rarely in life-long 'office'. Polynesia, in contrast, has had some of its greatest leaders honoured as kings and queens internationally. Tahiti's POMARE dynasty, Tonga's Tāufaʻāhau TUPOU I, and the Hawaiian queen, KAʻAHUMANU, have been prominent among them. Island complexes were noted for their systems of chiefly status and titles, for an order of priests (*kahuna*, *tahuʻa*, *tohunga*, *tufuga*, for example) within these ruling classes, and for rules of obeisance applying to commoners and slaves. On the margins of such leadership complexes, stratification is less intense, though in the smaller Polynesian groups (such as Tikopia) and Micronesian atolls, the same principles of claim to rightful leadership applied. Heirs of the first chiefly arriving voyager inherit seniority in leadership—unless it is blunted by bad personal qualities or through reversals of war. Warriors often played significant roles as heirs and powerful nobles (especially in the Hawaiian group), and on the Marquesas the female priesthood was rather more powerful than the male at the time of contact. There was a tendency for power to flow from the top, but some decentralization could occur; in Samoa, for instance, authority and ritual life were more evenly dispersed among many (great) families (SAMOAN MATAI TITLES).

In both warfare and exchange, Polynesian and Micronesian societies often saw the manipulating of commoners by the noble stratum, while more egalitarian Melanesian arrangements allowed for authority through experience and 'eldership'. A conviction pertained, however, that the flow of gifts with alliances, trade systems and humdrum daily exchange brought collective wellbeing, so long as one fulfilled obligations. Thus, although goods tended to flow towards the pinnacle to satisfy the sumptuary needs of the king or queen, the riches were expected to return downwards. At the Hawaiian New Year and connected Temple Renewal rite, when all came to witness the pivotal sacrificial act of the king (the noiseless dashing of a pig to the ground), the dispersal of cooked food must reach down (as the king announced) to 'the very little people' of the realm. The same principle prevails in Micronesia, as recently documented for Ujeland Atoll in Marshall Islands (though today food is lavished on and redistributed by Christian ministers). In the greater Melanesian sacrifices, such as the giant pig-kill ceremonies among the Wahgi and Chimbu peoples, or pig presentations among the Melpa and Enga, the big-men sponsors are also involved in crucial preliminary invocations and speeches, yet most of the festivities reflect the collectivity of host warriors and healthy young women, whose display of vital energies affirm in dance the relatively more egalitarian statement that 'we are a people'. Men who could contribute no pigs to the great kill or display, however, would be seen as 'rubbish'.—GWT

Traditional rulers

■ *Pomare I* Pomare I (c1743–1803), or Tu as he was known in Tahiti, and 'Otou' as Captain COOK recorded his name in 1769, was an ambitious young chieftain with great prestige in the northwest part of the island. His family had close links to the powerful Oro cult which emerged in Raʻiatea and later spread through Tahiti and Moorea; and his great-uncle, Tutara, chief of Atehuru, had defeated the forces of Amo, chief of Papara, and his wife, 'Queen' Purea, in 1768. On Cook's third visit in 1774, Pomare and his allies were attacking Mahine, paramount chief of Moorea, with whom they negotiated a truce. Cook assumed that Pomare was now 'king' of Tahiti and treated him with respect, not understanding the rivalries between five or six competing Tahitian tribal coalitions. When BLIGH came in October 1788, Pomare and his wife, Itia, came on board the *Bounty* at Matavai Bay. Bligh was told that Pomare had been defeated by some of his former allies in an attack from Moorea in about 1782, and that the title Tu had now passed to Pomare's eldest son. Later, after the MUTINY ON THE BOUNTY, Pomare offered shelter to those mutineers who chose to live on Tahiti, and this time, with English firearms and tactical support, the 17 years of fighting with Moorea ended in a final victory for Pomare and his friend, Hitihiti. By 1791 he had moved to live on Moorea—also claiming the Leeward Islands of Borabora, Ra'iatea and Huahine as his own—and his son, Tu, was being called Pomare.—KRF

■ *Kamehameha I* Kamehameha (c1752–8 May 1819; other names Paiea, Kūnuiākea) was born in the northern district of Kohala, Hawai'i. He inherited the title of war god (Kūkā'ilimoku) after the death of his uncle, the Hawaiian paramount chief (Mō'ī). This spiritual emphasis, coupled with his own personal ability and the support of solid advisers, enabled him to gain eventual control of Hawai'i. Inter-island battles for supremacy with Maui chiefs ended in 1795, at the Battle of Nu'uanu. Kaua'i Mō'ī ceded his island in 1810. Kamehameha was the first to unify the islands, to appoint governors to oversee each major island and to allow inheritance rights for lands under the control of trusted advisers. He established a reputation for being intelligent, fair, fearless and a staunch traditionalist. His descendants continued to control government until 1893. Kamehameha died at Kona.—TKY

■ *Ka'ahumanu* Ka'ahumanu (c1768–5 June 1832), one of the most powerful women in Hawaiian history, was the daughter of the high chief Ke'eaumoku of Hawai'i (a senior counsellor of KAMEHAMEHA I) and granddaughter through her mother, Nāmāhana, of the Maui paramount chief Kekaulike. She became the favourite wife of Kamehameha I, and was known as an extremely strong leader in her own right. With the death of her husband in 1819, she created the position of *kuhina nui* (regent) and co-ruled with Kamehameha II ('Iolani Liholiho). Breaking the centuries-old religious sanction of *'Aikapu*, the foundation of chiefly worship, she sat publicly to eat with him (*'Ainoa*), just six months after her husband's death. When Calvinist missionaries came from Boston to teach in Hawai'i, she not only encouraged them but also converted to Christianity herself in 1825, after learning to read and write with Hiram BINGHAM, and was baptized with the name Elizabeth. She proved a stalwart ally of the mission and continued as *kuhina nui* until her death.—TKY

■ *Pomare II* Pomare II (c1782–1821), who established himself as the first paramount ruler of Tahiti, gained the early attention of the LONDON MISSIONARY SOCIETY (LMS) evangelists who arrived in Matavai Bay on the *Duff* in March 1797. Although the missionaries made little initial headway in their religious aims, their dwindling presence was tolerated, and their influence with visiting traders helped to bolster Pomare II's standing. When a major challenge to his authority erupted in 1808, and he fled to Moorea, the Rev Henry Nott (1774–1844), a bricklayer from Birmingham, was the only one of the LMS band to stay with him in exile. The traders continued to call on Pomare in Moorea, while he prepared to regain power, and in 1811 his counter-attack on Tahiti met no resistance. He re-established his base on Moorea, where the remaining missionaries soon joined him. In 1812 Pomare announced his conversion to Christianity, and—in the name of Jehovah, and with the aid of European guns—led his growing band of supporters to victory in battle at Fei Pi in 1815.—KRF

■ *George Tupou I* Tāufa'āhau (1797–1893), later known as King George Tupou I of Tonga, grew up at a time of violent political struggles among local chiefs. His political career began in 1820, when his father (the Tu'i Kanokupolu) died and he assumed control of the Ha'apai group. A gifted natural leader, he asserted his traditional right to Tongan supremacy and openly challenged the rival royal line of the TU'I TONGA. He broke the ancient custom of allowing the eldest daughter of the *hau* (his sister) to marry the heir to the Tu'i Tonga, Laufilitonga, and later defeated him in battle in 1826. Over the next few years he developed a close association with the Wesleyan missionaries who had come to Tonga in 1797, and whose efforts had been invigorated by the arrival of Nathaniel Turner in 1826. Impressed with the superiority of their knowledge, wealth, goods and especially weapons, Tāufa'āhau accepted Christianity in 1831, taking the name George after George III of England. Convinced of the power of the Christian god, he became determined to eradicate heathenism, successfully converting many of his people. He extended his crusade to Vava'u and was accepted as its ruler after the death of the aging chief 'Ulukalala.

In 1833 he eloped with Lupe Pau'u, the principal wife of Laufilitonga, and they were later married by the missionaries. There were further battles against 'heathen' chiefs on Tongatapu in 1837 and 1840 before they capitulated on 26 June 1840. King George became Tu'i Kanokupolu on 4 December 1845, finally ruler of all Tonga. One last pocket of resistance among the Ha'a Havea chiefs on Tongatapu was fostered by the Roman Catholic mission, established in 1842. Encouraged by Marist missionaries who promised French naval support, the Ha'a Havea chiefs rebuilt their fortresses and declared their independence. This brief civil war was won by King George in August 1852, and the dissident chiefs were pardoned, converted to Wesleyan Christianity, and later became nobles.

The King had strengthened his position by encouraging his cousin Enele Ma'afu (a capable young chief with legitimate rights to the succession) to go to Fiji in 1847 and then to take control of a substantial part of the Fijian group. The King's ambitions led him to intervene in the Fijian wars of 1855, and he appealed for compensation when King CAKOBAU sought the annexation of Fiji by Britain in 1859. At the same time, he worked to ensure Tonga's independence by obtaining the recognition of the major powers. He visited Fiji and Sydney in 1853 and began to encourage European settlers to Tonga. He corresponded with Sir George Grey, Governor of New Zealand and with Charles St Julian, later Hawaiian Consul in Sydney. From 1860 he was advised by Shirley BAKER, a Wesleyan missionary who became a trusted ally.

In 1862 he updated his own earlier (1839) code of laws: a poll tax was introduced, along with a system of leasehold land tenure, and serfs were emancipated. In other farsighted moves, education became compulsory (and later, free along with medical services); and an army was established. In 1875 the new CONSTITUTION OF TONGA ensured that most land would remain in Tongan hands; and the creation of a landed nobility helped win the support of chiefs whose power was being undermined. In preventing land alienation by planters and companies, he was also maintaining Tonga's political independence. When he died in 1893, he left an orderly succession safely entrenched by hereditary rules of monarchy and land ownership.—KRF

Source/further reading

Latukefu, S, 1970. 'King George Tupou I of Tonga', in J W Davidson and D Scarr (eds), *Pacific Island Portraits*, Australian National University Press.

■ *Queen Pomare IV* Aimata, or Pomare IV (1813–77), was the sister of the boy king Pomare III, whose death in 1827 made her queen at 14. Inclined towards a 'wild' social life, she initially showed no interest in Christianity, to the despair of the aging Henry Nott and his LONDON MISSIONARY SOCIETY (LMS) missionary colleagues. In 1830 she indicated support for the breakaway Mamaia sect whose followers favoured promiscuity (see CARGO CULTS). Tahitian tolerance of the missionary community was dwindling, but finally it was the younger, more energetic, handsome and ambitious missionary, George PRITCHARD, who became her close adviser. She made a first attempt to have him appointed British consul in 1832, and persevered until his appointment was approved in 1838. By then Pape'ete was already a popular port of call for traders; French vessels had begun to visit, followed in 1836 by two Catholic priests, Fathers LAVAL and Caret. Encouraged by Pritchard, Pomare decided to forbid the establishment of a Catholic mission, and had the priests expelled.

The queen's support of Protestantism served only to complicate island politics and international

'The Queen's house at Papua (Pape'ete), Tahiti c1822'

relations. The priests complained to the French government, and the frigate *Venus* was despatched with Captain Abel Aubert du Petit-Thouars to collect a fine of 2000 Spanish dollars and obtain an apology. The queen, furious and mortified, insisted that Pritchard raise the money and then dismissed him as consul. France's power had been demonstrated, and soon Tahiti's submission was complete. A French Protectorate was established in 1842, and soon afterwards, Pritchard was deported from Tahiti.—KRF

■ *Kamehameha III* Kauikeaouli (1814–15 December 1854), the younger son of KAMEHAMEHA I, succeeded to the throne upon the death of his brother 'Iolani Liholiho. Only 11 years old in 1825 when he was declared king, his first years were in the shadow of KA'AHUMANU who ruled until 1832. When Elisabeta Kinau (1805–39), the king's half-sister, then became *kuhina nui*, the king reacted sharply, breaking with the Christian chiefs and entering into unrestrained pursuit of the drinking and gambling that had been prohibited with mission support. After two years, the king was reconciled with Kinau and the council of chiefs, and the remainder of his reign was noted for developments in constitutional and land reform, progress in education, and growth in commerce and industry. His advisers included two missionaries—William Richards and Gerritt Judd—who later resigned from the mission in order to join the fledgling administration, Judd serving as secretary of state. In 1845 the king moved the capital from LAHAINA to HONOLULU. His reign was also noted for the development of agriculture and cattle on a commercial scale and the first production of SUGAR.—KRF

■ *Naisiline Nidoish* Naisiline Nidoish (c1815–80) was great chief of the Si Gwahma tribe on Maré, one of the LOYALTY Islands, known for his exploiting of European religious and national rivalries. On his father's death in 1848, Naisiline out-manoeuvred other family members for the chieftaincy, and extended and consolidated Si Gwahma rule over much of Maré by supporting English Protestant missionaries and organizing an army of 'Christian soldiers'. He aspired to be the 'king of Maré'. Enemy tribes called upon French Catholic missionaries for support, leading to a series of 'wars of religion'. The French government, which had annexed neighbouring New Caledonia in 1853, was eventually able to control Maré in the 1870s. Unimpressed with Naisiline's self-proclaimed title 'Napoleon of Maré', it limited his influence to traditional Si Gwahma territory.—KRH

■ *Cakobau* Ratu Seru Epenesa, later known as Cakobau (c1817–February 1883), was the son of the Vunivalu of Bau, Ratu Tanoa Visawaga, and became the most powerful chief in 19th century Fiji. Ambitious and cunning, he developed strong political and military skills as he plotted to exert his power across Fiji. His authority in Bau was strengthened by his marriage to Adi Samanunu, a daughter of the Roko Tui Bau who had formerly opposed the Vunivalu. Having established his authority over the area that included the port of LEVUKA, which he valued as a source of European trade goods, he sent all foreigners into temporary exile from the island in 1844 after some of them assisted an adventurer he was pursuing. By this time a major part of coastal Fiji was acknowledging his supremacy and some Europeans had begun to address him as 'King Seru'. Over the next decade, however, his enemies continued to con-

Portrait of Cakobau made by officers of the HMS *Herald*, c1855

spire against him; his installation as Vunivalu of Bau (in July 1853) was challenged by the people of Kaba (on the southeast coast of Viti Levu); and some of the American traders were pressing claims to a considerable debt. In 1854, in need of allies, he finally agreed to conversion to Christianity by the Wesleyan Reverend Joseph Waterhouse, and was baptized with the name Epenesa. In 1855 the American demands for financial compensation for various Fijian misdeeds were investigated by the naval captain Boutwell, who forced Cakobau to sign for an inflated debt. Unable to pay it himself, Cakobau reached an agreement with the POLYNESIA COMPANY in 1868, and signed a charter granting 200 000 acres of land to the company. In June 1871, he was declared King (the Tui Viti) of a unified Fiji by colonists, and crowned at Levuka, but his government was inherently unstable, since it required equal support from both Fijians and foreigners. While much Fijian support was forthcoming, the Europeans at large wanted merely a puppet, a role he was not prepared to play. Aided by J B THURSTON, the Chief Secretary, he attempted to resist the idea of cession, but within four years, the islands had become a British Crown Colony. (See DEED OF CESSION.) Cakobau was treated with respect by the first resident governor, Sir Arthur GORDON, and he appeared to enjoy his role as elder statesman and loyal subject of Queen Victoria, until he died in February 1883, after suffering from asthma for several years.—KRF

Further reading

Scarr, D, 1970. 'Cakobau and Ma'afu: contenders for pre-eminence in Fiji', in J W Davidson and D Scarr (eds), *Pacific Islands Portraits*, Australian National University Press.

■ *Lili'uokalani* Lili'uokalani (2 September 1838–11 November 1917; other names Lydia Kamaka'eha) was born to the highly ranked Keohokālole, her father being the lesser-ranked chief Kapa'akea. Lili'uokalani married John Owen Dominis in September 1862, and in 1891 she became queen, succeeding her brother, David Kalākaua. Responding to the wishes of her people, she attempted to promulgate a new constitution for Hawai'i in 1892. Her actions drew opposition from American SUGAR interests, who favoured annexation, and whose supporters claimed that the lives and property of Americans were threatened. The US Minister John Stevens then ordered American naval forces to support the sugar interests and overthrow the Hawaiian government, demanding the queen's abdication. Lili'uokalani surrendered to the superior might of the United States on 17 January 1893. Knowledgeable regarding ancestral traditions, she was also a gifted composer. Her estate continues to support a children's centre that provides social services to disadvantaged Hawaiian families.—TKY

Further reading

Lili'uokalani, 1964. *Hawai'i's Story by Hawai'i's Queen*, Tuttle Press.

■ *Lauaki Namulau'ulu Mamoe* Lauaki Namulau'ulu Mamoe (c1845–14 November 1915) was a significant influence in Samoan politics and figured prominently as Samoa's greatest orator chief into the 20th century. Lauaki received the *tulafale*, or talking chief title of Lauaki from his father Lauaki Namulau'ulu Atamu, who was presented with it by the Tongan king Tuitonga Gigigigi in 1828. He drew freely from western influences, including adherence to the LONDON MISSIONARY SOCIETY and use of the Bible as a tool for his great oratory; his son was even named Tivoli after a hotel in APIA. But in politics Lauaki was renowned for his traditionalism and as a protector and king-maker for the Malietoa title and its chiefly holders. During the 1880s Lauaki also began to see himself as the defender of Samoan unity and tradition against the increasing interventions of European imperial powers. In 1898 he insisted on carrying out the last will of Malietoa Laupepa and conferring titular supremacy on Mata'afa Josefo of the rival Tupua lineage, as Samoa's best hope to unite against annexation. Partition was not averted and Lauaki became the centre of controversial challenges to the policies of German Governor SOLF. In 1908 he led opposition to Solf's policies of trying to break the traditional chiefly power-broking cartels, but was defeated by the arrival of the German navy and the collaboration of his Samoan enemies. Lauaki was exiled to Saipan with his family and followers and died from dysentery at Tarawa (Gilbert Islands) while being transported back to Samoa in 1915. Sometimes characterized as a conservative rebel, single-handedly taking on the Germans, Lauaki was the most talented, articulate organizer in Samoans' group defence of their political culture, deeply dedicated to the self-sufficiency and integrity of Samoan culture.—PJH

Further reading

Davidson, J W, 1970. 'Lauaki Namulau'ulu Mamoe: a traditionalist in Samoan politics', in J W Davidson and D Scarr (eds), *Pacific Islands Portraits*, Australian National University Press.

■ *Kwaisulia* Kwaisulia (c1850–1909), Solomon Islands Passage Master and BIG-MAN, was born on

Adagege artificial islet, Lau lagoon, Malaita (Solomon Islands). He grew to prominence through his early participation in the Queensland labour trade, 1875–81, probably at Rockhampton, and his almost 30 years as Lau's leading 'passage master', the person who controlled labour recruiting from the lagoon to Queensland, Fiji and Samoa. Kwaisulia was a classic Malaitan big-man, who rose to prominence through his own personality and abilities rather than any hereditary right. He was probably inspired to leave for Queensland by knowing Jack Renton, a Scot shipwrecked at the lagoon, 1868–75, but on his return his knowledge of Pidgin English enabled him to manipulate recruiting of coastal and inland peoples through the lagoon. By the time the first resident commissioner arrived (1897), Kwaisulia was the dominant force in north Malaita, having accumulated great power and material possessions. He was killed while dynamiting fish in 1909.—CM2

Further reading

Corris, P, 1970. 'Kwaisulia of Ada Gege: a strongman in the Solomon Islands', in J W Davidson and D Scarr (eds), *Pacific Islands Portraits*, Australian National University Press.

■ *Te'o Tuvale* Te'o Tuvale (1855–1919), a titled Samoan *matai,* was born in Feleasi'u, A'ana district on the island of Upolu. He was a member of the Petaia lineage and the son of a PASTOR of the LONDON MISSIONARY SOCIETY (LMS), Va'aelua Petaia, who had studied at the LMS seminary in Malua. After attending the same seminary Te'o Tuvale was appointed in 1878 as assistant secretary to the official indigenous Samoan government seated in Mulinu'u. He remained there or nearby through the rise and fall of successive Samoan regimes in the 1880s and 1890s. By 1900 when the western Samoan islands became German, Te'o had held positions as secretary of A'ana district, clerk to the Land and Titles Commission set up by the Berlin Conference, and chief judge at Mulinu'u. Like other church and political élites in his lineage he had travelled abroad, spending some years in Fiji during the wars of the late 1880s. In 1900 he led a troupe of traditional dancers to Germany where he met the Kaiser and received a gold watch. Te'o served as translator to the first German governor, Wilhelm SOLF, though his duties ranged more widely, as tutor on village affairs and protocol, adviser and mediator in disputes, and an active participant in the contests for power between the German colonial regime and traditionalist chiefs. Shortly before his death, he completed a history of

Te'o Tuvale (right) in 1897 with Vaiga (left) and Apelm (standing)

Samoa for the New Zealand military administration.—PJH

■ *Henry Nanpei* Henry Nanpei (1862–1928), the son of Nahnku, the NAHNKEN of Kiti chiefdom, Pohnpei, benefited from his father's patronage of the Protestant mission at Rohnkiti. Nanpei attended school at the main Protestant mission station at Ohwa in the neighbouring chiefdom of Madolenihmw. There, he learned to speak and write English, and became a member of a small group of mission-trained young men who would later use their literacy and other mission-derived advantages to exert considerable political change. While privileged by his father's rank, Nanpei held no prospects for advancement in the island's chiefly system because of the relatively low-ranking status of his mother's clan, the Dipwinluhk. Nanpei did benefit considerably from the unprecedented inheritance of his father's lands; the 'deeding' of these lands was conceived and arranged by Nanpei's maternal grandfather, James Headley of London, who worked as a pilot at Mwudok Harbor in the south of Kiti. Generally, upon the death of a titleholder, all land reverted to the *nahnmwarki* or paramount chief for his considered use or redistribution.

Nanpei used the advantages provided him by birth to open a store at Rohnkiti which provisioned the WHALING ships and other trading vessels that used to call there throughout the latter half of the 19th century. He added considerably to his land holdings by extending credit at his store to chiefs, and then negotiating for portions of their land rights as payment for their debts. Nanpei employed the same land-procuring tactic to even greater effect after the GERMAN COLONIAL ADMINISTRATION abolished chiefly control over land in 1907, and established a land tenure and inheritance system based upon primogeniture. Nanpei's land holdings were formally recognized by the Spanish colonial administration in 1896, and by the later German and Japanese regimes.

Nanpei showed himself a manipulator of both local and colonial political systems. He struggled for power within Kiti and against a larger chiefly group aligned with the Spanish Catholic Church. Nanpei's political machinations brought him into direct conflict with Spanish authorities who arrested him several times, and even threatened him with banishment. In the end, however, they needed his help to broker the 1898 truce among the competing factions. Both local and colonial histories suggest Nanpei also promoted rebellion against German rule in 1910 as a way to weaken his Pohnpeian rivals and to deflect German taxation of his extensive business operations at Rohnkiti that now included a COPRA plantation and the importation of labour from the Mortlocks. A measure of the power he acquired can be found in his assumption of the high chiefly title of '*nanpei*' as his family name. Some believe Nanpei's ultimate political ambition involved the establishment of an island-wide governing council modelled on the US Congress, staffed by mission-trained friends, and with himself as head. Viewed as either the good and holy patron of the Protestant church or as anti-colonial hero, Henry Nanpei actually seems a more complicated, even conflicted man whose activities had a truly significant effect upon the distribution of land and the nature of chiefly power on the island.—DH

Further reading

Howe, K R, 1984/1991. *Where the Waves Fall*, Allen & Unwin.

Scarr, D, 1990. *History of the Pacific Islands: kingdoms of the reefs*, Macmillan.

THREE EUROPEAN VISITORS: FIRST CONTACTS

Europe arriving

> We had nothing to do but to hasten our departure to some different island where our vices were not known, and where our extrinsic virtues might gain us another short space of being wondered at, and doing as we pleased, or as our tars expressed it of being happy by the month.
>
> —*John Ledyard, Hawai'i, February 1779*

The Pacific Ocean's penetration by 16th-century Spanish and Portuguese mariners, uncomfortable beyond their more familiar seas, meant a comparatively late arrival of unweatherly square-rigged ships around the great capes. They were commanded by men whose ability to write meant that passages, landfalls and new experiences were immediately and permanently recorded. In the end, European penetration meant Europe's appropriation of tropical coastlines' trade and eventually of their sovereignty, mitigated in the beginning (outside early-established entrepôts like Guam) by preoccupations in Europe or technical limitations elsewhere.

So the seafaring Dutch with their eyes on foreign trade were frustrated in a projected voyage of Pacific exploration in the 1670s by France's invading armies. Russia's presence on the far northwest Pacific coast was nullified because, until the early 19th century when they came in to retrace the famous passages of voyagers like COOK, Russia was hardly a seafaring nation. China was content to crawl coastwise to Manila in vessels that, to western eyes, looked like tea chests and sailed about as well. And in the end even Spain, some late 18th-century expeditions apart, became so obsessed with the capacity of South America's bullion to command the eastern world's commodities that Spanish seamen were evidently not even veering far enough south from the Acapulco-Manila galleons' post 1565 track to raise the mountains of Hawai'i.

When, as Peter Martyr put it at the time, Vasco Núñez de Balboa first 'scaled the mountains and saluted the ocean' from the Darien peak in 1513, this Mar del Sur was expected to be a mere channel between Darien and Asia, though that Ptolemaic preconception was immediately challenged by the 18-foot tide bringing back the sea for Vasco Núñez to wade in and take possession of for Spain. A very great sea indeed, the 'Spanish lake' revealed itself, in 1520–21, to the crews of Ferñao de Magalhães, alias MAGELLAN, on the 98-day passage from Magellan

Straits to the Philippines via Guam. 'And I believe that never more will any man undertake to make such a voyage,' wrote the voyage's chronicler, Antonio Pigafetta. Pirates followed the Spanish empire, though, including Drake. Among vessels captured by Drake in 1579 was the *Capitana* which Spanish seamen of 1568 had sailed into their Estrella Bay of Santa Ysabel, in the islands they called 'Solomon Islands', before losing them again to Europe for 200 years.

More land was always for the seeking, in the Renaissance world, and more gold. For all the priests who accompanied this and the two later Spanish expeditions into the western Pacific, and the women who went with the intention of founding colonies, they carried men-at-arms. Some of them—said Don Diego de Prado y Tovar, a commander on the final voyage—had lately been begging for alms in the hills behind Callao, sword in hand. Gold was there, on Guadalcanal, in the Louisiades, and in the Highlands of New Guinea which Don Diego was coasting with Luiz Vaéz de Torres in 1606. They parted company in Vanuatu with the main expedition led by the Portuguese Pedro Fernández de Quirós, and made their own way to Manila via Torres Strait, reflecting 'We have found only the black devils with poisoned arrows; what has become of the riches?'.

With 'Santa Ysabel' of the first expedition lost to western charts, the follow-up voyage of 1595 chanced instead upon their Marquesas—and charted them accurately enough for Cook to identify them nearly 200 years later; but came to grief from MALARIA and mutiny at Graciosa bay of their Santa Cruz (Ndeni). The *Almiranta* had sailed on in the night to oblivion on San Cristobal. The *Capitana* staggered with the survivors to Manila and was condemned 'because she was no longer part of this life but a mass of mud, so rotten that it horrified those were here and they saw clearly that God had brought us miraculously aboard her'. Another of this expedition's ships was reported aground on the Luzon coast. Until about 1767 when the frigate *Swallow* chanced upon Tahiti, the Pacific beyond the South American coast was always more present in the European mind than in western experience or charts.

Dutch East Indiamen entering in the 1640s from the east had been using outlines marked with the wandering Solomons, bits of New Guinea coast, enigmatic Tuamotu atolls, and some islands of the western Pacific sighted by Dutch mariners entering in 1615 by Strait Le Maire. Seeking the hypothetical southern continent, the two Dutch ships of the 1640s under Tasman made a 47-day passage to raise their Van Diemen's land, anchor on the New Zealand coast, call at Ata of Tonga, and sojourn at Tongatapu where Polynesian hospitality combined with common prudence to make women available to the strangers. Then they sailed due north through Fiji, amid blinding rain and great apprehension of the supposedly close New Guinea lee shore, before making for Batavia (Jakarta).

In 1675 the Middleburg merchant Arend Roggeveen proposed a further voyage; his son Jacob Roggeveen made it, in his 60s, in 1720–21 and concluded that English buccaneers who had lately spied the southern continent's outlier of 'David Land' had been piratical with truth also. Ranging ahead of the squadron, the shallow-drafted *Afrikaanische Galey* ran up on Takapoto reef in the night. Her alerted consorts 'tacked with all power of sail' to get safely to windward of these wickedly dangerous Tuamotu atolls 'in a stiff reefed topsails' breeze, accompanied by squalls, so that our foretopmast got a crack and the maintopsail tore apart'.

If the ocean was now bulking larger in European strategic thinking (as it was in France where Juan Fernandez was seen as a major potential base) it was linked to trade routes to Asia. In 1764 when Commodore John Byron, RN, sailed with secret orders to find 'Pepys's Island' and take possession of the Falklands as potential keys to the Pacific, the Admiralty's instructions might dwell on national honour but did not fail to mention 'the advancement of the Trade and Navigation' of Britain. 'Let us maintain trade,' the publisher of John Harris's influential *Complete Collection of Voyages and Travels* (1744) wrote, 'and there is no doubt, that Trade will maintain us.' The wonder, then, is not that the rising maritime powers should have sent out so many South Seas exploring expeditions in the 1760s–80s, but that they should have taken so long, and should have waited until the end of the Seven Years' War. Industrializing Britain, with its small domestic market, was export-driven; and La PÉROUSE's voyage in the 1780s had some of its origin in Cook's reports of the northwest Pacific coast's richness in furs.

No influential man's mind in 18th-century Europe was likely to be entirely an island of commerce, even so. Practical geography and natural philosophy held almost obligatory attractions, in the Age of Enlightenment. Moreover, launching all the expeditions into the Pacific ports from British ports in the 1760s and 1770s, culminating in the three under James Cook, probably cost no more than a single ship. And the international concern to compute the distance between earth and sun by observing the transit of Venus across the sun—that event occurring only twice each 113 years which sent Cook in the *Endeavour* to Captain WALLIS of HMS *Swallow*'s chance 1767 landfall of Tahiti—need not preclude the Admiralty's secretly ordering Lieutenant Cook to search once more for the southern continent from a newly available island base.

A base in the deep Pacific was the only way to make the ocean yield to exploration. Even with a base, the Pacific westward from New Caledonia never yielded to Cook, the ocean's most thorough European explorer. He was himself reduced in energy, perhaps in judgment too, by incessant shipboard living and intestinal parasites. Winds that were far from seasonally constant could always baffle square-rigged ships. Even major landmarks could deceive—Eddystone Rock off New Georgia in the Solomons could seriously be mistaken for a full-rigged ship. And though navigation had so improved with the accurate chronometer that *Resolution*'s officers might only be three miles apart in calculating their Dusky Bay landfall between the Cape of Good Hope and New Zealand in 1772, even three miles could be fatal, in thick weather on a dark night. La Pérouse discovered this among the reefs of Vanikoro one cyclonic night of 1788—leaving the explorer of coastal Australia, Captain Matthew Flinders, RN, to stumble on the plantation in Mauritius where La Pérouse had once lived, and reflect—'on this spot he once dwelt, perhaps little known to the world, but happy: when he became celebrated, he ceased to exist'.

An amiably sceptical man, La Pérouse is revealed by his journals, taking wry satisfaction in keeping clear of the cliché of an island paradise Tahiti. He bore testimony to long exposure on deck by predicting that his wife would take him for his grandfather; and like others, he disposed of the current Commerson-cum-Rousseauesque Romantic images of South Sea islanders. At Rapanui, he commented that 'No one who has read the accounts of the most recent travellers could take the South Sea natives for savage; on the contrary they are as corrupted as they can be, given their circumstances'. At the same time La Pérouse would take possession of, say, an island like Maui: 'This European practice is too utterly ridiculous, and philosophers must reflect with some sadness that, because one has muskets and cannon, one looks upon 60 000 inhabitants as worth nothing…'

Despite the intimacy of hammock-and-pillow researches, the Austronesian definite article 'O' went on being misapplied to Tahiti and personal names. Syphilis and gonorrhea followed upon the expression of that passion which, as the Connecticut-born marine, Corporal John Ledyard said as he dismissed common humanity and Cook's rules, with a fine trans-Atlantic republican derision, 'were not against the articles of war, and which like hunger would persuade stone walls'. As to the willing, long-accustomed female partners, on this last voyage of Cook, according to Lieutenant Rickman, those of the Society Islands had each picked out their man on board, for a price—'and those who still had something in reserve led a sad life till they shared it with them'. The Tahitian AHUTORU had left for Europe with Louis Antoine de BOUGAINVILLE in 1768 because he wanted to try out white women.

Pacific realities came to disturb the civil perception of Europe. 'Is it possible that the good Children of Nature can really be so wicked', breathed Jean-Jacques Rousseau, to the second in-command of the ship that was to have returned Ahutoru to Tahiti. (The commander, Marion du Fresne, was killed by New Zealand Maori because, by landing on a beach where Maori corpses had passed, some of his men had broken *tapu*.) Inner worlds ashore were scarcely and rarely fathomable, for all the efforts of *savants* then and now; but these same Maori were, at any rate, self-revealed as cannibals for all the initial scepticism of Cook's astronomer, the schoolmaster from Christ's Hospital, William Wales. At Tongatapu, the TU'I TONGA sat 'with so much sullen and stupid gravity' to Cook's own eye 'that I really took him for an ideot which the people were ready to worship from some superstitious notions'; yet this same Tu'i Tonga was the warrior, Pau, who died in battle in a succession dispute. Nails bought coconuts, fowls and the rest in the Marquesas, until a pig was paid for in red feathers from Fiji via Tongatapu, after which 'red feathers was what they wanted…'. And in the Society Islands too, after 10 or 11 years of steady trading, red feathers were still what 'they esteem of greater value than anything else we could offer then', in Midshipman Gilbert's experience. The initial effect ashore was often one of profound ambivalence, and remained so. 'Tangaroa has sent a ship, which has burst through the sold blue vault', sang the solo singer in a Mangaian song composed by a warrior and the chorus commented, 'A ship full of guests is here. What gibberish they talk!'

Not simply the professionally learned in natural philosophy like Commerson accompanied the 18th-century voyagers, much as priests had accompanied Mendaña and Quirós, and not merely the much-lampooned patron of science, Joseph BANKS, but draughtsmen and painters of genius too. In landings painted at Erromango and Tanna, weapons are levelled and ships may be wreathed in smoke from their great guns, but other figures went down peaceably in crayon and ink, often stylized, sometimes in drapery-folds such as *tapa* never achieved, yet rarely unrecognizable as credible forebears of islanders today. Tu glares, a tattooed Maori thrusts a tongue in defiance, a Vanuatu woman carries her child on her back. Tahitian *va'a* thrust curved prows high in the brilliant luminous paintings of Walter Hodges. Matavai Bay's hills and palms are painted against a recognizable Society Islands sunset. Archbishop Whateley's lecture *On the Origins of Civilisation,* with its theme that the 'liberty enjoyed by the savage consists in being left to plunder and oppress those weaker than himself', in the end was implicitly to enjoy rather wider currency in the islands than anything out of the Romantic Movement, but the ocean was at last recognizably established in European reality as well as in European mind. It had taken nearly 300 years.—DAS

Further reading

Kelly, C (ed.), 1966. *La Austrialia del Espiritu Santo*, Cambridge University Press.

Markham, Sir Clements (ed.), 1904. *Voyages of Pedro Fernandez de Quirós*, Hakluyt Society.

Dunmore, J (ed.), 1981. *The Expedition of the St Jean Baptiste to the Pacific*, Hakluyt Society.

—— (ed.), 1994. *The Journal of Jean-François Galaup de la Pérouse*, Hakluyt Society.

Gallagher, R E, 1964. *Byron's Journal of his Circumnavigation*, Cambridge University Press for Hakluyt Society.

Gilbert, G, 1982. *Captain Cook's Final Voyage: the journal of midshipman George Gilbert*, Christine Holmes (ed.), Caliban.

Ledyard, J, 1963. *Journal of Captain Cook's Last Voyage*, J K Munford (ed.), Oregon State University Press.

Nuttal, Z (tr. and ed.), 1914. *New Light on Drake: a collection of documents relating to his voyage of circumnavigation 1577–1580*, Hakluyt Society.

Pigafetta, A, 1975. *Magellan's Voyage*, Hakluyt Society.

Sharp, A, 1970. *Journal of Jacob Roggeveen*, Oxford University Press.

Spain and Portugal in the Pacific

Portuguese mariners were the first Europeans to venture into the Pacific Ocean, drawing on the inspirational example and navigational knowledge of the Infante Dom Henrique (Prince Henry the Navigator, 1394–1460), and there is some evidence to suggest that they may even have reached Australia's north and east coasts in the 16th century. The Spanish conquistador, Vasco Núñez de Balboa, first set eyes on the Pacific from its eastern shores in 1513, and claimed its islands for Spain. Only eight years later (1519–21), an expedition to cross the Pacific set out with the primary purpose of ascertaining whether the spice-rich Moluccas lay in the Portuguese or Spanish half of the world, as defined by the Treaty of Tordesillas of 1494.

This expedition left Spain under the command of Ferdinand MAGELLAN, sailing from the Strait of Magellan to Guam and the Philippines. After Magellan himself was killed in the Philippines, his ships *Victoria* and *Trinidad* reached the Moluccas. They set off, laden with spices, until the *Trinidad* was found to have sprung a leak, and the *Victoria* returned to Spain alone, reaching Seville in September 1522. Emperor Charles V of Spain was so pleased with its rich cargo that he ordered another expedition to the Moluccas at once, although its departure was delayed until July 1525 while Portugal and Spain argued fruitlessly over the title to those islands. The expedition, comprising seven ships commanded by García Jofre de Loaisa, proved to be one of history's great fiascos. Only the flagship reached the Moluccas, and no spices were obtained. One ship, the caravel SAN LESMES, became the first of Europe's LOST SHIPS in the Pacific. Two others disappeared in sailing from Mexico in 1527 to seek news of the expedition, and contrary winds prevented a third from getting back. Finally, Charles V cut his losses and ceded his claim to the Moluccas to the Portuguese for 350 000 ducats.

In 1543 a Spanish expedition from Mexico under Ruy Lopez de Villalobos sought to re-establish contact with the Philippines and open up trade. It also failed because contrary winds foiled its return to Mexico. The secret of making return voyages was only discovered in the mid 1560s when the expedition of Miguel de Legazpi established a foothold in the Philippines and one of his ships got back to Mexico by sailing far to the north of the then-unknown Hawaiian islands. This set the stage for the famous Spanish galleon trade between Manila and Acapulco which lasted until 1815. From Acapulco, the galleons took silver ingots to the Philippines via GUAM and returned with the luxuries of the Orient for onward shipment to Spain.

Meanwhile, the Spaniards in Peru had heard of islands of great wealth that reputedly lay in the South Pacific. The notion grew that King Solomon's riches had come from these supposed outposts of a great south land. In 1567, Alvaro de Mendaña, with two ships, left Callao to search for them. After about 11 weeks, he came upon several high volcanic islands to which he gave such names as Santa Isabel, San Cristobal and GUADALCANAL. In exploring them, some of his men fancied they found gold and wanted to stay. Mendaña wanted to keep searching for the southern continent. In the end, the poor state of his ships forced him to head for home. Mendaña was given a second chance in 1595 as commander of four ships with many would-be colonists. After discovering the Marquesas Islands, he reached the outliers of those now known as Solomon Islands where one of his ships disappeared in a fog. An attempt was made to establish a settlement on Ndeni (Santa Cruz), but it failed because of hostile islanders, internal dissension, MALARIA, and many deaths, including Mendaña's.

Another ship was also lost as the survivors made for Manila. In December 1605, Pedro Fernández de Quirós, Mendaña's chief pilot in 1595, led a third Spanish expedition from Peru to search for the great south land. He had two ships, a launch and 92 men. Eventually, the expedition reached present-day Vanuatu. With its double chain of islands overlapping each other as far as the eye could see, Quirós felt certain he had found the land he sought. He named it La Austrialia del Espiritu Santo in partial compliment to Mariana of Austria, Spain's queen. On 14 March 1606, at Big Bay in Espiritu Santo, Quirós took possession of all he had found as far south as the South Pole. He planned to build a city, New Jerusalem, but it came to naught. Many of his men became ill through eating poisonous fish and Quirós headed reluctantly for the Americas. His second-in-command, Luiz Vaéz de Torres, whose ship soon became separated from his, made one of the few significant discoveries of this era: the strait between New Guinea and Australia that now bears his name. The north coast of New Guinea had been visited 90 years earlier, by a Portuguese governor of the Moluccas, who called the frizzy-haired people he saw on his involuntary voyage *os papuas*, the source of the name Papua. The excursions of Mendaña, Quirós and Torres marked the end of Spanish exploration for more than 150 years, leaving the way open to the Dutch and the English to enter the 'Spanish lake'.—RL2

Ferdinand Magellan

Ferdinand Magellan, or Ferñao de Magalhães (c1480–1521), Portuguese navigator, was commander of the first European expedition to cross the Pacific. Magellan was born at Sabrosa, Portugal. He served in the East Indies under Affonso de Albuquerque and took part in the capture of Malacca in 1511. When the Portuguese reached the spice-rich Moluccas in 1512, Magellan thought his countrymen might have pushed so far round the world as to have trespassed into the Spanish hemisphere, as defined by Pope Alexander VI in 1494. Back in Portugal in about 1516, Magellan proposed to the king that the matter could be resolved by sailing to the Moluccas by way of South America to see if that was longer or shorter than the African route. Rejected, he renounced his citizenship and put the same proposal to the Spanish monarch, Emperor Charles V. He left Seville in command of five ships and 239 men. After wintering in Patagonia (Argentina), Magellan found the eastern entrance to the strait that now bears his name. Three of his ships passed into the Pacific on 28 November 1520 and began a hungry, 98-day passage across it. On reaching Guam, the expedition sailed to the Philippines where Magellan was killed in an affray. His ship *Victoria* later obtained a cargo of spices in the Moluccas and returned to Spain in September 1522 under a Basque seaman, Juan Sebastian Elcano—the first ship to circumnavigate the globe.—RL2

Further reading

Pigafetta, A, 1969. *The Voyage of Magellan: the journal of Antonio Pigafetta*, P Spurlin Paige (tr.), Prentice-Hall.

Dutch exploration

The Dutch began their explorations into the Pacific in the early 1600s. The religious wars against Spain had sharpened their seafaring skills, and when Spain blocked their trade with southern Europe, they launched a challenge to Spanish supremacy in the Orient. The Dutch East India Company, founded in 1602, became immensely powerful, quickly developing a fleet of 40 warships and 150 merchant vessels. Having taken a firm hold of Indonesia, the Dutch turned towards the Pacific. The journeys of Abel Tasman in 1639 and 1642–44, at the behest of the Governor General of the East Indies, Antoonij van Diemen, was the first significant Dutch venture into the southern Pacific. His discoveries included Tasmania (named Van Diemen's Land), New Zealand (named for a Dutch province), Tongatapu (Amsterdam Island), Nomuka (Rotterdam Island), and he also visited the Fiji Islands, Ontong Java and New Ireland on his way to Batavia (now Jakarta). Another Dutch expedition, 80 years later, was led by Jacob Roggeveen, who set out with three ships, and reached EASTER ISLAND, so named because it was on Easter Day, 5 April 1722. One of the ships, the *Africaanische Galey*, was later wrecked in the Tuamotu Islands, where the survivors became castaways and lived among the islanders.—KRF

Lost ships

In the two and a half centuries from MAGELLAN's entry into the Pacific in 1520 to Captain COOK's advent in 1769, nearly a dozen Spanish ships disappeared on trans-Pacific voyages. Evidence pieced together in recent years suggests that some reached or were wrecked on islands that were then unknown; that their crews took local wives; and that European genes and elements of culture were introduced to those islands long before they appeared on European charts. Deserters and marooned men from early Spanish ships also seem likely to have played such roles. In 1526, the caravel SAN LESMES, one of the Moluccas-bound fleet of the Loaisa expedition, became the first European ship to be lost in the Pacific. Two others in a flotilla of three that were sent from Mexico in 1527 to seeks news of Loaisa's ships in the Moluccas were also lost. They were the caravel *Santiago* (45 men) and the brigantine *Santiago* (15 men) which disappeared in a storm near the Marshall Islands. One or both seem likely to have ended their days at or near Fais or Ulithi in the Western Carolines. The first evidence suggesting this was recorded in 1543, when a Spanish ship arriving at Fais was greeted by men calling out '*Buenos dìas, matelotes*' (Good day, sailors).

In 1569, when an expedition from Peru under Alvaro de Mendaña spent several months in Solomon Islands, several of his men deserted there. On a second expedition in 1595, one of Mendaña's four ships, the frigate *Santa Isabel*, disappeared in a fog near Ndeni in the Santa Cruz group. A second, the frigate *Santa Catalina*, became separated from its companions as they headed northward to Manila following a vain attempt to establish a settlement on Ndeni.

Archaeological evidence found in 1971 indicates that the *Santa Isabel* sailed on to Pamua on San Cristobal and that its crew and passengers camped there for a time. After leaving Pamua, probably for Manila, the *Santa Isabel* may have been wrecked on low-lying Ontong Java Atoll, leaving the survivors to make the best of things with the local Polynesian-speaking people. As for the *Santa Catalina*, which was leaking badly when last seen, its complement seems likely to have been stranded on Pohnpei. Some five generations later, when 30 islanders from the Central Carolines drifted to Guam in two canoes, a Spanish priest wrote: 'The colour of some is like that of pure Indians: there can be no doubt that others are *mestizos*, born of Spaniards and of Indians'. He noted that the islanders' religion seemed to have Biblical elements in it and that they had learned some vague principles of astronomy from a teacher who used a globe to indicate the principal stars so that they would know the rhumb lines to follow at sea. Later European visitors to the Carolines noted similar details, suggesting that early Spanish influence was indeed evident. The galleon trade that was initiated between Mexico and the Philippines in the mid 1560s also produced its quota of lost ships besides 26 men from the galleon *San Jeronimo* who were marooned on Ujelang Atoll, Marshall Islands, in 1566. The first of the lost galleons, name unknown, was lost on a voyage from Acapulco to Manila in 1574. Five east-bound galleons also failed to reach their destination, namely the *San Felipe* (1576), *San Juanillo* (1578), *San Juan* (1586), *Santo Cristo de Burgos* (1693) and *San Francisco Xavier* (1705).

The complement of at least one of the early east-bound galleons seems likely to have ended their days in the Hawaiian islands. When Captain James Cook was there in 1779, some of his officers were convinced that Spanish castaways had preceded them. Three items of material culture suggested this: crested helmets, feather cloaks and small daggers made of iron that were seen among members of the chiefly class. To one officer, the helmets and cloaks were 'a singular deviation' from clothing worn elsewhere in Polynesia. The Hawaiian term for crested helmet, *mahiole*, has no cognates in other Polynesian languages. It seems to be derived from Spanish *morrion*, meaning an open, vizorless helmet such as Roman soldiers wore in Biblical times. Early Spanish missionaries in the Philippines used passion plays with actors portraying Roman soldiers to popularize Christianity. Spanish clerics from an early lost galleon may have introduced 'Roman' helmets and cloaks to Hawai'i with a similar motive.—RL2

Captain James Cook

James Cook (27 October 1728–14 February 1779), British navigator and explorer, was born in Yorkshire and began his seafaring career as an industrious 18-year old apprentice to a shipowner and coal merchant at the port of Whitby. After six years of sailing the North Sea, he was offered the command of a merchant ship but instead volunteered for the Royal Navy at 26. Two years later, during service in the Seven Years War, he earned promotion to ship's master and went in the *Pembroke* to Canada where he carried out the meticulous survey work (spending three years as master of the *Northumberland*) which established his reputation. His precise observations of an eclipse of the sun in 1766 brought him to the attention of the Royal Society.

Captain James Cook: portrait by Nathaniel Dance, c18--?

In 1768 he was sent by the Royal Society and the Admiralty to Tahiti, to observe a transit of Venus, and then to search for the legendary southern continent. His first expedition (1768–71, on the *Endeavour,* with the rank of lieutenant) carried two experienced and talented botanists, Joseph BANKS and Daniel Solander, and the artist Sydney Parkinson. Their detailed reports and drawings, together with Cook's methodical journal entries, provided a wealth of extraordinarily valuable material which heavily influenced the development of trading and settlement in Oceania. As well as circumnavigating New Zealand (and mapping its coastline), Cook employed the services of his interpreter, the Tahitian priest TUPAIA, to communicate with Maori tribes he encountered. He then sailed west to Australia where he named New South Wales, before returning home via Timor and Batavia, where he stopped for repairs.

On his second expedition to the Pacific (1772–75), Cook sailed on the *Resolution* with the rank of commander, accompanied by Tobias Furneaux on the *Adventure*. They travelled south to the Cape of Good Hope and to the ice shelf of Antarctica before eventually turning northeast to the Crozet Islands and then on to New Zealand, reaching the west coast of the South Island in March 1773. In June he set out for the Society Islands and Tonga, returning to New Zealand five months later, and continuing his exploration of the southern Pacific for another six months, this time reaching the Marquesas Islands and Tahiti in April 1774. After voyaging through Tonga, Fiji, New Hebrides and New Caledonia, Cook turned back to New Zealand once more, this time visiting and naming Norfolk Island. His detailed account of this expedition provided clear evidence that the long-sought southern continent did not exist.

His final voyage on the *Resolution*, begun in 1776, was directed at the northern Pacific, in a search for the northwest passage. He joined Charles Clerke in the *Discovery* at Cape Town and they sailed together to Tasmania and then New Zealand. In February 1777 they went north to Cook Islands and Tonga, and called in at Tahiti before visiting Christmas Island and the Hawaiian group, which he named the Sandwich Islands. He then continued east to the northwest coast of North America in March 1778, sailing to Alaska before turning back to Hawai'i. After an extended survey of these islands, he dropped anchor in Kealakekua Bay on 17 January 1779, where he rested for more than two weeks, enjoying the islanders' hospitality. After departing on 4 February, the two ships ran into a storm and had to return to shelter a week later. After two days in the bay, Cook took a landing party to investigate a stolen cutter. On the beach, there was a sudden eruption of violence: Cook and four marines were killed. The expedition then continued on, visiting China before arriving back in England in October 1780. Cook was survived by his wife, Elizabeth, who died in May 1835.—KRF

Further reading

Beaglehole, J C, 1974. *The Life of Captain Cook,* A & C Black.

Daws, G, 1968. 'Kealakekua Bay revisited: a note on the death of Captain Cook', *Journal of Pacific History,* 3.

Obeyesekere, G, 1992. *The Apotheosis of Captain Cook: European myth-making in the Pacific,* Bishop Museum Press.

Sahlins, M, 1981. *Historical Metaphors and Mythical Realities: structure in the early history of the Sandwich Islands kingdom,* University of Michigan Press.

——, 1995. *How 'Natives' Think—about Captain Cook for example,* Chicago University Press.

■ *Death of Captain Cook* Cook, making an enforced return to Kealakekua Bay, was infuriated when the Hawaiians stole a cutter. He attempted to take Kalani'opu'u hostage to get it back. The crowd around Cook and his marines became increasingly threatening. Cook fired his musket, killing one man. The crowd then overwhelmed him. There is no eyewitness account of events on the beach on 14 February 1779. Various expedition members wrote contradictory accounts based on rumour and speculation. Some blamed the marines for not protecting

Cook. Others blamed Cook himself for being too belligerent and firing unnecessarily into the crowd. In Europe, Cook became a secular saint of Enlightenment imperialism. He was deemed to have sacrificed himself by turning his back on the attacking islanders to signal to the marines on a nearby boat to cease fire.

A contrary tradition arose of Cook as evil. He came to his violent end either by the avenging agency of the Almighty, or by retribution of outraged Hawaiians, or both. Central to these explanations was the belief that Cook had allowed himself to be worshipped as the deity Lono by the Hawaiians. This notion was vigorously propounded throughout the 19th century, particularly in church and missionary publications in Hawai'i. In addition to his idolatry, Cook was said to be a fornicator, a blasphemer, and the murderer of the Hawaiian race through the introduction and communication of venereal disease.

The modern study of Cook has its origins in the 1950s. Cook becomes more recognizably human than the symbolically good or evil Cook. J C Beaglehole and others portray Cook on his third voyage as a tired man, sometimes quite ill, and periodically subject to violent outbursts of rage. His death resulted directly from loss of both his temper and judgment on the shores of Kealakekua Bay.

Only recently have historians considered the role of the Hawaiians in Cook's death. Gavan Daws and then Marshall Sahlins have argued that Hawaiians identified Cook as Lono. At a particular time in the *makahiki* cycle, just when Cook returned, Lono had to be ritually sacrificed. In short, given certain times and situations, the Hawaiians were culturally preprogrammed to kill Cook. A contrary view is now offered by Gananath Obeyesekere, who suggests that Cook as the god Lono is a myth fundamentally based on the western idea of the redoubtable European who is a god to savage peoples. Cook was killed not by ritual necessity, but because he acted so violently towards the Hawaiians on that fateful day.—KRH

French exploration, 1768–1815

Although there were various French traders or buccaneers who had sailed the Pacific from the 17th century, it was really Louis de BOUGAINVILLE in 1768 who awakened the ambitions of France in the great ocean. The expedition he led served the policy of a monarchy weakened by defeat in the Seven Years War (1756–63) and the loss of the principal French colonies in America and Asia, but also responded to the demands of its time, those of an Age of Enlightenment fascinated by scientific knowledge for its own sake. For Bougainville, exploring new sea routes, discovering new lands, observing the fauna, flora and exotic human societies, and continuing the quest for a vast southern continent were the main goals. With his voyage, France embarked on a 'quest for knowledge' in the Pacific, along with the English and in the wake of the Dutch, in order to lay the foundations of power and prestige. After Bougainville's triumphant return to France, all the great French expeditions of the end of the century followed the same pattern, and were supported by the state. In 1769 an expedition led by Jean-François-Marie de Surville set out for the Pacific in the *St Jean-Baptiste*. From the Philippines, he sailed into Melanesia and along the coasts of New Zealand, travelling at the same time as COOK, but in the opposite direction. On 18 October 1771 Marc-Joseph Marion du Fresne sailed from Port Louis with AHUTORU, in the *Mascarin* and *Marquis de Castries*. Ahutoru died on the voyage; and du Fresne met his death in New Zealand. These two expeditions were already a grave disappointment to France, but then the major voyage of La PÉROUSE (1785–88) ended in his disappearance, a mystery that was to last 40 years. Étienne Nicolas Marchand claimed a group of islands in the northern Marquesas (1791), and in 1791, still pursuing the dream of a French presence in the Pacific, Louis XIV approved an expedition to search for La Pérouse. Antoine Raymond-Joseph de Bruni d'Entrecasteaux was its leader, on the *Recherche*, accompanied by the *Espérance*, commanded by Huon de Kermadec, and carrying Jacques-Julien Houtou de la Billardière as the principal naturalist. D'Entrecasteaux made several discoveries in the Louisiade Archipelago in 1793, and still later, Nicolas Baudin was sent to explore Tasmania and South Australia in 1801.

Interest in the Pacific remained strong, but France's position was still only tenuous. England had already established itself at the beginning of the 19th century through its presence in Australia, the influence of its missionaries and the boldness of its whalers. The collapse of Napoleon's grand European dream at Waterloo (1815) was a severe blow to the expansionist desires of France. Driven back within its 1791 frontiers, France lost most of its colonies and was relegated to being a fifth-ranking colonial power behind England, Spain, Portugal and the Netherlands.—IM & KRF

Louis Antoine de Bougainville

Louis Antoine de Bougainville (12 November 1729–20 August 1811)—the first French explorer to circumnavigate the earth—was a well-educated nobleman, a fine mathematician and a professional soldier turned naval officer. He set out from Brest in December 1766 in the frigate *La Boudeuse*, meeting up with his supply ship *L'Etoile* in June 1767 at Rio de Janeiro, and sailing into the Pacific in January 1768, where he reached the Tuamotu group, which he named the Dangerous Archipelago, because of their low elevation. In early April, just 10 months after WALLIS, Bougainville reached Tahiti, which he named La Nouvelle Cythère (or New Cythera), where the local chief Ereti allowed them to stay nine days. Bougainville and the botanist/surgeon Philibert Commerson made detailed scientific notes of Tahitian customs, flora and fauna, and when they left the Bourbon Archipelago, Ereti's brother AHUTORU sailed with them. Continuing westwards, the ships reached the New Hebrides in May 1768—recognizing Espiritu Santo from de Quirós' description—and came to the southern coast of New Guinea, which they named the Louisiade Archipelago. They sailed on to the northern Solomon Islands where they named Choiseul (after the Minister of the Navy) and Bougainville.

After 18 days in New Ireland in July 1768, the two ships sailed on to Mauritius and finally separated for the return voyage to France, where Bougainville received widespread acclaim for his exploits. The published accounts of the expedition provided valuable information for increased understanding of the Pacific, although Commerson's romantic view that Tahiti might be the home of Rousseau's NOBLE SAVAGE reinforced stereotypical images of an idealized South Seas paradise. Bougainville later assisted with plans for the expedition of La PÉROUSE and eventually retired with the rank of rear admiral in 1802.—KRF

Further reading

Thiery, M, 1932. *Bougainville, Soldier and Sailor*, Grayson and Grayson.

Wallis and Carteret

Captain Samuel Wallis (1728–95), English explorer, was sent by the Admiralty in 1766 to search for the unknown southern continent. The *Dolphin*, which had been captained by John Byron for the 1764–65 expedition into the Pacific, was accompanied by the cumbersome *Swallow*, commanded by Philip Carteret (1733–96), who had been Byron's first lieutenant. The two ships sailed through the stormy seas of the Magellan Strait before being separated. In the Tuamotu Islands, Wallis collected fresh water and coconuts, then sailed on to the west to reach Tahiti—which he named King George III Island—arriving in Matavai Bay on 18 June 1767. The Tahitians were eager to trade, especially in iron nails which were unknown to them. Wallis spent a month in the area, fixing the position of the island with careful precision, and making notes on the people, vegetation and climate which were later published and widely read, including his misleading identification of the hospitable 'Oberia' (Purea, the wife of the local chief Amo) as a queen. He named Moorea Duke of York's Island, and visited some other nearby islands, before finding two islands in the northern Tongan group (previously sighted by Le Maire), and giving his own name to 'Uvea in the Wallis and Futuna group. He returned to England by passing to the west of the Marshall Islands, then to Batavia and around the Cape of Good Hope, arriving in May 1768.

Carteret had meanwhile searched for 'Davis Land', reported by Edward Davis in 1687, but instead found (and named) Pitcairn Island, and Moruroa (Tuamotu group), and reached the Santa Cruz Islands named by Quirós. The islanders were unwelcoming, and Carteret proceeded northwest into the eastern Solomons—naming the islands he sighted Gower's Island (Ndai), Carteret's Island (Malaita) and Simpson's Island (Manaoba)—and then to Buka (Winchelsea's Island). He sailed through St George's Channel, between New Britain and New Ireland, stopping to carry out repairs to the hull and to take possession of these islands in the name of King George, and then went on to name the Admiralty Islands, and make his way back to England as Wallis had done, via Batavia (Jakarta) and the Cape of Good Hope, arriving in May 1769.—KRF

La Pérouse

Jean-François de Galaup (23 August 1741–June 1788), known as Comte de la Pérouse, made a significant contribution to French exploration of the Pacific. Having joined the French navy in 1756, he served in numerous campaigns during the next 25 years in the long-running wars between France and England. After many months of careful planning and research, he led a major survey expedition into the Pacific with the personal support of King Louis XVI. Sailing from Brest in August 1785 on the *Boussole*, accompanied by the *Astrolabe* under the command of de Langle, they went from Chile in March 1786 to EASTER ISLAND, then to Maui in the Hawaiian group and on to the northwest coast of North America and Alaska. In late September 1786 they sailed from Monterey, California, and crossed the Pacific, discovering Necker Island and French Frigate Shoals and continuing west to Macao. For several months in 1787, they made detailed coastal surveys off Formosa, Korea and Japan, reaching southern Kamchatka in September, where fresh instructions awaited La Pérouse. Now promoted to commodore, he was to sail to Botany Bay where the French had heard that an English colony was to be established.

On reaching the South Pacific, La Pérouse arrived in the Samoan group—the first Europeans to land there—but one of the landing parties was suddenly attacked by islanders and de Langle and 11 men were killed in Tutuila on 11 December. After some further exploration of Samoa and also Tonga, La Pérouse visited NORFOLK Island (where he was unable to land) and at last reached Botany Bay in January 1788, to find that Captain Arthur Phillip's First Fleet had arrived a few days before. On 10 March the two ships set out again, planning to return to Tonga and to visit New Caledonia. The expedition then disappeared, in June 1788, leaving only speculation as to their fate for another 40 years, until some items from their wrecked ships were found in the Santa Cruz Islands of the Solomon group. (DUMONT D'URVILLE visited the little island of Vanikoro in the *Astrolabe* in 1828, and erected a memorial monument to La Pérouse.)

Various reports of their travels and La Pérouse's own journal had already been sent to France, so that their major achievements were documented, even though most of the drawings and natural history materials of the expedition were lost.—KRF

Mutiny on the Bounty

[HMS *Bounty* was a full-rigged ship built in 1783, formerly a coastal trader named Bethia, which was bought and refitted by the British Royal Navy in 1787. The ship sailed from Britain on 23 December 1787, captained by 33-year old Lieutenant William BLIGH and manned by 46 volunteers. After a 10-month voyage to Tahiti and a further wait of five months at Matavai Bay until the proposed cargo of breadfruit trees was ready to be transplanted, the *Bounty* sailed on—until the morning in April 1789 when Fletcher Christian seized the ship. After the mutiny, the *Bounty* was burnt at PITCAIRN Island on 23 January 1790, having been stripped of everything useful. The story of the mutiny is recounted below.—*Editors*]

The mutiny is over. On a calm sea in a launch crowded with 19 men, amid the chaos of clothing, personal belongings and five days' supply of food and water, William Bligh watches the *Bounty* sail off—he presumes, to Tahiti. It is 8.00 am, 28 April 1789. Bligh's ambitions for this voyage had been unbounded. Taking breadfruit to the slave plantations of the West Indies from Tahiti would be a voyage of discovery and science as notable as COOK's, he had hoped.

He turns to the frightened men around him and asks for paper. Peter Hayward, midshipman, gives him his notebook that he used for 'fagging' his navigational calculations. John Smith, Bligh's secretary, searches out some sheets of paper and quill and ink. The mutiny is over and Bligh begins to make history of it. He does not ask the men the cause of his mutiny. He thinks he knows the cause, the lecherous days at Tahiti. The conspiracy of it, that is what he wants to know about. How had it happened without so much as a whisper? The men in the launch had no answer to that question. Mostly that was because there had been no conspiracy to hear of, just spontaneous irresponsible passions built on a welling hatred of Bligh. And anyway, they were as sullen as they were frightened. They nursed their hatreds of Bligh, too.

Even as they sailed towards the white volcanic cloud of the island of Tofua, their first destination, Bligh takes them through a description of every man left on the *Bounty*, 'pirates' now as well as mutineers for stealing the ship. Bligh knows that the Admiralty for all its disinterest in this traders' enterprise will be interested now. Many more lives would be lost, and another ship, the *Pandora*, to bring back to justice the men he was picturing on paper.

Fletcher Christian first of all: 'Fletcher Christian. Aged 24 years. 5ft 9in High. Dark swarthy complexion. Complexion—Dark and Very Swarthy. Hair—Black or very dark Brown. Marks. Star tatowed on his left breast and tatowed on the backside—His knees stands a little out and may be called little bow legged. He is subject to violent perspirations and particularly in his hands so that he soils anything he handles.' There is hatred in that description, too. Christian is disturbing in his clammy-handed presence: he suffered from hyperhydrosis, later dermatologists will say; a breakdown in the sweat regulation mechanisms, likely to be triggered and augmented by emotional disturbance. Christian had always been disturbing, we have to assume, in his long acquaintance and friendship with Bligh. 'I am in hell,' he had said in response to Bligh's reminder on the deck of the *Bounty* that he had held Bligh's children on his knees.

If Bligh was making history in the launch, there was not much history being made on the *Bounty* itself; although two of the midshipmen, George Stewart and Peter Heywood, continued their midshipmen chores in keeping a journal. There had been some budding authors among the mutineers, too, hoping to market their South Seas experience. What happened to their efforts is not known. All papers were destroyed with the disappearance of the *Bounty* and the sinking of the *Pandora*, the vessel that came to catch them. But memories were good and James Morrison, the bos'un, would provide one of the most brilliant of all beachcomber manuscripts when he put on paper what happened to them on the *Bounty* and during their Tahitian stay. He wrote it all down when he had recovered from the trauma of his trial, his sentencing to death and the King's Mercy he earned. The manuscript was not published for 150 years. But the rumours of what was in this other history of the mutiny did Bligh great harm.

Bligh had his history well honed by the time of his return to England, 14 March 1790. Much was said at the time, and ever since, about his remarkable navigational skills in getting the launch from Tofua to Timor. One man had been killed by the islanders at Tofua. Four would die after the horrendous voyage. Their stay with the Dutch in Timor and Batavia was worse, if anything, than the rigours of the launch. It was filled with rancour and conflict as they looked accusingly at one another for the real cause of their sufferings. Bligh left them to go ahead to tell his story.

That story, *Narrative of a Mutiny*, was a bestseller by July. The theatre of his mutiny began even before that. By May, the Theatre Royal was producing a 'Fact, told in Action, called the Pirates Or, The Calamities of Capt. Bligh'. It included somewhat irrelevantly but for prurience's sake 'dances and ceremonies of the Hottentots'. Hottentot genitalia were of as much curiosity at the time as Tahitian sexual practices. The history of the mutiny on the *Bounty* began to be laced with soft pornography as authors raked the accounts of the voyages of discovery for colour and context.

The theatre of the stage had to bow to the theatre of the courts when the 14 men found at Tahiti by Captain Edwards of the *Pandora* were brought back for trial—or rather the 14 reduced to 10 by the sinking of the *Pandora*. Six would be condemned to death. Three were hanged from the yard of HMS *Brunswick* on the morning of 29 October 1792. Two won King's Mercy. One escaped on a legal technicality. Their trial was of national interest. By now the Revolution in France had shown how fragile institutions of power were. It was clear, and the prisoners were told as much when they arrived in England, that someone needed to die for the mutiny, no matter what their guilt.

The man really on trial, but not there, Fletcher Christian, had family and friends who had standing high enough in society to be sensitive to the stigma of the mutiny. Three bishops, a lord chief justice, a high sheriff, two members of parliament and a professor of law belonged to the Christian family, all connected to a long line of the Deemsters of the Isle of Man. Fletcher's friends, William Wordsworth among them, chaplains in the King's court, too, and other gentlemen of liberal belief had no time for a venture like the *Bounty* which seemed to abet slavery. So, if the theatre in the court demanded bloody justice, there was also a theatre of rumour and gossip that did no good for William Bligh. Even his naval colleagues believed that if there was a gentleman on the *Bounty*, it was not William Bligh. They would fete and promote the condemned but saved midshipman Peter Heywood, who had become, in the absence of Christian, the object of Bligh's rage.

Christian's own venture, meanwhile, had left a trail of blood and suffering all over the Pacific as he tried to satisfy his and his men's lust for women, meat and the good life. When a first settlement failed on Tubuai and the mutineers had killed more than 100 islanders in their unsuccessful effort to get women, Christian allowed those who wanted to return to Tahiti so long as he could have the *Bounty*. Then with eight of the core mutineers, 13 kidnapped Tahitian women and six islander men as slaves, Christian roamed the western Pacific looking for a suitable island. Finally, out of Bligh's Great Cabin library of books of discovery, he decided on Pitcairn across to the far east of the Pacific. A high island, deserted of its native population, but supplied with the subsistent vegetation that they had transported there, with no port, Pitcairn seemed ideal.

After four years of cruel treatment, the native slave men revolted and killed five of the mutineers, Christian among them. The four remaining mutineers then murdered the native men. Then in the next few years one mutineer was murdered for all their safety's sake. One committed suicide in an alchoholic madness. One died peacefully of asthma. The last, John Adams, living patriarchally with all the women and children of these early years, had a vision of Michael the Archangel and found God. He created a fundamentalist theocracy. The British navy finally found them in this blessed state in 1815. Pitcairn, then, for most of the 19th century became a living parable of Good triumphing over Evil. But there was pain in being the world's parable. The Pitcairnese were subject to a charity that declared they must leave their island for their own good. They suffered a cruel and disastrous diaspora to Tahiti. They returned to Pitcairn only by selling their sole capital, the metal they had rescued by diving to the sunken *Bounty*.

The theatre of the mutiny on the *Bounty* has been constant since the first news of it. Aquaballets, pantomimes, operettas, bogus letters from the absent Christian, novels—every form of dramatisation multiplied in the first few years. Samuel Coleridge, an acquaintance of the Christians, seemed to make a parable of Fletcher's dilemmas in *The Rime of the Ancient Mariner*. Lord Byron, an enemy of Coleridge, wrote *The Island* in praise of Bligh. The first of the histories, Sir John Barrow's *The Eventful History of the Mutiny and Piratical Seizure of HMS Bounty; its causes and consequences* appeared in 1831. Barrow was an acquaintance of the Heywood family and a secretary of the Admiralty. He had access to the manuscript of James Morrison that had quietly been suppressed by the navy. He thought along Admiralty lines: a captain made his own mutiny. In Bligh's case, this was because he lacked the natural authority of a gentleman.

Bligh, the 'Bounty Bastard', had other mutinies—in the launch itself, another at Great Nore, and the 'Rum Rebellion' in New South Wales. There is no evidence among his contemporaries to suggest that he had these four mutinies because of his violence. What offended his contemporaries, especially those of officer class, was his verbal abuse and aggressive gestures. And if statistics of floggings are some measure, he was the least violent British naval captain in the Pacific in the late 18th and early 19th centuries. The 'Captain Bligh' of our 20th century imagination does not come from history.

Our 'Captain Bligh' cliché comes from films. There have been five 'Mutiny on the Bounty' films: a 1916 silent movie directed by the Australian film pioneer, Raymond Longford; Charles Chauvel's 1932 docu-drama, *In The Wake of the Bounty*; the 1935 Metro-Goldwyn-Mayer classic, starring Charles Laughton and Clark Gable; Marlon Brando's and Trevor Howard's version of 1962; and Anthony Hopkins' and Mel Gibson's version of 1984. Film critics tend to rate only the 1935 version as historical. All the others have been deemed unhistorical because they omitted what the 1935 version invented. Our image of 'Captain Bligh' as the sadistic, almost pathologically violent man who flogged his men mercilessly, masted them, gagged them, keelhauled them, tortured them in irons comes from Charles Laughton's brilliant performance. How we have made a cliché of this film is a complex story, involving not just the script but the whole of Hollywood film culture. But there is a historiography in film, too. Brando makes the mutiny a struggle between a foppish dilettante and a populist captain, because he learned that Bligh was not a gentleman. Mel Gibson and Anthony Hopkins play out a broken homosexual relationship because a late 20th century narrative must open up the psyche.

There has been a *Bounty* musical, a television serial farce about 'Captain Bligh'. There are robotic re-enactments of the mutiny in museums. One can sail at dinner-time on a reconstructed *Bounty* around Sydney Harbour. The theatre of the *Bounty* has had its bicentenary. There is no indication that it has ended.—GD

William Bligh

Vice Admiral William Bligh (1754–1817), born in Cornwall, joined the Royal Navy and was with Captain James COOK on the second expedition (on the *Resolution*, 1772–74), which called at Tahiti. Later he served with Lord Howe, before being sent in command of the ill-fated voyage which ended in the MUTINY ON THE BOUNTY. With 18 companions, he survived the 5800 km journey in the ship's launch to Timor, returning to England in 1790. Exonerated in court-martial proceedings brought by the Admiralty, he resumed his naval career, but experienced a second mutiny, on the *Director* in 1797, during protest strike action involving several British ships. He took part in naval engagements against the Dutch, and won commendation in the battle of Copenhagen in 1801, but in 1805 he was reprimanded in court-martial proceedings for abusive language to a junior officer. Appointed in 1806 as Governor of New South Wales, he was overwhelmed and imprisoned by mutineers in 1808, and returned to Britain in 1810 to become a rear admiral and then in 1814, vice admiral.—KRF

Louis-Claude de Freycinet

Louis-Claude Desaulses de Freycinet (1779–1842), navigator and scientist, enrolled at 14 in the French navy with his older brother Henri and was a sub-lieutenant at 17. In July 1800 the two brothers were commissioned to take part in a voyage led by Captain Nicholas Baudin, which carried out a reconnaissance of the southwest coast of 'New Holland' (Australia) in the *Géographe* and the *Naturaliste*, and explored 'Van Diemen's Land' (Tasmania) six months later. In Sydney, Louis de Freycinet was given command of a light schooner, *Casuarina*, and completed a detailed geographic investigation of the Tasmanian coast and offshore islands. He later edited the account of the Baudin expedition, published as *L'Histoire du Voyage aux Terres Australes*. In

1817 he led a new expedition, on the *Uranie*, this time commissioned to investigate the customs, habits and languages of indigenous peoples, and taking Louis-Isidore Duperrey (1786–1865) as his surveyor. The ship called at several islands off Papua and in the Bismarck Archipelago, went on to the Admiralty Islands and the Carolines, and reached Guam in March 1819. Freycinet spent three months in the Marianas group, noting his observations on the language and culture of the inhabitants, and recording details of history and trading patterns. The expedition continued to Hawai'i and then turned south to the eastern islands of Samoa in October, and to Cook Islands. After this he sailed west, to Lord Howe Island and Sydney, spending a month in New South Wales before resuming the homeward journey across the southern Pacific. Although a shipwreck in the Falkland Islands ended the *Uranie*'s voyage, Freycinet returned safely to France in November 1820. Over many years he edited the official account of the findings of the expedition, the final sections being published after his death, but his wife Rose also kept a detailed journal of the three-year voyage (which she had joined as a stowaway) and it was published separately much later, in 1927. One of the founding members of the Geographical Society in 1821, Freycinet was admitted to the Academy of Sciences in 1826 and was a member of many other French and international scientific societies.—KRF

Further reading

Freycinet, R, 1996. *A Woman of Courage: the journal of Rose de Freycinet on her voyage around the world*, tr. S Rivière, National Library of Australia.

La Roquette, 1843. 'Historical notes on M M Henri and Louis de Freycinet', in *Bulletin de la Société de Géographie*, 2(20), Arthur Bertrand.

Dumont d'Urville

Jules Sébastien César Dumont d'Urville (23 May 1790–8 May 1842), French scientist and explorer of the Pacific, was born in Normandy. He joined the navy at 17 and pursued further botanical and language studies, eventually gaining a position as second-in-command and official botanist of Louis-Isidore Duperrey's expedition into the Pacific on the *Coquille* (1822–25) which visited the Tuamotus, Tahiti, Bora Bora, Niue, Solomon Islands, New Ireland, the Carolines, New Guinea and Java, before returning to France via Mauritius. The detailed scientific publications from the voyage included three botanical volumes in which Dumont d'Urville collaborated. A year later, he was appointed to lead a fresh expedition—on the *Coquille*, now renamed *L'Astrolabe*—when he was 35. They reached western Australia in October 1826, then Sydney in early December, before crossing the Tasman to New Zealand. After 10 weeks of scientific investigations, the expedition moved on to the Kermadec Islands and Tonga, then to the Fiji Islands, New Hebrides, Loyalty Islands, Papua New Guinea, and from there to the Dutch East Indies and south again to Hobart. Here Dumont d'Urville at last received news of a possible discovery by the Irish trader, Peter Dillon, of items relating to the disappearance of La PÉROUSE. He sailed for Tikopia and was guided to Vanikoro, in the Santa Cruz group, where he found anchors and cannon in shallow waters, and erected a memorial monument to the La Pérouse expedition on 14 March 1828. The *Astrolabe* returned to France on 25 March 1829, and Dumont d'Urville, now promoted to captain, devoted himself to publishing the many volumes of official and scientific reports of the voyage. His final voyage into the Pacific (1838–40) took him into the Antarctic as well as through the Polynesian islands once more. This time promoted to flag rank, he was beginning to be recognized for his scientific achievements when he was killed in a train crash near Versailles, 18 months after his return to France.—KRF

United States exploring expedition

This first major American government-funded exploration of the Pacific (1838–42), was a fleet of six US Navy vessels under the command of Lieutenant Charles Wilkes, which visited the Tuamotus, Samoa, Hawai'i, Tonga, Fiji, Tuvalu, Kiribati and Wake Island. A highly productive scientific and diplomatic success, the far-ranging voyage charted coasts and collected vast quantities of scientific information, including the first descriptions of Samoan flora and fauna. One of the expedition ships, the barque *Flora*, a supply vessel, transported the missionary Hiram BINGHAM and his family from Hawai'i back to the United States in 1840.—KRF

Further reading

Badger, G, 1988. *The Explorers of the Pacific*, Kangaroo Press.

Barclay, G, 1978. *A History of the Pacific*, Sidgwick and Jackson.

Dunmore, J, 1992. *Who's Who in Pacific Navigation*, Melbourne University Press.

——, 1997. *Visions and Realities: France in the Pacific 1695–1995*, Heritage Press.

The noble savage

French Enlightenment thinkers like Jean-Jacques Rousseau and Denis DIDEROT developed and promoted the idea that 'primitive' people from North America and the Pacific had certain noble qualities despite being 'savages', because they were as yet uncorrupted by the material vices of western civilization. Hence, some explorers of the Pacific, notably Louis de BOUGAINVILLE, expected to find people who still had qualities that Europeans had lost. When Bougainville reached Tahiti in 1768, indigenous leaders had already developed a strategy for 'taming' foreign warships by sending out women to offer themselves to European sailors. He and his crew were entranced by the 'paradise' they saw, where everyone supposedly loved freely, shared everything and fought no wars.

Several early European visitors to the Pacific kidnapped individual islanders whom they encountered or invited them to accompany them to other islands or even to Europe. Bougainville took AHUTORU to Paris, and COOK took OMAI to London, where he was taken to meet King George III. Such travellers were often ennobled in European eyes even when they lacked status in their own community (and indeed, they were sometimes sent along by their chiefs because they were considered expendable). When Omai was returned home, his status quickly diminished because he was of low rank in Tahitian society. 'Lee BOO' of Palau enjoyed favoured treatment but died of disease, as did Ahutoru. TUPAIA of Ra'iatea, a priestly navigator, helped Cook communicate with the Maori of Aotearoa/New Zealand, but he died on Java. Half a century later the Maori chief Hongi HIKA met King George IV in London and received prestigious gifts, including a double-barrelled shotgun and a suit of armour he used in wars back home. To an extent, these 'specimens' opened European minds to other ways of life, though their hosts usually measured their humanity by their ability to adopt European manners.—DC

■ *Ahutoru* Ahutoru, or Aoutourou (c1750–November 1771), the first Tahitian to visit Europe, was a brother of one of the chiefs on Tahiti who welcomed the French captain BOUGAINVILLE in April 1768. Keenly interested in the expedition and quick to acquire some French, the young Ahutoru was able to tell Bougainville of the visit by Samuel WALLIS several months before. Bougainville agreed to take him to visit France, and soon found him a valuable source of information and a useful interpreter. Creating a sensation in Parisian society in 1769, Ahutoru was widely seen as the embodiment of the NOBLE SAVAGE from a tropical paradise. In October 1771 Marion du Fresne sailed out of Port Louis with the *Mascarin* and the *Marquis de Castres*, one of the main purposes of the voyage being to return Ahutoru to Tahiti. They took on supplies in Madagascar, but Ahutoru had contracted smallpox in Mauritius, and died three weeks after the ship sailed.—KRF

■ *Omai* Omai, or Mai (c1753–c1780), went from Ra'iatea to Tahiti after his father died in battle. He witnessed the visit of WALLIS to Matavai Bay in June 1767, and was present when James COOK arrived in April 1769—the voyage on which the priest TUPAIA, also from Ra'iatea, sailed but failed to survive. When Cook returned to Matavai Bay in August 1773, he took a young man from Borabora, Odiddy (Hitihiti, of chiefly birth, who had a young servant), on board the *Resolution*, and Omai sailed with Captain Furneaux on the *Adventure*. In Tonga, neither young man could translate for Cook as Tupaia had, and when the two ships later separated, Odiddy was returned to Ra'iatea. Omai continued the voyage, as an able seaman ('Tetuby Homy' on the crew list).

In London in July 1774, Omai was cared for by Joseph BANKS, whom he knew from his Tahitian visit, and to whom he could speak in Tahitian. Introduced into society and taken to meet the king and queen, Omai's polite behaviour and smart clothing made a generally favourable impression. After the precaution of a smallpox vaccination, he was taken everywhere—to concerts, dances, theatre, opera, dinner parties, the House of Lords. He was painted by Joshua Reynolds, went horse riding and ice skat-

Omai: detail of portrait by Joshua Reynolds, 1774

ing, took English lessons, and wandered freely around London. On occasion, he made a Polynesian 'earth oven' to roast food for his hosts. Two years after his arrival, Omai said goodbye to the king and sailed with Cook on the *Resolution*. In New Zealand, they were joined by a young Maori named 'Tiarooa' and his servant. The ship then visited Cook Islands and Tonga, where Omai acted as interpreter, and finally reached Tahiti in August 1777. Cook, observing no welcome among Omai's relatives, offered valued red feathers and other gifts. He took Omai to Huahine, and prepared a house, garden and vineyard for him at Fare Bay, leaving several animals including two horses. The two young New Zealanders and some of the Tahitian crew stayed too. Omai's gifts from England included a suit of armour, a musket and several swords. No news of Omai's fate was known for 10 years, until, on the visit of the BOUNTY in October 1788, Captain William BLIGH was told that Omai and the two New Zealanders had died of illness about 30 months after Cook's departure.—KRF

Further reading

McCormick, E H, 1977. *Omai: Pacific envoy*, Auckland University Press/Oxford University Press.

■ *Lee Boo* Lee Boo (c1764–27 December 1784) was the son of the high-ranking chief or *rubak*, Abba Thulle, of Palau. After the *Antelope* commanded by Captain Henry Wilson was wrecked on reefs at Palau in 1783, on a voyage to China for the East India Company, Abba Thulle supplied the English sea trader with food while a new vessel was built, named *Oroolong* after the island on which they had found shelter. When they left on 12 November 1783, the king permitted his son and a servant to accompany them. After reaching Macao, Lee Boo spent several days in Canton before he and Captain Wilson joined another ship, the *Morse*, and arrived in Portsmouth on 14 July 1784. The Wilson family took him into their home in London, where he attended school for several months and took part in a range of social events and activities. Before arrangements could be made for his return to Palau, however, he succumbed to smallpox and died, being buried in St Mary's churchyard in London.—KRF

Further reading

Peacock, D J, 1987. *Lee Boo of Belau: a prince in London*, University of Hawai'i Press.

■ *Ruatara* Ruatara (c1787–1815), a chief of the Ngapuhi of northern New Zealand, spent several years on European ships before setting out in 1805 with the intention of calling on King George III in Britain. In Sydney he made the acquaintance of Governor Philip King and Reverend Samuel MARSDEN, and eventually reached London in 1809, although he was prevented from leaving the ship and completing his mission. Another ship brought him back to Sydney, where he then stayed several months at Parramatta, studying agriculture and improving his English. Having returned home at last in 1812 (by then in his mid 20s), he was able to put his agricultural lessons into effect and to demonstrate his knowledge of growing vegetables and wheat, and grinding flour. Having helped Marsden set up his New Zealand mission at the Bay of Islands in 1814—in Ruatara's own village of Rangihoua—he became the translator of Marsden's sermons and supervisor of all transactions between the missionary settlement and Maori, until his premature death.—KRF

Further reading

Belich J, 1996. *Making Peoples*, Allen Lane.

Scientists and observers

■ *Denis Diderot* Denis Diderot (1713–84), a French philosopher and encyclopedist, never visited the Pacific but wrote an influential commentary on Pacific and European society and their entanglement. His *Supplement au voyage de Bougainville* was written in 1772 and extensively read and debated, although not published until 1796. Using the journal of Louis de BOUGAINVILLE's 13-day visit in 1768 to Tahiti, Diderot constructed a series of dialogues between a Tahitian and Frenchman on free society, sexual liberty, corruption and the universality of nature. Diderot's noble islander, the simple savage, challenged the complicated, mechanized civilization of the European. Diderot borrowed from his friend Jean-Jacques Rousseau the idea of the 'good savage' and so was born two long-lived European conceptualizations of the Pacific—of the NOBLE SAVAGE and of FATAL IMPACT. Diderot's warning to the Pacific about encroaching European civilization, missionaries and rulers, that 'one day they will come with crucifix in one hand and dagger in the other to cut your throats or to force you to accept their customs and opinions; one day under their rule you will almost be as unhappy as they are,' is still quoted. Diderot also wrote a critical essay about Spanish colonial conquests and met the Tahitian AHUTORU in Paris. Although the *Supplement* was his one literary contribution, his name and ideas have a long association with the European imaging of the Pacific.—MQ

■ *Joseph Banks* Joseph Banks (1743–1820), botanist and administrator-entrepreneur-patron of the sciences, grew up at his family's extensive estate in Lincolnshire. Educated at Harrow, Eton and Oxford, he did not take a degree, preferring private tutoring in botany to the traditional education in the classics. While botany was the focus of his most intense scientific activities, Banks was neither an important botanical theorist nor a prominent taxonomist. Rather, botany was his stimulus for the larger scientific enterprises that marked his career; and his generous spirit and considerable private wealth as a member of the landed gentry made these enterprises not only possible but often sumptuous.

Banks established his position in the world of science initially as a voyager. His first expedition (1766) was to Labrador and Newfoundland, an experience that secured him both a fellowship in the Royal Society and the beginnings of his famous herbarium. Two years later he assembled and funded the scientific party that accompanied COOK's first voyage to the Pacific, aboard HMS *Endeavour*. With the assistance of the Linnaeus-trained botanist Daniel Solander, the artist Sydney Parkinson and others, Banks accumulated 30 000 specimens, including possibly 1400 new species, plus thousands of illustrations, during this three-year voyage to Tahiti, Australia and New Zealand. His ethnographic interests were sharpened by numerous encounters with Pacific islanders.

Joseph Banks, c1789, engraving by Joseph Collyer

The *Endeavour* voyage established Banks' reputation as a naturalist and ensured the support of those in high places, including King George III, through whom Banks worked to convert Kew Gardens into a botanical research institution. The voyage also supplied the initial stimulus for many of his non-scientific enterprises. His exploration of Botany Bay convinced him that Australia would be suitable for British colonization, especially by long-term convicts, and the plan he promoted for colonization was put into effect in 1788. He also took a keen interest in establishing economically important plants and animals outside their native range.

Banks' final voyage was to Iceland briefly in 1772. Thereafter his attention was focused principally on the London scientific community. As president of the Royal Society for an unprecedented 41 years, Banks earned his greatest fame, serving in office from 1778, aged only 35, until his death at 77. He patronized aspiring scientists and explorers, and his house in Soho Square became a mecca for informal scientific gatherings. Neither the productivity of London science nor the percentage of scientists among Fellows of the Royal Society improved substantially in his time, but he fostered a close international network of scientists, ensuring the exchange of scientific publications, especially during the American Revolution and Napoleonic Wars.

Banks was made a baronet in 1781 and knighted in 1795. Upon his death the remarkable Banksian collections passed first to his librarian, Robert Brown, botanist and veteran of Matthew Flinders' voyage, and thence to the British Museum where they became a foundation of the natural history collections.—PFR

Further reading

Carter, H B, 1988. *Sir Joseph Banks, 1743–1820*, British Museum.

Gascoigne, J, 1994. *Joseph Banks and the English Enlightenment: useful knowledge and polite culture*, Cambridge University Press.

■ ***Adelbert von Chamisso*** Adelbert von Chamisso (1781–1838) was a botanist, poet and writer whose studies and travels provide historical and scientific insights into the South Pacific. Born in France as Louis Charles Adélaïde de Chamisso de Boncourt, he and his family were driven into exile in 1792, in the wake of the Revolution. He became an accomplished linguist, living and reading widely in two languages, and achieving renown in his lifetime for his German poetry. After 10 unhappy years in the Prussian army, he was discharged with the rank of lieutenant in 1808 and returned to more literary pursuits. He later studied botany and medicine, and published a fairy tale, *Peter Schlemihls*, in 1814. Then in 1815, torn between France and Germany by the Napoleonic wars, Chamisso took part in a three-year Russian scientific expedition on the *Rurik* to the Pacific and Arctic, under the leadership of Otto von Kotzebue, aiming to explore a northern passage.

They travelled west from South America, visited Easter Island, and spent two months in the Marshall Islands—'gardens of bliss'—where Chamisso saw 'pure and uncorrupted customs, gracefulness and delicacy, and the lovely blossom of modesty'. Here he met Kadu, from the Ulea island group in the Caroline Islands, who became his friend and informant, accompanying Chamisso to the north and Hawai'i. Drawing on his knowledge of oral traditions and songs in various languages, Kadu provided answers to many geographical, linguistic and ethnological questions.

In Hawai'i, Chamisso perceived that trade-induced and foreign intrigues cleverly exploited old regional quarrels between rulers. He noted that the wealth and dominance of KAMEHAMEHA I came from the SANDALWOOD TRADE, 'while the oppressed people who are obliged to gather it, withdrawn from their agriculture and their arts, are becoming impoverished'. Chamisso recognized the onset of colonial monoculture and its consequences, portraying a society in transition.

Chamisso returned to Berlin with a rich harvest of experiences, ideas and a herbarium of 2500 plant species. His initial 'Notes and Opinions' on the three-year voyage were published as part of Kotzebue's record of the expedition, but Chamisso was not impressed with this official version and felt the need to refine and develop his observations into a longer narrative, as a 'journal' of his earlier travels. This major work, finally published as *Voyage Around the World (Reise um die Welt)* in 1836, combined botany, zoology, geology, geography, climatology, linguistics, ethnology and socio-political, religious and historical aspects, and wove these elements into a comparative analysis of human history. In this, he insisted that it was contact with Europe that led Pacific societies into the cultural decline and immorality that he had seen in Hawai'i. His botanical articles appeared in a number of scholarly journals, and in 1837 he presented a paper 'On the Hawaiian Language' to the Berlin Academy of Science.—HS

Further reading

Schutte, H, 1995. 'Adelbert von Chamisso and the South Pacific', in A Talu and M Quanchi (eds), *Messy Entanglements: the papers of the 10th Pacific History Association Conference, Tarawa, Kiribati*, Pacific History Association.

von Chamisso, A, 1986. *A Voyage Around the World with the Romanzov Exploring Expedition in the Years 1815–1818*, tr. and ed. Henry Kratz, University of Hawai'i Press.

■ ***Lajos Biro*** Lajos Biro (1856–1931), a little-known but respected Hungarian ornithologist, entomologist, collector and photographer, travelled widely in German New Guinea 1896–1902. His frank commentary and annotated photographs of New Guineans and Europeans in the early phase of colonial contact mark him as an unusual and perceptive observer. His reputation rests not on ethnography nor on two popular works and numerous articles in Hungarian, but on the several thousand ethnological objects and 200 000 natural history specimens in European museums he sent back from New Guinea. More than 200 species and genera have been named after him. Biro's voluminous notes, published articles on natural history and photographs have recently recaptured scholars' attention.—MQ

■ ***T J McMahon*** Thomas John McMahon (1864–1933), Australian journalist, author and photographer, published several hundred illustrated articles and a thousand photographs of the western and central Pacific in a prolific decade of travelling and writing. A journalist before going to Papua in 1915, he then toured the Pacific promoting European economic development, tourism and Australian colonialism in the region. In 1924, disappointed at not achieving fame and honours, he returned to Brisbane as a minor journalist and photographer on a city newspaper. His writing was undistinguished and rarely focused on the peoples of the Pacific, but his excellent photography captured the early days of the colonial era and forms an important record of early 20th century European activity.—MQ

■ ***Bronislaw Malinowski*** Bronislaw Kasper Malinowski (1884–1942), a Polish-born social anthropologist, dominated the discipline in Britain between the wars. He was a direct successor of the pioneering generation of British anthropologists (comprising Haddon, SELIGMAN and RIVERS, all veterans of the Cambridge Torres Strait Expedition) who began comparative studies of Melanesian societies. Malinowski studied mathematics, physics and chemistry at the Jagellionian University in Cracow (where he was awarded a PhD in 1908) and at the University of Leipzig. In 1910 in London, he studied ethnology and primitive sociology under C G Seligman and E Westermarck, and in 1914 travelled to Australia to attend the meetings of the British Association for the Advancement of Science. At the outbreak of war he was permitted to do fieldwork in Papua, though as an Austrian citizen he was technically an 'enemy alien' and liable to be interned. After brief survey-type fieldwork in Mailu on the south coast of Papua (resulting in *The Natives of Mailu*, 1915), Malinowski spent two lengthy periods in the Trobriand Islands between 1915 and 1918. His extraordinary gift for languages enabled him to master the vernacular, and the unprecedented depth and thoroughness of his investigations gave birth to the legend of Malinowski the consummate fieldworker. Prolonged, intensive fieldwork involving 'participant observation' was to become the hallmark of British social anthropology. Malinowski returned to teach in London in the early 1920s and in 1927 was appointed Professor of Social Anthropology at the London School of Economics, where his socratic seminars became famous. In a series of compelling monographs on ceremonial exchange (*Argonauts of the Western Pacific*, 1922); primitive law (*Crime and Custom in Savage Society*, 1926); courtship, marriage and family (*The Sexual Life of Savages*, 1929); horticulture, land tenure and the language of magic (*Coral Gardens and their Magic*, 1935), Malinowski examined many aspects of Trobriand life. These islanders remain among the best-known peoples in world ethnographic literature. Although the exigencies of funding obliged Malinowski to turn his attention to Africa during the 1930s, a number of his pupils also worked in the western Pacific: notably, Raymond Firth, Camilla WEDGWOOD, Reo Fortune, Ian Hogbin and Phyllis Kaberry. In 1938 Malinowski went to America, and later took a Chair at Yale. He died as he was about to embark on his third fieldtrip to Mexico.—MWY

Further reading

Malinowski, B K, 1929. *The Sexual Life of Savages in North-Western Melanesia*, Routledge and Kegan Paul.

■ *W H R Rivers* William Halse Rivers Rivers (1864–1922) was a pivotal figure in the emergence of modern anthropology. As a leading physiologist and psychologist, he was recruited by Alfred Cort Haddon to join the Cambridge Anthropological Expedition to Torres Strait (1898). Fascinated by Torres Strait islanders, his interests were radically reoriented. He began to address anthropological questions, and periods of 'survey fieldwork' in India and in Solomon Islands enabled him to initiate the modern study of kinship, as well as contributing to the more speculative field of culture history. Rivers was equally struck by the extent of DEPOPULATION in the islands of Melanesia, and marshalled anthropologists, missionaries and colonial officials to account for it and especially to reverse it.

Rivers' reputation suffered after his premature death, the intensive fieldwork methods of MALINOWSKI, and the obsolescence of culture history and the depopulation panic. He merits attention, however, as an exemplar of a relatively innocent era when anthropologists and missionaries were on friendly terms, and fieldworkers allowed their agendas to be shaped by islander informants.—DD

■ *C G Seligman* Charles Gabriel Seligman (1873–1940) trained in London as a physician. His interest in tropical medicine led Alfred Cort Haddon to include him in the Cambridge Anthropological Expedition to Torres Strait (1898). During that expedition Seligman (like RIVERS) found his medical enthusiasms overwhelmed by anthropological questions. In 1904 Seligman persuaded an American philanthropist to finance a research trip to British New Guinea, which gave rise to the compendious survey, *The Melanesians of British New Guinea* (1910). Seligman's survey methods were soon eclipsed by MALINOWSKI's intensive methods, and Seligman's work is now rarely cited. In his own time however, his work gave some social shape and substance to the previously pejorative term 'Melanesian'.—DD

Further reading

Kuper, A, 1973. *Anthropologists and Anthropology: the British School 1922–1972*, Allen Lane.

Slobodin, R, 1978. *W H R Rivers*, Columbia University Press.

■ *Sir Peter Buck (Te Rangi Hiroa)* Peter Buck (c1880–1951), New Zealand doctor, anthropologist, politician, administrator and soldier, established an international reputation for his ethnological work on Polynesia. Born at Urenui to an Irish father and Maori mother, of Ngati Mutunga of Taranaki, he took the name Te Rangi Hiroa as a young man and frequently used it in later life, particularly for his scientific publications. After working as a government medical officer for Maori Health, he entered politics when he was about 30, and spent five years in parliament, representing Northern Maori. He served in World War I (as a medical officer in Egypt and Gallipoli, and later with the infantry) and then resumed his former medical career, becoming director of Maori Health (1919–27). His growing interest in Polynesian anthropology then led him to the BISHOP MUSEUM, Honolulu, where he was employed as an ethnologist. His theories about the Polynesian voyagers who settled the Pacific were elaborated with painstaking research on traditions, material culture and social organization. He published a number of distinguished studies which won him prominence and awards, as well as several honorary degrees and fellowships. He died in Honolulu, but his ashes were returned to New Zealand for burial near his birthplace.—KRF

Further reading

Buck, P, 1938. *Vikings of the Sunrise*, A Stokes.

——, 1939. *Anthropology and Religion*, Yale University Press.

——, 1949. *The Coming of the Maori*, Maori Purposes Fund Board.

Hiroa, Te Rangi (P H Buck), 1926. *The Evolution of Maori Clothing*, Thos Avery & Sons.

——, 1927. *The Material Culture of the Cook Islands*, A Stokes.

——, 1930. *Samoan Material Culture*, Bishop Museum.

——, 1932. *Ethnology of Manihiki and Rakahanga, Bishop Museum.*

——, 1934. *Mangaian Society*, Bishop Museum.

——, 1944. *Arts and Crafts of the Cook Islands*, Bishop Museum.

——, 1945. *Introduction to Polynesian Anthropology*, Bishop Museum.

——, 1957. *Arts and Crafts of Hawai'i*, Bishop Museum.

Women anthropologists in Papua New Guinea

American anthropologist Margaret MEAD, who arrived on the island of Manus in 1928, following her *Coming of Age in Samoa* (1928), was the first in a succession of female anthropologists to work in New Guinea. Her fieldwork together with that of compatriot Hortense Powdermaker and British anthropologists Camilla WEDGWOOD and Beatrice Blackwood validated the participation of women in a discipline seen as difficult for them. The period of their fieldwork overlapped: Mead at Manus 1928–29, then at four mid-to-lower Sepik villages: Arapesh, Mundugumor and Tchambuli 1931–33, and Iatmul 1938–39; Powdermaker at Lesu 1929–30; Blackwood at Buka–Bougainville 1929–30, then amongst the Kukukuku 1936–37; and Wedgwood at Manam Island 1933–34.

To gain professional recognition, all four fought the conservatism of the universities and colonial society. Wedgwood, Powdermaker and Blackwood owed much to Bronislaw MALINOWSKI at the London School of Economics, while Mead was a protégée of Franz Boas. At the time there was much unease about female anthropologists living in villages because of the 'risks from male natives', a fear exacerbated by the passing of the White Women's Protection Ordinance in Papua in 1926.

The early research interests of all four focused on women, reproduction and family life in small-scale Melanesian societies. The strictly gendered division of Melanesian societies provided unique opportunities for female anthropologists. The Australian government hoped that their work would shed light on gender imbalance, low birthrate, sexual practices, abortion and their implications for fecundity. Australian Research Council grants were usually awarded to female anthropologists on this basis, though no female anthropologists were appointed to Papua in this period.

Anthropological research opened new insights into Melanesian village life, especially on the roles of women. All four women's careers were boosted by their fieldwork. Mead began her lifetime work at the American Museum of Natural History, but returned to Manus in 1953, 1964 and 1975 to document the effects of change. Powdermaker became president of the American College of Ethnologists, and Blackwood was awarded the prestigious RIVERS Memorial Medal in 1943. Wedgwood began a career in public administration in Australia, returning often to New Guinea in this capacity.—SK

Further reading

Blackwood, B, 1935. *Both Sides of Buka Passage: an ethnographic study of social, sexual and economic questions in the north-western Solomon Islands*, Clarendon Press.

——, 1978. *The Kukukuku of the Upper Watut*, C R Hallpike (ed.), Pitt Rivers Museum.

Powdermaker, H, 1966. *Stranger and Friend: the way of an anthropologist*, W W Norton.

■ ***Margaret Mead*** Margaret Mead (16 December 1901–15 November 1978), American anthropologist, conducted fieldwork in the Pacific islands in an outstanding career of almost 50 years, including 27 honorary degrees. Interested in applying her anthropological insight to universal social problems, Mead described her first nine-month study in SAMOA, when she was only 23, as an 'experiment to find out whether the difficulties of adolescent girls are due to physiological changes which take place at puberty or to the civilization in which they grow up'. Published in 1928 as *Coming of Age in Samoa*, it brought her instant fame in the United States where it was seen to have relevance to American youth. She was appointed an assistant curator at the American Museum of Natural History in New York—

where she remained all her life, in addition to a later teaching position at Columbia University.

After ending a student marriage to a young Protestant minister, Luther Cressman, Mead married Reo Fortune, a New Zealand psychologist whom she had met on her way home from Samoa. They embarked on fieldwork at Manus in PAPUA NEW GUINEA for six months. Returning to New York in 1929, Mead—always an energetic and extraordinarily fast worker—published her investigation of Manus childhood as *Growing Up in New Guinea*. In 1930 they returned to New Guinea to spend six months among the Arapesh, followed by a study of the Mundugumor people of the SEPIK RIVER. During this period, they met the English anthropologist, Gregory Bateson, and were persuaded to study another Sepik group, the lake people now known as Chambri.

Mead published her findings in *Sex and Temperament in Three Primitive Societies*, in 1935, by which time she had divorced Fortune and was about to marry Bateson. In 1936 she and her new husband set off for Bali, Indonesia, where they lived in a mountain village for two years, collaborating on a joint project finally published as a photographic essay called *Balinese Character* (1962). Their daughter Catherine was born in 1939.

In 1942 Mead conducted wartime sociological research and published a book, *And Keep Your Powder Dry*, which attempted to identify the American 'national character' for a popular audience. The publication of *Male and Female* in 1949 further enhanced her reputation as a guru and she became a television personality and magazine columnist. In mid 1953, now divorced from Bateson, she returned to Manus to investigate the effects and extent of social change, publishing another book, *New Lives for Old*, in 1960. After undertaking a trip to Israel to study the assimilation of immigrants from different cultural backgrounds, she used this material and her Manus experience to write *Culture and Commitment* (1970, revised and updated 1978).

For the last 25 years of her life she continued to travel frequently, often returning to Manus, and maintained a busy schedule of lectures and conferences. She published her autobiography, *Blackberry Winter: my earlier years*, in 1972 and continued to receive widespread public acclaim, although serious attacks on her ideas and the superficiality of her research had begun to emerge. Betty Friedan led the feminist criticism, arguing that Mead had used stereotypical images in *Male and Female*.

Her death in 1978 was followed by a reassessment of her work and ideas. Derek Freeman, an Australian anthropologist with considerable experience in Samoa, formed serious doubts about the findings of *Coming of Age in Samoa* in the early 1940s. He raised his concerns (about the exclusion of biology from theories of cultural determinism) with Mead in 1964, and they had continued to correspond while he prepared his proposed refutation. Freeman published his detailed charges—that her simplistic observations were based on limited data, because her fieldwork was subjective, superficial and gender-specific—in 1983. He became the target of outspoken and frequently personal criticism, but his book and the subsequent debate produced a deeper appreciation of both the strengths and weaknesses of Mead's prolific achievements.—KRF

Further reading

Freeman, D, 1983. *Margaret Mead and Samoa: the making and unmaking of an anthropological myth*, Australian National University Press.

Grossgurth, P, 1988. *Margaret Mead*, Penguin Books.

Mead, M, 1972. *Blackberry Winter: my earlier years*, William Morrow.

■ ***Camilla Wedgwood*** Camilla Hildegarde Wedgwood (1901–55) was a descendant of Josiah Wedgwood—of pottery fame—and Charles Darwin. Her parents, Josiah IV and Ethel Bowen were active Fabian socialists. They separated in 1911 and Camilla lived with her father who became a radical member of parliament and later a baronet. Educated at Bedford College, London, and Newnham College, Cambridge (in 1921, centre of a debate over degrees for women), she graduated with honours in English, anthropology and archaeology.

Wedgwood acknowledged A C Haddon, Bronislaw MALINOWSKI and fellow student, New Zealander Raymond Firth, as her mentors. Despite outstanding academic ability, Wedgwood found it difficult to gain a suitable position. After assisting Haddon and Malinowski in a semi-voluntary capacity, in 1928 she was appointed foundation lecturer at the Department of Anthropology, University of Sydney. In 1939 she won an Australian Research Council Fellowship to undertake fieldwork at Manam Island. Although living in a remote New Guinea village required exceptional courage, she considered fieldwork an essential part of an anthropologist's training.

Wedgwood's association with New Guinea continued when, having decided against an academic career, she took a post instructing cadet patrol officers at the Australian School of Pacific Administration and became a government adviser on indigenous affairs. She enlisted in the army during the Pacific War and afterwards worked with W C Groves overhauling the education system in Papua. She approached indigenous education by asking 'for what future then, were Papuan and New Guinean schoolchildren to be educated?' Like Hubert Murray, she feared the creation of a landless proletariat and sought to maintain the village unit. Wedgwood, who was remembered with the greatest affection by local people, was committed to protecting the quality of their lives. She died from cancer in 1955.—SK

Further reading

Hogbin, H I and Wedgwood, C, 1943. *Development and Welfare in the Western Pacific*, Institute of International Affairs.

Wetherell, D and Carr-Gregg, C (eds), 1990. *Camilla a Life: C H Wedgwood 1901–1955*, Sydney University Press.

The Pacific in European art

Despite their remoteness from Europe, the Pacific islands have loomed large in western culture since the 18th century. Oceania has had a presence in literature through voyage and travel books, through great canonical novels such as *Moby-Dick*, as well as many more popular works, from missionary tracts to R M Ballantyne's *The Coral Island* and Michener's *South Pacific*. The fact that Michener's romance is at least as well known as a film and a musical reflects the degree to which European imaginings of the Pacific have never been purely textual. From their inception, in fact, they were also visual and theatrical. Costume, image, artifact, and performance have been as vital to European conceptions of the Pacific as word and narrative.

The cultural category most often used to sum up European responses to the Pacific is that of the 'NOBLE SAVAGE'. This is unfortunate and misleading: although many western characterizations of islanders have been idealizing, the emphasis and motivation of affirmations of 'uncivilized' sociality have been so various that nothing is gained by grouping them together. The European response to the Pacific did not entail the imposition of ready-made stereotypes. Certainly, conventions, expectations, and prejudices conditioned the ways insular environments and indigenous peoples were imaged, and understood or misunderstood. But the images and texts that arose from personal encounters, in particular, are often nuanced, and frequently register the perplexed response of the observer before confusing circumstances. Representations of the Pacific places and peoples produced by European artists are therefore of enduring significance, not only because they reflect a succession of western responses, but also because artists recorded a great deal—through portraits of indigenous people, sketches of indigenous canoes, houses, and artifacts, and through depictions of indigenous RITUALS and ceremonies. Even if their subjects were frequently assimilated to western conventions, the power of indigenous self-presentation—the optical armour of TATTOOING, for example—is vividly conveyed.

Although images of the Pacific from Spanish and Dutch voyages are extant, European knowledge of the Pacific was dramatically extended during the last decades of the 18th century. The voyages of Captain James COOK were crucial for the emergence of a European visual culture of the Pacific, not only because Cook was accompanied by professional artists and draughtsmen, but also because the sheer range of places visited, and the range of contacts with populations previously unknown or little known to Europeans, was extraordinary. While Rapanui (Easter Island) and the Marquesas had been visited before, the extent of the voyagers' familiarity with other parts of Polynesia made it much easier for them to interpret and respond to local practices that had been hazy and bewildering for previous visitors such as Quirós and Roggeveen. Participants in Cook's voyages were also exposed to peoples of the western Pacific such as the Tannese and New Caledonians, who challenged their inchoate understandings of Oceanic ethnology, and enriched their sense of the variety of Oceanic cultures.

William Hodges produced wonderfully fresh sketches in the course of the voyage, including remarkable coastal profiles, distinctive portraits of individuals, and animated scenes of collective indigenous activity, notably of the gathering of the Tahitian canoe fleet in May 1774. He also painted in oil during the voyage; the views of Vaitahu in the Marquesas, Pickersgill Harbour in Dusky Sound, and Easter Island are among important works attentive to the environmental specificity of the places depicted. The Easter Island landscape is distinctive for the sombre but monumental treatment of the famous *ahu moai* stone figures, which had been described by earlier mariners, but were depicted artistically for the first time on this voyage.

Hodges' treatments of Pacific islanders are highly various. In his larger Tahitian oils, men and women alike appear indolent and voluptuous. The softness of air and light, and the luxuriance of palms and foliage, are attributes shared by their bodies. Not exactly a representation of noble savagery, it was consistent with the environmentalism of the anthropological thought of the period, which took people's physique and dispositions to be shaped by the climate they inhabited, and by their mode of life. In his portrait sketches, however, Hodges treated islanders as individuals rather than as exemplars of types. While representations of peoples of the western Pacific were generally negative, his images of Tannese, Malakulan, and New Caledonian men and women describe physical distinctness in non-racialized terms.

Hodges' works, and those of other Cook voyage artists, are important not only for their own complexity, but also because they provided source material for published engravings. A significant group of plates was published with the initial official editions of the voyages, which were freely adapted in popular reprints, such as George William Anderson's subscription edition of 1784–86. This group of images continued to be mined well into the 19th century;

'Temple du Roi dans la baie Tiritatea', hand coloured lithograph by Louis Choris; from *Voyage pittoresque autour du monde* (Firmin Didot, 1821–22)

Dominy de Rienzi's *Océanie ou cinquième partie du Monde (Firmin Didot Frères)*, an encyclopedic work translated from French into a number of European languages, incorporated many plates derived from Cook and from subsequent illustrated voyages.

The French and Russian voyages of the first half of the 19th century also produced much material of importance. Louis Choris's studies of Hawaiian carvings and temple precincts extended the interest in ethnographic artifacts and ritual sites that had been manifested in the Cook voyage corpus; visual art also began to document Polynesian adoptions of European dress, typically representing 'acculturated' islanders in ambivalent or negative terms. Portraits and depictions of artifacts encoded European concerns in various ways, but the effort to assimilate indigenous peoples into a larger moral and political narrative is most evident in images of situations of contact and interaction between Europeans and islanders. Characterizations of such scenes are highly various, ranging from the tragic nobility of the DEATH OF COOK in Hawai'i, initially painted by John Webber, but often reworked by other artists, through Russian images suggesting the licentious traffic between sailors and Marquesans, to more formal and dignified presentations of meetings between chiefs and naval officers.

As Bernard Smith noted in his foundational analysis, *European Vision and the South Pacific* (1960), a turning point in this genre of representation is marked by George Baxter's oil print of the death of the missionary John WILLIAMS, on Erromango in southern Vanuatu, in 1839 (pictured on page 196). This was the first print in which islander violence was not depicted in terms that retained some resonance of classical warriorhood; shorn of these dignifying associations, the Erromangans were presented as bloodthirsty, positively bestial cannibals. These evocations of belligerent savagery were to acquire great circulation in evangelical propaganda, and in other genres of popular illustration, and retained life long after the conflict that gave rise to them had been generally suppressed by pacification (for instance in the Benjamin Minns cartoons that accompanied Louis Becke's South Seas stories in the Australian *Bulletin* magazine).

During the later 19th century, however, a more picturesque approach to the Pacific emerged in Conrad Martens' bland Tahitian landscapes, and in the light and anecdotal works of Nicholas Chevalier. In Chevalier's paintings, the exoticism of Polynesia is diminished; we no longer encounter the mysterious and sometimes threatening indigenous carvings that so interested Hodges and Choris; we have no sense of any autonomous indigenous polity; and if the denigration of the 'ignoble savage' genre is absent, so too is any sense of indigenous power or threat. Instead, all that the eye encounters is charming. Chevalier was, at about this time, painting southern New Zealand in order to attract tourists. His island works may be seen in similar terms, and indeed anticipate the Polynesian tourist iconography that emerged in the 20th century.

It is against this background that the force and originality of Paul GAUGUIN's painting remains striking. Few artists have been the subject of quite as much mythmaking as Gauguin, and the tendency from an early point was to lurch between contradictory assessments. According to one view, the artist was a culturally sensitive proto-ethnographer whose residence in Polynesia enabled him to step beyond European conventions and prejudices. According to the other, he is an exploitative colonial voyeur and

'Pacific Islanders', from Dominy de Rienzi, *Océanie ou cinquième partie du monde* (Firmin Didot Frères, 1869)

retailer of primitivist stereotypes. Unfortunately much of this discussion referred again and again to the same works, and has never addressed the full range of Gauguin's artistic responses to Polynesia (a task made more difficult by the very widely dispersed character of the original work, and by the lack of a *catalogue raisonné*). Hence, while paintings such as *Manao tupapau* are clearly implicated (in however complex a fashion) in a distinctively colonial sexuality, much of Gauguin's other work is not susceptible to this reading at all. Not all his nudes are patently objects of sexual interest, and more importantly, many of his Polynesian portraits are not nudes at all. In many cases women are represented in the Tahitian dress of the period, in missionary-introduced Mother Hubbards, which they wear with dignity and presence.

While Alan Moorehead (in *The Fatal Impact*) and a number of other writers have taken Gauguin's *Nevermore* as an elegy for the Polynesian race, Gauguin was not the kind of primitivist who mourned the passing of an archaic culture. He was, to the contrary, conspicuously interested in the Polynesian modernity that he encountered. He frequently depicted signs of that modernity, in Polynesian Christianity as well as in the hybridity of colonial dress. His images encompassed both the overtly imaginary and the realities of the period, and in many cases these were merged in extraordinary compositions such as *Tehamana has many parents*. The painting suggests the young woman's deep connections with an ancestral religion and culture, evoked through the rows of stylized figures behind her, yet she is in no sense presented as a captive to the past or to a strange cult. In some respects, this insistence on the contemporaneity of cultural tradition, and the connectedness to tradition of the modern Polynesian subject, is broadly compatible with Polynesian self-representations, but this does not mean that Gauguin's understanding was especially profound or nuanced. The superficiality of his engagement with indigenous culture is manifest in the fact that the motifs are derived from a Rapanui (Easter Island) pictograph board, not from any art form that belongs to Tehamana's own Tahitian culture. As has often been pointed out, Gauguin's artistic allusions and symbolic references are as often to Hindu as Polynesian sources, in keeping with his broadly theosophical interest in ancestral cultural affinities that was unsurprisingly indifferent to ethnographic specificity.

There can be no definitive verdict upon Gauguin's work because it is so richly contradictory, and also because the criteria employed in any adjudication are themselves nebulous and contentious. Contemporary Polynesians and Polynesian artists respond in diverse ways to Gauguin's work. In some cases they are offended by images that are in fact voyeuristic; in others they are moved and empowered by paintings that point to the spiritual force of Oceanic sites, cultures, myths, and symbols. Gauguin's work remains fertile, because it is powerful and compelling as well as limited and superficial. To a greater degree than any other oeuvre, it exhibits both the content and the limitations of cultural exchange, the success and the failure of cross-cultural art.

Gauguin's work is distinctive, moreover, for its basis in direct experience in the Pacific. In this respect it differs from the work of most European modernists, who were inspired by Oceanic and African objects that they encountered in museums, without having direct experience of the regions or cultures which produced them. Important exceptions to this are the German expressionists, Emil Nolde and Max Pechstein, both of whom travelled in the Pacific shortly before World War I; Pechstein in particular was following Gauguin's example. Both produced work of considerable interest, including many portraits, and both adopted anti-colonial stances in their writings that were occasionally made visually explicit, such as Nolde's *The Missionary* (1912).

The Pacific was depicted not only by these avant-garde figures, but also by commercial artists whose work was closely linked with tourism, and particularly tourism to Hawai'i. Among the most spectacular instances are the images produced for menus by Matson Lines cruises during the inter-war and post-war period. Frank MacIntosh and Eugene Savage both revelled in a sensual exoticism, the former emphasizing generic dusky maidens, the latter depicting highly romanticized Hawaiian customs such as *luau* and *hula*, and scenes of Hawaiian history, such as the encounter between Kamehameha and Cook. The efflorescence of this type of imagery in musicals, Elvis Presley films, and on record covers is beyond the scope of this essay, but is significant for its reduction and reiteration of the sensual paradise cliché that was present in earlier representations, but generally only as one element in a more complex response.

It is important to recognize that Oceania continues to be represented by contemporary artists, especially by those in New Zealand and Australia. Both Nigel Brown and Vivienne Binns have been concerned to re-examine the historical legacy of Cook. Brown has produced several rich series of re-workings of Cook images and narratives (*Cook in Pacifica*, 1993). These emphasize the presence and power of indigenous cultural sites and forms in the landscape that the British navigator would trespass on, but nevertheless could be seen to reproduce rather than repudiate Webber's interest in a collision of peoples or cultures. The Australian painter, Vivienne Binns, adopts a more overtly postmodern and postcolonial attitude, reworking Hodges' famous *Tahiti Revisited*, in a fashion that incorporates barkcloth patterns and allusions to Australian art history.

The work of Robin White, of Maori and Pakeha New Zealander descent, and resident in Kiribati for more than a decade, provides a fitting concluding point. She is manifestly inspired by a tradition of European representation of Pacific islanders, but somehow shifts the vantage point, not from outside to inside, but from outside to a situation between, a situation on the beach ('Sainimele goes fishing'). Her islander men and women are classicized and dignified; her compositions are manifestly inspired by Gauguin, and less directly by Webber; but her vision

'Cook in Pacifica', 1993 lithograph by Nigel Brown; private collection, Canberra, courtesy Nicholas Thomas

is also remarkably quotidian. People appear true to the actions and movements of real islanders in the present. These works represent both a continuation and transcendence of the rich and beautiful, but often partial and exoticist, envisaging of the Pacific islands that European artists have worked and reworked.—NT

■ ***Paul Gauguin*** Paul Gauguin (7 June 1848–8 May 1903), a French painter of Peruvian ancestry, went to live in Tahiti in June 1891, escaping from 'rotten' contemporary society in pursuit of the imagined purity and innocence of the islands, and leaving his wife and family in France. He made a brief return visit to France (1893–95), trying to sell his paintings, and used his time also to work on a handwritten notebook with sketches and images of his sojourn in the islands, *Noa Noa* ('fragrant perfume'), subtitled *Voyage de Tahiti*. Gauguin then went to live in the Marquesas Islands where he spent the rest of his life, and it was only after his death that his work began to achieve its present fame.

Writing about the Pacific

In the past, Pacific literature has been understood as the writing about the islands of Oceania by western travellers, settlers and sojourners on tours of professional duty. The maintenance of this construction has served to perpetuate a vision of the islands as distant, exotic sites of white desires and disillusions in which local people are part of the scenic backdrop or supporting agents of dramas of the European mind. Such writings also erase or fix as museum curiosities and 'natural' objects of scientific observation the indigenous cultures that predate and survive white contact. Despite the emergence of an indigenous counter-voice within modern print cul-

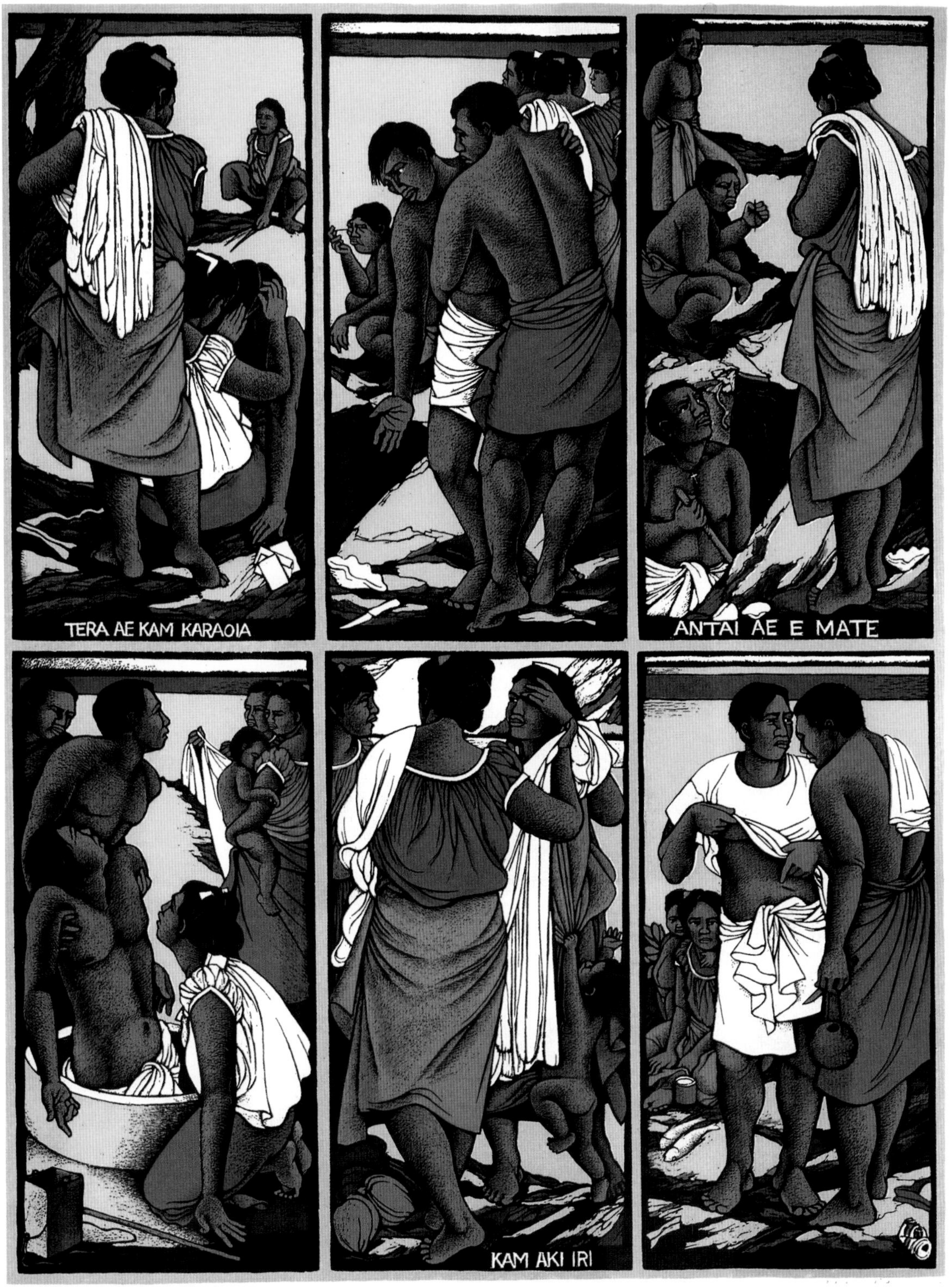

'Sainimele goes fishing', screen-print by Robin White; School of Art, The Australian National University, Canberra

ture, travelogues, romances and ethnographies continue to dominate the second-hand book catalogues and popular imagination of those who do not inhabit the Pacific islands.

The buccaneer adventures of William Dampier, published in 1697 as a bestseller (*A New Voyage Round the World*) stimulated 18th-century British interest in the 'South Sea' with his record of contacts with Chile, Peru, the Galapagos Islands, Mexico, Guam, the Philippines and China. Further inter-island visits by Dampier (1703–07 and 1708) retained public interest through the rescue of Alexander Selkirk—the source of inspiration for Daniel Defoe's *Robinson Crusoe* (1719) and Jonathan Swift's *Gulliver's Travels* (1726). Travel writing reached best-selling status with COOK's *Journals* in their various versions. These and the voyages of BOUGAINVILLE and WALLIS inspired poetry and popular theatrical parodies of island life as well as emulative travelogues installing the contradictory stereotypes of cannibal savages and dusky maidens symbolizing a society free of artificial conventions.

Either way, the Pacific was an inversion of European society used to dramatize a debate about the proper way for westerners to live. This function became entrenched in the 'imaginary voyage' literature of utopian vision, surviving at least until Samuel Butler's *Erewhon* (1872) and Jules Verne (1828–1905). More realistic romances such as Herman Melville's *Typee* (1846) draw on a genre elsewhere influential in literature (notably William Mariner's account of Tonga), the 'castaway' journal. The Pacific also became a popular site of children's fiction aimed at instructing European youth in natural history, survival skills and their supposedly inherent superiority over other peoples and ways of life. R M Ballantyne's *The Coral Island* (1858) is a famous example. W H G Kingston was also a prolific contributor of this genre.

Abstract musings on Oceania, even though based on explorers' accounts, were quickly mocked for their extremes and countered by those who knew the 'real' Pacific. Until World War II direct contact with the islands was entirely dependent on ships, and so a body of maritime writing holds a significant place in Pacific literature, full of the tropes to be expected from days mostly of sail: the storm (Nordhoff and Hall's *The Hurricane*, 1936), shipwreck and marooning (H de Vere Stacpoole's *The Blue Lagoon*, 1909, being a particularly saccharine version of the long-running 'Robinson Crusoe' tradition), mutiny (the story of the MUTINY ON THE BOUNTY, a lasting favourite), plus brief landfall in a variety of places with notes on the natural features of islands, on the customs of the people and on 'characters' encountered. The French romantic novel *Le Mariage de Loti* (1882) by the sailor-writer 'Pierre Loti' [Viaud] provides an influential if self-indulgently sentimental version of the idealized dalliance between a junior naval officer on shore leave and a teenage Tahitian princess (abandoned with sentimental regrets when he has to move on).

Literature of this type falls into two major categories: the travel sketch 'literature of passage' and the yarns of traders following more regular routes amongst the islands. Notable writers in the first category include Beatrice Grimshaw, Charles Bennett, Arthur Grimble (*A Pattern of Islands*, 1952), Willard Price (*Adventures in Paradise*, 1956) and Olaf Ruhen's writings. In the second group, Louis Becke's *By Reef and Palm* (1894) is a leading example. Later works in verse such as Kenneth Slessor's *Five Visions of Captain Cook*, James McAuley's *Captain Quirós*, Allen Curnow's *Landfall in Unknown Seas* and R D Fitzgerald's *Heemskerck Shoals* reflect on the age of European discovery in an attempt to forge founding myths for settler societies in the Antipodes. Scientific adventurers like Thor Heyerdahl tap into the literary tradition with KON-TIKI (1950) and *Fatu Hiva* (1974) as latter-day exploration and Crusoe narratives, while Peter BUCK's *Vikings of the Sunrise* (1954) and Bronislaw MALINOWSKI's *Argonauts of the Western Pacific* (1922) found a place for ethnographic history within popular tales of adventurous voyaging, a mix that seemed to integrate settler history with the Polynesian past.

Occasionally travel and trader narratives were successfully combined to literary effect as in Robert Louis STEVENSON's *The Beach of Falesa* (1892), Jack London's *South Sea Tales* (1911) and Somerset Maugham's *The Trembling of a Leaf* (1921). More sedentary contact allowed an impressionist gloss that swung between tropical idyll (Charles Warren Stoddard's *South Sea Idylls*, 1873; Robert Dean Frisbie's *The Book of Puka Puka*, 1923) and melancholic tedium (James Norman Hall, *The Lost One and Other True Tales of the South Seas*, 1952; 'Asterisk' [Robert James Fletcher] offers a particularly bleak view of plantation life in the New Hebrides, *Isles of Illusion*, 1923).

Fact jockeyed often uneasily with fiction in the 'yarn' mode of Pacific writing, but (allowing for selective colouring) comes to the fore in the memoirs of missionaries and colonial officers. Arthur Grimble administered the Gilbert Islands while he was writing his travel sketches; Lady Cumming wrote her diaries in Fiji where she was governor's wife. A no-nonsense picture of managing indentured labour on a Fiji cane farm comes from Walter Gill (*Turn North-East at the Tombstone*, 1969). The workers of the Empire were not generally literary types, but Papua New Guinea produced a number of widely read *kiap* memoirs (Jack Hides, Ian Downs, J K McCarthy) and various fictional versions as well, most significantly perhaps, Randolph Stow's *Visitants* (1979). Missionaries also wrote copiously and were written about often. Key figures include William Ellis, John WILL-

IAMS, James CHALMERS, George BROWN, Joseph DAMIEN and Hiram BINGHAM.

Resolutely resisting the less than sensational details of the everyday and the call of the divine alike, adventure romances set in the Pacific have proliferated. Guy Boothby, Jack McLaren, Sydney Walter Powell, Arnold Safroni-Middleton and a host of others (Friederich Gerstäcker and Ernst Löhndorff in German) have perpetuated the tradition which was given a new lease of life with the onset of World War II. Instead of 'the savage', the treacherous and violent foe became 'the Jap', but the plots and settings churned over in the same way. Notable works to emerge from this period are the stories of James Michener, and James Jones' *From Here to Eternity*. Michener also made his name for the blockbuster historical romance, *Hawai'i* (1959), a form attempted with less notoriety by O A Bushnell (also writing on Hawai'i) and Russell Foreman (on Fiji).

This entire body of writing has been mostly superseded by the advent of air travel and the onset of mass tourism but is still used as a nostalgic point of reference by modern travellers or resurrected by journalistic venturers such as Gavin Young (*Slow Boats Home*, 1986) and Paul Theroux (*The Happy Isles of Oceania: paddling the Pacific*, 1991). The early days of more leisurely CRUISE SHIPS produced regular visitors to and settlers in Hawai'i, resulting in a body of poetry not found elsewhere. (Don Blanding is a prolific example of its lyric wafts of tropic palms, etc: *Hula Moon*, 1930.)

Literary renditions of myths and 'local colour' sketches of native life and customs abound in Hawai'i, while Tahiti and New Caledonia have bodies of work in French by sojourners and European settlers (Paul GAUGUIN and Jean Mariotti are two notable instances). In Micronesia, William Peck has translated and remodelled traditional poetry (*I Speak the Beginning*, 1982). Non-literary ethnographic writings on the Pacific are legion and deserve their own discussion, but writers who have crossed into popular reading or influenced other literary forms are Bronislaw Malinowski, Margaret MEAD and Greg Dening. Another very influential text across many fields has been the art history of Bernard Smith (*European Vision and the South Pacific*, 1969).

With the exception of major national literary figures like Melville and Stevenson, the study of writing about the Pacific has been sketchy and for a long time dependent on the enthusiasm of a few figures. Editor, academic and bibliographer A Grove Day, based at the University of Hawai'i, has been a leading exponent of the field. Other studies by Bill Pearson (*Rifled Sanctuaries*, 1984) and Nigel Krauth (*New Guinea Images in Australian Literature*, 1982) are worthy of mention. With the advent of colonial discourse analysis and post-colonial studies in literature, the full range of writing about the Pacific is coming under scrutiny. Since the 1970s, this scrutiny has also included indigenous Pacific writers and scholars (see PACIFIC IDENTITIES, PACIFIC WRITING). The one-way 'speaking about' of past writing has become a contestatory 'dialogue with' a local view of the world. SUBRAMANI, Haunani-Kay TRASK and Albert WENDT in particular have sought to counter the old romantic clichés and prejudicial assumptions about island life and to reclaim or redefine some of the imaginative space that the Pacific has been written into.—PS3 & TGB

Further reading

Day, A Grove, 1987. *Mad About Islands: novelists of a vanished Pacific*, Mutual Publishing of Honolulu.

Dening, Greg, 1998. *Selections 1998: readings/writings*, Melbourne University Press.

Hides, Jack Gordon, 1935. *Through Wildest Papua*, Blackie.

Krauth, Nigel (ed. and intro.), 1982. *New Guinea Images in Australian Literature*, University of Queensland Press.

McCarthy, John Keith, 1963. *Patrol into Yesterday: my New Guinea years*, F W Chesire.

Martin, John, 1981. *Tonga Islands: William Mariner's account*, Vava'u Press.

Pearson, Bill, 1984. *Rifled Sanctuaries: some views of the Pacific islands in western literature to 1900*, Auckland University Press/Oxford University Press.

Smith, Bernard, 1969. *European Vision and the South Pacific, 1768–1850: a study in the history of art and ideas*, Oxford University Press.

Some European writers on the Pacific islands

■ *R M Ballantyne* (1825–94), born in Edinburgh, worked in northern Canada (1841–47) and wrote adventure stories.

■ *Louis Becke* (1855–1913), pen-name of George Lewis Becke, traveller and island trader, born in Australia, who wrote more than 30 books including novels, short stories, biographies and reminiscences; *By Reef and Palm* (London, 1894) was his first collection of short stories.

■ *Samuel Butler* (1835–1902), born in Nottinghamshire, spent several years (1859–64) as a sheep farmer in New Zealand.

■ *Lady Constance F Gordon Cumming,* English wife of the colonial administrator of the Fiji Islands wrote

A Lady's Cruise in a French Man-of-war (Blackwood, 1882), *At Home in Fiji* (A C Armstrong/Blackwood, 1882/1885), and *Fire Fountain: the kingdom of Hawaii, its volcanoes and the history of its missions* (Blackwood, 1883).

■ ***Allen Curnow*** (1911–), New Zealand poet, was commissioned to write 'Landfall in unknown seas'; it was published in *Abel Janszoon Tasman and the Discovery of New Zealand* (ed. J C Beaglehole, Department of Internal Affairs, 1942), and then in the collection of Curnow's poetry, *Sailing or Drowning* (Progressive Publishing Society, Wellington, 1943).

■ ***William Dampier*** (1652–1715), navigator, buccaneer and travel writer, born in Somerset.

■ ***Daniel Defoe*** (1660–1731), satirist and political pamphleteer, born in London, turned to fiction in his 50s and achieved fame with *Robinson Crusoe* (1719).

■ ***William Ellis,*** English missionary, wrote *Narrative of a Tour through Hawaii: manners, customs and language of the inhabitants* (Fisher & Jackson, London, 1827; republished in Honolulu in 1917), and *A Journal of a Tour around Hawaii, the Largest of the Sandwich Islands* (Crocker & Brewster, Boston, 1825).

■ ***Robert D Fitzgerald*** (1902–87), Australian poet, worked as a surveyor in Fiji and Tonga early in his career (1931–36), and his poem, 'Heemskerck shoals', was included in *Between Two Tides* (Angus & Robertson, 1952).

■ ***Robert James Fletcher*** used different pen-names (Asterix and Bohun Lynch) for his edited collection, *Isles of Illusion: letters from the South Seas*, which was published in 1923 by Constable in London and by Small Maynard in Boston.

■ ***Robert Dean Frisbie*** (1896–1948), American writer, settled in the Cook Islands and married a Cook Islander (see Florence (Johnny) FRISBIE).

■ ***Friedrich Gerstäcker*** (1816–72), writer and traveller, born in Hamburg, wrote colourful adventure stories.

■ ***Arthur Grimble*** (1888–1956), colonial administrator, described his travels in *A Pattern of Islands* (John Murray, 1952); the American edition, *We Chose the Islands*, was published by Morrow in 1952.

■ ***Beatrice Grimshaw*** (1871–1953), Irish journalist and travel writer, lived in Papua New Guinea for several years; she wrote *In the Strange South Seas* (Hutchinson, 1907), *From Fiji to the Cannibal Islands* (Nelson, 1907, with an American edition titled *Fiji and its Possibilities*), and *The New New Guinea* (Hutchinson, 1910).

■ ***James Jones*** (1921–77), born in Illinois, used his wartime experiences in Hawai'i to write his best-selling novel, *From Here to Eternity* (1951).

■ ***William Henry Giles Kingston*** (1814–80), English writer of more than 150 children's adventure stories, including *Peter the Whaler* (1851) and *The Three Midshipmen* (1862).

■ ***Jack London,*** pen-name of John Griffith Chaney (1876–1916), novelist, born in San Francisco.

■ ***Pierre Loti,*** pen-name of Louis Marie Julien Viaud (1850–1923), writer and naval officer, born in Rochefort, France, who used experiences and observations from his voyages in his novels.

■ ***James McAuley*** (1917–76), Australian poet and literary critic, published *Captain Quirós* in 1964 (Angus & Robertson).

■ ***Jack McLaren*** wrote a book of adventure stories, *Gentlemen of the Empire* (Hutchinson, 1940), which included a tale called 'Among the headhunters of the Solomon Islands'.

■ ***William Mariner*** (1791–1853) wrote *An Account of the Natives of the Tonga Islands in the South Pacific Ocean*, published by John Murray in 1817.

■ ***Jean Mariotti,*** French writer, published *Les Contes de Poindi* (Stock, Paris, 1941), which was translated into English by Esther Averill (*Tales of Poindi*, Domino Press, 1948).

■ ***Somerset Maugham*** (1874–1965), novelist, playwright and short-story writer, born in Paris.

■ ***Herman Melville*** (1819–1905), novelist, born in New York, sailed on a whaling ship in the Pacific, using his experiences to create popular works including *Typee* (1846), *Omoo* (1847, see OMAI), and *Moby Dick* (1851).

■ ***James A Michener*** (1907–97), born in New York, drew on his experiences as a naval historian in the Pacific region (1944–46) in many of his popular novels, including *Tales of the South Pacific* (Macmillan, 1947) and *Hawai'i* (Random House, 1959).

■ ***Charles Bernard Nordhoff*** (1887–1947) collaborated with James Norman Hall (1887–1951) on several books about the islands, including *Faery Lands of the South Seas* (1921, Harper & Bros.) and *Pitcairn's Island* (1935, Little, Brown & Co.).

■ *Willard Price*'s books include *Pacific Adventure* (Day Reynal & Hitchcock, 1936), *Rip Tide in the South Seas* (Heinemann, 1936), *Japan's Islands of Mystery* (Heinemann, 1944), and *Adventures in Paradise* (Heinemann, 1956).

■ *Olaf Ruhen* (1911–), born in New Zealand, worked in Australia as a journalist, using his wartime experiences and later travels in Papua New Guinea to write more than 30 books, including *Dahori: tales of New Guinea* (Lippincott, New York, 1957).

■ *Arnold Safroni-Middleton*'s travel tales include *Wine-dark Seas and Tropic Skies* (Grant Richards, 1918) and *Tropic Shadows: memories of the South Seas* (Richards Press, 1927).

■ *Kenneth Slessor* (1901–71), Australian poet and journalist, included the long poem, 'Five visions of Captain Cook', in *Cuckooz Country* (Angus & Robertson, 1932).

■ *Henry de Vere Stacpoole* (1863–1951), Irish physician, made several voyages as a ship's doctor; his many popular novels included *The Blue Lagoon* (1909), *The Pearl Fishers* (1915) and *Green Coral* (1935).

■ *Charles Warren Stoddard*'s books include *South Seas Idylls* (1873) and *Summer Cruising in the South Seas* (1881), published by Chatto & Windus.

■ *Randolph Stow* (1935–), Australian novelist, poet and librettist, worked as an anthropologist in Papua New Guinea; his first novel, *To the Islands*, (Macdonald, 1958, revised edition 1983, Pan Books/Secker & Warburg) is set in Australia, and *Visitants* (1979) is set in the Trobriand Islands.

■ *Paul Theroux* (1941–), novelist and travel writer, born in Massachusetts.

■ *Jules Verne* (1828–1905), writer, born in Nantes, France, wrote several works of popular science fiction including *Vingt Mille Lieues Sous les Mers* (1870, *Twenty Thousand Leagues Under the Sea*).

FOUR RELIGION AND CHRISTIANITY

Indigenous religious systems

Roughly one quarter of the world's known discrete (albeit small-scale) religious traditions come from Oceania. Generalizations are hazardous, and prior impressions make it difficult to reconceptualize the whole picture in a small compass. Prima facie and by archaeological implication, Melanesian traditions are older, and the apparently less structured nature of their religions has tended to suggest magic in western terms. The homogeneous Polynesian and Micronesian systems have met more common expectations of 'the religious'. These first appearances are deceptive, and yet there is no doubt that Polynesia is well known for its sacral rulers and priesthoods, and thus for more signs of 'religious propagation' from the top. Greater social stratification and the smaller island contexts of Micronesia and Polynesia produced a more vertical view of the world than is usually found in Melanesia. Since the Melanesian geocultural landscape constitutes the most complicated ethnographic scene on Earth, the language diversity itself contributes to the impression of a religious splinteredness—in fact, given the complicated nature of SEPIK RIVER societies, it turns out that there are slightly more Melanesian traditional religions than indigenous languages. Evidence of commonly held outlooks in Polynesia, however, such as the recognition of Hawaiki as a spirit home, reflect the populating of the region (FOOTSTEPS FROM ASIA) by voyagers sharing an Austronesian heritage. Possibilities for social coherence in Polynesia and Micronesia sometimes allowed for incipient imperialism (as with the YAP 'TRADE EMPIRE'). Some Voriana of central New Georgia set themselves up as overlords on eastern Bougainville, but their prime object was to link in with the long-distant raiding expeditions to take human heads. Their activity reflects the kind of in-and-out expansionism found elsewhere in Melanesia, as with the Marind-Anim of southeast Irian Jaya, who gained notoriety from their fearful and consistent headhunting incursions into what is now Papua New Guinea.

Territoriality was an important, if variably conceived, aspect of Oceanic religious life. Upon contact with the outside world, it is hard to find a local area unaffected by group or tribal conflict, so that indigenous religious traditions across the whole region make no sense without accounting for the pressures of military survivalism (or 'warriorhood religion') and the vitality involved in compensations and exchanges between allies (the 'religion of economics'). The ways by which conflict was perpetuated on one hand, and social balances maintained on the other, are as much data of religion as anything, often providing the key to any given picturing of the cosmos, the social and leadership structure, and the compositions of ritual life and creative artistry. 'Cultures' have been virtually synonymous with 'religions' (or life-ways in a world of spiritual as well as human agencies).

Melanesian cosmic picturing tends to be more 'horizontal'. Sky or high gods are fewer, and not necessarily acknowledged across whole culture areas. In east Enga of central Papua New Guinea, to take Melanesia's most populous language block, Aitawe as the heavenly un-worshipped, rather 'non-interventionist' sustainer of the cosmos is prominent; while in west Enga, the key idol was the unvenerated 'Man of Cordyline' or First Ancestor. In the large Massim complex of eastern Papua New Guinea, Joboahine figures as the sky-dwelling dispenser of punishments against tabu-breakers among the (southern) Bonarua Islanders, whereas on Normanby Island to the north, he is a rather testy and down-to-earth war god. Common among creator gods are those who start or 'put' the cosmos, and who were regarded more as a life force, while ritual attention was given to deities crucial for everyday affairs. What was generated by the Sek people's deity Dodo (of seaboard Madang), indicatively, was a world stretching horizontally just as their coastal strip and richly resourced islands do.

Across Melanesia, creation more often than not involved a variety of spirit-beings, including culture-heroes, whose movements involved a cosmic tracing of the known (micro) world. The goddess Jari/Jali, for instance, is shared by seaboard eastern SEPIK RIVER groups, and in urinating during her wanderings, great rivers were forged. The famed Manamarkeri, or fleeing scabaeous Man of the Biak coastal and island region in northwest Irian Jaya, was the 'namer' of key places of the world, as well as discoverer of the Realm of the Ancestors and their enriching power (Koreri). Across Melanesia, gods (or great Ancestors) of war abound. Success in war depended on their placation, or on a sacrificial rite (pig's blood smeared on sacred stones, for instance, in east Wahgi and west Enga). Great Ancestor Vlisuak of the Yuat River people (Sepik) had his skull placed in the central cult village of Andefukua with an extraordinary and famous mask over it; Vlisuak had to be fed regularly for success against enemies (and health), and war omens were taken by swinging betelnut before him. Fecundity, prosperity and welfare were also vital concerns behind the worship of various deities, including a fair range of fertility goddesses (the cult of Enda Semangko having the largest known following) spreading and growing into prominence among the central New Guinea Melpa and eastern Enga before contact. But in Melanesia it was above all spirits of the dead who were most commonly conceived as bringing success and benison. The more 'distant' dead (typically beyond 5–6 generations) were considered the most benign because one could not as easily fall out with them. The dead whose names were remembered were usually still seen as part of the community and their hurt feelings could bring trouble. Ghosts were often distinguished from the settled dead. For the Dugum Dani warriors (highland Irian Jaya), ghosts of men who died in battle required placating by killing one of the enemy; for the Roro of coastal Papua, one could expect difficulties from a family member killed suddenly (by a crocodile, a spear from behind or the like). Yet the ancestors, having reached the proper 'place of the dead', were the spiritual sources of help most often and consistently turned to.

In Polynesia and Micronesia, the pattern of divinities and the relationship of their creative energies to the social order follows far more definite generalities. Major deities (such as *aitu, akua, atea, atua* and *etua*) were personifications of nature or patrons of cultural pursuits. One or a pair is usually singled out as initiating Creation. Samoa's Sky Father Tagaloa-a-lagu, for example, lonely in the heavens, throws a boulder into the ocean to create the first island. In creative processes there occurs a cosmic separation; the Heavens hold the gods above, and an Underworld lies under the land and seas or under the visible world. In Micronesia's Makin Meang (Kiribati), the young hero Naareau has to kill the cosmic eel before the sky can be propped up, and defeat other powers before other creations can occur. The tiered effect makes for a comparatively vertical look at the world, complementing the social stratification of eastern and northern Pacific traditions. Apart from the prime mover, often involving a primal father and mother (with the parting of the heavenly Papua-una and the earth Mother Papa-aʻo through the creative power of Atea, according to Marquesan belief), there were also departmental divinities and local ones. Among pre-contact Maori, each tribal group knew their own particular deities, yet shared a nervous concern to please Tumatauenga, the war god. Compartmental gods were mostly male, and aside from war, forests and agriculture were prominent departments—the positive bio-cosmic areas against that of negative aggression. Female spirits were known to guard the Underworld, the great Kine-nui-te-po being best remembered. In Maori myth she brings an end to the culture hero Maui (widely extolled across the Pacific), because he dared to attempt to destroy her, with his failure spelling the inevitability of death. Across the board, the vital engagement in fulfilling obligations in war and production constitutes religious data. Stories were constantly told about warrior and trading exploits (such as the HIRI TRADING VOYAGES of the Motu to the Papuan Gulf); elation and disappointments were always connected to the blessings and anger of the spirits, and calculations were constantly being made as 'pay-back' logic applied.

As protectors and sustainers of families and lineages, the ancestors were no less important in the everyday life of the wider Pacific than they were in Melanesia. In Austronesian stratified societies, however, they could take on a distinctive prominence in bolstering chiefly power. GENEALOGY was crucial for Micronesia and Polynesia, where the tracing of one's ancestry to the first or senior canoe of discovery established politico-sacral priority. The great ancestors protected their land and fortresses (as Maori carvings on the latter illustrate). The startling statues of RAPANUI (Easter Island) are not of gods, but of ancestral chiefs, whose tombs generally lie behind their effigies, and who were made to sit looking on their heartlands, not the sea. (See also WHO CARVED THE STATUES OF EASTER ISLAND?) Over and above responses to gods and ancestors, the island region is known for beliefs about special places of spirit habitations, and a host of minor powers, such as sky people, trickster beings, ghouls and malevolences. These all reveal the general ceremonial or bio-cosmic interests of survivalist peoples, and social life was never independent of these, as totem groups, the naming of persons and things according to place and circumstances, and hunting procedures all combine to confirm.

Pacific religions were generally about the acquisition of 'spirit power'. The pidgin languages of Melanesia usually express this as *paua*, although the better known term *mana* (or *mina*) has come to denote this concept from the western Solomons to eastern Polynesia. The acquisition of wealth, closely linked to the reciprocal obligations of GIFT-GIVING IN MELANESIA, is almost invariably encouraged so that prestige can be enhanced by giving goods to put others in debt. In some of these societies, increase in power over wealth goes hand in hand with entering higher grades of 'secret societies' (as on Malekula, Vanuatu) while in others, wealth distribution upon death is crucial. (Among East New Britain's Tolai, for example, no one could enter the 'kingdom of the spirits' without collecting the required amount of *tambu* or shell money, which is recirculated during funeral rites.) Austronesian chiefly societies, Polynesian especially, enhanced social hierarchy instead and expected competition only within ranks. In Melanesia magical control was and still is a more prominent motif—with resources to love magic and the bolstering of one's chances with access to sorcery techniques or sorcerers—while in Micronesia and Polynesia, protection is stressed. In these latter regions invocatory prayers tend to value protection over success. The tattooed 'other body'—outstanding on the Marquesas—provided protection in hostilities and between genders. The *mana* of great and powerful people had to be guarded, protocols and the avoidance of social boundary-crossing (*tapu*/*tabu*) had to be strictly observed, because tribal life would disintegrate without strict customary rules of decorum and relationships. The mandate of *mana* was to be skilfully upheld.

Pacific islanders generally saw themselves within communities that extended beyond living humans. Most often the goal of the wise old survivor was the most attractive example of purpose in life; such a person had lasted out many battles and negotiated many transactions, and, whether chief or BIG-MAN or not, he was 'becoming spirit' (as the north-east New Caledonian Houailou would say). Becoming an ancestor without difficulty meant entering a world in which all movement was subtle and swift, and with the readiest capacity to mete out benefit or sanction. The salvation of the immortal soul was not the point of traditional Pacific religions. That was a radically disturbing new issue raised by the coming of the Christian missionaries. The traditional point was more often than not that one became in death more of an effective saviour of one's group than was usually achievable in life. Dreams about the dead were thus often the most powerful—for warning, for even changing the course of ritual life, and certainly for grasping what was finally in store for the soul-part after death. To die before due time, though, was to be avoided, and it was often the role of the diviner, healer or shaman to recall the wandering souls of sick persons, whose life energies could be debilitated by bad social relations or sorcery. The vision of becoming an effective ancestor was perhaps stronger in Melanesia than Polynesia, where the belief in a cluster of powerful deities and the overarching importance of kings and paramount chiefs usually made the role of ancestors as a group incompletely communal. A kind of fatalistic imaging—about not being able to get to the place of the dead except by finding precisely the right spot on the spirit journey—also lends a certain tragic element to Micro-Polynesian 'eschatology'. That the Melanesian dead could be collectively helpful was also going to lay the groundwork for beliefs that they could collectively return, perhaps not a common traditional view at all, but one crucial for the emergence of so-called 'CARGO CULTS' after contact with the outside world.—GWT

The spread of Christian missions

The island Pacific today has become a Christian majority area. The major—so-called mainline—churches derive from the spread of Christian missions, beginning in 1668 with the arrival of Catholicism in the Northern Mariana Islands and Guam, in the form of Spanish Jesuits from the Philippines. A more substantial diffusion of Protestant Christianity dates from 1796, when the interdenominational British Missionary Society (later known as the London Missionary Society) entered Tahiti. The LONDON MISSIONARY SOCIETY (LMS) and the Wesleyan METHODIST Missionary Society (WMMS), beginning in Polynesia, recruited and transported Pacific islander missionaries known as teachers or auxiliary missionaries, in a movement from east to west, eventually as far as New Guinea and its offshore islands. The conversion of Cook Islanders to Christianity can be traced to two converts from Ra'iatea, Isaiah Papeiha (or Papehia) and Vahapata, who were brought there by the LMS' John WILLIAMS in 1821.

Both the LMS and the WMMS were reinforced by missionaries from the British colonies in Australia and New Zealand. From 1820 onward the largely Congregational AMERICAN BOARD OF COMMISSIONERS FOR FOREIGN MISSIONS (ABCFM), working from its original stations in Hawai'i, trained and employed Hawaiians as ordained missionaries to the Marshall and Caroline Islands in Micronesia. In Melanesia and French Polynesia, the Paris Evangelical Missionary Society, representative broadly of the Reformed Presbyterian tradition, took over from the LMS in New Caledonia. In the New Hebrides (now Vanuatu) the majority Presbyterian Church was founded by Scots missionaries in 1848 from Nova Scotia, Scotland, Australia and New Zealand. (John G PATON represented the Reformed Church of Scotland.) No other areas of the Pacific islands were entered by Presbyterian missionaries. In 1886 LUTHERANS from Germany came, by way of South Australia, to New Guinea, becoming, through the deployment of New Guinean evangelists, a major presence in the populous New Guinea Highlands before World War II. The present complexion of Protestant church life is due to these origins—a steady process of diffusion by indigenous islanders who worked at village and hamlet level to establish nascent churches from the time of the earliest baptisms onwards.

Roman Catholic churches were founded and tended by missionary orders and congregations of religious men and women. They were slow to train ordained islander successors since their academic requirements and celibacy rules were uncompromising. They also came later than the Protestants in most places. From 1838 to 1844, the European French-speaking Society of Mary (Marists) sent 41 French missionaries to New Zealand and set up 12 missions under POMPALLIER's care. From this time, the Marists gradually formed churches in central Oceania. In eastern Polynesia, including Tahiti and Hawai'i, the French society of the Sacred Hearts of Jesus and Mary (Picpus Fathers) came first in 1834. In Micronesia, the Missionaries of the Sacred Heart (MSC) came to Kiribati and the Marshall Islands. In Melanesia, the Marists spread out into Solomon Islands, including Bougainville. In Papua and New Britain, the MSC contended against colonial government restrictions to put down roots of a Catholic Church early in the present century, while German-speaking missionaries of the Society of the Divine Word (SVD) came first to the vicinity of Madang and spread to the Highlands.—JG1

Malua Theological College near Apia, Samoa

London Missionary Society

The London Missionary Society (LMS), oldest of the Protestant societies working in the Pacific, was founded in London in 1795 by a committee of Calvinistic Methodists and Dissenters closely associated with the *Evangelical Magazine* (1793). Dr Thomas HAWEIS, who had attempted to send missionaries to Tahiti with William BLIGH, was responsible for the Society making Tahiti its first mission field. Samuel Greatheed prepared geographical histories of the Society, Friendly, Navigator, Sandwich and Marquesas Islands, and a new chart of the Pacific to assist missionary operations. The Society chartered a vessel, *Duff* (Captain James Wilson), which landed missionaries in Tahiti, Tonga and the Marquesas in 1797. Despite the departure and defection of some missionaries and the murder of three others in Tonga, a few converts were made in Tahiti in 1812. The conversion of the Tahitian chief POMARE II led to the formation of a Christian party. Following the victory of Pomare at the battle of Feipi in 1815, a Christian kingdom was established with Christianity as the nominal religion. Other chiefly confederations became Christian kingdoms on Ra'iatea, Huahine and Borabora. With a rapid increase in church membership, auxiliary missionary societies were founded in the islands, and approved converts were sent out to other island groups as 'native teachers'. Some went to Hawai'i to work with the AMERICAN BOARD OF COMMISSIONERS FOR FOREIGN MISSIONS (ABCFM), some went to the previously abandoned Marquesas, others were successful in Cook Islands and the far-flung islands of what is now French Polynesia. Some did pioneering work in Tonga, Fiji and Rotuma. In 1830 teachers were left in Samoa. Training institutions were set up at Rarotonga and at Malua (Samoa), and evangelization of Niue, the northern Cooks, Tuvalu, the southern Gilberts, New Hebrides, New Caledonia, and Loyalty Islands was shared between Cook Islands and Samoan teachers. Attempts to set up kingdoms in Samoa, Niue, Cook Islands and Loyalty Islands were only partially successful. Law codes were introduced in most groups, and in Cook Islands, the 'blue-laws' (1827) were so repressive due to chiefly influence that the missionaries were blamed.

The last thrust of LMS activity was into Papua via the Torres Strait Islands, again using islander teachers. The Society regarded all the 'isles of the sea' as its brief, but due to heavy financial and personal commitments in its other mission fields (South Africa, Madagascar, India and China), it reluctantly handed over much of its sphere to other missions: to the Wesleyans in Tonga, Fiji and Rotuma; to Anglicans in New Caledonia and Torres Strait; to Presbyterians in New Hebrides; and to the ABCFM and the Hawaiian Evangelical Association in Marquesas. The only field it took over was northern Gilbert Islands (Kiribati) from the ABCFM, since islands north of the line were part of the new colony of Gilbert and Ellice Islands. The Papuan station of Kwato broke with the parent society over its industrial mission policy and sought separate sponsorship.

Although the LMS became a Congregational missionary society when the Congregational Union of England and Wales was formed in 1831, it still retained its fundamental principle not to send episcopacy, presbyterianism or independency to the mission field, but to let the island churches decide for themselves. As it was, most island churches called themselves independent or congregational, but organized their assemblies on Presbyterian lines with the European missionaries frequently taking on an episcopal role.

From the beginning the LMS favoured comity arrangements and through Samuel MARSDEN's influence in Sydney, the Pacific field was divided into three spheres of influence (LMS, Church Missionary Society, and Wesleyan METHODIST Missionary Society). Despite this amicable arrangement, there was conflict in Samoa between the LMS and the Wesleyans, largely due to local politics and personalities. Also the LMS was reluctant to hand over its work in Loyalty Islands to the Melanesian mission on theological grounds. The most successful comity arrangements were those endorsed in 1890 by Sir William MacGregor in Papua New Guinea, which remained in operation for several decades although not recognized by Roman Catholics or SEVENTH-DAY ADVENTISTS.

Although many of the missionaries came out by convict ships, whaling or trading vessels, there was an early push led by individuals such as William Shelley, Samuel Marsden, and John WILLIAMS to have a ship belonging to the Society. Besides numerous small vessels serving in each region, the Society

London Missionary Society mission house at Avarua, Rarotonga (engraving)

furnished its own mission ship largely from funds raised by Sunday school pupils. The sailing ships were *Camden*, and three vessels named *John Williams*. Of the steamships, *John Williams VI*, launched by Princess Margaret in 1948, was the largest. The last ship of the line, *John Williams VII*, confined its activities to Gilbert and Ellice Islands (now Kiribati and Tuvalu).

At first the LMS had difficulty in maintaining contact with its agents and long delays frequently led to grievances. The practice of sending deputational visitors to the Pacific began in 1821–29 with the voyage of Daniel Tyerman and George Bennet, and was revived later in the century with deputations from England and Australia every decade from 1887. Local missionary deputations also visited the outstations.

As the various islands of the Pacific became independent and came to rely less on European mission input (the pattern throughout the mission field), the LMS went through a final transformation. At first renamed the Congregational Council for World Mission in 1966, it later amalgamated with other bodies and became the Council for World Mission in 1977. In the mission field many of the Congregational churches merged in other unions, the most notable in the Pacific being the United Church in Papua New Guinea and Solomon Islands (1968) in which the LMS (represented by the Papua Ekalesia since 1962) combined with Methodists and the Port Moresby United Church. The Kwato mission had already been reunited with Papua Ekalesia in 1964.

The LMS always favoured teaching in the vernacular, translating the Bible and a limited range of texts into the major dialects of each group, thus standardizing the languages. Until colonial governments were well established, local education and health were in the hands of missionaries. Although the LMS discouraged the involvement of missionaries in politics, circumstances sometimes led individuals to take actions they believed were in the interest of their flock—such as the anti-French activities of George PRITCHARD in Tahiti and John Jones in Loyalty Islands. In more recent times, missionaries acted as advisers to those serving in newly independent governments, or stood as candidates for island legislatures.

Missionaries such as John Williams of Ra'iaṭea and James CHALMERS of Papua contributed to exploration. Of the numerous missionaries who wrote scientific papers and contributed to ethnography, William Ellis, J M Orsmond, George Pratt, William Wyatt Gill, James E Newell, and J H Holmes stand out. Other justly famous missionaries include William Pascoe Crook, Charles Barff, George H Eastman, W E Goward, Cecil Abel and Percy Chatterton.—WNG

American Board of Commissioners for Foreign Missions

The American Board of Commissioners for Foreign Missions (ABCFM) was the first American mission society. Set up by members of the Congregational church in 1810 to support overseas mission activities, it was active in the Pacific islands up until 1961, when the Congregational Christian church merged with the United church, and it then became the United Church of Christ Board of World Ministries. In the 19th century, the ABCFM was responsible for sending more than 150 missionaries (ministers, teachers, doctors, farmers, printers) to Hawai'i and Micronesia. As their activities expanded throughout Micronesia, many mission stations and at least 50 churches were set up.—KRF

Methodists

The English Methodists came to the Pacific in the second wave following the Congregationalists, to Tonga, Fiji and Samoa. After their arrival in Tonga in 1826, Tonga became a strongly Protestant kingdom because of the support of Tāufa'āhau (George TUPOU I), who was converted in 1830. From Tonga, Methodism spread to Fiji. Tongans had a long background of contacts with Fiji through trade and warfare, and Tongan missionaries accompanied the English Methodists, first to the smaller eastern islands and then to the main island of Viti Levu. Most famous was Joeli Bulu, who settled permanently in Fiji and became one of the most venerated figures of Fijian Methodism. After CAKOBAU accepted Christianity in 1854, Methodism spread rapidly.

In Samoa too, Christianity was readily accepted. The first LONDON MISSIONARY SOCIETY (LMS) teachers in 1830 had paved the way for wider acceptance by 1836; but a rift developed within the new Christian community because of the efforts of an earlier group of Methodists from Tonga. Some chiefs supported the Methodist church against the Congregationalism of the majority. British missionaries arrived from Tonga to support them (1835–39), but then these were withdrawn by Britain, in response to reports of the division in Samoa, in favour of the LMS forces. The Samoan Methodists struggled on, and then in 1857 the Australian Methodists finally agreed to help them. From that time, Methodists became a well-established minority in Samoa, against the greater numbers of the Congregational church.

In Papua New Guinea, it was the British administrator in Papua, Sir William MacGregor, who invited both the Methodists and the Anglicans from Australia to add to the efforts of the LMS and Catholics in the field. A formal conference was held in 1890, and agreement was reached with the LMS on division of territory.

Once established in the islands, the Methodists made the transition to independence gradually, dropping all foreign help for their churches in Tonga in 1875, in Samoa by 1915, in Fiji by the late 1920s, in New Britain by 1937, and in Papua and Solomon Islands after 1950. An autonomous Annual Conference was established in 1964 in both Samoa and Fiji, and a complete break with the General Conference of the Methodist Church of Australasia came in 1977.—KRF

Anglicans

The Anglican church of England was established in Hawai'i in the 19th century, but in 1902, responsibility for its administration was transferred to the American Episcopal church. In Fiji the Anglicans had arrived in the 19th century not as missionaries but to serve the needs of the European community, having agreed after discussion with the METHODIST mission that they would not seek new converts among the indigenous Fijian population. Some of their successes occurred among the Fijian Indian community, however, which had been mostly Hindu, with a minority of Muslims (nearly 10 per cent).

Conflicting attitudes towards the proper role of the church in the Pacific islands emerged, with the controversial figure of Bishop Alfred Willis (formerly Bishop of Hawai'i) seeking a new missionary diocese. Bishop Neville of Dunedin, in New Zealand, supported him, having already provided assistance in Shirley BAKER's discredited attempt to found a competing Anglican church in Tonga; but Willis' involvement was opposed by a majority. The new Pacific bishopric was created in 1908, with the Reverend T C Twitchell becoming the first bishop of Polynesia. By the 1920s the Anglican missionaries in Fiji had overcome the initial prohibition of the COLONIAL SUGAR REFINING COMPANY against preaching to any plantation workers, and had established schools for the Indian community. The diocese remained under the auspices of the English church until 1925, when it was transferred to the Province of New Zealand. In 1913 the Anglican Diocese of Carpentaria took over the Torres Strait Islands.

In Papua New Guinea, the Anglican church in Australia was invited by Sir William MacGregor, Governor of (then) British New Guinea, to become involved in missionary work, alongside the already established LMS, and Catholics. A conference was held in 1890, at which the Methodists and Anglicans reached agreement on their respective areas of operation. By the turn of the century, the beginnings of Anglican activity were established along the northeast Papuan coast, and the first Papuan priest was ordained in 1917. A large cathedral was built at the Papuan headquarters, Dogura, in the 1930s, and the church's efforts in providing educational and medical services were greatly upgraded after World War II.

The Melanesian mission in Solomon Islands had operated from its headquarters on Norfolk Island, using its steamboat, the *Southern Cross*, to maintain its missionary training program. Pawa, the Anglican central school, was set up on Nggela in 1919, and the church remained involved in primary education in Solomon Islands until the end of 1974.

During the first half of the 20th century, Anglicans in the Pacific continued to be financially supported from outside, and progress in allocating church offices to local villagers was slow until after the war. By the 1960s, however, village priests were well established, and Anglican churches in the Pacific had formed a South Pacific Anglican Council. A number of autonomous dioceses were set up, and the first Pacific islander was appointed to the leadership of one of them (Hawai'i) in 1970.—KRF

French missions in the Pacific

Although the evangelization of the Pacific region had been discussed for many years, the predominantly Roman Catholic French missionary societies did not enter the Pacific field until after the long and bitter Revolutionary and Napoleonic wars. This coincided with a religious revival in France which produced a number of vocations during the 1820–40 period. By then English and American Protestant missionaries—Anglicans, Wesleyans and Presbyterians—were established in various island groups, and they did not view with any sympathy the arrival of their Roman Catholic rivals.

An attempt by the Congregation of the Sacred Hearts of Jesus and Mary (the Picpus Fathers) to establish a mission in the Hawaiian Islands in 1827 led to a bitter struggle which lasted over 12 years. The American missionary Hiram BINGHAM used his influence with Queen KA'AHUMANU to have the first priests expelled and to ban their religion. This led successive French naval officers to demand equality of treatment for French nationals, including missionaries.

Eventually, Captain Cyrille Laplace, of the *Artemise*, obtained freedom of religion and the release of all imprisoned Catholics, whether natives or European, in exchange for France's formal recognition of Hawaiian sovereignty. Within a couple of years, some nine priests had settled in the islands, there were over 2000 Catholics on O'ahu alone, and in 1846 Honolulu's Catholic cathedral was dedicated. Gradually, however, the missionary orders recognized that the English language was assuming a dominant role, and ceased to send French priests to Hawai'i.

The Gambier Islands proved easier for the French priests. When Fathers LAVAL and Caret arrived in 1834 the only opposition they met was from the LONDON MISSIONARY SOCIETY's David Darling, who pointed out that the LMS had discovered the island group in 1797 and invited the French to go elsewhere. This request was ignored and the French missionaries rapidly gained the support of the population and the chiefs.

However, an attempt by Laval and Caret to move on to Tahiti in 1836 met with the determined opposition of the LMS missionary George PRITCHARD, who had been in the island since 1824 and had gained an ascendancy over Queen POMARE IV. The two Frenchmen were expelled within a month and a situation developed which was almost a repetition of the Hawaiian crisis, with French naval officers pressing for equal rights for French nationals. The clashes in Tahiti were, if anything, more bitter, with the Tahitian ruler repudiating—almost as soon as the naval units disappeared over the horizon—agreements which their commanders had forced on her. This led, in 1842, to a re-statement of the rights of French and Polynesian Catholics to practise their religion, but this time with the proclamation of a French protectorate to enforce it.

After Tahiti became a French possession, the authorities realized that a substantial part of the population belonged to the Protestant faith, and took steps to ensure that French Protestant pastors were appointed. The Société des Missions Évangéliques took over from the LMS, the first pastor arriving in 1863 (see Charles VIÉNOT); within a few years the number of ordained ministers exceeded 50. Frédéric Vernier (1841–1915) played a significant role in reconciling the English and French Protestant churches.

The Picpus Fathers were fairly successful in establishing themselves in Marquesas Islands, partly because the first two arrived on a French warship, but also because the LMS had given up its attempt to set up a mission in 1797. Tribal disputes and general anarchy, however, did not make this archipelago a pleasant or easy mission.

The western Pacific had meanwhile been allocated to another religious order, the Society of Mary. Bishop POMPALLIER sailed from Valparaiso in 1827, crossing the Pacific with a group of missionaries; an attempt to establish a station in Tonga failed, as the islands had been evangelized by Wesleyan missionaries and the Tongan king refused the Marists the right to land. Pompallier was able to land several priests on Wallis and Futuna, however, (one of them, Pierre CHANEL, would soon become the Order's first martyr) and he found it relatively easy to establish himself in New Zealand which became his headquarters.

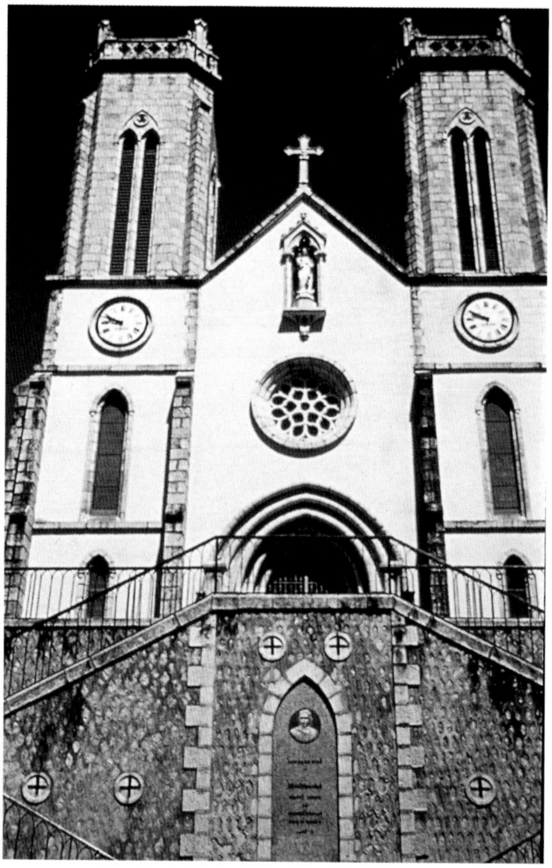

St Joseph's Cathedral, Noumea

A second attempt to land in Tonga was made in 1842. The French priests were allowed to settle and were relatively successful until 1847 when tolerance waned; the Catholic church was burnt down and a period of persecution began which lasted until 1853. A French naval unit called in 1858 to exact reparations for the damage suffered by the mission, but refused any compensation, asking instead for freedom of religion which was granted by royal order in 1861.

Fiji had been evangelized by Wesleyan missionaries and when the French Marists arrived in 1844 they were met with dislike and indifference. They made slow progress until 1858 when a French ship secured freedom of religion, and by the 1860s had five mission schools. Although the French were gradually replaced by English-speaking priests, the Marist press at LEVUKA continued to publish books in French for the Pacific missions for many years.

The LMS had settled in Samoa in 1830 and secured considerable influence. When the Marists arrived in 1845 they met official opposition from the

LMS, but were welcomed by a number of Samoans who resented the power and stern rule of the English missionaries. This at least enabled the French to establish a footing among the population: their success was always contested, but in time some 20 per cent of the population became Catholic.

New Caledonia and the New Hebrides presented other problems. An early mission station was opened at Balade on the north coast of New Caledonia in December 1843, but the shortage of supplies and attacks by the Melanesians forced the missionaries to leave in 1847. Several other attempts were made, with little success. This paralleled the problems encountered by the LMS in 1840 and 1841. The Society was more successful in the Loyalty Islands, especially in 1854 when two European missionaries were landed. Not long after, Marists arrived on Ouvea and Lifu and from there they were gradually able to settle on New Caledonia itself.

Other parts of Melanesia presented similar difficulties. Anglicans and Presbyterians were seeking a foothold in the New Hebrides: the French tried their luck on Aneityum, in the far south of the archipelago, in 1848, but this outpost lasted only three years. A more concerted attempt was made in 1887 on Malekula, soon followed by mission stations on some of the other larger islands. In time, missionary activities became entangled in the political problems of the Anglo-French CONDOMINIUM, with French-speaking Catholics and English-speaking Protestants and long-lasting suspicions on both sides.

The difficulties encountered in eastern Melanesia were compounded in Solomon Islands and New Guinea, with difficult terrain, numerous tribes and languages, and a general suspicion of all outsiders. In 1845, Bishop ÉPALLE led a group of Marists to Santa Isabel, but he was killed in December. Retreating to San Cristobal, the survivors were defeated by MALARIA and new attacks by the islanders. They gave up in 1852, handing over to an Italian order which found conditions equally unbearable. Missionary work was abandoned until the 1890s, by which time Solomon Islands were being taken over by Britain.

French missionaries did not start evangelizing New Guinea until 1881 when five priests sailed from France. Even so, they could go no further than Thursday Island, in Torres Strait, because British policy opposed different denominations operating in the same mission field. The French nevertheless smuggled themselves across to the Port Moresby area and by the 1890s their mission numbered 32 priests and brothers and 17 sisters. Protests by the Governor of Queensland led to the dispute on restricted religious spheres of influence being referred to London, where it dragged on until the 1920s. The policy was in time rejected as sectarian, but by then the number of French missionaries in New Guinea had dwindled into insignificance.

Sectarianism was often at the heart of the disputes which bedevilled missionary efforts in the Pacific, but it was also difficult for the missionaries, whatever their nationality, to avoid being drawn into colonial and political arguments. Residual suspicions between France and Britain after the Napoleonic wars and rivalry over colonizing ventures, affected the missionaries and caused many to espouse their country's interests and to call on their governments for moral and active support. For the French, the situation became further complicated later in the century by anti-clerical governments at home and occasional anti-clerical local administrators. These strains lessened as the years went by, sectarianism became less bitter, and the two countries found themselves united by common interests during the two world wars.—JD

Lutherans

The Lutheran mission in the Pacific islands originated in the work of two missions from Germany, which came soon after the German annexation of New Guinea in 1884 and established themselves in the Madang area. The Neuendettelsau Mission, led by Johannes Flierl in 1886, came from a small village in Bavaria—first to South Australia. It based its activities around Finschhafen on the Huon Peninsula, where it became the largest Protestant body in the country. Its effectiveness arose largely because of the carefully formulated mission method developed by one of its missionaries, Christian Keysser, who served from 1899 to 1921. Understanding the solidarity of village or tribal community groups, Keysser recognized the value of appointing community leaders to positions of mission authority, and allowing the congregations to decide ethical issues of church policy. His method produced vigorous and unified village congregations, soon sending thousands of their own dedicated members as missionaries into the inland areas. The second German body, the Rhenish Mission from the Rhineland, was much weaker. In the aftermath of World War I, the peace agreements initially required the Lutheran administration to be transferred to American and Australian personnel. After Australian rule was established, all German missions suffered because further immigration was halted until 1927, and the Rhenish Mission was struggling with inadequate financial resources. In 1932 the American Lutheran church took over its management and made great advances from this time. A small group of Australian Lutherans subsequently assumed responsibility for mission work in the Siassi Islands to the northeast.

German Lutherans were the first white people to enter the eastern Highlands in 1919 and 1920, and their coastal recruits followed in 1922. One of these early evangelists (40 were working in the eastern Highlands by 1930) was Gape'nuo, whose explorations revealed the existence of the traditional trading route into the Purari valley. The Kate language of the Lutheran evangelists became the church language for all the Lutheran parts of the Highlands. Among the Lutheran congregations, the practice also developed of creating a dramatization or enactment of a Biblical text, rehearsed by a small group and then presented within the church service. In the remote valleys between the eastern and western Highlands, the young German Wilhelm Bergmann and his wife Louise became the first white residents in 1931. The Lutheran mission began an air service for their inland stations in 1935, and operated a licensed radio for the mission air strips. Each teacher graduating from the Lutheran training college received some coffee seedlings to take home, thus ensuring the successful dissemination of coffee over a wide area of the northeast region, and enabling the mission to export its first shipment of coffee in 1938.

The Lutheran mission had a press for printing both religious and secular literature in native vernaculars. Operating under skilled indigenous supervision, this press was allowed to continue to print religious literature with the permission of the Japanese during the Japanese occupation in the 1940s. The press was later destroyed during air raids while the Allied Forces reoccupied the Finschhafen area. After the war the Lutherans expanded their activities in the Highlands, but now competing for new recruits alongside a dozen other missions. In the post-war missionary philosophy that supported the rapid establishment of an independent indigenous church, the Wabag Lutheran church was established in 1961, only 12 years after the large Missouri Synod Lutheran mission had arrived from the United States.—KRF

Lotu

The term Lotu is used in the central South Pacific for the Christian religion. The origins of the word, though not definitively established, are generally acknowledged to be Tongan. It is likely that the word *lotu* was carried to Samoa and Fiji by Tongan converts in the first three decades of the 1800s. In Samoa, Christianity was first known as Lotu Taita, because the first resident missionaries were eight Tahitians. Christianity in Fiji was first called Lotu Toga. METHODISTS in Fiji came to call themselves Lotu Wesele, while the Roman Catholic church is known as Lotu Katolika, and the SEVENTH-DAY ADVENTISTS Lotu Kavitu (*vitu* = seven).

The word was also used as a verb: to *lotu* means to convert to Christianity. There are slight variations to *lotu* in other languages, such as *rotu* in Rotuma. Pacific missionaries carried the word to Melanesia. The Mota language of northern Vanuatu uses *lotu*, and Anglican expansion from there took the word to Solomon Islands. In more recent times, development of vernacular scriptures seems to have led to a decline in the word's use in Melanesia.—AT2

New Zealand's involvement in Pacific missions

When the METHODIST missionary Walter Lawry went to Tonga in 1822, Maori converts accompanied him. White missionaries from New Zealand served in the Methodist missions of Fiji, Tonga and Samoa, George Brown being the best known. From 1922 the New Zealand Methodist church assumed responsibility for the western Solomon Islands, where John Goldie most notably served for 50 years. Later in the 20th century many New Zealanders served in Papua New Guinea.

The first ANGLICAN Bishops of Melanesia, John Coleridge PATTESON and George Augustus SELWYN, had their headquarters and training centre in Auckland. The present Diocese of Polynesia is part of the province of Aotearoa/New Zealand.

Most Pacific islands have received Roman Catholic missionaries from New Zealand, including the Marist Fathers (trained at Greenmeadows), the Marist Brothers (Timaru) and the Missionary Sisters of the Society of Mary (Heretaunga). Many New Zealand women have served in the Pacific with the Australian-trained Marist Sisters. Other New Zealand denominations with Pacific links include the Presbyterians, Congregationalists and the Brethren.—AT2

Hongi Hika

The formidable Maori chief Hongi Hika (c1777–1828), leader of the Ngapuhi of northern New Zealand, visited Sydney with RUATARA in 1814 to fetch Samuel MARSDEN and his Church Missionary Society (CMS) community and bring them to the Bay of Islands. He and a close relative, Waikato, later accompanied the CMS missionary, Thomas Kendall, to London in 1820, where he assisted in the compilation of a Maori dictionary. On his return in 1821, he brought 300 muskets (obtained in Sydney by trading presents he had been given in London) and then, wearing a suit of armour supplied by King George IV, he proceeded to slaughter several thousand of his ancient enemies. Hongi himself refused conversion to Christianity, claiming that it was unsuitable for warriors. After his death in 1828, the CMS made rapid progress throughout New Zealand, assisted by the release of Hongi's many captured slaves who had attended mission schools and become familiar with the Christian message.—KRF

Source/further reading

Belich J, 1996. *Making Peoples*, Allen Lane.

Mulipola Faueā

The Samoan *ali'i* chief, Mulipola Faueā, had been living in Fiji and Tonga for 10 years when he met John WILLIAMS in 1830 and offered to accompany him on the *Messenger of Peace* to Savai'i, Samoa, to introduce the missionaries to his people. They reached Sapapali'i, one of the home villages of Malietoa, in mid July, where Faueā's message—that acceptance of Christianity would be rewarded not only by peace but also shiploads of goods—won some immediate converts. Faueā had warned Williams that they would find their main obstacle in the chief Leiataua Tonumaipea Tamafaigā, of Manono. When it was found that the chief had been killed only a few weeks before the arrival of the missionaries, Williams credited his death as a major factor in the subsequent success of the mission.—KRF

Further reading

Gilson, R P, 1970. *Samoa, 1830–1900: the politics of a multicultural community*, Oxford University Press.

Influence of missions in Fiji

The first Christian missionaries in Fiji were three Tahitians—Tahaara, Arue and Hatai—of the LONDON MISSIONARY SOCIETY. A Fijian emissary of Tui Nayau, Takai, brought them from Tahiti to Lakeba. In 1835 the METHODIST missionaries David Cargill and William Cross came from Tonga to Lakeba and in 1838 took the Tahitians under their supervision. In 1839, after preliminary investigations by Josua Mateinaniu of Vulaga, Cross established a mission station on the island of Viwa in central Fiji. Progress was hampered by the frequency of warfare among Fijian confederations in the 1840s, though in 1845 Viwa experienced a Christian 'pentecost' through the work of John HUNT.

Cargill, Hunt and David Hazelwood were mainly responsible for the written Fijian orthography, the first vernacular Bible and the Fijian Grammar. Through the influence of Tongan missionaries and the Fijian high chief, Ratu Seru CAKOBAU, Methodism became the predominant Christian denomination by the 1880s, and the missionaries imparted literacy through a network of elementary village schools.

The Roman Catholics arrived in Fiji in 1844 and had most success on the islands of Ovalau and Taveuni. The ANGLICANS started in Fiji in 1869, and the SEVENTH-DAY ADVENTISTS in 1891. Today 75 per cent of Fijians are Methodists and 15 per cent are Roman Catholics. The Methodists also began Christian work among the Indo-Fijian population in 1892. Today 5 per cent of the Indo-Fijian population are Christian, divided among a number of denominations.—AT2

Pacific islander missionaries

It was John WILLIAMS, the celebrated LONDON MISSIONARY SOCIETY missionary, who first introduced islanders to the vision of missionary work, while George BROWN, the equally capable METHODIST missionary, consolidated Williams' initiative in Melanesia. Both men stand in the tradition notably set by Alexander de Rhodes, the 17th century Jesuit priest in Vietnam, and William Carey, the Baptist missionary in India. All of them appreciated the role that could be played by committed indigenous lay people (and later, PASTORS), desiring to put into practice Christ's great commission (*Matthew* 28:19–20) to 'go and make disciples of all nations'.

The first Pacific islander missionaries were Tahitians who went to Hawai'i, Cook Islands, Tonga, Samoa and Fiji. In turn, Hawaiians went as missionaries to Micronesia, Tongans to Fiji and Rotuma, Samoans to southern Vanuatu and Tuvalu, Fijians and Rotumans to New Britain and New Guinea, and many other Pacific islanders—including Niueans, Cook Islanders and the above-named groups—to Melanesia. Later in the 20th century, Melanesian missionaries served in the Highlands of Papua New Guinea and in northern Australia. The movement of Pacific islander missionaries formed part of a complex and substantial spreading of Protestant Christianity, a steady process of diffusion by indigenous islanders who worked at village and hamlet level to establish nascent churches. Details of their numbers cannot be given accurately, though a list in the PACIFIC THEOLOGICAL COLLEGE, not claiming to be definitive, contains more than 1200 names.

Their contribution was minimized for many years in published missionary literature. By contrast, oral traditions about Pacific missionaries remain very strong within island communities and legends quickly become established regarding the exploits of overseas workers—for example, the Tongan Semisi Nau's dramatic 'entry' into Ontong Java when he was left drifting in the lagoon for 90 days, before being permitted to land. Recently, a growing body of literature by and about Pacific missionaries has appeared, but Pacific islander scholars are only now beginning to explore vernacular sources such as island church newsletters, which carried reports from missionary letters.

Yet to be recognized and even more difficult to research is the work of missionary women, wives of ministers and teachers. They served unofficial roles as carers, women's leaders and nurses to the communities where their husbands worked. The death rate of the infant children of Pacific missionary families was unusually high, and many of these women never saw their homeland again once they had left it. They were, in the vivid expression of one missionary woman, 'outriggers to the canoe', their life's journey bound to that of their husband.

The observations of Stephen Neill, author of *A History of Christian Missions* (1986), most adequately summarize and give proper perspective to the achievements of Pacific islander missionaries.

Few marvels in Christian history can equal the faithfulness of these men and women, left behind among peoples of unknown speech and often in danger of their lives, to plant and build churches out of their own limited stock of faith and knowledge, supported only by the invigorating power of the Holy Spirit and the prayers of their friends. Many watered the seed with their own blood; but the churches grew, and far more widely than if reliance had been placed first and foremost on the European missionary.—AT2

Pastors

Pastors is the term used largely by Pacific churches descended from the LONDON MISSIONARY SOCIETY (LMS) Congregationalist tradition to describe indigenous missionaries ordained for the Christian ministry. In the Pacific, the first Protestant pastors began training under George PRITCHARD of Pape'ete in 1829. LMS pastor training institutions were later established on Rarotonga, Cook Islands (the Takamoa Institute) in 1839, and at Malua College near Apia, Samoa in 1844. In the United States from the early 1800s, Cornwall School in Connecticut was also providing religious education for islanders. Designed to inculcate Christian values among non-Christian peoples—Indians, Hawaiians and others—the school was a showcase for New England piety and philanthropy, and many of its teachers and students joined the early companies to the islands. From about 1841 the Protestant mission in Hawai'i began the practice of licensing natives to preach, but it was not until 1849 that a Native Hawaiian was formally ordained to the ministry and installed as pastor of an independent church. In Tonga the first METHODIST training institution was established at Neiafu, Vava'u, in 1841, with the support of King George TUPOU I. Its graduates were called native missionaries, rather than pastors. Islander pastors taught in their own home islands, but there was also a strong overseas impulse in the early Pacific churches. Many hundreds of newly converted 'native teachers' (as they were first known) and pastors played a significant pioneering role in the introduction of Christianity throughout the Pacific, risking their health and their lives, and many died of disease or were murdered. (See PACIFIC ISLANDER MISSIONARIES.)—AT2

■ ***George Sarawia*** George Sarawia (1845–1901), the first Melanesian clergyman—ordained deacon in 1868, and priest in 1873—came from Vanua Lava, Banks Islands (New Hebrides, now Vanuatu), and first met the Anglican missionaries George SELWYN and John PATTESON when their mission ship called at the island when he was 15-years old. In 1858 he was persuaded to attend the Melanesian Mission's winter school on Lifu (Loyalty Islands), and was baptized in 1863 by Bishop Selwyn, who named him George. After assisting at a mission school at Mota, in the Banks Islands for a few months each year, Sarawia with his wife Sarah and two other Christian couples—all former mission students on Norfolk Island—established a separate Christian village on their island, with Patteson's support. The settlement of Kohimarama (named for the Auckland school) was established in 1869, and Sarawia began a boarding-school for about 30 boys and young men. On Mota he enjoyed considerable prestige, but this rested on his high rank as head-man rather than as Christian priest. He was not an energetic church leader; his health was poor and he seldom left home, although he did attend the consecration of Bishop Cecil Wilson in Auckland in 1894. In the last years of his life, the Mota church was in decline.—KRF

■ ***Soakimi Gatafahefa*** Soakimi Gatafahefa (1838–96), known as Gata, was the first Pacific islander Roman Catholic priest. Born of Tongan parents at Lakeba in the Lau group, Gata spent most of his childhood in Futuna and was taken by the French priest, Pierre Bataillon, to Propaganda College in Rome to study for the priesthood. Ordained in 1865, he returned to a short and unsuccessful appointment in Tonga in 1867, where he apparently found a hostile reception. He was transferred to Samoa and then back to Futuna, where he eventually came into conflict with Bataillon, who accused him of trying to turn the Futunans against the European clergy. Another transfer to Wallis failed to resolve the problem and Gata was at last suspended as a priest and sent for retraining in Sydney. Later he went to New Zealand, where he lived for 20 years as 'Brother Joe', supposedly a Marist lay preacher.—KRF

■ *The first Hawaiian missionaries* When the first American missionary contingent sailed from Boston on the *Thaddeus*, there were four Hawaiian youths on board from Cornwall School. John Honolii, a Hawaiian sailor who arrived in the United States in the early 1800s, had been converted to Christianity by another Hawaiian in exile, Thomas Hopu (Hopoo), who had attended Cornwall School. Honolii taught the missionaries the rudiments of the Hawaiian language, and once in Hawai'i, he helped negotiate for permission for the mission to remain in the islands. William Kanui (Tenooee), who had sailed to Boston in 1809, went to New Haven and was befriended by Yale College students who sent him to Cornwall School. When he returned to Hawai'i with the pioneer mission, he was torn between Hawaiian culture and Protestant ideals. In the end the mission resolved his conflict, excommunicating him for persistent backsliding. George P Kaumualii (Kamooula) had also been a student at the Cornwall School, because he was the son of the King of Kaua'i. He became a labourer and later a seaman in the American navy. Bartimeus was a blind Hawaiian, much respected for his piety. One of the first converts to Christianity, he became a licensed preacher in 1842, a year before he died. His life, the essence of legend, was the subject of at least two biographical tracts, one written by Hiram BINGHAM, 'Bartimeus, of the Sandwich Islands' (1851).—KRF

■ *Mary Kaaialii Nawaa* Mary Kaaialii (14 January 1851–c6 April 1914), missionary teacher in the Marshall Islands, was born at Lahaina in Hawai'i and educated at the ABCFM-established Waialua Female Seminary on O'ahu (1867–69). On graduation, she married Simeon Kahelemauna, who had been accepted as a member of the Micronesian Mission, and they set out for the mission headquarters on Ebon, where they studied the language. Assigned to the tiny atoll of Mili in the Ratak chain in 1870, they opened the first schools and built a church, and their son was born in 1872. By 1875 the Mili Mission was reported as an outstanding success, and Simeon was ordained, but he became ill soon after and died in January 1876. Kaaialii was pregnant but she refused the ABCFM offer to leave Mili and instead indicated her determination to carry on the missionary work. She returned to Hawai'i for several months after the death of the new baby, and was encouraged to marry Simeon's brother, Samuel Nawaa, in order to be permitted to return to Mili—where an ordained Marshallese pastor, Jeremiah, was now installed—in October 1877. After three years in Micronesia, however, Samuel was recalled by the Hawaiian Board and dismissed from the ministry. He continued as a lay preacher and was ordained in 1884 as pastor of the Ewa church on O'ahu, but no further details of Kaaialii's life are known.—JL3

Further reading

Crocombe, R and Crocombe, M (eds), 1982. *Polynesian Missions in Melanesia: from Samoa, Cook Islands and Tonga to Papua New Guinea and New Caledonia*, Institute of Pacific Studies, University of the South Pacific.

Laracy, H, 1977. 'The Catholic Mission', in N Rutherford (ed.), *The Friendly Islands: a history of Tonga*, Oxford University Press.

Miller, C, 1988. *Selected writings of Hiram Bingham 1814–1869: missionary to the Hawaiian Islands: to raise the Lord's banner*, Edwin Mellen Press.

Munro, D and Thornley, A, 1996. *The Covenant Makers: islander missionaries in the Pacific*, Pacific Theological College and Institute of Pacific Studies, University of the South Pacific.

Neill, S, 1986. *A History of Christian Missions*, Pelican History of the church, 6, Pelican.

Missionary biographies

■ *Charles Abel* Charles William Abel (25 September 1862–10 April 1930), pioneer missionary in Papua, was born in London and worked as a clerk before migrating to New Zealand as a cadet farmer. Having become involved in missionary teaching among the Maori, he went back to England to train at Cheshunt College, and was ordained in 1890. He went to Papua in 1890, sent by the LONDON MISSIONARY SOCIETY (LMS) to Suau, but he moved to Kwato in Milne Bay to set up a mission station that was to become a community of 300 young Papuans. With the support of his accomplished wife, Beatrice Moxon, from 1892 Kwato was established as an industrial mission which taught practical skills in copra production, boat building, printing and other trades, and developed a 'settlement scheme' which brought promising children to be educated away from their families at Kwato. Innovative, forceful and often controversial, Abel broke the rules, ignored LMS meetings, and made extreme demands in his energetic pursuit of a model of Christian commercial activity. In 1918 he and his followers separated from the LMS, and he aligned himself with American Evangelicals with millennialist leanings in the 1920s, making a final break with the LMS in 1928. Abel returned to England on leave, following a fund-raising visit to the United States, and died in Surrey as a result of an accident. His elder son, Cecil (Seselo) Abel, (1903–) who had been educated at Cambridge, then led the mission closer to the Moral Re-Armament movement in the 1930s. He remained at Kwato through the war, resigning in 1951. Kwato finally collapsed in 1975, while Cecil Abel became a co-founder of the PANGU PATI and Member of Parliament for Milne Bay (1968–72), and was knighted in 1983.—KRF

Further reading

Wetherell, D, 1997. *Charles Abel and the Kwato Mission of Papua New Guinea 1891–1975*, Melbourne University Press.

■ *Shirley Baker* Shirley Waldemar Baker (1835–1903), a missionary who became Prime Minister of Tonga in 1880, was born in Gloucestershire and emigrated at 18 to Australia, where he studied pharmacy. Recruited to the WESLEYAN ministry, he was sent to Tonga in 1860. He helped King George TUPOU I draw up the 1862 code of laws and the 1875 Constitution, and obtained for the king a crown, a flag, a coat of arms, and a national anthem. As chairman of the mission in 1869, he became King George's political and financial adviser, as well as his personal physician. He supported the king's attempts to gain international recognition for Tongan sovereignty, persuading him to sign a treaty with Germany in 1876. This in turn forced Britain to negotiate and sign a treaty with Tonga in 1879; and the United States to follow suit in 1888. Meanwhile, Baker had so insinuated himself that he was able to resign from the mission and become premier. His position ruptured the king's formerly close relationship with the Wesleyan missionaries, leading to the creation of a breakaway independent church in 1885, the Free Church of Tonga, and the active persecution of the original mission by the Tongan government. Baker survived an assassination attempt in 1887, but his accusations (attempting to implicate first the Wesleyans, including even the king's daughter Sālote, and then the British Vice-Consul) eventually led to his downfall. Sir John THURSTON, High Commissioner in the Western Pacific, intervened and Baker was deported—with 12 days' notice—in 1890. Although he returned to Tonga some years later, attempting to set up the 'Church of Victoria' under an ANGLICAN banner, he never regained his former influence.—KRF

Further reading

Rutherford, N, 1971. *Shirley Baker and the King of Tonga*, Oxford University Press.

■ *Hiram Bingham* Hiram Bingham (30 October 1789–11 November 1869), a pioneer missionary who spent 20 years in the Hawaiian Islands, was a Calvinist Congregationalist from Vermont. With his bride, Sybil Moseley, Bingham arrived from Boston on the *Thaddeus*, reaching Honolulu in 1820, just one year after the death of KAMEHAMEHA I. A few months earlier, the king's son, Liholiho, had feasted with the widowed KA'AHUMANU, violating a sacred *kapu* (taboo) and thus challenging a series of interwoven traditional relationships underpinning the old religious order. Initially, Ka'ahumanu and Liholiho saw no need to establish ties to the fledgling mission, but in 1823, after the latter's death, the *Kuhina nui* and six high chiefs requested baptism. Bingham was content to accept this as a victory for Christianity, and to bear the brunt of the opposition of the foreign community to subsequent royal bans on prostitution, gambling and drunkenness. By the time Ka'ahumanu died in 1832, however, Bingham was no longer able to dominate the expanding activities of American missionaries in Hawai'i. When Kauikeaouli became king, the former proscriptions were overturned. By 1840, weary and concerned for Sybil's health, Bingham was close to defeat. The family returned to the United States and although they planned only a short stay, Sybil remained unwell and eventually died in February 1848. Bingham had resigned from the AMERICAN BOARD OF COMMISSIONERS FOR FOREIGN MISSIONS (ABCFM) in 1846, but he was unable to find a new post. Reduced to short-term 'locum' ministerial positions, he also wrote a semi-autobiographical account of the Hawaiian mission, *A Residence of Twenty-One Years in the Sandwich Islands* (1847). In 1851 he married Naomi Morse, head of a boarding school attended by two of his daughters. He and Naomi ran a small seminary and he saw his son, Hiram Bingham Jr (1831–1908), ordained as a missionary. In the last years of his life, he received an annuity from the ABCFM.—KRF

Further reading

Miller, C, 1988. *Selected Writings of Hiram Bingham 1814–1869: missionary to the Hawaiian Islands: to raise the Lord's banner*, Edwin Mellen Press.

■ *William Bromilow* William Edward Bromilow (15 January 1857–24 June 1929), Methodist missionary in Fiji and Papua, was the Australian son of a bricklayer, whose mother dedicated him to mission work before he was born. A schoolteacher before his ordination in 1879, he and his wife, Lilly Thomson, went to Fiji where they served 10 years, before arriving at Samarai in British New Guinea in 1891. Accompanied by the Rev George BROWN, the party included four more missionaries and 22 islanders, teachers from Fiji, Samoa and Tonga. As chairman of the New Guinea district mission, Bromilow remained at Dobu (D'Entrecasteaux Islands) for 17 years. A strong and authoritarian figure, he set up a training institution for Papuan pastors, and used his deep interest in language to work on a translation of the Bible into Dobu, completed in retirement. His wife fully supported him in the mission, establishing a group of Australian Methodist sisters whom she supervised zealously. In early retirement (1908) for health reasons, Bromilow continued to supervise further mission developments and ended his participation in the executive committee of the Mission Board only in 1928, about a year before he died in Sydney. His autobiography, *Twenty Years Among Primitive Papuans*, was published posthumously in 1929.—KRF

■ *George Brown* George Brown (7 December 1835–7 April 1917), a dominant figure in METHODIST missionary history in the South Seas after 1860, established a mission in New Britain in 1875. Born in England, he joined a ship in 1850 and spent several years in Canada and then New Zealand, where he became a Wesleyan missionary. Ordained in Sydney in 1860, Brown went with his wife to Samoa for 14 years where he built churches and involved himself in health and educational work. His vigorous advocacy of the need for a mission in New Britain at last won Mission Board support and he took a party of teacher recruits from Fiji and Samoa to the Duke of York Islands in August 1875. Over the next five years, he set up 10 mission stations in the district, relying heavily on the Fijian teachers especially in this work, and achieving the appointment of the first three local preachers. After retiring as chairman of the New Britain mission district, he took up an administrative role in Sydney and later became General Secretary to the Methodist missions (1887–1908). During this time he pursued the idea of opening a mission in British New Guinea (achieved by William BROMILOW in 1891), and in the New Georgia group, Solomon Islands, finally achieved in May 1902. Brown also first raised the possibility of recruiting women in 1890, and was largely responsible for the subsequent appointment of Methodist sisters, although he became disheartened by their sometimes brief careers. On retirement he published the results of his methodical ethnographical studies, *Melanesians and Polynesians: their life-histories described and compared*, in 1910.—KRF

■ *John Wear Burton* John Wear Burton (1875–1970), missionary statesman and social activist, was born in England but grew up in New Zealand where he was ordained as a missionary. He went to Fiji to join the METHODIST Indian mission in 1902, going to live at Nausori, 20 km east of Suva, in a small Indian Christian community near an area of sugar estates. Intelligent and energetic, he read widely, learned to speak adequate Hindustani and studied Indian philosophy and religion. He visited India to bring back six newly trained catechists from a theological college, established the Dilkusha (Happy Heart) orphanage and girls' home at Davuilevu near Nausori, and initiated technical and industrial training at the theological training college. Ahead of his time in asserting that his mission was motivated by the 'unhappy condition of people…ignorant of the good news' rather than the wish to save the heathen from damnation, Burton opposed the sugar plantations and became a staunch critic of the indenture system. He published his views in a pamphlet, *Our Indian Work in Fiji*, and a book, *The Fiji of Today*, that was circulated in Britain, Australia and India, upsetting planters and colonial officials and embarrassing the Methodists, but assisting the anti-indenture crusade. In 1912 the illness of Burton's wife took him to Australia and he moved into administrative work until his appointment as general secretary of the mission organization, Methodist Overseas Missions in Australia. He continued his own studies, wrote persuasively on many topics, and edited the Australian Methodists' *Missionary Review*. In his later years, his leadership role in the church and the influence of his writings made him one of the most famous missionaries of the Pacific.—KRF

Further reading

Burton, J W, 1949. *Modern Missions in the South Pacific*, Livingstone Press.

■ *James Chalmers* James Chalmers (4 August 1841–8 April 1901), pioneer missionary and explorer, was the son of a Scottish stonemason, who joined the United Presbyterian church in 1859, and was influenced by a conversation with George Turner (1818–91), a Scottish missionary from Samoa, to apply to the LONDON MISSIONARY SOCIETY. After his ordination in 1865, he and his bride, Jane Hercus, served in Rarotonga (1866–76) before achieving his long-held wish to work in Papua—in Suau, Port Moresby, Toaripi and Saguane—from 1877. His wife died in 1879, and Chalmers met with a violent death after visiting a remote part of the Papuan Gulf with a young colleague, Oliver Tomkins (who had been in Papua only four months), and 11 Papuans. They were invited ashore on Goaribari Island and taken to the ceremonial house where the whole party was clubbed to death and eaten. Chalmers published four books including *Pioneer Life and Work in New Guinea*, which contained many vivid portraits of the coastal Papuans he had encountered.—KRF

Further reading

Langmore, D, 1974. *Tamate—a King: James Chalmers in New Guinea 1877–1901*, Melbourne University Press.

■ *Pierre (St Peter) Chanel* Pierre-Louis-Marie Chanel (12 July 1803–28 April 1841), the first Catholic martyr of Oceania, was born at Cuet, Ain, in France, the son of a peasant farmer. He was ordained a priest in 1827 and soon joined the Marist Congregation. In 1836 he volunteered to join a group of missionaries for the South Seas under Bishop POMPALLIER who had been appointed Vicar Apostolic of Western Oceania. They left Lyons in October, making for Le Havre but were unable to sail until 24 December. Finally reaching Valparaiso on 28 June 1837, their voyage across the Pacific began in August, calling at the Gambiers, Tahiti, Vava'u (Tonga), Wallis Island, and on 8 November reached the nearby island of Futuna. Pompallier established a mission station, which he dedicated to St Francis of Assisi, and placed Pierre Chanel in charge. Assisting him was a catechist Marie-Nizier Delorme. Father Pierre Bataillon, whom Pierre Chanel had first met at the Lyons seminary, had been left on nearby Wallis, and the two were able to meet occasionally—in March 1838 for joint language studies and in May 1839 when a small group of Marists called on their way from Tahiti to New Zealand. It was clear that both priests were making progress in their mission field and Pompallier sent another catechist, Father Joseph Chevron, to assist them.

This success was to lead to Father Chanel's death. By 1841 a majority of islanders had been converted to Catholicism, but aroused bitter opposition from some of the older islanders. After Father Chanel converted the king's son and the youth refused to recant, the chief decided to dispose of Chanel. He sent out a group of men who attacked and killed him. Bishop Pompallier sailed to the islands the following year to fetch his remains. During his stay, Pompallier baptized some 1220 islanders, including the new king, Keletaona, who chose Peter (Petelo) as his baptismal name. Father Chanel's remains were taken to New Zealand and later sent to France, but they were eventually returned to Futuna. He was beatified in 17 November 1889 and canonized on 12 June 1954.—JD

■ *Robert Codrington* Robert Henry Codrington (1830–1922), pioneering Pacific anthropologist, was born in Wiltshire and educated at Oxford. Ordained in 1857, he came to work in the Nelson diocese, New Zealand, (1860–64) before joining John PATTESON when the Melanesian Mission moved from Kohimarama to Norfolk Island in 1867. Codrington spent 20 years as St Barnabas' headmaster, also as Acting Head of the Melanesian Mission immediately after Patteson's death in 1871. Using information obtained from his students and from his mission travels on the *Southern Cross*, he produced careful, methodical works in Pacific anthropology and linguistics including *The Melanesian Languages* (1885), *A Dictionary of the Language of Mota* (1896), and *The Melanesians* (1891). He returned to England to take up an appointment to the diocese of Chichester in 1887.—KRF

■ *Joseph Damien* Joseph Damien de Veuster (3 January 1840–15 April 1889) was born in Tremeloo near Louvain, Belgium. The son of a farmer, he joined his brother in the Congregation of the Sacred Heart of Jesus and Mary (popularly known as the Picpus Fathers). His brother was about to embark for the Hawaiian missions when he fell ill. Damien, who was then still only in minor orders, decided to take his place, sailing to the Pacific in 1863. He was ordained priest in Honolulu and served in the islands until, shocked by the deplorable living conditions of the lepers which the government deported to Moloka'i Island, he volunteered to minister to them. He laboured there from 1873 until his death in 1889. Besides attending to the spiritual needs of over 600 lepers, he struggled to improve their housing, water supply, sanitation and medical services, and the victualling of the settlement. He did this at first on his own, then with the help of other priests and of the Hawaiian government. He endeavoured to raise the morale of the people as well as their standard of living by encouraging agricultural ventures and local industry. Father Damien eventually contracted leprosy and died in 1889. He was the subject of a celebrated 'open letter' by the novelist Robert Louis STEVENSON.—JD

Further reading

Daws, G, 1973. *Holy Man: Father Damien of Molokai*, Harper and Row.

■ *Jean-Baptiste Épalle* Jean-Baptiste Épalle (8 March 1808–18 December 1845) was born at Marlhes, near Lyons in France. Ordained a priest, he joined the Society of Mary in July 1838 and in September sailed for the Pacific with two other missionaries. After a brief stop at Futuna, where they met the future martyr, Pierre CHANEL, the Marists went on to New Zealand. Épalle served under Bishop POMPALLIER at Whangaroa in the North Island and later in the Bay of Islands, until 1845 when Pompallier sent him to France to report and seek funds and new recruits. He was to return, not to New Zealand but to Melanesia. A Vicariate Apostolic of Melanesia had been set up in 1844, covering New Guinea, Solomon Islands and outlying islands. Épalle, appointed bishop and vicar apostolic, sailed from London in February 1845 with seven priests and six brothers. His original plan had been to establish his headquarters on Waigeo, eastern New Guinea, but it was later agreed that Solomon Islands would be more appropriate. Épalle hired a schooner, the *Marian Watson*, in Sydney in which he sailed on 23 October 1845 for New Caledonia, San Cristobal and Santa Isabel. The schooner put in at Thousand Ships Bay at the south of the island where Épalle spent several days trading with the islanders and planning a mission station. Underestimating the state of almost constant inter-tribal warfare in which the islanders lived, he ventured into an enemy tribe's territory and was promptly attacked. He died as a result of his injuries and was buried ashore.—JD

■ *Thomas Haweis* Dr Thomas Haweis (1735–1820), chaplain to the Countess of Huntingdon (who was the founder of Cheshunt, the theological college), was one of the first English Evangelicals to take a keen interest in the South Pacific. Haweis made several attempts to establish missionaries in the islands from the early 1790s. He played a major part in establishing the LONDON MISSIONARY SOCIETY and used his personal influence and financial support to persuade the directors to establish their first missions on three Pacific islands in 1797: at Matavai in Tahiti (Society Islands), at Tongatapu in Tonga (Friendly Islands), and at Tahuata in the Marquesas.—KRF

■ *John Hunt* John Hunt (1812–4 October 1848), METHODIST missionary in Fiji, was born at Hykeham, Lincolnshire, and after limited primary education, worked as an agricultural labourer from the age of 10. In 1828 he converted to Wesleyan Methodism and became a local preacher. His natural abilities impressed the Methodist hierarchy and he was admitted to Hoxton Theological Academy in 1835, where he studied for the ministry. Ordained in 1838, he married Hannah Summers and they were sent to Fiji as missionaries. The Hunts served at Rewa (1839) and Somosomo (1839–42), and then went to Viwa in 1842, where he was chairman of the mission. In 1848 he died from the debilitating effects of dysentery and was buried on Viwa. His widow and two daughters returned to England.

Hunt was principally responsible for establishing the Christian church in Fiji, though he was assisted by other able missionaries such as Jane Calvert, David Cargill, William Cross, Thomas Jaggar, Richard Lyth, Thomas Williams, Joshua Matananiu and Joeli Bulu. Hunt translated the New Testament into Fijian, established systematic training programs for an indigenous ministry, made initial contact with most parts of central and western Fiji, including Rotuma, and secured the conversion of prominent chiefs, notably Ravisa, also known as Vareni. He published two books, *Memoir of William Cross* (1845) and *Letters On Entire Sanctification* (published posthumously in 1853). Energetic in his labours, a committed Christian, devoted family man and statesmanlike in his approach to Fijians, Hunt has properly earned the title 'Apostle of Fiji'.—AT2

■ *Honoré Laval* Honoré Laval (1808–80) was born in France and joined the Order of the Sacred Hearts of Jesus and Mary, known as the Picpus Fathers from the street in Paris where their establishment was situated. By a decree of June 1833 Pope Gregory XVI had founded the Vicariate Apostolic of Eastern Oceania which he then allocated to the Picpus Fathers. Father Laval sailed from Bordeaux for Valparaiso in February 1834 with Father François Caret and obtained a passage to the Gambier Islands in an American ship, the *Peruvian*. They landed on Akamaru Island on 8 August. They met only mild opposition from the LONDON MISSIONARY SOCIETY and soon established a thriving mission in the islands. The local ruler Maputeoa was baptized in January 1836 with 160 of his people and adopted the name of Gregorio in honour of the Pope. Laval and Caret attempted to expand into Tahiti in February 1836, but although courteously received by Queen POMARE IV, they were expelled exactly one month after landing and sent back to the Gambiers. In 1837 Father Caret sailed for Paris and Rome; he worked tirelessly to obtain additional resources and was appointed Prefect Apostolic of the southern sector in 1840; he died in 1844. Father Laval's immediate superior, Bishop Rouchouze, also left, and died in 1843. Father Laval thus remained in full charge.

Honoré Laval's influence in the Gambiers became all-embracing. He banned a number of Polynesian customs that he felt infringed the tenets of Christianity or the laws of decency. Traditional songs and dances were replaced by religious hymns. A huge stone-block cathedral capable of seating 1200 people was built, as well as schools and offices. He clashed on a number of occasions with the French authorities, as he never hesitated to criticize them or ignore their edicts. He was finally removed to Tahiti in 1871. His devotion and self-sacrifice during 37 years in the Gambiers cannot be faulted, but his main legacy is his *Mémoires pour Servir à l'Histoire de Mangareva: ére chrétienne*, an impressive record of a vanishing world.—JD

■ *W G Lawes* William George Lawes (1 July 1839–6 August 1907), pioneer missionary, was born in Berkshire, son of a tailor. Inspired in 1858 by the preaching of William Wyatt Gill (1828–96) and Isaiah Papehia, a Raiatean PASTOR, (both visiting from the Cook Islands), he was ordained by the LONDON MISSIONARY SOCIETY (LMS) in 1860, and set off for Niue with his bride, Fanny Wickham. On Niue (1861–72), he made translations of the Bible, and became involved in teaching carpentry and agriculture as well as the training of local pastors. After returning to London for a year, Lawes arrived in Papua in 1874, stationed at Port Moresby where the Rev A W Murray had brought a group of Cook Islands teachers—including Ruatoka—in November 1873. Lawes set up the base for LMS operations in central Papua, and with Ruatoka's help, built the first training institution in 1882. Later he established the Vatorata Training College at Rigo in 1894. Taking students who had received elementary local schooling, it provided training in reading, writing and arithmetic as well as in theological subjects. In his 32 years in British New Guinea, Lawes continued to publish texts in Motu and other local languages, became a strong advocate for the British annexation of New Guinea, and took a formative role in the establishment of the British administration. With George BROWN, he participated in defining the separate spheres of influence for LMS, Anglican and Methodist missionary activity. Awarded an honorary doctorate by the University of Glasgow in 1894, he retired to Sydney in 1906.—KRF

■ *Maurice Leenhardt* Maurice Leenhardt (1878–1954) was born at Montauban, France, the son of a professor of theology. Ordained a Protestant minister in 1902, he sailed for New Caledonia and set up a school at Houailou on the main island, a base he retained until 1926. He developed several Protestant parishes in New Caledonia and trained a number of Melanesian catechists, but incurred criticism for his outspoken championing of the indigenous people. Settlers and especially traders disliked his educational policies—which included teaching Melanesians about the true cost of the goods they bought at inflated prices. His work and his sympathy for the Melanesians, however, greatly contributed to the success of the Protestant mission, and he played no small part in helping Melanesians to regain their self-respect and adapt to the modern world.

The settlers worked to undermine his standing with the Sociéte des Missions Evangéliques in Paris, and he was finally recalled in 1926 and appointed to a parish in Paris. His close association with Melanesian culture led to a number of publications which earned him a well-deserved reputation among ethnologists. These include *Notes d'ethnologie Néo-Calédonienne* (1930), *Documents Néo-Calédoniens* (1932), *Gens de la Grande Terre* (1937) and *Do Kamo* (1937). Leenhardt soon severed his ties with the Société des Missions Évangéliques and turned to lecturing, holding posts at the École Nationale des Langues Orientales, where he inaugurated the study of Melanesian languages, the École Pratique des Hautes Études, the École Nationale de la France d'Outre-Mer and the Institut d'Ethnologie. He served as adviser to the French government, travelling back to New Caledonia in 1938 on behalf of the Minister of Education, and the Musée de l'Homme, where he helped to set up the Département de l'Océanie. In 1947 he was appointed foundation director of the Institut Français d'Océanie. He died in Paris in 1954.—JD

Further reading

Clifford, J, 1982. *Person and Myth: Maurice Leenhardt in the Melanesian world*, University of California Press.

■ *Samuel Marsden* Samuel Marsden (24 June 1765–12 May 1838), the principal ANGLICAN chaplain of the convict settlement of New South Wales, was the son of a blacksmith, educated by an evangelical society in Yorkshire. As a director of the LONDON MISSIONARY SOCIETY (LMS), he was principally responsible for the resumption of the Tahitian LMS mission in 1811. Keen to start a mission in New Zealand, he obtained the services of three volunteers, all skilled tradesmen but untrained missionaries: William Hall, a carpenter; John King, a shoemaker; and Thomas Kendall, a schoolteacher. With the assistance and support of Hongi HIKA and RUATARA (who had visited him at Parramatta, New South Wales), he established an evangelical base for the Church Missionary Society in the Bay of Islands, New Zealand, where he preached the gospel for the first time on Christmas Day, 1814. Leaving his disciples to their task, he returned to Australia to establish a seminary at Parramatta in 1819, envisaged as a nursery for evangelical activities in the south Pacific region. Later he also took part in the opening of the Wesleyan mission in New Zealand between 1819 and 1822. His direction and policies had a major influence on the Church, and on the London and Wesleyan missionary societies in the South Pacific until 1826.—KRF

Further reading

Yarwood, A T, 1977/1996. *Samuel Marsden: the great survivor*, Melbourne University Press.

■ *John G Paton* John Gibson Paton (1824–1907), outspoken crusader against BLACKBIRDING, was a member of the Reformed Presbyterian Church of Scotland. Stationed in the New Hebrides (Vanuatu) on Tanna, where his wife died soon after she arrived, Paton was hardy and strong-minded. After the murders on 20 May 1861 of his colleague, G N Gordon, and Mrs Gordon (who had been stationed on Erromango since 1857), Paton and his second wife were threatened in a violent demonstration by islanders, and forced to escape to Aneityum. In 1862 he went on a highly successful fund-raising visit to Australia. On his return, he opened a new mission station on Aniwa, enjoying a more amicable relationship with the residents, and in 1870 printed a hymnbook in the local language. The first church built by islanders was destroyed in a hurricane and had to be rebuilt. Paton was the subject of another violent personal assault, but this time his local supporters recruited a bodyguard of 100 men to protect him. In 1873, after the death of a child and severe threats to the health of his wife and himself, the Patons left for New Zealand on holiday. After this, he began to focus his energy in the political arena, leading Presbyterian protests in the New Hebrides against French commercial interests in the region. These efforts contributed to the unusual compromise between Britain and France in 1878 that created an Anglo-French CONDOMINIUM. His son Fred J Paton, who died in 1941, gave nearly 50 years of service to mission work in Vanuatu.—KRF

■ *John Coleridge Patteson* John Coleridge Patteson (1 April 1827–20 September 1871), missionary bishop of Melanesia, was born in Oxfordshire. After attending Oxford, and Cuddesdon Theological College, he was ordained in 1854. Appointed as missionary chaplain to the Melanesian mission, he accompanied Bishop SELWYN—then returning with fresh funding—to New Zealand in 1855. Their exploratory voyages into Melanesia over the next few years established a wide range of friendly contacts, and enhanced Patteson's remarkable linguistic skills. He produced simple grammars, phrase-books and Biblical translations for a range of islands languages, and the Auckland mission school, moved from St John's College to Kohimarama in 1859, continued to attract as many new recruits as the mission ship, the *Southern Cross*, could carry.

In 1861 he was consecrated by Selwyn as the new Bishop of Melanesia, and began to develop systematic, long-term teacher-training courses at the Kohimarama school (St Andrew's). By 1867 he had also changed the language of instruction from English to Mota, already spoken by a group of older students from Banks Islands (New Hebrides, now Vanuatu), and easily learnt by other islanders. After considerable debate about alternative locations (such as Queensland) for the diocese headquarters, the Governor of New South Wales, Sir John Young, offered land on Norfolk Island and the move was completed by the end of 1867.

The location of the new mission school (St Barnabas) provided a more congenial climate as well as improved access to Solomon Islands. Patteson, maintaining a strong emphasis on regular worship, conducted daily chapel services with hymns that he composed himself in Mota, and insisted that all chores (kitchen, laundry and farming work) were shared equally among the whole missionary community.

Patteson's demanding responsibilities and the discomforts of frequent travel began to take their toll, and he became quite ill in 1870. In 1871 he went to the island of Mota, and after three months, sailed on to visit the Reef Islands (southern Solomons). On 20 September, anchored off tiny Nukapu, near Santa Cruz, Patteson went ashore with a chief who had welcomed him on a previous visit. For reasons that are still obscure, but widely interpreted as a response to some earlier BLACKBIRDING raid, he was attacked and killed in the village soon afterward.—KRF

Further reading

Hilliard, D L, 1970. 'John Coleridge Patteson: missionary Bishop of Melanesia', in J W Davidson and D Scarr (eds), *Pacific Island Portraits*, Australian National University Press.

■ *Bishop Pompallier* Jean-Baptiste François Pompallier (11 December 1802–21 December 1871) established the first Roman Catholic mission station in New Zealand in 1838. Born at Lyons, he was ordained priest in June 1829 and became associated with the nascent Society of Mary which, in 1836, was entrusted with the Vicariate of Western Oceania. In May of that year, Pompallier was appointed Vicar Apostolic with the title of bishop. He left France in December 1836 with a group of four priests and three Brothers. At Valparaiso, he obtained a ship which took him to the Gambiers and then Tahiti. There he hired a schooner, the *Raiatea*, which he sailed to Tonga, Wallis and Futuna, Rotuma and Sydney. On 10 January 1838 he reached New Zealand, to be his base for 30 years.

The country would have been large enough to take up all his energies without the added responsibility of founding mission stations on various islands of the western Pacific. He purchased a schooner, which he named the *Sancta Maria*, to travel around New Zealand and to the islands. His main voyage through the Pacific, in 1842, took him to Wallis and Futuna, where the missionary he had left behind, Pierre Chanel, had been killed, to Fiji and to Tonga where he was able to set up a mission station.

The New Zealand missions multiplied, requiring most of his attention and resources. By 1846, when he left for Europe, he was viewed as the leading Catholic churchman in New Zealand and his association with the Marists was about to come to an end. The Vicariate of Western Oceania was obviously too large, and as a first step towards splitting it up the Vicariate of New Caledonia was founded; further divisions of responsibility occurred later and Pompallier returned to New Zealand in 1850 to take charge of the secular clergy and most of the missions to the Maori people, while the Marists, under Bishop P J Viard, took over the new diocese of Wellington. His reputation continued to grow, and he struggled in the rapidly developing colony with a great deal of success—but funds were never adequate and he incurred considerable debts. Although a person of great charm, the problems he faced sometimes strained his relations with other priests. He left for Europe in 1868 and died near Paris in 1871.—JD

■ *George Pritchard* George Pritchard (1796–1883), missionary, merchant and British Consul, was born in Birmingham to working class parents. A Congregational preacher at 18, he was accepted for missionary work after four years at the LONDON MISSIONARY SOCIETY (LMS) theological college at Gosport, where he stayed with James CHALMERS. Pritchard and his wife, Eliza Aillen, arrived in Tahiti in December 1824, stationed at Pape'te in the Pare district, where he used his Gosport experience to begin the first training of islander teachers in the Society Islands in 1829. Quickly involved in trading ventures (including sugar), Pritchard dealt extensively with visiting ships, and began to live and entertain in style. His business activities alienated other traders, but his roles as interpreter and commercial agent also brought him into politics. As chaplain he had attracted the attention of Queen POMARE IV, and was soon a close adviser. Their mutually supportive relationship led to his appointment as British Consul to Tahiti in 1838. Pritchard ultimately resigned from the LMS although he remained an active clergyman, introducing the infant school system at Pape'ete after 1839, and taking on the young Tahitian-born John Barff (1820–60) as assistant. On a visit to Samoa in 1839, he also supported the efforts of Ebenezer Buchanan (1812–97) to set up an infant school at Apia. His consular post in Tahiti, however, ended in ignominy when his advice regarding the expulsion of the French Catholic priests, LAVAL and Caret, brought a French frigate to obtain an apology and compensation. Pritchard was powerless to protect the horrified queen, who—insisting that he raise the indemnity—then dismissed him. A French protectorate was established in 1842 and Pritchard was deported in 1844.

Disillusioned and humiliated, Pritchard returned to Britain, won a small payment for the loss of his Tahitian land, and turned to his role as Consul to Samoa. On Upolu, his political ambitions remained frustrated by his lack of personal influence among the Samoans. He was at first unable to obtain land for his consular headquarters, but he resumed trading activities, and used the support of visits from the *Juno* (1847) and the *Dido* (1848) to proclaim his consular authority. Over time, however, his misuse of his role (and his clumsiness in dealing with French competitors) alienated the Samoans and the British. When he defied the liquor ban in 1850 by importing a shipment of spirits into Apia, and repeated the offence in 1852, the LMS church expelled him. Pressure to remove him as consul was growing, and Pritchard at last resigned in 1854, returning to Britain. In his later years he rejoined the ministry and

Portrait of George Pritchard

became the LMS agent for Scotland and Ireland. His son, William Thomas Pritchard (1829–1909), became British Consul to Fiji from 1858 to 1863, and was involved in the preliminary moves leading to the DEED OF CESSION.—KRF

■ *Bishop Selwyn* George Augustus Selwyn (5 April 1809–11 April 1878), the first Bishop of New Zealand in 1841, was born in Hampstead, attended Eton and St John's College at Cambridge and was ordained in 1834. He used the voyage to New Zealand to study navigation and Polynesian grammars, and conceived the idea of a central missionary college that would draw in Pacific islanders. He set up St John's College in Auckland, a theological college that also served as bishop's residence, boarding-school, hospital and printing office, but most of his first years in New Zealand were spent in frequent internal travel, establishing his own authority over Church Missionary Society clergy and the organization of the Maori mission. In December 1847 he visited the islands for the first time, on a 10-week voyage on the HMS *Dido* that included Samoa, Tonga, New Hebrides (now VANUATU) and New Caledonia. Supported by Governor George Grey for his own purposes, Selwyn planned an Anglican mission to Melanesia, but he saw it operating as a Melanesian 'Native Ministry', using indigenous teachers.

In 1849 he began the first of several missionary voyages, initially to the southern New Hebrides, New Caledonia and the Loyalty Islands, bringing back five missionary recruits. Each trip returned trained young converts to their homes and collected fresh volunteers, over an expanding arc that soon included the northern New Hebrides and the southern Solomon Islands. By 1860, 152 Melanesians had attended the mission school in Auckland for at least one season, some of them returning two or three times. Amid criticism of the unconventional methods of his grandiose scheme, Selwyn failed to unify the various church groups in New Zealand, although he enjoyed some success in a fundraising trip to England in 1853–55, and gained a new mission ship, the *Southern Cross*.

In 1861 Selwyn won approval for a new ANGLICAN diocese of Melanesia, and consecrated his missionary chaplain, John PATTESON, as the first bishop. He himself returned to England in 1868 to take up his appointment as Bishop of Lichfield, surviving to see his son, John Richardson Selwyn (1844–98), elected as Bishop of Melanesia in 1877.—KRF

■ *Charles Viénot* Charles Viénot (c1840–11 June 1903) arrived in Tahiti on 25 February 1866 to take over the French Protestant mission on behalf of the Société des Missions Evangéliques of Paris. Proposals to transfer the mission to the control of French-speaking ministers had been made soon after the French protectorate was declared over Tahiti and its outlying islands. A favourable report had been drawn up in 1863 following the visit of Arbousset, and Viénot was selected to take charge. He was given a free hand—a necessary approach in view of the distance and problems of communication.

One of his first tasks was to re-establish Protestant schools: the first of a number opened in Pape'ete on 17 September 1866. He then turned to the restructuring of the various mission stations, a number of which had been languishing since the French takeover. Viénot's strong personality made itself felt throughout the Society Islands, including in areas which France did not yet control. Many Polynesians associated Protestantism with pro-British views and consequently with opposition to French rule, and Viénot's status—he soon became known as 'the Protestant Bishop'—earned him a considerable influence in parts of the Society Islands where French rule was still being contested.

In 1870 Viénot became head of the Conseil Supérieur des Eglises, a post he was to hold for 23 years. Governor Chesse appointed him to the Comité de l'Instruction Publique in 1876. He was also elected to the General Council, of which he became the vice-president. His political base continued to grow, partly as a consequence of the anti-clerical movement in France which was pressing for the setting-up of non-denominational schools. Viénot's own efforts were helped by his close links with Jules Ferry, the founder of the modern French secular system of education. Viénot's Conseil Supérieur became formally recognized by the government in 1884, a status which the Catholic missions were unable to acquire except in Tahiti itself. Viénot undoubtedly would have acquired even greater influence had French Polynesia enjoyed a greater degree of autonomy. Even so, he remained a force to be reckoned with until his death in 1903.—JD

■ *John Williams* John Williams (1796–14 November 1839), pioneer missionary and martyr, was born in

'The Massacre of the Lamented Missionary, the Rev John Williams, 1843', oil print by George Baxter

England. Only 18 when he was drawn to mission work, Williams was fairly typical of the lower middle-class craftsmen who were the backbone of LONDON MISSIONARY SOCIETY (LMS) fieldwork. After his ordination, he and his wife set off with three other missionaries for the Society Islands. With William Ellis (1794–1872), who used his printing press to produce books in Tahitian, Williams first served on Moorea and Huahine (1817–18). He moved to Ra'iatea (1818–27), where he supervised the building of a house and a church, as well as a system of roads and a coconut oil industry. Practical but restless, he enjoyed the challenge of evangelizing and created the practice of taking islanders as native teachers to other islands. He was responsible for bringing two Polynesian converts, Isaiah Papeiha (or Papehia) and Vahapata, from Ra'iatea to Aitutaki (Cook Islands) in 1821, while taking his sick wife to Sydney. After raising funds to buy a schooner, he was able to monitor the progress of his teacher recruits and subsequently brought them to Rarotonga in October 1823. Four years later Williams returned for several months (1827–28), bringing Charles Pitman and his wife to continue the pastoral work. During the remainder of his time in Ra'iatea (1828–31), he continued these voyages with Charles Barff (1792–1866), visiting Mangaia in the Cook group and then Tonga (where the Wesleyans were already in residence). They next sailed to Samoa, where they stayed only a week but left behind the first native teachers—several Tahitian Christians—at Sapapali'i in July 1830, to continue the job of spreading the gospel. After leaving Ra'iatea in 1831, Williams visited Samoa once more, pleased to find Christian services now installed and the chief Malietoa willing to adopt Christianity for a trial period. In Rarotonga (1832–33), he observed further cause for satisfaction; Aaron Buzacott (1800–64) was in charge of a flourishing mission and was publishing books and pamphlets. Having allowed himself a four-year fund-raising spell in Britain, Williams returned to the Pacific in 1838 to face a series of disappointments. Islanders were becoming disillusioned and antagonistic; diseases were spreading; serious disputes were emerging among different denominations. Finally he moved on to the islands of New Hebrides (now Vanuatu), reaching Tanna Island on 19 November 1839 with a number of Samoan missionaries. On the following day, he landed at Erromango, where he and John Harris were killed by islanders in apparent retaliation for previous activities of SANDALWOOD traders.—KRF

Further reading

Forman, C W, 1982. *The Island Churches of the South Pacific: Emergence in the twentieth century*, American Society of Missiology Series, Orbis Books.

Garrett, J, 1982. *To Live Among the Stars: Christian origins in Oceania*, World Council of Churches and Institute of Pacific Studies, University of the South Pacific.

——, 1992. *Footsteps in the Sea: Christianity in Oceania to World War II*, World Council of Churches and Institute of Pacific Studies, University of the South Pacific.

——, 1997. *Where Nets were Cast: Christianity in Oceania since World War II*, World Council of Churches and Institute of Pacific Studies, University of the South Pacific.

Gunson, N, 1978. *Messengers of Grace: evangelical missionaries in the south seas 1797–1860*, Oxford University Press.

Hilliard, D, 1978. *God's Gentlemen: a history of the Melanesian mission, 1849–1942*, University of Queensland Press.

Langmore, D, 1989. *Missionary Lives: Papua, 1874–1914*, Pacific Island Monograph Series, University of Hawai'i Press.

Laracy, H, 1976. *Marists and Melanesians: a history of Catholic missions in the Solomon Islands*, Australian National University Press.

The church in the Pacific today

The major churches of the Pacific have origins in Protestant and Roman Catholic missionary activity. Catholic churches in Oceania have been localized since the Second Vatican Council of the early 1960s and are now mostly led by indigenous bishops. The larger Protestant churches in Polynesia, Micronesia and Melanesia nearly all became autonomous earlier than Catholic churches, partly because Protestant missions, from their beginnings in Tahiti in 1796, employed volunteer PACIFIC ISLANDER MISSIONARIES. The descendants of their converts have, in most places, taken over from missions since World War II, as fully ordained church leaders. Protestant churches in the South Pacific have become self-governing, self-propagating, and in some cases self-supporting. In Melanesia, including Papua New Guinea, LUTHERAN and ANGLICAN churches have developed similarly. Foreign missions under colonial flags have been transmuted into independent churches in island states. Pacific Oceania is nominally a Christian majority area. Islander leaders in social and political life often publicly acknowledge their church membership as significant for their careers. The churches thus influence formulation of policy in relation to politics, HUMAN RIGHTS, the use of natural resources and debates on NUCLEAR TESTING issues.

Departure of foreign missions after World War II coincided with the spread of several world-wide movements in Christianity. The Ecumenical Movement focused on visible and practical forms of Christian unity; the Liturgical Movement encouraged forms of worship expressive of local cultures; Pentecostal and charismatic movements spilled over into the mainline ex-mission churches and led to 'speaking and praying in tongues'—which met a ready response in societies where forms of ecstatic behaviour and spirit possession had been present in pre-contact religions. After the emergence of the World Council of Churches in 1948 and the sessions of the Second Vatican Council in the early 1960s, islander church leaders sensed their common identity as islanders; they drew together formally in 1966 to constitute the Pacific Conference of Churches (PCC), which includes in its meetings and programs almost all the major churches in the Pacific islands—Catholic, Anglican and Protestant. Cooperation was facilitated when the Roman Catholic churches, acting together through the Episcopal Conference of the Pacific (CEPAC), joined the PCC. Local Catholic bishops also earlier endorsed coordination of resources for social action and the launching of the South Pacific Association of Theological Schools to raise standards of training and accreditation in colleges and seminaries. Priests and ministers are trained at advanced tertiary level at the regional and ecumenical PACIFIC THEOLOGICAL COLLEGE in Fiji and the adjacent Roman Catholic Pacific Regional Seminary. Both institutions are recognized by the UNIVERSITY OF THE SOUTH PACIFIC. Such international bodies as the Lutheran World Federation, the World Alliance of Reformed Churches, the Council for World Mission and the World Methodist Council facilitate multilateral aid for church activities through the World Council of Churches' Inter-Church Aid multilateral programs through a Pacific Advisory Group, which meets annually.

At the same time, influx of ecstatic behaviour into mainline churches through the charismatic movement has been developing, with varying degrees of acceptance, alongside the fast growth of dynamic Pentecostal and conservative Evangelical church groups which decline membership in the PCC, suspecting it of doctrinal liberalism, compromise with Catholicism, and left-leaning political and social activity. The largest and longest established Pentecostal church in the islands is the Assemblies of God, from America. Its first efforts were in Fiji, starting in 1926, but it attracted very little response until about 1960. Then it spread into Tonga, Samoa, New Caledonia, Vanuatu and Marshall Islands. Like all Pentecostal churches, it allowed for a free and emotional type of worship, which appealed to many people who were not satisfied by the formality of most of the Pacific churches. The SEVENTH-DAY ADVENTIST church, with origins in the United States and a substantial following in Australia and New Zealand, stems from within 19th-century Protestantism, but has doctrines of its own. Adventists are strongly represented in Papua New Guinea, where the Pacific Adventist College near Port Moresby offers accredited tertiary education. A dynamic and wealthy American group, the Utah-based Church of Jesus Christ of Latter-day Saints (MORMONS), has its own additional sacred books and revelations, which are unacceptable to older-established churches. The Mormons have grown rapidly in Polynesia since World War II and have recently entered Micronesia and parts of Melanesia. In Pohnpei, traditional religious preferences began to break down in the 1970s, when other groups such as the Seventh-Day Adventists, Mormons, Jehovah's Witnesses, Baptists and others began building church memberships from the two major churches. By 1995, more than 12 churches, including the Salvation Army, were established throughout the villages of Pohnpei island and Kolonia Town. Jehovah's Witnesses succeeded in gaining entry into practically every island group in Oceania during the 1950s and 1960s. Banned in Fiji when they first arrived in 1939, they have recently made considerable headway in Majuro (Republic of the Marshall Islands) as well as making inroads in Solomon Islands, Papua New Guinea and Fiji. In a similar way, some Pentecostal and conservative evangelical para-church groups have produced divisions and splits within mainline island churches. They attract converts by proselytizing and offer incentives to their adherents through education and travel.—JG1

Mormons

The Church of Jesus Christ of Latter-Day Saints ('Mormons') has a history dating back to 1844 in Polynesia, which became the first foreign mission field of the Mormon church of the United States. Mormons have a particular attraction in Polynesia because their strongly vertical cosmology stresses the sky, and takes the God of our Earth to be a 'divine man', literally propagating the souls on the earth through his heavenly wife from a planet named Kolob. This chimes in quite strikingly with the world-views of Polynesia's traditional religion. Up until 1939, however, their numbers were small, and they struggled to compete with the other major churches already operating in Polynesia. Mormons stand apart from conventional Christians in their belief that the Book of Mormon, revealed to their founder, is (like the Bible) the word of God. The church also teaches that Polynesians and Micronesians are descendants of the Lost Tribe of Israel. A belief that black-skinned people were spiritually inferior (not able to enter the priesthood or to hold positions of authority in the church) kept the Mormons out of Melanesia. Church policy changed in 1978 when God revealed to the Mormon president that black men could join the Mormon priesthood and now the church is vigorously expanding into parts of Melanesia.

Mormon missionaries were young, single men, often from a limited farming background. Lacking the educational and financial resources to set up schools and church buildings, they remained hardworking, dedicated evangelists, travelling in pairs from village to village. In the Tuamotu archipelago (where a fascinating Mormon 'kingdom' was established in the 1840s, before the cession of the Tuamotus to France and even before the founding of Salt Lake City), the Reorganized Mormons, known locally as Sanitos, became an important part of the population. More commonly, governments limited the number of Mormon missionaries, out of concern to minimize or avert the disorderly protests that sometimes accompanied their presence. A Tongan law banned them entirely (1922–24) and then permitted only five in the country at a time. When Samoa lifted its restrictions in the 1950s, complaints from the other churches quickly revealed that 120 Mormons had arrived, and the former quota was reinstated in 1958.

In spite of such restrictions, Mormon influence in the islands began to experience significant growth after World War II, as the church in America flourished and expanded, sending out increasing numbers of missionaries worldwide. With the new prosperity of the church, its missionaries were better dressed, better organized, and better trained. From the 1950s, American funding provided a substantial building program which produced impressive new churches in Samoa, Tahiti, Tonga, Cook Islands and Niue. The standard style of construction featured a large assembly hall for community functions, and included facilities for recreations such as American basketball. Not only did these leisure and entertainment facilities appeal to young islanders, but also the erection of churches offered the opportunity to acquire new carpentry and construction skills. Many young people responded with enthusiasm.

The Mormons' mission on Niue in 1953, strongly opposed by the congregations of the entrenched LONDON MISSIONARY SOCIETY (LMS), was supported by the New Zealand colonial representatives who wanted other churches to break the LMS monopoly. In Fiji, the government permitted the Mormons to erect a church in 1956; and in New Caledonia, they were allowed to enter for the first time in the 1960s. By the mid 1960s, as well as their new bases in these islands, the Mormons had extended their membership to 11 000 in Tonga, and 18 000 in Samoa.

The Mormon building program also included schools, as part of an extensive new formal educational administration, involving professional, salaried teachers, and managed after 1957 by a Mormon Board of Education in America. Primary schools were followed by secondary schools in Tonga,

Samoa and American Samoa; French teachers were brought in to open a Mormon primary school in Tahiti; and financial assistance was available to allow students to attend Mormon colleges in Hawai'i and elsewhere. As churches throughout the Pacific gained their independence in the 1970s, the Mormon church also gave indigenous leaders responsibility for the management of their own activities. In Kiribati, the first Mormon converts were students who had attended the Mormon school, Liahona College, in Tonga in 1976. Soon afterwards, an American Mormon missionary couple went to Kiribati from Tonga, and from 1978, a private school in Tarawa had Mormon teaching staff. In the 1980s, church funds provided chapels, classrooms and accommodation.—GWT, JB & KRF

Seventh-Day Adventist church

One of the long-established smaller churches in the Pacific islands, the Seventh-Day Adventists (SDAs) have relied since 1906 on financial support from outside. Australasian church members especially have provided generous financial support. The earliest and most successful base of the SDA church in the Pacific islands was Pitcairn Island, where American missionaries came in 1886 and 1890. Supported by occasional subsequent visits from America, where the church originated, and later by more regular workers on two-year terms from Australia, the SDA has remained the predominant religion of the island community. In Cook Islands, SDA missionaries had only a toehold, never usurping the authority of the LONDON MISSIONARY SOCIETY (LMS). Some also came to Tahiti, Tonga, Samoa and Fiji, but without great success. In Vanuatu, SDA missionaries have been active since around the turn of the century, but a recent estimate of the strength of the present church is only about 5 per cent.

One of the areas where the SDA had some of the first mission stations was Solomon Islands, where they arrived in 1914. At a time when METHODIST authority was growing, traders and administrators were keen to encourage alternative influences, and Adventists were willing to send workers into some areas where missions had not existed previously. They set up a major centre in the Marovo Lagoon of New Georgia, where Methodist influence was minimal, but elsewhere they remained a small minority. They believed firmly in creating separate, Christian villages and went further than any other mission in removing people from their old life and creating a new way of living. Cleanliness, dietary regulation, health services, small businesses, and English education were emphasized. In Papua New Guinea, the SDA church had begun work before World War II, with a station in the eastern Highlands in 1934. After the war they had as many as 64 missionaries established in a chain of missions across the whole length of the Highlands.

More strict than other churches in their observance of a taboo day (a Saturday), they found a harmonious arrangement in Tonga by failing to recognize the international dateline's diversion to the east, so that all churches worship on the same day. Like the New Caledonian Protestants and the Marshall Islands church, SDAs continued to oppose dancing, and smoking was adequate ground for exclusion from the church.

In the 1960s and 1970s, as URBANIZATION brought a cosmopolitan environment into Pacific towns, the Adventists became one of the fastest-growing churches in centres like Port Moresby and Kolonia Town, as well as in some of the rural areas where they had started early. They began to spread much more widely in scattered groups, and today they have become considerably more numerous in the islands than in Australia and New Zealand from where their missionaries came.—KRF

Baha'i

Among the recent new sectarian groups in the Pacific that are growing significantly, usually in the cities, are the Baha'i. Stemming from a reformist movement in Islam and appealing mostly to intellectuals in the west, with a message of inter-religious unity and international, interracial harmony, they might have seemed unlikely to appeal to vigorously Christian, practical peoples with little cosmopolitan experience. Among younger, educated urban residents, however, the Baha'i message has gained some response, particularly in Micronesia. Their missionaries have succeeded in gaining converts also among some village communities where they have settled, for instance in Fiji, Kiribati, Solomon Islands, Tonga, Samoa and Vanuatu. Probably their greatest single increase came in 1966 when they won the adherence of Tommy Kabu, leader of an important modernizing movement in the Purari River area of Papua New Guinea, along with many of his followers.—KRF

Hinduism

Most Indians who came to Fiji as indentured labour (GIRMITIYA) were of the Hindu faith, with much smaller numbers of Muslims and Sikhs. Among Indo-Fijians, the majority today are Hindus, most belonging to the more orthodox group, the Sanatanis, and a smaller number to the more reformist

Arya Samaj. In the early years, there were no missions to assist families and communities to maintain their cultural and religious heritage and identity. Religious and cultural revival took place after the end of indenture in 1920, with the establishment of a number of voluntary associations dedicated to that task. Temples and schools were built, important festivals celebrated (Diwali and Holi), and plays based on sacred texts (especially the *Ramayana*) were performed in village carnivals. Some aspects of Hinduism (the emphasis on family ties, social service and respect for elders) are familiar to Pacific islander communities, but Hinduism is not an institutionalized religion, and many of its rituals, ceremonies and spiritual codes are unique, contributing to the isolation of its members from the broader community.—BVL

Further reading

Ali, A et al, 1981. *Pacific Indians: profiles in 20 Pacific countries*, ed. R G Crocombe, Institute of Pacific Studies, University of the South Pacific.

New Christian movements

With the end of World War II, Christianity in the Pacific islands entered a 25-year period of steady growth and consolidation. Most of the remaining large groups of traditionalists, living in the New Guinea Highlands, accepted Christianity. By the mid 1970s, most of the Protestant missions had been replaced by national churches run by indigenous clergy and lay people. Most churches had come to embrace aspects of traditional culture that had previously been criticized and repressed. Fewer and fewer people could remember a time when church services and church-run schools and hospitals had not been part of daily life. Less than 200 years after its arrival in the Pacific, Christianity had become the 'traditional religion' for most islanders.

The forms of Pacific Christianity that came into being in the second half of the 20th century are now under increasing pressure, from within. Many members of mainstream churches—those which came from the old missions—criticize many things: the benefits enjoyed by some clergy, acceptance of some local customs, and church rituals and beliefs that seem to younger, better educated people to be out of touch with modern conditions. Pressures also come from without. Most people are no longer isolated from the outside world, moving easily between rural and urban areas. They hear about things they can buy and new groups they can join, on radio or television and by word of mouth. Many are leaving the mainstream churches to join churches that preach more radically individualistic forms of Christianity. Others seek to change their churches from within by sponsoring revivalistic crusades and introducing new forms of worship.

What does this new Christianity look like? We need to consider the main players in the new Christian movements. These can be divided into four categories: the MORMONS, who are the fastest growing non-Evangelical sect in the Pacific; the Evangelical church, including Pentecostals and Fundamentalists; Evangelical service organizations; and reform movements within the mainstream island churches.

The Church of Jesus Christ of Latter-Day Saints ('Mormons') began to experience significant growth after the Second World War. When God revealed to the Mormon president in 1978 that black men could join the Mormon priesthood, the church began a vigorous expansion into parts of Melanesia. Despite their separation from other Christian churches, Mormons share many practices and beliefs with the Evangelical churches, especially a stress on individual responsibility to God and His church.

Evangelical Christians hold that the Bible is the inspired and authoritative word of God and embrace the need for missionary outreach and renewal for one's personal salvation. Evangelicals include a huge range of churches in the region. Some, like the Baptist church in Papua New Guinea, are large, but many are very small indeed. Some are missionary churches with strong links to the United States and Australia and others are entirely locally-run congregations. Some are fairly accepting of Pacific customs and others find much to condemn. Evangelicals include two smaller groups which take more radical positions. Fundamentalists are theologically conservative Evangelicals who insist, among other things, that the Bible is literally true and who look forward to the bodily return of Jesus Christ to the world. Pentecostals are Evangelicals who place a strong emphasis on 'gifts' of the Holy Spirit such as prophecy, healing, and the ability to speak in ancient languages (glossolalia).

Evangelical churches receive a great deal of support from mission organizations that are not affiliated with any particular church. These include groups like Campus Crusade for Christ and World Vision International, which help organize Christian rallies and crusades. Many of these organizations are very large, with offices across the world. Some provide important specialized services. The Wycliffe Bible Translators (also known as the Summer Institute of Linguistics) are engaged in Biblical translation work across much of the Pacific. Pacific Missionary Aviation, also an Evangelical organization, has grown into one of the largest airlines in Papua New Guinea.

The Mormons and the different Evangelical, Fundamentalist and Pentecostal groups are the most visible of the new Christian movements. However, groups with similar beliefs have found homes within many of the mainstream churches as well. For instance, there are Anglicans and Roman Catholics known as Charismatics, who experience speaking in tongues and gifts of healing. Many churches sponsor youth fellowship rallies, which include much of the gospel music, testimonials and excitement found at Evangelical events. It is clear that the changes taking place in Pacific Christianity cannot be explained merely as a new missionary movement—that is, as a result of new missions 'stealing' members from the older churches. There is a far more widespread and deeper change occurring in Christianity in general.

Those critical of the new religious groups often claim that converts are attracted only by material benefits. Mormons and SEVENTH-DAY ADVENTISTS, for example, sponsor excellent schools. Many students go on to further education in the United States or Australia. Such criticisms are too simple. Members of these churches devote a tremendous amount of labour and money to support them, committing themselves to regular worship and strenuous missionary crusades and rallies. And they must resist 'temptations' that are enjoyed by non-believing friends and kin.

People accept certain beliefs or join particular churches for various reasons. However, the common elements of the new religious movements do provide some clues as to why they have become so powerful. All these groups stress the relationship between an individual and God: salvation comes not to communities but to individuals. Individuals, therefore, must take responsibility for their personal relationship to God. With the help of their faith in Christ, Christians must embrace a moral lifestyle, one that supports their family and their church.

This individualistic ethic has a strong appeal in many places. Islanders are less and less isolated from the global society. People face choices that their parents could not have imagined. Where will they live? What kind of work should they take on? What should they purchase? How should they respond to development projects that may provide jobs but damage the environment? These issues reduce people's dependence upon their ancestral communities. They have greater freedom to leave, or to disagree. But freedom also brings disruption and dangers. Sadly, many give in to the temptations of alcohol and other drugs; they fall into despair; they engage in violent acts. As the communal unity weakens, the new Christianity's message of personal responsibility for one's salvation becomes an attractive alternative. The new churches offer believers a moral discipline that may help them escape ALCOHOL AND DRUG ABUSE and other problems, creating a new sense of integrity for themselves.

There are two other attractions. The growing churches, with their emphasis upon the individual, offer members a far greater degree of participation in church affairs than many of the mainstream churches. One does not need permission from a bishop, or even much training, to preach or give testimonials in many of the new churches. Local congregations thus feel that they really have their own church. Finally, the new Christian movements are exciting. Adherents enjoy the music, the rallies, the emotional public confessions, the dramatic conversions. They know that they are part of a movement that is much bigger than themselves or their communities. Individualistic Christianity is, in fact, advancing in many parts of the world.

The great majority of Pacific islanders, however, still belong to mainstream churches, which have for the most part worked hard to accommodate local customs. In addition, many islanders have rediscovered traditions with the end of colonialism, and are openly embracing and encouraging them, with or without the support of the churches. But the future of a distinctive Pacific Christianity will depend far more on the hearts and minds of Christians in general. For two centuries now, islanders have created their distinctive religions out of the conflict and dialogue between western Christianity and local cultures. The same process is at work today, as ordinary people translate the teachings of the new churches into their own languages, historical experiences and local hopes and dreams. The churches in many rural areas, for instance, put a tremendous effort into healing sickness. As they root out sorcerers, protect themselves from angered ancestral spirits, and seek to appease God, villagers engage in a religion that shares much with older religions.

The world is becoming a smaller place. Christians, for all the different churches, sound more and more the same. The growth of new Christian movements in the Pacific is evidence (along with Pepsi and national anthems) that cultural diversity is declining around the world. Yet as long as the lives, languages and experiences of Pacific islanders remain distinct, they will contribute a distinctly Oceanic form of Christianity to the world.—JB

Further reading

Ernst, M, 1994. *Winds of Change: rapidly growing religious groups in the Pacific islands*, Pacific Conference of Churches.

Forman, C W, 1982. *The Island Churches of the South Pacific: emergence in the twentieth century*, American Society of Missiology Series, Orbis Books

——, 1986. *The Voice of Many Waters: the story of the life and ministry of the Pacific Conference of Churches in the last 25 years*, Institute of Pacific Studies, University of the South Pacific

——, 1992. *Island Churches: challenge and change*, Institute of Pacific Studies, University of the South Pacific.

Garrett, J, 1982. *To Live Among the Stars: Christian origins in Oceania*, World Council of Churches and Institute of Pacific Studies, University of the South Pacific.

——, 1992. *Footsteps in the Sea: Christianity in Oceania to World War III,*

——, 1997. *Where Nets were Cast: Christianity in Oceania since World War II.*

James, K and Yabaki, A (eds), 1989. *Religious Cooperation in the Pacific Islands*, Institute of Pacific Studies, University of the South Pacific.

FIVE TRADE AND LABOUR

Colonial labour trade

The Pacific labour trade emerged from early European networks of expansion into the region, when—from the 1790s until the 1850s—Pacific islanders began to supply labour for provisioning European ships, and as crew members. They also joined the fur trade in the American northwest, worked at early port and mission settlements in the islands, and became involved in the extraction and processing of SANDALWOOD and maritime products such as BÊCHE-DE-MER. Hawai'i, New Zealand, Samoa and Tahiti dominated this early use of labour. Polynesian chiefs found it profitable to organize local labour, harnessing it to European needs. This is reflected in one of the earliest industries, the production of salted pork in New Zealand and Tahiti, to feed sailors in the Pacific and the convict settlement in New South Wales. Between 1793 and the mid 1820s, 3 000 000 pounds (weight) of Tahitian salted pork was exported to New South Wales. The labour demands of the WHALING trade had a significant impact on islanders in Tonga, Tahiti, Rotuma, Fiji, Norfolk Island and New Zealand. From the 1840s the whaling trade moved into Melanesia, opening up labour markets. In Melanesia the development of the labour trade was overwhelmingly a male affair.

Intensive labour was also required to extract and process commodities which commanded high prices in east Asia, particularly sandalwood and bêche-de-mer. The SANDALWOOD TRADE made its initial impact between 1804 and 1830 in Fiji, Marquesas, Cook Islands and Hawai'i, and by the late 1820s in New Hebrides. The trade revived between the early 1840s and mid 1860s in New Caledonia, New Hebrides and Solomon Islands. Chiefs and BIG-MEN were important in raising and controlling the necessary labour force, in return receiving trade goods, particularly guns. As the sandalwood trade shifted into Melanesia, the role of European labour recruiters increased. The first recruitment of southern Melanesian labour for Queensland in the 1860s developed from the hiring of gangs for the sandalwood trade.

Bêche-de-mer, like sandalwood, was readily available in large quantities in some areas, but its production was labour-intensive. The brief but thriving bêche-de-mer trade lasted from 1804 in Fiji, 1812 in Hawai'i and from 1814 in the Marquesas, up to the 1820s and was then revived between the 1830s and 1840s when there was a slump in the sandalwood trade. By the 1860s and 1870s the bêche-de-mer trade had moved to Torres Strait and the southern coast of New Guinea. Other exotic commodities included tortoiseshell, pearls and pearl shell. The pearling industry became a mainstay of early maritime industry in Torres Strait and in the Louisiade archipelago off east New Guinea in the 1870s and 1880s.

The production of COPRA AND COCONUT OIL reflected a change in the commodity type exploited: coconuts were plentiful and renewable. During the late 1840s and 1850s coconut oil was sought for the manufacture of soap and candles, then copra became a basic material in the manufacture of vegetable oil after technological breakthroughs in the 1850s. Whalers also traded for coconut oil, and in Tonga particularly, large supplies of labour were organized so that Tongans could donate to the new Christian churches and barter for goods with missionaries.

The way in which islander labour was used changed in the second half of the 19th century, following the abolition of slavery. By the 1860s the extraction of labour as a commodity had been firmly established in the South Pacific. This led to the growth of a labour reserve, mainly in Melanesia and to a lesser extent in Micronesia, which, between 1840 and 1915, provided over 300 000 workers for employment under various schemes of indenture. External migration from the Melanesian and Micronesian reserve comprised about half of the indentures in the western Pacific during this period, the balance being mainly internal recruits within German New Guinea and Papua. Melanesians in Fiji and New Caledonia (except Loyalty Islands) did not participate in the external labour trade.

The demand for labour was related to swings in commodity prices and by the 1880s became subject to longer-term colonial interests. The supply of labour also reflected availability within reserves, determined not only by coercive forces but also reflecting the willingness of islanders to participate in contract labour. Forced labour obtained by outright coercion occurred, historians estimate, in about 10–15 per cent of the Melanesian labour trade, mainly in the unregulated years to the mid 1880s. Around 3600 Polynesians and Micronesians were also abducted between 1862–64 to work on plantations and GUANO mines in Peru. (See BLACKBIRDERS.) The majority of the Melanesians enlisted willingly, though some 'cultural kidnapping' occurred, as islanders were lured to participate by an unequal exchange of their labour for cheap European commodities.

Between the 1860s and 1880s economic activity in the Pacific moved from raids on rare commodities to the mass production of agricultural staples. In many island groups, particularly Hawai'i, Fiji, Samoa and Tahiti between the 1840s and the 1880s, foreigners secured long-term access to cheap land, establishing coconut and sugarcane plantations; the pattern was extended by mining in New Caledonia and cotton and sugarcane in Queensland. This heightened competition for labour, leading to colonial partition of the islands and the importation of Asian labourers. In Hawai'i, 1877–88, 2400 islanders were contracted to join the Hawaiian labour force, plus 5000 Chinese in the 1880s. Between 1863 and 1904, 62 475 mainly Melanesians were contracted to work in Queensland and 26 460 in Fiji, between 1865–1911. These statistics are a little misleading as many enlisted more than once (in Queensland the total number of individuals involved is probably around 50 000) and the figures do not include those who re-engaged in the colonies. Others migrated to work mainly on copra plantations: 5746 islanders went to Samoa, 1885–1913; over 2000 to New Caledonia, 1863–85; and at least 1700 to French Polynesia, 1850–85. Significant but smaller numbers were drawn from the Micronesian labour reserve: around 9400 Gilbert Islanders migrated to plantations in Fiji, Samoa, Tahiti, Queensland, Hawai'i, Central America and Réunion from the 1860s to 1900s.

A labour crisis developed from a commodities boom in the later decades of the 19th century and before the Depression of the 1930s: the SUGAR INDUSTRY was at a peak in the 1880s; copra industries developed in Solomon Islands and New Hebrides in the 1910s and 1920s; and the Wau–Bulolo gold field developed in New Guinea from the 1920s. Wages increased: minimum wages remained fixed, but higher amounts went to labourers renewing their contracts. These rising costs led to an expansion of recruiting areas away from the New Hebrides and towards Solomon Islands and Micronesia, the use of labour reserves outside of the Pacific, and to increased regulation of the labour trade.

More than 350 000 Asians supplemented or replaced Pacific workers between 1850 and 1917. Hawai'i, 1852–99, received 125 000 Chinese and Japanese indentured labourers, and a further 100 000 Japanese and 4000 Chinese over the next 17 years after the abolition of the indenture system in 1900, along with a further 30 000 Filipinos and Koreans. Fiji came to rely on the 61 000 Indians who arrived as indentured labourers, 1879–1916. French territories tended to draw their labour from French Indo-China, supplemented by Javanese, Chinese and Japanese: New Caledonia's NICKEL MINING was sustained largely by 22 000 workers, 1892–1915, from these sources. German Samoa attracted 3800 Chinese to its cacao and rubber PLANTATIONS, 1903–13, and German New Guinea imported around 4300 indentured Asians (1885–1914) and a further 2000 immigrant labourers from Asia (1901–14).

Competition by recruiters in Melanesia and Micronesia led to increased government supervision of all aspects of the labour trade. The final partitioning of the Pacific labour reserve between the 1880s and 1900 suited colonial interests and reflected the protectionist character of industrial capitalism. The British adopted labour regulations attempting to end illegal recruiting from the 1870s, used the *Masters and Servants Act* as a basis for labour regulation, and the Suva-based WESTERN PACIFIC HIGH COMMISSION (established in 1877) to oversee a loosely-knit system of government by protectorates. Solomon Islands was placed under a British Protectorate in 1893 and New Hebrides became a joint territory of France and Britain in 1906. More slowly, the French introduced labour regulations, land reserves and restricted mobility; and imposed a head-tax system in New Caledonia to help harness local labour to their enterprises. The Germans continued a system of company and colonial regulation, granting monopoly recruiting rights to the Deutsche Handels-und Plantagen Gesellschaft (DHPG) in the 1880s, enabling the company to draw labour to Samoa from eastern New Guinea archipelagos and northern Solomon Islands. The result of colonial partition and labour regulation was the virtual cessation of labour migration outside of island groups or colonial empires. World War I cut off most sources of Asian labour, forcing utilization of internal labour reserves. Between 1880 and 1941, 37 871 contracts were engaged in New Hebrides, 54 110 contracts were issued between 1913 and 1940 in Solomon Islands, 212 546 contracts were issued between 1909 and 1950 in Papua, and 309 499 contracts allocated within the (formerly German) Australian Territory of New Guinea, 1920–1950. (These figures need to be treated with caution as they include workers who re-engaged their indentures. Also the Papua and New Guinea data does not include labour statistics during and in the two years after the Pacific War.)

The recruiting process varied over time, from early years of forcible recruitment to later years when islanders enlisted voluntarily to obtain foreign goods, or to fulfil head-taxes imposed by colonial governments. The indenture system has been equated with slavery, and often called a new form of slavery. Indenture included penal sanctions which favoured the employer. The imposition of taxation and forced labour regulations is another debatable issue: taxation was usually a device to create a pliant, stable, motivated labour supply. Nonetheless, the whole recruiting system could never have been successful without the support of local indigenous leaders who aided and abetted the process, gaining considerable personal benefit in the process. This co-opted élite largely distributed their new wealth in traditional ways, benefiting mainly from enhanced prestige. Heightened Pacific mortality rates, caused by lack of immunity to many common Asian and European diseases, can also be associated with the manipulation of the labour reserve. Although labourers who survived developed immunity, the moving labour frontier and the circular nature of many labour migrations constantly exposed new individuals to alien disease, and brought home communities into contact with new diseases. The process was male-dominated: young adult males were removed from their home communities, paid a bachelor wage and eventually returned. Women and children largely stayed at home, subsidizing colonial labour by maintaining subsistence production and social obligations, and the care of children.

There was surprisingly little organized resistance to labour mobilization. Friction often occurred at the enlistment stage as local leaders negotiated to release men to the recruiters, but once away, indenture laws forbade protest, and the plantation system ensured that labourers were dispersed through rural areas, and lived in ethnically mixed groups, making it difficult to develop cohesive dissent. Mobilizing the labour reserve was the major way the colonial state and capitalism interacted with the indigenous people of the Pacific. Working for wages under indenture became the cement that enabled the colonial states to hold together.—JL1 & CM2

Further reading

Moore, C, Leckie, J and Munro, D (eds), 1990. *Labour in the South Pacific*, James Cook University.

Beach communities

The term 'beach communities' emerged from the common use of 'The Beach' as a reference to the aggregations of islanders and foreigners who lived around the shorelines of the more frequented harbours of the Pacific from the early 1800s. Once sustained European trading activities developed, beach communities heavily dependent upon them appeared. There were five beach communities—APIA, HONOLULU, PAPE'ETE, LEVUKA and KORORAREKA—which evolved at different times, but shared many characteristics and similarities which outweighed their differences.

With the development of WHALING and of regular trade in BÊCHE-DE-MER and SANDALWOOD, the major ports on the Pacific periphery (Sydney, Manila, Canton and Valparaiso) could no longer meet the immediate and multifarious needs of the new island trade complexes. Each of the five new Pacific beach communities reflected in its location the navigational requirements of sailing vessels up to 1000 tons—good anchorage, open approaches free from reefs, and ease of entry and exit with the wind in various quarters—as well as its proximity to trade products and trading routes.

Colonial vessels engaged in whaling and sealing in the late 1700s were attracted to New Zealand, and many of these ships were also involved in further trade at Tahiti or Fiji. The Bay of Islands lay on the most convenient route for sailing vessels leaving Sydney for the South Pacific, and as the seal trade declined, shipowners turned to New Zealand-grown timber or flax. Although Australian vessels dominated trans-Tasman trade, British and American ships frequently called at Kororareka for refitting and supplies. The sandalwood found on the southwest coast of Vanua Levu (Fiji) in the early 1800s attracted both Australian and American traders initially, although the Americans, who had direct access to Canton, gained a virtual monopoly from 1810 until Fijian supplies were exhausted four years later. The salted pork trade also brought traders and

BEACHCOMBERS to the Tahitian islands, and from the late 1820s Pape'ete provided a base for pearlshell expeditions, and trade in arrowroot and COCONUT OIL. By this time Honolulu had become a supply and refitting centre on the fur route to China, and sandalwood was systematically plundered in the mountainous regions of Kaua'i, O'ahu and Hawai'i from 1815.

With the discovery of the Japanese and equatorial whaling grounds in the early 1820s, whaling vessels were drawn to the islands to find places to refresh and refit. In the northern Pacific, Honolulu became the unchallenged centre for the whaling industry, while in the south whaling captains could choose between Pape'ete, Kororareka, Apia or the Marquesas, depending on which was most convenient. In Samoa, both Apia and Pago Pago offered anchorage and shelter, but the larger resources of Upolu made Apia more suitable as a supply centre, which grew slowly from 1840. After the early 1820s, although no single product had been discovered to replace the valuable fur and sandalwood cargoes, a variety of items were traded—primarily bêche-de-mer, but also tortoiseshell, pearls, pearlshell, edible birds' nests and coral moss. Fiji became the centre of the bêche-de-mer trade, controlled almost exclusively by Salem merchants. By the 1840s trade in coconut oil had also become established throughout the islands to meet the demands of manufacturers of soap and candles.

The traditional settlement patterns of the islands into which these Europeans arrived were essentially non-aggregated. Islanders were located in household groups or hamlets along the beaches, in valleys leading to the sea and, in Melanesia, in the more mountainous inland areas—reflecting the need for people to live within reasonable distance of their food supplies. While many islanders conducted elaborate and extensive trading operations, none of these required large trading centres. Only in Melanesia were central market places maintained, often on small islets, where mountain dwellers could exchange goods for coastal products.

Explorers, traders and beachcombers had neither the occasion nor the power to change the existing patterns of settlement. It was only when the earliest exploited products no longer guaranteed profitable margins that new commodities and trade patterns were instituted, stimulating the growth of beach communities. Honolulu, Pape'ete, Kororareka, Levuka and Apia were creatures of necessity, none of them having enjoyed any great importance in pre-European times. Islanders were receptive to European goods and travelled considerable distances to barter for axes, cloth or whatever else took their fancy. In addition, KAMEHAMEHA I, POMARE I and II, Whareumu and Tui Levuka all appreciated the advantages of European goods and skills.

The good relations established and maintained in the early beach communities owed much to a number of foreigners who had absorbed enough of the island way of life to become sympathetic and tolerant towards the norms of local society, and to act as mediators between the two worlds. Several of these were beachcombers who brought with them habits of cooperation with islanders, and used their knowledge to advise the chiefs in dealings with newly arrived and more influential foreigners. In Levuka and Honolulu, settlers depended on their ability to maintain good relations with their island hosts for their livelihood and their security of tenure. David Whippy, an American sailor who arrived in Fiji in 1825, became involved in organizing the bêche-de-mer trade, and was soon in demand for his navigational, negotiating and shipbuilding skills. In

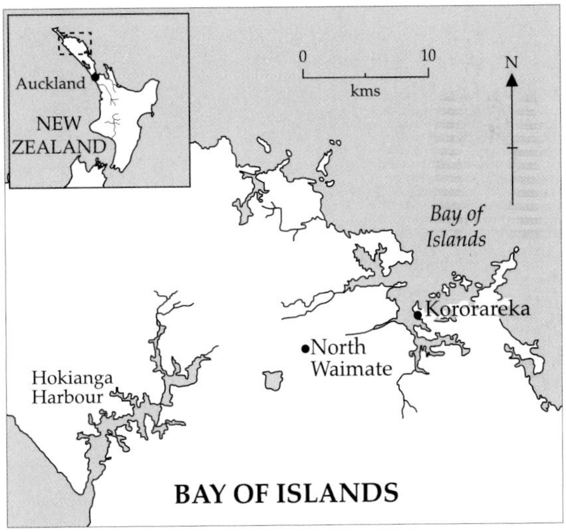

Hawai'i, Kamehameha I, who built a fleet of small western-style vessels to transport his army, appointed the English carpenter Boyd to assist him.

The foreigners in Pape'ete, Kororareka and Apia did not demonstrate any comparable sense of responsibility or concern. In Tahiti the foreign community was small and showed no great loyalty to the Pomare family, which was renowned for its parsimony to outsiders in their employ. Foreigners often disregarded the interests of Tahitians in their pursuit of economic gain. In Apia there was a similar attitude towards the achievement of a quick fortune and a return to the civilized world. The foreign residents of Kororareka had little contact with the Maori chiefs except for their immediate neighbours, the minor chiefs Whareumu and later Pomare and

Titore. Good relations between individual islander and foreigner still existed in these three settlements but the Tahitians, Maori and Samoans had no recognized beach mediators they could turn to.

As the beach communities became established and grew larger, their character changed. Later foreign arrivals introduced new tensions within the expatriate communities, which came to be dominated by the activities of consular agents, missionaries and company traders. Foreign economic development and consular encroachment into the preserves of island authority did not go unchallenged, but all too frequently, island leaders could do little more than voice their opposition and occasionally retard development for a limited period of time. Like the consuls, many of the company traders who established themselves in the beach communities were directed by decision makers in their home countries and were concerned with company profits and national prestige. Company traders brought with them the complex trading procedures and large establishments of western commerce, in which few islanders could find employment. Beyond the port towns, island labour was still used for pearl diving and to some extent in the COPRA AND COCONUT OIL industries, but on large company PLANTATIONS non-indigenous labour was increasingly used. Ownership of the major economic enterprises remained in foreign hands. Samoa, with its potential for coconut oil production, attracted the attention of August Unshelm in 1857, and within a few years Apia became the centre of the GODEFFROY company's Pacific empire.

With the exception of Honolulu, the early missionaries stationed in or near the beach communities rarely had any significant or sustained contact with the foreign settlers. In both Hawai'i and Tahiti, the Protestant faith became closely identified with the ruling chiefs, who felt dangerously threatened by the subsequent appearance of Roman Catholicism and reacted accordingly. In both places, the introduction of Catholicism gave foreign residents an unprecedented chance to enhance their power to islanders' detriment.

The predominantly egalitarian atmosphere which islanders, beachcombers, traders and missionaries created and enjoyed in the early beach communities was largely undermined by later foreign development and population increase. Over a period of about 40 years intensified foreign contact and activity in the beach communities and their hinterlands resulted in European domination in political, economic and religious spheres and the slow westernization of these and many other aspects of life. The beach communities were gradually transformed into port towns oriented almost exclusively to the demands of expatriate commerce and society. In New Zealand and Tahiti, annexation formalized European control long before the resident foreign populations of Kororareka and Pape'ete had become dominant. In Fiji annexation formally recognized that the interests and rights of the indigenous population were secondary to foreign development, and Levuka became Fiji's capital for eight years after 1874. In Hawai'i, despite the Great Powers' formal recognition of Hawaiian independence, American and English residents were firmly entrenched in Honolulu and their influence in the newly established parliament of the early 1840s facilitated legislation that fostered foreign development. Apia had no significant non-missionary population until the early 1840s, but by 1879 the number of foreign residents had increased greatly and included opportunists who had thrived in Levuka before annexation. With the active connivance of the consuls of Great Britain, America and Germany, the foreign residents obtained control over the land and harbour of Apia and all their economic and social activities.

The commercial enterprises built up by the pioneer settlers made it possible for later arrivals to settle in the port towns without the need to establish significant contact with the islanders. Beach community society gradually assumed western standards and conventions, creating a gulf between the foreign-dominated port settlements and the traditional villages. Finally the beach communities, with or without formal annexation, developed into port towns and became alien enclaves in which the rights and interests of the islanders were subordinated to the needs of expatriate development.—CR

Further reading

Ralston, C, 1977. *Grass Huts and Warehouses*, Australian National University Press.

■ *Kororareka* Kororareka, in New Zealand's Bay of Islands, provided good anchorage for South Sea whalers from the 1790s. It developed as a European settlement from 1827, and by 1838 there were 500–600 Europeans living there. Known as 'The Beach', it attracted a disreputable set of BEACHCOMBERS—mainly runaways from whaling ships—but it also contained a thriving small business community of merchants and traders, a doctor, a blacksmith, several sawyers, a British Resident (James Busby, appointed in 1833) and an American Consul (a local trader, J R Clendon). The Church Missionary Society had begun purchasing land, and a bank was estab-

Kororareka, Bay of Islands, New Zealand, c1837 (engraving)

lished in 1840. The importance of the tiny township—and its population—dwindled rapidly after 1840 with British annexation of New Zealand, confirmed in the signing of the Treaty of Waitangi. The first governor, William Hobson, moved his capital to Auckland—where he had purchased land from the Ngati Whatua chief, Te Kawau—and Auckland swiftly became the commercial centre of New Zealand, reaching a population of 2000 in 1841. At the end of 1844, Hone Heke (a nephew of Hongi HIKA, and the first Maori to sign the treaty) cut down the symbol of British sovereignty, the flagstaff at Kororareka, and then sacked and burned the township—an incident which triggered the first major conflict, fought in the Bay of Islands in 1845, in the wars between British and Maori. When the settlement was later rebuilt, it was renamed Russell. (See BEACH COMMUNITIES.)—KRF

■ *Lahaina* Lahaina, on the island of Maui, was the site of the Hawaiian royal residence, and became capital of the kingdom in 1819, used for government meetings between 1820 and 1845. The port was less popular than HONOLULU for whaling ships in the 1820s, but during the following decade the attractions of cheaper supply prices and more liberal entertainments at Lahaina brought it equal trade. The 1840s saw twice as many ships at Lahaina—probably because the availability of white potatoes

Lahaina, first capital of Hawai'i, in c 1851: Presbyterian church painted by James G Sawkins

drew sailors—and also because after the death of the Christian chief Hoapili, Governor of Maui, the prohibition laws were allowed to lapse, producing a proliferation of grog shops and prostitution. The potato boom was over in Lahaina by the mid 1850s, and with prostitution and the sale of alcohol flourishing in Honolulu, the recognized major port eclipsed its minor rival.—KRF

■ *Levuka* Levuka, on the eastern (windward) side of Ovalau, was the first European capital of Fiji. Between 1828 and 1835, the first period of BÊCHE-DE-MER trade, Levuka grew slowly, but after 1842 it became a shipbuilding centre and attracted new settlers. A Pacific port for traders and labour recruiters, its white community was denounced by Pacific missionaries in the mid 19th century for its social life and drunkenness. There was no mission station, but John Binner set up a Wesleyan school in the early 1850s. From 1870, growing concern about Fiji's insta-

Levuka, first capital of Fiji, in September 1875: from a painting by Constance Gordon Cumming

bility and the lawlessness of its European population brought demands for some form of recognized authority under European tutelage. An interim solution (urged by settlers) was to declare Fiji one kingdom, under King CAKOBAU, in 1872. The move towards full British annexation, eventually negotiated—with reluctance and under pressure from British representatives—by J B THURSTON who had accepted a commission as chief secretary, produced the DEED OF CESSION, signed in Levuka in 1874. Levuka remained the capital for another eight years, until SUVA replaced it in 1882, and by 1886 its population had dwindled to 500 as the merchants followed government to Viti Levu. It became a fisheries processing port in the 20th century and remains a place of nostalgia with an uncertain economic future.—KRF

China trade

From the late 1700s until the second half of the 19th century, when the British developed tea plantations in Assam and Ceylon, China virtually monopolized the supply of tea to Europe, America and Australia. China also supplied high quality ceramics and porcelains, silks, and a variety of specialized items such as camphor wood and carved ivory. European demand for these products was very great, especially as tea ceased to be a luxury item in the 19th century, and became a normal component of the working class diet. However, while Chinese goods were highly desirable to Europeans, China showed little interest in any European goods that could be supplied in return, and Europeans were forced to pay for their China goods with gold or silver instead.

The search for trade goods for the China trade was a major preoccupation for the tea merchants. American merchants dealt in Appalachian ginseng and beaver furs, while British merchants found a market in Canton for opium from Turkey. The search also drew merchants into the Pacific. SANDALWOOD, which was used by the Chinese in funerary rites, was the most important Pacific product in the China trade, although other exotic items, such as tortoiseshell, pearl shell and BÊCHE-DE-MER played a similar role in the trading process. A triangular system of trade developed, in which tea merchants bought sandalwood or other produce in the Pacific islands, took their cargoes to Canton, exchanged them there for tea, sold the tea in their home ports, and used part of the profits to purchase trade goods such as tobacco, metal objects and beads, to exchange for sandalwood and other items all over again.—MD

Blackbirders

Blackbirding referred to the recruitment of labour in the Pacific islands, but was used particularly to refer to the worst forms of kidnapping and FORCED MIGRATION, the virtual slave trading of islanders. This began with instances of illegal and forced recruitment and transportation of Melanesians to Australia after 1847 and of Polynesians to South America in 1862–64. (See also KANAKAS IN AUSTRALIA.)

Widespread opposition began to emerge in western countries, led by strong missionary protests. At the same time, island communities—especially in coastal areas, where the effect of population loss was often enormous—sometimes retaliated against blackbirding raids. The death of John PATTESON in 1871 was attributed to such retaliation, and opposition to blackbirding grew stronger. The Gladstone government in London finally took note and in June 1872 the Pacific Islanders Protection Act was passed to halt blackbirding. Five naval cutters were despatched to the South Pacific to see that the Act was enforced.—KRF

Peruvian slave trade

After the victory of the Andean republics over Spain in the war of 1863, Chile and Peru realized the importance of sea power, and the fact that the eastern islands of the South Pacific lay at their mercy. The large coastal plantations of Peru (producing sugar, cotton, olives, grapes and grains) turned to the islands for labour from mid 1862, after the abolition of both African and Chinese slave trading. Their activities became notorious for fraud and brutality. Over a period of about 14 months, some 3630 islanders were gathered up by BLACKBIRDERS, using varying degrees of persuasion, coercion, and kidnapping, and transported to Callao. Some failed to survive the voyage, others died soon after their arrival, and more than half were reported to have died within a year or two of landing. By 1864, Chilean and Peruvian blackbirders were operating as far west as Tahiti itself; and the French had intervened to check their depredations in Gambier and the Pomutus. Amid the international storm of diplomatic protests, which eventually succeeded in ending these recruitment practices, the decision was made to repatriate the last arrivals. About 1200 islanders accordingly began the homeward journey, but only 186 survived this experience and very few reached their own home islands.

Among the many Pacific islands that suffered heavily from these calamitous events, the little atoll group of Nukulaelae (Tuvalu) lost 80 per cent of its original population of 350; Puka Puka (Cook Islands) lost 25 per cent; and on Easter Island, the Peruvian episode is believed to have caused a 60 per cent loss to its estimated population of 4126 in 1862. About 1400 Easter Islanders were taken to work in the mines of the Andes, and a further 1000 later died of smallpox brought back by the 15 repatriated recruits.—KRF

Further reading

Maude, H E, 1981. *Slavers in Paradise: the Peruvian labour trade in Polynesia, 1862–64*, Australian National University Press.

Scarr, D, 1990. *History of the Pacific Islands: kingdoms of the reefs*, Macmillan.

Torres Strait seaway

Between 8000 and 6000 years ago, Torres Strait emerged in the form of sea channels through the swampy land bridge that once joined Australia and

New Guinea. As the ocean level rose, the bridge became islands—some on the western side merely cut-off sections of Cape York, others much lower, and some no more than mud and sand banks, all surrounded by reefs. Although the vast majority of migrating Pacific voyagers would have passed east along the north New Guinea coast, there must have been some who found their way into the South Pacific via the strait, as did more recent Austronesian settlers along New Guinea's southeast coast. The strait was named after Spaniard Luiz de Torres whose expedition was the first from Europe to pass between Australia and New Guinea in 1606. Macassan fisherman frequented northern Australia as far as the eastern Gulf of Carpentaria from the 16th to the early 20th centuries; some may have been blown off course through the strait. Once the Australian east coast was settled by the British, European voyagers began to venture through. Mapping of its islands, reefs and shoals took place between the 1790s and the 1840s. Although most of the strait is shallow, there are deep channels: the outer route around the northern end of the Great Barrier Reef, entering through the northeast channel; the middle route, passing through the Barrier Reef at several points opposite Capes Grenville and Direction; and the inner route, along the Queensland coast within the Barrier Reef, passing through the strait near Cape York.

By the 1830s sailing ships regularly passed east–west through the strait but the prevailing winds prevented regular west–east traffic until the advent of steam ships. From the 1860s the strait became a haven for pearling and BÊCHE-DE-MER fishermen, and the LONDON MISSIONARY SOCIETY established a headquarters there. The Queensland government set up an administrative base, first at Somerset on Cape York, then on Thursday Island from 1877, and the strait was incorporated into Queensland colonial territory in 1872 and 1879. Torres Strait islanders were brought into contact with the outside world through the opening of the new seaway, really the final communication link between the Indian and Pacific Oceans, which shortened sea voyages considerably.

Mail steamers plied from Brisbane to Batavia (Jakarta) from the 1860s and the Torres Strait Pilot Service has operated since the 1870s, guiding ships through the dangerous passages and down the Queensland coast. Since the 1950s the deeper draughts of ships have caused major problems, but new hydrographic surveys and precisely calculated tidal rises now provide safe passage for ships of up to 12.2 m draught.—CM

Whaling

Until the 1720s, the main target of whalers in Europe and along the northeast American coast was the right whale, so-named because it was the 'right' whale to catch: it inhabited coastal waters, moved slowly, did not put up much of a fight when harpooned, floated when dead, and provided both oil and whalebone. By the late 1700s right whales had been hunted virtually to extinction in the known whaling grounds. In the 1780s and 1790s, new Pacific whaling grounds were discovered—around Australia and New Zealand in the west, and Cape Horn in the east—and these gave new life to a declining industry. Sperm whales were hunted first from the New England coast from about 1712, and became a particular focus of the vessels based in Nantucket. Sperm whalers needed bigger vessels, longer voyages, and sought a larger and more aggressive quarry and their crews saw themselves as an élite among whalemen.

Whaling ship with whale in a cove, c1840 (oil painting)

Whale oil became more important with industrialization, its uses extending beyond heating and lighting into industry, being especially important in the development of high quality machine oils. Whale bone—baleen from the mouth of virtually all whales except the sperm whale—was in demand not just for corsets and skirt hoops, but for umbrellas and a range of domestic products. But changing women's fashions meant that corsets and skirt hoops became so popular in the early 18th century that some whalers only took the bone from captured whales and did not reduce the blubber for oil at all. The sperm whale was hunted not only for the oil from its body, but the spermaceti—a fine clear oil ideal for making candles—that was to be found within the 'case' that occupied the upper part of its head.

In 1819, the *Maro* under Captain Joseph Allen visited Hawai'i for provisions and then tested a rumour that rich whaling grounds were to be found in the North Pacific off Japan. Thus the 'off-shore' whaling industry was born, with vessels probing north into the 'Japan grounds' or the Arctic during the northern summer, returning to Hawai'i to repair their vessels and refresh the crews in October, heading westward 'along the line' to the central Pacific islands, or eastward to Californian waters or to the South American coast in the winter, visiting Hawai'i again in March or April before sailing north for another season. This pattern was forced upon the whalers by the migratory habits of the whales and because foreigners were forbidden to land in Japan. Similarly, the North Pacific grounds in the Bering Sea, discovered by New England whalers in 1848, gave a boost to the industry but there was no easy local source of food, water and firewood, thus further enhancing the importance of Pacific 'wintering' ports.

By 1846 there were some 735 American vessels engaged in the whale fishery—many of them by that time being New England-based but operating in the Pacific. By this time, too, British and French interest had declined, leaving the field to Americans. The industry peaked in the mid 1840s, and again in the mid 1850s. In the 1860s and early 1870s the sinking of some whaling vessels and the scuttling of others during the American Civil War brought disruption to an industry that was already in decline—partly because of diminishing whale stocks, and partly because of the challenge provided by petroleum products.

Between 1804 and 1876 (when the Pacific whale fishery had virtually come to an end), American whalers are estimated to have killed some 225 500 sperm whales and 193 500 right whales. The impending demise of off-shore whaling was hastened in 1871 with the loss of some 30 vessels but no lives in the Arctic ice. From the 1850s until the late 1860s, when try-works for rendering blubber were built on ship rather than shore, there had been few major changes in basic technology. The development of the explosive harpoon, compressed air to inflate whale carcasses, iron chase-boats powered by steam, and a factory ship that processed whales at sea made the fishery both efficient and lethal. At a time when sperm whales, like right whales, had almost been hunted to extinction, these new methods made vulnerable the rorqual whales—humpbacks, grey and blue whales that had previously been made safe by virtue of their speed through the water and the fact that they sank when killed. These species, and the newly discovered Antarctic ground, became the major focus of commercial whaling into the 20th century.

Hawai'i—being centrally located, and with several harbours (notably HONOLULU, LAHAINA and Hilo), agricultural productivity, supplies of firewood, repair and chandlery services and, for most of the 19th century, a reputation for the availability of liquor and women—was the most-visited of all island groups. The Pacific 'port towns' of KORORAREKA, PAPE'ETE, Pohnpei and GUAM were also major whaling towns, though none of them on the scale of the Hawaiian ports where the extent of contact with whaling vessels exceeded that of all other locations combined. The next most visited group was the Gilberts where contact was frequent (because of location) but brief, and there was little basis for trade beyond fish, coconuts, handicrafts and the services of women. These same patterns were repeated around the Pacific with the whalers having an impact socially and demographically because of their numbers and because by mid century up to a fifth of all crew were islanders. (See KANAKA SEAMEN.)

Where whaling centres like Honolulu emerged, the towns attracted rural people wishing to share the economic opportunity. Economic transformation was widespread with the demand for agricultural products, which affected customary patterns of land use, brought the commercial cultivation of new crops like potatoes, melons, oranges and pineapples, and affected the distribution of wealth and power. In Hawai'i, for example, returns to prominent chiefs from trade were a potent factor in politics, with constant tension between the desire by some to maximize returns and the desire by others to control the liquor trade, violence and prostitution that were inevitably associated with the presence of large numbers of whalemen. For Hawaiian merchants, the accumulation of capital through servicing the whaling industry laid the basis for later investment in SUGAR. By the 1870s, however, the trade was in decline. A major economic and social force that had brought great trade and travel opportunities to Pacific islanders gave way to locally based plantation industries, mining, labour migration, and enhanced subsistence as the basis of economic organization.—BM

Bêche-de-mer

Bêche-de-mer or trepang, the dried flesh of several edible species of sea cucumbers (*Holothurioidea*), had little local value in the Pacific but was considered to be a gourmet delicacy in China. It attracted European and American traders involved in the CHINA TRADE from the early 1800s (from 1804 in Fiji, 1812 in Hawai'i and from 1814 in Marquesas). Since it was thickly distributed on the shallow reefs of southeast Vanua Levu and the islands of the Koro Sea, the trade flourished in Fiji. Collecting bêche-de-mer was labour-intensive as the sea slugs had to be gathered from shallow reefs, gutted and boiled, and then dried and cured on neighbouring beaches for export. After the sun-drying process was replaced by a smoke-curing technique—taught to the Americans in 1827 by a crew who had mutinied from a Spanish ship—the trade expanded rapidly to become Fiji's leading export by 1830. By 1835 serious depletion of the sea slug on the reefs led to a lull in the trade, lasting until 1842. The second major trading period, 1842–50, was important for the development of LEVUKA. Since bêche-de-mer was not available in its earlier quantities on any one reef, many more fishing establishments had to be set up and it took much longer to collect a full cargo. Men from Levuka were hired to work the boats and the curing stations, some setting up their own businesses to sell to the traders, and a shipbuilding operation was established to provide fishing vessels. The large-scale bêche-de-mer trade declined after 1850, and in the 1860s and 1870s moved north, operating in Torres Strait and along the southern coast of New Guinea.

In 1992–93, Fiji, Solomon Islands and Papua New Guinea supplied about 14 per cent (930 million tonnes) of the total exports of bêche-de-mer to Hong Kong, the principal world market. Approximately 30 per cent of this production was re-exported, primarily to China. The Pacific island region also contributed about 15 per cent of the total bêche-de-mer exports to Singapore.—KRF

Further reading

Ward, R G, 1972. 'The Pacific bêche-de-mer trade with special reference to Fiji', in R G Ward (ed.), *Man in the Pacific Islands*, Clarendon Press.

Sandalwood trade

At the beginning of the 19th century, European countries were at a trade disadvantage with China, a large exporter of tea, silks, and lacquered ware (CHINA TRADE). The west had few products of interest to China, and resented having to pay for its imports with specie. When SANDALWOOD was found growing in the Pacific islands—a product that always found a market in China where it was burnt as incense by Buddhist acolytes—it became a prized item to western merchants.

Traders—mostly American—first found and exploited the scented wood in Fiji, between about 1803 and 1816, and in the Marquesas in 1814–17. Hawai'i was the scene of the next sandalwood rush from about 1816 through the 1820s. The British East India monopoly of the China trade ceasing in 1834, Australian traders were free to exploit stands of sandalwood found in Aneityum, Efaté, Erromango and Espiritu Santo in the NEW HEBRIDES and all around the coast of NEW CALEDONIA, the LOYALTY ISLANDS and the Isle of Pines from the 1830s until the wood was virtually cut out by the mid 1860s. Inevitably, there were disputes and violent fights between sandalwooders and islanders during the trade, in which the traders often came off worst. Considering the number of negotiations and contacts carried on between peoples very foreign to each other, however, the business was conducted remarkably smoothly on the whole.

The main significance of the sandalwood trade for Pacific history lies in the early—sometimes first—and regular contact with the island peoples in the above areas, and the social effects thereof. Islanders took an active part in the trade and were respected as hard bargainers. The language of exchange was the Pidgin used in the China trade which became known in the islands as 'sandalwood English', or 'BISLAMA' after the sea slug (BÊCHE-DE-MER) also picked up by the ships for export to China. In Fiji, the New Hebrides and New Caledonia this trade introduced the islanders to European goods, and everywhere iron and steel tools, muskets, drapery and tobacco became prized items of exchange. In most affected islands, metal knives, axes, hatches and fish-hooks completely supplanted their own stone tools, and were on-traded at profit by islanders to neighbouring places lacking sandalwood to exchange for them. In Hawai'i the monopolization of the trade by the KAMEHAMEHA family is supposed to have contributed greatly to the rise of this dynasty.

As the longest-lived trade in the New Hebrides it also prepared the population for the coming of the LABOUR TRADE. Labourers became used to leaving home to work for Europeans, 'cleaning' (taking off the outer layers of) the wood on stations set up in the islands, where the wood was picked up by Sydney and Hobart ships on their way to China. The spread of Pidgin in the area later considerably assisted the labour traders in their work. And the arousal of a desire for metal tools, muskets and tobacco was of prime importance to future labour recruiters.—DS1

Further reading

Shineberg, D, 1967. *They Came for Sandalwood*, Melbourne University Press.

Phosphate

The Pacific phosphate industry was crucial to the development of large-scale agriculture in Australia and New Zealand and, for a time, contributed to the intensification of agriculture in Japan. The importance of phosphatic fertilizers had long been known but demand grew rapidly in the 1800s with increased European settlement in the Southern Hemisphere. Without the availability of industrial by-products to form the basis of a fertilizer industry as in Europe, interest turned to alternative supplies. GUANO was mined on islands off the Pacific coast of Central and South America and, from the 1860s, mining had been established on several islands scattered through the Pacific especially in the Phoenix and Line groups. In the 1930s the activities of these early miners were to be used by the United States to acquire strategic sites for the development of trans-Pacific AVIATION.

By the late 1800s there was a shortage of guano. Moreover, the discovery that, once applied to the soil, other forms of phosphate were not easily accessible to plants had led to research on treatment of phosphate with sulphuric acid. The resulting superphosphate became fundamental to agricultural development, not only to pastoral farming but to the cultivation of crops like wheat and cotton. 'Super', based on phosphate supplied at well below world price until the late 1960s, was critical to economic development and rising living standards in Australia and New Zealand.

Distance from European and American suppliers and the cost of shipping made local manufacture imperative. Around the turn of the century, the situation was transformed by the discovery of large scale deposits of both alluvial and rock phosphate on Christmas Island (Kiritimati) in the Indian Ocean and on a number of islands—Nauru, Banaba (Ocean Island), Ngeaur (Angaur) and Makatea—in the Pacific. Most of these 'phosphate islands' were small, raised atolls a few square kilometres in area and rising only 70–80 m above sea level.

Ngeaur in the Palau group remained in production until 1955 and Makatea in French Polynesia for a decade longer. Both produced substantial quantities, with 200 000 tonnes a year being exported from Makatea during World War II, but both remain insignificant alongside Nauru and Banaba. Here, high-quality deposits were discovered in the late 1890s by Albert Ellis and quickly came under the control of the Pacific Islands Company for which he worked. The firm, with Baron Stanmore (Sir Arthur GORDON) as its chairman and J T Arundel as its driving force, soon abandoned most of its island trading business and was reconfigured as the Pacific Phosphate Company. Linked in a joint venture at Makatea, the company enjoyed a virtual monopoly of both the islands' phosphate trade and the supply of phosphate to both Australia and New Zealand—Ngeaur being closely tied to the Japanese market.

Under the 1886 Anglo-German demarcation of the Pacific, Banaba (then called Ocean Island) fell within the British sphere of influence, subsequently becoming part of the Gilbert and Ellice Islands Colony, and Nauru fell within the German sphere. With the seizure of Germany's Pacific possessions during the First World War, the future of Nauru became the subject of debate at the Versailles peace talks and rivalry between prime ministers W M (Billy) Hughes from Australia and William Massey from New Zealand. As a compromise, the League of Nations mandate for Nauru was given to the British Empire with Britain, Australia and New Zealand forming a consortium, the British Phosphate Commissioners (BPC), to manage the industry at both Nauru and Banaba. The BPC, for many years managed by the redoubtable Harold Gaze, became all-powerful in both the industry and in the colonial administration of both islands. With labour from the Gilbert and Ellice Islands and from Hong Kong, and European managers and engineers, the industry was increasingly mechanized with excavators, crushers, dryers, and cantilevered loading systems all strongly in evidence. With the stripping away of topsoil, and the excavation of the phosphate, the landscape was left dominated by stark coral pinnacles and a barren wasteland.

At their peak in the late 1960s, Nauru and Banaba exported 1.8 million and 450 000 tonnes of phosphate a year respectively, but the deposits at Banaba were exhausted in 1979—coinciding with the independence of Gilbert Islands (Kiribati). By then, the Banaban people had been resettled on Rabi Island in Fiji, and claims for Banaban sovereignty and compensation for environmental damage had been only partly resolved by a significant cash payment and some representation for Banaban interests in post-independence Kiribati. Nauruan refusal to accept resettlement off their home island and ultimately successful demands for ownership of the industry made for a troubled path to independence in 1968. A later action in the World Court led eventually to a substantial out-of-court settlement. Nauru remains the only significant source of phosphate within the Pacific region with deposits having, perhaps, a decade's supply at current rates of extraction.—BM

■ *Guano* Guano is the accumulated powder-dry deposits of seabird droppings which formed on barren coral islands over centuries, wherever seabirds had lived in sizeable numbers. Named from the Peruvian *huanu*, guano was first exploited in the Pacific islands just off the coast of Peru in the early 1800s. As a fertilizer, it became a seemingly miraculous cure for depleted soil.—KRF

Copra and coconut oil

After the process of making soap from COCONUT oil was discovered in the mid 1800s, coconut oil became a major trade item in the region. Oil was initially extracted from nuts gathered from existing groves but missionaries and governments later encouraged, and sometimes required, islanders to plant more palms for commercial production. Production, storage and transport became easier when copra, the dried flesh of the coconut, replaced oil as the form in which the product was exported. The ripe nuts are not picked, but simply gathered up off the ground and piled in heaps ready for splitting with a large knife or axe. The green copra is gouged out, and then dried—in hot air driers, in the sun, or smoke-dried.

The copra trade (for the industrial manufacture of soap and margarine) became the basis for much of the inter-island and international SHIPPING that linked the islands into the trade systems of Europe and North America. This trade was an important factor in the growth of ports such as Apia. Copra, being storable, was a very suitable commercial product for relatively isolated areas. It became the mainstay of European-owned PLANTATIONS in New Guinea and across the Pacific and the core business of major companies such as LEVER BROTHERS, GODEFFROY'S, DHPG, and BURNS PHILP. The demand for land for coconut plantations was a major factor in the process of land alienation in the latter half of the 19th century, and in the COLONIAL LABOUR TRADE.

For more than 100 years copra was widely established as a significant tradable commodity in the Pacific islands, and indeed, for many small islands, the sole commodity available for export. In colonial Gilbert and Ellice Islands (Kiribati and Tuvalu), officials levied tax in the form of copra rather than cash, and this 'tax copra' was then offered for sale by tender. Copra lost its dominance as commercial agriculture was diversified in the islands, and as international prices fluctuated and fell in real terms when temperate region alternatives such as soy bean oil captured a large share of the market. Nevertheless, the widespread importance of coconuts in the subsistence sector, and the status of copra as the only feasible commercial crop in many remote locations, ensure the continued role of coconuts in Pacific islands agriculture.—RGW

Polynesia Company

The Polynesia Company was a Melbourne-based land and PLANTATION development company which paid Ratu Seru CAKOBAU's American debt in 1868 in return for large land grants, which it hoped to subdivide and to sell to Australasian colonial investors and intending migrants and planters in Fiji. After a British Crown Colony was established in 1874, the company was hampered by its shady reputation, the nefarious activities of its directors and agents, and the collapse of the cotton boom. Although it lingered on until the 1880s, all land claims, except where occupation occurred, were rejected by the Fijian Land Claims Commission. Only 100 mostly unsuccessful shareholders settled on the Suva Peninsula, Viti Levu Bay and Natewa Bay. The company in Melbourne collapsed despite negotiating a deal with the government to provide land at SUVA for the development of the capital when it moved from LEVUKA. (See J B THURSTON.)—MQ

Japanese commercial interests

The Japanese refer to Micronesia as the Nan'yô or south seas. Business and commerce spearheaded Japanese economic development in the Pacific islands, with small groups of Japanese entrepreneurs, called 'mini-shosha' involved in commercial enterprises in Chuuk (Truk), Pohnpei and the Palau islands in the 1890s. With determination, resilience and skill, these commercial pioneers overcame isolation, lack of capital or support from their homeland, and the hostility of the German colonial administration, to exercise an economic influence out of all proportion to their numbers. From their small trading stores and from the decks of their handful of schooners, dealing in sundries in return for COPRA and other island products, they came to control a significant proportion of the trade of German Micronesia.

By 1908 several of these struggling ventures had merged to form the South Seas Trading Company (Nan'yô Bôeki Kaisha)—'Nambo' for short—with a growing commercial network, including copra production, a chain of retail outlets, and a fleet of five vessels transporting inter-island freight, mail and passengers. World War I offered a windfall for Nambo, as it did for much of Japanese commerce and industry. With the occupation of the German islands by the Japanese navy, and the later establishment of a mandate under the League of Nations, the company acquired a lucrative naval contract to transport provisions and naval personnel within the islands and between Micronesia and Japan. With heavy subsidies and government cooperation, its assets amounted to more than 3 000 000 yen by 1917. The Nan'yô Bôeki Kaisha was able then to acquire several small competitive firms operating in the islands, and by 1920 it had attained great prominence in the region.

The 1920s saw the firm expand into a variety of enterprises—general merchandise, fisheries, trade in fats and oils, and some construction—through its 32 branches throughout Micronesia. One of its principal ventures continued to be maritime transportation. Beginning in 1922, under arrangements with Japan's South Seas Government Office (Nan'yô-chô) at KOROR, the company maintained a regular inter-island service between the principal islands of the Mandated Territory and some of the adjacent British islands.

The majority of its merchants remained as single traders under contract to the company, who managed the small tin-roofed trading stores that became a ubiquitous feature of the Japanese presence in the South Seas. It was from these far-flung commercial outlets that the Nan'yô Bôeki Kaisha was able to establish itself in the village economies of Micronesia, introducing a range of Japanese goods and services which profoundly altered islander tastes and lifestyles.

The development of Japanese industry in Micronesia was very unsteady in the beginning. Soon after Japanese naval forces occupied Micronesia, the islands began to be seen as an attractive area for Japanese business development. SUGAR seemed a particularly promising crop, given the hot moist climate, the fertile soil of the Marianas, and Japanese success in sugar cultivation and refining in Taiwan. To take advantage of such an opportunity, several companies were formed, the Nishimura Takushoku and the Nan'yô Shokusan being supported by influential backers in Japan.

Both companies established themselves in 1916 on Saipan, bringing in Korean labourers, tenant farmers from the Bonin Islands, and fishermen from Japan, to serve as a workforce. After several years of failure caused by technical problems, corruption, and by a post-war world economic slump which slashed sugar prices, the companies were on the verge of collapse. By 1919, they had both withdrawn from Micronesia, leaving behind 1000 or more Japanese labourers and farmers. Questions were asked in the Japanese Diet and bureaucracy about these initial failures, advocating that Micronesia be abandoned. But the navy argued otherwise, and Japan remained.

It was with the arrival of Matsue Haruji, an entrepreneur possessed of determination, integrity, government backing, and technical skill in the sugar business, that Japanese industry gained a solid base in the South Pacific. Matsue—trained in the United States at Louisiana State University, apprenticed with the Spreckles Company and destined to be nicknamed the 'Sugar King' of the South Pacific—had made his name and his fortune in Taiwan. Just when he went to Saipan to investigate the potential of the Marianas for sugar, the first governor of Nan'yô-chô, Tezuka Toshiro, turned to the Oriental Development Company (a key player in the economic development of Korea), to revive the economy of Saipan for those Japanese abandoned several years before. With capital from this company and government approval, Matsue acquired the assets of Nishimura Takushoku and the Nan'yô Shokusan. Thus, in 1921, was founded the Nan'yô Kôhatsu Kaisha (South Seas Development Company)—familiarly known as 'Nanko', with Matsue as executive director. Employing the Japanese already on Saipan and bringing in more immigrants from Okinawa and the Tohoku region, Matsue cleared the land, showed the workers how to cultivate and harvest the cane, and built his refineries.

His initial efforts (1922–23) were ruinous: labour problems, delays in obtaining refining equipment from Germany, insect blight, carelessness in cultivating the sugarcane by tenant farmers, difficulties in constructing a narrow-gauge railway to the refinery, the plummeting price of sugar, and the destruction of his first small sugar shipment in a warehouse in Yokohama during a fire after the Great Kanto Earthquake of 1923. Not to be daunted, Matsue began to reverse his company's fortunes. By 1925 he had built an alcohol factory and ice plant on Saipan, planted over 3000 hectares of sugar, extended his operations to Saipan's neighbouring islands, Tinian and Rota, and by the end of the decade, brought more than 5000 workers to the Marianas, where sugar had indeed become king, the main impetus behind the economic boom which followed.

The rapid growth of Nan'yô Kohatsu was due largely to the aid that it received from the Nan'yô-chô: nearly rent-free use of land, subsidies to support land clearing and planting, a favourable tax policy, and an encouragement of sugar production in the Nan'yô. Nourished by such favoured treatment and propelled by Matsue's initiatives, the company became the dominant economic force not only in the Marianas, but throughout Micronesia. With government backing, Nanko began to move into other Micronesian island groups and ultimately into Melanesia and then the Dutch East Indies, diversifying into such enterprises as tapioca and coconut cultivation, marine products, PHOSPHATE, and warehousing along the way. By the early 1930s the company's sugar-related industries accounted for more than 60 per cent of the revenues of the Nan'yô-chô, largely through port clearance fees for its exports, and by the mid 1930s Nanko was a substantial investor in the colonial government's own industrial enterprises.

During the first decade of the mandate, the success of the two largest enterprises, the Nan'yô Bôeki and the Nan'yô Kôhatsu, aided by a friendly administration, had revived the fortunes of commerce, industry and agriculture in the islands, opening the way for increased business and commerce. The Nan'yô not only became a self-sufficient territory, allowing the government to terminate its annual subsidy, but also contributed to the support of the home government as a whole, its small but growing surplus being transferred to the general account of the metropolitan government.—DAB

German commercial interests

The Germans came to the Pacific as traders, broadened into other forms of economic activity—such as PLANTATIONS, labour recruiting and PHOSPHATE mining—and eventually became colonial administrators to protect these interests.

The first German trading company, J C GODEFFROY & SOHN, established an agency in Apia in 1857 and gained commercial ascendancy almost from the moment of its arrival. With massive capital backing from Germany the firm rapidly expanded and diversified and within a decade presided over Samoa's largest plantation system. Godeffroy's also entered other island groups and by degrees established a network of trading stations which, at its height, stretched from the Marianas to the Tuamotus. The firm also gained a competitive edge by introducing large quantities of debased South American coinage. By 1874, Pacific commercial life was dominated by German firms—in effect Godeffroy's—that controlled an estimated 70 per cent of it. Godeffroy's represented a departure from the methods of the small and often owner-operated trading concerns that preceded it. The firm was, as Harold Brookfield said, 'the model of the vertically-integrated, multinationally operating corporation that has since been widely replicated'. Sound management, economic efficiency and political protection were vital to its success.

In contrast, the second largest German firm was a fiasco. The New Guinea Company was formed in 1884. A chartered company, it ran the newly created colony on behalf of the Reich by a consortium of German bankers, largely as a land speculation. The Protectorate of the New Guinea Company was run by remote control from Berlin. Given this lack of on-the-spot knowledge so vital to Godeffroys' success, it is not surprising that the New Guinea Company failed to realize its objectives. It never became the envisaged settler colony. Forced then to become a plantation colony, the company unwisely centred its operations on the New Guinea coast rather than in island New Guinea, was never self-supporting, and eventually, in 1899, the Protectorate of the New Guinea Company was replaced by a conventional imperial administration.

Godeffroy's also experienced hard times. Following the bankruptcy of the parent company, the profitable Pacific segments were reconstituted into two separate joint stock companies—the Société Commerciale de l'Océanie based in Tahiti and the Deutsche Handels-und Plantagen Gesellschaft (DHPG) based in Samoa. Badly affected by the fall in world copra prices from the early 1880s, the DHPG had its profitability curtailed, while competition from British recruiters meant that its plantation labour lines were often stretched thin. In response, the firm reduced its activities. Over the next decade it ended its involvement in the seaborne copra trade and concentrated on its plantations in Samoa and Tonga, where it purchased native-produced copra. The DHPG also sold its Micronesian interests to another German firm, Robertson & Hernsheim, in 1887. The merger resulted in the JALUIT GESELLSCHAFT, on whom the German government conferred numerous privileges, including exclusive right to unoccupied lands. A chartered company, the Jaluit Gesellschaft administered Marshall Islands on behalf of Germany, thus being strategically placed to drive out foreign competition.

The elimination of serious competition was a preoccupation, almost an obsession, of German trading companies. With too many players in relation to exploitable resources, mercantilist solutions were increasingly sought. The DHPG, for example, was exceedingly hostile towards its largest competitor in Samoa—H M Ruge & Co, another German firm—and contributed to its demise in 1888. The DHPG and the New Guinea Company competed for labour in the New Guinea islands, the DHPG coming out the winner by decree of the German government. At the same time, German firms were prepared to enter into pragmatic compromises. In 1901, for example, the Pacific Island Company's Marshall Island trading stations were taken over by the Jaluit Gesellschaft in return for a licence to the British company to mine phosphate in Marshall Islands. The Jaluit Gesellschaft also entered into a joint venture with the same company to mine phosphate at Nauru in 1906.

The close ties between some German firms and the German authorities was another feature of German commerce. In Samoa, the local German consul gave the firm a free hand in the recruitment and employment of plantation labour, his primary objective being the DHPG's survival and profitability in difficult times. Whether or not German firms received such privileged treatment, all benefited by lack of restraint on the part of their home government. Unfettered by humanitarian concerns or philanthropic pressure groups, the Germans could afford to be far more single-minded than the British in their pursuit of profit. A reflection of this was the willingness of Germany, after 1884, to declare colonies and to protect its nationals and their commercial interests vigorously by force of arms.

With rising commodity prices from the early 1900s, German plantations became profitable once again and their future looked bright. But the outbreak of World War I resulted in Germany's Pacific colonies being occupied by expeditionary forces from Australia (New Guinea and Nauru), New Zealand (Samoa) and Japan (Micronesia), and German property was expropriated. After the war, the occupying forces were granted League of Nations Mandates over these territories, and became beneficiaries of the solid economic foundations established under German influence.—DM

Further reading

Brookfield, H C, 1972. *Colonialism, Development and Independence: the case of the Melanesian islands in the South Pacific*, Cambridge University Press.

Firth, S, 1973. 'German firms in the western Pacific islands, 1857–1914', *Journal of Pacific History*, 8.

——, 1983. *New Guinea Under the Germans*, Melbourne University Press.

Hempenstall, P, 1978. *Pacific Islands Under German Rule: a study in the meaning of colonial resistance*, Australian National University Press.

■ ***J C Godeffroy & Sohn*** Johann Caesar Godeffroy was a wealthy merchant and shipowner in Hamburg, Germany, whose interests included a passenger steamship service from Europe to Australia and trading branches in Hong Kong and Valparaiso. In 1856 Godeffroy agents first opened a trading station in Apia as their South Seas headquarters and were soon operating successfully throughout the southern Pacific—sometimes the only western traders (in Marshall Islands, eastern Caroline Islands, and Gilbert and Ellice Islands). In the early days, Godeffroy operations were backed by private German financiers seeking commercial dominance. The company's British and German agents were highly competent, empowered to offer planters low freight rates and a fast, efficient service to Sydney, Hong Kong and Germany. One of the most successful of these was Adolph Capelle, in the Marshall Islands, who subsequently started his own company and began a copra plantation.

In Samoa, Godeffroy's planned a leading role for itself in the Pacific islands cotton boom in the aftermath of the American Civil War. It bought up Samoan copra and acquired land (some 25 000 acres by 1872), even securing the support of a German warship in a land dispute in 1874. Godeffroy agents dominated trade in the central Pacific by the 1870s, although at home the French blockade of Hamburg was sending the company into liquidation. Other German companies moved in to secure the flourishing Pacific trade interests, and by 1879 Godeffroy's had been succeeded by Deutsche Handels-und Plantagen Gesellschaft (DHPG). As German agents in the Pacific took on consular responsibilities, their influence on the government's colonial policies increased.

In the early 1870s Godeffroy company agents had made the first inroads into New Britain, off the coast of New Guinea, trading in coconuts and pearl shell. Within 10 years several German traders were establishing coconut plantations in northeastern New Guinea, and by 1884 Germany was persuaded to support the Neu Guinea Kompagnie (the successor to Godeffroy's original development) to the extent of annexation. In the following year, Bismarck's government also took possession of Marshall Islands, where the former Godeffroy affiliate was now the commercially successful JALUIT GESELLSCHAFT.—KRF

■ ***Jaluit Gesellschaft*** Jaluit Gesellschaft, a German trading company that began as an affiliate of J C GODEFFROY in Marshall Islands, dealt in COPRA, pearl shell and GUANO fertilizer. Company agents succeeded in negotiating a trade agreement with a powerful chief, and subsequently this 'treaty' helped persuade the Bismarck government to establish a protectorate over the island group in 1885. For many years following annexation, the islands' administration was left to Jaluit, in return for generous trade concessions. Other large production and mercantile firms eventually merged with Jaluit, and the support of the German government gave them a virtual monopoly in both Marshall Islands and eastern Caroline Islands.—KRF

■ *Burns Philp* Burns Philp & Company Limited was created in the 1870s, when its founding partners, James Burns and Robert Philp (both from Scotland), established a regular shipping line between Sydney and Townsville to supply their own trade stores. In the 1880s the company took on wider shipping agencies and expanded its branch activities along the Queensland coast, soon moving into pearling in Torres Strait and establishing a steamship run between Port Moresby and Thursday Island. While carrying passengers and trade for the Morobe gold fields, Burns Philp ran the mail service to New Guinea and set up trading branches at Port Moresby and Samurai in 1890–91. By 1896 the company had established itself as carriers for (then German) New Guinea, and was driven out by Nord Deutscher-Lloyd (NDL) in 1900 only because the administration was able to support a German company with massive subsidies.

Following similar expansion into the New Hebrides, Burns Philp further extended its area of interest into the central Pacific, opening branches in Tonga (1899), and an agency in Samoa (1912), acquiring a Fijian company in 1916, and opening depots in Solomon Islands (1910) and Gilbert Islands (1912). Extensive business was also conducted with planters and traders on its ships, used as floating shops where goods from Australia might be traded for COPRA and other island products.

Plantation ownership (copra production) became part of the company's Pacific mercantile activities, while both copra and tourism ensured the continued success of the shipping operations. Successful efforts to sustain and extend its dominance in the Pacific through the 1930s and 1940s included the establishment of subsidiary companies to manage operations in the New Hebrides and other non-Commonwealth areas of the Pacific, and major expansion in New Guinea.

For 75 years Burns Philp ships were household names in the South Pacific—including the *Bulolo*, *Burnside*, *Macdhui*, *Malaita*, *Malekula*, *Mamatu*, *Marella*, *Marsina*, *Matunga*, *Merkur*, *Montoro*, *Morinda*, and *Neptuna*. In World War II, eight company ships were requisitioned and six were lost in enemy action. Many of its Pacific branches ceased operating and Burns Philp took on a wartime role as agent for the United States Army Small Ships Command.

Since the war, retail trading and manufacturing have become increasingly significant activities for the company. Burns Philp's shipping interests virtually ended with the sale of the *Montoro* in 1970, following the decision of the Australian government in the 1960s to withdraw its shipping subsidy. By 1998 the company had absorbed substantial abnormal losses from its forays into the international herbs and spices industry and the antibiotics market, and was relying for survival on the sale of its terminals group, operating bulk storage facilities in Australia and New Zealand.—CP & KRF

Further reading

Buckley, K and Klugman, K, 1981. *The History of Burns Philp: the Australian company in the South Pacific*, Allen & Unwin.

——, 1983. *'The Australian Presence in the Pacific': Burns Philp 1914–1946*, Allen & Unwin.

Pritchard, C, 1992. 'Chronicle', *Burns Philp and Company Ltd*, Noel Butlin Archives Centre, N115.

■ *Lever Brothers* Lever Brothers, a large British company with important COPRA trading and planting interests in the South Pacific region, developed from a family grocery business which became involved in soap manufacture in England in the mid 1880s, using the trademark name 'Sunlight'. William and Elizabeth Lever came to Australia in 1892, setting up a vegetable oil mill (1897) and then a soap factory (1899) at Balmain. On his next visit in 1901, Lever made the acquaintance of a Pacific property dealer, J T Arundel, and began to purchase a chain of island trading stations and copra PLANTATIONS. Lever's Pacific Plantations was formed in 1902, aimed initially at stimulating copra production and thus lowering prices.

In Solomon Islands, an early burst of enthusiasm saw the company buy up 18 870 acres from Solomon Islanders in 1905, acquire another 51 000 acres from the islands trader Captain O Svenson, and in 1906 take over the 99-year occupation leases granted by the Colonial Office to Sir Arthur GORDON, foundation High Commissioner for the Western Pacific. Problems soon emerged: production costs were higher than anticipated, and recruitment of staff among small expatriate BEACHCOMBER communities was unreliable. The company ran its own shipping service as well, but in 1916 Lever was still bemoaning the unprofitability of copra, and then wartime exigencies forced him to transfer the largest ship *Kulambangra* to the vegetable oil trade between

West Africa and Britain. Although a policy of substantial coconut planting was pursued, Lever's Pacific Plantations only began to show a profit in the late 1920s, after a merger with J Kitchen & Sons, when the company's emphasis switched from copra to dessicated coconut.

Sir William Lever, the first Lord Leverhulme, died in 1925, and Lever Brothers Pty Ltd merged with Unilever in 1937. World War II put a temporary halt to the company's Pacific operations. All expatriate staff were evacuated from Solomon Islands in 1939 and the little inter-island trading ship *Kurimarau* collected the last white residents of the community in 1942 and, hugely overcrowded, managed to deliver them safely to Australia. W Hulme Lever died in 1949.—KRF

Source/further reading

Bak, C, 1988. *A Lever & Kitchen Album*, Lever & Kitchen Pty Ltd.

Reader, W J, 1980. *Fifty Years of Unilever, 1930–1980*, Heinemann.

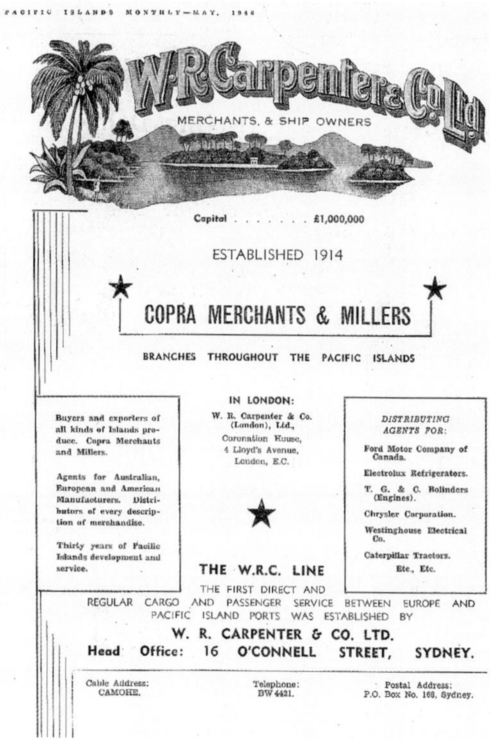

Advertisement for the Carpenter Group, *Pacific Islands Monthly*, May 1946

■ *Carpenter Group* W R Carpenter & Co Ltd, the trading company which became a household name in the Pacific islands from the 1920s, was established in Sydney in September 1914. Its founder, Walter Randolph Carpenter (1832–1954), was the son of an American-born sea captain. He was subsequently joined by his two brothers, J A and W H Carpenter, and still later by his two sons, R B and C H Carpenter. In Papua New Guinea the company established trading and inter-island shipping operations, and became involved in copra PLANTATIONS after 1920, when Australia took over the administration of what was then known as the Mandated Territory of New Guinea.

One of the larger companies involved in coconut plantations (alongside the earlier established LEVER BROTHERS and BURNS PHILP), Carpenter's took the same approach as Burns Philp in regarding copra production as only one phase in a wider mercantile operation. The company's activities grew rapidly in the period between the wars, with plantations set up in Solomon Islands and Gilbert and Ellice Islands (now Kiribati and Tuvalu), and in New Guinea. In 1938 Carpenter's inaugurated an air link between Sydney and Lae, flying via Brisbane and Port Moresby. Once the Pacific War interrupted all trading and shipping operations, Carpenter's was unable to maintain or defend its plantations, stores, ships and shipping facilities and the company suffered substantial losses. After 1945 the whole character of the company's structure changed, with the parent company reducing its involvement in direct trade and becoming largely a holding company.

Following the death of Sir Walter Carpenter in 1954, his elder son R B Carpenter became chairman of directors. In 1956 the Carpenter Group purchased MORRIS HEDSTROM Ltd of Suva, a retail company established in Fiji in 1898 which already had subsidiary companies in Samoa and Tonga. The Carpenter Group thus gained a controlling interest in the central and eastern part of the South Pacific. It continued to expand and diversify from this time, and in 1965 was the first commercial company to begin a management training scheme for young Papua New Guinean employees.—KRF

■ *Hennings* F & W Hennings, the trading company established in the late 1850s in Fiji, was founded initially on credit from J C GODEFFROY & SOHN. Frederic Hennings, an agent for Goddefroy, went into partnership with his two younger brothers, William and Gustave, who had followed him to the islands from Germany. Involved in commercial development and especially PLANTATIONS, the company was interested in cotton, BÊCHE-DE-MER, and the COPRA AND COCONUT OIL trade. Hennings acquired its early influence by allowing high-ranking Fijians, and the Tongan Enele Ma'afu, to run up accounts at its stores. By January 1870, it had several large plantations in cotton and coffee, and it was printing its own currency and offering advances on cotton. Several firms acted as bankers to the European community, but the strategically placed Hennings stores (Frederic at LEVUKA, William at Lomaloma, and Gustave on the Rewa River) were the biggest.

Godeffroy's withdrew from Fiji in 1867, and the Sydney firm of Rabone, Feez and Co, managed by Carl L Sahl, took over the role of creditor to F & W Hennings. There were substantial debts by 1871, and Sahl, who for some time delayed foreclosing on the mortgages totalling £50 000 on all Hennings' property, at last put the company into liquidation in March 1874. The Hennings brothers struggled to re-establish themselves in the late 1870s and 1880s. Frederic and Gustave maintained an interest in sugar, supplying cane to the COLONIAL SUGAR REFINING COMPANY, while William returned to trade with Apia, reviving his connections with Godeffroy's (later replaced by the DHPG), and joined by two more younger brothers. He built up his business, maintained close personal connections with Fijian society through his de facto marriage to Adi Mere Tuisalalo, and successfully won a series of government contracts for copra, always striving for a monopoly.

Although they managed to appear as successful merchants in Levuka, the Hennings brothers continued to live on credit. Gustave succumbed to drink, and when Frederic died in 1891, he owned nothing more than a small store at Lakeba. Charles died at sea in 1896, leaving only debts, and the youngest brother, Christian, who had made money during the 1890s from his trading stores, took his own life in 1906. The Lau trading network was taken over by another trader in the 1890s, and by 1901 was owned by Henry Marks, one of Fiji's successful merchants.—DAS & KRF

■ *Morris Hedstrom* Morris Hedstrom Limited had its origins in the trading company founded by Sir John Maynard Hedstrom in Fiji in 1898. Sir John's son, John Maynard Hedstrom (born at Levuka, 16 May 1908, and educated in Australia), joined Morris Hedstrom Ltd as a junior clerk in 1934. After retiring as general manager in 1958, he served as chairman of directors. In 1920 when Henry Marks amalgamated his mercantile interests (which had begun with the acquisition of part of the commercial operations of the former Fiji Trading Company, 1875–92, and by the 1920s included HENNINGS) with Morris Hedstrom and Company, it became the largest trading company in Fiji and had subsidiary companies in Samoa and Tonga. It was purchased in 1956 by the CARPENTER GROUP. The company's retail premises in central Suva, a well-known and much-photographed landmark, were destroyed by fire in 1998.—KRF

■ *Ben Boyd* Benjamin Boyd (c1797–1851) was the first capitalist to import Pacific island labour into Australia for his pastoral activities. (See COLONIAL LABOUR TRADE.) The second son of a landed Scottish family, Boyd worked in London as a stockbroker, and in 1840 established the Royal Bank of Australia to raise money to invest in Australia's pastoral and maritime industries. He arrived in Australia in 1842, and established Boydtown in southern New South Wales as a port for the Pacific and whaling trades. In 1847 his first shipment of about 65 islanders (from Loyalty Islands and New Hebrides) arrived.

Boyd's speculations in New South Wales failed, and in October 1849 he escaped his creditors by setting sail for the Californian gold fields in his private yacht, *The Wanderer*. In June 1851, Boyd left San Francisco again for the South Pacific, together with several companions including John Webster, who subsequently recounted the events in *The Last Cruise of the Wanderer* (185?). In apparent pursuit of an earlier objective to found a 'republic' in the South Seas (an idea raised in a letter to the Colonial Office in 1840), Boyd set out for Solomon Islands. In September he reached Stewart Island, on the eastern side, which he 'purchased' from its occupants for $1000 worth of merchandise. He then sailed on to San Cristobal, where he named Wanderer's Bay, and dreamed of establishing a trading station at Makira Bay. On 5 October Boyd negotiated a similar 'purchase' of Makira Bay, for A$2000 in merchandise.

On 11 October *The Wanderer* sailed on to Guadalcanal. Boyd went ashore to shoot birds and was never seen again. His companions subsequently came ashore and burned several villages in punishment, before sailing back to Australia. Rumours persisted of Boyd's survival on Guadalcanal, and in 1854 HMS *Herald* was sent to investigate his death and to punish those responsible. According to oral testimonies from Guadalcanal, Boyd was killed because he ventured too near the women's quarters.—MD

■ *John Higginson* John Higginson (13 November 1839–24 October 1904) was an enterprising businessman who played a significant role in NICKEL MINING in New Caledonia. Born in England of Irish parents who brought him to Australia in 1841, he went to Noumea at the age of 19 in search of adventure. After a series of odd jobs, he eventually came to represent the French shipping company Panclonnet and by 1870, controlled a regular shipping service to Australia. His next venture was in SUGAR, first with a mill in Bourail and then at Moindou. He acquired land and continued to diversify, becoming involved in copper mining in 1872 (with an Australian partner, William Morgan) soon after the discovery of gold at Fern Hill. In 1876, having became a French citizen, he established the Société le Nickel (SLN), astutely perceiving its potential for New Caledonia. In recognition of his good works, he was made a *chevalier* of the Legion of Honour in 1878, and gained substantial financial backing from the Rothschild Bank, which later took over SLN.

His second major area of interest—emerging from his involvement in recruiting labour for the nickel mines—was to prevent the annexation of the New Hebrides (Vanuatu) by Britain, to which end he set up the Caledonian Company of New Hebrides and successfully raised some half a million French francs to purchase large areas of land there. By 1886 the company could claim almost half the land area, but as soon as French settlers started arriving to take up their holdings, it became apparent that islanders had not in fact wanted or intended to sell their land. Even as Higginson lobbied for a French take-over of the island group, the scheme was falling apart. The Caledonian Company collapsed under the weight of disappointed investors, and those who had gained secure land-holdings (bought from planters) converted it to a French company. When Higginson died in Paris, the French Minister for the Colonies attended his funeral service, and then—as he had requested—his body was returned to Noumea for burial.—KRF

■ ***Robert Louis Stevenson*** 'Rain, calms, squalls, bang—there's the foretopmast gone; rain, calm, squalls, away with the staysail; more rain, more calm, more squalls: a prodigious heavy sea all the time, and the *Equator* staggering and hovering like a swallow…' So in a letter of December 1889 the novelist, short-story writer, essayist and, despite lifelong tuberculosis, constant traveller, Robert Louis Stevenson (13 November 1850—3 December 1984) wrote, *en route* to Samoa from Gilbert Islands aboard a Honolulu-based trading schooner after 18 months afloat and ashore in the ocean that gave him comparative good health.

The 'place of schooners and island', he called the Pacific. If he were alert to self-criticism the ocean taught him he had been wrong ever to suppose he had handled his own schooner *Hispaniola* without public shame. The classic *Treasure Island* and Jim Hawkin's unlikely tacking of the *Hispaniola* through tricky shallows single-handed lay behind him now, along with the engaging *Inland Voyage* and *Travels with a Donkey*, the major commercial success *Dr Jekyll and Mr Hyde*, the minor masterpiece *Kidnapped* with its thin sequel *Catriona*, and the commonly underrated *Black Arrow*. Ahead there lay, according to his plan, a big book about the South Seas as he believed he alone knew them—the rather dull *In the South Seas*; short stories, including the Samoa-set novella *The Beach at Falesa* which he claimed told more about the Pacific than a whole library, and does give a small trader's voice; and above all *A Footnote to History*, his atmospheric excursion into the contemporary history of Samoa with its indigenous politics complicated by the imperial ambitions of Germany and counterbalancing presence of Britain and America.

There he settled in splendour to live, as he said, and to die, as a 'servant of the High Commissioner' who found him one more European meddler in an already complicated Samoan scene. Samoa with all the grotesque Great Power involvement brought out the submerged Stevenson, eager to be active in the world—not merely through his book and in letters to the press but by actual though covert excursions into politics on behalf of Mata'afa Iosefo. Mata'afa was the better candidate for the kingship, but with the Powers committed at Germany's insistence to his rival Malietoa Laupepa, the only effect of private Europeans' encouraging Mata'afa was to lead him into captivity.

In short, Stevenson's activity—secretly and through an intermediary going so far as to encourage Samoans to stop paying taxes to Malietoa—was rather after the manner of the man who lit moss on a tree on the fringe of a bushfire in California to see whether the tree would catch light. Samoa burned too, under warships' gunfire, and Stevenson had to lay *Weir of Hermiston* aside to write sadly to Mata'afa about the deaths and Mata'afa's approaching exile under the Germans. 'That you have played a part in recent Samoan events is not I think questioned', High Commissioner Sir John THURSTON told Stevenson privately; 'whether a wise one or not is to say the least not free from doubt…' Neither of them succeeded in getting Mata'afa out of German hands and sent in more comfort to Fiji, but Stevenson's tomb above Apia is well kept, and Samoans tend to remember him now as one *pa'langi* who was very much on their side.—DAS

Further reading

Furnas, J C, 1951. *Voyage to Windward: the life of Robert Louis Stevenson*, William Sloane.

Mackenzie, K S, 1979. 'The last opportunity: Robert Louis Stevenson and Samoa', in D Scarr (ed.), *More Pacific Islands Portraits*, Australian National University Press.

Stevenson, R L, 1892. *A Footnote to History: eight years of trouble in Samoa*, Cassell.

——, 1894. 'My First Book', *Idler* (August).

——, 1911. *The Letters of Robert Louis Stevenson*, S Colvin (ed.), 4 vols, Methuen.

Scarr, D, 1973. *I, the Very Bayonet*, Australian National University Press.

SIX LAND TENURE AND ALIENATION

Customary land tenure

The land tenure systems of the Pacific islands before the colonial and commercial impacts of the 19th and 20th centuries were varied, and sometimes complex. In most island countries they are still important as, with the exception of New Caledonia and Tonga, most of the land remains under some form of customary tenure. In most countries less than 20 per cent of the land has been alienated. The present land tenure systems operating on non-alienated land are frequently referred to as 'traditional' or 'customary'. These terms are used below although most systems have been modified to meet the requirements of new forms of economy, technology and social or political organization. A new system of LAND TENURE IN TONGA was introduced in the late 1800s, placing all land under the control of the Crown. Estates were then allocated to nobles who were required to make lifetime and inheritable allotments available to all adult males. Most land thus came to be held under permanent usufruct by individual allotment holders. This system is now often considered 'traditional' within Tonga. The process of LAND ALIENATION IN NEW CALEDONIA means that land remaining in indigenous hands under customary tenure is restricted to that which was set aside as 'reserves' in the 19th century.

Customary tenure in the region is important not only because it is still widespread, but also because the tenure system has close links with social and political structures. Group or individual right of access to land through customary processes is often one of the main components of ethnic and national identity. It was and is an important component of island cosmologies, and land has spiritual as well as economic value. Thus land and its control is imbued with considerable political and social force.

Traditional land tenure systems evolved in association with subsistence economies within which households or small kin groups produced most of their own food and other material requirements from the areas of land and water to which they had access. Some long-term crops were grown, such as coconuts in coastal areas, but most agriculture was based on shifting cultivation. Short periods of cultivation for root crops were separated by long periods of fallow. If not burned too frequently, land would revert to woody growth, and ultimately to forest unless re-cleared for more cultivation. In these conditions, land tenure systems had to meet several requirements. Each household or kin group required access to a variety of ecological sites from which all the needs of the group might be obtained. These included areas for hunting, collection of building materials and firewood, gardening, fresh water sources, housing and, in coastal areas, the reef and sea for gathering marine foods and fishing. Planters needed security of use over their garden plots until all their crops had been harvested. This was normally a period of three or four years but could be much longer for tree crops. After a period of cultivating specific plots, farmers needed access to areas for new gardens as the old ones were left to fallow. The systems needed to be flexible to allow for the inevitable changes in the relative size of groups, and for land to be transferred from the control of one group to another as needs changed.

One result of these subsistence strategies was that different groups often held a variety of rights over the same area. These might include rights to hunt and collect, to transit an area, to take water or fish from a stream, to gather shellfish from a reef, or to clear and plant forest or fallow land. In the last case, it was common for the previous planter of a plot to have a degree of priority over its re-use after fallow. If land were left unused for a lengthy period, such rights of priority would weaken. In some cases, one group might control an area of land although the crops growing on it were the property of another group or household. Within the broad area over which a group claimed control, there was variation in the intensity and degree to which small subgroups might claim rights. The widest area, much of which might be forested, would be acknowledged as being controlled, or even 'owned' by the group. The borders were usually defined only vaguely, although boundaries would be more precise near the settlement itself, or where the land of neighbouring groups abutted closely. All members of the group might exercise rights to hunt and collect over this broad area. Where land had been cleared for cultivation, usufruct, if not ownership, would be acknowledged to lie with an individual planter or family as long as the plot was cultivated or the intent to re-use it was clear. House sites might be recognized as virtually the personal property of a family or household. Land in which a great deal of labour had been invested to create permanent assets might also be regarded as akin to permanent property. This could be the case with irrigated taro terraces, pits dug for root crop cultivation on atolls, or raised garden beds created in swampland. In some societies, particularly those with chiefly structures, pieces of land could be gifted to individuals (and their descendants) who had performed notable service or distinguished themselves in other ways in the eyes of recognized land controllers. Land, or at least the usufruct of land, could normally be given to refugees or people who married into the group. Thus most societies had acknowledged processes for transferring land from one user to another.

In the larger islands of Melanesia many inland communities did not have access to the coast, and ridges, rivers or bands of marchland might delimit the territories of neighbouring groups. On the smaller islands of Polynesia and Micronesia, territories of lineages or settlement groups were frequently laid out in a manner which allowed each to have access to the variety of land and water resources available. Thus, on the atolls of Tokelau and Kiribati, holdings tend to run right across the island from ocean shore to lagoon. In the Marshall Islands and Carolines a kin group's holdings would normally be scattered over several reef islets (motu) and would thus provide access to different productive areas. On high islands, with generally more varied and richer environments, territories commonly extend from lagoon and shoreline to the central peak or ridges. On roughly circular islands lineage territories often have a triangular or pie-slice shape. Within such a territory each household or family would control the usufruct over a scatter of garden plots which would rotate over time through areas of bush fallow.

Some colonial governments, as in Fiji and Cook Islands, sought to codify customary tenure, to survey the holdings claimed by indigenous groups, and to record the members of the claimant groups. This was done for a variety of motives. In some cases these included a desire to ensure the indigenous peoples were not deprived of their land (as had happened in Hawai'i and Australia, for example). Customary land was sometimes declared to be inalienable. Another aim was to delimit areas which were not claimed or needed by the indigenous people and which, as waste and vacant land, might become state land or be allocated as freehold or leasehold to new settlers. Whatever the motives, codification and survey removed the pragmatic flexibility of the older systems. It became more difficult to adjust holdings as the relative size of groups changed. In former times permanent emigrants from a community would lose their rights to land and in practice cease to be regarded as members. By recording all descendants regardless of residence, the group of potential claimants might now expand exponentially even if not all were present and contributing members of the community. One result can be difficulty in getting agreement on allocation of land and its use by particular members of the group. Tensions between resident and non-resident members of landowning groups have been reported in several Pacific island countries. Other changes in customary tenure have occurred where codification has not been imposed. This is not a new phenomenon as pragmatism was a major feature of the day-to-day practice of customary tenure.

In recent decades, however, a number of new trends have emerged. Most are linked to the spread of the commercial sector of the economy and related changes in agricultural systems and social organization. In commercial farming, planted land usually remains in cultivation for much longer periods than under subsistence and shifting cultivation. Commercial tree crops, or pasture, may keep plots under the control of the same individual or family for several decades. There is a growing tendency for farmers of such land to regard it as their own, rather than accepting that their rights are restricted to temporary usufruct. By clearing and maintaining communal land, people can in fact establish virtually permanent usufruct, which they may wish to will to their children. Thus communal land is often being privatized in some respects, and not recycled into the general community reserve through the fallowing process. Such holdings are often much larger than would have been the case under a subsistence economy, and with some members of a group having large holdings, others may no longer be able to obtain sufficient land even for subsistence use. Because particular people may hold the usufruct of areas for much longer, chiefs and BIG-MEN, who would traditionally have had some control over land allocation or re-allocation, may now rarely perform this function which was one of their key community roles. The change to wage labour, and away from mobilizing help on farms on a basis of reciprocity and kinship ties, may also weaken a group's social relations and reduce the influence of traditional leaders. Thus, in practice, land may play a reduced role in binding society together.

Much scholarly literature on development and economic planning in the Pacific islands views customary land tenure as a constraint on development. This criticism stems largely from a belief that such tenure cannot provide security of tenure to users. In fact customary usufruct can be very secure. However, most banks and credit providers prefer to have land as the main security against loans. Because customary land is generally not alienable, it is often thought to be difficult to provide credit to indigenous farmers using such land. Some lending agencies have found ways to overcome this problem without compromising the inalienability of customary land and such strategies could be adopted more widely. When the demand is for the use of customary land by non-indigenous, or non-land owning interests, most countries have systems under which leasing of customary land may be allowed. (See FIJI NATIVE LAND TRUST BOARD.) At present, however, not all such arrangements are effective.

Despite the changes that have occurred in the modern practice of customary tenure, the political rhetoric in most Pacific island countries aims to reinforce the supposedly unchanged traditional structures in which leadership has close links to ideologies in which land tenure is a key component. In some countries, notably Vanuatu, customary land tenure has been given a key place in the independence constitutions, explicitly enlisting land and land tenure as forces in the creation of modern national identities. This development, along with the changing nature of island societies and economies, means that governments will eventually have to face the reality that many current land tenure practices diverge from older traditions. The new practices are often justified on the basis of supposed conformity with tradition or custom. However, when customary land tenure becomes embedded in the written law it becomes necessary to define it more precisely, and this very act of definition may nullify many of the pragmatic strengths of the older systems.—RGW

Further reading

Crocombe, R G (ed.), 1987. *Land Tenure in the Pacific*, 3rd ed., University of the South Pacific.

Ward, R G and Kingdon, E (eds), 1995. *Land, Custom and Practice in the South Pacific*, Cambridge University Press.

German colonial land policies

German colonial law from the 1880s respected the private property rights of indigenous people. From 1903, all land in Germany's Pacific colonies was governed by an imperial ordinance, which was less concerned with individual rights than with the public interest. Hence, colonial authorities could acquire land or land rights from natives subject to special conditions, or prohibit it altogether.

In the 'Old Protectorate' of German New Guinea, tens of thousands of hectares had already been claimed by non-natives by 1885 when a charter granted the Neu Guinea Kompagnie (NGK) monopoly rights to acquire native and ownerless land. It was assumed that most land in Melanesia was legally ownerless, and, in order to protect the NGK monopoly, acquisition of native or ownerless land by other non-natives was prohibited, although existing *bona fide* land claims were to be protected. The exercise of the monopoly was regulated in an 1887 ordinance which provided that land so acquired was to be registered not as private acquisition, but by means of a public certificate issued by its administrator. When the NGK surrendered its charter in 1899, its land acquisition monopoly was transferred to the *Fiskus* of the colony, the colonial state in its property-owning capacity. The company was compensated with 4 million marks for its past efforts, and was permitted to acquire an additional 50 000 hectares of land because it had not used its monopoly.

The new imperial government sought to negotiate with non-native claimants, including the NGK, a voluntary reduction of their claims in order to satisfy indigenous land needs. When the demand for plantation land increased, the 'general conditions' for land transfer became the most important instrument of land administration. Key provisions related to setting aside native reserves large enough to satisfy indigenous subsistence needs, and imposing comparatively onerous improvement conditions on non-natives acquiring land. It was the aim of the government not to profit from its monopoly but to promote overall economic development.

The colonial land law of Marshall Islands was modelled on that of the Old Protectorate, but the alienation of land was handled differently—reflecting the differences between a potential plantation colony and a trading colony and, in particular, the different roles played by the NGK in New Guinea and the JALUIT GESELLSCHAFT in Marshall Islands. The latter had been unwilling to govern the colony under an imperial charter although it was prepared to cover financial shortfalls agreed between the Jaluit Gesellschaft and the German government. For this 'guarantee' the Jaluit Gesellschaft was granted the exclusive right to acquire ownerless land, assumed to exist in large quantity. By contrast the acquisition of native land was totally prohibited by an ordinance of the imperial commissioner in 1887. The general prohibition remained in place until 1905 when it was replaced with a general land acquisition monopoly of the *Fiskus* in line with the position in the Old Protectorate.

In the Island Territory of the Carolines, bought from Spain in 1899, the governor of German New Guinea had a free hand to create a provisional system of colonial law, but the manner in which he exercised his powers in relation to land shocked the authorities in Berlin. Using the system already operating in the Old Protectorate (allowing the government to acquire native and ownerless land), he went further by authorizing heads of local administrations to sell up to 800 hectares of land so acquired to individuals or companies and by reserving for himself the right to approve the transfer of even larger areas. The colonial department was upset that his action interfered with its negotiations with the Jaluit Gesellschaft, which included a possible land acquisition monopoly as in Marshall Islands. It therefore promptly repealed the governor's ordinance and issued a total prohibition. A year later the prohibition was replaced by a general land acquisition monopoly of the *Fiskus* in line with the Old Protectorate.

In Western Samoa, the 1889 *Samoa Act* assumed that no land was ownerless. After it became a separate German colony in 1899, a governor's ordinance of 1900 decreed that some key provisions in the Samoa Act and much of the existing local legislation were to remain in force. This effectively prohibited any alienation of land by Samoans to foreigners outside the municipal district, although the lease of agricultural land for up to 40 years was permitted, subject to the written approval of the authorities. This prohibition was not affected by the 1902 imperial land ordinance and remained essentially in force until the end of German colonial rule.

There was a good deal of additional, protective paternalism. The governor could order that any payments due to Samoans for land sales or leases—including regular payments of rent—had to be made to the Land and Titles Commission, in which case its chairman was also entitled to pursue these claims *ex officio* against non-native debtors. The Land and Titles Commission was a key institution with no counterpart in other German colonies. In 1900 the governor had introduced a system of Samoan self-administration, but had also placed Samoans under the jurisdiction of German colonial courts. Between 1903 and 1911, a temporary special commission operated, consisting of the district judge, two assessors and a number of Samoan advisers, to deal with 'Samoan law and Samoan customs and habits'. In 1911 it was reconstituted as a 'permanent' commission whose Samoan assessors, appointed by the governor, now became officials of the 'Samoan self-administration'. Its jurisdiction extended to all cases within the Samoan law of real property, the family and inheritance relating to land, titles and similar matters. Within two years, however, an ordinance transferred its powers to the administrative districts of APIA and Savai'i, although the governor could still deal with all relevant matters himself, as well as alter decisions, and delegate to a commission.

The political climate was changing in the German colonies. As part of a fundamental reform of customary socio-political organization on Ponape (now Pohnpei) between 1908 and 1913, changes to traditional land tenure were enacted. These reforms not only introduced individual ownership and decreed that the land in question would pass on, undivided, to the closest patrilineal male relative of the owner, but it also gave all male relatives of the owner who had no land, and all female relatives who had no husband, the right to use the land. Further, they stipulated first that the owner needed the approval of both his *nahnmwarki* (high chief) and the district commissioner if he wanted to transfer the land or part of it, and second, that all land not held by individual title belonged to the tribe and could only be allocated to an individual jointly by its *nahnmwarki* and the district commissioner. The *nahnmwarki* could punish a non-compliant landowner (who already had to work for him without pay one day twice a year) in the first instance with five days of unpaid labour, in the second instance with 10 days and in the third instance by application to the district commissioner to have him banished—thereby also forfeiting title to his land.

This strict regime was to serve as a model for Marshall Islands and eventually for the rest of the island territory. Within an overall process of creating a uniform system of law and government, the plans for Marshall Islands were revolutionary. Indigenous people were to be encouraged to develop their agricultural potential in the south of the group, while the northern islands were to be developed by non-native enterprises, predominantly the Jaluit Gesellschaft. However, the land was only to be leased to these enterprises so that the developed land would later become available for allocation to Marshall

Islanders if the population increased and the southern areas were fully developed.

At the beginning of 1913 a total of only about 4300 hectares of land had been alienated for agricultural purposes (with just over 3000 hectares cultivated) in the entire island territory. This was minor compared with about 10 000 hectares in German Samoa and about 32 000 hectares in the Old Protectorate, but the speed of plantation development was picking up in the island territory, since one-third of the planting had occurred in 1912 and 1913. In the Old Protectorate almost 5000 hectares were taken into cultivation during the same period. Still the Old Protectorate had only exported the same amount of copra in 1912 as German Samoa and less than twice as much as the island territory. This discrepancy demonstrates the continuing commercial importance of coconuts grown on 'native' land throughout the German Pacific. But whereas no substantial increase in 'trade copra' was expected, a dramatic increase in the production of 'plantation copra' was certain in the Old Protectorate, where well over 20 000 hectares had already been planted with young trees by the end of 1913. A doubling of agricultural production in New Guinea was therefore likely during the next decade, while production would probably remain more or less the same in German Samoa, in spite of the plentiful availability of agriculturally useable native land. This economically depressing state of affairs was in large measure owing to the 1889 prohibition of alienation of Samoan land. Whether it was on balance a positive result is another question. German administration in the region ended in 1914, at the start of World War I.—PS1

Land alienation in New Caledonia

The earliest alienations of land rights to non-Melanesians were of use rights for Protestant missionaries on LOYALTY ISLANDS and Catholic missionaries on the northeast of Grande Terre (main island). SANDALWOOD TRADERS, such as James Paddon at Dumbea, claimed to have purchased the freehold of much larger areas. The Melanesians would not have seen their early agreements with missionaries or traders in such terms but with the annexation of New Caledonia by France in 1853, European views of land tenure were imposed.

The French authorities did not regard Melanesian customary land tenure as conferring full proprietorship of any land at all. Even village sites and cultivations, although recognized administratively, could be acquired by official fiat, without compensation. Uncultivated land was at the disposal of the state. Lacking resources for colonization, however, the French authorities at first encouraged settlement only around the military barracks and headquarters at NOUMEA and outposts at Balade, Canala and Wagap. They supported the traders and the small clusters of settlers in the clashes with Melanesians which grew as the settlers tried to expand their holdings.

Serious settlement began from 1858 when large concessions of about 1000 to 4000 hectares were granted to investors in the southeast plains around Noumea, mainly for cattle ranching. From 1862 Governor Guillain switched to a policy of granting smallholdings of a few dozen hectares, many of them by lease with a right of purchase if development conditions were met. Convicts were sent to New Caledonia from 1864 and they too were granted 'concessions' to grow coffee. In fact many of the concessions continued to be acquired by absentees, who ran them with convict labour.

The rapid expansion of settlement and the destruction of Melanesian gardens by wandering cattle were the major causes of widespread Kanak resistance, followed by military repression and confiscation of fertile valley land. The KANAK REBELLION led by Atai in 1878 in the region of Boulapari and La Foa was the most serious.

Although some 240 000 hectares of freeholds and 53 000 hectares of leaseholds had been granted to settlers by 1893, close settlement did not thrive. The dry west coast was more suited to ranching than to coffee, while the indifferent farming practices of the convicts did not favour the crop. With the discovery of rich minerals in the 1870s and 1880s, investors and free settlers became much more interested in NICKEL MINING, often on large land concessions in the mountain chain, rather than in farming.

In 1895 a new governor, Feillet, made a fresh effort to promote small farming based on grants to free, rather than convict, labour. Again the Kanak clans paid the price, the land largely being taken from their reserves, which were reduced from 320 000 hectares to 120 000 hectares between 1895 and 1903. This *cantonnement*, or bundling of clans together on land not traditionally their own, increased the tensions and malaise in Kanak society. It led also to further revolt, notably in the northeast in 1917, and thence to more repression. By the 1920s the Melanesians were confined to their reserves and obliged to give labour service on public works or to settlers to pay a poll tax. Nevertheless the coffee crop failed to compete with rising costs (convict labour no longer being available) and competition from Brazil.

history

Land tenure and alienation

By 1939 New Caledonia had settled to a pattern of large-scale ranching, on land largely owned by the big business houses in Noumea, and mining. In 1939 the Melanesian population of about 28 000 was confined to about 128 000 hectares on Grande Terre (less than 9.6 per cent of the island), plus Loyalty Islands and the Isle of Pines, most of which had been reserved to Melanesians after the ending of convict settlement. Private settlers owned about 270 000 hectares of the Grande Terre while the remaining million hectares (approximately) was domaine land of the territory or the state, much of it granted in mining concessions.

At the end of World War II the Melanesian people were freed from their reserves and enfranchised. More land was urgently needed for their rapidly growing population and the reserves were extended to 167 000 hectares by the 1970s. But new immigration from France and other French overseas territories increased competition for land, and private holdings increased to 370 000 hectares by 1975. One third of this land was owned by only 18 people. This more intense competition for land coincided with a recession in mining. In 1976 clashes between Melanesians and settlers on precious valley land resumed, and the Kanak campaign to recover land became an integral part of the movement for a Kanak-led independence (NATIONALISM IN FRENCH TERRITORIES).

Green hills and river on east coast of New Caledonia

In an attempt to achieve a more equal distribution of land, the French administration, through the Rural Land Management and Development Agency known as ADRAF, began repurchasing private estates in the 1980s and returning the land to Kanaks, largely in private title to clans as legally incorporated groups. Another state agency provides development finance. The policy was in part overtaken by direct occupation of land by the Kanak independence front in the 'events' of the mid 1980s, and their own attempts to restore a form of customary title.

Since then, concerted efforts have been made to promote rural development in the Kanak-dominated northern and islands provinces. There is nevertheless a trend towards urban migration and economic growth focused on Noumea and the southern province. The NOUMEA ACCORD, signed in May 1998, provides for a review of the role and functions of ADRAF, in land reforms that will include the surveying and development of customary land.—AW1

Further reading

Néaoutyne, P, 1994. 'Land policy and economic development in Kanaky', in R Crocombe and M Meleisea (eds), *Land Issues in the Pacific*, Macmillan Brown Centre for Pacific Studies, University of Canterbury, and Institute of Pacific Studies, University of the South Pacific.

Saussol, A, 1988. 'The colonial chimera', in M Spencer, A Ward and J Connell (eds), *New Caledonia: essays in nationalism and dependency*, University of Queensland Press.

Land alienation in Hawai'i

Present land tenure and alienation in Hawai'i follows western concepts of property common to the rest of the United States. Most private land is owned in fee simple and registered either in the common law tradition or under a land court system virtually indistinguishable from the Torrens system prevalent in Australia. Except for a small percentage owned by Native Hawaiians under homestead laws or by the state Department of Hawaiian Home Lands as trustee for Native Hawaiians, and a larger percentage owned by the Kamehameha Schools/Bishop Estate (KS/BE) in trust for the education of Native Hawaiians, private land is owned and transferred in the English common law system. Much of the land owned by KS/BE is leased to residential and commercial lessees to provide income to the trust. Large landowners own much of the private land. State or federal government agencies own well over half the state's land area, particularly the mountain regions which are extensive on all four major islands.

Although occasionally described as communal, early land tenure in Hawai'i was essentially feudal until the late 1700s. A reigning king parcelled out large landholdings (*ahupua'a*, triangular pie-shaped blocks extending from the mountains to the sea) to faithful nobles (ALI'I) in exchange for various non-military services and produce from the land and sea. Commoners were free to move about from one *ahu-*

pua'a to another, but had no legal rights in land. Fee simple was unknown in Hawai'i until the 1800s.

After western contact in the late 1800s, the king was under increasing pressure to provide security of tenure to an emerging foreign landholding and merchant class. Such pressure culminated in the GREAT MAHELE or land division of 1848, by which King KAMEHAMEHA III divided the lands of Hawai'i roughly in half between the king and about 240–250 chiefs. The king's land was separated again almost immediately into crown lands (his), and government land. Most of the land was subject to rights of commoner tenants who actually resided on the land. However, in order to perfect title to their lands, the chiefs (*konohiki*) and tenants were required to record their interests. Many lost title in this process, and large landholdings ended up in the hands of those familiar with western methods of title registration and perfection. Among the largest such landholdings today are those of the Estate of James Campbell, consisting of thousands of acres formerly planted for sugar but now the site of a 'second city' northwest of PEARL HARBOR, and the scattered but more substantial holdings of the Bishop Estate, established by the will of the last descendant of Kamehameha for the education of Native Hawaiians. Much of this land—up to 10 per cent of the private land on O'ahu—is leased to residential and commercial lessees. Much of the government land (2 million acres) was ceded to the United States upon annexation, and was returned to the state government (except for several military bases) in the 1950s. About both the return of the lands and the income from it, there is much debate, with Native Hawaiians claiming that the land should have been returned to them and not to the government.

The picture of land tenure is incomplete without brief reference to two phenomena, both without precedent in the rest of the United States. First, Hawai'i is the most regulated of states with respect to the use of land. Not only do the four counties of Hawai'i (the only units of local government—there are no cities, villages or towns) exercise local zoning, subdivision and other land development controls, but also the state of Hawai'i regulates land through a state Land Use Commission. Established by the same 1961 statute which divided all the land in the state into agriculture (currently 48 per cent), conservation (48 per cent), urban (a little over 3 per cent) and later rural districts, the commission has the statutory authority to shift the boundaries of the districts upon petition by government or private landowner. Meanwhile the state controls absolutely the use of land in the conservation district, shares with counties such control in the agricultural districts, and defers to the counties in the urban districts only.

Second, a 1978 state constitutional provision guarantees certain customary and traditional rights to Native Hawaiians, subject to regulation by the legislature. The state's supreme court has interpreted this provision and Hawaiian history to mean that a Native Hawaiian may enter any land, public or private, developed or undeveloped, for the purpose of exercising such customary and traditional rights as fishing, gathering, hunting and religious worship. Local title companies have since inserted clauses in all title insurance policies noting that alienation of land is or may be subject to undefined Hawaiian access and use rights. There is, moreover, a substantial HAWAIIAN SOVEREIGNTY movement, various forms of which range from seeking the return of the kingdom and separation from the United States to the establishment of a state within a state or, at the very least, return of certain government lands to Hawaiians. Land rights and security of tenure in the western sense are therefore, in the words of the Hawaiian Supreme Court, 'not universally applicable' in Hawai'i.—DLC

Further reading

Callies, D L, 1994. *Preserving Paradise: why regulation won't work*, University of Hawai'i Press.

Chinen, J J, 1958. *The Great Mahele: Hawaii's land division of 1848*, University of Hawai'i Press.

Kame'eleihiwa, L, 1992. *Native Land and Foreign Desires*, Bishop Museum Press.

■ *Great Mahele* The *Mahele* was the division of all land in the Hawaiian kingdom in 1848, with full records being made in the *Mahele* Book. The first major step was to divide the lands into two categories, those belonging to the king and those belonging to 240–250 chiefs or *konohiki*. Then, in order to satisfy the agreed government claim for about one-third of each, King KAMEHAMEHA III divided his lands again into two, retaining one part for himself ('crown lands') and giving up the slightly larger part as a public domain ('government lands') to be controlled by a legislature. The next step in the process of land reform was to deal with the rights of the tenants in the lands held by each group. The *konohiki* could surrender part of their lands to the government, in exchange for clear title to the rest, and many did. The decision was then made, in 1849, to grant fee simple titles, known as *kuleana* grants, to all commoners, varying in size from 1–40 acres (0.4–16 hectares).—KRF

Land tenure and alienation

Land tenure in Tonga

In 1862 George TUPOU I abolished the traditional servitude exacted from commoners by chiefs. Instead, he granted a series of property rights designed to break the power of the chiefs opposed to him, and to bind the people directly to the crown. All land became the property of the crown; no land could be alienated to foreigners and there was no freehold. The former aristocratic chiefly system was dismantled although certain remnants remain socially salient. From among the 200 or so chiefs, only 20 titles were ennobled, a number that later rose to 33, with the rest assuming the legal status of commoners. To each noble title was attached in perpetuity an estate (*tofi'a*) of tracts of land throughout the kingdom. The noble estates varied greatly in size. The rest of the land was divided into royal and government estates. Adult commoner male taxpayers over the age of 15 years became eligible to apply for 3.3 hectares (8.25 acres) of garden land (*'api tukuhau*) and a smaller house site (*'api kolo*) from an estate. Once registered with the government, the land could be inherited in the senior male line in successive generations so long as rent was paid to the estate owner and tax to the government. Women were rather poorly served in the matter of land rights since it was expected that men, as husbands, fathers or brothers, would continue to provide for them. Widows were given a life interest in their deceased husband's land and unmarried daughters the right to be supported from their father's. Noble titles and the crown were also to devolve according to the principle of male primogeniture.

Although the provisions of the 1882 *Land Law* have never been implemented perfectly, and the rapid rise of population has made it impossible to provide an allotment to every adult male, nevertheless, the institution of individualized land holding so early in Tonga's modern history exerted a profound influence on other social institutions and promoted a sense of autonomy among commoner families. Recent legislation has made it easier for both men and women to lease land from the hereditary *'api*.—KEJ

Fiji Native Land Trust Board

Within Fiji's traditional chiefly system (FIJIAN CHIEFLY STATUS), land (*vanua*) remains a strong binding force, possibly the strongest unifying factor amongst Fijians. Before cession in 1874, all lands came under the chiefly leadership as part of the complex and interdependent set of traditional rights and responsibilities. The English term 'ownership' was applied to this system of CUSTOMARY LAND TENURE, and the alienation of native land was prohibited from 1875. Today, most land in Fiji (83 per cent) is communally owned by indigenous Fijians in inalienable right.

The Native Land Trust Board (NLTB) is charged with the administration of this land. It was established in 1940 through the Native Land Trust Ordinance No. 12, to preserve indigenous ownership of land on one hand and to allow the best use of land in the national interest on the other. For a long period the NLTB was led by one of the best educated indigenous Fijians of his time, Dr Rusiate Nayacakalou, who had trained as a social anthropologist under Raymond Firth at the London School of Economics. He had also assisted O H K Spate in his report on the social and economic problems and prospects of the Fijian people, reinforcing a deep empathy for his people and the imperatives of modern development.

In recent times the NLTB has managed native Fijian land within the framework of the *Agricultural Landlord and Tenant Act*. Of the total rent, the NLTB retains 25 per cent for its operational expenses; the three leading chiefs of the owning group share 22.5 per cent; and the commoner owners share 52.5 per cent. In 1997 the NLTB received F$4.3 million native land rent poundage, with a further F$331 273 in timber and F$79 403 in river gravel royalties. It also received F$329 695 in premium and miscellaneous charges. Still, despite its substantial income base, the NLTB needed a government salary subvention of F$1.3 million.

The NLTB has a well-developed Geographical Information System which enables it not only to manage rents more efficiently, but also potentially to plan much better. It is decentralizing its estate management, and generally preparing to become leaner and more efficient. The current operations of the NLTB are governed by the *Agricultural Landlord and Tenant Act* (ALTA) under which tenants have been given short-term 30-year leases, which began expiring in 1997. A parliamentary joint committee was set up in February 1998 to determine the most appropriate arrangements under which native land would be leased. ALTA was recommended by the Burns Commission in 1959 and set up in 1966 as the Agricultural Landlord and Tenant Ordinance. Enacted in 1976, ALTA has provided a framework to govern relations between landlords and tenants. It has attempted to provide greater security to tenants while safeguarding the ownership of the landlords and securing returns acceptable to all parties. It has allowed the projection of the national interest in Fiji's land policies.

The NLTB has undertaken surveys to determine the land-lease situation of tenants. The final report of the task force was completed in April 1997, and its recommendations have been accepted by the Great Council of Chiefs, though they remain to be approved by parliament. Although there is some discussion of changing the administration of native Fijian land to reduce or eliminate the role of the NLTB, it is likely that it will manage native land for some time to come.—RC

SEVEN COLONIAL RULE

Colonial rule: administrative styles and practices

In general, colonial rule was underpinned by three crucial objectives. The first was economic expansion—to exploit resources, create markets and make a profit for the home country and its settlers. The second was to affirm national power by carving out spheres of influence and defence against competing nations. The third was to modernize, convert and educate indigenous populations in the image of the west.

Despite these uniform characteristics, Pacific empires displayed wide variations in their operations and had highly variable impacts on different communities. At one extreme—the harshest—were the settler colonial states: Australia, New Zealand, France in New Caledonia, and America in Hawai'i. Settler states extinguished, or attempted to extinguish, native rights over land, marginalizing islanders as a labour force, sometimes confining them to segregated areas (Australia and New Caledonia) and, in the case of Australia, even trying to breed out racial characteristics. Extreme *laissez faire* imperialism in Hawai'i removed community restrictions on the transfer of land and resources and replaced communal patterns of growth and control with a philosophy of individual opportunity. At the other extreme was the kingdom of Tonga, where there was no serious European settlement, nor even formal annexation, though Britain practised an informal over-sight through a treaty of protection. Tongan chiefs continued to control land, labour and behaviour; and capitalist development was minimal.

Between these extremes, ways of ruling Pacific peoples differed from nation state to nation state. Even within one empire, colonial rule varied enormously. A good example was Germany's fragments of empire. Germany came late to colonies: the first annexations took place in 1884 and they were all lost immediately on the outbreak of war in 1914. GERMAN COLONIAL ADMINISTRATION had to start from scratch, creating a colonial office and putting administrators into the field; there was no ministry dedicated to its colonies till 1907.

German Samoa was a compact, homogeneous hierarchical society of 40 000 people, with a few hundred German settlers, as well as small numbers of British, New Zealanders and Australians. The 10 years of Governor Wilhelm SOLF's rule can be read as a continuing contest between his attempts to insert German legal and bureaucratic structures into Samoan society, altering them towards more rationalist, organized ends, and the Samoans' proto-nationalist struggle to retain their decentralized political culture. Solf had no military force: he relied on 40 Samoan police and the occasional warship which could take six weeks to come from its Asian base. He also had to contend with militant settlers unwilling to cooperate with him and demanding tougher policies which would put Samoan land and labour more firmly in their hands.

German New Guinea with over 1 000 000 people and hundreds of pockets of autonomous, linguistically fragmented and mutually hostile local populations was a more complex proposition for Governor Albert Hahl. The colony had begun life under chartered company rule but its conspicuous failure to develop a secure administration and commercial economy led the Reich to assume full control in 1899. Hahl acted like a particularly aggressive warlord to conquer New Guinean communities in the islands and on the mainland. Stations were extended by using mobile police columns to pacify local districts, then installing local agents to 'manage' the area till the Germans next returned. The Germans, and the Australians who took New Guinea from them in 1914, simply could not engage the total populations of the societies they 'governed'. Direct rule operated where the regime could reach, alternating with watchful neglect of remaining areas. Only where there was a thriving PLANTATION economy, on the Gazelle Peninsula in New Britain and on New Ireland, were more stable, indirect forms of colonial rule in place by 1914.

In Micronesia, German rule was relatively relaxed and benign, though the people of the Marshall Islands vigorously protested their economic exploitation, and on Pohnpei the Germans suffered their most serious revolt in the Pacific over attempts to change the land tenure system. The German administrator and his colleagues were killed and only a massive amphibious operation by German marines defeated and executed the rebels. Thus the German colonial state was far from monolithic or well-coordinated. It relied on the active collaboration of officials, business interests, missionaries and local agents negotiating their own agendas, as well as relatively passive acceptance from the colonized populations.

Colonialism throughout the Pacific rested on this formula, with variations. Like all the European powers France came to the Pacific looking for commercial and strategic opportunities, but national glory kept her actively engaged in both Melanesia and Polynesia after other empires had ended. French images of Melanesian peoples as inferior to Polynesians determined harsher methods of rule and exploitation. New Caledonia, annexed in 1853, felt the full force of French imperialism, becoming a penal colony and colony of settlement not only for the French but also for immigrants from Asia and other parts of the French Pacific. Two parallel societies emerged in New Caledonia, the European and a

Village official (*tultul*) on left, on a visit to Salamaua in 1937, wearing the hat of administrative authority, photographed by Sarah Chinnery

Melanesian or Kanak community (from a Polynesian word meaning man). Melanesians had an inferior legal status via the *Régime de l'indigenat*, a set of 'native regulations' which had their counterpart in other colonies such as Australian Papua. The French system removed Melanesians from the scope of civil law, tightly restricted their movements, subjected them to a poll tax and obliged them to provide free labour to the state. New Caledonia was deeply colonized under this regime. European migrants were granted the best land, colonial administrations continually re-defined what could remain in Melanesian possession so that by the end of the 19th century Kanaks on the dry, sub-tropical west coast plains had lost much of their land and been confined to reserves, often in mountainous areas of poor soil. These expropriations contributed to the KANAK REBELLION of 1878, a second large revolt by Kanaks in 1917, and growing political mobilization and violence in the 20th century.

The intensity of colonial pressures varied within the French empire, even in Melanesia: the LOYALTY ISLANDS attracted fewer settlers and local social structures were able to absorb pressures more effectively. In the New Hebrides, Efate and Espiritu Santo were closely settled, the rest of the group less affected. Resistance from British, Australian and New Zealand settlers prevented Britain from agreeing to France's annexation, and the Pacific's only joint colonial administration—the CONDOMINIUM—was set up in 1906 with parallel regimes of administration, law and education. Eastern Polynesia (Society and Marquesas Islands, and Tuamotu archipelago), French since the mid 19th century, stayed firmly in the hands of missionaries and *gendarmes*, its politics becoming more dominated by mixed European-Polynesian *demi* groups.

The British structure of colonial rule in the Pacific differed from both the German and the French. The élite of colonial ranks displayed much more class homogeneity and social cohesion. Less specifically trained for colonial service than German administrators, they were often men who could draw on Britain's experience in ruling foreign peoples over centuries. A sense of obligation towards 'backward' people was more widely shared among the British population at home than was the case on the continent. The anti-slavery movement and the evangelical revival both influenced colonial style. Nonetheless, or perhaps because of them, the notions of parenthood featured in the language and practices of imperial rule. The largest settler colonies in the Pacific, Australia and New Zealand, developed along lines of more rigid conquest, gradual occupation of land leading to violence and long-lasting frontier wars.

But in Fiji, Sir Arthur GORDON, of wide experience in colonial administration, set a new tone for colonial policy by protecting the land and labour of the indigenous community and using its capacities for self-government. The compensation for the growing sugar economy was the importation of indentured Indian labour which introduced new layers of rule and resistance to the colonial history of Fiji. (See GIRMITIYAS.) Though Fiji became a template for systems of indirect rule, Gordon intended that the state, by constant engagement with the community through his own person, and monitoring all activities, should be seen to transcend ordinary social conflicts and partial interests. This was a crucial objective of colonial rulers: to overcome what they regarded as decentralized chaos and put in its place orderly, bureaucratized power structures that reflected western images of proper state formation.

A trinity of ruling instruments was vital to this process: the Christian missions and their workers, police forces drawn from indigenous populations but led by Europeans, and the institutions and processes of labour represented by the plantation system. Christian missionaries often prepared the way for annexation, and a partnership with the colonial state developed naturally in most Pacific colonies. In New Guinea the Germans built their roads following the bridle tracks laid by evangelists and left whole regions alone where the LUTHERANS had organized communities into Christian congregations. In Papua between the wars, missions provided the bulk of health and schooling facilities. The relationship between colonial governments and missionaries was always problematic, however. Islanders recognized them as different from other westerners. Often missionaries acted as the primary protectors of island communities, mediating conflicts over labour demands and acting as brokers of peace with hostile neighbours.

Colonial police forces were also a problem in some areas. Colonial states relied on them in Melanesia as the linchpin between governors and the governed. In French colonies the *gendarme* held communities together, combining law and order with a range of functions. In Papua and New Guinea, the *kiap* acted as patrol officer, census taker, magistrate, medical dispenser, labour recruiter—and symbolized the moral power wielded by government. At his right hand were indigenous police who were used to conquer new groups and ready them for the ordered demands of labour and taxation. In Samoa the police were a small, largely decorative outlet for the sons of chiefs, acting as messengers and security officers in the town. On Melanesian frontiers, they could develop their own agendas, traditional and modern: the pursuit of wealth, status and power. Police were indispensable if risky intermediaries in colonial transactions.

The plantation was the economic pivot of colonial empires, rising and falling with world prices for the Pacific's major commodities—sugar and copra. In Fiji, sugar and one large company, the COLONIAL SUGAR REFINERY (CSR), dominated the economy. COPRA AND COCONUT OIL plantations required little skilled labour, and planters dealt with their work forces less as managers than as jailers or parents of recalcitrant children. Corporal punishment, confinement and reduced rations were all means of controlling the work forces that drove the economic imperatives of empire. At moments of crisis like the RABAUL STRIKE of 1929, all the allies of the colonial state, including the missionaries, cooperated to intimidate and defeat the wage claim and industrial rights of the 2000 labourers.

Colonizers ultimately determined the organization of empire, not only through guns and troops and ships, but also through the powerful belief that they possessed the right to rule 'inferior' peoples. A racist syndrome of rule coloured Pacific empires; force, intimidation and legislated discrimination went hand in hand with social distance and paternalistic attitudes. No Pacific colony was, however, a simple police state. Bluff was a regular feature of European demands on islanders, and anxiety in the face of alien cultures dogged every colonizers' community. As well, adequate spaces survived in all colonies where islanders could work their resistance and manipulations of western power to share in the wealth and power that colonial transactions brought.—PJH

Further reading

Aldrich, R, 1990. *The French Presence in the South Pacific 1842–1940*, Macmillan.

Bulbeck, C, 1992. *Australian Women in Papua New Guinea. Colonial passages 1920-1960*, Cambridge University Press.

Hempenstall, P J, 1978. *Pacific Islanders under German Rule: a study in the meaning of colonial resistance*, Australian National University Press.

Lewis, D C, 1996. 'The plantation dream: developing British New Guinea and Papua, 1884–1942', *Journal of Pacific History*.

Macnaught, T, 1982. *The Fijian Colonial Experience: a study of the neotraditional order under British colonial rule prior to World War II*, Pacific Research Monograph 7, The Australian National University.

Spanish expansion, 1675–1899

In the early period of exploration and rivalry between SPAIN AND PORTUGAL IN THE PACIFIC (1519–1605), contacts with Pacific islanders were limited to trade, occasional landings and shipwrecks which introduced the survivors to some knowledge of Pacific cultures. From the mid 17th century until 1819, however, the Philippines became a major outpost of Spanish influence, with the dual roles of sending Asian goods to Spanish colonies in the Americas, and fostering the conversion of the population to Christianity. For more than two centuries, the *Manila Galleon* crossed the Pacific Ocean between Manila and the port of Acapulco in Nueva España (Mexico), on an annual basis. Contacts with Chamorros became regular as the ships anchored in GUAM on the way to Manila, and made occasional expeditions into Micronesia from the Philippines.

The first Order of Jesuits mission in the Pacific was established on Guam in 1668. Father Sanvitores played a key role in pushing Spain to claim the islands which became known as the Marianas, when he convinced Queen Mariana of Austria and won her sponsorship for the conversion of Chamorros. Sanvitores' failure and death led Spain to establish a permanent presence, embarking on a conquest in 1672 which was achieved by 1685. Continued resistance to the foreign rulers decided Spain to concentrate all Chamorros in Guam for strategic reasons, leaving the northern Marianas almost uninhabited until the mid 19th century, when Chamorros and

Spanish wall, Kolonia, Pohnpei, FSM

BEACHCOMBERS found their own way to the islands. A combination of sporadic fighting and introduced illnesses also diminished the population, leaving only a handful of pure-blooded Chamorros.

Remoteness from Spain and the slowness of communications left Guam in a state of quasi-independence, however. The so-called *Gobernador Político-Militar*, who combined all civil and military responsibilities, took his salary and his authority from Mexico. He issued edicts or *bandos* and acted as judge and chief of police. Under the governor, the highest authorities in the districts (each defined by having a church) were the *alcades*. Missionaries (the Jesuits were followed in 1769 by the Augustinian Recollects) held considerable power among Spaniards as well as Chamorros, and acted as intermediaries through their mastery of language as well as their length of residence. There was some trade with the Philippines, mainly in grass mats (*petates*) and ships' sails made in the Marianas.

Spanish colonization of the Caroline Islands was planned, with Francisco Lazcano following Sanvitores' example to the extent of naming the islands after King Carlos II in 1686. However, the attempt was unsuccessful. Missionaries were unable to convert significant numbers of islanders to Christianity, partly because the Manila authorities failed to set up any authority. Developments in Easter Island (Rapanui) were similar; an expedition from Peru claimed possession for the Crown in 1770, but insufficient attention was paid to subsequent colonization.

From 1820–98, after the Americas won their independence, the Spanish empire was widely dispersed, with colonies in Latin America (Cuba and the Dominican Republic), Africa (Morocco and Equatorial Guinea), Asia (Philippines) and Oceania (Micronesia). Mexican independence ended the voyages of the *Manila Galleon* and thus also the significance of Guam and Micronesia on a route through the Pacific. They remained linked to Manila, but offered Spain no more than prestige. In the 1850s and 1860s, when Spain felt strong enough to expand from the Philippines, expeditions set off for Indochina with France—the opposite direction from Micronesia. Only at the end of the century was Micronesia to acquire fresh strategic importance for the Spanish empire, once the Panama Canal opened up a route between Cuba and the Philippines.

The Berlin Conference of 1884, relating to sovereignty over territories not yet colonized, provoked Spain to confirm its right to the Micronesian islands with formal occupation at the same moment that Germany moved to add new territories to its empire. Two ships arrived at the island of Yap almost simultaneously to take formal possession for two different empires. The technicalities—the Spanish ship *San Quintin* arrived four days before the German *Yltis*, but the Spaniards had still not planted their flag when the Germans did—created lively discussion and even demonstrations in Europe, though not in Micronesia. The conflict was resolved through the mediation of the Pope, in an agreement which gave Spain formal sovereignty but the Germans (and later the British) won total economic control.

Madrid established two divisions in Micronesia, Yap for the western Carolines and Pohnpei for the eastern islands, both headed by naval officers and directly dependent on Manila. The Spanish imperial regime collected no taxes, but extracted its colonization expenses in the form of compulsory native labour. Herein lay the origins of difficulties in the

Catholic (Spanish mission) bell tower, Kolonia, Pohnpei, FSM

occupation of the Eastern Carolines, where there was an already established copra trade—mainly in the hands of the German company, JALUIT GESELLSCHAFT—and a strong Methodist church presence, the AMERICAN BOARD OF COMMISSIONERS FOR FOREIGN MISSIONS. Rebellions sprang up soon after the arrival of Spanish and Filipino troops; the governor, Posadillo, was killed and Spain was unable to complete its occupation of Pohnpei, much less to start establishing contact with other islands in the area, such as Kosrae. The Western Division in Yap was more peaceful, and regular contact was set up between Yap and Palau, albeit with fewer appointed personnel. Spanish officialdom, paying more heed to strategic defence than to economic development, banned immigration from Japan, although no action could be taken against the influx of Germans and other westerners.

After the Spanish–American War in 1898, the Treaty of Paris gave Washington control of Guam and the Philippines, while the remaining Micronesian islands were sold by Spain to Germany for 25 million *pesetas*. From 1899 Madrid ended its official involvement in the Pacific region. From this time, the only visible Spanish presence was the activities of the Jesuits in Micronesia after the German period, the Capuchins in Guam, and the Benedictines in Australia.

The Spanish period in the Pacific has left different legacies. In the Federated States of Micronesia and Palau, there remain only a few family names and the Catholicism of part of the population. In the Marianas, where the Spanish language was retained by some inhabitants until the Pacific War, Chamorros have embraced the Catholic religion as their own and it may be said that traditional Spanish customs such as the praying *novenas* are more vividly adhered to than in present-day Spain. (Arguably, this reflects the decisive role of the religious motivations of Spanish decision makers.) The larger role of Mexico in cultural links with Micronesia has not been considered.—FRG

French expansion, 1817–1939

The late 17th century voyages of FRENCH EXPLORATION, supported by the state, were conducted in a climate of strong interest in the Pacific, despite the hazards posed by the French Revolution and the problems it brought with it. The defeat at Waterloo (1815) continued to weigh heavily on the foreign policy of the Restoration (1814–30) and the July Monarchy (1830–48), closely watched by the dominant power of the day, Great Britain. Beset by internal problems, Charles X and Louis-Philippe dreaded 'colonial adventures' that might endanger diplomatic arrangements or financial stability. While not averse to policies that might bring prestige to brighten a tarnished escutcheon, they saw colonies as a luxury that had to enhance national pride at no risk and no cost.

Paradoxically, France's vague wish to expand was, from the 1820s, mostly focused on the Pacific, on the other side of the world. It chose those distant seas dotted with islands and atolls as the place to begin a slow recovery of its rank and position in the world. The paradox is only apparent, for more than any other part of the world, the Pacific admirably suited the cautious strategy of the Restoration and the July Monarchy. In this peripheral zone, far from the hot spots of rivalry where the English would not compromise, France could follow an imperialist policy without too much risk. The seas as well as the lands were the object of aspirations, since the goal was to restore the essential instrument of power, the navy. Under cover of scientific research, the Restoration in 1817 revived the the tradition of great discoveries—FREYCINET (1817–20), Duperrey (1822–25), Bougainville's son (1824–26)—but also gave the navy the opportunity to rebuild and expand. From

1826, with the expeditions of DUMONT D'URVILLE (1826–29 and 1836–39), Vaillant (1836) and Petit-Thouars (1836–39), political goals emerged, including the search for ports of call or territories to conquer. The navy, which played the part of an active lobby, justified its activities in the Pacific by the need to support French Catholic missions. These missions blossomed at the end of the 1820s under the impetus of Pope Leo XII, the Picpusians being responsible for the evangelization of Polynesia and the Marists that of Melanesia. Together they formed the frontier of French presence in Oceania, justifying the navy's voyages as an essential lifeline of supplies, and arousing the interest of the French government in lands hitherto largely unknown. The state eventually sought to establish itself in places where its missions were located—in the Marquesas, in Tahiti, in New Caledonia and Wallis and Futuna, but gave up its claims in Tonga, Samoa, Fiji and New Zealand.

A naval presence, a religious presence and the need to acquire ports of call were enough to justify a policy of annexation by France which, in the absence of sufficient numbers of nationals in support, could not create an informal empire in the English style. This explains the annexation of the Marquesas in 1842, the attempted annexation of New Caledonia in 1843—abandoned following the PRITCHARD affair, but confirmed in 1853 by Napoleon III—the protectorate over Tahiti in 1844, and extensive French influence in the Gambiers, the Tuamotus and Wallis and Futuna. But France also had another objective in the Pacific: the quest for a penal colony. Dissatisfied with the way its prisons and naval *bagnes* operated and mesmerized by the experiment of British transportation to Australia, it gave the navy the task of finding a land suitable for receiving its convicts. In 1863, New Caledonia was chosen as the place for French transportation in the Pacific.

The French presence in the Pacific was consolidated during the great partition of the world in the 1880s. The protectorate over Tahiti was then converted into a formal annexation, extended in 1881 to include the Gambiers, the Austral Islands and the Tuamotus, together forming the colony of French Polynesia. In 1886 a protectorate was proclaimed over Wallis and Futuna, formally annexed in 1913. Finally, as the result of the efforts of a francophile British speculator, John HIGGINSON, together with the development of a plantation economy, the New Hebrides began to appear to the settlers of New Caledonia as a natural extension of their colony. After acrimonious negotiations with the English, a unique form of joint colonial administration was born, the Anglo–French Condominium of the New Hebrides, established in 1906. Some 30 000 convicts, political prisoners from the Paris Communard uprising, and exiles were sent to New Caledonia between 1864 and 1897 (when French transportation ended). In an attempt to create a 'little France' in the south, a smaller number of free French migrants also settled in the colony to grow coffee while others went to the New Hebrides to develop coffee, cotton and copra. Parallel to this settler colonization, which was essentially rural, France exploited the mineral resources of New Caledonia, particularly with NICKEL MINING. French Polynesia followed a different path, attracting few immigrants apart from civil servants and missionaries. Colonial agriculture remained marginal, and between the two wars the only true wealth of Tahiti lay in the exploitation of PHOSPHATE in Makatea.

The active role played by France in the Pacific in the 18th century gave way to indifference throughout the first half of the 20th century. The initiative of the state, which in spite of difficulties spurred the settlement of New Caledonia and the New Hebrides, dried up in 1900, reviving feebly in the 1920s with the arrival of migrants, the so-called Nordistes, from the northern parts of France devastated by the Great War. For the French, Polynesia retained only its classical image of a tropical paradise, the refuge of painters and writers such as Paul GAUGUIN, Segalen and Loti. Not until after the Second World War and the changes it brought did France renew its interest in these distant islands. The Pacific seemed destined to be of only intermittent interest to France; it was a small distant patch that it was fond of but often forgot.—IM (tr. by DS1)

Kanak rebellion, 1878

When France annexed the main island (Grand Terre) of New Caledonia in 1853, it was mainly for use as a penal colony. Within 20 years, many of the released convicts had chosen to stay and wanted agricultural land, and growing numbers of French settlers were arriving. Contacts between settlers and the Melanesian population had been mainly hostile from the outset, with numerous localized bursts of violence followed by fierce reprisals. When colonization extended along the west coast, there was large-scale LAND ALIENATION IN NEW CALEDONIA, and forced labour was introduced to supply the plantations. Resistance against the invaders suddenly became a major insurrection in 1878. It was led by a significant chief named Atai, whose tribe owned lands in the La Foa valley on the central west coast of the island. His charismatic leadership became a focus of opposition to further loss of land to French settlement, and the associated issues of growing concern to Melanesians: widespread damage to village gardens by colonists' cattle, and the desecration of burial sites. When several chiefs of his region were imprisoned following the murder of a French settler family (a former convict with a Melanesian wife, who had become involved in a tribal dispute over a local woman), Atai directed an attack on the gendarmerie on the night of 24 June, which killed the police and freed the chiefs. The two major tribes of the area then attacked the village of La Foa and the nearby coastal military post.

The uprising spread further afield, involving a series of massacres of French colonists and convict workers. Atai united most of the central island tribes, encouraging them to destroy many more settlements and launch attacks on the military. The French troops despatched against them successfully recruited support from among traditional enemies of the rebel forces, and concentrated on destroying rebel villages. Finally it was some of the French-allied rival tribesmen from the Canala (north coast) region who betrayed and killed Atai and his son. Another stage in the rebellion then erupted further to the northwest, in Poya and Bourail, in September and October, but the French had largely regained control of the La Foa region by then, and all fighting ceased by April 1879. When the official state of siege was lifted from Bourail and Bouloupari in June 1879, the death toll stood at 200 French and probably 1000 Kanaks. In the repression which followed, there was widespread dispersal of the former rebels. Nearly 1000 were deported (to the Isle of Pines and Belep), and the administration took over large areas of land in the Bourail region without paying compensation. A new decree in July 1887 made Melanesians French subjects, placing them under the arbitrary authority of the colonial administration, and requiring them to seek permission to leave their reserve lands.—KRF

German colonial administration, 1884–1914

Germany's colonial empire in the Pacific consisted of four parts: the 'Old Protectorate' of German New Guinea, comprising the northeastern quarter of New Guinea and the Bismarck Archipelago, annexed in 1884, to which the northern section of Solomon Islands was added in 1886; Marshall Islands, also annexed in 1884, to which Nauru was added in 1888; the 'Island Territory' of the Carolines, including Palau, and the Marianas (initially excluding Guam, which was bought from Spain in 1899); and Western Samoa, acquired during the same year on the basis of a treaty between Germany, Britain and the United States, which also involved a cession of part of the northern Solomon Islands by Germany to Britain.

In 1906 the Marshall Islands were incorporated into the Island Territory which had been placed under the governor of the Old Protectorate from the beginning and was itself increasingly integrated into 'German New Guinea', whereas German Samoa remained a separate colony. However, after 1900, German colonial law was generally 'centralized' in the sense that the colony-specific legislation characteristic of the pre-1900 period was replaced in key areas with imperial enactments which applied to all German colonies.

These imperial ordinances reflected a dual system of law, one for 'natives' and another one for 'non-natives', typical of German colonial law from its inception in the 1880s. It was taken for granted that the private property rights of natives—in contrast to their public political rights—were to be legally respected. The substance of these rights, however, was not determined by customary law, but rather 'translated' into the rights provided for under the introduced colonial law. The customary law on which they were based was generally not legally recognized, although it was not abolished. There existed a legal twilight zone in which customary law was tolerated as long as the colonial authorities did not exercise their legislative or executive powers to modify or abolish it. Natives were denied the same legal freedom as non-natives but they were given special protection and privileges, if the authorities deemed it to be in their best interests.

Under the dual system of law, natives remained outside the jurisdiction of the 'regular' colonial courts. The administration of justice in relation to them was seen as an administrative rather than judicial task, and the executive had unlimited discretion as to how it chose to exercise its powers. A 1908 imperial ordinance confirmed and clarified the position, extending this administrative discretion to cases of so-called 'mixed jurisdiction', as well as to the customary native law.

In the Old Protectorate and in Marshall Islands, although special courts for natives were soon established with an exclusively criminal jurisdiction, the treatment of civil disputes involving natives remained a matter of administrative discretion until the end of German colonial rule. While the legal position was the same in German Samoa, the scenario looked quite different because in 1900 the governor had introduced a system of Samoan self-administration. However, the entire system remained subject to his discretion and he had bluntly stated that he alone was giving orders in

German Samoa and that his powers extended to 'you Samoans' as much as to foreigners. But the German authorities were prepared to operate cautiously. Thus the governor's fundamental ordinance placed Samoans 'for the time being' under the jurisdiction of the regular German courts: the supreme court and magistrates court.

For a time, special land and titles commissions made use of Samoan assessors appointed by the governor (see GERMAN COLONIAL LAND POLICIES), but by 1911 it became clear that the governor would deal with any politically sensitive cases himself—the Samoan assessors were only playing an advisory role; and no longer was there an express reference to 'Samoan law or Samoan customs and habits'. The political climate was certainly changing, although it is not clear how deeply and speedily these changes would have affected Samoan law and self-administration.

In the Island Territory the situation had also begun to change, starting on Ponape (now Pohnpei), where a fundamental reform of the customary sociopolitical organization and land tenure system had begun in 1908 and was completed in 1913–14, after a 'rebellion' had been put down by a combined naval and police force in 1911. It is significant that these reforms—like the establishment of Samoan self-administration—did not take the form of legislation but were merely summarized on the back of the title documents issued to the new owners. This strict regime was to serve as a model for Marshall Islands, where things were just beginning to move at the end of German colonial rule, and eventually also for the rest of the Island Territory, whereas the non-hierarchical, traditional land tenure systems in Melanesia were of little concern to the German colonial authorities at the time.

The German colonial state was a rudimentary formation compared to the practised colonial cultures of Britain and France. Governors in German colonies had broader powers than their British and French colleagues but regulation from Berlin was stricter, while militant settler communities in Samoa and New Guinea constantly wrestled with governors over the priorities of economic development. Germany's Pacific colonies were less militarized than those in Africa. The governors were civilians and (unlike the larger African colonies) could not rely on standing colonial armies. There were no standardized patterns to colonial rule but the general principle was to change the local scene permanently in accord with the cultural mission that Germany carried to the corners of its empire. The overall goal was clear: the gradual creation of a uniform system of law and government in the metropolitan German mould into which people fitted on the basis of their class, wealth and education rather than their ethnic background. German colonial administration in the Pacific was essentially neither racist nor nationalistic. It was concerned with economic development and administrative efficiency. After the outbreak of war in 1914, Australian, New Zealand and Japanese authorities took possession of Germany's Pacific colonies, ending German administration in the region.—PS1 & PJH

Japanese activity in Micronesia, 1885–1945

While Japan briefly dominated the central and western Pacific during World War II, its occupation of Micronesia in the period between the world wars constituted its only sustained and formal presence in that ocean. Japanese interest in Micronesia arose in the late 1800s as part of a brief Japanese public enthusiasm for a 'southward advance' (*nanshin*). A nebulous mixture of romanticism, political idealism, and sense of national mission, the southward advance idea was promoted by a variety elements—novelists, politicians, entrepreneurs, journalists and even the Japanese navy—all of whom advocated Japanese expansion into the Pacific before it suc-

Man of Toloas, Truk (Chuuk), photographed by Matsumura in 1915

cumbed completely to western occupation. An unauthorized effort to annex Marshall Islands in 1885 proved abortive and in the subsequent decade a small number of Japanese traders and adventurers turned their attention to the central and western Carolines. Operating without the protection of their government and under the difficulties of distance from their homeland and the suspicion and hostility of the occupying power—Spanish until 1898 and German until World War I—a cluster of tiny Japanese trading companies established themselves, limpet-like, in the Carolines and, by the decade prior to World War I, came to dominate the region's inter-island trade.

Competing Japanese and American strategies in the Pacific in the first decade of the 20th century and the emerging strategic importance of Micronesia formed the backdrop to Japan's sudden *démarche* in the late summer of 1914. By joining Britain in its war on Germany, Japan justified a naval expedition to the central Pacific which swiftly and bloodlessly occupied all the islands of Micronesia (except the American territory of Guam). During the course of World War I, through discreet diplomatic manoeuvering, Japan was able to gain Western acceptance of its retention of the islands when hostilities ended. At Versailles, despite initial Australian and American opposition, Japan was awarded all of Micronesia (minus Guam), as a Class C mandated territory under the League of Nations.

During the six years that it remained in Micronesia, 1914–22, the Japanese navy displayed considerable zeal and energy in administering the islands, undertaking a variety of public works, setting out laws and regulations, and supervising justice, education, and hygiene. But in 1922, under the terms of the mandate, its last officers departed and turned over control of the islands to a South Seas Government Office (Nan'yô-chô) with headquarters at KOROR in Palau Islands.

Though a lesser agency in the Japanese colonial hierarchy, the South Seas Government, like the other four colonial governments in Japan's overseas empire, was heavily bureaucratic and authoritarian. It remained virtually untouched by external interference from either the Japanese Diet or the League of Nations Mandates Commission or by any internal resistance from a generally passive indigenous population. Its governor held all executive, legislative, and judicial power which he exercised through six district governors in the western Carolines (at Koror), in the Marianas (on SAIPAN), on Yap, in the central Carolines (on Truk), in the eastern Carolines (on Ponape) and in Marshall Islands (on Jaluit). At the community level, the South Seas Government exerted its authority through a manipulation of village chiefs and a ubiquitous police presence, both Japanese and Micronesian.

Japanese economic development and exploitation of its newly acquired territories began even before the South Seas Government had been established, though the initial processes were marred by the failures of would-be profiteers through ignorance and recklessness. By the mid 1920s, however, other entrepreneurs, more skilful, more persistent, and better prepared, had begun to lay the foundations of a sound economic foundation for the colony and thus to transform it from a drain on the Japanese budget to a paying colony. In this process the Japanese government played a significant role by backing those enterprises it regarded as sound. While industries, particularly mining, did develop in Micronesia, economic expansion took place largely in trade and agriculture, each represented by a dominant Japanese firm.

Trade came first, and here the lead was taken by the South Seas Trading Company (Nan'yô Bôeki Kaisha) which arose out of the cluster of small trading firms in the central Carolines prior to 1914. By the end of the 1920s, the company had established a network of trading posts throughout Micronesia, had come to dominate inter-island freight transport, and had begun to move into other fields—retail commerce, refrigeration, warehousing, and marine products—not only in Micronesia, but also in the Netherlands East Indies.

But it was agriculture, or rather a single agricultural industry, that became the basis for the economic development of the Japanese mandated territory as a whole. In the 1920s, the 'Sugar King', Matsue Haruji, head of the South Seas Development Company (Nan'yô Kôhatsu Kaisha), after numerous difficulties and setbacks, successfully began to harvest and refine sugar in the Marianas. By the mid 1930s, sugar had indeed become king in Micronesia, had brought thousands of immigrants into the islands, and by itself provided the mandate with a favorable balance of trade. From sugar, the company also moved out into various other ventures—marine products, phosphates, coconut cultivation—in the East Indies, as well as in Micronesia.

At the beginning of the Japanese occupation of Micronesia, in numbers and impact, Japanese emigration to the islands was slight. It was Matsue's sugar enterprise that turned a ripple of immigrant interest into a rip-tide migration. Heartened by the success of the first wave of sugar workers and by the encouraging conditions of settlement in the Marianas offered by the South Seas Development Company, a growing number of Japanese, mostly poor farmers, came to cultivate the cane or work in the mills. By 1925, more than 5000 Japanese were settled in the islands, out of a total Japanese population of 7000 in Micronesia. For reasons of proximity and poverty most of these came from Okinawa and most settled in the Marianas. There they eventually outnumbered the indigenous population. The Carolines filled up with Japanese engaged in other occupations, principally fishing, and even Marshall Islands, furthest east, felt the ripples of this tide of Japanese immigration. Throughout the 1930s, the number of Japanese in Micronesia more than doubled every five years, so that by 1941 it climbed past 93 000 and in 1942 it reached a high water mark of 96 000.

The unrestricted inflow of Japanese settlers into Micronesia during the inter-war years is fundamental to any assessment of the Japanese record as a mandatory power. Japan had assumed its mandate under the League with the explicit charge that it held a sacred trust to work for the wellbeing of the Micronesian people and the implicit understanding that it would tutor them toward their eventual emergence as a free, self-governing people. By the end of its occupation of Micronesia, it must be said that Japan had made only modest progress on the first task and almost none on the second.

It is true that the colonial government undertook a range of initiatives—in public health, in education, in public works, and in land survey and registration—that benefited the island peoples in varying degrees. The coming of Japanese trade and industry meant a higher standard of living and economic gain for the Micronesians as they were gradually brought into a modern commercial economy. But these initiatives and advances were either so limited or so weighted in favour of the Japanese immigrant population that the totality of their impact on the indigenes was slight. More than anything else, the sheer numbers of Japanese who poured into the islands in the inter-war years, in combination with later Japanese policies which aimed at the forced assimilation of the island peoples, meant that the prospects for eventual Micronesian self-determination grew dimmer by the year.

As the Japanese grip on Micronesia increased in the 1930s, so did suspicions that Japan was secretly violating its international pledge not to fortify the islands. In fact, there is little evidence that, until the last several years prior to the Pacific War, Japan had constructed fortifications in Micronesia in the pre-air age sense. Japan openly admitted the building of airfields and seaplane ramps on various islands beginning in the mid 1930s, claiming that these were for commercial purposes.

It was from those airfields that the Japanese navy despatched air units to attack British and American island territories in the central Pacific in December 1941. During the next two years of fighting in the Pacific, the Japanese position in Micronesia remained inviolate. In the autumn of 1943, however, Japanese armed forces in Micronesia hastened to shore up their defences in preparation for the American counter-offensive. In early 1944, the main Japanese bases in Marshall Islands were overrun by American amphibious forces. During the spring of that year Japanese bases in the Carolines were destroyed from the air and then bypassed. In the summer of 1944, Japan's 'absolute defence zone' in the Pacific was breached with the loss of the Marianas, and many in Japan considered the war as good as lost. The Japanese garrisons on the remaining islands, now defenceless and starving, were surrendered to American naval forces at the end of the war in September 1945.—MRP

Further reading

Peattie, M, 1988. *Nan'yô: the rise and fall of the Japanese in Micronesia, 1885–1945*, University of Hawai'i Press.

Deed of Cession

The Deed of Cession was the document, signed on 10 October 1874, by which Ratu Seru CAKOBAU, self-styled Tui Viti and Vunivalu of Bau, and 12 other chiefs, including the Tongan Enele Ma'afu, ceded Fiji to the British monarchy. Cession itself was a way out of the threatening instability which had engulfed Fiji in the mid 19th century, following European demand for land, labour and greater political control over the islands and the failure of the chiefdoms to tame the new forces of change to their purposes. Fiji was 'conjointly and severally' ceded by the chiefs to Queen Victoria who was asked to take 'possession of and dominion and sovereignty over the whole of the said islands and over the inhabitants thereof'. The stated purpose of cession was the desire to secure 'the promotion of civilization and Christianity and securing of trade and industry'. The cession was unconditional, the chiefs reposing their trust in the 'justice and generosity' of the British monarchy. For his part, Sir Hercules Robinson, Lieutenant Governor of New South Wales, who accepted the instruments of cession from the chiefs on behalf of the Crown, agreed to scrutinize and deal with the financial debts of the colony, investigate claims to land by Europeans and claims to pensions and allowances by the chiefs, and recognize the rights and interests of the chiefs in so far as they were 'consistent with British Sovereignty and Colonial form of government'. In time, the Deed of Cession came to be invested with meanings and symbolism far beyond the original intent, among them the oft-repeated claim that the deed promised to maintain the 'paramountcy of Fijian interests' in Fiji's body politic.—BVL

Guano Act of the United States

In 1856 the 34th United States Congress passed the *Guano Act*. While it had global dimensions the Act presaged American colonial presence in the central and south Pacific. Of the 101 islands, keys and rocks acquired by the United States for exploitation of GUANO, 70 were located in the Pacific. Eight were kept by the United States. The discovery of guano in the early to mid 1800s came when the American economy—and especially the value of slaves in the South—was heavily based on agriculture. A guano 'mania' produced a 'guano crusade'. Guano was not available in any quantity in the United States, and its extraction from Peruvian offshore islands was inhibited by an Anglo-Peruvian guano monopoly. Peaceful attempts to break the monopoly were unsuccessful. In December 1850 US President Millard Fillmore said that Peruvian guano was so desirable that it was a 'duty of the Government to employ all the means properly in its power for the purpose of causing that article to be imported into the country at a reasonable price'.

After many failures, several key American political figures, including Daniel Webster and William H Seward, demanded action. During the next presidency of Franklin Pierce the 1856 *Guano Act* was adopted. The Act empowered US citizens to take 'peaceable possession' of 'any island, rock or key not within the lawful jurisdiction of any other government' for the purpose of obtaining guano. Apparently 'any other government' did not apply to indigenous rule, but only to such nations as France, Great Britain or Spain. The island, key or rock could 'at the discretion of the President of the United States, be considered as appertaining to the United States', and the guano was to be exploited specifically for the 'use of the citizens of the United States'. It authorized the president to 'employ the land and naval forces of the United States' to protect the exploitation of guano. In 1860 and 1873 there were some minor revisions that did not change the fundamental intent, and in 1890 the US Supreme Court in *Jones v United States* confirmed the constitutionality of the *Guano Act*.

The majority of occupations under the *Guano Act* were in the Pacific, including Kiribati, Tuvalu, Tokelau and Cook Islands. Once exhausted, many Pacific guano possessions were abandoned. In 1898 French Frigate Shoals was joined to Hawai'i and in 1925 Swains Island to American Samoa. A few were reoccupied in World War II for strategic and military purposes. One served as a support island in the hydrogen bomb test and another as a missile tracking station. One (Howland) is famous because of the Amelia Earhart saga in 1937. (The pioneer aviator disappeared between Lae in Papua New Guinea and Howland Island, where an airfield had been hastily prepared for her arrival.) The situation changed with the emergence of independent island nations. By 1983, after several years of debate in the US Senate, the United States—in treaties with Kiribati, Tuvalu and New Zealand—had relinquished rights to most of the islands, keys and rocks claimed under the *Guano Act*. Six Pacific islands (Baker, Howland, Jarvis, Kingman Reef, Palmyra and Johnston Atoll) remain in US possession and are classified as 'Unorganized American Territories'.—CWA

Further reading

Arnade, C W, 1994–95. 'The great guano rush: a review article', *Bolivian Studies*, Vol. 5, Institute of Bolivian Studies, University of Akron.

Skaggs, J H, 1994. *The Great Guano Rush: entrepreneurs and American overseas expansion*, Macmillan.

Condominium

The Anglo–French Joint Condominium Administration of Vanuatu, 1906–80, was a compromise that emerged out of the rivalry between Australian settlers, British missionaries and John HIGGINSON's Caledonian Company in the New Hebrides. In 1878 the British and French governments had agreed that neither would annex the islands without consultation, and they established a joint naval commission in 1887 to protect the interests of planters and to regulate trade. Higginson required French assistance in 1894 and again in 1904, by which time the British and French had decided to appoint resident commissioners to guard against possible German annexation.

The condominium system of government established in 1906 represented joint rule, with each commissioner looking after his own nationals. Each headed a separate administration that built its own hospitals and managed its own schools, teaching Melanesians in its own language. It subjected villagers to an unwieldy division of power and an expensive duplication of services, leading to wide use of the description 'pandemonium'. The condominium brought stability, but little economic benefit to islanders, for whom the establishment of a joint court simply legalized the loss of their best agricultural land to foreign plantations.

Political self-consciousness was slow to develop because of linguistic diversity and settlement dispersion. Nationalism was manifested by the John FRUM cult, and the NAGRIAMEL movement, while religious differences also influenced political decision-making. Britain appeared more ready to accept the prospect of independence, but the condominium agreement required a joint departure. The French administration resisted, and since it relied completely on expatriate officials, had also failed to train Melanesians for the task of taking over. When political parties were eventually being formed from 1971, the Francophone groupings were much weaker than their Anglophone counterparts, particularly the Vanua'aku Pati which built up a strong support structure closely allied to the dominant Presbyterian church. The entrenched interests of French settlers, who owned most of the PLANTATIONS, could not withstand the appeal of a party platform that called for the return of all alienated land to its customary owners. The administration was obliged to accept a provisional government led by Walter LINI that drafted a constitution and in 1979 organized elections which produced a convincing victory for the Vanua'aku Pati. In spite of Nagriamel's last-minute attempt at secession, the achievement of independence for Vanuatu occurred on schedule in July 1980.—KRF

Western Pacific High Commission

With its seat in Fiji, where the governor was high commissioner and consul-general, and the chief justice was chief judicial commissioner, the Western Pacific High Commission was established by Orders in Council of 1877 under authority of the *Pacific Islanders Protection Act 1875*, giving it extra-territorial jurisdiction over British subjects resident in or resorting to a long list of specified island groups.

The Pacific islands had always been considered ideal for expediency in British colonial policy designed to avoid expensive territorial responsibility. Kidnapping and Fiji occupied the popular mind in 1874–75, as a result, among other things, of lobbying by a member of parliament with very mixed motives, the islands trader and prominent Wesleyan layman (Sir) William McArthur. The annexation of Fiji which ensued was no particularly rapturous event even for Disraeli's cabinet apart from Lord Carnarvon. On the assumption that British subjects could in future be held accountable to British law, extra-territorial jurisdiction was established while at the same time the independence of the islands was recognized.

No high commissioner intervened with quite the success foreseen (not least because the role was ill-defined and resources slim) except in relation to supervising the labour traffic, where alert naval commanders acted as deputy commissioners. The High Commission was to guide relations with islanders, and where this in effect meant punishment for attacks on British subjects, act of war by the Royal Navy remained the only practical as well as legal recourse. Where it meant conducting relations with island governments, as consul-general he must advise and control British subjects whose interests might lie in retailing prohibited, but staple, trade goods like arms, ammunition, dynamite and alcohol. In the case of the Reverend S W BAKER in Tonga, early officials rarely did justice to his motives; by the time Sir John THURSTON, who understood him, became high commissioner in 1887, Baker was dominated by a desire for vengeance on his detractors among old Wesleyan colleagues.

Where island élites were too independent for High Commission advice or too weak to act on it, or when islands were under French, American or German influence, the high commissioner had limited powers. At the same time, High Commission attempts, by refusing recruiting licences and registration of land claims, to discourage British subjects from opening plantations west of Fiji were nullified by international competition and the use of foreign flags. Competition, again, led in the 1890s to Britain's declaring protectorates.

Now the High Commission changed its character, except that in the early years of protectorate administration the Fiji principles of island self-government were followed. The Ellice and Gilbert atolls produced enough COPRA to pay for skeleton administration, but Solomon Islands required administrative encouragement of tax-yielding firms like LEVER's Pacific Plantations. Henceforth, big firms' welfare had to be balanced against islanders'. In the case of the Pacific Phosphate Company on Banaba after 1900, islanders' interests were entirely subordinate. In Solomon Islands, the basis of land policy came to be the assumption that islanders were anyway doomed to extinction, until at last, in the 1930s, medical science showed that the anthropologists' 'racial degradation' through 'decay of custom' was not what was operating. Disease and food-deficiency were the causes, in a vicious cycle often promoted by concentrations of people in big mission villages on low-lying foreshores. Tuberculosis and dysentery were now as widespread in Solomon Islands as in Europe, and, along with YAWS, were in the end fought with some success. In the New Hebrides, an extreme case under its CONDOMINIUM administration, the Presbyterians constantly fought the French Residency over issues like recruiting, and the British Residency wore kid gloves.

At least civil as opposed to mission government meant a diet so much richer than indigenous carbohydrates that, as on plantations where government-decreed rations were actually provided, jail could be a comparatively healthy place, physically speaking. Not even a well-run plantation was healthy, psychologically-speaking—very few if any labourers on Solomon Islands plantations were women in 1938 and, said the visiting high commissioner darkly, 'some day when some one takes an interest in the Pacific there will be a scandal about it'. In the view of this man, Sir Arthur Richards, later Lord Milverton, there was much scandal on view, and much shaking up to be done to replace amateur administration in the Western Pacific territories.

All across the western Pacific, Australia-based companies sought monopoly powers, Levers in planting and trade, BURNS PHILP and W R CARPENTER in trade, shipping and planting. Australian-administered Papua New Guinea did not much discourage them, the High Commission opposed and deplored. While Chinese cut prices, a single European-owned store on 100 miles of Solomon Islands coast could mean six boxes of matches cost islanders a shilling when the Tulagi price was about seven shillings a gross to Europeans. At the same time, a seaborne empire from Papua to Christmas Island like Burns Philp's meant careful management of costly shipping. In the 1920s–30s, company profits were threatened by schooners from Japanese-run Micronesia.

War, the first war really to touch the High Commission territories, made itself felt directly in December 1941 when German raiders from Japanese bases shelled Nauru and sank five phosphate ships. Nauru suffered under Japanese occupation, and even more so Banaba, direct High Commission responsibility. Evacuation was under consideration when the Japanese landed. Westward, the small Australian fighting-force at Tulagi looted the place before abandoning it in haste; and planters mostly fled. Coastwatchers went to work; and, contrary to myth, the administration remained underground too, in skeleton form, until the American counter-attack, with its Fijian, Tongan and New Zealand guerrillas, cleared the way for the High Commission's return.

As the new colonial world developed in the post-war period, economic and social reconstruction was the watchword, and remained so up to and after the time when the Western Pacific High Commission diverged from the Fiji government in 1952, and established headquarters in the new capital of the British Solomon Islands Protectorate at Honiara. In 1974 the office ended its role, and the high commissioner became the governor of the Solomon Islands.—DAS

Further reading

Scarr, D, 1967. *Fragments of Empire*, Australian National University Press.

——, 1973. *I, the Very Bayonet*, Australian National University Press.

■ ***Sir John Thurston*** Sir John Bates Thurston, CMG, KCMG, FLS, FRGS (31 January 1836–7 February 1897), was High Commissioner and Consul-General for the Western Pacific, and Governor of Fiji. He made trading voyages to Fiji and Gilbert Islands in the 1860s, was wrecked on Rotuma in 1865 while botanizing, joined the British consulate in Fiji as clerk, became acting consul in 1867, chief secretary to King CAKOBAU's and the Ad-Interim Government, 1872–75; Trusted and Special Adviser to Cakobau over Cession, 1874–5; Auditor-General in the Crown Colony; colonial secretary, administrator, lieutenant-governor; and then governor from 1887 with all the Western Pacific offices.

Under Cakobau, he put a respectable Scottish planter in jail, and proposed to govern by an assembly which would not have been white-dominated. Europeans, in his view and that of the WESTERN PACIFIC HIGH COMMISSION in general, were for the most part better kept out of the islands where, even missionaries, or writers like Robert Louis STEVENSON, could not be trusted to behave like rational beings.

'We are, as a race, a race of robbers and spoilers', Thurston once commented privately, having been a planter and made a recruiting voyage to the New Hebrides too; and, in public: 'the mission of the civilized man to the semi-savage is pretty much the same all over the world. It is to overreach him in business, and to overcome him in war!'.

Government's own financial needs exacted a moral price, even so. The COLONIAL SUGAR REFINING COMPANY (CSR) was to be attracted to Fiji: 'It would be a good thing if they invested, but not if they got all they want.' Recognized by the company as an enemy, even he found it hard to deny them, in the end. Labourers from Melanesia could be banned from sugar plantations, which killed them; but he learned how hard it was to interest CSR in the care or even the high mortality of the Indian indentured labourers who replaced Melanesians. Not until after his death, though, were Indian indentured numbers more than quadrupled by vastly increased immigration.

His system, adopted by Sir Arthur GORDON as first governor, depended on recognition of Fijian structures as hierarchical, communal and perfectly valid in an imperial world to be ruled by a sense of relative values or not at all. It depended on taxes in produce not money, to stimulate Fijians' production and yield them more actual cash from refunds than could have been earned from wage-labour or selling to merchants direct. It meant control on the debt that Fijians could contract, and limiting their absence from hearth and home. It meant self-government through the Fijian Administration with its tier of councils, inevitably led by hereditary chiefs but with able commoners encouraged. Thurston's view was functional as well as relativist. His age put a premium on evolution; and his practice was so unpopular among Europeans that it was appropriate that, as he once grimly said: 'I was brought up at sea, and I preferred stormy to fine weather.' He died at sea, and is buried in the Melbourne General Cemetery.—DAS

Further reading

Scarr, D, 1973. *I, the Very Bayonet*, Australian National University Press.

——, 1980. *Viceroy of the Pacific*, Australian National University Press.

——, 1984. *Fiji: a short history*, Allen & Unwin.

■ ***Sir Arthur Gordon*** Arthur Hamilton Gordon (26 November 1829–1912), was born in London, the youngest of four sons of the fourth Earl of Aberdeen. He entered Trinity College, Cambridge University, in 1847, becoming president of the Cambridge Union in 1848–49. After rejecting a career as a country clergyman, and motivated by (in his biographer's words) the 'desire for useful work, eminence, power and public recognition', Gordon at 31 accepted an appointment as lieutenant-governor of the Canadian province of New Brunswick. He later served as Governor of Trinidad and Mauritius, before going to Fiji, where he became the first substantive governor from 1875 until 1880. His term laid the foundations of modern Fiji. His 'native' policies shielded the Fijians from the pressures of development to enable them to progress at their own pace. His policy of 'indirect rule' devised a separate system of administration, involving indigenous leaders through the Council of Chiefs. His land policies, even if mistaken, placed 83 per cent of land in Fijian hands. Realizing that Fiji's future lay in large-scale PLANTATION agriculture, Gordon invited the COLONIAL SUGAR REFINING COMPANY (CSR) to Fiji to lay the foundation of the SUGAR INDUSTRY which came to dominate the economy. With previous experience in two sugar-producing colonies, he turned to Indian indentured labour (GIRMITIYA) to provide a cheap and reliable workforce for the industry. Gordon left Fiji to become Governor of New Zealand (1887–90), before returning to London. He joined the House of Lords as the first Baron Stanmore in 1893.—BVL

Further reading

Chapman, J K, 1964. *The Career of Arthur Hamilton Gordon: First Lord Stanmore*, University of Toronto Press.

Legge, J D, 1958. *Britain in Fiji: 1858–1880*, Macmillan.

■ ***F J Moss*** Frederick J Moss (1829–1904), New Zealand author, planter, journalist, was the first administrator of COOK ISLANDS, 1891–98. His books *A Month in Fiji* (1868) and *A Planter's Experience in Fiji* (1870) were responsible for much of the enthusiasm in the colonies during the cotton boom and Fiji 'Rush', and he later served on trade commissions and inquiries as New Zealand contemplated a colonial role in the Pacific. His book *Through Atolls and Islands* (1889) was based on these travels. Although Moss was not regarded as an administrative success in Cook Islands, two articles he wrote on the group remained standard works long after his death.—MQ

■ ***Wilhelm Solf*** Wilhelm Solf (1862–1936) was the first Governor of German Samoa. An urbane and thoughtful Berliner, he was a scholar of Indian languages, a civilian lawyer and judge who served as an interpreter for the German Foreign Office in Calcutta and as a judge for the emerging colonial administration in German East Africa. In 1899 he was appointed president of the municipality of APIA in the Samoan islands. After Samoa was partitioned between Germany and the United States, he became governor of the German colony. His conception of colonial rule revolved around guiding Samoans into the channels of German civilization and protecting them from rapacious development. His method was to engage with Samoan culture, mimicking Samoan chiefly style and values, competing for rhetorical and political dominance with the great chiefs. In 1910 he was made State Secretary for Colonies in the Kaiser's administration and remained in charge till the end of the war. He was also foreign minister in 1918 and later ambassador to Japan during the Weimar Republic. He actively resisted the development of National Socialism in Germany in the 1930s.—PJH

EIGHT WORLD WAR II

Islander experiences in the Pacific war

The thousands of islands and atolls stretching across the Pacific Ocean were affected in so many different ways by the Second World War that generalization is impossible. For example, in Papua New Guinea where coastal areas experienced massive military invasion and sustained aerial bombardment, isolated groups in the Highlands remained unaware that the war was even taking place. In staging areas outside of the war zones, many islanders found that the war added excitement and new opportunities to their lives. But in those islands and atolls that became battlegrounds, people suffered every form of deprivation and degradation, ranging from the simple inconvenience of severed communications to the devastation of entire communities.

In most cases, Pacific communities were profoundly affected by the war in ways that would set the course of change for decades to come. Perhaps the dominant theme in these experiences was disruption—specifically, disruption of the colonial order (or rather multiple colonial orders). But just how this unsettling was effected, and with what consequences for local populations, was extremely diverse.

Even the dates of World War II in the Pacific are difficult to pinpoint. In official military history, the war can be said to begin with the Japanese invasion of Guam on 8 December 1941 (and PEARL HARBOR, on the other side of the dateline, on 7 December). Land fighting in the Pacific began with the Allied counter-invasion of GUADALCANAL on 7 August 1942. From that time until the Japanese surrender on 2 September 1945, the entire Pacific region became a war zone where some of the most intense battles in the history of human warfare were fought.

The end of the Pacific war is even more difficult to locate. The surrender of Japanese garrisons and the closing of Allied military bases—which had a greater impact on local populations than the formal Japanese surrender—stretched out for several years. In the view of some Marshall Islanders, whose home atolls were appropriated by the United States for the purpose of NUCLEAR TESTING in the 1950s and which continue to be used as a missile test range, the war in fact has never ended. In terms of the visible and active presence of military weaponry, the war even escalated during the Cold War period to the present, with severe consequences for populations forced off their atoll homes, some suffering the effects of radiation sickness caused by nuclear fallout.

During the period 1942–45, daily life in the war zones became harsh and regimented. In areas where men were recruited for war work, women coped the best they could to sustain a subsistence economy and family welfare in the face of constant threats as varied as immediate bombardment to malnutrition caused by failing gardens. For people who find their identity in the land, forced movement away from villages and ancestral homes was one of the bitterest experiences. In European colonial territories invaded by Japanese forces, many coastal people

Sergeant Katne's patrol reports to an Australian captain, on return from Oro Bay, Papua New Guinea

abandoned their settlements and took refuge in rugged inland regions, in some cases carving out a marginal living for years.

As battles raged, areas occupied by the Japanese were cut off from supply lines, bombed incessantly and, in some cases, invaded with massive force. As Japanese troops became increasingly desperate, their relations with islanders deteriorated badly, often leading to further suffering and death. In the case of the Nauruans on Chuuk, which was 'isolated' and neutralized by American strategy, 473 of the 800 people taken there to work died before the end of the war. The death toll of islanders killed by the warring powers, either accidentally or deliberately, will never be known. Allied forces eager to make an example carried out bombing missions against native communities suspected of collaboration with the Japanese. It is estimated that in Papua New Guinea alone, 15 000 people perished in the fighting, bombings and executions carried out by both sides.

If separated from sources of supply, servicemen were taught to 'live off the land', which usually meant off people's gardens and domestic animals. With tens of thousands of Japanese in New Guinea cut off from their supply lines, desperation led to the exploitation of native communities and numerous atrocities. One of the most ignominious war-time fates suffered by islanders was that of the Arapesh individuals who were killed and eaten by starving members of the 18th Army in 1945. In many of the Japanese bases in Micronesia where large populations were isolated by the Allied 'island hopping' strategy, islanders suffered starvation alongside the Japanese.

The reversals suffered by the Japanese in many areas frequently led local populations to take on a more aggressive posture in gathering intelligence

American Memorial Park, Garapan (Saipan, Northern Marianas), with Flag Circle, a war memorial

and carrying out guerrilla actions. These in turn evoked punitive actions that worsened local misery. In Irian Jaya, where local cult activity was widespread during the war and Japanese occupation was actively resisted, hundreds were killed in executions and punitive massacres. Testimony at the post-war trial of the Japanese commander on New Ireland revealed that 40 New Guineans had been executed under his command. And after the Allied victory, with the resumption of their own control, Australian authorities hanged 10 Papuans for treason.

Formal military units were organized in nearly every colony and territory. In areas away from the front lines, police forces and militias were expanded and put through accelerated training. For example, in Vanuatu, more than 2000 men, mostly from the island of Malekula, joined the New Hebrides Defence Force. In American Samoa, not only was the US Navy's indigenous Fitafita guard expanded, hundreds of Samoans were for the first time allowed to volunteer for military service, either as Navy or Marine Corps Reserve.

Recruitment of a greater number of islanders into military roles, with many given the ranks of corporal and sergeant, transformed expectations on both sides of the colonial relationship. Although some units were outfitted with uniforms resembling the shirtless style of dress common among plantation labour, many served in the same type of uniforms worn by Allied or Japanese units. Although the prestige of the European colonial powers suffered greatly because of reversals at the outset, their weakened position offered islanders opportunities to assert themselves in the critical contexts of war. In Tahiti, Polynesian villagers turned out in droves requesting to be sent to Europe to help de Gaulle liberate the 'mother country'. Enlistment in Pape'ete had to be stopped within a week due to shortage of uniforms and rifles.

In Papua New Guinea and Solomon Islands, where the most sustained jungle fighting occurred over a period of years, both sides recruited local scouts and trained island military units. The Allies recruited more than 3500 Papuans and New Guineans into the Pacific Islands Regiment, made up of the Papuan Infantry Battalion (PIB) and the First and Second New Guinea Infantry Battalions. The first company of the Papuan Infantry Battalion was raised in June 1940 and was soon thrown into the breach when the Japanese landed at Buna in 1942. These men played an important role in stopping the Japanese advance southward toward Port Moresby across the KOKODA TRACK. Recruits were 'enlisted' on the trail and their training consisted of bearing arms in action. Despite this lack of training, many distinguished themselves as decorated veterans. Official losses for the Papuan infantry were 43 killed in action, 110 wounded, 64 dying otherwise, and 11 missing, presumed killed.

Although newcomers in Papua New Guinea, the Japanese also inducted islanders into military service and labour groups. Their landing posed a dilemma for New Guineans in occupied areas and many communities experienced divided loyalties, sometimes along lines of traditional rivalries. The Japanese offer to provide education and training was attractive to many. Michael SOMARE recalls in his autobiography (1975) that in his home around Wewak the Japanese gave military training to adolescent boys. Adult men were recruited into the Japanese police force, the *kempeitai*, some with officer rank. Where both the Australians and Japanese recruited from the same local population, villagers sometimes found themselves on opposite sides of military encounters. On Bougainville, not only were New Guineans fighting New Guineans, but Fijians and Solomon Islanders lined up with Allies against Japanese and their island recruits.

Encouraged by their chiefs and staunchly loyal to the British cause, more than 2000 Fijians joined new military battalions. Ratu Sir Lala SUKUNA, a paramount chief, urged recruitment with the view that 'Fijians will never be recognized unless our blood is shed first'. And shed blood they did, during months of tough jungle fighting in Solomon Islands and Bougainville. While unfamiliar with modern warfare at first, the Fijian units gained wide notoriety among the Allied forces as 'Ghurkas of the Pacific'.

The Japanese also recruited loyal islanders to assist with their New Guinea campaign, drawing recruits from their colonies in Micronesia. Although small in numbers, these recruits played significant roles and took grievous losses. A group of Pohnpeians called the *Kessitihai* was recruited in May 1942 and sworn to die for Japan. Most of them did. Twenty were sent to New Guinea in July that year and only three returned. Termed the 'Pohnpeian death band' by a Japanese veteran who knew them (Mitsuo Watakabe), these men were first sent to Rabaul in New Guinea, and then split up and assigned to various Japanese units later annihilated in the fighting around Buna.

Palauans also volunteered for service with the Japanese army. 'Survey groups' (*Chosatai*) of 60 men each were sent to New Guinea where they could apply their knowledge of the tropics in providing logistic support. In addition, 29 Palauans formed a military unit (*Teishintai*, 'devoting one's life') that served with the Japanese in Irian Jaya. The *Teishintai* who returned to Palau, together with new recruits, were selected to serve as guerrillas in the defence of Palau. They were assigned to suicide missions against the US Marines, although these were never carried out.

The longest war journeys were undertaken by the Maori Battalion (28th Battalion of the Second New Zealand Division) and the Bataillon du Pacifique made up of Tahitians and New Caledonians. Both fought with the Allies in Europe. The Maori Battalion took more casualties than any other unit in the New Zealand Expeditionary Force. The record of the 300 volunteers in the Bataillon du Pacifique is similarly distinguished. One third of them were killed in action in North Africa, Italy, France and Germany.

In Solomon Islands, preparations for war began with the formation of the Solomon Islands Defence Force in 1937. An initial plan to recruit only Europeans and Chinese was quickly abandoned and Solomon Islanders serving in the police force were inducted into the Solomon Islands Defence Force (SIDF) and given military training. Touted as the 'youngest combatant unit in the [British] Empire', the SIDF comprised nearly 400 recruits at peak strength. When the British administration evacuated the capital at Tulagi, these recruits formed the primary support for European coastwatchers who remained behind Japanese lines to provide strategic information to the Allies. While statistics for such a dispersed force are sketchy, one (admittedly biased) coastwatcher tallied the record of SIDF as 350 Japanese killed and 43 taken prisoner, with 7 of the Defence Force killed in action.

Those who distinguished themselves in combat were honoured with medals for bravery. Among the 120 Fijians participating in the recapture of New Georgia, 11 were killed and 20 wounded. Medals received by Fijians in the Solomons campaign

Cover of *Pacific Islands Monthly* in 1945, featuring Ratu Lala Sukuna of Fiji

include one posthumous Victoria Cross, two Military Crosses, four Distinguished Conduct Medals, 16 Military Medals, and two US Silver Stars. A sampling of awards for Papua New Guineans decorated for bravery turns up a number of remarkable cases, such as the citation for Sergeant William Matpi of Manus Island which notes that he was officially recognized for killing 110 of the enemy. In some instances, the heroic exploits of certain individuals, such as Sir Jacob Vouza of Guadalcanal or Sergeant Yauwika of Bougainville, were singled out for prominent attention by the Allied military and media. But for each Vouza there are scores of others whose stories were never recorded.

At least as important as the formal military units were the thousands of islanders who contributed as 'coastwatchers'. Most of these worked with Allied networks—either in rear areas such as Vanuatu and New Caledonia, or behind Japanese lines in Papua New Guinea and Solomon Islands. Small groups of island recruits supported military officers with radios transmitting information to Allied command centres. Many islanders proved to be adept in the arts of deception and intelligence gathering. There are countless examples from Papua New Guinea, Solomon Islands and elsewhere of men who gained access to Japanese camps and bases by offering to sell food or provide labour. In the Guadalcanal campaign, the first Allied offensive, reports supplied by coastwatchers proved to be critical, as officers hiding in occupied islands to the north radioed advance notice about ship and plane formations headed south from the Japanese stronghold in Rabaul. In the words of the American Admiral William Halsey, commander of Allied forces in the South Pacific, 'The coastwatchers saved Guadalcanal and Guadalcanal saved the Pacific'. And, one might add, 'native scouts saved the coastwatchers'.

Japanese anti-aircraft guns at Gaan Point, in Agat, Guam

Although Halsey was referring to the small squads of European and Islander coastwatchers with military or police status, these groups were in fact supported by untold numbers of ordinary men and women who formed an invisible network providing logistic support and surveillance of Japanese movements. Villagers and scouts rescued hundred of pilots—for both sides—downed in remote areas. More Allied planes were lost over Papua New Guinea than in any other campaign in any war. In Solomon Islands it is estimated that about 188 Allied airmen were returned by coastwatching networks.

Although established as a passive intelligence-gathering operation, some coastwatchers engaged in guerrilla actions that were highly effective in harassing and confusing larger forces. One of the best known of these, headed by a former district officer named Donald Kennedy, operated in the New Georgia area of Solomon Islands. 'Kennedy's army' lost no men in its various operations, but others were not so fortunate. On New Ireland, near the Japanese base at Rabaul, 36 coastwatchers, European and Melanesian, lost their lives during the occupation. One of these was a respected New Ireland elder, Boski, who was betrayed by local rivals and beheaded by the Japanese in a public ceremony. Of 12 men landed by submarine at Hollandia to reconnoitre enemy positions, three were killed on the first day and only seven survived after dispersing into the jungle. One of these, Yali Singina, did so by making an epic three-month trek covering 120 miles back to Allied lines at Aitape.

The great majority of islanders who participated directly in the war did so through labour recruitment. The Allied and Japanese war efforts demanded manpower, replacing plantations as the major source of employment. Micronesians were recruited by the Japanese; Polynesians by the Allies; and Melanesians by both sides.

Strategic and supply bases throughout the Pacific were constructed and maintained with substantial help from native labour corps. Islanders offloaded, transported, stored, and distributed the tons of supplies and equipment ('cargo') that made battles possible. Local workers performed a wide range of services, including carrying supplies; stretcher-bearing; cultivating food crops; constructing roads, airfields and buildings; mosquito abatement; laundry and clean-up details. By the end of 1942, for example, 500 islanders were at work draining 40 square miles of mosquito breeding grounds near Milne Bay in Papua New Guinea.

The US military employed 1500 New Caledonians out of an indigenous population of 30 000. Preparing their forces to counter-attack Japanese positions to the north in the Solomon Islands and New Guinea, the Americans next moved into Vanuatu where they employed more than 1000 men on Efate and over 500 on Espiritu Santo. In Fiji, 1375 men had joined the First Battalion, Fiji Labour Corps by the end of 1942. A company of these men eventually travelled to Bougainville to work as stevedores at the American base at Torokina. In Solomon Islands, at least 3200 men worked on Guadalcanal,

Russell Islands and Tulagi. Men on Guadalcanal were joined by 400 I-Kiribati. Monthly labour strengths in Papua New Guinea peaked at nearly 38 000 in June of 1944, nearly equal to the pre-war total of 50 000 laborers working in the plantation economy. This figure does not count those working for the Japanese, nor an unknown number of workers recruited directly by the Americans and by the Japanese in Irian Jaya.

The labour needs of both sides were a major source of disruption, with extraordinary numbers of young men recruited out of their home villages. Despite colonial policies to the contrary, recruitment left some villages and islands depopulated of able-bodied men, leaving mostly women, children and the aged. In one of the more extreme examples, more than half of the population of Nauru (800 out of 1700) was taken by the Japanese to work at Chuuk, over a thousand miles away.

Colonial authorities attempted to regulate recruitment so as to mitigate the depopulation of local communities. Recruiters for the Australian New Guinea Administrative Unit (ANGAU) were initially instructed not to recruit more than 25 per cent of the adult male population. However, as fighting grew fiercer and military needs grew, this limit was often ignored and recruitment levels sometimes reached 100 per cent.

The war gave new meaning to the word 'cargo'—the pre-war term most often applied to manufactured goods of European origin. The Allied and Japanese military machines both established elaborate transportation networks to bring an incredible variety of goods into remote Pacific islands unaccustomed to such trade links. Islanders witnessed the establishment of supply bases, depots and dumps where huge amounts of materiel and equipment poured ashore in unprecedented quantities. Working alongside port and quartermaster companies, Island labourers hefted and stacked much of the war's material lifeline. This was the war's 'cargo'.

The amount of military supplies that moved through the Pacific was tremendous—a point of pride even in the Allies' own propaganda. From 1942 to 1945 the US Army alone shipped over 4 million tons of cargo from American ports to Pacific destinations. Another 1.7 million tons were procured from Pacific sources, primarily Australia and New Zealand.

Saipan alone had more than 1.8 million square feet of warehouse space constructed to accommodate supplies destined for that island. At the same time, military installations on Guadalcanal sprawled across more than 1800 acres. In some cases such as Solomon Islands, military bases established the site for national capital cities after the war, where towns grew up around the base infrastructure of roads, airfields, docks, hospitals and Quonset huts.

In addition to the sheer spectacle of massive amounts of modern weaponry, the often nonchalant treatment of their cargo on the part of military personnel left deep impressions among island observers. Americans, Australians and others frequently gave away food rations, clothing, cutlery, blankets and other supplies. And at the end of the war, vast amounts of supplies were bulldozed into the sea. It was easier and less expensive to ditch the contents of island warehouses than to ship them home. There is more than one beach near the site of wartime bases, like Espiritu Santo's 'million dollar point', where skin divers today swim through the decaying remnants of World War II's military might. At Kukum docks in Guadalcanal, the army burned, buried or dumped at sea 58 831 tons of cargo worth US$19 888 587 at the end of the war.

For many islanders, one of the greatest disappointments of the war came from witnessing this wholesale destruction of war equipment. Even more bitterly resented was the confiscation of property acquired by labourers. Colonial authorities attempted to re-impose pre-war expectations by limiting the amount of material that labourers could retain for themselves. Members of the Solomon Islands Labour Corps were allowed to keep only those goods which could fit in a single patrol box for their return home. Everything else was confiscated. Islanders decades later still complained of colonial agents taking away the money, uniforms, and other goods acquired as gifts or in trade with servicemen.

World War II deployed an array of new communications technologies across the Pacific. Areas whose communication capacity had been limited to mail delivered on occasional mission or plantation boats now witnessed the installation of radar, radio and telephone links. As bases developed, complex telephone networks were established, often with the help of island workers accustomed to climbing palm trees. Base newspapers such as Papua New Guinea's *Guinea Gold* were also established. Photography, film and tape-recording also arrived in force with military personnel interested to record their progress, develop propaganda images, and keep their troops entertained. The war also brought cinema to the Pacific, just as it helped bring the Pacific into the theatres of America and the rest of the world. Most military bases had numerous movie screens where newsreels and Hollywood films were shown. Espiritu Santo reportedly had 43.

Wartime encounters between islanders and military personnel continually threatened to undermine established relations between natives and colonizers. Pre-war norms required distinctly different styles of dress and conduct, usually symbolizing the subordination of islanders. A whole system of signs and symbols had evolved to maintain European dominance. Much of this was tied to the plantation economy, such that the sudden infusion of new sources of income had important cultural as well as material effects.

The concentration of troops around bases and staging areas created new economic demands for goods and services. Islanders responded to these opportunities by going into business as workers, traders and salesmen. The military and colonial administrations attempted to regulate this inflationary economy by setting low wage limits and price controls. In some cases authorities attempted to cut off all trading, such as the New Hebrides Joint Regulation No. 1 of 1944 which prohibited all 'sale of native curios', on penalty of fine and/or six months in jail.

In many instances these regulations proved impossible to enforce. Freewheeling exchanges took place in and around most military bases. A US dollar in wartime Tonga could buy 48 pounds of corn, oranges, pineapples or watermelon, 144 pounds of papaya, or 84 pounds of sweet potatoes. The other major sector for native entrepreneurship was in the production and sale of tourist souvenirs. Servicemen snapped up baskets and mats, weavings, spears, bows and arrows, walking sticks, carvings, and the ubiquitous grass skirt. These exchanges during the war set the pattern for island tourism for decades to come. Indeed, some of the tourist art seen in Pacific airports today has its origins in the wartime trade for souvenirs where islanders refined their understandings of foreign tastes for native artifacts.

The diverse ways in which islanders and military personnel interacted for all sorts of mundane reasons posed a constant threat to the colonial hierarchy. Every time an islander and soldier did the same job, ate the same food, played the same game, watched the same film, wore the same clothes, or addressed each other with familiar nicknames like 'Joe' or 'mate', the colonial code suffered another setback. The problem so alarmed colonial authorities that they made official entreaties to Allied military commanders to enforce more strict codes of separation. These efforts included publication of a 1943 booklet of guidelines titled *You and the Native: notes for the guidance of Members of the Forces in their relations with New Guinea natives*. Written by an Australian officer of the Southwest Pacific Allied Command, the booklet set out 100 points of advice outlining pre-war codes of conduct.

In Melanesia, where the colonial order was colour-coded in terms of black/white oppositions, the appearance of black American troops wearing the same uniforms and performing many of the same tasks as white soldiers made a deep impression and breached the rigid oppositions that had characterized the colonial order. Approximately 200 000 black US military personnel served in the Far East and the Pacific. Since many were in service units (quartermaster, transportation, Seabees), they had considerable contact with island labour corps. Apparently the segregation of the American military was less noticed than the obvious abilities and achievements of the black Americans.

Despite efforts to regulate interaction between military personnel and natives, many men who went to work on American bases recall informal interactions with servicemen for purposes of trading, earning extra income by doing laundry, or attending the same church services. These interactions were frequently lubricated by American generosity with military-issue food, cigarettes, clothing and equipment. Food and other items were not only swapped, they were sometimes consumed jointly, marking the formation of new relations of familiarity. Throughout the Pacific, the act of exchanging goods, especially food, is imbued with wider social meaning. In can be argued that perceptions of friendship and expectations for continued cooperation helped establish the views of a generation of islanders who subsequently pushed for DECOLONIZATION in the post-war period and the eventual establishment of independent Pacific states.—GMW

Further reading

Cooper, H, 1946. *Among Those Present: the official story of the Pacific islands at war*, Her Majesty's Stationery Office.

Lindstrom, L and White, G M, 1990. *Island Encounters: black and white memories of the Pacific war*, Smithsonian Institution Press.

Somare, M, 1975. *Sana: an autobiography of Michael Somare*, Nuigini Press.

White, G M and Lindstrom, L (eds), 1989. *The Pacific Theater: island representations of World War II*, University of Hawai'i Press.

Papua New Guinea in the war

In 1939 world war seemed remote from the Pacific islands, but suddenly in December 1941, Papua New Guinea was mid-point between two armies. The day after PEARL HARBOR was bombed, Japanese reconnaissance planes flew over Rabaul and Kavieng. War against Japan, long-feared by the Australians in New Guinea, had come quickly. White women and children were evacuated in December 1941, but mission women and nurses were given the option of staying. Asian women and civilian men not of military age and not in essential services were left to face invasion. Even before Singapore—the bastion of British defence in the east—had fallen, the Japanese occupied Rabaul on 23 January 1942. The 1500 Australian troops in Rabaul, by far the strongest force the Australians had in all of Mandated New Guinea, were soon desperately trying to escape along the north and south coasts. Demonstrating the poverty of Australian power then in the area, the troops on New Britain could not be reinforced, supplied or rescued. Only about one-third of the Rabaul troops reached safety.

Extending from their major base in Rabaul, the Japanese occupied the New Guinea islands, Bougainville and the northern Solomon Islands, and the north coast of New Guinea. Under the duress of war the Australian civil administration in the Mandated Territory of New Guinea handed control to the Australian Army, and in Papua, after confusion, the army also assumed control. From early 1942 the two Australian territories were combined, and the Australian New Guinea Administrative Unit (ANGAU) was given responsibility for what had been the tasks of civilian companies and government.

Raphael Oimbari, of Oro District, Papua New Guinea, guides a wounded Australian soldier to safety near Buna, Christmas Day 1942

From May 1942 the critical turning-point battles were fought: Coral Sea, Midway, Kokoda, Milne Bay and Guadalcanal. By the end of September the Australians had defeated the Japanese at Milne Bay and were advancing on the KOKODA TRACK. At the end of 1942 the Japanese were defeated by combined American and Australian forces at Buna and Gona. In 1943 the Allies recaptured Salamaua, Lae and Finschhafen on the mainland and made landings on Bougainville and New Britain. The Americans had begun their 'island hopping' north, bypassing many of the strongest Japanese bases and leaving them without ship or air links to Japan. Through 1944 Australians fought along the Ramu Valley to Madang and the Americans leap-frogged ahead to Aitape and Dutch New Guinea. By the time the Japanese surrendered in August 1945 the Australians were confining the Japanese on the Gazelle Peninsula and attacking them on Bougainville and in the SEPIK District. The final battles in New Guinea liberated some villagers from hunger and violence, but have been criticized for the high cost of lives when the decisive battles of the war were being fought far to the north.

The war transformed New Guinea's relationship with the outside world. Nearly 1 000 000 Americans, over 300 000 Australians, 300 000 Japanese and lesser numbers of New Zealand and Fijian troops went to New Guinea. In addition the Japanese shipped thousands of conscripted and volunteer Indian, Chinese and Malays to labour for them. In terms of death rates the Japanese suffered appallingly: over 150 000 Japanese had died in New Guinea before the last soldiers were repatriated. Their labourers suffered even higher mortality. The Australians, who had the highest death rate among Allied soldiers, lost nearly 9000 dead. Many of the government officers and planters from the New Guinea islands had been killed, and nearly 300 foreign-born missionaries were dead. Just how many Papua New Guineans died is uncertain. In areas of intense bombing or ground fighting and long Japanese occupation, such as the Gazelle Peninsula and Bougainville, the population dropped by a quarter. Most deaths were not a result of the violence of war, but of deprivation.

The war fell unevenly on the villagers. Along the coast of the Gulf of Papua and into the Western Division people saw no battles, but nearly all fit adult men were conscripted to work for the army, and communities had to allow male-controlled activities such as trade and initiation ceremonies to decline and women took over the subsistence tasks of men. In parts of the Highlands, except for the increase in the number of aircraft that flew overhead and rumours that passed from community to community, people knew nothing of the war. In Port Moresby there were numerous air raids, coastal villagers were evacuated, and a massive military base was developed. After a brief and violent battle the people of Milne Bay had to learn to live alongside a giant Allied base. In the north, villagers spent periods between two armies, visited by rival patrols and subjected to rival propaganda. In some places tribal fighting re-surfaced amid the battles of a world war. On New Ireland and the Gazelle Peninsula the people lived for over three years under Japanese occupation. As the Japanese themselves became short of supplies and feared an Allied invasion, so their demands for food and labourers increased and they became more brutal in the suppression of what they assumed were acts of defiance.

Over 3500 Papua New Guineans served in the Pacific Islands Regiment, 3000 in the Royal Papuan Constabulary, 955 were medical assistants, and others served as armed soldiers with the coastwatchers and 'M' Special forces. But most Papua New Guineans worked as labourers and carriers for the Japanese and Allied armies. By the end of the war more Papua New Guineans had worked for cash than ever before, they had travelled further, encountered more and a greater variety of foreigners and seen more of the foreigners' engines of destruction and construction. With cash earned during the war and payments under the Australian scheme for war damage compensation, Papua New Guineans also had more money than before.

The war had directed Australian attention to their north: nearly one in 20 Australians had gone to New Guinea in uniform. Australian perception of Papua New Guineans had been transformed: from 1942 Papua New Guineans were recognized as the 'Fuzzy Wuzzy Angels'. Conscious of a debt to Papua New Guineans, Australians proclaimed new policies and the Australian parliament was willing to subsidize development. Although granted better labour laws, improved health and education services, and more chances to earn cash, many Papua New Guineans who heard that their war services were to be rewarded were disappointed in the post-war. Movements that they themselves initiated—by Tommy Kabu and Paliau Maloat, for example—failed, and by the mid 1960s when real opportunities opened up for Papua New Guineans, it was the next and better educated generation who moved into the positions of power.—HN

Further reading

Nelson, H, 1980. 'Taim bilong pait: the impact of the Second World War on Papua New Guinea', in W McCoy (ed.), *Southeast Asia Under Japanese Occupation*, Yale University Press.

War in Fiji

The news of the outbreak of World War II broke in Fiji on 4 September 1939, and the colony, like the rest of the British Empire, was at war. The principle that 'might is right' had to be defeated to protect 'settled peace and security of justice and liberty among nations', the governor informed the people through an emergency radio broadcast. Immediately, the colony was put on a war footing; censorship was imposed on all postal and telegraphic communication, the movement of enemy aliens restricted, and a Necessary Foodstuff and Controls Committee established to prevent profiteering. Early in 1940, individual and residential taxes were increased by 25 per cent and corporate income taxes by 50 per cent. By early 1942 these increases had produced £110 000 in additional revenues. Eventually, Fiji's war expenditure amounted to nearly £5 million, the largest of any comparable colony in the empire, and nearly half the total local revenue raised during the wars. Voluntary contributions enlarged this contribution by significant but unknown amounts. The Patriotic Knitting and Sewing Society, led mostly by European women, was an effective raiser of funds. Fijian men and women performed traditional dances and Indo-Fijians staged soccer and singing competitions to raise funds for the war.

The first contingent of foreign troops, from New Zealand, arrived in November 1940; their numbers were augmented at the end of 1941, when New Zealand assumed responsibility for the defence of the colony. After the onset of the Pacific War following Japanese attack on PEARL HARBOR on 7 December 1941, much larger forces, totalling 8000 troops, mostly Americans arrived. Nadi, in Western Viti Levu, became home for a large number of infantrymen, a fighter aerodrome, a trans-Pacific airport, and a command station, as well as the base for coastal, field and anti-aircraft artillery units. The resulting concentration of people and activity infused significant amounts of cash into the local subsistence economy, which brought about its own changes. The rowdy presence of American soldiers in the hotels, streets and cinemas caused concern to the colonial officialdom keen to maintain the colonial social protocol of limited interaction among the principal ethnic groups.

Fijian response to the war effort was enthusiastic and their service distinguished. The government's Fijian recruitment campaign was facilitated by the hierarchical organization of the Fijian society. Fijians, furthermore, were no strangers to warfare; bravery and courage in battle were values upon which their society placed great emphasis, and physical prowess demonstrated in war was an important rite of passage. Of Fiji's 262 war dead, there were 139 indigenous Fijians, 29 of whom were killed in action while the rest died from wounds, sickness and disease. The soldiers returned as heroes from Solomon Islands, many decorated for bravery. The highest award, the Victoria Cross, was presented posthumously to Corporal Sefanaia Sukunaivalu in November 1944 for his bravery in the Solomon Islands campaign. The Indo-Fijian response to the war effort was lukewarm, partly because of an ineffective recruitment drive and partly because Indo-Fijian leaders, standing on the principle of equal pay, equal worth, equal risk, demanded the same compensation and allowances as European soldiers. Membership in the British Empire was no badge of honour for them. The COLONIAL SUGAR REFINING COMPANY, the main employer of Indian labour, discouraged recruitment among its tenants. The government itself wanted Indian farmers to make their war contribution through increased production of foodstuffs. Europeans also opposed the recruitment of Indians as soldiers, suspecting their loyalty and holding them responsible for the gathering pace of anti-colonial events on the Indian subcontinent which they could not fathom but which they detested intensely.

In the 1950s, partly because of the reputation as skilled jungle fighters they gained during the war, Fijians were sent to Malaya to combat communist insurgency there. The First Battalion of the Fiji Military Forces, which had been reconstituted early in 1950 under a 1948 defence agreement between Fiji and New Zealand, left in January 1952, initially on a commission of two years, which was later extended to four. By 1953 there were 850 men from Fiji in Malaya, of whom 800 were Fijians (0.6 per cent of the total Fijian population). Not surprisingly, Fijians covered themselves in medals once again: two Orders of the British Empire, one Member of the British Empire, one British Empire Medal, two Military Crosses, two Distinguished Conduct Medals, five Military Medals and 24 Mentions in Despatches. Unrealized at the time, the absence of able-bodied Fijian men from their villages cost the Fijian people valuable productive time in a period of rapid change.

The war ended Fiji's isolation and enhanced its position in regional affairs. The wartime aerodrome at Nadi was declared an international airport in May 1950, becoming a transit point for Tasman Empire Airways Limited (TEAL, now Air New Zealand), Pan American Airways and Qantas. Fiji Airways, formed in 1954, linked the two main islands of the colony. CRUISE SHIPS began to visit Fiji with increased frequency. Internally, a regular and scheduled transportation system began to take shape. Suva was declared a city in 1953, after being a town for 72 years. Three years later, living up to its new image and responsibilities to multiracial taxpayers, the city opened its once exclusively European Suva Sea Baths to all races, and the city's affairs were once again, from January 1949, managed by a fully elected council. Organized, colony-wide multiracial competitions in soccer, rugby, tennis and cricket began to bring the various ethnic groups together in ways that might not have seemed feasible before the war.—BVL

Further reading

Lal, B V, 1992. *Broken Waves: a history of the Fiji Islands in the 20th century*, University of Hawai'i Press.

Ravuvu, A, 1974. *Fijians at War*, University of the South Pacific.

Tonga in the war

On 3 September 1939 Tonga (population 33 000) declared war on Germany, and Great Britain handed over the responsibility for the defence of TONGA to New Zealand, a responsibility taken over by the United States on the outbreak of the Pacific War. Virtually every Tongan male volunteered to join the newly formed Tonga Defence Force (with Tongan and New Zealand officers), which eventually sent a platoon to Solomon Islands and another to Bougainville. Thirty thousand US servicemen passed through Tonga during World War II, at times more than doubling the adult population of Tongatapu. The numbers, wealth, superior technology and youthful high spirits of the US forces undermined Tonga's subsistence economy and hierarchical society, bringing (together with the greatly increased prices for copra) unheard-of wealth to ordinary Tongan people.

The example and influence of Queen SĀLOTE meant that Tongans did not lose their heads completely or develop the sort of CARGO CULT that was common elsewhere in the Pacific after the war. Her exhortations and example meant that Tonga's financial contribution to the war effort was outstanding among Pacific and small nations. Her government allocated an average £20 000 for defence each year of the war. As well as supporting the Red Cross and Tongan Comforts Fund, Tonga collected enough money during the war to buy four Spitfires for Great Britain's Royal Air Force. The three planes commissioned were named the *Queen Sālote, Prince Tungī,* and *Tupou I*, and the first two planes were flown in combat. Two members of the Tonga Defence Force died in Solomon Islands, and a much greater number in war-related accidents in Tonga itself.

In the early years of the war, relations between Tongans and the US forces were good, but as the war receded, relations soured, and the officers of the US advanced naval base sometimes acted in despotic ways. A very real benefit was that US Army doctors set up clinics and treated the people for injury and illness and gave practical lectures on public health. However, the advent of a cash economy, with its emphasis on individual ownership of property, led to a slow but steady decline in the Tongan ideal of communalism.—EW-E

Sources/further reading

Hornabrook, J S, 1951. New Zealand and the Tonga Defence Force 1939–1945, MA thesis, Victoria University of Wellington.

Wood-Ellem, E, 1999. *Queen Sālote of Tonga: the story of an era, 1900–1965*, Auckland University Press.

Kokoda Track

The Kokoda Track is a single-file track crossing the Owen Stanley Ranges of Papua New Guinea, joining Port Moresby in the Gulf of Papua with Kokoda, an administration outpost, on the foothills inland from Popendetta, Dobudura and Buna on the northern coast. The track rises to 2250 m and takes four to six days to traverse. Relatively insignificant for Papuans, it became an icon for Australians when an advancing Japanese army was forced to retreat and was eventually beaten in late 1942 after several months' exhausting and costly jungle warfare involving Australian and Papuan infantry. Papuan carriers earned the gratitude of Australians, as well as the enduring name 'Fuzzy-Wuzzy Angels' because of their hairstyles and heroism. The recapture of the Kokoda Track and outpost was an early sign that the war had turned against the Japanese. (See PAPUA NEW GUINEA IN THE WAR.)—MQ

Guadalcanal

World War II encroached directly on Solomon Islands soon after the attack on PEARL HARBOR on 7 December 1941, but the build-up to the heavy fighting there was slow and gradual. Most European residents evacuated the group during February 1942. Japanese aircraft had bombed the island of Gavutu on 22 January, but it was not until 3 May that Japanese troops occupied the neighbouring administrative centre of Tulagi. On 27 May more troops began landing at Tenaru on nearby Guadalcanal. On 6 July they began building an airfield at Lunga on the largest plain in the Solomons. Meanwhile, 'coastwatchers' in the hills above observed the construction work and relayed progress reports to US military authorities in Vanuatu.

The airfield was designed to give the Japanese a strategic advantage in the contest for control of the southwest Pacific. Its completion could have represented a serious threat to the security of Fiji, New Caledonia, eastern Australia and the American shipping in the area. Accordingly, on 7 August, when it was almost finished, a large US naval and marine force invaded Guadalcanal and captured the airport which they named Henderson Field, after a hero of the Battle of Midway. The Japanese response was swift and fierce. For the next six months they sought to dislodge the Americans with a series of assaults by land, air and sea. The Americans defended with desperate vigour. Losses were huge on both sides. The Japanese counter-attack began with the bloody but indecisive naval battle of Savo Island on the night of 8–9 August. It continued with bitterly fought land actions, notably at Tenaru (21 August) and Bloody Ridge (12 September); and further naval actions at Cape Esperance (11 October) and Santa Cruz (25–26 October). Meanwhile, the American defenders were also subjected to steady air attacks, which they managed to withstand mainly because of early warnings provided by coastwatchers on islands to the northwest. At length, conceding a tactical defeat, the Japanese abandoned Guadalcanal. During 1–7 February 1943 they withdrew 10 000 troops, but strengthened their positions further north and maintained air attacks on the island until June.

The contest for Guadalcanal was crucial to the Pacific War. It marked the end of the southward advance of the Japanese. Conversely, it was the point from which the US and its Allies would change from defenders to attackers. It was also the most prolonged single campaign in the Pacific War. Guadalcanal became a synonym for American bravery and endurance under fire.—HL

Pearl Harbor

Pearl Harbor, a lagoon on the Pearl River on the island of Oʻahu, Hawaiʻi, was first proposed to be ceded to the US government for use as a naval station in 1873 during the reign of Lunalilo. Its strategic location was intended to tempt the Americans into a reciprocity treaty, but initial opposition from Native Hawaiians caused the offer to be withdrawn. Later, in the reign of Kalākaua, the exclusive right to use it as an American naval coaling and repair station was included in the treaty and was finally approved by the American senate on 20 January 1887. After assurances that this posed no threat to Hawaiian independence, the treaty was ratified by Kalākaua on 20 October 1887.

In the late 1890s, even as the treaty of annexation of Hawaiʻi was before Congress, the start of the Spanish–American War brought an enthusiastic reception to American soldiers in Hawaiʻi, and Pearl Harbor became a convenient mid-ocean stopover for troops involved in the Philippines. In 1898 and 1899 lands adjacent to the harbour were officially designated as 'Naval Station, Honolulu' and the channel was widened and deepened. Other nearby areas were later occupied by US military establishments—the first of these, Fort Shafter, becoming the army headquarters. More forts were developed to guard Honolulu and Pearl Harbor, and a dry-dock was completed in 1919. By the end of World War I, these defence outposts and a network of supporting roads were in place, and the first airfield was established, Luke Field on Ford Island. Three more airfields followed, including Hickam Field, adjacent to Pearl Harbor, which became Hickam Air Force Base, headquarters for the Pacific air command.

The surprise Japanese attack on Pearl Harbor on 7 December 1941, just before 8.00 am, involved bomber units striking from south and north. The first wave of dive bombers was followed by 40 torpedo bombers, then 50 horizontal bombers and 45 fighter planes. In that first 15-minute attack, almost the entire air strength of Oʻahu was wiped out and enormous damage was done to the US Pacific Fleet. One or two ships managed to get clear but only until the second wave of dive bombers arrived. Total casualties (killed, missing and wounded) were 3435. Very little damage had been caused in the city and the population was immediately mobilized. Civilian doctors and nurses rushed to assist the wounded at Pearl Harbor and at the emergency hospital. Hawaiʻi remained headquarters for the Pacific War as well as an important supply area, providing recreation and recuperation facilities to many thousands of American personnel, and Pearl Harbor has since retained its strategic military value.—KRF

NINE POST-WAR PACIFIC

Cargo cults

Cargo cults were acts of protestation as well as of high expectation, characteristically non-cooperative and altercatory. People grouped afresh to be independent from missions that presented the new faith in too foreign a fashion and from governments demanding head-tax and productivity for international markets. The dream of the cargo cult is for a transformation in which the subversions of the intruders will become irrelevant: the new goods being accessible to all and the locals regaining the power—total and 'sacro-political'—that they had lost. The outward forms of cargo cultism, however, vary according to cultural context and take on different aspects in the passages of colonial and neo-colonial history. The most famous early cargo movement was dubbed the 'VAILALA MADNESS' (1917), and this name was often used for comparable movements before the term 'cargo cult' was popularized by Lucy Mair.

Twenty years later, World War II brought dramatic repercussions to the Pacific. The bombing of PEARL HARBOR by the Japanese marked their entrance into the war (1941), but Hawaiʻi had already been experiencing rapid social change as a US territory since 1900. In far less developed Melanesia, Japanese expansion towards Australia involved military incursions all along the north coast of the large New Guinea island, through Manus and the Bismarck Archipelago and on into Solomon Islands as far as GUADALCANAL. Some Micronesian islands important for Japan were also taken, although in fact they received League of Nations mandate of the Marianas and Marshall Islands after World War I. Various islands witnessed astounding, if short-term, manifestations of high technology through the Allied and (most noticeably) the American repulsion of Japan's advance, especially Solomon Islands and the New Guinea coastal and island areas. At Momote on Loniu in the Admiralty group alone, for instance, at least 1 000 000 black and white American servicemen passed through the air base in one year (1944–45). Carrier ships disgorged large numbers of tanks and amphibious landing-craft (known as DUKWs) there, a four-lane highway was built down the centre of the island, and Manus experienced a sudden influx of American dollars. Other significant places with large camps included Saidor on the New Guinea coast east of Madang, and Meokwundi Island off Biak in Irian Jaya. Madang, Biak and Manus all experienced well-known cargo cultist outbursts.

Yali Singina of Sor (in the hinterland from Saidor) was an Australian-trained native coast-watcher and war hero who remained faithful to the Allied cause because he had been promised that the Australian government would radically improve the living conditions of his people after the war. He became the object of intense cargoist expectations, and, after falling disillusioned with Catholic and Lutheran missionaries (for criticizing his sexual laxity) and the post-war administration (for not keeping its aforementioned promise), he began his own 'work' (*wok bilong Yali*). The tentacles of his well-organized movement—held together by lieutenants and 'law bosses'—stretched from Manam Island to the west towards the Huon peninsular in the east (a few Yali missionaries even operating near Goroka in the Highlands). The cult splintered after Yali's death in 1975.

Among the Biak peoples in Irian Jaya, a movement seeing the promise of *Koreri* or 'eternal life' (of riches) in the teachings and healings of the Insumbabi island prophetess Angganita, turned to magico-military action when the Japanese invaders kept her in custody. The 'AB' Army, formed to secure her release, was decimated by Japanese troops in October 1943 (when Angganita had already been killed). The army's anagram, 'America Blanda', showed the high hopes pinned on the Americans as rumoured saviours, whose awesome forces came to Meokwindi—as if miraculously—in 1944, an event which reinforced this most popular of Koreri movements for a further 10 years. Meanwhile, on Baluan Island, south of Manus, one Paliau Maloat returned from his time as chief of police in Rabaul, New Britain, under both Australian and Japanese rule. On this obscure outlier he began preaching a new fashion (*nupela pasin*) of social organization and thought, both deliberately opposed to government and mission. For the early post-war years, cargoist hopes were also pinned on Paliau, but he was himself more interested in building upon a Manus trust fund (albeit for his own manipulations), setting up a local government, and founding an independent church.

During the 1970s many well-known cargo movements were actually tending towards independent churches, and by then various such churches had emerged without having much of a cargoist basis. Some of these local movements to set up alternatives to the mission denominations were highly syncretic (mixing traditional and Christian movements), or split-dimensional (claiming the Bible was for the whites and a new version of the traditional past for islanders). In the latter cases they could be neo-traditional or nativistic rather than Christian in message, yet using the altars, ranks of 'ministers', church buildings, blackboards and written sloganing from the world of the missions. Syncretistic movements or attempts to create independent churches have not been confined to Melanesia; they have a much larger history in the wider Pacific.

The earliest sizeable collective action of religious rebellion in the Pacific was the Mamaia movement on Tahiti (1828–33). While a military conflict continued between the exiled POMARE II and custodians of the old war cult of Oro, prophet-diviners claimed combined—or 'synthesized'—access to Jesus and traditional mana so as to usher in a new rule of freedom. Mission moral restrictiveness was to give way to sexual licence, and there was talk of cargo coming 'from the skies' (with Polynesian vertical cosmology always tending to stress the descent of power from above). Something comparable occurred on the Samoan group as a result of the freelance missionary prophet Siovili of Eva, whose effects lasted for some 40 years (especially 1830–65) and who achieved an adherence of some 5000 persons. Siovili and his prophetesses had many characteristics of the old mediums, yet their messages were about the imminent return of Sisu, God's son, along with a cargo ship sent by 'the king of the skies'.

The first formal independent church among Pacific islanders was also in Polynesia. In 1852, Tāufa'āhau (George TUPOU I) had managed to combine the 'secular' and 'sacred' chieftainships of the Tongan group into his own person, and then had to overcome the anomaly of not being head of a burgeoning Wesleyan church. His solution came through the missionary Shirley BAKER's suggestion that Tonga split from Australian Methodism, which the ruler achieved by creating the Free Church of Tonga in 1875, with his kingship now involving divine as well as constitutional properties. Not long after, the Maori prophet Te Kooti's 'Ringatu' movement presented as a 'Maori Christian church', the first in a cluster of smaller Maori breakaways from mainstream churches. The Ratana church (founded in 1928, and now 20 000 strong), is outstanding among them. Around 25 such indigenous-inspired independents can be found across Micronesia and Polynesia today, the most sensationalist of recent ones surrounding Mrs Piho of Rakahanga in Cook

Islands. A healer, she self-designates as Jesus, and attempted to use New Zealand television to raise money for her following.

The independent churches of Melanesia make up a more complicated scene. From 20 more or less classic cases by 1990, the spread of Charismatic or Pentecostal style worship has generated many splinter congregations (mainly in the Papua New Guinea Highlands and mimicking a host of sectarian foreign missions). Of the better known independents, some recall parallel phenomena in black Africa. Silas Eto or the Holy Mama of New Georgia (1905–84), for example, wore long white robes and a turban, and like Simon Kimbangau of the Congo, his name has been incorporated into the liturgy along with the members of the Trinity. On Fiji, 'Vuniwai' Loaniceva, (1921–), a healer-prophet like Eto and one who also broke from Methodism, encourages his close followers to wear robes like himself in worship. Eto separated in 1960 heading the Christian Fellowship church, Loarnieva in 1953 with the Congregation of the Poor.

A number of cargo cults have metamorphosed into independent churches. Perhaps the most famous is the Peli ('hawk') Association. Originating with indigenous apocalypt Matias Yaliwan in 1969, and backed by a managerial side-kick Daniel Hawina, the Peli dream focused on Mt Hurun and a great event presaged there for the date 7/7/1971. Yaliwan ascribed lack of fertility in the Mt Torricelli region to the fact that American geodesic markers had been placed on Hurun. With thousands of people involved in their removal on the above date, it was collectively understood by Peli subscribers that cargo would miraculously come out of the mountaintop, not just the effects of re-fertilization. About 30 000 people rallied to the newly built village to await the results and join in the related rituals. When nothing dramatic occurred, Hawina skilfully used the presence of in-and-out Canadian Apostolic church missionaries to start a new church (Nie Apostolik), building on the prior Peli constituency and flouting the Catholic majority in the east Sepik hinterland.

While other cargo cults also shifted towards church status, others again have had different histories. Strictly speaking, Paliau was the first to found an independent church in Melanesia—the Baluan Native Christian United church, in 1946. Its teachings were based on his indigenous theology of 'new fashion', which contained the prospect of divine retribution against Australia through the Americans if the former did not do the right thing by his people. The success of Paliau's movement carried high cargoist hope in its train among Manus islanders, but it eventually settled down as a complete alternative way, with its own ecclesiastical pretensions side by side with claims to third-level government. Politics, cargoism and independent churches have by now had a long history of interrelation. MAASINA RULE in Malaita and Guadalcanal just after the last war, for instance, organized itself very much on the basis of previously imposed church rules as it constituted itself into a protest movement for islanders' independence from the British. Other maverick political enterprises were also organized religious forces. The ni-Vanuatu NAGRIAMEL movement for land distribution, led by part-Tongan Jimmy Stephens, was a self-declared independent United Church. Satellites of the anti-Presbyterian, anti-British John FRUM movement on Tanna, southern Vanuatu, were close to the same.

There have been quite direct connections between older new religious movements and modern rebellions. The tragic massacre of the 'AB' army in 1943 provided the inspiration of veritable martyrdom for the anti-Indonesian ORGANISASI PAPUA MERDEKA (OPM, the liberation forces for West Papuan independence founded 1962). Before the emergence of the Bougainville rebellion, John Teosin had become a symbol of possible future instability for Australian holdings on Bougainville with his anti-tax protest on Buka in 1962 (organized non-cooperation which was coupled with rituals and dreams looking to cargo, and which also eventually led to the founding of the Hehela Church). Inspired by Teosin, Damien Damen founded the Ten Shilling movement among the central Bougainvillean Nasioi, also in 1962. This was to provide the ideological stronghold for neo-Luddite protest against the effects of the great copper mine at Panguna. Francis Ona, Damen's frontman on behalf of Mekamui ('Sacred Island'), was behind the formation of the Bougainville Liberation Army, from the start in 1989 of the BOUGAINVILLE CONFLICT AND PEACE PROCESS to its virtual end in 1998. Ona preferred to operate (later with a satellite-connected computer) from the headquarters of what had become the 'Fifty-toea Movement'.

Cargo cults as discrete outbursts in which groups expect the miraculous arrival of the new goods are now infrequent, small affairs confined to Melanesia. Disillusionment over extravagant dreams and with the trickster element revealed in cult leadership have blunted the effects of cargoist innovators. The consolidation of native churches has come to provide a more reliable source of total and spiritual directedness. Promising new and attractive possibilities of modernity, however, raise expectations that are 'cargoistic' (offering the promise of quick development and a rapidly acquired higher standard of living). Education is looked to this way in many districts. And the same applies to politics. Hopes of material improvement are recurrently tied to elections throughout the whole region. Even in earlier days some cargo leaders played on the periodic winding up of election forces. Koriam Urekit, perhaps the earliest national in the new Papua New Guinea Assembly in 1962, developed the technique of combining traditional festival cycles and electioneering among the Pomio and other East New Britain coastal peoples under his aegis, and this explains why the Pomio Kivung has firmly outlived him and remained viable in modern Papua New Guinea politics. Many different quests for 'religious power' have absorbed the old cargoist energies, as the pain of relative deprivation eases, access to new goods widens through monetization, and the talk of Christianity circulates in more literate and highly debated forms.

In Micronesia and especially Polynesia, spiritual power (mana) always counted for as much as material blessing, and the old alternatives of separatist movements had more to do with a sudden turning against mainline churches, such as when administrator Arthur Grimble had to suppress the 'Swords of Gamaliel' of the Onotoa prophet Ten Naewa (Southern Gilberts), men who were sent by Ten to kill Catholics on an already 'Protestantized' atoll (1930–32). But now the quest for spiritual power works itself out more in competition between well-established, conservative island churches and strong newer sectarian groups offering 'more complete' packages of mana.

In Melanesia, by comparison, preoccupation with the material fruits of religiosity have lessened over time in favour of secular-materialistic tendencies on one hand, and yearnings for the visible manifestations of spirit power on the other. Earlier forms of collective violent protest may have their longer-term extensions in the form of the great armed rebellions of modern times, so that one could write a history of armed uprisings from Navosavakandua's Fijian hill-tribes insurrection of 1883–85 to the Bougainville liberation fighters. But the main lines in the history of the relationship between religion and protest have been towards politicization. In older neo-Marxist terminology this has been described as a journey from the proto-political or pre-modern political to modern politics, yet in reality the whole of the Pacific has seen a fascinating mixture of continuing traditionalism and tribalism within the constraining forum of councils and parliamentary assemblies over the last three decades. The emergence of political parties and the coalitions of such are the main order of the day, and at times the influence of the religious vision shines through in a solidarity against neo-colonial conditions. As for the Pacific churches, they have attained a steady religious predominance, but they have been tested and chastened by cargo cults and other new religious movements across Oceania for not shedding foreignness or integrating as authentically and as healthily with indigenous cultural impetuses as they might have since pioneer missionary days. Certainly cargo cults and other new religious movements are worth serious study and attention, rather than cynicism and socio-political repression, for they reflect collective 'rites of passage' or adjustments—whether acculturative or reactionary—mediating between small-scale traditional cultures and new globalist ways of operating.—GWT

Further reading

Lawrence, P, 1964. *Road Belong Cargo: a study of the Cargo movement in the southern Madang district, New Guinea*, Manchester University Press.

Lindstrom, L, 1993. *Cargo Cult: strange stories of desire from Melanesia and beyond*, University of Hawai'i Press.

Mair, L P, 1963. *New Nations*, Weidenfeld & Nicolson.

Worsley, P, 1968. *The Trumpet Shall Sound: a study of 'cargo' cults in Melanesia*, Schocken Books.

Nuclear testing

Foreigners tested nuclear bombs in the Pacific islands for half a century, from 1946 to 1996. They were tested there because the islands were remote from the populations of the testing powers: the United States, the United Kingdom and France. The islands were not remote from Pacific island populations; they were, instead, in American, British and French overseas territories whose peoples could not stop nuclear testing because they lacked the formal political sovereignty to do so. Colonialism and nuclear testing went together.

The driving force behind nuclear testing was the arms race that accompanied the Cold War. Competition between the nuclear powers centred first on developing the atomic bomb (an American monopoly until 1949), then on creating the vastly more destructive thermonuclear or hydrogen bomb, and later refining bombs to make them smaller and easy to deliver. Pacific testing helped the nuclear powers to reach all these objectives and—in the face of worldwide protest—it continued even after the end of the Cold War, when France conducted a final series of underground explosions in 1995 and 1996.

■ *US nuclear tests, 1946–62* The United States exploded bombs over BIKINI and Enewetak atolls in Marshall Islands from 1946 until 1958, moved to Johnston Atoll and Kiritimati (Christmas Island) in 1962 and then stopped all atmospheric testing under the terms of the 1963 Partial Test Ban Treaty. No further American tests took place in the Pacific.

The first effect of the American testing program was the relocation of people living on atolls in the northern Marshall Islands. To make way for the testing, the Americans evacuated people from their home islands, either temporarily or for what turned out to be decades. For the first tests in 1946, for example, the Americans evacuated the people not only of Bikini Atoll where the bombs were to be exploded but also of the nearby atolls of Enewetak, Rongelap and Wotho. The military commander of Marshall Islands, Commodore Ben H Wyatt, had the task of explaining to people why they had to leave. He recounted the Biblical story of the flight of the Israelites from Egypt, when God showed them the way with a pillar of smoke by day and a pillar of fire by night, and said America, under the guidance of God, was developing something just as effective, something that could be used 'if in the future any nation attacked the peoples of God'. A Bikinian chief, Lore Kessibuki, later recalled that 'we didn't feel we had any other choice but to obey the Americans'.

The second effect was radioactive contamination, which began in 1946 and will endure in some parts of the Pacific for thousands of years. The 1946 test, code-named Baker, was an underwater explosion which created a column of 2 000 000 tonnes of water more than 1 km high over the Bikini lagoon and which blanketed the entire area with radioactive spray.

From Baker onwards Bikini Atoll lost its pristine environment. Indeed a nuclear test there in 1954 created the worst contamination in the history of the American testing program. Code-named Bravo, the test was one of a series of thermonuclear explosions in Marshall Islands that year, all with explosive yields hundreds of times greater than that of the Hiroshima bomb. Bravo, a gigantic bomb, spread radioactive fallout over all atolls to the east of Bikini in northern Marshall Islands, most seriously over Rongelap, whose people were exposed to a snowfall of radioactive particles which fell gently on their islands for a period of hours. People further to the east on Utrik Atoll experienced a finer mist of fallout when the radioactive cloud generated by Bravo reached them the following day.

The people of Rongelap and Utrik suffered both short-term and long-term injuries from radioactive fallout. Many of the Rongelapese experienced immediate radiation sickness. They had burns on exposed parts of the body, they vomited and their hair fell out in tufts. Then they recovered. Long-term injuries appeared years later in the form of stunted physical development of some children, miscarriages, stillbirths, an extraordinarily high proportion of thyroid growths, and—insidiously—a fear that all illnesses were a consequence of the bomb.

As the political sophistication of the Marshallese grew, so did their demands for clean-up and compensation. A campaign by the people of Enewetak, site of many 1950s tests, led to an attempted decontamination of the atoll in the late 1970s at a cost of US$100 million. A similar clean-up of Bikini occurred in the 1990s. After the new Republic of the Marshall Islands entered into free association with the United States in 1986, the US government funded compensation and a health care program for the people of the four recognized 'radiation atolls', Bikini, Enewetak, Rongelap and Utrik. Tens of millions of dollars have since gone to hundreds of individuals who suffer from one of 25 medical conditions presumed to result from radiation exposure.

The political sequel to American testing was the world's first NUCLEAR-FREE CONSTITUTION, drawn up by the US territory of Palau in 1979 in advance of a new political status. Palauans gave their constitution overwhelming popular support when it was first promulgated, but the United States objected, fearing restrictions on its military forces. The result was a stalemate for 13 years during which, in successive referenda on their constitution, Palauans consistently failed to vote by the constitutionally required majority of 75 per cent to abandon the nuclear-free provisions. The deadlock was finally broken in 1992, when the hurdle to be cleared changed to a simple majority. On that basis, Palauans agreed to free association with the United States on the terms the Americans wanted and Palau gained independence in 1994.

■ *British nuclear tests, 1957–58* British nuclear tests in the Pacific were on a much smaller scale than those of the Americans. The United Kingdom exploded thermonuclear weapons over Kiritimati and Malden Island in the Gilbert and Ellice Islands Colony in 1957 and 1958. About 300 Gilbertese plantation labourers were on Kiritimati at the time, and for some tests, though not others, they were taken on board Royal Navy ships for protection. At least 39 Fijians joined the British force of 21 000. Research on the health effects of the tests remains inconclusive, despite alarming anecdotal evidence, and in 1998 the European Court of Human Rights rejected a claim for compensation by British test veterans.

■ *French nuclear tests, 1966–96* France moved its nuclear tests to French Polynesia after being forced out of the Sahara by Algeria, which won independence in 1962.

The French built testing facilities on two uninhabited atolls in the Tuamotu archipelago, Moruroa and Fangataufa, and exploded as many as 190 nuclear bombs there over a period of 30 years. For the first nine years, from 1966 to the end of 1974, French bombs exploded in the atmosphere, usually suspended from balloons at levels which created radioactive fallout. Regional anti-nuclear protests then compelled the French to switch to underground explosions conducted in deep shafts dug beneath the land surface of Moruroa Atoll. After land sites grew scarce, the shafts were drilled and bombs detonated beneath the base of the atoll lagoon.

Strict military secrecy for 30 years ensures that much less is known about French than about American tests, but some firm conclusions can be reached. The atmospheric trials created fallout that sometimes blew east towards Latin America and sometimes, tracked by New Zealand monitoring equipment, west towards the countries of the South Pacific. The French authorities built fallout shelters for islanders within the danger zone, such as Tureia and Mangareva, and told them to take precautions. Underground tests, while safer, were not without hazard. A bomb stuck half way down the shaft in 1979. When exploded, it produced a tidal wave that swept over Moruroa. A storm in 1981 dislodged plutonium-impregnated tar on the northern rim of the atoll, and pounding seas took it into the lagoon and the open ocean. The islands of Moruroa sank metres as they settled over the nuclear caverns beneath. France never admitted to causing radioactive injuries and consistently claimed a virtually perfect safety record for the entire period of testing. For this reason France has not paid compensation, and the health effects of French testing remain disputed. A 1998 report by the International Atomic Energy Agency found no significant radioactive contamination at Moruroa.

Nuclear testing made French Polynesia a nuclear dependency economically and a pro-French dependency politically. The tests brought thousands of army personnel to French Polynesia, thousands of jobs and a lot of money. *La bombe* created an economy of transfer, in which funds flowed freely from the other side of the world in return for strategic services. Subsidization, on a staggering scale, propelled French Polynesia from villages, subsistence and cash crops into urbanization, wages and modernity. If we treat that subsidy as foreign aid, French Polynesia was receiving 354 times as much aid per capita in 1992 as the average for developing countries. The result is a standard of living among the highest in the South Pacific.

French military spending left the pro-independence political parties without arguments likely to convince people whose livelihoods depended on it. Such parties have never won more than minority support in elections for the territorial assembly. Government television from Paris has conveyed a relentlessly pro-French cultural message, and the education system has done the same in the schools.

■ *Nuclear-free Pacific* French testing in the rest of the Pacific islands had the opposite effect politically. French tests inspired a nuclear-free movement that became part of the region's post-colonial identity (REGIONAL COOPERATION AND INITIATIVES). As territories gained independence, they expressed their anti-colonialism by condemning French nuclear tests and embracing the goal of a 'nuclear-free Pacific'. Reflecting popular sentiment, island governments called for an end to French testing from the first meeting of the SOUTH PACIFIC FORUM in 1971. As the Forum expanded, so did the number of countries opposed to France's nuclear tests. By 1985 the Forum had produced the South Pacific Nuclear-Free Zone Treaty, under which signatory states agreed not to acquire, possess or test nuclear weapons in the Forum area.

Two events, one in 1985 and the other in 1995, mobilized anti-nuclear feeling in the South Pacific. The first was the Rainbow Warrior affair, when France sent secret service agents to New Zealand. These agents set off explosions beneath the Greenpeace vessel *Rainbow Warrior* in Auckland Harbour, where it was berthed before a protest voyage to Moruroa Atoll. The explosions sank the vessel and killed a Greenpeace activist, Fernanda Pereira. The French government initially denied involvement, but New Zealand police arrested a man and a woman who turned out to be French agents. The revelation that France had organized 'state terrorism' in defence of its nuclear tests produced a wave of anti-French feeling in the South Pacific.

The Greenpeace ship *Rainbow Warrior I* after its sinking in Auckland Harbour, 1985

The second event was the announcement by the French President Jacques Chirac in June 1995 that France, having suspended tests in 1992, intended to conduct a final test series. The French decision stirred popular and official protests within French Polynesia, throughout the Pacific, and soon throughout the world. Thousands of people took to the streets in Tahiti in an anti-nuclear demonstration larger than any since 1973. A delegation from the SOUTH PACIFIC FORUM protested formally in Paris. Anti-French fever gripped Australia and New Zealand. When the Greenpeace vessel *Rainbow Warrior II* entered the exclusion zone around Moruroa Atoll on 10 July 1995, 10 years to the day since the sinking of its namesake, French naval commandos stormed aboard, provoking a new level of regional protest. The first nuclear test a few months later caused a major riot in Tahiti, where demonstrators looted and burnt part of the territory's capital Pape'ete.

Under the pressure of world opinion France concluded its tests ahead of time in 1996, and soon afterwards signed the protocols to the South Pacific Nuclear-Free Zone Treaty, together with Britain and the United States. All five declared nuclear powers now endorse the treaty, and the era of nuclear testing in the Pacific islands is over. Yet the nuclear legacy lives on in the strong nuclear-free sentiment of the people of the region, in the injuries done to islanders and their descendants and in the contamination of atoll environments.—SF

■ ***Bikini Atoll*** In 1946 Bikini Atoll was selected as the United States' first post-war NUCLEAR TESTING site in the Pacific. The atoll's remote location in the northern Marshall Islands was ideal for American purposes, and its small community of about 170 people was relocated on Kili Island in the south. Between 1946 and 1958, 23 nuclear tests were conducted at Bikini, and large parts of the atoll suffered radiological contamination. Bikini Islanders have never adjusted to their unwanted relocation and have demanded a return to their ancestral homeland. A clean-up and resettlement of Bikini is being planned for early in the 21st century. The famous French bathing suit that also exploded on the world scene in 1946 was named after the atoll.—RCK

Decolonization

Decolonization, unlike independence, emphasizes the metropolitan power's policies and initiatives in restoring sovereignty to (or conferring it upon) dependent peoples. There have been several significant anti-colonial movements in the Pacific islands; but decolonization has sometimes occurred in their absence, and it is not a necessary consequence of a community's demands. Great Power politics have sometimes proved more consequential. When the Netherlands departed from West Papua, the United Nations endorsed an 'act of free choice' which made it (as Irian Jaya) an Indonesian province.

Decolonization was not inevitable, nor was it unconditional. Until the 1940s, dominion status seemed the only possible outcome in British dependencies, and then probably for settler societies only. The Balfour Declaration of 1926 stated that the settler dominions were 'autonomous communities within the British Empire, in no way subordinate to one another in respect of their domestic or external affairs, though united by a common allegiance to the Crown, and freely associated as members of the British Commonwealth of Nations'. The independence of Asian and African colonies broadened the options, and the process was encouraged by the 1960 Declaration of Granting of Independence to Colonial Countries and Peoples issued by the United Nations. Britain abandoned the assumption that small populations could not sustain a viable independence, but nevertheless, decolonization was hedged by conditions, including (Westminster-style) parliamentary democracy, an independent public service and judiciary, and mechanisms for financial accountability. The potential government had to win an electoral mandate and demonstrate its capacity to provide a stable government.

Those British requirements were readily met in the Pacific once the larger ex-colonies of Africa and Asia created new precedents. Britain decolonized as soon as credible successor governments were available: Fiji in 1970, Solomon Islands and Tuvalu in 1978, Kiribati in 1979. Tonga re-emerged from its protectorate in 1970. In 1980 the Anglo–French CONDOMINIUM of the New Hebrides became the Republic of Vanuatu, though that process was impeded by

French obstruction and secessionism. French policy had changed direction since the 1946 constitution recognized 'peoples and nations' in overseas France, and allowed them to create political parties. Until the 1950s, therefore, French Polynesia made steady moves towards autonomy, and even full independence seemed possible (NATIONALISM IN FRENCH TERRITORIES). Pouvana'a A OOPA's *Rassemblement Démocratique des Populations Tahitiennes* aspired to autonomy in association with France. That prospect—and the mechanisms of partial autonomy—were put into reverse with the installation of Charles de Gaulle's Fifth Republic and the initiation of NUCLEAR TESTING.

France was equally determined to retain sovereignty in New Caledonia. Since Kanaks were a minority, and the settler-dominated majority resolved to maintain French authority, politics grew violent in the 1980s, reaching a climax in May 1988 when French troops stormed the cave where Kanak militants held hostages. Three soldiers and 19 Kanaks died. That tragedy provoked negotiations leading to the MATIGNON ACCORD which deferred a decision on independence, by referendum, until the 1998 NOUMEA ACCORD. France retains sovereignty over Wallis and Futuna Islands as well.

New Zealand's decolonization strategies were precocious and innovative, accommodating unusually intimate relations with the peoples of the dependent territories. Very large numbers of Samoans, Cook Islanders and Niueans live in New Zealand, permanently or for much of their working lives. These demographic and economic circumstances necessarily affected the form of political relationships. Discussions with Western Samoa began as early as 1948, leading to independence in 1962—the first of the Pacific islands to reach this status. Again, New Zealand pioneered the intermediate status of 'free association' with the Cook Islands in 1965, whereby Cook Islanders hold dual citizenship. This was the model for free association between Niue and New Zealand in 1974, and it was adapted for island groups in the United States Trust Territory of the Pacific Islands.

The Northern Marianas achieved United States Commonwealth status in 1976. Yap, Chuuk, Pohnpei and Kosrae formed the Federated States of Micronesia (FSM). The FSM and the Republic of the Marshall Islands entered free association with the United States in 1986, and Palau did the same in 1994. Citizens of associated states enjoy free access to the United States. Neither free association nor full independence covers all cases; the United States maintains the territories of American Samoa and Guam, and New Zealand is still responsible for the tiny population of Tokelau.

Free association might have been thought appropriate for the Australian dependent territories, but the 'white Australia' policy, which prevailed until the late 1960s, made this option unthinkable by Australian governments. Nauru achieved full independence in 1968. Papua New Guinea's status and destiny were ambivalent for many years. Several expatriate and indigenous political leaders assumed that as an Australian territory (analogous to the Northern Territory) it might become Australia's seventh state. That possibility was finally extinguished only in 1972, when a conservative government decided to press towards decolonization. Later that same year, Australians elected the Labor Party to office. Prime Minister Whitlam was determined to decolonize within three years; and Papua New Guinea's election of 1972 produced a House of Assembly which was willing to cooperate towards that outcome.

In one perspective, decolonization is the logical end of colonization. In recent years a longer-term view has emerged. A spur to rethinking these relationships was the adoption by the World Bank and many other aid donors, of an interest in human rights issues generally, and 'good governance' in particular. Since the late 1980s, in terms of this agenda, aid donors have become increasingly keen to attach conditions to their aid. This conditionality has been represented as an assault on the sovereignty of independent countries which receive financial support: even, perhaps, recolonization. Since the concerns of good governance include democratic institutions and practices, financial accountability, and a broad range of human rights issues, observers are irresistibly reminded of the conditions which applied to decolonization. On that view, decolonization was not the end of a narrative but merely one episode in a much longer saga of unequal international relations.—DD

Fiji coups, 1987

The Pacific islands' first modern military coup took place in Fiji on 14 May 1987 when the National Federation Party–Fiji Labour Party Coalition was ousted from power by the then Lieutenant-Colonel Sitiveni RABUKA, the third-ranking officer in the Fiji Military Forces. The coalition had won independent Fiji's fifth general election in April. An interim military-installed regime comprising the long-reigning but recently defeated Alliance Party headed by former Prime Minister Ratu Sir Kamisese MARA ran the country until the second coup of 25 September, which derailed delicate constitutional negotiations between the major political leaders then under way. To reinforce his demand for total Fijian political control, Rabuka declared Fiji a republic on 7 October, just three days short of the 113th anniversary of the cession of the islands to the United Kingdom. The new status did not bring the expected respite, however, which led Rabuka to return the country to civilian rule by installing a new president, Ratu Sir Penaia GANILAU who, in turn, appointed Mara as the interim prime minister. 1990 saw the promulgation of a new constitution which, although bitterly opposed by the opposition for its many discriminatory provisions, brought a semblance of constitutional normalcy to the country. That racially-weighted constitution was reviewed by an independent CONSTITUTION REVIEW Commission in 1996 and replaced by another much more broadly acceptable one in 1997.

The debate about the reasons for the military coups of 1987 continues. For some the coup was little more than an indigenous Fijian backlash against an Indian-dominated coalition government, an attempt to protect the paramountcy of Fijian interests in the polity of Fiji. Others saw it as a class struggle between the élite and the masses, with the eastern chiefly establishment of the Koro Sea and their supporters refusing to heed the verdict of the ballot box to relinquish power to political leaders from traditionally subordinate areas. Yet others saw the coup as a political struggle in which ethnicity was used, both as an expression of identity as well as a political tool, to return power to the Fijian establishment.

Whatever its causes, the coup was severely criticized by the international community, and Fiji's membership of the British Commonwealth was allowed to lapse. Pacific leaders, however, saw the coup as essentially an indigenous uprising against an economically successful and numerically preponderant immigrant community. For Fiji, the coup was a traumatic event, a turning point. Even though it was a bloodless affair, the coup unleashed forces which threatened the fabric of society, compromised processes of accountability and transparency in governance, and undermined investor confidence in the economy. It also caused the migration of an estimated 70 000 people, mostly Indo-Fijians, to Australia, New Zealand and North America. The 1997 constitution promises to halt the decline and mark the beginning of a new era in Fiji's political evolution.—BVL

Further reading

Lal, B V, 1988. *Power and Prejudice: the making of the Fiji crisis*, New Zealand Institute of International Affairs.

Lawson, S, 1991. *The Failure of Democratic Politics in Fiji*, Clarendon.

Robertson, R and Tamanisau, A, 1988. *Fiji—shattered coups*, Pluto Press.

Scarr, D, 1988. *Fiji, the Politics of Illusion: the military coups in Fiji*, University of New South Wales Press.

Bougainville conflict and peace process, 1988–98

Violent conflict in the Bougainville province of Papua New Guinea erupted in November 1988 and continued to 1997 (see CHRONOLOGY OF A CRISIS). The conflict was of such complexity that it defies simple analysis.

An island province east of the Papua New Guinea mainland, Bougainville consists of two adjoining large islands, Bougainville (8646 sq km) and Buka (598 sq km), five main atoll groups and many smaller islands. Its total area of 9438 sq km is about 2 per cent of Papua New Guinea's land area. Its population of about 170 000—approximately 4.5 per cent of the Papua New Guinea population—speaks 19 main languages, and is divided into numerous small and still semi-traditional societies. Before the conflict the national economy was heavily dependent on production from the vast copper mine at Panguna in the mountains of south-central Bougainville which operated from 1972 until closed by the conflict in 1989. Bougainville also produced significant levels of agricultural commodities, notably cocoa and copra, with a high proportion of smallholder production.

Bougainvilleans' sense of a distinct identity is based on the characteristic black skin colour of most Bougainvilleans, traditional and church organization links with neighbouring Solomon Islands and shared grievances about colonial neglect and the imposition of the Panguna mine for the benefit of a remote national government. Internal tensions arising from rapid social and economic change also contributed to resentment of outsiders seen as dominating the Bougainville economy or benefiting from it unfairly. The limited returns to Bougainville from the Panguna mine, the minority position of Bougainvilleans in the mine workforce and the flood of people from elsewhere in Papua New Guinea seeking to gain from opportunities associated with the mine were also factors.

However, significant internal divisions also existed, based on culture, language, religion and wealth. Even before colonial intrusion, there were marked cultural variations in Bougainville, related largely to the differing economic returns of the main environmental niches occupied by particular groups—coast, valley and mountains, with coastal people being most open to outside influences. Colonial and post-colonial experience favoured the coast.

Disparities in war reparation payments, smallholder cash cropping and other economic activity produced uneven patterns of material prosperity. Rapid population increases and diversion of land from subsistence agriculture to cash cropping resulted in land pressure, growing economic inequality and increased conflict within and between groups due to increasing competition for resources. The Panguna mine complicated the picture, bringing employment, business opportunities as well as payments of land rents and compensation to groups whose land was required for mining and associated purposes. The fabric of what had hitherto been largely egalitarian societies was weakened. Limited

Former Prime Minister Bill Skate (right) and Joseph Kabui at cease-fire signing, April 1998

opportunities for economic advancement for young males contributed to their increased social alienation.

It is no surprise that ethnicity involving a sense of uniqueness and resentment of outsiders and situated in a clearly defined area remote from the national centre should be associated with secessionist sentiment. Support for Bougainville's independence, widespread by the late 1950s, was intensified by the late 1960s conflict over development of the mine. Disagreements from 1973 over Bougainvillean demands for provincial autonomy culminated in a unilateral declaration of Bougainville's independence in September 1975. Agreement on a constitutionally protected provincial government system resolved the conflict in 1976, and Bougainville's provincial government was subsequently highly effective. However, most Bougainvilleans continued to support independence, although there was little evidence of active political mobilization around that goal between 1976 and 1988.

This background provides some insights into the central issues concerning the conflict, necessary to explain first, how inter-generational conflict among Panguna landowning groups about distribution of mining rents was transformed into a civil war. The failure of the national government to respond to concerns of the landowners about environmental damage and distribution of mine rents caused bitterness, especially among the younger generation of landowners who received few material benefits. Ethnicity became a key issue because of generalized violence against Bougainvilleans by PNG security forces (police riot squads and—later—army units). Initial destruction of mine property elicited ill-judged responses by the security forces—assaults, rapes, murders, and destruction of villages. Anti-Papua New Guinea and pro-independence sentiment became the basis for mobilizing support for landowner leader Francis Ona and his group, especially among alienated young men, soon known as the Bougainville Revolutionary Army (BRA). Nevertheless, many Bougainvilleans opposed or were ambivalent about the BRA.

A second issue is why bitter conflict developed among Bougainvilleans from 1990. It was largely related to pre-existing divisions in Bougainville, BRA fears of opposition from Bougainvillean elements, the rapid escalation of violence as the means of dealing with conflict established by both the BRA and the PNG forces, and the limited centralized organization and discipline within the BRA. Ona sought to legitimize his leadership by resort to 'custom', inclusive of economic equality. After the withdrawal of the PNG forces in 1990, the loosely organized BRA took revenge on perceived enemies, inclusive of the educated and the wealthy, and often used the BRA to carry on local conflict unconnected with independence. Organized groups opposing the BRA emerged gradually. Known as the Resistance Forces, they were used by the national government as it slowly re-established some control over parts of Bougainville, beginning with Buka in September 1990. The conflict divided Bougainvilleans into those bitterly opposed to the national government and supporting independence, and those opposing the BRA and fearing independence under BRA leadership.

A third issue is why Bougainvilleans agreed to cease fighting and participate in a peace process from the middle of 1997. Part of the explanation lies in the deep war-weariness of most Bougainville communities and the heavy reliance of the fighting elements on community support. Numerous efforts had been made from 1988 onwards to find a peaceful solution, with many female leaders and women's organizations playing prominent roles.

Following the collapse in March 1997 of PNG government efforts to engage foreign mercenaries to destroy the BRA, new national leadership supported negotiations between opposing Bougainvillean groups. Beginning with a meeting at Burnham in July 1997, the New Zealand government facilitated the process through provision of venues, transport and facilities. Subsequent meetings involved the Papua New Guinea government, and produced a truce and later a cease-fire, monitored by a regional force comprising representatives from New Zealand, Australia, Fiji and Vanuatu, with most funding from Australia. To the end of 1998, efforts were mainly concentrated on reconciliation among Bougainvilleans, leaving the question of the political future of Bougainville until the process was more established.

As to the impacts of the conflict in Bougainville, withdrawal of the security forces in March 1990 resulted in a breakdown of administration and government services. Loss of services, national government land and sea blockade of BRA-controlled areas from April 1990 to September 1994, and widespread armed conflict caused great hardship for many. At times more than half the population was living in refugee camps ('care centres'). Overall estimates of deaths from the civil war range from unsubstantiated claims of 20 000 down to more credible figures of 3000 to 5000. The continuing prevalence of armed violence is likely to be one of many longer-term legacies of the conflict. As at January 1999, progress towards establishing an elected Bougainville reconciliation government was being made. However, serious areas of disagreement exist, both among Bougainvilleans and between Bougainvillean leaders and Port Moresby, making the future of the peace process uncertain.—AJR

Further reading

Dinnen, S, May, R and Regan, A J (eds), 1997. *Challenging the State: the Sandline Affair in Papua New Guinea*, Pacific Policy Paper No. 30, National Centre for Development Studies and Department of Political and Social Change, The Australian National University.

Spriggs, M and Denoon, D (eds), 1992. *The Bougainville Crisis: 1991 update*, The Australian National University and Crawford House.

Chronology of a crisis

1988

March–October Panguna landowners demand compensation for land and environmental damage, and the transfer of Bougainville Copper Ltd (BCL) to Bougainville control within five years. Demonstrations in Arawa against the mine operation.

November–December Negotiations between the PNG government and Francis Ona, leader of the new Panguna Landowners' Association (PLA), break down, leading to disruptions and sabotage of mining operations. Riot police brought in.

1989

January–March Violence escalates, with attacks on government buildings and foreign-owned plantations. All-night curfew imposed from 23 January. Ona demands the closure of BCL. First Papua New Guinea Defence Force (PNGDF) soldiers arrive.

April–June Plantation workers and squatters are repatriated to the PNG mainland. Deaths occur in fighting between landowners and security forces. The PNG government offers to develop provincial infrastructure and share mine equity with North Solomons provincial government. A Bougainville group proposes provincial government control of the mine, autonomy for Bougainville, a truce with the Bougainville Revolutionary Army (BRA) and amnesty for Ona. This is rejected by the BRA. The mine closes, BRA is outlawed and a state of emergency in Bougainville is declared.

July–September The PNGDF begins resettling mountain villagers. Catholic priests in Bougainville call for reconciliation. Prime Minister NAMALIU announces a public peace ceremony. The mine reopens briefly, but shuts after shots are fired at workers.

October–December A public meeting in Arawa, attended by the prime minister, the premier of North Solomons provincial government (Joseph Kabui), government ministers, church leaders and traditional leaders, supports peace and reconciliation. Ona rejects the 'peace package'.

1990

January–March Amnesty International reports human rights abuses by security forces. A cease-fire between PNGDF and BRA takes effect. The Namaliu government restricts air and sea links to the island.

April–June BRA agrees to negotiate. International observers arrive to monitor the security force withdrawal and surrender of weapons by BRA. On 17 May, Ona makes a unilateral declaration of Bougainville's independence. The BRA's political wing, the Bougainville Interim Government (BIG), led by Kabui declares the Republic of Meekamui ('sacred land'). The PNG government imposes a full economic and communications blockade, while offering greater autonomy to North Solomons.

Peace talks are held on board the New Zealand naval ship *Endeavour* between the national government and Bougainville delegations. The Endeavour Accord provides for restoration of services, but defers decisions on Bougainville's political status. The North Solomons provincial government is suspended.

July–October The PNGDF returns but is restricted to Buka, where there are reports of heavy loss of lives among BRA and civilians, and torture of villagers. Buka leaders sign the Kavieng Agreement, calling for the restoration of order and services on Buka.

1991

January–March The 'Honiara Declaration' is signed by the government and Bougainville delegations. It provides for annulment of the declaration of independence, an armistice, lifting of the blockade and restoration of services, establishment of a multinational supervisory team, and amnesty for the BRA. The BRA/BIG repudiates the agreement soon after, and the BRA turns away a ship carrying medical and other supplies to Kieta. Kabui leads a BIG delegation to the UN Committee of Rights of Minorities and Indigenous Peoples in Geneva.

Bougainville women singing at cease-fire signing April 1998

November–December Local chiefs and leaders in areas under PNGDF control set up interim district authorities in an attempt to restore some form of administration.

1992

January–March The MV *Cosmaris* carrying medical supplies for Arawa hospital is destroyed by the BRA at Kieta. BRA members attack Rorovana villagers suspected of collaborating with the PNGDF. A PNGDF raid on a BRA fuel depot in the Shortland Islands leads to tensions between the PNG and Solomons governments.

July–September Meetings take place between the PNG government (now led by Paias WINGTI) and BRA/BIG in Honiara. Church leaders and chiefs from Central Bougainville propose a Pan-Bougainville Peace Conference but it fails to eventuate. Another cross-border incursion by PNGDF ends in the deaths of two Solomon Islanders. Violent encounters between PNGDF soldiers and local militants continue.

October–December North Solomons provincial government building is burnt down.

1993

January–July Bougainville Leaders Forum (including 150 traditional leaders) meets on Buka, seeking reinstatement of the provincial government. The PNGDF recaptures Arawa, but a BRA ambush kills eight soldiers. Ken Sauvia, BIG minister, is killed by PNGDF soldiers. Churches and women's organizations call for peace.

November–December Amnesty International report, *Under the Barrel of a Gun: Bougainville 1991–93*, alleges human rights abuses by PNGDF and BRA.

1994

January–March The Wingti government announces its intention to reopen the BCL mine. Deputy prime minister Sir Julius CHAN seeks to have proposals for a multinational peace-keeping force discussed at the SOUTH PACIFIC FORUM meeting.

April–July Widespread voluntary surrender by members of the BRA occurs in PNGDF-controlled areas. The peace and reconciliation process gains momentum.

August–October Wingti's government discredited by 'War is Won' claim, and Sir Julius becomes prime minister. Broad agreement is reached with BIG representatives in Honiara for a peace conference, which eventually takes place in Arawa in October. Senior BRA/BIG members refuse to attend. BRA field commander Ishmael Toroama, after speaking at the conference, is shot at by PNGDF soldiers.

November–December The prime minister and Bougainville leaders sign the *Mirigini Charter for a New Bougainville*.

1995

January–March National Executive Council establishes Bougainville Transitional Government (BTG), and ends suspension of North Solomons provincial government.

April–June North Nasioi leader, Theodore Miriung, becomes leader of the BTG, with temporary headquarters on Buka. Negotiations produce agreement on amnesty for BRA members and others guilty of criminal acts, and on future restoration programs.

July–December BRA/BIG and BTG representatives meet in Cairns, Australia, followed by a further meeting jointly chaired by representatives of the secretaries-general of the United Nations and the Commonwealth Secretariat.

1996

January–March The prime minister cancels the planned peace talks amid further violence. Honiara headquarters of BIG spokesman, Martin Miriori, is fire-bombed, and the BRA undertakes retaliatory military action in the north and on Buka. Sir Julius addresses the nation, resolving to reach a military solution. The cease-fire is ended.

April–October The PNGDF launches an unsuccessful offensive to take Aropa airport, leaving casualties on both sides. The national government and the BTG agree to explore other aspects of the peace process. The BRA raids a PNGDF camp in Buin, killing a dozen soldiers and taking five PNGDF hostages. Miriung is killed on 12 October in his own home, probably by PNGDF soldiers and members of the Resistance force.

November–December A PNGDF mortar bomb attack kills 10–12 civilians in a Buin Catholic church. Several deaths occur in a PNGDF raid on a village in Siwai.

1997

February The hiring of mercenaries by the PNG government through the British military consultants Sandline International becomes public.

July The Burnham Talks (5–18 July), hosted and sponsored by New Zealand, are held between the BRA/BIG and the BTG. A reunited Bougainville spirit is rekindled, with the declaration outlining all parties' commitment to unity and reconciliation.

October Further talks (1–10 October) and 'Burnham Truce' reaffirm the Burnham Declaration, agreeing on the peace process and a neutral regional monitoring group.

November–December The Truce Monitoring Group's requirements and the sharing of responsibilities in Bougainville are agreed. Members of the first Truce Monitoring Group, including Australia, Fiji and Vanuatu, arrive on the island.

1998

January The 'Lincoln Talks' (18–23 January) between the PNG government, BTG, and BIG/BRA in New Zealand are facilitated by NZ Foreign Minister Don McKinnon. The Lincoln Agreement provides for a permanent cease-fire, a peace-keeping force, and a Bougainville reconciliation government to be set up by June 1998 with December elections. Signing is witnessed by Solomon Islands prime minister, Bart Ulufa'alu.

March Further discussions are held in Canberra between the PNG government, the BIG/BRA, the BTG and the Resistance, on the implementation of the cease-fire.

April The cease-fire agreement is signed in Arawa on 30 April by Joseph Kabui (BIG vice president), Gerard Sinato (premier of BTG), and Sir John Kaputin (PNG chief negotiator). Ona disassociates himself from the cease-fire.

December Leaders of the three main parties agree to set up a Bougainville reconciliation government to be known as the Bougainville People's Congress, and Prime Minister Bill Skate indicates that it will be endorsed by his government.—RSS

Defence forces in the Pacific

Since World War II, the only disputes involving Pacific island states have been internal, either connected with independence movements (Papua New Guinea, New Caledonia) or with civil disruption (Fiji, Vanuatu). Generally, outside forces have not intervened in local issues. There have been exceptions: France, as the colonial power, has been involved in New Caledonia and French Polynesia, and Papua New Guinea assisted Vanuatu to restore order in 1980. There have been no significant neighbourly territorial disputes and only minor military confrontation—between Papua New Guinea and Solomon Islands over transit to and from Bougainville, and between Papua New Guinea and Indonesia on the Irian Jaya border (see WEST PAPUAN NATIONALISM).

In the South Pacific, France is the only external country maintaining a permanent defence presence. There are significant United States forces based and operating in the northern Pacific, since—under constitutional agreements with the Federated States of Micronesia, the Republic of the Marshall Islands and Palau, and the covenant with the Commonwealth of the Northern Marianas—the United States of America is responsible for defence. Both Australia and New Zealand provide limited support and training to those Pacific island countries with a military capability.

Few island countries maintain defence forces. Only three—Papua New Guinea, Fiji and Tonga—have structured military forces. Two others—Vanuatu and Solomon Islands—operate paramilitary units (as a 'Police Field Force') within their police structures. A further seven—Cook Islands, Kiribati, Federated States of Micronesia, Marshall Islands, Palau, Samoa and Tuvalu—have patrol boats for coastguard and resource protection. About 20 large, lightly armed patrol boats were provided to 12 island states by the Australian government, between 1987 and 1995.

■ *Papua New Guinea* The Papua New Guinea Defence Force (PNGDF) comprises two infantry battalions of the Pacific Islands Regiment, with signals and engineer support; an air unit with both small transport aircraft and four helicopters; and a naval unit of four Australian-built patrol boats and two landing craft. The total strength of the PNGDF is about 4000 personnel. The PNGDF was deployed to Vanuatu in 1980.

■ *Fiji* The Republic of the Fiji Islands Military Forces (RFMF) has two components—a well-equipped land force (3000 personnel) comprising three infantry battalions with engineer and signals support, and a naval division (300 personnel) operating three Australian-built patrol boats and six smaller craft. Fiji also maintains reserve infantry forces. The RFMF is actively involved in United Nations and regional peacekeeping. RFMF personnel have served in the United Nations Interim Force in Lebanon (UNIFIL) since 1978 (and in 1998 provided the Force Commander, Major-General Jioji Konrote), the Sinai Multinational Force and Observers (MFO) since 1982, and the Iraq-Kuwait Observation Mission (UNIKOM). Fiji forces have also performed peacekeeping functions in several other countries including Bougainville, Croatia, Pakistan, and Angola.

US Navy ship at Apra Harbor, Guam

■ *Vanuatu* The paramilitary Mobile Force (MF) of 300 personnel supports the Vanuatu Police Force. It has a light infantry configuration. The Maritime Wing of the MF undertakes maritime surveillance with an Australian-built patrol boat. Vanuatu MF personnel have been a part of the Bougainville peace monitoring force.

■ *Solomon Islands* The National Reconnaissance and Surveillance Force (NRSF), about 200 personnel, supports the Royal Solomon Islands Police Force. It has a land element of three mobile platoons; a Maritime Surveillance Force with two Australian-built patrol boats and several smaller inshore vessels; and uses a small aircraft for local coastguard support. The NRSF has not been deployed outside Solomon Islands.

■ *American Samoa* The United States is responsible for the defence of American Samoa. Pago Pago was a US naval base until 1951, but there are now no naval or military forces stationed in American Samoa. The Pago Pago port administration operates the coastguard service.

■ *Guam* Naval and air force personnel of the United States continue to operate the naval base, which was established in 1898, and the naval air station. Defence installations occupy one-third of all land.

■ *Hawai'i* Hawai'i is the military command centre of the US Pacific forces, with headquarters at Camp Smith, near PEARL HARBOR. Extensive military installations occupy one-quarter of land on O'ahu.—KRF

Further reading

Henningham, S, 1995. *The Pacific Island States: security and sovereignty in the post-Cold War world*, Macmillan/St Martin's Press.

four

politics

Contributors

Article contributors

AH	Alan Howard
AJR	Anthony J Regan
BD	Bronwen Douglas
BVL	Brij V Lal
CGP	Guy Powles
CM2	Clive Moore
DA	David Akin
DAS	Deryck Scarr
DH	David Hanlon
DT	Darrell Tryon
EW	Eric Waddell
EW-E	Elizabeth Wood-Ellem
FR	Fred Radewagen
GH1	Graham Hassall
HN1	Hiroshi Nakajima
HS	Heinz Schütte
JAP	John A Piper
JD	John Dunmore
JKO	Jonathan Kamakawiwo'ole Osorio
JRH	John Haglelgam
JVD	Jon Van Dyke
KE	Leiataua Kilifoti Eteuati
KRF	Kate Fortune
LWM	Larry W Mayo
MG	Michael Goddard
MP2	Malcolm Philpott
PJH	Peter Hempenstall
RA	Roderic Alley
RAH1	Richard A Herr
RCK	Robert C Kiste
RGC	Ron Crocombe
RJM	Ron May
RS2	Rosaleen Smyth
SBCLF	Sharlene B C L Furoto
SD	Sinclair Dinnen
SL1	Stephanie Lawson
SM	Steve Mullins

Photo contributors

Alexander Turnbull Library (National Library of New Zealand, Wellington): P McKnight Collection: 301

Australian National Archives (Canberra): photograph by F E Williams (1893–1943): 303

British Central Office of Information (London): 279

Canberra Times, 1983: photographed by Michael Porter: 293

Cunningham, Lawrence J (University of Guam, Mangilao): 267

Fortune, Kate (Wellington): 299

Office of the Prime Minister, Government of Solomon Islands (Honiara): 300

VexVentures (Melbourne), flags courtesy Ralph G C Bartlett: 280, 303, 306

Watanabe, Ing & Kawashima (Honolulu): 288

Wellington Newspapers Ltd (New Zealand): 281, 284, 286, 287, 295

ONE LEADERSHIP

Politics in the Pacific: an overview

Politics in the Pacific comprises a distinctive blend of tradition, culture, and modernity, but Pacific expectations about what politics ought to provide are not unique. Like everyone else, islanders look to their leaders and governments to deliver essentials such as security, basic public services, social justice and equity, and some hope for emerging generations. As a means of facilitating the funding and management of core public needs, how has politics performed in the Pacific? Regardless of variations that differentiate cultures, constitutional systems, representative institutions, and individual styles of governance, how have the Pacific's political processes affected the life chances of its citizens?

Apart from significant French, and some American, territories the Pacific is now largely decolonized (DECOLONIZATION). Independence has accorded international status, access to legitimacy, and the levers of internal control. To these attributes of sovereignty should be added the responsibilities of stewardship. While much political activity has been geared to gaining the rewards of office, what of its performance in stewardship? Governance as collective responsibility invites questions about who participates in public decisions, acting in response to which kinds of constituency, and subject to what form of accountability.

Most Pacific institutions of political representation permit open, competitive contests for popular support through regular election (PACIFIC CONSTITUTIONS). In a majority, the executive is accountable to the legislature. Contrary to claims that it is an alien imposition, representative government has coexisted with indigenous cultural systems and facilitated peaceful political succession. Representative government has prevailed despite fissures in its constitutional architecture, as in Papua New Guinea (overt challenge by the military to an elected government); politicized appointment and removal of governors general (Tuvalu and Vanuatu); Fiji's 1987 military COUPS; and gross abdication of fiscal responsibility through manipulation of the public purse for private advantage (Cook Islands). Although these strains have been serious and are likely to persist, consensus prevails about the desirability of retaining the essentials of representative government. Where that principle has been seriously distorted, as with Fiji's post-coup constitution, expectations have emerged to favour reform. Although the standing of representative government has been shaken, it retains the faith of its practitioners; in the interests of workability, international legitimacy, common sense and fair play, they support its retention. That expectation is separate from questions about actual system performance and the adequacy of methods of electoral representation.

Constitutional formulae handed down by former colonial masters or rules agreed at self-determination have not been immutable. Changes have occurred, driven either by strain on traditional systems (abusive proliferation of SAMOAN MATAI TITLES leading to Samoa's adoption of universal adult franchise in 1991); aftermath of crisis (attempting constitutional rehabilitation in post-coup Fiji); or response to palpable system failure (1995 abolition of provincial representation in Papua New Guinea).

Much representation is preoccupied with local, village, and CLAN or extended family demands, creating a vacuum in public life of the national constituency interest. Local affiliations are intensified by island separation and personal following, Tuvalu, Kiribati and Tokelau providing examples. Parochial pressures subject political careers to incumbent fragility, perceived failure in meeting local 'pork barrel' demands often punished at the elections. In Melanesia, the proportion of sitting members losing their seats at election can run higher than 40 per cent, a situation that penalizes an accumulation of legislative experience needed to carry out ministerial responsibilities. Turnover of legislative representation is reinforced where numerous candidates contest a constituency under simple 'first past the post' methods of election. Political groupings are not often treated as instruments to promote policy, but as mechanisms for gaining office and gratifying immediate sources of electoral support. Political party formations lack organizational depth, rendering them vulnerable to capture by dominant personalities or a few key financial clients. Party discipline within legislatures is often shallow, contributing to executive instability or unstable coalition arrangements.

Associational representation, having access to centres of decision, is primarily economic and professional, and heavily concentrated in urban areas. The better educated, those with standing as corporate taxpayers, landowners or lease-holders, or members of established community-based institutions, are best positioned to gain the ear of government. Distinctly under-represented are the rural landless, urban poor, growing numbers of unemployed youth, and some ethnic and migrant minorities.

The representation of women in legislatures remains poor. Apart from Guam (29 per cent) and Wallis (10 per cent), female members of island legislatures are fewer than 10 per cent—and even lower in Papua New Guinea, Solomon Islands, New Caledonia, Cook Islands, French Polynesia, Nauru, Kiribati and Palau. Opportunities for women to participate fully in electoral activities and politics throughout much of Melanesia and Micronesia are impeded by barriers in education, training, employment and income. Hard-earned seniority in public bureaucracies by women is jeopardized should they enter politics. Women are active in other spheres of public life. In Vanuatu and Fiji, organized campaigns have engaged women in local government, while their advocacy has extended beyond health, welfare, educational and family concerns to include campaigning against NUCLEAR TESTING, environmental degradation and DOMESTIC VIOLENCE. The violation of women's rights is now more openly acknowledged as a public issue.

Standards of legislative representation in the Pacific have not been sufficiently high to scrutinize the conduct of governments. This shortcoming is compounded by inadequate servicing and support arrangements for parliaments. Surveillance by legislative committees of government policy and expenditure remains weak (LEADERSHIP CODES), and related functions such as the offices of OMBUDSMEN not fully developed.

A further focus of political activity concerns access to the allocation of particular goods, including foreign assistance, rent, public revenue and, less tangibly, legitimacy and status functions. By international standards, the Pacific's quantum of external assistance is substantial, although there is some dispute about its appropriate scope, distribution, and supervision. Political careers are advanced for those not only known to facilitate access to external assistance, but to deliver it in a form appreciated by constituents. Although donors have become disinclined, the capacity to maintain external funding for public sector establishments is a highly regarded local political attribute. Another is the ability to channel external assistance intended for disaster relief towards general constituency needs—house construction or road repairs being examples.

Politically motivated decisions have been made regarding rent from key areas such as mining, fishing, forests, land and tourism. Excessive logging—notably hardwoods in Melanesia—has become notorious, inviting condemnation from conservation lobbies in and beyond the Pacific. Papua New Guinea's support for large-scale commercial production is criticized for doing little either to encourage smaller, local operations or to maintain traditional forest food for rural communities. Local critics regard exploitation as a wider problem of agriculture and mining causing damage to land and food grounds, while lowering health and nutritional standards. Other conservation problems neglected by political processes include over-fishing, sewage and fertilizer pollution, landfill and sedimentation damage, mangrove destruction, and lagoon pollution. Toxic waste and hazardous substance damage, through source pollution or poorly managed disposal from urban areas, have compounded health problems. (See NATURAL RESOURCES AND INTERNATIONAL DEVELOPMENT and SUSTAINABLE DEVELOPMENT.)

The 1994 *Pacific Human Development Report* criticized Solomon Islands for its deforestation practices failing to give adequate attention to environmental costs, and a loss of revenue through under-reporting of volumes and values. By the mid 1980s it was evident that the forestry industry in Papua New Guinea was out of control, involving widespread corruption, resource plunder and fraud against traditional landowners. The SOUTH PACIFIC FORUM's Logging Code of Conduct, intended for member states with significant forestry assets (Australia, Fiji, New Zealand, Papua New Guinea, Solomon Islands and Vanuatu), was approved only after a dispute in 1994 saw its intended enforcement powers reduced to those of exhortation.

Pecuniary gain by some politicians from rents such as forestry concessions or licences has overshadowed efforts made by others to support conservation goals, such as those spelled out in a 1992 plan designed by the South Pacific Regional Environmental Program. (See REGIONAL COOPERATION AND INITIATIVES.) This encouraged governments to devise national environmental policies that linked controls over local pollution with building standards, and land use inside coastal zone management frameworks. Opposition to resource rent-exploitation by politicians has pitted them against international non-governmental organizations motivated by environmental concerns, and some local communities disillusioned by poor rates of return. Gaining access to public revenue has seen political activity designed to exact concessions and subsidies for urban land incorporations (Vanuatu); maintaining pressure for government spending that outpaces revenue, and retaining 'slush fund' schemes (Papua New Guinea); denying central bank warnings to adjust prices in the face of a weakening currency, declining reserves, and excessive demands for credit

(Solomon Islands); unacceptably high levels of debt (Western Samoa Trust Estates Incorporation); exploiting lax supervision of government-owned banking and credit facilities (Fiji); or connivance in tax fraud or suspect tax-haven activities (Cook Islands).

Political leaders collaborate with non-governmental bodies, church groups and professional associations to enhance revenue for social, health and educational spending. This remains a difficult exercise, with caution towards and delay of welfare reform often revealing Pacific politics at their most conservative. As Fiji's Dr Timoci BAVADRA discovered after winning office in 1987, campaigning for and planning reforms viewed as threatening by established élites may provoke extreme retaliation.

The power to allocate status, approval or recognition is a considerable resource in Pacific politics. Despite migration, urbanization, and interdependencies of communication, taste, travel or consumption, the prerogatives of public appointment according to ascriptive or traditional cultural criteria remain. They are also used to deploy extended family connections to positions of influence, particularly for women entering public life. Historically such responsibilities have entailed reciprocities of stewardship to commoners, obligations now eroded by mobility, individualization of interest under the cash economy, or political rewards bearing little relationship to needs originally conceived as group entitlements. Structures of traditional political authority remain, but their original justification as systems of support and reciprocity has declined. Accordingly the capacity to control status allocation has been tenaciously retained, particularly for authorizations affecting land holding, resource use, or citizenship. Flexibility here has reached a point where beneficiaries may reside offshore, indicating how cultural norms have been stretched to take advantage of an increasingly interdependent Pacific and commercially driven international environment.

Politics in the Pacific is inextricably entwined with public service functions. Often these activities have clashed, dissonance caused by incompatibility between the demands of personal loyalties, kin, electorate or friendships promoted by politicians, and the need to operate public bureaucracies according to principles of law and probity. A related source of strain is nepotism and use of public service employment to provide a 'fair shares' allocation of jobs between competing districts or islands. Where politicians prevail, personal dynasties have colonized bureaucratic systems, as in Cook Islands. When stalemated, these forces can precipitate industrial action, as in Samoa. Where they clash, disputes can fester for years, as in Vanuatu where the role of so-called 'political secretaries' has been a source of unresolved tension.

In very small states, it is difficult for senior public service officials to maintain arms-length relationships with political masters, or to provide alternative policy advice or evaluation. Partially fulfilling those functions are religious, academic, legal, news media and other non-governmental voices—although this cannot match the strengths of the public service apparatus and political establishment. Whether in conflict or collusion, this combination exerts a preponderant presence across the public landscape.

Public management systems often exhibit incoherence in their planning, budgetary and resource allocation functions. Data gathering, statistical evaluation, internal audit and forecast systems are either weak or non-existent. Public enterprises have been indifferently managed, producing poor rates of return on capital. Trained personnel frequently depart to the private sector or placements abroad. The absorptive and transformational capacity needed to maximize advantages from external assistance is often lacking. These problems are compounded because few ministers or controlling operatives have had opportunities to develop public management skills outside cumbersome, unreformed local bureaucracies. Public officials who gain career experience abroad and then return, often assume quasi-political functions as policy innovators with independent or private sector agencies.

Roots of local government are often shallow, rendering decentralization problematic. An ethos of public service professionalism emphasizing teamwork and pride in accomplishment is lacking. Judicial independence cannot be assumed (COURTS AND LEGAL SYSTEMS), while politicians and officials do not always back enforcement of the law, for instance because of cultural constraints in land disputes. Corruption is increasingly a fact of public life, while news media investigation and reporting is actively discouraged as governments attempt to avoid public scrutiny. Although not endemic, neither are these afflictions episodic.

Another difficulty is the weakened accountability that may accompany donor–recipient development assistance relations. Confronting adverse economic circumstances, Pacific islands governments may enforce cuts to local funding of recurrent costs to (possibly overly ambitious) aid-assisted capital projects. Local skill acquisition measures are postponed, international agencies 'backstopping' completed projects with expatriate personnel. Governments may also accept assistance packages for reasons unrelated to current priorities. According to the *Pacific Human Development Report*, excessive concentration on securing additional resources at aggregate levels has eroded needed investment in human development. That bias has been encouraged by political processes that fail to facilitate local consensus about development objectives.

Encouragement for community participation and plural civil society functions do not occur in a political vacuum. As women of the South Pacific have found, public argument about values unsettles governments reluctant to tolerate opposition. Such contest has proven feasible where it is sanctioned by law, where constitutional safeguards protect essential liberties, and where the news media remains uncensored. While the region's record in maintaining constitutional rule has been generally good, its accumulation of secular, civil society functions has been slow.

Exposure to commercial and economic interdependencies has provided islands' leaderships with scope to advance the interests of their people and further private advantages. Internationalization has also subjected domestic political developments to closer scrutiny, which has provided added traction for local interests seeking reforms and challenging traditional values. This has been manifest in abuse of resource rents and over related environmental questions. Political and public management skills have yet to develop the versatility and capacity needed to pilot vulnerable, economically weak countries into a new century. Facing the future, a major challenge for politics in the Pacific will be the difficult but necessary task of divorcing private interest from public responsibility under constitutional government and the rule of law.—RA

Further reading

Drage, J, 1994. 'Women's representation in the Pacific islands', in W vom Busch and F Alailima (eds), *New Politics in the South Pacific*, Institute of Pacific Studies and University of the South Pacific.

Larmour, P, 1994. 'A foreign flower? Democracy in the South Pacific,' *Pacific Studies*, 17(1) March.

Taafaki, T, 1996. *Governance in the Pacific: the dismissal of Tuvalu's governor general*, Working Paper 19/5, Research School of Pacific and Asian Studies, The Australian National University.

United Nations, 1994. *The Pacific Human Development Report*, United Nations Development Programme.

Traditional leadership today

The persistence of chiefly authority has profound significance for today's Pacific island states. Histories of much of the Pacific region are rich with accounts of the status, functions and exploits of chiefs (EARLY SOCIETY AND AUTHORITY SYSTEMS, ALI'I AND HAWAIIAN CHIEFLY STATUS and TONGAN CHIEFLY STATUS AND THE TU'I TONGA). Nevertheless, it was expected that the forces of modernity in the contemporary world would ensure the replacement of tribal and feudal styles of leadership with the universalistic, rational forms of the nation state and its methods of government. Instead, westernization has been accompanied by doubts over the global applicability of such principles as democracy and individual rights, particularly where they confront the chief as the icon of local tradition and identity, or the contemporary political leader whose legitimacy is underwritten by notions of traditional chieftainship.

Pacific societies are frequently categorized according to styles of traditional leadership. The term 'chief' (borrowed from the Scottish highlands) replaced the earlier use of 'king' to describe influential island leaders observed by European visitors. It appeared that greater power was being exercised in the hierarchical systems of Polynesia and Micronesia (ARIKI, POHNPEIAN CHIEFDOMS, NAHNKEN and TRADITIONAL SANCTIONS AND LAWS). Because of its association with widespread influence, 'chief' was not the term chosen for use in much of Melanesia, particularly the New Guinea Highlands. There, the term for customary leaders is 'BIG-MEN'.

Today, shifts in the incidence of the involvement of chiefs in government are occurring at opposite ends of the state structure. At the upper end, in relation to the positions of head of state and membership of upper legislatures and councils (PACIFIC CONSTITUTIONS), the role of chief is becoming more formalized and less traditional. The modern marriage of hereditary chiefly authority and constitutionally sanctioned political power is most clearly exemplified in Tonga, but also remains in Fiji, Samoa and parts of the Federated States of Micronesia.

Across the societal landscape, however, in other countries as well as these, the titles, functions and traditional authority of chiefs and elders constitute a substantial body of customary law which has played a large part in encouraging recognition by the state of the usefulness of traditional institutions in local administration and land matters (CUSTOMARY LAND TENURE). Chiefs are thought to possess the knowledge and authority necessary to resolve disputes in these areas (COURTS AND LEGAL SYS-

TEMS). In some countries, chiefs employ traditional authority to administer the affairs of CLANS and extended family groups, and councils of chiefs govern villages and districts.

As a source of political influence which is not readily made accountable to the public at large, chiefly authority may interfere with governmental processes (MICRONESIAN LEADERSHIP AFTER WORLD WAR II) and help create environments conducive to official corruption (LEADERSHIP CODES).

Conversely, traditional chieftainship has been eroded and distorted by, and sometimes re-invented in response to, the pressures of colonial administrations and subsequent statehood. In some countries, the numbers of chiefs have multiplied considerably, undermining traditional status. For example, in Samoa, where the right to vote was originally limited to chiefs as the heads of extended families (SAMOAN MATAI TITLES), proliferation in numbers since independence swelled the ranks of registered chiefs from 4000 to 24 000 (1996 population—165 000). In 1991 the legislature was persuaded to introduce universal adult suffrage, but retained the requirement that candidates for election must be *matai*.

Today, chiefs are frequently carrying out semi-official government functions at village, island or provincial level. Some countries rely heavily on the administrative work of chiefs to provide essential infrastructure. Rather than fading away as obsolete, pre-modern political figures, chiefs are vital elements, sometimes formalized, sometimes not, within the apparatus of the state.—CGP

Further reading

Douglas, B, 1979. 'Rank, power, authority; a re-assessment of traditional leadership in South Pacific societies', *Journal of Pacific History*, 14.

Godelier, M and Strathern, M (eds), 1991. *Big Men and Great Men: personifications of power in Melanesia*, Cambridge University Press.

Lindstrom, L and White, G, 1998. *Chiefs Today: traditional Pacific leadership and the post colonial state*, Stanford University Press.

Powles, G and Pulea, M, 1988. *Pacific Courts and Legal Systems*, University of the South Pacific.

■ *Big-men* A literal translation of the term for 'leader' in many vernacular languages, 'big-man' is used in TOK PISIN and was adopted by anthropologists to classify achieved, informal leadership in the very small-scale egalitarian societies supposed to be typically Melanesian. Big-men typically were skilled orators and manipulators who relied on their own abilities and forceful personalities (rather than any formal social status) to achieve the wealth that ensured their influence (GIFT-GIVING IN MELANESIA).

Big-men were compared and contrasted with chiefs, the latter being considered typically Polynesian. The precise categorizing of big-men and chiefs in the context of an assumed Melanesia–Polynesia division had racial, evolutionist implications from the time of its systematization in the 1830s. This dichotomy has been contradicted by the widely varied complexity of Polynesian societies; by the consideration of aptitude and success as well as genealogy in determining Polynesian chiefly status; by the significant incidence of hereditary principles and small-scale chieftainship in Melanesia, especially in coastal and island areas; and by the mixture of chiefly types in Micronesia.

Over 150 years later, contrast between the terms big-man and chief has shrunk to a more pragmatic distinction between, on one hand, Papua New Guinea (especially the Highlands) and, on the other, the Austronesian-speaking societies of much of coastal and insular Papua New Guinea, island Melanesia, Fiji, Polynesia and Micronesia. In Solomon Islands and Vanuatu, chiefs have been reconfigured and constitutionally enshrined as epitomizing tradition (CULTURE, KASTOM, TRADITION). It seems that egalitarian ideologies widely professed in Melanesia may in fact hide serious social inequalities, especially between male and female.—BD

Micronesian leadership after World War II

After the Pacific War, the Americans created a three-tier government in Micronesia, then officially known as the Trust Territory of the Pacific Islands. Heading the Trust Territory administration was the High Commissioner, appointed by the US President and under the direct supervision of the Secretary of Interior. At the second level were the five district administrations, with boundaries drawn along ethnic and traditional ties, ensuring the recognition of traditional chiefs. Each district was headed by an administrator who was appointed by the High Commissioner and directly responsible to him. At the lowest rung of the Trust Territory administration hierarchy were the municipalities. Like the districts, the municipal boundaries were based on traditional perimeters. Some municipal chief magistrates were elected and others were the highest traditional chiefs. The American administration initially encouraged self-rule through the established traditional political system. In the mid 1950s municipal governments were established, following the traditional boundaries which preserved the customary jurisdiction and power of the traditional chiefs.

In Marshall Islands, Palau, Pohnpei and Yap, traditional leaders were given formal roles in their respective island municipal councils. Pohnpei created a legislature with two chambers: a house of nobles and a house of commons. For the other three island groups, chiefs who served in their respective legislatures were appointed by their peers. More often than not, the highest traditional leaders were selected to represent their peers. In Chuuk, the traditional political system was too fragmented to forge a consensus for inclusion of traditional leaders in the legislature; there was no traditional basis for including chiefs.

In the early 1960s when district-wide legislatures were created, the Trust Territory government opposed the automatic inclusion of traditional leaders as undemocratic. Running for election was probably appalling to the traditional chiefs and, in general, they stayed away from their legislatures. There was a general consensus among Micronesians that chiefs should not subject themselves to the politics of the election: they are chiefs by birthright, and also they should stay above political wrangling. However, chiefs used their customary power to support their favourite candidates.

At the Micronesian Constitutional Convention in 1976, 11 traditional chiefs appointed by their peers served as fully-fledged members. The basic argument for including them in the convention was to ensure that there were advocates for custom and tradition. They may not have been able to codify their formal role in the constitution, but they were able to push for the inclusion of two provisions that (1) recognized and protected their traditional rights and privileges; and (2) allowed each of the Federated States of Micronesia (FSM) to set aside one of its two-year term congressional seats for the traditional chiefs. The latter was a compromise, avoiding a separate chamber for traditional leaders at the national level, and embodying the general feeling among Micronesians that the best place for traditional chiefs is at the local level. This was confirmed by the overwhelming rejection of a proposed amendment to the FSM Constitution in 1991 to create a separate national council of traditional chiefs. No state in the FSM has set aside one of its two-year term seats in the national congress for the chiefs.

The formal role of traditional chiefs is defined as a prescribed function by law or in a constitution at any level of governance. After the approval of the FSM Constitution, all four states convened conventions to draft their constitutions. With the exception of Kosrae which no longer had chiefs, all these conventions required the participation of traditional leaders. In Chuuk, the convention produced a draft constitution that created a council of traditional chiefs as a part of the state governance, but this was rejected by voters. The main objection was the inclusion of a formal role for the traditional chiefs in the state government. Chuuk never had a cohesive traditional structure linking the islands into a political unit.

On each island, the highest political units are the villages, each with its own highest chiefs. Chuukese felt that no traditional basis for their chiefs' formal inclusion in government existed, and that it was better to confine them to their traditional village base. The Pohnpeian state constitution makes no specific mention of a formal role for traditional leaders. Like Chuuk, Pohnpei has no traditional base for a chiefly role within the state borders. Paramount chiefs were, and still are, undisputed rulers. The boundaries of the five municipalities followed the traditional boundaries of the old kingdoms, ensuring the authority and legitimacy of the paramount chiefs remain unquestioned, despite the election of municipal chief magistrates. Traditional chiefs in Pohnpei have created their own council which allows them to exert influence on state policy, and particularly to reinforce it. For instance, when Pohnpeians went into panic mode over the downsizing of the state government, the chiefs played a positive role in calming fears and reassuring people that the reform was needed.

In Yap, traditional leaders have formal roles in government. The Yap state constitution created two councils of chiefs: one for the main islands of Yap and one for the outer island chiefs. These councils are empowered to review and disapprove an act of the state legislature if it violates custom and tradition. They have disapproved a few appropriation bills as violating custom and tradition. The legislature cannot override the veto but can incorporate the objections and return an amended bill for review. So far the councils have used their power sparingly. They have also expanded their power to review policy of the executive branch, which has forced the governor and his cabinet to justify their policy to the councils. In addition, the whole state administration is accountable to the two councils, and hearings have been effectively used to question state policy. They are in essence public watchdogs, making sure that elected officials and bureaucrats are doing their job, although their effectiveness is limited by the members' relative lack of education.

In Palau, a council of traditional chiefs was created to advise the president. Unlike their counterpart in the FSM, therefore, the Palauan traditional chiefs have a formal role at the national level, albeit an advisory one. However, the council has complained that the president ignores their advice on policy matters. Of course, the power to advise does not carry with it the power to modify or formulate policy, and the Palauan traditional chiefs' power to influence public policy is minimized by this restriction. In Marshall Islands, traditional leaders are accorded a formal role in the national congress. As members of the national parliament, they have a direct impact on policy and governance.

Traditional chiefs also have an informal role and influence on the political process in Micronesia—informal in the sense that it is not formally prescribed by law or constitution. Traditional leaders can seek election to municipal, state, or national office, although so far only a small number have won election to national office, reflecting the prevalent attitude that they will be more effective at the local levels because of the legitimacy of their traditional leadership role at these levels. The exception to this rule is Marshall Islands, where the first president of the Republic was one of the highest chiefs who had served in the Congress of Micronesia. Although his administration had been described as authoritarian and corrupt, he brought stability to Marshall Islands and was widely respected and revered by his people. His legitimacy to govern was enhanced by his traditional role as a high chief, because the power of the traditional chiefs was absolute (like the Kosraean highest chief in Micronesia). A previous holder of the chiefly title was recognized by the Germans as the paramount chief of Marshall Islands. The power of the Marshallese chiefs could expand or shrink depending on personal bravery, cunning, or other personal attributes. So in the view of Marshallese leaders, the first president had the traditional base and legitimacy to the highest office, and he governed unchallenged.

Few politicians can win election in Micronesia without the support of traditional leaders, although their influence varies from state to state. In Pohnpei, traditional chiefs play a crucial role in swaying election results in favour of a particular candidate. Every candidate seeks the blessing and support of his traditional chief(s). In the 1995 election for the FSM Congress, the traditional chiefs in Pohnpei told a candidate who had previously never lost an election to withdraw; he ignored the chiefs' injunction and lost the race by a wide margin—due to a combination of factors, but the chiefs' lack of endorsement may have proved decisive.

In Yap, the support of the two councils plays a very important role in the election of the governor and the lieutenant governor. Since the implementation of the state constitution in 1984, the two councils have essentially selected the candidates for governor and lieutenant governor and stopped others from opposing them, so that the councils' preferred candidates always run unopposed. Some traditional chiefs in the outer islands have been known to cast votes for people who stayed away from voting. They were observed opening ballots for voters and instructing them to vote for certain candidates. The chiefs feel that it is their right to instruct their people in this way. Few Yapese expressed opposition to the traditional councils' and individual chiefs' involvement in the election. Most take an ambivalent attitude and laugh it off as a practical joke, apparently expressing a deep-seated feeling that voting is a foreign concept imposed by the outside world. Yapese do not consider voting as a right. The councils, individually or jointly, have forced members of the state legislature to resign. In one instance, a particular member who had made a public remark against the traditional chiefs was forced by a council to resign. The traditional chiefs' role in governance in Yap is so important that a popular joke has it that no Yapese will miss the governor and the lieutenant governor if they get lost at sea.

In Chuuk, chiefs have little influence on state governance and politics. Traditionally, the basic political power in Chuuk was, and still is, the head of the lineage. Members of a lineage are usually the children of females of closely related families. The head is usually the oldest son of the most senior ranking female in the group. The heads of the lineages have more influence on the voting process than the highest ranking village chiefs. Generally, lineage heads control elections in Chuuk and decide their outcomes. They might specifically instruct their lineage members on which candidate to support. Sometimes they might divide their lineage support between two or more candidates. The factors that can prompt lineage support are personal, social, traditional and other relationships to the candidate(s); and a promise of support, usually financial, by the candidate. A candidate who garners enough support from the lineage heads usually wins. This reduces the influence of the traditional chiefs on voting in Chuuk. It has also polarized and fragmented Chuuk politics and prevented the emergence of consensus among leaders. These problems make governance difficult and chaotic. Chuuk is now the most problematic state in the FSM in regard to good governance.

For those holding political office in Micronesia, dealing with traditional chiefs can be quite difficult, requiring skill and patience. They guard their traditional privileges jealously. Two patterns seem to be emerging in regard to the influence of traditional chiefs on governance in Micronesia. First, in areas where no consolidated traditional leadership exists, chiefs are excluded from government. They still wield considerable power in local and national elections. Second, Micronesians have incorporated the role of their traditional chiefs as a part of the formal governmental structure where a strong, cohesive traditional leadership foundation exists. In these areas, the chiefs serve either as advisers or active participants in government. They are a formal part of government and at the same time they can still exert influence on the voting process. Marshall Islands is an extraordinary case: one of the highest traditional chiefs has served as head of government and head of state.

Although the Micronesian traditional leaders' influence on modern governance has varied in form and degree from state to state, they will continue to be a powerful force in politics and to a lesser extent in contemporary governance. The chiefs' ability to influence the political process is attributable mainly to their close customary affiliation with the people and the fact that most Micronesians are still culture-bound to follow their orders. On the other hand, they lack the education to be major players in policy formulation and governance. The chiefs are generally uninterested in policy matters. Even in Yap, where they are formally incorporated into government, chiefs' councils have only limited impact on state governance. This might have something to do with the general view among Micronesians that policy and modern governance are outside the customary power of the chiefs. However, it is a prudent policy to brief and consult with them on a regular basis regarding policy and governance. Recently the chiefs have assisted in implementing crucial public sector reform.—JCH

Further reading

Haglelgam, J, 1998. *Traditional Leaders and Governance in Micronesia*, State, Society and Governance in Melanesia Discussion Paper 98/1, Research School of Pacific and Asian Studies, The Australian National University.

Leadership codes in the Pacific

Four Pacific island constitutions contain codes of conduct for leaders, namely Papua New Guinea, Solomon Islands, Vanuatu and Fiji Islands. The codes apply to a wide range of elected and appointed officials, specifying broad principles governing the conduct of leaders and forbidding certain kinds of potentially corrupt conduct. Such codes are unusual, there being few constitutions which take this approach to promoting accountability of leaders. The thinking underlying the Pacific leadership codes is found in the 1974 Final Report of Papua New Guinea's pre-independence Constitutional Planning Committee which envisaged the success of an independent Papua New Guinea depending largely on the quality of its political and administrative leadership.

In each of the four countries the constitution states the principles of the code, leaving it to other legislation to set out details. The Papua New Guinea code has operated since 1975 and the Solomon Islands code since 1980. The statute to implement the relevant provisions of the 1980 Vanuatu Constitution was passed in 1998. Legislation to implement the 1998 Fiji Islands Constitution 'Code of Conduct' provisions had not been passed at the time of writing.

The codes apply to all members of parliament and to heads of departments and statutory bodies. In Papua New Guinea and Solomon Islands, they also cover all members of provincial and local governments. As a result, those codes extend to about 7000 and 10 000 persons, respectively.

The codes for Papua New Guinea, Solomon Islands and Vanuatu require leaders to conduct themselves in both public and private life so as to avoid conflicts of interests, conduct demeaning public office, conduct allowing their integrity to be called into question, and conduct which could cause respect for or confidence in the integrity of government to be diminished. In Fiji the code is less stringent, for while it is based on the same principles, they apply only to the performance of public duties, and not to the private lives of leaders. Certain kinds of conduct inconsistent with the principles on which the codes are based are breaches of the codes (referred to as 'misconduct in office' in Papua New Guinea and Solomon Islands). Leaders are required to make regular disclosure of their financial affairs—annually in Papua New Guinea and Vanuatu and biannually in Solomon Islands. Failure to make disclosure and the making of a false disclosure are breaches of the codes.

Responsibility for administration of the codes is vested in independent bodies with wide powers of investigation (the OMBUDSMAN in Papua New Guinea and Vanuatu and the Leadership Code Commission in Solomon Islands). Proceedings for breach of a code are referred to the public prosecutor and dealt with in the normal courts in Solomon Islands and Vanuatu and in a specially constituted leadership tribunal in Papua New Guinea. Penalties for breaches of a code vary, and include reprimand, suspension from office, fine, imprisonment and dismissal from office. In Papua New Guinea and Vanuatu dismissal from office for breach of the code carries grave consequences—in Papua New Guinea disqualification from holding elected office for three years, and in Vanuatu disqualification from any leadership office for 10 years.

In Papua New Guinea a total of 34 cases of misconduct in office have been referred to the public prosecutor. Some leaders have used a loophole in the code, resigning leadership positions to avoid being subject to the code. To the end of 1998, 12 leaders accused of misconduct in office have been found guilty and dismissed from office, six have been found guilty and received penalties other than dismissal from office, three have resigned from office after a finding of guilt but before penalty was determined or imposed, six resigned before the leadership tribunal was convened or made a determination, four lost office before they could be prosecuted, and only three were found not guilty. Complete statistics for Solomon Islands are not available, but few leaders have been referred to the public prosecutor for breaches of the code. The Vanuatu *Leadership Code Act 1998* applies only to conduct and actions of leaders after 1 July 1998 and no referrals to the public prosecutor had been made by the end of 1998.

There is a public perception in each of these four countries that corrupt behaviour by leaders is increasing. The bodies administering the codes carry heavy administrative loads in just managing the disclosures required from leaders let alone investigating allegation of breaches of the codes. Limited resources are available to undertake the work involved. While leadership codes may have had a limited impact on corruption, in Papua New Guinea most observers agree that the situation would have been far worse without the code.—AJR

Political biographies

■ *I'iga Pisa* I'iga Pisa (1882–1965), a significant figure in SAMOA prior to independence, grew to fame as a composer of poetry and songs. Volatile and prone to enthusiasm, as a young *matai* in 1909 he acted as lieutenant to LAUAKI Namulau'ulu Mamoe, the orator chief from Safotulafai in Savai'i who challenged Germany's rule under Governor SOLF. Lauaki sent him to American Samoa to garner support, for which he was imprisoned by Solf. When Lauaki was exiled to Saipan, I'iga Pisa went with him and settled down to learn German. Instead of returning with other exiles in 1914, Pisa made a dramatic lone canoe voyage to Guam where he worked for the American navy, learned English and travelled to Hawai'i. Back in Samoa he served under a series of New Zealand secretaries of Native Affairs as translator and bureaucrat, becoming a particular friend of C G A McKay, later Secretary of Island Affairs in Wellington. I'iga Pisa served on the Constitutional Convention of 1954, was a *faipule* in the parliament, a member of the Board of Agriculture and recorder of Samoan histories. Last of the exiled *matai* left alive at Samoa's independence, he dictated a history of Lauaki's opposition movement which has been translated into English.—PJH

■ *Samuel Wilder King* Samuel Wilder King (17 December 1886–12 March 1959), the 11th governor of Hawai'i, was born in Honolulu, and attended the US Naval Academy (1905–10). He was appointed to the Territory Tax Commission, reporting to the Board of Supervisors of the City and County of Honolulu, and later served with the Home Rule Commission. He was elected delegate to the US Congress (1934–48), attempting in January 1935 to introduce the necessary legislation to enable Hawaiians to form a state government, although Congress deferred a decision for several years. When he was appointed the 11th governor of the territory (1953–57), he was the first Hawaiian ruler since Queen LILI'UOKALANI of Hawaiian descent. His term of office was devoted to the task of preparing for Hawaiian statehood.—KRF

■ *Marou Mimi* Marou Mimi (1886–1968), Torres Strait Island Councillor and civil rights activist, was born on Mer. He worked on luggers, farmed on the mainland and trained for the Anglican priesthood before returning to Mer to work as an assistant teacher. In 1928 he was elected to the Mer Council, becoming chairman in 1931. He was dismissed from office by the Queensland administration for his leading role in the 1936 Maritime Strike, which nevertheless won Torres Strait Islanders considerable concessions from the government. He is credited with having persuaded the Commonwealth to form the Torres Strait Defence Force in 1942, in which almost all physically fit Torres Strait Islander men served. After the war Marou advocated transfer of control of Torres Strait Islander affairs from Queensland to the Commonwealth, but was once again ejected from office in 1950 when two-thirds of Meriam electors petitioned against him. Marou served a final term on the Meriam Council from 1953 to 1956.—SM

■ *Ratu Sir Lala Sukuna* Ratu Sir Josefa Lalabalavu Vanaaliali Sukuna, KCMG, KBE, *Croix de Guerre, Médaille Militaire*, BA (Oxon), (22 April 1888–30 May 1958) was a Barrister-at-Law of the Middle Temple in Fiji, who became the first Speaker of the Legislative Council (1956). *Turaga na Tui Lau* when he succeeded to Ma'afu's title in the late 1930s, *Turaga na Talai* as he was known to his people when he became Secretary for Fijian Affairs in 1943–44, he was eldest son of Adi Litiana Maopa of Lakeba and Ratu Joni Madraiwiwi from Bau. Ratu Sukuna was at Oxford when World War I broke out. He joined the French Foreign Legion, and was wounded in action in 1915. His distinguished administrative career began with appointment as Provincial Commissioner, Lau (1932), where he gave voice to Fijians' feeling that mere numbers would swamp them if they accepted democratic principles of election. Nomination to the Legislative Council (as a Native Member) followed in 1937, then Member of the War Council (1940), Commissioner of the Native Land Commission (1940), Adviser on (later Secretary for) Fijian Affairs (1943) and first Speaker of the Legislative Assembly (1956). He was married to Adi Maraia Vosawale Tatawaqa. Ratu Sukuna died at sea, on a voyage to Britain, and lies buried at Lakeba.—DAS

Extracts from Sir Lala Sukuna's selected writings, published under the title *Fiji: the three-legged stool*

Report for 1950 of the Secretary for Fijian Affairs

—Though we see indisputable signs of Native progress, the Fijian is still at heart a subsistence agriculturalist with a simple conception of life—his clan institution and the thatched houses of his boyhood, his land and the peace and leisure of his koro. In the use of natural resources of which in this country the soil is the principal, he is a long way behind his Indian neighbour. It is true that in a period of high prices his interest in cultivation, in extending crops, in marketing products is noticeably at a high level; but it is only the very few that save for a purpose. At such times as this, native mushroom stores come to light, hawkers appear from round the corner, traders come from across the sea—all out to attract his money before he has decided what to do with it. To get him to save, the only effective method is to lead him to a savings bank before he has begun to think of the things he is going to buy. But he never forgets that he has a double economy and that what he loses in the swings he gains in the roundabouts. A number of Fijians—and a small number at that—do not fit into this picture; but very few of them ever ignore a levy by the clan or the group. But times are changing and the Fijian Affairs Board must lead and point the way to larger production and purposeful savings, to better villages and better houses which it is proposed to pay for from voluntary deductions being made from copra proceeds. And in the course of the next 50 years, *quo vadis*? At the beginning of a long journey, the Fijian has assets which should help him along—his willingness to learn, his friendly attitude—which is not unreciprocated—towards Europeans, and his new attitude towards economic production.

Cession Day Address, Levuka, 1954

—I have just spoken of loyalty as one of the highest and most important of the social qualities. In a country such as this, populated by three major races, we all have our duty to perform. We have each to contribute to the Colony's life, its good life, by being first and foremost loyal to each other; and we must see to it that we do nothing to defile the well-being of these islands…And, further, no community should be allowed to take more than its just share of our resources by neglecting to think of others.

Further reading

Macnaught, T J, 1982. *The Fijian Colonial Experience: a study of the neotraditional order under British colonial rule prior to World War II*, Australian National University.

Scarr, D (ed.), 1984. *Fiji: the three-legged stool, selected writings of Ratu Sir Lala Sukuna*, Macmillan Education for Ratu Sir Lala Sukuna Biography Committee.

——, 1980. *Ratu Sukuna: soldier, statesman, man of two worlds*, Macmillan Education for the Ratu Sir Lala Sukuna Biography Committee.

■ *Marcel Pouvana'a A Oopa* Marcel Pouvana'a A Oopa (10 May 1895–10 January 1977), leader of the Tahitian nationalist movement of the 1950s, was born on Huahine, French Polynesia. Recruited into the army by the French administration to serve in the Pacific Battalion in World War I, he first began to agitate for political rights in the early 1940s, making sufficient protest to persuade the French governor, Colonel Georges Orselli, to exile him to his home island. He returned to Tahiti at the end of the war in 1945 to the enthusiastic support of 300 war veterans, and this time—in the general mood of reform in the wider world at the end of World War II—the French government was ready to grant his claim that all Tahitians should be entitled to French citizenship. In 1947 his supporters formed the Comité Pouvana'a, aiming at greater local autonomy, but when they organized a shipside protest against the disembarkation of metropolitan French officials arriving to take up positions in the colonial bureaucracy, the 'revolt' was taken seriously and quickly suppressed. Pouvana'a and some of the others spent several months in custody, but the publicity won him greater support and he was elected in 1949 as a deputy (*deputé*) to the French parliament. His party (later known as the Rassemblement Démocratique des Populations Tahitiennes, RDPT) won a majority in the national assembly in 1953 and 1957. When Pouvana'a campaigned vigorously in 1958 for secession from France, however, his popularity dwindled. The RDPT-supported independence proposal won only a little over one third of the popular vote, and a few days later Pouvana'a and several associates were arrested on charges of arson, attempted murder and illegal possession of arms. Convicted in October 1959, he served an 8-year prison sentence, which was to be followed by 15 years of exile from Tahiti. His cause was taken up briefly by his son, Marcel Pouvana'a, who was elected as a *deputé* in 1960, but died in Paris a year later. Then fresh support came from John Teariki, a chief from Moorea. Although the RDPT was banned in 1963, in response to its protests against NUCLEAR TESTING, Teariki made a personal plea to President Charles de Gaulle in September 1966, to release Pouvana'a. Tahiti's radical politicians maintained the pressure until de Gaulle relented, issuing a decree on 11 November 1968 allowing Pouvana'a's return. Although suffering the effects of a slight stroke, he was able to stand again for public office after President Edouard Pompidou issued an amnesty for all political crimes. Pouvana'a was then elected to the French senate in 1971 for a 9-year term, but he died early in 1977, aged 81.—KRF

■ *Queen Sālote Tupou III* Queen Sālote of Tonga (13 March 1900–16 December 1965) was born of a marriage that divided the kingdom, her father being Tāufa'āhau Tupou II and her mother Queen Lavinia Veiongo. Educated for five years in Auckland (privately and at the Diocesan School for Girls), she returned to Tonga in December 1914, acquiring the skills necessary for a high chiefly woman: knowledge of GENEALOGIES and other determinants of status in complex ranking systems; the history and value of the royal *koloa* (women's wealth); and the rituals in which the ranking of individuals was demonstrated. She used this knowledge to good effect in managing the ambitions of the chiefs (women and men) of the kingdom.

In September 1917 Sālote married the high-ranking chief, Uiliami Tupoulahi Tungī Mailefihi, afterwards known as Prince Tungī. Upon the death of her father, on 5 April 1918, she succeeded to the title Tu'i Kanokupolu, and was thereafter known as Queen Sālote Tupou III. At the time of her accession, Sālote decided to accept the proffered alliance (so strongly resisted by Tupou II) with the British, and benefited from the advice of successive British Agent and Consuls in internal as well as external affairs. In 1923 the queen appointed her consort as her premier, and

Queen Sālote of Tonga, in London for the coronation of Queen Elizabeth II, June 1953

thereafter gradually came to be seen by Tongans as the female sacred ruler who could not be openly defied. Tungī assumed the role of secular ruler, carrying the day-to-day burdens of European-style government, although (behind the scenes) the queen remained actively involved, ruling in the Tongan way. She showed that their loyalty to each other was strong when members of the largely ineffective parliament attempted to impeach Tungī and his Tongan ministers in 1940. Sālote had a gift for organization, and this was demonstrated in Tonga's outstanding contribution to the Allied cause in the European and Pacific theatres of war. When the main island of Tongatapu was virtually occupied by US forces in 1942, the queen and her subjects left the capital, Nuku'alofa, maintaining her rule by personal influence (TONGA IN WORLD WAR II).

Sālote's life was marked by great sorrow. Her mother had died when she was 2-years old, her father when she was 18, her only half-sister in 1933, the second of her sons in 1936, and her consort in July 1941. Sālote and Tungī had three sons: Tāufa'āhau (born 1918), later known by his chiefly titles of Tupouto'a (1936) and Tungī (1945); Tuku'aho (1919–36); and Sione Ngā (born 7 January 1922), known from 1945 by his chiefly title of Tu'ipelehake.

Royal standard of Tonga

By the time the crown prince returned to Tonga in December 1942, after completing his education, the kingdom was secure, as was the Tupou dynasty. The queen appointed him as Minister of both Education and Health (reflecting her own deep concerns), and then as premier (in 1949). The crown prince was determined to westernize Tonga, and the queen now found a major role as the defender of tradition. She wanted Tongans to enter the modern world with a strong sense of their Tongan identity. Throughout her life she was the mainstay of church organizations such as the Ako Lotu (Christian Endeavour), village Bible studies and women's groups. In 1954 she founded the Komiti Talafakafonua (Tonga Traditions Committee) and the Langa Fonua'a e Fefine Tonga (Nation-building by Women). Although women did not have the vote in Tonga until 1960, Sālote promoted the education of girls and the status of women, particularly their traditional status in the family and in areas of health and perpetuation of traditional arts.

During her lifetime the queen was invested with the DBE, GBE, GCVO and GCMG by the British. She was a gifted orator (a constant theme being 'peace and unity') and poet. Many of her poems were set to music and some choreographed, and are still popular in Tonga today. Sālote's distinguished descent, exceptional intelligence, strong religious faith, willingness to learn from advisers, and warm personality all made her a wise and much-loved leader whose 47-year reign brought Tonga a period of peaceful, gradual and closely controlled development. Her health began to decline in the early 1960s. She died in Auckland, and was buried in the royal cemetery in Nuku'alofa on 23 December 1965, marked by universal mourning.—EW-E

Further reading

Wood-Ellem, E, 1999. *Queen Sālote of Tonga: the story of an era, 1900–1965*, Auckland University Press.

Queen Sālote, *The Poems and Songs of Queen Sālote*, in preparation.

■ *A D Patel* Ambalal Dahyabhai Patel (13 March 1905–1 October 1969) was, along with Ratu Sir Lala SUKUNA, one of the preeminent political leaders and public figures of colonial Fiji. Born in Kheda district of Gujarat (India) and a Barrister-at-Law of the Middle Temple, Patel was sent to Fiji in October 1928 by emissaries of Mahatma Gandhi to provide leadership to a disorganized Indo-Fijian community then emerging from the shadow of indenture. The colony's most successful criminal lawyer and its most brilliant advocate, Patel was also a tireless advocate of equal, non-racial franchise, and common roll remained his lifelong commitment, much to the bewilderment of his opponents who supported a communal roll for Fiji. He led the cane-growers' strike against the COLONIAL SUGAR REFINING COMPANY (CSR) in 1943 and again in 1960. His persuasive advocacy before the Denning Arbitration led to a report which caused the CSR to withdraw from Fiji. Patel was a member of the legislative council, 1944–50, and 1963–69. He was a member of the executive council, 1948–50 and again from 1964–67 as member for Social Services. He founded Fiji's first political party, the National Federation Party, in 1963, and in 1967 became Fiji's first leader of the opposition. He also founded newspapers, schools and several voluntary organizations.—BVL

Extracts from A D Patel's writing

From The Pacific Review, *12 February 1954*

Time and again British statesmen in England have reiterated that the ultimate goal of British rule in the Crown colonies is self-government for the territories concerned. If that is really the goal, the least the British government can immediately do is to stop ruling these territories for the benefit of Great Britain and make the interests and welfare of the colonies the supreme objects of their rule.

On opposition to communal (racial) rolls

Communal Rolls can be a serious obstacle to the successful operation of parliamentary democracy. The elected representatives of a racial or religious sub-community cannot afford to subordinate the interests and prejudices of their people to those of a larger community. Whether elected as independents, members of a communal party, or even as members of a party professing to transcend communal lines, they will not accept party discipline in a way to offend the group upon whose support their political future depends. It will inhibit the formation of secular parties. Success in politics will depend upon reflecting exactly the communal interests and prejudices. Compromise will be rendered difficult and relative party strength may be frozen for long periods because a party can grow only with an increase in the size of the community upon which it is based. In such a case, government formed by one or more of these communal parties, may not be able to meet the challenge of urgent social problems and a breakdown of representative government may occur because the legislators and executives are prevented by communal loyalties from attacking problems in a common-sense fashion.

Further reading

Lal, B V, 1997. *A Vision for Change: AD Patel and the politics of Fiji*, National Centre for Development Studies, The Australian National University.

■ *Albert Henry* Albert Royle Henry (11 June 1907–1 January 1981) was the first premier of Cook Islands. Educated at Anaura School, Aitutaki, he worked as a clerk, teacher, labourer and storeman before becoming involved in the labour movement in New Zealand. Returning to Rarotonga, he founded the Cook Islands Party in 1964 and led it to victory in the first general elections for the Legislative Assembly of the Cook Islands on 20 April 1965, although he himself lacked the necessary residential qualifications to stand as a candidate. The new government quickly amended the constitution; his sister, Marguerite Story, resigned her seat; and Henry won the by-election and became premier of the Cook Islands in June 1965. He continued in office until July 1978 when, following allegations of electoral malpractice, eight members of the Cook Islands Party, including Sir Albert Henry, were charged with corruption. He was subsequently banned from politics for three years, and the Queen withdrew his knighthood. He married Elizabeth Connel in 1927.—KRF

Further reading

Crocombe, R, 1979. *Politics in the Cook Islands: the inside story*, Polynesian Press.

■ *Wilson Inia* Wilson Fagmaniua Inia (1908–83), Rotuma's first senator in the post-independence Fiji legislature, was the son of a Rotuman METHODIST minister. Educated at Davuilevu Teachers' Training Institute in Fiji, in 1931 he took a position there as tutor. He stayed for 15 years, tutoring in English, mathematics and hygiene. He went on a deputation as Methodist preacher to Australia for two years (1938–39), and represented Fiji at a World Meeting of the International Missionary Council in Madras, India (1938). He married Elizabeth Kafonika in 1947, shortly before being appointed headmaster at Richmond School on the island of Kadavu—the first non-European to hold that post. In 1947 he was appointed Justice of the Peace for the Southern District of Fiji, and a member of the Methodist Synod of Fiji, which he served until 1952.

He returned to Rotuma in 1953 as headmaster of Malhaha School and in 1958 was appointed headmaster of Rotuma High School, which he founded. In 1965 he received a Certificate of Honour from Queen Elizabeth II for public service to education in the colony. Inia also became the guiding light for Rotuma's fledgling COOPERATIVES movement, which had begun four years prior to his transfer. Convinced that the key to the cooperatives' success was bookkeeping, he formed, along with a Fijian trainer, a bookkeeping class that he taught without compensation. In 1958 he was given a scholarship by the British Council to study the operation of cooperatives in England and Scotland. Under his guidance the Rotuma Cooperative Association became one of the most successful in the Pacific region. A natural leader, Inia was elected to the Rotuma Island Council, assuming a major role in formulating policy for the island's development. In June 1969 he became a Member of the British Empire (MBE), and the following year was chosen as one of three men to represent Rotuma's interests at the conference on Fiji's independence in London. Following independence he served as senator for 13 years, until his death in 1983. He served as vice-president of the Methodist Conference in Fiji during 1977–78.—AH

■ *Sir Robert Rex* Robert Richmond Rex (25 January 1909–13 December 1992), the longest-serving head of government in the Pacific islands, was born at Hamula, Alofi, Niue Island, son of Leslie Rex (a school inspector who served as official interpreter for the Niue government from 1952) and educated at Tufukia government school. Having worked in business and set up his own company, he entered the Niue Island Assembly in 1966, becoming Leader of Government Business in 1974 and then premier after the introduction of self-government later that year. His wise and steady leadership over 16 years relied on consensus and minimized the politicization of the public service. A new opposition party, formed in 1990, was unable to unseat him in the 1991 elections nor in an attempted no-confidence vote in parliament, and he remained in office until his death. He was succeeded as premier by Young Vivian, first in an acting capacity and then elected by parliament.—KRF

■ *Sir Fiatau Penitala Teo* Fiatau Penitala Teo (July 1911–), first Governor General of Tuvalu, was born at Funafuti, son of Teo Vali, and began teaching (1930–32), before entering the colonial administration as a clerk and interpreter (1932–37). He then served in administrative positions on Banaba (Ocean Island, 1937–42), Tarawa (now Kiribati, 1943–44), and Tuvalu (1944–58), interrupted by war service (1944–45), during which he was promoted to second lieutenant. From 1959, he served as District Officer, and later District Commissioner in both Ellice Islands and Gilbert Islands, and finally ended his distinguished public service career with the appointment as Governor General from 1978, when Tuvalu became independent, until 1986.—KRF

■ *Francis Sanford* Francis Ariioehau Sanford (11 May 1912–), first head of government of French Polynesia, is a Tahitian of American ancestry. Born and educated in Pape'ete, he began his career as a teacher (1929–32), before entering the administrative service. At the start of the Pacific War, he was Administrator of the Gambier (Mangareva) District (1939–41), during which time he rallied support for Free France. He enlisted for military service, and was appointed liaison officer for the American forces stationed on Bora Bora, receiving several citations. After the war he returned to teaching, rising to Director of Education and then holding several other important administrative positions, before becoming involved in politics in 1959. He was elected the first mayor of the municipality of Faa'a, near Pape'ete, in 1965, and then won election in March 1967 as a deputy (*deputé*) in the French parliament, in the first of four consecutive terms to represent French Polynesia in Paris. He formed a radical political party, Te E'a Api no Polynesia, which won a majority in the September 1967 elections to the territorial assembly on a platform of internal self-government, and successfully achieved a pardon for the exiled rebel politician, POUVANA'A A OOPA, in November 1968. During the 1970s Sanford's opposition to NUCLEAR TESTING included returning his war service medals to France. Sanford then became vice-president of the new government council, which first met on 22 July 1977, ending his political career in May 1982.—KRF

■ *Malietoa Tanumafili II* Malietoa Tanumafili II (4 January 1913–) was born in Apia, the son of Malietoa Tanumafili I, and was educated at Leififi, Apia, St Stephen's College and Wesley College, Auckland. Elected to the title of Malietoa in 1940, he became Fautua (one of the two high chiefs) and was one of the Samoan representatives who appeared before the United Nations session in New York in 1958. With Tupua Tamasese Mea'ole, he was joint chairman of the Working Committee on Independence, and later of the Constitutional Convention of 1959. Awarded the CBE in 1959, at independence in 1962 he became a joint Head of State with Mea'ole (who died in April 1963) and remains sole Head of State for his lifetime. He was married to Lily Molioo Setu in 1940; and after her death, to Patu Tauvela Hunter in 1962.—KRF

■ *Sir John Guise* John Guise (1914–91), Papua New Guinea politician and Governor General, was born in Gedulalara village, near Dogura, Milne Bay District. His grandfather was Reginald Guise, an English adventurer who reached Papua in the 1880s, settled as a trader and married locally. John Guise received four years of formal education from 1923, and at age 14 began work on Samarai as a waterside worker for BURNS PHILP, remaining in this job until war broke out, after which he joined the Australian New Guinea Administrative Unit (ANGAU) as a clerk in Signals. In 1946 he joined the police force, rising over 10 years to the rank of sergeant-major, then spent five years in the Department of District Services in Port Moresby, often clashing with the colonial administration. He first travelled to Australia in 1949, making a further four trips to Anglican Synods over the next few years, and visiting London in 1953 as part of the police contingent at the coronation.

Guise's first overt political activity was in the Port Moresby Mixed Race Association, of which he became president in 1958. He found its élitism distasteful but it brought him to the attention of the administration which chose him to represent local opinion on the Central District advisory council. Guise entered the legislative council as member for East Papua in 1961, becoming the most successful early indigenous politician, also developing connections with the COOPERATIVE movement and helping found the Milne Bay District Workers Association. The administration chose him to represent Papua New Guinea at the 1962 South Pacific Commission conference at Pago Pago, and later the same year and again in 1965 sent him to New York as special adviser to the Australian delegation to the United Nations Trusteeship Council.

His pre-independence political career included chairmanship of an important select committee on constitutional development, the positions of Speaker of the House of Assembly, Deputy Chief Minister, and the portfolios of Lands, Agriculture, and the Interior. The first Papua New Guinean to be honoured by an honorary doctorate from the University of Papua New Guinea, he was knighted in 1975 when he became Papua New Guinea's first Governor General. Ultimately frustrated by his vice-regal position he resigned in 1977 and at age 63 returned to politics. Failing in his bid to form a ruling coalition to oust the Somare–Chan government, he was for a time deputy leader of the Opposition and remained in the House until 1982. A cunning lone wolf of Papua New Guinea politics in the 1960s and 1970s, Guise died in 1991.—CM2

■ *Kondom Agaundo* Kondom Agaundo (c1917–66), was a tribal leader from Kundiawa, Chimbu (Simbu), who served in the Papua New Guinea legislative council, 1961–64, representing almost one million Highlanders. Born before outsiders entered the Highlands, the son of a war leader, but orphaned in childhood, Agaundo became one of the youngest *luluais* (native government officials) under the Australian administration. He involved his people in coffee in the 1950s and was himself involved with the Waiye local government council, of which he became president in 1959. Agaundo had numerous wives (estimates vary from 7–14) and up to 40 natural and adopted children. Although he never learnt English and was not fluent in TOK PISIN (Melanesian Pidgin), he was a great orator. In the legislative council he was constantly frustrated, a token Highlander, dignified and progressive but bewildered by the foreign procedures. He lost his bid for the Chimbu Open electorate in 1964 and, tragically, was killed in a car accident in 1966. Agaundo epitomized the generation of Highlanders who bridged the pre and post-colonial eras.—CM2

■ *Sir Thomas Davis* Thomas Robert Alexander Harries Davis, or Pa Tu Terangi Ariki (11 June 1917–), doctor, scientist, writer and politician; the second premier of Cook Islands. Tom Davis was educated at King's College, Auckland, in the 1930s and gained a medical degree from Otago University in 1945. After four years in the Cook Islands medical service, he continued his studies in Australia (Diploma of Tropical Medicine, 1950) and the United States (Master of Public Health, 1952). He was a member of the research staff of the Harvard School of Public Health (1952–55) and continued working in the United States (in various research and administrative positions) until 1971. On his return to Cook Islands, Dr Davis became involved in politics and founded the Democratic Party, while operating a private medical practice (1974–78). In 1978 he was elected as premier of Cook Islands, following the removal of Albert HENRY from office for electoral corruption. He held the position until March 1983, when the Cook Islands Party returned to power, but parliament was dissolved a few months later on constitutional grounds and he became premier once again, in a coalition government. Now Sir Thomas Davis, he survived the election in 1985 but lost the leadership in late 1987. His first wife, Lydia, was co-author of his novel *Makutu* (1956, see COOK ISLANDS LITERATURE); he later married Pa Tepaeru Ariki, who died in February 1990.—KRF

Further reading

Crocombe, R, 1979. *Politics in the Cook Islands: the inside story*, Polynesian Press.

Davis, T and Davis, L, 1954. *Doctor to the Islands*, M Joseph.

■ *Tāufaʻāhau Tupou IV* Tāufaʻāhau Tupou IV (4 July 1918–), King of Tonga, was born at Nukuʻalofa, the eldest son and heir of SĀLOTE and Uiliami Tungī. As Prince Tupoutoʻa, he was educated at Tupou College (Tonga), NEWINGTON College (Sydney), and at the University of Sydney where he obtained a double degree in arts and law (1942), the first Tongan with a university degree. On his return home, he became Minister of Education (1943–49) and then Prime Minister (1949–65). Many of the major changes in education, health and economic development during the later years of Queen Sālote's reign are attributable to Prince Tupouto'a and his determination to modernize the country. After the queen's death at the end of 1965, he became king, with his formal coronation on 4 July 1967. Under his rule, Tonga ended its dependent relationship with Britain in 1970 and joined the United Nations as an independent state. He served as the first chancellor of the University of the South Pacific (1970–73). Honours and awards he has received include a CBE, KBE, DCMG, GCVO, and a D Litt (1973, University of the South Pacific). He married Princess Halaevalu Mata'aho 'Ahome'e, and they have three sons and a daughter.—KRF

King Tāufa'āhau Tupou IV of Tonga on a visit to Wellington, October 1979

■ *Ratu Sir Penaia Ganilau* Ratu Penaia Kanatabatu Ganilau GCMG, DSO, OBE (28 July 1918–December 1993) was Governor General (and later President) of Fiji from 1983 until his death. Born into the paramount Ai Sokula chiefly line of Cakaudrove, and educated at Queen Victoria School, he began his career as a clerk in the public service (1937–41), then served in the Pacific War, rising to the rank of company commander in 1944. He later attended an administrative service course at Oxford, United Kingdom. He became a district officer in 1948 and then returned to military service in Malaya (1953–56), for which he was awarded the DSO for outstanding leadership. His involvement in politics began when he was appointed to the legislative council (1957), then elected to the executive council (April 1963); he became Secretary for Fijian Affairs (1965) and a member of cabinet (1967). Serving first in the senate (leader of government business, 1970, and Minister for Communications, Works and Tourism in 1972), and then elected to the house of representatives (1973), he became Deputy Prime Minister (1973–77), and held various portfolios including Home Affairs, Fijian Affairs and Rural Development, before being appointed Governor General. He became the first President of the Republic of Fiji after the link with the British monarchy was severed in October 1987. (See FIJI COUPS.) He was installed as Tui Cakau in April 1988. He was married in 1949 to Adi Laisa Delaisomosomo; after her death, to Adi Davila; and finally to Bale Mavoa.—DAS & KRF

Further reading

Tarte, D, 1993. 'Turaga: the life and times and chiefly authority of Ratu Sir Penaia Ganilau', *Fiji Times*.

■ *Peter Coleman* Peter Tali Coleman (8 December 1919–28 April 1997) was born in Pago Pago, American Samoa, where he attended primary school. He graduated from high school in Honolulu, joined the National Guard and enlisted in the United States army at the outbreak of World War II. Stationed in Solomon Islands and Vanuatu in addition to Hawai'i, he rose to the rank of captain and was later the first Samoan to be inducted into the US Army Officers' Candidate School Hall of Fame in Georgia (1982). After the war he completed a Bachelor of Science degree in economics (1949) at Georgetown University in Washington, DC. While in college, Coleman began his civilian, federal service as a Congressional staff member (1946–47) and later served with the US Capitol Police (1948–51). After brief service in the Office of Territories at the US Department of Interior (1951–52), he returned to American Samoa, where he became public defender, then attorney general, and also established a private law practice.

In 1956 he was appointed Governor of American Samoa, serving in this office until May 1961, followed by nearly 17 years in the administration of the US Trust Territory of the Pacific Islands (TTPI): heading the government in Marshall Islands (1961–65), Northern Marianas (1965–69), then appointment as deputy high commissioner of the TTPI in Micronesia (1969–76), and finally acting high commissioner (1976–77). Upon his return to American Samoa, Coleman served two terms as the first popularly elected governor (1978–85) and then, barred by law from serving a third successive term of office, he returned to his law practice for three years, while continuing to carry out a range of international and Pacific assignments for the US Administration. Reelected for a further term as governor in 1988, his retirement on 3 January 1993 brought to an end a distinguished record of Pacific leadership and government service in war and peace that had spanned five and a half decades.—FR

■ *Ratu Sir Kamisese Mara* Ratu Sir Kamisese Kapaiwai Tuimacilai Mara, GCMG, KBE, MA (Oxon), (13 May 1920–), President of Fiji. Born in Lau, his chiefly titles include Tui Lau and Tui Nayau. He was educated at Otago Medical College, New Zealand, and at Wadham College, Oxford, and later gained a Diploma from the London School of Economics. He became the first Prime Minister of Fiji at independence in 1970, and his Alliance Party held power for 17 years, until the election in April 1987 of the National Federation Party–Fiji Labour Party coalition, led by Dr Timoci BAVADRA. The new government was deposed by military coup on 14 May 1987, but Ratu Mara was reinstated by Ratu Sir Penaia GANILAU as 'interim Prime Minister' on 5 December 1987. (See FIJI COUPS.) Major General RABUKA became Prime Minister in 1992, and after Ratu Penaia's death in December 1993, Ratu Mara became President of Fiji. He is married to Adi Lady Lalabalavu, Roko Tui Dreketi.—KRF

Extracts from the 10th Dillingham Lecture, presented in Hawai'i on 30 July 1975, when Ratu Mara was Prime Minister

Oceania

I have called my talk 'Currents in the Pacific' for various reasons. First, it reminds us that we are oceanic peoples, with all the advantages and disadvantages that this brings. We can harvest the seas and the reefs and the lagoons for our protein needs—at least as long as we can avoid pollution of all the kinds that threaten us nowadays.

The 'Pacific Way'

Clearly there must be the fullest possible development of agriculture and fisheries. Quite apart from the income and employment it provides for our own people, I believe that there is a moral duty on us all to develop to the utmost the natural advantages we have been given in the way of fertile soil and benign climate, together with seas abounding with fish, always provided there is sound exploitation and wise conservation...Care for others, and sharing are an integral part of Pacific custom and tradition and we have never limited this within a narrow selfish pattern. Our general landholding pattern enjoins sharing...

On Pacific societies

Our village and countryside environment are simple and the means of controlling it are a matter of traditional knowledge passed down over the centuries. On social support, the closely knit traditional village community provides a degree of social support not available in an industrial society where a young adult leaves home and makes his way, probably in another social world. On satisfaction of drives contributing to physical well-being it might be thought we are at a disadvantage, but a village community, perhaps particularly one on the sea coast, has all the factors required for a good diet—and those of you who have had the good fortune to see rugby teams from the Pacific would certainly not call them undernourished. On aesthetic and sensory drives, one has perhaps only to look at the beauty of our islands, but the wonderful Pacific Festival of the Arts held in Suva in 1972 showed not only the kaleidoscopic variety of our cultural heritage but also the joy of those engaged in it.

Further reading

Mara, Ratu Sir Kamisese, 1975. *Currents in the Pacific*, Dillingham Lecture Series.

——, 1997. *The Pacific Way: a memoir*, University of Hawai'i Press

——, 1977. *Selected Speeches*, Fiji Government Printer.

■ *Fiamē Mata'afa Mulinu'u II* Fiamē Mata'afa Faumuinā Mulinu'u II (1921–75), first Prime Minister of (Western) Samoa, was the son of Mata'afa Faumuinā Mulinu'u I (a man of great influence in the colonial administration, who died in 1948), and thus a descendant of one of the four *tama'aiga*, high chiefly families of Samoa. Educated at the Marist Brothers school in Apia, his political aspirations were made public on the final day of the Constitutional Convention held in December 1954, when he criticized the decision to elect Tupua Tamasese and Malietoa TANUMAFILI as joint Heads of State. In the newly reorganized legislative assembly of 1957, Mata'afa became Minister for Agriculture. When the former position of 'leader of government business' became prime minister in 1959, Mata'afa was the first incumbent, leading Samoa into independence in 1962 and remaining in power until 1969 (succeeded by Tupua TAMASESE Lealofi IV), and then serving a further term 1972–75, ended by his death in office. Associated with the early development of COOPERATIVES in Samoa, Mata'afa was also closely involved in the Congregational Christian church, being elected chairman during his term as prime minister. He married Fetauimalemau Fuatino La'ulu (Masiofo Fetaui Mata'afa), who became the first pro-chancellor of the University of the South Pacific (1970–76), and then entered parliament after her husband's death. Their daughter, Fiamē Naomi Mata'afa, is also a politician, and is the present Minister for Education.—KRF

■ *Jonathan Fifi'i* Jonathan Fifi'i (1921–90), Solomon Islands political leader, was the son of Buumae and his wife Dafua, from near 'Oloburi, Sinalagu harbour, in the Kwaio district of Malaita. Born a pagan, he was educated by the SEVENTH-DAY ADVENTIST Mission until 1938 when he went to Tulagi to work as a house-servant until 1941. He returned to Malaita during the war, then joined the Solomon Islands Labour Corps, working for the American forces on Guadalcanal. It was here that he met the other men who were to become leaders with him of the MAASINA RULE Movement, 1944–52, a sustained political protest which brought changes to British policies although it did not directly lead to independence for the Protectorate. Fifi'i became head chief of the movement in east Kwaio, one of nine head chiefs on Malaita. Arrested in 1947, Fifi'i and other leaders were tried under the 1799 *Unlawful Societies Act*, sentenced to six years imprisonment, finally released in June 1950. A member of the first Malaita Council, Fifi'i became an important custodian of Kwaio culture, working with anthropologist Roger Keesing, with whom he visited the United States in 1966–67. In 1968 he was elected to the new legislative assembly and became Minister for Home Affairs in 1972–75. Fifi'i travelled widely overseas on government business, continuing in parliament after independence in 1978, until his defeat in the 1980 election. During 1982 he recorded his life story, published in 1989.—CM2

Further reading

Fifi'i, J, 1989. *From Pig-Theft to Parliament: my life between two worlds*, tr. and ed. R M Keesing, Solomon Islands College of Higher Education and University of the South Pacific.

■ *Prince Fatafehi Tu'ipelehake* Prince Fatafehi Tu'ipelehake (7 January 1922–10 April 1999) was born in Tonga, the younger son of Queen SĀLOTE and Prince Tungī. He was educated at Tupou College, Tonga, NEWINGTON College, Sydney, and Gatton Agricultural College, Queensland. In his early political career he became Governor of Vava'u (1949) and served in ministerial posts as Governor of Ha'apai and Minister for Lands and Agriculture. When his brother became king in 1965, he was made Prime Minister of Tonga, a position he retained until he retired in 1991, and also held the portfolio of Foreign Affairs. He was married to Princess Melenaite Tupaimoheafo, who died in Auckland on 16 March 1993, and they had six children.—KRF

■ *Tupua Tamasese Lealofi IV* Tupua Tamasese Lealofi IV (8 May 1922–9 July 1983), who served two terms as Samoa's prime minister, was a sensitive and articulate leader. He was the eldest son of high titleholder, Tupua Tamasese Lealofi III, who was leader of the Samoan resistance movement known as *ole* MAU, and who had been killed when police opened fire on Mau marchers on 'Black Saturday', 28 December 1929. Lealofi's uncle, Tupua Tamasese Mea'ole, inherited the title and became a member of the Council of State from 1949. At independence in 1962, Mea'ole became a joint Head of State with Malietoa TANUMAFILI II. Lealofi, who had attended the Marist Brothers' School and Malifa High School in Apia, went to Suva to study medicine. He returned to work as a doctor for the Health Department, and was employed at Apia Hospital until 1969. After his uncle's death on 5 April 1963, Lealofi inherited the Tupua and Tamasese titles; and in 1968 he was appointed to the Council of Deputies (which acts in the absence of the head of state). In 1970, Tupua Tamasese Lealofi resigned from the Council to stand for parliament, and when the Legislative Assembly met, he was elected prime minister, defeating Fiamē Mata'afa MULIUNU'U II, who had held office since 1959. Mata'afa returned to power in 1973, but when he died in office in 1975, Malietoa appointed Tupua Tamasese immediately, without waiting for the assembly to declare its nomination. After the 1976 election Tupuola Efi was elected prime minister, and Tupua Tamasese then resigned from the legislature and returned to the Council of Deputies.—KRF

Extracts from Tupua Tamasese Lealofi IV 1970 address, *Western Samoa Faces the Modern World*, shortly after he became Samoa's second prime minister

Samoa's belief in her own ways is demonstrated in those aspects of government unique to itself. When the United Nations Organisation learned about the proposal that only the *matai* [chiefly titleholders] would be given the right to vote, it could not accept this as a view supported by the majority. So a plebiscite was taken and the will of the people was confirmed. A *Malo Tutotasi* [independent government] was established which is an embodiment of an intricate blend of the Samoan and the foreign. This improbable marriage appears to be working reasonably well...Despite the fact that the first two Prime Ministers are also *tama-a-aiga* [of royal descent], I believe that a Prime Minister that is not a *tama-a-aiga* will be elected to office in my own lifetime.

Even though Western Samoa is small and technologically under-developed, her population is highly literate in the mother tongue and most of the people under 40 years of age understand, even if they do not speak, English. The average villager in Western Samoa is a sophisticated person, quite capable of dealing with his everyday world—in other words, the differentiation between town-dweller and peasant which exists in some under-developed countries, is absent in my country...I find Samoa's confidence in itself and its own ways extremely comforting and even inspiring.

Further reading

Lealofi, Tupua Tamasese IV, 1970. *Western Samoa Faces the Modern World*, address to the Wellington Branch of the New Zealand Institute of International Affairs, 30 September, Institute of International Affairs, Wellington.

■ *George Mye* George Mye, MBE, OAM (1923–), Torres Strait Islands Councillor and ATSIC Commissioner, was born on Erub. After leaving school he joined the Queensland government's Islands Industry Board and in 1948 was sent to manage its store on Mer. He was elected to the Mer Council in 1953 and retained the position until he returned to Erub in 1976. Mye was the Eastern Islands Representative to the Islander Advisory Council established in 1972, and Chairman of its successor, the Islands Coordinating Council, from its establishment in 1984 to 1988. He was a member of the Commonwealth's National Aboriginal Consultative Committee (1973–77), and its successor the National Aboriginal Conference (1977–85). From 1990 to 1994 he was a commissioner on the Aboriginal and Torres Strait Islander Commission (ATSIC). Mye chaired the Border Committee, which led a successful campaign against the partitioning of Torres Strait between Australia and Papua New Guinea in the 1970s. He has been a staunch advocate of land and sea rights for Torres Strait Islanders, and an influential advocate of self-government.—SM

Further reading

Beckett, J, 1987. *Torres Strait Islanders: custom and colonialism*, Cambridge University Press.

■ *Hammer DeRoburt* Hammer DeRoburt (25 September 1923–July 1992), first President of Nauru, was born and educated on Nauru, later attending Geelong Technical College in Australia before returning to Nauru as a schoolteacher (1940–42). One of the 1200 Nauruans deported by the Japanese, he survived the term of forced labour (1942–46) and after the war entered the Nauru public service in educational administration (1947–51). He then became a member of Nauru's Local Government Council (1955–68), rising to the position of chairman and Head Chief of Nauru in 1965. In 1968 DeRoburt became chairman of the Transitional Council of State, and then president, his first term lasting until 1976. He headed the opposition for the next two years and began his second term as president in 1978. A skilful and practical politician, he co-opted three opposition members into his cabinet in 1983, including Bernard DOWIYOGO, a former president (1976–78) and the leader of the Nauru Party. DeRoburt served as the second Chancellor of the University of the South Pacific (1973–76) and received an honorary doctorate from USP in 1976. He was serving a fourth term as president when he died in office in 1992.—KRF

■ *Tofilau Eti Alesana* Tofilau Eti Alesana (4 June 1924–20 March 1999) became Samoa's fifth prime minister on 30 December 1982. He relinquished the post on 29 December 1985, and then resumed the office on 25 March 1988. Tofilau led the Human

Rights Protection Party (HRRP) which has won every general election since 1982. Internal party dissension after the general election in March 1985 saw several senior HRRP members of parliament vote with the opposition to defeat Tofilau's budget in December 1985, a process leading to his replacement as prime minister by Va'ai Kolone who was leader of the dissident HRRP members.

Apart from the high chiefly title of Tofilau, he was bestowed with four others, the first when he was 23 years old, very young for a chiefly title. He was an exceptional exponent of Samoan oratory, the most revered of Samoan arts. Tofilau was born in Vaitogi, American Samoa, to the Reverend Alesana Faivae (a longtime missionary to Papua New Guinea) and Vaoita Malaitai of Samoa. Educated in both countries, he was descended from eminent Samoan families whose members have played prominent roles in local and national politics and church affairs in Samoa as well as American Samoa.

A successful planter and businessman, Tofilau was first elected to parliament in 1957 under the high chiefly title of Luamanuvae and became the youngest member of Samoa's first cabinet in 1959, being entrusted with the difficult Health portfolio. From 1988 Dr Tofilau presided over a vigorous drive to develop public facilities throughout the country, as well as implementing major reforms in many areas, particularly in the economic and financial sectors. Determined to prepare Samoa for the challenges of the next century, which is expected to be dominated by the World Trade Organization and globalization, he successfully won the strong support of Samoans as well as the international community for his reforms. In November 1998, suffering from terminal cancer, Dr Tofilau resigned as prime minister, nominating Tuilaepa Sailele Malielegaoi as his successor.—KE

■ *George R Ariyoshi* George Ryoichi Ariyoshi (12 March 1926–), was the third Governor of Hawai'i (1974–86), and the first American of Japanese descent to become a governor in the United States. Born in Honolulu, he is a graduate of Michigan State University and has received six honorary degrees from international universities and been awarded the Order of the Sacred Treasure, first class (1985) by the Japanese government. He was elected to the Territorial House of Representatives in Hawai'i in 1954, and then became a member of the Territorial and State Senate (1958–70), serving as Lieutenant Governor of Hawai'i (1970–74), Acting Governor (1973–74), and then Governor. He also became president of the Bar Association of Hawai'i in 1969, and was president and founder of the Hawai'i Bar Association (1969–70), and the Pacific Basin Development Council (1980–81). Governor Ariyoshi currently chairs the board of governors of the EAST–WEST CENTER and holds a number of directorships, while continuing his law career in international business consulting.—SBCLF & KRF

■ *Amata Kabua* Amata Kabua (17 November 1927–20 December 1996), first President of the Republic of the Marshall Islands, was descended by adoption from Kabua the Great, the paramount chief (*iroi'lapalap*) of the Ralik or southern chain of the Marshall Islands who died in 1910. Kabua the Great's power resulted from his distinguished lineage, force of personality, political acumen, leadership skills, and his ability to construct mutually beneficial alliances with German traders and colonial officials in Marshall Islands. In many ways, Amata Kabua's life mirrored that of his accomplished ancestor. Born on Jabor Island, Jaluit, Kabua attended Mauna College, Hawai'i, and then served as an elementary and intermediate schoolteacher on Majuro. In 1951, he was appointed Superintendent of Schools in Marshall Islands (after two years as assistant superintendent), a position he held until 1953. An accomplished musician and singer, he received an Associate of Arts degree in 1955 in Hawai'i.

On his return, Kabua served in several administrative positions with the Marshall Islands Congress. In 1956, he won election to that body's House of Iroij, and remained a member for nine years. He also served during this period as president and manager of the Marshall Islands Import-Export Company. Kabua represented Kwajalein Atoll landowners in their earliest negotiations with the United States military over the use of their atoll for American missile testing. At Kabua's insistence, landowners rejected the United States' initial offer of indefinite use for a lump sum payment of US$300 000. A settlement was finally achieved in 1964 when the Kwajalein landowners agreed to a 99-year lease and a one-time payment of US$750 000.

In 1965 Kabua was elected one of the four Marshallese representatives to the first Congress of Micronesia. An early critic of the American administration of the islands, Kabua adopted a less combative profile after winning election in 1969 as

President of the Senate of the Congress of Micronesia. In 1973 Kabua again changed course, leading efforts to separate Marshall Islands from the rest of Micronesia. Under Kabua's leadership, a constitution was drafted in 1977 and later ratified by popular vote. In 1979, Kabua was elected president of the new republic, holding this office until his death. Kabua in the later years of his presidency came under increasing criticism for the waste, corruption and nepotism said to characterize his government. Particularly appalling to local, regional and international critics was Kabua's willingness to entertain plans to accept contaminated foreign soil as landfill and to use some of Marshall Islands' more remote atolls as dumping sites for nuclear wastes from Japan and the United States.—DH

■ *Ricardo J Bordallo* Ricardo Jerome Bordallo (11 December 1927–1990), who served two terms as elected Governor of Guam, was born in Agana (Hagatna), and educated at George Washington High School, Guam, before attending the University of San Francisco (1947–50). From 1956, he combined business (proprietor of Ricky's Enterprises, and publisher of a newspaper) with a political career with the Democrat Party in the Guam legislature (1956–70), before becoming governor in 1974. He then moved into building and real estate, and was involved in a wide range of community and business organizations, before being elected to a second term as governor (1983–86). He failed to win a third term of office after charges relating to corruption were brought against him. The Republican candidate, Joseph F Ada, won the election, and Bordallo, who was later convicted, took his own life in 1990. His widow, Madeleine Z Bordallo, is a Democrat senator and the present Lieutenant Governor of Guam.—KRF

■ *Toalipi Lauti* Toalipi Lauti (28 November 1928–), first Prime Minister of Tuvalu, was born in Papua New Guinea, attended Queen Victoria School, Fiji, and completed his education in New Zealand, at Wesley College and the Christchurch Teachers Training College. When a new constitution was adopted in Tuvalu in October 1975, Lauti became chief minister, and then prime minister from independence in 1978 until 1981 (succeeded by Dr Tomasi Puapua). Lauti's parliamentary career also included terms as Minister for Finance and Minister for Foreign Affairs.—KRF

■ *Sir Albert Maori Kiki* Albert Maori Kiki (21 September 1931–), from Orokolo in the Gulf district of Papua New Guinea, was educated at the London Missionary Society village school and then at Sogeri after the war (1948–51). Kiki was accepted for medical training in Fiji and gained a diploma in pathology. After returning to Port Moresby, he established the New Guinea Workers Association and began to work for removal of discriminatory laws and increased indigenous participation in the legislative council. He also set up the first Rugby Union Association. His growing sense of the injustices of the Australian administration increased during time spent in Buka as a welfare assistant (1961–63), and on his return to Port Moresby his political consciousness developed during a course at the Administrative College (1964–65) which eventually led to the formation of the PANGU PATI in June 1967, and to Kiki's resignation from the public service. Unsuccessful in the 1968 elections, Kiki remained national secretary of the Pangu Pati and after the 1972 elections, he entered parliament as Minister for Lands and Environment in SOMARE's cabinet. He served as deputy prime minister (1975–77) and received the award of KBE in 1975.—KRF

Extracts from Sir Albert's 1968 autobiography, *Kiki: ten thousand years in a lifetime*

The two years at the administrative college were very important years in my life, not only because I learned Pacific History, English, Political Science and even bookkeeping, but mainly because it was there that I met many of the men who were my closest allies in my present struggle. Perhaps the most stimulating course was Cecil Abel's political science class, where we discussed different forms of government and speculated which of these would be most suitable for an independent Papua–New Guinea. Many of us felt that a presidential system would suit us better than the Westminster model because in most of our traditional societies we looked up to one strong leader. However, it was clear to us that the Australians were most likely to give us the only form of government they knew themselves, which was the Westminster type. We spent many hours after lectures speculating on the type of changes we might want to introduce after independence. Those were restless years in 1963 and '64, with racial and political tension gradually mounting.

Among the many issues we [Pangu Pati in 1968] shall press for are the unification of Papua–New Guinea into one country, and the straightening out of the land problems...Many government offices and schemes are on land that was never properly acquired from native owners...Furthermore, we shall revive the issue of the local officers pay arbitration case. We cannot accept two rates of pay for expatriate and local officers...We shall look at the housing situation in great detail. We cannot tolerate a set-up which virtually sets aside certain areas for white residents only. In residential areas like Boroko, the rents are put up deliberately to keep potential native tenants out...Such discrimination will have to be stopped. Most important of all, the Pangu Pati will have to take a close look at the Department of District Administration. The patrol officer may have been a useful person in the early days when the country was being opened up, but nowadays many districts have their education officer, their doctor, their agricultural officer, their police station and their magistrate. The Kiap in such areas is a complete anomaly...These are just some of the immediate problems Pangu will have to tackle. Our most important claim will remain immediate home rule leading to eventual independence...I feel very optimistic about the future of the country. That alleged tensions between Papua and New Guinea will prove insurmountable has been proved wrong by the very existence of Pangu Pati...At this moment in our history I can see my country's future mapped out. We know where we want to go and I think we know how to get there.

Further reading

Kiki, A M, 1968. *Kiki: ten thousand years in a lifetime, a New Guinea autobiography*, F W Chesire.

■ *Tosiwo Nakayama* Tosiwo Nakayama (23 November 1931–) was the first President of the Federated States of Micronesia. He was born at Piserach, Chuuk and attended the University of Hawai'i (1955–58) before being appointed as an adviser to the US Delegation to the United Nations in 1961. Entering politics in 1963, he was elected to the Chuuk District Legislature in 1963, and became a member of the Council of Micronesia which was elected in 1965. When a constitutional government was installed in the FSM in May 1979, Nakayama became the first president, remaining in office until 1987 (succeeded by John Haglelgam, from Yap). In 1990 he was a delegate to the constitutional convention.—KRF

■ *Gaston Flosse* Gaston Flosse (1932–), President of the territorial government of French Polynesia, was born in rural Rikitea in the Gambier group, the son of a French COPRA trader. Beginning his career as a schoolteacher, his developing interest in politics led to his election to the territorial assembly in 1967, and he emerged in the 1970s as leader of conservative, anti-autonomy opinions. In 1980 he and his Tahoeraa Huira'atira party changed tack, campaigning for some degree of local autonomy, and winning 30 per cent of the vote in the 1982 elections. The awakening reassertion of Tahitian identity was accompanied by the introduction of new legislation in France in 1984 providing increased autonomy for the territory. Flosse became a dominant figure in French Polynesian politics: first elected to lead the territorial government in 1986, he was also an elected representative (*deputé*) in the French parliament, becoming a junior minister in Jacques Chirac's cabinet as Secretary of State for Pacific Affairs (1986–88). The conflicting demands of his various duties and business interests produced growing allegations of corruption and mismanagement, and in January 1987, Flosse stood down as president in favour of his loyal ally, Jacky Teuira. By the end of 1987, a new opposition coalition had formed, and Alexandre Léontieff took over the presidency, which he retained until the March 1991 elections. Then Tahoeraa Huira'atira swept back to power in coalition with the centrist party, Ai'a Api. Flosse resumed the presidency, further supported by the dismissal of all cases brought against him, and continues in this office, enjoying a further expansion of powers and privileges recently granted by the national assembly.

Flosse is a gifted orator with impressive political skills, and has been an enthusiastic participant in regional diplomacy. His mixed French and Tahitian ancestry has allowed him to benefit from the recent revival of Maohi culture while also taking advantage of his familiarity with French politics and law to achieve maximum financial aid from the French government, and his party's dominance is reinforced by its control of the capital, Pape'ete.—KRF

Further reading

von Strokirch, K, 1998. 'Gaston Flosse: a recipe for longevity in Tahitian politics', in D R Shuster, P Larmour and K von Strokirch (eds), *Leadership in the Pacific Islands: tradition and the future*, Pacific Policy Papers 29, National Centre for Development Studies, The Australian National University, and MARC, University of Guam.

Henningham, S, 1992. *France and the South Pacific: a contemporary history*, Allen & Unwin.

■ *Ellie Gaffney* Ellie Gaffney (1932–), community activist, was born on Thursday Island. Gaffney's early education was interrupted when her family was evacuated south during the war. She spent several years working in Brisbane cafés, before returning to Thursday Island where she became an assistant nurse at the local hospital. After studying at night to complete her schooling Gaffney left for Brisbane to train as a Registered Nurse. She gained her qualifications at the Royal Brisbane Hospital, and did midwifery at Brisbane Women's Hospital, before returning to work at the Thursday Island Hospital in the early 1960s. She worked at Yarrabah from 1963–65, and then in Darwin for most of the 1970s. Gaffney returned to Thursday Island in 1980, gave up nursing and joined Aboriginal Hostels Ltd. For three years she worked to set up the Jumula Dubbins Hostel, until being employed to establish the Torres Strait Islanders Media Association (TSIMA) and train local broadcasters for Radio Thursday Island. The TSIMA office opened in 1985. Gaffney served as a director of the Torres Strait Co-operative Society from 1981 to 1993, and as its chairperson from 1989–93. She is also a member of the Aged Care Project and Mura Koska Women's Shelter.—SM

Further reading

Gaffney, E, 1989. *Ellie Gaffney, Somebody Now*, Aboriginal Studies Press.

■ *Jacques Lafleur* Jacques Lafleur (1932–), prominent conservative politician in New Caledonia, is the son of the first senator to represent New Caledonia in the French parliament (1946–55). Henri Lafleur (18 April 1902–October 1974, born at Noumea) who owned large NICKEL MINING and grazing interests, had founded the Rassemblement Calédonien (RC) in 1958, representing conservative Noumea mining and business interests. Putting aside earlier differences, the RC merged with the Union Démocratique in 1968, but Henri Lafleur left it in 1972, together with Roger Laroque (1910–85, long-serving Mayor of Noumea), because of personal rivalries, and formed another grouping. After his father's death, Jacques Lafleur became leader of yet another reformed version of this grouping, the Rassemblement Pour la Calédonie in 1977, and in the following year, again led the way into a still larger grouping of conservative parties, the Rassemblement pour la Calédonie dans la République (RPCR), which gained the patronage of prominent Gaullist politician Jacques Chirac, and came to represent the dominant conservative opposition to Kanak nationalism.

Around 1980, Lafleur began to express support for a moderate degree of self-government, however, and the fresh approach to a political compromise achieved by Michel Rocard in June 1988 rested heavily on an interim settlement negotiated in Paris between Lafleur and Jean-Marie TJIBAOU. The combined support given to the MATIGNON ACCORDS by the RPCR and the Front de la Libération Nationale Kanak et Socialiste (FLNKS) was essential to its acceptance, and made further economic reforms possible. In 1990 Lafleur, whose inherited mining and business interests have made him a multimillionaire, fulfilled a commitment to Tjibaou to assist Kanak participation in the nickel industry, agreeing to sell his company, the Société Minière du Sud Pacifique, to the FLNKS-controlled government of the northern province, which obtained French government funding for the purchase. During the 1990s he also played a significant role in achieving a consensus solution to the scheduled referendum on independence among major political groups, which resulted in overwhelming support for the NOUMEA ACCORD.—KRF

■ *Paul M Calvo* Paul McDonald Calvo (25 July 1934–), the third elected Governor of Guam, was born in Agana (Hagatna) and attended George Washington High School, Guam, and then the Peacock Military Academy in San Antonio, Texas, and the University of Santa Clara, California. He embarked on a business career in his family's insurance company from 1958, also entering politics in the 1960s, becoming elected as a senator (1965–66), and chairing the government Committee on Finance and Taxation. In his two further terms as senator (1970–74), he was parliamentary leader of the Republican Party, and was elected governor in 1978, his term ending in 1982.

■ *Dr Timoci Bavadra* Timoci Uluivuda Bavadra (22 September 1934–3 November 1989), from Viseisei on the west coast of Viti Levu, was a medical doctor and a politician. Having entered politics through involvement in trade unions (President of Fiji Public Servants Association, 1978–85), he was the founding President of the Fiji Labour Party (FLP) in 1985 and became leader of the National Federation Party–FLP Coalition in 1987. He was elected Prime Minister of Fiji in April 1987, but a month later, he was deposed by military coup (see FIJI COUPS). He subsequently entered into negotiations which produced a political solution in the Deuba Accord, signed on 23 September 1987, but a second coup occurred two days later, and a republic was declared on 7 October 1987. In March 1988, Dr Bavadra was diagnosed with spinal cancer and died in 1989. His wife, Adi Kuini Vuikaba (a member of the Great Council of Chiefs and her husband's short-term successor as leader of the National Federation Party–FLP Coalition) played a significant role in Dr Bavadra's political career.—KRF

Extracts from Timoci Bavadra's speeches

First address as Prime Minister, 13 April 1987

We recognise that the welfare of our nation is linked to the inter-dependence of nations, particularly our neighbours in the South Pacific and those nations with which we have historical, economic and democratic ties. I have no doubt that today their best wishes are with Fiji and its people. My fellow citizens, the dawn of the new era is upon us. Together let us write the new chapter which, God willing, will be one which we and our children will be proud of.

Extract from speech at Brent Hall, London, 8 June 1987

I would like to stress once again that the multiracial society of Fiji has been responsible for the prosperity of our country. If the people of Indian origin had not been brought into Fiji as labourers 100 years ago, it would clearly have been the indigenous Fijians who would have been exposed to the horrors of plantation work in those primitive colonial times. It would indeed not be an exaggeration to say that the coming of the Indians to Fiji has allowed a continuation of Fijian traditions and customs and for them to be retained intact. If the indigenous population had, on the other hand, been forced into plantation labour, it would surely have resulted in the decimation of the small Fijian population due to the hardships and diseases to which they would have been exposed.

Further reading

Bain, A and Baba, T (eds), 1990. *Bavadra: Prime Minister, Statesman, Man of the People: selection of speeches and writings, 1985–1989*, Sunrise Press.

■ *Lazarus Sali'i* Lazarus Sali'i (1936–20 August 1988) was the second President of the Republic of PALAU, elected in 1985. A strong supporter of the United States, Sali'i had been educated at the University of Hawai'i at Mānoa. He served in the administration of the US Trust Territory of the Pacific Islands (TTPI) at SAIPAN, was a member of the Congress of Micronesia, chaired the Congress Committee on Future Political Status, and was an advocate of the Compact of Free Association with the United States, approved by the US Congress in November 1986. Intense political infighting over the compact, PALAU'S NUCLEAR-FREE CONSTITUTION, and allegations of government corruption plagued Sali'i's administration. He was found dead after an apparent suicide, aged 52.—RCK

■ *Edward Mabo* Edward 'Koiki' Mabo (1936–92), land rights activist, was born on Mer, the son of Robert and Poipe Sambo. His mother died soon after his birth and he was adopted by Benny and Maiga Mabo. He worked on luggers from 1953 to 1957, then in the cane-fields, railways and wharves of north Queensland. From 1967 to 1975 he was a gardener at James Cook University of North Queensland, where he often participated in classes. An active trade unionist since 1960, he was secretary of the Aboriginal Advancement League in 1962 and a member of the Federal Council for the Advancement of Aborigines and Torres Strait Islanders (FCAATSI). In 1970 he resigned from FCAATSI and became president of a rival organization, the Council for the Rights of Indigenous People. He was a founder of the Black Community School in Townsville and its director from 1973 to 1985. Throughout the 1980s Eddie Mabo served in numerous organizations dedicated to the promotion of indigenous and in particular Torres Strait Islander rights.

In the late 1970s Mabo became aware that legally he had no title to his family land on Mer, and in May 1982, with a number of others, took a claim to the High Court of Australia. Despite a determined effort by the Queensland government to block the claim, in June 1992 the High Court eventually found in favour of the plaintiff in *Mabo and others* v *the State of Queensland*, which recognized the existence of native title in Australia. This landmark case is usually referred to as the Mabo Decision, or more simply as 'Mabo'. Eddie Mabo died of cancer in Brisbane in January 1992, just months before the decision was handed down. He was buried in Townsville, but on 3 June 1995, his tombstone was desecrated. On 18 September 1995 he was reburied on Mer, near his ancestral land at Las.—SM

■ *Sir Michael Somare* Sir Michael Thomas Somare (9 April 1936–), the first Prime Minister of Papua New Guinea, was born in Rabaul, the son of a policeman and heir to a Murik (SEPIK) chieftaincy. Educated at a Japanese primary school in the Sepik during the war, and at Wewak and Finschhafen, he graduated from Sogeri Teachers College in 1957. After a visit to Australia, several years' teaching, and work as a radio journalist and broadcaster, Somare's growing interest in politics involved him in the foundation of the PANGU PATI in 1967. He was elected member for East Sepik in 1968 in the second house of assembly, and became chief minister—leading a coalition government—in the third house of assembly in April 1972, and then prime minister upon independence on 16 September 1975. His government fell in a motion of no confidence in March 1980, but he returned to power after the 1982 elections, until he was replaced by Paias WINGTI in 1985. His attempt to form another coalition after the 1987 elections was unsuccessful, and he remained as Leader of the Opposition until deciding to step down from leadership of the Pangu Pati in late May 1988. Becoming foreign minister in Rabbie NAMALIU's government (1988–92), and later Minister of State in Julius CHAN's government, he has continued to represent East Sepik, and is currently leader of the National Alliance Party. Somare is a consensus leader who has survived because he is not dogmatic, but willing to compromise, and negotiate to a resolution. Defeated in his bid to become prime minister after the 1997 elections, he has taken a back seat as elder and respected statesman of the nation. He was awarded the KBE in 1990.—CM2

Extracts from Michael Somare's 1975 autobiography, *Sana*

It took me months to get the self-government date of 1 December 1973 passed by the House of Assembly, but only 45 minutes to set the date for Papua New Guinea's independence. It was one of the happiest days of my life. With some of my colleagues, I had laboured for three years to effect the constitutional changes necessary to bring Papua New Guinea to nationhood. When I decided to go into politics in early 1967 the one purpose I had in mind was to be instrumental in bringing the country to self-government and eventual independence...In spite of the mounting political pressures and numerous crises we are faced with from time to time I am still optimistic about the country's future. Despite what we used to be told in the past, Papua New Guinea is a country of very rich and abundant resources. There is no shortage of firms and investors eager to develop those resources...The conflicts and tensions between various groups, sometimes moving them to the brink of secession, have been one of our most difficult problems. Like most other third world countries that have thrown off colonial rule and been faced with the problem of forging numerous language groups and cultural traditions into one nation state, we are faced with two options. We could create an all-powerful central government and force dissident groups to fall into line, using force if necessary. Our other option is to adopt a tolerant attitude towards local interests and to recognize the existing variety of patterns. The first alternative is relatively easy for a government willing to rely on force. But it is highly undesirable because it means imposing on the people a way of life based on some abstract ideology that is alien to them. The government would necessarily remain remote from the people. The second alternative is far more difficult, but it is the only possible way for this country. It is a difficult way because the central government may often appear weak. It puts the central government into the awkward position of having to arbitrate constantly between different local interest groups and between different regions of the country. It involves the danger that, if the government cannot resolve the issues and local pressure groups become too strong, the country could fall apart. However it is the wise way to take and the one congenial to our own traditions.

Further reading

Somare, M, 1975. *Sana: an autobiography of Michael Somare*, Niugini Press.

■ ***Jean-Marie Tjibaou*** Jean-Marie Tjibaou (1936–May 1989), influential political leader and architect of the Kanak cultural renaissance, left his home village at Tiendanite near Hienghene, New Caledonia, at the age of nine to be educated by the Marist Brothers in Canala and the Isle of Pines. It was his subsequent training for the priesthood and his experience at the cathedral in Noumea which made him conscious of the injustices which his people experienced and their sense of desperation. Inspired by the beginnings of a Melanesian political consciousness, the libertarian and egalitarian principles of post-war France, and the transcendental vision of the world provided by Christianity, he left for Europe in 1968. There he moved into the social sciences, finding inspiration in the work of missionary-anthropologist, Maurice LEENHARDT, and of Roger Bastide. The kind of anthropology he found—concerned with issues of development and social justice—equipped him with the knowledge, understanding and analytical tools to return to his Kanak people at 35, to explore a new future based on direct social and cultural action.

Having abandoned the priesthood, married and re-established himself as an active member of the Tiendanite and larger Melanesian community, Tjibaou began to enter into a dialogue with the other inhabitants of New Caledonia, first initiating a program of seminars directed at Europeans and then in 1975, organizing a major Kanak cultural festival, *Mélanésia 2000*. He made his first move into politics in 1977, at the local level, becoming Mayor of Hienghene, but then emerged rapidly on to the national stage as leader of the Front de la Libération Nationale Kanak et Socialiste (FLNKS), a key actor in the search for a political solution to the New Caledonian drama. While the country came close to massive bloodshed in the 1980s, in part this was averted because Tjibaou adopted an international, statesmanlike role as 'President of the Provisional Government of Kanaky', systematically avoiding violent confrontation, affirming the cultural and historical legitimacy of the independence movement, and stressing that Kanaky's future would be a shared one. Captivating fellow Kanaks and French political leaders alike, he drew on time-honoured French presidential strategies of open communication, while introducing Melanesian codes and oratorical practices, searching for consensus. The virtues of Melanesian pacifism were confirmed, active sympathy with Kanak aspirations was revealed, and material support from sympathizers in France (notably, the development of cooperatives and legal assistance) was assured for the Kanaks in their struggle.

Tjibaou died at the hands of Djubelly Wea, a fellow Kanak nationalist, on Ouvea in May 1989, essentially for having compromised on the issue of outright and immediate independence for his country, and for having opted for dialogue rather than confrontation with the loyalist (essentially settler) Caldoche community. A man of enormous charisma, unswerving commitment and exceptional integrity, Tjibaou—looking far into the modern world from the perspective of his village in the northern interior of the country—left as his legacy the almost single-handed creation of a national Kanak identity, and the establishment of a new territorial basis for the exercise of political and economic power by the Kanak people within New Caledonia.—EW

■ *Carlos Sablan Camacho* Carlos Sablan Camacho (27 February 1937–), former Governor of the Commonwealth of the Northern Mariana Islands, was born at Garapan, Saipan, and attended the University of Hawai'i and the Fiji School of Medicine (now part of the University of the South Pacific), qualifying as a doctor and working in medicine (1963–67) until he entered politics as an elected member of the Congress of Micronesia (1967–68). He served as chief medical officer of Public Health (1969–77), also being appointed to the Northern Marianas Constitutional Convention in 1976, and becoming president of the Saipan Democratic Party (1975–77). He was elected governor in 1978, serving until 1981.—KRF

■ *Sir John Kaputin* John Rumet Kaputin (7 July 1939–), a Tolai from Matupit Island, East New Britain, was educated in Papua New Guinea and Australia. He began a teacher-training course and worked in a series of jobs in Australia, returning to Port Moresby to work as interpreter in the House of Assembly, training as a Clerk of the House. He then pursued two years of university studies on scholarship to the EAST–WEST CENTER, at the University of Hawai'i. On returning to Rabaul, he became manager of the European-owned savings and loans society, and set up the New Guinea Development Company (NGDC) in East New Britain in 1970, on behalf of the newly formed MATAUNGAN ASSOCIATION. An outstanding orator, he was elected to parliament in 1972, becoming Central Planning Minister in Michael SOMARE's 1977 cabinet. Then in 1979, he spent 10 weeks in jail after being convicted of failing to lodge company returns for the NGDC. Abruptly demoted by Somare to Minister of Education in 1980, Kaputin joined John MOMIS in forming a new party, the Melanesian Alliance, and both switched their support to Julius CHAN who then became prime minister. As Minister of Finance in the early 1980s, Kaputin introduced the policy of fixing the value of the kina against a basketful of currencies represented in imports. He became foreign minister in Paias WINGTI's cabinet in July 1992 and was knighted in 1997. In 1998, Sir John was the special state negotiator representing the PNG government during the BOUGAINVILLE CONFLICT, and in this capacity led the signing of the Bougainville Truce agreement at Arawa. (See also PACIFIC ISLANDERS' SPORTING ACHIEVEMENTS.)—KRF

■ *Sir Julius Chan* Julius Chan (29 August 1939–) was born at Tanga, New Ireland, to a New Ireland mother and Chinese father. In 1954 he went to the Marist Brothers College at Ashgrove, Queensland, and afterwards to the University of Queensland. His family was heavily involved in shipping and accommodation in the New Guinea islands, and after he was elected for Namatanai, New Ireland, in 1968 in the second house of assembly, he founded the People's Progress Party, representing business interests. He joined the coalition formed by Michael SOMARE in 1972, and was appointed Minister for Internal Finance (and at independence, the country's first Finance minister), responsible for the introduction of Papua New Guinea's own currency in April 1975. He withdrew from the Government at the end of 1978, but became prime minister in March 1980 with the support of four MPs from Bougainville, when Somare lost a no-confidence vote in parliament. Sir Julius lost power again after the 1982 elections, but he became Finance and Planning minister and deputy prime minister in the cabinet of Paias WINGTI in 1985 until the vote of no confidence in July 1988 which installed Rabbie NAMALIU as prime minister. After an election victory in August 1994, Sir Julius enjoyed a second term as prime minister (replacing Wingti) but lost his seat in the 1997 elections, after widespread criticism of his involvement in the controversial 'Sandline' affair, in which mercenaries were brought into Papua New Guinea in an apparent attempt to resolve the long-standing BOUGAINVILLE CONFLICT. He was awarded the KBE in 1980.—KRF

■ *Solomon Mamaloni* Solomon Mamaloni (c1940–), former Prime Minister of Solomon Islands, was born on Makira (San Cristobal). He entered politics in 1970, and was elected to the governing council, representing Makira/Ulawa. Under a new constitution adopted in 1974, the governing council became the legislative council, and Mamaloni was appointed the first chief minister, leading the Solomon Islands into self-government on 1 January 1976. He resigned from parliament in 1977, after failing to win re-election as chief minister in 1976, but was returned in the general election of August 1980. He then became prime minister (leading a coalition government), and has held the office three times: 1980–84, 1989–93, and 1994–97. One of the first measures introduced when he came to power in 1980 was the introduction of the *Provincial Government Act*, which decentralized a number of administrative powers and functions. In 1989, however, his failure to deliver the expected federal government was seen as a major back-down on campaign promises. Mamaloni, facing the threat of a no-confidence motion on his style of leadership, resigned from the People's Alliance Party and formed a new government—the first time that a personal rather than a political coalition held power.

During this second term of office, relations between Solomon Islands and Papua New Guinea deteriorated with friction generated by the BOUGAINVILLE CONFLICT. Mamaloni was succeeded by the less combative Francis Billy Hilly after the 1993 elections, but returned to office in October 1994. Immediately after the 1997 elections, he was obliged to stand down as leader of the National Unity party, and was replaced by Danny Philip. In the parliamentary vote for prime minister, Bartholomew ULUFA'ALU was elected in a new coalition government. (See also LOGGING IN SOLOMON ISLANDS.)—KRF

■ *Walter Lini* Father Walter Lini (1942–21 February 1999), an Anglican priest and first Prime Minister of VANUATU, led the former Anglo–French CONDOMINIUM of the New Hebrides to independence as the Republic of Vanuatu on 30 July 1980, and was awarded a CBE in that year. He was prime minister for 11 years from 1980. In 1991 his Vanuaaku Party (which he had played a leading role in founding in 1974) suffered a major split. As a result Lini established a new political party, the National United Party, in opposition to the Vanuaaku Party.

Father Lini was born on Pentecost Island. He undertook his theological training at St Peter's Theological College in Solomon Islands, and at St John's Theological College in Auckland. From January 1974 he was granted leave by the church to devote himself to his full-time role as President of the Vanua'-aku Party (formerly the New Hebrides National Party). In 1976 he and Ati George Sokomanu presented the New Hebrides case for independence to the United Nations Committee of 24. In 1977 he led his party in a boycott of the New Hebrides Representative Assembly elections in protest against Condominium slowness in moving towards independence. However, 1979 saw his party win an outright majority in the Assembly (26 out of 39 seats), which was to become the first parliament of the Republic of Vanuatu.

The 'Father of Independence', as Father Lini was widely known in Vanuatu, achieved stable government during much of his time as prime minister, in contrast to the often tempestuous coalitions which have beleaguered Vanuatu since 1991. Lini's National United Party has been a coalition partner in government since 1991, first under the majority leadership of first Maxime Carlot Korman and then Rialuth Serge Vohor, both Union of Moderate Parties (UMP, Francophone), and now in coalition with the Vanua'aku Party.—DT

■ *John Momis* John Momis (1942–) has been member of parliament for the Bougainville Provincial seat in Papua New Guinea since 1972. Born in Salamaua, Morobe Province, he attended Buin Primary School in Bougainville and St Brendan's College in Yeppoon, Australia. He entered the Holy Spirit Seminary, Madang, in 1963, and was ordained as a Catholic priest in 1970. Elected to the first house of assembly in 1972 as the member for Bougainville (North Solomons), he chaired the constitutional planning committee (1972–75). On the eve of independence, concerned about Bougainville's future, Momis resigned his seat to form a secessionist movement in 1975. After the North Solomons won the right to set up a provincial government, however, he returned to national politics, was re-elected in 1977, and subsequently joined John KAPUTIN to launch a new party called Melanesian Alliance. In return for support for SOMARE's coalition, Momis was appointed Minister for Decentralization. He retained this post until 1982, serving the last two years in the cabinet of Prime Minister Julius CHAN, after Momis and the other Bougainville Members of Parliament supported Chan against Somare in a vote of no confidence in March 1980. When Somare returned to power in March 1985, he made Momis Deputy Prime Minister and Minister for the Public Service. In his parliamentary career since then, Momis has been Deputy Leader of the Opposition (1985–87 and 1987–88), Minister for Provincial Affairs (1988–92), Shadow Minister for Bougainville Affairs (1992) and Provincial Affairs (1993), Deputy Leader of the Opposition (1994), and Minister for Information and Communication (1994). He was granted dispensation to leave the priesthood and marry in 1993.—KRF

■ *Sir Iambakey Okuk* Iambakey Okuk (1943–1986), Papua New Guinea politician and businessman, was born at Pari, Chimbu Province, and adopted as a child by his uncle, a corporal in the police force, after the death of his father, Palma, a Kamanegu fight leader. His early schooling was in Mount Hagen, Goroka and Port Moresby where he was a Form Three student at Sogeri High School in 1965. Okuk then completed an apprenticeship as a motor mechanic in Port Moresby before returning to Wabag to work in the department of Public Works. After unsuccessfully contesting the Western Highlands Regional seat in 1968, and a by-election for Simbu in 1970, he entered the national parliament in 1972, representing Simbu until 1982 and Eastern Highlands from 1983 until his death. In 1970 Okuk created his own political base, the National Party.

Okuk held three portfolios in SOMARE's government between 1972 and 1976: Agriculture, Stock and Fisheries, then Transport, and Education. Dismissed from the ministry in 1976, Okuk became Leader of the Opposition in 1978. Between March 1980 and August 1982 he was Deputy Prime Minister and Minister for Civil Aviation and Transport in Chan's government. Losing his Simbu seat in 1982 he won an Eastern Highlands electorate in a 1983 by-election, but was disqualified from the seat in December 1984, regaining it in May 1985. He then became Minister for Primary Industry in the WINGTI government from November 1985 until his death from cancer.

Knighted in 1986, Sir Iambakey was the most prominent Highlands leader, his untimely death leading to riots on Port Moresby, Lae and the Highlands towns. A man of great personal charisma and contradictions he was self-serving and manipulative, advocating free enterprise and government assistance for national capitalists. His political philosophy is summed up in his 1978 statement: 'If you are not hungry for power then you should be working for the missions and reading the Bible all day.' Two of his most famous political acts occurred in 1981: the Dash-7 deal he did with De Havilland in Canada to re-fleet Air Niugini, without any Cabinet approval; and his personal intervention in the airing of a NBC radio program, by driving to the studio and ripping the tape out of the machine.—CM

■ *Kuniwo Nakamura* Kuniwo Nakamura (1943–), current President of PALAU, is descended from Japanese pre-World War II settlers to Palau, and speaks Japanese. A businessman whose family has wide-ranging commercial interests, he began his political career in 1970, and won election to the presidency in 1992 on a platform supporting the Compact of Free Association with the United States, which brings substantial funding to Palau. In his first term of office, a significant foreign affairs focus was on cultivating Japanese and Taiwanese corporate investment, especially in hotel development and commercial tuna fisheries. He has also been committed to the development of roads and infrastructure to open up and resettle Babeldaob, the least populated island, to reduce the overcrowding of KOROR.—KRF

■ *Sir Peter Kenilorea* Peter Kenilorea (23 May 1943–), first Prime Minister of Solomon Islands, was born at Takataka, Malaita. He completed a teacher-training course in New Zealand and was a teacher at King George VI Secondary School (Solomon Islands) from 1968 to 1970, before entering the public service. As he embarked on his administrative career, he gained a Certificate in Public Administration and qualified as a magistrate. He was then transferred to the position of deputy secretary to cabinet and secretary to the chief minister (1974–75), which he left to become district commissioner of the Eastern Solomons (1975–76). Moving on to the national political stage, he entered parliament in 1976, and was immediately elected chief minister. In this position, he was responsible for the introduction of the Solomon Islands National Independence Constitution, and became prime minister in 1978, at independence. He served two further short terms as prime minister in 1980 and 1984 (succeeded each time by Solomon MAMALONI), and became increasingly involved in international trade and fisheries negotiations on behalf of Solomon Islands. In 1986 he assisted in negotiations and later signed two important REGIONAL TREATIES, the South Pacific Nuclear Free Zone Treaty and the South Pacific Regional Environment Programme (SPREP). His knighthood (KBE) was awarded in 1982.

Sir Peter resigned his political career in 1991 (his leadership of the United Party being taken over by Ezekiel Alebua) to take up an appointment as executive director to the Forum Fisheries Agency in Honiara. During this period (1991–94), he negotiated the successful extension of the MULTILATERAL TREATY ON FISHERIES, signed in May 1992. In 1996, he was appointed to the office of OMBUDSMAN of Solomon Islands, on a five-year term.—KRF

■ *Dame Josephine Abaijah* Josephine Abaijah (1944–) was the first woman elected to parliament in Papua New Guinea in 1972. Her education began at the first government school in Misima, Milne Bay, the only girl in her class in 1950, followed by secondary schooling in Queensland. In 1960 she was part of the first intake of students at the new Papuan School of Medicine. After completing a Diploma in Health Education in London, she studied in the Philippines and returned to Port Moresby to become principal of the new Institute of Health Education, where she worked until winning the regional seat for Central District in the third house of assembly (1972). She formed the PAPUA BESENA political party in June 1973, with Papuan autonomy as its key issue, and made a symbolic declaration of independence for Papua on 16 March 1975, with the support of the Port Moresby City Council. In August, one month before Papua New Guinea's independence, her close friend and mentor, Dr Eric Wright, was deported. Abaijah left the country with him, remaining overseas for several months, and then continued to spend periods of time in Australia, returning to Port Moresby for each parliamentary session. When Wright died in Sydney, Abaijah brought back his ashes to scatter in Papuan waters. She became the member of parliament for the new National Capital District of Port Moresby, and was re-elected in 1977, along with a number of Papua Besena supporters. She lost her seat in 1982, stood unsuccessfully in 1987, then left the political arena to pursue business interests, being made a 'dame' in 1990. She was subsequently returned to Parliament in the 1997 elections, representing Milne Bay, and has become Governor of Milne Bay.—KRF

Further reading

Abaijah, J and Wright, E, 1991. *A Thousand Coloured Dreams*, Dellasta Pacific.

■ *Nidoish Naisseline* Nidoish Naisseline (1944–), leader of early Kanak nationalism, is the eldest son of Henri Nawossé Naisseline (1911–), high chief of Tadine on Mare (Loyalty Islands). One of the first Melanesians to attend the Sorbonne in 1962, he completed a masters degree in sociology. His radical student experience (as a participant in the May 1968 uprising) led him to organize the *Foulards Rouges* (Red Scarves) in 1969. Drawing on the KANAK REBELLION of 1878 for inspiration, group members wore red scarves marked 'Kanak' or 'Atai' (the 1878 rebel chief), and led a revival of pride in Kanak culture and identity (see NATIONALISM IN FRENCH TERRITORIES). Their protest activities created tensions and drew reprisals. Naisseline was convicted of subversive activity and sent to France in 1970, and then arrested again in 1974, when he and several others, including Déwé Gorodney and Suzanne Ounei, were imprisoned on various charges. At the end of 1974, when the movement was attracting popular support from diverse ethnic groups, members redefined their political goals to set up four regional groups, one of which included Déwé Gorodney's newly formed *Groupe 1878* on Grande Terre. From these groups, the new socialist political party known as PALIKA (*Parti de Libération Kanak*) was formed in May 1976. It called for the nationalization of NICKEL MINING, industries and banks, and Naisseline was one of its two members elected to the territorial assembly in 1977. PALIKA became a founding member of the Independence Front (*Front Indépendantiste*) in 1979, but differences emerged in June 1981, when Naisseline and his more moderate supporters left PALIKA to form the LKS (*Libération Kanak Socialiste*), refusing to support radical proposals to reorganize the Front into the FLNKS (*Front de Libération Nationale Kanak et Socialiste*) and to boycott and obstruct the 1984 elections. Support for the LKS dwindled when the fast-growing FLNKS campaigned against it, and Naisseline (continuing to represent Mare) was left as its only successful candidate in the 1985 elections. He continues to hold the position of president of the provincial assembly of Loyalty Islands.—KRF

■ *Bernard Dowiyogo* Bernard Dowiyogo (14 February 1946–), former President of Nauru, was educated in Nauru and Ballarat, before graduating from the Australian National University in Canberra as a lawyer. A former schoolteacher, he was secretary of Nauru General Hospital and general manager of the Nauru Cooperative Society. He entered parliament in 1973, becoming leader of the Nauru Party, and then Nauru's second elected president for six months (1976–77). He was appointed as Minister of Justice (recruited from the Opposition bench) in the cabinet of Hammer DeROBURT in 1983, and held the Health and Education portfolio under Kenas Arioi in 1989. After Arioi suffered a severe stroke, Dowiyogo defeated DeRoburt in the election for the presidency in December 1989. DeRoburt later resumed the presidency, but after his death in July 1992, Dowiyogo was again elected president. In 1995 he was a strident critic of French NUCLEAR TESTING, calling for the expulsion of France from the Pacific.—KRF

■ *Sir Rabbie Namaliu* Rabbie Langanai Namaliu CMG (3 April 1947–), a Tolai from Raluana, East New Britain, was one of the first students at the University of Papua New Guinea (UPNG) in 1966. He then completed a masters degree in Canada and returned to teach at UPNG for a year before being recruited by Chief Minister SOMARE in 1973 as his principal private secretary. In 1976, after a visiting fellowship at the University of California, he became provincial commissioner of East New Britain, and subsequently chairman of the PNG Public Services Commission. He was elected to represent Kokopo in the 1982 elections, and Somare appointed him Minister for Foreign Affairs and Trade. He succeeded Somare as leader of the PANGU PATI in 1988, and was elected prime minister in July that year, when the new session began. He remained prime minister until the end of the parliamentary term, but failed to form a successful coalition in the 1992 parliament. He was appointed speaker of the house of assembly in 1997.—KRF

Extracts from a speech on *The Papua New Guinea–Australia Relationship* at a public meeting arranged by the Institute of National Affairs in Port Moresby on 17 March 1983, when Namaliu was Minister for Foreign Affairs and Trade

We are a small, developing country in the early days of our transition from traditional fragmented village societies to a modern integrated nation. Australia is a large modern industrialized nation by comparison and it is inevitable that our national interests will differ at significant points.

We are more and more determined as a government to develop our domestic primary production and manufacturing capacity. We…are determined to create more job opportunities and develop the level of skills within our society. One obvious approach to primary and secondary industry expansion is import replacement and that is already affecting our imports of certain goods from Australia. Chickens, flour and sugar come easily to mind…Australian firms will need to adjust to the loss of a 'captive' market but they still have the advantage of geographical proximity in their competition with other sources of imports.

Australian investment also constitutes an important part of the special relationship between our two countries. In earlier years that investment occurred within the plantation, commerce, forestry and mining sectors. More recently there has been a shift away from plantations into mining and minerals exploration, such that mining and forestry are now the areas of greatest Australian investment interest...I believe there are too many obstacles in the way of a foreign investor wishing to establish a business in Papua New Guinea. Those of you who operate here already are well aware of our problems of high wages and transport costs, expensive electricity and lengthy land acquisition procedures...The government acknowledges that a comprehensive approach is now necessary to improve the climate for new investment and growth.

Source/further reading

Namaliu, R, 1983. *The Papua New Guinea–Australia Relationship*, Institute of National Affairs Speech Series 20.

■ *Sitiveni Rabuka* Major-General Sitiveni Ligamamada Rabuka OBE (Mil) (13 September 1948–), former Prime Minister of Fiji. Born in Nakobo village on the south coast of Vanua Levu, into the Navatu clan, after leaving school, he became a member of the Royal Fiji Military Forces, attaining the rank of lieutenant colonel at the age of 31. On 14 May 1987, Rabuka carried out a military coup to depose the newly elected coalition government led by Dr BAVADRA, and followed this with a second coup in September to remove the caretaker administration set up at the instigation of the Governor General, Ratu Sir Penaia GANILAU. (See FIJI COUPS.) A METHODIST lay preacher, Rabuka introduced a strict Sunday observance policy, banning all trading, organized sporting activities and public transport on Sundays. He then formally revoked the 1970 constitution, and declared Fiji a republic on 7 October, naming himself as head of state. On 5 December 1987 he announced the formation of a new civilian administration, with Ratu Sir Penaia as president and Ratu Sir Kamisese MARA as interim prime minister. The new cabinet included Rabuka as Minister of Home Affairs—responsible for internal security, defence and immigration. Rabuka became prime minister after the 1992 elections, and resigned in May 1999.—KRF

Extracts from *Rabuka: no other way*

The Fijians openly declared the May 14 action as an act of God to save them in their own land. They felt, when the news of the coup broke, that it was the greatest thing that had happened to them since Christianity was brought to the islands in the 1830s.

What I did in May and September this year, I did for Fiji. I did not do it to achieve political power for any person or group of people. My officers and men who have supported me, shared with me the desire to prevent what we have seen over the last few years as the gradual erosion of the Fijian way of life, with threats to the customs and traditions of Fijian people, our social principles and values, threats to the identity of the Fijian people and threats to their economic well-being...The result of the April 1987 election was not the beginning. It was the moment when the threats became intolerable...What I champion is above party politics or political movements. The name of our Lord Jesus Christ, Fijian customs and traditions, the Fijian way of life, should not be the subject of party politics.

Source/further reading

Dean, E and Ritova, S, 1988. *Rabuka: no other way*, Doubleday.

■ *Ieremia Tabai* Ieremia Tienang Tabai (16 December 1949–), first President of Kiribati, was born at Nonouti, and attended primary school in Tarawa and then secondary school (St Andrews College) in Christchurch, New Zealand. He continued his studies at Victoria University of Wellington, graduating with a BCA degree in 1972. He joined the public service in the ministry of Finance (1973–74) before being elected to parliament in 1974. Chief minister from March 1978 (before independence), he then became *beretitenti* (president) in July 1979 and was awarded a CMG. He provided wise leadership through the first years of Kiribati independence, and remained in office until 1990 when the constitutional requirement for a maximum of three terms obliged him to stand down, although he continued to hold his seat for the Nonouti electorate. Tabai was awarded an honorary doctorate of laws from Victoria University of Wellington in 1990, and later became secretary-general of the SOUTH PACIFIC FORUM. He was also awarded a GCMG—an honorary title only, as he is a citizen of a republic.—KRF

■ *Bartholomew Ulufa'alu* Bartholomew Ulufa'alu (25 December 1950–), the present Prime Minister of Solomon Islands and leader of the Liberal Party, was born in Laulasi, in Malaita Province. He attended school in Solomon Islands and then the UNIVERSITY OF PAPUA NEW GUINEA, where he gained a degree

in economics. On his return home in 1974, he set up a community sawmill project at Bina, and in the following year, founded the Solomon Islands National Union of Workers, later becoming its president. He entered parliament in 1976 representing East Honiara, and as leader of the National Democratic Party (NADEPA) he became leader of the opposition. In his second parliamentary term from 1980, he was Minister of Finance in the coalition government of Solomon MAMALONI, and in his third term after 1984, he moved from NADEPA to the Liberal Party. During his fourth term he resigned to contest the Aoke/Langalanga seat, but was unsuccessful. After employment as an economic consultant, he was returned to parliament in 1997, representing Aoke/Langalanga, and was elected Prime Minister of Solomon Islands in 1997.—KRF

■ *Paias Wingti* Paias Wingti (2 February 1951–), former Papua New Guinea Prime Minister, was born near Mount Hagen (Western Highlands). He interrupted his study for an economics degree at the University of Papua New Guinea to stand in the 1977 elections, winning the Mount Hagen Open seat and joining Michael SOMARE's PANGU PATI. Minister for Transport and Civil Aviation in 1978, Wingti shared defeat in the fall of the Somare government in 1980, and then became deputy prime minister to Somare in 1982. He and 15 others withdrew from the Pangu Pati in early 1985, and set up the People's Democratic Movement. Wingti then became prime minister later that year after winning a parliamentary no-confidence motion. Re-elected prime minister after the 1987 election, he held power for 11 months, with Julius CHAN as deputy. After two short-lived attempts to form a major coalition with the Pangu Pati, Wingti lost a no-confidence vote in July 1988. Two unsuccessful attempts to reinstate Wingti as prime minister occurred during 1989. Then he became prime minister once more in the 1992 elections, and was able to retain power until 1994 when Sir Julius defeated him in a no-confidence vote. He failed to retain his seat in the 1997 elections.—KRF

■ *Paul Néaoutyine* Paul Tyaou Néaoutyine (12 October 1951–) was born at St Michael, near Poindimie, New Caledonia, and educated at Catholic schools at Poindimie, Paita and Noumea. He attended the University of Lyons, France, in the early 1970s, graduating with a master's degree in economics. On his return to Noumea he taught economics at the Lycée La Pérouse (1978–85), while also becoming active in the socialist political party known as PALIKA (*Parti de Libération Kanak*) which had been formed by Nidoish NAISSELINE in 1976. Appointed by Jean-Marie TJIBAOU to head his cabinet in the northern region, Néaoutyine visited New York twice in 1987 for the United Nation's debates on New Caledonia. He then won election as Mayor of Poindimie in March 1989, and three months later, was elected to represent the FLNKS (Front de Libération Nationale Kanak et Socialiste) in the new Northern Province assembly and the territorial assembly. After Tjibaou's death in 1989, Néaoutyine was elected president of the FLNKS in March 1990. He was later replaced by his former deputy, the Union Calédonienne candidate, Roch Wamytan.

Source/further reading

Colbert, E, 1997. *The Pacific Islands: paths to the present*, Westview Press.

Craig, R D and Clement, R T, 1980. *Who's Who in Oceania, 1980–81*, Institute for Polynesian Studies, Brigham Young University–Laie.

Craig, R and King, F (eds), 1981. *Historical Dictionary of Oceania*, Greenwood Press.

Crocombe, R, 1989. *The South Pacific: an introduction*, 5th ed., Institute of Pacific Studies, University of the South Pacific.

Dorney, S, 1990. *Papua New Guinea: people, politics and history since 1975*, Random House.

Ghai, Y and Cottrell, J, 1990. *Heads of State in the Pacific: a legal and constitutional analysis*, Institute of Pacific Studies, University of the South Pacific.

Henningham, S, 1992. *France and the South Pacific: a contemporary history*, Allen & Unwin.

Tudor, J, 1968. *Pacific Islands Year Book and Who's Who*, 10th ed., Pacific Publications.

TWO PARTIES, POLITICS AND PROTEST MOVEMENTS

Protest: proto-nationalist movements

Violent resistance has often been at the centre of histories of encounters among Pacific islanders and between them and western invaders since the 18th century. Examples abound in the invasion of the Australian continent where wars and violent death accompanied settler colonialism after 1788. In New Zealand thousands of Maori died in the wars of the

1860s against the British Crown, tens of thousands more in the decades preceding. Punitive raids, pacification expeditions and pay-back campaigns claimed an unknown number of lives throughout Melanesia as colonial empires were established.

But violence is often the reading first chosen by western interpreters, whereas armed struggle was a small part of more fundamental encounters over issues of political economy. Pacific islanders engaged in more sustained political contests for power and a share in new wealth through manipulative strategies. This contesting for power began the moment Samuel WALLIS, the first European to contact Tahiti, stepped ashore in 1767 and it continued unabated through the Polynesian wars of dynastic succession in Tahiti, Hawai'i, Tonga and New Zealand during the early 19th century—all of them also encounters with growing numbers of Europeans. In Melanesia the same competition for local power, prestige and territory went on around Europeans as they developed coercive systems of colonial rule. Island protest was often about social survival and change: the struggle for a share in new wealth and the right to contribute to the formation of new societies.

Opportunities for such manipulative protest varied around the Pacific, depending on the ability of colonial regimes to deploy the power at their disposal. Kanaks in New Caledonia had little room to move, whereas Tongans enjoyed an arms-length relationship with Britain their protector which enabled them, through shrewd chiefly initiatives, to maintain control of their land and social structures as an independent kingdom. In between were a range of paths and levels of participation in new state formation. Fijians were protected on their lands, taxed in produce, and given an all-Fijian native administration. A multi-racial state with imported Indian labourers resulted with its own dynamics of continuing inter-communal struggle. New religious movements also offered alternative values to counter European dominance. In Papua New Guinea early colonization by pacification and management via occasional patrols provided minimal avenues for political protest. It grew however, in the form of millenarian movements and the protest

Tupua Tamasese Lealofi III (in white) and the Mau committee, in front of their headquarters, c1928

that flowed from missionary and government hostility to these experiments with change (see VAILALA MADNESS). After World War II Papua New Guineans, especially in the areas of oldest settlement—Papua and the Gazelle Peninsula—gradually evolved communal associations and political parties in the face of continued Australian resistance to decolonization. Micro-nationalist movements and separatist campaigns by provinces were part of the march towards nation state formation in several parts of Melanesia (Bougainville, Papua, New Hebrides/Vanuatu).

One of the longest struggles for national autonomy was in (Western) Samoa under both German and New Zealand colonial regimes. Among Samoans a sense that Samoa was an embryonic state with natural boundaries and a fixed cultural profile had been growing for centuries. Colonial rule after 1900 was for them a continuing struggle to retain their decentralized political culture against European attempts to insert legal and bureaucratic structures into Samoan society. Political movements of opposition, economic attempts at independence and confrontation leading to nationalist martyrdom of leading chiefs lasted from the 19th century till 1962 when Samoa became the Pacific's first independent nation state.

Protest took a variety of forms in the Pacific. Conflict coexisted with cooperation and accommodation, people were cowed by foreign regimes and the harshness of rulers, and élites who worked through the colonial systems for the betterment of their communities were also guardians of tradition and proto-nationalist activists.—PJH

■ *Mau a Pule* Ole Mau a Pule or the Opinion of the Traditional Leaders of Savai'i, was the name given to the challenge made by the traditional Samoan authorities, led by prominent Savai'i orator-chiefs, to the newly established German administration in SAMOA during the first decade of the 1900s. Germany had annexed the western islands of the Samoa archipelago in 1900 following an agreement with the United States, which annexed the eastern islands, and with Great Britain, which withdrew claims to Samoa in return for concessions in Tonga and Solomon Islands. The Samoans did not have any say in this agreement. They accepted it however, as it was backed by overwhelming military force.

The Samoans at this time had just emerged from a particularly ferocious civil war in which warships and soldiers from the United States and Germany had taken an active part. The forces loyal to Mata'afa Iosefo, the paramount chief who had been dominant in Samoan affairs over the last two decades and who had the support of Germany, were victorious and were claiming the right to rule the country. In foreign eyes, however, this war and the continuous Samoan internal confrontations which repeatedly attracted foreign involvement, had been highly damaging and expensive to overseas commercial interests, particularly German companies which owned very large PLANTATIONS and conducted a thriving and lucrative trade in tropical produce in the western islands. They wanted political stability and they believed that annexation would deliver it.

From the beginning, there were clashes between the new administration and the dominant Samoan leadership. Mata'afa and his supporters installed themselves at the seat of the Samoan government at Mulinuu and asserted the right to run the government in conjunction with the head of the administration, Governor Wilhelm SOLF. They did not get their full demands. They soon moved on to support the operations of a company called *Oloa*, owned by local whites and Samoans, to buy and sell Samoan COPRA, the most lucrative commercial operation in the islands. They asked the Samoans to sell all their copra to this company and they also tried to impose a levy of between four to eight German marks on all adult male Samoans to go to the *Oloa*. The new administration stopped this direct challenge to German commercial interests after several Samoan leaders had been imprisoned and some later deported.

The biggest confrontation occurred in late 1908 and early 1909 when Lauaki Namulau'ulu MAMOE, the leading orator-chief at the time from Savai'i, set out to organize a nation-wide movement, based on the traditional power centres (Tumua and Pule), to try and force Governor Solf to give the traditional Samoan leadership a more prominent role in the political and administrative structure of Samoa being established by the Germans. In the event, when Solf and Lauaki came face to face at Vaiusu, near Apia on 18 January 1909—with the meeting venue surrounded by hundreds of Lauaki's warriors all painted, armed and ready for war—the Upolu groups (Tumua) were absent, having withdrawn their support from Lauaki and transferring it to Solf and were indeed preparing to go to war against Lauaki. Savai'i and Manono were left confronting the German administration, thus the name Ole Mau a Pule.

Solf's sensitive and diplomatic handling of this confrontation and Lauaki's astute and realistic assessment of the situation (neither man wanted war), averted another episode of destruction engulfing the country. Lauaki and his forces returned to

Savai'i thereby effectively ending their challenge to the new administration. Several weeks later, three German warships carrying some 700 soldiers arrived in Samoa, and Lauaki and the other leaders of the Mau a Pule submitted themselves peacefully for deportation to Saipan, Marshall Islands. The confrontation between Solf and Lauaki was inevitable. Solf needed to impose the authority of the colonizing power while Lauaki, as the leading orator-chief from the traditional power centres in Samoa, was duty-bound to defend and assert the right of the Samoan leaders to rule in Samoa alongside the German colonizers.—KE

Further reading

Hempenstall, P J, 1978. *Pacific Islanders under German Rule*, Australian National University Press.

Davidson, J W, 1970. 'Lauaki Namulau'ulu Mamoe: a traditionalist in Samoan politics', in *Pacific Islands Portraits*, J W Davidson and D Scarr (eds), Australian National University Press.

■ *Vailala Madness* Vailala Madness was the name given to a famous early millenarian movement (CARGO CULTS) in Papua New Guinea in 1917. Diary materials reveal that the Vailala movement began among the Elema (Papua Gulf) with gifts of money to the LONDON MISSIONARY SOCIETY at Orokolo station. The suggestion of entering into reciprocity with outsiders, combining spiritual and material goals, is strong. Over (uneventful, unfulfilling) time, however, the heightened anticipations were diverted by one Evara, who emceed collective trance states and xenophobic behaviour, encouraged the destruction of native ceremonial items, claimed to be contacting the dead through a make-believe wireless, and allowed for hopes that a cargo ship manned by the ancestors would soon loom over the horizon. The autonomic bodily jerking and curious speech convinced the government anthropologist F E Williams, who arrived late on the scene (1920), that the situation was pathological. The phenomena of trance and possession, so common in small-scale black religious traditions, eluded him; and it was the catching on of these altered states that made the movement spread along to Toaripi country in the eastern Gulf.—GWT

Vailala village 'office' c1921, photographed by F E Williams

■ *John Frum movement* Tanna, in the southeastern group of the islands of VANUATU, is the home of the John Frum movement, a kind of messianic, revivalist cult which has grown and developed since World War II. The identity of John Frum—a pale-skinned figure first sighted in 1938—remains mysterious, but the early John Frum followers advocated a return to traditional ways, rejecting the currency, religion and the presence of Europeans on the island. The British administration responded by arresting ring-leaders and forbidding mention of the name of John Frum,

Flag adopted by John Frum followers on Tanna

but the subsequent arrival of US troops in the 1940s provided a wealth of material to supplement the creation of a mythical saviour who was an American. Devotees claim that John Frum will one day appear, perhaps by plane (for which event villagers once prepared an 'airfield' with bamboo control towers) or possibly emerging from the Yasur volcano on a motorcycle, bringing gifts and rewards for those who have faithfully waited for him. (See CARGO CULTS.) John Frum celebrations have regularly included folk songs to the cowboy spirits which may assist communication, and are accompanied by the decorative imagery of American flags and the letters 'USA'. In 1957 the commander of the American warship *Yankee* was prevailed on to visit and attempt to explain that no such person as John Frum existed in the United States. The crowds listened and then dismissed him as false. Throughout the 1960s, about 1000 continued to honour John Frum on Friday nights, dancing until dawn at Sulphur Bay, and on 15 February celebrating the anniversary of the release of all followers from jail in 1957. By 1980 adherents had dwindled to possibly 300 or 400, although small sub-groups have continued to appear.—KRF

Further reading

Bonnemaison, J, 1994. *The Tree and the Canoe: history and ethnogeography of Tanna*, University of Hawai'i Press.

■ *Maasina Rule* Maasina Rule (or Marching Rule) was a political movement that emerged on the island of Malaita in 1944 and dominated the politics of the southeastern SOLOMON ISLANDS for many years. The movement's founders had laboured on American military bases on Guadalcanal and Gela where they met black American soldiers with seemingly high status, and whites who ignored and even condemned the colonial racial code. Solomon Islanders had long resented their status within the colonial system and the war experience was a catalyst for collective resistance. These men organized their communities and by 1946 Maasina Rule dominated Malaita (and also neighbouring Makira and parts of Guadalcanal, where the movement took somewhat different forms).

Maasina Rule's agenda was to radically reorganize and unite Malaitans to improve their condition and make collective demands on government. Followers moved to large coastal villages where they worked on communal gardens and building projects, raised taxes for the movement, compiled a detailed census, and codified 'custom' laws to enforce in local courts. These activities resembled projects previously encouraged by government social engineering schemes, except that they were now under Malaitan control. A complex hierarchy of 'chiefs' was established to govern and ensure compliance. Malaita became politically united for the first time.

Europeans had thought Solomon Islanders incapable of serious political organization and district officers were woefully unprepared to cope with a unified, resistant populace. They tried to direct and control movement activities but by mid 1947 many movement leaders were demanding British withdrawal from their island. Most serious for Europeans was a movement labour strike that threatened to cripple the plantation economy and government's post-war reconstruction plans. Colonial policy shifted from negotiation to suppression and in August 'Operation De-Louse' began raiding movement villages and seizing leaders. Government officers mistakenly believed the chiefs ruled by intimidation and that the movement would collapse with their arrest. Although the movement soon fragmented, defiance became more open and determined. A massive campaign of civil disobedience in northern Malaita overflowed colonial prisons and paralyzed British rule into the 1950s. Aspects of Maasina Rule ideology remain central to Malaitan politics today.

Many Maasina Rule adherents maintained unrealistic hopes (including beliefs that America would assist the movement and oust the British) and expectations of impending apocalyptic events. The relative importance of these varied from place to place, and over time, and this later spawned considerable debate about Maasina Rule's true nature. Earlier writers, primarily former district officers who had suppressed the movement, described it as having been regressive, irrational, and dangerous. More recently, scholars have rejected these portrayals and stressed the movement's progressive political goals. Each side has tended to ignore or deny aspects of Maasina Rule that complicate its arguments, and the movement is better understood as having encompassed a complex mixture of diverse and sometimes contradictory perspectives and goals.—DA

Further reading

Laracy, H, 1983. *Pacific Protest: the Maasina Rule movement, Solomon Islands, 1944–1952*, Institute of Pacific Studies.

■ *Nagriamel* Nagriamel, a nativist movement that emerged on the island of Espiritu Santo in Vanuatu in the 1960s, was set up by Jimmy Stephens (also spelt Stevens), to campaign for respect for customary traditions (*kastom*) and support for the customary ownership of land. The name Nagriamel refers to the 'magical' *namel* and *nagria* leaves. As Nagriamel gained momentum, it concentrated on lands held by the Société Française des Nouvelles Hébrides (SFNH), the company supported by the French government which claimed more than half the total land area. In 1965 Stephens was joined by a *kastom* chief, Paul Buluk, who had spent several months in jail after a violent protest against the fencing and clearing of land just north of Luganville (later Santo Town). Buluk and Stephens prepared a proclamation, the 'Act of Dark Bush', forbidding settlers from extending their properties into the cooler, higher inland areas of *dak bus* (dark bush) which were held in *kastom* ownership.

Stephens is of mixed ethnic origins, the son of a Tongan woman from a chiefly family and a Scots sailor. Barely literate, he speaks some English and French, but is a charismatic orator in BISLAMA (Pidgin). Employed as a supervisor in the hospital gardens on Espiritu Santo during World War II, he later worked for a Santo trader, then operated a bulldozer, and was employed by the British administration.

Stephens and Buluk set up a village which they named Tanafo, about 30 km north of Luganville, in 1967, and were both imprisoned for 6 months on a charge of trespassing. The immediate result was a surge in popular support for both Stephens and Nagriamel, and by the early 1970s, he had been joined by hundreds of followers who helped to turn Tanafo into a model settlement. Stephens claimed to represent more than 20 per cent of all ni-Vanuatu, and it is possible that his supporters numbered 15 000 at their peak.

Nagriamel became increasingly political in its aims, and Stephens—who had hired an Indo-Fijian lawyer to assist him in 1968, and who was impressed by Fiji's attainment of independence in 1970—petitioned the United Nations in 1971 to support independence for the New Hebrides within a year. Other political parties were being formed, with the New Hebrides National Party (later to become the Vanua'aku Pati) also concentrating initially on *kastom* and land issues, and Francophone parties representing conservative expatriate interests. These accumulated pressures helped persuade the British and French governments to set up a constitutional framework for self-government, with elections to be held in November 1975.

While the National Party's strongly nationalist platform gained growing support, Stephens (who had been taken to Paris and introduced to President Giscard d'Estaing) began agitating for Britain to leave the islands. Nagriamel's following dwindled, and its alliance with one of the Francophone parties achieved only two seats in the new assembly, compared with 17 for the National Party. Stephens, claiming electoral irregularities and supported by French and American business interests, led a large protest rally in late December 1975 at which he announced the imminent independence of Santo as the Nagriamel Federation. Almost immediately his alliance partnership dissolved, and Stephens was obliged to yield before the paramilitary police forces sent by the CONDOMINIUM administration.

Nagriamel's next move on the national stage was a more serious secession attempt in 1980, after the Vanua'aku Pati had triumphed in the elections of November 1979. Refusing to accept the validity of their electoral losses on Santo, Stephens announced the formation of an independent state, the Republic of Vemerana, and some of his militant supporters occupied the British administrative offices. French officials blocked attempts to use police to restore control, but the new independent government of Vanuatu (taking office on 30 July 1980) refused to make concessions. Order was restored with the help of 450 troops supplied by Papua New Guinea. The Santo rebellion ended with one death, the son of Jimmy Stephens, but there were many injuries and arrests. Hundreds of expatriate supporters were expelled, weakening the credibility of various Francophone and *kastom* opposition groups, and causing a significant set-back to the economic development of Santo.—KRF

■ *Hawaiian sovereignty: 100 years as a colony* In 1993 President Bill Clinton signed a resolution acknowledging the United States' role in the loss of Hawaiian independence 100 years before. Committing America to a reconciliation process, the 'Apology Bill' has opened a legal door to a continuing Native Hawaiian sovereignty movement, now over 10 years old. Citing not only the illegal overthrow and annexation but socioeconomic ills that plague Hawaiians up to the present, many Native Hawaiian leaders have come to believe that only sovereign control of their land and resources will prevent the culture from disappearing altogether. About 20 per cent of the population of Hawai'i, Native Hawaiians consistently represent over half of the incarcerated felons, and less than 10 per cent of the college student population. The health statistics are even more frightening, leading every other ethnicity by large margins in the incidence of heart disease, DIABETES, ALCOHOL AND DRUG ABUSE, and the concomitant threats to childbirth and child rearing.

Treated as an American minority and wards of the government, *Kanaka Maoli* (the True People) prior to the rise of the sovereignty movement could only look forward to either complete assimilation into American society, and gradual estrangement from their ancestral culture, or fruitless and pitiful defiance, usually accompanied by poverty and prosecution. Meanwhile TOURISM, which overtook and then replaced SUGAR as the industry of Hawai'i, has brought up to 7 million visitors a year into the islands, creating tremendous economic pressure on water, land and ocean resources. As ancient sacred lands are turned into resorts and golf courses, Hawaiian culture and arts are appropriated and reissued as attractions for tourists from America, Japan and Europe.

Nevertheless, Hawaiians are optimistic that they will be a nation again. The Hawaiian language is making a comeback and is now one of the two most popular language courses at the University of Hawai'i. Hundreds of young people are being educated in Hawaiian language immersion schools with the expectation that this will grow into the thousands in the next decade. There are now many sovereignty initiatives and a high percentage of the Native population believes that it is a possible reality in their lifetime.

Currently, there are about a half dozen well-known and established bodies whose collective membership is around 30 000. Their aims and national aspirations range from limited self-government to full independence from the United States. Even the State of Hawai'i has recognized the legitimacy of Hawaiian sovereignty and tried to sponsor its own version with the 'Native Hawaiian Vote' in the 1996 elections. Less than 30 per cent of the ballots were returned, partly out of fears that even participating in the state-sponsored balloting might invalidate *Kanaka Maoli* claims before international bodies, such as the World Court and the United Nations. Despite differences in their respective visions, all pro-sovereignty groups support the Hawaiian language and the *Kanaka Maoli* access to the forests and

Flag representing the Hawaiian sovereignty movement

beaches, besides acting as watchdogs over wetlands, forests and coastal areas threatened by urban development. The achievement of Hawaiian sovereignty will demonstrate that self-determination is accessible to even the smallest and most vulnerable of peoples.—JKO

■ *West Papuan nationalism* In the period from the 1930s to the 1950s, some Melanesians in what was then Dutch New Guinea joined the nationalist movements which sought independence for the Netherlands East Indies. At the end of the Pacific War, Indonesian nationalists proclaimed independence on 17 August 1945 and claimed the western half of New Guinea, leading to a prolonged period of conflict with the Dutch government. From the early 1960s, however, encouraged by developments in neighbouring Papua New Guinea and by the accelerated pace of change under the Dutch colonial administration, the Melanesians of West New Guinea focused instead on the prospects for an independent West Papua. Several commentators have linked these nationalist aspirations to earlier quasi-millenarian popular movements which emerged during the Dutch colonial period.

In 1961 Melanesian members of the newly-established New Guinea Council formed a National Committee and created a flag, an anthem and a constitution for an entity they named Papua Barat (West Papua). The 'morning star' flag was first raised in that year.

Following the creation of the United Nations Temporary Executive Authority (UNTEA) and the progressive Indonesian takeover of West New Guinea in the period prior to the 'Act of Free Choice' in 1969, Melanesians opposed to Indonesian rule coalesced around the ORGANISASI PAPUA MERDEKA (OPM, Free Papua Movement), an organization initially headed by Markus Kaisiepo and drawing its principal support from the Arfak people of the Manokwari area.

After 1969 the Indonesian military increased its efforts to suppress any expression of West Papuan nationalism, and a number of OPM supporters fled to Holland, Papua New Guinea and Senegal. But atrocities committed by the Indonesian military strengthened popular support for the OPM. In 1971 a group of OPM supporters within Irian Jaya unilaterally declared West Papua independent, under the 'presidency' of former Indonesian army officer Seth Rumkorem.

In subsequent years factional strife within the movement, the loss of leaders through surrender or voluntary exile, lack of significant external support, and continued harassment by the Indonesian armed forces have restricted the OPM's activities to a token resistance movement, operating a low-level propaganda campaign with assistance from supporters mostly from outside Indonesia. But West Papuan separatist sentiments remain strong, and in the aftermath of the May 1998 uprising against President Soeharto, and the admission by the Indonesian military that atrocities have been committed in Irian Jaya, there has been some strengthening of West Papuan nationalism and calls for some form of self-determination or autonomy.—RJM

■ *Torres Strait independence movement* Sovereign independence for Torres Strait was first proposed by the Torres United Party (TUP), founded in 1976 by expatriate Torres Strait Islanders living in Townsville. In 1978 Carlemo Wacando, a founder of TUP, unsuccessfully brought a High Court action challenging the validity of the original annexation of the islands to Queensland, and a number of appeals were made to the United Nations to have Torres Strait placed on the agenda of the Committee on Decolonization. Although the Australian government was embarrassed by these appeals, nothing came of them and TUP fell silent in 1981. The independence issue resurfaced in 1987, this time advocated by George Mye, a senior member of the Islands Coordinating Council, at that time the superior representative body in Torres Strait. In June Mye cabled delegates to the SOUTH PACIFIC FORUM meeting in Samoa seeking support for Torres Strait independence. In the same year the issue received considerable publicity when it was promoted during festivities to celebrate the 50th anniversary of the first meeting of Torres Strait Councillors. The TUP was reactivated and its leaders, Wacando and James Akee, shifted their activities to Torres Strait proper. The independence movement was now more broadly based, and at Thursday Island an Independence Working Party Committee was established in 1988. In the early 1990s attention turned to the Murray Island Land Case (see MABO), first brought before the High Court of Australia in 1982, which in June 1992 confirmed the continuing existence of Native Title on Murray Island (Mer). Although the High Court ruled that sovereignty remained with the Commonwealth, the Mabo decision inspired the movement, and James Akee declared Murray Island (Mer) secession twice: in September 1993 and August 1995. Akee was imprisoned for embezzlement in 1996, but the moderate Torres Strait Islander leadership continues to press the Australian government for some form of self-government by 2001, the anniversary of Australian Federation.—SM

■ *Pro-democracy movement in Tonga* Change of government by constitutional means has occurred in most Pacific states, indicating that one of the most important aspects of a democratic system of government has become reasonably well established. Tonga's form of government, however, is monarchical, and although some parliamentarians are elected by commoners, these are outnumbered by representatives of nobles and appointees of the monarch. The Westminster system comprises a blend of political institutions and practices, and although the Tongan political system has become far more democratic—and the monarchy and its surrounding nobility appear far more conventional—the mass of commoners are still excluded from effective participation in government. Under the present constitution, it is impossible that the government could actually change following a general election (see CONSTITUTIONAL DEVELOPMENT IN TONGA).

This system has come under challenge from an active pro-democracy movement which is seeking, among other things, greater accountability in government due to widespread perceptions of corrupt practices. Inspired by the example of pro-democracy movements elsewhere, its leaders and supporters have campaigned strongly for a range of political reforms. Since 1987 a number have succeeded in gaining election to parliament as people's representatives. But the responses of the entrenched political élite have indicated that there is little prospect of significant reform in the near future. Moreover, pro-democracy leaders and Tonga's more critical mass media have been subjected to a range of political and legal tactics, including court actions and withdrawal of publishing licences, which effectively suppress calls for reform and intimidate critics.

In the broader context of contemporary debate about culture and democracy, an interesting aspect of these developments is the basic justification used by the political élite, that the present system reflects a set of long-established Tongan cultural traditions. Indeed, the monarchy and the nobility are sometimes represented as the very embodiment of Tongan cultural traditions—of all that makes Tonga a unique and distinctive society. A persistent conservative theme has been that these traditions stand in distinct contrast with those of 'the west'. It has therefore been argued that western democracy is unsuitable for Tonga, that it is an alien political form lacking resonance with local cultural traditions.

In fact, however, the very cultural traditions which appear to support the Tongan élite in power had their origins in the not-so-distant past. Tonga was never formally colonized, but its system of government, including the constitution which sets out the rights and privileges of the royal family and the nobility, was influenced very strongly by external models. By themselves, such exercises in reinventing cultural traditions are not especially remarkable, but they warrant critical attention when they are used by these élites to denounce democracy as a western impost, and calls for more democratic participation are coming from within their own societies. The Tongan movement has persevered, with a convention on constitutional reform organized by political and church leaders in 1992 and consideration of a draft revision in early 1999.—SL1

■ *Nationalism in French territories* Not swayed by the steps being taken towards post-war DECOLONIZATION by the four other powers in the Pacific, France remained firm in its intention to maintain control of its overseas territories, integrating them constitutionally, politically and economically with metropolitan France. It resisted the momentum towards independence in the New Hebrides, although the CONDOMINIUM was disrupted by secessionist pressures, complicated by British and French differences in language, religion and politics. In the three remaining colonies, however, there was considerable support for the position adopted by France, that French Polynesia, Wallis and Futuna, and New Caledonia should be regarded as overseas territories, simply distant parts of France. It was only after World War II that the indigenous inhabitants of the French Pacific gained the full democratic rights that allowed them to express their potential political strength.

In French Polynesia, the focus of early demands for local automony was a *maohi*, Marcel POUVANA'A A OOPA, whose argument for French citizenship for all Tahitians emerged just as the French government was ready to acknowledge colonial participation in Free French forces. A constitutional amendment changing the status of the indigenous inhabitants of French colonies from French subjects to French citizens was duly passed in 1946. Demands for more political rights were taking a variety of different forms in the post-war Pacific, and occasionally overlapped with the organized activities of emerging TRADE UNIONS. Tahitian workers had begun to set up 'syndicates' which avoided aggressive STRIKES AND INDUSTRIAL ACTION, but when Pouvana'a organized a protest against the metropolitan French officials who were taking up positions in the colonial bureaucracy, the 'revolt' was taken seriously and quickly suppressed. Nevertheless Pouvana'a was elected in 1949 as a deputy (*deputé*) to the French parliament, and formed a new party, the Comité Pouvana'a (later the Rassemblement Démocratique des Populations Tahitiennes, RDPT), which won a majority in the national assembly in 1953 and 1957. When the RDPT began to propose secession from France, General Charles de Gaulle offered all French territories the opportunity to vote on independence. Pouvana'a campaigned vigorously in 1958, but his efforts were rewarded with only 36 per cent of the vote. He himself was imprisoned soon afterwards on charges of arson and attempted murder, and the RDPT was banned in 1963 because of its opposition to NUCLEAR TESTING. For the most part, the more numerous *demi* population—half Polynesian, mixed with European or Chinese ancestry—steadily won positions of influence in politics, business and administration in the immediate post-war period.

In New Caledonia, the general post-war reformist mood led to much wider enfranchisement of the Melanesian population in 1951, and the newly formed Union Calédonienne (UC, the Caledonian Union) polled strongly in the July elections. Emerging as the popular voice of proto-nationalism for the 1950s and 1960s, it was led by Maurice Lenormand, a last-minute candidate, who broadly sympathized with and supported Melanesian interests and aims. A French-born businessman, married to a Lifu Islander of chiefly descent, Lenormand proposed liberal policies for economic and social reforms under the slogan 'Two Colours: One People'. The party aimed to unify New Caledonian society, with integration of Kanaks as its goal rather than a separate political status, and it achieved genuinely multiracial representation. A more liberal statute (*loi-cadre*) introduced by the French socialist government brought a measure of self-government, on the strength of which the UC campaigned in favour of continued territorial status for New Caledonia—tied to a continuation of French aid—in the independence vote offered in the 1958 referendum. An overwhelming majority in New Caledonia rejected independence, but almost immediately their embryonic autonomy was curtailed by the newly elected conservative government in France, headed by General Charles de Gaulle. As Lenormand began to lose authority, bombs were used in violent attempts by two UC members, apparently to disrupt the conservative opposition; Lenormand was implicated and deprived of office. Roch Pidjot replaced him, but the UC had suffered a severe blow and the opportunity for orderly progress towards its political goals was lost.

In the 1970s and 1980s, with the emergence of new leaders of nationalist sentiment in the French Pacific, issues of indigenous identity and political autonomy came strongly to the fore. At the same time, connections to a tradition of anti-colonial violence were deliberately evoked to validate the origins of the movement. In French Polynesia, Oscar Temaru, leader of the anti-nuclear, *indépendentiste* FLP (Polynesian Liberation Front), linked himself with the Tahitian resistance of 1844–47, when he erected a monument at Faa'a to commemorate one of the battles. In New Caledonia, where the Melanesians remained a demographic and electoral minority, Nidoish NAISSELINE sought inspiration from the KANAK REBELLION of 1878 in organizing the Foulards Rouges (Red Scarves) movement in 1970. Another more militant nationalist organization, the Groupe 1878, was formed by Déwé Gorodney and Elie Poigoune in 1974. Naisseline's group of young radicals also took the formerly derogatory term *Canaque* and proclaimed 'Kanak' as a term of nationalist pride.

Several violent incidents brought growing tension in New Caledonia. The Groupe 1878 developed into a political party, the Parti de Libération Kanak (PALIKA, the Kanak Liberation Party) in 1976, and when the UC also announced its support for independence, albeit in line with Christian influences which promoted largely non-violent political and reformist goals, it became clear that a Melanesian majority had adopted a nationalist position. Kanak leaders organized a boycott of the 1978 referendum on continued territorial status, and relations between Kanaks and Caldoches (the white rural settler population) grew bitter and violent. As promised reforms failed to appear, the pro-independence forces united in the Front de la Libération Nationale Kanak et Socialiste (FLNKS, the Kanak Socialist National Liberation Front) under the leadership of Jean-Marie TJIBAOU in 1984. They boycotted the November 1984 elections, and instead proclaimed a Provisional Government of Kanaky on 1 December.

As political unrest led to violence in 1984–85, the French government attempted to find a political solution, offering greater autonomy and another election in 1985. The Rally for New Caledonia in the Republic (RPCR), led by Jacques LAFLEUR, which had become the major party representing the conservative (Caldoche) opposition, gained a substantial victory, and brought temporary stability. By the end of the second bout of political unrest that occurred in 1988, however, more than 50 people had died, leaving a legacy of resentment and suspicion. Fortunately, the election of a new French socialist government and the appointment of Michel Rocard as French prime minister in May 1988 allowed a fresh approach to be made. The prompt negotiation of the MATIGNON ACCORDS, later confirmed in a national referendum, provided a compromise, which then proved to be sound enough to survive the murder of Tjibaou and his deputy, Yeiwene Yeiwene, in May 1989. Both the FLNKS and the RPCR came to acknowledge the Accords as a basis for both economic and political development, and the subsequent NOUMEA ACCORD of 1998 appears to have justified their faith. Lafleur, an immensely skilful politician, continues to receive wide support.

In French Polynesia, the calls for autonomy by Pouvana'a's sucessors, John Teariki (who died in October 1983) and Francis SANFORD, had achieved some limited powers of local self-government by 1977. The campaign to extend these powers and to secure maximum economic concessions from France was greatly assisted in 1980 when Gaston FLOSSE and the conservatives changed tack and began to assume a leading role. This permitted the development of a broad pro-autonomy consensus which has encompassed the revival of Tahitian culture and a sense of separate identity. The political conflicts of the 1980s were less violent than in New Caledonia, but one person was killed and several others were injured in a serious riot that developed in the centre of Pape'ete in October 1987, following a labour dispute. Against a political majority support for greater autonomy, Oscar Temaru's FLP (Front de Libération de la Polynésie) has maintained its pro-independence stance, rejecting the legislative reforms passed by the territorial assembly in 1995 and endorsed in France in 1996.

The preoccupation with political change has not extended to Wallis and Futuna, where executive power is shared by the traditional rulers and the French-appointed administrator. There have been no obvious nationalist pressures in the small and isolated French territory, where French financial support is recognized as essential to the predominantly subsistence economy, and conservatism is represented by the maintenance of traditional culture and the influence of the Roman Catholic church. The population rejected independence in a referendum in 1959, expressing an overwhelming preference for territorial status. Since 1961 the territorial assembly has permitted a small measure of autonomy, with the three traditional chiefdoms being established as administrative districts, and the privileged position of the three paramount chiefs seems unlikely to be threatened by constitutional reform in the immediate future.—KRF

■ *Mataungan Association* The Mataungan Association (MA) is a political organisation that started in 1969 on the Gazelle Peninsula of Papua New Guinea, as a Tolai alliance extending beyond clan and regional animosities and appropriating as its symbol the Tubuan mask as an expression of traditional authority. It emerged as a village-based movement attempting a comprehensive change of Tolai cultural, economic and social life.

The Mataungan response (*Mataungan* means being alert or watchful) was prompted by threats that the Local Government Council would become multiracial, and the Tolai Cocoa Project a public company with foreign investors—both considered control agencies of outside political and economic domination. Structurally, discontent was nourished by a population explosion and limited available land, almost 40 per cent of which had been taken from indigenous control by colonial interests. Already in 1967, Oscar Tammur who was to become parliamentary patron of the Mataungans, had occupied alienated plantation land with fellow villagers. The Mataungans boycotted the new council and withheld taxes, and in 1970 John KAPUTIN—equipped with a blackboard to explain the Tolai position in the colonial cobweb—went from village to village in the Gazelle Peninsula to propose a cooperative venture, the New Guinea Development Company (NGDC), to give Tolais a larger share of investment in business and property. In the beginning, everyone was to contribute three coconuts which yielded A$1120, thus emphasising self-reliance and fostering mobilisation of surplus produce with the labour of unemployed youths; then small shares were issued. By 1972, the NGDC had accumulated substantial capital which was used to establish Tolai-run local businesses and, it seems, Australian investments. Kaputin, who had cemented his reputation locally, was elected to parliament when Mataungan spokesmen won 3 out of 4 Gazelle seats.

The entrepreneurial Tolai were at the time considered the most 'modernized' group in the Territory, professionally and economically; Kokopo and Rabaul had been the seats of the German colonial administration and the centres of its influence. In its organisational structure (with village meetings, council and sub-committees for example) and its aspirations (freedom from outside domination, self-determination for a small nation), the MA reflected traditional policy (authoritative BIG-MEN reliant on persuading a retinue of followers, organizing communal works and achieving personal wealth and status) as well as the utopia of the western left of the 1970s (grass-roots democracy, peasant mobilization, student revolt). While the world market showed no interest in Tolai copra, some MA spokesmen manifested their Big-Men qualities, moving into national politics and taking up business opportunities; others contented themselves with time-proven local political, economic and church activities (notably Melchior ToMot). The MA was the first radical mass political movement in Papua New Guinea, exerting an important mobilizing function in that it alerted New Guineans to the possibility of national politics. It also conveyed a new image of Papua New Guineans to Australia, as astute political actors rather than 'fuzzy-wuzzy angels' and children needing the guiding hand of the colonial parent.—HS

Further reading

Schütte, H, 1973. 'Village-based development in Niugini: the Mataungan Association', *Asia Quarterly*, 2.

■ *Organisasi Papua Merdeka* (OPM) The Organisasi Papua Merdeka or Free Papua Movement emerged in 1963 among the Arfak people of the Manokwari area of Irian Jaya, many of whom had been trained by the Dutch for the Papuan Volunteer Corps. They fought the first OPM armed resistance action in 1965 and sustained the struggle for two years.

Indonesian expansion into West Papua began in 1963, when the Dutch pulled out and allowed West Papuan self-determination to be decided on a 1969 'Act of Free Choice'. When the United Nations peace-keeping force withdrew in 1963, more than 15 000 Indonesian troops were stationed in West Papua or Dutch New Guinea. Land disputes began to occur almost immediately. Because the outcome of the referendum appeared inevitable, the OPM called it the 'Act of No Choice', and continued to challenge Indonesia's authority over its 17th province.

The OPM has grown considerably larger since the 1960s, and has based its public relations activities in Dakar, Senegal, where several of its supporters fled after 1969. However, leadership disputes (particularly, in the 1970s, between a 'Pemka' faction led by Jacob Prai, and the 'Victoria' group led by former Indonesian army officer Seth Rumkorem), lack of significant external support, and continued harassment by the Indonesian armed forces have limited the capacity of the OPM to do more than offer token resistance to the Indonesian military and maintain a low-level propaganda campaign with assistance from expatriate West Papuans and sympathetic supporters mostly from outside Indonesia.—RJM

■ *Pangu Pati* Pangu Pati, the first real political party in PAPUA NEW GUINEA, was formed in June 1967 in preparation for the elections for the first House of Assembly. Emerging out of the informal 'Bully Beef Club' at the Administrative College, key founding members included Albert Maori KIKI, who became the party's Secretary-Treasurer, and Michael SOMARE, who was then employed as a government information officer in Port Moresby. About 25 candidates campaigned on the party platform and nine were elected in 1968. Kiki was unsuccessful, but Pangu won a number of significant victories: Tony Voutas defeated the Speaker of the former House of Assembly, H L R Niall (Morobe Regional); Michael Somare defeated sitting member Frank Martin (East Sepik); and Cecil Abel, son of missionary Charles ABEL, defeated Elliott Elijah (Milne Bay). Another prominent European party member was Barry Holloway (Kainantu Open).

Somare was elected Leader of the party, which then organized itself as an official Opposition in the

House of Assembly, with Paul Lapun as Deputy Leader and Pita Lus as Party Whip. Calling for internal self-government and demanding target dates for independence, Pangu stressed the need for a steady program of economic development in which all Papua New Guineans would participate and criticized the level of spending proposed for tertiary education. The party platform also had national unity as an important objective. In the 1972 elections, Pangu was able to form a government through a coalition with the People's Progress Party headed by Julius CHAN. It continued to be the ruling party through independence in 1975 until 1980, when Somare lost a motion of no-confidence and Chan became prime minister for the next two years. In the June 1982 elections, a well-organized campaign brought resounding popular support for Pangu Pati (34 per cent of the national vote) and Somare's third term as prime minister commenced amid optimistic prophecies that Pangu might remain the dominant political party in Papua New Guinea. Within three years, however, the defections had begun. Somare was replaced in 1985 by Paias WINGTI (who had by then left Pangu with a group of back-benchers to form the People's Democratic Movement), and five more MPs—three of them ministers and including founding member Barry Holloway—left Pangu. Somare attempted to form another coalition after the 1987 elections, when Pangu won 26 seats, but he was unsuccessful. He decided to step down from the party leadership in late May 1988 and was replaced by Rabbie NAMALIU, who was able to put together a coalition government which held power from July 1988 until 1992. The Pangu Pati, still headed by Sir Rabbie, has been unable to lead a successful coalition since 1992, when the new parliamentary session elected Wingti as prime minister. Sir Julius Chan replaced Wingti in 1994 for the remainder of the parliamentary term, and after the 1997 elections, Bill Skate (National Party) came to power, appointing Sir Rabbie as Speaker.—KRF

■ *Papua Besena* Papua Besena, a Papuan anti-colonial movement, was formed by Josephine ABAIJAH in June 1973, while she was the elected member for Port Moresby in the third house of assembly. With the prime objective of achieving self-determination for Papua, the organization produced a series of noisy protest marches and mass rallies, culminating in the 'women's demonstrations' in Port Moresby in June 1974. One group of women forced their way into the chief minister's conference room, damaging furniture and breaking a door. The Port Moresby City Council passed a resolution on 18 June 1974 that Papua should be a free and independent country and that there should be no political union between Papua and New Guinea. On 16 March 1975, Abaijah made a unilateral declaration of Papuan independence, but in August, one month before Papua New Guinea's independence, she left the country when her close friend and mentor, Dr Eric Wright, was deported. Although seven members of Papua Besena were elected in 1977, including Abaijah, the movement lost momentum, with its adherents drifting off to join other parties.—KRF

Further reading

Abaijah, J and Wright, E, 1991. *A Thousand Coloured Dreams*, Dellasta Pacific.

Colbert, E, 1997. *The Pacific Islands: paths to the present*, Westview Press.

Crocombe, R G, Neemia, U, Ravuvu, A and Vom Busch, W, 1992. *Culture and Democracy in the South Pacific*, Institute of Pacific Studies, University of the South Pacific.

Dorney, S, 1990. *Papua New Guinea: people, politics and history since 1975*, Random House.

Henningham, S, 1992. *France and the South Pacific: a contemporary history*, Allen & Unwin.

Hoadley, S, 1992. *The South Pacific Foreign Affairs Handbook*, Allen & Unwin.

King, P (ed.), 1989. *Pangu Returns to Power: the 1982 elections in Papua New Guinea*, Political and Social Change Monograph 9, The Australian National University.

Lawson, S, 1996. *Tradition Versus Democracy in the South Pacific: Fiji, Tonga and Western Samoa*, Cambridge University Press.

Robie, D (ed.), 1992. *Tu Galala: social change in the Pacific*, Bridget Williams Books and Pluto Press.

Stephen, D, 1972. *A History of Political Parties in Papua New Guinea*, Lansdowne.

Media management and the foreign policy process

The media have a pervasive influence in the foreign policy process—opening it up to non-government players and enabling governments to go beyond formal diplomatic relations to attempt to reach the people of other nations over the heads of their governments. Two recent examples demonstrate ways in which the media have been used to enact a political debate in the policymaking process in Papua New Guinea and Australia. A particularly testy period in the public relations between these two governments arose in 1995–96, when government officials publicly criticized each other through the media in an increasingly bitter dispute which led an editorial in *The Australian* (13 September 1996) to declare that Australia's relationship with Papua New Guinea was in urgent need of repair. In the heat of the debate both sides demanded to know why the other side was using the media to publicize their grievances rather than voicing them through normal diplomatic channels.

In making such comments both sides chose to ignore the great changes that have taken place in how government-to-government relations have been conducted since the rise of mass democracies and the communications revolution have given greater power to public opinion to affect the behaviour of governments. In earlier times, governments conversed privately, but today they have to consider their audience. On one hand their domestic audience may include groups who have an active interest in foreign policy issues and use the media to publicize those views and bring pressure on a government. And on the other, there may be groups in the country whose policy the government is seeking to influence. In the United States, the term 'public diplomacy' refers to these influences on the policymaking process. It has been defined by the chairman of the US Advisory Commission on Public Diplomacy as 'diplomacy in pursuit of our national interest aimed not only at foreign governments but at foreign publics'.

The Papua New Guinea government's series of public criticisms may have been seeking to influence groups in Australia who have a sense of special obligation to Papua New Guinea to bring pressure to bear on the domestic foreign policymaking process; as well as to attentive publics in Papua New Guinea who may enjoy seeing their government stand up publicly to Big Brother, the former colonial ruler. When Australia's then Minister for Foreign Affairs, Gareth Evans, chose to respond in August 1995, in the pages of the *Australian*, to the barrage of criticism by PNG leaders, he was seeking to reach those among the readership of that paper who may have been sympathetic to the PNG government's position.

In 1994 when the Minister for Pacific Island Affairs, Gordon Bilney, broadcast by satellite to the Pacific islands the Australian government's message about good governance, he was not only seeking to communicate a message to aid-dependent Pacific island governments that they should implement economic and structural reforms—that message, after all, can be conveyed by more traditional diplomatic means—but was also aiming at other audiences: Australian taxpayers and Pacific island voters. The latter were being informed by the major aid donor in the region of the shortcomings of their governments. As voters in their national elections, they would be in a position to demand greater accountability and exercise their ultimate option of voting their governments out of office. While the Australian government may not have raised the question of national elections in this and other public statements about the performance of Pacific island governments, an editorial in the *Australian Financial Review* on 2 August 1996 was much more blunt. It declared that Australia should take up Papua New Guinea's idea of a review of aid arrangements

> to redeploy Australia's assistance more strategically in the Asia Pacific region, taking into account how welcome it is to the recipient. Then at the next June election, the country's village-dwelling majority will be able to record its own verdict on its government's performance.
>
> The emergence of public diplomacy does not mean that it has replaced government-to-government diplomacy; both forms coexist, with traditional diplomacy now a much more open process because of the role of the media and public opinion in what were once private negotiations. The need has democratized traditional diplomacy.

A second example occurred in 1995, when students at the UNIVERSITY OF PAPUA NEW GUINEA (UPNG) used the media to launch a grass-roots activist campaign to arouse public opinion against the World Bank/International Monetary Fund's structural adjustment program, particularly as it related to land mobilization. The relationship between the media and a grass-roots activist movement is a thoroughly dynamic process. News media need stories that are full of drama and conflict to attract and boost circulation and ratings. The leaders of activist movements need publicity to command attention for their issue, to attract grass-roots support and persuade decision makers to adopt their solution to the problem. This was the process at work when UPNG students, allied with members of non-government organizations (NGOs) in Port Moresby and others, used the media to launch a protest with the aid of a sudden dramatic act—the burning of a government vehicle during a protest meeting at the Waigani campus.

Their success was two-fold, not only in capturing instantaneous headlines for their cause but also in exerting some influence on the way the issue was subsequently framed. In this they were assisted by the fact that there is considerable freedom of the press in Papua New Guinea and that there was sympathy for their cause among sections of the media in Port Moresby, among some university staff, and

nated, in 1997, in the present constitution. Constitutional reviews have also taken place in the Federated States of Micronesia and Kiribati, but with less significant consequences. Papua New Guinea's constitution has undergone partial review. Debate on constitutional reform has proceeded elsewhere (in Vanuatu, and the PRO-DEMOCRACY MOVEMENT IN TONGA), with little outcome.

Throughout the region, issues of effective governance (including accountability and adherence to the rule of law), and equity (especially provision of services to outer regions) remain critical issues. Papua New Guinea has operated a 'decentralized' form of government, although this system of 'provincial governments' was reformed in the 1990s in an attempt to remedy the system's failures. Only the Federated States of Micronesia has explicitly adopted federal principles. Failure by governments to provide services to remote areas has been a constant concern, but also points to the high levels of self-sufficiency maintained by some of these communities, frequently through traditional systems of organization and leadership.

Pacific island legislatures range from 12 (Tuvalu) to 109 members (Papua New Guinea). All are based on universal suffrage, but in Samoa, only chiefs may be elected to parliament (SAMOAN MATAI TITLES). The Fiji and the FSM parliaments have upper houses, and some countries also have a chamber of chiefs, empowered to advise on matters affecting custom, such as Cook Islands House of ARIKI. Fiji's Council Bose Levu Vakaturaga, and Marshall Islands' Council of Iroij have other functions (MICRONESIAN LEADERSHIP AFTER WORLD WAR II). Fiji's chiefs are empowered to select the Head of State (CONSTITUTION REVIEW IN FIJI). Vanuatu's Council of Chiefs (Malvatu Mauri) is influential but is not constitutionally recognized. Fiji's parliament allocates seats according to ethnicity as well as constituency. Elsewhere, ethnicity is a significant issue in elections and politics without being entrenched within the constitutional framework.

In parliamentary systems in the region, executive power is held by a cabinet, derived from and responsible to the legislature. Since the executive is often regarded as the most powerful branch of government, it is the most coveted by political interests, and subject to the most scrutiny by other public bodies, particularly the legislature, but also the courts (when application is made to them—see COURTS AND LEGAL SYSTEMS), and other offices which may be in place such as the OMBUDSMAN, LEADERSHIP CODES tribunal, and auditor-general.

Most island legal systems share many similar post-colonial features. Written constitutions provided an opportunity to specify sources of law, and a hierarchy of laws. The constitution is the supreme source of law, followed by statutes created by parliament, the 'received' laws in place at the time of independence, and customary law and common law. Diversity characterizes the ways in which these elements of the legal system are ranked and interact with each other. At independence there was, for some, a vision of national parliaments replacing the foreign 'received' law with more relevant enactments, and of national courts contributing law based more firmly on custom. Papua New Guinea's constitution expounds the doctrine of the 'underlying' law, an indigenous common law that parliament and judiciary were to create. This has not been the post-colonial experience, however, with programs of law reform faltering, and courts explaining that judgments based on custom were dependent on the quality of arguments placed before the courts that relied on such custom. In the French Overseas Territories, law is based on civil codes rather than the common law. Pacific constitutions provide for higher courts which usually have specific constitutional responsibilities, such as upholding the constitution and enforcing HUMAN RIGHTS, while the lower level of courts handles most of the day-to-day work of the legal system.

Some former Commonwealth countries (Solomon Islands, Papua New Guinea, Tuvalu) retained the British monarch as head of state, represented by a governor-general appointed by the queen on the advice of the executive. In Kiribati, Nauru, Palau and Marshall Islands the head of state is also head of the executive. In Tonga the monarchy is possessed in perpetuity by the king's heirs. Samoa came to independence with joint heads of state who possessed two of the highest *tama'aiga* (chiefly) titles, and after the death of both of them, the position will be determined by parliamentary election. The Vanuatu and Papua New Guinea parliaments each elect heads of state who, following the British model, hold mostly ceremonial powers. Uncertainty concerning the extent of the head of state's authority has resulted in constitutional crises in Papua New Guinea, Solomon Islands and Vanuatu in the 1990s.

Legislative elections are held throughout the Pacific islands. Most general elections use a 'plurality' system by which the candidate with the most votes wins the seat. However, when votes are cast over a large number of candidates standing for the same seat, the highest number of votes may fall well short of a majority (50 per cent)—as has frequently occurred in Papua New Guinea. The French Overseas Territories use proportional representation, and Kiribati a majority system. In Vanuatu a modified form of proportional representation is used. The French Overseas Territories and areas under American jurisdiction also elect representatives to metropolitan legislatures (although the representatives to the US Congress from Guam and American Samoa cannot vote). The elaboration of legislatures along Westminster lines has encouraged the formation of political parties in most, but not all, islands. In Tuvalu and Nauru, for instance, the polities have been regarded as too small to sustain a party system. In the larger states, electoral campaigns have become a major periodic feature of public life, and the stability of any parliamentary majority is now dependent on political relationships. One clear trend in post-independence politics has been the fragility of party systems, and the continued significance of independent members of parliament. In some states governments more often fail than succeed in running a full term in office, due to shifts in party and member allegiances.—GH1

Further reading

Ghai, Y (ed.), 1988. *Law, Government and Politics in the Pacific Island States*, Institute of Pacific Studies and University of the South Pacific.

—— and Cottrell, J, 1990. *Heads of State in the Pacific: a legal and constitutional analysis*, Institute of Pacific Studies and University of the South Pacific.

Ntumy, M (ed.), 1993. *South Pacific Islands Legal Systems*, University of Hawai'i Press.

Powles, C G and Pulea, M (eds), 1988. *Pacific Courts and Legal Systems*, University of the South Pacific.

Saunders, C and Hassall, G (eds), 1993. *Asia-Pacific Constitutional Yearbook*, from Vol. 1, Centre for Comparative Constitutional Studies.

vom Busch, W and Alailima, F (eds), 1994. *New Politics in the South Pacific*, Institute of Pacific Studies, University of the South Pacific and Pacific Islands Political Studies Association.

International law and the Pacific Ocean

One of the most significant aspects of international law in the Pacific islands relates to jurisdiction of the marine environment, extending beyond exclusive economic zones (EEZ). Greater awareness of the importance of global action on environmental matters has led to increasing international activity. The International Whaling Commission has created whale sanctuaries; and the United Nations Conference on Environment and Development, the UNCED 'Earth Summit' held at Rio de Janeiro in 1992, took a number of steps to establish principles for sustainable development.

For Pacific islanders with limited bilateral influence, active involvement in multilateral agencies is often the most effective means of achieving international objectives. The case taken to the International Court of Justice by New Zealand in 1975, in an attempt to halt French NUCLEAR TESTING, was supported by Australia, Samoa, Solomon Islands, Marshall Islands and the Federated States of Micronesia. Through their SOUTH PACIFIC FORUM, island nations have used the South Pacific Regional Environment Program (SPREP) and other international negotiations to ensure that their environmental concerns are heard (REGIONAL COOPERATION AND INITIATIVES). The Global Conference on the Sustainable Development of Small Island Developing States, held in Barbados in 1994, was one such example, and the establishment of the International Coral Reef Initiative is another: a collaborative effort to ensure the conservation and sustainable use of coral reefs and similar ecosystems.

Of particular relevance to Pacific islands is the United Nations Convention on the Law of the Sea (UNCLOS), which was signed on 10 December 1982, and took effect in 1994. The convention provides for international institutions such as the International Sea-bed Authority (for management of deep-sea resources extending beyond national borders), and the International Tribunal for the Law of the Sea, established as a means of compulsory dispute settlement.

Building on UNCLOS provisions relating to cooperation between coastal and distant-water fishing nations in matters of conservation and fisheries management, a new agreement was signed on 4 December 1995: the Agreement for the Implementation of the Provisions of UNCLOS Relating to the Conservation and Management of Straddling Fish Stocks and Highly Migratory Fish Stocks. This agreement—which will come into force when 30 nations have ratified it—is aimed at ending the dramatic over-fishing which has decimated fish stocks in many parts of the world. It provides opportunities and challenges for island nations, especially in relation to the effective control of the oceanic regions outside of individual EEZs. Apparently requiring island nations to work together with distant-water fishing nations in an existing or new fisheries organization, the agreement should permit island nations to monitor fisheries catches beyond their own boundaries, and ensure that these do not differ significantly from their own catches. While the Forum Fisheries Agency (FFA) is an effective and dynamic organization, working vigorously to maximize the benefits of the TUNA resource for islanders, the FFA nations have been reluctant to admit distant-water fishing nations into their membership, or to incorporate them in a new formal grouping.

Under the new agreement, member nations must determine conservation (or limit) reference points, providing levels of fisheries stock populations that must be maintained, to ensure the maximum sustainable yield. Data collection requirements (including species caught, amount discarded, types of fishing methods and locations of fishing vessels) will entail revolutionary changes in the fishing industry, relating to unprecedented sharing of information in a 'timely manner'. Management procedures will allow member nations to monitor one another and take action in the event of 'serious violations'. Underpinning the agreement is the 'precautionary principle' (set out within the UNCED Earth Summit's Agenda 21), which follows the established norm of international law that no state has the right to engage in activities within its borders that cause harm to other states. The precautionary principle requires users of the ocean to exercise caution by undertaking relevant research, developing non-polluting technologies, and avoiding activities that present risks to the marine environment. The new agreement is a significant step forward to bringing order to high-seas fishing, although it will require hard work and good will to achieve it.—JVD

Courts and legal systems

Courts are one way in which disputes are resolved and order is maintained. They are part of a legal system, found in every Pacific country today, which combines old and new techniques. Traditionally, as people looked for ways to avoid warfare and destruction, formal rules were developed to determine a growing range of matters—such as where responsibility lay (not necessarily the question of guilt or innocence), the nature of communal obligations, and issues of leadership and land rights. There would also be rules governing punishment, compensation and restitution, and for deciding ways to restore social balance. In many societies, chiefs, elders or headmen, or councils of such leaders, constituted courts. In some cases, the role of orator or advocate was well established.

European law and courts were introduced into different parts of the Pacific at different times and in different ways. In most of Polynesia (including Fiji), British, American or French style courts began operating over 100 years ago, while parts of Melanesia have had little exposure to formal courts until the last two decades. The constitutions of most Pacific island states recognize the existence of both indigenous and introduced elements of the legal system (PACIFIC CONSTITUTIONS), but have generally failed to provide guidance as to when, where and how the contrasting elements should be managed.

This duality distinguishes Pacific legal systems in a fundamental way from those of Britain, the United States and France. While the latter are essentially homogeneous in terms of legal culture, each Pacific state and territory now presents a legal tapestry woven in sharply contrasting threads. The number of different colours may depend on the diversity of indigenous cultures. This results in a very complex pluralism, but the sharpness of contrast will reflect the extent to which introduced and indigenous concepts are still recognizably distinct. The depth of time over which introduced and indigenous ideas have interacted within a society is seen in the resulting perceptions of what is old and what is new. Such perceptions are relevant for the legitimacy of laws and courts. Radical land distribution laws enacted in Tonga in 1882 based on English and Biblical precedents and applied in the land court are regarded as Tongan. Also, the Land and Chiefly Titles court of Western Samoa established by Germany in 1903 is jealously protected as traditional. As ideas and practices from different origins are adapted, they may merge to produce tightly woven combinations, even new creations, the individual threads of which become almost indistinguishable.

The fact of legal pluralism confronts people working in the courts with conflicts, inconsistencies and seeming incompatibilities. These include

- between traditional ideas and Christian teaching, as to what is right and wrong, or just
- between group-based and individual-oriented societies, as to notions of responsibility
- between unwritten customs and written statutes, as to both the way they are expressed and the content of what they say
- between the authority of local chiefs, elders and councils, and that of the courts and agencies of central governments, often called upon to deal with the same matter
- between courts dealing once-and-for-all with the particular act or offence in isolation, and traditional processes which address the wider context of disputes, often without attempting to achieve finality
- between customary manners and methods of communicating, and formal court procedures
- between local attitudes to statements which are accepted as proof of facts, and strict rules of evi-

dence such as the exclusion of hearsay and the burden and standard of proof

- between the different backgrounds and training of personnel, as judges and lawyers, within the same jurisdiction
- between the function of the court as the arbiter of isolated breaches and disputes and its function as an agent of social or government policy.

Typically, first level courts are established to serve villages, towns and smaller islands. As extensions of government, such courts in remoter areas may represent sources of authority but, at the same time, opportunities for local adjudicators to adopt them as fresh contexts for the exercise of power, in a manner not envisaged by those who designed the court system (VILLAGE COURT SYSTEM OF PAPUA NEW GUINEA).

Most of the case-load of the courts of a country is undertaken by the first level courts, yet the processes and outcomes of these courts are usually the least well understood and the most difficult to manage. In Papua New Guinea, Solomon Islands and Vanuatu, these courts apply customary law as well as the criminal law of the land. First level courts may be expected to attach primary significance to the settlement of disputes but in Solomon Islands, traditional chiefs have a gate-keeping function in land disputes, which means that a party cannot have the matter heard in the court unless the chiefs certify that the dispute is unsuitable for settlement or that attempts to settle it have failed.

In Samoa and Solomon Islands, certain courts are established to apply customary law, particularly in relation to land. A difficult question for policymakers is whether the law should allow the decisions of such customary courts to be appealed to or reviewed by the higher courts which are usually conversant only with the common law.

There is often a second level of district or senior magistrates courts which deals with more serious matters and handles appeals from the first level. Pacific countries generally have two further levels of courts at the apex of the hierarchy. There is the high court or supreme court, which is usually presided over by the chief justice or a single judge, to deal with important, but often routine, civil and criminal cases. Under the common law system which originated in Britain, this court exercises unlimited jurisdiction, which means that not only can it deal with the most serious cases but its power to reach down and review the decisions of lesser courts is unlimited—unless there are special provisions protecting a customary law court. In many countries, there is only one further appeal possible, mainly to the court of appeal, which (due to the small number of local judiciary) often comprises judges visiting from Australia, New Zealand and other island states, who are brought together periodically for a list of cases.

Lack of consistency across the Pacific in the naming of higher level courts can make comparison confusing. In ascending order of importance, Papua New Guinea has a national court and supreme court, Fiji has a high court, court of appeal and supreme court, Samoa and Vanuatu have a supreme court and court of appeal, and Kiribati has a high court and court of appeal. In addition, the citizens of Cook Islands, Kiribati and Tuvalu enjoy a further limited right of appeal to the judicial committee of the British privy council in London. The former United States territories place their supreme courts at the pinnacle of the system.

The judiciary of Pacific states carry a significant responsibility under their constitutions, including the obligation to ensure that legislation conforms with constitutional principles, to enforce the HUMAN RIGHTS provisions of the constitution and to review the actions of government where allegations of abuse of power are made, or a breach of natural justice has occurred.

The senior judiciary share many common problems. Regular meetings such as the triennial South Pacific Judicial Conference and regional programs concerned with sentencing for drugs, family issues, and judicial independence are highly regarded. The independence of the judiciary is seen as a fundamental constitutional principle (PACIFIC CONSTITUTIONS) essential to stability of government and maintenance of the rule of law. Contributing to regional consideration of these problems and issues is the annual Pacific Islands Law Officers Meeting, or PILOM. At PILOM the senior government lawyers of each country receive reports from the Legal Division of the London-based Commonwealth Secretariat, and from the SOUTH PACIFIC FORUM Legal Division and the Pacific Forum Fisheries Agency, and discuss public policy concerning the courts as well as technical and professional legal matters (see REGIONAL COOPERATION AND INITIATIVES).

Common understanding of Pacific legal systems, and deeper appreciation of the uniqueness of each, will be further enhanced as graduates from the relevant law school curricula at the UNIVERSITY OF THE SOUTH PACIFIC and the UNIVERSITY OF PAPUA NEW GUINEA advance their careers in the region.—CGP

Further reading

Powles, C G and Pulea, M (eds), 1988. *Pacific Courts and Legal Systems*, University of the South Pacific.

Ntumy, M (ed.), 1993. *South Pacific Islands Legal Systems*, University of Hawai'i Press.

Human rights

Most PACIFIC CONSTITUTIONS include a Bill of Rights expressing the fundamental rights of citizens. These typically provide for the freedoms of life, liberty, speech, assembly, association, residence, movement, expression, religion and belief, and rights in relation to the criminal process and fair trial. A significant element is the anti-discrimination provision, which exists to protect individuals, usually those who are in a minority in society because they have been discriminated against on such grounds as race, ethnicity, place of origin, GENDER, sexual orientation, birth, primary language, economic status, opinions, beliefs, age or disability. The key to a Bill of Rights lies in the effectiveness of machinery for its enforcement. Application may usually be made direct to the senior courts (COURTS AND LEGAL SYSTEMS). The ideal method is a human rights commission which will investigate complaints and also, most importantly, will disseminate educational material aimed at raising public awareness of human rights issues. Fiji, in its 1997 Constitution, is the first and, so far, the only example of such a commission in the Pacific.

Although the phraseology of most Bills of Rights is derived from the United Nations Declaration of Human Rights and subsequent international covenants, every Bill is different, ranging from the detailed provisions of the Constitution of Papua New Guinea to the terse summary of rights in the Vanuatu Constitution. The political implications of Bills of Rights have sometimes been muted to suit the objectives of the architects of particular constitutional systems. For example, the Tongan 'Declaration of Rights' in the 1875 Constitution (CONSTITUTIONAL DEVELOPMENT IN TONGA), the first in the Pacific and the only one derived from the United States model through the short-lived Hawaiian Constitution, declares that the law shall be the same 'for all people of this land', chiefs and commoners alike, while the same Constitution entrenches political supremacy for the chiefs. The successive constitutions of Fiji (1970, 1990 and 1997) reserve certain powers for the Great Council of Chiefs who are mainly hereditary, thus discriminating on grounds of birth. In the 1980s a major discrimination court case was fought in Samoa, alleging that the electoral law reserving the right to vote to chiefs was contrary to the constitutional Bill of Rights. The action failed because the court of appeal believed that the chiefs' pre-independence prerogative was intended to survive the 1962 Constitution. In due course, Samoa introduced universal suffrage for chiefly candidates in 1991, and it applies today.

The provisions of Bills of Rights are often called 'fundamental freedoms' or 'universal rights'. In countries where local customary norms require primary allegiance to the group, and individual members have duties to it rather than rights against society at large, the acceptance of universal rights through international covenants may seem irrelevant. Concern to preserve the essential effectiveness of village government around the traditional authority of local chiefs moved Samoa to legislate in 1990 to support the enforcement by village councils of the customary obligations owed to councils by village members. The people of Tuvalu took a more comprehensive approach and in 1986, rewrote their 1978 Constitution to reflect more specifically their concerns for Tuvaluan traditions and values. Nevertheless, no Pacific country has gone as far as the African Regional Charter of Human Rights and Obligations, which spells out the duties of individuals, parents, children, families and other groups.

A regional charter of human rights for the Pacific was proposed in the mid 1980s. Governments have not offered support, and one of the obstacles may be that the draft charter includes some of the 'social and economic rights' which citizens may claim against the state. In this regard, it is interesting to note that the 'National Goals and Directive Principles' of the Papua New Guinea Constitution include statements of such state obligations, and that the Fiji Constitution of 1997 is the first in the Pacific to provide that 'every person has the right to basic education and to equal access to educational institutions'.

Courts are increasingly resorting to the Bill of Rights, as citizens and judges alike become more familiar with the usefulness of such remedies. Lawyers trained in Australia and New Zealand, where they have not learned about constitutional Bills of Rights, have been slow to understand its significance. Ironically, the citizens of Pacific states are less likely to enjoy the protection of international human rights law, as not all states have become signatories to the international covenants, and reporting abuses to international agencies is not easy for citizens in small and remote jurisdictions.—CGP

Ombudsmen

The ombudsman institution, which originated in Sweden in 1809, has been welcomed in the Pacific. The first national level ombudsman was established in Fiji in 1972. Since then, they have been established in Papua New Guinea (1975), Solomon Islands (1980), Cook Islands (1984), Samoa (1988) and Vanuatu (1995). The ombudsman is a single member institution in each case except Papua New Guinea where there is a three-member Ombudsman Commission.

In Sweden the ombudsman was an independent parliamentary appointee with responsibility to investigate complaints by citizens about maladministration by government officials or agencies, and to make non-binding recommendations for remedial action. New Zealand in 1962 was the first English-speaking common-law country in the world to establish an ombudsman. Since the 1960s, the institution has been adopted and adapted in many countries, at national, state and local levels, as well as in state agencies, universities and the private sector.

The Cook Islands and Samoa ombudsmen are similar to ombudsmen institutions in Australia and New Zealand in following key aspects of the original Scandinavian model. They are parliamentary appointees, and their functions are limited to investigation of citizen complaints. The other four Pacific ombudsmen hold constitutional offices. Procedures for their appointment aim at wide consultation to ensure appointees are both highly qualified and acceptable to government and opposition. They enjoy a high degree of constitutionally guaranteed independence from direction, control or influence by other arms of government.

In exercising the traditional ombudsman role (investigating complaints of maladministration), the Pacific ombudsmen are in the same position as most ombudsmen elsewhere in having limited enforcement powers. They can argue for the need for change or redress and can also publicize their reports and recommendations.

Ombudsmen in Fiji, Vanuatu and Papua New Guinea have significant additional roles. Under the 1997 Fiji Constitution the Ombudsman chairs the Human Rights Commission. The Papua New Guinea Ombudsman Commission has administered a code of conduct for leaders since 1975 and the Vanuatu Ombudsman has done so since 1998 (LEADERSHIP CODES). The Vanuatu Ombudsman also has responsibilities in relation to the constitutional provisions for 'multilingualism'. The ombudsman deals with citizens' complaints of breaches of rights to receive government services using whichever of the three official languages the citizen uses, and is required to make an annual report to Parliament about the observance of multilingualism. The Papua New Guinea Ombudsman Commission is also responsible for anti-discrimination legislation, and has subsidiary functions, including: power to refer questions of constitutional interpretation to the Supreme Court; a role in judicial appointments through the Chief Ombudsman's membership of the Judicial and Legal Services Commission; and a role in ensuring that the non-justiciable National Goals and Directive Principles set out in the preamble to the Constitution are not without effect.

Major reports of the Vanuatu and Papua New Guinea ombudsmen on corrupt practices in government have resulted in both institutions being seen as having anti-corruption roles. In Papua New Guinea, that perception has been reinforced by the Ombudsman Commission's active role in administration of the Leadership Code. As a result, these ombudsmen have often been at the centre of political controversy. Indeed, several attempts have been made by politicians to abolish the Vanuatu ombudsman. The high degree of constitutional protection enjoyed by the institutions has been important for their survival, but they also enjoy strong popular support largely as a result of their anti-corruption activities. The concentration of limited resources on anti-corruption roles has probably detracted from the capacity of these ombudsmen to carry out effectively the traditional ombudsman role of investigating complaints by individual citizens.

Declining state capacity has contributed to situations where many maladministration complaints are made by government officials against their own agencies. Ombudsmen have little capacity to deal with such systemic maladministration problems. Limited resources have made it difficult for ombudsmen institutions to decentralize their offices and conduct effective public awareness campaigns. As a result the rural-based majority in these countries has limited knowledge of the work of the ombudsmen and restricted access to their services.—AJR

Further reading

Gilling, B, 1998. *The Ombudsman in New Zealand*, Dunmore Press.

Criminal justice in Papua New Guinea

Colonial rule in Papua New Guinea introduced an alien regulatory system into an environment occupied by a profusion of indigenous legal systems (TRADITIONAL SANCTIONS AND LAWS). The process was gradual and extremely uneven, actively negotiated at local levels. In the early colonial period a two-tiered system was established with separate courts and laws for foreigners and indigenes. Until the 1960s there was no discrete system of criminal justice *per se*. Instead, policing, judicial and penal powers were part of a largely undifferentiated system of native administration. The key figure was the European patrol officer (*kiap*) who was responsible for maintaining order at district and sub-district level. Among other things, patrol officers, assisted by an armed Native Constabulary, investigated crime, apprehended suspects, and heard cases as magistrate in the Court of Native Matters (Papua) or Court of Native Affairs (New Guinea). Prison sentences were generally short and served at small rural lock-ups. Prison labour was widely used on a variety of public works projects. While colonial authorities believed this system would play a significant role in the social and economic transformations initiated during this period, its practical impact was invariably mediated through the diverse and remarkably resilient forms of customary social regulation in local communities.

The adoption of the 1960 Derham Report on Judicial Administration led to the gradual dismantling of colonial district administration and its replacement with a centralized system of criminal justice based upon an institutionalized division of labour between police, courts and prisons. With independence in 1975, many experienced Australian officials departed and public service positions were rapidly localized. Lack of adequate training and supervision compounded the human resource problems of the criminal justice system. Growing law and order problems added to the pressure. Serious deficiencies in institutional capacity became increasingly apparent after independence with particular problems associated with investigative police work, prosecutions, case management in the courts, and security at prisons. The introduction of the VILLAGE COURT SYSTEM in the mid 1970s and later establishment of probation and parole represent the most significant innovations in Papua New Guinea's criminal justice system.

The main functions of the police under the constitution are to preserve peace and good order, and to maintain and enforce the law in an impartial and objective manner. The police are a national force with their administrative headquarters in PORT MORESBY. For operational purposes the country is divided into five regions, each with a divisional commander. In addition, each province has its provincial police commander and police headquarters. The size of the force has not kept pace with population growth and escalating lawlessness in many parts of the country. In 1975, when crime rates were generally low, the national population was slightly more than 2 million with a police force of 4100—a police/population ratio of 1:476. By 1996 the population had doubled to 4 million, while the number of police personnel remained at approximately 5000 uniformed staff and 300 civilian support staff. The police/population ratio stood at 1:800, with crime a major concern.

The institutional weakness of the police is reflected in the uneven coverage provided, with many rural areas having little police presence. Lack of financial resources has been a major constraint. It is not unusual, for example, for police vehicles to be immobilized owing to lack of funds for fuel or maintenance. Serious discipline problems are another feature of policing practice and have given rise to regular allegations of human rights abuses, as well as numerous compensation claims in the civil courts.

Village Courts, Local and District Courts, and the National Court each have jurisdiction at different levels over specified criminal matters (COURTS AND LEGAL SYSTEMS). Local and District Courts, presided over by professional magistrates, deal with summary offences. A Juvenile Court has the power to hear offences committed by children under the age of 18. The National Court sits with a single judge and handles serious indictable offences. Decisions from the National Court can be appealed to the Supreme Court.

While the performance of the superior courts has generally attracted praise, the judicial system has not been immune to the shortage of resources affecting all state institutions. Difficulties with case management have also led to congestion in many courts and consequent delays in hearings. The Public Solicitor's Office provides legal aid and assistance. In practice this work is restricted almost entirely to indictable trials before the National Court where a defence counsel will be made available. The legal aid offered in other cases takes the form of advice on legal problems and representation in court where necessary. If defendants have no funds, assistance is free. As with other parts of the system, shortage of funds remains a constraint.

Prisons are the least visible arm of criminal justice and have suffered from more serious financial neglect than either the police or courts. Complaints are often aired about the state of particular prisons, regarding hygiene, food and physical maintenance, as well as the poor quality of warder accommodation. Mass escapes are relatively frequent and recapturing escapees adds to police workloads.

Allegations of human rights abuses by prison authorities are occasionally made, and violence between prisoners is not uncommon. While imprisonment remains the most common punishment for crime, capital punishment was re-introduced for the offence of wilful murder in 1991. Since then the death sentence has been imposed in several cases before the National Court but appeals have either been successful or remain pending. No executions have occurred.

The limited success of institutionalized criminal justice in general and policing in particular, has led to the practice of supplementing 'normal' criminal justice processes with extraordinary measures such as curfews and special policing operations. Police are often joined by defence force and correctional services personnel in larger operations. These are aimed at restoring order in high-crime areas through a combination of restrictions on movement, police raids and orchestrated displays of militaristic strength. Such displays belie the actual capacity of PNG security forces to control crime and disorder on any significant scale.

For the vast majority of rural villagers, the introduced system of law remains socially (and often physically) remote. Primary allegiances reside in highly localized CLAN and sub-clans, and collective responsibility is a fact. Tension is evident between local perceptions and expectations and the principles of individualized criminal justice embodied in the state system. Customary forms of conflict resolution, adapted to the vagaries of change, continue to operate in most village communities.—SD

Village court system of Papua New Guinea

Papua New Guinea's village court system was introduced by legislation at the end of the colonial era in a climate of criticism of the Anglo-Australian legal system which, indigenous representatives claimed, was not accessible to rural communities and which oppressed customary regulatory systems. The 1973 legislation provided that village courts should sit informally when and where disputes arose in communities, that magistrates should be selected by villagers from among themselves rather than being specialists trained in the law, and that the courts should follow custom as far as possible in procedures and decisions.

The system began to spread through rural areas in 1974 but there were soon signs that the courts were diverging from the intentions of the legislation. Some communities began building bush-material court houses imitating the structures of formal courts that had been operating in the country since the beginning of the colonial period. Village courts came to be held at regular times rather than in the *ad hoc* manner set out in the legislation; and a variety of formal procedural elements, such as flag-hoisting, bowing to magistrates, opening and closing announcements and prayers, became common. The customary disposition of the village courts had been a romantic ideal on the part of the planners, and had been partially negated from the outset by the legislation (itself non-customary) which stipulated the kinds of cases to be heard, provided for supervision by members of the formal judiciary, and required records to be kept. Not surprisingly, some commentators noted that village courts were drifting toward the formal legalism which a grassroots justice system had been intended to counter.

Rural communities themselves were complicit in this drift. Customary dispute settlement in kin-ordered societies had often been necessarily a matter of compromise rather than clear and final decisions. A degree of bias was recognized as inevitable among dispute adjudicators obliged to take into account such factors as the relative social status of disputants, kin-group antagonisms and long-standing contentions of which individual disputes were momentary manifestations and often strategic in themselves. The introduced legal system, which idealized objectivity and clear, unbiased judgement, seemed a desirable alternative to potential disputants in changing times. Thus pressure to reproduce structural and procedural characteristics of formal legal institutions came also from the community.

Nevertheless, village courts have not simply come to be smaller versions of district or local courts. Magistrates' lack of training in the law and the legislative exclusion of lawyers are among the elements preventing village courts from capitulating completely to legal formalism. And the fact that the village court magistrates are members of the communities they serve and are particularly sensitive to local issues has also had a bearing on procedural style and decisions in individual courts, so that each court demonstrates a unique blend of legal formalism and local social influences. This has occasionally resulted in some well-publicized controversy such as the intervention of a national court judge in a village court's jailing of a woman in accordance with allegedly discriminatory local custom. The issue of friction between custom and law appears to have been exaggerated by the media. The legislation's recommendation that village courts should follow custom was not grounded in any rigorous analysis of the ever-changing and often contestable nature of local custom. In practice those influences on village court decisions which are sometimes glossed as 'custom' are simply commonsense, or matters of the attitude of sitting magistrates. The legal strictures on what kinds of cases village courts may hear, what penalties they may impose, and how those cases are to be entered in records ensures that for the most part village courts follow 'law' rather than 'custom', and controversial decisions are few. So far as alleged discrimination against women (under customs regarded by outsiders as sexist) is concerned, research suggests that women have confidence in the village courts and prosecute disputes in them as successfully as men. It has to be said, though, that village court magistrates are overwhelmingly male—less than 2 per cent are women.

Some few legal researchers, anthropologists and sociologists have been studying village courts since their inception, observing individual village courts around the country. The diversity of court procedural styles and local circumstances means that research findings vary depending on which court (out of more than 1000 by the mid 1990s) is observed. In-depth studies are increasingly necessary in the face of poorly informed negative publicity and a degree of hostility among legal professionals toward village courts. Although the system is administered through the Attorney-General's Department, which keeps records and publishes intermittent reports and statistics, unforeseeable idiosyncrasies have made official sources an inadequate point of reference. For example, the legislation provides that magistrates can attempt to settle disputes by mediation, bringing the dispute to court only if this strategy fails. In practice this option and the absence of rigorous strictures on court procedure have led to some traits which subvert efforts to monitor case-loads and types. While all disputes and their outcomes are supposed to be documented for official records by court clerks (also chosen by the community and in some areas the only reasonably literate official in the court) research indicates that mediations are rarely recorded. Further, many disputants simply drop complaints after an initial court appearance, having used the court only to publicize their annoyance with someone, and there is also a tendency for magistrates to persuade disputants toward out-of-court resolution after an initial hearing and 'adjournment'. Such outcomes are common and are rarely recorded by court officers, so that official statistics tend to under-represent case numbers and court work.

At an early stage the village court system began to spread into towns, where it served not only urban village communities but also the steadily growing migrant settlements within town boundaries. This urbanization of the system has shifted village courts closer to the formal courts hierarchy in Papua New Guinea, and away from a custom-oriented alternative to the introduced legal system. Regardless of the debate about the direction village courts are taking, however, this successful and locally popular justice institution has provided a necessary dispute settlement forum at grassroots level. Their responsiveness to the varying social patterns of the communities they serve ensures that they remain the most dynamic and innovative element in the country's regulatory system. (See also TRADITIONAL SANCTIONS AND LAWS and CRIMINAL JUSTICE IN PAPUA NEW GUINEA.)—MG

Constitutional development in Tonga

The Constitution of Tonga, proclaimed on 4 November 1875, remains in force as the oldest constitution in the Pacific region. It was based on previous law codes (of 1839, 1850 and 1862, the last including the Edict of Emancipation) and on the short-lived Constitution of Hawai'i. European (especially missionary) influence is clear, but the ideas of Tāufa'āhau (George TUPOU I) relating to land reform and the restructuring of Tongan society are evident in the legal codes. The constitution was an attempt by Tupou I to establish Tonga as a responsible, self-governing country, and to protect it against European powers that had annexed other island groups.

It begins with a Declaration of Rights—guaranteeing freedom of religion and speech, the sanctity of the Sabbath, freedom from slavery and arbitrary arrest; prohibition of punishment without trial and retrospective laws; and providing for the right to trial by jury and free elections. The constitution also declares that the sovereign owns all the land, great male chiefs (designated nobles and six other estate-holding chiefs) are trustees of the land, and all adult males are entitled to a farm and village allotment. This arrangement was undermined by the introduction of the law of primogeniture, which now determines the leadership of family groups, and legislation of 1915, which made male hereditary estate-holders virtual landowners.

The king's powers were strengthened by amendments to the constitution in 1882, which entrenched sovereignty within the Tupou family. The king is not accountable to anyone for his actions, he appoints ministers who protect his interests, and presides over the privy council, from which legislation emanates. Although parliament can amend legislation, the king may refuse to sign the amended bill. He can also suspend habeas corpus, sign treaties, and declare martial law. The sovereign is immune from impeachment and legal challenge.

The authority of the sovereign is not subject to the unwritten conventions of Westminster government conferring effective power on elected ministers. The sovereign presides over the privy council, which is the highest executive authority and until 1990 was the final court of appeal. The sovereign appoints the premier, the ministers, and the governors of Ha'apai and Vava'u, who form the privy council. Between sessions of parliament, the privy council may pass ordinances, which must be affirmed or amended by the next session of parliament. Members of the privy council other than governors are also members of cabinet, presided over by the premier, who almost always has been a close relation of the sovereign.

The premier, ministers, and governors sit in the sole chamber of parliament. At first, parliament also included all the nobles and an equal number to represent the people, but in 1914 the constitution was amended to reduce the number of members to seven representatives of the 32 nobles and seven representatives of the people. The numbers were recently increased to nine of each, together with the members of the privy council.

Since 1914, elections have been held every three years. Adults over 21 (including women since 1960) elect the people's representatives. Voting is by secret ballot, and is not compulsory. Parliament's principal power is to delay or block legislation, including supply. It can also impeach privy councillors and judges. There have frequently been petitions under a procedure that allows subjects to bring grievances to parliament or the sovereign, but there is no requirement on government or sovereign to act, or even to respond. The constitution may be changed by simple act of parliament and has been amended from time to time, without affecting the power of the sovereign. Only the nobles in parliament may discuss and vote on matters affecting their own and the sovereign's interests.

Tupou I was capable of disregarding his own edicts when it suited him, as when he forced Tongans to join his new Free Church of Tonga after 1885, in spite of the constitutional guarantee of freedom of religion and speech. Tupou I's successor, his great-grandson Tupou II, ignored those parts of the constitution that restricted his privileges, but his daughter, Queen SĀLOTE TUPOU III, respected the constitution and laws, recognizing that they protected her rights and powers and provided a stable framework of government within which she could continue to exercise many of the traditional powers of a ruling chief. The queen rejected British advice to appoint enough ministers to secure the passage of legislation that she deemed important, realizing that it would undermine the respect of chiefs for the constitution and laws.

The constitution has primacy over the laws, but in 1900 Britain declared Tonga a 'protected state' and the Treaty of Friendship with Great Britain gave the Agent and Consul (sole representative of the British government resident in Tonga) considerable powers, which were re-interpreted from time to time. In 1958 all previous agreements were replaced by a treaty concerned only with defence and external affairs, and this, in turn, was replaced in 1970, when Tonga regained full independence and became a member of the British Commonwealth.

Since 1987, growing concern for reform of the constitution has been reflected in the election to parliament of representatives of the PRO-DEMOCRACY MOVEMENT IN TONGA. A convention organized by political and church leaders in 1992 examined the document in detail with a view to substantial reform. A draft revised form of the constitution has been prepared and circulated, leading to a further convention on the draft document in January 1999.—EW-E & CGP

Sources/further reading

Papers of the WESTERN PACIFIC HIGH COMMISSION, held in Foreign and Commonwealth Office, Milton Keynes, United Kingdom.

Powles, G, 1993. *Asia-Pacific Constitutional Systems Yearbook*, Centre for Comparative Studies, University of Melbourne.

Constitution review in Fiji

Following a unanimous resolution of the Fiji house of representatives on 22 September 1993, the president, Ratu Sir Kamisese MARA, appointed a three-member Constitution Review Commission in 1995 to review the 1990 constitution. That constitution, which had been decreed into existence with no popular participation in its formulation or its implementation, included a provision for its review seven years after the date of its promulgation. The commission was headed by Sir Paul Reeves, former New Zealand governor general and archbishop, its other members being former speaker of the house and Alliance Minister Tomasi Rayalu Vakatora, the government nominee, and Fiji-born, Canberra-based historian Brij Vilash Lal, the opposition nominee.

The commission's terms of reference required it to recommend constitutional arrangements which would meet the present and future needs of the people of Fiji, and promote racial harmony, national unity and the economic and social advancement of all the communities in Fiji. Those arrangements had to guarantee the full protection and promotion of the rights, interests and concerns of the indigenous Fijian and Rotuman people, have full regard for the rights, interests and concerns of all ethnic groups in Fiji, and take into account internationally recognized principles and standards of individual and group rights. In accomplishing its task, the commission was expected to ascertain the views of the people and suggest how the provisions of the 1990 constitution could be improved upon to meet the needs of Fiji as a multi-ethnic, multi-cultural society.

In September 1996 the commission presented its 800-page report to the president, containing some 694 recommendations covering the electoral system and the composition of parliament as well as the functioning of parliament; the relationship between the executive and the legislative branches; institutions of government and the mechanism for improving accountability and transparency in them; the administration of justice, citizenship, ethnic and social justice issues; rights of communities and groups; the operation of local government bodies; public revenue and expenditure; emergency powers; and bill of rights.

The commission recommended that progress towards the sharing of power among all communities was the only way to resolve Fiji's pressing constitutional problems. Such arrangements should protect the rights and interests of all citizens, particularly of the indigenous communities. And they should provide incentives to political parties to move gradually but decisively away from the communal system of political representation. The principle of Fijian paramountcy should be recognized, as in the past, in its protective role, in securing effective Fijian participation in a multi-ethnic government, along with members of other communities, and in securing the fruits of affirmative programs of social and ethnic justice based on a distribution of resources broadly acceptable to all.

The report was referred to a joint parliamentary select committee which, after working through it, accepted the great majority of its recommendations, with certain notable exceptions. On the advice of the select committee, the bill for the new constitution was drafted and presented to parliament, and adopted in 1997.

The commission recommended a 70-seat house of representatives, 45 of which were to be contested from 15 three-member open (non-racial) constituencies and 25 from reserved (communal) constituencies (12 for Fijians, 10 Indo-Fijians, 2 general electors, 1 Rotuma). The new constitution reversed the order. Similarly, it rejected the commission's proposal for a fully elected upper house in favour of an appointed body made up of the nominees of the great council of chiefs, the prime minister and the leader of the opposition. The commission's recommendation that the president (and the vice-president who would be the president's running mate, as in the American system) should be elected without debate by the electoral college, comprising both houses of parliament, from a list of three to five names submitted to it by the great council of chiefs, was also rejected. The constitution provides for the president and the vice-president to be nominated by the great council of chiefs in consultation with the government. Even more significantly, the new constitution provides for a mandatory power-sharing through a multi-party cabinet comprising political parties with more than 10 per cent of seats in the house of representatives. The new constitution, which is a marked improvement on its earlier counterparts, came into effect in July 1998.—BVL

Palau's nuclear-free constitution

The Republic of Palau became a self-governing state in free association with the United States in 1994, the last of the four political entities to emerge from the UN Trust Territory of the Pacific Islands (TTPI). Palau was then admitted as a member of the United Nations. A nuclear-free constitution had been adopted on 1 January 1981. The Belau people chose to provide in it that their government could not permit the storage in, or passage through, Palau of nuclear weapons, unless a plebiscite of all citizens approved such action by a majority of 75 per cent of votes cast.

The Compact of Free Association agreed between the United States and Palau in 1986 gave the islands independence subject to defence being the responsibility of the United States for 50 years. Successive referenda in Palau, however, failed to produce the 75 per cent majority required by the constitution to approve the compact provisions which were otherwise inconsistent with it. Incompatible with American perceptions of its defence interests, Palau's nuclear-free constitution long delayed a mutually acceptable Compact of Free Association. In 1987, Palau voted to amend the constitution to allow approval of the compact by a simple majority. In a subsequent plebiscite, 73 per cent of the votes were cast for the compact, but the Palau supreme court ruled this invalid in August 1988.

The court also ruled there were inconsistencies between the compact and Palau's nuclear-free constitution, which was incompatible with the US defence policy. The impasse was broken when Palau revised its constitution. Agreements with the Bush administration in 1989 provided aid in paying off foreign debt and funds for new development. On 9 November 1993, a 68 per cent majority voted in favour of the compact.

After this vote, Palau achieved self-government on 1 October 1994. Kuniwo NAKAMURA, a former teacher elected president in November 1992, managed the country's change of status, achieving an agreement by the United States to pay Palau compensation over 15 years for military and political control rights for 50 years. Palau received US$450 million for the first year. Today, Palau has authority over its affairs, except that defence and other strategic prerogatives remain in the hands of the United States. In exchange, the United States continues to provide substantial financial subsidies for the first 15 years of the compact, which must be re-negotiated in the year 2009.—RCK

Matignon Accords

The Matignon Accords are the agreements and associated legislation negotiated between France and NEW CALEDONIA in 1988, which provided a framework for settlement of New Caledonia's constitutional future. In the previous decade, the French Territory had endured bitter conflicts and escalating violence, with the conservative government of Jacques Chirac, which sought to marginalize the Kanak nationalist movement, unable to resolve the crisis. Michel Rocard, his successor, moved immediately to negotiate a prompt settlement. On 26 June 1988 at the Palais de Matignon, he signed the foundation agreements together with Jean-Marie TJIBAOU, leader of the nationalist FLNKS (Front de la Libération Nationale Kanak et Socialiste) and Jacques LAFLEUR, leader of the 'loyalist' anti-independence RPCR (Rassemblement pour la Calédonie dans la République). These agreements were subsequently ratified by a national referendum in France in November 1988.

Accordingly, the territory abandoned arrangements for a modest level of self-government and instead came under direct rule from Paris for a year until elections were held in June 1989. New governments were elected for each of the three new provinces created from July 1989, comprising the northern and southern portions of the main island and the outlying Loyalty Islands. France undertook to carry out a substantial program of public spending on economic and social development, improving infrastructure and services in disadvantaged areas, and providing improved educational and training opportunities for Melanesians.

The final commitment was to hold a referendum on the territory's constitutional future in 1998, in which only those who had been eligible to vote in the 1988 referendum and their descendants would be eligible to participate. Following the signing of the Accords, calm was restored in the Territory, although immediate tensions led to the murder of Tjibaou and his deputy, Yeiwene Yeiwene, in May 1989.—KRF

Noumea Accord

The Noumea Accord for New Caledonia, which was signed on 5 May 1998 at the opening of the JEAN-MARIE TJIBAOU CULTURAL CENTRE, was a significant step in the constitutional evolution of the French territory, following on the earlier commitment of the MATIGNON ACCORDS. Agreed to by the French government, the FLNKS (Front de Libération Nationale Kanak et Socialiste) and the conservative RPCR (Rassemblement pour la Calédonie dans la République), it confirms a set timetable for the progressive and irreversible transfer of sovereign powers, and represents a commitment to hold a referendum in 20 years on full sovereignty. The Accord includes in its preamble a substantial acknowledgement of the rights and aspirations of the Kanak people, recognizing the loss of identity, the disruption to social organization, and the repression of artistic heritage caused by the imposition of colonial rule. (See NATIONALISM IN FRENCH TERRITORIES.) Territorial elections for the new government will be held under the new legislation in mid 1999.—KRF

Further reading

Henningham, S, 1992. *France and the South Pacific: a contemporary history*, Allen & Unwin

——, 1994. 'The uneasy peace: New Caledonia's Matignon Accords at mid-term', *Pacific Affairs*, 66(4).

FOUR THE REGION AND THE WORLD

Regional cooperation and initiatives

Discussion of the achievements of Pacific island states in developing common approaches to regional problems should begin with a reminder of the region's diversity. This goes beyond the obvious differences in ethnicity, culture, language and colonial inheritance. For example, the Polynesian states of Samoa, Tonga and Cook Islands have tended to be more conservative politically, and less interested in taking the critical, anti-colonial approaches often favoured by Papua New Guinea, Vanuatu, and Solomon Islands, and sometimes Fiji. These four formed the 'Melanesian Spearhead Group' in 1986. Also, the independent states of the region have clearly distinguished themselves from the territories which are still dependencies of the United States and France. There is the further division between the larger, wealthier states and the smaller ones which are more reliant on former colonial powers as well as on international and regional inter-governmental agencies.

Early cooperation between the colonial powers brought into existence in 1947 the South Pacific Commission, which subsequently admitted independent states and dependent territories (see PACIFIC COMMUNITY). The most significant development in Pacific island affairs has been the birth in 1971 of the SOUTH PACIFIC FORUM and the evolution of this politically dynamic relationship of the heads of government of 16 member countries. Tension between colonial and self-governing states had caused some of the latter to form the Pacific Island Producers' Association as the region's first special purpose organization in 1965, and the UNIVERSITY OF THE SOUTH PACIFIC followed in 1970.

Members of the South Pacific Forum and the South Pacific Commission, sometimes in conjunction with international agencies, have been responsible for a series of multilateral agreements within the region covering a range of activities in which cooperation was seen as essential. The South Pacific Regional Shipping Council formed in 1974 led to nine states and New Zealand establishing the PACIFIC FORUM LINE in 1977. The South Pacific Regional Civil Aviation Council of 1976, however, did not lead to the formation of a regional airline (see AVIATION).

Other councils and committees which have been of benefit to members include

- the Pacific Island Tourism Development Council (1975) which led to the TOURISM COUNCIL OF THE SOUTH PACIFIC (1983)
- the Regional Committee on Trade, leading to the South Pacific Regional Trade and Economic Cooperation Agreement, known as SPARTECA, in 1980
- the Pacific Island Development Program established in 1980 to act as the research, publishing, policy advice and training arm of the South Pacific Conference
- the Pacific Island Law Officers Meeting, inaugurated in 1981, to bring together senior government legal advisers (see COURTS AND LEGAL SYSTEMS)
- the South Pacific Telecommunications Development Program which was formed in 1983.

Three significant areas of regional cooperation are those concerned with fisheries, coastal and submarine minerals, and protection of the environment. As to the first, the lengthy international processes leading to the United Nations Convention on the Law of the Sea (UNCLOS) prompted Pacific island states to reach agreement on a common position which would protect their position, particularly in relation to the major fishing nations. Over the objections of the Polynesian governments and Australia and New Zealand, which favoured including the United States in regional fishing arrangements, the Melanesian governments in 1979 persuaded the balance of the then 12 members of the South Pacific Forum to establish the Forum Fisheries Agency in Honiara. Now operating with substantial professional and support staff, the Forum Fisheries Agency's (FFA) functions include the collecting, evaluating and disseminating of statistical and biological information as well as information relating to the shipping, processing and marketing of fish. It also provides technical assistance in the development of fisheries policies and in the negotiation of licences and matters relating to the surveillance of marine waters. A major achievement of the FFA was to secure agreement with the United States in 1987 on a treaty with Forum members over the control of highly migratory fish species (see MULTILATERAL TREATY ON FISHERIES). Shortly afterwards, the FFA began to tackle the problem of long driftnet fishing carried out by Japan, South Korea and Taiwan. The culmination of a vigorous campaign to ban this fishing technique was the Convention for the Prohibition of Fishing with Long Driftnets in the South Pacific which was signed in 1989. This collective action, supported by Australia and New Zealand, and subsequent United Nations declarations on the issue, was instrumental in inducing Japan and the other offenders to stop driftnet fishing by 1992. (See INTERNATIONAL LAW AND THE PACIFIC OCEAN, NATURAL RESOURCES AND INTERNATIONAL DEVELOPMENT and SUSTAINABLE DEVELOPMENT.)

Second, concern to manage the potential wealth of coastal and submarine minerals led to the establishment in 1972 of a committee for coordination of joint prospecting for mineral resources in South Pacific offshore areas. Based in Suva, this became an autonomous regional organization in 1984, subsequently renamed the South Pacific Applied Geoscience Commission (known as SOPAC). Considerable offshore resource mapping has been completed and mineral deposits located.

Third, concern for better management of the environment led, in 1978, to a comprehensive environmental management program. By 1980, the South Pacific Forum and the South Pacific Commission (SPC) had agreed to establish the South Pacific Regional Environment Programme, with a secretariat funded by the SPC. Known as SPREP, the secretariat was instrumental in securing agreement in 1983 for management of the natural resources and environment of the South Pacific region, followed by the adoption in 1986 of the Convention for the Protection of Natural Resources and Environment of the South Pacific Region (the SPREP Treaty). This treaty deals with such issues as the effect of climate change, watershed and water quality management, pesticide hazards, the protection of areas and species, natural resources management and pollution control. It also includes protocols prohibiting the dumping of radioactive wastes and testing nuclear explosive devices. In 1990, SPREP was itself established as an autonomous regional organization with its headquarters in Apia.

One of the best-known achievements in regional cooperation was the South Pacific Nuclear-Free Zone Treaty which followed a long period of regional opposition to NUCLEAR TESTING and nuclear waste dumping. From 1971, this was the first and most consistent example of collective advocacy on the part of members of the South Pacific Forum. Ultimately, the treaty was signed in Rarotonga in 1985, and came into force in December 1986. It prohibited the manufacture, stationing or testing of any nuclear explosive device, as well as the dumping of nuclear waste at sea, within the treaty area. However, it stopped short of banning the passage of nuclear armed or powered vessels through the region. The all-important protocols to the treaty were signed first by the Soviet Union and the People's Republic of China and then, in 1996, after the cessation of French testing, by Britain, the United States and France.

Bilateral treaties of friendship and cooperation within the region have characterized relationships between some Pacific island states and their former colonial powers. Examples include Tonga/United Kingdom, Samoa/New Zealand, Nauru/Australia and the compacts between the Micronesian states and the United States. Post-colonial relationships are considered in separate discussions of the relationships of Australia, New Zealand, the United States and France with the region (see PACIFIC ISLANDS AND THE WORLD).

Pacific island states have increasingly participated in international organizations, ranging from specialized agencies such as the Universal Postal Union, through financial and aid bodies such as the World Bank, the Asian Development Bank and the International Monetary Fund, to general purpose organizations such as the United Nations, the Food and Agricultural Organization, and the World Health Organization. Forum members are also parties to international treaties, particularly those which have immediate impact on the region such as UNCLOS. Members have seemed less interested in the international conventions on HUMAN RIGHTS.

Other regional non-governmental bodies to have significant impact on political and social developments in the Pacific region include

- the Pacific Conference of Churches, founded in 1966, which has tackled social justice issues across the region and took a stand on the once-planned incineration of chemical weapons on the US possession, Johnston Atoll
- the Nuclear Free and Independent Pacific movement (NFIP), a loose coalition of activist groups which had its origins in the 1975 Nuclear-Free Pacific Conference in Suva and the 1983 Port Vila Charter for a Nuclear Free and Independent Pacific, and which has shifted its focus to issues of indigenous rights, particularly in relation to New Caledonia, French Polynesia, Hawai'i and New Zealand
- Pacific Concerns Resource Centre (PCRC), which retains a small but effective infrastructure based in Suva, with a range of social justice initiatives in the region
- the Pacific Islands Association of Non-Government Organizations (PIANGO), founded at a Pago Pago conference in 1991 to help develop Pacific identities, cultures and well-being and to facilitate communication and provide a common voice at regional forums, and which, as the name implies, is a regional coordinating body representing national umbrella organizations of NGOs.—CGP

Pacific Community (South Pacific Commission)

The South Pacific Commission (SPC), which changed its name to the Pacific Community in February 1998, was established in 1947 when representatives of the six Pacific colonial powers—United States, Great Britain, Netherlands, France, Australia and New Zealand—met in Canberra at the 'South

Seas Commission Conference' and signed the Canberra Agreement which created the new organization. Aware of the importance of achieving regional security and stability after the Pacific War, the six participating governments were acknowledging the value of international cooperation in the administration of colonial territories. The Dutch withdrew in 1962 when the former territory of Dutch New Guinea (now Irian Jaya) was transferred to Indonesia. The United Kingdom relinquished its membership in January 1996.

The first formal change in membership occurred in 1951 when the Canberra Agreement was amended to admit Guam and the United States Trust Territories of the Pacific Islands.

In 1962 (Western) Samoa became independent and was ineligible for membership. The membership criteria were subsequently changed to allow any territory within the SPC's area of influence to become a full member, if invited. Under the new Amending Agreement, Samoa became the first island state to join as a full voting member on 17 July 1965, followed by Nauru (1969), Fiji (1971), Papua New Guinea (1975), Solomon Islands and Tuvalu (1978), and Niue and Cook Islands (1980).

As its membership grew, the character and scope of the SPC evolved to incorporate the indigenous peoples of the Pacific in its decision-making process. Originally, each of the six governments was represented by two commissioners and they established the South Pacific Conference—meeting every three years until 1967 and thereafter annually—to provide a forum for island participation. The first Conference met in SUVA in 1950 and its role, up until 1983, was to make recommendations to the SPC. In 1983 all the remaining governments and self-governing administrations of the region were accorded full membership, and since then the Conference has become the governing body of the organization now known as the Pacific Community.

In 1999 the Pacific Community (with 26 members) is an established institution in the region, with an integrated work program that caters for the development needs of its membership. The focus has changed from research to technical assistance, with significant achievements including work on combatting mosquito-borne diseases, dissemination of public health information, and programs for the eradication of agricultural pests and diseases such as rhinoceros beetle, fruit fly and taro leaf blight. Other ongoing activities are community education services, fisheries development and training programs. The routine work of the Pacific Community has been managed by a Secretariat based in NOUMEA since 1949. Until 1995 the SPC was accommodated in the former American military headquarters known as the Pentagon, but a new building was completed in time to be officially opened for the 35th South Pacific Conference in 1995. Programs and projects are funded by annual contributions from member governments as well as special grants made by member and non-member governments and by international aid agencies.—KRF

South Pacific Forum

The South Pacific Forum has been the premier regional association of the Pacific islands for more than 25 years. Its authority derives from the fact that the representation of its 16 member countries (in 1998) is at head-of-government level. Formally, it is not an inter-governmental organization since it lacks a foundation treaty to give it international legal standing. Nevertheless, the Forum's importance in the Pacific is such that it is often treated as inter-governmental. The annual meetings of the Forum not only set the region's political agenda, they also manage the affairs of a significant family of agencies which operate under the aegis of the Forum or report to it.

The South Pacific Forum owes its origins to the incapacity of the regional countries to 'decolonize' the South Pacific Commission (SPC—see PACIFIC COMMUNITY) in the latter half of the 1960s. Difficulties became apparent in 1965 when three regional polities—Fiji, Tonga and (Western) Samoa—were forced to go outside the SPC framework to pursue their common economic ambition of higher commodity prices for their agricultural exports. The resulting Pacific Islands Producers Association was the region's first indigenous inter-governmental organization. A variety of influences contributed to mounting dissatisfaction with the SPC during the 1960s but French objections to discussion of the environmental hazards of NUCLEAR TESTING proved the final stumbling block. Matters came to a head in 1970 with the independence of Fiji. A review of the SPC in that year rejected reform, and the newly independent government determined to strike out on an independent course.

Five independent and self-governing countries met with Australia and New Zealand in Wellington in August 1971 to consult at a heads-of-government level on the entire gamut of regional issues. This meeting helped to promote a permanent association when it decided to meet again in Canberra in February 1972. The second Forum added to its institutionalization when it resolved to establish a South Pacific Bureau for Economic Cooperation (SPEC) to support the development aims of its members. The third Forum in SUVA later in 1972 approved the administrative arrangements for SPEC and agreed to annual Forum meetings in future. Although initially not intended to serve as the Forum's secretariat, this administrative responsibility was delegated to SPEC in 1975 and, ultimately, in 1988, this function was more formally recognized in a change in the organization's name from SPEC to the Forum Secretariat (ForSec).

SPEC's primary mandate was to assist the export capacity of member states. Thus in 1973, the independent island states found themselves in control of two regional economic development agencies with very little to distinguish one from the other in terms of formal responsibilities. The amalgamation of SPEC and the Pacific Islands Producers Association in 1974 may have inadvertently set in train a process which dominated the institutional dimension of regionalism in the South Pacific for the next 15 years—the single regional organization concept. The idea of transferring the functions of the SPC to SPEC appealed to a number of SPEC members not only on the grounds of economic and administrative efficiency, but, even more in the minds of the SPC's critics within the Forum, because it would eliminate the colonial vestiges of SPC.

Despite its own reservations, however, the Forum demonstrated the impracticality of the single regional organization concept in 1979 when it established the South Pacific Forum Fisheries Agency (FFA). The FFA was an autonomous regional organization which, like SPEC, reported to the Forum, but was wholly independent of SPEC. The catalyst for this development was the progress made by the United Nations Third Conference on the Law of the Sea (UNCLOS III) which rewrote the global marine agenda during the 1970s. Indeed, UNCLOS III was to add significantly to the regional ecology, directly or indirectly, by promoting the development of other inter-governmental organizations and agreements under the direction of the Forum during the 1970s and 1980s. Amongst these were included the Committee for Coordination of Joint Prospecting for Mineral Resources in South Pacific Offshore Areas which changed its name in 1989 to the South Pacific Applied Geoscience Commission (SOPAC); the South Pacific Regional Environment Program (SPREP); and a variety of specific measures to give Forum members greater control over, and protection of, their extended marine zones.

The 1987 Forum began an important period of reform within the association, which probably had the effect of restructuring South Pacific regional organization as comprehensively as anything envisaged by the single regional organization concept. Anticipating the collapse of the Cold War, Forum members sought to extend its influence beyond the boundaries of the South Pacific. A report tabled by the Forum's Committee on Regional Institutional Arrangements (CRIA) borrowed the concept of 'dialogue partnerships' from ASEAN (Association of South East Asian Nations) to enable interested extra-regional states to engage the Forum as a body. Dialogue partners were to be invited to attend post-Forum meetings with elements of the Forum from 1989 to discuss issues of mutual relevance. Initially, six governments—Canada, China, France, Britain, Japan and the United States—were so designated.

A second significant CRIA proposal, which was implemented in 1988 by the Forum after approval by other regional bodies, established the South Pacific Organizations Coordinating Committee (SPOCC). This effectively ended the long-running single regional organization campaign and, over the years since, it has worked to rationalize the relations amongst the regional bodies to ensure less competitiveness and greater efficiencies. Since 1996, by agreement, the Forum Secretariat has chaired SPOCC's annual meetings, so adding substantially to the Forum's coordinating role in the region.

While control and management of the region's political agenda have accounted for much of the procedural impact of the Forum over its life, the substantive outcomes of its deliberations have arguably been just as important. Annual Forum meetings have been responsible for such significant decisions as those to create a regional non-reciprocal trading arrangement between Australia and New Zealand and the islands, known as the South Pacific Area Regional Trade and Economic Cooperation Agreement (SPARTECA), and the 1985 South Pacific Nuclear-Free Zone Treaty which was essentially a security measure to isolate the region from Cold War rivalries. The Forum has given endorsement to numerous programs, projects and activities, large and small, covering a vast array of issues ranging from economic development and environmental protection to transport and telecommunications. Most have been entrusted to its economic arm, the Forum Secretariat/SPEC. Economic pressures and changed priorities in the 1990s (post-Cold War), however, have caused the Forum to re-evaluate the commitments of its family of agencies and embark on its current rationalization process.—RAH

Further reading

Hoadley, S, 1992. *South Pacific Foreign Affairs Handbook*, Allen & Unwin.

Pacific islands and the world

■ *Australia and the Pacific* Since the early 1800s the Australian colonies, and later the Commonwealth of Australia, have had extensive contact with the Pacific islands. People from the colonies have been prominent in commerce and trade, sealing, whaling, missionary activity, plantations, shipping, mining development, and various forms of education and the public service. The overall legacy is one of ambivalence after successive phases of often single-minded pursuit of commercial advantage, characterized, for example, by the recruitment of islands labour for the sugar industry of Queensland, and the exploitation of plantation crops and mineral and phosphate resources in the islands. These developments were followed by much more enlightened policies towards the treatment of local labour, and increasing recognition of the political and economic aspirations of the island peoples. Australia remains the region's principal trading partner, and a major source of essential fuels, foodstuffs and machinery, aid, investment, technology, service industries and tourism, responsible for over a third of total trade and FOREIGN AID flows to the independent countries of the region, ahead of Japan, France and New Zealand. It is a full partner, as is New Zealand, in all the institutions of regional cooperation, and a major and lead contributor to their programs.

Australian political leaders, from the early days of British settlement, have traditionally viewed the crescent of islands from Papua New Guinea in the north to the Polynesian islands in the east of the South Pacific as a defence perimeter against all potentially hostile powers. Colonial leaders pressed the British government to extend its territorial acquisitions to head off other 'imperialist' powers like France, Germany and the United States for the cause of Empire, trade or missionary support. Such pressures contributed to pushing an often reluctant and parsimonious Great Britain, with more immediate priorities in Africa, to acquire control over Fiji (1874), the southeast coast of New Guinea (1886) and Solomon Islands (1892), and into a clumsy form of joint Anglo–French control in the New Hebrides (1887).

The British Royal Navy from its base in Australia was the main instrument for British control, and although its jurisdiction extended only to British subjects it tempered some of the excesses of the COLONIAL LABOUR TRADE, and occasionally bombarded recalcitrant native communities who had committed crimes against British subjects. Concern to develop a more coherent approach to the South Pacific islands played a role in pushing the Australian colonies towards Federation in 1901.

Germany's defeat in the First World War enabled Australia, through the assertive advocacy of Prime Minister Hughes at the Versailles Peace Conference, to secure in 1919 responsibility for the administration, under League of Nations Mandate, of ex-German New Guinea and its islands, and of Nauru, on behalf of the other mandatees Great Britain and New Zealand. These acquisitions consolidated Australian commercial expansion with the exploitation of the New Guinea estates taken from the Germans; well-established shipping and trading companies like BURNS PHILP, Steamships, and the CARPENTER GROUP; and control of the FIJI SUGAR INDUSTRY by the Australian COLONIAL SUGAR REFINING COMPANY, using indentured Indian labour. Australian investment, banking and insurance expanded. The mandated territories of New Guinea and Nauru, and the colony of Papua, were administered with paternalistic good sense but without generosity, relying mainly on Christian missions to deliver education and health services.

The post-war emergence of the United Nations Trusteeship system (successor to the League), and demands for self-government or independence for all colonies, moved Australia to more active promotion of political and economic change. A more assertive Australian approach emerged in the Australia/New Zealand Agreement of 1944, which also foreshadowed the establishment of the South Pacific Commission (PACIFIC COMMUNITY). Criticisms in New York and by United Nations Visiting Missions, notably the Foot Mission of 1962 to Papua and New Guinea, jointly administered since 1945, accelerated the process of political and economic development. Nauru, where the phosphate deposits had made a substantial contribution to Australian agriculture but were becoming progressively exhausted, achieved independence in 1968. Independence for Papua New Guinea, strongly promoted by the 1972–75 Australian Labor Government, came in 1975, leaving behind some unreconciled separatist demands, notably on Bougainville, but with much goodwill and generosity of spirit on both sides.

Successive Australian governments welcomed and promoted practices of regional consultation (REGIONAL COOPERATION AND INITIATIVES). These included the launching of the SOUTH PACIFIC FORUM by the independent island countries, to which Australia and New Zealand were admitted as full members in 1972. Australia substantially increased its aid to the South Pacific from the mid 1970s, and later provided preferential non-reciprocal trade access for the islands region (SPARTECA) and Papua New Guinea (PATCRA). These were of diminished value as overall tariff levels declined. Such initiatives were widely regarded as designed, in a Cold War context, to head off outsiders, in particular the Soviet Union, which had signed fisheries agreements with Kiribati (1985) and Vanuatu (1987), not renewed by those countries. Australia, while promoting the South Pacific Nuclear-Free Zone Treaty, was critical of New Zealand's refusal from 1987 to permit US nuclear-powered or armed ships or aircraft to enter New Zealand, an issue which divided South Pacific countries and led to suspension of US defence cooperation and security guarantees to New Zealand under the ANZUS Pact signed between Australia, New Zealand and the United States, known simply as ANZUS (see UNITED STATES AND THE PACIFIC). France's role in the region is now welcomed by Australia after periods of tension arising from internal conflict in New Caledonia in the mid 1980s, and resumption of French NUCLEAR TESTING before its suspension in 1996. Australia has also welcomed the increased role of Japan and other Asian partners in the region, with cautions about the commercial practices of some Asian logging companies and other enterprises. Australian policies in some areas, for example on global warming, have divided it from others in the region (CLIMATE CHANGE).

In the face of a number of recent internal political crises in the islands, Australia has been a concerned onlooker, well-meaning but often not adroit, promoting peaceful and democratic outcomes, but restrained from any direct intervention by island insistence on respect for their sovereignty, and by other uncertainties. Such was the case at the time of the two military COUPS IN FIJI in 1987; the closure of the Panguna mine on Bougainville in 1988 and subsequent armed separatist resistance to the PNG Government (BOUGAINVILLE CONFLICT AND PEACE PROCESS); and periods of political instability in Solomon Islands and Vanuatu. In the 1990s Australia, while maintaining its aid flows to the region, became a vigorous advocate of reforms in the South Pacific countries, directed to reducing the public sector and tariff protection, and to achieving more sustainable development and a better return to the islands from their natural resources.—JAP

■ *The French Pacific in the 20th century* At the end of the 1890s, France controlled a vast colonial empire which included much of eastern Polynesia (the *Établissements Français d'Océanie*, EFO), New Caledonia and, in association with Britain, the New Hebrides. In size these possessions looked impressive; the EFO covered an area of 4 million sq km, and indeed, since the introduction of the 200-mile exclusive economic zone, France controls more ocean than any other nation. The economic value of the EFO, however, and their potential as European settlements were limited, especially in comparison with French-controlled territories in Africa and the West Indies.

The First World War eliminated Germany from the Pacific, but France made no claim for the former German possessions which fell, under League of Nations mandates, to Britain, Australia, New Zealand, the United States and Japan. The war, however, did affect the French territories: French nationals were subject to the general call-up, and Polynesian and Melanesian volunteers joined them to serve in various theatres of war.

The veterans came home with a new insight into French life and the inter-relationships of world powers, while for their part the French authorities were forced to recognize the contribution they had made to the war. The French also began to crystallize their theory of empire. Opinions had ranged widely, from a belief that colonial settlements should remain commercial and cultural outposts to the more committed imperialism of full integration and assimilation. Consensus favoured a French empire with a dual culture, in which the local peoples retained their own traditions while acquiring a knowledge of the French language and French laws.

This view was expressed in the great colonial exhibition in Paris in 1931, embodying this theme of diversity in unity. At the same time, colonial administrative structures were reformed, with greater local autonomy, a more unified legal system and greater emphasis on education. The times were not propitious for costly reforms. After the war, France faced problems of reconstruction, a deadly influenza epidemic, a world-wide depression and, eventually, the rise of the dictators in Europe. The Pacific was not immune from these problems: influenza killed over 2500 people in the EFO alone, the recession stifled economic growth, including a nascent tourist industry, caused a drastic fall in commodity prices and saw unemployment emerge in islands where hitherto there had been a shortage of labour.

World War II brought other problems. When France fell in 1940, the Pacific territories were torn between the Vichy Government and General de

Gaulle's Free French. Clashes occurred between the senior administrators, who felt still bound to their superiors in Vichy, and the great majority of French residents. The pro-Vichy Governor of the EFO was overthrown on 2 September 1940, and the governor of New Caledonia on the 19th; the resident commissioner in Wallis and Futuna held out, largely ignored, until May 1942. The first contingent of military volunteers left in May 1941; they were to form the 'Pacific Battalion' (nicknamed the Guitarists' Battalion) which distinguished itself in North Africa and in Italy.

Meanwhile, the situation in the Pacific was changing. The Japanese attack on PEARL HARBOR heralded a series of concerted attacks on island groups close to the French territories, but it also brought the United States into the war. Large contingents of American troops arrived in the EFO and in New Caledonia, eventually averaging a total of 35 000, of which 22 000 were stationed in the EFO. They injected money into local economies, opening new windows on social attitudes—and on modern consumerism.

After the war, the role played by France's overseas territories needed to be recognized: they had provided the early framework for the Free French movement and had supplied thousands of volunteers for the fighting forces. Rearguard actions by conservatives to maintain the old colonial structures in Indo-China and Algeria led to protracted conflicts and to De Gaulle's election as president of a reconstituted republic in 1958.

Post-war governments had already begun to transform the old empire. Their *Union Française* provided for local elected assemblies and for representatives of the colonial territories in the Paris parliament. De Gaulle's reforms went much further. A referendum was held through the Union, asking the local populations to choose between immediate independence and greater autonomy, with 'Territorial Assemblies' and representatives in the French lower and upper Houses, all within a new 'French Community'. The EFO (to be renamed *Polynésie Française*), New Caledonia and Wallis and Futuna became *Territoires d'Outre-Mer* ('TOM', overseas territories).

The local assemblies received increased powers, a process which continued steadily over the next 30 years, and substantial funds were made available by Paris for education, including the setting up of a *Université Française du Pacifique*, medical services and public works. Increasing attention was paid to local traditions, with Polynesian and Melanesian cultural institutes and courses in local languages, and to customary laws. All this fitted into the ideal of a *Francophonie*, a world-wide network of former colonial territories linked together by a common understanding of the French language and the French way of life.

Local assemblies, however, led to rapid politicization. Parties proliferated, merged, vanished and reappeared. Pressures for greater autonomy turned in some cases into a demand for full independence. This was particularly marked in New Caledonia where Melanesians and European settlers, their numbers evenly balanced, sought different forms of autonomy serving their personal interests; the result was a bitter struggle, with often bloody clashes, which ceased only in 1988 when a new referendum was promised, after a 10-year period which would allow tensions to subside (MATIGNON ACCORDS and NATIONALISM IN FRENCH TERRITORIES).

In the New Hebrides, the British and the French failed to agree on a suitable formula for independence. The latter supported an unsuccessful attempt at secession by islanders from Santo, the situation being exacerbated by religious rivalries. The consequence was that when the archipelago gained independence under the name of VANUATU, French settlers and their supporters went through a period of expulsion and exclusion which did not end until late in the 1980s.

In French Polynesia, the pressure for independence was more moderate. In 1958 two-thirds of the voters had favoured joining the French Community, the 'Yes' vote rising to 85 per cent in the Gambiers and 90 per cent in the Marquesas. The opening of a nuclear base in French Polynesia, the *Centre d'Expérimentation du Pacifique* (CEP), in the mid 1960s was to have far-reaching consequences, economically and politically. The United States and Britain were beginning to wind down their own local bases, so that by 1971 France was the only power carrying out NUCLEAR TESTING in the Pacific. Opposition from anti-nuclear campaigners and a number of Pacific states forced France to switch to underground tests, but protests multiplied until 1992 when the tests were suspended. Their resumption in mid 1995 caused an even greater furore which did not abate until their final suspension in early 1996.

The economic impact of the CEP on French Polynesia's economy was considerable. An entire infrastructure had to be provided, not only in the uninhabited atolls of Moruroa and Fangataufa, but also in Tahiti where the main administrative base was set up. By 1966, close to 14 000 workers were employed by the CEP, in addition to some 5000 military and naval personnel. Substantial immigration occurred, mostly to PAPE'ETE and its adjoining working-class suburb, Faa'a. Internal politics were similarly affected, independentists linking up with protest movements abroad, while those favouring continuing links with France warned of serious economic consequences if the tests ended. When the CEP closed down, France had to promise to continue providing financial aid for at least 10 years.

The majority parties which favoured links with France used the situation to gain constitutional concessions which brought full internal autonomy, or the ideal of 'independence-in-association', much closer. The model many had in mind was the relationship which Cook Islands enjoy with New Zealand, rather than total 'floating' freedom. A complicating factor was a growing hostility between the outlying archipelagoes, Marquesas and Gambiers in particular, and Tahiti, especially the Pape'ete urban district which wields considerable power because of its large population.

It is possible to draw a parallel between these archipelagoes and Wallis and Futuna, which have few European settlers, are strongly Catholic and pro-French, and where traditional customs still rule. Wallis and Futuna enjoy all the benefits predicted by the proponents of the 'overseas territories' formula: a local assembly, representatives in the upper and lower houses in Paris and substantial funds for education and development. In the 1959 referendum, 94 per cent of the islanders had voted in favour of the French Community proposals; such an overwhelming majority would be unlikely today, but support for the status quo is still widespread.

The future of the French Pacific cannot be predicted. Whatever happens, the links with the French-speaking world will continue, and the centuries of interaction will not be erased. The French imprint—over language, institutions, legal and political practices, and even genetic elements—will remain.—JD

Further reading

Aldrich, R, 1993. *France and the South Pacific since 1940*, University of Hawai'i Press.

Dunmore, J, 1997. *Visions and Realities: France in the Pacific 1695–1995*, Heritage Press.

Henningham, S, 1992. *France and the South Pacific: a contemporary history*, Allen & Unwin.

Maclellan, N and Chesneaux, J, 1998. *After Moruroa: France in the South Pacific*, Ocean Press.

■ *Japan and the Pacific* One of the earliest probable contacts between Japanese and Pacific islanders was in 1171, when a boatload of strange people drifted ashore at Okinoshima, in Izu—the present-day Prefecture of Shizuoka. The event was described in *Kokon Chomon Jyu* compiled by Tachibana-no-Narisue in 1254. These strangers were possibly from Melanesia, if we can rely on the descriptions of their features and equipment. A link with Hawai'i was forged some 600 years later, after the Japanese Naval Academy was established in Tokyo in 1869. The first long training cruise for cadets, made on HMS *Tsukuba* in 1875, included a visit to Honolulu in January 1876. A few years later, when Hawaiian King David Kalākaua arrived in Yokohama on 4 March 1881, the Japanese military band performed the national anthem of Hawai'i as the first performance for a foreign head of state in Japan.

Large numbers of Japanese settled in Hawai'i from this time, where they often intermarried, and their descendants have since assimilated. Today, a significant number of third and fourth generation descendants of Japanese SUGAR plantation labourers are employed in the fields of law, elementary education, secretarial services, medicine, and dentistry. (George ARIYOSHI, who served as third governor of Hawai'i from 1974 until 1986, was the first state governor of Japanese descent in the United States.) Much smaller numbers of Japanese migrants came to other areas—Papua New Guinea, Samoa, Fiji—where they often struggled with overt discrimination, low-paying jobs, unfair laws, and sometimes bachelorhood.

Following the involvement of Japanese entrepreneurs in the Nan'yô or South Seas in the 1890s, JAPANESE COMMERCIAL INTERESTS in the region led to its occupation from as early as 1915 in the former German Micronesia (JAPANESE ACTIVITY IN MICRONESIA, 1885–1945). Even during the German era most of the overseas trade was with Japan. Under the highly efficient Japanese administration, the Marianas were transformed from being the greatest liability to the richest asset of all Japanese Micronesia. Saipan and Tinian were converted into sugar plantations with the help of liberal subsidies and concessions from the government. Thousands of Japanese and Koreans were brought in as agricultural labourers and settlers, and soon outnumbered the Micronesians. In spite of the effects of drought, damage to most crops by noxious insects, and finally the post-war recession of 1920, the sugar industry was profitable from 1925. This success was largely due to the vital leadership of Matsue Haruji, whose South Seas Development Company (a trading and shipping company, Nan'yô Kôhatsu, later known as NBK or Nanbo), had operated in Micronesia and other parts of the Pacific since 1883.

In Palau the Japanese took over the German phosphate mines on Angaur and expanded them considerably. During the 1930s the Japanese also started bauxite mining on Palau. Pohnpei became a large Japanese colony, providing a base for Japanese fishing fleets, and it was also developed as an agricultural station. Economic development forged ahead, and all foreign interests, including Burns Philp, were driven out of Micronesia. A large bureaucracy was installed, and compulsory schooling quickly introduced Japanese language and the Shinto religion, as well as improved health services. In New Caledonia, there were about 1500 Japanese settlers—mostly small traders—and also a Japanese iron mine, established in the 1930s.

Immediately after World War II, on 30 September 1945, General Headquarters of the Allied Forces ordered the closure of Nan'yô Kôhatsu and it was later liquidated. In 1950 former employees of Nan'yô Bôeki, with the assistance of Tokuichi Kuribayashi, the last president of Nan'yô Kôhatsu, then established Nan'yô Bôeki Kabushikikaisha again to revive trade between Japan and the Pacific islands.

During the 1980s Japan's growing economic interests in the region began to revive the strategic concerns of the policymakers, and the government declared its intention to undertake increased responsibility for the defence of sea-lanes in the Pacific up to 1600 km from its shores. With some concern to ensure regional stability, and encouraged by the United States to increase its spending on overseas development aid, Japan then began to consolidate and expand its links with many Pacific island states.

In a speech delivered in Suva in January 1987 by the then Foreign Minister Tadashi Kuranari, Japanese support for the independence and autonomy of the small island states was confirmed, together with assurances of increased aid and cultural links. Following his commitment, Japan issued an invitation for the Chairman and Secretary-General of the SOUTH PACIFIC FORUM to visit Tokyo in 1987, a practice which has continued every year since then. Japan has embassies or consulates in all the larger island states, and Papua New Guinea, Fiji and Nauru have offices in Tokyo.

In FOREIGN AID, Japan is a major contributor in the region. According to the annual report of the Foreign Ministry, Japan's official development assistance amounted to US$14.72 billion in 1995, up 9.3 per cent from the previous year, which made Japan the top donor in the world for the fifth consecutive year. The Pacific islands receive about 1 per cent of the total Japanese aid budget. Japanese investment in the region has continued to rise, especially in forestry and fishing (NATURAL RESOURCES AND INTERNATIONAL DEVELOPMENT), and it has become a major market for raw materials from the Pacific islands. In support of the growing trade, investment and tourism between Japan and the Forum island countries, the PACIFIC ISLANDS CENTRE, the Tokyo office of the South Pacific Forum for trade and tourism promotion, was set up in October 1996. The Japanese government pays 90 per cent of its operating costs.—HN & SBCLF

■ *Latin America and the Pacific* The first contacts were made either when Polynesians reached the west coast of what is now Latin America, or when people from there reached eastern Polynesia; and probably both occurred—as confirmed by oral traditions, some cultivated plants of South American origin, and some elements of material culture. As the percentage of Mormons in Polynesia is higher than in any other part of the world, the MORMONS' belief that Polynesians originated from Latin America is important today.

From 1521 until the 1800s, Spanish ships provided contact between some Pacific slands and Latin America (SPAIN AND PORTUGAL IN THE PACIFIC). Spain attempted to establish colonies in Solomon Islands, Vanuatu and Tahiti, all of which included some American Indian people. These attempts all failed. Guam, however, became focal to the Spanish trade from the Philippines to Mexico for 250 years. Elements of Latin American cultures were absorbed, such as the Latin American loom and cloth used in central Micronesia, where a Spanish vessel was lost (see LOST SHIPS). From the early 1800s Valparaiso was the most important port for trade between Polynesia and the outside world. The Chilean peso became the main currency in central and eastern Polynesia. From 1869 the Suez Canal provided a shorter route from Europe to Sydney and Auckland, which then became the main foreign ports for Polynesia.

In the era of BLACKBIRDERS, some 3320 slaves were taken to Peru from Polynesia, and 312 from Kiribati, in 1862 and 1863. Only 148 of them survived the epidemics, malnutrition and ill-treatment, and returned to the Pacific islands.

Contact between the two regions was minimal for nearly a century, except for Easter Island, which Chile annexed in 1888, and the Galapagos, which Ecuador acquired in 1832. LAN-Chile opened an air service to Easter Island and Tahiti in 1971 with connections to Cook Islands, Samoa, Fiji, New Zealand and Australia. Shipping from Valparaiso to several island ports resumed in the 1980s. Most trade is from Chile and in timber, foods and other primary products. Brazil's Bandierante and Brasilia are among the most popular small aircraft in the South Pacific. Drugs from Colombia and Peru move westwards through the islands, and some drug money from these countries is laundered through Pacific islands' tax havens.

The Permanent Commission for the South Pacific (of Chile, Colombia, Ecuador and Peru, with Mexico, Panama and Costa Rica likely to join), interacts with the SOUTH PACIFIC FORUM, the PACIFIC COMMUNITY and the South Pacific Regional Environment Programme on marine, aviation, environment, nuclear and other issues (REGIONAL COOPERATION AND INITIATIVES). The Pacific Basin Economic Council, the Pacific Economic Cooperation Council, and the Pacific Science Association and other organizations now include Mexico, Chile and Peru along with Forum islands countries. Chile is a member of the FESTIVAL OF PACIFIC ARTS and has observer status in the Forum Fisheries Agency and the Pacific Community. Several Latin American nations have diplomatic relations with islands countries, accredited through embassies in Canberra, Wellington, Jakarta, Manila or Tokyo. Some have honorary consuls where they are not accredited. Islands nations handle their accreditations either from home or from their United Nations or Washington embassies.

Awareness of the Pacific islands in Latin America has increased with growing interest in the Pacific Basin. Islands' awareness of Latin America, however, remains minimal, although some schools in the region now teach Spanish. Latin American tuna fishermen now frequent island ports, and some islander crews fish from Latin American bases in the off season. Latin American priests and nuns have long worked in the islands, and since the 1980s some islander Catholic, Mormon, METHODIST, Youth with a Mission and other missionaries work in Latin America.

The Pacific's relations with Latin America are growing but will be constrained by limited common interests except in marine exploitation, environment, rural technology and tourism.—RGC

■ *New Zealand and the Pacific* Since 1840 when a central government was established in New Zealand, interaction with the Pacific islands has steadily intensified. One of the first expressions of an embryonic colonial interest in the region came from Sir George Grey (1812–98), governor and later premier of New Zealand. He conceived an extended role for the infant colony as a natural centre for British expansion in the South Pacific, and attempted during 1848 to persuade the colonial office of the commercial, strategic and political value of the immediate annexation of Tonga and Fiji. Bishop SELWYN's role in the Melanesian mission may perhaps have provided a basis for New Zealand's spiritual responsibility for islanders, but New Zealand settlers mostly wanted Great Britain to secure enough territory in the central Pacific to protect their interests against the German or French. Great Britain ignored the offer of Sir Robert Stout (1844–1930) to annex Samoa in 1884, and also similar dreams of imperial expansion in the Pacific from Sir Julius Vogel (1835–99). The idea that New Zealand might be entrusted with the administration of some of Britain's island possessions was pursued vigorously by Richard John Seddon (1845–1906), the longest-serving prime minister in New Zealand's history. Where his predecessor, John Ballance (1839–93), had asked the British government to control the Cook Islands' liquor trade, Seddon suggested that the islands should be annexed to New Zealand. Equally interested in Samoa (offering a New Zealand protectorate) and Tonga (proposing annexation), he countered the perceived lack of British interest in Pacific territories with expressions of New Zealand's willingness to pay towards administrative costs. His advocacy of 'federation' with Fiji was ignored, but New Zealand was allowed, in 1901, to annex Cook Islands—which, for administrative convenience, then included Niue. Tokelau, formerly under British jurisdiction, was also entrusted to New Zealand in 1925. Although New Zealand's colonial officials were not well-equipped for the task, the administration was generally well-intentioned, and for most of the first half century, it was supervised by Maori ministers—Sir James Carroll, Sir Maui Pomare, and then Sir Apirana Ngata.

Western Samoa, seized from the Germans at the outbreak of World War I by NZ troops, became a League of Nations Mandate. Although the first decade of New Zealand's administration was marked by political unrest and Samoan passive resistance (MAU A PULE), the relationship improved, and in 1946 the newly formed United Nations granted New Zealand trusteeship responsibilities. New Zealand's determination to discharge these responsibilities in accordance with the wishes of the Samoan people and to the satisfaction of the Trusteeship Council brought about an early and harmonious transfer of authority, and Western Samoa became the first independent state in the region, in 1962.

For the smaller populations of Cook Islands, Niue and Tokelau, New Zealand found it difficult to discern their best interests. The government began sponsoring limited immigration of Tokelauans to New Zealand in 1963; all three island peoples saw the advantages in maintaining close relations with New Zealand, and having easy access as New Zealand citizens. Cook Islands (1965) and Niue (1974) chose 'free association' with New Zealand as their formal constitutional status, and Tokelauans have been encouraged to adopt the basic machinery of self-government within a traditional Tokelauan format.

In trade, the Pacific region is now an important market for New Zealand for a wide range of food and beverage products (40 per cent of total exports to the region) and manufactured goods (41 per cent). New Zealand's involvement was at first mainly with Polynesia and Fiji, but in the 1990s trade with Papua New Guinea has become significant, and exports to New Caledonia have been growing steadily. For the most part, it is tropical produce from the islands that flows south. An exception was Cook Islands' garments exported from the 1950s to the 1980s, and from Fiji and Tonga from the 1980s. Nauru and Ocean Island phosphates were important to New Zealand agriculture for half a century, but are no longer so.

New Zealand investment in the islands began last century. It has been significant in Fiji, Samoa and Tonga, but only in Cook Islands and Niue has it been the main source of foreign investment. Pacific islands' investment in New Zealand is largely a phenomenon of the present generation, and although no statistics are available, it will not be surprising if it now exceeds the reverse flow, as many island retirement, insurance and other funds have been held in New Zealand, and many island businessmen and others have invested in New Zealand, especially in real estate and in shares.

Remittances from islanders working in New Zealand to relatives at home constitute a major source of income for Tonga and Samoa. Such remittances are much studied and commented on, but there does not appear to be any study of the reverse flow of funds from the islands to New Zealand, and it is generally assumed to be non-existent. There is good reason to believe, however, that for Cook Islands and Niue at least, it is higher. Many Cook Islanders and Niueans, as well as many New Zealanders working or doing business in those places, seem to remit more to New Zealand. This may also be so for Fiji, and the reverse flow is significant for Samoa.

FOREIGN AID from the New Zealand government was at first exclusively to its former territories, Samoa, Cook Islands, Niue and Tokelau. From the 1970s it slowly expanded to include Fiji, Kiribati, Tonga and Tuvalu, with substantial increases to Melanesia in the 1980s, and token amounts to French territories and to Micronesian states. The New Zealand government concentrates most of its aid in the Pacific region. Voluntary aid from church-related and secular organizations in New Zealand is extensive.

The flow of people from the mid 1800s to the mid 1900s was mainly of New Zealanders to the islands, but today there are many times more PACIFIC ISLANDERS IN NEW ZEALAND. Short-term interaction in both directions includes people visiting relatives, touring, or on business. Church workers used to be mainly from New Zealand but now more come from the islands to New Zealand. Volunteers flow only northwards, as do consultants and specialist staff in education, health, construction, transport, communications, technology, and other fields. Many Pacific islanders attend educational institutions in New Zealand, and many have earned a place in New Zealand representative sports teams (PACIFIC ISLANDERS SPORTING ACHIEVEMENTS).

Diplomatically New Zealand is more widely represented in the islands than any country except Australia, and eight island nations have high commissions or consulates in New Zealand. New Zealand's representatives in the region have exerted considerable influence in matters of common concern, such as AVIATION, SHIPPING, the regulation of fishing, and protection of the environment. Being joined in the SOUTH PACIFIC FORUM, the PACIFIC COMMUNITY, the Forum Fisheries Agency and some other regional organizations, there is close interaction in most areas of common interest (REGIONAL COOPERATION AND INITIATIVES).

On NUCLEAR TESTING and particularly the policy issues of the use of NZ waters by nuclear-armed or powered vessels, New Zealand split with Australia, and there were some differences in island viewpoints which divided the region. (See AUSTRALIA AND THE PACIFIC.) In negotiations leading to the South Pacific Nuclear-Free Zone Treaty, New Zealand drove the proceedings as a matter of the highest priority, but finally conceded the issue of nuclear visits in the interests of securing agreement and encouraging the United States to sign the protocols. New Zealand, and in particular its Foreign Minister Don McKinnon, has played the lead role in developing a peaceful resolution of the Bougainville crisis in Papua New Guinea (BOUGAINVILLE CON-

FLICT AND PEACE PROCESS). New Zealand is not the largest external interest for any Pacific islands except Cook Islands, Niue and Tokelau. Although it will remain important for some others, its overall significance will continue to decline slowly in response to the growing East Asian presence in the region.—RGC & CGP

■ *The United States of America and the Pacific* The United States has had dealings with Pacific islands and their peoples since its emergence as an independent nation. Whalers, mainly from New Bedford and Nantucket, Massachusetts, were forced by the British to enter Pacific waters during the American Revolution of 1776 and the War of 1812. American WHALING vessels became predominant in the region throughout the 19th century, and thus it may be said that the first major presence of Americans in the Pacific was by fishermen. The second major presence was by fishers of men: missionaries.

Also from Massachusetts, clergy of the AMERICAN BOARD OF COMMISSIONERS FOR FOREIGN MISSIONS based in Boston sailed to the Pacific to save souls by converting islanders to Protestantism. First establishing themselves in Hawai'i in 1820, Boston missionaries eventually reached the Marshall, eastern Caroline, and Gilbert Island groups, although their greatest impact was on the Hawaiian Kingdom. Missionaries greatly influenced Hawaiians, introducing not only new religious and moral values, but also western social, economic and political modes of life. Over time, some became key political advisors to the indigenous monarchy, while others ventured into commercial and agricultural enterprises.

American traders established themselves in the Pacific not long after whalers entered these waters. Common to many industrializing western nations toward the end of the 18th century was the desire for trade relations with China and other Asian countries (CHINA TRADE). But in order to trade they had to have something Asians wanted. One item was SANDALWOOD, discovered in Hawai'i by westerners in 1790. By 1805, sandalwood became the principal commodity for trade in the islands, and American traders were predominant. They exchanged various materials or dollars for the wood, which was then shipped to China and traded for goods for the US market.

The SANDALWOOD TRADE and visits by whaling ships to Hawai'i for provisioning during the first half of the 19th century led to the emergence of several American-owned mercantile firms, to supply the visiting vessels with local and imported goods. Furthermore, the establishment of commercial centres in HONOLULU, Hilo and LAHAINA drew increasing numbers of Hawaiians away from their traditional villages and lifestyles, and toward western-oriented patterns of life in these fledgling towns.

SUGAR became a major commodity for commerce in Hawai'i in 1835. Led by American and British entrepreneurs, hundreds of acres of land were acquired and planted with sugarcane. In addition to displacing native Hawaiians from the land, the sugar industry promoted an influx of immigration (including Filipinos, Japanese and Chinese) to the islands to fill the newly created demand for labour. This immigration began the ethnic diversification of the islands for which they are now acclaimed.

American commercial interests were not limited to Hawai'i, although Americans took the lead in commercial enterprises there. As America's industrial might began to exert itself during the mid 19th century, new markets were needed. Attention turned to the Far East, focusing on China. Following the path of many other western nations, the United States set out to establish trade with China and other Asian countries. Commodore Matthew Perry's intrusion into Japan in 1853 was a first step in this process. The American Civil War interrupted the push toward Asia, but it resumed in the 1890s, led by American strategic interests. Ports were needed across the vast expanse of the Pacific for naval vessels protecting shipping lanes, for coaling stations to supply these vessels (this was the era of steam-powered ships), and for a proposed trans-oceanic communications cable. All these goals were accomplished just before the turn of the century, precipitated by the Spanish-American War.

The war with Spain afforded the United States opportunities to exert its power in the Pacific. Besides engaging Spanish military forces in Cuba, where the conflict began, US naval vessels were sent to capture the Philippine Islands, then a Spanish colony. Capturing the Philippines would give the United States a much desired base from which to initiate commercial and strategic policies in Asia. In May 1898, Commodore George Dewey, with orders to engage Spanish forces in the Pacific, defeated the enemy in Manila, and the Philippines came under American control. Another fleet of US war ships *en route* to the Philippines in June 1898 stopped at GUAM in the Mariana Islands, also a Spanish colony. Finding the island's small garrison unprepared for battle (and unaware that their country was at war with the United States), American forces easily captured Guam. Although Spain then claimed all the islands in Micronesia (the Caroline, Mariana, and

Marshall island groups), the United Stated failed to lay claim to these after acquiring Guam. Initially declared only as a US possession, Guam became a US territory in 1950.

Elsewhere in the Pacific, American representatives in SAMOA persuaded local chiefs to grant the United States landing rights in the archipelago's best harbour, PAGO PAGO in eastern Samoa. Great Britain and Germany were also vying for landing rights in the islands. Internal conflict among the Samoans afforded the foreign powers excuses to intercede, and win favour for their respective positions. American and British forces allied against the Germans, and only a tropical storm (striking the harbour at Apia) prevented warfare. Subsequent negotiations at the Three-Powers Convention of 1899 resulted in an agreement to partition Samoa, the US obtaining eastern Samoa and the western islands, including Apia, going to Germany. It was not until 1926, however, that the US Congress formally approved the acquisition, making AMERICAN SAMOA a territory.

Meanwhile, US citizens in Hawai'i were steadily consolidating their spiritual, commercial, and political influence throughout the islands. In 1875 American planters were successful in a movement to establish closer political ties with the United States. Increasing American power and numbers in the islands allowed them the ability to overthrow the monarchy in 1894 and proclaim a republic. By 1898, they convinced the then US President William McKinley to claim Hawai'i as an American territory. At the turn of the century, then, the United States had acquired full sovereignty over the Philippine Islands, Guam, eastern Samoa and Hawai'i. It would later add claims to dozens of islands in the central Pacific for mining GUANO (see GUANO ACT OF THE USA) and still more when airplane travel necessitated acquisitions of islands for stops (including Midway, Baker, Jarvis and Howland islands). This would not, however, be the extent of American territorial expansion in the Pacific.

During the Pacific War the United States captured from Japan several islands—including the islands of Micronesia (having by-passed the earlier opportunity to acquire them in 1898 following the Spanish-American War). Japan had secured the islands and stationed a large portion of its Pacific fleet there during the war. The United States captured Micronesia from Japan in the overall process of liberating Guam, which had fallen to the Japanese at the same time PEARL HARBOR was attacked in 1941. Once in US hands, the islands became the staging area for attacks against Japan, including the bombing missions resulting in the dropping of atomic bombs on Hiroshima and Nagasaki. Strategically, Micronesia became valuable in the post-war period.

American military activity was also prevalent in the South Pacific during the war, but rather than acquiring islands for a permanent military presence, a greater impact was the personal interactions between American soldiers and islanders. These encounters afforded inhabitants of the islands opportunities to learn about the world beyond their shores, bringing them new ideas, social arrangements, and material goods—particularly in the form of infrastructure and communications facilities left behind—that would influence their lives well after the war.

Because Americans paid a high price in blood for capturing the islands of Micronesia, military and some political leaders believed the islands should permanently remain under US control after the war. Up to this time, the United States had very limited experience with overseas territorial possessions. In the Philippines, the desire for independence among Filipinos led to a revolt early on under US rule. Although they lost the battle, Filipinos won a promise of eventual independence, which was obtained in 1946. But annexing Micronesia posed a problem: it went against the American political value of political freedom. America did not view itself as an 'imperialistic' nation, but this would indeed be the case if Micronesia were claimed; and hypocritical in light of US opposition to the expansion of the Soviet Union in eastern Europe after the defeat of Germany. Those who argued against annexation proposed a compromise: the concept of a strategic trusteeship under the supervision of the newly formed United Nations.

In 1947 Micronesia was designated a 'strategic trust' under the UN Trusteeship System, with the United States as the administering authority. Under the trusteeship agreement, the United States was obliged to promote social, economic and political development in Micronesia. Known formally as the US Trust Territory of the Pacific Islands, Micronesia was a unique entity within the UN Trusteeship System. Unlike other trust territories, designation as a strategic trust allowed the United States to maintain military bases in the islands, and limit access into the region. BIKINI ATOLL, and other atolls in Marshall Islands, became the main sites for American NUCLEAR TESTING. Because of its strategic value during the Cold War era, many scholars believe the United States was reluctant to fulfill its obligation toward Micronesia under the UN trusteeship agreement, specifically with regard to fostering economic self-sufficiency and political independence. But after numerous policy changes and more than a decade of negotiations, the trusteeship was eventually terminated by the United States in stages beginning in 1986. It did not end, however, with Micronesia becoming totally independent. Instead, all but one of the new political entities that emerged—the Federated States of Micronesia (FSM), the Republic of the Marshall Islands, and the Republic of Palau—became self-governing with continued political ties to the US under a treaty called the Compact of Free Association. (For Palau's opposition to the US reservation of military rights, see PALAU'S NUCLEAR-FREE CONSTITUTION.) Under the compact, the islands became independent states but are guaranteed economic and military support from the United States. The Northern Mariana Islands had in 1975 established a closer relationship with the United States, becoming a commonwealth, a political status just a few degrees away from statehood. The United States' claims to the various guano islands and airway points were waived, and most of these islands became part of the Republic of Kiribati in 1983.

American activity in the South Pacific during and after World War II was often in concert with other nations with colonial or territorial interests in the region (REGIONAL COOPERATION AND INITIATIVES). The United States was a founding member of the South Pacific Commission (SPC, see PACIFIC COMMUNITY), formed in 1947 to promote social and economic development in the region, and a few years later, in 1951, joined Australia and New Zealand to form a mutual defence treaty called ANZUS. United States participation in the SPC is ongoing, but American security arrangements with New Zealand under the ANZUS Pact fell apart in the mid 1980s due to disagreement between the two nations concerning nuclear weapons (see AUSTRALIA AND THE PACIFIC, NEW ZEALAND AND THE PACIFIC).

The US presence in the Pacific remains strong. Hawai'i was granted statehood in 1959; eastern Samoa and Guam remain territories, but Guam is seeking commonwealth status like the Northern Mariana Islands. The compact agreements between the United States and the Marshallese, FSM, and Palauan governments ensure continued links if renewed. But lacking resources for economic independence, these governments cannot afford to go it alone. Conflict over nuclear weapons disrupted ties between the United States and New Zealand, and could affect future relations with other island nations who support a nuclear-free Pacific.—LWM

Further reading

Oliver, D L, 1989. *The Pacific Islands*, 3rd ed., University of Hawai'i Press.

Kiste, R C, 1994. 'United States', in K R Howe, R C Kiste and B V Lal (eds), *Tides of History: the Pacific islands in the twentieth century*, University of Hawai'i Press.

five

economy

Contributors

Article contributors

ADC	Alistair Couper
AT3	Anna Tiraa
BG	Bill Gammage
BVL	Brij V Lal
CH	Christy Harrington
CK	Chris Kissling
CM2	Clive Moore
CY	Charles Yala
DG2	Desh Gupta
GB	Geoff Bertram
JL1	Jacqueline Leckie
JO	John Overton
KRF	Kate Fortune
MTS	Michael T Skully
ND1	Ngaire Douglas
PD	Peter Dauvergne
PK	Peter Kiely
PL	Padma Lal
RAH1	Richard A Herr
RC	Rajesh Chandra
RGC	Ron Crocombe
RL2	Robert Langdon
SF	Stewart Firth
ST	Sandra Tarte
WCC	William C Clarke
YN	Yoshiharu Nishioka

Photo contributors

Australian Agency for International Development (AusAID), Department of Foreign Affairs and Trade (Canberra): 349, 350, 356, 367, 369, 374, 378, 380, 391

Bourke, Michael (The Australian National University, Canberra): 357, 358

Coleman, Neville (Australasian Marine Photographic Index, Springwood, Queensland): 399 (top left)

Cunningham, Lawrence J (University of Guam, Mangilao): 382

Hendrie, Peter (Pacific Journeys, Melbourne): 341 (detail), 353, 354, 366, 376, 381, 386, 389

Hope, Geoffrey (The Australian National University, Canberra): 370

Kiste, Robert C (Center for Pacific Islands Studies, University of Hawai'i–Manoa, Honolulu): 390

McPhetres, Samuel F (Saipan, Commonwealth of the Northern Mariana Islands): 385, 400 (top right)

Marshall Islands Visitors Authority (Majuro, Republic of the Marshall Islands): 400 (left)

Ministry of Foreign Affairs and Trade (Wellington, New Zealand): 383, 387

Ministry of Information, Republic of the Fiji Islands (Suva): 399 (right)

Panholzer, Thomas C (College of Micronesia–FSM, Pohnpei): 377, 392, 401

West, Richard (Canberra): 368, 371

ONE AGRICULTURE

Agriculture

Pacific islanders practise agriculture in environments ranging from frost-prone mountain slopes at 2600 m elevation in Papua New Guinea to tiny ATOLLS scarcely above the waves in the warm equatorial ocean. Similarly, rainfall varies from virtual desert to places that are constantly humid; and soils may be derived from young volcanic and alluvial materials of high fertility or from the parent material available on atoll islets, which is no more than rough, highly alkaline coral rubble, with a very low water-holding capacity, little organic matter and few available nutrients. Traditional agriculturalists adapted to these conditions with a wide range of agronomic techniques and crop combinations, which enabled food production on all but the most barren islets or at the highest elevations of the larger islands. Most of today's islander families still work the land with a wide variety of agricultural practices that continue to provide many of their daily needs and at least some of their cash income.

Among Pacific peoples, the production of food remains a social endeavour: no ceremonial activity is considered complete without a presentation of ample amounts of food. Gifts of food should always be the best and the most one can afford. Traditional foods such as taro and yams, fresh fish, whole carcasses of pork and indigenous greens are still presented at ceremonies—together with introduced foods—and any inadequacy is a matter for shame (see FEASTS). The land itself has greater social meaning than it does in western societies. Planting a garden or establishing a tree garden of breadfruit and pandanus, a grove of coconuts, or an excavated taro garden on an atoll islet are more than isolated acts of land management; they involve participation in a community, as reflected in land tenure systems, which maintain in modified forms the traditional patterns, based on the idea that kinship groups held communal rights to land. Within the communal land, individuals or extended families held rights of use, either generally or to specific plots because of prior use or because they have planted trees there. Few individuals have absolute rights over land; all use and users are bound into a community, tied together by reciprocal rights and obligations—a system that is often seen as an obstacle to individual economic enterprise.

■ *Indigenous cultivation systems* Traditional agriculture in the Pacific can be divided into six cultivation systems, including animal husbandry, which may involve crop production. Each cultivation system has its distinctive techniques, cropping frequency, and crop inventory. The six traditional systems are not necessarily segregated spatially. Often they are or were found on a single community's land holding. The six systems are: arboriculture (tree gardens or mature fallow forests) and agroforests; shifting cultivation in forest or bush, sometimes alternating with tree gardens or agroforests; water control: irrigation and drainage, including wetland taro systems and drainage for sweet potato; intensive dry-field, open-canopy cultivation, including cultivation systems in fern and grass savannas; houseyard gardens; and animal husbandry.

■ *Arboriculture and agroforestry* A distinguishing characteristic of the earliest agriculture of the western Melanesian region is its emphasis on arboriculture—the culture of trees, which were domesticated following a history of use during a pre-agricultural hunting-gathering stage dating back more than 10 000 years. Archaeological evidence for a well-developed arboriculture at least 3500 years ago comes from the Mussau Islands, north of New Ireland, where the coconut, Pandanus, 'Tahitian chestnut' (*Inocarpus fagifer*), Canarium 'almond', and several other trees, including hardwoods prized for carving, were in use. Many of these trees and others from Southeast Asia such as breadfruit—which perhaps also has origins in western Melanesia—were transported Pacific-wide, carried by voyaging colonist-cultivators, begetting the diverse and beautiful tree groves and orchards rich in useful trees that still typify Pacific villages and landscapes almost everywhere.

■ *Shifting cultivation* Shifting cultivation (also known as swidden and slash-and-burn cultivation) is found on almost all high islands and raised limestone islands with some secondary forest. More technically elaborate forms of agriculture exist within an integument of shifting cultivation. Shifting cultivation can be very sophisticated biologically, as well as intellectually, as it often involves a manipulation not only of a diversity of annual or near-annual crop plants but also of the intervening forest fallow, which acts to suppress weeds, crop pests, and diseases, and to renew the soil with organic matter and nutrients. By selective weeding and planting, the cultivators encourage some tree species and discourage others so that a highly useful tree-garden fallow results.

■ *Irrigation and drainage* Of the three main starchy staples that dominated indigenous cultivation systems—aroids (the taro family), several species of yams, and the sweet potato—some of the taros are the most water-tolerant. Yams grow only under dry-land conditions and require a dry season. The sweet potato, which tolerates a greater range of soil type and climate than yams, grows well in fertile swamp-land soils if provided with adequate drainage. Massive systems of ditches to provide drainage for taro and, later, sweet potato were constructed in the swamplands of highland New Guinea. On a smaller scale, sweet potatoes and sometimes yams were planted in mounds, ridges, or ditched beds for purposes of drainage as well as to loosen heavy soils or to maintain fertility by throwing ditch spoil onto the bed. In some places, the contrasting moisture tolerances of taro compared with yams and sweet potato were complementary, with taro grown in the pits excavated to make mounds or ridges for the other two crops.

Pacific islanders had a variety of techniques for irrigating the true taro (*Colocasia esculenta*), which is also planted in dry-land shifting gardens, given moderately high rainfall. It yields better, more permanently, and freer from weeds and some insect pests when grown in water. Irrigation techniques included the use of natural ponds, construction of small dams to pond a stream, erection of bamboo aqueducts to carry water to hillside sites, making taro 'islets' in swampy areas, and construction of extensive canal systems that brought water to elaborate hillside terrace systems such as those of New Caledonia, Fiji and Hawai'i.

In Palau, the southern Cook Islands, and elsewhere, *Colocasia* taro was the traditional prestige staple, with many myths and rituals associated with its cultivation. The taro swamps, which, like the irrigated terrace systems, were labour-intensive, with the fields visited daily and green manures added to the soil, were said to be the 'mother of life'. But the abandonment of wetland taro cultivation is the rule today. In some areas (such as in Samoa, where taro had become an important export crop in the early 1990s), taro leaf blight (*Phythophthora colocasiae*) has made taro cultivation problematic, whether irrigated or dryland.

The decline of irrigated and swamp taro cultivation has meant the loss of one of the highest-yielding and ecologically sustainable Oceanic agricultural subsystems. Estimates of production vary from 30 to 60 metric tons per hectare, making irrigated taro capable of producing a substantial surplus, a potential understood by the Hawaiian chiefs, who sought to develop and control such systems for political purposes.

The other traditional aroid grown in wetland conditions is the giant swamp taro *Cyrtosperma chamissonis*. Not of great importance in Polynesia, *Cyrtosperma* taro was present in Melanesia in coastal swamps from northern New Guinea to Fiji, where it was a significant traditional staple. *Cyrtosperma* was extremely important in the atolls of Micronesia. There, swamp taro was capable of producing sustained yields of staple food by means of a distinctive and ingenious system of cultivation whereby a pit was excavated to reach the freshwater lens and soil was created by composting the leaves of breadfruit and several other trees as well as seaweed, pumice, and other materials. The 'seed' corm is planted together with the compost of leaves in a bottomless basket that reaches below the water level in the pit. The pit continues to be composted at least four times a year until harvest, two or three years after planting. Some varieties, grown mainly for prestige and ceremonies, may be cultivated for 10–15 years.

■ *Intensive cultivation* Given a choice between practising shifting cultivation in the forest or cultivating in open grasslands, tropical cultivators worldwide will generally choose to cut the forest and garden the newly cleared land because, compared with grassland soils, forest soils are relatively more fertile, more friable, and freer of pathogens and pertinacious weeds. But as the human population grows and the density of shifting gardens increases, the forest is replaced by grass-fernland-scrub complexes.

In dry-field, open-canopy cultivation, the polycultural richness of species and varieties found in forest-fallow shifting gardens usually declines sharply, with fewer crops planted, and crop segregation becoming the rule. Fallow times also diminish, often being shorter than or equal to the cultivation period. Tillage almost always increases compared with the minimum of soil working and disturbance typically associated with shifting gardens in the forest. In Yap, the savannas of the interior are known as the *tayid* or *ted*. Here sweet potatoes are grown in a manner not unlike the extensive open fields of sweet potato in ditched and sometimes mounded beds found in the Eastern Highlands of Papua New Guinea. The Yapese ditched beds are rectangular in shape and surrounded by ditches closed at the ends. The beds are prepared by slashing the grass cover or merely flattening it with a layer of grass cut from around the perimeter of the bed. Then, blocks of soil and grass are dug up around the perimeter of the garden bed and placed upside down on the bed, and then covered with a layer of soil excavated from the ditches. Other vegetative litter from the surrounding area may be added.

Dry-field intensive systems were widely spread across the Pacific, including Hawai'i and Easter Island. Such systems are assumed to have developed from an intensification of shifting cultivation. Such a developmental sequence has been demonstrated archaeologically for the Kohala field system on the island of Hawai'i. In many islands following European contact and the decline of indigenous populations and changes in the economy and settlement patterns, the intensive dry-field systems have undergone dis-intensification or fallen wholly out of use, a process that also happened to most irrigated taro terraces—and to many excavated pit gardens in atoll Micronesia.

■ *Houseyard gardens* These may also be named kitchen gardens, dooryard gardens, or backyard gardens and are present traditionally throughout Oceania and remain important today in both rural areas and in towns. They contain a wide assemblage of trees, shrubs, herbaceous plants and vines contributing a wide variety of products, including staple foods, fruits, spices, medicines, stimulants, ornamentation, shade and perfumes. Often disregarded in assessments of agriculture, houseyard gardens are important spatially, nutritionally, and with regard to aesthetic amenity. Pacific island towns and villages reveal the wealth of productive beauty created by the ubiquitous plantings of mangoes, breadfruit, coconuts, citrus, bananas, hibiscus, *Cordyline* and *Codiaemum*, the annatto tree, betelnut in places where that habit prevails, fig species, bamboo, soursop, lemon grass, peppers, sugar cane, the paper mulberry, trees and shrubs with edible or colourful leaves, plants with fragrant bark or flowers, taros and yams, cassava, beans, cabbages and much more.

■ *Animal husbandry* The only pre-European domestic animals were the pig, dog and chicken, all of Southeast Asian ancestry; although the cassowary native to New Guinea was tamed to some extent. All three were not present everywhere. The pig and dog were absent from Easter Island, and the pig and chicken from New Zealand; and various atolls lacked one or another, indicating either a failure of initial dispersal or a failure to survive in harsh environments. Generally, the dog and chicken occupied a scavenging or foraging niche and were not important agriculturally. The pig, on the other hand, was often of great significance agriculturally as communities built up herds for major ceremonies and presentations. A large part of food production, especially of sweet potato, was directed towards the pigs—exceeding 60 per cent in some parts of Papua New Guinea. So great a demand for food for pigs requires a considerable expansion or intensification of agriculture. The increasing numbers of marauding pigs cause damage to gardens. Caring for and feeding the animals brings a disproportionate increase in women's work, at least in Melanesia. In many forested areas, feral pigs remain an important food resource and are highly esteemed.

Since European contact, other domestic animals, notably horses, cattle and goats, have been introduced to most larger islands but to few atolls. Where cattle have been introduced, they have sometimes caused considerable dislocation to cultivation systems. In many countries there is now battery production of chickens (for meat and eggs) and pigs, based on imported or partly locally produced feeds and on improved imported poultry and pig breeds. In Fiji, self-sufficiency in poultry products for urban markets was achieved early in the 1990s before the global move towards a free market economy began to allow imports of foreign chickens. In Papua New Guinea, New Caledonia, Vanuatu and Fiji, large-scale cattle ranching based on improved breeds and pasture has been established, as has also a small local dairy industry in Fiji.

■ *Contemporary production systems* Agriculture can be subdivided on the basis of the purposes and the socioeconomic organization of production. Such a classification also depicts important elements in the history of agriculture in the Pacific, as illustrated by the four basic agricultural production systems.

The oldest of these is the integral subsistence system, in which virtually all the requirements of the community are produced locally, cash cropping is absent, and the producers and consumers are the same people. The pure integral subsistence system is now rare, found only in very remote parts of the largest islands. Elsewhere, it has given way to the second production system, mixed subsistence-cash cropping, which began shortly after the coming of the first permanent European settlers.

With the presence in the islands of European traders, missionaries, and administrators, islanders began to add introduced crops to their traditional inventory and to sell their products (for cash or barter) to visiting European ships or the resident Europeans. Coconuts particularly expanded quickly in response to government or missionary edict, or perceived market opportunities, with the additional production facilitated by the introduction of steel tools, the reduction in intergroup warfare, and the diversion of labour from more labour-demanding traditional crops or cultivation systems.

The third agricultural production system, the PLANTATION or estate, was entirely foreign to the Pacific. Apart from its requirements for land and labour (the recruitment and movement of which had enormous impact on Pacific islanders), plantations operated in isolation from the indigenous production systems. Foreign-owned and managed, plantation production was directed almost entirely toward export crops. Unlike traditional agriculture, the units of production were large, and mono-cropping predominated. Spatially, coconut palms came quickly to be the major plantation crop across the coastal lands. Although plantations remain important in parts of the Pacific, they are no longer a favoured form of production, as independent island governments see foreign-owned plantations as a remnant of colonial exploitation. The balance of ownership has shifted towards individual nationals or groups of nationals, in some cases totally, as in Vanuatu, where all freehold-land ownership was abolished in 1980, and the alienated land returned to its 'custom owners'. Existing large-scale plantation production tends to be owned jointly by governments, foreign companies, local landowners, or, as is the case with a major OIL PALM plantation in Solomon Islands, agencies such as the Commonwealth Development Corporation.

The fourth and most recently emerged production system involves a 'plantation mode of management' but not necessarily plantation production tied to large-scale land holdings under single ownership or control. Economies of scale are achieved through the aggregation of smallholder production under centralized marketing and management control. The most outstanding example of this approach is FIJI'S SUGAR INDUSTRY. With the collapse in the 1910s of the indentured labour scheme, the industry converted to a system of smallholder tenant farmers, producing under the general direction of the sugar milling companies which provided economies of scale in credit facilities, research, extension, and transportation as well as some agronomic inputs and large-scale processing. Currently, about 22 000 cane farmers, most with contract areas of about 4.6 hectares, operate under an umbrella of centralized management and marketing in the Fijian industry. This system provides acceptable quality control and a reliable supply of the product. Under the coordinated system, individual farmers may also come closer to achieving desired levels of income. Another example of umbrella management is the smallholder tobacco industry in Fiji. It provides tobacco for local cigarette manufacture under the centralized management of the Southern Development Company, which provides economies of scale in credit facilities, research, seedling supply, transport, processing and marketing. With the recent decline in tobacco acreage, the company has extended its smallholder management and extension capability to developing papaya (pawpaw) exports. Oil palm and some other crops are also grown under similar management systems in several countries.

■ *Farming's future* Throughout the Pacific, the urban population is growing faster than the rural population so that agriculture's relative significance in providing livelihoods will diminish—though the function of agriculture in supporting large rural populations will remain critically important for a long time, especially in Papua New Guinea, Solomon Islands and Vanuatu. Efforts to increase productivity will have little success, given constraints of low levels of technical skill among farmers, inadequacies in agricultural extension services, deficiencies of transport infrastructure, and the farmers' motivation. It is not that islanders still enjoy 'subsistence affluence' but that for many commercial crops, a day's agricultural labour is not rewarding enough to entice rural people into cash-cropping as a full-time occupation. Rather, they practise a mixed economic strategy, being part-time commercial farmers, part-time subsistence horticulturalists, and also seeking income from wage labour, remittances, gift exchange, and small-scale trading. They want cash but because the returns from commercial farming are often so low, smallholders concentrate on subsistence activity to ensure food security for their family. On the other hand, when new niche products promise high prices or when prices of traditional exports rise, rural people quickly invest labour in the opportunity, as exemplified over the past few years by the rush into squash (butter pumpkin) farming in Tonga when a seasonal window was discovered in the Japanese market, or when, in early 1998 in Fiji, the price of copra suddenly rose markedly.

Although they encourage agricultural development, back the search for successful niche products, and urge an increase in agricultural exports, most island governments give little practical support to agriculture, or to matters of environmental sustainability. Thus, for example, success in developing exports such as squash from Tonga, pineapples from Cook Islands and ginger from Fiji, has also caused damage to the physical resource base by erosion or other forms of land (and reef) degradation. The increase in the area under sugarcane in Fiji since independence has meant an expansion into marginal sloping land unaccompanied by conservation measures. In consequence, erosion has been severe, with a recent estimate costing the loss conservatively at F$10–20 million a year from increased fertilizer use and production losses.

Widespread causes of erosion—which most Pacific countries currently list as an environmental problem—include not only the increase in commercial cropping but also the associated expansion of subsistence agriculture onto marginal land, the shortening of bush or grass fallow periods, and efforts by individuals or families to claim unused land by planting it with coconuts or other cash crops, a process that has resulted in dramatic forest loss in Samoa. Agricultural chemicals remain a largely unmanaged source of pollution in the Pacific countries. Fertilizers are generally not used as heavily as in some developed countries, but on atoll islets, even their frugal use can contaminate the underground supplies of freshwater. And everywhere, because of the high proportion of coast and reef to land surface, there is likely to be marine pollution and damage from the runoff of both agricultural chemicals and eroded soil.

Formal land-tenure arrangements that give full authority to local communities inhibit the development of effective land use policies and are often seen to impede commercial agricultural development on both a large scale (because of the difficulty of acquiring large tracts of land) and small scale (because smallholders cannot acquire loans without individual title to a piece of land). There are, however, many informal mechanisms for acquiring and using land if profitable opportunities present themselves, although the benefits from successful ventures may not be distributed evenhandedly within the landholding group. A great value of the current tenure systems is that most rural people still have access to land and may enjoy the security of food for their own subsistence and to meet social obligations. From a global perspective, small Pacific economies remain agricultural price takers, vulnerable to the costs of distance and smallness, and now the threats of free trade.—WCC

Further reading

Clarke, W C, 1994. 'Traditional land use and agriculture in the Pacific islands', in J Morrison, P Geraghty and L Crowl (eds), *Science of Pacific Islands Peoples: land use and agriculture*, vol. 2, Institute of Pacific Studies, University of the South Pacific.

Kirch, P V, 1994. *The Wet and the Dry: irrigation and agricultural intensification in Polynesia*, University of Chicago Press.

Ward, R G and Proctor, A (eds), 1980. *South Pacific Agriculture: choices and constraints. South Pacific Agricultural Survey 1979*, Asian Development Bank/The Australian National University.

Ward, R G and Kingdon, E (eds), 1995. *Land, Custom and Practice in the South Pacific*, Cambridge University Press.

Plantations

The plantation is a device to rationalize the production of crops. It is also a social system, typically dependent on an unskilled, exploited and oppressively regulated labour force. In the Pacific as elsewhere in the tropical world, the plantation played a large role in incorporating pre-capitalist economies into the global economic system. Plantations employed far more Pacific islanders and Asian migrant labourers than any other commercial enterprises in the 20th century Pacific. Except in the Northern Marianas, plantations were never important in the smallest countries of the Pacific such as Kiribati, Tuvalu, Cook Islands, Tonga, Marshall Islands, Federated States of Micronesia, Palau and the French territories. They were and are to be found instead in Hawai'i, Fiji, Papua New Guinea, Solomon Islands and Vanuatu, which have sizable areas of land, especially flat coastal land.

The key plantation crops in the Pacific have been SUGAR and COPRA. The first plantations in the islands were a few small sugar estates in Hawai'i, laid down in the 1830s. Plantations on a large scale came later, driven by the high cotton and sugar prices that accompanied the American Civil War. The 1860s boom caused rapid growth of plantations in Hawai'i, the main source of sugar for the population of the Pacific coast of the United States and British North America, and a flow of settlers to Fiji, where they grabbed what land they could for cotton. Germans laid down the first plantations in Samoa at the same time, pioneering what was to become the characteristic Pacific planting enterprise of the 20th century, the copra plantation.

Hawai'i and Fiji—and for a short time Northern Marianas—were the sugar territories of the Pacific. In the case of Hawai'i, the turning-point was the 1875 Reciprocity Agreement, which granted Hawaiian sugar access to the American market, forcing up its price by as much as 50 per cent. Plantations multiplied and by 1890 Hawai'i was exporting 10 times as much sugar as in 1876. Sugar plantations generated the profits that underlay the economic and political dominance of the Big Five companies in Hawai'i—Castle & Cooke,C Brewer, American Factors, Theo H Davies and Alexander & Baldwin—and their thirst for labour brought a stream of immigrants on indentured labour contracts from Japan, China, the Philippines, Puerto Rico and even Portugal. As an American territory from 1898, Hawai'i was under the rule of King Sugar, and its economy diversified only after World War II.

In Fiji the turning-point was cession to the British Crown in 1874. Cession brought an end to uncontrolled plantation development by settlers, most of whom lost their land claims. Instead, in a deliberate attempt to save the Fijian people from extinction, Governor Sir Arthur GORDON prohibited the sale of Fijian land and induced the COLONIAL SUGAR REFINING COMPANY (CSR) to invest in sugar plantations. He then brought plantation labour from India (GIRMITIYA), which was the origin of 60 000 migrant labourers who came to Fiji from 1879 to 1916. Like the Big Five in Hawai'i, the CSR dominated the economy of Fiji. The colonial government assisted by subjecting labourers to an oppressive supervision of their working lives. The CSR shifted from plantations to a small farm system of sugar production in the 1920s. Sugar remains vital to Fiji's economy today.

Under Japanese supervision, the sugarcane plantations of Saipan and Tinian in the Northern Marianas were producing two-thirds as much sugar as Fiji by the late 1930s and were worked mainly by labourers imported from Okinawa. But World War II and the expulsion of the Japanese ended the plantation period in Marianas' history.

The first planters in the Pacific tried all sorts of crops from tobacco to vanilla, cacao, rubber and hemp. But the COCONUT became the islands' staple crop. Copra needed less labour and less skill to be cultivated successfully. The history of copra plantations in the Pacific is one of an initial investment boom, mostly before World War I, followed by a long slow decline punctuated briefly by periods of high copra prices. With its low level technology and unskilled and often dragooned labour force, the copra plantation was never a route to development. The Samoan copra plantations laid down by the Germans in the late 19th century covered thousands of acres, employed thousands of Melanesian, Chinese and eventually Samoan labourers, and remained important after independence in 1962. The Germans were also responsible for establishing a string of copra plantations along the coasts of New Guinea, and by World War II Australian New Guinea was the largest copra exporter in the region. LEVER BROTHERS and BURNS PHILP ran plantations in Solomon Islands, while Australian settlers leased land for coconut palms in Papua on estates that grew fast at first but hardly at all after 1918. Plantations remain in the Pacific but, in more diversified economies, they have lost their economic centrality, and landowners in a number of Melanesian countries have reoccupied them and returned them to traditional uses.—SF

Further reading

Corris, P, 1973. *Passage, Port and Plantation: a history of Solomon Islands labour migration*, Melbourne University Press.

Firth, S, 1983. *New Guinea under the Germans*, Melbourne University Press.

O'Meara, T, 1990. *Samoan Planters: tradition and economic development in Polynesia*, New York.

Lal, B V, Munro, D and Beechert, E (eds), 1994. *Plantation Workers: resistance and accommodation*, University of Hawai'i Press.

Rural change and development

Despite centuries of migration, agricultural adaptation, landscape modification and social transformation prior to the arrival of Europeans in the Pacific, the most profound changes in the rural Pacific have occurred in the last 200 years. Contact with new markets, technologies and transport systems, coupled with new forms of governance and control, precipitated a series of fundamental and related changes in the social, economic and environmental spheres of rural life. To a large extent, these resulted from incorporation of Pacific production systems into global markets and the subsequent commodification of labour, land and daily exchange. Yet they were also affected by ideologies of progress, modernization and development that were promoted and shaped in particular ways by the state and implemented by a range of agencies.

Pacific islanders were quick to react to the opportunities that resulted from contact with the wider world from the late 18th century. Whether through supplying pork to the new colony in New South Wales, SANDALWOOD or BÊCHE-DE-MER to Asian markets, or through involvement in the COLONIAL LABOUR TRADE to Australia or South America, island production systems began a response in labour organization, resource use and technological change that continues to the present. The trade in land had a further major impact. Good coastal land often changed from supporting diverse subsistence gardens to single crop PLANTATIONS. Such land, as in Fiji, Samoa, Tahiti and Hawai'i, was

Copra processing in Tonga

permanently alienated from customary communal ownership to freehold title traded by new European owners. Labour—often imported from overseas—became another commodity, controlled, disciplined and specialized. In response, village agriculture frequently was forced to retreat to more marginal land, commonly aided by population decline that followed the introduction of new diseases.

The plantation mode of production led to the appearance of island commodities, principally COPRA, on world markets, yet it also yielded a flow (if hardly reciprocal) in the other direction with cloth, books, tinned food and steel tools appearing on the shelves of the trade stores that began to be seen in rural areas. Such material goods (later supplemented by videos, rice and chemical herbicides), together with the imposition of colonial taxes, stimulated a desire for cash: a desire that could be met either by engaging in wage-labour or producing and selling cash crops, such as copra or bananas. Thus, there was no simple dual economy, no clear distinction between plantations and village agriculture, for both to varying degrees were linked to the global economy.

Plantation and village cash-crop production characterized and determined rural change in the Pacific, until about the 1970s. They were accompanied by major economic and social changes, but, over time, they also exposed the costs as well as the benefits of such a rural development strategy. From its introduction as a commodity, copra provided the major source of income for many rural dwellers across the whole Pacific region. It allowed people to engage in the global economy and gain access to new goods and services whilst, outside the plantation sector, maintaining sovereignty over their land. Yet, as an agricultural commodity, it proved a fickle friend. Returns fluctuated often wildly and what might bring a good return one year was barely worth the bother of selling the following. Over the decades it also became apparent that more and more copra (or SUGAR or COFFEE) was required to purchase the same quantity of manufactured imports. When prices fell to very low levels, it exposed the emerging rural economy to crisis, for dependence on a single commodity for the income of a company or household could leave many without the means of support. Plantation companies weathered such market crises worse than village producers who could revert to subsistence production. Many companies gradually withdrew. Others, such as the sugar industry in Fiji, underwent major restructuring, in this case in the 1920s switching to a primarily processing venture, passing production (and subsequent vulnerability to price fluctuations) to smallholders.

In response to the declining fortunes of specialist commodity production for the world market, island agriculture gradually transformed itself in the post-colonial era, moving away from a dependence on single export commodities. Diversification was encouraged, into such export products as COCOA, vanilla, passionfruit, PALM OIL, timber or fish. Rapid urbanization created new local opportunities as new urbanites wanted their old foods (taro, yams, cassava, sweet potato, KAVA, fruit and vegetables) and municipal markets became attractive outlets for surplus rural production. Many village producers, especially those within reach of the expanding towns and cities, realized that such local markets were more lucrative and reliable than overseas ones and supplying them meant much less in the way of disruptions to their production systems. Such a move to more inward-looking rural change was encouraged by many newly-independent governments. Concerned at the rising cost of food imports in the 1970s and after, yet anxious to boost rural incomes, agricultural protectionism began to reshape the rural economy. Tariffs and quota on imported foods such as rice, beef and dairy products, coupled with subsidies for fertilizers and other inputs, raised returns for local producers and encouraged a move to a more diverse and self-sufficient national economy, even if it meant that individual producers were becoming more specialized 'farmers' with their own titles to land and a concentration of effort on particular commodities.

Alongside this import substitution strategy in the 1970s and 1980s was an attempt in several places to deal with the problem of export price fluctuations. Schemes were established to even out returns to producers by creating reserve funds, saving surpluses in good years and paying out extra in poor. There were also attempts, as with the copra industry in Vanuatu, to even out returns to different regions so that distant islands were not unduly penalized by higher freight costs. Another strategy was to seek protected markets abroad. Under the Lomé Convention, for example, Fiji was able to secure a reliable market for its sugar in Europe and it received a subsidized return well above the open market price.

Agricultural tractor at work in Tonga

These twin rural development strategies of local market orientation and protected export markets did much to promote a period of rural expansion and a fundamental rural transformation in the Pacific. There was intensification, as producers specialized in certain crops and boosted their production through the use of fertilizers, chemicals and, occasionally, machines. There was 'extensification', as new areas were brought under cultivation and forest was turned to agriculture. And there was heightened resource use as natural reserves of timber, minerals, fish and in many cases natural soil fertility were exploited for commercial return. Throughout these processes of change the nation state was prominent, negotiating market access, supporting research and extension, imposing local tariffs and quota, providing credit and subsidies and, in many cases, encouraging foreign investment in resource extraction industries.

This phase of largely state-sponsored rural development may be approaching an end in the Pacific. Global trade liberalization and neo-liberal economic development philosophies in the 1990s are gradually having an impact in the rural Pacific. Economic restructuring, as in Fiji, has led to the dismantling of many agricultural subsidies and various protectionist measures, opening local product to internal competition. Some local import-substituting industries, such as rice, are proving not to be viable in the face of such free trade. Of perhaps greater concern is the potential loss of protected international markets. A general fall in trade protectionism worldwide has made vulnerable old agreements which have secured access for Pacific island produce in Europe and elsewhere. The small-scale nature of Pacific island production and the very high relative costs of shipping products to world markets from the region mean that the prospects of successful competition by Pacific commodities on open world markets are poor indeed. An end to the sugar protocol of the Lomé Convention, for example, could have dramatic implications for the FIJI SUGAR INDUSTRY, hitherto the most successful and longstanding agricultural export industry in the Pacific. The next phase of rural change in the Pacific could thus be one of contraction and retreat, at least in commodity production, from the global economy.

Rural change has been intimately linked with wider processes of social transformation in the Pacific. Some of the major shifts in production and market orientation noted above have contributed in major ways to social changes such as increased individualism and social inequalities but in other ways they have responded to different processes such as population change and mobility. The major link between rural and social change has been in the way key economic and social relations have been commodified.

Land, for the most part in the Pacific region, remains under various forms of communal CUSTOMARY LAND TENURE. This prevents alienation and limits the ability of individuals to exploit, degrade or even enhance the land without group consent. Land laws have protected communal tenure and customary rights of access to land. Yet the everyday practice of land tenure in the face of urban expansion, commercial agriculture or logging has often acted to extend commercial relations and land transactions into the sphere of communal land. Where land has economic value, especially where it is deemed to be in short supply, there have long been pressures to exchange use rights for land, if not freehold title. Pressure on land has been exacerbated by population pressure: in some cases, such as Tonga, this has resulted from increased numbers of local people seeking rights to land; in others, such as Samoa, migration may have eased local population growth but it has not lessened the pressure on land as expatriates have sought to affirm rights to land 'at home'. In response to demand, some government laws have allowed for official leases of customary land to be granted to outsiders whilst protecting the rights of communal landowners. Such measures have assisted in the provision of agricultural credit, for individuals with a lease have collateral even if they do not own the land. However, such government policies have usually proved inadequate in dealing with the pressures over land. Recent studies in Samoa, Vanuatu, Tonga and Fiji have shown that there has been *de facto* individualization of land tenure with 'landlords' and 'tenants' negotiating directly, often outside the official (if not the customary) law, to bring land into production and to share the benefits.

Labour has similarly become a commodity. In colonial times, the use of imported labour on plantations and laws to prevent migration from villages to the towns kept a brake on overt labour markets. However, with post-colonial expansion of the rural economy and enhanced employment opportunities in the towns and overseas, island labour is often in short supply. Whereas non-monetary reciprocal exchange of labour in the past worked in customary tasks such as house-building and bush clearing, and communal labour was used for village projects or fishing, it is increasingly common to find wages being demanded for agricultural work outside the context of the immediate household or extended family. Furthermore, in societies where mobility is high and people have access to relatively highly paid jobs in the cities or in Pacific Rim countries, the shadow price of labour can be high, being related more to urban wages than rural productivity. Therefore, while rural life in the islands may appear to be 'traditional' and unchanging this may often relate more to the form than the substance of village life.

One of the most pervasive elements of rural change in the Pacific has been the belief in 'rural development', of its pressing need, its efficacy and its nature. Fundamental to this has been the view held by colonial and present-day officials, foreign observers and consultants, and not a few local people, that the rural Pacific should progress from its static, lethargic and conservative past towards a more modern and 'developed' state which will provide for the new material needs of its people and, thereby, provide a counter to the obvious economic and social attractions of the city. In addition, because of the limited natural resources in many island states and because authorities want to minimize the disruption that is often seen to follow urbanization, rural-centred development has been seen as perhaps the leading instrument in economic development strategies. Thus, the state embarked on itspolicies of support for agriculture, its search for secure markets and its efforts to increase rural productivity. These efforts were mirrored by individual strategies: using traditional land rights as a basis for commercial agriculture (or fishing or acceptance of logging) was an attractive alternative for many compared to the perils of urban wage labour or entrepreneurial activity.

The ideology of rural development was matched by concerns over social policy. In some cases, particularly during the colonial period, there was a strong element of social conservatism behind rural development strategies. Lessening social disruption, minimizing urbanization, using customary polities and, thus, keeping the costs of social control as low as possible were neatly in accord with policies which used subsistence agriculture and communal land tenure as a basis from which gradually to encourage cash cropping. Such social conservatism persists not only on the part of the state but also by many in society who want to retain security in the land and retain values and protocols which help them deal with the pressures of the outside world. On the other hand, rural development has been seen by others as an instrument for social change. Again recognizing the importance of maintaining a sense of identity and realizing that communal tenure cannot be dismantled, these officials and observers—from the late colonial years to the present—have seen the modernization of agriculture as a means to bring about gradual social transformation: greater individualism, increased mobility, specialization of labour, commitment to the market and achievement-orientation. The ideal pursued in this strategy was not communal societies but communities of smallholder farmers. Modernization was, and still is, believed to be necessary and seen as providing the most effective means for islanders to achieve their new material aspirations and engage in the global economy. The desired aim of this social change discourse is a new rural society, one that will still have inequalities but these will be the result of differences in skill or industry rather than birthright. Once again, such a strategy has been followed not only by officials but also by individuals who see rural development as a means for personal and familial advancement.

Attitudes to society paralleled attitudes to the environment. The putative need for rural 'development' was based on the assumption that the natural resources of the islands—its timber, soil, minerals, reefs and oceans—could provide the material foundations for social change and economic progress. Resource exploitation was thus a justifiable basis for development. Development plans put much store on extending and intensifying agricultural production, developing industries based on catching the supposedly bounteous supply of fish or felling timber, and boosting rural incomes. Despite the fact that many such resources were fragile or in short supply, especially in the small island states of Polynesia and Micronesia, there was a discernible cornucopian flavour to many rural development strategies in the 1970s and 1980s. This contrasted markedly with other attitudes to the environment both old and new. The recent interest in sustainable development, though often reluctantly recognized by island governments, has sought to question the resource exploitation strategy and it has suggested some alternative strategies such as ecotourism, sustainable forestry and organic agriculture. Significantly, within this new discourse of sustainability has been a recognition of the past: of ancient—and occasionally extant—island production systems, practices and values which are marked by guardianship of the environment, established resource management practices and minimal impact technologies. This discourse has much in common with (though some important differences from) those which seek social conservation and which question the very need and nature of 'development'.

To a large extent the competing discourses outlined above have been mediated through a further set of contrasting narratives, those involving the differing roles of the state, the market and custom. We have seen how the state came to assume a prominent role in rural development after the 1960s. Whilst ostensibly 'protecting' communal land tenure and customary social order, it encouraged rural development through resource exploitation, agricultural intensification, and specialization of production. Through its development plans, extension officers, and trade and pricing policies it promoted change. It sought to regulate and intervene in the market, through tariffs and subsidies, but it wanted rural people to engage more in commercial enterprise. It saw 'development', both economic and social, as not only desirable but also imperative. This approach has recently been under attack on both global and national levels and there has been a retreat of state involvement in rural development, with further retreat still to come. In its place, many have set store on the market. This has not only involved a view that sees an unfettered market as the best mechanism for promoting economic growth and allocating resources most efficiently, but also one that places emphasis on capital. Private capital is seen to be in short supply in the region and capital (whether in the form of foreign investment, local savings or credit facilities), it is believed, will help the region find a new place in the global economy. It is an approach which goes hand in hand with calls to develop a new entrepreneurial culture in the Pacific where village-based subsistence agriculture and cash cropping will give way to rural commercial enterprises—farms, businesses and private sector employment generation. In the way of such capital-led development lies the supposed communalism and conservatism of rural people and it is these attitudes that are seen to be in particular need of change. It is a vision that foresees the most radical transformation of the rural Pacific. It is a vision as yet far from achieved but which is being actively promoted.

In response to the competing discourses of the state and the market many rural dwellers in the Pacific islands have become confused and wary. At various times they have embraced change, adopting new crops, new ideas, new markets and new social relations. At other times they have resisted change, refusing to give up land, enforcing codes of social conduct, and both passively and actively resisting the development efforts of the state. For most, rural change is something to be negotiated: because people retain sovereignty over their land they have the power to resist, yet the attractions of material wealth and the promise of modernity are often overwhelming. To make sense of change and to help inform and guide their decisions, most Pacific island people still hold fast to what are seen as the 'old ways'—customs, codes, history and values. Though these are themselves flexible and not unchallenged they do at least give some context for change. It has allowed them sometimes to keep the state at arm's length—the power of the village *fono* in Samoa, for example, means that state agencies have to negotiate with the community and at their level if they wish to promote government activities in the rural areas. In other ways custom can also help shield people from the market. Keeping their land and retaining the means of subsistence provides a useful welfare safety net for many and it also means that commitment to the market does not have to be complete.

Therefore custom—variously *kastom*, *fa'a Samoa*, *vaka vanua* etc—has survived, albeit itself continually changing, not because it is an inviolable, uniform and non-contentious model for rural livelihoods, nor because it resists change. It survives because it allows change; it allows people to regulate, negotiate and make sense of change. As long as sovereignty over land is maintained and as long as that is primarily communal rather than individually-based, rural people will be able to incorporate some changes but resist others. Thus, despite the long history of rural change in the islands and the concomitant transformations of island economies, societies and environments, despite the continual advance of western material culture into all walks of rural life, and despite the inevitability of future pressures for change, it is probable that rural societies will continue to be characterized by an adherence to 'tradition' and 'custom', however these might be construed.—JO

Further reading

Brookfield, H C and Hart, D, 1971. *Melanesia: a geographical interpretation of an island world*, Methuen.

Burt, B and Clerk, C, 1997. *Environment and Development in the Pacific Islands*, National Centre for Development Studies and University of Papua New Guinea Press.

Overton, J and Scheyvens, R (eds), 1999. *Towards Sustainable Development: Pacific island experiences*, Zed Books.

Schoeffel, P, 1996. *Sociocultural Issues and Economic Development in the Pacific Islands*, Asian Development Bank.

Sugar

Sugarcane (*Saccharum officinarium*) probably originated in New Guinea, and grew widely in the Pacific before western contact. It was cultivated: early European visitors noted that Hawaiian villagers often had a small patch of cane growing nearby, serving as a windbreak as well as a supplementary food, chewed for sweetness. As early as 1802 a Chinese immigrant in Hawai'i set up a simple stone mill on Lāna'i and turned out loaf sugar in small quantities for about a year. The early missionaries of the London Missionary Society in Tahiti set up a sugar mill in 1817 as one of the embryonic industries which they hoped would provide cash incomes for the islanders, but the enterprise did not last long. In New Caledonia, sugarcane was cultivated from 1865 to 1890, but it failed due to milling difficulties as well as labour costs. When sugar was first developed as a large-scale industry in the Pacific, non-islander labour was sought for its cultivation, while in the cane-fields of Queensland from the 1860s, islanders (KANAKAS IN AUSTRALIA) were brought in considerable numbers. FIJI'S SUGAR INDUSTRY dates from the late 1800s.

From 1835 in Hawai'i commercial production began when some American and British settlers recognized the need for new products to replace sandalwood and whaling. Many acres were converted to cane growing but it was only in 1842 that sugar of reasonable quality was being produced. Over time, further steps were taken (in land tenure reforms, capital, and technical advances in both agricultural production and processing) to ensure that it became an established industry. From 1848 onwards, the Hawaiian sugar industry gradually won a healthy share of the American market, in spite of problems at home with occasional severe drought, and in the United States with tariff barriers. The Treaty of Reciprocity—allowing Hawaiian unrefined sugar into the United States without tariffs from September

Sugarcane plantation, Kaua'i, Hawai'i

1876—more than doubled the output of sugar in four years. The industry made more advances: huge irrigation projects; and rationalization of a large-scale, efficient mass-production organization. Immigrant labour, mostly Chinese, was brought in from 1877, and after 1881 also from Japan. (See MULTI-ETHNIC POPULATION OF HAWAI'I.) The severe economic setback caused by the McKinley Tariff Bill of 1890 (removing tariffs on all raw sugars into the United States and giving a bounty to American sugar producers) brought renewed business arguments in favour of Hawaiian annexation. This was achieved in August 1898, and followed by a boom in speculation in sugar.

Further advances were made in agricultural production in the 1930s, notably with improved varieties and pest control, and in 1932 the sugar harvest reached one million tons. Hawai'i was recognized as a 'domestic sugar producing area' in the *Sugar Act* of 1937, which initiated the concept of a percentage for

Hawaiian cane sugar in the domestic national quota. Major companies have continued to dominate Hawaiian sugar in recent years, with five corporations estimated to control about 95 per cent of all sugar production. STRIKE ACTION IN HAWAI'I has affected the sugar industry on a number of occasions in this century, resulting in improved wages and conditions but accompanied by a continued impetus for mechanization.

In Micronesia, sugar became the basis for the economic development of the Japanese mandated territory in the 1920s, when the dynamic Matsue Haruji, head of the South Seas Development Company (Nan'yô Kôhatsu Kaisha), after numerous initial difficulties and setbacks, successfully began to harvest and refine sugar in the Marianas. By the mid 1930s, sugar had brought thousands of immigrants into the islands, and by itself provided the mandated territory (JAPANESE COMMERCIAL INTERESTS) with a favourable balance of trade.

In Papua New Guinea, sugar has been a relatively new cash crop, commercially produced by Ramu Sugar in the upper Ramu valley of Madang Province, as a government venture set up in partnership with British investors—particularly the Commonwealth Development Corporation. The first export shipment (about 5000 tonnes) was made in late 1983. Although the Ramu project is able to provide the country's sugar needs, it has relied on protected pricing for its competitiveness.—KRF

Fiji's sugar industry

In Fiji, as in other islands of the Pacific, there was an indigenous variety of sugarcane, but the country's sugar industry dates from the late 19th century, when sugar plantations were developed with imported indentured labourers (GIRMITIYAS) from India. With the abolition of the indenture system in 1920, and the collapse of the sugar market, the sugar industry was restructured on a smallholder basis which has continued to this day.

The sugar mills were initially started by different companies, but by 1926 the Australian-owned COLONIAL SUGAR REFINING COMPANY Limited (CSR) had out-manoeuvred its rivals to become the sole miller of cane. Today four sugar mills process Fiji's sugar: Rarawai, Penang, Lautoka and Labasa.

Following the sugar dispute in 1960 and the Eve Commission Inquiry, the CSR formed a subsidiary in 1962, South Pacific Sugar Mills Limited (SPSM), to manage its Fiji operations. In 1973, the Fiji government purchased the SPSM and the Fiji Sugar Corporation (FSC) took over its operations. The FSC continues as the monopoly miller of Fiji's sugarcane.

Canefields, Viti Levu, Fiji

The sugar industry has been the backbone of the Fiji economy for more than a century, second only to tourism as the country's largest foreign exchange earner. Unlike tourism, the sugar industry has a low leakage factor and it provides employment for a very large number of people, directly and indirectly. In 1996 the industry employed 22 304 growers and their families, and a further 15 000 cane cutters, apart from those employed indirectly in the fertilizer industry, transportation, marketing and farm implement garages.

Sugarcane is grown in the coastal areas of the two main islands. Most of the growers are Indo-Fijians. The government has, however, been assisting indigenous Fijians to become more active in the sugar industry, where they now form a sizeable part.

Fiji's sugar industry has benefited from the various Lomé Conventions, which have paid Fiji a price substantially higher than the prevailing world market price. Of the total of 409 000 tonnes of sugar sold in 1996, 34 per cent went to the United Kingdom under the high Lomé price. The balance of the sugar was sold to a handful of countries, including Malaysia, Japan, United States and South Pacific countries.

An announcement in early 1998 suggested that the European Union (EU) would continue to give preferential treatment to sugar from Fiji (and other African, Caribbean and Pacific countries whose relationship with the EU was established under the Lomé Convention) even after the dissolving of the Lomé Convention in 2000. The sugar protocol of the Lomé Convention continues for the moment, but Fiji must expect future difficulties not only because the EU is likely to press for changes and a potential loss of subsidies when Lomé V is negotiated at the end of this century, but also because World Trade Organization rules preclude discriminatory pricing. Thus the sugar industry is under severe pressure to restructure itself, and a strategic plan is being discussed.

The future of the sugar industry is also tied closely to the critical and currently unresolved issue of the leases of the native land upon which sugarcane production largely rests. (See FIJI NATIVE LAND TRUST BOARD.) As of February 1998, a Parliamentary Joint Committee had been established to resolve the land problem.—RC

Colonial Sugar Refining Company

The Colonial Sugar Refining Company (CSR), founded by Edward Knox in 1855, was built into a giant Australian enterprise by his son Edward William during his 40-year reign as general manager beginning in 1880. The company started with refineries but in the 1860s began to produce raw sugar, building three large and profitable mills in 1869 in northern New South Wales. Ten years later, it began exploring expansion into Queensland and Fiji. In 1880 the CSR reached an agreement with the Fiji government to extend its operations to the colony. The government promised to sell it 1000 acres of land on the Rewa at £2 an acre, and reserve another 1000 acres in Savusavu Bay. In return, the CSR agreed to erect a mill on the Rewa by the start of the 1882 crushing season. The first mill was built at Viria that year, followed by one at Rarawai in 1886, Labasa in 1894, and Lautoka in 1903. Penang, the fifth mill to be operated by the CSR, was bought by the company from a rival in 1926. From then until it withdrew in 1973, the CSR was the sole miller of sugarcane in Fiji, buying cane from mostly Indian small farmers, processing it into raw sugar and exporting it for refining overseas.

At first, the CSR had produced practically all of its sugarcane with Indian indentured labour. In 1909 it began leasing some plantations to independent contractors, mostly former company officers, a practice that collapsed with the labour shortage caused by the end of indentured immigration in 1916 and of the indentured labour system itself in 1920. Faced with this situation, the company decided to get out of cane cultivation. From the 1920s onwards, it began dividing its extensive holdings—132 886 acres of fee simple and lease land—into 10-acre parcels, leased out to Indo-Fijian tenants. By 1941, 97 per cent of all cane acreage was in smallholdings, with CSR tenants accounting for 52 per cent of the total, and independent contractors 45 per cent. The company's fee simple land was converted to Crown fee simple at the time of its departure from Fiji.

The CSR ran the sugar industry with a firm hand, and its dominant place in the economy ensured its broader influence on colonial policy. Close supervision of the growers and tight control over their labour remained the hallmarks of the smallholding system, which periodically plunged the industry into industrial strife. The first of the major strikes took place in 1921, followed by one in 1943 and another in 1960. Reforms recommended by various commissions of inquiry improved relations between the growers and the company, though many sources of friction remained. In 1969 an independent inquiry into the sugar industry headed by Lord Denning, Britain's Master of the Roll, made far-reaching recommendations for profit sharing between growers and millers, long a major bone of contention. Unable to accept the terms of the contract recommended by Denning, the CSR withdrew from Fiji. For more than 100 years, sugar remained the mainstay of Fiji's economy. It accounted for over—usually well over—half of the total exports each year. It provided direct employment for about 30 per cent of the economically active population outside subsistence agriculture in 1966, and nearly one-fifth of the gross domestic product each year. The sugar industry under the CSR played a central role in shaping the history of modern Fiji.—BVL

Sources/further reading

Moynagh, M, 1981. *Brown or White? A history of the Fiji sugar industry, 1873–1973*, Pacific Research Monograph 5, The Australian National University.

Lowndes, A G, 1956. *South Pacific Enterprise: the Colonial Sugar Refining Company*, Angus & Robertson.

Pacific cash crops

■ ***Palm oil*** Oil palms grow in low-lying areas (up to 500 m above sea level) in many parts of the Pacific. Producing fruit all year, the plant lives for almost 30 years and has been widely cultivated in coastal PLANTATIONS. Palm oil is extracted from the small fruit clusters, and used in the commercial production of soap, cooking oil and margarine. After the first commercial crop was developed in West New Britain in 1967, Papua New Guinea, because of its high rainfall, has become a successful producer of palm oil, achieving steadily growing export quantities since the late 1980s. In Solomon Islands, the palm oil plantations and milling plant on Guadalcanal are jointly owned by the government (40 per cent), the Commonwealth Development Corporation (56 per cent) and landowners (4 per cent).

■ ***Rubber*** The rubber tree produces a thick white fluid that can be collected by tapping a cut in the trunk at any time of year, once a tree is at least 5–6 years old. Growing well at low altitudes (up to 450 m above sea level), it requires well-drained soil and about 2000 mm of annual rainfall. Rubber plantations were introduced into Samoa and Papua in the late 19th century, and later in Solomon Islands. Immediately after World War I, extensive rubber planting was carried out in Fiji, but the attempt was discouraged by low international prices in the 1920s and 1930s. The Papua New Guinea rubber plantations (near Port Moresby) were flourishing by the late 1970s, exporting their entire crop to Australia.

■ *Cocoa* A valuable cash crop, cocoa comes from the cacao tree which grows well in tropical climates up to 600 m above sea level. The seeds are collected, then fermented and dried before roasting and grinding to produce cocoa butter (used in sweets and medicines) and cocoa powder (used in chocolate). There is moderate production of cocoa in Solomon Islands, but in Papua New Guinea, cocoa exports are second only to COFFEE. More than three-quarters of the crop is grown in East New Britain and North

Harvesting cocoa in Papua New Guinea

Solomons, mostly by smallholders. When commercial agricultural activities were interrupted by the BOUGAINVILLE CONFLICT, however, cocoa production was abandoned in North Solomons, and became more significant in Madang.

■ *Coffee* Introduced into the Pacific as a cash crop, coffee grows in two main varieties in Papua New Guinea: *robusta* (in low-lying areas up to 600 m above sea level), and *arabica* (1000–2000 m above sea level). About one-third of rural households grow some coffee, picking the coffee berries for sale to processors, and in the past these smallholders have produced up to three-quarters of the total crop. The fermented beans then have to be dried and sent offshore for roasting and grinding. The industry was previously regulated by a quota system required by the International Coffee Organization, but no quotas have been applied since 1990. The Coffee Industry Corporation now licenses the exporters and regulates the quality and prices of coffee being exported. Coffee remains an important crop for Highlanders.

Coffee—mostly the *robusta* variety—was introduced into New Caledonia by French settlers, and it has been successfully grown since then. Kanaks grow the coffee and sell the beans for commercial processing and marketing by large French companies. An early attempt was made to grow coffee in Fiji in the 1880s, but the plants were affected by disease. In French Polynesia the development of a small coffee industry was interrupted by the loss of labour (to meet the demands of the NUCLEAR TESTING program) in 1965, but it is now able to supply about 20 per cent of the local market.

■ *Rice* The Chamorro peoples of the Marianas were the first Pacific islanders to cultivate rice. Commercial production, usually on a small scale, was a much later development, first attempted by the Japanese in Micronesia. In Fiji the Fiji-Indian community began to produce rice to meet their own food needs, mostly on mixed farms where smallholders also grew sugarcane. The government then decided to encourage the production of rice, and large areas of irrigated cultivation were developed at Navua, on the southern coast of Viti Levu, and along the Dreketi River in Vanua Levu in the 1970s and 1980s. Rice has been successfully grown in Solomon Islands since the 1970s, on the plains of northern Guadalcanal. In Papua New Guinea rice planting was introduced into the yam-growing areas of the SEPIK RIVER region by the Australian administration in the 1950s, and the country's first COOPERATIVES were set up to market rice. It is perceived as a difficult crop, however, vulnerable to weather and insect pests, and it has not become widely established, although it is grown in Central District and further north around Afore (Oro District).

■ *Tea* Tea, which grows best in mountain areas, was introduced into Fiji in the 1890s and flourished for a time in the 1920s. It was grown in Papua New Guinea in the 1930s but it remained only a minor crop until a tea factory opened in Morobe Province

Picking tea, Kindeng, Papua New Guinea Highlands

in 1962. Now it is grown mostly on PLANTATIONS in the Southern Highlands and the Western Highlands, since processing of the young leaf tips needs to be done promptly.

TWO LABOUR

Trade unions

Trade unions developed late in the Pacific, in part because industrial and capitalist development was unevenly spread, and subsistence economies remained central to many communities. Proletarianization came much earlier to Hawai'i and Fiji than the rest of the islands. In Fiji the early development of the SUGAR INDUSTRY from the 1870s and gold mining after the 1930s resulted in a larger non-subsistence sector than in other islands. As a result workers' organizations developed earlier and more coherently than elsewhere. Hawai'i had the first trade union in the entire Pacific in 1884, and by the early 1900s trade unionism was well established there. In the 1920s many urban unions declined as the Hawaiian state introduced criminal laws against syndicalism and picketing, and then revived from the mid 1930s, when organizers from the US mainland assisted Hawaiian stevedores. The International Longshoremen's and Warehousemen's Union (ILUW) successfully helped organize PLANTATION and cannery workers in a lengthy strike during the 1940s (STRIKE ACTION IN HAWAI'I).

In Fiji an early attempt to unionize in 1916 by the Fiji Wharf Labourers' Union failed, but by the 1930s sugarcane growers and workers there had formed their own organizations, such as Kisan Sangh and Mazdur Sangh. Meanwhile indigenous Fijian gold mining workers also began to combine and take industrial action. Until the 1940s colonial governments resisted unionization but encouraged compliant professional organizations such as the Association of European Servants, formed in Fiji in 1921. Some Europeans, with Indo-Fijians and ethnic Fijians, broke away in 1943 to establish what eventually became one of the strongest unions: the Fiji Public Service Association. Teachers' unions in Fiji began in the early 1930s. In New Hebrides there was a British Civil Servants' Association but membership did not include locals until the late 1950s. The British Solomon Islands Civil Servants' Association, formed in 1954, was racially divided with a separate branch for local Solomon Islanders.

World War II had a profound effect, particularly on the growth of organized labour (ISLANDER EXPERIENCES IN THE PACIFIC WAR). Demand exceeded supply for both new and established industries. Labourers supplied raw materials, such as sugar and PHOSPHATE, when other sources were cut off. Communications' infrastructure was boosted by war demands, and islanders provided a range of services to Allied military. As islanders worked for and alongside overseas servicemen, they grew conscious of workers' rights, unionism and the value of their labour. The latter was also enhanced by a rising cost of living in many islands. Colonial officials tended to blame workers' unrest on outsiders rather than addressing issues in the local workforce. Workers in Fiji demonstrated their refusal to accept low wages and poor working conditions in several strikes during the 1940s. Gold mining workers at Vatukoula engaged in various forms of labour resistance including strikes in 1938 and 1947, before forming the Fiji Mineworkers' Union in 1948. In response, management tried to set up a 'company union' dominated by traditional leaders, to control industrial unrest.

Waterside workers in Tahiti established the first union there in 1946. Twelve other unions, organizing seamen, machinists, printers, nurses, police and teachers, formed the Trades Council, affiliated to the *Confédération Générale du Travail* (General Confederation of Labour) in France.

With the exception of Hawai'i, trade union development within Polynesia and Micronesia was weak in comparison to Melanesia. In some states, such as Tonga, there is still no legal provision for workers' organizations, although two established associations are the Tonga Nurses' Association and the Friendly Islands Teachers' Association. In Cook Islands, trade unions date back to World War II, although these were mainly in the public sector. Unionization in Samoa's civil service became relatively strong after the Western Samoa Public Service Association (WSPSA: Faalapotopotoga Tagata Faigaluega Malo Samoa i Sisifo) emerged in 1969 from the Western Samoan branch of the New Zealand Public Service Association. The Teachers' Association was established in the 1950s.

Industrial unrest and the demand for labour during and after World War II was a catalyst for labour legislation in British and New Zealand colonies. Labour legislation was advocated by the British Colonial Office, with the *Colonial Development and Welfare Act (1940)* stipulating that aid would be given only if a colony had fair labour conditions and laws to recognize trade unions. Fiji was the first Pacific colony to follow this directive with the formation of a department of Labour in 1942 and the passing of an Industrial Associations Ordinance and Industrial Disputes (Conciliation and Arbitration) Ordinance to recognize trade unions, collective bargaining, conciliation and arbitration. Other legislation followed to recognize unions as collective representatives of workers and protect their right to collective bargaining.

Rice growing near Madang, Papua New Guinea

Immediately after the war, *Trade Union Ordinance (1946)* was introduced in Gilbert Islands. The first union registered under this in 1953 was the Civil Services Association, an affiliate of the British Civil Service Association. Both local and expatriate civil servants were members. Unions were absent from Solomon Islands until the Labour department began in 1960. The commissioner of labour encouraged the formation of the British Solomon Islands Workers' Union to represent ports and COPRA workers, although Solomon Islands workers had long wanted to improve their pay and conditions. Many founding members of this union had been active in the MAASINA RULE movement. State control over the operation of trade unions was solidified with the 1966 Trade Unions Ordinance.

Trade union legislation in Papua New Guinea stemmed from the 1963 Industrial Relations Ordinance and Industrial Organizations Ordinance, which changed labour policy from preventing workers' representation to channelling it along 'acceptable' paths. Following Australian models, the legislation legalized trade unions, and established industry councils, boards of inquiry, industrial negotiation and compulsory conciliation and arbitration. However, colonial labour legislation remained in place long after independence in 1975. In Vanuatu, the Joint Regulation of 1969 stipulated certain conditions of employment in the private sector and provisions for the registration of trade unions.

Even after the legalization of trade unions, the Cold War years of the 1950s–60s were a testing period in the few Pacific territories where unions had taken root. In Hawai'i during the 1950s, the downsizing of sugar and pineapple plantations drastically reduced the size of the ILUW, although it recovered to some extent by organizing workers in the escalating hotel industry. This was also a volatile period for sugar and other manual workers in Fiji. The government responded with force, co-opting some union leaders and enacting legislation to deal with industrial unrest in the sugar industry. In Cook Islands by the 1950s the once-promising strong union movement had become a weak arm of the state. In Samoa there is still no legal provision for the registration of trade unions. Workers' freedom of association is guaranteed under the constitution, however, while the 1972 Labour and Employment Act refers to workers 'united in association'.

Some Pacific territories encouraged the development of a national or central union, ostensibly to strengthen union structures but in fact to put unions into one compliant body. In 1951 Fiji's colonial officials encouraged the Fiji Industrial Workers' Congress, later renamed the Fiji Trade Union Congress (FTUC). By the 1970s it was affiliated to the then anti-communist International Confederation of Free Trade Unions (ICFTU). The FTUC was sporadically tested by factionalism and attempts to establish general unions outside the national centre. In 1972 Apisai TORA, general secretary of the Airport Workers' Union, set up the rival Fiji Council of Trade Unions, which attracted brief support from some blue-collar unions.

Greater obstacles impeded the formation of a peak union in Papua New Guinea. Australian administrators supported the Federation of Workers' Associations (FWA) during the mid 1960s, but it was largely ineffective. Tensions between the Solomon Islands Public Employees' Union and Solomon Islands National Union of Workers (SINUW) also hindered local and international acceptance of a central union. SINUW had grown out of the Solomon

Islands General Workers' Union, consolidated in 1975 by Joses Tuhanuku and Bart ULUFA'ALU. In 1986 several unions launched the Solomon Islands Council of Trade Unions. Kiribati had a national centre in the Kiribati Trade Union Congress (KTUC), subsequently affiliated with ICFTU. During the 1990s efforts were made to constitute the Cook Islands Workers' Association and a national centre in Samoa. The Western Samoa National Union of Workers (WSNUW: Falapotopotoga a le Aufaigalueaga Tumaoti) was founded in 1994 to cover private sector workers.

Greater regional union participation came with the establishment of the Pacific Trade Union Forum in 1981, renamed the Pacific Trade Union Community (PTUC) in 1986. The forum had a strong commitment to social change, a nuclear-free Pacific, anticolonialism, union solidarity and cooperation. The most ambitious project to strengthen regional union links was the South Pacific and Oceanic Council of Trade Unions (SPOCTU), formed in 1990. The focus has been on trade union education, rights and empowerment. SPOCTU has responded to political, economic and ideological changes within the islands and the growth of global labour markets and production in recent decades. Connections between regional labour movements have followed the relocation of manufacturing from Australia, New Zealand and Japan to Pacific islands.

The concept of trade union imperialism has attracted much discussion. Colonial officers, employers and island leaders have argued that trade unions were a foreign intrusion, unsuited to Pacific cultures. It has been suggested that Pacific unionists are victims of trade union imperialism or have 'sold out' to foreign interests, perpetuating another level of imperialism over regional workers. Although external influences were important, workers' protests were often responses to genuine local needs.

International links have been particularly important among maritime workers. When some New Zealand and Australian trade unionists attended World Federation of Trade Unions (WFTU) conferences during the 1980s, fears emerged of a growing Soviet influence in Pacific unionism. South Pacific unionists were more nervous about rising American interest in their affairs, especially after the sponsorship of the Labour Committee for Pacific Affairs by the Asian–American Free Labor Institute. This committee was alleged to have links with the US Central Intelligence Agency and with unionists considered politically conservative by New Zealand and Australian workers.

The FIJI COUPS of 1987 provided the biggest test for international union solidarity when Fijian unions clashed over requests for international direct action. Union organizations outside Fiji were willing to offer support but they received conflicting mandates from Fijian unions. The ICFTU maintained international pressure by trying to open dialogue and monitor conditions through annual visiting missions, 1987–90. Unions in Fiji frequently threatened to reinstate international union bans to protect human and working rights.

Debates over unionism have considered the way that cultural and ethnic issues have both constrained and supported union development. In Fiji ethnicity was rationalized by authorities to inhibit the establishment and operation of trade unions. Unions have been dismissed as a foreign import, antithetical to chiefly Fijian tradition. Similar arguments persisted in Polynesia where unions have been considered alien to the 'PACIFIC WAY'. There are few workers' organizations in Tonga, where the weight of tradition and hierarchical authority is particularly strong. Alternatively, ethnicity has been used to promote compliant unions. Ethnic Fijian unions were encouraged by some employers and chiefs in the aftermath of the industrial unrest of 1959–60. Some unions revived after the 1987 coups but did not attract sustained support.

Kinship loyalties have also tested workers' cohesion. Conflict emerged along kinship lines during the 1981 PUBLIC SERVICE STRIKE IN SAMOA. Industrial action and challenging the prime minister was perceived as not just against *fa'a Samoa* or Samoan culture but as a threat to kinship ties.

Trade unions have been both general, covering workers in different sectors, and also confined to specific industries. Their representation has reflected the complexity and size of the workforce, as well as state concerns to direct the politicization of organized labour. In Fiji, the British model of the state discouraged the formation of large general unions among workers in the private sector. After the leading role of the Wholesale and Retail Workers' General Union in the FIJI STRIKE OF 1959, the government resisted large general unions which might amass industrial and political strength. In contrast, big unions were permitted in the public sector.

General unions were facilitated by British officials, as in the British Solomon Islands Workers' Union and from 1973–74, the New Hebrides General Labour Union. The French did not support general unionism in the Joint CONDOMINIUM Administration (1906–80). Despite official opposition, the

Botakin Karikirakean Aroia Tan Makuri (BKATM) was registered in Kiribati in 1972. The New Zealand government was adamant that one general union be formed in Cook Islands in 1947: the Cook Islands Industrial Union of Workers. It was claimed that the workforce was too small to warrant separate unions, but another agenda was to weaken political and industrial organization among those Cook Island workers associated with socialists in New Zealand.

The small size of unions has been a problem. Although there was a substantial increase in the number of unions in Fiji from three in 1944 to 31 by independence in 1970, most were very small or short-lived. Similar patterns developed among unions in Papua New Guinea. The small populations of the islands has not stopped union development, however. In the early 1990s Tuvalu (population 10 000) has four unions: Civil Servants' Association, Nurses' Association, Overseas Seamen's Union (TOSU) and the Teachers' Union.

In contrast, in Papua New Guinea the colonial administration allowed large regionally based general workers' associations to register as unions. These covered all workers in their region not classified as permanent public servants. Scattered and small workplaces impeded strong development except among workers on wharves or in public works. An exceptionally powerful union during the 1970s was the Bougainville Mine Workers' Union under the leadership of Henry Moses.

There has been considerable controversy over the political role of trade unions, partly because working conditions and remuneration are rarely separate from the political and economic context. Workers' organizations have been an important avenue for political expression in the absence of political parties and suffrage through much of the colonial Pacific. Regional unions have been aligned to and instrumental in democratic movements in the post-colonial Pacific. Trade unions have been integral to the growth of regional social movements, especially anti-nuclear and anti-colonial movements. This began in the early 1960s with protests and boycotts by unions of French goods and services in the Pacific. The *Union des Syndicats des Travailleurs Kanak et Exploités* (Union of Kanak and Exploited Workers, USTKE) split from other unions in New Caledonia to advocate independence and the welfare of Kanak workers. As late as 1995, a general French Polynesian union, *A Tia i Mua*, was proactive in community protests about NUCLEAR TESTING, which resulted in general secretary Hirohiti Tefaarere being jailed for four months.

Some unionists became political leaders within independent Pacific states. For example, Kiribati's Abete Merang, the original organizer of the main union, BKATM (a former source of political opposition within the house of assembly), became Minister of Labour in the new government. Ieremia TABAI, the first President of Kiribati, had close links with trade unions when he was leader of the opposition. This connection with BKATM changed after independence, particularly after the 1980 strike. Similarly in Vanuatu, Prime Minister Walter LINI reversed initial overtures towards unions in the independent state. In Cook Islands, Albert HENRY, a pro-independence leader and exponent of unionism during the late 1940s, adopted a less sympathetic position after he became premier. Such a turnaround by the first wave of political leaders with union connections evoked popular cynicism about the political ambitions of union leaders.

A wave of political assertiveness by unionists came in the 1980s–90s, when social democratic, labour parties and pro-democracy movements became stronger. Best known was the founding of the Fiji Labour Party in 1985 and its election victory in coalition with the National Federation Party in 1987. Much of the impetus for the Fiji Labour Party came from the FTUC, following a unilateral wage freeze by government and erosion of workers' rights. Almost a decade later the Vanuatu Council of Trade Unions reactivated the Vanuatu Labour Party after a four-month public service strike, 1993–94.

The Solomon Islands General Workers' Union facilitated the first political party with working class support (1975–76): the Nationalists' Party, later renamed the National Democratic Party. In 1989 the Solomon Islands Council of Trade Unions organized the Solomon Islands Labour Party and Tuhanuku became leader of the opposition. Former unionist Bart Ulufa'alu is the present prime minister.

Other Pacific unions attempted to engage in business ventures. During the 1970s–80s, central union leaders James Raman of Fiji and Tony Ila of Papua New Guinea, were attracted to the US style of business unionism. Through Ila's focus the PNG TUC developed ties with the Asian–American Free Labour Institute and the American Federation of Labor Congress of Industrial Organizations (AFL–CIO). This brought allegations of American union imperialism.

Pacific unions have also provided welfare services for members and the general public. For example, Tuvalu's Overseas Seamen's Union operates a public transport system. The FTUC's Women's Wing identified a lack of child-care facilities for working mothers and set up a children's day-care centre. The Cook Islands Public Service Association has negotiated trade discounts with local retailers for members. Credit societies and welfare subsidies, covering for example, maternity, sickness and funerals, have become significant union functions in societies where the state provides limited assistance. Since 1981 Fiji's Federated Airline Staff Association has taken members' welfare in a different direction by providing one of the few examples of worker participation in the Pacific. Union and government each hold half the shares and have equal representation on the management board of Air Terminal Services at Nadi airport.

The meaning and practice of HUMAN RIGHTS has been under extensive debate in the Pacific. This embraces trade union rights. With an increasingly globalized labour and investment market, working conditions of islanders were seriously eroded by changing employment patterns and, in some countries, government policy responses. Restrictions were placed on union activities during the 1990s. Several decrees promulgated by Fiji's post-coup administrations infringed the rights of trade unions. Public sector unions faced restrictions in Vanuatu after a 1993–94 strike. Industrial conflict has also focused on public sector 'structural adjustment' which has produced substantial worker redundancies. Nevertheless, unions continue to exist in major island societies and are gaining more acceptance in smaller ones, such as Cook Islands and Samoa. Much of the growth in new employment is among women, especially in the manufacturing and service sectors where jobs are often poorly paid and have little security of tenure. Currently women are under-represented within unions, both in numbers and leadership. The right to form collective organizations has been an important gain by paid workers, but this right is by no means secure. Unions will continue to represent workers on employment issues but have a wider role as non-government community organizations, especially as advocates of human rights and democratic development.—JL1

Further reading

Moore, C, Leckie, J and Munro, D (eds), 1990. *Labour in the South Pacific*, James Cook University of Northern Queensland Press.

Hess, M, 1992. *Unions under Economic Development: private sector unions in Papua New Guinea*, Oxford University Press.

■ *Apisai Tora* Apisai Vuniyayawa Mohammed Tora (5 January 1934–), trade union organizer, was born at Vunidawa, Fiji, son of Ratu Kalivati Tora. Educated at Queen Victoria School, he joined the Fiji Artillery in 1952 and served in Malaya (1954–56). He then joined the Fijian public service as a clerk in 1957 and became involved with the Wholesale and Retail Workers' General Union (WRWGU) in 1959, becoming president in 1960. Co-leader of the 1959 industrial dispute with the Shell Oil and Vacuum Oil companies, Tora also established the Natalau Cooperative Society in 1960 and was elected as chairman. During the 1960s he became general secretary of the WRWGU, president of the Fijian Federation of Labour, and a member of the Sugar Advisory Council and the Wages Council. He organized the Fiji Banana Planters and Agricultural Producers' Association and was elected secretary (1962–63). He helped establish the Fijian Western Democratic Political Party and was elected secretary in 1963. Instrumental in the merger of the National Democratic Party with the Federation Party in 1968, leading to the creation of the National Federation Party (NFP), Tora was elected to parliament in 1972. He resigned from the NFP in 1978, and was elected on the Alliance ticket for the Ba-Nadi Communal Seat in 1982, becoming minister of state without portfolio, then minister of state for Rural Development; and finally Minister for Communications, Transport and Workers, 1985–87, and in the interim administration, 1987–91. He was a founding member of the Taukei Movement and the founding president of the All Nationals Congress (1992).—KRF

Labour reserve

From the mid 1800s, Pacific villages were developing the characteristics of a labour reserve: they supplied labour on demand as needs arose, but the subsistence economy was still basically responsible for the maintenance of the labourers and their families. Two million Pacific islanders and half a million Asians worked for wages in the region up to the Pacific War. Using the concept of a labour reserve gives a unified perspective to the different colonial policies. It partly explains the pattern and motivation of colonial partition of the islands, the various uses of labour within island groups and externally, and the introduction of Asian labour into some colonies in the second half of the 19th century, followed by local alternatives to external labour migration as PLANTATIONS and cash crops were developed. The indenture system was failing by the 1940s and was abolished in most parts of the Pacific by 1950, but the subsistence sector still continued to act as a reserve from which periodic migratory labour was drawn.—CM2

Further reading

Newbury, C, 1980. 'The Melanesian labor reserve: some reflections on Pacific labor markets in the 19th century', *Pacific Studies*, 4(1).

Strikes and industrial action

Pacific islanders took various forms of 'industrial action' long before they were legally permitted to form trade unions. Labour protest has been demonstrated in forms of resistance such as absenteeism, go-slow, accidents, feigned sickness, theft and industrial sabotage. Much industrial action by islanders is unrecorded and falls within culturally bounded forms of resistance.

Migrants working on the Pacific's early plantations and mines engaged in direct labour protest. In Samoa, workers at GODEFFROY's Mulifanua plantation stopped work in 1875 and 1882. Fiji's first recorded strike by GIRMITIYAS occurred in Rewa, 1880. Early strikes in New Caledonia's NICKEL MINING industry over dangerous conditions and wages included Japanese workers in 1892 and Vietnamese mineworkers in 1927 and 1945. Throughout the Pacific, employers would play off one ethnic group of workers against another to impede concerted protest. This did not stop striking in 1919 by Japanese workers on Ocean Island (Banaba) spreading to other Pacific island workers in the PHOSPHATE industry there. The same year in French Polynesia, returning soldiers fomented a strike with local wharf labourers (NATIONALISM IN FRENCH TERRITORIES).

World War II accelerated regional labour unrest, following a dramatic increase in the paid workforce, increasingly dependent on the cash economy but facing mounting inflation. Post-war demand for labour continued with the expansion of new industries. Many forms of industrial unrest escalated during and immediately after the war, including petitions, demonstrations and strike action. Industrial unrest was heightened in Fiji with cane-growers boycotting the 1943 harvest and workers striking elsewhere. Other Pacific territories were not immune; see also LABOUR–COOK ISLANDERS.

Although strikes had many causes, pay and conditions of work were fundamental. This was clear during a major strike in 1920 in Fiji by public sector and sugar workers. In 1929 in New Guinea, colonial settlers were astounded when approximately 3000 employees stopped work to seek a pay increase (RABAUL STRIKE, 1929).

A second key issue has been recognition of trade unions and the right of collective bargaining. An early strike in Fiji during 1916 by stevedores employed by the COLONIAL SUGAR REFINING and Union Steam Ships companies was sparked by not only unreasonable pay, heavy work and dangerous working conditions but also the employers' refusal to recognize a union. Over 70 years later in 1990, gold mining workers at Vatukoula staged Fiji's longest strike, over similar grievances. These included company recognition of the union, an issue still occurring in the 1990s especially in heavily feminized industries, such as export manufacturing. The same issue arose among striking garment workers in Fiji and a strike in 1993 at Yazaki Samoa, an automotive assembly parts plant in Apia.

The 1980s saw major strikes by public sector workers. This reflected the growth of the public sector, rising inflation, monetization of the economy and political tensions within newly independent nations. When the Botakin Karikirakean Aroia Tan Makuri union (BKATM) stopped work for five weeks in Kiribati during 1980, public services were severely curtailed. The resulting violence included arson, sabotage of public property and a union member being shot by police.

Workers in Solomon Islands have taken lengthy strike action in recent years. In 1989 the Solomon Islands National Teachers Association (SINTA) organized a three-month teachers' strike, mainly over discrepancies between their pay scale compared to the general public service. Solomon Islands Public Employees' Union (SIPEU) struck a year later when government substantially increased permanent secretaries' salaries and benefits. A nine-week strike involving up to 4000 civil servants erupted in April 1991, after government withdrew recognition of SIPEU. Public servants did achieve a 16 per cent pay increase but the dispute persisted. A four-month strike by Vanuatu's public sector unions (1993–94) began over salaries grievances but also concerned the right to collective bargaining, dispute procedures and reinstatement of strikers.

Most Pacific states have legislation to control industrial action or have assumed that traditional authority would dampen unrest. Yet even in Tonga nurses, frustrated over work grievances, stopped work for 15 days. Public support was overwhelming, as it was also when nurses in Fiji went on strike in 1991 over inadequate transportation. Strike action has not been taken lightly but continues to be an ultimate protest by islanders to protect working rights.—JL1

Further reading

Moore, C, Leckie, J and Munro, D (eds), 1990. *Labour in the South Pacific*, James Cook University of Northern Queensland Press.

Newbury, C, 1980. *Tahiti Nui: change and survival in French Polynesia 1767–1945*, University of Hawai'i Press.

■ ***Fiji strikes of 1920 and 1921*** Fiji's first major strike of the 20th century began on 15 January 1920 when the Indo-Fijian employees of the Public Works department walked off their jobs in Suva, refusing to work 48 hours a week instead of the customary 45. The workers also demanded more wages to meet the increased cost of living, which the government was reluctant to grant even though an appointed commission of inquiry confirmed that the prices of basic Indo-Fijian food items had increased significantly since the war. The government ordered the striking workers back to work before it would consider their grievances. The strikers refused, leading the government to use European and Fijian constables to restore law and order. The confrontation climaxed in a tragic encounter near Suva when an Indo-Fijian striker was shot dead and several wounded. The show of force won the day for the government, straining race relations. While the strike failed, it signalled that the Indo-Fijians, recently freed from GIRMITI, would be more assertive than in the past in resorting to direct action to secure their economic rights. An important feature of the strike was the role Indo-Fijian women played in preventing their menfolk from crossing the picket line.

The 1920 strike was confined to southeastern Viti Levu. No sooner was it quelled than Indo-Fijian workers in western Viti Levu struck, this time against the COLONIAL SUGAR REFINING COMPANY (CSR). The company's tenants and workers demanded better wages (12 shillings a day), specified work hours, adequate housing, medical and pension benefits, educational facilities for children, and small plots of land on which to keep milk cows. Their situation was compounded in 1921 by the CSR's decision to alter its procedure in buying cane, no longer valuing it according to its sweetness at individual rates, but at a flat rate for farms grouped into 300–400 acre blocks. The CSR resisted the demands and the government refused to intervene in the dispute. Once again the strike was broken by force, which this time included 250 specially commissioned Fijian constables from Bau, deployed for political reasons rather than for their services. Sadhu Basisth Muni, a recently arrived Sanatani (orthodox) Hindu priest, falsely rumoured to be an agent of Mahatma Gandhi, was deported.

Peace was restored, but the embittered Indo-Fijians became further alienated from a government they considered more sympathetic to their employers. The 'Indian problem' was thus born. More significantly, the two strikes saw the (assisted) emergence of an accord between Fijians and Europeans which would provide the basis of future political alignments in the colony.—BVL

■ ***Rabaul strike 1929*** On the dark, stormy night of 2 January 1929, Rabaul's town workers struck for more pay. They were led by Sumsuma, from Boang Island in the Tanga group off New Ireland. Captain of the Melanesian Company's motor schooner *Edith*, he was 'a most extraordinary and outstanding native', his employer thought, and the mandated territory's highest-paid New Guinean. His chief ally was N'Dramei, from Pitylu Island, Manus, the senior sergeant-major of police. Yet the strike was decided by consensus: Rabaul's boss-boys and police NCOs agreed to demand £12 a month for every worker. N'Dramei told 19 police to remain on duty protecting key points, then 200 police and 3000 workers, everyone except possibly the Tolai on whose land Rabaul was, walked out of Rabaul. A thousand men gathered at Malaguna Methodist Mission two miles from town, and 2000 at Rapolo Catholic mission a mile further on. They expected the missionaries to pass on to employers their pay demand, but the missionaries urged them back to work. At Rapolo almost all stayed; at Malaguna most agreed to return, and by dawn were walking back to Rabaul.

Rabaul's Europeans woke to find the town almost deserted. A few were merely 'totally surprised'; most were fearful. European police officers armed themselves, swore in white special constables and hurried to Rapolo. 'Why are you armed?', strikers called, 'Do you think we wanted to kill you? We could have done that last night if we wanted to.' The officers called out police one by one, and slowly the crowd gave way. Men ran into the bush or set off for Rabaul. The strike was over.

Among Rabaul's whites fear became fury. 'MUTINY. RABAUL NATIVE LABOURERS ON STRIKE. POSITION VERY GRAVE', screamed the *Rabaul Times* headlines on 4 January. Angry residents formed the New Guinea Citizens' Association and demanded that missionaries be deported, senior police officers be dismissed, and employers be allowed to flog workers. They wanted the strike leaders harshly treated. They were. Sumsuma, N'Dramei and 19 others were sentenced to three years' prison, 12 leaders got lesser sentences, many strikers were sacked and some were forced to become carriers on the tough mountain track from Salamaua to the Wau gold fields. In prison strikers were beaten, and on release most went home, bitter that a reasonable demand was treated so brutally. N'Dramei died on Pitylu about 1940. Sumsuma became a progressive leader on Boang but his ventures failed. He died in 1965.

The strike was extraordinary. Led by New Guinea's best-paid workers, who would gain least and lose most by striking, it wanted the same wage for all. It included the police, an achievement rare in strikes anywhere in the world, and it united workers, some of them traditional enemies, from throughout New Guinea. It appealed to the new society emerging in the white man's town. It failed not from want of planning, but because its leaders misjudged the fury of the European reaction. Sumsuma particularly was exceptional—a people's champion, with the vision to see that all his countrymen, whoever they were, deserved better.—BG

Further reading

Gammage, B, 1975. 'The Rabaul strike, 1929', *Journal of Pacific History*, 10(3–4).

——, 1981. 'Oral and written sources', in D Denoon and R Lacey (eds), *Oral Tradition in Melanesia*, University of Papua New Guinea.

■ ***Strike action in Hawai'i*** Strikes in Hawai'i have been extremely volatile and persistent. Major plantation strikes occurred in 1909, 1920, 1924, 1946 and 1958. In 1909, 7000 Japanese plantation workers under the Higher Wages' Association struck on O'ahu. Workers' solidarity was tested by ethnic divisions but in 1920 Japanese and Filipino workers stopped work for 165 days. A strike in 1924 by 13 000 Filipino workers—affecting 23 out of 45 SUGAR plantations—erupted in serious violence with 16 strikers and six police killed. In 1938 protesters peacefully supporting an inter-island shipping strike were brutally attacked by police in the 'Hilo Massacre', also known as Hawai'i's 'Bloody Monday'. Strikes flared after World War II. In 1946 the International Longshoremen's and Warehousemen's Union organized a 79-day strike resulting in better wages and working conditions and union recognition. Another dock strike followed in 1949 when stevedores in Hawai'i successfully sought equal pay with dock workers on the US mainland.

From the 1940s employers also organized to present a united front, and the Hawai'i Employers Council had 223 members (representing most businesses) by 1958. Union activity since the war has been directed towards acquiring political influence, and significant labour legislation has been effected.—JL1

Further reading

Beechert, E, 1985. *Working in Hawai'i: a labor history*, University of Hawai'i Press.

Puette, W, 1988. *The Hilo Massacre: Hawai'i's Bloody Monday, August 1st, 1938*, University of Hawai'i Press.

■ ***Fiji strike of 1959*** The five-day 1959 Fiji Strike was one of the most militant industrial actions in the colonial South Pacific. The Wholesale and Retail Workers' General Union instigated this after oil companies rejected wage increase demands from workers. The strike reflected deeper frustration of social and economic disparities. It included two days of serious violence and threatened to escalate into a general strike. The colonial government suppressed the strike using reserve soldiers, riot police, smoke grenades, a curfew and the Public Safety Ordinance. Interpretations of the strike have dismissed it as racial riots or a communist plot by Indians, or celebrated it as anti-colonial and anti-capitalist: a demonstration of inter-ethnic working class solidarity. It was directed at European control over industry and workers' lives and threatened the traditional authority of Fijian chiefs. The union achieved some pay increase, but after 1959 the state hardened its stand against militant general unions.—JL1

Further reading

Lal, B V, 1992. *Broken Waves: a history of the Fiji Islands in the twentieth century*, Center for Pacific Islands Studies, University of Hawai'i.

■ ***Public service strike in Samoa*** During the Samoan Public Service Strike in 1981, Western Samoa Public Service Association (WSPSA) members stopped work for 13 weeks. The dispute was over wages and the high cost of living, but related issues were the lack of any provision to recognize service organizations and the need for a tribunal to arbitrate in disputes between public service workers and employers. The association linked these issues to political criticism of the state. Public demonstrations were mainly peaceful and included a large protest march, rallies and a petition to the head of state. Outside agencies were asked for help, with the WSPSA president appealing to unions in New Zealand, and the prime minister of Samoa urging his New Zealand counterpart to help break the strike. The dispute was resolved but left a controversial legacy. WSPSA was strengthened but distrust of unionization remained.—JL1

Further reading

Snell, R, 1992. 'Western Samoa trade unionism: the 1981 public service strike', *New Zealand Journal of Industrial Relations*, 17.

Public sector employment

Throughout the Pacific islands the public sector has been dominant, the provider of essential social services and often the main employer. In 1994 an estimated 40 per cent of paid work in the region came under the public sector. It proliferated in countries such as Solomon Islands, where despite small populations, a provincial system of administration coexisted with the growth of central government. The public service is virtually the only industry in many island economies, playing a key role in fostering development and implementing donor aid. Employment in the public sector offers security not just for the individual but for the wider kin group.

Contemporary public services in the Pacific emerged from colonial structures which were dominated by expatriate Europeans, leaving hierarchical principles of colonial control in much of the public sector. The system has also been open to patronage. Many civil servants also find it difficult to separate traditional and kin commitments from public roles and status. This sometimes leads to corruption, mismanagement and political interference in the public sector, affecting personnel, finances and policy.

Changes in the public sector have far-reaching consequences, particularly in small communities. Since the mid 1980s the public sector has been restructured using foreign models, and in response to pressure by international lending agencies. Changes have included restructuring, corporatization, privatization, cost-cutting, redundancies, greater efficiency, accountability, industrial relations reforms, hiring officials on contracts, and charging the public for services. These measures are part of overall structural adjustment programs to promote environments more conducive to private sector investment. Corporatization and privatization have been implemented in Cook Islands, Vanuatu, French Polynesia, Solomon Islands, Fiji, American Samoa and Papua New Guinea.

Fiji implemented aggressive measures to restructure its public sector. Here public sector restructuring was associated with political as well as economic and institutional issues. Plans to privatize began in the mid 1980s but the 1987 FIJI COUPS and the subsequent economic climate facilitated major shake-ups in the public sector. Radical restructuring has also been in place in Papua New Guinea since 1989, with the loss of 4500 positions from the public service in 1995. Massive redundancies and slashing of public service salaries also occurred in small states such as Cook Islands which faced a serious financial crisis during the mid 1990s.

In many island states the public sector is the main site of organized union activity. Often unions have not just acted to preserve and enhance their members' economic interests but have been watchdogs of policy and practice within the public sector. The localization of civil service positions was a key issue addressed by unions prior to and immediately after political independence.

Public sector restructuring has generally been hostile to the operation of strong trade unions, with serious implications for unions in countries where unionization is non-existent or weak. Restructuring for efficiency and cost-cutting has adversely affected union organization. Privatization, corporatization and the widespread practice of out-sourcing public services have also weakened unions. For example, in Fiji the Public Service Association has lost many members with the corporatizing of posts and telecommunications services. A further constraint faced after the coups has been restrictive legislation in the public sector, such as removing rights of appeal.

Despite global and regional cutting of public sector employment, workers in many island states continue to have strong international union, educational and professional links with, for example, Public Services International, Education International, World Confederation of Organizations of the Teaching Profession, Commonwealth Nurses' Federation, International Transport Federation, International Journalists' Federation, and Postal Telegraph and Telephone International.—JL1

Unemployment

Conventional definitions of unemployment in the Pacific islands have relied upon official registration statistics, which apply only to those actively seeking or available for work but not in paid, subsistence or informal employment. This means that unpaid workers—females especially—have been excluded from official figures. Most islanders produce for subsistence and exchange but require cash. Paid work may be seasonal or sporadic. There is usually no monetary assistance for the unemployed, although increasingly job search agencies, especially for youth, are being established. These cater only to a tiny proportion of the unemployed. Figures are typically understated because extended families are expected to care for members not in paid work.

The discrepancies between definitions of unemployment, official statistics and economists' estimates are best illustrated in an example from Fiji. In 1995 the official unemployment rate was 6 per cent; academic estimates for overall unemployment over 19 per cent; marginal unemployment rate (isolating new entrants into the labour market) at 36 per cent. This acknowledges the inability of regional economies to provide job opportunities for school leavers, compounded by youth population growth rates and migration from rural to urban areas.

Unemployment is also becoming common in villages, especially when migrants return home after failing to find work or being made redundant. Women in the rising number of female-headed households are vulnerable to unemployment or pressure to accept wages well below poverty levels. In 1994 the United Nations Development Programme estimated that economic growth sufficient to create 498 000 waged jobs would leave 75 per cent of the projected Pacific islands labour force in the year 2010 without paid employment.—JL1

Labour—Cook Islanders

Cook Islanders began to work for Europeans on WHALING and merchant ships and in COPRA production during the 1800s; recruitment for GUANO on Malden (Kiribati) continued until 1927. By the early 20th century large numbers of Cook Islanders were migrating from outer islands to take up paid work on Rarotonga. Thousands of Cook Islanders worked in the phosphate mines on Makatea in French Polynesia from the early 20th century until the late 1950s. Although earnings were good, some Cook Islanders and New Zealand unionists called it an exploitative 'Frontier Forsaken'. Families migrated to Makatea but by 1946 this was stopped to meet Cook Islands' domestic demand for women's labour in subsistence and citrus production.

One of the most direct interventions by outside unions in Pacific island affairs came from the New Zealand Federation of Labour (NZFOL) during the late 1940s in Cook Islands. New Zealand's prime minister insisted workers there forgo a wage increase until a union was formed and affiliated to the NZFOL. This requirement did not apply to New Zealand workers. By 8 November 1947 the Cook Islands (except Niue) Industrial Union of Workers was established but many Cook Islands waterside workers continued to agitate for a separate union.

From World War II an increasing number of Cook Islanders migrated to New Zealand for work (see PACIFIC ISLANDERS IN NEW ZEALAND). Young women were sponsored to work as domestics in private homes and hospitals. Others entered more lucrative employment in factories. Cook Islands, Niuean and Samoan women formed the vanguard of massive Pacific islands labour migration to New Zealand in the post-war period, reflecting both the employers' preference for cheap, female labour and some island families encouraging daughters to emigrate.—JL1

Further reading

Scott, D, 1991. *Years of the Pooh-Bah: a Cook Islands history*, Cook Islands Trading Company, with Hodder & Stoughton.

THREE FISHERIES, FORESTRY AND MINING

Natural resources and international development

The natural resources of the Pacific islands have always proved attractive to outside trading and investment interests, although the bulk of the resource extraction is of recent duration. Small island economies tend to rely on the export of resource products and tree crops in exchange for manufactured goods and processed food imports. The benefits from such extraction are not reflected in improvements in social and economic conditions, even though volume and value of exports have increased.

Fisheries

The islands are rich in fisheries resources. They have an enormous sea area, with exclusive economic zones (EEZ)—and therefore fishing grounds—extending over more than 30 million sq km, compared to just over half a million square kilometres of

Tuna fish at market

land area. Moreover, the sea area is spread more evenly between individual island states than is the land area. Kiribati, the Republic of the Marshall Islands and the Federated States of Micronesia, for instance, occupy a significantly smaller combined land area than Papua New Guinea, but have a sea area of 3.55 million, 2.13 million and 2.98 million sq km respectively; while Papua New Guinea's sea area is 3.12 million sq km. Commercial fishing and access fees are thus particularly important as a source of revenue for these island nations.

Actual and recorded commercial exploitation of these resources in the post-war period was perfunctory and, more recently, has become dependent on the activities of the distant fishing nations. This reflects the increased use of transshipment from catcher boats to career vessels by the larger Pacific Rim nations, and limitations on research, monitoring and licensing capacities of the island states. It also reflects a shift to purse-line fishing from pole-and-line fishing. The latter, from being a dominant form of fishing in these waters in the first half of the 1970s, had disappeared by the late 1980s. In addition, domestic commercial fishing collapsed because of depressed prices in the 1980s. Islands became increasingly dependent on licensing agreements with Japan and the United States. Japan cut its fisheries aid to Fiji when Fiji refused to sign a bilateral fisheries agreement, and it withdrew Japanese vessels from PNG waters after Papua New Guinea raised licence fees to compensate for under-reporting of catch and price. The vacuum created by the Japanese was filled by other Asian nations, such as South Korea, Taiwan and the Philippines

Tuna fishing in New Caledonia

It was only in 1988 that the United States signed a MULTILATERAL TREATY ON FISHERIES with the SOUTH PACIFIC FORUM's 16 member countries. Under this agreement, a fixed annual sum of US$18 million is paid for access; only a quarter of this is paid by the American tuna industry, and the balance by the US government. The bulk of this payment is distributed to the member countries on the basis of catch. (See also INTERNATIONAL LAW AND THE PACIFIC OCEAN, and REGIONAL COOPERATION AND INITIATIVES.) In several Pacific countries access fees paid by foreign vessels have become a major source of government revenue: fishing accounts for 45 per cent of revenue for Kiribati, and 25 per cent for Marshall Islands and the Federated States of Micronesia. In 1996 over US$66 million was paid out to Pacific island nations, with Japan paying about 38 per cent of this, the United States about 14 per cent, and Taiwan about 15 per cent. Papua New Guinea, Kiribati and Marshall Islands received the largest share of the licensing fees.

There is considerable under-reporting of tuna catch. Even so, current catch levels are below potential yield in the case of tuna and barely tapped in the case of coastal pelagic fish, and reef and lagoon fish—the latter being fished mainly in small quantities for subsistence. Nevertheless, given global pressures generating over-fishing, there is an urgent need to manage the licensing of tuna fishing (SUSTAINABLE DEVELOPMENT). Whereas the considerably larger tuna industry is in the hands of foreign owners, the smaller prawn fishing has become increasingly localized in the 1980s and 1990s.

Member countries of the European Union have been a significant market for canned tuna produced in the Pacific. Canned tuna exports from canneries in Fiji, Solomon Islands and Papua New Guinea enjoyed a 24 per cent tariff preference over the most-favoured-nation rates of the European Union. Without the preferential tariffs, the Pacific islands could not compete with countries such as Thailand, Philippines and the United States. Today the bulk of the recorded tuna exports goes to the US Tuna Cannery, with increasing exports to the Japanese sashimi market. Prawn exports are mainly for the Japanese market. There is considerable value-added profit from prawns and tuna, and some US companies plan to locate in Papua New Guinea. Nevertheless, demand for tinned mackerel has increased along with pressures for import substitution. Papua New Guinea responded by giving protection to International Food Corporation to can mackerel in Lae. In 1997–98 as the value of the PNG kina slumped and the cost of imported material inputs increased, the company became increasingly non-competitive. The value-added gain is limited to employment, which fell in 1998.

Forestry

Out of a total Pacific land area of approximately 525 000 sq km, Papua New Guinea has 462 243 sq km. Most island states, including Kiribati and the Federated States of Micronesia, have a land area of less than 1000 sq km. Apart from Papua New Guinea, only three others have a land area of more than 10 000 sq km: Solomon Islands, Fiji and Vanuatu. It is not surprising, therefore, that most of the international forestry investment interest has been centred on Papua New Guinea, although large-scale logging is permitted in Solomon Islands. (See Table 5.1.) Forestry plays a particularly significant role in Solomon Islands' economy (see LOGGING IN SOLOMON ISLANDS), accounting in 1993 for 55 per cent of total merchandise exports; in Papua New Guinea, Vanuatu and Fiji it accounted respectively for 16 per cent, 13 per cent and 7 per cent. Until the 1970s there was little logging in Papua New Guinea, and the revenue base of Solomon Islands, without a mining industry, was weaker. That increased the lure of the timber companies, particularly from Malaysia. In Papua New Guinea, the downturn in commodity prices in the 1980s led to similar developments. But the revenue benefits to the Melanesian economies were small. The economic surplus was

Processing rubber trees for timber export, Papua New Guinea

Table 5.1 Forest and timber statistics, 1993

	Papua New Guinea	Solomon Islands	Vanuatu
Total forest area (million ha)	34.0	2.4	0.43
Commercially productive area (million ha)	7.0–7.5	0.48	0.12
Allowable yield under licences now issued (million cu metres)	8.0	3.3	0.2
Current harvesting yield (million cu metres)	3.5	0.7	0.03
Sustainable yield (million cu metres)	3.5	0.3	0.038–0.052

Source: Author's calculations.

captured by the logging companies, which underreported export price and volume, leading to widespread corruption and malpractice. Later, Papua New Guinea hired a Swiss firm to monitor the price and volume of log exports, but Solomon Islands did not. Therefore, though both Papua New Guinea and Solomon Islands continued to suffer revenue losses, they were relatively much larger for the latter—35 per cent of gross domestic product compared to 5 per cent for Papua New Guinea.

Table 5.1 also shows that timber licences issued and logging contracts signed exceeded estimated sustainable timber yields. It is possible that, at the logging rates prevailing in 1994, the forests in Solomon Islands could be cut out in 15–20 years. With the increase in approved licensed quota, its forests could be liquidated in as little as eight years.

With the rising international log prices in the early 1990s (prices doubled in 1993 over 1992), and with export bans imposed in Sabah, and reduced logging quotas in Sarawak and western North America, international investment interest and logging increased in both Papua New Guinea and Solomon Islands. Vanuatu imposed a ban on log exports from 1990–94, although this was designed as much to encourage local processing as to control logging. But with the lifting of the export ban in 1994 and an increase in logging licences, logging has increased to an unsustainable level.

Between 1991 and 1993 export volumes doubled in both Papua New Guinea and Solomon Islands. Until 1992, the logging interests in both countries were almost exclusively from Malaysia. Papua New Guinea's Investment Promotion Agency data over the 1993–97 period show that proposed new timber investment is flowing from almost all members of the Asia Pacific Economic Forum. Nevertheless 35 out of 78 proposals are from Malaysia, though by far the largest is from Canada (K310.7 million). How many of these proposals are likely to materialize remains uncertain. This is because of the fall in international prices, the restriction to an annual cut rate of 3 per cent of the permit area to ensure a sustainable forest strategy and the introduction of a stumpage system. Under the latter, a minimum or base stumpage fee of K20 per metre is added to an appraised logging cost, together with a minimum profit allowance specified as 20 per cent of logging costs. In order to capture a major part of the economic surplus, the sum of the above is subtracted from the free-on-board price. A substantial part (85 per cent) of the difference has to be paid by the company to a representative body appointed by the owners; a 25 per cent forestry withholding tax is paid on the latter. There is also a royalty payment of K10 per cubic metre and a variable project development levy ranging from K2 to K13 per cubic metre, depending on the free-on-board (fob) price of logs. Of the total project development levy, 40 per cent will be paid directly to resource owners and 60 per cent retained in a project development fund. The new system benefits landowners, but the price risk to them and the government has increased. At the same time the pressures on landowners to allow more than the 3 per cent cut of the permit area are likely to lead to a breach of this rule. As prices recover, there will be an increase in new investment and expansion in logging from existing and new investments, making the objective of sustainable logging more difficult to achieve.

More than 95 per cent of the log exports from Papua New Guinea and Solomon Islands are sent to Japan and South Korea. Between 1991 and 1993, export values increased almost fivefold because of a substantial jump in both price and volume. Log exports, from being one-sixth to one-third in value of tree crop exports, had by 1993 reached parity with tree crops in value. Since then, log export volume has stabilized, especially after 1994; and log prices have fallen, because of the recessed conditions in Japan and Korea. As demand recovers in the Asian economies, prices will recover—together with renewed pressure on landowners to allow increased logging by the international companies.

Mining and petroleum

Apart from the mainly NICKEL MINING in New Caledonia, and some gold mining in Fiji (see MINING IN THE PACIFIC ISLANDS), there is limited mining activity outside Papua New Guinea. Since the war, Banaban PHOSPHATE has been exhausted and Nauru phosphate nearly so. The Banabans received little revenue or royalty and had to resettle in 1945 on Rabi, as phosphate and land were exhausted. Though the Nauruan share increased progressively between 1922 and 1964, they received little in the way of royalty until 1964. From 1965–66, under concerted pressure from Nauruan negotiators and the UN Trusteeship Council, the royalty was increased substantially. Australia, New Zealand and Britain benefited most from cheap imports of phosphate. Phosphatic fertilizers were essential to the agricultural productivity of Australia and New Zealand. The International Court in 1993 ruled that compensation for environmental damage be paid to Nauru. The Australian government agreed to pay A$57 million in three installments over 12 months and A$2.5 million per annum for 20 years indexed at 1993 prices in rehabilitation and development.

Exploration and mining revived and expanded greatly in Papua New Guinea from 1964, when commercial quantities of low-grade copper were identified in the Crown Prince mountain range of Bougainville, centred on the tiny pre-war gold-mine of Kupei. After protracted and vexed negotiations over the ownership of sub-surface ores, and appropriate levels of compensation and royalty payments to national and provincial authorities, the Panguna mine was commissioned. Bougainville Copper Ltd (BCL), the operating company, was created by the Australian mining companies Conzinc Riotinto of Australia (CRA), which provided two-thirds of the capital, and New Broken Hill Consolidated (NBHC). CRA in turn was 85 per cent owned by the giant Rio Tinto Zinc Corporation of London. The first copper was exported in 1972. Gold and silver were significant by-products which occasionally yielded greater value than the copper.

Phosphate mining in Nauru

The *Mining (Bougainville Copper Agreement) Ordinance* was negotiated and enacted in 1967. One of its striking features was that the Papua New Guinea government was entitled to purchase 20 per cent of equity at par. The agreement was immediately criticized on two grounds: that the national government should gain more revenue (as opposed to dividends) from an earlier date, and that landowners should receive substantially more compensation and royalty payments. Revision of the agreement was one of the first items addressed by Michael SOMARE's coalition. Re-negotiation in 1974 gained for the government almost all its demands, including a resource rent tax which worked like an additional profits tax. The new provincial government also made some fiscal gains, but the interests of the direct landowners were ignored. The revision provided for reviews every seven years, but these also were neglected.

Opposition to the mine was apparent from the beginning of prospecting in 1964 (see BOUGAINVILLE CONFLICT AND PEACE PROCESS). Various *ad hoc* agreements defused or contained this opposition, but landowners remained dissatisfied with royalty and compensation payments. Their anger was exacerbated by the increasingly evident destruction of large areas of land, for the mine itself and for the disposal of overburden and tailings. There was also profound tension over the distribution of funds among landowners. In 1989, once Francis Ona and the New Panguna Landowners' Association had overthrown the first generation of landowner representatives, they initiated the physical violence which brought the mine to a close in May 1989.

While the national government was renegotiating the Bougainville Agreement, it was also resisting an ultimatum from the American giant Kennecott Corporation, concerning the gold and copper ore in the Star Mountains which later became the Ok Tedi mine. The lease was taken over and brought into production in 1982, by a syndicate which included the Australian company Broken Hill Proprietary (BHP) as the leading component. Ok Tedi, the first Highlands copper mine to come on stream, endured a series of grave disputes with immediate landowners, provincial governments, expatriate employees and national employees. The most serious, however, involved landowners along the FLY RIVER, protesting against massive environmental damage to the river, and therefore to their livelihood. When the Papua New Guinea government blocked their access to the national courts, they took their case against BHP to the Australian court system, creating a major new precedent in international environmental litigation. In 1996 BHP agreed to a very large compensation payment. That, in turn, formed a precedent for Amungme landowners in Irian Jaya to approach the courts in New Orleans with their case for environmental compensation from Freeport mine.

Carstensz Meadow, Irian Jaya, in 1973: main ore body; now the site of (Freeport) copper mine

In each successive royalty and compensation negotiation, the national government has gained less, and direct landowners have gained more. The national government has also withdrawn from areas where mining takes place, and provincial governments have shown little enthusiasm for filling the gap. When landowners demand schools, roads and similar services, therefore, the mining company is pressed to provide them.

This has been the background for the new oilfields developed in the prospecting boom of the 1980s, the Lake Kutubu oil project (1992) in the Southern Highlands, and the Southeast Gobe oil project between the Gulf District and the Southern Highlands. To ensure the safety of the oil pipeline for the Gobe project, the government had to agree to fund a road project for the landowners whose land the pipeline traverses. At Kutubu the local people demanded the construction of a new road in addition to the large airport which the developers needed. These conflicting arguments over the need for expensive but temporary infrastructure and the involvement of local companies have defied easy resolution. The Lihir gold project being managed by Rio Tinto Zinc had to accept 15 per cent of the equity being available to the landowners.

Lihir, a tiny island off the eastern coast of New Ireland, was first explored only in 1982. The enormous potential of its gold resources was recognized, but some of Lihir's coastal deposits are engulfed in boiling water because of the extreme heat of the caldera. On the island of Misima, Placer Niugini began operating the open-pit mine (gold and silver) in 1989. Early progress was brought to a halt in conflict over the development process, and, particularly, over the developers' preference for a rotational workforce. Environmental concerns also remain unresolved, as Lihir and Misima are permitted to continue the direct discharge of tailings into deep water.

At Mt Kare, north of Tari in the Southern Highlands, alluvial gold was discovered during exploration by CRA, launching thousands of prospectors into an unruly scramble (1987–90) for millions of dollars worth of gold. Land disputes, overcrowding, disease, prostitution, gambling, and alcohol abuse all took a heavy toll before CRA was able to enter into a joint venture with several landowners. The company's plans were short-lived, however, collapsing before the local community's demands for roads, schools and hospitals, and the attempts of a number of additional thwarted landowners to lodge time-consuming claims.

The Porgera mine in Enga Province began production in September 1990. By 1996 pollution of the Fly River catchment area had become a major environmental concern. Direct discharge of mining tailings from Porgera into the Strickland River, and from Ok Tedi into the Fly, have not been contained, with the major companies—BHP, Placer Pacific, Goldfields Limited, Highlands Gold—denying allegations of toxicity in the river systems.

In the 1960s, throughout the developing countries, mining companies were fearful of strong post-colonial states which would nationalize profitable mining operations. Conversely, they expected no trouble from small numbers of ill-organized landowners. In Papua New Guinea, therefore, they were caught by surprise when the state proved weak and the landowners have become increasingly militant and astute. The major mining investors are from Australia, including subsidiaries of multinationals based there. The Kutubu oilfield was developed by Chevron Niugini, which then joined up with the PNG petroleum company, Barracuda, to develop the Gobe oilfield. Out of 79 new mining proposals over the 1993–97 period, 49 were from Australian companies. Papua New Guinea has vast, unexploited gas resources, and in petroleum, where potential investors are fewer, the main players are American (notably the giant Exxon Corporation and Du Pont Group). The internal market is small, and mining companies have not yet been drawn towards specific gas projects.

In 1995, mining accounted for more than 70 per cent of Papua New Guinea's exports, and is likely to grow as the Lihir mine assumes production and other mines come on stream. Gold is exported to Australia for refining or for re-exporting. Papua New Guinea is the seventh largest gold producer in the world, and was also, before the closure of the Panguna mine, a significant producer of copper. Copper exports mostly end up in Japan, Germany and South Korea. Oil is taken to refineries around the region.—DG2 & CY

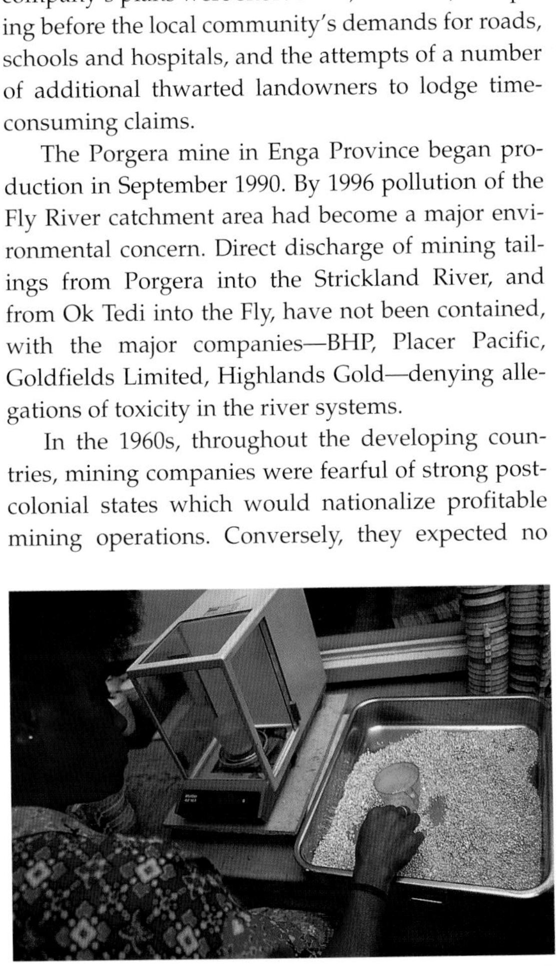

Gold processing, Port Moresby, 1997

Further reading

Denoon, D, Ballard, C, Banks, G and Hancock, P, 1995. *Mining and Mineral Resource Policy Issues in Asia-Pacific*, The Australian National University.

Duncan, R C, 1995. *Melanesian Forestry Sector Study*, International Development Issues No. 36, AIDAB.

Gupta, D, Deklin, T and Yala, C, 1995. *Issues in Mineral Exploitation in Papua New Guinea*, Discussion Paper 85, National Research Institute.

Latukefu, A, 1995. 'Statistical annex', *Pacific Economic Bulletin*, 10(1), July.

Temu, I (ed.), 1997. *Papua New Guinea: a 20/20 vision*, Pacific Policy Paper No. 20, National Centre for Development Studies, The Australian National University.

Waugh, G H, 1993. 'Strategies for development of fisheries', in *PNG Economy: prospects for sectoral development and broad based growth*, IDI 30, AIDAB.

Weeramantry, C, 1992. *Nauru: environmental damage under international trusteeship*, Oxford University Press.

Mining in the Pacific islands

Before the colonial era brought a new scale of mineral exploitation, mining activity was confined to the quarrying of stone for axes or building blocks, and the excavations of Palau by Yap Islanders (see YAP 'TRADE EMPIRE' AND STONE MONEY) from about the 17th century. By the end of the 19th century, the prospect of PHOSPHATE mining had drawn British and Australian companies to Micronesia, and then, more successfully, to Ocean Island (now Banaba) and Nauru. Phosphates were also mined on Makatea, in French Polynesia, from 1908. The only significant mineral resource in French Polynesia, the deposits were exhausted in 1966, and the mine closed. Many small uninhabited islands were mined, but elsewhere islanders were simply deprived of their land, and not involved in the production process.

The discovery of gold in the islands emerged as an extension of gold prospecting in Australia, and in its early days involved only alluvial mining. In New Caledonia, gold was found on the Diahot River in 1870, before NICKEL MINING became a major industry in 1874 and copper became more significant. Up until the 1950s there was also coal mining at Dumbea, Moindou and Goro (mainly small-scale), cobalt mining at Tiebaghi, and some phosphate mining on Walpole Island. Papua New Guinea in the 1870s first attracted small-scale gold prospectors, although later mining became the business of major investors (NATURAL RESOURCES AND INTERNATIONAL DEVELOPMENT). Small alluvial gold deposits were found in the islands off the southeastern coast (Misima and Woodlark islands) and at isolated mainland locations. There was a short-lived gold rush in 1878 which brought white miners into the hinterland of Port Moresby; and in 1888, a discovery on Sudest Island of Milne Bay. Further discoveries occurred on the southeastern mainland, but then the first development of the Bulolo River region of Morobe Province began in 1926. This was soon recognized as the richest alluvial goldfields of the country. Air transport was introduced between Salamaua and Wau, large companies eventually replaced the individual prospectors, and substantial goldmining communities became established at Wau and Bulolo. Gold became Papua's main export, and Lae, briefly, was the busiest airport in the world.

In Fiji, there was some gold found in the Tavua district on Vanua Levu, and two more major deposits in Colo Province of Viti Levu, which began production in 1935 when the Depression had helped to raise gold prices. The rights of Fijian landowners were bypassed. Australian investors set up Fijian companies to secure mining rights, and by 1938 the mines produced more than a quarter of Fiji's exports. During World War II, gold was more valuable than the SUGAR INDUSTRY. The latest phase of mining in Fiji has involved Placer Pacific, the developer of Porgera and Misima mines in Papua New Guinea, in the huge Namosi copper mine, 35 km from Suva, where exploratory drilling began in 1992.

In Solomon Islands, gold was found in the upper reaches of Kichia Creek in the early 1990s, and the first gold mine, Gold Ridge, was officially opened in September 1998. There had been individual prospecting in this area of central Guadalcanal for some years, and the government had to overcome legal challenges from conflicting landowner disputes before the Australian company, Ross Mining, was able to proceed. Environmental concerns have been given attention, and it is the first mine in Melanesia to contain all tailings and waste on site. There is an area of nickel and cobalt that has been identified in the Isabel Islands, and also bauxite deposits on Rennel Island.

The physical challenges of the inhospitable and remote terrain of many parts of Melanesia, where infrastructure is absent, can be overcome when global prices support further exploration. In Papua New Guinea, the relatively inaccessible Porgera mine in Enga Province is 2300 m above sea level, with annual rainfall of 3600 mm. Many of the new deposits of gold, oil, natural gas, copper and other minerals—including platinum—which have been located in commercial quantities, have been epithermal mines, closely associated with hot springs and ancient volcanic activity at the mobile junction of the Australian and Pacific geological plates.

The development of mining often brings huge disruption to specific localities. Although resource development generates revenue, it requires massive capital and sophisticated technologies. Instead of providing economic self-sufficiency for new nations, mining enterprises have been largely foreign-owned and operated, and attempts to achieve local participation have been unsuccessful.

Negotiations between mining conglomerates and independent island governments have had to enter new territory, and particularly to reconsider earlier attitudes to land rights and royalties. In both Irian Jaya and Bougainville, the original mining agreements involved only the companies and the respective governments. Subsequent events, including armed resistance—notably the actions of the guerrilla organization, ORGANISASI PAPUA MERDEKA (OPM, Free Papua Movement), at the Freeport mine at Ertsberg, and the closure of the Panguna mine in 1989 (BOUGAINVILLE CONFLICT AND THE PEACE PROCESS)—as well as growing local and international environmental concerns, are dictating new approaches.—KRF

Further reading

Emberson-Bain, 'A, 1994. *Labour and Gold in Fiji*, Cambridge University Press.

Henningham, S and May, R J (eds), 1992. *Resources, Development and Politics in the Pacific Islands*, Crawford House Press.

Howard, M C, 1991. *Mining, Politics and Development in the South Pacific*, Westview Press.

Nelson, H, 1976. *Black, White and Gold: mining in Papua New Guinea 1878–1930*, Australian National University Press.

Williams, M and Macdonald, B, 1985. *The Phosphateers*, Melbourne University Press.

■ *Nickel mining* New Caledonia's substantial mineral resources include one-quarter of the world's nickel resources, as well as chromium, cobalt, iron, manganese, gold, silver, lead, and mercury. When steel manufacturing raised the value of nickel, chromium, cobalt and manganese, the ore-bearing mountains provided the basis for a thriving mining industry. The presence of rich deposits of nickel had been first confirmed in the 1860s by Jules Garnier, a mining engineer, and exploitation began in the 1870s. By the 1890s the French colony had become the world's largest producer of cobalt, nickel and chromium. Up to 1939, the nickel sold to France and Belgium, and the chromium sold to the United States, France and Australia remained the economic mainstay of the island. Japan and Germany also took large quantities of crude nickel ore, and from the 1930s up until the start of World War II, iron-ore was mined by Japanese and shipped direct to Japan.

Early mining in New Caledonia used cheap Asian labour—5000 Tonkinese and many of the 9000 Javanese who lived in the colony—working at isolated locations with the most rudimentary facilities. Mostly on short-term contracts (3–5 years), they were housed in primitive work camps and paid minimal wages. The nickel mines have been labour-intensive, usually involving digging out the mountains with bulldozers, and conveying the ore to the coast by road. New immigrants have continued to take most of the jobs created in the expanding mining sector, especially Polynesians from Wallis and Futuna, and French Polynesia.

Because New Caledonian nickel is low grade, it has to be delivered to NOUMEA for refining and export. Several smaller companies, owned by local French businessmen, operate mines, but most have remained in the hands of overseas interests. The Société le Nickel (SLN, formed in 1880 through the merger of companies established by Jules Garnier and John HIGGINSON) controlled the only refinery and the largest mines. It was the target of Kanak protest activity in the 1980s (see NATIONALISM IN FRENCH TERRITORIES) but probably more because of environmental concerns than because the company's considerable profits left the colony. In 1990 Jacques LAFLEUR sold his family company in the north of New Caledonia, the *Société Minière du Sud Pacifique*, to the Kanak-controlled government of the northern province.—KRF

Further reading

Connell, J, 1987. *New Caledonia or Kanaky? The political history of a French colony*, Pacific Research Monograph 16, National Centre for Development Studies, The Australian National University.

Henningham, Stephen, 1992. 'Nickel and politics in New Caledonia', in S Henningham and R J May (eds), *Resources, Development and Politics in the Pacific Islands*, Crawford House Press.

Logging in Solomon Islands

Logging companies in Solomon Islands have been able to operate with little scrutiny and almost no restraints, while state capacity to control dismal environmental practices has decreased over the last two decades. The serious problems of national-level timber management are a result of political instability, inadequate technical and financial resources, conflicting loyalties of state members, legal constraints on state actions, and direct corporate bribes and pressure.

Forests cover about 85 per cent of Solomon Islands, mostly on steep slopes and small islands, but commercial logging is only appropriate or viable on about 480 000 hectares. Customary landowners control around 87 per cent of the total land area. In the mid 1990s, about 80 per cent of logging occurred on customary land. The *1969 Forest and Timber Act*—amended several times and renamed the *Forest Resources and Timber Utilization Act* in 1984—is the core of national forest legislation, but actual rules for timber management can be obscure. Forest management is the responsibility of the Ministry of Forests, Environment and Conservation. The Ministry of Finance issues log export licences and grants export tax exemptions. The Foreign Investment Board approves applications and sets minimum financial, employment and infrastructure development criteria for foreign investors. The division of Inland Revenue is responsible for collecting taxes.

However, there are insufficient financial and technical resources for monitoring multinational timber investors, and for effective supervision of logging sites and timber exports. Inland Revenue

Logging in Solomon Islands

has limited powers to prevent corporate tax evasion schemes. Serious flaws also exist with government policies to capture timber rents. Fees imposed on foreign loggers—log export taxes, royalties to landowners, provincial forest charges and corporate taxes on royalty payments and profits—are inconsistent, or can be avoided by tax breaks for 'reforestation programs' and 'community development', and by partial or full tax exemptions. (One such exemption was allowed for Somma, a landowner company linked to Solomon MAMALONI, prime minister for most of the post 1978 independence period.)

Multinational companies have dominated logging in Solomon Islands. At first (1963–81), three foreign loggers controlled the industry: Levers Pacific Timber, a subsidiary of United Africa Company; Allardyce Lumber Company of Australia; and the American-funded Kalena Lumber Company. Levers Pacific Timber was the largest, accounting for two-thirds to three-quarters of total logging. Although environmental rules and management were limited, annual log production was below theoretical sustainable levels, averaging around 260 000 cubic m. This changed in the early 1980s. Under the first Mamaloni government (1980–84), the number of licences quadrupled and foreign firms moved into Guadalcanal, Malaita and Makira-Ulawa. Annual log production escalated, exceeding sustainable levels between 1981 and 1986. The increase in licences and log production, the move to customary land, and the spread to more islands stretched state capacity to monitor and regulate foreign timber investors. At the end of the 1980s, Levers Pacific Timber's departure provided temporary relief, and aggregate production again fell below a sustainable level. From 1991, however, an influx of Malaysian investors brought a proliferation of logging licences, often with highly favourable investment terms. State officials succumbed to corporate pressures and bribes, stalling environmental reforms, eroding implementation of forest management rules, and leading to generous tax breaks. In 1995 log production from natural forests was 826 000 cubic m, more than double that of 1991. At this rate, commercial forests will be depleted in 13 years—or if the rate continues to increase, in less than a decade.

The state's limited legal powers to manage commercial forests—in particular to regulate foreign investment and approve logging licences—have had little impact on aggressive investors. The application process involves approvals from provincial governments and area councils (the latter including landowners) before a series of negotiations leading to a Standard Logging Agreement. In theory, the Forestry Division is supposed to monitor negotiations, ensuring that proper procedures are followed, that legal appeals are settled, and that the final logging agreement and the area council certificate are consistent, but in practice effective monitoring fails. Far too many logging licences have been approved for foreign investors, sometimes even before formal agreements with landowners. Although unlikely, if all of these licences became active, loggers could harvest 4 million cubic m a year, depleting commercial timber in only three years.

The inadequacies of the system—exploited by highly trained corporate negotiators—have generally allowed multinational timber companies to benefit. For example, the Standard Logging Agreement and the Forest Act recommend a royalty rate of 17.5 per cent of free-on-board (fob) value; yet the average royalty rate in 1994 was only 11.5 per cent of fob value. Moreover, timber investors have distorted or broken many agreements with landowners. They have largely ignored environmental rules outlined in Standard Logging Agreements, setting aside promises to provide 'lasting development' such as roads, bridges, medical clinics, or schools. Often considerable damage is left behind. Companies log areas outside their licence; damage or cut undersized and protected trees; build temporary and inappropriate roads and bridges; leave pools of stagnant water that spread malaria, pollute and disrupt food and water sources; disregard reforestation duties; violate sacred sites; and ignore obligations to consult landowners. Some corporate groups, such as Malaysia's Kumpulan Emas, have little logging experience. Others, especially from Sarawak Malaysia, have terrible records at home. A logging site operated by Malaysia's Silvania has been condemned as the most extensive degree of canopy removal and soil disturbance in any logging operation in tropical rainforest in any country.

Prime Minister Billy Hilly's government (1993–94) initiated reforms and increased efforts to verify log export prices, grades and species. It embarked on new national forest legislation, proposed banning log exports in 1997, and investigated foreign assistance to strengthen surveillance and compliance. These moves were quickly thwarted. Since October 1994, when Billy Hilly's government fell, environmental protection and control over foreign investors has further weakened. Mamaloni's third government (1994–97) lowered log export taxes, postponed the log export ban until at least 1999, removed foreign advisers, abolished moves to strengthen logging surveillance, and agreed to cancel four forestry aid projects including one created in 1993 to monitor log grades, species, volumes and prices.

Foreign loggers have pressured and bribed state officials to provide generous tax breaks. The *Solomon Star* reported that from 1993 to 1995 Integrated Forest Industries distributed SI$7 million and supplied generous perks to government ministers and powerful bureaucrats—and in 1995 the company paid no taxes. According to the 1995 *Forestry Review*, tax breaks combined with lower international prices produced a drop in government revenue from log export taxes to SI$12.6 million in 1995, even though log exports jumped by 88 000 cubic m.

Foreign logging companies also evade royalty payments, export taxes, and corporate taxes on profits. They forge species names and log grades, and conceal high-grade logs in low-grade shipments. Schemes to under-record log export prices (by 25 per cent to 30 per cent) may have cost the government up to SI$94 million in 1993. The 1995 *Forestry Review* noted that in a year when Somma realized an average price of SI$458 (from Makira logs which 'are generally smaller and of lower quality to those on other concessions'), the overall average export price from all foreign logging was a mere SI$366. A 1995 report also drew attention to under-pricing of log exports, calculating that the average Japanese import price of Solomon Islands logs in 1994 was US$33.90 per cubic m higher than the declared export price; in Korea, it was US$32 per cubic m higher. Even though log exports account for about half of government export earnings in Solomon Islands, foreign logging companies continue to make windfall profits, while the government captures only a relatively small portion of timber revenues.—PD

■ *Jant wood chipping* In Papua New Guinea there are 36 million hectares of enclosed forest, of which about 15 million hectares of high quality tropical hardwoods are suitable for development. Timber operators currently harvest only around 1.5 million cubic m of the estimated 375–450 million cubic m of available timber. About 85 per cent of the annual harvest is still exported as unprocessed logs. The largest domestic processing operation is the Jant wood chipping facility at Madang (approximately 200 000 cubic m). Jant was established in 1971 as a joint venture between the Papua New Guinea government and Honshu Paper Company of Japan.

After 24 years of operation, both sides revised the original project agreement for the Trans Gogol concession area in Madang Province in 1995, for a term of 15 years. The new deal is based on reforestation and is geared to sustainable forest development to bring more benefits and more jobs to landowners. The company also supplies seedlings for tree farming to the concession landowners. Jant has been plagued over the years by landowners protesting against environmental damage and lack of benefits. The revised agreement involved a complete downstreaming processing operation, combined with nearly 10 000 hectares of plantation for a sustained renewable resource of low-grade timber processed by 1998.—YN

Subsistence and domestic fishing

Subsistence fishing is an important source of protein for most island communities. The Food and Agriculture Organization estimates the regional per-capita consumption of fish at about 55 kg per year, compared with about 13 kg for the rest of the world. Islanders in Kiribati, Tokelau, Palau and Tuvalu are among the highest consumers of fish, eating over 100 kg per capita per year. In all the islands except Tonga, subsistence catches far outweigh the commercial harvest, including tuna catches.

Island coastal dwellers (often women, in countries like Fiji and Papua New Guinea) fish regularly for home consumption, selling the surplus locally for cash. In Solomon Islands, over 80 per cent of coastal households fish primarily for domestic consumption; in Vanuatu, it is 35 per cent of rural households, and in Kiribati 99 per cent. In Solomon Islands in 1995, subsistence fishing—amounting to US$7.7 million—was equivalent to about 60 per cent of the value of their canned fish exports. About US$8 million in Fiji's foreign exchange savings is due to subsistence fishing. Subsistence catches equate to about 44 per cent of the retail value of the total artisanal catches in Fiji where, as in Vanuatu, it is about three times the value of local commercial and artisanal catches.

Artisanal fishing in island reefs, estuaries and lagoons is low-capital and labour-intensive, involving the use of mainly gill nets or hand lines, and in some limited cases, traps. In Fiji, Kiribati and Solomon Islands, deep sea demersal fishing is also important. Much of the near-shore catches are for domestic consumption, with the exception of Kiribati where they provide about 65 per cent of fishery exports. In Fiji, Solomon Islands and Marshall Islands, near-shore fisheries, including non-fin fish species such as BÊCHE-DE-MER, pearl oysters and trochus, provide about 10 per cent of the total fish export. These non-fish species have played an important role in the history of the Pacific islands, and today they continue to serve as an important source of income.

Gathering shellfish, Tongatapu, Tonga

■ *Island fisheries* The fisheries sector in the Pacific islands comprises near-shore coastal and off-shore subsectors. The coastal waters are the main source of SUBSISTENCE AND DOMESTIC FISHING, and off-shore catches of PELAGIC FISH are largely for export. During the boom period of the late 1970s, tuna was caught by American, Japanese and Taiwanese fleets, both purse-seiners and pole-and-line vessels, while attempts to establish domestic island fisheries involved pole-and-line fishing. In 1995–96 over 1300 vessels were registered to fish in the region, the overwhelming majority of them from Japan, the United States, China, Taiwan and Korea. Of these, only 400 were actually based in the Pacific, and only 15 carried any Pacific island flag. However, offshore fishing—primarily tuna—is now an important source of government revenue, employment and improved household income, while export earnings from tuna are also important for many Pacific islands. Direct employment on tuna vessels and in the processing plants has grown steadily, with mostly women engaged in processing. The handful of tuna canneries in the Pacific alone employ 4 per cent of all women in the formal workforce. By 1993, direct and indirect employment in domestic fishing represented about 8 per cent of all wage-earners in Solomon Islands, the probable level of participation in offshore fisheries for all Pacific islanders in the region.

The Pacific region is the most important source of tuna in the world, contributing more than a third of the world's total sold as fresh or frozen or canned product. Income from the offshore fishery plays a vital role in the region's economy. The value of tuna catches in the mid 1990s represented about 10 per cent of the combined gross domestic product of all nations, or one-third of all exports from the region.

Much of the fisheries management in the Pacific is carried out by the relevant fisheries departments under their various fishery legislation, with some assistance for inshore and pelagic fisheries from the former South Pacific Commission (PACIFIC COMMUNITY) and for their tuna resources from the Forum Fisheries Agency (FFA). Commercial catches of key fish species are managed by restricting either the size of fish caught and marketed, or the type of fishing gear, or by imposing closed seasons—strategies most suited to single-species fishing, but not necessarily to the multi-species fishing conducted in lagoons, reefs and estuaries. In the absence of adequate management, much of the sedentary fishing for export markets has shown a 'boom–bust' cyclic phenomena. A good example of this can be seen with the BÊCHE-DE-MER exports from the Pacific.

The biggest constraint to effective management of multi-species coastal fishing is the absence of an appropriate management framework and a lack of adequate technical and socioeconomic strategy to underpin fisheries development. Poor enforcement capacity is also a problem in the islands. Management strategies have often also neglected the traditional resource ownership patterns and collaborative management regimes. In some areas, such as in Samoa, this is changing and collaborative fisheries

Fishing boats at Commercial Harbor, Pohnpei, with international airport at rear

management regimes incorporating the traditional resource custodians are gradually being developed.

The management of offshore fishing is the responsibility of individual countries. However, FFA provides management and logistical assistance in relation to licensing, management controls and surveillance in the region. Tuna fishing in the central and western Pacific is managed under various agreements, including the Nauru Agreement, Niue Treaty, and the Palau Agreement. Even though the region is not considered to be biologically over-exploited, active measures are necessary to effect greater compliance, and to obtain better reporting of catches and by-catch discards so that Pacific nations will achieve better returns for their fishery industry and prevent over-exploitation.—PL

Further reading

Waugh, G, 1992. 'The politics and economics of fisheries in the South Pacific' in S Henningham and RJ May (eds), *Resources, Development and Politics in the Pacific Islands*, Crawford House Press.

■ *Multilateral Treaty on Fisheries* The Multilateral Treaty on Fisheries with the United States of America in 1987 successfully ended an extended and serious dispute with the membership of the Forum Fisheries Agency (FFA) over the regional control of the region's resources of highly migratory fish. Under its 1976 *Magnusson Act*, the United States could not accept coastal state jurisdiction over tuna and this engendered violations of the extended maritime zones of Papua New Guinea and Solomon Islands. Papua New Guinea seized the US vessel *Danica* in 1982, and Solomon Islands seized the US purse-seiner *Jeanette Diana* in June 1984. The latter incident provoked counter sanctions by the United States and was only resolved by the negotiation of a five-year multilateral access agreement between the FFA members and the United States. This agreement provided a regional approach consistent with the Magnusson Act. A 10-year, US$180 million extension of the treaty was secured in May 1992. (See also INTERNATIONAL LAW AND THE PACIFIC OCEAN, and REGIONAL COOPERATION AND INITIATIVES.)—RAH

■ *Solomon Taiyo Limited* Fishing makes a major contribution to the economy of Solomon Islands, both on a commercial and non-commercial basis. Fishing as part of the daily way of life in the coastal villages has always contributed to the nation's subsistence economy. Commercial fishing made little economic input until the establishment of Solomon Taiyo Limited (STL) in 1973—a joint venture between the Solomon Islands government and Taiyo Fishery Company (now Maruha Corporation) of Japan.

The venture allows Solomon Islands access to Maruha's fishing and marketing expertise, while the industry provides a major source of wealth for Solomon Islands, creating employment (STL is the second largest employer after government) and export earnings. Maruha gains access to the tuna fish resource of the Solomons' exclusive economic zone (1.3 million sq km), providing a further source of fish for its growing markets and a base for rapid processing of tuna, close to the fishing grounds.

The operations of STL are managed and administered from the company's head office in HONIARA on Guadalcanal. Tuna processing has been consolidated with the development of a large modern cannery at Noro, on the island of New Georgia, Western Province.—YN

Sustainable development

The Pacific islands are characterized by small land masses dispersed over vast tracts of water, considerable ecosystem and species diversity, an extraordinary level of endemicity, and a high degree of economic and cultural dependence on the natural environment. They are thus highly vulnerable to natural and human-induced disturbances to their local and global environments.

Many Pacific islands face rapidly growing populations with changing needs, wants and aspirations, and an increasing rate of urbanization. Until recent times, agriculture and fisheries provided the main source of food and income for most people. In smaller states, FOREIGN AID and, particularly in Polynesia, remittances from islanders abroad form an important part of the economy. In the larger economies of Fiji, Papua New Guinea and Vanuatu, the industrial and manufacturing sector is becoming important as a major source of income. Nonetheless, the scope for greater reliance on the manufacturing and industrial sector is small because of the islands' remoteness from large trade and investment centres in Australasia and the limits imposed by the size of domestic markets.

Most Pacific islands have little choice but to rely on economic growth based on natural resources exploitation. AGRICULTURE, forest and fisheries have been and will remain the main economic activity of the Pacific, and often the main source of export earnings. Encouraging economic growth and development to meet the needs of the current generation without jeopardizing the ability of future generations to meet theirs, is a challenge facing island nations.

Subsistence and monetary economies exist side by side, across the Pacific. Amongst the major export earners are SUGAR, COFFEE, COCOA and PALM

Intercropping in Tonga

OIL. COPRA AND COCONUT OIL are also important in some parts, along with the export of taro and other cash crops. The subsistence economy is expected to remain an important source of livelihood, although the monetary economy is becoming important as well. Agriculture and fisheries generally, and forestry in Papua New Guinea, Solomon Islands, Vanuatu and Fiji will continue to provide the backbone of the monetary and subsistence economy. In this context, the environmental issues facing the Pacific nations become important. Degradation of land and coastal marine resources, deforestation and loss of biodiversity, the disposal of solid and liquid wastes, localized industrial pollution—these are high on the list of local issues in many places. At the global level the biggest source of concern is climate change and the rise in sea level.

Sources and causes of land degradation vary. In rural areas, where more than 80 per cent of the region's 5.8 million people live, loss of soil fertility is a major concern. This is particularly so in those regions where population growth is rapid (parts of Papua New Guinea) and where institutional rigidities constrain the availability of arable land for agriculture. Increasing reliance on cash economy coupled with population pressure and constraints imposed by the traditional indigenous land tenure system (Fiji and Samoa) encourage agricultural incursion into marginal land. Much marginal land is on steep slopes and thus highly susceptible to soil erosion. Commercial farming for sugarcane in Fiji has gradually moved into marginal and erodable lands. Eroded soils have been washed down rivers into the coastal areas smothering coral reefs and causing an apparent decline in fisheries catches. In Papua New Guinea and Solomon Islands, the small area of land cleared for agriculture is intensively used. Such intensive cropping is likely to result in loss of soil fertility as fallow periods are reduced with increasing population pressure.

Deforestation is a growing problem. Commercial logging in excess of sustainable yields, agricultural plantation development and expansion and swidden agriculture are the main causes of forest loss, the extent of which is difficult to determine because of the paucity of spatial or temporal data. Clearing of forest for agricultural development and logging to fund the construction of roads, bridges, schools and medical centres are justifiable. But in many instances, timber licences issued and logging contracts signed are excessive. Incomplete information about the extent of timber resources hampers landowners from negotiating a fair price for their timber. The problem is exacerbated by the influx of foreign logging companies and malpractice by the logging contractors. In some cases, competing demand for land for other uses, including urban and agricultural developments, has been a main cause of deforestation, particularly of wetlands. In Fiji, where there is an artificial shortage of land because of the customary land tenure system, large areas of mangroves have been reclaimed to 'create' land for other uses.

The islands are renowned for their natural beauty, and high levels of terrestrial and marine species diversity and endemism. Species diversity and endemism is the highest in Papua New Guinea and decreases eastwards. Endemic species are threatened by deforestation and the loss of major habitats. About 75 per cent of the mammal and bird species that have become extinct in recent times were island dwellers. With increased deforestation, the risk of losing potentially valuable endemic species is high. Poorly managed logging and soil erosion from agricultural developments on logged lands can have major impacts on the adjacent coastal coral reef systems and coastal fisheries productivity.

Island states manage their forestry resources under their respective Forestry Acts which vary in strength. At a minimum, forestry logging is controlled using licences with concessionaires paying royalty to the government, which can also raise revenue through company licences. None of the licence fees or taxes have levies totally hypothecated for reforestation purposes. Logging planning procedures can be found only in Fiji and Vanuatu. In countries such as Papua New Guinea, although a revised code of logging practice has been introduced, a broader view of the forest resource management is yet to develop. Only Fiji has attempted to develop forest management plans. Despite the fact that much of the forest resources in the Pacific is in private (communal or individual) ownership, landowners are not—except in Vanuatu—involved interactively in planning for the use and management of resources.

Some countries have used resources provided by the World Bank under its global environment facility to declare areas for biodiversity conservation. In the Pacific, this effort has been coordinated by the South Pacific Biodiversity Conservation Area project. Some 13 countries have declared 16 conservation areas under this scheme. However, many of these do not reflect the multiple uses which communities have made of these areas, and which has led in some countries to the gradual erosion of preservation areas. Systematic planning for the use and management of forest resources, including identifying areas for logging, multiple uses and biodiversity reserves, is almost non-existent, although Vanuatu, Solomon Islands, Papua New Guinea and Samoa have begun to develop detailed resource assessments.

The western Pacific has the world's highest marine diversity, with up to 3000 species being found on a single reef. The thousands of islands in the Pacific Ocean are surrounded by a rich and complex ecosystem including fringing and barrier reefs, mangroves and estuarine lagoons, and seagrass beds. The productivity of coastal waters has been reduced over time by a host of factors, including over-fishing and the use of explosives; toxic wastes; sedimentation from deforestation, agriculture and beach mining; lagoon dredging; mangrove damage or swamp reclamation for garbage dumps; and unsustainable logging of mangroves for poles and firewood.

Most island states have implemented fisheries management under their fisheries legislation, although it tends to focus on commercial fisheries. Coastal fishing has largely been managed through regulatory means. Social or economic aspects of management of the coastal fisheries for subsistence purposes have often been ignored. Nor have traditional fishing rights been explicitly considered in designing fisheries management strategies, leaving local communities with substantially depleted coastal resources.

Economic sustainability of natural resources has not been given much priority except where foreign access fees are involved. Many Pacific islands rely on tuna fishing fees for much-needed foreign exchange. With the help of the PACIFIC COMMUNITY (formerly the South Pacific Commission) and the Forum Fisheries Agency, island nations have adopted a regional management approach in regulating international fishing efforts in the Pacific, surveillance of fishing and monitoring of tuna stocks.

With rapid urbanization and changing lifestyles caused by increasing consumption of processed foods—causing a rapid rise in demand for imported canned, plastic-wrapped or bottled goods—the disposal of solid wastes is becoming a problem. Because of limited availability of suitable disposal sites around many urban centres, mangrove wetlands and coastal beaches are being used for the disposal of domestic and urban solid wastes. The environmental consequences of waste disposal in coastal areas are serious, particularly as the local reefs, lagoons and inshore waters are vulnerable to pollution. Point source pollution from industrial wastes, sewage, and disposal of toxic chemicals are also significant contributors to coastal pollution and degradation. In smaller atolls, pollution of groundwater, the main source of freshwater other than rain, is of particular concern. In Tokelau, the only freshwater sources, rain and the groundwater lens below the surface, are believed to be contaminated.

Recognizing the potential gravity of the problem, many islands have identified the national priorities for waste management and pollution prevention in their national environmental management strategies (NEMS). A regional waste minimization and management and pollution-prevention program has been compiled by the South Pacific Regional Environment Programme (SPREP) and agreed to by member countries. Much will depend on the implementation of these resolutions.

Samoa and the Federated States of Micronesia already use environmental regulations covering waste management. Some countries use financial incentives to encourage recycling to reduce solid wastes. Papua New Guinea and Samoa, for example, use a deposit/refund system for aluminium cans. For human wastes, new technologies such as biological toilets are being trialled in the Federated States of Micronesia, Kiribati and Palau with the assistance of Australia, New Zealand and Canada and international and regional organizations.

Sustainable development is a viable option in the Pacific provided that a balance is maintained between economic growth and the integrity of the natural ecosystems. Such a balance is particularly critical to those islands that do not have the resource alternatives to underpin continued economic growth to provide the necessary incomes to meet the needs of growing populations and service their external debts. Controls on absolute population levels will be an important precondition for success. Sustainable development goals will be achieved only if resource allocation and management decisions involve both the users and the government adopting a multi-disciplinary analytical framework. This would require, among other things, the devel-

Repairing a sea-wall, Betio Island, Kiribati

opment of national policies, strategies and plans reflecting explicit considerations of economic, social and environmental goals and strengthening national capacities in integrated decision-making. Because of the geographical proximity of the inland areas to the coastal regions, limited resource endowments, a reliance on coastal and marine resources for their livelihood and export earnings, sustainable development is vital for their long-term existence.—PL

■ *Environmental concerns in Cook Islands* Major environmental impacts on the islands of the Cook group can be divided into natural and anthropogenic. Among the natural events, CYCLONES and DROUGHT have had impacts in recent years. Cyclone Sally damaged Rarotonga extensively in January 1987. In November 1997, Manihiki was devastated by Cyclone Martin, destroying about 90 per cent of the houses and killing nine people with a further 10 missing. Since 1996, the southern Cook Islands have experienced severe drought. Many households have been without water for long periods, and agriculture was severely affected. Although defined as natural, these impacts have also been linked to global warming brought about by emission of industrial (greenhouse) gases, as well as the EL NIÑO event. (See CLIMATE CHANGE.)

The anthropogenic environmental impacts have been diverse. Because of the small landmass—237 sq km spread over 15 islands—human activities on land have had an impact on the lagoon and associated coral reef system. One problem is soil erosion, which results from poor land management. Agriculture and deforestation washes soil into the lagoons smothering coral and freshwater spawning sites, especially on the high islands. On Rarotonga, housing on the inland slopes, with poorly planned land clearing and road construction, sometimes causes extensive soil erosion.

Waste management is a problem common to all Cook Islands, but especially Rarotonga where effluent seeps into the lagoon from household septic tanks, tourist resorts, pig and chicken farms. Poorly planned sewage systems and overflowing septic tanks are the major culprits. In most cases there is no sewage collection from pig pens and chicken sheds, even though pigs outnumber humans on the island. On Rarotonga, most inorganic rubbish is dumped at the already overflowing landfill site. Residents also dump rubbish on the beaches and inland valleys. Apart from an aluminium can-crushing centre on Rarotonga, which exports metal to New Zealand for recycling, there is no recycling scheme in Cook Islands. There have been recent steps by environmental non-government organizations and importers to initiate a kerbside rubbish sorting system to reduce waste going into the landfill, and facilitate recycling of plastics and glass. A stockpile of hazardous agricultural chemicals that are no longer used is a threat to the environment. A safe method of disposal is required.

Over-harvesting of certain marine species including tridacnid clams, reef fish, and coconut crabs also contributes to environmental problems. Beach mining (for the construction industry, which requires sand, coral and gravel aggregates) contributes to coastal erosion. The *Environment Act (1994–95)* prohibits this practice on Rarotonga, but infringements occasionally occur. Reclamation of land for construction and inappropriate sea-walls are another major problem, especially on Rarotonga and Aitutaki.

With the economic crisis and the effect on the Environment Service of wider public service contraction, it has become imperative that communities and community organizations participate in solving environmental problems. Intensive and long-term commitment to environmental education and awareness is needed. Recent initiatives by local communities on Rarotonga include the establishment of five marine *ra'ui* (periodic closure) sites around the island to allow marine resources two years to recover, and the establishment of the inland Takitumu Conservation Area by the landowners. On the outer islands the Takutea wildlife sanctuary was established by the people of Atiu several years ago, and some northern group islands continue with their traditional *ra'ui* practices, especially for land areas.—AT3

FOUR TRANSPORT

Shipping

Pacific island countries depend on maritime transport. This links them with overseas sources of manufactured goods and markets for island products, it provides connections between many of the states, and it is the essential transport mode for economic, social and political integration within each country. Common features of maritime trade in the Pacific include the great distances involved, the relatively small quantities of cargo loaded and unloaded (no more than 1 per cent of world seaborne trade), imbalances in exports and imports involving empty haulage, and long chains of collection and delivery requiring intermediate handling, storage and transshipment.

Regular schedules and patterns of trade are dictated mainly by the delivery of manufactured goods, foodstuffs and fuel; there is less regularity in exports. The trade patterns can be best outlined under the three broad but overlapping categories of shipping carrying out these functions, namely deep sea transport, regional shipping, and domestic intra-insular shipping.

The deep sea transport sector includes very large and technically advanced container ships moving unitized cargo between the Pacific Rim countries in North America and Asia. These have coordinated schedules and operate a 'hub and spoke' pattern calling at a very few hub ports from which relatively smaller but equally sophisticated vessels radiate to a series of other large ports. This activity has virtually no impact on the Pacific islands—other than some calls at Hawai'i.

There are intermediate size deep sea container vessels which call regularly at several main ports in Papua New Guinea, and at Noumea, Suva, Guam, and ports in French Polynesia, from Australia, North America and Europe. They unload about 3 000 000 tons of containerized general cargo at these island main ports, and load some 1 000 000 tons of return cargoes (fresh produce, fruit juice, fish, cocoa, coffee, palm oil, garments and other small manufactured items). In addition, deep sea bulk carriers load sugar in Fiji, and minerals at terminals in Papua New Guinea, New Caledonia and Solomon Islands, while logs and timber products are loaded in Solomon Islands and several of the other high Melanesian islands. A tanker trade with crude oil, and in the future natural gas exports, has been developing from Papua New Guinea.

Unloading ship, Hakahau, French Polynesia

In regional shipping, a number of unitized (container and roll-on roll-off—often known as 'RoRo') vessels which do not need port container crane facilities are engaged in trunkline services from Australia, New Zealand and United States ports specifically to a wide range of Pacific island main and intermediate ports. Their schedules are changed from time to time but typical itineraries for the PACIFIC FORUM LINE (PFL) are round trips from (i) Auckland–Lautoka–Suva–Apia–Pago Pago–Nuku'-

alofa; (ii) New Zealand (three ports)–Brisbane–Port Moresby–Lae–Honiara; (iii) Sydney–Brisbane–Lautoka–Apia–Pago Pago–Nuku'alofa (with transshipment to Rarotonga); and (iv) Suva–Funafuti–Tarawa–Majuro.

Two other lines have operated over several years from New Zealand to all main Pacific ports, with special services to the Cook Islands and Niue and two regional lines run from Australia to Papua New Guinea. There have also been services direct from Hawai'i to Samoa (East and West), Tonga and the Cook Islands. Cargo liners call on a regular basis from Japan and Southeast Asia to Papua New Guinea and Fiji, and there are regular vessels from American west coast ports to the Trust Territories of Micronesia. There are few backloads for these vessels and little intra-regional trade based on island products. The exception in the latter case is Fiji, where items such as locally produced beer, cigarettes and soap are traded to other territories.

Neiafu, Vava'u, Tonga

The main pivotal ports of the Pacific islands are well served by deep sea liner shipping from overseas. The most difficult places to service reliably and economically on a regional basis are the small ports in the several island states made up of the atolls and chains of Micronesia and Polynesian coral islands. In Kiribati, for example, there are about 70 000 people of whom 40 per cent live in the area of Tarawa atoll and the others on 30 or so atolls and reef islands, many of which are at great distances from Tarawa.

A PFL vessel has carried out a service to Tarawa on a six-weekly basis. It has provided this regional link with transshipment of deep sea cargoes from Suva, and calls at Funafuti in Tuvalu, then Tarawa and periodically to Jaluit in the Marshall Islands. This service has involved a one-way distance of about 2900 km. There is little backload of cargoes and the service requires subsidization, which has usually been met by payments from Australia and New Zealand.

Container ship and gantry at Apra Harbor, Guam

The intra-domestic shipping services have even more problems. Many small vessels link the ports which receive direct cargoes from overseas, and by transshipment, with the villages in the outer islands. Distances range from 80–1100 km. The closer, bigger and more productive islands have jetties and landing places for RoRo (roll-on roll-off) vessels and barges. They receive regular services and as they usually have roads there is produce collection and onward truck movement of imports. By contrast, small island villages are visited irregularly and work boats carry cargo to and from a domestic vessel anchored in the lagoon or lying in deep water beyond the outer reefs.

Domestic shipping is characterized by delivering small quantities of a large range of vital goods to outer islands and receiving minimal backloads mainly of COPRA. Passenger carriage is also very important in the domestic trades. Some of this has been eroded by air services, but the domestic vessels are favoured with their lower fares, and the ability of passengers to carry with them large quantities of baggage, goods and live animals such as pigs and fowls as they travel between their distant small island villages and the main port towns. These services are vital also for secondary school children who need to reside at principal towns during term times.

The outer islands generally have small populations (some of them aging) and few products for markets other than copra. The shipping services are often uncertain and even in the nearer islands this constitutes a great disincentive for production and for staying on the island. In many cases distances are very great. In Micronesia, trips of 1600 km may have to be undertaken. Kiribati has the problem of servicing Phoenix Islands over 1600 km from Tarawa, and Christmas Island and the northern Line Islands about 3200 km. In Vanuatu small islands lie at distances of 600 km from Port Vila, and in Solomon Islands, servicing the peripheral islands can involve 800–1100 km voyages.

Costs of transport in Pacific shipping are already high in the deep sea sector before goods are carried onwards by inter-island vessels. The isolation of the region from world markets and the paucity of return liner cargoes are reflected by high levels of freight charges which are added to commodity prices. The world average freight cost measured as a percentage of import (cif) values is 5.27 per cent. The goods carried by ship to main island ports are more than double this world average, being (1995) 12.1 per cent to French Polynesia, Guam and Vanuatu; 13.14 per cent to Fiji; and 16.42 per cent to Solomon Islands. Transport costs could be doubled again by the time transshipments are made from the international hubs to regional feeder ships, and from these to small domestic vessels serving the remote outer islands.

Much of these transport costs for imports are passed on to island communities as higher prices. The return export cargoes, which are fewer and of lower value than the imports, also incur high transport costs, which often have to be deducted from the market price of island products. Islanders thus remain vulnerable to escalating freight rates.

The PFL is the principal shipping corporation in the islands. Several government ships operate within island groups (some donated as FOREIGN AID) and generally there is a mixture of public and private owned vessels. Table 5.2 shows the fleets of vessels above 100 tons registered in the islands. There are in addition to these hundreds of small craft below 100 gross tonnage serving the domestic trades.

Table 5.2 indicates that Vanuatu and Marshall Islands appear as major ship-owning states in world terms, and Tuvalu has a significant tonnage under its flag. These are flag of convenience ships, however, with no genuine link between the ship-owners and the flags the ships fly. Pacific states obtain registration fees and other payments as income for the use of their flags. In the case of Vanuatu and Marshall Islands, the registries are run primarily from New York.

Kiribati Shipping Corporation

There is only a little employment generated from the flag of convenience international trading ships registered in the three island states, but Pacific islanders are employed on domestic vessels and partly on the regional ships operating from Australia and New Zealand to Pacific island ports. As small island states with many people having a strong affinity to the sea, the employment outlet for seafarers should be significant. There are several maritime colleges in the Pacific which facilitate employment, including large establishments at Suva and Lae. Smaller training schools are located in Solomon Islands, Tarawa, Tonga, Funafuti and in the French Pacific. As a result some Pacific islanders have found employment in world shipping, enabling valuable remittances to be made to home islands. The German Columbus Line has many I-Kiribati as seafarers, and islanders serve on South Korean fishing vessels and even on chemical carriers in the North Sea. Pacific islanders have spread internationally as seafarers, but the numbers are well below the potential demand even in the Pacific trades, especially for people who are capable of becoming senior officers.

Table 5.2 Merchant fleets of ships over 100 tons deadweight registered in Pacific island countries, 1996 (in deadweight tons), Marshall Islands (1998) GRT

	Tonnage
Fiji	29 219
Kiribati	7 094
Marshall Islands (GRT)	6 300 000
Samoa	6 501
Solomon Islands	6 775
Tonga	14 555
Tuvalu	84 936
Vanuatu	2 093 163

Sources: United Nations Review of Maritime Transport (1997); International Registries (UK) Ltd London.

Other maritime transport-related employment includes port workers, employment in the ship repair industry, storing in main ports and increasingly in some principal ports the provision of cruise ship services.

It has been recognized for many years that the advances in maritime transport technology which have involved high-cost containerization, economies of scale and centralization at massive terminals have had some adverse impacts by isolating small island communities. At the same time island people have become more dependent on sea transport and trade in their requirements for day-to-day consumer goods, fuels and basic equipment. It has been impossible in highly fragmented Pacific nations to achieve economies of scale and to develop efficient low-cost shipping able to overcome distance and isolation, and be economically viable in the back hauls of small quantities of low-value products from remote islands for onward shipment to world markets. Only in the cargo and passenger services between the main port towns and the nearer bigger islands has it been possible to develop good RoRo and container operations.

Attempts to introduce energy-efficient sail-assisted vessels to island transport, and simpler tug-and-barge systems as low-technology alternatives, have met with limited acceptance and economic success. More efficient small port construction and better operational procedures have also been devised for some islands, as well as improved storage and marketing techniques. However, there are aspects of Pacific geography which will always entail high costs in cargo and passenger transport. But shipping is for island communities what roads are for remote rural people in areas of contiguous land, and road transport infrastructure costs are normally borne by the nation as a whole. This should apply to island shipping, but with so many islands to be supported in this way by the poorer small states, long periods between vessels are bound to remain features of life for the more remote islands.—ADC

Further reading

Couper, A D, 1990. *The Problems of Inter-Island Transport*, UNCTAD/RPD/LCD:32.

—— (ed.), 1992. *The Shipping Revolution*, Conway Maritime Press.

Aviation

In the early 1970s, two basic groups of airlines provided the island nations with international air services. In the first group were the 'pioneering' airlines of the metropolitan nations, Australia (Qantas), New Zealand (Air New Zealand), France (UTA), Canada (Canadian Pacific), and the United States (Pan American and Continental Airlines). In the second group were found the fledgling carriers of the relatively recent independent nations, Fiji (Air Pacific), Western Samoa (Polynesian Airlines), The Republic of Nauru (Air Nauru), Papua New Guinea (Air Niugini). Other island microstates also aspired to acquire their own unique tail-fin logo expressions of independence. These were justified on such grounds as foreign exchange earnings, employment, the transfer of skills, support for Pacific TOURISM developments, and service guarantees made possible by having carriers under the control of island governments rather than by remote foreign businesses.

In recent years, once-revered names such as Pan American have collapsed. Other US carriers like Continental, American, South Pacific Island Airways and Hawaiian have also departed. UTA gave way to Air France and an expanded role for the New Caledonian based Air Calédonie International. Canadian Airlines (formerly Canadian Pacific) have pulled back in favour of interline hub arrangements at Honolulu.

Both Air New Zealand and Qantas continued through the 1980s to use the islands gateway airports of Nadi (Fiji) and Pape'ete (French Polynesia) for some of their trans-Pacific routes. Air New Zealand also made use of the improved infrastructure at Faleolo airport (Samoa) for some of its South Pacific services. However, technological developments have encouraged the overflying of previous way points as end-to-end traffic dominates and dictates route networks. It is no longer necessary to refuel as aircraft have the capacity to fly non-stop between opposite points of the Pacific Rim. Qantas has rationalized further in the late 1990s, preferring to code-share with islands carriers like Air Pacific, in which it holds equity, rather than to deploy its own equipment on island routes.

The first signs that island interests could not rely upon external carriers to provide minimum air services necessary to support their tourist-based economies came with the oil price shocks in the 1970s. Poor yields on 'thin' routes in the Pacific saw some metropolitan carriers look to other parts of their networks to maintain their viability. Some were never to return.

Natural cyclonic disasters have all too often devastated island tourist destinations with consequent problems for recreating images of tranquillity and abundant sunshine. Two military coups in Fiji played a destabilizing role, while the global economic recession saw would-be tourists looking for vacations closer to home to conserve dwindling discretionary dollars. The Pacific islands were vulnerable and in danger of being severely marginalized.

Thus in the 1980s and through into the early 1990s, niche players in the Pacific filled some of the void created by metropolitan airline departures. The risks have been high. Any losses from unsuccessful national airline operations can severely disrupt national budgets given that the cost of buying or even leasing modern jet aircraft can represent the single biggest call on national resources. Most of the islands carriers have passed through very difficult financial circumstances. Without government backing, some would not survive. This has been true for international carriers such as Air Niugini, Air Nauru, Polynesian Airlines and Air Pacific as well as smaller feeder airlines. Without recourse to expatriate management expertise, individual airlines overreached on both schedules and destinations, flying too many empty or promotionally discounted seats. Individual island governments could not continue to support such loss-making dreams.

Early attempts by the island states to compete with the metropolitan airlines in the international aviation business failed. Their governments were unskilled in negotiating favourable bilateral air service agreements. The few likely lucrative sectors were already occupied by carriers with 'grandparent' rights. Metropolitan governments were usually able to confine island carriers to subordinate feeder roles.

Most passengers to the islands came from the Pacific Rim countries or beyond, with relatively small contributions from island nationals. Metropolitan airlines with their mature penetration of national markets could ensure that most travellers flew on their services and used their ticket paper, even if indulging in side trips with island carriers. Accordingly, metropolitan carriers had the benefit of collecting total fares and using the money until settlements through the International Air Transport Authority clearing house mechanisms were due.

In the 1980s governments could not continue supporting their loss-making airlines. They could quit the airline business altogether leaving the skies to foreign airlines. They could compromise their sovereignty and cooperate with neighbouring islands in a single regional airline serving their joint interests. They could rationalize their equipment needs through coordinated leasing of aircraft to ensure nationally identified but internationally integrated services. They could seek foreign equity and with it foreign management expertise to put their individual national airlines into a sound financial position. Invariably they chose the last option (Air Niugini, Air Pacific, Polynesian Airlines). New entrant Air Vanuatu was also launched with an external management contract with Australia-based Ansett International.

What the foreign interests in islands airlines did prove in the 1980s was that innovative management and tight financial controls could sustain viable airlines. Ansett International has come and gone as a management force, having demonstrated whilst active how the aviation interests of various islands could be met through coordinated use of shared equipment. The management ties between Ansett Australia, Air Vanuatu, and Polynesian Airlines saw maximum utilization of Polynesian's B737 'Sina', and later replacement aircraft. For a time, the Ansett factor helped produce perhaps the best ever inter-island east/west sector links that the region has always needed to complement the primary north/south long-haul trans-Pacific sectors. It initiated interlocking services in a way that individual governments found too hard politically.

Island governments saw that the airline business could be made to work. They wanted earlier dividend returns than the foreign investors wished to yield before those investors had themselves extracted their risk capital. Confrontation over contract renewals for Air Vanuatu saw the Ansett International management depart and the tourism industry in Vanuatu falter badly until stable air services were restored. Pacific tourism needs good air services to prosper. A few cruise ship visits helps, but the industry is sustained by international civil aviation services.

Saipan International Airport (Saipan, Northern Marianas), which handled more than 600 000 tourists per year prior to the Asian financial crisis in 1997

Not all the success can be attributed to new management regimes. Concurrently, the mood to liberalize air service agreements was taking hold. Metropolitan governments, once paranoid about how island states might exercise their traffic rights using other than their own 'substantially owned and effectively controlled' equipment, were changing their attitudes. It is now commonplace for international airlines to lease-in much of their aircraft capacity. It is also commonplace to code-share and sell seats on another company's aircraft as if it belonged to the ticket-selling company. Each airline still sells their own 'paper' retaining the advantages that that brings through the IATA clearing system. Inter-airline agreements may see two companies parcel out sectors to each other and code-share rather than compete head-to-head. They also take advantage of interlining with each other at an intervening offshore territory such as in Singapore, or Honolulu. Global alliances are becoming increasingly important in the 1990s.

One factor probably contributing significantly to the success of the foreign-managed island airlines in the 1980s and 1990s was the substantial rise in tourism, accompanied by increases in infrastructure to cater for them. It is continuing, but never fast enough for either tourist operator or airline manager, each of whom seeks capacity in the other before they feel comfortable to invest themselves.

Perhaps more importantly, airport and communications improvements have removed what were

Airport at Atiu, Cook Islands

serious impediments to aviation developments in the 1970s. Runway lengths and strengths allowing full payloads, navigational aids, and airport lighting for night operations have improved markedly. Unlike some metropolitan airports, aircraft noise is not socially unacceptable to island communities reliant upon tourist trade. The disease of airport curfews does not plague island destinations.

Aircraft technology enables the complete overflying of island destinations once vital as 'stepping stones' across the Pacific. That same technological thrust has produced reliable twin-engine aircraft of a size more suited to the needs of island states. No longer are they restricted by the old 90-minute rule, requiring over-water flights in twin-engine aircraft never to be more than 90 minutes from an airport which could receive them in an emergency. B767 'twins' can now fly the long-haul over water routes. This means that an aircraft with a capacity better matched to some South Pacific needs on relatively 'thin-traffic' routes is available.

New air navigation technical capability will allow flight paths to follow great circle routes that take advantage of weather systems rather than having to fly at set altitudes along fixed corridors. The application of satellite-based air navigation systems that act like secondary radar are starting to be deployed in the late 1990s, replacing antiquated radio communications vulnerable to atmospheric conditions. Significant savings in aircraft separations can be achieved safely. Air traffic control can be provided efficiently from a few locations, none of which need be based in the Pacific islands. This prospect alarms some island governments in that they derive significant income from fees paid for passage through their flight information regions. Unless they can broker membership in some joint ventures that will provide the new air navigation services, they will again be the losers.

Island-based carriers in the 1990s have far better access to routes connecting them very directly to their major source markets on the Pacific Rim. By the 1990s it became possible for South Pacific island nations to secure valuable fifth-freedom traffic rights trans-Tasman. For a short period a Cook Islands airline exercised rights from Rarotonga via Auckland to Sydney but that service has ended.

The restrictive bilateral deals of the 1970s and early 1980s that continued to favour non-island-based airlines have largely gone, not without some acrimonious exchanges along the way—seen when Fiji moved to obtain rights to Japan for Air Pacific and told New Zealand that Air New Zealand's flights to Japan using fifth-freedom traffic rights via Fiji were to be curtailed. Air New Zealand could fly directly, and now does.

In 1974 five airlines occupied the Honolulu/Nadi sector. They were Air New Zealand, Canadian Pacific, Qantas, Pan American, and British Airways. In the early 1990s only Air New Zealand for a time remained. United Airlines, which picked up routes from the defunct Pan American, had no interest in the sector. Canadian code-shared with Air New Zealand. Fiji's Air Pacific was reluctant to get burnt a second time on the sector having jeopardized the airline's existence with its attempts to open a route between Nadi, Honolulu and Los Angeles. Air Pacific was more interested in the developing Asian markets, especially Japan.

Given this apparent vacuum, Polynesian Airlines (Samoa) in its post-Ansett management embarked in 1994 on major expansion with two services non-stop to Honolulu and to Los Angeles. It also exercised newly acquired traffic rights south. It could fly direct to Sydney or indirectly via the Kingdom of Tonga and Auckland to Sydney and directly to Auckland. Polynesian Airlines could also extend one of the direct Auckland services to provide a one-stop service to Melbourne. Polynesian Airlines had the requisite airport facilities and leased aircraft to open alternative paths across the Pacific to challenge the traditional gateways of Pape'ete and Nadi. It was a brave attempt. Going it alone without partners in the major source markets for tourists meant the numbers never added up. Samoa could not afford the marketing effort to penetrate these long-haul markets unaided. The outcome was severe financial strain on the Samoan economy and a political scandal. Polynesian Airlines was only turned around financially when it reduced its fleet for international long-haul routes to one aircraft and again called in expatriate management.

A key to any future success strategy for an expanding island carrier in a step up into the long-haul markets will be an ability to form strategic alliances with carriers who can provide feed traffic and who themselves need a partner to provide an attractive trans-Pacific connecting service. Air Pacific has a strong relationship with Qantas involving equipment, management, and code-sharing arrangements. Qantas is part of a much bigger global alliance with British Airways and American Airlines. Such a situation can be expected to assist the small Fijian airline to garner business from the others in the alliance even though it is not itself a member or contributor to frequent-flyer benefits. An international event like the Sydney Olympics in 2000 offers the chance to provide long-haul travellers with some add-on destinations in the Pacific islands.

Cooperation is emerging among the small airlines, as well as between such airlines and larger metropolitan-based carriers. Aircraft are shared between airlines in different countries. Economic realities are over-riding sovereign aspirations. Tonga and Fiji share aircraft used on regional services. Island airlines that share appear to have a better track record financially than those determined to operate independently. There is much saving in pooling spare parts, joint training, and interlocking promotion.

Cooperation has not required the surrender of identity. Aircraft have two sides. They can be painted in the insignia of several cooperating carriers. Often there is insufficient work in one small country to keep a jet aircraft like a B737 fully occupied. By coordinating the schedules in neighbouring countries, the aircraft can be fully utilized. Management control does not have to be centralized. Coordinated schedules, demonstrated by Ansett International's integration of Air Vanuatu, Polynesian Airlines, and Ansett Australia, also facilitate interconnection between neighbouring island nations. The more that happens, the less is the need for travellers to take excessively roundabout routes between adjacent island destinations. It should also help joint marketing of multi-country multi-destination packages, provided tourist wholesalers can be convinced that inter-island scheduled air services are sufficiently frequent and are stable to be marketed with confidence 12 months or more in advance.

Air Pacific has a decided advantage over other Pacific airlines in that its home base, Fiji, is at a strategic crossroads with an already well-developed tourist industry. Fiji can offer a convenient break point for both North American and north Asian visitors to New Zealand and Australia. It has successfully exploited its geographical advantage in the past and doubtless will continue to do so.

Trilander at Bonriki Airport, Kiribati

More liberal air service agreements in the region are opening more opportunities for Pacific island airlines to string together viable route structures which can service their tourist-oriented economies. Regional aviation facilities in the 1990s pose relatively minor technical impediments compared with the 1970s. Pacific island microstates face a changing pattern of metropolitan airline competition with only a few traditional carriers like Air New Zealand remaining firmly entrenched on key South Pacific sectors. Their biggest concern must be the strength of the economies that supply most of their tourist clientele. The Asian economic flu will impact on island tourist destinations and the health of island airlines that serve those distant markets. Strategic alliances will become vital as will cooperation between carriers in the South Pacific. Continuing liberalization of aviation agreements, and increasing political willingness to look for regional as well as national solutions suggest that the aviation outlook is not all bleak, but the temptation to over-reach available resources will likely remain a cyclical feature of national civil aviation in the SOUTH PACIFIC FORUM economies.—CK

Further reading

Findlay, C, Sien, Chia Lin and Singh, K (eds), 1997. *Asia Pacific Air Transport Challenges and Policy Reforms*, Institute of Southeast Asian Studies.

Kissling, C C, 1984. *Transport and Communications for Pacific Microstates: issues in organisation and management*, Institute of Pacific Studies, University of the South Pacific.

Peter Roberts Aviation and Tourism, with Keith Walsh & Associates P/L and Travis Morgan P/L, 1994. *Rationalisation of Air Services in the South Pacific*, AIDAB Report, December.

Flying boats

Flying boats were used in the Pacific region from the 1920s. Parts of Papua were explored by flying boat in 1922, and one was used to carry mail and passengers to Fiji in 1930. In these early days, there were no base facilities, and no radio aids to navigation. Then the Depression stifled this seemingly promising form of Pacific transport until 1937 when Pan American Airways began a San Francisco–Manila flying boat service via Honolulu, Wake Island and Guam. Political problems and two lost 'clippers' delayed a San Francisco–Auckland service until August 1939, but then both these services ceased after the start of the Pacific War.

Though the flying boat had a particularly useful role in the Pacific islands, it was eventually replaced by land-based aircraft on trans-ocean and other international airlines because of its relatively slow speed and costly performance as a flying machine. It had great advantages in space and comfort for passengers, but its requirement for propeller clearance over the water dictated a deep hull which cost power and money to drive through the air. It was also costly to operate because of the complicated, over-developed facilities which often grew up around its bases. So after the Second World War, the structure of international airlines was built upon the foundation of land airports for the highly efficient four-engined transports recently developed and then in service. The flying boat was retired.

The substantial investment in land airports increased steadily throughout the post-war period of piston-engined, propeller-driven aircraft. With the advent of the gas turbine with jet propulsion, and therefore the removal of the propeller, the potential of the flying boat immediately reappeared. Without the need for a deep and aerodynamically inefficient hull, and with the operational water base available without cost, the flying boat conception had very definite advantages, including economy in overall operating costs (including bases), and safety in take-off, approach and landing requirements due to the length of water runways available. However, land airports and their increasingly magnificent terminals had become major prestige symbols of the cities and international centres they served; the return of the flying boat would threaten the huge investment already made. Therefore the flying boat was diverted to specialized military and other services which can be fulfilled only by a water-based aircraft.

From 1951 until 1960, Tasman Empire Airways Ltd (TEAL) of New Zealand ran a monthly Solent flying boat service between Auckland and Tahiti, via Suva, Apia and Aitutaki. Flying boats were used extensively within French Polynesia in the 1950s and 1960s to link Pape'ete with other island groups. Flying boats were also used by Trans Oceanic Airways in Sydney. Mostly these were two-engined Catalina flying boats, used in the war. However, there were also four-engined Sandringham class boats. The British Overseas Airways Corporation (BOAC) had a fleet of flying boats, Sandringham VII, Bermuda class, built for the Baltimore/Bermuda run, to compete alongside Pan American for the wealthy resort traffic. At least one of these was purchased for use on charter cruise trips in the Pacific.—RL & KRF

Further reading

Taylor, G, 1964. *Bird of the Islands: the story of a flying boat in the South Seas*, Cassell Australia.

Passenger liners and cruise ships

The development of a trans-Pacific steamship service was given impetus in the mid-19th century by the discovery of gold in Australia and then New Zealand. Once the provision of comfortable first-class accommodation became established, the stage was set for tourists, and companies such as the Cunard Line and the Peninsular & Oriental Steam Navigation Co (now the P & O Line) trace their present-day luxury cruise trips back to these passenger steamship origins. As early as 1895 sightseers could take round trips from Auckland to Fiji, Tonga and Samoa in the ships of the Union Steam Ship Company. Beatrice Grimshaw publicized such opportunities in her booklet, published anony-

Cruise ship, Yasawa Island, Fiji

mously, *A Cruise in the Islands*, around the turn of the century.

By the early 1920s tourists could enjoy a holiday by cruise ship to almost every island group in the Pacific, and this market—catered to by the Oceanic Steam Ship Co, which later became known as the Matson–Oceanic Line—flourished in the 1930s. After a lull caused by World War II and its shipping losses, Pacific tourism revived strongly from 1956 when the Matson Line began to offer San Francisco–Sydney round trips with calls at the main islands. By the 1970s fast, passenger-only luxury liners were catering to this booming holiday market and it became possible to include spots as remote as Tikopia, Rapa and Easter Island, while converted troopships provided budget-priced tours to the main western Pacific ports.

In the 1990s the cruise market was again undergoing steady expansion. In 1998 the Cunard Line boasted a growth rate of 28 per cent in its Asia–Pacific operations, by paying particular attention to the niche market of luxury tourism. It had a fleet of three major liners, the *Queen Elizabeth II* (built in 1967 and accommodating 1750 passengers), the *Royal Viking* and the *Vistafjord*, as well as two superyachts, *Sea Goddess I* and *II*.—RL2 & KRF

Pacific Forum Line

The Pacific Forum Line (PFL) is a regional shipping service which supports economic development, particularly export objectives, by providing an appropriate maritime infrastructure. It is a joint venture corporation, owned by the governments of Cook Islands, Fiji, Kiribati, Marshall Islands, New Zealand, Nauru, Niue, Papua New Guinea, Samoa, Solomon Islands, Tonga and Tuvalu.

After several economic studies and in the shadow of an industrial dispute involving New Zealand's Maritime Union and the Nauru Pacific Line, it was established in 1977—under the auspices of the SOUTH PACIFIC FORUM—through the South Pacific Bureau for Economic Cooperation (SPEC). Its incorporation created some political controversy; New Zealand and nine island governments were united in their support, but Australia was reluctant. However, despite misgivings about the concept of a regional shipping line because of the perceived financial risk, Australia agreed to provide aid and technical assistance, and West Germany provided two 4000-tonne roll-on roll-off container vessels, constructed under favourable loans. Named the *Forum Samoa* and *Fua Kavenga*, they have served the PFL since 1979. Four cargo liners have been supported by Australia and New Zealand.

Management offices for PFL were set up in Apia (Samoa) when operations commenced in May 1978 with three services. One linked New Zealand with Fiji, the two Samoan groups and Tonga; the second connected Fiji with Tuvalu, Solomon Islands and Papua New Guinea; and the third linked Australia with Fiji, the two Samoas and Tonga.

The first years were loss making for PFL, and in 1982 substantial capitalization was undertaken. The South Pacific Forum accepted a loan from the European Investment Bank (US$6 million), and a further US$12.6 million was provided by New Zealand, Australia and seven island shareholders.

Policy for the PFL is set by annual meetings of the participating Ministers of Transport and executed through a board of directors chosen by the member countries. While the memorandum of understanding which established the PFL requires the operation of a regular and viable shipping service, rationalizing shipping costs, containing escalating freight costs, and providing essential services on commercial routes, the PFL now operates on a commercial basis, and aims to provide a return on shareholder funds. Following its first recorded surplus in 1985, it returned a profit in several subsequent years, and in 1988 and 1996 paid a dividend to each of its shareholders.—PK

Further reading

Nightingale, T, 1998. *The Pacific Forum Line: a commitment to regional shipping*, Clerestory Press.

FIVE FINANCIAL AND ECONOMIC DEVELOPMENT

Banking and finance

Banks and other financial institutions play an important role in the economies of Pacific island countries. They mobilize savings from the local residents, and businesses and allocate them to those best qualified to use them. Banks operate the local payments systems (clearing cheques and cash payments) and help handle the import and export of goods and services.

Commercial banks are by far the most important and usually the oldest type of formal financial institution in the islands. Foreign (or foreign-owned) banks are usually the most prominent. Two Australia-based banks, the Westpac Banking Corporation and the Australian and New Zealand Banking Group, and one American bank, the Bank of Hawai'i, dominate the local industry in most countries. Where local-owned banks do exist, they are usually owned by the government or government entities. The National Bank of Fiji and National Bank of Vanuatu, for example, are both wholly government-owned. Other state-owned lending institutions include Amerika Samoa Bank, Banque de Tahiti, Bank of Guam, Bank of Nauru, Banque de

PNG Banking Corporation building, Port Moresby, Papua New Guinea

Nouvelle-Calédonie, Bank of Palau, and Papua New Guinea Banking Corporation. In contrast, the National Bank of Solomon Islands is a joint venture between the Solomon Islands' National Provident Fund (49 per cent) and the Bank of Hawai'i (51 per cent). Others, such as the National Bank of Samoa and the Bank of the Marshall Islands, have a range of individuals and government bodies (national provident fund/social security office) as shareholders. The Bank of Kiribati, Bank of Tonga, and National Bank of Tuvalu are joint ventures between the respective governments and overseas banks.

As most bank deposits have a relatively short-term maturity, commercial bank lending is seldom for more than one to three years. Some very selective term loans may be for up to 5–7 years when secured by real estate. Consumer finance is similarly short term, but more banks now make home loans from 7–10 (and sometimes up to 15) years.

Longer-term finance for agricultural and other businesses is often provided by government-owned development banks. These institutions raise their funds mainly through long-term debt issues or other borrowings (often from the Asian Development Bank, World Bank, or European Investment Bank) and so can lend to their clients on better terms than commercial banks. This type of lending is fairly risky and most development banks have had a fairly mixed earnings history as a result, though they have played an important role in developing local industry. More recently, some of these (like the Development Bank of Vanuatu) have been merged with government-owned local commercial banks.

Another increasingly common government-owned institution is a national provident fund. These collect by law a percentage (typically 3–7 per cent each) from both employers and employees within the country, funds which are then invested and held for the employees' retirement. As the funds mature, they accumulate a large pool of assets which is available for investment. Initially these funds were invested in bank deposits and government securities, but most of them have now purchased investment property as well as offshore foreign equity investments. Some funds also allow their members to pledge a portion of their contributions to a bank as part of the down-payment for a housing loan.

These three types of financial institutions are supplemented by much smaller institutions such as life insurance companies, venture capital firms, general insurance companies, finance companies, credit unions, credit cooperatives, and a range of even smaller informal micro finance institutions.

The commercial banks and finance companies are regulated by the government, typically through a central bank which also issues the country's currency. Not all countries have found this necessary, however. For example, Kiribati, Nauru and Tuvalu all use Australian dollars, while Palau, Federated States of Micronesia and Marshall Islands use US dollars. Most independent Pacific island currencies, such as Papua New Guinea's kina and the Fijian dollar, have undergone substantial changes in value (in US dollar terms) over the last decade. The Asian financial crisis of 1997–98 did not spare the Pacific, and many countries have had to devalue the currencies accordingly so that their prices remain competitive.

Besides the above-mentioned financial institutions, the two largest Pacific economies, Fiji and

Papua New Guinea, have some additional features: a stock exchange (Suva Stock Exchange and the proposed Port Moresby Stock Exchange) and unit trusts. The latter hold shares in the larger local companies that trade (or will trade) on these exchanges.

A tax-haven-based international finance centre is found on Vanuatu and, to a lesser extent, Samoa. The tax haven business was once important in Cook Islands' economy, earning about A$4.6 million a year in fees and taxes. Marshall Islands and Northern Marianas gained some brief notoriety with offshore banks. Tonga, Nauru and Guam have similarly had some involvement with tax havens, and most island countries have at least considered the idea. Tax havens offer overseas depositors a tax-free location to place their funds or to run overseas transactions through these offshore centres to minimize the tax paid elsewhere in the world. They provide some local employment as well as fee income to the island government, but the funds themselves have little involvement with the local economy. As the name suggests, most of the impact remains offshore.—MTS

Further reading

Skully, M T, 1997. *The South Pacific: finance, development and the private sector*, Australian Agency for International Development.

——, 1986. *Financial Institutions and Markets in the South Pacific: a study of New Caledonia, Solomon Islands, Tonga, Vanuatu, and Western Samoa*, Macmillan.

Tax free zones

Tax free zones, which aim to attract foreign investment by offering incentives to capital, have been implemented as part of a recent effort by island governments to replace import substitution with an export-oriented approach. While tax free zones exist all over the world, the only tax free zone in the Pacific islands is in Fiji. Following World Bank advice, the Fiji government implemented the Tax Free Factories/Tax Free Zone Scheme (TFF/TFZ) after the 1987 coups. Where tax free zones are a collection of factories in a particular location, tax free factories are individual entities enjoying the same concessions, but not necessarily within the zones. Some pre-existing industrial zones in Fiji have been designated as TFZ, while other new zones are being set up.

The TFF/TFZs in Fiji enjoy concessions including a 13-year tax holiday, freedom to repatriate profits, and duty-free importation of raw materials and components. In order to qualify for tax-free status, investors initially had to export 95 per cent of their annual production, but this has been lowered to 80 per cent. Enterprises involved in the general areas of manufacturing; mixing, blending and packaging; assembly; and exportable professional services, are eligible for tax-free status. Some locally-owned companies have qualified for tax-free status, and other tax-free enterprises are joint ventures with foreign investors, or are entirely foreign-owned. The TFF/TFZ Scheme attracted investment from Australia and New Zealand initially, with the most significant influx in the area of garment manufacture which now employs at least 14 000 workers. More recently, investment has come from Asia, with the Asian firms bringing in 800 'guest workers' from China and the Philippines to labour in the TFF/TFZs.

Other island governments offer similar incentives to export-oriented ventures although these have not been formalized into official TFZ programs. Samoa's incentives include a tax holiday of up to 15 years for enterprises exporting at least 95

Factory workers in Samoa

per cent of their annual production. The incentives program attracted Japanese firm Yazaki Samoa in 1991, employing 2600 workers by 1998 in the assembly of automotive wire harnesses. Chinese firm Ningbo Jingong Woolen Mill Company also negotiated with the government of Samoa to establish a garment factory potentially employing 300 Samoans and 50 Chinese workers, and the firm's permit was approved in 1998.

The Northern Marianas (CNMI) and American Samoa have attracted manufacturing investment by offering partial tax exemptions. The CNMI garment industry developed in the 1980s, and by 1998 comprised 27 garment factories, primarily Chinese and South Korean-owned. The industry employs 13–15 000 workers, mostly Asian guest workers. In America Samoa, BCTC-Samoa began garment manufacture in 1995. By 1998 BCTC employed 700 workers, of whom 300 were Chinese guest workers. Another garment firm, South Korean Daewoosa-

Samoa, was preparing to bring 150 Vietnamese workers into American Samoa to start up a garment factory, and had future plans for cardboard and shoe factories. American Samoa's success in attracting manufacturing investment was short-lived, however. BCTC announced the closure of its American Samoa factory, scheduled for November 1998. Daewoosa-Samoa's plans also looked increasingly uncertain by the end of 1998.

Low wages are a primary attraction of these island economies to foreign investors. Minimum wages in the garment industry are F$1.10/hour in Fiji, US$2.45/hour in American Samoa, and US$2.90/hour in the CNMI. The minimum wage for Yazaki workers in Samoa is US$0.43/hour. Women workers predominate in all of these industries, in keeping with global trends. Working conditions have been the subject of much controversy, particularly in the garment industry in Fiji and the CNMI. Workers in Fiji have staged strikes relating to low wages, long hours of work, sexual harassment, and denial of overtime pay, maternity leave and annual leave. In the CNMI, allegations are rife regarding violations of labour laws and health and safety regulations.

Market access is another key attraction for foreign investors. Manufacturers in Fiji and Western Samoa enjoy preferential access to the world's major markets under three trade agreements: to the Australian and New Zealand markets under SPARTECA, to the European Community under the Lomé agreement, and to the US market under the Generalized System of Preferences (GSP). Manufacturers in the CNMI and American Samoa receive duty-free access into the US market. American Samoa-based manufacturers additionally receive preferential treatment in the Australian, New Zealand and Japanese markets under GSP. The future of export-oriented manufacturing in these island economies is uncertain as trade liberalization around the world reduces the preferential market access on which the industries depend.—CH

Sources/further reading

Osman, W M, 1996. *Fiji Economic Report*, Bank of Hawai'i Economics Research Center.

——, 1997. *CNMI Economic Report*, Bank of Hawai'i Economics Research Center.

——, 1997. *American Samoa Economic Report*, Bank of Hawai'i Economics Research Center.

——, 1997. *Western Samoa Economic Report*, Bank of Hawai'i Economics Research Center.

Post Office and Philatelic Bureau of the Federated States of Micronesia

Philatelic bureaux

Postage stamps from the Pacific islands are popular with collectors, and many of the smaller island economies (notably Cook Islands, Kiribati, Niue, Norfolk, Pitcairn, Solomon Islands, Tonga and Tuvalu) have succeeded in generating significant revenue through stamp sales. A wide range of flora, fauna, traditional dancing, tropical scenery and artifacts have featured on numerous issues, but also, in the attempt to exploit every marketing possibility, many non-Pacific themes have been used to attract collectors.

Stamp dealers acquiring monopoly rights in small countries can distort the political processes. Albert HENRY's Cook Islands Party in the 1978 elections was assisted by an American stamp dealer, although the High Court later deposed the government and the company was prosecuted. The Cook Islands government has continued to find revenue opportunities, including separate stamp issues from the islands of Aitutaki and Penrhyn, overprinting of unsold issues with commemorative events unrelated to Cook Islands' history, and above-average face values.

Tonga issued its first stamps in 1886, using a portrait of King George TUPOU I. The country maintained conventional postage stamps until the issue on 15 July 1963 of the first gold-foil stamps. This was followed by other foil issues in the shapes of hearts and maps, and a new series of unconventional shapes (representing tropical fruit and birds) printed as self-adhesive postage stamps (1968–81). Tonga also has issued stamps from the northern island of Niuafo'ou since 1983, making use of its novel postal history, from the days when island mail was delivered in kerosene tins, thrown overboard by passing vessels. The name 'Tin Can Island' was used by a trader, Walter George Quensell, who developed colourful postmarks that were welcomed by collectors.

Tuvalu drew criticism in the 1980s for its exceptional number of stamp issues: 373 in 1985, and 245 in 1986—the highest number produced by any stamp issuing authority in the world. Solomon

Islands allowed a private company to market a gold stamp (face value A$5) featuring the America's Cup race, in 1987. Although old stamps reflecting the colonial era, such as Samoan issues of overprinted New Zealand stamps and Solomon Islands canoe stamps (issued in 1908), remain valuable collectors' items, the emergence of less reputable practices has diminished the investment value of stamps even from island countries with conservative philatelic policies.—KRF

Cooperatives

In the post-war period of economic development, cooperatives were seen as a means to offer opportunities to islanders, and they grew rapidly, particularly in the 1950s and 1960s. In Kiribati and Tuvalu, cooperatives took over almost all commercial enterprises, filling the vacuum left by foreign companies (displaced by the Pacific War) which were persuaded not to return, in return for becoming wholesalers to the cooperatives.

In every area of the Pacific—though to a lesser extent in the French territories—the cooperative movement has played some part in the growth of commercial activity.

Cooperatives provided specific skills, a boost to self-confidence, and meaningful economic participation in economic systems for islanders who had little education and almost no experience in business affairs. Many successful island businessmen received their first training in commerce and bookkeeping as cooperative managers and secretaries. A number of the first heads of national governments—notably Fiamē MATA'AFA, Hammer DeROBURT and Albert HENRY—emerged in the political arena from a background of involvement in promoting cooperative enterprises.

By the 1970s, however, the early promise of significant commercial development (even as a possible alternative to foreign investment) had failed to materialize. Realistic assessments of the cooperative movement have acknowledged that collapses have occurred in spite of substantial government subsidies, and in the absence of deliberate undermining by business competitors. Where post-colonial cooperative movements have continued to survive, they handle only a small percentage of total trade, and they are in receipt of favourable treatment and extensive subsidy. With their limited potential for buying and selling goods (and their almost total failure as a means of producing goods), cooperatives have been only a moderately successful movement, now widely eclipsed in part by credit unions, savings and loans societies and other such institutions, but vastly more so by private enterprise.—RGC

Further reading

Crocombe, R, 1989. *The South Pacific: an introduction*, Institute of Pacific Studies, University of the South Pacific.

Singh, S, 1972. *Cooperatives in Papua New Guinea*, New Guinea Research Bulletin, Australian National University Press.

Foreign aid

Foreign aid or Official Development Aid (ODA) plays a key role in the economies of almost all Pacific island countries. In a region marked by often extreme diversity, one common characteristic of most Pacific island economies is heavy reliance on aid to finance development programs. The ratio of development assistance to GDP is more than 20 per cent for many countries and for a few (Tuvalu for example) it is as high as 70 to 80 per cent. This reflects the small export base in many countries and low levels of domestic savings. Fiji, with a relatively large export base and higher savings rate, has an aid-to-GDP ratio of only 5 per cent. Over the region in 1993, aid per capita was estimated (South Pacific Forum figures) at US$246, by far the highest among developing country regions.

Aid finances the bulk of capital expenditure in Pacific island countries and has sustained high levels of funding in the public sectors and in infrastructure development. As a result of ready access to aid, most island countries have enjoyed relatively stable balance of payments positions. But it has also been observed that aid may have contributed to inefficiencies in the public sectors, allowing governments to postpone or avoid economic and financial adjustments.

Aid donors to the region fall into two categories: bilaterals and multilaterals. The bilateral donors, in turn, may be divided into two groups: those donors who are members of the Development Assistance Committee (DAC) of the Organization of Economic Cooperation and Development (OECD) and those who are not DAC member countries. The leading donors to the region belong to the first group and are Australia, Japan, Britain, New Zealand, the United States, France, Germany and Canada. Donors belonging to the second group are less prominent. They include the People's Republic of China, Republic of Korea and Taiwan. The principal multilateral donors to the region are the European Development Fund of the European Union, the Asian Development Bank and the United Nations.

In 1993 the region received US$689.2 million as ODA. Of this, approximately US$555.5 million was provided as bilateral aid, via country to country programs, by DAC member countries. Australia and Japan were the largest bilateral donors by far, contributing US$279.2 million and US$130.6 million respectively. Within Australia's aid program, the largest share (about US$221.8 million) was provided to Papua New Guinea, leaving US$57.4 million to be shared by the other island countries. Papua New Guinea, while the largest recipient of Japan's South Pacific aid, consumed a far smaller share (US$27.4 million). This left US$103.2 million that was distributed among the other Pacific island countries. The United States was the next largest bilateral donor, providing US$72 million. The bulk of this (US$69 million) was provided to Federated States of Micronesia and Marshall Islands. New Zealand provided US$37.4 million, Britain US$15.8 million, Germany US$10.8 million and France US$9.7 million. Multilateral donors to Pacific island countries in 1993 were the Asian Development Bank (US$42.4 million), the European Development Fund (US$32.1 million) and various United Nations agencies (US$32.4 million). In 1992 the non-DAC donors were the People's Republic of China (A$3.9 million) and Republic of Korea (A$113 000).

In addition to country-to-country programs, some donors channel significant amounts of aid through regional organizations and programs. Australia is the leading donor to a number of regional organizations, including the SOUTH PACIFIC FORUM Secretariat, the PACIFIC COMMUNITY (formerly the SPC), the Forum Fisheries Agency (FFA), the UNIVERSITY OF THE SOUTH PACIFIC, the South Pacific Regional Environment Programme and the South Pacific Applied Geoscience Commission. In 1993–94, A$32.9 million was allocated to regional organizations and programs. On the other hand, Japan provides very limited support to regional forums, its largest donation being to the Forum Secretariat. This is due in part to a policy of not providing aid to organizations of which it is not a member. But there is also a strong preference in Japan's ODA system for country-to-country project-based aid.

The United States provides support to the South Pacific Commission (about US$1 million) and to the South Pacific Regional Environment Programme (about US$90 000). But its main contribution is through the MULTILATERAL TREATY ON FISHERIES. Between 1988 and 1992, the United States provided US$66 million to the region under this treaty, as payment for access to the region's exclusive economic zones. Cash grants to countries on the basis of fishing efforts took up 85 per cent of these funds, while 15 per cent was apportioned equally among all parties to the treaty, as fisheries-related technical assistance. This latter portion was coordinated by the FFA. The fisheries treaty was extended for a further 10-year period in 1992, with an annual payment to the region of US$18 million. This constitutes the main body of US aid to the region since all other US bilateral aid to the South Pacific (except for Federated States of Micronesia, the Marshall Islands and Belau) was phased out in 1994.

The Forum Secretariat attracts the widest range of foreign donor support. It also acts as the regional authorizing officer for the disbursement of European Union assistance under the Lomé Convention and for Canadian assistance. In 1996 the principal donors to the Forum were Australia (F$3.27 million), New Zealand (F$1.1 million), European Union (F$1.48 million), Japan (F$845 000), United Nations Development Programme (F$753 000), Canada and France (each F$385 000), Taiwan (F$346 000), Korea (F$140 000) and People's Republic of China (F$120 000).

Official development aid to Pacific island countries mainly comprises technical assistance, capital grants and soft loans. This aid is generally given 'in kind'—as goods and services and infrastructure development, often supplied by the donor. Most countries also receive small amounts of budget support. Papua New Guinea has been the main anomaly in this regard, receiving most of its aid in the form of budget support from Australia. However, since the mid 1990s Australia has moved progressively towards providing program and project aid, and by 2000, all Australia's aid to Papua New Guinea will be in the form of program aid.

Japan does not provide budget support or non-project-tied aid. The only exception is the annual contribution to the Forum Secretariat, which began in 1989. Almost all Japanese aid to the region tends to be bilateral and project-based. There is a preference in the Japanese aid system for large-scale infrastructure projects. This means that Japan's aid to individual countries may fluctuate quite significantly from year to year, depending on whether a major infrastructure project is being implemented. The policy of providing only project-tied aid is rationalized on the grounds that it ensures accountability of aid monies. It also ensures the involvement of Japanese companies in the delivery of aid projects and thus the recycling of aid monies in Japan. Also important is the fact that the aid administration in Japan is structured around the delivery of aid on a case-by-case, project-by-project basis.

The sectoral distribution of aid varies from donor to donor. The largest sectoral component of Australia's aid to the South Pacific (excluding Papua New Guinea) is education (approximately one-quarter). Health and management of natural resources are also priority areas. Britain has narrowed the emphasis of its bilateral aid to the region to two sectors: education and good government. Since becoming an aid donor to the region in the mid 1970s, Japan has devoted the bulk of its assistance to the fisheries sector. This emphasis shifted in the late 1980s, and Japan's aid now encompasses health, education, transport, fisheries, energy and water supply. Japan has also provided yen loans to Papua New Guinea to support structural adjustment.

■ *Aid rationale and philosophy* In the post-colonial 1970s and 1980s, donor effort was largely driven by a combination of political, commercial and strategic factors. With DECOLONIZATION, metropolitan states undertook, in most cases, to maintain economic assistance to their former colonies. These commitments ensured the growth and consolidation of the post-colonial state. An underlying rationale of this support was to maintain political stability in the region which was seen as crucial in order to safeguard the commercial and strategic interests of donors.

The Cold War encouraged high levels of aid to the region, especially in the 1980s. Strategic concerns also helped to convince some donors to adopt quite innovative policies that responded to the demands of island states. An example was the US MULTILATERAL TREATY ON FISHERIES, which aimed to counter Soviet inroads into the region while securing fishing access for the US tuna fleets. The Soviet Union had concluded two fisheries agreements in 1985 and 1986, with Kiribati and Vanuatu respectively. The US treaty was an unprecedented achievement in regional cooperation, providing island states with a far greater return on the catch taken by American fishing vessels than they had previously received. It also put increased pressure on Japan to enter into a similar arrangement and pay higher access fees under bilateral arrangements; pressure which Japan's fisheries policymakers resisted. In order to defuse island demands, Japan channelled increased amounts of fisheries aid to the region.

Resource security, and specifically securing access to the region's tuna, was the original motivation and rationale for Japan's aid to the South Pacific. In the 1980s Japan also grew concerned about possible Soviet influence in the region and in early 1987 the Japanese foreign minister visited Fiji and announced a major increase in Japan's aid to the South Pacific. The intention was in fact to double Japan's contribution to the region. This policy was motivated by geopolitical considerations, as well as a desire to demonstrate Japan's allegiance to the United States and its willingness to assume a 'security burden'. There were tensions, however, between the political strategic goals of Japan's South Pacific aid diplomacy and its traditional fisheries interests in the region. Pacific island countries expected Japan's 1987 declaration of support for the region's development to include greater cooperation in the fisheries domain—specifically by addressing their grievances in respect to fisheries agreements. But these expectations were not fulfilled, which undermined the goodwill Japan sought to build through its aid contributions. Goodwill was also undermined by Japan's reticence about providing aid to regional organizations; its insistence on providing only bilateral project-tied aid (usually large-scale infrastructure projects); and its cumbersome and unwieldy aid procedures.

Australia's aid policy was also shaped by geopolitical considerations and concern about keeping the Soviet Union out of the region. But Australia also had a broader conception of regional security, which included securing the exclusive economic zones of the island states from illegal fishing by distant water fishing nations. This underpinned its program, under its defence cooperation scheme, of providing patrol boats to the island states as well as assistance to the South Pacific Forum Fisheries Agency to enhance regional fisheries management and surveillance capabilities. Such cooperation was viewed by Japan as challenging its own fisheries operations in the region, thus fuelling tensions between Japan and Australia.

The end of the Cold War spelled a shift in donor policies. For some traditional donors there were no longer compelling reasons for providing aid to the region. This, and the rise of new priority areas for donors, led to a scaling back of some programs to the region. In 1994 Britain announced that it would withdraw from the South Pacific Commission. It ended its bilateral aid to Fiji in 1995 and narrowed the focus of its remaining Pacific aid to two sectors (education and good government). The United States announced the closure of its South Pacific aid office in 1994 and the termination of its bilateral aid programs.

The guiding philosophy of Australia's aid to the Pacific in the post-Cold War era was the need for island countries to 'adjust' to changing international circumstances, in particular the possibility that donors would no longer be as willing to provide financial assistance to the region. This made it imperative that the island states demonstrate commitment to domestic reforms aimed at improving the efficiency of their economies. In order to promote its 'reform agenda', Australia put increased emphasis in its aid program on what was termed 'policy and management reforms', sustainable resource use and development of the private sector.

Australia has been closely involved in moves to streamline regional organizations (especially the SPC and the Forum Secretariat) and to promote greater donor coordination and dialogue. This has taken the form of periodic Development Partners/ Pacific Island Countries meetings, hosted by the Forum Secretariat. Four were held between 1991 and 1995. A product of this dialogue has been the drawing up of a regional strategy, which aims to ensure the efficient use of available aid resources.

As the two leading donors, Australia and Japan have engaged in aid coordination both through parallel aid projects and, in Fiji, a joint aid project. This was part of a process begun in the late 1980s by Australia to draw Japan into the region and also reform Japanese aid procedures. Japan regarded aid coordination with Australia as a useful way of learning more about the region while demonstrating its commitment to cooperation with Australia. However, aid coordination, especially joint programming, has been marred by problems of accommodating two very different aid systems, with very different approaches to implementing and disbursing aid. Japan has also been reluctant to impose policy conditionally, unlike Australia, in order to promote domestic reforms in Pacific island countries.

Japan's aid to the South Pacific in the 1990s has been sustained at relatively high levels, motivated by a combination of commercial, resource and political interests. In the latter category are Japan's interests in securing the support of the Pacific island states in international forums, where the region comprises a significant voting bloc. While continuing to emphasize large-scale infrastructure projects, Japan has also provided increasing numbers of small grants for 'grass-roots development'. This has encompassed aid to non-government organizations (NGOs), mainly in the environment area. Environmental aid is the fastest growing component of the Japanese aid budget. Such aid, however, tends to be bilateral and project-based; it also aims to promote particular economic interests. For example, environmental aid in the fisheries sector, a recent innovation in aid policy to the region, aims to demonstrate Japan's concern for conservation of fish stocks and to improve its image as a fishing nation. It thereby also aims to gain membership of regional fisheries management bodies.

France is the only donor to announce a significant increase in its South Pacific aid since the end of the Cold War. Following the cessation of its nuclear testing program in 1996, France announced it would more than double its development cooperation to the region, from FF10.7 million (F$2.7 million) to FF25 million (F$6.35 million). About half of these funds would be channelled through the Forum Secretariat. France also announced it would step up military cooperation, including a military exercises program with Vanuatu, Tonga and Fiji. The aid announcement was timed to influence Forum countries on the issue of readmitting France to the Post Forum Dialogue, from which it had been suspended because of the resumption of nuclear testing. More generally France aimed to demonstrate its commitment to remaining in the region and to consolidate its role in regional affairs.

■ ***Problems and prospects*** There are growing tensions between some donors and recipients in the South Pacific because of changing aid policies. The shift to program aid by Australia has not been welcomed by Papua New Guinea. In 1996 Papua New Guinea's foreign minister announced a review of Australia's aid program, stating that 'aspects of this program' were not in Papua New Guinea's best interests and gave Australia a continuing advantage over Papua New Guinea. The Papua New Guinea prime minister also mooted a review of Australia's defence cooperation with the possibility of its termination. This was in reaction to Australia allowing members of the Bougainville independence movement to be based in Australia. Also fuelling tension was Australia's support for the World Bank's suspension in 1996 of a structural adjustment loan to Papua New Guinea, worth US$210 million. This was due to World Bank concern about the pace of domestic reform in Papua New Guinea and the failure of the PNG government to act in accord with a structural adjustment agreement reached with the bank and other donors in 1995.

There were also tensions between Australia and Solomon Islands due to conflict over the Solomon Islands government's logging policies, and in 1995 Australia suspended forestry aid to Solomon Islands. The European Union also froze aid to Solomon Islands because of the failure of the Solomon Islands government to utilize the funds available to it under the Lomé Convention. Problems of disbursement were not uncommon in the region and the European Union warned that other countries faced the prospect of aid suspensions if they could not put the aid to 'proper use'.

Donor policies created various problems for the region. Pacific island countries struggled to cope with high recurrent cost burdens on the aid they received. Some donors such as Japan refused, in principle, to fund these. Island governments were often provided with goods and services at inflated prices. Problems also arose due to inadequate consultation, the refusal by donors to provide commercial aid, and the political pressures to which donors at times subjected island governments.

The overall trend in aid flows to the South Pacific is a decline in real terms (estimated at 2 per cent between 1983 and 1993). Donors are also adopting more intrusive and interventionist aid policies, in order to encourage reforms in recipient countries. Pacific island states are thus in an unenviable position, caught between a rock and a hard place. The future challenge will be in striking a balance between maintaining Pacific island sovereignty and meeting the countries' continuing need for development assistance.—ST

MIRAB economies

MIRAB, an acronym (from MIgration, Remittances, Aid and Bureaucracy) was coined by Geoff Bertram and Ray Watters in 1984 to identify a new social formation based on the migration process; the massive flow of aid, remittances and other invisibles; and the dominant role of government in several small Pacific island economies. The island economies covered by the model shared, to varying degrees, certain economic characteristics. A significant proportion of the islands-born labour force lived and worked offshore, regularly sending back to their home communities remittances in cash and kind which financed a substantial part of consumption expenditure, especially the purchase of imported consumer goods. The government sector was typically the largest source of local employment, and the government budget the principal local source of cash incomes. Government expenditure on infrastructure, education, health, and the delivery of a number of other services which underpinned material standards of living in the islands, was supported by large inflows of official aid which held the government budget well above the size that could have been sustained on the basis of revenues available from the local economy.

Although most islands were commodity exporters, producing a variety of agricultural, mineral and fish staple products, their export earnings exhibited cycles around a stagnant long-run trend rather than functioning as leading sectors for economic growth. Living standards had risen steadily during the decades following the Second World War, with increasing import requirements, but except for pre 1979 Kiribati, this import growth was paid for by official aid and private remittances, not rising exports.

The availability of foreign exchange income from aid and remittances contributed to stagnant exports, just as booming oil revenues caused de-industrialization in some European economies in the 1970s (the so-called 'Dutch Disease'). Export production, and industrialization in general, is usually unprofitable in small MIRAB island economies because of high wages (indexed to the wages workers could earn abroad as migrants) and fixed exchange rates (all the economies in the original study formed part of either the New Zealand or the Australian currency areas). Financial transfers into these small island economies and labour migration out of them have the effect of making capitalist private-sector activity mostly unprofitable in traded-goods production (especially manufacturing and agriculture) because of the resulting combination of strong exchange rates and high wages.

The coexistence of high material living standards, compared to other economies at similar levels of development, with the absence of 'leading sectors' producing tradeable goods has resulted in low rates of privately-financed capital formation, high dependency ratios (since many productive-age workers were absent as migrants), and stagnation of the agricultural sector due to poor incentives for production of a marketable surplus.

None of these characteristics are necessarily problems or evidence of economic failure. The MIRAB paradigm highlights the inadequacy of a conventional concept of development which restricts its attention to the evolution of economic production within a politically-delimited geographical space. In MIRAB models the focus is not on gross domestic product (the central development indicator for conventional models) but on the level and sustainability of material welfare enjoyed by the relevant community of islanders, including that community's migrant offshoots located in other countries and often comprising the economically dynamic part of the 'transnational corporation of kin'. Such migrants account for much of the income generation and wealth accumulation of islander communities. In MIRAB models, therefore, development is conceived of as development for the geographically dispersed target community defined in terms of kin, village and ethnic affiliation—not simply as maximization of marketed output within the island locale.

In a MIRAB economy the indigenous population maximize their material well-being by globalization. Subsistence production from land, most of which remains unalienated under CUSTOMARY LAND TENURE, puts a floor under living standards by providing for basic needs, and possibly also for some modest cash sales of produce to urban or export markets. However, it is the release of family members and family savings from village agriculture and fishing, and their outward movement not merely to other sectors, but to other islands and other countries, that opens the way to securing higher incomes and wealth. Released factors and cash are allocated across the geographical and economic space to which the local population has access, with the resulting income shared between migrants and their home communities by means of remittances. Employment in the large aid-supported government sectors puts additional cash into the hands of all households with members engaged in such employment.

Besides its critique of modernization models of development, the MIRAB model stands also in opposition to the dependency approach which argues that any community in an economically and/or politically dependent relationship with a larger patron will tend to be worse-off in development terms than it could have been under a regime of greater autonomy. The MIRAB model suggests that, on the contrary, political dependence offers major economic and social gains for small-island communities, because of the positive effects of dependent status both on flows of budgetary support (aid) and on migrant access to metropolitan labour markets. DECOLONIZATION *per se* is therefore neither necessary nor sufficient for economic development understood in terms of material welfare and social cohesion. On the contrary, so long as informal-sector transnational kin enterprises remain firmly under islander control, political integration with metropolitan economies opens a wider horizon of opportunities on which those enterprises can capitalize effectively.

The central issue in policy debates concerning the MIRAB process has been whether it represents a sustainable development model or a temporary and unstable condition from which a transition must in due course be made to a more conventional model of economic development. The most striking empirical result from research on the migration-remittance nexus in the Pacific has been the persistence of individual remittance effort at high levels for several decades after migration, indicating that this leg of the MIRAB system is indeed sustainable. The sustainability of official aid flows, the other main prop of the MIRAB economy, rests upon a number of political and geopolitical imperatives which are likely to remain powerful at least in the case of the smaller island economies. Larger MIRAB economies may well become increasingly dependent on the continuing success of their 'transnational corporations of kin' in generating income and wealth offshore, if aid flows taper off in future.

The easiest MIRAB economies to identify are those which are small, open, politically integrated, and import-led in an absolute sense. Outside the New Zealand sphere of influence where it was first formulated, the MIRAB model with appropriate modifications seems applicable to French Polynesia, the Federated States of Micronesia, the Marshall Islands and other small US-associated former Pacific Trust Territories, Tonga and Samoa, Chile's Pacific outpost of Easter Island (Rapanui), outlying islands of Papua New Guinea and Solomon Islands, Tuvalu and Kiribati. Even Hawai'i exhibits certain MIRAB features—a large government and defence sector supported by budgetary subventions from mainland United States, a substantial current-account deficit in interstate and international trade, and a large migrant community resident in the US mainland states.—GB

Further reading

Ahlburg, D, 1995. 'Remittances and income distribution in Tonga', *Population Research and Policy Review.*

Bertram, G and Watters, R F, 1984. *New Zealand and its Small Island Neighbours: a review of New Zealand policy toward the Cook Islands, Niue, Tokelau, Kiribati and Tuvalu*, Institute of Policy Studies, Victoria University of Wellington.

Fleming, E M and Hardaker, J B, 1995. *Pacific 2010: strategies for Polynesian agricultural development*, Pacific Policy Paper No. 15, National Centre for Development Studies, The Australian National University.

Hooper, A, et al. (eds), 1987. *Class and Culture in the South Pacific*, Institute of Pacific Studies, University of the South Pacific.

Tourism

Tourism in the Pacific islands is suffused with myth, especially that of an earthly Paradise, a condition which has its historical basis in the journal of the French explorer Louis Antoine de BOUGAINVILLE. Encountering Tahiti in 1768, Bougainville gave expression to peculiarly European fantasies, writing that he felt transported to the Garden of Eden. For

Sunset at the Marlin Bay Resort in Beqa Lagoon, Fiji Islands

him, Paradise had been disclosed, and the term, or a variation of it, became in time the most overworked expression in the lexicon of travel, particularly Pacific travel. In the late 20th century, catering to European tourists' expectations of paradise has enabled tourism to become the backbone of the economy in states such as Fiji, Hawai'i, Guam, Saipan and Cook Islands. Others—Vanuatu, Samoa and Solomon Islands—would like it to achieve a similar status. Still others appear ambivalent about pursuing the tourist dollar—Tonga and Papua New Guinea, for example. The factor shared by most, however, is that in an increasingly competitive global economy, they have few resources other than their geographic, climatic and cultural attributes over which they maintain control and which can be exploited. Tourism is the single product that can package all three items and which appears to be in increasing international demand.

A snapshot of the size and contribution of tourism in the region varies according to the source used for statistics. Pacific Area Travel Association (PATA) membership includes Hawai'i, Guam and Saipan but not French Polynesia. According to PATA statistics, in global terms the South Pacific region accounts for 0.3 per cent of international visitor arrivals and these generate some US$2.7 billion, less than 1 per cent of the world total. SOUTH PACIFIC TOURISM COUNCIL (SPTC) membership does include French Polynesia but not the others, which between them accommodate some 7.6 million visitors annually. Their statistics indicate that the region hosts less than 0.15 per cent of world arrivals, contributing US$600 million each year in tourism receipts, representing between 5 and 10 per cent of GDP and about 8 per cent of total government revenue. The major tourist generating markets for the region are Australia (19 per cent of the total), New Zealand (15 per cent), USA (14 per cent), Japan (12 per cent) and France (9 per cent). The picture is thus determined by the interests of the photographer. Whichever view of the size and value of tourism is used, however, there are a number of issues which are common throughout the region. These include the extent of economic, social-cultural and environmental impacts.

It is a common belief that tourism contributes unerringly to many economic goals including increasing foreign exchange earnings, reducing balance of payments deficit, generating employment, and assisting the development of regional areas and the development of supporting infrastructure. In some countries this has occurred to some degree. Tonga, Fiji, Vanuatu and Samoa now have tourism receipts which are significantly higher than income from their commodity exports: these range from 70 per cent to 25 per cent of all exports. But the significance of these figures must be viewed within the context of other information about the type of tourism industry present in each country and it is generally acknowledged that many tourism figures are estimates at best and perhaps unreliable. High imports in construction materials, machinery, food and other tourism-related requirements means high leakage, estimated by some economists to be up to 80 per cent in some isolated, undeveloped areas. Heavy reliance on expatriate management also con-

Tourists visiting Indian market stall, Fiji

tributes significantly to the leakage factor. Employment creation is perhaps the most significant economic contribution. Approximately 12 per cent of all jobs in the region are tourism-related. Although some would argue that the positions are at the lower end of the scale, requiring only semi-skilled or unskilled labour, with little opportunity for advancement and subject to seasonality, it is indisputable that in a region where unemployment is high and other opportunities for paid employment are few, tourism can create jobs.

Social and cultural impacts are more difficult to assess than those on the economy, but all are closely related. Tourism does not occur within a vacuum and its effects upon a community must be considered within a complex web of political, economic, environmental and historical factors, many of which have been powerful agents of change well before the introduction of tourism. Christianity, colonialism, education, URBANIZATION and the demands of a

Robert Reimers Enterprises Hotel, Majuro, Marshall Islands

cash economy have been affecting Pacific communities at various levels for some 200 years. Indeed, the attempt to separate tourism as an independent and more profound agent of change—a task which increasingly occupies tourism academics—is not only exceedingly difficult, it may be ultimately pointless. Tourism in a form substantial enough to make significant impacts has only infiltrated Pacific communities (Hawai'i excluded) in the past 40 years or so and even then only a relative few. The extent and nature of impact depend on the host/guest ratio, rate of development, the degree of cultural difference between hosts and guests, the distribution and visibility of tourism and the extent of foreign ownership. For some Pacific countries tourism development on any significant level will never amount to much more than inflated rhetoric on the part of foreign consultants, entrepreneurs and some indigenous politicians.

There are, however, parts of the Pacific where tourist numbers exceed residents in staggering proportions and the demands of tourism have had a

Hafadai Beach Hotel, on Beach Road, Garapan (Saipan, Northern Marianas)

dramatic impact on host communities. Hawai'i is the most obvious example of this, accommodating over 6 000 000 tourists annually, the majority of whom stay in the tourist enclave of Waikīkī. With a huge proportion of its land devoted to resorts and golf courses, Hawai'i now imports most of its food and there is an increasing loss of sense of place among indigenous Hawaiians.

Ownership of land in the Pacific is mostly communal and problems of social displacement have occurred where rights to land have been traded by a few rather than by the community as a group. The Sheraton resort development on Rarotonga in Cook Islands is a good example. Disputed ownership of the site has contributed to the project remaining incomplete and the withdrawal of Sheraton several years after its approval. A *tapu* was placed on the site by opponents and several accidents followed, although non-believers have pointed to the combination of poor economic planning and political debacles which dogged the project from the outset.

Pacific tourism is confined to two identifiable areas. The first and most common is the designated capital island, which offers immediate access to necessary infrastructure and labour pools; the second is the small, isolated, sometimes unpopulated island where developers can maintain an 'environmental bubble', thus minimizing outside contacts and ensuring control of all factors. The capital islands of Viti Levu (Fiji), Efate (Vanuatu) and Rarotonga (Cook Islands) are prime examples of the former cluster developments where the majority of the indigenous populations have very little contact with tourists, simply because they do not live in proximity to the tourist enclaves. Developments in the second type of location can be so insular and self-contained that tourists may be unaware that they have actually visited a particular Pacific country, being able to identify only the name of the resort. Fiji is particularly notable for the number of small, exclusive island resorts, the guests of which are

Pohnpei Tourist Office, Kolonia Town

unlikely to see any other part of the country except the airport.

Other areas of discussion concerning socio-cultural impacts include the so-called 'demonstration effect', whereby hosts seek to imitate guests—although occasionally the reverse takes place, if only briefly—and the commoditization of culture and cultural artifacts. Throughout the Pacific changes in most aspects of living are apparent. For example, rice is preferred to yams, tinned fish to fresh, instant noodles to tapioca; but these are neither the introductions nor the preferences of tourists. Rather they are contemporary products, the purchase of which may symbolize wealth, modernization and status to other members of the community. Tourism alone can hardly be blamed for the dietary changes which have resulted in the increase of diabetes and heart diseases. Similarly, the argument that tourism has bastardized cultural artifacts by demanding that they conform to the weight limit imposed by international airlines ignores the obvious fact that all cultures are dynamic and that Pacific islanders have experienced several centuries of selectively assimilating outside influences. Tourism and its requirements are merely the most recent aspect of a relentless continuum of change.

Images of a pristine tropical environment are the cornerstone of marketing for South Pacific tourism. In an increasingly polluted world it is the natural environment which is the region's most valuable resource and the one which needs the most monitoring in order to promote sustainable tourism development. Just as it is difficult if not impossible to separate tourism's socio-cultural impacts from other instigators of change, so it is with its environmental impacts. Overpopulation, non-sustainable agricultural practices, inadequate pollution controls and poor waste management techniques have had considerable negative effects in many areas. To try to isolate tourism's real or perceived negative environmental impacts is to ignore far greater urgencies faced by the region, such as global warming, depletion of fisheries and forestry resources and the rapid growth of populations. Ecotourism of the 'take only pictures, leave only footprints' kind is being promoted by the SPTC as an economically viable and sustainable alternative to current resource use, but it is a slow process to convince many cash-needy landowners of the long-term benefits to be gained.

Notwithstanding the previous observations, it is possible to identify some environmental impacts which if not caused solely by tourism are at the very least exacerbated by it. One of the most serious is the destruction of mangroves, regarded by developers as impediments but essential as a source of food and shelter to much marine life, and hence a source of food and fuel to many villagers. Most Pacific tourism development is coast-based and requires facilities such as marinas and sandy beaches for leisure activities. However, following mangrove clearance, fragile coastal fringes are left exposed to the vagaries of the sea and violent weather. Coral reefs, among the most desirable resources for tourism in the Pacific and also among the most vulnerable, are affected not only by tourists seeking souvenirs or by the constant tramp of reef-walkers but also by blasting for construction and sedimentation caused by waste disposal. All too often environmental impact assessments are not seen by island governments as a necessary prerequisite for development, and tourism, as one of the more visible and recent factors affecting the environment, may be made a scapegoat for environmental destruction for which it is only partly responsible.

There are a number of features which will continue to constrain tourism development in the region for some time to come: the fragmented and scattered nature of the islands, their poor accessibility, their distance from major tourist-generating markets, a lack of regional cooperation—despite the pretensions in that direction—a high leakage factor, and an absence of managerial skills among indigenous people. However, in an increasingly complex and industrialized world, the islands are still seen by many as destinations which offer a chance to experience a simpler, cleaner, more peaceful environment. The myth of Paradise—perhaps the Pacific islands' major export—persists.—ND1

Further reading

Britton, S and Clarke, W C (eds), 1987. *Ambiguous Alternatives: tourism in small developing countries*, Institute of Pacific Studies, University of the South Pacific.

Douglas, N, 1996. *They Came for Savages: 100 years of tourism in Melanesia*, Southern Cross University Press.

Graburn, N N H, 1976. *Ethnic and Tourist Arts: cultural expression from the fourth world*, University of California Press.

Hall, C M and Page, S J (eds), 1996. *Tourism in the Pacific: issues and cases*, International Thomson Business Press.

■ ***South Pacific Tourism Council*** The South Pacific Tourism Council (SPCT) began as a United Nations Development Programme/World Trade Organization study during 1980, into the need for a regional tourism development program. Initially called the Tourism Council of the South Pacific (TCSP), it emerged from this planning process in 1983. The SPCT operated informally and without a formal infrastructure until 1986 when the South Pacific Bureau for Economic Cooperation (SPEC) secured Lomé Convention funding for the Pacific Regional Tourism Development Program. At a meeting of South Pacific Ministers of Tourism in August 1988, SPCT severed the relationship with SPEC by adopting a Memorandum of Association which formally established the SPCT as an intergovernmental organization governed by annual meetings of a council composed of national representatives; a management board responsible for the management of the TCSP; and a secretariat. The SPCT Secretariat remains based in Suva. In 1992 the Forum agreed to SPCT becoming a member of the South Pacific Organization's Coordinating Committee (SPOCC).

In 1995/96, its full membership was: Cook Islands, Fiji, French Polynesia, Kiribati, Marshall Islands, New Caledonia, Niue, Papua New Guinea, Samoa, Solomon Islands, Tahiti (sic), Tonga, Tuvalu and Vanuatu.—RAH

■ ***Pacific Islands Centre*** The SOUTH PACIFIC FORUM Secretariat's long-standing proposal to establish an office in Tokyo was finally achieved in October 1996 with Japanese government funding. The office, known as the South Pacific Economic Exchange Support Centre, increased the Secretariat's network of overseas trade offices to three, complementing the South Pacific Trade Commission offices in Sydney and Auckland.

Private sector development in Forum island countries based on the expansion of exports, foreign investment and tourism, is critical to the enhancement of the economic and social wellbeing of the peoples of the South Pacific. The size of island countries and the smallness of their private sector enterprises restricts their ability to establish on-the-ground presence in overseas markets to support private sector activities. Promotion of Forum island countries within the Japanese market in particular has suffered from a lack of resources, needing a concerted, long-term marketing thrust to enable it to reach its full potential. The establishment of permanent representation for the South Pacific region in Japan provides an effective conduit for promoting trade, investment and tourism opportunities between Forum island countries and Japan.—YN

six

society

Contributors

Article contributors

ACW	A Crosbie Walsh
AR1	Asesela Ravuvu
AR2	Alan Rumsey
AT2	Andrew Thornley
BF	Ben Finney
BH	Bruce Horsfield
CAG	Chris A Gregory
CEH	Colin E Hindson
DAKW	David A K Watters
DD	Donald Denoon
DHR	Donald H Rubinstein
DR	Dale Robertson
FYAJ	Felix Y Attah Johnson
GD2	Gary Dowse
GMcC	Grant McCall
GWT	Garry W Trompf
HB	Heather Booth
HCM	Honor C Maude
'IFH	'I Futa Helu
IJ	Ian Johnston
JDV	John D Vince
LC	Linley Chapman
LES	Larry E Smith
LL	Lamont Lindstrom
MA	Michael Alpers
MG	Michael Goddard
MJ	Margaret Jolly
MM	Mac Marshall
MP1	Megan Passey
MQ	Max Quanchi
MRO	Michael R Ogden
MSC	Maria Sylvia Codecasa
MTC	Marjorie Tuainekore Crocombe
NB	Niko Besnier
NJP	Nancy J Pollock
PH	Philip Hayward
PP	Peter Pirie
PS2	Penelope Schoeffel
RAH2	Robert A Hooper
RC	Rajesh Chandra
RCK	Robert C Kiste
RL2	Robert Langdon
RS1	Richard Scaglion
SD	Sinclair Dinnen
SL2	Suzanna Layton
SN	Sirus Naraqi
VL	Victoria Lukere

Photo contributors

Alexander Turnbull Library (National Library of New Zealand, Wellington): A M Rutherford Collection: 459 (bottom left)

ANU Photography (The Australian National University, Canberra): 425, 426; photograph by Akira Matsumura reproduced from *Contributions to the ethnography of Micronesia*, (University of Tokyo, 1918): 455 (bottom left); courtesy Robert Langdon: 476, 477; courtesy Philip Hayward: 478

Australian Agency for International Development (AusAID), Department of Foreign Affairs and Trade (Canberra): 446

Australian National Archives (Canberra): photographs by F E Williams (1893–1943): 455 (right), 456

Besnier, Niko (Victoria University of Wellington): photograph by Tod Kent: 417

Cunningham, Lawrence J (University of Guam, Mangilao): 420, 429, 449

Hendrie, Peter (Pacific Journeys, Melbourne): 403 (detail), 412, 419, 457 (top left), 458 (top right), 459 (right), 461

Kiste, Robert C (Center for Pacific Islands Studies, University of Hawai'i–Manoa, Honolulu): 441

Lawrence, Helen Reeves (Papua New Guinea): 407, 409 (top left)

McCall, Grant (Centre for South Pacific Studies, University of New South Wales, Kensington): 428

Marshall Islands Visitors Authority (Majuro, Republic of the Marshall Islands): 405

National Library of Australia (Canberra): 460

Netball New Zealand (Auckland): 457 (bottom right), 462

Panholzer, Thomas C (College of Micronesia–FSM, Pohnpei): 465, 469

Samoan High Commission (Wellington): courtesy Vincent Fepulea'i: 463

Waters, Sheila (Melbourne): photograph by Sarah Chinnery (1887–1970): 409 (right)

West, Richard (Canberra): 447, 451, 458 (left)

ONE GENDER AND FAMILY RELATIONSHIPS

Family

The English 'family' appears in many Pacific languages as a 'loanword'—for instance, *famili* in Tongan, *pamili* in Dobuan. But the processes of cross-cultural translation and historical transformation of families are not so simply labelled mere loans. Familial and kinship patterns in the Pacific were not only very different from those many Europeans or Americans take to be natural or universal, they also differed dramatically from each other. There have been profound changes in the patterns of Pacific domesticities, although the character and the causes of such changes have been much debated.

There has been a tendency in some social theory as in daily life to posit the family as a universal, and to idealize or naturalize the elementary or nuclear family, of husband, wife and children. Yet both as an empirical reality and as a social ideal, the nuclear family is both more recent and more evanescent than this. Extended family forms persisted into the early 20th century in Europe, North America and Australia (usually 'extended' to include single or married adult siblings or parents of husband or wife). In such countries today, the statistical and normative dominance of the nuclear family has been eroded by a proliferation of single parent families, of 'mixed' families, with children of prior unions living together, heterosexual couples without children, homosexual couples with children and households composed of friends or colleagues who claim no kinship connection. This poses the important question of the difference between a 'family (those who claim kinship or affinal connection by local definition) and a 'household' (those sharing a domestic space, which usually entails living—eating, sleeping and, hopefully, talking—together).

Broader conceptions of 'family' and the disarticulation of family and household are pervasive in the Pacific. Throughout most of the Pacific a far more extended sense of family prevails to the present. Despite the extraordinary diversity of kinship patterns and familial forms, there is a far broader definition of 'family'—both kin with whom one claims connection of substance (either through birth or adoption and nurture) and affines with whom one observes a link through marriage. Whether the local form of descent reckoning privileges patrilineal or matrilineal connections or both, there has been a pervasive tendency to 'extend' the boundaries of kinship to larger kinship collectivities like lineages and CLANS. Many Pacific kinship terminologies embrace collateral relatives with the same terms as lineals. Thus the father's brother may be called 'father', or the mother's sister, 'mother'. In some systems, the kin terms for parents, siblings and children are extended over generational cohorts, to adjacent or alternate generations. Thus in one kinship system in Vanuatu, a man calls his father's father 'elder brother' and his son's son 'younger brother', while his father's father's father is called by the same word as 'father'.

In those parts of the southwest Pacific where separate men's houses prevailed, men and adolescent boys often lived there for protracted periods rather than in the household dwelling with wives and children. In some parts of Papua New Guinea, in the Gulf region for instance, men's houses co-existed with longhouses—where several families lived together, although maintaining separate sleeping quarters and hearths. Apart from such dramatic

Family groups at Japanese Memorial Park, Majuro

disjunctions of family and household, there were frequently patterns whereby children moved between their own and other households, not just through processes of ADOPTION and fostering but through the high velocity of daily visiting. Such 'abnormal' families attracted the interest of all foreign observers and the reforming zeal of most missionaries.

Anthropologists have also studied the relationships between family members. Thus MALINOWSKI's early ethnography of the Massim not only insisted that the Trobriand family was structurally different from that of his own European experience, he also claimed that the 'structure of feelings', the emotional relations of parents and children, were very different from that proclaimed as universal by Freudian psychoanalysis. The Trobriand father, he asserted, was a 'stranger' not a genitor to his child, who was seen as the conjunction only of maternal blood and matrilineal ancestral spirit. Any physical resemblance between father and child was attributed to nurture, as the palm of a hand imparts a shape to yam paste. Moreover, he claimed, because material support of, and authority over, children derived more from their mother's brothers, fathers gave to their sons and daughters only the gift of love. His claims about Trobriand families—about procreation beliefs, emotions and power—have been hotly debated ever since. Weiner, for instance, insists that Trobriand fathers are not powerless strangers, and are seen to 'grow' their children through nurture and gifts emanating from their own matrilineages. Thus exchanges between matrilineages, involving women's wealth—grass skirts and banana leaf bundles—not only secure the reproduction of persons over generations but are foundational to the chiefly system.

The continuing debate about this early and influential analysis of a Pacific 'family' illustrates the fundamental point—about not projecting the ideal of the nuclear family onto the region. But of course it was not just the relations of parents and children which European observers found so different and various, but conjugal and sibling relations. In many parts of the western Pacific—Papua New Guinea, Solomon Islands, Vanuatu, New Caledonia and Fiji—POLYGYNY was practised, not necessarily by all men, but by those of greatest wealth, rank or seniority. Where polygyny was pronounced, lesser men might be unable to marry until late in life or, rarely, be forced to remain bachelors. It has been suggested for the eastern Pacific, and for Marquesas Islands in particular, that the sexual and marital relations of high-ranking women constituted a kind of polyandry. Even where 'monogamy' prevailed, as in many parts of Polynesia, serial monogamy ensued from successive divorces and remarriages, and/or pervasive sexual freedom suggested that having one spouse did not entail having one lover. In Hawai'i and Tahiti, sexual and marital relations, especially among the high-ranking, were rarely eternal or faithful, and such sexual 'promiscuity' excited the ire of missionaries there, as in parts of the Massim, like the Trobriand Islands.

Moreover, foreign observers noted the establishment of a marriage often depended not so much on the desires of the prospective couples as the desires and strategies of the respective families. Forms of infant betrothal and arranged marriages prevailed in many places, and although the desires of the prospective spouses were not thereby completely ignored and 'love matches' were negotiated through forms of institutional elopement or even bride 'capture', the broader interests of both families were essential to making, sustaining and breaking marriages.

Very often goods were exchanged and thought crucial to affirming or legitimating the union. Bride wealth, or as it is often dubbed 'bride price', entailed the movement of goods—like pigs, shells, pandanus mats or *tapa*—from the kin of the husband to the kin of the bride, often in exchange for the sexual, productive and reproductive aspects of her person, securing attachment to his kin group. He thereby usually had rights over her labour and over children born to the marriage. There was often some reciprocal movement of goods in the other direction. Some commentators argue that 'bride price' is a misleading term and that missionary critiques of it, as rendering women as objects for sale, fail to recognize the value or honour thus conferred on women and evince a capitalist, commodity logic, with its strict separation of subjects and objects.

Bride wealth still prevails in many regions of Papua New Guinea, Solomon Islands and Vanuatu, where increasingly it is paid in cash rather than indigenous valuables and where the amounts paid are vastly escalating, and are responsive to shifts in the wealth and power of the women's ethnic group or region. Some indigenous women suggest that it is indeed a 'price' now and even seen by some as a 'licence' for a man's violent control over his wife. Masing in her poem *Braed Praes* (in Bislama, the pidgin of Vanuatu) says that bride price makes her feel like a speed boat or a truck for sale, while bride price is implicated in contemporary justifications of DOMESTIC VIOLENCE in Papua New Guinea, Solomon Islands and Vanuatu.

Missionaries criticized not just bride price but many practices of Pacific families—the stress on collective rights of families rather than the 'free will' of the couple, and especially the bride; the celebration of clan and lineage relations over those of the nuclear family; the fact that many households were not 'true families', and that polygyny, polyandry, promiscuity and divorce compromised the Christian ideals of marriage as an eternal bond, divinely ordained. Missionaries and colonial states were very critical of undisciplined parenting (especially mothering) as much as unbridled eroticism. They often combined to curb the latter, through a combination of moralizing sermons, confessions and colonial legislation, including laws designed to control prostitution and the spread of venereal diseases, while disciplined mothering was promoted through sanitation, public health regimes and, most vigorously in Fiji, through state surveillance over infant mortality, abortion and infanticide.

There has been a profound transformation in family forms throughout the Pacific over the last 100 years or more. Generally this has been towards a more nucleated family pattern, a diminution of the more strenuous demands of kinship collectivities—of lineages and of clans—and an associated tendency to the celebration of the conjugal and parental relations at the expense of equally important relations between siblings, between grandparents and grandchildren, and those whom English labels aunts, uncles and cousins. In part these changes were in response to missionary pressures, but they are also partially due to the impact of DEPOPULATION, pacification, the intrusions of colonial and independent states and the emergence of an economy dominated by commodity rather than gift relations. Let us briefly consider three examples of familial transformation in Solomon Islands, Tonga and Tahiti to suggest the complexity of these changes and the complicated array of influences which are at work.

Dureau, in her history of Simbo gender relations in the western Solomon Islands, notes that whereas, in the past, the sibling relationship of brother and sister (*luluna*) was the critical gender relation, it has now shifted to that of husband and wife. Up until British pacification and Methodist conversion at about 1900, brothers exercised a violent control over their sister's sexuality and fertility. A woman who had sex or a child outside marriage could not only be violently disciplined but even killed by her brother, since this was thought to imperil his own life in war and especially in head-hunting raids. In that era, husbands and wives lived separately for long periods, and the protracted sexual abstinence, coupled with indigenous practices of fertility control and perhaps poor nutrition, kept the average family to the ideal of two. Missionary reforms, enacted by local converts, not only entailed the co-residence of husbands and wives, and a dramatic increase in the number of living children per woman, but also diminished the power of brothers over sisters at the expense of the husband. Husbands today exercise a violent control over their wives—a violence which both parallels the powers of *luluna,* but which some men legitimate by Biblical quotations. Dureau perceives the greater salience of the nuclear family as partly due to Christian conversion, but also deriving from the shortage of material resources, cash and available land which forces many to privilege close family over more distant kin.

Dureau challenges an earlier claim in the literature about Polynesia, and especially Tonga, that the shift from a stress on the sibling relation to the conjugal relation necessarily entails a shift from women's equality to male domination. In Simbo this shift was rather from one mode of male domination to another, since the relation of brother and sister was patently one of female subordination, not equality. In Tonga, in the past and still to some extent today, the brother–sister relation was characterized by respect and avoidance, especially among higher-ranking families. Her claim that the combination of Christian conversion and of capitalist penetration led to the 'domestication' of Tongan women and the loss of the significance of the sister in favour of the wife has been challenged. The brother–sister relation is now more relaxed, and the powers sisters assume varies by rank and denomination, but they have not disappeared. Critics attest to the continuing high value of Tongan women, especially as sisters, the continued significance of extended families in Tonga itself and diasporic communities overseas, even

Children of Tauhunu village perform a drum dance (*hupahupa*) at a welcoming ceremony, Manihiki, Cook Islands

where nucleated family households predominate. Moreover, they challenge Gailey's related claim about the devaluation of 'women's wealth' with the substitution of imported cloth for indigenous textiles. Cloth is still crucial to Tongan kinship exchanges—even if *ngatu* are sometimes made with calico, paper and house paint rather than the bark and earth ochres of the past.

There have also been familial transformations in French Polynesia. It is argued that the combination of capitalist intrusion and Christian patriarchal ideology has 'domesticated' Tahitian women as the family form has become more nucleated. Through violent early contact, drastic depopulation and the continuing impact of French control in Tahiti, the indigenous structures of chiefly hierarchy and family life which conferred on chiefly women, in particular, great powers and privileges were dramatically changed. In this process, women lost the authority they had both in the domestic and the public sphere, where men prevailed in the new organizations of church and state. On Tubuai, the Christian ideology of the male as the head of the family is accepted, and women are relegated to 'family' life. Although women contribute much to both subsistence and commodity production, men control the cash in families and the commodity economy at large. Elliston has challenged this view on the basis of her research on Huahine and in Pape'ete. She suggests that it is women who are more regularly connected to the cash economy both through wage and salaried employment and through the selling of craft goods, while men have more invested in the 'traditional' values of Polynesian exchange. Moreover, women are still often named as titleholders of family land, and many households are matrifocal and dominated by women. Young men move between households, living with different relatives and offering labour for food and accommodation. Young women are more attached to one household, often retaining a room in their natal household even when they move out. These gendered differences in attachments to households and modes of belonging to localized or dispersed places, Elliston argues, explain young men's greater enthusiasm for nationalist ideals.—MJ

Further reading

Dureau, C, 1998. 'From sisters to wives: changing contexts of maternity on Simbo', in K Ram and M Jolly (eds), *Maternities and Modernities: colonial and postcolonial experiences in Asia and the Pacific*, Cambridge University Press.

Elliston, D A, 1997. En-Gendering nationalism: colonialism, sex, and independence in French Polynesia, Doctoral dissertation, Department of Anthropology, New York University.

Gailey, C Ward, 1980. 'Putting down sisters and wives: Tongan women and colonization', in M Etienne and E Leacock (eds), *Women and Colonization: anthropological perspectives*, Praeger.

Jolly, M, 1994. *Women of the Place: kastom, colonialism and Christianity in Vanuatu*, Harwood Academic Press.

—— and Macintyre, M, 1989. *Family and Gender in the Pacific: domestic contradictions and the colonial impact*, Cambridge University Press.

Lockwood, V S, 1993. *Tahitian Transformation: gender and capitalist development in a rural society*, Lynne Reiner Publishers.

Masing, H, 1992. '*Braed Praes*', in Grace Mera Molisa (ed.), *Who Will Carry the Bag?*, Vanuatu National Council of Women.

Strathern, M, 1984. 'Women as subjects, women as objects', in R Hirschon (ed.), *Women and Property, Women as Property*, Croom Helm.

Toft, S, (ed.), 1985. *Domestic Violence in Papua New Guinea*, Law Reform Commission of Papua New Guinea.

Weiner, A B, 1988. *The Trobrianders of Papua New Guinea*, Holt, Rinehart and Winston.

Rituals of the life-cycle

Pacific cultures maintained social and bio-cosmic regulation through rituals. At births there are characteristic ritual showings. Among the coastal Madang Bargan, the newborn child is held up to the nearby forest and loudly named, so that spirits dwelling there would know it and refrain from assault. Infants are kept away from certain sacred spots; even a toddler touching the tabu pole in front of the Mekeo chiefs' *ufu* house would be put to death. Initiation rites were fundamental for instilling the law and tabus of the security circle. In Melanesia young men commonly faced ordeals to prove their bravery and worth as new adults—the young Wahgi initiates pushed closer and closer to a fire in the men's house until virtually dehydrated, or the youth of the Duke of York Islands made to swim across shark-frequented waters. At a cathartic moment the basic rules of the group would be revealed, often by a masked figure, and more intense teaching later began in a period of seclusion before boys could appear, fully decorated, as men. In many cases participation in attacking or killing enemies was part of the initiation procedures. Young girls were instructed in nursing wounds and concocting herbal remedies, as well as in midwifery. Analogies are found in Micronesia and Polynesia but greater and earlier social changes have left them less well documented.

In stratified chiefly societies, of course, rituals involving chiefs were pivotal. A chief's installation

Men and women of Tūkao village singing *hīmene tuki tapu*, known as *ʻīmene tuki* in Rarotongan, at a tombstone unveiling ceremony, Manihiki, Cook Islands

had to confirm worthiness, as suggested by the awesome avowals Roro and Mekeo chiefs had to make on such occasions. Deaths of great ones were momentous; Maori chiefs' last verbal wills and testaments were heavily ritualized and a dying ruler, propped up, had to name his successor. Among certain Maori groups a chief was carefully entombed to make sure of his passage to become a star.

Funerals were obviously more important for the living than the dead. They involved liminal situations in which various groups had to be satisfied with wealth distribution; the pathway of the dead had to be carefully secured so that ghostly trouble for kin would not ensue; time had to be set aside for funeral ceremonies when younger warriors and allies could be itching for revenge; while a powerful man might find himself temporarily out of circulation, and put on a strict fast for having accidentally touched a corpse. Rites for the dead varied across the Pacific. Exposure to the atmosphere, with dripping pits and the wearing of dried bones as memento was more the Melanesian fashion; outstanding tombs or monuments at graves better exemplified from Polynesia. Unproductive, perhaps crippled persons could be quickly buried in Melanesia, as among the Wam (SEPIK RIVER hinterland). Commoners' graves were insignificant in Tonga, ordinary folk being expected to live a lowly underground life eating vermin. Occasionally the grave sites of 'good' and 'bad' people were separated (as among some New Guinea Chimbu), yet for most Pacific cultures any group's collective deceased were expected to share the same conditions. Heavens and hells make few appearances. The Papuan inland Erave believed men fighting on the field of battle, and women supporting them, would go to a Vailala-like red place, and the rest to a dull brown one. In the far western Micronesian outlier culture of Wuvulu, malefactors would have to put up with a temporary hell, being defecated on by punitive Puela spirits, until such a time as they were called to the main body of the dead.

Rituals of the life-cycle, and associated beliefs, require comparison with great periodic festivities, and with a wide variety of sacrificial acts to secure special benefits. In many places, from the Kabu harvest festival among the Ngaing (in the Madang hinterland) to the Makahitii New Year and Luakini Temple Renewal festivals on Hawaiʻi, great feasts were annual. In many other cultures, the periods between a group's bigger events were longer, roughly 12–15 years between Wahgi tribes' *Kongar*, for instance, or about 25 between the exciting *hevehe* ceremonies on the Papuan Gulf, when the mask of the threatening sea-monster was burnt and cast into the brine. Sacrifices in Melanesia were less 'classic-looking' for not being made on high altars, though some such altar-making was known, for example, among the Toambaita on north Malaita (Solomon

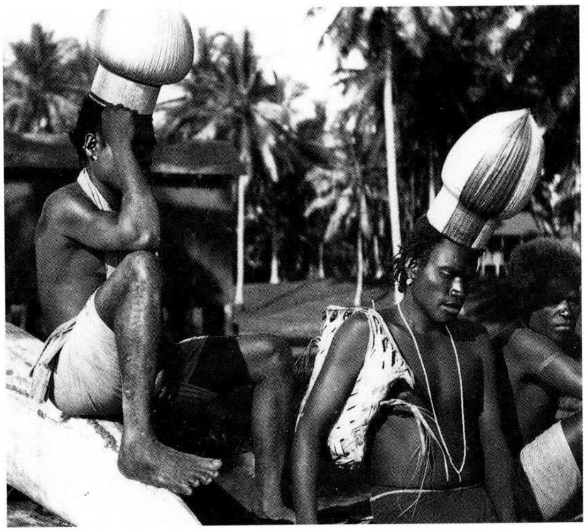

Young men on Bougainville in 1933 wearing the bulbous hats—made of pandanus, tied to the head and not to be removed—that were part of their traditional initiation procedure, photographed by Sarah Chinnery

Islands). In Micronesia and especially Polynesia, stone platforms open to the air (*malae/marae*, on which sacrifices were made) are well known, perhaps indicating a lack of familiarity with temple building, while Melanesia experienced a greater range of temple architecture. The great high-pinnacled *rau* and *eravo* cult houses among the Purari and Elema were the tallest structures of Melanesia (and in the *eravo*, Hiri traders arriving with their pots would first have to leave offerings to the goddess Kaeva-Kuku), while the Sepik *tambaran* houses, though more richly decorated, come second in their uplift. In such a high *tambaran* house the Yuat River 'ancestor-god' Vlisuak had to be fed daily. Everyday depositing of offerings in large shrines such as these was matched by leaving food remainders out for the dead after the night meals in houses (and even if cockroaches and other scavengers took away the bits and pieces, as Trobriand Islanders tell, it was the dead who were thought to participate in the meal through these small 'messengers' or manifestations).

Forms and objects of sacrificing make for intriguing comparative study. Human sacrifices were more prominent in eastern Melanesia; Fijians would kill caught victims in a sacred enclosure before delivering them to cannibal feasts for trade points; and western Solomonese Roviana used to run the newly carved hull of their headhunting canoes across a stack of dead victims. Temple dedications in Polynesia could involve human sacrifice, typically with the hairs carefully picked off, but of only one or two people. From Vanuatu to central Polynesia, KAVA was not only ceremonially drunk for friendship and negotiation, but also often poured on the ground in sacrificial libations. Sexual acts were sometimes ritually and publicly performed, women 'sacrificing' themselves this way on Malekula (Vanuatu), so that priests would be properly 'made', under the shadow of the remarkable megaliths. A form of Melanesian sacrificial 'suttee' was known, the Lemakot widows of New Ireland being thrown on their husbands' funeral pyres.

Ritual and ritual sites for enclosures bespeak also creative artistry. 'Art', like 'religion', is perhaps an inappropriate term in most Pacific cultures, for the skilful making of decorated objects in 'creative participation'. The erection of significant buildings; the patient preparation of patterned and serrated weapons; the making of canoe prows (as with the Papuan Gogodala, or the Trobriand Islanders); the design-making of great shields (as with the southwest Irian Jayese Asmat); the feather headdress decorations from New Guinea's Melpa warriors to Tahitian nobles; the carved shell armlet of the Motuans to the carved *tiki* amulets of the Maori; TATTOOING designs; the varieties of masks and sculptured figures; painted and notched musical instruments; kites, net-bags and pots: these expressions of material culture are also integral to religious life. They are the investments of a vital warrior outlook, which makes sure that all important items for survival are 'ritually prepared'. They are tokens of identity and symbols of wealth or a good name. It is wrong to exaggerate the theory that Melanesian artists were 'slaves to tradition', but certainly they were often under pressure to keep to established rules and a clan's characteristic designs.—GWT

Divination

For thousands of years, all over the world, divination has inspired interest and awe in many, while it has been despised by the élite. As a philosophy of religious significance, or a sacred ritual, divination rests on the principle of a divine concept of universal harmony underlying the surface of chaotic reality; the diviner knows subtle ways to exclude chance and omit meaningless illusions, in order to identify the path along which a society may progress in intimate and positive relationship with its territory.

On Pacific beaches we can salvage only a few wrecks of this ancient philosophy: we meet questionable interpreters of birds' flights, or shamans with their hands dripping blood from the entrails of sacrificed victims (the liver was as important in Hawai'i and Tahiti as it was in Babylon or ancient Rome); or with their eyes fixed on twigs with orange leaves (in Kosrae, Micronesia); or throwing pairs of oyster shells to get an oracle from the coupling of concave or convex sides. Pacific islanders have had three distinctive divination systems, detailed in early missionary reports and in the monumental documentation of the German Süd-See Expedition (1908–10). The first and most primitive method, familiar to Polynesians, is used for trivial matters: the diviner checks whether the folding of a coconut leaf, cut at random, does or does not coincide positively with the width of the questioner's hand. A second system, practised mainly in Nauru, was the modern and sophisticated derivation of the Arabic divination method, known in the west as geomancy, and widely applied in Europe after the Crusades. The third type of divination is peculiar to Micronesia and Marshall Islands. Known as *bue* in Chuuk, *bua* in Haluk, *wei* in Yap, and *foa* in Kosrae, it involves the leaves of the coconut palm, which has sacred value since it is essential to survival. Four leaves are thickly knotted at random, and inserted between the fingers; after four knots have been counted off on each leaf, the surplus knots only will be kept in sight, poking above the back of the hand. Then the leaves are paired, two by two, and the resulting couplets of numbers (for instance, 3–1, or 0–2) will be recorded, repeating the knots on a string. Reciting a catch-phrase, the diviner quotes names corresponding to sailors of a mythical canoe that visited Micronesia to teach people true understanding; from those names, they will know how to behave.

Such intricate processes aim at creating a fluid yet orderly complex of connections, matching the complexity of ordinary life and imposing on it a humanly acceptable framework. The universal occurrence of the number 4 is not fortuitous; it is a way of controlling chance, since chance is subject to the four dimensions of space. This is why in Yi Ching, sticks are counted off by four, just as divination rosary beads are counted in Tibet. Fortune-telling dice had four sides in Rome as well as among the Bantu; and 4 is the sacred number in Chuuk, just as 8, its double, is sacred in Melanesia.—MSC

Feasts and the symbolism of food

Feasting represented one end of the oscillation between plenty and scarcity that marked many societies before the 20th century. But in the Pacific the social gathering was important as well as the material aspects of the food eaten at feasts. Feasts have been part of celebrations of a particular event for a very long time. They celebrated a visit by a neighbouring CLAN or tribe (such as the feasts called *malaga* in Samoa), the death of a particular person, or a victory over circumstances such as DROUGHT or over an opposing clan. Food has usually been available in abundance, and in great variety. Major feasts such as the *'inasi* in Tonga, or a *magiti* in Fiji, caught the eye of Captain COOK and other visitors for the displays of food, such as the 'wall of pigs'. In their view such 'prodigal abundance' was wasteful. Feasting in the Pacific, according to the Victorian or Christian ethic, was marked by over-indulgence.

Feasts marked a break in the daily routine. Not only was it necessary to gather and prepare large amounts of food in greater variety than was normally eaten, but such work necessitated cooperation between households and extended family members who did not eat together on a regular basis. They were notable for the change in the daily round. Preparing for a feast may take a week, or longer, if we take into account the planting cycle that allowed for such irregular calls on those food crops.

Food, however, was only one part of a feast. It was very necessary and subject to much comment about the types of foods (such as turtles) or the abundance of particular foods. But drinking KAVA, certainly in Polynesia, and dancing (as in SINGSING IN PAPUA NEW GUINEA) also made the whole event memorable. A kava ceremony was included as part of any feast, and entertainment, especially dancing for the guests, was an essential feature. So feasts were complex social events.

Certain foods were deemed culturally suitable for feasts. The importance of the starch foods, such as yams, taro, or sweet potato, over the protein foods, particularly pigs, is hard to ascertain for those times before western influence put higher value on the protein content of such events. Pig kills in Highland Papua New Guinea have been much noted as have the large numbers of pigs killed for a feast in Fiji or Tonga. Certainly turtle has always been an important feast food, symbolizing chiefly food. At the other end of the scale, recently introduced foods such as cassava are not deemed appropriate for a feast; they are 'just family food'.

Abundance is a key feature of any feast. Today, amounts suitable to the occasion are calculated, with each family involved being asked to contribute a given amount. For a Tongan feast, a family will be asked to provide a *pola*, a coconut basket food tray on which yam, taro, a chicken or a large fish and two or three drinking coconuts are placed. The term *pola* is linked to the term *polapolo*, which referred to the presentation of first fruits. Formerly the amounts were left to the family or household to provide as they deemed fit to represent their status. A *tapu* was sometimes placed on a particular crop to ensure enough would be available for an up-coming feast. Contributions to feasts thus represented the extreme values of sharing food, where generosity was paramount.

Much of the food presented at a feast was not eaten at the site. Rather those present might eat a little of what was before them, with the bulk of the coconut basketful being sent back to the house. The persons seated at a feast were the representatives of families invited as guests. Their families though not physically present participated in sharing the food after the main event. The person whose task it was to divide the food at a feast held a high rank in Polynesian societies, sometimes a chiefly title. Thus the size of the participant group at a feast could not be judged from the numbers of persons present. More important were the social ties between visitors and the hosts as expressed through distribution of the contributions.

As well as being occasions of social solidarity, feasts were also competitive. On Goodenough Island, people manipulated their social relationships through feasts, many of which had the purpose of supporting up and coming BIG-MEN. A feast was thus important for the contrast it provided to the normal daily round of activities, including eating. It marked a high-point in people's memories, especially where the abundance and variety occurred after a time when food had been short. Feasts necessitated a lot of work—the status of the host group was at stake. The honour for the success of the event accrued to the host group rather than to any one individual. Groups competed to provide more special foods, thus escalating or inflating the value of the occasion. This inflation has continued to the present time, especially where food is used as part of 'treating' for political recognition.

The contrast between feast and famine was particularly marked in Pacific societies. Irregular supplies of food due to environmental circumstances were mitigated by occasional feasts to mark special events. And breaks in daily routines were welcomed, especially for the social enhancements of dancing, good food and drinking kava. The strength of feasts as social occasions has thus carried them through into modern times when the food supply is more regular, and the occasions for feasts are more frequent. Thus feasting combines both material and symbolic aspects.—NJP

Further reading

Mennell, S, 1985. *All Manners of Food*, Basil Blackwell.

Pollock, N J, 1992. *These Roots Remain*, IPS and University of Hawai'i Press.

Young, M, 1971. *Fighting with Food*, Cambridge University Press.

Kava

Kava (*Piper methysticum*), a member of the pepper family, is a handsome shrub growing up to 3 m tall. Chemical and genetic evidence suggests that *Piper methysticum* consists of sterile cultivars cloned from a wild progenitor, *Piper wichmannii*, in an ongoing selection process. This evidence also suggests that kava most likely was domesticated in northern Vanuatu around 3000 years ago. It spread from farmer to farmer throughout Vanuatu and eastwards into Fiji and most of Polynesia except New Zealand, Easter Island, Rapa, Tuvalu and the Tuamotus. People also brought kava to two Micronesian islands, Pohnpei and Kosrae. From here, perhaps, it made its way south to a number of isolated locales in New Guinea, including Admiralty Islands, coastal areas near Madang, and the southern border region of Papua New Guinea and Irian Jaya.

While kava use has declined or disappeared in some areas (such as Kosrae, Tikopia, Hawai'i and French Polynesia), it remains strong elsewhere (Vanuatu, Fiji, Samoa and Tonga). Kava-drinking has also spread into new regions, including urban Noumea in New Caledonia and some Australian Aboriginal communities. The drug is increasingly popular, as well, in Europe and North America where it is sold for medical or recreational purposes. Kava is an important cash crop within several Pacific island agricultural economies, such as Vanuatu and Fiji where growers provide kava roots, often dried and powdered, for urban kava bars and retail sale. They also produce kava for export to the international pharmaceutical industry.

Kava ceremony, Yasawa Island, Fiji

The plant's active principles are a series of kavalactones that are concentrated in its rootstock and roots. Users ingest these chemicals by drinking cold-water infusions of chewed, ground, pounded, or otherwise macerated kava stumps and roots. Given the plant's complex and subtle psychoactivity, it is difficult to categorize in terms of common drug typologies, although it is often described as a narcotic or a sedative hypnotic. Kava may induce sociability, feelings of peace and harmony and, in larger doses, sleep; or it may fail to produce relaxation and provoke nausea. Typically, however, kava evokes an atmosphere of relaxation and easy sociability among drinkers. It is non-addictive and has no side effects except for causing skin scaliness in heavy users.

Kava retains important religious, political, and economic functions in all societies in which it is used. The drug serves as a means of religious inspiration and knowledge production. It acts to connect drinkers with the realm of ancestors and gods. Kava drinking also signals good fellowship. By sharing kava, people create new relations with strangers and repair these relations when they falter. Bowls of kava lubricate island political systems, as men and women assume chiefly rank by acquiring traditional titles, enemies make peace, law-breakers seek forgiveness, and leaders attract supporters. The everyday details of drinking kava signal the state of important social relationships and mark the identities and roles of the people involved. Typically, men's greater access to and use of kava differs from that of women, and chiefs' from that of commoners. In Fiji, Samoa, and Tonga, in particular, an elaborate etiquette of kava preparation and consumption marks the status of drinkers within social and political hierarchies.—LL

Clan

Clan refers to a range of kin-based social groups commonly found throughout the Pacific, and among many other peoples around the world, including some Australian Aborigines, Native Americans, and ancient Scots, from whom the term originates. Though diverse in form, all such groups establish membership mainly or entirely by having a parent who is a member of the group. Marriage is generally forbidden between members of the same clan—that is, it is exogamous.

Among some peoples, such the Iatmul of the Middle Sepik, and in much of Polynesia, it is the father's clan affiliation that determines that of the children; while in other places such as Dobu, Trobriand Islands and Chuuk (formerly Truk), it is the mother's. In some places it can go either way, depending on where the child actually grows up, lives and works. This is true, for example, of much of the central Papua New Guinea Highlands, though in practice clan affiliation there more often follows that of the father than the mother. Elsewhere, such as among the Duna of Papua New Guinea's Southern Highlands, people can be fully identified with more than one clan, through both the father and the mother, or even a parent's father and mother, and so on. The number of clans with which a person can be affiliated in such a system obviously depends on how many ancestors they keep track of. Among the Duna it is very many—genealogies 8–10 generations deep are not uncommon.

Clans also differ in where people live. Given that marriage within the clan is forbidden or immoral, and that husbands and wives generally live close together, no clan can be an entirely compact residential group. Its members will always be found somewhat interspersed among people of other clans. In some places, such as the middle SEPIK and Chuuk, there is little connection between where you live and what clan you belong to. But elsewhere it is common for each clan to be identified with a specific area of land, which people of that clan have the main rights to use and to make available for the use of others. This is sometimes true even in systems such as the Duna one, where a person is affiliated with more than one clan, in which case the person has potential rights in many clan lands, which can be variously activated over a person's lifetime, or even after a lapse of several generations.

Clans are often internally differentiated into smaller segments, named by anthropologists as subclans, sub-sub-clans, etc; and grouped into higher level units, known as tribe and phratry. Sometimes the relations among these more and less inclusive levels are organized in terms of descent from more and less remote common ancestors, but this is perhaps less usual in the Pacific than elsewhere.—AR2

Polygyny

Polygyny was a common practice in most Pacific societies in the past, but today it survives in only a few locations. The most common element of polygyny was that it served as a marker of high masculine status; thus the arithmetic of polygyny was that high-ranking men had a number of wives and low-ranking men had one or none. The rationale of polygyny differed between ranked and egalitarian societies. In the ranked societies of Polynesia and Micronesia, its primary purpose was to maximize the genealogical connections between high-ranking descent groups. Thus men of chiefly rank took a succession of wives from other high-ranking families. The giving of secondary wives or concubines to men of high rank by those of lower rank was also motivated by the honour of such advantageous connections. This assisted the formation of political alliances between chiefdoms, and contributed to the 'breeding' of aristocratic men and women to perpetuate dynastic successions. In Samoa, for example, the most genealogically qualified young virgin women were installed ceremonially to *taupou* titles, taking the name of a famous female ancestor, and signalling their availability for an aristocratic match. Courting parties on behalf of chiefs, or the heir apparent, would then compete to arrange a marriage. Such marriages were usually of relatively brief duration. When a child was born to the union, a further such marriage would be sought for the chief, and the wife would return to her own people. In Samoa, she could not remarry unless the rank and power of her kin exceeded that of her former husband, although in Tonga and Hawai'i, chiefly women could and did make a succession of marriages as they saw fit. Indeed in Marquesas Islands, aristocratic women took secondary husbands or male concubines as a perquisite of their status. The exchange of valuable property which attended chiefly marriage was also of considerable importance. Highly valued goods such as fine MATS and red feathers flowed between the highest ranking families of Samoa, Tonga and eastern Fiji via marriage alliances.

In Melanesian societies, there was a tendency to attribute generic superiority to males and inferiority to females. Alliances motivated by genealogical considerations were thus less common, and there was a highly developed notion that women themselves were a valuable currency. This was emphasized by the common practice of gifts from the wife-takers to the wife-givers at marriage, in contrast to the practice in Polynesia where the gifts of highest value were given by the wife-givers. The labour of his wives contributed to an ambitious man's store of wealth, through which he could sponsor FEASTS and distributions of property to enhance his reputation and build his quest for public renown. However, the function of marriage in pursuit of alliances was of major importance, often being the principal mechanism by which different groups cemented coalitions for various purposes, or restored peaceful relations after fighting. Polygyny was (and still is) regarded by most Christian churches as an impediment to church membership. Missionary opposition was fierce and effective in the 19th century in most of Polynesia and Micronesia, with the result that the practice had been virtually discontinued by the early 20th century. In those areas of Melanesia that were evangelized in the late 19th and early 20th century, polygyny has become relatively uncommon. Those societies that refused Christian conversion, such as the Kwaio of Malaita, have continued the practice, as have other groups in Melanesia who have encountered Christianity more recently.—PS2

Adoption

Adoption and fostering of children is a social institution in many Pacific societies, particularly in Polynesia. Its purpose was to strengthen extended family ties, to enable adults to have children of the needed age and sex in their households; and in some cases, to maximize the social standing and rank of a family. An adopted child was usually referred to as a 'made child'. Adoption was almost always among kin, so that a child developed an expanded rather than a new family identity, and retained knowledge of and some degree of interaction with its natural parents. In eastern Polynesia younger women who had not settled into a conjugal relationship would typically give their child to relatives who, by fostering the child, were acknowledged to have a special but not exclusive relationship with it—as in Cook Islands, where a foster child is termed a 'feeding child'. Children were an economic asset from the age of about 7 or 8 years, and older couples, widows and widowers would often foster older children, who in return would perform their chores. In western Polynesia, where great emphasis was laid on the complementarity of brothers and sisters, it was considered desirable for boys to have sisters, and families deficient in children of one sex would adopt from close relatives to balance their families. Children were also often transferred to kin with high social status so that the children might render service while gaining the benefits of living in a high-ranking household.

In Melanesian societies, adoption does not seem to have been institutionalized to the same extent. Some societies practised infant betrothal, in which young girls were raised in the households of their prospective husbands. The predominance of unilineal systems of descent in Melanesia and Micronesia, where group membership rights were transferred through only one parent (rather than both parents, as was common in Polynesia), influenced practices of adoption in the case of orphaned children; ideally such children were adopted by relatives of the parent from whom they inherited rights. In both non-unilineal and patrilineal Pacific societies there was an ideal that widows should remarry a close kinsman of their deceased husband in order to keep the children in his descent group. Generally the rights and status of adopted children were little different to those of children raised by their natural parents, since adoption was usually amongst kin. In terms of succession rights to chiefly office in Polynesian societies, pre-Christian principles laid primary emphasis on the genealogical rank of the natural father and mother. Adopted children could not inherit social rank and chiefly titles unless their genealogical qualifications fitted the prevailing social and religious prescriptions. European missionaries in the 19th century tended to disapprove of adoption and fostering practices. The teaching that children were a 'gift from God', and admonitions from the pulpit that the transference of infant children with living parents was an 'unnatural act', has tended to weaken the institutional nature of adoption in Polynesia. The growth of market economies and universal education has also had an impact on the practice, as children become more of an expense and less of an immediate asset.—PS2

Prostitution

Early explorers in the Pacific incorrectly perceived the propensity of island women to offer themselves to visiting sailors as evidence of indigenous prostitution. The romantic notion of eastern Polynesia as a region of 'free love' grew out of this misunderstanding of early contact relationships. Throughout most of Polynesia in pre-contact times, independent women of the lower ranks were free to form temporary liaisons with men visiting their settlements, a practice which some foreign observers have described as prostitution. But such relationships appear to have been voluntarily initiated by women and there is little evidence that they were motivated by economic considerations. It is more likely that the practice was required of lower-ranking women as a public duty to provide hospitality to guests. It quickly developed an economic character in some islands during the early contact period in eastern Polynesia. Women were initially sent out to the ships to placate potentially dangerous foreigners, and possibly to try to acquire the supernatural powers initially attributed to them. Women offering themselves to sailors were given gifts for their services—iron nails and fishhooks were an early currency. This exchange of favours rapidly developed into well-established 18th century patterns of interaction between islanders and foreign seafarers, introducing venereal disease to the Pacific and contributing to population decline in some places. Practices analogous to prostitution arose in WHALING and trading ports in the 19th century when women were contracted as temporary wives in exchange for money and trade goods given to their kin. There were Melanesian practices of prostitution in which women captured in war, or regarded as delinquents, became 'public' property for sexual purposes, but such practices did not attain the legendary dimensions of Polynesia. The exception may be Trobriand Islands, although the 'free love' initiated on festive occasions by young women has no overtones of prostitution.

In the contemporary Pacific, prostitution is fairly widespread. It is not organized on the scale it is in the west, or in some Asian countries, although recent concerns have been voiced that sex tourism, including those catering to paedophiles, is on the increase in some island countries. The more common pattern is casual 'pickup' sex for gifts, involving women, young men and transsexuals, centred upon night-clubs and ports in major towns. In Papua New Guinea, prostitution became established on the Highlands highway in the 1970s, where young women '*pasendia meri*' sought to escape oppressive marriages by forming liaisons with truck drivers and moving into a life of prostitution. In Fiji and Solomon Islands, there has been a well-established system of temporary liaisons between local women and Asian contract fishermen. Prostitution is also associated with urbanization, increasing poverty, and the plight of near-destitute women in squatter settlements in several countries in the region, where there are organized brothels. The apparent growth in prostitution in the Pacific is a major public health concern because of its role in the spread of HIV INFECTION/AIDS.—PS2

Gender

Gender, once defined as a grammatical term only, has undergone a transformation and expansion of its meaning, in part as a resistance to the biological determinism implicit in the word 'sex'. Although Margaret MEAD (in *Sex and Temperament in Three Primitive Societies*, 1935) first mooted the idea that 'woman' and 'man' were cultural constructs rather than natural, it was not till the late 1960s that feminist scholars distinguished sex, the biological differences between men and women, from gender, the social constructions of masculine and feminine. This distinction has since been challenged by those who argue that the body is not so readily transcended by mind and that the distinction relies on a facile view of the social. It has also been challenged by those who doubt the universality of 'sex' as biological difference. Paradoxically a stress on the social construction of gender has often coexisted with forms of biological determinism. The 'nature' implicit in sex has been challenged by anthropologists who claim this is a recent western folk model which fixates on the genitals as signs of interior differences—fluids, hormones and chromosomes—and on the reproductive relation of men and women as the basis of their difference. The very notion of nature entailed in the concept of sex has been proclaimed a western cultural construct.

General premises about sex and gender have various relationships to indigenous meanings in the Pacific, involving cross-cultural translation and historical transformation. Marilyn Strathern has argued that there are fundamental differences in Melanesian constructs of gender and that many anthropological accounts of gender in Melanesia had imported foreign notions of the person grounded in western individualism. She challenges the relevance of gendered oppositions like nature/culture and domestic/public and suggests that Melanesians, unlike western 'individuals', are permeable and partible. Personal relationships are composed through debts to others, male and female, and thus persons are not readily 'sexed' as male or female by their anatomy, but rather gendered 'masculine' or 'feminine' through the processes of social life. Melanesian gender is not just a language pertaining to persons, but other beings, artifacts, events and processes are gendered masculine or feminine, and perhaps equally important, same-sex and cross-sex.

Her analysis has been influential, although many perceive the difference as overdrawn, too reliant on a dichotomy between the west and Melanesia which denies the historical relations pertaining between these worlds, relations configured by a colonial history of exploration, missionary projects, capitalist penetration and state formation. There are many ways to approach pasts of Oceanic gender relations. In reconstructing ancestral native views of gender many have relied on the oral historical traditions of genealogy, stories and chants. Throughout the eastern Pacific, there are variants of the primordial story of Sky Father and Earth Mother—which construct the difference between male and female origins and relate the difference not just to sky and earth, but also to light and dark. Such stories of primordial conjugation, incest and infanticide yield fascinating insights not just into the gender and sexual scripts of ancient Polynesia, but into how rank articulated with gender. In Melanesia the origin stories of sexual difference are equally rich but more diverse—with women variously emerging from a parthenogenic male belly, a castrated younger brother or from plants or birds. Such narratives often explain not just sexual difference but justify customary practices—the separation of men and women in eating or housing, local variants of male or female initiation, the enduring forms of kinship and spatial attachments and appropriate work relations of women and men.

But as well as spoken stories about the past, there are other sources from which we might discern earlier patterns of gender relations—textual, material, corporeal. In some parts of the Pacific, indigenous peoples, with the guidance of Christian missionaries, rendered their stories as texts in their own languages and in translation. Such texts often combined or opposed ancestral and Christian models of gender—thus effecting early transformations as is perhaps attested by the translation of indigenous eroticism in Hawai'i as 'promiscuity' and the patterns of *kapu* (segregation or taboos between genders and ranks) as based on notions of 'pollution'. Spatial culture—the remains of house forms, ritual grounds and temple structures—can witness how men and women lived, ate, celebrated and worshipped in the past, together and apart. In the Christian villages of Vanuatu, men and women now eat and sleep together, while traces of exclusive men's houses, paths and dancing grounds are still visible in the earth. Artifacts may reveal common or differentiated patterns of labour—the bows and arrows of Melanesian male fishing and hunting as against the same-sexed digging stick of Melanesian horticulture; the mallets used by women in making *tapa* in Polynesia and parts of Melanesia; the famous earth ovens whose baked and steamed food were the culinary specialty of men. Clothing and ornament also yield insights into the indigenous practices and aesthetics of sexual difference and of rank—grass skirts and penis wrappers, *tapa* wraps, flax and feather cloaks, the elaborate hairdos of Tannese and Fijian men, and greenstone ornaments of Maori men and women. And perhaps most graphically for a foreign spectator, brilliant body art—from the evanescent primary colours painted on the bodies of men in the Highlands of Papua New Guinea (BILAS), to the permanent marks of TATTOOING which mark the difference between and the connection of male and female bodies (as well as the differential embodiment of rank). Thus gender is told not just through stories or conversation but through the languages of bodies and of things.

These past patterns of Oceanic genders are known not just through excavation but recuperation and transformation. HAWAIIAN HULA with its associated erotic chants has been revived after decades of suppression and is performed not just for the tourists at Waikīkī but for local audiences in annual competitions like the Merrie Monarch Festival. Women throughout the Pacific are making textiles with both the old materials of *tapa* and pandanus, and with introduced cloth. With these fabrics they create beautiful baskets, mats, dresses and quilts. The pasts of gender liminality, of *mahu* in Tahiti for instance, is in dynamic relation with imported ideas of gender identity and sexual orientation (see TRANSVESTISM). Thus we often know the gendered patterns of the past through how they are reinscribed and reinterpreted for the present.—MJ

Further reading

Besnier, Niko, 1994. 'Polynesian gender liminality through time and space', in G Herdt (ed.), *Third Sex, Third Gender: beyond sexual dimorphism in culture and history*, Zone Books.

Strathern, M, 1988. *The Gender of the Gift*, University of California Press.

Transvestism (transgenderism)

In many societies in the Pacific, there is a category of individuals who adopt certain characteristics of members of the opposite gender. Men who fall in this category may dress up as women more or less routinely, perform work normally associated with women, adopt women's demeanour, and regularly socialize with women rather than with men, against normal expectations. They often engage in sexual intercourse with ordinary men, during which they generally adopt a passive (that is, 'woman-like') role. Women can also follow the reverse pattern, namely to dress, work, and act as men, and conduct sexual relations with other women as if they were men. Because it involves much more than simply

Contestants in 1997 Miss Galaxy fakaleitī beauty pageant in Nuku'alofa, Tonga: such pageants are held regularly in many urban centres of the Pacific islands, providing a context in which transgendered identities come into full bloom

dressing like a member of the opposite gender (implied by the term 'transvestism'), the phenomenon should be referred to with the vaguer descriptors 'transgenderism' or 'gender liminality' ('liminality' signifying states and individuals who are 'betwixt and between' social categories). The local terms that refer to such individuals differ greatly from one language to the other: transgendered males are called *mahu* in Tahitian and Hawaiian, *fakaleiti* (or *fakafefine*) in Tongan, *fa'afafine* in Samoan, and *binabinaaine* in Gilbertese. (The phenomenon should not be conflated with patterns of gender reversal that characterize certain rituals in some traditional Melanesian societies.)

The dearth of information on transgenderism in Pacific societies makes it difficult to assess precisely its geographical and historical attestations. It appears to be a quintessentially Polynesian phenomenon, although it is also found in urban areas of Melanesia and Micronesia, where it may be of relatively recent vintage. Even in Polynesia, its distribution is uneven in both time and space: it is very salient in larger and more urbanized societies like Tahiti and Samoa, but not reported in more remote Polynesian societies like Tikopia. There is unequivocal historical documentation of its existence in Tahiti at the time of first contacts with westerners; in Tonga, early European travellers explicitly remarked its absence, even though it is today prevalent there. While transgenderism is considered to be an integral part of 'tradition' in much of Polynesia, it is not necessarily of great antiquity, nor pervasive in the region.

Little serious research has been conducted among transgendered Pacific islanders, and no research has focused on transgendered females. Anthropologist Robert Levy proposed in the early 1970s that the presence of transgendered males in Tahiti was related to a lack of clear differentiation between men and women. Transgendered men display to other men a model of what not to be, something which Tahitian society fails to provide. The functionalist logic underlying this hypothesis has now been set aside although it is generally recognized that transgendered Pacific islanders do mediate between certain aspects of womanhood and certain aspects of manhood. Contemporary research shies away from attempting to explain the presence or absence of the phenomenon, and instead focuses on the social, political and cultural position of transgenderism in Polynesian societies. Transgenderism in the Pacific is not a unified phenomenon, in that it can differ significantly across individuals and across societies, in its characteristics and its social significance, so that providing a list of diagnostic attributes is impossible. However, certain patterns recur across the Pacific societies where transgenderism is witnessed. First, transvestites are never considered members of the opposite gender in the more consequential aspects of society, such as the reckoning of kinship. Second, they are the object of diverse representations and conflicting attitudes, both admiration and loathing, depending on context and the particular aspects of liminality. Third, transvestites are particularly receptive to social change and the increasing internationalization of Pacific societies, processes in which they often act as catalysts and mediators.—NB

Further reading

Besnier, N, 1997. 'Sluts and superwomen: the politics of gender liminality in urban Tonga', *Ethnos*.

Mageo, J M, 1992. 'Male transvestism and cultural change in Samoa', *American Ethnologist*, 19:443–59.

Ritualized homosexuality

The practice commonly referred to as 'ritualized homosexuality' consists of non-reciprocal genital contacts between a younger and an older male, usually in the form of fellatio (or, more rarely, sodomy), practised in the context of initiation rituals. Certain kinship relationships between the two participants are often favoured for these relations. The practice is prescriptive, in that every male must partake in it, first as a receptive participant and later as an active agent. Most men go on to marry and engage in heterosexual activity after a period of ritualized homosexual practice, although, in some societies, homosexual practices continue alongside heterosexual marriage. Ritualized homosexuality had a limited geographical distribution: it was found in societies that occupy the southwest border of the Papua New Guinea Highlands and the southeastern coast of Irian Jaya, as well as isolated areas of insular Melanesia (such as Malakula in Vanuatu). The practice appears to have been abandoned in most areas today, a process in which progressive mission influence in the Melanesian hinterlands since the 1920s, and subsequent colonial control, has played a significant role.

The rituals associated with such homosexual practices were complex, elaborated and protracted, with strong religious connotations. Many involved the ritualized hazing of initiates. For example, the initiates were often terrorized with mysterious flutes played in the bush, and threatened against revealing any imparted secrets to women. They might be forced to induce nose-bleeding and vomiting by inserting grasses and bamboo slivers in their noses and throats. Homosexual practices thus occur in a context of terror and pain for the initiates. It is noteworthy that societies which practise ritualized homosexuality are embedded in a larger cultural area in which male initiations and hazing rituals, but not necessarily ritualized homosexuality, are found. Why certain societies include or even centralize same-sex practices in rituals of manhood while neighbouring societies do not remains a mystery.

Underlying ritualized homosexuality is the belief that male adolescents must ingest the semen of older men in order to grow into full-fledged adult men. Semen is comparable to mother's milk, but while mother's milk is seen as sufficient to ensure the normal growth of women and pre-adolescent boys, it is inadequate for the production of men, a process which requires the ingestion of semen. Semen ingestion is found in societies in which men believe in the polluting and debilitating power of women, which must be counteracted through such purifying practices as induced nose-bleeding, which they continue to engage in even after initiation in many of the societies concerned.

Anthropologists who have studied ritualized homosexuality disagree about the relative importance of erotic aspects for the participants. Certain aspects of the ritual suggest that, for the younger participant at least, it is devoid of erotic meaning: for example, the climate of fear and intimidation in which the practice takes place, and the fact that some adolescents, who initially refuse to fellate their seniors, have to be forced to do so. Yet pleasure can play an important role in the ritual, as is attested by the fact that, in some societies, adults continued to engage in playful homosexual contacts beyond the ritual stage, and the evident pleasure that many initiates take in talking about semen ingestion. Thus the practice may have had multiple meanings—some overtly erotic and some concerned with growth and fertility—which coexist, or differ between individuals, across the various societies which formerly engaged in the practice.—NB

Further reading

Herdt, G (ed.), 1993. *Ritualized Homosexuality in Melanesia*, 2nd ed., University of California Press.

Knauft, B, 1994. *South Coast New Guinea Cultures: history, comparison, dialectic*, Cambridge University Press.

TWO EDUCATION

Introduction of formal education

The introduction of formal schooling in the Pacific islands was an integral part of the evangelizing activities of Christian missionaries. One aspect of this was the transcription of vernacular languages, in order to produce translations of Biblical texts and religious tracts (but which also facilitated the later work of printing traditional oral literature). Schools also produced assistants trained in literacy and numeracy skills, health and hygiene, as well as in biblical studies. Instruction in practical skills—house building, furniture making, boat building, and various crafts such as printing for the young men; domestic pursuits, handicrafts and childcare for the young women—soon followed. From the earliest days of mission work, elementary schooling followed conversion.

■ *Education in Hawai'i* When the American Protestant missionaries (of the AMERICAN BOARD OF COMMISSIONERS FOR FOREIGN MISSIONS) arrived in Hawai'i in 1820, the establishment of schools was given priority. Kamehameha II encouraged the teaching of reading and writing, and a number of schools for adult students opened in the first decade, exposing most of the adult population to elementary schooling, and using Hawaiian as the language of instruction. By 1830, the first teacher training institution appeared on Maui, followed by the setting up of mission schools for children. A private school opened in Honolulu in 1833, established by a charitable trust, and the Hilo Boarding School—teaching manual and technical skills—opened in 1836. The first Catholic school was established on O'ahu in 1844. The Hawaiian government became involved in education from the 1840s, and established a public school system which made steady improvements in administration from the 1880s. Strongly influenced by American educational philosophy, a system of 'progressive education' was imposed even before annexation to the United States.

■ *Education in Tonga* The first missionary training institution in Tonga—at Neiafu, Vava'u, in 1841—was established with the active support of King George TUPOU I. In 1847 the Scottish missionary, Richard Amos, arrived and introduced the 'Glasgow system' of teaching in Nuku'alofa, producing 8000 students able to read the Bible and about 5000 able to write by 1853. The king made instruction in schools for children compulsory in 1862, and the Wesleyan mission opened Tupou College in 1866, thus producing a steady stream of educated men and women, not only teachers and ministers for the mission but also government officials and community leaders. Schools used the Tongan language as their medium of instruction, and taught English as well as history, geography, arithmetic and religious subjects. At college level, students learned philosophy, astronomy, geometry, algebra and physics.

Tongan schoolchildren

■ *Education in Fiji* Methodist missionaries set up the first central training institution in 1856 at Davuilevu. It comprised primary and secondary schools, a technical school and a theological college, and an agricultural college was established at Navuso. The Roman Catholic mission followed suit, with five schools open by 1863, and later there were ANGLICAN and SEVENTH-DAY ADVENTIST schools. Public schools first opened in 1879, originally intended for the children of European settlers, first at LEVUKA and in 1883 in SUVA. Government involvement was marginal (except for the provision of funding for Queen Victoria School and the provincial schools) until 1916, when a Department of Education was set up to coordinate the educational system under a Superintendent of Schools. After 1924, a formal scheme of cooperation with the New Zealand school system was introduced, accompanied by active recruitment of New Zealand-trained teachers to Fijian schools.

■ *Education in Solomon Islands* All missions were involved in education from the time they arrived in Solomon Islands, although the level of education was low. In each village the pastor or catechist taught a small school, and there were district schools for somewhat more advanced instruction. Pawa, the central school of the Anglicans, and the Methodist central school were the most outstanding. The Methodists put more into education than any other mission and were able to claim by 1926 that all the children in the Western Solomons could read and write. All Melanesians who were employed in the civil service during the period before World War II were products of the Methodist schools.

The government grew dissatisfied with the missions' approach which, in most schools, tended to put religious instruction ahead of general education; only arithmetic was clearly not a form of religious teaching. In 1930 the Resident Commissioner began to make proposals for improvements and for small government grants-in-aid. The missions, other than the Seventh-Day Adventists and possibly the Methodists, regarded the grants as inadequate, particularly when they also entailed government interference. A conference between government and missions in 1934 failed to resolve their differences, and the proposals were dropped. The old system continued intact until after World War II, and it was only in 1957 that the government played any real part, beginning to plan new educational policies which have been implemented in secondary education and teacher training since the late 1960s.

■ *Education in French Polynesia* The arrival of the LONDON MISSIONARY SOCIETY in the early 1800s marked the beginning of formal education in French Polynesia. Missionaries established a standardized written form of the Tahitian language, which was used in the preparation of printed Biblical extracts and mainly religious texts. With the support of POMARE II, who was one of the first Tahitians to learn to read and write, several schools were established throughout the islands. The first French Catholic school in Pape'ete in 1854 met fierce objections, but a French public school was opened by the Dames de Cluny in 1857, and the children of the royal families began attending a French school in the 1850s. From 1860 Catholic schools became widely established, receiving some support from the French government after annexation in 1880. Secular education first appeared in 1882, officially within the French public school system, and this provided the main basis for the subsequent educational development of the islands, although a number of private schools—including Chinese schools—have continued to compete for students. From the late 1960s, private and public schools were standardized to a French curriculum, with education becoming compulsory from 6 years to 14.

■ *Education in New Caledonia* The early Marist missionaries did not have the resources to establish schools, and the first small advances made in the formal education of the Melanesian population were through the efforts of the Protestant LONDON MISSONARY SOCIETY missionaries in the LOYALTY ISLANDS, and especially Mare and Lifu. By the 1880s, a wider network of Catholic and Protestant mission schools were operating, except in the more remote villages, using either English or French after the colonial administration banned the use of local languages in mission schools. The educational achievements of Maurice LEENHARDT in the early 20th century included sending Loyalty Islanders to work on Grande Terre, but many rural communities still lacked access to elementary schooling until the 1960s. Secondary education became available to Kanaks only in 1958. By the 1960s both state and church schools offered an education system that was similar to that found in metropolitan France. In the resurgence of the Kanak nationalist movement, from the late 1970s, the idea of Kanak schools (*Écoles populaires Kanaks*) received some support and led to the development of a small number of schools in 1985 which used vernacular languages at junior levels.

■ *Education in Papua New Guinea* In Papua New Guinea, the first Europeans to enter some villages were missionaries, and formal education was left in their care until the 1950s. The post-war Australian government administration planned to introduce universal primary education, but the level of funding was inadequate to the task. Even with missions continuing to play an important role in primary schools, no more than half the children of primary school age attended school by 1970. In 1998 education was still not compulsory, and the target date for universal primary education had been extended to the year 2000. The education system includes government schools and schools nominated by other education agencies which meet defined criteria. Village schools provide a preparatory year and two years of primary instruction using local languages; community schools and provincial high schools teach in English.—KRF

School bus on the road in Guam

■ *Education in Cook Islands* Formal education was begun by Tahitian teachers of the LONDON MISSIONARY SOCIETY in the 1820s. Higher education began with Takamoa Theological College on Rarotonga in 1839. Until the end of that century all formal education was by missions. Government provided a little subsidy and operated some schools thereafter, but missions were the main educators until the 1950s. Religious instruction was a major component of all teaching and academic standards were low, as they were in government schools.

A church high school opened in 1895 but was closed in 1911 after the church could no longer finance it and the government was not prepared to. No secondary education was available within Cook Islands again until 1954, although the government provided scholarships for selected students to New Zealand high schools. Today there are secondary schools on most islands and education levels are probably the highest in the SOUTH PACIFIC FORUM region, although they are not adequate to equip students for their future at home or abroad.

Most students migrate to live in New Zealand, Australia and elsewhere, raising questions about appropriate curricula. Teaching of Cook Islands language is emphasized in principle, but often not adequately supported in practice. Moreover, with over 80 per cent of Cook Islanders living abroad and many young people aspiring to join them, and with television, video, books and other media overwhelmingly in English, the quality of the language keeps declining. Dance and drumming, however—something of an international hallmark for the nation—are taught at all schools and maintain and enhance their quality and uniqueness (COOK ISLANDS TRADITIONAL MUSIC AND DANCE).

It is difficult to maintain standards in the conventional academic subjects, especially on the smaller, more isolated islands which do not readily attract teachers and where low roll numbers make it necessary to combine students of several class levels into one. Teacher salaries and morale are low, partly because many with qualifications of a standard acceptable in New Zealand or elsewhere emigrate for the much higher salaries and better conditions. The economic crisis of the mid 1990s had a major impact on education. For a time teachers' salaries were cut by 15 per cent, then by a further 50 per cent. Previous pay rates have now been restored but some of the best teachers have emigrated. Materials and equipment have not been supplied to schools, and maintenance of school buildings has been allowed to lapse. Parents are expected to bear a larger share of the costs, when their own incomes have been reduced. Another impact of the economic crisis is falling enrolments as a result of emigration. In 1998 a new policy of deregulation took the schools on all islands except Rarotonga out of the control of the Ministry of Education and transferred their administration to the local communities concerned, with government subsidy provided through the Ministry of Outer Islands Development.

For post-secondary education, a Hospitality Training Centre runs short courses to train staff for the tourist industry, and a Small Business Enterprise Centre runs short courses in a range of topics relevant to commerce. The Nursing College survived thanks to a grant from the World Health Organization, but the Teachers Training College faces an uncertain future. Two theological colleges operate on Rarotonga.

At tertiary level, the UNIVERSITY OF THE SOUTH PACIFIC maintains an extension centre in Rarotonga, offering credit and non-credit short courses. Some students of Massey University and other universities and polytechnics in New Zealand and elsewhere also take extension courses in Rarotonga. For full-time higher education, most students go to New Zealand, and others to Fiji, Australia and elsewhere. An increasing number of parents, not only those with higher incomes, now send their children to New Zealand or Australia for secondary education.—MTC

Educational planning in the Pacific

The search for educational direction in the Pacific region illustrates the difficulties underlying formal planning processes. Pacific countries accepted the Western model of education, partly because it had been imposed by the colonial powers, partly because national leaders and new emerging élites were products of such systems, and partly because political leaders, and parents, saw such a model as providing the 'cargo' of economic rationalism. The objective of preparing manpower for independence has been successful, but schemes designed to involve schools in a broader role in development were less effective. Research identified four main areas of conflict that eventually resolved themselves in different ways in different countries: concerns about the possible adverse effects of growth on the quality of education; moves to a more local form of education and pressures to retain the Western model; unease with the academic nature of schooling and desires to see a more vocational/practical emphasis; and attempts to establish a balance between economic and social aims in education.

Particular studies of educational planning at junior secondary level in Fiji and Kiribati in the decade 1970–80 established that these were issues of general concern, to be taken into account in developing plans for those countries, but that certain difficulties arose in each country to confuse the planning process.

In Fiji, the problems included a lack of government control over the schooling system, since most schools were run by community or religious groups. The need to cater for cultural diversity was an ongoing issue, and is still a major topic of debate, particularly at tertiary level. Tensions also focused on urban/rural socioeconomic differences. 'Alternative' junior secondary schools tended to be set up in rural areas, but were not very well accepted. Finally, there was opposition to change in the well-established examination system, because the extensive system of formal examinations had been so thoroughly accepted by parents.

In Kiribati, very real confusion emerged over the proposed nature of the curriculum changes—should schooling be preparatory or pre-vocational? The immediate question of vocational prospects for students was a key issue in a system where very few went on to secondary school, and employment opportunities were limited. There were also unique physical problems in managing a single school system spread over 24 islands and 3.5 million sq km of ocean—'the biggest little system in the world'. The very real and direct influence of planners and decision makers became a part of the wider debate. While this influence is apparent elsewhere, it tends to be diffused in larger systems. In Kiribati during the period examined, individuals, particularly expatriate advisers, played key roles and had much influence.

A more recent case study of the basic school system (primary and junior secondary levels) in Vanuatu further illustrated that local tensions can upset the well-intentioned nature of educational planning. Vanuatu became independent in 1980 after nearly 80 years of joint colonial rule (the Anglo–French CONDOMINIUM). Despite its relatively small population, Vanuatu is one of the most culturally diverse countries in the world, and has the highest number of languages per capita of any country. Until 1980 there were two formal education systems, anglophone and francophone, two distinct philosophies of education, and two separate curricula. English and French still coexist as the principal languages of education, though BISLAMA (Pidgin) is more and more used as a means of official and administrative communication. In 1996, there was a single administration for education, with schools teaching in either English or French with some bi-lingual primary and secondary schools. About 40 per cent of the students attend francophone schools and 60 per cent anglophone schools.

Since independence, two major questions have dominated educational planning: the unification of the curriculum and the expansion of secondary education. Over the years, sub-committees in various subject areas began to draft a common curriculum for anglophone and francophone schools and to discuss the validity and content of teaching programs. Development of a common lower secondary curriculum was difficult because secondary schools were geared to examination systems and educational philosophies imported from Britain and France, but by 1993 curricula at the secondary level had been produced for the core subjects, and common examinations were held for the junior secondary Year 10 Certificate. The main problem at secondary level is the demand for more places, and the need to establish a clear policy on the numbers to proceed beyond the Class 6 level, about 22 per cent in 1996.

An Australian aid project (1991–93) encouraged unification of the primary curriculum, but due to local political problems and a change of government in 1991, little was achieved. Such problems and delays were due to factors outside the education process itself. Educational planning was always going to be a political exercise, due to the two-language situation and the carryover from the former split system. Changes from an anglophone-dominated government (1980–91) to a francophone-dominated government (1991–96) have not helped consistency in planning in recent years. A coalition government (anglophone-dominated) was elected in early 1996.

A number of factors have thus influenced the progress of educational planning in Vanuatu. The recent planning confusion, and the *ad hoc* decision-making will certainly continue until clear policy directions emerge. The factors which have influenced this approach to planning have parallels in other Pacific countries, the important difference being the unique two-language policy and the difficulties this imposes on planning. The main tensions lay in the colonial inheritance of a two-language system and disagreement about unification, and in political indecision resulting from instability of the government—itself reflecting the basic split in the political community between anglophone and francophone interests. The direction of education policies veers between two competing groups, and it is difficult to satisfy both sets of interests. The general aim is clear: a system that is ni-Vanuatu in character. There is broad agreement on this, particularly when discussions are in Bislama. The legacy of colonial influence clouds further definition of clear direction when the colonial languages are the vehicle for discussion and for instruction. Unless there is some resolution of this basic dichotomy, either by some very formal and clearly delineated debate and agreement on some compromises in policy or by the clear political domination of one group, these tensions will remain the key factor in educational planning for the foreseeable future.

As these examples indicate, the 'actualities of context' need to be given far more attention in educational analysis. Educational planning is important, but island countries need to recognize that progress will not be always as expected. Consideration of particular local tensions and their impact will help planners, advisers and education authorities move towards improved educational planning.—CEH

Further reading

Baba, T, 1985. 'Education in the Pacific islands in the Year 2000', in R C Kiste and R A Herr (eds), *The Pacific Islands in the Year 2000*, University of Hawai'i Press.

Hindson, C, 1991. 'Education and developing countries—a framework for analysis', in R Burns and A Welch (eds), *Contemporary Perspectives in Comparative Education*, Garland.

——, 1995. 'Educational planning in Vanuatu—an alternative analysis', *Comparative Education*, 31(3).

Higher education for Pacific islanders

The emergence of tertiary institutions has been an encouraging feature of widespread educational development in the Pacific since World War II. The rapid development of higher education is of great significance for Pacific islanders. The educational ferment in the post-war Pacific represents a move towards more equitable distribution of resources, reflecting the concerns of the departing colonizers.

Academic doctrines linked to various theories of 'modernization' and 'development' were devised to meet the challenges of decolonization and reconstruction, and were conceptually packaged neatly around the known features of the situation in the islands: Pacific peoples perceive education in purely utilitarian/materialistic terms; and foreign aid is most readily available if donors are satisfied that potential projects are suitably 'developmental' in intent.

Most PACIFIC UNIVERSITIES were set up on this principle, that they not only contribute to but also take a leading role in the economic development of the islands. This is reflected in curricula, which are dominated by 'relevant' programs. Ultimately, the end-product of this type of education is the raising of gross national product. Graduates emerge with a specific qualification, better prospects of acquiring a job, and the satisfaction of making a contribution to the economic reconstruction of their country. This is a reasonable outcome, it is true—but it still leaves a lot to be desired. What is missing from the higher education offered in the Pacific is the fundamental quality of 'general literacy' provided by a traditional formal education—where open learning is not directly related to vocational goals. This, of course, is true not only of Pacific universities; it is a worldwide phenomenon. Granting, for the sake of argument, that the development credo is appropriate for Pacific island countries, what are the major flaws in its implementation?

The general program provided by the World Bank for restructuring in developing countries ranks general needs as: first, development of natural resources; second, technical transfer; and third, human resources development. Because higher education and training started late in the Pacific region, it will take time for the islands to provide the trained manpower equal to the tasks. This means that development of natural resources will continue to be implemented by foreigners—investors and developers, development 'experts' and advisers. Indigenous peoples will play little part in their own development, apart from supplying unskilled labour. The World Bank prescription, then, will keep islanders out of any effective participation in the development of their own local resources. It is clear that we must invert this whole program, and put human resources development first, then technical transfer, and lastly the development of natural resources. If not, then by the time islanders are ready to tackle their own development, the resources will be much depleted or gone altogether.

The second weakness relates to the abysmally low standards and inadequate content of courses offered at many Pacific tertiary institutions. They simply cannot match the development needs and especially the required levels of expertise (sophistication, durability and general quality) now demanded by island governments and their growth targets, to say nothing of the personal needs of islanders. People trained in Pacific institutions, especially in the theoretical and technical fields, are likely to emerge as technicians who will require further training to be able to contribute to Pacific development. And those scholarship holders who study overseas too often opt for some esoteric course that may be easily undertaken but is little use in the islands. We are thus building a pool of basic technicians who are increasingly employed by foreign companies as trained skilled labour.

What is the solution then? First, we must stop believing that educational and training levels must be tied to the apron strings of 'society's needs', and realize that people's expectations and needs proceed in spurts. A good rule of thumb here would be: always set levels and standards as high as possible. In this way, we take care of needs, but they do not set the standards. Second, we must institute top quality theoretical courses in the technical subjects taught at Pacific universities. Third, we should establish a good research centre for both physical and social sciences at some central location, such as the UNIVERSITY OF THE SOUTH PACIFIC. Finally, we need a first-class polytechnic for the region. It is a well-known principle that for industry to thrive, 'pure science' must be pursued and given full autonomy, but the polytechnic, which makes physical transformations and embodies a theoretical framework in its technological focus, is the ideal bridge between research and industry.

This program will incur a phenomenal outlay of resources, both capital and human, but if we are serious about development, then Pacific universities and training institutions must be adapted along some such lines. Australia has been proposing that postgraduate training of Pacific islanders should be conducted exclusively at island institutions. This could have disastrous consequences—producing ever slighter levels of competence—in the absence of the overhaul that I suggest.—'IFH

Pacific universities

Prior to 1945, there was only one university in the Pacific islands: the University of Hawai'i—established in 1907, when Hawai'i was a US Territory. The 1960s saw rapid changes in tertiary education. In

Irian Jaya (West New Guinea), the new Indonesian administration set up Universitas Cenderawasih (UNCEN) in Jayapura in 1964, teaching in Bahasa Indonesia. This encouraged the creation of the UNIVERSITY OF PAPUA NEW GUINEA (UPNG), founded in 1965, in Port Moresby (Waigani). The University of Guam (which had been established as a degree level college in 1963) opened in 1968, as did the UNIVERSITY OF THE SOUTH PACIFIC, in Fiji. 'Atenisi University (which developed from an experimental university class at 'Atenisi Institute in 1971) was established in 1975. The 1980s saw other Pacific universities emerge—the National University of Samoa (Le Iuniversite Aoao O Samoa I Sisifo) in 1984; the Université Française du Pacifique (1987) incorporated the existing Vice Rectorat (a consortium of six French universities), which had campuses in Noumea, New Caledonia (since the 1970s) and Pape'ete, Tahiti (1983); the Solomon Islands College of Higher Education (SICHE), established in 1985. By 1987 there were 10 universities offering degree courses in the Pacific islands.

Alongside this development, several universities teaching in the Japanese language have been established in the Ryukyu Islands, including Meio University in Okinawa. Papua New Guinea's University of Technology at Lae was first established as the Institute of Technology in 1967. The University of the South Pacific has offered extension courses for several years, establishing several research centres in the late 1970s, beginning with an Extension Centre in the Solomon Islands, built in 1975. The Community College of Micronesia, set up in 1970, has campuses at Pohnpei, Majuro and Palau, and began offering degree-level courses in 1989. The American Samoa Community College, set up in 1970, began offering a degree course in education in 1988. The former UPNG campus at Goroka, which provides teacher training, is now a university.

Reflecting the almost exclusive role of THEOLOGICAL COLLEGES in higher education in the Pacific islands until the late 1920s, several of the tertiary institutions that have been established emphasize religious training, rather than a specifically academic education. Most notably, the PACIFIC THEOLOGICAL COLLEGE in Suva opened in 1965, but religious universities include the Pacific Adventist College in Papua New Guinea in 1984, and the Mormon Church's Brigham Young University which opened a campus at Laie in Hawai'i (BYU-H). There is also the Divine Word Institute (Roman Catholic) in Solomon Islands, and Pacific-Asia Christian University in Tonga. Hawai'i now has the Catholic Chaminade University and Hawai'i Loa College. Seventh-day Adventist tertiary training begins with diploma-level courses at Fulton College (in Fiji) and Sonoma College (in Papua New Guinea). Other tertiary institutions offering specialist studies (for example, diploma courses in MEDICAL TRAINING and agriculture) are the Fiji School of Medicine (formerly the Central Medical School, which opened in 1928), the Fiji College of Agriculture established in 1972, Alafua Agricultural College in Samoa, and Vudal Agricultural College in Papua New Guinea, now a university. The National University of Samoa opened its new campus on 5 September 1997, built under a major Japanese aid project, and one of the largest buildings in the country.—KRF

Further reading

Crocombe, R and Meleisea, M (eds), 1988. *Pacific Universities: achievements, problems, prospects*, Institute of Pacific Studies, University of the South Pacific.

■ ***University of Papua New Guinea*** The University of Papua New Guinea admitted its first 81 degree students in 1967, after a preliminary (pre-matriculation) course in 1966. The University Council had met for the first time in September 1965, and resolved to begin teaching at once. Haste was evident in the temporary accommodation around Port Moresby's show-ground, and in the scarcity of students from the country's few high schools. Only in 1971 could local high schools offer students matriculation directly into the university. The hardship of the first year is celebrated in narratives of pioneering cherished by the first graduates, although the new campus at Waigani was very soon ready for occupation. Equally important was the intimacy of a small academic enclave on the fringe of Port Moresby. As late as 1970 there were only 772 students, 99 academics, and 307 other staff. On such a small and residential campus most people knew everyone else at least by sight, and social distinctions were unusually blurred and permeable. Half of the students and all academic staff were expatriates, mainly Australian.

Higher education was proposed by the United Nations 'Foot Report' of 1963, alongside economic development and a representative parliament. These issues became intertwined: many early students were activists for decolonization, or for economic development, or both. The university was independent, and lecturers devised their own responses to national priorities as they saw them. Early courses therefore included Physics, Prehistory and Creative Writing, as well as more overtly career-oriented fields of Medicine, Law and Education. The first cohorts of students—sure of careers in government

University of Papua New Guinea, aerial view taken in mid 1980s

or politics—could indulge their wider enthusiasms. The campus therefore enjoyed a virtual monopoly of Port Moresby's creative writing and play production.

The ethos of the university changed after the pioneering phase. Student numbers peaked at about 2000 in the 1980s, reducing intimacy. Rabbie NAMALIU was the first national academic in 1973, before he left to join Michael SOMARE's staff. For similar reasons, localization proceeded slowly until the 1990s, when citizens formed the great majority of academic staff. Independence in 1975 put a new perspective on student politics, which gained in rowdiness what it lost in coherence. This turbulence reflected the fact that the university could not isolate itself from social and political conditions in the rest of the country. The integration of campus and town is facilitated also by the encirclement of the campus by Gerehu, now the country's third largest settlement, but unknown in the 1960s.

The university reflects its social context also in (for example) the persistently low ratio of women students (never more than one in four) and staff. The university shares the pain of the country's budget. European Community grants have funded a clinic, a building for a large and growing Distance Education faculty, and facilities for the Creative Arts Centre, but the original buildings are run down and, as the kina declined, the library lost its ability to maintain its book collections. Blockages in national political and bureaucratic systems also delay responses to all the universities' needs for new legislation and approaches to the divisive issue of a dual salary structure. As student protests in the early 1990s tended to alienate parliamentarians, the institution seemed to be locked into a spiral of declining budgets, falling morale and poor performance.

During the 1990s, however, Council appointed a new Vice Chancellor and adopted concerted measures to streamline administration, rationalize courses, encourage better teaching, build physical security, and enforce social discipline. When Goroka Teachers' College became a separate university in 1998, the university returned to manageable numbers and only two campuses (the Medical Faculty at Taurama, and the main campus at Waigani). About 4000 students study by distance mode (the great majority attempting adult matriculation), while almost 3000 are full-time resident students.—DD

■ *University of the South Pacific* The University of the South Pacific (USP) is a regional university established in 1968 to provide higher education for 11 Pacific island countries and territories: Cook Islands, Fiji, Kiribati, Nauru, Niue, Samoa, Solomon Islands, Tonga, Tokelau, Tuvalu and Vanuatu. In 1992 the membership increased to 12, when Marshall Islands joined.

The University Council, the highest decision-making body, includes regional ministers of education, representatives of the university, of the governments of Australia and New Zealand, of the Privy Council, and of regional organizations, as well as representatives of staff and students, together with co-opted members. Academic decisions are taken by the University Senate.

There are five schools (equivalent to faculties): School of Agriculture (at Alafua, Samoa); School of Humanities; School of Pure and Applied Sciences; School of Social and Economic Development (all at the main campus, Laucala Bay, Suva); and the School of Law at the newest campus, Emalus, in Port Vila, Vanuatu. The USP also maintains University Centres in all but one of its member countries. Its strong outreach role is supplemented by seven institutes: Institute of Agricultural Research, Extension and Teaching (Alafua); Institute of Marine Resources (Honiara); and in Suva: Institute of Education, Institute of Applied Sciences, Institute of Social and Administrative Studies, Institute of Pacific Studies, and the newest, Institute of Justice and Applied Legal Studies. The university also has a Centre for Development Studies and the Oceania Centre for Arts and Culture (both in Suva), and the Pacific Languages Unit in Port Vila.

In 1999, the university currently had about 9200 students, representing the equivalent of 5300 full-time students. About 37 per cent are enrolled in the distance education program. The largest concentration of students is from Fiji (68 per cent), but all member countries send students. Students also come from some other Pacific islands, as well from countries outside the region.

The university offers first degrees in most natural and social sciences, in law, and in the humanities. It also offers postgraduate diplomas, masters degrees in arts, science and agriculture and doctoral programs. In 1997, 981 students graduated.

There are approximately 600 staff, of whom about 290 are academic. About 60 per cent of the academic staff are from the member states (referred to as regional staff). Many of the most senior positions are now held by regional staff, and the university is widely seen as a model organization in the Pacific islands. The USP still recruits from the international market, however, and wishes to ensure that its staff always contains a sizeable number of international staff to ensure intellectual vibrancy.—RC

■ *Specialist medical training* The earliest initiative in the medical training of Pacific islanders was taken in Fiji where the first Native Medical Practitioners graduated in 1889 after three years of hospital training. They were then posted to the provinces, and in some instances to other island groups, and a number of these practitioners became highly respected in both indigenous and European circles. Later the program was expanded to fill a greater regional role. The Central Medical School was founded in 1929 and received additional students from Tonga, Samoa, Solomon Islands and other islands. After World War II, medical training was further upgraded. From 1947 small numbers of students from Papua New Guinea were selected by the Australian administration to train in Suva. The Fiji model influenced the development of medical training in these dependencies.

Today specialist medical training is available in two medical schools run by the UNIVERSITY OF PAPUA NEW GUINEA (UPNG) and the Fiji School of Medicine. Both schools offer a four-year Master of Medicine degree to doctors who have gained an MBBS and completed their internship. Specialist training was introduced in Papua New Guinea in the early 1980s and over 25 surgeons have now been produced, as well as slightly fewer specialists in child health, obstetrics and gynaecology and internal medicine. The first otolaryngologists, ophthalmologists, pathologists and psychiatrists have been trained. The postgraduate program in the School of Medicine in Fiji began in 1997 and prior to that two orthopaedic specialists were trained under the auspices of the Australian Orthopaedic Association. Specialist medical training has also taken place in Australia, New Zealand and Europe. Throughout the region there are few specialists, although a small number of Solomon Islanders have been trained at UPNG. Micronesia developed a different system of undergraduate medical training with the University of Hawai'i, for students not intending to proceed to postgraduate medical training within a university system.

Sub-specialist training in orthopaedics, urology and head and neck surgery was introduced in Papua New Guinea in 1994 and takes two years for someone with an MMed degree in General Surgery. Five specialists had been trained by the end of 1997 in a system which seeks to produce appropriately trained specialists able to work in their own country after the standard six years of supervised training that occurs in developed countries.—DAKW

■ *Theological colleges* Most Pacific island churches have their own theological colleges to prepare clergy for ordination. The first college, the Takamoa Institute (Cook Islands Christian Church), was established in 1839 by the LONDON MISSIONARY SOCIETY at Rarotonga. Other major colleges include Malua (Congregational), near Apia in Samoa, established in 1844; Bishop Patteson (Melanesia Anglican) established in Honiara in 1970; École Pastorale de Bethania (Église Evangélique), New Caledonia in 1862; École Pastorale d'Hermon (Église Evangélique), French Polynesia in 1927; Fulton College (SEVENTH-DAY ADVENTIST), Fiji in 1940; Kanana Fou (Congregational) in American Samoa in 1983; Marshall Islands (United Church of Christ) on Majuro in 1976; Davuilevu and Deaconess Theological Centres (Methodist), Fiji in 1908 and 1967; Moamoa (Roman Catholic Diocese of Western Samoa) in 1935; Pacific Regional Seminary (Catholic Bishops of the Pacific), Suva in 1972; PACIFIC THEOLOGICAL COLLEGE (PTC Council) Suva in 1966; Piula (Methodist), Samoa in 1868; Officer Training School (Salvation Army) in Suva in 1980; Sia'atoutai (Methodist) in Tonga in 1948; St John's (Polynesia Anglican) in

Takamoa Theological College on Rarotonga, Cook Islands

1952; Talua (Presbyterian) in Vanuatu in 1988; Tangintebu (Kiribati Protestant Church) in 1961.

The colleges are accredited by the South Pacific Association of Theological Schools, which has its headquarters in Suva. The largest college libraries are Bishop Patteson (25 000 books), Pacific Regional Seminary (21 000) and Pacific Theological College (21 000).—AT2

■ *Pacific Theological College* Pacific Theological College (PTC) in Fiji was the first degree-granting institution in the islands. It is an ecumenical centre for training Protestant clergy for diploma, bachelor and master's degrees in theology. The major Protestant churches in the region authorized the founding of the PTC in 1961 and the first classes began on a site at Laucala Bay, Suva, in 1965. The college moved to its own buildings at Vetuto in 1966. The inaugural principal was Rev Dr George Knight, followed by Rev Alan Quigley. The first Pacific islander principal was Rev Dr 'Amanaki Havea of Tonga, succeeded by Rev Drs Sevati Tuwere (Fiji), Sione Latukefu (Tonga), Faitala Talapusi (Western Samoa) and Jovili Meo (Fiji).

Students are sent from churches throughout Melanesia, Micronesia and Polynesia. The teaching faculty comprises four main departments: Biblical studies, Church history, ministry and theology. The PTC is active in promoting women's theological education as well as theological education by extension.—AT2

■ *Newington College* Newington College, a secondary school for boys in Sydney, was founded by the Methodist Church in 1863. The first principal, and later President of the College, was Rev Dr James Egan Moulton. As a result of Moulton's many years in Tonga as a missionary, Newington was attended by Pacific island students, mainly sons of chiefly families in Tonga and Fiji. Well-known students attending the college in the 1930s were the present King of Tonga, Tāufa'āhau TUPOU IV, and the late Governor General of Fiji, Ratu Sir George Cakobau—both descendants of the high chiefs instrumental in consolidating Christianity in Tonga and Fiji respectively (Tāufa'āhau George TUPOU I and Ratu Seru CAKOBAU).—AT2

■ *Center for Pacific Islands Studies* The Pacific Islands Studies Program (PIP) was launched at the University of Hawai'i at Mānoa in 1950 as a cross-disciplinary Master of Arts (MA) degree and research seminar. For many years, university support was small, and PIP was sustained by a few committed faculty members. In the early 1970s, PIP was recognized as a National Resource Center with a grant from the US Department of Education. It is the only such centre in the United States that focuses on the Pacific islands.

In 1986, PIP became the Center for Pacific Islands Studies (CPIS). Today it has a core of six faculty and staff. A faculty of 30 offers over 60 courses on the Pacific islands, and about 25 students are enrolled in the MA program. The centre sponsors conferences, a teacher training program, and a vigorous publication program that includes the Pacific Islands Monograph Series, the South Seas Books (first published in 1989) and the journal, *The Contemporary Pacific: A Journal of Island Affairs*.—RCK

■ *East–West Center* The East–West Center is an international educational institution established in Hawai'i by the US Congress in 1960 to 'promote better relations and understanding between the United States and the nations of Asia and the Pacific through cooperative study, training and research'. The centre is directed by the Board of Governors of a public, non-profit educational corporation—known as the Center for Cultural and Technical Interchange Between East and West, Inc—created by the Hawai'i state legislature in 1975. The US Congress provides basic funding for centre programs and a variety of scholarships, fellowships, internships and other awards. Additional support is provided by private agencies, individuals and corporations, and by more than 20 Asian and Pacific governments. The centre is situated on land adjacent to, and provided by, the University of Hawai'i, which also conducts classes and grants degrees for East–West Center students. In addition to their university degree, these students can earn the East–West Center Leadership Certificate through the centre's program on Education and Learning. This certificate aims to develop participants' capacities for leadership in multicultural contexts. The South Pacific Islands Scholarship Program provides a limited number of scholarships to individuals from the Cook Islands, Fiji, Kiribati, Niue, Papua New Guinea, Samoa, Solomon Islands, Tonga, Tuvalu and Vanuatu to pursue baccalauréate and master's degrees. In other centre programs researchers address issues of contemporary significance in international economics and politics, the environment, population, energy and mineral resources, journalism and Pacific islands developments. The *Pacific Islands Report* web-site [http://pidp.ewc.hawaii.edu/PIReport/] is a recent addition to increase awareness of news in the Pacific islands region.—LES

■ *Institute of Pacific Studies, Suva* The Institute of Pacific Studies, one of the seven original institutes of the UNIVERSITY OF THE SOUTH PACIFIC, was established in 1976, to represent and serve Pacific islands communities within the university region. The institute has gained a reputation for its publication of more than 500 books on Pacific islands topics, written mostly by Pacific islanders and covering a variety of subjects, including the social and physical sciences, linguistics, poetry and art.

The institute offers short courses in Pacific studies for university students and others visiting from the United States, Europe and Asia. It has produced ethnographic videos and films on the Pacific islands' traditional subsistence and cultural activities. Institute staff developed and currently teach a university course in Pacific studies, and institute staff have also supervised Masters and PhD students in Pacific studies.—AR1

■ *Institute for Polynesian Studies, Hawai'i* The Institute for Polynesian Studies (IPS) was established in 1977 to research and preserve Oceanic history and culture. The IPS has produced ethnographic films, held conferences, supported research, and published books, pamphlets and a quarterly journal, *Pacific Studies*, a multidisciplinary scholarly journal which publishes historical and contemporary articles on island nations of the Pacific. The IPS is sponsored by the Polynesian Cultural Center (PCC) and Brigham Young University–Hawai'i Campus, and carries out research and documentation on their behalf.—DR

■ *Centre for South Pacific Studies, UNSW* The Centre for South Pacific Studies was established in 1987 to collect, collate and distribute information from a diversity of disciplines in printed and electronic form about the peoples and places of the Pacific islands. Within the University of New South Wales (UNSW), the centre acts as a home for research in the Pacific region, coordinating projects, furthering such investigations and attracting outside funding both for this research and related activities, including postgraduate, visiting and research associateship programs.

Outside UNSW, the centre monitors work done in Australia and overseas on the Pacific islands and contributes to the national database in a variety of disciplines involved in that region. About 100 academics at UNSW research and work in the Pacific islands, from business and commerce to mining and post-colonial literature. Faculties of Medicine and Engineering are represented, as is the Australian Defence Force Academy. The centre has organized conferences on 'Australia and the Pacific', 'Pacific Islander Migration' and 'Kava', all resulting in publications. Since 1987 some 100 occasional seminars have been given, with speakers from the region and elsewhere contributing research on a range of topics from a variety of academic disciplines.

Rapanui artist Pedro Atan carved a one-third size (0.8m) replica of the *moai* at the British Museum and presented it to the Centre for South Pacific Studies. It is on display in the Arts and Social Sciences Faculty at the University of New South Wales, Sydney

The centre publishes a newsletter that is sent to nearly 4000 individuals and institutions in over 80 countries. The Pacific Studies Monograph Series counts over 20 volumes (in 1998) on topics such as Pacific islander migration, Pitcairn ethnobotany and aspects of economic development in selected countries and in the region as a whole. The foundation director was anthropologist Grant McCall (1987–92), followed by economist John Lodewijks (1993–).—GMcC

■ *Research School of Pacific and Asian Studies, ANU* The Research School of Pacific and Asian Studies (RSPAS) was one of four original research schools comprising the Australian National University when it was established in Canberra in 1947. The school emerged out of growing awareness that Australia needed a sound understanding of the problems of both its Pacific island neighbourhood and the 'near north' Asian region. Its Pacific focus involves research and graduate training on the societies, economies and physical environments of the Pacific islands, and on the Pacific–Australia relationship. Its research deals with contemporary and historical issues concerned primarily with social sciences—anthropology, archaeology, history, geography, linguistics, political and social change, international relations, peace, defence and strategic studies—and the environmental sciences of biogeography and geomorphology and Quaternary research. The school has about 120 academic staff, supported by research assistants and technical and administrative staff.—KRF

■ *South Pacific Bureau for Educational Assessment* The South Pacific Bureau for Educational Assessment (SPBEA) provides advice, assistance and a Form 6 (year 12) examination for member countries seeking educational assessment expertise. Founded in 1981 through the South Pacific Commission (PACIFIC COMMUNITY), SPBEA grew from an organization offering advice only to seven member countries, to a multi-focused assessment organization offering training, advice and assistance to 11 Pacific island countries—Cook Islands, Fiji, Kiribati, Marshall Islands, Nauru, Samoa, Solomon Islands, Tonga, Tuvalu, Tokelau and Vanuatu. Governed by a board comprising the chief executives of island Education ministries, and funded by member contributions together with assistance from Australia and New Zealand, a secretariat operates out of offices in Suva.—IJ

■ *Micronesian Area Research Center* The Micronesian Area Research Center (MARC) was established by the Guam legislature in 1967 as a unit of the University of Guam. The centre has a threefold mission: to develop a major collection of Micronesian and Pacific area materials; to conduct social and historical research on Guam and Micronesia; and to communicate the results of this research through publications, teaching, and public lectures. The MARC collections now constitute one of the most extensive repositories of Micronesian library holdings in the world, although much needs to be done to modernize the organization and access to the collection. Current MARC research priorities include contemporary applied research on migration, fisheries, tourism and social change. All MARC full-time research faculty are heavily involved in teaching in the newly established Micronesian Studies Master of Arts program.—DHR

■ *Centre for the Contemporary Pacific* The Centre for the Contemporary Pacific was established by the Australian National University (ANU) in 1998 to tap the university's well-known strengths of Pacific research and to enhance its regional outreach activities. The centre was mandated to develop and promote Pacific studies within the university; to develop links with government agencies, institutions and universities within Australia and the Pacific region; and to act as a focal point for their access to Pacific studies at ANU. The centre performs this role by coordinating Pacific activities at the ANU, hosting major annual workshops and conferences on topical issues and concerns in the contemporary Pacific, facilitating collaborative projects, and administering a visiting fellowship program which brings senior Pacific island leaders and opinion makers to Australia. The centre's tri-annual newsletter, *Talanoa*, describes its activities and programs.—BVL

College of Education, Mangilao, Guam

■ *Macmillan Brown Centre for Pacific Studies* The Macmillan Brown Centre for Pacific Studies was established in 1988 at the University of Canterbury. It was founded through a bequest from the late Professor John Macmillan Brown (1846–1935), a founding professor of the University of Canterbury and a former vice chancellor of the University of New Zealand who spent a considerable time travelling and studying the countries of the Pacific. Under the terms of Professor Macmillan Brown's will, the Centre was set up to facilitate the 'investigation and research of the history, traditions, customs, laws, and ideas of the peoples of the Pacific generally'. It is administered by the Director, Dr Ueantabo Neemia-Mackenzie, and an advisory board appointed by the University Council.

The Centre is adjacent to the Macmillan Brown Library, which holds a collection of approximately 80 000 books, journals, microfilm, periodicals, archival material and pamphlets with special emphasis on the anthropology and ethnology of New Zealand and the Pacific Ocean regions, available to researchers. The Centre's main activities focus on a research and visiting scholars program, and an active publications program which began in 1992.—KRF

THREE SOCIAL ORDER

Traditional sanctions and laws

In recent years the study of law and society has been dominated by two major paradigms or models: the rule-centred approach and the processual approach. The rule-centred approach is based on the idea that social life is governed by rules. Advocates of this approach, which seems to work particularly well for analyzing hierarchically-ordered societies such as

Western cultures, believe that social groups develop rules or norms of behavior in order to regulate the lives of their members. When people break these rules, counteraction by the legal institutions of society becomes necessary. This view of law has its roots in Anglo-American legal theory. Law is seen as a discrete subject, able to be studied in its own right. The legal process is thus seen largely as a matter of rules, courts, tribunals, and judges.

However, when anthropologists and other researchers began examining the nature of law and law-like institutions in certain Pacific island societies where there were no chiefs, courts or judges, they observed that local people seemed much more interested in mediating social relationships than in observing formal rules of behavior. Particularly in Papua New Guinea, where there are a great many politically decentralized societies, local people often cannot articulate any formal set of legal rules for their group at all. Instead, they are concerned about the practical management of social conflicts. Disputes between people are handled on a case-by-case basis, sometimes through consensus solutions based on notions of fairness or equity, and sometimes by various sorts of political manoeuvering. Scholars working in these types of societies have tended to adopt a processual paradigm, in which attention is centred not on legal rules, but on the actual processes through which disputes are resolved. From this perspective, law is seen as intimately intertwined with the broader fabric of society, rather than as a discrete entity unto itself. Scholars taking a processual approach therefore take a very broad view of law and society, and examine many different types of social institutions in order to understand how dispute management actually occurs.

Interestingly, of the two distinct groups of peoples inhabiting the Pacific, one is structured more like western society and consequently can be readily analyzed using a rule-oriented paradigm, whereas the other tends to lack formal rules and is more easily examined by employing a processual approach. The former group, often called the Austronesians (see FOOTSTEPS FROM ASIA) settled in the Pacific only within the past several thousand years. They were almost certainly fairly complex societies, characterized by hierarchy and well-structured normative orders, when they first entered the Pacific region. Because of their presumably common background and their relatively rapid and recent dispersal throughout the Pacific islands, the Austronesian peoples of the Pacific all have relatively similar languages and cultures today.

Representatives of the second group, already resident in the Pacific by 50 000 years ago, colonized only Australia, New Guinea and a few nearby islands. These earlier peoples nowadays have strikingly diverse cultures and languages, and probably had multiple origins. More because they contrast with the Austronesians than because of any clearly distinguishing characteristics of their own, they are often placed in a residual category labelled simply, 'non-Austronesians'. Today, most non-Austronesians live in the interior of larger Melanesian islands, including New Guinea, and on the Australian mainland. Whereas Austronesians tend to have hierarchically-structured social organizations, non-Austronesians almost uniformly have egalitarian social structures, based on reciprocal relationships, that have resulted in widely different types of customary political and legal organizations. Because the non-Austronesians lack formal rules and legal structures, they have lent themselves particularly well to legal analysis using the processual approach.

In a very influential article, Sahlins (1963) contrasted the Polynesian (Austronesian) chief and the Melanesian (mostly non-Austronesian) 'BIG-MAN' as models of leadership in the Pacific islands. For the most part, Polynesian chiefs occupy formal (often hereditary) offices, or hold titles which are formally bestowed. As with centralized leadership found in hierarchically-ordered cultures, they have authority over certain resources, and can allocate or redistribute them. People recognize their legitimate right to collect tribute, sponsor ceremonies, organize labour, adjudicate disputes and punish wrongdoers. In contrast, Melanesian big-men have no such authority. They do not command but merely exert influence through their reputations and by their persuasive abilities. Sahlins playfully styled them as 'harangue-utans', because they often get what they want by verbally bullying their followers. Their role in conflict management is limited to negotiation and mediation; they do not have the authority to adjudicate. Unlike the chiefs of many Pacific societies, whose power depends upon succession to ascribed, hereditary office, big-men are free-enterprising individualists whose charisma, beguiling manner, and accomplishments earn them a following. In such societies, individual leaders rise and fall, and the social groups over which they have influence are constantly shifting. However, big-men rarely exercise influence beyond a small group of kin and supporters, and in these cultures there are no traditional forms of authority transcending the local level.

When Europeans first made contact with Pacific islanders, these differences between the legal systems of Austronesian and non-Austronesian societies did not go unnoticed. Because the legal systems of Austronesians in Micronesia and Polynesia resembled those of contemporary European societies, colonial authorities understood how they operated. During the colonial era, the legal and political structures of these groups were often pre-empted and modified to facilitate colonial rule. This did not occur with non-Austronesian groups. The traditional forms of conflict management in egalitarian societies, while effective in the smaller, more personal contexts in which they developed, were considered unsuitable and inadequate in the colonial context, and indigenous legal systems were superseded by hierarchical models of law.

These differing approaches to customary law were employed by colonial governments in Samoa and New Guinea. As early as 1903, the German colonial government in Samoa established a Land and Chiefly Titles Court to hear disputes related to MATAI (chiefly) titles and local land matters by applying relevant Samoan custom. This court, which still exists in independent Samoa, is comprised of Samoan judges, who are traditional chiefs appointed for three-year terms, and assessors, who are also senior chiefs. Traditional Samoan laws and customs are followed in hearings. Although the German colonial government in Samoa recognized and empowered local chiefs very early, the reaction to local leadership in German New Guinea was quite different. Realizing that no formal political offices existed at the local level, the German colonial government attempted to establish local non-traditional authorities by introducing titles of leadership (*luluai* and *tultul*) in village contexts. Not surprisingly, their authority was generally not recognized by local people. Later, the Australian colonial government in the Territories of Papua and New Guinea set up local courts presided over by Australian magistrates who also employed a rule-oriented western legal model. It was not until the *Village Courts Act 1973* that local big-men were appointed as magistrates, and empowered to act in a panel and follow customary law in arbitrating disputes, the outcomes of which were finally recognized in a formal legal sense.

This dual pattern of legal development has been repeated in many other parts of the Pacific. In much of Polynesia and Micronesia, traditional ruling élites continue to have considerable influence in the legal and political process. In the Kingdom of Tonga, for example, the current king is a direct lineal descendant of the TU'I TONGAs or traditional paramount chiefs of Tonga, and the parliament is controlled by hereditary chiefs. The senate of American Samoa is controlled by *matai* (chiefs), and the village courts, which administer customary law, are presided over by associate judges who are also *matai*. In the Republic of the Marshall Islands, a council of 12 *Iroij* (chiefs) is selected by custom, and chiefs also resolve local disputes and maintain order according to custom. In Palau, the council of chiefs advises the president on matters of traditional laws and customs.

Although not highly regarded by colonial administrations, the conflict management systems of egalitarian non-Austronesian cultures have always been of considerable interest to legal scholars precisely because the ability to maintain social control without chiefs or formal laws fundamentally challenges rule-oriented notions of law. For most social scientists, social control refers to the various ways by which individual action is constrained by society. This occurs through the application of sanctions, which range from informal pressures such as ridicule and gossip to painful physical punishments mandated by law. But sanctions may also be positive and take the form of rewards and incentives, such as praise, recognition, deference and respect for socially approved behavior. Leopold Pospisil examined some of the ways in which the sanctions of the Me (Kapauku) people, a big-man society of western New Guinea, differ from those of western society. For the Me, psychological punishments such as public reprimands are thought to be just as severe as physical punishments. Various sanctions employed by the Me indicate that a preoccupation with physical punishment and, in fact, with coercive aspects of social control in general, may be more characteristic of western or complex societies, and can be much less important in non-Austronesian cultures. The withholding of positive sanctions that would have otherwise been granted, such as failing to help a person, or refusing to carry out reciprocal obligations, are examples of sanctions that are not physical or directly coercive, but can be acutely painful in Melanesian and Australian societies.

Exchange is of paramount importance in most Melanesian cultures, and in his classic studies of the Trobriand Islanders of New Guinea, Bronislaw MALINOWSKI showed how voluntary, reciprocal obligations of individuals are a critical component of social control. People perform mutual services because there is an expectation of reciprocal favours. Civil law in the Trobriands consists of a 'body of binding obligations, regarded as a right of one party and acknowledged as a duty by the other, kept in force by a specific mechanism of reciprocity and publicity inherent in the structure of their society'. Individuals willingly comply with social norms, not so much for fear of negative sanctions, but for internal, self-regulatory reasons consistent with their own best interests. Melpa big-men gain status through a system of escalating exchange called *moka*. Large ceremonies are staged in which pigs, cassowary birds and other valuables (which in more recent times have included cash and land cruisers) are given away to rivals. The donors gain prestige at the expense of the recipients, who must then stage return *moka*s in which even more valuable goods are returned. Technically, *moka* refers to the extra that is given: the 'return' on the 'loan'. These sorts of reciprocal obligations are enforced only through 'self-regulation'. Through enculturation, people come to hold beliefs that incline them to adhere to customary behaviors. Notions of honor, morality, guilt and shame are examples of self-regulation, which needs few controls, since traditional behaviors are highly valued by society.

The contrasts between chiefs and big-men, hierarchical and egalitarian societies are distinctions that have conditioned the responses of colonial governments to customary legal systems in the Pacific and have shaped the resultant legal syncretism, or blending, of systems of laws. But such dichotomies do not adequately convey the complexity and richness of the legal process in any particular local situation. In Austronesian societies, the authority of chiefs may be questioned, negotiated, and restricted. And big-men sometimes exercise considerable influence and can wield power. Although rules are more formally inscribed in hierarchical societies, egalitarian societies may also have quite complicated normative orders which are important in shaping how cases actually get resolved. While many legal scholars believe that the rules of law in complex societies are clear, predictable, and determine the outcomes of cases, legal realists and legal anthropologists see 'law' as much less certain, with rules that are highly variable, sometimes vague, and often contested and manipulated.

The diverse and contrasting systems of customary law and legal sanctions in the Pacific islands have made for the development of interesting legal structures today. A striking characteristic of 'law' in most contemporary island nations is 'legal pluralism', the simultaneous existence of different types of legal systems within a single setting. Many countries have legal heritages that include 'custom law' together with a legal system introduced during the colonial era. While attempts to reconcile these models of law have often been made, the story of contemporary legal institutions in the Pacific is very much a story of negotiation and reconciliation between and among competing models of law, authority, and morality. The blending of introduced and customary systems of law presents a great challenge for Pacific nations as they struggle to create unified and equitable national legal systems in the contemporary context.—RS

Further reading

Feinberg, R and Watson-Gegeo, K A (eds), 1996. *Leadership and Change in the Western Pacific*, London School of Economics Monograph 66.

Malinowski, B, 1926. *Crime and Custom in Savage Society*, Routledge and Kegan Paul.

Nadel, S F, 1953. 'Social control and self-regulation', *Social Forces*, 31.

Pospisil, L, 1958. *Kapauku Papuans and their Law*, Yale University.

Powles, G and Pulea, M, 1988. *Pacific Courts and Legal Systems*, University of the South Pacific.

Scaglion, R, 1996. 'Chiefly models in Papua New Guinea', *The Contemporary Pacific*, 8.

——, (forthcoming). 'Law in the Pacific islands', in M Rapaport (ed.), *Geography of the Pacific Islands*, Bess Press.

Strathern, A, 1971. *The Rope of Moka*, Cambridge University Press.

Gift-giving in Melanesia

The competitive giving of gifts for which Melanesian BIG-MEN are renowned is often contrasted with the chieftainship and redistributive (or tributary) gift-giving found in Polynesia. While this contrast says much about the respective indigenous political economies, it is important to remember that chieftainship is also found in Melanesia, that women and 'rubbish' men also engage in various forms of gift exchange, and that many indigenous forms of economic and political activity have effloresced under the impact of colonization. This is because the principle of reciprocity has its basis in family organization, and while colonization has transformed family relations in Melanesia their distinctive cultural form remains.

Competitive gift-giving is a form of symbolic warfare and it often arises out of actual tribal warfare. The battle is about prestige. The aim of a big-man is to crush his rival with a large gift, and to impress onlookers with the brilliance of his oratory. The size of these gifts has grown rapidly in recent years and the fame of some Melanesian big-men has become international. Such is the case of Ongka, a big-man from the Melpa tribe near Mount Hagen (Papua New Guinea). Two films have been made about his exploits, many books have been written about his people by anthropologists, and he has published his own memoirs. One film deals with a big *moka* he made in 1975, which included 8 cows, 12 cassowaries, 600 pigs, a Landrover, and A$10 000.

Redistributive gift-giving is a form of tribute given to chiefs. In Trobriand Islands, brothers are obliged to give yams to their sister's husbands at harvest time. These exchanges maintain relationships between affines but, because chiefs tend to have many wives, annual exchanges enable chiefs to accumulate large quantities of yams that they display in elaborately designed storehouses as symbols of their status. These may be left to rot or they may be given away by chiefs in special ceremonies.

Less spectacular, but no less important, is the non-competitive form of gift exchange that occurs between 'rubbish' men (those with little prestige) and women. The variety here is bewildering: apparently every kinship relationship is marked by gift of a special symbolic kind. An important distinction is made between cooked and uncooked food, the former used in exchange relationships between close relatives and the latter in exchange relations between more distant kin. Another important distinction is between women's wealth and men's wealth. Women not only engage in daily exchanges of utilitarian items, they have also developed elaborate exchange systems of their own. In Trobriand Islands, for example, women spend long hours scraping patterns on banana leaves, which are tied up in bundles and given away in complex mortuary rituals whose exchange cycles may last many years.

These indigenous forms of polity and economy now contradict, now complement, the imposed parliamentary political system and associated money economy. Not all big-men are politicians but many politicians are big-men because a man who has little prestige is unlikely to attract many votes. It has been said that big-men were 'pre-adapted' to capitalism, but the film, *Joe Leahy's Neighbours*, recording the travails of capitalist/big-man Joe Leahy, suggests that the key to success is the opportunistic switching between value regimes. It also reveals, somewhat tragically, that tribal warfare can just as easily substitute for gift exchange as the other way around.

Some churches have successfully adapted indigenous exchange systems to suit their own fundraising ends. Such is the case with the Uniting Church in Elavala, the coastal village now part of Port Moresby. Today these villagers are devout Christians and are almost totally dependent on the market economy for their survival. They have experienced the impact of colonization as no other PNG villagers have done, but their family relations are stronger than ever. CLAN leadership here is in the hands of church deacons who compete in a yearly gift-giving competition called *boubou*. This achieves a ranking of clans and raises large amounts of money—over K90 000 in 1996—for the upkeep of the church.

Gift-giving in Melanesia is a fluid and dynamic process that will persist for as long as the Melanesian family persists. Though gift-giving exists everywhere, its particular colouration and form in Melanesia derives, for the most part, from the culturally specific forms of kinship, marriage systems, and clan politics.—CAG

Further reading

Gregory, C A, 1982. *Gifts and Commodities*, Academic Press.

Strathern, A, 1971. *The Rope of Moka*, Cambridge University Press.

Strathern, M, 1972. *Women in Between: female roles in a male world*, Seminar Press.

Ongka, 1979. *Ongka: a self-account by a New Guinea big-man*, tr. A Strathern, Duckworth.

Weiner, A, 1976. *Women of Value, Men of Renown: new perspectives in Trobriand exchange*, Queensland University Press.

Domestic violence

Domestic violence in various forms was a culturally legitimate practice in many Pacific societies. Typically it had normative functions to reinforce expected social roles and behaviour in households, although this was justified in many different ways. For example, in western Polynesia, physical force is accepted as a legitimate means for older members of a household to enforce obedience among younger members, whereas in Melanesia the focus was more commonly upon the enforcement of the dominance of men over their wives. Despite such patterns, women were not completely powerless, and both formal and informal mechanisms existed to protect wives from abuse. In most Polynesian and in some Micronesian societies, a wife had the right to leave her husband. In western Polynesia, women could claim rights to protection from their brothers, particularly if they were of high personal rank. In those societies of Melanesia in which bride-price was paid, it was difficult for a wife to leave her husband, however women could use sanctions of shame to protect themselves against ill-treatment, even where they had minimal formal power. For example, attributed supernatural powers to 'pollute' men, or knowledge of how to shame men with particular words or actions, was greatly feared. In extreme cases women might even commit suicide to shame or to provoke supernatural revenge upon abusive husbands.

Binge-drinking in the late colonial and post-colonial period, predominantly among males, has been shown to be a significant factor in increasing the prevalence of domestic violence in many Pacific societies. Another contemporary social trend contributing to domestic violence may be an increasing tendency towards nuclear family households where disputes between spouses, or between parents and children, are less likely to be moderated by the presence of other relatives. In Papua New Guinea, studies of domestic violence by the PNG Law Reform Commission in the 1980s found that two-thirds of women have been beaten and two-thirds of men admit to beating their wives, indicating that it is a common problem for women at all levels of society. The use of weapons for marital violence is regarded as less acceptable. In rural areas such marital violence is most frequently explained as the result of women's failure to perform their expected duties for their husbands, and sexual jealousy. In urban communities, the perceived causes are alcohol, conflict over money, and sexual jealousy. When men are injured by a spouse it is normally due to retaliation or self-defence.

Since the adoption of formal codes of law, domestic violence in the form of spousal assault is illegal, however it has been difficult to persuade police and magistrates to prosecute such cases. Furthermore many PACIFIC CONSTITUTIONS give some degree of recognition to customary law, which may defend a man's right to beat his wife under certain circumstances, or parents' rights to beat children. In Papua New Guinea, Fiji and Vanuatu, there have been campaigns to raise public awareness of women's rights and the illegality of wife-beating. Fiji has an established non-governmental organization, the Fiji Women's Crisis Centre, which provides legal advice and counselling to abused women and which campaigns to change attitudes among the police and judiciary. In Papua New Guinea, Samoa, Cook Islands and Vanuatu, non-government organizations with similar concerns for the rights of women and children have been established.—PS2

Urban crime and social status

The most significant reportage of urban crime in the Pacific islands comes from Papua New Guinea. Media coverage of Papua New Guinea's 'law and order' problems focuses largely on the activities of RASKOLS, popularly portrayed as products of squatter settlements in the main towns. Unemployment and social dislocation linked to urbanization are commonly assumed to be the causes of urban gang crime, and *raskols* themselves, who become notably available for interviews whenever investigative journalists from overseas visit urban centres, reinforce this with a practised 'Robin Hood' rhetoric that they are driven to crime by poverty and that corrupt politicians and public servants are the real criminals.

Much analysis of *raskol* crime, however, is based on fairly superficial research and often uses models of gang crime and concepts of gangs developed in relation to urbanization, social disintegration, and lack of economic opportunity in industrial western society. While some street crime is a response to urban poverty, the crime phenomenon in Papua New Guinea is more complex than many commentaries imply and needs to be understood in a local context in which many social traditions remain fairly resilient against western influence. In particular, gifting and reciprocal obligations, which remain a driving force in Melanesian social life and status, are an important factor in *raskol* behaviour. Crime in Papua New Guinea, especially that involving theft, might be better understood as a kind of growth industry rather than a pathological response to the disruptions of urbanization and social dislocation.

Traditional GIFT-GIVING IN MELANESIA, which can enhance the status of an individual or group, now includes money and consumer goods. In urban areas especially, where land for gardening and pig grazing is scarce, theft is a quick way to obtain cash, or goods which can readily be sold for cash. The cash then becomes a resource which can be used, not for the accumulation of personal wealth, but for gifting in pursuit of status. A significant feature of urban gang crime is the speed at which stolen money is dispersed, not in payment for lasting luxury items, but in distribution to acquaintances or in orgiastic beer parties in which huge amounts of money are drunk away. By these magnanimous gestures an individual can enhance his status (the gangs are overwhelmingly male) and draw others into his debt. Chronic material poverty is not the driving factor behind this phenomenon. Recent research into the social background of *raskols* in Port Moresby has found that they do not come exclusively from the ranks of the unemployed, but from a range of socio-economic positions. Some remain in legitimate employment, and some leave jobs in the formal economy to concentrate on a more lucrative career in crime. However, just as traditional aspirants to high status enjoyed different rates of success, there are very successful *raskols* (in terms of status, not of accumulated wealth) and a range of aspirants with mixed fortunes.

The so-called gangs are mostly loose agglomerations of people involved to a greater or lesser degree in criminal activity centred around individuals who have developed high status through successful gifting of resources obtained through crime. Unlike gangs in industrial societies, they do not usually have rules of entry or stringent initiation rituals and 'members' can leave simply by giving up criminal activity. The term 'gang', therefore, applies only in its loosest sense to the *raskol* groups, and a more useful analytical focus would be the individual gang 'leaders', highly successful *raskols* who are organizers of large thefts such as bank heists and have developed networks of relationships enabling them to enlist appropriate individuals for specific 'jobs'. The growth of this type of crime exploits the well-reported lack of resources and training of the country's police force. Unless they are caught more or less red-handed, *raskols* are rarely apprehended.

The notion that gangs are the product of impoverished squatter settlements is based partly on the observation that they flee into such habitats when pursued and gather in them at other times. Their presence alarms settlement dwellers as much as anyone else, for it brings police raids which often victimize law-abiding inhabitants. Settlements are confusing places to outsiders; the dwellings often appear to be haphazardly arranged and the lack of well-defined through-roading contributes to a sense of disorientation. The popular term 'squatter settlements' is inappropriate in view of the variety of types of settlements in urban areas, but they do share the characteristic that they are enclaves of migrant groups and thus give an initial impression of insularity. All these factors make outsiders cautious about entering and for this reason some settlements have become handy gathering points for *raskol* gangs. Individual members of the gangs are not exclusively products of squatter settlements, and only some actually live there.

Finally it should be noted that while occasional attacks on élite citizens or overseas visitors gain major press coverage, most victims of crime in Papua New Guinea are much poorer, live in settlements, cannot afford security guards and are chronically vulnerable to attack. Far from being Robin Hood figures, most *raskols* victimize ordinary citizens for petty cash and hard-earned meagre possessions, and there has been a disturbing increase in recent years in gratuitous violence associated with personal thefts. Only a few *raskols* attain the kind of high status referred to above, developing connections and resources enabling them to concentrate on major heists. Petty criminals vie for fame in a variety of ways, including representing themselves as 'gang leaders' when they are in fact minor figures (or sometimes not *raskols* at all), appearing on films made by visiting camera crews and falsely claiming responsibility for publicized major heists. Behind the rhetoric of oppression and outrage at the excesses of the élite, *raskolism* has itself become a perverse vehicle in the search for prestige, a complex phenomenon in which notoriety serves as fame and the ethos of introduced capitalism is inverted as instant wealth is dispersed. It is unlikely that the so-called law and order problem will be solved by existing strategies such as periodic urban curfews and police raids on settlements (both of which penalize the innocent and encourage temporary relocations of criminals to other, vulnerable, communities). A more likely avenue of success may be the pursuit of strategies based on Melanesian regulatory mechanisms and communal modes of intervention. (CRIMINAL JUSTICE IN PAPUA NEW GUINEA.)—MG

Further reading

Norwood, H, 1984. *Port Moresby Urban Villages and Squatter Areas*, University of Papua New Guinea Press.

Youth and crime in Papua New Guinea

Young male migrants have been linked with street crime in Papua New Guinea since the rise of rapid urbanization during the mid and late 1960s. (See RASKOLS.) While the quality of criminal justice data in Papua New Guinea is poor, available figures confirm this. Police arrest statistics, for example, indicate that between 1986 and 1992 approximately 60 per cent of annual arrests were of children and young persons (overwhelmingly male) between the ages of 13 and 25. Likewise figures from the Department of Correctional Services indicate that between 1983 and 1988 an average of 41 per cent of all annual admissions to prison, including remandees and convicted prisoners, were aged between 10 and 20, while approximately 68 per cent were between 10 and 25. The youthful character of *raskolism* is partly a reflection of demographic factors. Approximately 43 per cent of the national population of 4 million are under the age of 15, while 50 per cent of the population of PORT MORESBY are under 20.

The emergence of *raskolism* against a background of rapid social and economic change has encouraged a modernist view of *raskol* crime, perceiving it as a response to marginalizations of recent origin. Unemployment is widely regarded as a key factor underlying juvenile crime in Papua New Guinea, and is regularly cited as a legitimation by *raskols* themselves. Over 50 000 youngsters leave school annually, most without having completed their formal education. Many leave because their parents cannot afford the school fees or because of the difficulties encountered with the western-oriented education system. The small formal economy, in turn, is incapable of absorbing the large numbers of annual school-leavers. It might appear that crime is one of the few options available to under-educated youth in this situation.

Nevertheless, most Papua New Guineans continue to operate outside the formal economy, mainly as subsistence farmers in rural villages. The relationship between crime and unemployment is less straightforward than in an environment where most individuals are dependent on the wage sector for survival. Many active criminals are, in fact, employed, some have deliberately abandoned employment for crime, and others have never actively sought employment. Unemployment may be an important factor in some cases but it does not explain criminal choices in every instance, nor does it explain why the majority of technically 'unemployed' youth do not become *raskols*. The appeal of crime to youth lies in a mixture of social and economic factors.

Lack of legitimate opportunities to acquire material resources adds to the attractions of crime, particularly in the fully monetized urban environment. The weakness of state controls—relatively low levels of popular allegiance to state law and a seriously under-resourced police force—provides another factor enhancing the appeal of criminal choices. The quest for cash and other commodities is also evident in the innovative strategies for exiting crime that have been developed by youth in recent years. Such strategies include 'walkathons', where youth groups walk great distances in order to seek financial assistance from government officials, business houses and political leaders for a variety of self-help development projects. They also include the distinctly Papua New Guinean phenomenon of mass surrender, where groups of self-professed criminals give themselves up, normally in return for the commitment of resources towards their chosen reform strategy.

Crime has also created new opportunity structures for youth, a notable example being the booming private security industry. With the limited capacity of state controls and escalating lawlessness, openings for private security services have grown exponentially. The relationship between the security industry and *raskolism* is essentially symbiotic. The industry is clearly dependent on high levels of crime and personal insecurity. Employment in the security industry, in turn, provides opportunities for *raskols* and ex-*raskols*. The practical skills of *raskolism*—requiring toughness and aggression—are generally consistent with those expected of security guards. In addition, such positions require few, if any, formal qualifications.

The rhetoric of social injustice used by *raskols* has convinced some observers that *raskolism* is a form of nascent resistance by socially marginal groups. Anger is often expressed at members of the social élite, who are viewed as neglecting—or cheating—their less fortunate counterparts. This sentiment appears to be based on perceptions about the unfairness (corruption or nepotism) by which élite groups have secured their privileged positions, rather than being about inequality *per se*. Such rhetoric represents crime as a way of combating these fundamental injustices, and might be expected to result in criminal activity that selectively targets the rich. The evidence, however, indicates that it is the poor who are more likely to be victimized.

In addition to its value as a relatively accessible means of acquiring cash and other material resources, *raskolism* offers the prospect of excitement, adventure and collective identity to the adolescents and young men involved. The social organization of *raskolism* and, in particular, the relationship between criminal leaders and their followers, suggests that crime provides an important strategy for building individual prestige and standing. (See URBAN CRIME AND SOCIAL STATUS.) The same dynamics can be seen in post-*raskol* strategies such as mass surrenders, as, indeed, they can in many other legitimate social occupations in contemporary Papua New Guinea.

Another dimension of *raskolism* is the way in which criminal identity and commitment are constituted through interactions with the institutions of criminal justice. Violent encounters with the police, for example, form a staple ingredient in *raskol* induction. Police beatings are commonplace and often referred to as 'the panel beat shop'. Such encounters provide youth with another way of building individual reputations within criminal groups, as well as a means of eliciting sympathy from the wider community. Imprisonment can also serve to increase solidarity within and between criminal groups, and advance the standing of individual criminals. Bomana Prison, outside Port Moresby, is referred to colloquially as 'the college', where inmates 'graduate' with enhanced criminal skills, contacts and commitment.

The violence of *raskol* crime is, in part, a consequence of the widespread availability of modern firearms and their routine criminal use. It also reflects the relatively high level of tolerance of violence in the wider environment, and connects with older social traditions pre-dating state formation, whereby interpersonal violence was a legitimate strategy for resolving conflict and maintaining dominance. Violence remains a major problem in modern Papua New Guinean society. It is by no means confined to *raskols* and is evident, in varying degrees, within many ordinary households (DOMESTIC VIOLENCE), as well as in the workings of state institutions themselves.—SD

■ *Raskols Raskol*—a TOK PISIN word derived from 'rascal' and applied by Papua New Guineans to anyone involved in crime involving theft with violence, from knife-point mugging to major bank raids or murder, but excluding white-collar crime. Mostly operating in groups, *raskols* arm themselves with a variety of weapons from knives and axes to home-made shotguns and high-powered rifles and usually wear masks. *Raskolism*, the euphemism for street crime in Papua New Guinea, is predominantly a youthful, masculine and group activity.

Juvenile criminal gangs emerged during the mid and late 1960s against a background of rapid URBANIZATION. Urban growth coincided with the removal of colonial restrictions over social movement in the lead-up to independence in 1975. De-prohibition of alcohol consumption in 1962 was another factor in early gang formation. The first gangs were primarily mechanisms for coping with the dislocative effects of socioeconomic change and, in particular, the challenges facing young male migrants in unfamiliar urban environments. Criminal activities were initially confined to the theft of desired commodities, mainly food, beer and cash.

Today, portraying *raskols* as the product of unemployment and urban squatter settlements is no longer sufficient for adequate analysis. Modern *raskols* come from a wide range of socioeconomic positions, rich and poor; *raskolism* has spread to many rural parts of Papua New Guinea and criminal activities have become increasingly more violent.—SD & MG

Urban squatting in Fiji

The root causes of Fiji's urban informal housing—squatting, as it is popularly but not always accurately known—are similar to those of squatting in developing countries: gross rural–urban and income disparities; areas of unused urban land; a history of inappropriate and unaffordable official building standards; and land and official housing, both government-supported and private, priced beyond the reach of poor migrant and urban families. Many locations are also similar, with early settlements on city marginal land—steep slopes and mangrove edges—close to menial and casual work in the downtown industrial and commercial areas, and more recent settlements established, or relocated as official developments replace them, in the peri-urban area.

The distinctive features of squatting stem from Fiji's colonial heritage. Towns were European creations and urban tenure either crown or private. Native tenure was expunged and native Fijians were relocated to urban villages outside town boundaries, where an essentially separate Fiji Administration (and later NATIVE LAND TRUST BOARD, NLTB) sought to isolate and thereby protect Fijian, and chiefly, interests. The labour lines, and later residences, of the indentured Indo-Fijian were also located just outside the early town boundaries, and Kai Solomoni (part-Fijian descendants of indentured Solomon Islanders) established informal settlements on Anglican church land at or beyond the city perimeter. SUVA was a typical colonial town where ethnicity, class and residence coincided. Many of its early features are evident in today's urban landscape.

Table 6.1 Estimated informal dwelling populations in Fiji's urban areas (per cent)

	Total 1996	Informal dwelling	Urban village[1]	Total informal[2]
Suva	186 903	14.1	4.7	18.8
Lautoka	43 274	19.9	1.9	21.8
Nadi	30 884	14.3	10.0	24.3
Labasa	24 095	12.6	1.9	14.5
Nausori	21 617	8.5	3.7	12.2
Ba	14 716	14.4	3.2	17.6
Sigatoka	7 682	8.6	30.4	39.0
Vatukoula	7 079	21.4	2.5	23.9
Savusavu	4 970	19.4	3.4	22.8
Rakiraki	4 836	29.9	2.6	32.5
Navua	4 183	6.2	-	6.2
Levuka	3 746	13.2	15.9	29.1
Tavua	2 419	9.4	16.8	26.2
Korovou	318	39.3	-	39.3
TOTAL	356 902	14.6	5.1	19.7

Notes: Areas not included: Pacific Harbour (pop. 1607); Nabouwalu (592); Seaqaqa (394).
[1] includes officially recognized 'urban villages' (those with traditional land rights) and other Fijian urban 'settlements' where residents are not traditional owners.
[2] These figures compare with Port Moresby (25 per cent, 1984) and Honiara (23 per cent, 1990).
Source: Percentages (of the 1996 total population) are based on aerial photograph interpretation (Walsh 1996).

This mix of historical circumstances led to the creation of informal settlements based on ethnicity (and within them, on islands or villages of origin) in which most older residents make some claim to extra-legal tenure. Fijians, whose settlements are mainly on crown or NLTB land, have presented *tabua* to city councils or the land-owning CLAN. They pay rates or rent, and meet their traditional obligations. Indo-Fijians, mostly on private land, generally pay rent. Refusal to accept rent usually heralds land development and ultimate eviction or resettlement. Kai Solomoni contribute towards Anglican church rates payments.

The 1960s and 1970s saw the rapid expansion of the Fiji urban economy, and with it considerable rural–urban migration and suburbanization. Fijians became a significant component of urban populations for the first time. A Housing Authority was established to house those low-income workers with permanent employment. By the late 1970s, nearly one-fifth of Suva's urban households lived in rented or mortgaged Housing Authority accommodation, but a further one-fifth could not afford even subsidized accommodation. A small number of destitute families were accommodated by the Fiji Council of Churches' Housing Authority Relief Trust (HART) but the fast-growing informal settlements, within and beyond the city boundaries, accommodated most poor and destitute families. Suva's size and youthfulness forestalled the emergence of significant inner city slum development.

An estimated 20 per cent of Fiji's urban population at the time of the 1996 census (some 70 000 people) lived in informal housing. Of the estimated 35 000 in the Suva urban area, 8800 lived in Fijian urban villages or settlements. Table 6.1 shows the estimated extent of informal housing in 14 of Fiji's 17 urban areas.

Very little substantial research has been undertaken on Fiji's squatting. There have been occasional civic surveys of head counts, housing and sanitation in Suva and Lautoka. The Lands Department polices some Suva settlements to deter new construction and establish settler credentials for resettlement. The churches and university undergraduate students have conducted settlement surveys. Some useful case studies have focused on poverty and environmental issues, there is a comprehensive census analysis and sample survey (1978) of 12 Suva squatter settlements, and an update carried out in 1998 (A C Walch forthcoming).

Most squatter houses (73 per cent) are built of tin, with sizes ranging from a 3x3 m single room (typical of recent arrivals, Indo-Fijian widows and the chronically poor) to much larger houses, expanded as household size and income increased. Some 5 per cent of households rent from other squatters, and about 20 per cent pay some form of land rent. Although many settlements show signs of improvement, at least 10 per cent of dwellings are grossly inadequate. In 1998, 16 per cent of dwellings had one room (31 per cent in 1976). One in five lack adequate toilets and close access to reticulated water (80 per cent had pit toilets and 59 per cent inadequate water access in 1976).

Contrary to public perception, squatting is not a consequence of ongoing rural–urban migration. One in three of both Fijian and Indo-Fijian household heads were born in Suva, and many more have lived there most of their lives. Most expect or wish to stay, saying that if evicted, they will move to other squatter areas. (Many older Fijians say they will return to their village.) Sixty per cent of households are nuclear. Many include 'extra' members (nephews, nieces, cousins and non-relations) and a significant number are 'incomplete' in that they lack key members such as husbands or wives. Females head nearly 20 per cent of Indo-Fijian (and 13 per cent of Fijian) households.

Fijian squatter settlements are typically more cohesive than Indo-Fijian settlements. Extensive kin-based mutual help systems are common, whereas among Indo-Fijians help more typically extends only to parents. Most Fijian settlements are still organized on traditional lines with a *turaga ni koro* (village leader) and the church active symbols of their unity. There are, however, increasing signs of stress in all squatter settlements, with many residents complaining about noise, drunkenness, drug abuse and violence, usually associated with unemployed Fijian youths. However, crime is also an increasing problem in non-squatter suburbs. Squatters are not especially politically active (as in some developing countries), but they have on occasion proved to be adept at using their political connections. Most former Indo-Fijian squatter areas are now ethnically mixed, and Fijian sub-renters are far less significant than Fijian house-owners.

The typical squatter is poor, far poorer than the average city dweller. Fijians especially rely heavily on gardening and fishing to supplement low incomes, and many squatters are engaged in informal sector activities. Employment in insecure casual or menial activities is typical, and unemployment levels are high. Better-off households receive incomes from several members; and women, both daughters and wives, make significant contributions to wage incomes. Women's informal activities contribute to nearly one-third of households. Fourteen per cent of households report significant contributions from relatives, in Fiji and abroad, and 12 per cent receive some income from pensions and welfare agencies.

Not all squatters, however, are abjectly poor. The mean weekly household head's income of F$96 slightly exceeds the urban household poverty line, but the standard deviation of F$85 is almost as great, and most households have more than one income. A wide—and probably increasing—income range exists among squatters, confirmed by the proportion of squatter households which can afford electricity (42 per cent), refrigerators (48 per cent), television (56 per cent), telephones (35 per cent), or cars (7 per cent). Some 65 per cent of squatters report some savings—usually for children's education—but a disturbing trend is the number of households at some time in debt for food (10 per cent) and hire purchases (44 per cent).

Squatters indicate a strong preference for proximity to Suva and secure tenure. Some 13 per cent have been asked to move, and 30 per cent (37 per cent Indo-Fijian) think they may be evicted or asked to move in the near future. Most are willing to contribute in cash or labour for secure tenure and settlement upgrading.

Current policies towards squatters (and informal activities generally) are more tolerant than in pre-independence days. Resettlement is preferred over eviction. Recognition is given to long-standing tenants. Official housing practices are increasingly based on realistic site-and-service provision in the peri-urban area. Some city squatter settlements are being upgraded but, over time, one might expect to see most moved out of the city. Such a move will relocate—but will leave substantially unresolved—a significant problem whose root cause is the poverty which continues to affect a significant proportion of the Fijian and the Indian Fijian urban and rural populations.—ACW

Further reading

Bryant, J, 1993. *Urban Poverty and the Environment in the South Pacific*, University of New England.

Walsh, A C, 1996. *Informal Dwellings in Urban Fiji: a report for the UNDP Fiji Poverty Study*, University of the South Pacific.

Suicide in the Pacific islands

Suicide is not new to the Pacific, but rates have increased dramatically in some populations in recent decades. These increases have occurred at young ages, such that Pacific suicide is characterized by its youthfulness. Some Pacific island youth suicide rates are the highest in the world (youth is defined as age 15–24 years).

The populations with high levels of youth suicide include the Indian population of Fiji, Guam, the islands of Federated States of Micronesia, Marshall Islands and Palau (collectively referred to here as Micronesia) and Samoa. Global comparison shows that male youth suicide in all four populations exceeds current levels reported elsewhere in the world. This is also true of female youth suicide in Samoa and the Indian population of Fiji.

The average age at suicide is 18 to 25 years for females and 22 to 28 for males, depending on the population in question. In all populations, females are at least two years younger on average than males. In Micronesia and Western Samoa, age at suicide is becoming younger for both sexes.

Pacific suicide has generally been regarded as an issue concerning males. Indeed, when suicide at all ages is considered, male rates exceed female rates in all populations. However, at youth ages there are two exceptions to this gender imbalance: in Samoa and among Indo-Fijians, female youth suicide rates slightly exceed male rates. This is unusual since in almost all other populations of the world, male rates exceed female rates by a considerable margin.

In most populations, hanging is the most common method of suicide. Hanging accounts for 70–80 per cent of suicide deaths in Micronesia, Fiji and French Polynesia. In Samoa, however, ingestion of the highly toxic herbicide, paraquat, accounts for about 75 per cent of suicides. Paraquat also accounts for about a quarter of suicides among Indo-Fijians, but is not commonly used elsewhere in the Pacific.

Fatality rates (the proportion of suicide attempts resulting in death) differ according to method. Low fatality rates are associated with ingestion of toxic substances such as household bleach and medicinal

Figure 6.1 Trends in suicide rates in selected Pacific populations, 1960–95

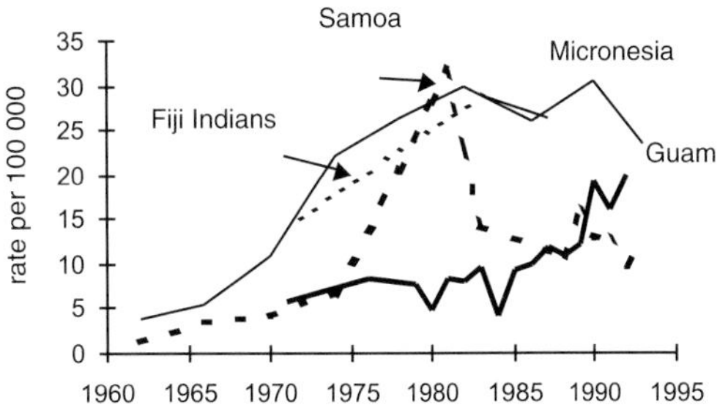

Note: dotted lines indicate less reliable data.
Source: Author's research.

drugs, and with hanging in Micronesia (since this often takes the form of leaning into a noose from a standing or sitting position). High fatality rates are associated with hanging (as usually defined) and paraquat ingestion. Thus, in Micronesia, less than 20 per cent of serious suicide attempts are fatal, whilst amongst Indo-Fijians almost 40 per cent are fatal, and over half are fatal in Samoa.

The higher suicide rates in males, found in most populations, are a result of gender differences in suicide behaviour. In fact, females usually attempt suicide more frequently than males but use less effective methods. Pacific examples of this include French Polynesia and Tonga, where females comprise 50–60 per cent of reported attempts, but have much lower fatality rates (6–7 per cent compared to 30–40 per cent in males). Amongst Samoan youth, however, males and females are equally likely to attempt suicide and equally likely to use paraquat ingestion, with roughly equal effect, resulting in the slightly higher female rates already noted.

Other factors associated with suicide include ethnicity, religion, culture and geographic location. These are often inter-related. Ethnicity is particularly important in Fiji, where rates for Indians exceed those of indigenous Fijians. Amongst Indo-Fijians rates are higher for Hindus than Muslims. Culture is associated with differences between the constituent populations of Micronesia and of Papua New Guinea. The association with geographic location varies between populations: higher rates are found for Indo-Fijians living in rural areas, in urban areas in Papua New Guinea and in peri-urban areas in Micronesia and Samoa.—HB

■ *Youth suicide in Micronesia* Suicide rates since the 1970s have risen to epidemic proportion among young Micronesian men aged from mid-teens to mid 20s. The increase in suicides has been especially alarming in Chuuk and Marshall Islands, where annual rates of over 200 per 100 000 are among the highest in the world. The suicides display considerable cultural patterning in method, motive and precipitating events. In Chuuk, the most common suicide scenario is a young man who hangs himself near home, after receiving a scolding or rebuff from a parent or other close relative. In Marshall Islands, suicides triggered by jealous anger towards a wife or girlfriend are the most common type. Researchers surmise that recent changes in family structure and adolescent socialization have greatly exacerbated traditional stress upon young men, and that suicide has arisen as a culturally patterned response to conflict with close kin.—DHR

Further reading

Booth, H, 1999. *Gender, Power and Social Change: youth suiide among Fiji Indians and Western Samoans*, Gender Relations Project, The Australian National University.

Haynes, R, 1984. 'Suicide in Fiji: a preliminary study', *British Journal of Psychiatry*, 145.

Hezel, F X, Rubinstein, D H and White, G M (eds), 1985. *Culture, Youth and Suicide in the Pacific: papers from an East–West Center conference*, Pacific Islands Studies Program, University of Hawai'i.

Karim, I and Price, J, 1975. 'Suicide in Fiji: a two-year survey', *Acta Psych. Scand*, 52.

Macpherson, C and Macpherson, L, 1987. 'Towards an explanation of recent trends in suicide in Western Samoa', *Man*, NS, 22.

Ree, G H, 1971. 'Suicide in Macuata Province, Fiji', *Practition*, 207.

FOUR HEALTH

Traditional food and nutrition

Food played a prominent role in the everyday lives of Pacific islanders. The term *kainga*, or *'aiga* in many Polynesian languages literally translated as 'those who ate food together', and is usually translated as the household, or extended family. Food was thus the symbol of integration of social groups. Eating together was a major symbol of social cohesion and wellbeing. Food was—and still is—an essential part of any social gathering. It formed a conspicuous part of any social event, however big or small. The types of foods, the way they were prepared, amounts available, and the precedence of some foods over others all form part of the picture of food consumption.

Pacific islanders' concept of food is complex. Individual food items such as taro or fish can be named, but they are not considered real food, *kakana dina* in Fijian, unless they are consumed in the appropriate cultural manner. This complex concept of food applies throughout Polynesia and eastern Micronesia. It is also found in Southeast Asia, for example in the Hanunoo of the Philippines. The edible items regarded as 'real food' also vary across the region, though there is more homogeneity in the eastern Pacific. Twelve MAJOR STARCH FOODS, together with fish and birds, can be distinguished as the 'main' foods, from secondary foods such as Bele or edible Hibiscus, nightshade or dog. 'Fall-back foods' are those eaten when none of the first two categories of foods are available. The 12 main starchy foods were both roots and fruits—the only grain crop, rice, did not penetrate much beyond Guam until it was reintroduced by Europeans in the 20th century.

A rich array of foods has developed over time. All the food plants had been introduced, most of them through Southeast Asia (see FOOTSTEPS FROM ASIA). Those plants originating in the Americas, such as coco-yam (*Xanthosoma*), cassava (*Manihot esculenta*), and sweet potato (*Ipomoea batatas*) are all 19th century introductions. Pacific islanders took food plants as gifts when they travelled to other islands, as borne out by the names used for species, such as Taro Tonga, known as *Xanthosoma* in Fiji. This reproduction of new species may have been accidental, through a discarded piece of taro or yam corm, for instance, or deliberate when planting material, such as taro tops or kava root, was donated for reproduction.

Accompaniments to the starch foods consisted of a range of items from salt water to coconut, either fresh or grated. Some of these items may have been eaten raw, while others required cooking. A starch food was not eaten alone if it was to be considered a 'real food'. Other accompaniments were fish, birds and 'packet' foods—that is, those wrapped in leaves—cooked in an earth oven. Pork was not an everyday meal but reserved more for FEASTS. A beverage accompanying a meal, such as coconut milk or water, was not sufficiently important to turn the starch food into a meal, and liquid accompaniments like salt water were used as a dipping sauce rather than a beverage.

■ *Cooking* The earth oven and pottery were two widespread modes of cooking. The earth oven—called *lovo* in Fiji, *umu* in Maori and *imu* in Hawai'i—was an all-purpose way of cooking all ingredients in one fire. The taro, or yams and cassava, together with fish and any 'packet' foods were all placed over prepared coals and the whole covered with leaves and then earth to be steamed for two hours or more. This mode of cooking conserved scarce fuel supplies and avoided acrid smoke in the cooks' eyes. Long cooking in the earth oven also ensured that toxic foods such as taro and cassava were well cooked, and retained nutrients in the foods.

Roasting food in the coals was the second most common form of cooking. Whole breadfruit and fish were frequently cooked this way. The breadfruit were turned from time to time and the ash scraped off until they were cooked, which would take about an hour.

Boiling required receptacles which were scarce in those societies that did not make or exchange pottery. Starchy food was cut into pieces and mixed with water, and sometimes coconut cream, before plugging the neck of the receptacle to steam the food. Such forms of cooking were more appropriate for small groups than for large extended-family households. When Europeans brought iron pots, boiling became more common. Liquids were also boiled or heated by plunging a hot stone into them.

Men prepared the earth oven. In pre-contact times an earth oven full of food may have been prepared only two or three times a week; the household and guests then ate the food available, or did not eat until the next oven was prepared. There was no cultural necessity to make an oven every day. Women prepared the food and made any packet foods, but men cooked most of the food in many societies of central Polynesia. For large-scale events such as ceremonies and feasts, men did the bulk of the cooking in many island societies. Restrictions on cooking

Street market, Port Vila, Vanuatu

food for their husbands applied to menstruating women in many societies. More elaborate restrictions on cooking were in place in specific cultures, such as Yap where complex levels of eating classes operated.

The amounts eaten were deemed 'prodigious' by European standards. The basic premise behind food offerings was (and is) that there should be more than enough food available for those who usually eat together as well as enough for any visitors. A 'good feed' was the synonym for wellbeing. This factor is seen negatively by present-day evaluations of nutrition, and is considered to contribute to obesity. That high status persons ate very large amounts of food was recorded by visitors who watched a Tahitian chief eat several whole breadfruit, and a custard, as well as several fish at one sitting. The amounts ordinary people ate were not so detailed, and presumably depended on what was available. Men generally ate more than women and children. They not only ate first and separately in the house, but they were wont to eat a fish or two, raw, as they caught them, or pick fruit as they were moving about in the bush. Ordinary men and women were expected to provide for their chiefs on a regular basis, sometimes at their own expense.

Amounts varied from month to month—some starches such as breadfruit and arrowroot were seasonal, while others were prone to natural disasters such as cyclones and flooding. The main safeguards were to plant a range of root and tree crops, with varieties maturing at different times, and to have some food stored. Irregularity of food consumption was a feature of early food habits. This has been given negative connotations nutritionally, though other human biologists have argued that islanders possessed a gene which allowed them to adapt to long periods without eating. The meal as a regulator of consumption was introduced by missionaries in an attempt to control what they saw as gluttony, and associated sloth. But the locally devised system of eating food when it was available was the best answer to whims of nature.

Surplus food was stored both as a protection against future need and because of the taste of that food. Pit fermentation of fruits such as breadfruit and bananas introduced new flavours into a bland diet. Yams and sweet potatoes were stored above ground in storehouses, not always for later use, but also as a status symbol. Having a range of foods, both roots and tree starches, meant that some could be stored until needed. Two other less conventional ways of storing food were practised. One was in the form of body fat, which may have been widespread before food became available on a regular basis. (It is possible that this introduced regularity has contributed to high frequency of DIABETES in modern populations.) Second, when food was scarce for long periods, some societies had a system of visiting their relatives in other villages (*malaga*) where they lived and were fed, reciprocating the hospitality as and when it was needed.

■ *Nutritional value of earlier diets* Today these early dietary habits are commended for their high fibre and low salt and fat content. The active lifestyle of the common people also probably contributed to their expenditure of calories proportional to their intake, in contrast to high status individuals who were fed lavishly and may have been less active in food production and other activities. The food pattern certainly contributed significantly to people's sense of wellbeing. The restricted range of foods is a matter of debate. If we consider the 12 starchy foods available in most island societies, together with the many varieties of those starches and different ways of cooking them, there was considerable variety in scope if not in taste.—NJP

Endemic and introduced diseases

Most Pacific islands were not very densely populated at the time of European contact, and it is likely that they lacked a wide variety of diseases prevalent in other parts of the world, even those prevalent in other tropical areas of Eurasia and Africa. The only diseases we are sure preceded contact are YAWS in those areas with a tropical rainforest climate, probably several types of helminth, but certainly HOOKWORM, filariasis and, in western Melanesia, MALARIA in the lowland areas of all the larger islands but not in some of the remote smaller ones. All of these diseases are more often debilitating than fatal. The earliest explorers repeatedly remark upon the robust and healthy appearance of Pacific islanders particularly in Polynesia.

The DEPOPULATION that occurred after contact involved a wide variety of bacterial and viral diseases that had previously been restricted in their spread by enormous trans-oceanic distances. However, these introductions vary a great deal as to timing, just what was introduced, and the subsequent processes of their spread. Detailed examination shows that each case is different, but in general, mortality levels were usually raised whenever and wherever alien visitors came into continuous or even sporadic contact with Pacific islanders. It may also be true that the more prolonged the period of contact, that is the earlier it began, the greater the cumulative effect on population numbers.

In some cases there was an epidemic of deaths following the initial introduction of some new viral or bacterial agent, which could rise to catastrophic levels as observed in the cases of smallpox, measles and influenza epidemics in specific instances, and cause mortality levels to fluctuate wildly from year to year, season to season or event to event. In other cases, diseases—after the first epidemic phase—became established and remained prevalent in a population, causing a general raising in mortality level but also often developing a measure of immunity in the group. Tuberculosis is perhaps the best example in the Pacific of the power of an endemic disease to raise mortality levels, often insidiously and over a prolonged period.

Each island group—and often each island, or even each separate valley—had its own unique history of contact with foreigners, disease introduction, and reaction to infection. The pattern of effects was therefore uneven. Mortality related to the introduced diseases was undoubtedly the major cause of depopulation, but in a few special cases venereal diseases, notably gonorrhoea, caused declines in fertility that contributed to depopulation (SEXUALLY TRANSMITTED DISEASES). Recovery, and the beginnings of population increase, also varied in time. Some island populations (such as Samoa) began to increase in the 1860s, more the result of increasing natural immunity than any medical intervention. Other populations (as in Marquesas Islands) continued to decline into the third decade of the 20th century.—PP

Traditional healing practices

In traditional islands societies, most cases of sickness, injury and death were attributed to supernatural causes. Traditional healing practices involved RITUAL procedures (sorcery, religion and magic) but also incorporated a wide variety of medicinal plants used to treat simple ailments as well as to effect cures for illnesses.

The cotton of *Hibiscus tiliaceus* was used to bathe a cut or scratch, and soothing and/or antiseptic solutions for cuts and wounds were produced from a wide range of plants, by crushing the stem, leaves, flowers or roots in water, or by applying the leaves or bark directly. Burns were treated with masticated bark of taun (*Pometia pinnata*) in coastal New Britain, and in many other areas, with crushed gingers (Alpinia and *Zingiber zerumbet*), with shredded taro leaves or with the sap squeezed from a sweet potato. Many different plants were used to relieve toothache.

In most areas of Papua New Guinea, women knew about plants that were considered to be oral contraceptives, abortifacients, or able to cause sterility. Used in association with closely guarded rituals and magic, extracts of the leaves or stems of *Callicarpa*, *Hemigraphis*, *Ludwigia adscendens* and *Scaevola taccada* had contraceptive properties, and infertility could be caused by eating the leaves of *Caldesia parnassifolia* or the stems of *Flagellaria indica*.

Plants that were poisonous in large doses might be used as ritual poisons, or as emetics to cure acute stomach pains or to counteract the effect of ritual poisoning. Such uses for *Alstonia scholaris*, *Alstonia spectabilis*, *Euphorbia buxoides*, *Piptadenia novoguineensis*, *Dysoxylum*, the fruits of *Drymaria cordata* and *Ternstroemia*, and the seeds of *Pipturus*, *Cycas circinalis*, and *Barringtonia* have been recorded. Minor stomach pains, dysentery and diarrhoea were often treated by a solution made from extracts of chewed leaves, stems, roots or fruits of specific plants, including a soup made from banana leaves and shoots, or bananas eaten with *Hibiscus manihot* and *Phyllanthus*, or the cooked leaves and stalk of taro.

Liniments were made from *Alphitonia*, *Dodonaea viscosa* and *Endospermum* for body aches, sore muscles and joints; bark and various leaves—heated or cold—might be applied to the aching parts; and headaches might be treated with fruits or plant extracts (to be eaten), or the head bathed with a solution made from *Ageratum conyzoides*.

In New Caledonia, the *niaouli* tree, related to eucalyptus, has a white papery bark and leaves which yield an oil used for various medicinal purposes.

The provision of basic health care was an accepted role of the early missionaries. Before government health services were established in the Pacific islands, the missions were responsible for providing hospitals and trained nursing staff. Improved standards in gardening and fishing also helped improve health in the Pacific islands.—KRF

Fertility and family planning

The view that large families were typical in traditional Pacific island societies has recently been challenged by the argument that populations were relatively stable and fertility levels were kept low by restrictions on sexual relations—separate men's and women's houses in Melanesia, postpartum taboos, prolonged breast-feeding, abstinence, physical techniques, herbal remedies—and abortion, high infant mortality, and, occasionally, infanticide. If this is correct, today's preference for large families is not based on traditional values. Pacific islanders' ancestors practised fertility control.

Fertility data on Pacific island nations leave much to be desired. Statistical routines stemming from five different colonial regimes pose reconciliation problems. Vital rates registration is incomplete. Government department records are of uneven quality. Population figures have to be calculated from censuses held every 5–10 years. Estimates and projections based on these sources, and the small population numbers involved, cause erratic and improbable changes from one year to the next. Family planning data, based on health department records and occasional surveys, need to be treated even more cautiously. Table 6.2 uses data variously recorded between 1986 and 1995.

Differences in geography, history and culture have resulted in the 21 countries reviewed entering the fertility transition at different times. Polynesia and Fiji started the transition over 20 years ago. From high crude birth and total fertility rates in the 1960s and 1970s, total fertility rates have fallen sig-

Table 6.2 **Pacific islands fertility related statistics**

	Last census	Crude birth rate *	Crude death rate *	Pop. 0–15 yrs (%)	Total fertility rate	Maternal deaths *	Contraceptive prevalence rate (%)	Life expectancy
American Samoa	1990	38.0	4	34.1	4.5	..	..	..
Cook Islands	1991	30.5	8	45.6	3.5	1.89	34.0	69.8
Micronesia (FSM)	1994	23.8	8	42.7	4.7	1.21	28.0	64.1
Fiji	1986	24.9	5	38.2	3.0	0.41	40.0	63.1
French Polynesia	1988	30.0	6	36.0	3.1	..	..	69.0
Guam	1990	30.0	4	30.0	3.5	..	..	73.0
Kiribati	1990	28.9	13	40.2	3.8	2.23	30.2	60.2
Marshall Islands	1988	49.0	9	51.0	5.7	1.09	37.0	63.0
Nauru	1992	24.0	5	41.8	7.5	..	..	55.5
New Caledonia	1989	24.0	6	32.6	3.0	..	37.0	72.0
Niue	1991	19.7	5	36.7	3.5	..	37.0	66.0
Northern Marianas	1990	30.0	3	23.8	5.6	..	..	65.0
Palau	1990	21.4	8	30.3	3.0	2.67	46.6	67.0
Papua New Guinea	1990	30.3	12	41.8	5.4	8.00	20.0	56.0
Samoa	1991	25.4	8	40.6	4.8	0.90	38.5	69.0
Solomon Islands	1996	38.0	8	47.3	5.3	5.49	20.0	60.7
Tonga	1986	27.1	7	40.6	3.7	1.26	33.0	69.0
Tuvalu	1991	25.5	11	34.7	3.0	4.34	45.0	67.2
Vanuatu	1989	37.0	9	44.1	5.3	0.68	22.0	62.8
Wallis and Futuna	1990	31.0	6	41.9	4.6	..	..	..

Notes: * rate per 1000; .. not available.
Sources: South Pacific Commission, 1995. *Population Statistics Bulletin*, 42; United Nations Development Programme, 1994. *Pacific Human Development Report*; United Nations Development Programme, 1996. *World Development Report*.

nificantly but most have now levelled off, and most remain high compared with developed country levels. Micronesia started the transition in the 1980s and many of its countries still have very high levels of fertility. Parts of the Papua New Guinea Highlands still have low pre-transition fertility levels but the rest of Melanesia, excepting Fiji, displays high early transition levels. Fertility has fallen from its peak in all Pacific island nations. Over the past decade, there have also been substantial reductions in fertility in Solomon Islands, Vanuatu, the Federated States of Micronesia, Kiribati and Palau but, as was the case earlier in Fiji and Polynesia, rates of decline appear to have slowed. None has reached the 'low regime' of 2 per cent or less when a population stabilizes or declines. Low and negative population increases—in Fiji (Indo-Fijians) and much of Polynesia—are due to emigration, not lowered fertility.

Modern family planning was introduced into most maternal and child health programs during the 1960s and 1970s as a means of improving maternal and infant health. Government policies focused on health issues and only implicitly on population control. These early moves met with opposition on religious and traditional grounds, and those dependent on outside sponsors initially foundered.

These influences are still evident but most officials now agree in principle with family planning, differing only on matters of access, method, and level of commitment. Growing concern about employment for young and fast-growing populations; increasing levels of rape, incest, violence against women; teenage pregnancy; HIV INFECTION/AIDS; and the influence of regional and international conferences, have done much to modify official and public attitudes. There is, however, still a reluctance, among men especially, to talk about sex, and male contraceptive participation rates are low. Teenagers (and unmarried women in some countries) have limited access to contraception, and there is little to no sex education in schools. In some countries women need their husband's consent for sterilization. Abortions are illegal, except on medical grounds, and for rape and incest in Vanuatu. Health worker efforts are focused on women who are too old (over 35 years); those with too many children (4 or more); and those who have had children too closely (less than 2 years apart). They also need to focus on the too young (under 18 years).

Modern family planning has had some effect on fertility, particularly among those aged 20–35 and the better educated, but in the absence of adequate data and research, it is not possible to assess its contribution relative to other causes of fertility decline. Lifestyle changes conducive to lower fertility—more education for girls, later age at marriage, somewhat less rigid religious observance, changes in family structures and expectations, far greater exposure to outside values, increased mobility, and higher levels of urbanization—and changing demographic structures due to these factors, have been major factors in fertility decline.

Contraceptive coverage rates are still generally low, and national figures conceal considerable variation spatially, socially and ethnically. National figures in Pacific island countries with significant European and Asian immigrant populations (which have accepted family planning more readily) are particularly misleading. Discontinuance rates are high. Coverage for teenagers and the over-40s are of special concern. Teenage pregnancies, attributed to changes in family values, little school or parental sex education, and limited knowledge or access to family planning, account for an increasing number of pregnancies.

The extent of contraceptive use is measured by the contraceptive prevalence (or percentage coverage) rate. Although broad patterns can be seen across the Pacific, the fact that expected rates often differ from the crude birth rate and total fertility rate, and these two from each other, indicate a probable high level of unreliability. The contraceptive prevalence rate is generally based on hospital and clinic attendance. Sales of condoms and the contraceptive pill from private doctors, chemists and family planning associations are not included. Inaccurate reporting is also due to including discontinued users, confusing new and cumulative figures, double counting where women attend two clinics, and the inclusion or exclusion of the ovulation (Billings or Mucus) method in countries such as Fiji, Samoa, Tonga, Cook Islands, Solomon Islands, Tuvalu, Vanuatu, eastern Micronesia and the French territories where the Catholic church is very active.

A wide range of contraceptives is available cheaply or at no cost from government hospitals and clinics, but often only for married women, and the choice is generally limited to the pill and the condom at sub-national levels. Female sterilization—usually for women with four or more children—remains an important means of fertility control throughout the region. The pill, injectibles, and, in some cultures or countries, the condom, are the most generally used methods. Norplants, not accessible in all countries, are gaining in popularity; the use of the intra-uterine device (IUD) is decreasing, and the post-coital pill is used only in emergencies. The female condom is on trial in Papua New Guinea. Vasectomy is the least popular method, except in Kiribati where a well-run campaign countered male fears of impotence at the outset. The condom is in increasing use, especially in the 15 countries where HIV/AIDS cases have been reported. Illegal abortions, a major cause of infertility and maternal deaths, are increasing. Preferred methods, however, differ considerably between countries and cultures. The pill and Depo Provera (injectibles), for example, are reported to account, among ever married women, for 75 per cent of Samoan use; tubal ligation and Depo Provera for 72 per cent of ethnic Fijian use; and tubal ligation and the condom for 66 per cent of Indo-Fijian use. The condom was used by 21 per cent of Indo-Fijians but less than 4 per cent of ethnic Fijians and Samoans.

An increase in present contraceptive prevalence rates will require changes at four levels. For individuals, levels remain low due to large family preference (surveys showed Indo-Fijians thought 6 children 'too many', ethnic Fijians 8, and Samoans 10), religious values, fear of side-effects, the equation of contraception with promiscuity and vasectomy with impotence, low male participation, and a reluctance to talk about sex and sexual relations. Improved supply and service issues concern reliability and range of contraceptives at the primary level; adequate follow-up; better information and access for all at risk, most particularly teenagers and the unmarried; and the introduction of sensitive sex education in schools.

At government level, positions differ. There is 'official' support for family planning on maternal health or fertility control grounds (and some governments have set fertility targets), but many officials hold less supportive personal views on the issue, and population numbers remain important in countries with multi-ethnic populations and those losing population through emigration.

At the macro-level, lifestyle changes associated with 'modernization', exposure to international conferences, and promptings by international agencies, their own family planning associations, and each other, will continue to move Pacific island nations through the fertility transition. Nevertheless, contraceptive prevalence rates over 50 per cent and total fertility rates close to 2 per cent are still a long way off.—ACW

Further reading

Pirie, P, 1995. 'Pacific transitions: population and change in island societies', *Asia Pacific*, 20 (July).

Seniloli, K L, 1992. The socioeconomic and cultural dimensions of ethnic fertility differences in Fiji, PhD thesis, The Australian National University, (unpublished).

Nursing

Both the history of nursing and aspects of its current predicament vary considerably. The forerunners of the profession were local women trained and engaged by Christian missions as midwives and sick attendants. The formal training of indigenous nurses in government hospitals began in some island groups during the early 1900s. Fiji, for instance, started training Native Obstetric Nurses in 1908 and the American naval administration in Guam introduced a native nursing school in 1912. During the inter-war era efforts were made in nearly every administration to organize or improve some kind of hospital-based training for islander women. Broadly speaking, the American, British and New Zealand administrations in Polynesia and Micronesia did the most, though even within these spheres of control, some island groups were relatively disadvantaged and as a whole, medical infrastructure in the Pacific islands was scanty.

Developments since World War II have improved local training facilities, established regional centres of nursing education and raised professional standards. In the independent states, nationals generally hold the highest positions in nursing which were formerly reserved for expatriates. A qualification in basic nursing now usually requires three years of study, though entry criteria and curricula vary. New Zealand and Hawai'i provide health services and training of a kind routinely found in developed countries and, within the Pacific fold, support the largest nursing workforce (by 1994 figures, 44 780 and 8552 respectively). Both have for long had a role in Pacific nursing education, particularly in associated island groups. Suva remains an important centre of MEDICAL TRAINING for the southwest Pacific; and the annual intake of 120 students at the Fiji School of Nursing includes many from outside Fiji. The School of Nursing and Allied Health Services within the University of Guam in Majuro and the School of Nursing in Papua New Guinea are other institutions of regional significance. All island states, however, with the exception of only the tiniest, offer some form of nursing training. International organizations and foreign aid, which have become major factors in the development of Pacific medical services over the last 50 years, continue to contribute to nursing education and support.

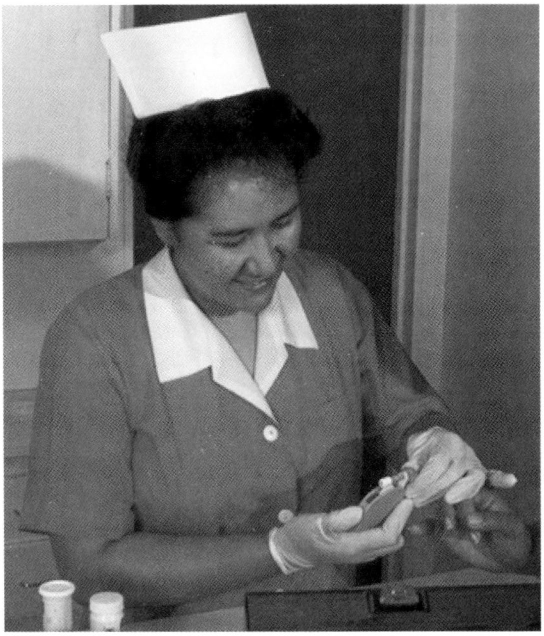

Nurse in Tonga taking a blood sample

Nurses in some islands can number as few as 59 (Cook Islands), and the ratio of nurse to population may range from 1:264 (Commonwealth of the Northern Marianas) to 1:778 (Solomon Islands). Yet in the Pacific as elsewhere, nurses by virtue of their numbers relative to other categories of medical professional, and their work in capacities of greater sustained contact with ordinary people, are crucial purveyors of health services and ideas. Financial constraints, difficult working conditions, cultural and social considerations and marked shifts in Pacific disease patterns all pose challenges to a profession which in the past has been able to draw on a strong ethic of service and a certain prestige as a career for Pacific islands women.—VL

Child health in the Pacific

Basic indicators of child health include infant and under-five mortality—the numbers of children who fail to reach their first and fifth birthday respectively, per 1000 live born.

The figures in Table 6.3 are estimates, and considerable variation exists between different provinces and between urban and rural sectors. Infections are the leading cause of death in Pacific children. The most important are pneumonia, perinatal infection (infection acquired around the time of birth), malaria, diarrhoeal diseases and meningitis. There is a high prevalence of tuberculosis in some Pacific countries and typhoid is common in Papua New Guinea. In some countries, dengue haemorrhagic fever is significant and often fatal. All indications are that HIV INFECTION/AIDS will become common and cause major problems for the region's health services. High hospital case fatality rates—for example 5–10 per cent in pneumonia and about 25 per cent in confirmed bacterial meningitis in Papua New Guinea—are often the result of delay in seeking medical attention. While disorders of affluence affect children in small sectors of one or two Pacific

Child with ulcerated toes, Papua New Guinea

Table 6.3 Infant mortality rate (per 1000 live births)

	Infant mortality rate	Under-5 mortality
American Samoa	11.0	..
Cook Islands	26.0	28
Micronesia (FSM)	22.0	28
Fiji	21.0	25
French Polynesia	13.0	..
Guam	10.0	..
Kiribati	57.0	77
Marshall Islands	45.0	92
Nauru	26.0	..
New Caledonia	11.0	..
Niue	10.0	..
Northern Marianas	9.0	..
Palau	21.4	35
Papua New Guinea	57.0	102
Samoa	20.5	54
Solomon Islands	26.0	31
Tonga	13.0	20
Tuvalu	40.0	56
Vanuatu	44.0	58
Wallis and Futuna	13.0	..

Note: .. not available.
Sources: South Pacific Commission, 1995. *Population Statistics Bulletin*, 42; UNICEF, 1997. *State of the World's Children.*

two Pacific countries, poor nutritional status is common in others, compounding the high mortality rates, and anaemia is a major problem in the malaria endemic areas. In Papua New Guinea, between 20–25 per cent of babies are of low birth weight, in part an indication of poor maternal health and nutritional status. The Pacific region is involved in important community health initiatives. Papua New Guinea, for example, has been a pioneer in the development and use of standard treatment manuals, and the training of postgraduate paediatric nurses. It was also the first country to legislate to protect breast-feeding. The use of baby/child health record books has been used effectively in many parts of the South Pacific. Often, there are village clinics attended by district nurses, but major difficulties arise in providing and maintaining health services in rural areas. A private non-profit foundation, Marimed, was established in Hawai'i in 1985, to conduct field clinics in scattered, remote communities like Marshall Islands, working with local health professionals. Church health services also play a vital role in isolated communities. Whilst the whole spectrum of paediatric disorders is seen throughout the region, resources for managing children with chronic diseases are limited.—JDV

Alcohol and drug abuse

Defining 'drugs' as 'pharmacologically active substances primarily taken for non-medicinal purposes', only two were widespread in the Pacific islands before western contact: KAVA and BETELNUT. Defining 'abuse' as the 'use of such substances in a manner that harms the user or others', neither kava nor betelnut was abused by islanders.

Islanders did not make and drink alcoholic beverages before Europeans came among them, and there was little knowledge of alcohol production or access to trade alcohol until the 19th century. With imposition of colonial control came prohibition laws that banned access by 'native peoples', with a result that commercially manufactured alcohol was a rare commodity in all but the settler societies of Hawai'i and New Zealand until decolonization following World War II. Consequently, alcohol abuse—despite missionary alarms over islanders' 'drunken excesses'—was equally rare. With independence of the former Pacific colonies came elimination of the legal prohibitions against alcoholic beverages. Most new island nations have been pulled into the global economy and urban centres have burgeoned with migrants from rural areas in search of education, employment and entertainment. Today, commercial alcohol, principally beer, is widely available, and locally made beer is a source of pride and identity. Contemporary islanders quaff 'national' brands such as 'South Pacific', 'Tusker', 'Hinano' or 'Fiji Bitter'. Aggressive marketing and improved systems of distribution by manufacturers have made beer more widely accessible in greater quantities than before. Predictably, some drinkers drink regularly to excess, and their subsequent behaviour contributes to problems that might be labelled abuse: brawls, drink-driving crashes, DOMESTIC VIOLENCE and occasional homicides, and the economic opportunity costs of substantial cash expenditure on beer. Alcohol abuse in the islands may also involve chronic physical harm such as alcoholic cirrhosis, cardiomyopathy, delirium tremens, and other well-known symptoms of long-term heavy drinking, but there are few studies to substantiate this. What is known is that Pacific drinking is primarily a male pastime, and only recently have many women become regular drinkers (with the possible exception of New Zealand and Hawai'i).

Other drugs are not yet a large problem in Oceania. Two that are widespread, both introduced in the post-contact period, are tobacco and cannabis (marijuana). Tobacco entered New Guinea from the west, carried via Malay traders from the East Indies where it was brought from the New World by Spanish and Dutch colonists. It also reached Mariana Islands via the Spanish in the late 1600s, from whence it spread to the western Carolines. Everywhere else tobacco became readily available as an integral component of the trade that sprang up between islanders and Europeans in the 19th century. Tobacco has been widely used throughout the region for the past 150 years. Given what we know about tobacco's negative effects on physical health, particularly when smoked as commercially manufactured cigarettes, most tobacco use is also 'abuse'. With tobacco, however, unlike with alcohol, the effects of abuse are primarily the illnesses linked to regular smoking.

Marijuana is a recent addition to the array of drugs easily available in the Pacific islands, most post-dating the 1960s. Everywhere illegal, its use is often furtive, and reliable information on its availability is spotty at best. Other than its possible association with organized URBAN CRIME in places like Papua New Guinea, the negative effects of marijuana use mirror those for tobacco: it contributes to a variety of chronic physical diseases, especially those affecting the cardiovascular and respiratory systems. How widely it is 'abused' in the islands remains an open question.

Other drugs have gained a toehold in Oceania, and in some instances these have been abused, but they are not found throughout the region. These include 'ice' (crystal methamphetamine) in Mariana Islands, heroin in Palau (use of which seems now to have subsided), and an array of 'street drugs' like crack cocaine and LSD in Hawai'i, Guam and New Zealand. Alcohol and drug abuse in the islands is much less of a problem than in other parts of the world, and the main 'drugs of abuse' remain tobacco and alcohol.—MM

Trauma

Trauma is a major health problem in the Pacific. Injuries are the fourth most common cause of death for all ages in the Highlands of Papua New Guinea and the single most common cause in the age group 15–44 years (3–4 cases per 1000 in this age group per year). In the same areas, injury is the leading cause of death after the first five years of life, overtaking acute pneumonia and childbirth, and responsible for 11.5 per cent of hospital admissions. Trauma is also the leading cause of surgical death in hospital, but about two-thirds of injury-related deaths occur before the patient reaches hospital. Head injuries are responsible for 60 per cent of deaths for trauma.

The common causes of injury are road accidents, DOMESTIC VIOLENCE, criminal assault, accidents (at home and at work), burns and falls. Tree-related injuries occur in rural areas and include falls from coconut, betelnut and mango trees and head injuries from falling coconuts. Exotic injuries which gain attention in the international medical press include tribal fights, tree and coconut injuries, penetrating wounds by swordfish, pig bites and grass-skirt burns. Snake bite is the most common reason for emergency assisted-ventilation in Port Moresby General Hospital because a neurotoxin in the venom causes respiratory paralysis.

In Papua New Guinea, the number of road traffic accidents increased by over 400 per cent between 1968 and 1978 but it then declined from 6867 in 1981 to 4906 in 1990. The number of accidents per annum is similar to that in New Zealand, but per road kilometre or per registered vehicle, the accident rate is about 50 times higher. Studies in the 1970s and 1990s showed that over a third of weekend drivers involved in accidents had blood-alcohol levels above 80 mg per 100 ml. Open-backed utility vehicles are responsible for many accidents, with occupants being thrown out of the vehicle. There is no legislation to make roll bars or cages compulsory.

Tribal fights persist in the Highlands of Papua New Guinea. They usually arise out of land disputes but may also be due to disagreements over property or women. Injuries due to tribal fights accounted for 24 per cent of all trauma admissions to Mendi Hospital in 1993. Although traditionally the weapons are bows and arrows, the use of firearms is increasing and a fifth of tribal fight injuries are now due to firearms. Bush thoracotomy, a practice favoured by some traditional healers, involves cutting open the chest and inserting herbs for medicinal purposes. It

Guam Memorial Hospital, Tamuning, Guam

has a significant complication rate, particularly infection (empyema) of the pleural cavity.

Throughout the islands, wounds, fractures and head injuries account for the majority of hospital attendances. Injuries to the abdomen, chest and spine are numerically less important but are normally serious and consume a lot of medical resources. The average length of admission for trauma patients is around 10–15 days. Half of all trauma hospital admissions are due to fractures. Poor fracture management results in much deformity, disability and prolonged hospital stay. At the beginning of 1988 there were only three trained orthopaedic surgeons in Papua New Guinea, three in Fiji and one expatriate in Solomon Islands. The Australian Orthopaedic Association is helping to train orthopaedic specialists in their own country.

Chronic MALARIA often causes enlarged spleens, which are therefore prone to injury. All spleen injuries must be admitted to hospital but not all require surgery. Many ruptured spleens are managed non-operatively, successfully so in 80 per cent of cases. In malaria-endemic areas, it is important to conserve the spleen to optimize resistance to malaria. One study on incidence of malaria and other illness after splenectomy in the tropics showed that 88 per cent of splenectomized patients had malarial parasites in their blood film on follow-up 1–10 years after splenectomy compared with 18 per cent of those whose spleens were conserved.

Head injuries are the commonest cause of death from trauma. The lack of computerized equipment makes surgical treatment difficult. There are no trained neurosurgeons working in the islands so that head injuries must be managed by general surgeons or general practitioners. Patients with spinal injuries do poorly because there is no spinal unit, no spinal registry and very limited facilities for rehabilitation. They must be treated in general surgical wards, often with inadequate numbers of nurses, and they can develop many pressure sores and urinary tract complications. Burns victims also suffer because of lack of a dedicated unit with specialized nursing.

Despite a lack of resources throughout the Pacific, injuries can usually be properly treated with simple measures that are widely available. The introduction of sub-specialist skills in fracture management and neurosurgery and the development of dedicated spinal and burns units would do much to improve the management of major injuries. To improve primary trauma care the health system depends on downstream support and education for health workers manning aid posts, health centres and rural hospitals. Ambulance services and communications will also need to be improved to enable a more efficient system of trauma care to be developed.—DAKW

Mental health

Mental diseases affect the mind, making people feel sad or constantly tired, and perhaps feel physical aches and pains. Some patients stop thinking, never want to do anything, do not feel like interacting any more. Some children have difficulty in learning at school. In some cases, convulsions can occur or be associated with mental illnesses. Mental health problems are common in all societies. Even diagnosable severe mental illness is relatively common. Many studies have revealed a lifetime prevalence of schizophrenia (a serious and disabling disorder) of about 1 per cent. In 1998 the World Health Organization reviewed epidemiological data for the year 1990. In established market economies including Australia, Japan and New Zealand in the western Pacific region, the number of cases present at any one time has been estimated at 11.6 per 1000 adult males and 11 per 1000 adult females. In comparison, for the 'other Asian and island nations' group which includes the Pacific islands, the estimates are 9.5 and 8.4. Depression was reported to be the fourth leading cause of disease-burden in 1990, and by 2020 will be the single leading cause.

In Papua New Guinea mental health services were first established in 1959 by Dr G Burton Bradley as part of the national health service, operating outreach services to all provinces and districts of the country.—FYAJ

Burkitts tumour

Among the many paediatric malignant diseases seen in the Pacific region, there is a high prevalence of Burkitts lymphoma in Papua New Guinea—the only country outside Africa where this tumour appears to be endemic. As in African countries, Burkitt's tumour initially responds well to single drug treatment with cyclophosphamide, but there is a high relapse rate and aggressive and prolonged multi-drug treatment is now recommended. The incidence of 'common' acute lymphoblastic leukaemia appears to be low, but may be increasing with improving socioeconomic status. While facilities for intensive management of children with malignant disease are not well developed in most Pacific countries, the disease is potentially curable with locally available expertise and relatively inexpensive chemotherapy.—JDV

Diabetes

There is clear evidence that modernization and urbanization of Pacific island populations have resulted in an increased incidence of several non-communicable 'lifestyle' diseases and conditions, including type 2 (non-insulin-dependent) diabetes, obesity, gout, hypertension, coronary heart disease, stroke and certain cancers. There is sufficient anecdotal and documentary evidence to suggest that diabetes either did not exist or was extremely rare in these populations at the time of first contact with Europeans. Type 2 diabetes as seen in the Pacific tends to occur at an early age (not uncommonly in the third decade of life) and is often poorly controlled. This is reflected in high complication rates, including renal failure, diabetic gangrene leading to amputation of lower limbs, and retinopathy leading to blindness.

High rates of diabetes have been documented in Micronesians of Nauru, Kiribati and Marshall Islands, and in most Polynesian populations, including Samoans, Maori, Hawaiians, Tokelauans and Cook Islanders. In Melanesian populations, diabetes is common in Fijians and some coastal Papuan New Guinean communities, but is unusual in PNG Highlanders, Solomon Islanders and ni-Vanuatu. Such a pattern of distribution gives rise to the theory that non-Austronesian Melanesians may be less susceptible to the disease than those with Austronesian (the forebears of today's Polynesian and Micronesian populations) genetic admixture. In most instances, prevalence, incidence and/or mortality rates for diabetes and its complications in Pacific island populations far exceed those seen in Pacific Rim countries. For example, the age-standardized prevalence of diabetes in adults aged 25 years and over has been reported as 39.5 per cent in Micronesian Nauruans, and 37.3 per cent in the Melanesian Wanigela people of coastal Papua New Guinea, compared to 3.1 per cent in European-origin Australians.

The marked susceptibility of island populations to type 2 diabetes has been explained in terms of the 'thrifty genotype hypothesis'. This suggests that in these populations which were subject to regular periods of 'feast and famine' associated with events such as droughts, hurricanes, crop failures and long migratory canoe voyages, there was a selective genetic advantage favouring those with a metabolism which allowed storage of available energy with maximum efficiency. In modern times, when there is an assured supply of calories from energy-dense refined and fatty foods, coupled with a sedentary lifestyle and cultural factors which promote feasting, the thrifty genotype has become a disadvantage. It results in obesity and resistance of the tissues to the effects of insulin, which leads to relative failure of the ability of the pancreas to produce insulin, and ultimately to type 2 diabetes. Fragile island economies and their already stretched health systems are ill-equipped to meet the burden of high morbidity and mortality associated with diabetes and related chronic conditions. There is a need to develop primary and secondary prevention strategies to encourage early diagnosis, effective treatment and appropriate patient education, by extending clinical services to more isolated areas.—GD

HIV infection/AIDS

Acquired Immuno-deficiency Syndrome (AIDS) is caused by the human immuno-deficiency virus (HIV) which belongs to the retrovirus group. It is transmitted by sexual contact (among heterosexuals as well as male homosexuals), by contaminated needles (medical or drug addiction) and surgical instruments, by trans-placental route (pregnant mother to foetus) and by blood (or blood product) transfusion. In Australia, New Zealand and Hawai'i, HIV infection/AIDS follows a pattern similar to that of Europe and North America. HIV infection was introduced into the Pacific islands in the 1980s, and by early 1998 more than 800 cases had been diagnosed in Papua New Guinea alone (Table 6.4). Most of the cases are due to heterosexual transmission. Close to 50 per cent of all HIV infected patients are diagnosed when AIDS is evident clinically. Males and females are equally affected. The majority of patients suffer chronic diarrhoea and weight loss.

There is a great danger for rapid spread of AIDS in all three major population groups, Melanesian,

Table 6.4 Reported cases of HIV infection/AIDS in the Pacific

	Report date	HIV	AIDS
American Samoa	1999	0	0
Cook Islands	1999	0	0
Federated States of Micronesia	1999	2	2
Fiji Islands	1999	43	8
French Polynesia	1999	174	54
Guam	1999	108	49
Kiribati	1999	20	4
Marshall Islands	1999	9	2
Nauru	1999	1	0
New Caledonia	1998	171	66
Niue	1999	0	0
Northern Marianas	1999	15	7
Palau	1999	1	1
Papua New Guinea	1999	1556	577
Pitcairn	1997	0	0
Samoa	1999	9	6
Solomon Islands	1999	1	0
Tokelau	1999	0	0
Tonga	1999	19	14
Tuvalu	1999	0	1
Vanuatu	1999	0	0
Wallis and Futuna	1999	2	1

Source: Islands Pacific Business, April 1999.

Micronesian and Polynesian. It has already become a major public health problem in some island nations, with cases increasing at an alarming rate. AIDS will definitely affect adversely the high incidence of tuberculosis (TB), both pulmonary and extra-pulmonary, and of cryptococcal meningitis already present in previously healthy islands populations. The death rate of HIV infection immediately following diagnosis is relatively high at about 40 per cent in some areas of the Pacific. This may be partly due to late detection and lack of sophisticated therapeutic measures. Health education on sexually transmitted diseases and on safe sex practices are the main tools available to the public health authorities in the region for controlling the spread of the disease. Anti-viral drugs are too expensive for widespread use in island countries with limited budgets.—SN

Publicity campaign, AIDS awareness, Cook Islands

Hookworm

Hookworm is a parasitic infection of the human gut caused by either of two nematode worms. The adult worm attaches itself to the lining of the small intestine. Eggs are shed with the faeces into the environment; the larvae then penetrate the skin to transmit infection to new hosts. Hookworm infection leads to significant blood loss and causes anaemia and debility, especially in children. Major campaigns to control hookworm in the tropics and subtropics were conducted in the past, but the disease is still widespread on most Pacific islands. It responds to drugs but re-infection soon occurs.—MA

Kuru

Kuru is a fatal disease of the nervous system. It causes progressive loss of coordination and tremors leading to total incapacity of motor functions. Death inevitably ensues about a year after onset. An epidemic of kuru occurred in a remote area of the Eastern Highlands of Papua New Guinea which by the 1950s was killing 200 people a year, mostly women and children. It was transmitted through the ritual mortuary cannibalism of dead relatives. Since this practice ceased the disease has declined dramatically, but occasional cases still occur because the incubation period may exceed four decades. Kuru is a form of Creutzfeldt-Jakob disease (CJD), which occurs worldwide. These diseases are not contagious but in the 1960s were shown to be transmissible experimentally and therefore caused by an infectious agent. The same kind of infectious agent causes scrapie of sheep and 'mad cow' disease. The agent is a self-replicating disease-producing variant of a normal host protein. CJD has been transmitted by 'modern cannibalism', for example corneal transplants and growth hormone derived from the dead. Kuru is dying out but remains important because research on it initiated new concepts of infectious disease and led to the discovery of a new infectious agent.—MA

Malaria

Human malaria is a tropical disease caused by four species of the blood parasite Plasmodium. Spanish explorers named it malaria ('bad air') when they encountered it in Solomon Islands in 1568, believing that it was connected to the dank atmosphere of the swamplands. It is transmitted by the *Anopheles* mosquito, and causes more serious sickness, worldwide, than any other disease. Though the smaller Pacific islands are malaria-free, it is a major debilitating disease of Melanesia. Malaria is characterized by high fever, rigors, severe malaise and an enlarged spleen. Anaemia and debility are chronic effects. In non-immune persons the brain and liver are often affected and malaria can be rapidly fatal. A dormant liver form of the parasite causes relapsing malaria. Many parasite strains have developed resistance to the drugs used to treat and prevent malaria. Avoiding mosquitoes after dusk is the best preventive measure. People from malaria-endemic areas inherit genetic variations which confer innate resistance to malaria; those who reach adulthood acquire anti-malarial immunity. Scientists are working towards a vaccine to provide this protective immunity but have not yet succeeded.—MA

Pig bel

Pig bel (*Enteritus necroticans*) is the name given to the condition of necrotising enteritis—literally inflammation of the intestine resulting in death of intestinal tissue—in Papua New Guinea. The name derives from the association with eating pig meat at traditional Highlands feasts. First described medically in 1959, it is well recognized locally, and was the second most common cause of death in Highlands children. The classic patient is a child with severe abdominal pain, vomiting and distended abdomen presenting within five days of eating pig meat. The elucidation of its aetiology, which involves a complex interaction between an abnormally high protein input (occuring through contamination of food by a toxin-producing Clostridial bacteria), and inadequate levels of toxin-destroying enzymes as a result of normally low production compounded by enzyme inhibition by substances in sweet potato (the local staple) and produced by the gut roundworm, Ascaris, is a fascinating medical detective story, with a happy ending—the production and administration of a highly successful toxoid vaccine.—JDV

Sexually transmitted diseases

Sexually transmitted diseases (STDs) were introduced to Pacific peoples by outsiders. Syphilis came to Europe after Columbus returned from America and rapidly spread through the movement of armies. Eventually, together with gonorrhoea, it travelled the world with sailors. Syphilis and gonorrhoea are bacterial diseases. Syphilis has an acute form with an ulcer (chancre) and a chronic form which affects many systems and may mimic other diseases. Gonorrhoea leads to genital discharge. Though often without symptoms in women it is still infectious and can cause infertility. Chlamydia is a widespread and very common bacterial STD with effects similar to gonorrhoea. Donovanosis is another bacterial STD which causes ulcers. A major outbreak of donovanosis occurred in southwest New Guinea and it is still common in Papua New Guinea, though rare elsewhere. Viruses may also cause STDs. Herpes-virus infection leads to ulcers. Human papilloma-virus infection of one kind causes warts but a more insidious variant causes cancer of the cervix. The most serious viral STD is the most recent: AIDS. AIDS has reached the Pacific—and Papua New Guinea in particular faces a growing epidemic. Parasites may also be transmitted sexually; one of the commonest genital discharges is caused by trichomonas infection.—MA

'Swollen baby' syndrome

In the late 1970s, the link was made between infestation of young infants in a remote mountainous area of Papua New Guinea with the parasite *Strongyloides Fulleborni var Kelly*, and high infant mortality primarily from a protein-losing enteropathy resulting in hypoalbuminaemia and 'Swollen baby' syndrome. *Strongyloides fulleborni* is recognized as a parasite of primates which can maintain its life-cycle in humans, but had not hitherto been found in countries without non-human primates. Following extensive attempts at identification, the Papua New Guinea *Strongyloides fulleborni* was given its own identity—variety *Kelly*, after the veterinary parasitologist who first described the embryonated ova. The mode of transmission to the very young affected infants has not been clarified, but heavy infections build up quickly, almost certainly because of the custom of nursing babies in a *bilum* (string bag) lined with leaves. The discovery of the aetiology of 'Swollen baby' syndrome led to the introduction of highly successful treatment with Thiabendazole.—JDV

Tropical ulcers

Tropical hospitals and clinics are full of patients being treated for ulcers. An ulcer is a break in the continuity of an epithelial lined surface, in this case the squamous epithelium of the skin. Ulcers should be differentiated from wounds (a break in the continuity of the surface of a structure), sinuses (a blind-ended tract opening on to an epithelial surface), and fistulae (an abnormal communication between two epithelial lined surfaces). Tropical ulcers are due to a combination of TRAUMA and infection with organisms such as *Borrelia vincentis*, Fusiform bacteria, Corynebacterium diptheriae and Streptococcal infection. Probably many other organisms can also be responsible. Trauma (including bites and stings) probably plays a part in the aetiology. Typically, the ulcer starts from a small prick or pimple with surrounding redness and inflammation. It is usually tender. Humidity and failure to rest probably favour its growth. Inflammation leads to ulceration. The ulcer is usually responsive to antibiotics (erythromycin) and resting the limb. Skin grafting may also be required if skin loss is extensive. A tropical ulcer should be differentiated from a chronically infected wound or burn which fails to heal because of inadequate treatment or continuing injury.

The Buruli ulcer is a progressive, aggressive skin ulcer on the limbs, occasionally at the site of an insect bite or other minor trauma. It often causes extensive destruction of the soft tissue of a limb resulting in serious disability. The amount of soft tissue death exceeds that which can be appreciated from inspecting the skin, the infection spreading far beyond and beneath the edges of the ulcer. It is the third most important mycobacterial infection (Mycobacteria cause tuberculosis), the organism responsible being *Mycobacterium ulcerans*. The infection was first described in 1948 in Gippsland, southeast Australia, although it had been previously recognized in Uganda and Zaire. It is prevalent throughout Africa and the South Pacific, particularly close to large rivers. In Papua New Guinea it is most commonly encountered in the SEPIK RIVER basin.

Marjolin's ulcer is the commonest malignant ulcer of the skin in the Pacific, arising in an area of the skin with a depigmented scar, chronic ulcer or old burn. The cancer is a squamous cell carcinoma which develops 20–30 years after the insult causing the scar. The cancer grows slowly and indolently and tends to spread to the lymph nodes late. It commonly affects the leg, and in advanced stages the only possible treatment is either for the patient to hide the huge ulcer under dressings or to have an amputation.

The basal cell carcinoma or rodent ulcer common in fair-skinned Caucasians in Australia is almost never seen in dark skins of the Pacific. Malignant melanoma is also uncommon but when it occurs it does so on the sole of the foot, the least pigmented area of the skin. Other malignant ulcers are likely to arise from advanced breast or head and neck cancers which are so advanced that they burst through the skin causing a foul-smelling, bleeding, rapidly growing ulcer which is usually incurable. Other conditions which cause ulcers in the Pacific include DIABETES, malignancy, syphilis and YAWS. Lack of sensation may result in ulceration from persistent injury in patients with leprosy, diabetes or spinal problems.—DAKW

Cancer in Papua New Guinea

The incidence of cancer in the South Pacific is rising, probably a true rise rather than due to better recording of data or an improvement in the health services. In fact, tumour registration may be declining. In many ways the identification of cases in rural areas may have declined in the last decade rather than improved. However, the information available comes only from central tumour registries (in the central hospitals) and often includes only those cases analyzed by biopsy rather than cases where cancer has been diagnosed clinically. The breakdown of rural health services means many cases are not referred. This has always been so but is probably as true now as when tumour registration was begun in Papua New Guinea in 1958 (Table 6.5).

The common cancers appeared to be related to chronic inflammation and viral infection. Most cancers present at an advanced stage when the options for treatment are limited and cure is unlikely. Surgery, anti-cancer drugs and hormonal manipulation are the management methods available. The only hospital providing radiotherapy in the South Pacific is in Lae, Papua New Guinea.

Oral cancer is the commonest cancer in males and third commonest in females in Papua New Guinea. The incidence is higher in coastal and island areas than in the Highlands. The differences parallel the habit of BETELNUT-chewing which in the past was less common in the Highlands. Epidemiological studies have suggested that the combination of betelnut and cigarette-smoking is more carcinogenic than betelnut alone. The type of lime used is also thought to be important; commercial building lime is worse than that from fresh-water shells. Oral cancer induced by betelnut develops in a slightly different site in the mouth from that in western countries where it occurs most often under the tongue. In Papua New Guinea, the cancer occurs most frequently at the angle of the mouth or on the inside of the cheek. The major steps in its pathogenesis are thought to be chronic inflammation (due to BETELNUT, lime and tobacco) which leads to the premalignant change of leukoplakia, which is followed by squamous carcinoma. The treatment of oral cancer in Papua New Guinea is by a combination of anti-cancer drugs (methotrexate) and radical surgery for those who present early without invasion of the jaw (trismus). The training of national surgeons in oral cancer began in earnest in 1995 when the first surgeon from the Pacific, John Beaso, completed his

Table 6.5 **Common cancers in Papua New Guinea (per 1000)**

	Possible cause	1958–70	1984–88
Females			
Cervix (womb)	Virus (Herpes II)	2.1	6.7
Breast	Unknown	1.3	2.6
Mouth	Betelnut, tobacco	1.2	3.1
Liver	Hepatitis B virus	0.6	1.3
Ovary	Unknown	0.6	1.3
Males			
Mouth	Betelnut, tobacco	3.0	5.9
Liver	Hepatitis B virus	1.8	1.3
Stomach	Heliobacter pylori	0.7	1.0
Lymphoma	Unknown, viral	1.2	2.3
Skin (squamous)	Pre-existing scar	3.5	3.1

Sources: Martin, W M, Sengupta, S K, Murthy, D P and Barua, D L, *The Spectrum of Cancer in Papua New Guinea*; Parkin, D M, 1986. *Cancer Occurrence in Developing Countries*, IARC 75, OUP.

higher postgraduate Diploma in Head and Neck Surgery, two years after gaining his MMed (Surg) from the University of Papua New Guinea.

Breast cancer in the Pacific (and in African developing countries) has a different pattern from that in industrialized countries. The proportion of fibrocystic disease (a benign condition) is lower, whilst that of inflammatory and malignant disease are higher. In Papua New Guinea, over 50 per cent of all breast biopsies were malignant and in Solomon Islands, 19 per cent. The incidence of breast cancer appears to be rising. In the first 40 years of the Papua New Guinea tumour registry, the incidence rose from 1.75 per 100 000 in the late 1950s to 5.3 in the 1980s until, in Port Moresby in the years 1992–97, the incidence exceeded 10 per 100 000 women. The incidence also rises until the age of 50 years and then steadies, similar to the pattern seen in South African blacks. In western countries the incidence rises progressively after the age of 50 years, the age at which free screening mammography becomes available. Pacific women do not have the same risk factors as their western counterparts: in the South Pacific, women with breast cancer have all had children, breast feed, and almost never report other members of their family to have been affected. The presentation of disease is also different in the South Pacific compared with Australia and New Zealand. At least two-thirds of Pacific patients are pre-menopausal and 60 per cent present late with large tumours and advanced disease, often with *peau d'orange* (an orange-skin appearance to the breast). The prognosis is poor with mortality for up to 50 per cent of women within one year of diagnosis. Research into the molecular biology of breast cancer in the tropics will indicate whether the tumour in the South Pacific is different from that seen in western countries where the risk factors and age-related incidence are different. Early studies have shown a difference in hormone receptor status, with a low incidence of oestrogen and progesterone receptor positivity in tumours in Papua New Guinea.—DAKW

Typhoid fever

Typhoid fever is a potentially lethal disease caused by infection with a bacterium, *Salmonella typhi*, which is spread by contaminated food or water, or by dirty hands. The bacterium is excreted in the faeces of people with the infection during active disease and convalescence; a few patients develop a chronic carrier state in which they excrete the organism indefinitely. The infection enters the body through the gut then spreads in the blood to become generalized. The disease usually has an insidious onset and the most common symptoms are fever, headache, lassitude and abdominal pain. However, because the infection affects any part of the body many different symptoms can occur. Typhoid fever is an ancient disease and previously occurred widely throughout the world. Now it has been largely eradicated in industrialized countries through the introduction of improved sanitation and water supply systems, together with isolation and treatment of typhoid patients with effective antibiotics. Typhoid fever is no longer common in Pacific island countries. However, in Papua New Guinea typhoid fever has become a major problem, especially in the Highlands and the large coastal cities, after the first documented outbreak there occurred in 1977 in a residential high school.—MP

Yaws

Yaws is an ancient tropical infection of skin and bones caused by a spirochaete. This bacterium is so similar to the Treponema which causes syphilis that immune responses to them cannot be distinguished. Nevertheless, the mode of transmission is different, with yaws being strictly through non-sexual contact. Yaws begins with a proliferative skin lesion which ulcerates. An eruption with berry-like papules (framboesia) may follow. Extensive and chronic ulceration occurs, often in the nose and feet. Chronic yaws in long bones causes a characteristic 'sabre shin'. Yaws is very susceptible to penicillin and has been largely eradicated by mass treatment campaigns.—MA

FIVE SPORTS AND GAMES

Traditional sports and games

Every Pacific society has a tradition of leisure activities ranging from children's games (such as STRING FIGURES, known to all societies) to highly structured and organized competitive sports, often intended as entertainment for spectators. Part of growing up was to acquire skills, strength and coordination for adult activities such as fishing and hunting, and so swimming prowess and accuracy in spear-throwing might be learned by islanders in childhood and tested in various games. Some sports (or particular variations) were permitted only to the chiefly classes.

Hawaiians enjoyed a great variety of sports and games, including swimming and SURFING. Coasting down steep hill courses on narrow sleds was a daring sport practised by chiefs. Children practised a similar version of sledding on ti-tree leaves and coconut fronds, a game still popular today. Skilled contact sports included boxing, wrestling and foot-racing. A form of bowling was played; several kinds of darts and throwing games; guessing games and something called *konane*, rather like checkers.

In Tonga, games played by young girls included juggling small gourds or wooden balls, usually to the accompaniment of chanted verses. Boys often played a form of stilts, balancing each foot on the half-shell of an empty coconut with a string threaded through, passed between their toes and drawn up to keep the shell in place. Water sports were popular, and Tongans enjoyed a kind of underwater football, using a large heavy stone which had to be lifted and propelled towards a team's 'goal line', marked by posts set in the seabed some 50–100 m apart. Foot-racing was common, as was shooting arrows at a target, or hurling spears to strike a small piece of wood set on a 2 m pole. Coconut spinning had several variations, but it was used among women to settle minor disputes. Another game played at different levels involved two seated players holding five counting sticks. As played in its simplest form (by the lower classes) it was called *matua*, but the more complex variant called *liagi* required not only rapid hand movements but also a deeper knowledge of possible sequences of play and an ability to memorize past moves. Popular contact sports, normally performed to a large audience, included wrestling, boxing and club-fighting.

Children's game at Koror, Palau, photographed by Matsumura, c1915

Traditional games were often an extension of inter-tribal rivalries which underpinned the warrior culture. In Fiji, sports such as wrestling, tug-of-war (using vines or *magimagi*), throwing a form of javelin (like the *veitiqa*, a wooden spear with a polished knob), and mock fights tested the strength of the performers while entertaining onlookers. A contest of coordination and courage (called *lutuvakaugane*, 'men falling down') involved hurling fruit at an opposing team.

Early hockey game in Papua c1920, photographed by F E Williams

In Papua in the 1920s and 1930s, anthropologist F E Williams observed a number of games played by children. One called 'wasp' involved a seated group stretching out their hands into the centre of a circle, forming a rounded pile like a wasp nest, and making humming noises like wasps, before suddenly attacking one another. Another beach game involved teams throwing balls of sand. Williams also photographed a form of hockey played with a wooden ball.

In French Polynesia, the ancient custom of *amoraa ofai*, or stone lifting, has been practised on the island of Rurutu for centuries. People from the three main villages used to keep their stones, known as *pa'oro'oro*, in special enclosures, bringing them out when required, to be oiled in preparation for the competition. The huge stones (60 kg for women and 140 kg for men) had to be lifted to chest level, then hoisted to the shoulders. Originally a kind of fitness contest for warriors, it became part of the traditional festivities held on New Year's Day, and included chants, dancing and feasting. In 1982 it was for the first time included among the events of the Tahitian HEIVA.—KRF

String figures or 'cat's cradles'

String figures are a worldwide recreation, which in its finest examples approach an art form. The patterns or representations are made with a closed loop of string, plaited hair or other medium of varying lengths using hands, neck and occasionally both teeth and toes as auxiliary aids. The objects portrayed are very diverse and the variety of manipulations required to make them seemingly endless, resulting in literally thousands being recorded in drawings or photographs. It would be hard to find a single area, tribe or community in which they are not made or known to have been made; while different areas are found to use different construction techniques, the Pacific islands constituted a distinct area of its own, in sharp contrast to surrounding regions. Some figures require two players while others are serials and proceed from figure to figure. Many of the designs represent persons, birds or fish; activities such as making sago; or everyday things such as a well, canoe or a bed.

String figures in Papua, c1920, photographed by F E Williams

Historically, string figures were known to exist in early and medieval Europe, but the first mention in the Pacific was by Captain BLIGH in his log of the BOUNTY, where he said that he saw the children of Tahiti 'taking a piece of line in a variety of shapes off one of the other's hands'. Anthropologists often spoke of them in their cultural descriptions and occasionally photographed the final figures, but nothing could be done to enable others to make them until Professors RIVERS and Haddon in 1905 devised an anatomically based method of describing the construction of string figures in Torres Strait Islands. This has been universally adopted for use in general, regional and local works which by now amount to many hundred, though a few recent books use various shorthand descriptions to save space.

For the Pacific islands there are now published monographs on the figures of almost every island group in Polynesia, Micronesia and Melanesia, as well as many of the tribal areas in New Guinea and Australia. These have resulted in the identification of particular construction techniques favoured by islanders and named, such as the Murray Opening in Torres Strait, Tao and Ta on Tikopia and the Caroline Extension in Micronesia. String figure enthusiasts are now greatly helped by the foundation of the International String Figure Association (headquarters are in Pasadena, California), which publishes annual and quarterly serials and works such as Tom Storer's *String Figure Bibliography*. Would-be beginners in this fascinating game can commence their studies in confidence by reading such books as the classic *String Figures for Beginners* or one of a dozen more recently published books for the novice.—HCM

Further reading

Maude, H C and Maude, H E, 1958. *String Figures from the Gilbert Islands*, Polynesian Society.

Contemporary sports

Many Pacific islanders have the natural advantages of height, strength and speed which help them excel in contact sports. The popularity of a sport and the opportunity to compete in it, however, varies across the region, usually reflecting the particular range of sports introduced into the islands by different immigrant groups, or more often, the dominant sporting interests of the colonial nation. The British brought

Soccer football in French Polynesia

CRICKET, various forms of football, hockey, tennis, rowing, swimming, cycling, golf, polo and horse racing. Rugby union, which originated at Rugby School in England, became popular in New Zealand from the 1860s, and was also an early part of the colonial experience in (Western) Samoa, Cook Islands, Tonga and Fiji—where it was first played in 1884. The Fiji Rugby Union was established in 1913, and the Western Samoan Rugby Union followed in 1927. Both countries now have strongly competitive national rugby teams, and the sport has a large following. New Zealand's All Black rugby team has included resident Pacific islanders for many years, as has the Australian Wallaby side more recently. The abbreviated seven-a-side version of the game has also become entrenched throughout the region, with island teams and particularly Fiji regularly reaching the finals of the annual Hong Kong Sevens tournament.

Soccer took longer to become a popular sport in the islands, although a fairly chaotic (barefoot) version of the game emerged in Fiji in the 1920s, encouraged by chiefs as a form of inter-village competition. Among Indo-Fijians soccer was played at local club level from the 1920s, encouraged by the COLONIAL SUGAR REFINING COMPANY, which provided playing fields adjacent to their mills. Sugar workers and farmers made up teams for weekly competitions. Mission schools (both Marist Brothers and METHODISTS) tended to organize soccer teams for their students also. After the formation of the Fiji Indian Football Association in 1938, the formal game developed steadily, although it was the 1960s before Fijians began to participate in their own soccer associations. The name change to Fiji Football Association occurred in 1961. From the end of World War II, multiracial competitions developed in a number of sports across Fiji, and by the 1970s many sporting organizations were multiracial.

Tahiti and New Caledonia, supported by French coaches and financial backing, have dominated

Pacific regional soccer. One of the first New Caledonians to break into French professional soccer was Marc Kanyan, in 1963, but several others have since followed. The success of soccer among the island nations also produced strong teams in Vanuatu, Papua New Guinea and Solomon Islands. (Among the islanders studying at the various tertiary institutions in Suva since the 1960s who have joined Fijian club teams are many Solomon Islanders, New Caledonians and ni-Vanuatu.) Charlie Dempsey, a former chairman of the New Zealand Football Association, took up the presidency of the Oceania Football Confederation in 1983, and continues to supervise the growth and development of soccer in the region. Futsal, the fast and skilful five-a-side version of soccer, has also become a regular feature of regional competition.

Australians brought cricket, rugby, soccer and rugby league to Papua New Guinea. Colonial officials and missionaries took the view that sport was a healthy pursuit that could usefully replace tribal warfare, and sport quickly became an accepted community activity serving a range of social functions. Before World War II, cricket was played in Papua especially, and there was some soccer played in Rabaul, but it tended to take the form of *ad hoc* social encounters between tribal groups. It was only after the war, too, that sporting clubs ceased to be divided by race, although some mixed race competitions

Netballers, including Pacific islanders, in a game between New Zealand and England, in New Zealand

were held in Port Moresby in the 1930s and 1940s. Organized sports emerged in the post-war years, in urban areas, and soccer soon attracted widespread interest. Today the most popular participant sports in Papua New Guinea are basketball, rugby league, soccer and volleyball, with netball played in Port Moresby.

Rugby league has become better known in Papua New Guinea through the influence of televised matches from Australia. The Papua New Guinea national rugby league team, the Kumuls, has an enormous following, and since the 1980s has defeated visiting international teams (England and France). In Australia there are numerous Pacific islanders playing in Australian clubs, including the Cook Islander brothers, Kevin and Tony Iro; Fijian Noa Nadruku (who came from representing Fiji in rugby union, 1986–91 to league in 1993); and Papuan New Guineans Marcus Bai, Adrian Lam and David Westley.

Canoe racing in Papua New Guinea

Horse racing in French Polynesia

Netball has become the most popular women's sport in a number of island countries since the 1970s, especially in Cook Islands, Fiji and Samoa. The sport was established in New Zealand by 1924, and New Zealand's representative team (the Silver Ferns) now regularly includes resident Pacific islanders. The first to be selected for the Silver Ferns was Margharet Matenga (Cook Islands) in 1979, and the next, three years later, was Rita Fatialofa (Samoa). Both took part in two successful world championship tournaments, and have been named among the top seven players in New Zealand's netball history. Since the 1980s, Pacific islanders selected for the New Zealand team include Jane Sulia (now an umpire), April Ieremia, Bernice Mene, Linda Vagana and Angela Pule. New Zealand began providing coaching and umpiring clinics for the Cook Islands Netball Association in the 1980s. Islands representative teams continue to develop and benefit from regional competition. In the South Pacific Games, Cook Islands teams achieved their first victory (over Fiji) in 1983, and have maintained their strong performances regularly since then.

In Hawai'i, sumo wrestling was introduced by Japanese immigrant workers in 1885 (encouraged by King David Kalākaua, who had already visited Japan in 1881) and sumo demonstrations quickly became popular events. The first islander to reach the highest levels of the sport was Konishiki (born Salevaa Atisanoe, in American Samoa, but raised in Hawai'i), who won his third Japanese national tournament in March 1992.

In American Samoa in 1968, when CRICKET, baseball, rugby and soccer had already taken firm hold, the introduction of American football won immediate converts. In recent years, American Samoans in Hawai'i have been regularly recruited into both Hawaiian and mainland US gridiron teams, with Jesse Sapolu, Junior Seau and Dan Saleaumua becoming notable achievers.

The successful introduction of various sports into the Pacific islands, such as Australian football into both Papua New Guinea and Nauru, and rugby union in Tonga and Samoa, has been significantly boosted by the showing of sport on TELEVISION. The former colonial sporting associations have been reinforced by the programming decisions and the result illustrates the close connection between sport and nationalism or CULTURE AND IDENTITY. In the island countries, greater national significance is given to the prowess of sports players in Australia (Bai and Lam), in the United States (Sapolu, Seau and Saleaumua) or in New Zealand (Jonah Lomu) who are seen as popular heroes.

Although contact team sports attract the most competitors and spectators, a number of Pacific islanders have excelled in individual sporting events. The first gold medal in a major competition won by a Papua New Guinean was in lawn bowls, when Geua Tau (who had taken up the sport only in 1982) won the women's singles lawn bowls at the 1990 Commonwealth Games in Auckland. Golf does not attract many indigenous participants in the islands, but Fijian Vijay Singh became a top-level international player on the professional golfing circuit in the 1990s. American Samoa's Fas Maselino reached the boxing quarterfinals in both the 1988 (Seoul) and 1992 (Barcelona) Olympics, and Fijian Tony Philp has excelled in board sailing and was the world champion in windsurfing in 1992.—KRF

Further reading

Prasad, M, 1998. *Sixty Years of Soccer in Fiji 1938–1998*, Fiji Football Association.

Cricket

Cricket, introduced into the Pacific by early missionaries, became a popular islander sport. Rules were generally flexible. Teams were not limited to their usual regulation size, but could accommodate as many players as were interested in joining the game.

LONDON MISSIONARY SOCIETY missionaries brought cricket to Loyalty Islands, where it became a major recreational activity, transformed into local variants by islanders. It has become the principal summer game of New Caledonia, where it is still dominated by Loyalty Islanders.

In both Samoa and Tonga, cricket had become such a craze in the late 1890s that men played for

First Malifa cricket team, Samoa, 1921

weeks on end and food production was seriously affected. The missions finally made cricket-playing a disciplinary offence, and the administration took action to limit playing to one day a week in Samoa and two days a week in Tonga, with heavy fines for those who were caught playing at other times.

In Fiji, cricket was one of the organized sports being played at Levuka in the 1880s, but it remained an activity for expatriates. By the early years of the 20th century, there was regular competition at the district level, and its popularity grew steadily, but islander involvement was secondary and separate. The first indigenous Fijian cricket league emerged in the early 1920s, with a separate Indo-Fijian league soon afterwards.

In the Trobriand Islands of Papua New Guinea, cricket evolved into a distinctive village competition, adapting the original British format into an indigenous version involving 50 players on each team, with a game lasting for 8 or 9 hours. A chief or

Samoan village cricket

hamlet leader instigated the tournament, inviting other villages to participate. Each team had its own chants and dances, full of sexual imagery, which were performed at the start and end of each innings. The cricket players were elaborately painted and decorated and the female spectators also wore their most splendid apparel. The cricket tournament might last for weeks until all the matches had been played; then the host team provided a huge feast, distributing pigs, yams and betelnuts as in traditional dancing performances. However, since the rules demanded that the host team won, it was always possible that the apparent 'losers' might behave badly, by objecting to the umpire's decisions or even starting a fight.—KRF

Further reading

Snow, P A, 1997. *The Years of Hope: Cambridge, colonial administration in the South Seas and cricket*, Radcliffe Press.

South Pacific Games

The first South Pacific Games took place in Suva in 1963. Set up as a regional event, for competing countries from the South, central and southwest Pacific, they have provided an impetus to sport in the Pacific islands. Held every three years for the first few years, they have sometimes been scheduled every four years more recently.—KRF

Origins of surfing

Surfing, the art of sliding down or riding waves—using a canoe, a board (or equivalent) or one's own body for a planing surface—is a quintessentially Pacific islands sport. Although surfing apparently also evolved independently along the coasts of Peru and West Africa, the sport reached its highest indigenous development in the Pacific islands, and from there spread across the world in the 20th century.

The best known and most highly developed form of the sport is surf boarding—here simply called surfing. In its simplest form it is a casual pastime practised primarily by children and youths who use a short wooden plank (or the broad stem of a coconut tree frond or, on wood-poor Rapanui, a tightly bound bundle of reeds) to ride an oncoming wave. Reports of this form appear all over the Pacific, indicating that surfing is probably part of the common heritage of those seafarers who, starting around 1500 BC, spread from Southeast Asia over the Pacific.

Surfing, at Lahaina, Hawai'i, c1855 (Watercolour, James G Sawkins)

From this widespread pastime evolved an advanced form of surfing, wherein adults rode the waves standing up on full-sized surfboards. This development apparently began in east Polynesia and reached its highest form in the Hawaiian Islands. There men and women as well as youths and children rode long boards, devoting their leisure hours to the sport. So popular was surfing that one early observer wrote that when the waves started running, 'the thatch houses of a whole village stood empty', and 'daily tasks such as farming, fishing and tapa-making were left undone while an entire community—men, women and children—enjoyed themselves in the rising surf and rushing white water'. Members of the chiefly class excelled at surfing, and according to some authorities had the sole right to surf on the giant *olo* boards that averaged five to six metres in length, as well as to the rolling surf breaks for which these boards were adapted. Both chiefs and commoners used the shorter, thinner *alaia* boards in the steeper, fast-breaking surfs around the islands. Surfing featured in Hawaiian oral traditions, particularly in romantic encounters, and at least one *heiau*, or stone temple, was dedicated to the sport: Kuemanu on the Kona coast of Hawai'i Island.

Hawaiian surfing almost died out during the 19th century. Massive DEPOPULATION from introduced diseases, general cultural disorganization and then the opposition of missionaries (alarmed at the idea of men and women surfing together nude or almost so and then enjoying each other's company afterwards), plus the attraction of new sports and other activities, almost extinguished the sport. By the late 1800s it had become rare to see surfers.

But surfing did not die out. Around the turn of the century it was revived both by Hawaiians who wanted to enjoy the surf as their ancestors had, and by immigrants who adopted the sport. From Hawai'i, the revived form of the sport spread to California, Australia and many other places with surfable waves.—BF

Surfing today

Hawaiian royalty had surfed the waves well before it was recorded by European explorers. (See ORIGINS OF SURFING.) With the development of tourism particularly at Waikīkī, and the shaping of long solid and later hollow skis and boards, surfing rapidly became a popular sport among Euro-Americans. In the 1960s the use of balsa and later synthetic materials, the introduction of the Malibu and then short boards, all made surfboard riding a worldwide phenomenon. Body surfing continued to grow and variations such as sailboarding, wind-surfing, the surf ski and the boogie-board have allowed all ages to participate in all kinds of wave and wind conditions. Several winter surf locations in Hawai'i have legendary status, including three north shore breaks on O'ahu—Waimea Bay (with waves up to 10 m), Sunset and the powerful Banzai Pipeline. Local and international competitions there attract huge crowds and a pack of photographers servicing a large and

Manu Samoa rugby team in Apia (1989) before setting off on a tour of Europe

senior, joined Manly. In 1995, after selection for the NSW 'State of Origin' team, he was named in Tonga's proposed squad for the World Cup, but was then persuaded to represent Australia instead.

■ *Beatrice Faumuina* (1974–), born in Auckland of Samoan descent, won the gold medal in discus at the 1997 World Games at Athens. In the lead-up to the games, in July 1997, she recorded her best throw of 68.52 m. She won a silver medal in the 1994 Commonwealth Games in Victoria, Canada, and gold in the 1998 Commonwealth Games in Kuala Lumpur.

■ *Akebono*, the sumo wrestler who featured in the opening ceremony of the Winter Olympic Games in Nagano, 1998, is Hawaiian-born Chad Rowan, whose weight is 232 kg. He was the first non-Japanese-born grand champion, or *yokozuna*, in sumo wrestling.

■ *Joeli Vidiri* (1975–), Fijian-born rugby player, represented Fiji in five matches during the 1994 tour of New Zealand, and then played in two tests for Fiji against Samoa and Tonga. A New Zealand resident, who plays for Auckland, he successfully won selection for the All Blacks, after waiting the necessary three years to qualify, and made his debut as a New Zealand winger in 1998 against England, followed by inclusion in the Bledisloe Cup match against Australia in July.

■ *Jonah Lomu* (1975–), a New Zealand-born Tongan who grew up in Auckland, was selected for the Auckland rugby team and then became the youngest ever member of the All Black team in 1994. His speed and strength as a winger were demonstrated over three seasons (1994–96), and he then made a successful return to the New Zealand side in 1998, after recovering from a rare kidney complaint.

SIX COMMUNICATIONS

Development of telecommunications

Pre-contact indigenous communication systems were primarily oral, and limited by the proximity and mobility of islander populations. Oratory, chant, storytelling and gossip were augmented by messages broadcast by drums or wind instruments, sometimes used to announce ceremonial activities and regulate daily routine. Western-style communications media were introduced into these indigenous communication 'micro-networks' by European and American missionaries in the early 1800s. While trying to keep pace with the rest of the world, Pacific islands business enterprises and colonial administrations likewise introduced 'modern' telephone systems, the first of which was installed on Maui in the Hawaiian kingdom in 1878—two years after Alexander Graham Bell introduced his new invention to the world. The COLONIAL SUGAR REFINING COMPANY in Fiji built their own private network in 1898. By 1910 Honolulu had nearly 6000 subscribers and the first public telephone exchange was opened in Suva, Fiji with much fanfare.

However, overseas communication was more problematic. From the arrival of the missionaries until the establishment of regular postal services in the 1870s, exchanging letters with home was the only means of staying in touch with the world. Outgoing mail was usually dispatched by arrangement with the captain or crew of visiting European or American sailing vessels and was infrequent at best. Letters were most often sent collect and took months to be delivered, while incoming mail was even less reliable. In 1874, with postal services established in most island colonies and the proliferation of steamship routes enhancing international mail services, the Universal Postal Union was formed (eventually claiming as members nearly all the world's nations). The basic treaty, the Universal Postal Convention, regulated the exchange of international mail and has been carefully tended and modified as circumstances warrant, up to the present.

The first reliable electronic communication links across the Pacific were undersea telegraphic cables. The Pacific Cable, completed in 1902, connected Asia and Australia with North America and island-hopped its way across the vast Pacific Ocean making land-fall at only a few geographically strategic colonial centres. The rate for sending a cablegram in the early years was quite high, over US$1.00 per word. Thus, outside of important administrative or business communications, the international postal system would remain the main mechanism of overseas communications for many years.

In 1957, nearly a century after the first telephones were introduced in the Pacific, the first undersea telephone cable was installed between Hawai'i and the west coast of the United States. However, it was not until the mid 1960s that trans-oceanic telephone cables (COMPAC in 1963–64, SEACOM in 1967) connected North America with Asia, Australia and New Zealand. Even in these instances, it was only the islands within the routing path of the undersea cables that were fortunate enough to have land-based relay stations—namely, Hawai'i, Guam, Fiji and Papua New Guinea.

The real watershed of telecommunications services in the Pacific occurred in the late 1920s with the development of high frequency (HF) radio technology. Indeed, until the Japanese bombing of PEARL HARBOR in 1941, a large and growing network of radio communications was expanding hand-in-hand with the new-found strategic and political importance of the island territories. Furthermore, post-war developments in HF radio-telephony greatly improved this means of communication whereby most of the Pacific islands soon had internal HF radio systems run by their respective administrations. Such radio links were established throughout the Pacific initially for wartime purposes, but soon they were being improved and built upon for peaceful activities. The HF radio medium quickly became the most economical means of maintaining contact with metropolitan governments, colonial offices and rural village administrations.

Despite these improvements, few rural villages had access to telephones for even domestic communications, let alone international. Likewise, island reliance on HF radio-telephony for international connectivity—once a boon—soon limited their traffic and saddled them with old, outmoded networks. Furthermore, colonial administrations spent little on infrastructure development prior to independence, leaving much of the existing equipment in poor repair. As a result, the newly independent island nations inherited grossly inadequate communication infrastructures in relation to the requirements of modern businesses and government.

Such inadequacies in telecommunications were soon recognized as presenting serious obstacles to achieving economic development and became an important agenda item for discussion among leaders of the island nations gathered in Wellington, New Zealand, in 1971 for the first meeting of the SOUTH PACIFIC FORUM. As a result of this meeting, the South Pacific Bureau for Economic Cooperation (SPEC, later the South Pacific Forum Secretariat) was created and charged with—among other things—the coordination of developments in telecommunications infrastructure within the region. The United Nations, at the request of SPEC member countries, funded a feasibility study for a regional telecommunications network. The study's main recommendations included immediate steps to upgrade the existing system across the board. However, in an environment of limited resources—and given the aid-dependent nature of many island economies—highest priority was given to improvements in their respective international telecommunication services. Thus, SPEC began the supervision of international aid-funded upgrades to HF radio transmissions as well as telegraph and telex circuits. Satellite and undersea cable technologies available at the time were ruled out as being far too expensive.

Too late to be considered in the initial regional telecommunications study, the International Telecommunications Satellite Organization (INTELSAT), a global provider of satellite services, changed its long-standing pricing policy in 1976, allowing smaller and thus cheaper earth stations access to its satellite network at a reduced rate. The telecommunication study's calculations were quickly re-examined and for all but the smallest of island countries, satellite communications immediately became more attractive. SPEC thus initiated the phased introduction of satellite operations using the INTELSAT Stand-

FSM Telecommunications Center, Kolonia Town, Pohnpei

ard B configuration. Furthermore, riding on the wave of urgency reported in the Maitland Commission Report (*The Missing Link*, 1984), efforts were redoubled to connect developing countries to modern international telecommunication services. In 1984, Kiribati was the last island country to be provided with a Standard B earth station while even smaller earth stations (Standard D) brought affordable satellite communications to the smallest of island nations by the early 1990s.

From the mid 1970s through the early 1990s, island governments placed the force of political will behind the construction of international gateways as satellite communications became a part of everyday life in the islands. Currently, almost all of the Pacific islands have satellite gateways for international telecommunications (see Table 6.6) and many have embarked upon ambitious modernization plans following the restructuring of their own telecommunications organizations. Some island nations have even entered into joint-venture agreements for the management of their international and domestic communications (see Table 6.7) in an attempt to 'leap-frog' from their out-dated infrastructure into the 21st century.

One outcome of this effort has been the interconnection via satellite of isolated outer islands previously reachable only by HF radio links. As the digitization of transmission technology advances and as on-board power for satellites increases, there has been a concomitant decrease in the cost of connection. Plans are currently underway to make use of new developments in satellite technology to connect even the most remote rural and outer island communities to the domestic, regional and international communication networks. One such effort initiated in the late 1980s is the PACT (Pacific Area Cooperative Telecommunications) Network, a regionally focused and operated satellite service. Likewise, Papua New Guinea's domestic satellite project is expected to carry a national television service, 2 Mbps restorative digital carriers, and a thin-route telephony service. Not to be outdone, Tonga has embarked on an ambitious venture to build a Pacific region satellite service based on its proposed TongaSat system of repurposed, refurbished and/or new satellites—generating substantial international attention in the process.

Thin-route, repeaterless fibre optic technology is also making inroads as costs come down, spanable

Table 6.6 INTELSAT earth stations in the Pacific islands

	Location	Type	Owner	Installation
Cook Islands	Rarotonga	Std B	TCI[1]	1980
Micronesia (FSM)	Yap, Chuuk, Pohnpei, Kosrae	Std B	FSMTC[2]	1983
Fiji	Wailoku Vatuwaqa	Std A Std A[5]	FINTEL	1975 (decom 1987) 1987
Kiribati	Tarawa	Std B	Kiribati Telecom	1983
Marshall Islands	Majuro, Ebeye	Std B	NTA[3]	1983
Nauru	Yaren District	Std B	Dir of Telecoms	1975
Niue	Alofi	Std D[1]	Post and Telecoms	1989
Papua New Guinea	Port Moresby	Std B	Post and Telecoms Corp	1985
Samoa	Afiamalu Maluafou	Std B Std A[5]	Post and Telecoms	1980 (decom 1991) 1991
Solomon Islands	Honiara	Std B	STCL[4]	1975
Tonga	Nuku'alofa	Std B	Cable and Wireless	1975
Tuvalu	Funafuti	Std D[1]	Telecoms Dept	1990
Vanuatu	Port Vila	Std B	VANITEL	1979

1 Telecom Cook Islands Ltd (TCI), formerly Cook Islands Telecommunications Corp., took over the operation of the international gateway from Cable and Wireless in 1991.
2 In 1988, the FSM Telecommunications Corp. (FSMTC) purchased each of the four earth stations originally installed and operated by Comsat.
3 The National Telecommunications Authority (NTA) of the Marshall Islands purchased the two Comsat earth stations in 1987.
4 Solomon Telekom Company Ltd (STCL), joint venture between Cable and Wireless and the Solomon Islands Government.
5 New 13 m INTELSAT Standard A earth station antenna.
Source: South Pacific Forum, 1991. *Regional Telecommunications Report*.

distances increase and bandwidth demands rise. Even wireless communications, with promises of high-quality voice and data services, are making their debut in the Pacific islands (see Table 6.8) with expectations of rapidly declining costs.

Whereas telephone densities (number of telephones per 100 population) and subscriber waiting lists in the Pacific islands (see Table 6.9) have greatly improved since the mid 1980s and are much better than in other developing countries, overall telephone penetration rates remain low despite detailed master plans and extensive aid funding of infrastructure developments. Only two island countries meet or exceed 20 per cent telephone penetration (French Polynesia and New Caledonia, at 20 per cent and 22 per cent respectively) while the average for the entire Pacific islands region is only 2.1 per cent. Still, the bulk of the telephones remain concentrated in only a few urban centres while most island populations resident in the rural hinterlands or on isolated outer islands languish without service—further widening the access gap.

It has been widely recognized that such disparities in access cannot long exist without exacerbating already volatile urban–rural inequalities or placing additional burdens on already over-strained economies. Efforts have been initiated to rectify these disparities, but there has been little improvement on the 7:1 urban-to-rural telephone ratio. Indeed, no substantial results have yet been reported on rural, thin-route communication initiatives in the Pacific. This task has proved more arduous than first assumed since Pacific nations need to make up for under-investment in telecommunications at a time when traditional funding sources are under increasing pressure, and other basic needs such as housing, roads, hospitals and schools remain.

In the midst of this access debate, the Internet burst upon the world scene. It should be noted that for many islanders outside of Hawai'i and perhaps Guam, the Internet remains a remote concept. Yet, as the rest of the world is 'jacking in' to the Internet at a ferocious pace—over 43 million host computers on the Internet as of January 1999 and growing at a rate of more than 65 per cent per year—the Pacific

Table 6.7 Organizational changes in Pacific islands telecommunications administration

	1984	1994
Cook Islands	Government department	Government holding company, joint venture operating co.[1]
Micronesia (FSM)	Government statutory agency	Government owned corporation
Fiji	Government department	Government owned corporation
Kiribati	Government department	Government holding company, joint venture operating co.
Marshall Islands	Government department	25% government owned 75% public owned authority[2]
Nauru	Government department	Government department
Niue	Government department	Government department
Papua New Guinea	Government corporation	Government corporation
Samoa	Government department	Government department
Solomon Islands	Government department	Joint venture company[3]
Tonga	Government department	Government corporation
Tuvalu	Government department	Government department
Vanuatu	Government department	Joint venture company[4]

1 Following the 1991 forced contract termination and acquisition of Cable and Wireless operations by legislative act, Telecom Cook Islands Ltd took over domestic and international telecommunications as a 60:40 joint venture between the Cook Islands government and Telecoms New Zealand International.
2 The Marshall Islands government holds a 25 per cent share in the privatized National Telecommunications Authority and retains control over all unsold public shares.
3 Domestic and international telecommunications is owned and operated by Solomon Telekom Company Ltd, a joint venture between Cable and Wireless and the Solomon Island government.
4 Telecom Vanuatu Ltd is the privatized domestic carrier set up as a joint venture between VANITEL, which is in charge of international telecommunications (owned and operated by Cable and Wireless), and the Government of Vanuatu.
Source: Author's research.

Table 6.8 Pacific island cellular telephone networks, 1996

	Operators	Subscribers	System	Supplier
American Samoa	Office of Comm.	2 500	AMPS	Motorola
Fiji	Vodafone	2 350	GMS	Ericsson
Guam	Guam Cellular	14 500	AMPS	Motorola/ NovAtel
Marshall Islands	NTA	400	AMPS	AT&T
Nauru	Telecom Office	650	AMPS	Plexsys
New Caledonia	PTT	500	GMS	Alcatel
Papua New Guinea	PTC	100	AMPS	Stanilite
Solomon Islands	STCL	250	AMPS	Stanilite
Tonga	TTC	100	AMPS	Stanilite
Tahiti	Tikiphone	1 300	GMS	Alcatel
Vanuatu	Telecom	150	AMPS	Stanilite

Notes: AMPS: Advanced Mobile Phone Service, analog cellular radio; GMS: Groupe Speciale Mobile, anglicized to mean Global Standard for Mobile Communications, a pan-European cellular digital system.
Source: Asia-Pacific Mobile Communications Report, 1996.

Table 6.9 Paficic islands telephones, 1990

	Total telephone	Pop.	Tel. per 100 pop.	Wait list
Cook Islands	2 540	18 552	13.7	245
Micronesia (FSM)	2 400	112 000	2.1	700
Fiji	68 532	726 000	9.4	11 500
Kiribati	1 130	68 828	1.6	133
Marshall Islands	1 193	42 108	2.8	1 500
Nauru	1 600	9 053	17.7	160
Niue	390	2 267	17.2	-
Papua New Guinea	73 068	3 600 000	2.0	1 491
Samoa	4 335	181 984	2.4	2 600
Solomon Islands	5 976	329 000	1.8	130
Tonga	3 984	95 810	4.2	680
Tuvulu	150	8 624	1.7	60
Vanuatu	6 480	159 830	4.1	88

Source: South Pacific Forum, 1991. *Regional Telecommunications Report.*

islands do not wish to be left behind. Such phenomenal worldwide growth has captured the interest of island governments, businesses and urban residents alike and reports of the Internet's growing usefulness and popularity elsewhere has opened up demand for Internet service providers in the Pacific. However, despite the fact that most island countries have primarily digital international and domestic telecommunication infrastructures, telephone densities still remain among the lowest in the world. Even if one has a reasonably reliable power supply, a good computer, appropriate software and a modem, a telephone line is still needed to connect to the Internet. Therefore, the relatively low telephone densities reported for even the most 'modernized' island countries represents a substantial entry barrier to accessing the Internet—especially if the average wait for a telephone in the capital city can be six months to a year, or longer.

Nevertheless, in early 1996 a consortium consisting of Telecom Fiji Ltd (formerly, Fiji Posts and Telecom Ltd), Fiji International Telecommunications Ltd (FINTEL), Telecom New Zealand Ltd, the University of the South Pacific and the Telecommunications Program of the South Pacific Forum initiated a six-month trial Internet service accessing the University of Waikato's Internet gateway in New Zealand. FINTEL and Telecom New Zealand provided a 64 Kbps (kilobits per second) circuit for the duration of the trial period and Telecom Fiji provided the router. Within months of operation, the trial had 143 modem users and six leased-line users while traffic reached over 900 megabits per second per month. This rapid adoption, understandably, piqued the interest of other island telecommunication service providers studying the feasibility of offering Internet access. (See ELECTRONIC NETWORKING.)

As computer-based communication technologies diffuse throughout the Pacific, some fundamental questions need to be addressed. At issue is the perceived value of such communication technologies and whether or not their 'value' matches or exceeds their 'cost' for islanders to connect. Among island states, issues of equitable and open access to information as well as the more basic issues of computer-based resource awareness and/or relevance as necessary public service priorities are not being adequately discussed. Furthermore, will schools in island nations integrate 'computer literacy' into the curriculum to prepare students for jobs in the next millennium? How many islanders will be able to afford computers, modems, software and the online connections without some sort of subsidy? While technology has the potential to promote economic growth, job creation and other social benefits, without a guiding social contract the information revolution will only aggravate underlying inequalities and may further bifurcate island societies as well as widen the gap between developed metropolitan countries and their less developed neighbors. Likewise, it is important for island governments to remain vigilant in order to ensure that communication and information technologies do not play a corrosive role in island society but, instead, empower islanders to preserve their culture. Indeed, these communication technologies offer as many opportunities to erode indigenous language, traditions, and history as they do opportunities to preserve and strengthen. As island nations begin to overhaul existing telecommunication and information systems to meet the demands of the information age, it is imperative that inequalities do not become codified for the next generation.—MRO

Further reading

Cutler, T, 1994. *Telecommunications: the Pacific link*, a Green Paper report for the Pacific Forum on the development of the telecommunications sector in the region, Cutler & Company, April.

Maitland, Sir Donald, 1984. *The Missing Link: report of the Independent Commission for World-wide Telecommunications Development* [Maitland Commission Report], ITU.

Ogden, M R, 1995. 'Pacific islands, information technology and universal access: it's not just about wires', *Development Bulletin*, Special Issue: Information technology and development, 35 (October).

Radio broadcasting

All Pacific island nations and territories have at least one government-owned radio station, except Hawai'i, Guam and the Northern Marianas (CNMI) in the North Pacific, and American Samoa in the South, each of which has between two and five commercial stations (Hawai'i has 62 commercial radio stations). This commercialization of the radio industry is unusual in the islands, and reflects differential attitudes toward government ownership of the broadcast spectrum in the United States compared with former British colonies.

In many places in the Pacific—Easter Island, Kiribati, Nauru, Niue, Solomon Islands (though a new commercial station is expected soon), Tokelau, Tuvalu, Vanuatu, and Wallis and Futuna—the government is the only broadcaster. Whereas government radio stations in Cook Islands, Palau, Papua New Guinea and Samoa share the market with a single private station, and in the Federated States of Micronesia and Tonga with a single religious station, the government broadcaster remains the major source of news and information for its citizens and typically the only station with national coverage. The remaining island nations and territories support a vibrant and competitive radio broadcasting environment with at least one government station and two or more private stations providing a variety of music, entertainment and news programs. A 1993 study found that 62 per cent of Palauans and Marshallese surveyed said radio was their primary source of information, particularly for local news bulletins. This survey convincingly illustrated previous, mostly anecdotal, reports that radio is perhaps the only true 'mass' medium in the islands because it uses both the local language and English and is accessible to anyone who has an AM radio and batteries. In the francophone Pacific, primarily French Polynesia and New Caledonia, the Radio France *d'Outre-mer* network tends to dominate the airwaves. Independent radio stations have struggled to reflect the views of indigenous nationalists and a few commercial stations have met with modest success.

Economic difficulties in the 1990s, however, have led to the increasing rationalization of government support for the broadcast sector. Radio stations now must seek commercial advertising and sponsorship to maintain services, and are chafing under continuing government restriction. One example is the Fiji Broadcasting Commission (FBC), which operates three networks in English, Fijian and Hindi. Long the main news and information source for rural Fijians, cutbacks in government funding and the competition posed by the private radio broadcaster Communications Fiji Ltd, which operates English and Hindi stations in Fiji and the commercial station Nau FM in Papua New Guinea, led to a reorganization of the FBC in the mid 1990s.

International and inter-regional broadcast news and information in English within the Pacific has been primarily received almost exclusively via the 'Big Four'—the British Broadcasting Corporation, Voice of America, Radio Australia and Radio New Zealand—although the overseas broadcasts from France are important in the French-speaking Pacific as well. Among the Big Four, Radio Australia stands out as the most received international broadcast service primarily because it has the strongest signal targeting the Pacific region and because it is the only one that maintains correspondents in the islands. The Voice of America is the primary international broadcast service in Micronesia, owing to the extent of the American presence (and influence) in this region since World War II. However, Radio Australia's dominant role as the main news and information provider for islanders was highlighted in a 1987 survey of Pacific island radio station managers conducted by the EAST–WEST CENTER. The response from Pacific broadcasters involved in the study clearly pointed out that news and public affairs programs were then—as they are today—the most listened to and widely rebroadcast service offered by Radio Australia. It should be noted that very few islanders possess shortwave radio receivers and therefore rely instead on the rebroadcast of international news and information services via primarily government owned AM, and to some extent commercial FM, radio stations. This has raised concerns regarding 'single-source' news reporting as well as issues of balanced and fair reporting of Pacific issues and events and has remained a sore point between island governments, foreign correspondents and local journalists.—MRO

Further reading

Richstad, J, 1987. Use of international broadcasts in Pacific islands radio services: dependency? cultural imperialism? practical necessity?, Institute of Culture and Communication, East–West Center, (mimeo).

Thomas, P, 1990. 'Communication policy and planning in the Pacific', in Yash Ghai (ed.), *Public Administration and Management in Small States: Pacific experiences*, Commonwealth Secretariat and University of the South Pacific.

Vusoniwailala, L, 1987. 'Radio in today's Pacific', *Pacific Islands Communication Journal*, 15(1).

Television and video

In the early 1980s, many Pacific island nations faced important policy decisions regarding the proliferation of communication and information technologies being offered to them by enterprising foreign private interests eager to forge new business alliances. Improved satellite services as well as terrestrial broadcast technologies also removed impediments to the establishment of national television services; remoteness from capital cities, rugged terrain, and small, isolated rural populations were no longer the barriers they once were. Early on, the comparatively larger populations of Papua New Guinea and Fiji, combined with the proliferation of new technologies, made the potential market for commercial television in these two nations attractive to some Australian and New Zealand entrepreneurs. One reason for the incursion of Australia and New Zealand broadcast businesses into the Pacific region was due to the limited size of their domestic markets and the desire to promote the export of their own programming and services. Perhaps also, the perceived advantage of being first to lock out competition in marginally profitable Pacific locales, or the ability to field test new technology and marketing approaches in relatively small, 'low-risk' markets might likewise afford experiences that could directly translate into the competitive and potentially lucrative Asian markets. In any case, increased competition among satellite providers in recent years as well as the proliferation of satellite-delivered television programming has resulted in a new wave of entrepreneurs trying to secure television deals with island governments. This has raised concerns over the percentage of locally produced content and the extent to which national governments would be able to control television. Indeed, it has been such external forces, along with the perceived lack of government policy and commitment compounded by insufficient funding and inadequate training, which have been blamed for constraining the potential of indigenous video and television production from the very beginning.

Broadcast television is now becoming widespread throughout the urban Pacific, although until the late 1980s, only seven island states had television—all territories of either France or the United States. In the US territories, American television programming—complete with commercials for products available in the United States—are still received via videotape cassette (taped directly from US West Coast or Honolulu broadcasts) or delivered by satellite transmission for subsequent terrestrial rebroadcast. The situation is similar in the French territories where satellite and videotaped programming is provided directly from Paris to the French Pacific. Outside the US and French territories, television developed more slowly, its pace quickening in the 1990s. Today only Tuvalu, Kiribati and Tokelau are without a broadcast television facility of some kind.

Most television broadcasters in the Commonwealth Pacific are at least partially owned by the government, and in the cases of Nauru, Niue, Tonga, Vanuatu and Samoa, the government is the majority shareholder. All, however, are increasingly exploring commercial operations due to the cost of maintaining broadcast services in an era of budget constraints. Much of this cost is due to programming, the vast bulk of which is imported from the United States, France, New Zealand and Australia. The newer Pacific television stations have had time to reflect on the US and French TV models and have responded to these by emphasizing the importance of local content—that is, content appropriate to the

Shopping area and video rental store in Kolonia Town, Pohnpei

social, economic, political and cultural interests of their countries. The stations established in the last several years have all stressed their intent to produce local material. However, a UNESCO survey in the early 1990s found local production levels averaging only about 5–10 per cent: primarily coverage of news, cultural or official events, and sports. Though the cost of metropole program packages is a significant portion of the television budget, locally made programs—such as the soap opera produced by Albert Toro for local broadcast in Papua New Guinea—can cost up to 10 times that of a foreign product due primarily to production underwriting of the latter. In addition, foreign-made programs often have the highest ratings, particularly in larger societies with an emerging middle-class keen to see how 'the other half lives'.

Thus, 'Hollywood-style' movies continue to be popular in the Pacific region, even though few are screened in movie theatres any more due to the pervasiveness of video. About 20 years ago, Marshall Islands had eight theatres and Palau three. By the late 1980s, there were none. Likewise in Cook Islands, seven of the capital's eight movie theatres closed following the advent of video. The remaining theatre was unaffected by the introduction of broadcast TV because it was regularly patronized by Rarotonga's teenagers. As videotape technology swept the region in the 1970s, it proved so popular that by the mid 1980s there were reported to be in excess of 60 000 video cassette recorders (VCRs) in Fiji alone. Suva itself has more than 50 rental shops, many with a 'rental' network which sends video tapes into remote villages. Access is multiplied by extended family and communal relations and village social organization. Whereas television reception has been concentrated in the urban and peri-urban areas, TV and videotape systems are spreading rapidly throughout the Pacific region. Most of this expansion has taken place alongside the expansion of electrification and/or satellite-based domestic communication services into rural and outer island areas. Likewise, the increasing availability and ubiquity of the 'mom-and-pop' video rental shops has further extended video and television's diffusion and acceptance. Where television and/or video systems are not present in rural areas, it is more likely due to poor reception or lack of power rather than purely economic reasons. In Palau, 15 video rental shops cater for the greater Koror area—including many areas accessible only by boat—with the average family renting 3–4 tapes per day and typically more on weekends. In Cook Islands, the introduction of broadcast television actually increased the video market by 33 per cent, because people purchased both television sets and VCRs to watch TV and boosted the videotape rental market.

To counteract the influx of 'culturally insensitive' videotape programming, some island governments introduced local television with programs for younger people, hoping to counter the attractions of overseas video programs—many of which are 'action movies' containing a great deal of violence and/or nudity. Such programming has already been blamed for perceived 'modern' social ills in society, causing a great deal of concern. Obviously, wherever and whenever television has been introduced, its impact has been readily observable. Yet, cause and effect cannot be easily demonstrated in the islands context (or any other developing society), especially when television and video were introduced at a time of rapid social transformations as a result of post-colonial modernization. Many effects of television are subtle, but taken together, may contribute to considerable changes in society.

Since 1987, renewed interest in the social impact of television in developing societies has seen a growing number of ethnographic studies conducted in the islands where 'natural experiments' of television's introduction are being monitored. Early reports indicate that islanders have attributed to television a number of unwelcome changes to traditional gender, social and familial roles, as well as changes in community structures of interaction, attitudes and values. Although many of the early research reports provide tantalizing data, results are inconclusive. Still, these studies have raised concerns perhaps best expressed by Ratu Inoke Kubuabola, Fiji's Minister for Information, Broadcasting, Television and Telecommunications. At the Pacific Regional TV meeting in 1989, sponsored by the Asia-Pacific Broadcast Union and the South Pacific Commission (SPC), he stated, '…the introduction of television services in the Pacific islands will be, for most of us, a new industry. A development which I believe may have greater impact on the community than any other single development in our history. The overall extent of this impact has yet to be made fully manifest.' However, at the same meeting in 1989, Atanraoi Baiteke, then Secretary-General of the SPC, said

> We don't fully understand television yet, this strange new creature. We must learn its needs and wants, what it eats, and most of all, what our families think of it. What effect will it have on our precious cultures and values?…We need to know how it can affect our lives…Many [island leaders] are faced with the questions of when and how concerning television, whilst looking for ways of serving their people. [To me] TV is what you make of it.

His address held out hope that television would not be a purely corrosive influence.—MRO

Further reading

Ogden, M R and Crowl, L (eds), 1993. 'Television and video in the Pacific islands', *Pacific Islands Communication Journal*, Special Issue, 16(1).

Asia-Pacific Broadcast Union and South Pacific Commission, 1989. *Report of the Pacific Regional TV Meeting*, 27 November–1 December.

Stewart, J, Horsfield B and Cook, P, 1993. 'Television and dependency: a case study of policy making in Fiji and Papua New Guinea', *Contemporary Pacific*, 5(2).

Waqavonovono, M, 1981. 'Who manipulates Pacific media? Influences on newspapers and television', *Pacific Perspective*, 10(1).

Impact of television in the Pacific islands

The socio-cultural and economic impact on island nations of the introduction of new communications media, particularly televisual forms such as terrestrial, satellite and video cassette television, has been of continuing interest to Pacific researchers. Motivated by the unexpected policy reversal of the government of Fiji to allow Australia's commercial TCN9 television network into Fiji, researchers of the Department of Mass Communication at the University of Southern Queensland (USQ), in later collaboration with academics at the University of the South Pacific, the University of Guam, the University of Texas at Austin and the University of Hawai'i at Mānoa, conducted the Pacific Telecommunications Project (PTP) from 1989 to 1992. The PTP aimed to survey Pacific islanders to assess social, cultural and economic changes—if any—resulting from the introduction of television into their communities. Project researchers also sought data on the political economy of the establishment of foreign television companies in these nations to extend their understanding of the contexts of television's alleged social impact.

The PTP used ethnographic methodology, choosing only field researchers with sound local knowledge and/or a high degree of cultural sensitivity in order to avoid systematic errors in social impact data collection due to cultural ignorance. Dependency theory, world systems theory, discourse theory and the literature of media effects studies informed variously the analyses of data collected in Cook Islands, Kiribati, Fiji, Papua New Guinea, Samoa, Solomon Islands, Vanuatu, Torres Strait Islands, Guam, Marshall Islands, Yap, the Northern Marianas and Palau. The island communities of French Polynesia, being the political responsibility of Paris, were treated as a different media effects category and were not included in the survey.

The PTP research identified a consensus of micro and macro-social, cultural and economic effects, both 'positive' and 'negative', linked with island consumption of one or more forms of television. Positive effects included gaining knowledge about the outside world, formal and informal education and training, enhanced self-dignity and assertiveness in women, an increased sense of national unity and communality, improved control over intra and international migration flows, increased tourism, the creation of culture industries, and an expectation—usually unrealistic—of economic development leading to a rise in the standard of living.

The negative micro effects included erosion of social routines and rituals, weakening of the authority of the village chief and parents, loss of respect for grandparents, increased immorality, adverse effects on family structures and family interaction, reduced social visiting, poor school performance, reduced literacy, reduction of the status of traditional foods and increases in the importation of expensive foreign foodstuffs, implying a validation of alien ideologies of consumerism and leading to a sharp increase in environmental pollution from non-biodegradable packaging. Major concern across almost all of the islands surveyed focused on sexually explicit and violent television and VCR programs, which were regarded as affecting both the individual and the society in general—for example, by breaching the widespread taboo barring males and females of the same family from seeing the same sexually explicit scenes together. Displacement affects, which blamed video and television for disrupting important work and normal leisure activities, were also regarded negatively. Interruptions to domestic routines, intra-village conflict over VCR viewing times, negative feelings toward children and the aged because of their nuisance value during viewing, and absenteeism and poor performance at work were also noted. Reduction in church attendance and falling participation in community activities were attributed to the advent of video and television in these islands. Other negative social impacts from television included the development in islanders of poor opinions of the people and lifestyles of other countries, the weakening of local dialects, the widening of the social gap between rich and poor, and the weakening of rituals such as the KAVA ceremony.

The undermining of traditional cultures and ways of life was also blamed on television. In Cook Islands, video was blamed for a perceived decline in the performing arts. Television and video were also held responsible for the weakening of self-image of many islanders. Fijian informants described a sense of inferiority about their own culture compared with western consumer cultures shown on television. Also, village and family economies were sometimes greatly strained by purchase or hire of video equipment and cassettes. This was apparently not offset by the emergence of small video businesses or, in some islands, by the establishment of local television stations. The reported displacement by television and video of domestic vegetable gardening and fishing, combined with larger expenditures from family budgets for home video, had a noticeable impact on many families.

Some negative macroeconomic effects of television were detected. The micro-effect of the reduction in self-reliance and self-respect was seen by PTP researchers as creating the wider, more general macro-effect of cultural and economic dependency on alien, imported cultures. In this context, deals between foreign television entrepreneurs and island governments made the development of local production industries very difficult to support financially and politically. The political economy of the introduction of television tended to favour the interests of foreign television owners and entrepreneurs rather than the individual country. For example, the persuasive rhetoric of national economic development (improved agricultural methods, community health and educational levels) that usually cloaked the bid by foreign television interests to establish television in an island nation and which typically was used by island governments to overcome local opposition to the introduction of television was usually mocked by the subsequent poor economic performance and cheap foreign programs of the new television enterprise.—BH

Further reading

Horsfield, B, Stewart, J and Plange, N, 1992. *The Socio-Cultural Impact of Satellite and Alternative Television and Communication Needs in the Pacific Region for the Division of the Free Flow of Communication and Information, Unesco*, Pacific Telecommunications Project, University of Southern Queensland.

Stewart, J, Horsfield, B and Cook, P, 1993. 'Television and dependency: a case study of policy making in Fiji and Papua New Guinea', *The Contemporary Pacific*, 5(2).

Television development and training

The arrival of satellite services in the Pacific islands has focused attention on local broadcasting. Small Pacific services have to redefine themselves in response to expanding satellite and cable programming availability, and eventually Internet programming via computer. With few resources, little infrastructure and a pervasive dependency on foreign sources for everything from trained personnel to programming and spare parts, Pacific broadcasters will face many of the same market-driven forces changing the face of broadcast media worldwide.

Many Pacific broadcasters have been struggling to fill 5 per cent of their schedules with local programs. Interest in local program production has increased dramatically, however, as new national television services have begun broadcasting with imported programming. Island broadcasters are beginning to look to developed nations to provide technical and production training for their indigenous staff. As they begin to employ new technologies, emerging program producers and broadcasters often attempt to emulate western styles and formats. The introduction of western training and production technology, however, can lead to cultural conflict when traditional relationships are challenged. Television cameras and video editing machines are not neutral technologies. The intrusion of television cameras in traditional ceremonies and the subsequent manipulation of images in the editing room can lead to subtle reinterpretations of relationships, with unpredictable consequences for the community.

With these new technologies, indigenous producers and editors must now decide how the statements of traditional chiefs and elders, as well as those of powerful government officials, will be edited and aired. Editing techniques commonly used to tighten up interview sequences, including the use of cutaways and reaction shots, have been reported to violate the cultural protocols accorded to traditional leaders, offending both the leaders as well as the indigenous television audience. Government officials who are also high-ranking traditional chiefs present a particularly serious challenge to lower-ranking indigenous producers and broadcasters. Broadcasters have reported severe repercussions for attempting to edit even minor parts of legislative hearings, and particularly the political orations of legislators.

Conflicts between cultural values and broadcast methods occur throughout the Pacific. In some cultures, routine sound recording techniques using overhead microphone booms are viewed as disrespectful, particularly in the case of chiefs and others of high rank. Fortunately, by repositioning the microphones from below, professional quality audio recording is permitted without offending the indigenous subjects; but other television production methods pose more serious dilemmas. Western trainers and educators must be especially sensitive and resourceful when instructing islanders in using this powerful medium within their own cultures.

A dearth of television engineering expertise and technical infrastructure, including equipment maintenance and spare parts, is responsible, not only for many failures of local broadcasting, but for the pervasive dependency of Pacific island broadcasters on expatriate consultants and foreign sources of supply. UNESCO's Pacific Regional Television Survey Project (PACTEL 1993) reported only Guam, American Samoa, Papua New Guinea and Fiji as having trained engineering staff—all expatriates. For some of the smaller island broadcasters, the malfunction of a single camera or editing deck can halt local production for weeks. While developed countries already possess the infrastructure to accommodate media technologies, island nations require considerable ancillary support to create an infrastructure from the ground up.

To acquire broadcast expertise and infrastructure many island governments initiate television services by entering into agreements with broadcast organizations in Australia, New Zealand, the United States and France. It is far cheaper for Niue, Nauru, Fiji, Cook Islands and Samoa to use previously licensed programs provided by Television New Zealand (TVNZ) than to produce local programs which require trained staff, infrastructure and a reliable source of funding. Broadcasting services typically tend to adopt the technical broadcast standard of their former colonizers, who are usually the suppliers of equipment and trained engineers. The incompatibility of broadcast standards in effect splits the Pacific along former colonial patterns and ties nations to their former colonizers.

Like other small broadcasters, islanders cannot compete with the economies of scale enjoyed by the industrialized nations in providing a vast array of programming at low cost. What they can do better than anyone else is to utilize the stunning diversity of their environments, the histories and cultures of their peoples, and the unique viewpoints of islanders. While aspects of culture and custom may indeed conflict with production methods introduced by outsiders, this presents an opportunity to expand the art and craft of television production by adapting these techniques to reach diverse Pacific audiences effectively. Possessing the technology of production, and the training to apply it effectively, creates the potential for presenting small island communities in their own voices—for themselves initially, and eventually for the world outside the Pacific islands.—RAH

Newspapers

Newspapers were introduced into the Pacific islands by European and American missionaries in the early 1800s. The first news-sheets, *Te Faaite Tahiti* (1836) and *O Le Sulu Samoa* (1839), were both published by missionary groups. Within a few decades, increased European activity in the islands led colonial administrations into publishing, to promote the government viewpoint on contentious issues and events. Commercial newspapers appeared with the influx of merchant capital during the 1870s. Often fiercely partisan, they represented planter and trader interests at a time when colonial administrations were struggling to reconcile indigenous and expatriate interests and establish political legitimacy. Many appeared only briefly before succumbing to financial pressures, or disappeared when their publishers were forced out of the colony. Those that survived prospered through close links with territorial administrations and expanding business interests.

World War I introduced the issue of nationalism into colonial media. Newspapers founded by islanders began to reflect a growing nationalist sentiment. Leaders of the 1920s MAU movement in Western Samoa instigated a program of civil disobedience that included publishing the weekly *Samoa Guardian*. The *Guardian* so angered the administration that it eventually had the paper's *afakasi* Samoan editor exiled to New Zealand. He resumed publication there, and smuggled copies of the *Guardian* back into Samoa. This tradition of using New Zealand as a base to escape government pressure at home continues today, with Tongan editor Kalfi Moala publishing the pro-democracy *Taimi o Tonga* from Auckland. In the 1960s and 1970s nationalist publishers in Papua New Guinea (*Pangu Pati Nius; Dialogue*, edited by Leo Hannett), Solomon Islands (*Kakamora Reporter*), and Vanuatu (*Viewpoints*, published by Walter LINI's Vanua'aku Pati) were instrumental in setting the independence agenda in their countries. In Fiji, the dominant position of the Australian-owned *Fiji Times* was challenged by the rival *Pacific Review*, owned and operated by Indo-Fijian businessmen who advocated an alternative to the government's political agenda.

In the post-independence period, government focus on localization, training and education stimulated rapid development in newspaper publishing. Tertiary journalism education in the region began with a one-year diploma course at the UNIVERSITY OF PAPUA NEW GUINEA in 1975, followed by similar courses at the UNIVERSITY OF THE SOUTH PACIFIC in Fiji and Divine Word Institute in Madang. Workshops, seminars and short courses were organized through regional and international development organizations such as UNESCO, AusAID, the South Pacific Commission, Friedrich Ebert Stiftung, the Asia Foundation, the EAST–WEST CENTER, the Commonwealth Federation of Journalists, the Australian Journalists Association and the Thomson Foundation.

Newspaper organizations went from mainly one and two-person operations in the 1970s to three-tier organizational structures resembling community papers in the developed western nations in little over a decade. Indigenous ownership also increased (from 6 titles in the 1970s to 14), indigenous editors began to outnumber their expatriate colleagues

(56 per cent), and the number of full-time journalists increased fourfold (to 241).

Today, 24 Pacific nations and territories publish at least one local newspaper. Ten have two competing general-interest papers along with a variety of specialist periodicals (American Samoa, Northern Marianas, Guam, Fiji, French Polynesia, New Caledonia, Papua New Guinea, Samoa, Solomon Islands, Tonga). Some 35 per cent are privately owned, 30 per cent government-owned, 24 per cent owned by churches and 11 per cent owned by non-profit organizations such as the Solomon Islands Development Trust. Privately owned newspapers and magazines, however, represent more than two-thirds of the regional circulation.

The biggest newspapers are dailies located in the major English-speaking markets: the *Papua New Guinea Post-Courier* (41 000), the *Fiji Times* (31 000) and the *Pacific Daily News* on Guam (25 000). Dailies in the French territories are also sizeable in regional terms: *La Dépêche de Tahiti* (12 000) and *Les Nouvelles Calédoniennes* (13 000). All five are owned by foreign-based media corporations. Gannett Corp has owned the *Pacific Daily News* on Guam since 1970. In 1986, Rupert Murdoch's News Ltd gained majority shareholding in the *Herald* and *Weekly Times* titles in Papua New Guinea and Fiji, and Robert Hersant's Groupe Pacifique Presse Communication has owned *Les Nouvelles Calédoniennes*, *Les Nouvelles de Tahiti* and *La Dépêche de Tahiti* since the late 1980s.

Some of the best newspapers in the region are quite small; in 1996 the PINA Media Freedom Award was given to the *Cook Islands Press* (1500). Microstate government newspapers include *Te Uekera* (1500) in Kiribati and the recently defunct *Tuvalu Echoes* (260). A small private-sector press operates in Nauru with *Central Star News* (400) and in Niue with the *Niue Star* (500). Weekly newspapers too are important in the regional media economy. Weekly circulation is nearly twice that of dailies and represents one out of three newspaper copies in the region. Though newspapers primarily serve an urban audience, the TOK PISIN-language weekly, *Wantok* (15 000), has a significant peri-urban and rural circulation. Church and non-government organizations publish most of the smaller weekly, and monthly newspapers, such as *Ko e Tohi Fanongonongo* (500) in Tonga and *Mere Save* (500) in Solomon Islands.

English remains the most common language of publication in the region (60 per cent of circulation). French is next at 9 per cent, with Neo-Melanesian third at 8 per cent. The use of Asian languages, however, is on the rise for the first time since the Japanese colonial era, due to tourism development and migration. In the mid 1990s, the *Guam Chinese News* (1993, 2500) and the Kyodo News Service joined the three older Asian-oriented titles on Guam—the *Guam Shinbun* (1986, 2000), the *Korean Community News* (1984, 2000) and the *Korean News* (1982, 1700).

Technology, too, has revolutionized the Pacific newspaper industry by introducing desktop publishing in the mid 1980s. This reduced production costs, increased the frequency of publication, and dramatically improved newspaper appearance. The introduction of the facsimile machine at about the same time allowed regional news-sharing initiatives such as PACNEWS to balance the flow of Western news agency copy with newspaper coverage of Pacific issues and events. More recently, the technology of the Internet has been seized by Pacific newspaper publishers seeking a global readership. In November 1995, the *Tonga Chronicle* established a regular web presence with the help of a Tongan national studying in the United States, followed by the Papua New Guinea daily, *The National*, in September 1996. Newspapers in Samoa and American Samoa went online in 1997.—SL

Publishing

Publishing in the Pacific islands is characterized by its small scale, its informality and relative freedom from the constraints imposed by tradition in large metropolitan publishing houses, its vitality, and its persistence. In many ways, it is similar to the small presses of the United States: operating outside the metropolitan centres with insufficient capital, makeshift facilities, semi-skilled or volunteer labour and sometimes outdated or inappropriate equipment. Supplies may be erratic, print runs small and deadlines irrelevant, but with patience and time, books do appear and are eagerly received.

Since the first mission press began operating in Tahiti in 1817, the scale of publishing in the Pacific islands has always been, and likely will remain, minuscule. The reasons are diverse, but focus around the small populations (under 7 million people in all of Melanesia, Micronesia, and Polynesia); small land areas, often divided among a scattering of islands; and limited financial, physical and human resources. In addition, irregular transportation and humid climates pose difficulties for maintaining supplies, as well as for distributing books. Most Pacific islanders are rural dwellers, few of whom complete high school. Literacy is estimated to range from 23 per cent for Solomon Islands and 52 per cent for Papua New Guinea to 99 per cent for Tonga and Tuvalu. In Melanesia, where multiple languages are the norm (more than 700 in Papua New Guinea alone), publishing in English means choosing the second or third language of most readers, after vernaculars and Pidgin. Low incomes and purchasing power, as well as competition from television and video, restrict the demand for books, which generally are poorly marketed and distributed informally.

Early mission presses were introduced to print religious materials in the vernacular languages and later produced government documents and educational materials. Some of this early printing had an enormous effect on language, by taking one dialect and 'instituting' it as the standard. (In some islands, Catholics and Protestants used different alphabets.) Gradually, the non-religious items were taken over by private or government presses, and all had to struggle against insufficient funds and uncertain supplies. Prior to the Second World War, agricultural societies, commercial groups, and planters' organizations published newsletters and trade information. Until the 1950s, the materials published overwhelmingly served the needs of colonists, settlers, traders, and missionaries, although islanders were quick to grasp the value of the new form of communication and keen to learn to read and write.

With the post-war establishment of regional universities and the encouragement of creative writing, islanders began, from the late 1960s, to publish poems, short stories, plays and novels (CREATIVE LITERATURE BY PACIFIC ISLANDERS). Publishing programs became established in Papua New Guinea, Fiji and Guam, as well as Tonga, Samoa and Solomon Islands. Frequently they owe their origins to key individuals such as Ulli Beier, Ron and Marjorie Crocombe and Albert WENDT. Among the literary and scholarly journals that appeared were the *Micronesian Reporter* (1951–c1974), *Kakamora Reporter* (1970–75), *Pacific Perspective* (1972–85), *Yagl-Ambu* (1974–), and *Mana* (1977–). Such publishing programs serve island audiences by attempting to meet their demand for information, stories and educational materials about their islands, all preferably written by and affordable to islanders. In addition to literary efforts, they publish opinion and commentary, records of traditional songs and stories, myths, legends and cultural lore. Multi-author national histories have been written by islanders under the guidance of western academics, such as Hugh Laracy for Solomon Islands.

As well, island publishers provide materials for use in schools and literacy projects, and disseminate information on diverse topics, including agricultural techniques, environmental protection, family planning, nutrition, and record-keeping for small businesses. Publishing permits islanders to control content, quality, price and timing, thereby strengthening self-reliance and lessening dependence on outside suppliers. Because they are aware of local needs, local publishers are willing to assume the risks of small print runs that would be seen as uneconomic by metropolitan publishers. Many items are produced by non-profit groups that rely on volunteer labour for such tasks as editing, proofreading, design and inputting. An example is the South Pacific Creative Arts Society, based in Suva, which publishes *Mana* and shares office space with the Institute of Pacific Studies.

Working with inadequate capital and little government recognition (if not suspicion or attempts at censorship), island publishers must tolerate the difficulties, delays and high costs of doing business. They must also overcome the uncertainties associated with maintaining stocks of such basic materials as paper and ink and obtaining spare parts, all of which may be subject to steep import duties. Delays and work stoppages may be attributable to a lack of trained personnel and management skills, often exacerbated by aging or ill-maintained equipment. Information is needed about manuscript preparation, editing, design, contracts, copyright protection, royalties, agents and the publication process. Even where owners or managers are aware of the training programs available in Fiji, Papua New Guinea, Australia, New Zealand or Hawai'i, shortages of both funds and replacement personnel may prevent their taking advantage of opportunities.

Despite the obstacles, island publishers continue, sometimes with the aid of grants or subsidies from diplomatic missions, international funding agencies, or governments. They recognize a niche in which they are able to meet needs of island audiences that are viewed as too small, uneconomic, or irrelevant in metropolitan terms. Visitors to their islands may be surprised and rewarded by the results.—LC

Further reading

Pacific Islands Communication Journal 1985–86, 14(1) and 14(2).

Crowl, L, 1996. 'Book publishing in the Pacific islands,' *Fiji Library Association Journal*, 35.

Chapman, L, 1992. 'Publishing options of Pacific island writers', *Mana*, 9(2).

Mana, South Pacific Creative Arts Society, Fiji.

Storyboard; a journal of Pacific imagery, Storyboard Association, Guam.

Yagl-Ambu, Papua New Guinea.

Magazines

For nearly 50 years, PACIFIC ISLANDS MONTHLY (PIM, circulation 8000) was the dominant news magazine covering the Pacific. PIM moved from Sydney to Suva in late 1988 after purchase by Rupert Murdoch's News (Pacific) Ltd. It was joined in regional coverage by *Pacific Magazine* (10 000), published in Hawai'i, in 1975. In the early 1980s English-language news magazines such as *Guam Business News* (1983, 2500), *Islands Business* (1984, 8000) and *Matangi Tonga* (1986, 2000) began appearing in the islands themselves. In the French overseas territories, magazine development came slightly later, perhaps due to the strength of the Paris-based magazine publishing industry. *Tahiti-Pacifique* was founded in the early 1990s, and has a circulation of 3000. With the exception of *Matangi Tonga*, all are owned by non-indigenous interests and, with the added exception of PIM, all are edited by non-indigenous people.

The 1990s has seen indigenous and non-European magazine development in many parts of the Pacific. *The Review* in Fiji (1994) and *Talamua* in Samoa (1995) are news magazines targeted toward a national readership. In New Caledonia, *Mwa Vee* (1993, 2500) is published by the Agence de Développement de la Culture Kanak as a Kanak cultural review. On Guam, *Latte* (1995), founded by Pulitzer-prize winning photographer Manny Chrisostomo, focuses on the Chamorro lifestyle, while *Manila Manila* caters to a middle-class Filipino readership.

As tourism has developed in the region, the number of titles catering to this market has risen. On Guam, Fiji, New Caledonia and Tahiti 'drive guides' distributed through car rental agencies now complement the in-flight magazines of the airline industry and the various free 'beach press' publications oriented to tourists. The spread of broadcast television has similarly given rise to 'TV Guide'-type periodicals such as *Tele 7 Jours* and *Coco TV* in New Caledonia.—SL

■ ***Pacific Islands Monthly*** This long-established news magazine, popularly known as PIM, first appeared in Sydney in August 1930. Its founder and first editor was Robert William Robson (1885–1984), a New Zealand-born journalist, who noted on a tour of the Pacific in 1914 that the people of each island were always eager to hear news from others. The first 16 issues of PIM were in broadsheet newspaper format. Pacific Publications, which was founded to produce it, later became the publisher of the *Pacific Islands Year Book* and other handbooks. Robson, a strong advocate of free enterprise, was PIM's editor for 30 years. His successors (as joint editors) were

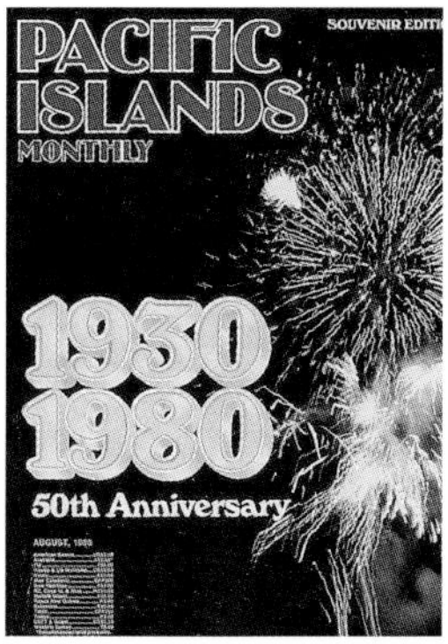

Judy Tudor (1910–97), a New Zealander, who had joined PIM during World War II, and Stuart Inder (1926–), an Australian, who had been the first radio journalist in Papua New Guinea after the war. Inder was sole editor from 1964 until 1975 and again in 1979–80. There have been numerous editors since then. PIM experienced lean times during the depression and after Japan entered the war. Its heyday was from about 1960 to 1970 when each issue ran to 150 pages at least—more than 2½ times as many as in recent years. Melbourne interests acquired Pacific Publications outright in 1975. The *Herald and Weekly Times*, a later owner, became part of Rupert Murdoch's publishing empire in 1987. PIM has been published from Suva since 1988.—RL2

■ ***Islands Business*** *Islands Business* is the main business news magazine of the Pacific islands region, the flagship publication of the Islands Business International publishing group in Suva. Carrying information on political and economic trends and events in the Pacific, it has been published monthly in English since 1974.

Managing director: Godfrey Scoullar. Publisher: Robert Keith-Reid. Editor-in-chief: Peter Lomas. Editor, *Islands Business*: Laisa Taga. Other titles produced by Islands Business International include *Air Fiji Inflight*, *Fiji Accountants Journal*, *Fiji Islands Business*, *Islands*, *Lulu Tai*, *Pacific Fishing*, *Pacific Power*, *South Pacific Aviation*, and *South Pacific Tourism*. Website: http://www.islandsbusiness.com/

■ ***Perfect Beat*** Established in 1992, and published biannually, *Perfect Beat* is a research journal dedicated to the study of the music and cultures of indigenous and Euro/Asian/North American migrant cultures in the Pacific since the late 1800s. In its focus on contemporary music and popular culture, it differs from more traditional ethno-musicological studies by addressing a range of outcomes of cultural, political, economic and technological contact and 'development'. The journal's principal regional focus is on Australia, New Zealand, Hawai'i, Papua

PACIFIC TRADE PROSPECTS

Fiji-Samoa-Tonga

A STRONG SPIRIT OF OPTIMISM

Written for The Pacific Islands Monthly by Sir Maynard Hedstrom

I CAN SPEAK, on trade developments and prospects, only of the three groups in which I am personally interested—Fiji, Samoa and Tonga.

Business in Fiji is depressed by the very low price of our primary products; but there are other factors which give hope for the future.

Though our sugar is selling at, or below cost of production, the Colonial Sugar Refining Co. Ltd. continues its policy of expansion and consolidation, and continues to expend money in improvements which are intended to effect permanent reduction in the cost of production. The policy of establishing peasant farmers as growers of sugar is working out very successfully, so that when the pendulum swings and world production and consumption become more nearly balanced, the Colonial Sugar Refining Co. Ltd. will be in an excellent position to take advantage of the improvement in market conditions.

The copra producer, also, is having a rather "thin time" and, in the case of the small man, the selling price is almost below the cost of production. On the other hand, the output of the Colony is steadily increasing—partly owing to the successful work of the entomologists of the Coconut Committee. Producers will have to study economy during the present period of depressed prices and, when the market recovers, they will benefit substantially by the increased production per acre.

Owing to floods, last December, banana shipments have been greatly reduced; but that is a temporary condition, and shipments will be back to normal about the end of the year.

BUTTER AND PINEAPPLES

Our little dairy factories are fully supplying local requirements, and we are exporting regularly to Honolulu and Canada.

The shareholders in the two small pineapple factories have confidence in the ultimate success of that industry. Probably, by January next, the Hawaiian Pineapple Co. Ltd. will have come to a decision as to whether they will commence operations on a commercial scale on the land over which they hold options. They have studied the proposition very carefully and, if they decide to establish themselves in Fiji, there can be little doubt that the venture will be successful.

Our aim here is to get greater variety in our products, so that we may not be entirely dependent upon one or two lines, but build our prosperity on a broader basis.

Public finances are very sound, but undoubtedly the Government will have to cut down expenditure during the next year or two, in this period of low prices. Because our exports are always substantially in excess of our imports, producers have benefitted considerably by the exchange position.

The number of tourist visitors increases year by year, and, this year, we have been favoured with exceptionally good weather, which has delighted our visitors.

POSITION IN SAMOA

In Western Samoa the financial position is not unlike ours in Fiji—they depend upon copra and cocoa, and trade is affected by the low prices of these two products.

On the other hand, their export of bananas is increasing steadily, and the shortage in Fiji has given Samoa an excellent opportunity of competing in the New Zealand market.

TONGA'S GOOD RECORD

The little island kingdom of Tonga is entirely dependent for revenue upon its copra production — consequently it feels the results of the depressed market more severely than either of the other groups.

Sir Maynard Hedstrom

Here, also, the Government is endeavouring to encourage the production of bananas. There is no difficulty about producing excellent fruit. The trouble is transportation, and the Tongan Parliament has indicated that it is willing to consider a small subsidy to any vessel which will carry bananas regularly to New Zealand.

Owing to careful administration, under the guidance of the British Agent and Consul, the Tongan public finances are in a very sound condition — it is probably one of the few governments in the world which has an actual cash balance in the Treasury.

Speaking generally, it seems probable that these three groups will, in the future, do an increasing volume of trade with Great Britain, Canada and New Zealand, which countries give some preference to their products.

N.G. TARIFF

Canberra, Aug. 16.

A number of alterations have been notified in the New Guinea Customs tariff. The following are the principal changes:

	Was	Is Now
Tobacco, manufactured, per lb.	2.6	4.8
Automobiles and Accessories	10 p.c.	20 p.c.
Linseed Oil	3 p.c.	10 p.c.
Aeroplanes and Parts	3 p.c.	10 p.c.
Mining Machinery and Parts	3 p.c.	10 p.c.

The other items are unimportant.

The duty on trade tobacco remains unaltered at 2/6 per lb.

DEATH OF "AUNT" NINNIE YOUNG

Descendant of Bounty Midshipman

From Our Own Correspondent

Norfolk Island July 25.

I HAVE just returned home from one of the most moving and picturesque ceremonies I have ever witnessed—the burial, after sudden death, of one of the remaining Pitcairners.

Old Miss Young—or Aunt Ninnie, as she was generally and most affectionately known—was actually born upon Pitcairn, and brought to Norfolk when she was only two or three years old, when the descendants of the Bounty mutineers were transferred from their overcrowded island to Norfolk

Her father, who was appointed first magistrate and leader of his people upon their arrival here, was grandson of the Midshipman Young, who together with the First Lieutenant Christian, led the mutiny upon the "Bounty," cast adrift the captain and other officers, sailed the "Bounty" back to Tahiti, where they took native wives—magnificent women of a magnificent race—and sailed further on to Pitcairn, where they sank the ship and settled ashore.

Young came, no doubt, from a middle-class, conventional family, where the children were taught to speak almost reverently of their parents; and that tradition was evidently maintained in the succeeding generations, for dear old Miss Young would talk to me of "Dear Papa" and "Dear Mamma" in the best Victorian manner, and I loved to listen to her.

Her name, all her life long, was synonymous with charity, goodness and the deepest religious feeling and, islanders and mainlanders alike, we all had tears in our eyes as we stood around her grave this morning in the quaint old cemetery, set beside the wide blue sea, beneath the wide blue sky, and joined in the singing of that wonderful anthem, "I was an-hungered and ye gave me meat. . . I was sick and in prison and ye visited me. . . ."

Those words might have been written for the dear old lady and, sung in the rich, warm, colourful voices, harmonising and blending in the passion of grief of her lifelong friends and neighbours, were almost intolerably moving.

It is a memory I shall carry with me wherever I may go.

Recent Visitors to San Francisco

These two Fijian village headmen created much interest in San Francisco recently when they arrived to attend the International Conference of Seventh Day Adventists. Residents of Fiji, to whom they are well known, will be interested to learn that the American papers said their names were "Ratu Jiali Tikowale and Setareki Shadrack Cevaca"; that they were the grandsons of cannibals; and that they were "dressed in English coats with smart cravats and short skirts instead of trousers." They dressed and posed for this photograph in San Francisco.

RADIO LINKS THE PACIFIC

Life In The Islands Has Been Revolutionised By Wireless

CENTRES OF THE PACIFIC NETWORK

SUVA (to Sydney, Samoa, Tonga, New Caledonia, New Hebrides, Gilbert & Solomon Is., Hawaii, and San Francisco).
3 sub-stations in Fijian Islands.

RABAUL (to Sydney, Gilbert, Solomon, Caroline, and Marshall Is.).
7 Sub-stations in Mandated Territory.

PORT MORESBY (to Australia).
1 Sub-station in Samarai.

NOUMEA (to Sydney, Suva, Vila).
Sub-stations in Allied Is.

NUKUALOFA (to Suva, Apia).
1 Sub-station in Tonga.

APIA (to Suva, Wellington and Hawaii, Cook and Hervey Islands).
6 Sub-stations in Samoan Islands.

TULAGI (to Rabaul and Suva).
1 Sub-station in Solomon Islands.

OCEAN ISLAND (to Rabaul, Nauru and Suva).
3 Sub-stations in Gilbert and Ellice Islands.

RAROTONGA (to Suva, and Wellington).
4 Sub-stations in Cook Is.

TAHITI (to Apia).
3 Sub-stations in Society and Marquesas Islands.

TRUK (to Japan & Rabaul).
Sub-stations in Marshall, Caroline and Marianne Islands.

PRACTICALLY all the Europeanised towns and settlements in the Pacific Island, and many plantations and trading stations, now have direct communication with the rest of the world.

The complete isolation of "the Islands," which early in this century was at once their greatest charm and their most serious handicap, is a thing of the past. The economic importance of this development, and its effect on the future of the Pacific, cannot be exaggerated.

TWENTY years ago, a man who lived in Bougainville or Vanua Levu, or Aitutaki, was almost as inaccessible as if he were buried in Darkest Africa. A letter written in London, or Sydney, or New York, might reach him six months after it was posted. To-day, a resident of almost any of the Pacific Islands, unless he is very remotely situated, can send a message to Europe, or America, or Australia, and receive a reply within twelve hours. To-day, people who reside in Rabaul or Vila, Suva or Nukualofa or Rarotonga, are little, if any more isolated, in relation to world affairs, than if they lived in New Zealand, Natal, or Newfoundland.

The magic of radio has revolutionised life in The Islands. Europeans may make their homes in the South Seas, enjoy the benefits of climate, soil-fertility, cheap labour, and the charm of sunshine and colour, while suffering none of the disadvantages of complete separation from their friends or their business principals, which residence in the Pacific entailed for so many decades.

The coming of wireless, and the development of the internal combustion engine, have removed from Islands life whatever terrors previously existed by reason of isolation and loneliness, and have greatly reduced the element of risk in the operations of planters and merchants. Even residents on the outer islands of the groups need be no more isolated than an Australian inland squatter. Radio takes the place of the squatter's long-distance telephone; and, instead of the grazier's motor-car, the planter has a fast-travelling, petrol-driven launch, which conveys him easily to the trading centre and the route of the mail-steamers.

Few people realise how completely the Islands are covered, now, by a network of wireless stations.

In the eastern and north-eastern Islands, nearest to Australia, there are three main wireless centres, which have direct communication with Australia, on the one hand, and, on the other with the smaller "feeder" stations in the Islands round about. Northwards, in the Marshalls and Carolines, and eastward in Samoa, the Cook Islands, Tahiti, etc., there are other similar radio organisations.

The history of what has happened in the nearer Islands provides an example of radio developments throughout the Pacific.

In 1914, when war broke out, Islands radio stations were just beginning to be commercially valuable. Already, a few had been established. It will be remembered that the first Australian casualties occurred when the Australian force was seizing the German wireless station at Rabaul; and that the Emden was trapped at Cocos Island, on November 9, 1914, because the radio operator got a message away to H. M. A. S. Sydney before the Germans could get ashore and destroy his apparatus. There was a German wireless station at Apia when the New Zealanders took possession of Samoa in September, 1914.

Radio Station at Bita Paka, near Rabaul

But it was not until after the War that the Governments of Britain, France, United States, Australia and New Zealand, as administrators of Islands territories, began to link up the fertile and beautiful lands of the South Pacific with a real network of wireless.

In 1922, while he was in England, Mr. E. T. Fisk, managing director of Amalgamated Wireless (Aust.) Ltd., interviewed the British authorities, and urged that, for purposes of efficient co-ordination and operation, the whole of the British radio stations in the South-western Pacific should be controlled by A.W.A. It was pointed out that other nations were becoming active in the installation of wireless stations in their Pacific Islands possessions, and that,

SEE MAP WITH CONTINUATION OF THIS ARTICLE ON PAGE 2

Pacific Islands Monthly (facsimile edition of first issue)

New Guinea and the island nations of the South Pacific Forum. A common theme in many of the articles published has been the development of new styles of popular music by indigenous peoples and their relationships with the technologies and institutions of 20th century media and music industries. Various articles have also addressed topics such as the global diaspora of Hawaiian music styles, and the discussion and promotion of various regional musics and musicians through the medium of the Internet.

Indigenous musicians and cultural activists contribute to the journal through interviews and co-authorship of individual studies. The editors have endeavoured to maintain a continuing relationship with musicians, communities and cultural groups who have been the subject of study—distributing copies of the publication to interested individuals and bodies, and publishing research updates on previous material (often at the invitation or instigation of the subjects of the preceding research). This commitment to involvement and dialogue has also resulted in key Pacific figures, such as leading Australian Aboriginal musician and activist Mandawuy Yunipungu and Papua New Guinean cultural entrepreneur Greg Seeto, writing material for the journal.—PH

Further reading

Hayward, P (ed.), 1998. *Sound Alliances: indigenous peoples, cultural politics and popular culture in the Pacific*, Cassell.

Perfect Beat, Centre for Contemporary Music Studies, Macquarie University, Sydney, NSW 2109 Australia <http://www.perfectbeat.mq.edu.au>

Foreign media

Foreign coverage of the Pacific islands is stereotypically exotic. Travel pieces form the bulk of copy, and even in hard news reports the exotic persists—coverage of a landowner dispute with a mining company, for example, is usually embellished within a discursive frame of deeply jungled terrain and primitive weapons.

Outside interest in the region diminished considerably in the 1990s due to the end of the Cold War, with the exception of the media of those western nations in Oceania: Australia, New Zealand, the United States (Hawai'i and Guam) and France. Renewed attention has come, however, as the French overseas territories of New Caledonia and French Polynesia accelerated toward a new political relationship with France.

Due to costs associated with maintaining a foreign bureau, few correspondents are based in the region. The Australian Broadcasting Corporation (ABC) and Australian Associated Press (AAP) have correspondents in Port Moresby, the *Australian* newspaper has a correspondent in Honiara, news agencies AAP and Agence France Presse have correspondents in Suva, and the Associated Press (AP) Pacific Bureau is based in Hawai'i. The ABC's international shortwave service, Radio Australia (RA), has two travelling correspondents, plus five journalists in its French service, and 5–10 in its *Tok Pisin* service, along with a network of stringers in the islands. Radio New Zealand International has a core Pacific staff of about six, and a similar network of stringers.—SL

PACNEWS

PACNEWS is the radio news exchange initiated in September 1987 by the Pacific Islands Broadcasting Association, through funding from Friedrich Ebert Stiftung. It aims to provide a regular news service to inform Pacific islanders of events in the region, to balance overseas coverage of regional events and provide 'development' news, to establish a free and indigenous flow of information and to inform an international audience more accurately and fully about Pacific life. Member stations include public broadcasters in Cook Islands, Fiji, FSM, French Polynesia, Hawai'i, Kiribati, Marshall Islands, New Caledonia, Niue, Norfolk Island, Palau, Papua New Guinea, Samoa, Solomon Islands, Tokelau, Tonga, Tuvalu and Vanuatu.

PACNEWS was dogged by controversy in its early years. In May 1990 the news exchange was forced to move from its Suva premises following Fiji's displeasure with 1989 Pacific Islands News

Association (PINA) conference resolutions calling for freedom of information legislation. It moved to a temporary base in the Auckland studios of Radio New Zealand before relocating to Honiara in December 1990. Housing shortages in the Solomon Islands capital once again forced a move in late 1993, this time to its current headquarters in Port Vila.

PACNEWS' current priority is to become self-funding—independent of overseas aid. Technology is assisting with this; originally news stories were disseminated by telephone and/or telex, then fax. In mid 1996, members' stations began trialling an email service.—SL

Media associations

The Pacific Islands News Association (PINA), a non-governmental organization representing the majority of regional media outlets (both print and broadcast) grew out of the Fiji Press Club in 1972. It has three stated aims: protecting media freedom, coordinating training, and fostering professional fellowship and cooperation. The Pacific Islands Broadcasting Association (PIBA), a consortium of the region's national broadcasters, was established in 1988 to oversee multilateral aid projects such as the PACBROAD training project and the PACNEWS broadcast news exchange.

Many rank and file journalists see PINA and PIBA as representing management interests. There may be some truth in this; 15 years ago newsroom staffs were small or non-existent. Today staff numbers a sizeable professional class, and one with its own objectives. The Pacific Journalists Association (PJA) was founded in 1989 to improve working conditions through trade union development, and to 'safeguard media freedoms' that neither governments with their political interests, nor media proprietors with their commercial interests can be trusted to preserve.

National media associations have in most cases followed the establishment of the regional bodies, and are more or less modelled on PINA. Though they receive little outside funding, they conduct training and provide professional support, and are quick to react to instances of government pressure. Press councils are also being discussed in the region, though with some delicacy given their popularity with regional governments. The PNG Press Council, founded in 1975, is the only such organization currently active.—SL

Electronic networking

At the end of 1996, the best estimate was that there were approximately 45 million people worldwide using the Internet, with roughly 30 million of those in North America, 9 million in Europe, and 6 million in Asia/Pacific. In the Pacific islands, Internet services have now become an integral part of the communications environment in an increasing number of countries. By November 1996, Fiji had over 400 dial-up modem users and 10 leased line users with several dozen web pages online. Solomon Islands reported over 80 dial-up users within the same time period while Vanuatu reported over 50 dial-up users and was experiencing a downturn in fax traffic as customers began using electronic mail (email) for their communication needs. Likewise, Internet services were initiated in Palau as part of Palau's *Light-Net 2000 Plan* to meet demand for Internet services primarily in the capital city of Koror.

The Internet also provided a means for rapid dissemination of information on and about the Pacific islands. In the early years of the World Wide Web (WWW or Web), academics with interest in the Pacific islands region began collecting large lists of hypertext data concerning the Pacific islands. Each list provides connection to a wealth of information on Pacific islands including weather, ocean temperatures, business opportunities, tourist information and 'chatty electronic exchanges' where many people exchange stories of their Pacific island homes and/or adventures. However, these and other informative web-sites were almost exclusively maintained on host computers affiliated with universities in western metropolitan countries.

First among the Pacific islands to go online was the government of Samoa with their 'Cradle of Polynesia' web-site developed and maintained for them by a company in the United States. Additional sites, like the Republic of the Marshall Islands web-site 'RMI Online', and the Tourism Council of the South Pacific also saw advantages to being early adopters, going online in early 1996 with their respective web-sites maintained on host computers in the United States and Australia.

In August 1996, the Fiji Visitors Bureau was the first in the Pacific with its own home page providing information on everything from a simple listing of hotels and the usual tourist information, to more adventurous activities 'off the beaten track'. Many businesses in the Pacific are also starting to come online, seeing potential benefit in marketing their products to people around the world. How successful this will be as a mechanism of generating additional trade and investment in the Pacific islands has yet to be seen and much will depend upon the success of introducing 'electronic commerce' on the Internet in general. However, a possible harbinger of things to come may be the development of offshore interests gaining permission to 'sell' Internet domain names under Pacific island national registrations or establish 'Internet casinos' for online gambling in the Pacific islands where secrecy laws protect such companies from close scrutiny.

Indigenous expertise in Internet publishing is also developing alongside improved Internet infrastructure in the islands. A number of indigenous web-site managers have discussed the need for an improved Pacific news service on the web, and for a regional news and current affairs web 'zine'. The vitality and diversity of migrant Pacific island communities around the world, as evidenced by the various discussion forums of Taholo Kami (Kava Bowl, Wantok Forum, Bula Forum, Melanesia Forum), Al Aiono (Polynesian Cafe) and 'Alopi Latukefu (SPIN Forum), ensures that projects such as these will soon come to fruition.—MRO

■ *Internet resources*

CocoNET Wireless.
[http://www.uq.oz.au/jrn/coco.html].

Cradle of Polynesia.
[http://www.interwebinc.com/samoa/].

Kava Bowl Forums.
[http://www.netstorage.com/kami/wwwboard/kavabowl.html].

Pacific Islands Internet Resources (PIIR).
[http://www2.hawaii.edu/~ogden/piir/].

RMI Online.
[http://www.clark.net/pub/rmiemb/].

South Pacific Online.
[http://www.infocentre.com/spt/].

WWW Virtual Library: Pacific Studies.
[http://sunsite.anu.edu.au/spin/wwwvl-pacific/index.html].

Every attempt has been made to ensure accuracy, however, such documents are ephemeral, with frequent URL (Internet address) changes.

seven

culture

culture

Contributors

Article contributors

AKS	Amy Kuʻuleialoha Stillman
ALK	Adrienne L Kaeppler
AP	Alison Pasciuto
AT1	Allan Thomas
AW2	Albert Wendt
DG1	David Goldsworthy
EKV	Emma Kruse Vaai
HRL	Helen Reeves Lawrence
JAB	Joshua A Bell
JFM	Jane Freeman Moulin
JM	Julian Makaʻa
JV	Joseph Veramu
KLC	Keith Lujan Camacho
KN	Karl Neuenfeldt
KRF	Kate Fortune
KS	Karen Stevenson
LB	Lissant Bolton
MAM	Michael A Mel
MJ	Margaret Jolly
MP2	Malcolm Philpott
MTC	Marjorie Tuainekore Crocombe
ND2	Norman Douglas
NJG	Nicholas J Goetzfridt
PH	Philip Hayward
PS3	Paul Sharrad
PSH	Phyllis S Herda
RGC	Ron Crocombe
RH	Richard Hamasaki
RM	Richard Moyle
RN	Robert Nicole
RW	Reina Whaitiri
SC	Susan Cochrane
TD	Tom Dutton
VH	Vilsoni Hereniko
WNG	Niel Gunson

Photo contributors

ANU Photography (The Australian National University, Canberra): 516; photographs by Akira Matsumura reproduced from *Contributions to the ethnography of Micronesia,* (University of Tokyo, 1918): 492, 554 (right)

Bell, Joshua A (Wyndmoor, Pennsylvania): 556

Fortune, Kate (Wellington): 540, 548, 549, 550, 551; photograph by Neil McLeod: 553 (top left)

Hendrie, Peter (Pacific Journeys, Melbourne): 491, 498, 501, 554 (left)

Hope, Geoffrey (The Australian National University, Canberra): 493

Kiste, Robert C (Center for Pacific Islands Studies, University of Hawai'i–Manoa, Honolulu): 555

Lawrence, Helen Reeves (Papua New Guinea): 494, 496, 497, 509; photographs by Yvonne Underhill-Sem: 495

McCall, Grant (Centre for South Pacific Studies, University of New South Wales, Kensington): 547

Mel, Michael (University of Papua New Guinea, Goroka): photographs by Richard Cornish: 483, 488, 489, 490, 503, 504, 505, 506

Ministry of Information, Republic of the Fiji Islands (Suva): 511

Ministry of Foreign Affairs and Trade, New Zealand: 486

National Library of Australia (Canberra): 542

Palau Visitors Authority (Palau): 553 (right)

Potter, Rosie (National Aboriginal Cultural Institute–Tandanya, Adelaide): 539

Saint Publishing Ltd (Auckland): reproduced courtesy of John Pule and Gow Langsford Gallery, Auckland: 538

Taylor, Carol (Canberra): 481 (detail), 485

Te Awekotuku, Ngahuia (Victoria University of Wellington): 509 (right)

Thomas, Allan (Stout Research Centre, Victoria University of Wellington): photograph by Helena Hughes: 500

Waters, Sheila (Melbourne): photographs by Sarah Chinnery (1887–1970): 552

ONE CULTURE AND IDENTITY

Culture, kastom, tradition

Culture is contested in contemporary Oceania, viewed by some as a lifeboat for survival, the canoe which connects pasts, presents and futures, and by others as the flotsam of traditions which must be passed by. A little word but a capacious concept, culture is used to account for differences between islanders and others, as well as differences between islanders. It is a concept with European origins, but it has been indigenized and internalized by Pacific peoples. Notions of culture relate to pre-existing ideas of difference between islanders, and 'culture' has been indigenously translated and reconceptualized, for example as *kastom* ('tradition' in Vanuatu, Solomon Islands and Papua New Guinea), *fa'a Samoa* ('the Samoan way'), *vaka vanua* ('the way of the land' in Fiji). (See THE PACIFIC WAY.)

'Culture' has its Western genealogy in the emergence of natural history in the late 18th century, combining a study of the natural world with that of human history. In seeking to account for the differences between peoples encountered in the exploratory voyages to the Americas, Asia, Africa and Oceania, scholars deployed concepts of race, of nation and of 'manners' or customs. Johann Reinhold Forster developed a philosophy and a typology of human differences based on his observations of Pacific peoples on COOK's second voyage. He differentiated between the 'two great races' of the Pacific, in some respects prefiguring the later 19th century labels of Polynesians and Melanesians. Although he talks much of the colour, stature and aesthetics of bodies, of faces, skin and hair, unlike the later racial sciences of the 19th century 'race' was for him not so much an immutable essence, a corporeal certainty, as something equally formed by environment and habit. Thus although Maori people were classified in the 'first great race' (whom DUMONT D'URVILLE would later label 'Polynesians') their being at the lowest level therein was seen to derive as much from the austerity of climate as from their isolation from ancestral origins. Enlightenment theories often conjoined biological, ecological and cultural determinism rather than separating and opposing them, as became common in later European social theory.

The later emergence of a concept of 'culture' is indistinguishable from an argument about the autonomy of culture, its floating free from the 'nature' of human bodies or ecological forces. German, French and British scholars from the mid 19th century stressed how the very different forms of human sociality and diverse patterns of ideas meant that 'culture' was autonomous with 'nature'. Yet although divorced from nature, it was still often seen through the image of the organism, as a functioning totality, as a whole characterized by differentiated integration and by interdependence, even harmony. Culture was moreover simultaneously seen as created by humans and as an overarching 'collective consciousness', deeply determining of actions and thoughts. Increasingly analogies were made with language—with the arbitrary and contingent connection of words and things, the signifier and the signified in later parlance, co-present with the compulsions of unconscious rules of language, to make sense (or nonsense). The culture concept has for the last century or so been central to the academic discourses of anthropology, sociology and cultural studies. But it is also part of everyday talk, and an especially potent and recurrent word in Pacific conversations.

From oral histories, material forms and linguistic patterns we know that in ancient Oceania the worlds of nature, human culture and divine ancestral forces were seen as one, as indissolubly connected. There were no doubt perceptions of difference between islanders long before Forster's typologies or later ethnographic accounts of Pacific 'cultures'. Ways of making gardens, fishing and cooking, forms of carving, making pots or cloth, styles of tattooing, genres of myth and ritual, divergent political patterns, differences in language—all such differences were likely adduced by islanders in discriminating between different peoples. Such differences were explained not as stages in an evolutionary development nor the diverging paths of human cultural creativity but most likely as disconnections ordained by ancestral actions, as differences which ensued from intimate attachments (and detachments) between

Bilas for female Mekeo dancer, Papua New Guinea

peoples and places, as recounted across the Pacific in stories of origin and of movement. Culture moreover was perhaps seen not so much as a shared way of life as a sacred trust, as something revealed from the past and prophesied for the future rather than created by living people. This did not preclude extraordinary innovation and change nor impede lively exchanges of knowledge, rituals and artifacts between islands and valleys, across culture zones, but it de-emphasized the willed creativity of living individuals or collectivities in that process, situating Pacific peoples as custodians of culture as of their land, rather than as authors or owners. This viewpoint has relevance for contemporary debates about cultural property or copyright.

The relationship between such pre-existing genealogies of Oceanic difference and the introduced concept of 'culture' has been fraught. Islanders probably first became aware of the foreign concept of 'culture' not from reading the texts of the Enlightenment era but from later, more proximate conversations with Christian missionaries. Although foreign and islander missionaries were primarily concerned with conversion in the spiritual sense, conversion also involved cultural transformation, towards ways of life and habits of thought grounded in the Outlands. In mission rhetoric, certain pagan practices were especially targeted—war, cannibalism, POLYGYNY, widow-strangling, KAVA-drinking, pig-killing and erotic dancing. In insisting on the converts' potential for change, missionaries often adduced a notion of 'culture', a way of social life which although it might have divine or devilish origins, was amenable to human action and willed transformation. 'Culture' was then perhaps first introduced to many islanders as something to be left behind, an obstacle to the future of Christian and material salvation. The narrative of culture as 'tradition' to be overcome, still a recurrent plot in contemporary developmentalist writing in economics and political science, arguably had its Oceanic origins in missionary ideas about progress through the dawning light of Christ.

Of course such a negative view of Oceanic 'culture' has itself been abandoned. Pacific peoples' attitudes to past or indigenous practices are complex, contextual and contested, and, in the last few decades especially, a process of celebration, reassertion and recuperation of 'culture' across the Pacific has occurred. This is patent not just in the cultural extravaganzas of regional and national arts festivals, the proliferation of museums and cultural centres in towns and villages but the way local political forms, predicated on rank, age and gender hierarchies have been defended against introduced models, how rituals once abandoned have been revived and how indigenous languages have been recorded, transcribed, analyzed and transmitted with renewed vitality. Some Pacific people, with evangelical faith in God and/or development, are opposed to such recuperations—perceiving the revival of fertility rites or HULA dances, the contemporary carving of ancestral images, the renewed TATTOOING of bodies as signs of resurgent savagery or satanism—the work of the Devil. However, most islanders today positively avow at least some aspects of indigenous culture while they simultaneously sustain a contextual and fluid negotiation of what is desirable and even what is 'indigenous'. Christianity, more often than capitalist economics or parliamentary politics, is usually given the generous mantle of indigeneity.

How Pacific peoples are daily negotiating 'culture' anticipates and even goes beyond some recent academic critiques of the culture concept. These have, in various ways, challenged the notion that culture is a static, organic or homogenous whole, and affirmed dynamism, diversity and contesting values and powers in creating culture. There are four large questions here. What is indigenous and how does 'indigenous' relate to 'traditional'? How do we get beyond a view of culture as a totality, while not resorting to an image of bits, of shards of culture, irredeemably fractured? What of those who see ancestral or traditional cultures as simply lived and who dismiss self-consciousness and reflexivity as inauthentic? And if culture is always critically reflected upon and not just lived, whose interpretations prevail? Contests over legitimating 'culture' can divide old and young, men and women, chiefs and commoners, those who live 'at home' and those 'away' in the towns of the region and the cities of the rim.

First, although there is still a tremendous recourse to the past and the 'ways of the ancestors', 'the past' for many islanders is seen in dynamic relation with present and future rather than as an epoch fixed in time. As Binney has shown so beautifully, contemporary Maori embody and speak and do not just represent or echo the voice of the ancestors in their 'redemption songs'. Moreover the pasts which become presents are not just the deep time pasts of ancient Austronesian voyagers but the pasts of Christian missions, of plantations, of colonial states and of foreign armies. Many Pacific peoples celebrate the first arrival of missionaries to their islands as an affirmation of local or national culture, not colonial intrusion. The stories of the labour trade to Queensland, of anti-colonial movements and of

World War II, are as much a part of the 'living culture' of older Solomon Islands men as the scripts of male cults. What is indigenous then is not just the 'traditions' of those generations before foreign contact, but the lived and retold experience of more recent ancestors, women and men. Although in some contexts the difference between the indigenous and the exogenous, the 'people of the place' and the foreigners is rhetorically stressed and insisted upon, many introduced artifacts have become icons of Pacific identity—Christian hymns, steel bush knifes, Mother Hubbard dresses and lavalavas are as quintessentially 'Pacific' as ritual chants, stone adzes, grass skirts or tapa BARKCLOTH.

It is not then a story of one culture—Oceanic—being displaced or supplanted by another culture—Western. Both such 'wholes' are gaping holes in our capacity for imagining culture. Yet although some find the alternative discourse of fractures and fragmentation alluring, contemporary Pacific cultures are also much more than a series of 'bits'—where Christian hymns and ritual chants, steel bush knifes and stone adzes, calico and tapa cloth jostle in serried ranks. In lieu of the idea of culture as a knowing totality, or relentlessly fractured, we might perhaps best think of culture on the model of conversation, of talk which has privileged contexts and speakers, but which spreads beyond the limits of one speech community and the borders of villages, islands or countries in enchained dialects connecting Pacific peoples who live in the region with those large diasporic communities of Polynesian and Micronesian peoples in Aotearoa New Zealand, Australia and North America. Both through the movement of persons and things, and increasingly through telephones, videos and the Internet and through the creations of literature and the visual arts, conversations are sustained about how to be Tongan, Samoan, Rotuman, Niuean.

In some discussions of contemporary culture and identity, it is often imagined that in times past or in remote villages, 'culture' was not the subject of conscious awareness nor critical reflection. Probably the intrusion of powerful foreigners with mercantile, mission and state projects to colonize and change Pacific peoples precipitated a greater self-consciousness and occasionally a codification of 'culture', as in colonial legislation about customary land tenure, or prescriptions about the authority of traditional chiefs or big-men. This process of codifying and even commoditizing culture has assumed new and different forms with those performances which are essential to tourist packaging of the Pacific. New forms of cultural TOURISM and ecotourism take people beyond the circuits of luxury hotels and resorts, the spectator sports of Fijian fire dances or *haoli hula*, to more intimate, quotidian spaces to see not just how the locals dance, but how they live, the daily arts of domesticity, and of harvesting land and sea.

Performances of culture are moreover not just for foreign audiences. Increasingly Pacific peoples are spectators to each other, most obviously in the reciprocal postures of being dancers and audiences, artists and viewers in the national and regional contexts of the South Pacific Arts festivals, the Asia-Pacific Triennial, the Pacific Wave in Sydney. But even the smaller Pacific weeks or nights held on university campuses or schools in Honolulu, Suva, Auckland and even Canberra foster a self-conscious performance of identity. Hau'ofa has observed that such performances can inflame a sense of insularity and particularity, of ethnic chauvinism, rather than promote mutual understanding and that connecting sense he desires, 'the Ocean in us'.

Although we may lament the 'loss' of culture or feel horror at its commercial aspects in tourism and cultural displays, this does not render such manifestations of culture 'inauthentic'. To suggest so, posits that there was/is a genuine culture, in times past or

'Face paint': Huli (Highlands) woman at a *singsing* at Mount Hagen, Papua New Guinea

remote zones, which was simply lived. This denies Pacific peoples, past and present, their human capacities for creative agency and critical reflection. It suggests that while transformations of European culture are readily interpreted as development or even progress, Pacific cultures can only move from being more Pacific to more Western.

Pacific peoples themselves use the language of genuine and false culture, of authentic and inauthentic expressions, where issues about authenticity suggest contests about culture. For Vanuatu, Grace MOLISA declared that the language of *kastom* or tradition was a Frankenstein's corpse revivified to intimidate women. Although in general very sympathetic to reconciling 'traditional' and 'modern' values, she exposed a gendered politics about whose interpretation of culture prevails, a politics which has been in part redressed by ni-Vanuatu women claiming more power in *kastom* in recent time. In some places men are more powerful than women, old people more powerful than young, and chiefly or high-ranking more powerful than 'commoners' or ordinary people, in pronouncing what is legitimate customary practice. But let us listen to the range of voices in such conversations about culture rather than presuming that certain voices have authority or hegemony. In the film *An Act of War,* we see prominent women leading many of the movements for sovereignty and the revival of language, arts and ancestral religion in Hawai'i. In the film *Kilem Taim,* we see young Vanuatu men and women articulating sympathetic attitudes to traditional forms of discipline, preferring *kastom jifs* (custom chiefs) to the police, perhaps expressing more sympathy for *kastom* than some of their parents drilled in the modernist values of missions and some millenarian movements. And we witness some older Tongan men like 'I Futa Helu, espousing democratic values rather than those of hierarchy and royalty. Such is the contested ground of culture in the contemporary Pacific.—MJ

Ni-kiribati children, South Tarawa

Further reading

Binney, J, 1995. *Redemption Songs: a life of Te Kooti Arikirangi Te Turuki*, Auckland University Press.

Clifford, J, 1988. *The Predicament of Culture: twentieth century ethnography, literature and art*, Harvard University Press.

Forster, J R, 1996. *Observations Made During a Voyage Round the World,* 1778, N Thomas, H Guest and M Dettelbach (eds), University of Hawai'i Press.

Hau'ofa, E, 1998. 'The Ocean in us', *The Contemporary Pacific*.

Jolly, M, 1994. *Women of the Place: kastom, colonialism and Christianity in Vanuatu*, Harwood Academic Press.

Keesing, R M, 1992. *Custom and Confrontation: the Kwaio struggle for cultural autonomy,* University of Chicago Press.

Molisa, G M, 1983. 'Custom', *Black Stone*, Mana Publications.

Morton, H, 1996. *Becoming Tongan: an ethnography of childhood*, University of Hawai'i Press.

Pule, J, 1998. *Burn My Head in Heaven = Tugi a ulu haaku he langi*, Penguin NZ.

Trask, H-K, 1993. *From a Native Daughter: colonialism and sovereignty in Hawai'i*, Common Courage Press.

White, G, 1993. 'Three discourses of custom', in G White and L Lindstrom (eds), *Custom Today, Anthropological Forum*, Special Issue, 6(4).

The Pacific way

The 'Pacific way' is a term used in a general sense to refer to a way of behaving that is considered to be appropriate for Pacific islanders. It has developed out of the various notions of CULTURE, KASTOM, TRADITION and especially TRADITIONAL SANCTIONS AND LAWS that are individually referred to as 'the Samoan way', 'the Melanesian way', and so on. It suggests a way of communicating comfortably and effectively with others, requiring a form of consensus in manners and attitudes, emphasizing shared cultural values such as courtesy, respect for parents and elders, generosity towards others, and generally 'Christian' ethics. Beyond this loosely agreed set of values, it also tends to be used to include reference to enjoying life in the form of feasting, dancing, games and sports.

The expression gained wide currency during the 1970s, after it was used in an address to the United Nations General Assembly in 1970 by Fiji's prime minister, Ratu Sir Kamisese MARA. It appealed especially to the mobile élite of the Pacific islands—politicians, senior government officers, leading churchmen and businessmen. When Tuiatua Tupua Tamasese Efi, Prime Minister of Samoa (1976–77), gave 'The 1976 Pacific Way Lecture' at the University of the South Pacific, he spoke about the Samoan way and its basic values and principles.

> I am convinced that for far too long we have imitated and inherited imported forms of development, life-styles, ethics, dress, thinking, etc. Over the years, these have taken a heavy toll of the vitality of our own ways, of our pride in our inheritance, and of our self-confidence and self-respect. I am equally convinced that we must rediscover and reaffirm our faith in our values—the vitality of our past, our culture, so that we may develop our own uniqueness, our own way of doing things, our own solutions to our problems...When the *alii matua* (senior chief) or the *tuua* (senior orator) senses that the end is near, he will perform the farewell ritual, [making] many references to the word *tofi*...*Tofi* is more than the right to land or to a title. It means the right to our way of life—our cultural and spiritual values, our work ethic...a work ethic that places the highest priority on service to the community.

Fijian lawyer Julian Moti pointed out in 1992 that the consensual ideology inherent in the Pacific way had a useful application in mediation and arbitration of disputes, because islanders were already comfortable with the concept of alternative dispute resolution. He argued that islanders have traditionally preferred to resolve disputes informally, without the aid or intervention of the official legal system (see also VILLAGE COURT SYSTEM OF PAPUA NEW GUINEA), having long recognized the importance of preserving ongoing relationships and maintaining a dialogue.

Ati George Sokumanu, the first president of Vanuatu (1980–89), has discussed the continuing role in the life of the modern nation of the democratic sharing of power, communal effort, and tribal and clan support.

> In the European way, you put up your hand to vote for a motion...The Pacific way can often be seen operating in an organization such as the South Pacific Commission. 'All in favour?' asks the chairman. There is total silence, and the motion is passed. This may puzzle the European because he thinks his way is democratic and that of the Pacific islander is not. Little does he know that many islanders have lived with democracy since time immemorial...Again the European tends to build a separate home for his grandmother or mother to live in when she is old. It is the European way of dealing with family ties. The Melanesian way is different...It is not only an extended family tie but a custom that has been practised from generation to generation. Grandmother or mother lives with you until she dies. This Pacific or Melanesian way...is a basic cultural and traditional entity, showing how traditional principles play their part in the daily life of the people...The task must be...to evolve a way of life, particularly a system of government, that is congruent with key principles of our traditional cultures, while adapted to the needs of the growing nation, and compatible with interaction with the rest of the world.

—KRF

Sources/further reading

Crocombe, R G, 1976. *The Pacific Way: an emerging identity*, Lotu Pasifika.

Efi, Tuitua Tupua Tamasese Taisi Tupuola Tufuga, 1995. *Englishing My Samoan: selected speeches and letters*, University of the South Pacific.

Moti, J, 1992. 'Settling disputes the Pacific way', *Pacific Islands Monthly* (June).

Sokomanu, Ati George, 1992. 'Government in Vanuatu: the place of culture and tradition', in Ron Crocombe et al (eds), *Culture and Democracy in the South Pacific*, Institute of Pacific Studies, University of the South Pacific.

■ ***The pan-Pacific person*** The term refers to persons who have a multicultural, multinational orientation, who have a strong affinity with the whole Pacific islands region. All of them also have an identity with one (and sometimes more) nations within it. They are most evident in the over 300 Pacific regional organizations, and most come from the tiny minority of their home population who were born and at least partly brought up in the islands but have spent long periods abroad. (Of the half million Pacific islanders who live in New Zealand, Australia, the United States, Canada, Europe or elsewhere, only the smallest fraction has returned to the islands to live).—RGC

■ ***Wantok*** This is a TOK PISIN (New Guinea Pidgin) word derived from English which literally means 'one language'. Originally used to refer to anyone speaking the same language as oneself, it is now used to refer to any friend, mate or acquaintance, and in certain situations may be used to express unity or solidarity amongst a group of strangers who are in conflict with another, non-Tok Pisin speaking, group. The word is so regularly used that it has now passed into Papua New Guinea English with its 'friend' or 'mate' meanings. It is also used as the title of a weekly newspaper in Tok Pisin, published by Word Publishing Company which is owned by the four major churches of Papua New Guinea—the Catholic, Lutheran, Anglican and United churches.—TD

Greetings from the Pacific islands

Aloha (Hawai'i)
Amole (Irian Jaya)
Apinun/ia namo (Papua New Guinea)
Bula/namaste (Fiji)
Fakalofa atu (Niue)
Iakwe (Marshall Islands)
'Ia orana (Tahiti)
Kaselehlie (Pohnpei)
Kia ora (New Zealand)
Kia orana (Cook Islands)
Konichiwa (Ryukyu Islands)
Malo e lelei (Tonga)
Mauri (Kiribati)
Talofa (Samoa)

TWO DRESS AND DECORATIVE ART

Body decoration (*bilas*) in Papua New Guinea

Various forms of body decoration are practised by all peoples. Clothes, shoes, earrings, hairstyles, wigs, make-up, tattoos, hats, masks, rings, feathers and a host of other odds and ends are combined to decorate the body. In Papua New Guinea body decoration is known in TOK PISIN as *bilas*. *Bilas* relates to both the items used in decorating and the process of decoration. *Bilas* as a social practice is engendered by people and its meaning and significance must be given by the participants. The *bilas* described here is merely a partial survey of the cornucopia of PNG *bilas*.

Dancers of the mid-Wahgi area, Papua New Guinea

Dancer from the Morobe Province, Papua New Guinea, with striking head-dress

Papua New Guinea has had many cultural communities. Each group had its own language, laws, values, beliefs and *bilas* which governed their lives and gave them a sense of place. There was *bilas* for boys, girls, men and women. There was *bilas* for everyday wear and for specific occasions. *Bilas* today is not the same as that of a few years ago or even 100 years ago.

TATTOOING and skin cutting represent an aspect of *bilas* from our past. The skin and parts of the body were used for some of the most personal yet symbolic and spectacular *bilas*. In the SEPIK cicatrices were made on men, particularly on the chest and the upper back, as part of initiation ceremonies, in designs relating to their own traditions. The incised skin when cured became raised scars and formed beautiful and symbolic body patterns. Facial and body tattooing were popular among other groups. Some of the more spectacular tattoos were made in and around Central and Oro Provinces. Women in particular had their entire body covered with intricate patterns. Piercing of the nose, particularly the nasal septum and nostrils, took place in Central Highlands and further west towards Irian Jaya. Ornaments were attached to the ear lobes. Some areas cut and pierced the ear lobes, and in parts of Morobe Province entire earlobes were cut

Dancers from New Britain, Papua New Guinea. The laplap, introduced in the colonial era, is now worn for performances

but there was emphasis on other *bilas*. Grass skirts were a feature of *bilas* in many coastal regions—usually for women, but in some areas men also wore styles of grass skirt for particular occasions. The design, patterns and colours on the skirts varied greatly. In the Highlands men wore woven knit-bags in front and cordyline leaves behind. Women wore several strands of finely strung twine with marsupial fur front and back with layers of woven belts around the waist. Kina shells, shaped into a crescent moon and strung around the neck, were worn by men and women. Beads made from plant seeds, or animal teeth (often dogs) were also worn.

Other groups have been noted for the masks and structures carried by dancers as part of their *bilas*. Most notable were the Sepik masks in the interior of East Sepik; the head-dress structures from the region between Madang, Morobe and West New Britain; the Dukduk and Tubuan masks of the Tolai, and the masks of the fire-dancers from the Baining area, both in the East New Britain Province. The Malanggan masks of New Ireland, and the Upe hats from the North Solomons were notable. These hats shaped like elongated vases were put on young boys and were only removed after they were initiated and became members of their community.

and then carefully wound around the rest of the ear. In some areas of Papua, women shaved one another's heads in decorative patterns.

Facial painting and the use of colours in combination with wigs and head-dresses is another aspect of traditional *bilas*. Face painting combined intricate designs with a wide variety of colours—from natural ochres and from plants. Traditional colours ranged from black to red, yellow, brown and white. Some spectacular facial designs can be attributed to the Mekeo area in Central Province, Central Highlands and parts of Western Highlands, Enga and Southern Highlands. Facial decoration accompanied wigs and spectacular head-dresses of feathers from parrots, lorikeets, birds of paradise and cassowary, and fur from marsupials like cuscus and tree kangaroo. Some styles of facial design, wigs and feathers were for women and others were specifically for men.

Other groups focused on a specific pattern with particular colour. In Milne Bay and on some outer islands, the facial design was usually a diagonal strip across the face in black and white. The body would be covered with coconut oil and plant fragrances. For others body colour was not so strong,

Female dancer from Enga Province, Papua New Guinea, wearing coloured plastic beads which are often part of modern *bilas*

From the Highlands perhaps the most recognizable were the spectacular *kankar* from the Goroka area. A *kankar* could vary in length from 2–4 m. A male dancer carried it on his back. Similar to the *kankar* but different in meaning and purpose were the Aida masks from the Gogodala area on the west coast of the Gulf province. The Asaro mudmen, also from the Goroka area, were noted for their facial masks of clay. Male dancers were adorned with clay masks that completely enveloped their heads. The rest of their bodies were caked in the same clay, and they wore sharpened bamboo fingernails. The dancers then moved very slowly with deliberate hand movements that seemed to be brushing away flies from their face.

The contemporary face of *bilas* has changed considerably, beginning with the change to Western clothes. Missionaries who told villagers to cast away their *bilas* (considered heathen), and encouraged them to wear white garments, were a significant influence. When government officials recruited people as labourers, carriers, interpreters and policemen, recruits were supplied with cloth to wear as a *laplap*, and some were given uniforms. Gradually with the influx of stores and goods coupled with political and economic changes, people began to buy and wear Western clothes.

Dancers from Central Province, Port Moresby area. Washable ink has been used to tattoo the dancers' bodies

Today people wear a variety of modern clothes. The *laplap* with an accompanying top called *kolos* or *meri blaus* has remained popular with women. Men sometimes wear the *laplap* but most choose shorts and shirts. In urban centres people wear a range of Western clothing, and *bilas* are usually worn only on special occasions, such as when new buildings are opened or a foreign dignitary visits. Inevitably the context in which dances and *bilas* emerged has changed. The items forming part of *bilas* have also seen numerous additions and deletions. Introduced objects have been ingeniously incorporated. Face painting has taken on new non-indigenous colours. Head-dresses are given added bits of colour using plastic and/or a page of a colourful and glossy magazine. Nylon and synthetic cotton in their various colours provide enticing alternatives to traditional *bilas*. Tattooing, a painful and time-consuming process before, has seen interesting changes. Dancers today have their bodies decorated with washable markers. For Papua New Guineans these new *bilas* and the performances serve as reminders of their history and heritage.

There is little doubt that the face of *bilas* will continue to change through contact with new cultures, ideas and art forms. Traditional *bilas* is shifting as people take on board interesting odds and ends substantiating the changing face of PNG culture. Today's dances and performances are located in fresh contexts, and what matters is that the local people have seen things and made choices relating to what is worthwhile and suitable for themselves.—MAM

Further reading

Strathern, A (ed.), 1981. *Man as Art: New Guinea body decoration*, photographs by Malcolm Kirk, Thames & Hudson.

Tattooing

The word 'tattoo' comes from the Tahitian term, *tatau*, noted by Captain COOK in 1769. Throughout the Pacific islands, there were forms of the art of tattooing the body in a permanent decoration that served ceremonial and social purposes. All adult men and women were tattooed in Polynesia, with a variety of specific designs that reflected social, political and economic standing. The extent of the tattoo's coverage varied also; often women were less tattooed than men; sometimes the ornamentation was restricted to thighs, hands and feet. In Micronesia, the traditional geometric designs used to decorate houses were often tattooed on arms and legs; women were tattooed on the lower legs and on the backs of their hands. In Marquesas Islands, tradition called for full body ornamentation, with intricate geometric designs. In New Zealand the facial tattoo (*moko*) indicated noble rank and provided an identification of ancestry; the right to wear it was strictly controlled.

The usual technique in most parts of Polynesia involved puncturing the skin with a broad comb, dipped in pigment, which was hammered with a wooden mallet. Ancient Maori tattooing used a small chisel (made of bone) to make a groove in the skin to which pigment was then applied. Metal chisels and thick needles have since replaced the bone chisel.

European missionaries opposed the practice and under their influence the prevalence of the art diminished considerably. In Tonga, for instance, missionary disapproval reflected a view of tattooing as a defacement of God's creation, and King George TUPOU I was persuaded that it should be outlawed in his first law codes introduced in 1839. There has been a contemporary revival of the art form, among young Pacific islanders particularly, but the 1990s renaissance has included developments that are non-traditional and therefore controversial. In Samoa, Aotearoa New Zealand and Hawai'i the practices of tattooing have been revived with novel forms and contexts, and with new meanings of masculinity and femininity (see GENDER). The *moko* is no longer a symbol of traditional status; and the practitioners of tattooing may even be women.—KRF

■ *Tattooing in Samoa* Historical accounts of tattooing in Polynesia are varied and conflicting. Problems in tattoo description arose because many early Western visitors let their beliefs influence their attitude towards tattooing, seldom referred to as an art form. Often, the art of tattooing was not recorded at all because it was not perceived as significant. Further, when tattooing was recorded, it was often noted that the practice would die out once people came to learn 'superior' Western ways. However, it is possible to compile from numerous sources an account of tattooing in Polynesia and Samoa which helps provide a deeper understanding of why the art of tattooing in Samoa, and Polynesia as a whole, is still such an important aspect of life.

No exact date for when tattooing entered the Pacific can be confirmed, nor is it clear if, when Polynesians arrived in Samoa, the art of tattooing was already a part of the culture brought from Southeast Asia. Evidence from LAPITA pottery found at archaeological sites throughout the Pacific provides a useful estimate of dates (between 1600 BC and the start of the Christian era), since Lapita pottery is marked in similar style and method to Polynesian tattooing. It is highly likely that these art forms migrated through the islands simultaneously.

According to legend, two Samoan women (goddesses, born as Siamese twins and later separated), Tilafaiga and Taema, were sent by King Tui Manu'a to visit his daughter on Fiji. In Fiji, they observed the custom of tattooing women, and decided to transplant it to Samoa. On departure the two women were given, as a gift from the royal family of King Tuifiti, a tattooing instrument. Tilafaiga and Taema began their long swim home. On their journey they carefully held their gift, while continuing to sing a chant the Fijians had given them: 'tattoo the women, but not the men'. Through the arduousness of their journey, or because they became distracted by diving for a beautiful shell on the ocean floor, the women became tired and confused, and inadvertently reversed the words of the chant. Back home in Samoa, they repeated the instructions as 'tattoo the men, but not the women'. This is why Samoan men today are more heavily tattooed than the women.

Oral history records that the first Samoan man to be tattooed was Tuiaana Tamaalelagi. The completion of his tattoo was celebrated for many weeks, and the most beautiful virgins came from all parts of Samoa to Tamaalelagi's house to see the tattoo and offer proposals of marriage. Not surprisingly, Tamaalelagi became one of the most married chiefs in Samoa. His last wife bore him a daughter, Salamasina, who became the first queen of all Samoa. Whatever the truth of the tale, its date (in relation to the origin of tattooing) may be obtained from tracing the names of the two women in Samoan genealogies. This places Tilafaiga and Taema around 1210 AD. Whether or not tattooing entered Samoa from migrations from Southeast Asia, a visit to Fiji, or via independent invention, one thing is clear: the art of tattooing has persevered.

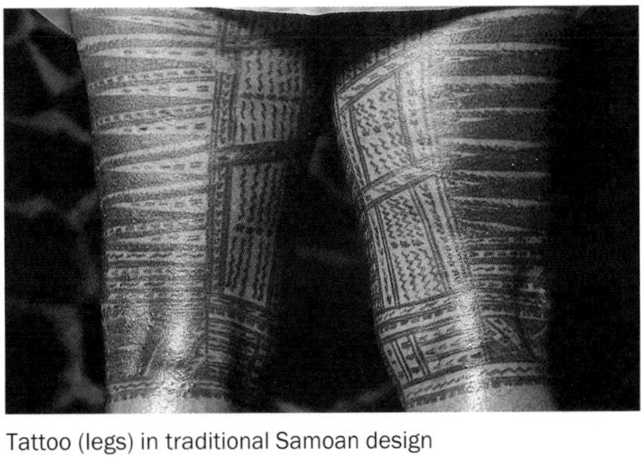

Tattoo (legs) in traditional Samoan design

The operation of tattooing was performed on young boys aged 12–15. It served as an initiation into manhood, and was cause for celebration. Usually, a young chief and other boys in his age-grade would be tattooed at the same time. A number of *tufuga*s (tattoo artists) were summoned for the occasion. This was often a costly procedure, with many fine mats being presented to the *tufuga* as payment. The tattoo on the young chief would be done before the others, and was of higher quality. In effect, the other boys served as sketch pads for the apprentice *tufugas*.

Instruments used were mallets with handles of bamboo or light wood, to which were lashed heads of tortoise shell with attached flat combs of pigs teeth or human bone. There were eight to twelve of these tools (called *'au*) with varying widths at the toothed end, ranging from about 10–60 teeth. The combs were dipped into the pigment, a mixture of water and ashes of the candle-nut (*Aleurites triloba*). This was then pounded into the skin with the wooden mallet.

The tattoo operation was painful and could take up to three months. Songs were often sung by family members to help the patient endure the pain. The small of the back was tattooed first, in a canoe design. Once the lower back was completed, the legs were tattooed. The final place to be tattooed was just above the navel, said to be the most painful part of the process. Completion was marked by a ceremony called *O le Lulu'unga-o-le-tatau* (the sprinkling of the tattooed), during which lighted torches were all extinguished simultaneously and a water-bottle was dashed to pieces. This was followed by the sprinkling of water from coconuts over each newly tattooed youth, a custom apparently intended to re-admit the previously sacred boys into society.

The *pe'a* or tattoo that extends from a man's back to his knees is linked to the passage into manhood. Instead of a circumcision, Samoan boys underwent tattooing. The *pe'a* represents the high status of the tattooed man—it was a mark of distinction, and without it the man was seen as unworthy. It has been suggested that the pain of tattooing during the initiation of manhood mirrors a girl's painful initiation into womanhood through childbirth. Both practices involve immense pain and bloodletting.

Many Samoan tattoo designs come from the environment, but usually in stylized or abstract forms. As well as the canoe motif, patterns often contain objects such as jellyfish, worms or caterpillars, starfish, birds, nets, and stripes resembling the lashing or rafters on a house. A tattoo was also used for identification. A man's *pe'a* immediately identified him as a person of status, and a tattooed man who died in battle would be easily identified. Finally, once a man had a tattoo he was identified as eligible for marriage. The *pe'a* is also viewed as a form of decoration, and is certainly a source of pride to many tattooed Samoans. Men are tattooed to increase their attractiveness to women, and the *pe'a* functions in a similar manner to clothing—as decoration. Further, being able to endure the pain of getting tattooed served as proof to women of how manly and strong a man was.—AP

Further reading

Gell, A, 1992. *Wrapping in Images: tattooing in Polynesia*, Clarendon Press.

Introduction of European clothing

Early European voyagers to the Pacific islands mostly accepted the great variety of clothing or lack of it which they noted. Generally they placed those wearing woven garments and clothes made of beaten BARKCLOTH in the scale of civilization while those wearing penis gourds, penis pins and scanty 'grass skirts' were regarded as 'savages'. As 'savages' were likely to be disregarded or fired upon in any dispute, perceptive islanders soon saw advantages in wearing European clothing. At first the new garments were a novelty. William BLIGH reported in April 1792 (25 years after European contact with Tahiti) that 'the quantity of old clothes left among these people is considerable'. He lamented the lack

Three Chamorro girls in Garapan, Saipan, c1915

Father and son with penis gourds and carrying an umbrella, in Irian Jaya, c1975

of the elegant barkcloth garments worn previously now replaced by 'a dirty shirt and an old coat and waist coat' saying that they were 'no longer clean Otaheitans, but in appearance a set of ragamuffins'. Nevertheless European clothing soon came to be regarded as symbols of status and rank, especially after visiting naval officers and other officials began making presentations to the local leaders of full dress uniforms and insignia of rank.

Although the first missionaries are sometimes blamed for forcing islanders to wear health-threatening clothing, this was certainly not so in early times and in all missions fields. The first LONDON MISSIONARY SOCIETY (LMS) missionaries were often reduced to rags while chiefs and islands sailors were fully accoutred. Some more enlightened missionaries argued that too much clothing was harmful and even as late as the 1830s the missionary John WILLIAMS was more amused than otherwise when received in audience by 'five naked queens' (the wives of Malietoa) in Samoa.

In regard to missionary teaching, Christian decorum only required decency in dress (satisfied by covering the private parts) and the covering of the head by female converts in church. When bonnet making was introduced in the 1820s as a means of meeting the Pauline injunction, some missionaries were shocked at the excesses of female finery worn to church. For their part Tahitian and other chiefly women had seen illustrations in the *Ladies Magazine* and fashion-plate prints from Europe. It was inevitable, too, that commerce followed the church as part of its civilizing mission. Cotton print garments and bales of Manchester calico soon put an end to barkcloth manufacture in the northern and eastern Pacific though it managed to survive in the central Pacific. For a short time in the 1820s the LMS attempted to establish a cotton industry in the Society Islands. Island women learnt to sew very early in the contact period and soon became adept at transforming coloured prints to their own designs. Whether or not the loose-fitting dress adopted by the islands women was a restrictive Mother Hubbard or a cool and comfortable *muumuu* depended on the prejudice of the beholder. Certainly in Victorian times, partly due to the development of photography, clothing did tend to become restrictive as evidenced by the daguerreotypes of missionaries often seen wearing tight-fitting clerical suits of missionary provenance.

Some distinctive customs and usages developed. In Tonga the ministers of the three main Methodist churches can be distinguished by their dress, ministers of the chiefly Church of Tonga wearing trousers rather than the traditional *vala*. In 1953 Queen SĀLOTE of Tonga standardized Tongan official dress by decree, combining practical European garments with symbolic Tongan items such as the distinctive *ta'ovala* or apron. The wearing of European dress is itself restricted by custom in many parts of the Pacific and at the end of the 20th century it is usually the islanders who are offended by the standard of dress of Europeans.—WNG

THREE PERFORMANCE

Cook Islands traditional music and dance

For Cook Islanders, music and dance are essential to everyday life. Apart from some forms of vocal religious music unaccompanied by musical instruments, most music genres are associated with dance or incorporate some dance gestures. Like other Polynesian music cultures, Cook Islands music and dance are closely associated with text; song texts and chants form part of the repository of oral literature. Because of the competitive nature of dance teams, Cook Islanders tend to view dance as a sport, rather than as art, although artistic presentation and other aesthetic considerations are important aspects of dance performance.

Since self-government in 1965, ideas about nationhood have led to the establishment of a number of national events, the most important being the annual celebration of Constitution Day. Held in Rarotonga, it usually lasts a week or more in August, and includes competitive performances of music, dance and drama, for which representative groups travel from the outer islands to participate. Other national events include Dancer of the Year (a competition for solo dancers) and an annual competition for school students—the latter aimed at promoting excellence in the performance of music and dance, and in fostering an interest in Cook Islands culture among young people. Gospel Day, celebrated annually on 26 October, commemorates the arrival of the first missionaries in the southern Cook group in the early 1800s. This religious festival is marked by pageantry, the singing of Christian songs

Members of Tauhunu Rua drum group performing at a wedding reception, Manihiki, Cook Islands. Upright footed drum, *pahu matatahi* (right), known as *pa'u mangō* in Rarotongan; and the *tini* (left), cabin-bread tin—both beaten with two sticks

and hymns, and dramatic performances (*nuku*) of stories relating to biblical themes or mission history.

The Cook Islands National Arts Theatre (CINAT) goes on tour overseas, and gives presentational performances within the Cook Islands. Members of CINAT perform songs, chants and dances from various Cook Islander music cultures. After a severe economic crisis in the mid 1990s, the government disbanded CINAT and cancelled the national constitution celebrations in Rarotonga; it also was unable to sponsor dance teams to perform at festivals overseas, such as the FESTIVAL OF PACIFIC ARTS.

Soon after the attainment of self-government, the government in Rarotonga made a conscious attempt to establish a national cultural identity. It set up a cultural division within the Department of Social Services, and firm rules for the national competitions in dancing and singing were established. In the 1980s, the cultural division was replaced by a Ministry of Cultural Development (Tauranga Vananga). This ministry is responsible for the continuing development of national collections of cultural material, maintenance of cultural heritage (including music, dance, drama and the associated material culture), and upholding national standards of performance and costuming. Its role has led to a strengthening of the Rarotongan hegemony, at least in the performing arts. In 1992 the ministry supervised the preparations and organization of the 6th South Pacific Arts Festival, held in Rarotonga. It has been influential in Cook Islands cultural revival and recreating traditional performing arts, such as the use of the previously obsolete nose flute and the *ka'ara*, an old type of slit drum from the southern Cook Islands from which two or more notes of different pitch could be produced.

In the atolls of the northern group, Manihikian and Tongarevan languages (spoken in Manihiki/ Rakahanga and Penrhyn respectively) are eastern Polynesian languages; Pukapukan language (spoken only in Pukapuka and its closely allied atoll, Nassau) is more closely associated with the languages of western Polynesia. Languages and dialects of the islands in the southern group are eastern Polynesian. The official language is Rarotongan (Cook Islands Maori). All government documents are in Rarotongan, as are the Bible and the Cook Islands Christian Church (CICC) hymnbook. As a result, Cook Islanders sing hymns and compose songs with Rarotongan texts, as well as performing and composing hymns and songs with texts specific to their individual island or atoll language/dialect. As the islands were a former dependency of New Zealand, many islanders speak and write English. Contemporary songs, both secular and religious, occasionally have texts in the English language.

Although each island group has its own chants, songs and dances, there are several music genres that are today common to all Cook Islanders. For

Manihikian dance group, dressed in costumes of white *rito* decorated with pearlshell and other shells, perform a drum dance (*hupahupa*) in the *'ura pa'u* competition held during the Constitution celebrations in Rarotonga, Cook Islands

competitions at the national level, the shared categories are: drum dance (*'ura pa'u*); hymn singing (*'īmene tuki*); a choral song with dance gestures (*ūtē*); action song (*kaparima*); and a dramatic presentation of a legend or historical account (*peu tupuna*). A choir competition also forms part of the program. Although each category is referred to in the program by its Rarotongan name, each competing group has its own style and technique, and costumes that identify its particular cultural origin. Costuming is generally genre-specific and, for national competitions, is made of locally produced materials.

Within individual communities, the performing arts serve important social functions. Secular songs and chants may be performed for praise, boasting, ridicule, welcoming an important visitor, social or political comment, fund raising, accompanying drinking parties, or simply for entertainment. Music and dance may serve as agents for emotional and psychological release, or for expressing ideas and behaviour that are normally not acceptable in other contexts. Children's play also frequently includes songs or chants. Singing and dancing often mark the major events in family life: a boy's first birthday, a boy's haircutting ceremony, a 21st birthday, or a marriage. These events are held in connection with feasts to which members of the extended family and friends are invited. Dance is generally presentational, and is performed by a group. Choreographed solo dancing is rarely performed in the village context; most solo dances are impromptu performances that enhance a particular occasion, such as a gift-giving ceremony to honour an important visitor.

Young people's songs incorporate elements of popular Tahitian, Hawaiian and Western songs. Many of these could be described as 'pan-Pacific pop' or as having been influenced by this type of music. The texts of such songs cover a wide range of subjects, including romantic love and courtship, the natural environment, and nostalgia (for people and/or places). Such popular songs are accompanied by an acoustic 'string band' (guitars and ukuleles) sometimes with the addition of a large skin drum or a tea-chest bass. In communities where electricity is not rationed, popular songs may be accompanied by an 'electric band' (electric guitars, drum machine and keyboard), although usually only for formal social occasions. In tourist locations, some groups regularly perform at hotels and other venues.

For religious services and ceremonies, unaccompanied hymns from two broad categories are performed: a homophonic European-style Protestant hymn (*'īmene āpī sāpati*) with Rarotongan texts from the CICC hymnbook, and a more complex, polyphonic hymn (*'īmene tuki*) with vernacular texts usually adapted from the Bible. The latter is similar in structure and musical style to a type of secular song (*'īmene metua*), but differs in textual content and performance practice. Additionally, modern evangelical songs, accompanied by guitars, are sung by young people; these Christian songs often have texts in English or Rarotongan.

Dancers from Manihiki pose for an action song (*kaparima*) at the Constitution celebrations in Rarotonga, 1985. The bodice of the garment is made of the fibrous leaf stipule of the coconut palm, as is the undergarment of the skirt or kilt. The skirt consists of threaded segments from the white inner stem of the *ngahu* plant (*Scaevola sericea*), a seaside shrub, and some segments have been dyed red and black. Polished pearlshell and strings of smaller shells decorate the dancers' necks and headdresses

Dances are accompanied by musical instruments, singing, or by a combination of the two, depending on the genre being performed. The *'ura pa'u* (and related drum dances of the Cook Islands, such as the *hupahupa* of Manihiki and Rakahanga) is a partnership between dancers and drummers. These vibrant dances are performed by groups of men and/or women who combine gender-specific movements in choreographed formations. The drumming ensemble usually consists of one large skin drum (*pa'u*), one or two footed drums (*pa'u mangō*), and several wooden slit drums (*pātē*), constructed in different sizes to obtain different tunings. In some villages, a 'cabin bread' tin (*tini*) or a wooden box is used as a drum, and is included in the drum ensemble to add a distinctive sound; such inclusions are not permitted for national competitions. In drum ensembles in the northern atolls, rhythms are often based upon the rhythms of chants, sometimes composed especially to act as mnemonic devices for the drummers. Chant texts may also serve to provide a theme for a drum dance and its choreography; dance movements may therefore have meaning, in relation to the original text. For southern Cook Islanders, drum dance movements are generally more abstract.

Action songs (*kaparima*) are also group dances, usually performed at a slow or moderate tempo, accompanied by guitars, ukuleles and a *pa'u*. The song is provided by a separate group of singers

Dancers and drummers of Tauhunu Rua group performing a drum dance (*hupahupa*) at a wedding reception in Tauhunu village, Manihiki, Cook Islands

and/or by the dancers themselves who perform synchronised movements that illustrate the song text; the interest lies mainly in the movements of the arms and hands. The *kaparima* was introduced to the northern atolls from Rarotonga. It is sometimes performed in combination with a drum dance to form a dance sequence.

The *ūtē* is generally believed to have been introduced from Society Islands to the southern Cook Islands, probably in the late 19th century. It is performed only infrequently by peoples of the northern group. The *ūtē* is a polyphonic choral song, performed by a group of men and women, either unaccompanied or accompanied by musical instruments such as a *pa'u* and guitar. The singers ornament the song with hand and arm gestures; occasionally, an individual will perform spontaneous dance move-

This double-headed drum, *pahu matarua*, known as *pa'u ma'ata* in Rarotongan, has its own name, Paravae, and is beaten with a single wooden mallet. Made more than 100 years ago, it is the oldest and most resonant drum in Manihiki. The maker was probably Kai Aranga who died c1920. The drum was restored in c1987 for the drum group in Tauhunu village, Manihiki, Cook Islands

ments to the side or front of the group, thus enlivening the overall presentation. Other kinds of chants, songs and dances are specific to individual island and atoll cultures; they are not performed at the national level.

Civilian brass bands have been a feature of musical life in Rarotonga for nearly 100 years. Smaller bands, such as the Boys' Brigade Band in Manihiki, also exist in the outer islands. Their function is a formal one and is often processional, to accompany wedding processions, or perform in parades on church days and national holidays.

The earliest audio-recordings of Cook Islander songs are phonograph cylinder recordings made by Alfred Knocks at the Christchurch International Exhibition (1906–07) in Aotearoa New Zealand, where invited groups from Mangaia, Aitutaki and Rarotonga performed. The greatest number of field recordings were made from the 1960s onwards, by various researchers; the majority of these recordings are housed in the collections of the Archive of Maori and Pacific Music at the University of Auckland. The Cook Islands National Archives (Rarotonga) also holds visual materials (photographs, films and videos) and audio recordings of music and dance.

Recordings that are commercially available have, in the past, often been made in New Zealand studios and released on various labels, such as Ode Records and Hibiscus. A recording studio in Rarotonga in the early 1970s consisted of a room containing basic recording equipment, and acoustically lined with cardboard egg cartons. Some Cook Islands recording studios have included Peter Story and Sons, Electrotek and Capricorn Studios, but these recordings were difficult to obtain outside Rarotonga. More recently, the Cook Islands Broadcasting Corporation and the Ministry of Cultural Development have been involved with commercial productions of audio-cassettes and videos: popular recordings or 'traditional' music, or selections of both.—HRL

Further reading

Buck, P H [Te Rangi Hiroa], 1944. *Arts and Crafts of the Cook Islands*, Bulletin 179, Bishop Museum.

Gill, W W, 1977. *Myths and Songs from the South Pacific*, Henry S King & Co, 1876; reprinted Arno Press.

McLean, M, 1980. 'Polynesia: 2. Cook Islands', in Stanley Sadie (ed.), *The New Grove Dictionary of Music and Musicians*, Macmillan.

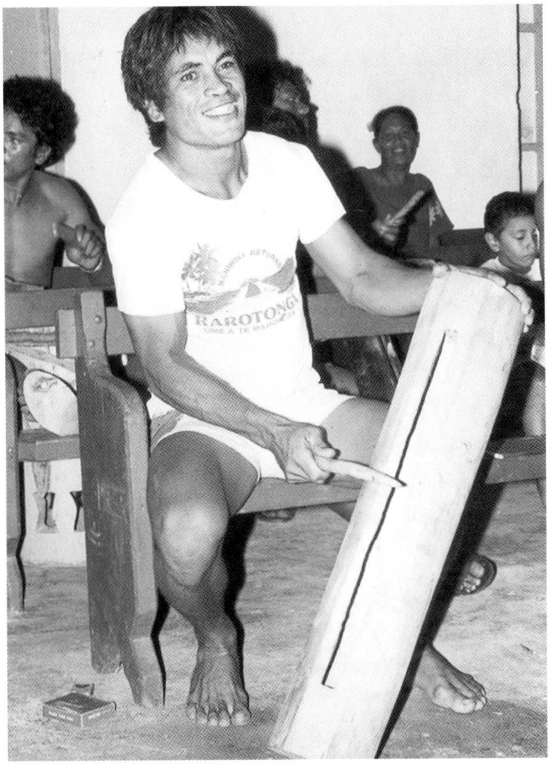

Tangi Toka, playing a large, low-pitched slit-drum during a rehearsal in the Sunday School building, Tauhunu village, Manihiki, Cook Islands. In the southern Cook Islands, *pātē* are generally beaten with two sticks; Manihikian drummers take pride in using a single stick just as rapidly

Music and dance in French Polynesia

Music is immensely popular in French Polynesia, in both the public and private realms, attracting performers and audiences from across the socioeconomic spectrum. A wide range of musical styles is enjoyed and supported, from traditional Tahitian dance songs to contemporary music such as techno or reggae, and choral singing in indigenous, introduced or hybrid styles. In addition, minority groups nurture their own musical traditions. The Conservatoire Artistique Territorial and the concert society Musique en Polynésie, for example, provide performances of European classical music; Chinese cultural associations stage occasional public appearances and competitions highlighting Chinese music and dance. Despite this broad scope of activity, however, the focal point of the performing arts remains firmly on those genres that Tahitians embrace as indigenous or indigenized.

Popular culture and the local recording industry acknowledge and promote well-known solo singers, such as Gabilou, Esther Tefana and Bobby Holcombe, who were among the stars of popular music from the 1970s into the 1990s. Within the world of traditional arts, however, Tahitians view music and dance as participatory group activities rather than virtuosic solo exhibitions. Islanders may recognize outstanding artists such as choreographer Coco (Jean Hotahota), musician Iriti Hoto or dancer Makau Foster, but know these individuals through their work with performing groups—not as soloists. Music and dance unite people in collective goals and experiences and, as such, contribute to the social and artistic life of the community. Music accompanies worship, private or public celebrations and relaxation; music and dance together are an important part of community festivities, official receptions, school programs, social events sponsored by various organizations, and any occasion when Tahitians wish to highlight the richness of their cultural heritage.

Tahiti tends to represent French Polynesia in the eyes of the world, despite the fact that the territory includes 128 islands grouped in five archipelagos, each with its own distinct culture and arts. Appreciation of this cultural plurality is slowly emerging, but Tahitian culture remains the predominant image in both islander and outsider views of French Polynesia. This image establishes Tahiti as the artistic centre for the territory, which in turn contributes to the continued hegemony of Tahitian music and dance.

In music, such dominance means that Tahitian song types are widely-known and performed throughout the islands. These genres include: *hīmene tārava* (large group polyphonic songs with either sacred or secular texts and up to nine vocal parts), *hīmene rū'au* (indigenized songs strongly associated with the Protestant hymn-singing tradition and having two to five parts), *'ūtē* (satirical songs for one or two singers accompanied by a small group of ukulele and guitar players who also provide back-up vocal parts), and popular entertainment songs (island tunes sung in Tahitian and accompanied by the typical Polynesian string band of guitars and ukuleles).

Tahitian dancing, an important ingredient of most large-group performances, generally features two main genres—*'ōte'a* (group dances performed to the rhythms of a drumming ensemble) and *'aparima* (story-telling dances accompanied by string band and bass drum). Less frequently-performed dance types include the *pā 'ō'ā* and the *hivinau*, both circle dances that incorporate a leader-response recitation to rhythms supplied by a drumming ensemble. The gender-specific dance movements that distinguish Tahitian dance (*'ori tahiti*) include revolving hip movements for women (*fa'arapu*) and a scissors-like opening and closing of the knees for men (*pā'oti*). When these movements occur in social couple dancing, Tahitians refer to the dance as *tāmūrē*.

Tahitians generally learn music and dance by joining an established group and repeating complete compositions in a rehearsal setting under the guidance of a music or dance *ra'atira* 'director'. New methods of instruction, however, include formal classes offered by private music or dance schools and the government-sponsored conservatory. In these class settings there is greater focus on the individual's acquisition of technique and a subsequent isolation and codification of dance steps and instrumental techniques.

Musical instruments range from the electronic, used in global contemporary popular music, to those associated with traditional performance. This latter group includes a standard drumming ensemble consisting of three to five wooden slit-drums *tō'ere*, a single-membrane *fa'atete* drum (played with two mallets), and the double-membrane *pahu* (played with one padded mallet). In the 1980s and 1990s, musicians expanded this ensemble to comprise as many as 20 drummers, especially for grand occasions, and revived earlier instruments such as the tall single-membrane drum *pahu tupa'i rima* (struck with the hands), *ihara* (struck bamboo rattle), *vivo* (flute), and *pū* (shell trumpet). Ukuleles and guitars accompany *'aparima* dances and popular songs. Locally produced ukuleles (*'ukarere*) provide inexpensive alternatives to imported instruments. Both four and eight-string models exist, with or without a membrane, and body shape varies widely; innovative double-necked versions appeared in the mid 1990s.

Contemporary performances of traditional music and dance reflect a complex interaction of Pacific-wide concerns and local practice. The performance is, in essence, a social stage on which the community simultaneously incorporates international ideas or trends and yet affirms its unique cultural history and specific local identities. On this stage, Tahitians not only define themselves in relation to their neighbours, they also refine the oppositional forces of maintaining traditions and desiring novelty. The joint processes of negotiating regional or local identities and weighing the respective value of tradition or innovation are fundamental challenges facing French Polynesian performing arts in the late 1990s.—JFM

Tahitian dancers, 1996 Heiva at Bora Bora

Further reading

Moulin, J F, 1979. *The Dance of Tahiti*, Christian Gleizal/Les Editions du Pacific.

——, 1996. 'What's mine is yours? Cultural borrowing in a Pacific context', *The Contemporary Pacific*, 8(1).

Hawaiian hula

Hula—Hawaiian dance—spans a range from sacred dances for the gods, honorific dances for royalty, and dances for entertainment. In pre-European Hawai'i, all phases of hula training and performance were surrounded by rituals to hula's deity, the goddess Laka.

In contemporary practice, hula is divided into two categories, on the basis of performative characteristics. In 'ancient hula', called *hula kahiko*, chanted poetic texts provide the basis for choreographic interpretation, and indigenous percussive instruments provide rhythmic accompaniment. In 'modern hula', called *hula 'auana*, dances are performed to the accompaniment of sung poetic texts and Western stringed instruments such as guitar, steel guitar, ukulele, bass (upright or electric), and even piano.

Named categories are also distinguished according to attributes of sacredness and poetic format.

Hula pahu are dances accompanied by the *pahu*, a sharkskin-covered log drum. Pieces in the pre-Christian repertoire are dedicated to the most sacred gods, and movements are thought to derive from activities during state rituals in outdoor temples. *Hula ʻālaʻapapa*, also held to be sacred, are dances accompanied by the double gourd *ipu*; these dances honor prominent historical figures. The *hula kuʻi* emerged sometime in the 1860s. These dances are performed to poetic texts that are divided into stanzas of uniform length, usually two or four lines, and accompanied by stringed instruments. When poetic texts in this format were chanted and accompanied by the *ipu* or other indigenous percussive implements, the dances were classified as *hula ʻōlapa*. It is in the *hula kuʻi* and *hula ʻōlapa* that the skirt of shredded leaves or grass, imported by labourers from Gilbert Islands, came into vogue, initially augmenting, then replacing, barkcloth or fabric skirts. Finally, English-language songs, called *hapa haole* songs, appeared by the early 1900s, and were used in hula performed mainly in tourist venues.

Poetic texts called *mele* provide the basis for gestural interpretation; choreographies are set to precomposed texts. Hula movements consist of hand and arm gestures that depict key aspects of poetic texts, and named lower-body motifs whose primary function is to maintain a motoric rhythm. In *hula pahu*, *hula ʻālaʻapapa* and *hula ʻōlapa*, there is a division of labour between dancers, called *ʻōlapa*, who execute the choreographies, and chanters, called *hoʻopaʻa*, who recite the text and provide rhythmic accompaniment. In *hula ʻōlapa*, seated dances require that dancers recite the text themselves, often while manipulating hand-held percussive implements. These implements include feather-decorated rattles called *ʻulīʻulī*, split bamboo single-node poles called *pūʻili*, rhythm sticks called *kālāʻau*, and waterworn pebbles called *ʻiliʻili*.

Hula is passed from teacher, called *kumu hula*, to student, called *haumana*, in schools called *hālau hula*. Since the 1970s, hula competitions have provided the major venue for performance. Initially established to encourage the perpetuation of repertoire from prior generations, hula competitions have also stimulated the composition of new texts and choreographies. Innovations in movement styles include quicker tempos and a highly drilled militaristic style popular among men's groups. The pre-eminent annual event is the Merrie Monarch Hula Competition, held over three nights in Hilo on the island of Hawaiʻi during the week following Easter.—AKS

Further reading

Barrere, D, Pukui, M K and Kelly, M, 1980. *Hula: historical perspectives*, Pacific Anthropological Record 30, Dept of Anthropology, Bishop Museum.

Kaeppler, A, 1993. *Hula Pahu: Hawaiian drum dances, 1: Haʻa and Hula Pahu: sacred movements*, Anthropology Bulletin 3, Bishop Museum.

Stillman, A K, 1998. *Sacred Hula: interpreting the historical hula ʻalaʻapapa*, Anthropology Bulletin 8, Bishop Museum.

Dance in Tokelau

The principal dance performed by Tokelau island communities is the *fatele*. Although it has much in common with Tuvaluan *fatele* which spread from the Ellice Islands to become the *batere* of Kiribati and other dances of the region, yet Tokelauans regard this as a special 'national' dance of their islands.

Fatele may be performed informally at cricket matches, where the batting side sing and dance to encourage (*lape*) their players, and at any communal gatherings such as those of women weaving mats. *Fatele* are also sung in other social contexts in the home, in a canoe, and elsewhere. But the major performances of *fatele* occur at *fiafia* or evening entertainments in which two or more groups perform alternately. The typical *fiafia* in Tokelau communities involves a contest between two sides (*faitu*) of a village, who also compete in sports. The sports and *fiafia* together with feasting mark special saints days and other important occasions such as the arrival of official visitors or interisland *fono* (meetings), and the Christmas–New Year season.

In a *fatele* a short text, with its melody and choreography, is repeated several times—three, four or more. The text is sung in two to four musical parts (*malu*, *tena*, *ato*, *uhu*) accompanied by the box drum (*pokihi*) and sometimes the tin drum (*apa*). Some dance gestures (*taga*) express images or ideas in the text, other gestures are decorative. The text draws from Bible stories, events of current interest or traditional activities, or (as in the example below) a traditional tale.

Tala o kakai mai anamua
Te ulugaliki na olo fagogota
Tokalalaga ma Hina
Oho ake ai te aitu Holopuga
Fakaino ia Hina ki lalo o te tai
Tagi faikaukau ko Hina
Tagi Hina Tokalalaga tuku mai te vaka e.

A legend from olden times
Of the couple who went fishing
Tokalalaga and Hina

But the spirit Holopuga
Pushed Hina out
Hina went swimming and crying:
Tokalalaga bring me the canoe.

The principal musical feature of the *fatele* performance is an acceleration of tempo in the repetition of the *fatele*. After an initial slow rendition, the verse is repeated to accelerating tempo; associated changes with the acceleration are a rise in pitch, an increase in the volume of singing and drumming, and a greater dynamic in the dance gestures and dance movements. Instrumental in achieving the desired acceleration and the excitement which it engenders is the *fakamatagia*—cries of encouragement—through which performers signal their own state of excited involvement and support. This change in the *fatele*, from an introverted, quiet opening to a dynamic and noisy conclusion, is the main feature of the performance. The smooth transition is a matter of dancing experience and performers' pride. It also reflects a social feature, expressing the dynamics and personality expectations within Tokelau society.

The *fatele* itself is a short dance usually only 4–5 minutes in length though the performance can be lengthened by interludes and interpolations which act as introduction (*taki*), finale (*tuku*) or a line-changing interlude (*hui unu*) in which one of the lines of the performing group comes to the front in a sung-and-danced section of the performance. The origin and development of these dance routines within the *fatele* performance is scarcely known, although names suggest links with other such phenomena in Polynesia. The line-changing routine is frequently used; in an evening performance each of the lines of the group will perform in the front row, reflecting the egalitarianism of Tokelau society.

The *fatele* is the predominant dance in Tokelau, but some other music and dance forms are given a place at *fiafia* and other gatherings. Samoan dances (an introductory *laulausiva* and a final *tau'oluga*), Cook Island dance CLOWNING (*upaupa*), and the stick dance from Wallis and Futuna (called here the *hake*), all originate in the specific historical links with neighbouring islands particularly during the mission period and early contact.

An earlier stratum of songs and dances is particularly valued for its ancient lineage. These accord with the general types found elsewhere in Polynesia but have here a specific Tokelau form: the dance with paddle-like implements (*tafoe*), old dances (*hiva hahaka*), and old songs (*pehe anamua—haumate, viki, tuala* and *vale*).

Tokelau Islanders performing at the Pacific Drum Festival, 1989, in New Zealand. The costume and ornaments—skirt (*titi*), head garland (*pale*), and neck garland (*fau*)—are all made from modern materials, using traditional designs

Many Tokelauans compose *fatele* but only those of long experience are recognized by the term *pulotu*. Composers are influential and individual forces within the traditional music system. As in other Polynesian composition, the text is the first element created and a melody is envisaged for the words. The choreography of gestures may be developed by the group or by the composer. Other elements such as the part singing, the acceleration, and the dance movements which mark time are added in the customary way by the performers. Once a work has been performed it may be copied (and slightly altered) by any other group. *Fatele* spread rapidly from one group of performers to another, and between the islands and New Zealand.—AT1

Further reading

Thomas, A, 1996. *New Song and Dance from the Central Pacific: creating and performing the fatele of Tokelau in the islands and in New Zealand*, Pendragon Press.

Samoan traditional music and dance

American Samoa and Samoa, although divided politically into two countries, present an essentially single cultural profile in traditional music and dance. Traditional melodic instruments such as the nose flute and panpipes have been obsolete since the early 1900s, when their principal function of private entertainment was supplanted by the arrival of gramophone records and, later, a variety of audio-visual devices. Only one type of song-accompanying instrument first noted in the early years of European contact is still in use: the *fala*, a rolled floor mat beaten with two light sticks to accompany group song. By contrast, the hand-held *pātē* slit drum was introduced from Rarotonga by 19th-century Christian converts acting as 'native teachers'.

One distinctive form of song/dance accompaniment is body percussion, in the form of hand clapping and body slapping. By clapping in unison with the hands held flat and parallel (*pati*) or at right-angles and cupped (*pō*), a seated Samoan choir accompanies its own singing, principally for dance songs, while the standing choir leader signals both the style and frequency of the clap. Body slapping is normally restricted to the men's *fa'ataupati* dance, with dancers executing a series of synchronised and very fast slaps to their chests, sides, thighs and feet. The sounds of these forms of contact, together with stamping, constitute the dance's accompaniment.

In the specialised *siva* called *taualuga*, a solo dancer performing relatively small, slow movements centre-stage is surrounded by other dancers performing vigorous actions, which have frequently been misinterpreted by outsiders as clowning. Such dancers are, however, deliberately creating a wide contrast between their own movements and those of the centre-stage dancer in order to highlight the gracefulness of the soloist, these two styles representing one reflection of the division of secular authority into 'chiefs' and 'orators'. This aspect of the *taualuga* was retained when the dance was introduced to Tonga in the early 20th century.

Missionaries were responsible for the abandonment of several cultural activities, including the *pōula* or 'night dance', whose associated activities offended British moral standards. The cultural vacuum created by the loss of the *pōula* appears to have been filled by the prompt creation of a new dance genre, the *siva*, which soon became the generic term for the individualistic and non-choreographed style of dancing now performed nationally at formal and informal events. A wide variety of songs is used to accompany the *siva*, ranging from nationally-known items composed 50 years ago to one created especially for a particular occasion, and musical forces may be a cappella choirs, string bands or electric ensembles.

When the *mā 'ulu'ulu* dance was created towards the end of the 19th century, it was performed by young men and women and consisted of an introductory song, a *sāsā* dance, and finally the *mā 'ulu'ulu* proper. During the 1960s, these three components were separated and performed in their own right, and the performers tended to be young women. Further refinements in the 1990s have included a move from a seated position to a mix of seated, kneeling and standing, and a trend away from synchrony of all dancers' movement to brief divisions of the dancers into two or more sections, each performing separate sets of actions. The *mā 'ulu'ulu* is arguably the most dynamic of contemporary Samoan dances, both in Samoa itself and among expatriate Samoan populations. Its song poetry is usually composed for a particular occasion, and is reflected in choreographed dance movements through a combination of stereotyped and more individual gestures. The dance was introduced into Tonga less than 100 years ago.

The *sāsā* is a wordless dance performed by seated performers synchronizing their movements to the beating of a mat, small slit drum or tin drum in a fast, steady rhythm. Interspersing their synchrony with brief sections in which they create paired, interactive lines, dancers may also shout brief rhythmical calls of welcome to the audience.

Introduced dances such as the Futunan *'ailao* and *sākē* are infrequently performed and are associated with particular regions of Samoa having historical links with the country of origin. The so-called fire dance, known in Samoa as *'ailao afi* (*'ailao* with fire), has developed from an item in one nightclub in the 1960s to a showbiz spectacular widely imitated throughout Polynesia, and beyond. Until the establishment of European games taught in schools, a wide variety of indigenous games incorporated songs or rhythmic recitations, and several forms of play activities similarly incorporated songs. Although these activities have now largely ceased, many of the songs survive in a medley of items performed on stage as part of a rehearsed regrouping of performers between formal items in a concert.

Samoan dancers, contemporary performance

The chief function of Samoan song was, and still is, the transmission of the uttered word, with the village continuing to be the main social unit represented. In song, village identity normally overrides political and religious affiliations, and choirs featuring all able-bodied men rehearse and perform what are essentially statements of corporate identity. Although individual items may be given titles such as songs of welcome, farewell, and so forth, most function to support social institutions and the social hierarchy by way of praise, and for this reason the genre of *vi'i* (praise) song is widely considered of greatest social importance. Because they are poetically linked to specific events and political perspectives, most songs are not repeated after the official performance(s) or adopted by other choirs, although recording and subsequent radio broadcast may extend the period of national exposure. A few songs, nonetheless, have survived the passing of time and broadened their appeal to the extent that they are now considered as belonging to Samoa as a whole. A song describing the volcanic eruptions on Savai'i in the early 20th century and several items composed during World War II are examples.

Typical performance organization has a seated choir facing inwards in a tight U-shaped formation surrounding a standing conductor on three sides. The conductor has a repertoire of stock gestures which may include quasi-miming of specific poetic references while those words are sung; although these movements may appear as 'dance' to an outsider, a local audience will consider them as 'conducting' (*fuātaimi* or *taimi*). Should the song include hand clapping, the conductor will use exaggerated demonstration to indicate the style and timing of these claps. During such singing, individuals from the choir or audience may stand and perform stock dance movements in a spontaneous gesture of support or exhilaration. Similarly, one or more individual may perform as clowns (*fa'aaluma*), moving around the performance area and creating a contrast between their own behaviour and that of the official performing group and generally enhancing audience appeal. (See CLOWNING.)

Although Samoan choir singing is now heavily infused with European characteristics, elements of indigenous style are still evident, such as stereotyped cadence formulae, spontaneous *melisma* by one or more individuals singing an upper voice-part, and a bass part focusing on two pitches a 4th apart.

The greatest concentration of expatriate Samoans lives in New Zealand (c70 000) and there are substantial numbers living on Australia's east coast, in Los Angeles and Hawai'i. At most locations, the church has replaced the village as the large social unit, and has assumed responsibility for teaching both secular and religious songs, as well as locally-created dances. The flow of cultural information is two-way as, for example, a steady flow of village-based concert parties visits New Zealand on fund-raising tours and New Zealand-born Samoans are encouraged to visit their cultural homeland. Within Samoa, annual national events such as Flag Raising Day in American Samoa, and Independence Day in Samoa incorporate non-competitive performance of newly created songs and dances. By contrast, the competitive element is incorporated in Samoa's *Teuila* Festival, initiated in 1992. However, although the competitive element encourages groups to move beyond conventional repertoires of dance movements, such innovations are balanced by a more conservative approach to song poetry, which continues to recognize respect for traditional cultural values and structural elements such as rhyming lines. It is a measure of the strength of Samoan culture generally that, despite an emphasis on novelty and innovation, the underlying social and creative principles have remained largely intact.—RM

Further reading

Moyle, R M (ed.), 1984. *The Samoan Journals of John Williams: 1830 and 1832*, Pacific History 11, Australian National University Press.

——, 1997. *Tongan Music*, Auckland University Press.

——, 1988. *Traditional Samoan Music*, Auckland University Press.

Dance in Papua New Guinea

Ceremonies and festivities were an integral part of the life of many cultural groups in Papua New Guinea, and dance formed a basic part. Dance as a generic term for a particular activity as commonly understood, however, could not be applied to Papua New Guinea. This is largely because a particular ceremony or festivity was a combination of various processes and practices involving notions of dance, singing, story-telling, oration and spirituality. Marriage, birth, initiation, exchange and mortuary occasions brought together these processes, for example. What were these activities and how did dance fit into them? How have these ceremonies and festivities changed? The *mokail* ceremony from the Mogei in Western Highlands can shed some light on these issues.

A notable feature of many Highlands groups was their exchange ceremonies, well documented by anthropologists. In the Mogei there was an exchange ceremony called *mokail*. The *mokail* involved exchange of shells, feathers, pigs, cassowaries and other valuables between tribes. One *mokail* could take several years of planning and negotiations and then culminate in a week or two of dance and festiv-

Female dancer from the Mount Hagen area, Papua New Guinea

ities. It also served various aspects of the community's social, political, economic and spiritual needs.

During the *mokail* there were several dances. One called the *weld* was for women. It elevated the status of women and their contribution in bringing together the gifts for the exchange. Women (including teenagers and mothers) were richly decorated with an assortment of BILAS. In the *weld* women stood side by side in a single line gradually forming a semi-circle. One of the dancers would begin a song and gradually others followed. The dance was accompanied by *kundu* drums. Then in unison the dancers bent each knee inward and then flexed following the rhythm of the song and drums. At the completion of a song the dancers stopped briefly to catch their breath and started again. Usually there were many songs composed to accompany a *weld*, but its style and form did not change much.

The *mur* dance involved men. Sometimes a few young marriageable women joined in, and each dancer wore a great deal of *bilas*. The *mur* did not vary a great deal from the *weld* except for a difference in bending of the knees. The *mur* involved bending both knees at the same time and then flexing them as in a half-plié. Gradually the *mur* would taper off with dancers lifting their heels off the ground rhythmically. The songs in the *weld* and *mur* sometimes praised the group's capacity to put together the *mokail*. Other songs would tell stories of previous deeds or events which eventually led to the *mokail*. Sometimes the songs would mock other tribes or even a person.

The *weld* and *mur* took place earlier in the *mokail*. *Oont mbu* was a dance that came later, performed mostly by the men, before the recipients came to see the gifts and prepare to take them home. *Oont mbu* involved columns and rows of men 'marching' up and down the ceremonial grounds while stamping their feet. During a day of the *mokail* the *weld*, *mur* and *oont mbu* would usually be followed by the *malya*. There were two variations in this dance, one involving only women. The other *malya* which was very popular for courting involved young men and women from both sides (givers and recipients) of the *mokail* and other neighbours. Both types of *malya* were performed in circular formation with arms linked from the elbows and clasping each others palms and jumping up and down rhythmically to songs.

The *mokail* was also a platform for great orations by leaders of groups giving in the exchange and those receiving. These oratory spectacles focused on the tribe's capacity to do the *mokail*, recounting its

Papua New Guineans from Milne Bay Province performing a dance from the Trobriand Islands

history and challenging the other to match and make an early repayment. A speech involved clever juxtaposition of words, images, poetry and story-telling which entertained, informed, challenged, rebuked and praised. People flocked to a *mokail* not only to see the dances and dancers but also to see, hear and judge the oratory skills of the leaders.

The *mur* and *weld* were elaborate and gentle dances in style, and did not involve quick or dynamic movements. This is not to say that the dances were not dynamic in their own way. Part of their complexity related to the *bilas* for each dance, comprising feathers and other finery. To avoid dishevelment the dancer had to be careful not to turn too sharply or duck too quickly. The *oont mbu* required dancers to move quickly and stamp their feet, so that sometimes men shortened the aprons (*baalg*) they wore. The *malya* dances in comparison were very lively. The singing and movements of both dances were faster and more energetic. The *bilas* for this dance was less cumbersome, typically cockatoo feathers made into a pompom and pinned on to the wig (*wuna*). In the middle of the pompom was a marsupial tail stiffened with a stick. As the dancer jumped, pompom and marsupial tail flagged up and down and to and fro rhythmically.

Men from Mount Hagen area, Papua New Guinea, decorated for *Mur* dance and *Oont Mbu*

Mekeo dancers at the 1994 Goroka Show

The different forms of the *mokail* did not change much, nor did the *bilas* for each dance. One village's *mur* was much the same as that of the neighbouring village. Mothers taught their daughters the same *weld* they had danced. The structure of the songs also remained the same but the words could be changed by the singers. On one level the dances were static in style and form, without change. As a performance, however, the *mokail* and its accompanying aspects of dance—exchange, orations and so on—are actual experiences both for the onlooker and the dancer.

Today many dances and SINGSING performed in villages, hotel foyers, showgrounds and festivals are not part of the traditional institutions like the *mokail*. The context has changed: dances like the *mur* or the *weld* have become tourist spectacles. Show organizers (at Goroka, Hagen, PORT MORESBY and Lae) give cash and goods for performers to exhibit their traditional culture. Clans and tribes have given way to collectives called cultural groups representing a particular area. To collect monies and goods proffered the cultural groups have become itinerants, moving with their *bilas* from one show to another. Popular groups like the Huli dancers of Southern Highlands or Manus dancers are usually invited and marketed by show organizers as draw-cards.

Very few *mokail*s take place, but they have perhaps evolved rather than been lost. The showground and the hotel foyer serve as the new ceremonial ground at which Papua New Guineans can acknowledge their history and find a place for themselves in an ever-changing world. In that sense both the *mur* and the *weld* can never be seen entirely as historical icons. In the Mogei, dance was a performance not a ritual. The *mur* and the *weld* at the showground today provide a window into Mogei history and at the same time a glimpse of future possibilities. It is this sense of ambivalence (and also incommensurability) that surrounds dance and indeed identity in Papua New Guinea today.—MAM

Further reading

Cochrane, S, 1997. *Contemporary Art in Papua New Guinea*, Craftsman House.

Singsing in Papua New Guinea

Ceremonies or festive occasions marking the birth of a child, coming of age, marriage, death, harvest, or exchange were usually marked by songs, dances, stories, and exchanges of gifts, with each occasion given a different name. Today the various celebrations and festivities involving BILAS, dance and songs are collectively called *singsing*. *Singsing* has become a ubiquitous term referring mainly to the dances and celebrations put on by different cultures for various purposes. But to be able to understand *singsing* as a reference to a particular process it is useful to appreciate the way the word evolved.

During the colonial era when the early missionaries and government representatives went into a community, one of the first things they did was to impose some order and bring people under their control. Villagers were given new beliefs, values, ways of social conduct and behaviour; new laws; new clothes to wear; new tools to work with; and different food. People were told to discard their ways of seeing and doing things including their *bilas*, songs, dances and ceremonies. Missionaries wanted people to discard their evil and heathen practices and become Christians. Government representatives wanted to institute a common law and bring the people under one rule. They saw that traditional practices could be avenues for insubordination and social anarchy, and they banned them. Many young men and women were recruited to work as evangelists, policemen, interpreters, servants and plantation labourers. The effect of these changes in people's lives contributed to the lack of continuity of their *singsing*.

Surprisingly, while both missionaries and government representatives admonished the people for their cultural practices they were also fascinated by them. This was made manifest in two significant ways. Firstly, fascination coupled with a desire for the unique, different and the exotic led the colonial emissaries to collect a wide variety of objects, and to photograph, film and write about the cultures. This material was then sent back to their home countries as evidence of the different people and their weird and wonderful ways of living and celebrating life.

Secondly, the colonial powers began a process of 'appropriation' of the various cultural practices. On a special day like the king's birthday, or a visit from a government dignitary, government officials rounded up villagers to prepare what they called a *singsing* for the occasion. Visitors were welcomed with the *singsing* and shown some native culture. In centres like Mount Hagen and Goroka, government officers organized annual shows and cultural groups show-cased their cultures. These cultural shows were advertised around the colony and abroad for visitors to come and see the natives' culture, and indeed the way the government was bringing civilization to the country.

Missionaries fascinated by the cultures began to take some of the practices and incorporate them into their work. Some missionaries learnt a local language and then translated the Bible and hymns into that language. They also trained teachers and evangelists who taught the local people the new beliefs and values in the language. In some areas where the particular language was not known the teachers taught the villagers the 'new' language as they began to teach about the church. Also there were specific days which required special celebrations and observances. For instance occasions like Christmas, Easter, Corpus Christi or even the feast day of a

North Solomon Islands bamboo band ensemble. Collection of bamboos of varying lengths gathered in raft formation and beaten on one end with a thong

saint or other spiritual icons of the church were celebrated with *singsings*.

Today a *singsing* is a celebratory occasion where traditional *bilas* is worn and dances are performed for annual shows and for tourists. The context in which these dances were performed has changed. Does that mean that the PNG *singsing* is less authentic today? Have people lost their traditions? Do these changes lessen the value and significance of the *singsing* today compared with those of the past?

Papua New Guineans, and even outsiders, may on the one hand view the traditional *singsing* to be seen at a showground or hotel foyer as reflecting an authentic culture. On the other hand, the shows and performances may be seen as commodities and the performers as driven by economic needs. These are important political and cultural propositions, but for contemporary Papua New Guineans as well as for outsiders the *singsing* continues to cater to a deep desire and fascination for the exotic and the different. In addition, for Papua New Guineans *singsing* has become a vehicle to search for an authentic cultural anchor—a metaphoric anchor that is antithetical to 'Western' culture. From that perspective *singsing* is and will be a very strong feature of contemporary Papua New Guinean culture.—MAM

The *kankar* structures of the Goroka area, Papua New Guinea, usually carried by male dancers

Tongan music and dance

Modern Tongan music is a composite of various strands of sound and movement that have evolved from pre-European Tongan performances under a variety of influences from the Western world, other Pacific islands, and more recently, the Caribbean Islands. Tongan performances are based on poetry conveyed through indirectness (*heliaki*, 'to say one thing but mean another') in the sung poetry itself as well as in the movements that accompany it. The sound component of music is primarily the vehicle for conveying the poetry, and the resulting melodic/rhythmic motifs and phrases may be stereotypic and repetitious. The lower body movement motifs primarily keep the time, while the hand/arm motifs convey the poetry.

Performances in Tonga include the following genres.

- *Me'etu'upaki*, an ancient dance in which paddle-like implements are twirled and manipulated, is performed by men from the village of Lapaha on special occasions as an identity marker of their association with the highest line of kings and the fertility rituals of old. Sung in a poetic idiom no longer understood, it is accompanied by a struck idiophone and chorus that face the dancers.
- *Fa'ahiula*, a traditional women's dance, begins seated in a curved row (*'otu haka*); then one or more female dancers stand and perform (*ula*). The singing is accompanied by a percussion instrument consisting of lengths of bamboo rolled in a mat.
- *Lakalaka*, a contemporary dance form, is usually village-based and can be characterized as a sung speech with choreographed movements. The basic element is poetry, through-composed in stanzas which are usually repeated. The poetry is set into a polyphonic musical setting consisting of *fasi* (melody or leading part), *laulalo* (bass or underlying part), and one or more additional parts. The performers, often 100 or more, stand in two or more long lines facing the audience, the men on the right (from the observer's point of view), the women on the left. The dancers also sing and a chorus of men and women stands behind to augment the sound. The audience must hear the poetry clearly in order to understand it and how the movements enhance the meaning of the poetry.
- *Ma'ulu'ulu* often draws its participants from a school or church. The poetry is structured in verse–chorus alternation, and it is usually sung in two or three parts. The poetry is conveyed visually by the arm movements. Performers may be

all female, all male, or both—seated in curved lines (or the second and consecutive lines may be raised by kneeling, standing, or elevated on benches). The number of participants ranges from 10–500 individuals. Sung poetry is preceded by a long introduction of complicated drumming on one or more *nafa* membranophones and elaborate hand/arm movement motifs; next a verse of poetry is sung without movement or drum accompaniment; then the rest of the verses and choruses are sung with hand/arm movements that make allusions to the poetry and with (less complicated) drum accompaniment. Finally, the introduction is repeated.

- *Hiva kakala*, sweet songs, are accompanied by string bands composed of ukulele and guitars (and sometimes banjos, one-string bass, etc). Structured in verse–chorus alternation, the melodic line and harmony are more Western, but unmistakably Tongan. The poetry is topical about places, people, and Tonga as a paradise. The sung poetry is accompanied by *tau'olunga* dance movements—hand/arm movement similar to those used for *lakalaka* and *ma'ulu'ulu* but with a wider variety of lower body movement motifs. The movements may be pre-set or spontaneous and may be performed as a solo or by a number of women. These principal dancers may be accompanied by one or more secondary dancers (male or female) who spontaneously join in with virile movements to emphasize the graceful movements of the women.
- *Kailao*, a men's club-dance imported from 'Uvea, has no singing. Its complex movements are structured according to rhythmic motifs struck on an empty biscuit tin with additional sounds from ankle rattles.
- *Sōkē* combines sung poetry with the striking of short and long sticks in complex patterns. It is performed by a large number of male or female participants in sets of four that combine into larger and larger groupings.—ALK

Further reading

Kaeppler, A L, 1993. *Poetry in Motion: studies of Tongan dance*, Vavu'u Press.

Kaeppler, A L and Love, J W (eds), 1998. Entries on Tonga, 'Australia and the Pacific Islands', Vol. 9, *Garland Encyclopedia of World Music*, Garland Publishing.

Moyle, R, 1987. *Tongan Music*, Auckland University Press.

Clowning in the Pacific

Clowning, in the form of spontaneous mimicry, 'silly behaviour', flirting, or humorous antics designed to make people laugh, is a universal human phenomenon. In the Pacific, it can be verbal as well as physical, rehearsed or improvised, brief or lengthy. It is usually associated with celebrations, and as dancing is the most popular form of entertainment, clowning is often part of dance. Its formal origins can be traced back to a tradition of ritual clowning, which brought humour into serious ritual occasions of religious ceremonies and sacred festivals in the Pacific islands. Formal rites connected with the weather, seasonal cycles, warfare, fertility and life transitions had a supernatural basis and a spiritual significance. Within this context, ritual clowning appears to have emerged as a means of exploring complex emotional conflicts and mediating tensions. Inverting normal order—by role reversal, parody, sexual innuendo, and simulation of low bodily functions, ritual clowning encompasses ambiguities and contradictions which serve to underline and reinforce the established social controls and authority structures that are being mocked.

The performance elements central to traditional sacred rites—drama, dancing and songs, involving elaborate costume and body decoration, masks and music—are often part of ritual clowning. In Rotuma, the ritual clown known as *hān mane'ak su* is always a female, past child-bearing age, who is non-threatening outside the boundary of privileged licence. Her status is lower in everyday life than that of chiefs and most men. At wedding receptions, wearing an extra skirt of leaves and carrying a stick (with multiple symbolic meanings including a phallus, a digging stick and chiefly authority), she inverts the dominant Rotuman values of humility, restraint and respect. Where Rotumans usually communicate indirectly, using pleasantries on sensitive matters, the clown is often blunt and direct. Men from the groom's side are harassed by her—a woman from the bride's side.

Ritual clowning is known to have occurred during festivals associated with agricultural fertility. On Vanua Levu, Fiji, at the time of the yam harvest, masked performers (males who were priests) represented named spirits or *veli* who were associated with agricultural productivity, and they were permitted to make fun of earthly authority.

In Hawai'i, the solemn ceremonies of the annual harvest festival, *makahiki*, in honour of Lono, one of the gods of fertility, featured uninhibited sexual expression in dances and chants. The celebrations, lasting three or four months, involved feasts, sports, games, dancing and other entertainment. There was sexual licence also in the Hawaiian mourning rites after the death of an important chief. The *oli* chants of ancient Hawai'i, a favourite form of amusement, used ridicule and mimicry to entertain an audience, and another form of clowning occurred in the *hula ki'i* of ancient Hawai'i (which probably developed out of the HULA), a comic performance using puppets about 50 cm tall to represent human figures. The puppet shows were satirical, and often critical of members of the audience, using dialogue and gestures to amuse.

In Papua New Guinea, clowning occurred during funerary rites among the North Mekeo, and among the Murik peoples of the Sepik region, who were thus induced to laugh during a time of grief and mourning. Among the Orokaiva people of Oro Province, clowns called *samuna* took part in complex dances in which masked figures represented fish and animals. In other regions of Papua New Guinea, ritual clowning performances recorded within the past 40 years have included masks, elaborate costumes and explicit sexual displays. Examples are the *naven* clowning among mothers' brothers of the Iatmul, the fertility ceremony of the Umeda villagers of the Sandaun Province, and the *niyel* 'curing' carnival among the Wape.

In Tokelau, women clowns still entertain and diffuse tension by performing brief comic sketches (involving role reversal) at social gatherings and during work group activities. In the Samoan dancing known as the *siva*, the dignified and restrained female dancer at the centre is accompanied by disorderly male dancers whose impulsive antics may include jumping, rolling about and shouting. In both Samoa and Tonga, the role of a 'jester' (always a male of low rank) could be part of the royal or chiefly retinue, a clown who made fun of people, dressed oddly, and made witty comments. In societies where social harmony is valued and few avenues exist for criticism of authority figures, the comic sketch serves as a vehicle for social comment and introspection, informing even as it lampoons and entertains. Tongan dance performances often include satirical and ribald comic sketches. In Samoa, the *fale aitu* (originally 'spirit house') refers to a comic sketch in which the lead comedian adopts an ambiguous dramatis persona and uses verbal or physical humour to defuse potential threats to the social and cultural equilibrium. Its origins lie in the performance (held within the community spirit house on traditional *poula* 'teasing' nights) which included a wild sexual frenzy preceding the comic sketches. The lead comedian is an untitled male who parodies a traditional spirit.

In Tahiti, the *arioi* society (a group of young people who toured the islands performing dances and comic sketches) lampooned authority figures and mocked non-conformists. In formal rituals based on worship of the god 'Oro, their founder and protector, the *arioi* society's activities ranged from uninhibited sexual orgies to elaborate gift exchanges, and included performances in which a member of the company was anointed with oil, highly perfumed and dressed to represent the god of paradise.

In Cook Islands, the historical pageant of myths and legends called *nuku* might often include village humorists who accompanied the chorus of songs with exaggerated gestures such as mimicry, poking out the tongue and thumbing the nose. Today the *nuku* has become a Biblical pageant, similar to the smaller-scale Biblical dramas performed in Tonga, Samoa and Rotuma. Part of the new tradition of Biblical dramas popular throughout the Pacific, there are also the *thukma* or *bina boli* sketches performed in Santa Isabel, Solomon Islands. Performed at feasts and celebrations, these dramatic presentations use parody, exaggeration and caricature for comic effect, and can be seen to explore ambivalent feelings about the arrival of Christianity and the process of missionization.

The role of the ritual clown no longer carries its former spiritual potency. Clowning continues to exist in the Pacific, as a recognized part of both formal and informal occasions, but its religious significance has been severely eroded. Now contemporary ritual clowning—apparently subversive, but enacted within defined limits of permissiveness—still has a role that goes far beyond entertainment and satire, reminding its audience of the rules and rulers in real life.—VH

Further reading

Hereniko, V, 1995. *Woven Gods: female clowns and power in Rotuma*, Center for Pacific Island Studies, University of Hawai'i Press.

Musical instruments

Music and dance-drama were an essential ingredient in traditional life in all the islands. The dance ground was the ritual and commercial centre of a village. Voices, dance movements and a wide range of instrumental sounds combined to inform and entertain. Some musical instruments are specific to particular music cultures, but the most commonly used were drums, pan-pipes and flutes, with bull-roarers and rattles containing seeds used in some regions, and trumpets made from bamboo, wood or tree-fern stems. Children today still make and play their own instruments: leaf oboes (made of pandanus or coconut palm leaves); small Jew's harps

Maihia Tupoufarapotea, a drum maker of Rakahanga, constructs a wooden slit-drum on Manihiki from a *fano* log (*Guettarda speciosa*). Working through the slit he has created through the top of the planed surface, Papa Maihia chisels wood out to form a cavity. His legs hold the log firmly

(made of a strip of palm leaf); slit tubes (made of a hollow stem of papaya); and various improvised instruments such as a wooden stick held to the mouth, which serves as a resonator, and beaten with another, smaller stick.

Slit-gong drums are made from local woods such as *Guettarda speciosa* (fano logs, Cook Islands), *Albizia, Intsia bijuga* or *Vitex cofassus* (garamut drums, Papua New Guinea). Hand drums are made from *Hernandia nymphaeafolia, Pterocarpus indicus* and *Araucaria*, or from bamboo. Pan-pipes, flutes and the Jew's harp made from bamboo are widely used. Whistles were sometimes made from small coconut shells, and from bamboo. Traditional Kanak percussion instruments such as bamboo stamping tubes (*bwanjep* or *jō*) and concussion bark bundles (*jêpak*) are used in the current revival of CONTEMPORARY KANEKA MUSIC OF NEW CALEDONIA.—KRF

Festival of Pacific Arts

Festival activity is firmly rooted in the Pacific past and is a vehicle of Pacific identity/culture. The concept of festival is very much linked to cultural identity. The importance of forging or creating a cultural identity within the Pacific region has grown exponentially as new nations have emerged. Drawing upon their cultural heritage, island leaders have created national symbols as well as localized symbols of identity. Using these as rallying points diverse groups and agendas meld together in the creation of a cultural and political identity accomplished through the concept of the festival.

The Festival of Pacific Arts, earlier known as the South Pacific Arts Festival, has become an important venue for the perpetuation of Pacific arts and cultures. Representatives to the South Pacific Commission felt that the values embodied in the arts and culture of the Pacific had been neglected during a century of colonial rule and that if left to themselves these island cultures would disappear. To counter that, the first festival was held in Fiji in 1972 followed by Rotorua (1976), Port Moresby (1980), Papeete (1985), Townsville (1988), Rarotonga (1992) and Samoa (1996).

Each festival has its own theme, and the host country adds its unique touch, introducing ideas and events which demonstrate the importance of the festival as both a cultural and political event. In this way the festival can promote cultural and artistic values, and do so in a political arena. As such the festival offers a consolidated political voice and identity. Beginning with cultural groups and artisans in Fiji, the festival has evolved to include the art

These young *taupou* (ritual virgins) escorted each national delegation to the opening ceremonies of the Seventh Pacific Festival of the Arts, held in Apia, Samoa, 1996

of navigation, contemporary art, and the literary arts. Learning from differences and sharing cultural similarities is the essential focus of the festival. Important issues have come to the fore as a result, and symposia have been organized to facilitate a dialogue between delegates.

The festival enables government agencies to promote Pacific art and culture. Often politicians do not admit the manipulation of cultural and political identity as created through festivals. However, the use and creation of composite national symbols (the vaka, dance, tattoo) in a multi-national festival reinforces the cultural and artistic identities.

The emphasis in the festival has been on the past. The performing arts are the focus, but also included is the festival village where the 'traditional arts' (weaving, plaiting, carving, tattoo, food, healing and medicine) are highlighted. Other venues include a book; postal, and photography exhibitions; a film/video series; and, lately, a seminar series. The festivals in Rarotonga and Samoa expanded upon those of the past, recognizing the importance of the body arts (*tatau*, see TATTOOING), literary arts and contemporary Pacific art, thus incoporating a recognition of the present and future of Pacific arts.

The issue is no longer re-establishing what is in danger of being lost, but how to interpret and harness the energy of the arts as they approach a new millennium. The value of the festival has been the establishment of strong cultural and political identities that have infused life into the arts. The arts are now firmly embedded in contemporary Pacific culture. The result is the institutionalization of an ideal—the festival—whose goal is to preserve and encourage the arts and cultures of the Pacific.—KS

Heiva

Heiva i Tahiti is a festival that takes place during a two-week period each July. It is a celebration of the artistic and cultural traditions of Tahiti, spanning more than 100 years. In the past it has often been linked with French independence (*La Fête Nationale* or *La Bastille*), obscuring its importance to Tahitian art and identity. Many of the events associated with the *heiva* have historical antecedents in traditional Tahitian culture which have evolved over the past century, but have remained constant in their appearance during this festival. Three events—marae reenactments, *umu-ti* (firewalk) and tattoo—have been introduced within the past 40 years and are rooted more firmly in current political and economic rhetoric. These activities represent the conscious creation of a spectacle whose ultimate effect is to instruct Tahitians about their traditional heritage.

The history of the *heiva* begins with the precariously balanced relationship between the French and the Tahitians. The annexation of Tahiti by France in 1843 was followed by six years of civil unrest. To reiterate their colonial position, the French government in Tahiti attempted to organize a festival in 1859 to correspond with festivities in France, honouring Napoleon III's victory over Italy. This was an overt attempt to assert political dominance. However, the Tahitians reinterpreted this festival for themselves, incorporating their cultural and artistic practices. The result was a festival comprised of French parades, games, ceremonies; and Tahitian activities—dance competitions, singing, and outrigger canoe, horse and foot races.

No further festival was organized until 1881. Again the French attempted to assert their colonial position by tying the festival to the cession of Tahiti to France. This attitude was countered by a dominance of Tahitian activities during the festival which led the participants to associate the festivities with traditional practices. This event mimicked the role of a *heiva* in pre-contact Tahiti. Often defined as entertainment, *heiva* incorporated dancing, singing, and sporting events that were accompanied by the presentation of gifts to venerate the *ari'i* (chiefs) and their guests. As such, the *heiva* became a venue for the perpetuation of traditional festival activity during the colonial period. It was a celebration of Tahitian culture, not French imperialism.

The name of the festival—*La Fête Nationale* or *La Bastille*—had remained the same until 1977 when the Tahitian language was accepted as an official language by the French. *Tiurai*, the Tahitian word for July, was used, thereby giving the festival a more explicitly Tahitian association. In 1986 *Heiva* was put into place, ideologically disassociating the festival both from July, *La Fête*, *La Bastille*—and more importantly, the French.

The contemporary *heiva* continues to focus on dance, and is supported by a variety of TRADITIONAL SPORTS events (outrigger canoe racing, javelin throwing, running and lifting events), subsistence activities and artistic competitions. The art of TATTOOING has become an important factor as have the more theatrical productions of marae reenactments and the *umu-ti*. The *heiva* today is seen as a Tahitian festival put on for and by the Tahitians. Its role as purveyor of Tahitian cultural values is implicit in the events that constitute the *heiva*. The result is an annual festival that fosters the creation of a Tahitian identity and provides a venue for the perpetuation of the arts and culture of Tahiti.—KS

Fijian traditional dancing (*meke*) remains an important part of ceremonial events and feasts, and tourist performances. These performers, in traditional dress, use a log drum

Contemporary Pacific music

Beginning with initial contact with Western explorers, merchants and missionaries, and accelerating with the systematic imposition of colonialism, various forms of indigenous Pacific music have been influenced by and modified through their exposure to Western innovations and influences. Significant factors in the development of contemporary Pacific music include the introduction of Western tonal systems, melodic and chordal structures; new instruments, such as, most notably, the guitar; various forms of technology (such as music recording, amplification and radio broadcast); and, most recently, particular genres (such as rock, country and western, and reggae).

While a range of 'syncretic' practices (involving the gradual incorporation of Western elements into traditional musical styles, and vice versa) took place in the Pacific in the 1800s, mostly in a small-scale, local and unheralded manner, international attention turned to one particular musical style, and its originating locale, in the 1920s. The music style in question was that developed in Hawai'i by a combination of local and North American musicians and composers. This involved the marriage of elements of traditional Hawaiian music, including vocal and instrumental glissandi (sliding between notes) and the use of vocal techniques such as falsetto, with established styles of Western pop songs. From the 1920s–50s Hawaiian music enjoyed a global vogue, with local styles of Hawaiian-influenced music being performed in Europe, Asia, North America and Australasia.

This vogue was also followed by the shorter, but nonetheless significant, international popularity of the style of musical exotica developed in Hawai'i by the North American instrumentalist and bandleader Martin Denny and local vibraphone player Arthur Lyman (which reached its peak in the late 1950s and early 1960s). The 1970s saw a major revival in traditional forms of Hawaiian music as part of what has been termed the Hawaiian 'renaissance'. Virtuoso instrumentalists such as slack key guitarist Gabby Pahinui achieved local and international fame, and a broad-based movement ensured a continuation of traditional styles through the 1990s.

In the 1980s Hawaiian music also developed another distinctive style, a mixture of Western song genres, contemporary Hawaiian vocal and instrumental approaches and a reggae-derived rhythm. This style became referred to as Jawaiian (referencing both Jamaica, home of reggae, and 'Jah', the Jamaican Rastafarian cult's term for God, together with Hawai'i). This localization of aspects of Jamaican music and religious association with Pacific styles was not just confined to Hawai'i. Following Jamaican reggae star Bob Marley's rise to prominence in the mid 1970s, and the subsequent success of pop-oriented reggae acts, such as the British reggae band UB40, reggae became firmly established across the Pacific as shared musical idiom. Almost without exception, this adoption of reggae was accompanied by a modification of the strong rhythmic accent on the second and fourth beats (deemed a 'signature' element of its sound), for a smoother, more regularly accented rhythmic structure. In the music of bands such as New Zealand Maori ensemble Moana and the Moa Hunters, or Jawaiian acts such as Ho'aikane, the combination of reggae-derived rhythms (and sparse instrumental arrangements) and rich melodic harmonies has created a subtle and inventive musical style. Fijian artist Danny Rae Costello has also produced another notable inflection of this, incorporating calypso and other Southern Caribbean elements on albums such as *Jungle Walk* (1996), produced for the California-based label, West Maui Records.

In the 1990s, following the innovative work of Australian band Not Drowning, Waving with musicians from Rabaul on the *Tabaran* album (1990)—and the marketing of various non-Western musics under the 'world music' category—a number of cross-cultural musical collaborations have occurred in the western Pacific region. These have primarily been instigated by Western artists working with indigenous musicians to produce recorded versions of traditional-derived music likely to be attractive to Western consumers. The most notable examples of this to date have been Australian producer Anthony Copping's *Siva Pacifica* album (1997) which featured

Samoan-Australian vocalist Robyn Loau with various Solomon and Cook Islander performers; and *Te Vaka* (1997), New Zealand producer Malcolm Smith's collaboration with Tokelau singer-songwriter Opetaia Foa'i. While the dance mix version of the traditional Hawaiian song *Aloha Oe* released by Siva Pacifica enjoyed considerable airplay in the islands, especially in Fiji, these albums have had little impact in the Pacific and have achieved only modest sales and airplay in Western markets.

Despite continuing anxieties over the swamping and destruction of Pacific cultures as a result of the continuing trends towards globalization and westernization, the principal characteristic linking the various music cultures of the Pacific region in the late 20th century has been their readiness to engage with and modify outside musical influences, producing new, distinctly local forms and styles.—PH

Further reading

Hayward, P (ed.), 1998. *Sound Alliances—indigenous peoples, cultural politics and popular culture in the Pacific*, Cassell.

—— (ed.), 1999. *Widening The Horizons—exoticism in post-war popular music*, John Libbey and Co.

Kanahele, G (ed.), 1979. *Hawaiian Music and Musicians—an illustrated history*, University of Hawai'i Press.

Contemporary Kaneka music of New Caledonia

A distinctively regional brand of popular music in New Caledonia, known as *kaneka*, developed in the 1980s, fusing indigenous Melanesian elements with features of Western popular music. This conscious process of infusing a tradition with indigenous elements in order to make it more regionally specific and representative, and achieve Kanak cultural identity through a popular music medium, may be termed 'indigenization'. *Kaneka* music is not widely known outside its homeland and neighbouring islands, but tours to New Zealand, Australia and other Pacific nations in the 1990s have secured some international fame for bands such as Vamaley and Mexem.

Prior to the development of *kaneka*, most popular music in New Caledonia was basically European or American style music with a Kanak 'flavour'. Song texts were often in French; some songs mixed French and Kanak, a few used a local language. English-language songs also became common. Love themes dominated and a basic voice, guitar and drums set-up was employed with little use of keyboard or percussion, and no brass. The most important influences on popular music in New Caledonia were American folk rock and blues. Some pre-*kaneka* bands, however, developed regionally-specific styles reflecting distinctive musical aspects such as vocal production and harmonies, as well as employing vernacular languages in their songs.

The late 1970s and early 1980s witnessed the formation of several groups which were to become the vanguard of the *kaneka* music style, including Kirikitr, Témââ, and Bwanjep. From this period dates experimentation with the incorporation of traditional instruments and rhythms in popular music from the indigenous ceremonial music and dance traditions (generically called *pilou*).

Kaneka songs are usually in Kanak languages, but some are in French and a few are macaronic, combining Kanak with French or English words. The texts of many songs are concerned with moral, social and political issues. In particular, some bands focus on the theme of French oppression or Kanak identity and liberation. Some songs have humorous texts, and love themes are still important but do not predominate as in other popular music styles.

Indigenous Kanak ceremonial music and dance traditions have provided instruments, rhythms, and in some cases, melodic chants for *kaneka* songs. Although many regional *pilou* rhythms exist, one common rhythm—crotchet-quaver, crotchet-quaver—has become the pan-Kanak rhythmic base for *kaneka*. In *kaneka*, a battery of percussion instruments may be used to create this rhythmic base.

The social context and function of *kaneka* would also appear to be related to pre-European traditions. Large-scale concerts and festivals are the main performance contexts for *kaneka* bands. These occur infrequently (once or twice every six months), and are often long, drawn-out, multi-stranded events, organized in conjunction with some fundraising purpose, for example, for a football club. These infrequent and lengthy performance events linked to modern cultural institutions assume a ceremonial dimension, not unlike that of traditional *pilou* performances and quite unlike performances of other popular music in New Caledonia. The dress, movements and song arrangements at live gigs also tend to reflect the operation of the indigenization process. Musicians may dress in traditional costume and 'dance' while playing on stage. Their song arrangements at these concerts bear little relation to the short standard popular song format. Lengthy versions of songs with percussion breaks, improvised sections, and in many cases, links between songs, predominate in their performances, again suggesting similarities to traditional *pilou* performances.

A major external source of inspiration for *kaneka* musicians has been reggae. From the late 1970s, reggae and its associated cultural baggage has influenced popular music in New Caledonia. Many of the younger male generation (including several *kaneka* musicians) cultivate dreadlocks and some smoke marijuana in addition to performing and consuming reggae music, both imported and local. Rastafarian religious practices, however, have not penetrated the New Caledonian cultural scene. Kanak musicians have identified with the larger picture of black solidarity and anti-hegemonic activity provided by reggae in their pursuit of their own specific goals, for which the reggae musical style provides an appropriate expressive framework and outlet. Many *kaneka* songs are permeated by reggae rhythms and instrumental patterns. Some bands, such as Mexem, adopt a primarily reggae style, which, nonetheless, is very closely congruent with the pan-Kanak rhythm mentioned above.

Kaneka songs also have other aspects derived from Western popular music. These include instruments (guitars, keyboard, brass, congas, bongos and drum kit), standard Western keys (major or minor), and melodies/harmonies which clearly follow the patterns of Western popular music, with triadically-based vocal melodies, symmetrical phrasing, and a basic, three-chord harmonic format. Many *kaneka* songs follow the common verse–chorus form of Western pop songs.

Kaneka is a clear example of conscious construction of cultural identity through music. This pan-Kanak socio-musical identity has been fashioned from existing resources and structures (both foreign and indigenous). Kanak musicians have deliberately invoked 'tradition', that is, indigenous elements of pre-European Kanak music, which in combination with introduced musical features, represent this emergent identity.—DG

Contemporary music of Polynesia: Cook Islands

Polynesia has experienced the development of several regional popular music styles in the 20th century. Each tradition has its own individual linguistic and musical traits, but some aspects are shared throughout the region. These include common themes for texts (love, beauty of nature/homeland and bereavement), accompaniment by 'string band' (usually guitars/ukuleles and optional percussion), and several features derived from Western popular music such as diatonic melodies and harmonies.

Popular music in Cook Islands is typical of the region. Rarotongan (Cook Islands Maori) is the favoured language for songs, but some groups use a local regional dialect. Some songs are in English or combine English and Rarotongan words/verses. Older-style popular music is acoustic—homophonic songs sung by vocal groups and accompanied by strummed guitars and ukuleles. It is played at private functions/parties, 'bush beer' drinking clubs (especially in the outer islands), and as a prelude to dance shows at hotels and resorts. More recently, popular music has acquired an electric dimension (electric guitars and bass, amplified ukulele, drum machine and keyboard) and an associated music industry. Commercial recordings of modern groups and soloists produced in studios in Rarotonga or New Zealand may include other instruments—sax and synthesizer—and exhibit the use of studio production techniques. Some new performance contexts have evolved—competitions, festivals and hotel/club gigs for entertainment of tourists and locals.

A basic repertoire of songs is common to both acoustic and electric groups, but the latter tend to play more recent 'originals', experimental/fusion pieces, or covers of Tahitian, reggae, and Western pop songs. Rahui Vaka's 1996 solo album, *Blue Highway,* for example, includes traditional string band songs and original tunes as well as Western pop songs, such as Tracey Chapman's *Give Me One Reason,* all presented in a unique fusion of blues and Cook Islands string band style. As in other parts of the Pacific, tune appropriation is common and 'authorship' is a flexible concept. Many older-style string band songs have no known/remembered composer. In some cases, the appellation 'composer' may apply to the text (not to the borrowed tune). Some songs of recent origin do have a known composer of both words and melody.

The presence and role of one or two ukuleles defines the essence of Cook Islands style popular music. The ukulele often commences the song alone, sets the tempo and rhythm, and strums chords in distinctive syncopated patterns throughout the song. In acoustic bands, the guitar(s) also strum chords, but electric guitars usually adopt the divided lead, rhythm and bass functions of Western pop groups.

Songs may be in slow or fast time. Slow songs are either 4/4 time ballads *(ula),* or waltzes. A number of fast beats, identified by dance terms used in Latin or Tahitian music (such as *samba, kaina* and *tamure*), are realised by the ubiquitous drum machine in electric bands. Some slow string band songs are performed for dance shows as 'action' songs in which the hand gestures illustrate the song text. People also sometimes dance to electric bands in clubs and bars, and may use steps and knee/hip movements of COOK ISLANDS TRADITIONAL DANCE.

Melodies of popular songs tend to set texts syllabically and musical phrasing is often text-determined. Melodies usually exhibit evidence of a Western triadic structure. Many songs employ only the three basic chords of Western diatonic harmony—tonic, subdominant and dominant—with occasional secondary dominants or a minor chord. Keys are invariably major. The tonic chord often has an added sixth (basic ukulele tuning) and this constitutes a distinctive harmonic feature of Cook Islands style. Modulation may be used as a contrastive device both within and between songs (in medleys). Some aspects are not derived from standard Western harmonic practice—these include asymmetrical and extended harmonic phrases. Most songs are set in the standard 'verse–chorus' form of Western pop songs, and include instrumental intros and breaks. A common practice in both live and recorded contexts is the medley where two or more songs are presented without a break.

Some musical aspects of these songs have persisted from indigenous traditions. Songs may include the bass rhythmic interjections (*tuki*) often found in Cook Islands religious choral music (*imene*). Modern composers such as Tepoave Raitia have used older chant and secular song styles (*pe'e* and *ute*) within a popular music context. Recent song compositions (for example, the T-Bones' 1997 album) indicate a continuation of this trend of fusing older styles with new sounds.—DG

Contemporary music in Papua New Guinea

Papua New Guinea's popular music represents several stages of historical development. Pre 1870 was 'truly traditional', 1870–1945 was a time of 'early external influence', 1945–75 was 'recent external influence', and arguably the post-independence years mark the beginnings of a third stage of 'emergence and new beginning'.

The distinctive sound of traditional instruments has become an active ingredient in the output of post-independence musicians, pioneered by a group of National Arts School graduates who performed as Sanguma in the late 1970s. The stage of 'early external influence' reflects forms introduced during the colonial era by missionaries and teachers. The still-popular hymnody was introduced, in part and especially in the island provinces, from Samoa and Fiji, and the Fijian slit-log *(lele)* is still used to summon worshippers in the eastern islands. Gospel music releases remain a regular feature in the catalogues of all the PNG recording studios, and church music is an important part of Sunday programming by both the national radio and television networks.

World War II marks a watershed in the development of popular music. American servicemen helped popularize the guitar and ukulele, and introduced a taste for new exotic folk and country forms. The Australian Broadcasting Corporation (ABC) introduced its Papua and New Guinea Service on 1 July 1946, adding yet another mediator to the music mix. Drinking became legal for nationals only in 1962, but quite rapidly urban beer garden venues began to resonate to the sound of amplified music and electric guitars. The product was largely imitative of overseas material, most early commercial recordings being mere cover versions of other people's music.

Enthusiasm for string band music making was particularly strong on the central Papuan coast adjacent to Port Moresby, and young men from villages and schools began to record their own songs, in Motu or English. Credit for the establishment of a new chapter in local music making must go to the Paramana Strangers founded as a trio in 1967, then as a larger group in 1972. The first band to travel overseas, they did not break up until 1983, when another group—Sanguma, this time from the islands and highlands of New Guinea rather than Papua—introduced a fascinating blend of traditional with Afro-American styles. Sanguma's use of traditional instruments, perfected during the late 1970s and early 1980s, influenced others—for example the group Tumbuna '84 and, in the 1990s, Tambaran Culture. Another group, this time of pop-rock exiles from Irian Jaya—The Black Brothers—were also influential before their deportation in 1979, and ethno-musicologists Webb and Niles have noted 'the reggae sound which they incorporated into their own music influenced the direction of some PNG bands'. Rock and 'island reggae' have spread with improvements in transport and communication leading to the emergence of regional styles, particularly in the Gazelle Peninsula of East New Britain Province, Momase and the Highlands.

In the years leading up to independence, and for perhaps the next 15 years, indigenous popular music in Papua New Guinea was affected by a predominantly one-way flow of cultural products, and the threat of a cultural 'grey-out'. Local popular music lost some of its traditional authenticity and social relevance in the move to accommodate and mimic alien musical forces and forms. However, with the benefit of hindsight, the post-independence years may now be viewed as a new beginning, forged by the combined efforts of the mediators—local broadcast music presenters, and major recording studios and sound engineers. The music industry also has reason to be grateful for the wider dissemination of local cultural product by radio (the National Broadcasting Commission and Nau FM), as well as tele vision (EM-TV).

The growing confidence in and appreciation of local music can be judged by the popularity of the NBC *Kalang* Service's PNG Top Twenty show, and EM-TV's video-clip *Mekim Musik* and *Fizz* programs. The major recording studios, Chin H Meen and Pacific Gold, have promoted local stadium performances and Pacific tours by popular soloists. Both have capitalised on the improved sound technology installed, and entrepreneurs have provided both rehearsal space and a productive learning experience for local musicianship. Sadly both lost their important Gazelle Peninsula studios when volcanic eruptions obliterated Rabaul in 1994. The national broadcaster also provides an avenue for local talent through its *Kalang* label, and there are smaller production studios in the north at Madang, and in the highlands at Goroka. Further encouragement to the local music industry is provided by the weekly English-language *Times of Papua New Guinea*, now *The Weekender*, which carries a regular music review column, and another full-colour national magazine, *Music*, was launched by a group of Tolais from East New Britain, in August 1995. It may be too early to state categorically that Papua New Guinea has arrived as a distinctive contributor to the world music stage, but there is certainly an emerging creativity and a growing self-confidence.—MP

Further reading

Webb, M, 1993. *Lokal Musik—lingua franca song and identity in Papua New Guinea*, Papua New Guinea National Research Institute.

See also the *Music Archive for the Pacific* at the Library of Southern Cross University, Lismore, New South Wales: http://www.scu.edu.au/

Indigenous popular music in Australia

Popular music is one of the main means of musical expression for Australia's indigenous peoples, Aborigines and Torres Strait Islanders. It is an important and vibrant part of the indigenous expressive culture that has emerged over the last few decades and now circulates within the global cultural economy.

Indigenous popular music is broadly defined here as contemporary music that adopts and adapts a combination of musical and poetic forms, and conventions of presentation and production from both indigenous and non-indigenous cultures. It also has considerable ongoing application and availability both for its indigenous and non-indigenous creators and audiences. For indigenous musicians, popular music is a medium of individual expression and a site of group identity. Some of the songs become important parts of the soundscapes and humanscapes of indigenous and non-indigenous communities. Importantly, popular music produced on cassette (and CD) is affordable, transportable and represents a wide range of artists, agendas and abilities.

The repertoire of indigenous popular music in Australia is eclectic. It ranges from more traditional song styles and genres (which feature traditional instruments and percussion) to the most up-to-date ones (which feature standard Western rock-pop instrumental/vocal ensembles). There are artists and groups who successfully bridge the two influences. Perhaps the best example of syncretic indigenous popular music is Yothu Yindi, a band with Aboriginal, Anglo-Australian and Papua New Guinean members who nonetheless are considered to be the most successful indigenous group to date. The band operates out of a small, isolated community in Arnhem Land in the Northern Territory (Yirrkala) yet tour and market their recordings internationally. Like some other indigenous bands Yothu Yindi operate successfully on at least three levels. They are part of local socio-cultural, economic and political agendas. They are part of the Australian music scene where they contribute to national identity through their performance styles and the important issues to which they draw attention, such as social justice, human rights and land rights. And they are also part of the 'world music' scene and act regularly as overseas musical ambassadors for Australia.

There are many bands and soloists who have enjoyed success locally, nationally and internationally in the 1980s and 1990s. Some of the better known bands are Amunda, Blekbala Mujik, Coloured Stone,Mixed Relations, Sunrize Band, Tiddas, Tjapukai, Tribal Link and Warumpi Band. Well known singer-songwriters are Christine Anu, Kev Carmody, Ruby Hunter, Toni Janke, Roger Knox, Jimmy Little, Archie Roach, Frank Yama and Dougie Young. Didjeriduists who record, teach and perform include Mark Atkins, Alan Dargin, David Hudson, Kerry McKenzie, Adrian Ross and Richard Walley. All these bands and soloists write original material and promote their music in live performance and recordings. Many of them work full time as musicians, while others combine music with other talents and occupations such as arts administration, painting, dancing, teaching and play-writing.

Indigenous populations in Australia are spread across the nation in rural, small town and urban communities. A major outlet for indigenous popular music is through indigenous media, primarily radio stations, which provide a network of contacts as well as broadcast performance royalties for writers. Some of the bands and artists, such as Yothu Yindi and Kev Carmody, are especially active in support work and donate time and energy to community projects and educational initiatives.

Of special note are two tertiary level educational institutions that have trained many indigenous musicians and singers, who now pursue music, media, teaching and community work careers. The Aboriginal-Islander College of Music in Perth, Western Australia, and the Centre for Aboriginal Studies in Music at the University of Adelaide, South Australia, have degree granting programs in contemporary music. The Central Australia Aboriginal Media Association in Alice Springs has a large catalogue of recordings. A useful source of information on both popular and traditional indigenous music is the Australian Institute of Aboriginal and Torres Strait Islander Studies (AIATSIS) in Canberra.—KN

Cover of *Nuanua*, published by Auckland University Press, 1995

FOUR LITERATURE

Pacific identities, Pacific writing

Pacific literature has been inventing and defining itself since the 1960s, clearing a space for itself in relation to colonial (and other) literature. It is not surprising that it began and gained euphoric power and mana within and alongside the movements for political independence in the region; movements which worked to decolonize island countries and to forge national identities rooted firmly in island ways of life and island pasts. Post-colonial literature was part of the drive for roots, cultural revival and rebirth. (Its most recent political phase is the attack on corrupt élites and the injustices perpetuated by neo-colonialism.) And as island political movements were inspired by other anti-colonial movements, this literature was inspired by and learned from the post-colonial literatures that emerged out of those movements.

Pacific literature puts islanders at centre stage, using island accents, dress, dreams and visions. Much of this literature is nationalistic, angry, protesting, lamenting a huge loss. That loss is defined differently from country to country. The literature attempts to reconstruct what has been lost or changed. Consequently much of it is a fabulous storehouse of anthropology, sociology, art, religion, history, dance and music. Novels like *The Crocodile*, *Maiba*, *Potiki*, *the bone people*, *Leaves of the Banyan Tree* and *Dr Wooreddy's Prescription for Enduring the Ending of the World* show this well.

Much early Pacific writing saw the colonial and the indigenous as an irreconcilable opposition: the colonial was the evil destroyer, and no benefits were seen in colonialism, or in the emergence of blends and mixtures and fusion of the indigenous and foreign, even though the literature itself is living proof of that. It is often modernist and uses the realist mode, reflecting the influence of Western art, literature and education on island writers. Now we have a complex and expansive blend of realism and magic realism in Pacific writing, but at its heart are the traditional ingredients: the techniques of oral storytelling and other oral traditions; art, dance and music; and indigenous philosophies and visions.

The literatures in indigenous island languages continue to flourish and grow. Oral literatures, which stretch back hundreds of years, are astounding collections of mythologies, genealogies, poetry, stories, songs, chants and incantations. These are still the richest Pacific treasures even though most of them have not been recorded or passed on to young people through island education systems. Many Pacific writers continue to draw their strength from oral traditions; some reuse or reinvent ancient mythologies to map the present, some use the techniques of oral storytelling and recitation and oratory. In a range of new, striking and energetic ways, Pacific writing continues to explore the possibilities of language, revealing island identities and the forces shaping island ways of life.—AW2

Source/further reading

Wendt, A, 1995. *Nuanua: Pacific writing in English since 1980*, Auckland University Press.

Creative literature by Pacific islanders

Imaginative writing for publication in print came to the fore in the 1960s, first at the UNIVERSITY OF PAPUA NEW GUINEA where local writers, facilitated by Ulli Beier, became 'vocal' to a national and international audience through publishing poems, plays, novels and political writings in both English and Pidgin. There were parallels in the visual arts. Several years later the UNIVERSITY OF THE SOUTH PACIFIC opened in Fiji with students from 11 countries. The South Pacific Creative Arts Society (SPCAS), founded in 1972, took a leading role in facilitating creative writing workshops for playwriting, poetry and prose. The best contributions were published. At first all the writing was in English, but later some wrote in Pidgin and local languages. The majority has been in English however, partly because most writers prefer it—giving them the opportunity to reach a wider audience—and sometimes because they are saying things that might not be acceptable in their home communities.

Commercial publishers at first were not interested in the writings of young Pacific writers. The market was very small and untried, the writers first-time amateurs. However, the PACIFIC ISLANDS MONTHLY carried an SPCAS literary supplement in each issue from 1972 to 1975, when the literary talents were more widely recognized and a wider range of outlets was available. The *Pacific Islands Monthly* made a small payment to enable the society to undertake further workshops and publications, and also published each year's collection as a separate volume which sold well. The society also established its own publishing program of books and the literary journal *Mana* (from 1976).

Many of these works have been reprinted many times by SPCAS or others. Some have been translated and published in China, Russia, France, Germany, Japan and elsewhere. Others have been reprinted in anthologies in Australia, New Zealand, Hawai'i and Europe. The demand for creative writing by islanders continues to grow. Pacific literature is now taught in many countries in the region and outside it, and publishers are much more willing to publish it.—MTC

New Zealand Maori literature: from fringe to centre

New Zealand publishes more books per capita than any other developed country in the world. Although the number of Maori being published is already comparatively large, their publications are increasing with every passing year. Perhaps more importantly, an increasing number of Maori writers are choosing to write in *te reo*, the Maori language. Writing in Maori used to be more a political statement than catering to a demand, but as the generations of young Maori educated totally in *te reo* reach maturity, the demand for literature in Maori is increasing. So rich and diverse is the range of Maori writing today that students entering the University of Auckland, for example, can take New Zealand literature at year one, two, and three, at undergraduate level, as well as postgraduate. At every stage, in both New Zealand and Pacific literature, Maori writers and writing contribute a substantial portion of the set texts.

Like the writing of many other indigenous peoples, Maori literature has come into its own. In Aotearoa New Zealand, it is now recognized across the primary, secondary, and tertiary education sectors that Maori have something unique to say and are saying it in new, exciting, and diverse ways. A recent survey of the literature being taught in New Zealand schools shows that Maori and Pacific island writers such as Witi IHIMAERA, Keri HULME, Alan DUFF, Patricia GRACE, Mihi Edwards, Hone TUWHARE, Alistair CAMPBELL, Albert WENDT and Sia FIGIEL are being taught along with Austen, Shakespeare, Swift and Keats.

Maori continue to write in the classical genre of *waiata*, *haka*, *karakia*, myths and legends, but now they also produce literature of every kind and in a variety of styles. Their work appears on stage and screen, both large and small, in poetry and short fiction anthologies, in collections of essays and plays, in journals, both national and international. An issue of *Mānoa* (Vol. 9, 1997), a journal of new writing from America, the Pacific and Asia, published in Hawai'i, features writing by Maori.

The first Maori fiction writer to be published was Jacqueline Sturm whose short story 'The Old Coat' appeared in *Numbers* in 1954. In 1964 Hone Tuwhare published *No Ordinary Sun*, the first book of verse from a contemporary Maori writer. Witi Ihimaera's groundbreaking collection of short stories, *Pounamu Pounamu*, appeared in 1972. Patricia Grace's collection of short stories, *Waiariki*, published in 1975, was the first by a Maori woman. Excerpts from this collection have been dramatized and made into a documentary on Grace and her work, now used as a teaching resource in secondary and tertiary institutions. Keri Hulme's *the bone people* (1983) achieved international recognition when it won the Booker Prize in London in 1985.

The number of publications by Maori continues to grow. Patricia Grace's latest collection of stories, *Sky People*, joins Apirana Taylor's *Ki Te Ao*, Ngahuia Te Awekotuku's *Tahuri*, and Bruce Stewart's *Tama and other stories*. Witi Ihimaera's list of novels includes *The Matriarch*, *The Dream Swimmer*, *Bulibasha* and *Nights in The Gardens of Spain*. Grace's latest novel, *Baby No-Eyes*, follows her previous novels, *Cousins*, *Mutuwhenua* and *Potiki*. Alistair Campbell, best known for his poetry, has written three novels: *The Frigate Bird*, *Tia* and *Sidewinder*. The poet Hone Tuwhare continues to produce new work; his latest collection is entitled *Shape Shifter*. Robert Sullivan will add *Star Waka* to his two previous collections of poetry: *Jazz Waiata* and *Pike Ake*. Jacqueline Sturm recently published her first collection of poetry, *Dedications*. Roma Potiki's *Shaking the Tree* follows her first collection of poems, *Stones in Her Mouth*. As well, there are new and exciting writers percolating to the surface encouraged and nurtured by Witi Ihimaera and Albert Wendt's creative writing course. New plays are being written, including Hone Kouka's *Waiora* (also performed at the Henley Regatta in England), and the one woman show *Nga Pou Wahine* written by Briar Grace-Smith, directed by Nancy Brunning and Tina Cook and starring Rachel House, all of whom are Maori. Scripts for stage and screen, librettos for opera, lyrics for popular songs, and many other popular literary forms are being written by Maori. The film version of Alan Duff's novel, *Once Were Warriors*, New Zealand's highest grossing film, won international acclaim for Maori director, Lee Tamihore, and actors, Temuera Morrison and Rena Owen. (See FICTIONAL FILMS.)

Witi Ihimaera (courtesy Heinemann Reed)

Maori writing is also reaching out to other Pacific peoples and re-establishing ancient links. Maori travelling to other parts of the world rediscover those common bonds which were all but lost. Maori of Aotearoa/New Zealand are rediscovering their Polynesian heritage and reconnecting with the senior genealogical lines, and this is happening most notably through literature.

Many young Maori are strong in *te reo* and soon there will emerge a new literature totally in Maori. This will finally complete the circle and once again Maori will be able to enjoy the beauty and uniqueness of being, thinking, reading, and writing in *te reo*. The demand for children's literature written in Maori is already far exceeding that being produced. This is a new growth area and Maori writers are rising to the challenge by producing a wide range of beautifully illustrated literature for children of all ages.

The influence Maori have had, and continue to have, on the wider literature of Aotearoa is also growing. Pakeha (non-Maori) New Zealanders are using more Maori in their writing, they are discovering that Maori is a culture worth exploring and worthy of inclusion. For years, Maori have been waiting in the wings, learning, observing, gathering strength and experience, and now it is Pakeha who are learning, many for the first time, about the culture surrounding them. Pakeha are also discovering that they are defined by outsiders more and more in their relationship with Maori. Writers of fiction from both cultures are taking risks. They face each other as literary equals and the energy and creative spirit emanating in the space between is proving beneficial.

More anthologies of poetry and short fiction will follow *Lali* and *Nuanua*, edited by Albert Wendt, and *Into the World of Light* and *Te Ao Marama* edited by Witi Ihimaera. There are currently calls for writing by Maori and Pacific islanders for new publications. The current project of those 'greats' of Polynesian writing and editing, Albert Wendt and Witi Ihimaera, assisted by Robert Sullivan and Reina Whaitiri, is anthologies of poetry and short fiction by Polynesians.—RW

Cook Islands literature

A wide range of types and styles of 'oral literature' has existed in Cook Islands—prose, saga, chant, song and poetry of various forms, much of it relating to migrations and other origins, legendary or historical characters and events, natural history, theology, values and moral teachings. The Polynesian Society has perhaps the largest collection of recorded oral tradition waiting for Cook Islands scholars to translate, annotate and publish.

Until writing was introduced by the LONDON MISSIONARY SOCIETY in the early 1800s, oration was a refined and valued art form. The missionaries were amazed to find that once reading was taught, many people learned whole chapters of the Bible by heart and could stand and recite them. Many families used writing to record their genealogies and traditions, but few survived because of hurricanes, fires, mildew, and some jealous chiefs who collected all records of their subordinates and burned them so that chiefly authority would not be compromised. The early Tahitian missionaries also suppressed the oral traditions as antithetical to Christian teachings.

Most of the preserved material was collected by a few later English missionaries and stored abroad. Some of them encouraged their Cook Islands counterparts to write about the pre-Christian era and the post-Christian as well. The most copious writers were Ta'unga (who wrote over 30 manuscripts, some of them very extensive), and Maretu (who wrote one book-length work) in the 1800s. Some foreign researchers recorded the knowledge of the traditional high priest Teariki Taraare and others.

The colonial era from 1901 to 1965 was a sterile time for writing by Cook Islanders. Only the noted New Zealand Maori ethnographer, Te Rangi Hiroa (Sir Peter BUCK), recorded the traditions and culture of the peoples of Manihiki, Rakahanga, Tongareva, Aitutaki, and to a lesser extent, the other islands. These he published in his capacity as director of the BISHOP MUSEUM in Hawai'i. Since 1965 there has been a surge in formal education and in writing. Over 140 books have been written by Cook Islanders in the past 30 years and there are probably more. Many articles, poems, dramas and other writings have been published in newspapers, journals, magazines and various outlets. Most writing is in English because it reaches a wider audience. The next largest category is in Rarotongan (Cook Islands Maori), plus several books in the Manihiki dialect, one in Atiuan, and one in Pukapukan, a separate language. With a national population of only 18 000—almost all of whom can read English as well or better than the Cook Islands languages—it is uneconomic to produce small print runs for a vernacular market only. Moreover, with over 80 per cent of Cook Islanders living abroad and many of them not fluent in their island language, English is more accessible.

The most prolific author was the late Taira Rere, who wrote 77 small books, mostly about the history and culture of Rarotonga. He worked for some years as a full-time writer for the Ministry of Education. He was unusual in that he travelled little, for most Cook Islands writers have spent long periods abroad. Almost all, if not all, are of multiple ancestry and multicultural. Alistair Te Ariki CAMPBELL has spent most of his life in New Zealand, but still publishes poetry and prose on Cook Islands themes, particularly on his mother's island of Tongareva. Sir Tom DAVIS (Pa Tuterangi Ariki) spent nearly 30 years in New Zealand and the United States before returning to become prime minister. His major historical novel, *Vaka*, about canoe voyaging in Polynesia, supplements his autobiographical and scientific writings. The late Kauraka KAURAKA (who died in 1997) spent much of his life in New Zealand, Fiji and Hawai'i, but wrote exclusively and extensively of the Cook Islands, mainly about his father's island of Manihiki which he had only visited. Kauraka was perhaps the only Cook Islands writer who often published in both English and either Manihiki or Rarotongan languages. Almost all others write in one or the other. Florence 'Johnny' Frisbie spent much of her adult life in New Zealand before returning home to Rarotonga. She writes novels and short stories of island life, and published a family biography. Jon JONASSEN, who has spent many years abroad as a professional performer of Cook Islands dance and drumming, and later working in international organizations and diplomacy, writes stories, legends, history, poetry, songs, chants and music. Va'ine Rasmussen Wichman, who travelled the Pacific for the South Pacific Commission (now PACIFIC COMMUNITY) writes short stories and poetry, mainly about issues of identity and culture in the Cook Islands. Makiuti Tongia, who spent most of his adult life in Fiji, the United States and New Zealand, writes poetry, short stories, and material on Rarotongan culture. Marjorie Tuainekore Crocombe, who spent more of her life in Fiji, Papua New Guinea, New Zealand and Hawai'i than in Rarotonga, writes history and stories based on history (for adults and children), mainly on Cook Islands themes. She was founder and president of the South Pacific Creative Arts Society (SPCAS) which promoted hundreds of islands writers.

Other modern Cook Islands writers who emphasize cultural themes include Tepoave Raitia and the late Turepu Turepu, both of whom travelled abroad as professional Cook Islands artists and choreographers, and are composers of drama, song and chant. John Herrmann composes and publishes song and writes on current affairs; Tai Turepu Carpentier writes on language and culture; Naomi Iro's main creations have been in song and chant; Vereara Maeva writes mainly song and legend, but also of

Cook Islands culture. Teupokoina Utanga Morgan writes music and poetry and created a folk opera. Teata Makirere, who travelled the region for some years as communications adviser to the Pacific Conference of Churches, is a noted composer (mainly of secular songs) and poet. Paiere Mokoroa writes extensively and exclusively on the culture of his island of Atiu, as does Merota Ngamata of his home island, Pukapuka. Tere Tarapu and Tepaeru Tereora compose song, chant and poetry with a strong emphasis on the theme of cultural retention; while More Rua writes of traditional religious, medical and cultural practices. The late Tangata Simiona concentrated on legendary based stories of Atiu. Florence Syme-Buchanan has published poems and short stories. Irai Wilkin and Nanette Woonton both write poetry and stories. Mona Matepi is unique as the only Cook Islander (perhaps the only Pacific islander) to have created a 52-episode children's television program, *Mokopets*, as well as having published short stories.

The above list of contemporary Cook Islands writers omits many who have not published. Many people who create song, chant and drama do not keep written records, let alone publish their work. Although much of this material is sung and performed on radio and television in the Cook Islands and Tahiti, and some is now available on cassette and CD, there are many more pieces—songs widely known and sung, or drama created for a particular occasion, performed and then abandoned—that form part of Cook Islands 'literature'. This unrecorded segment of popular culture is extremely important and merits further study.—MTC

Chamorro literature

The richest sources of Chamorro literature are to be found in oral traditions, ranging from legends and folk tales to a variety of musical forms. A wide range of Chamorro legends stress cultural values such as respecting one's elders and helping one another in reciprocal relationships. Many of the folk tales describe Chamorro ways of living in pre-colonial times as well as during the Spanish occupation of Mariana Islands between the 16th and 19th centuries. Chamorro literature is also embodied in various musical genres, including the *Kantan Chamorrita*, which is a four-line poem spontaneously composed and sung by two competing individuals or groups. Chamorrita singers, male and female, sing their original verses along beaches, after fishing trips, at political rallies, or just for fun. Some of the songs convey themes of courtship and many emphasize a competition between singers as to who can respond more quickly, with more humorous lyrics, and with more poetic and metaphorical imagery. Today one can also find Chamorro literature written in both Chamorro and English.

Since the 1960s there has been a gradual emergence of indigenous Chamorro creative writing. The University of Guam has played a role in promoting literary writing with the publication of two literary journals, *Xanadu* in the 1960s and 1980s, and *Storyboard: A Journal of Pacific Imagery*, in print since 1991. Both these journals express a multicultural (rather than exclusively Chamorro) literary consciousness within Mariana Islands, as well as within the larger Micronesian region. To date there are no established Chamorro creative writers. The only Chamorro novel is Chris Perez Howard's *Mariquita*, published in 1986 by the University of the South Pacific. In *Mariquita*, Howard narrates the life story of his mother during the pre-war and World War II years on Guam. His novel attempts to convey the importance of familial relationships as expressed by certain Chamorro families under both the American and Japanese occupations of the island, and it invites the interest of readers concerned with the impact of World War II in the Pacific (ISLANDER EXPERIENCES IN THE PACIFIC WAR).

The future of Chamorro literature as an integral part of the contemporary culture of the Mariana Islands appears bright. The current momentum, linked to an insurgence of cultural pride and consciousness, encourages young people and elders to put their thoughts and experiences on paper as well as to make use of film and music. The growth of mass media opportunities and popular cultural resources in the islands will undoubtedly contribute to the flourishing of written literature as a vehicle for the expression of Chamorro culture and identity.—KLC

Contemporary writing in Fiji

It seems paradoxical that in spite of its prominent economic and social position in the Pacific region, Fiji has not produced a strong body of literary works in the main indigenous languages of Fijian and Fiji Hindi. Fiji has the highest literacy rate and standard of living in the region, and yet in literary output it lags far behind its Pacific neighbours. This is surprising for a country which has endured much suffering during the GIRMITIYA period and during the two military FIJI COUPS: events which might have inspired enduring literature. One reason for this absence has been the overly exam-oriented education system which has not nurtured budding writers. Also, Fiji's integration into the global market economy has pressured many parents to have their children become accountants, doctors or lawyers and certainly not writers, a fringe profession often seen as frivolous. Third, although oral traditions are important, the indigenous peoples have not developed a taste for patronizing literary arts, preferring to use their hard-earned money on Hollywood or Bombay-made movies, for example.

Contemporary writing in the Fijian language has been mainly of a didactic nature. Most literary works are partly fiction and fact combined. The plot is often interrupted to allow author intrusion for a sociological account of culture or a spirited theological treatise as a commentary on the action. Many of the better known novels in Fijian touch on themes of respect for chiefs, filial love or the need for wives to show devotion to their husbands in these post-modern times. With the new millennium drawing near, recent works have exhorted readers in this decadent world to place more faith in Jesus.

Many other literary works in Fijian are an extension of oral literature with retelling of old myths and legends. There is a thriving audience for this type of material in primary schools. They are still didactic because contemporary writers have added moral lessons in stories to reflect their Christian affiliations. Much Fijian-language material offers simple, moralist messages, perceived by its readers as almost Biblical.

Writing in Hindi has not been a continuous development, though the wish to recount and create can be traced back to the indenture period when life was governed by the material needs of an insecure existence. The important book of the period of the indenture system was Totaram Sanadhya's *My Twenty One Years in the Fiji Islands*, published in India in 1914. This book—a political treatise—launched a Fiji Hindi literary tradition, and continues to influence contemporary Hindi writers.

Fiji Hindi writing blossomed in 1992–93. J S Kanwal wrote his novel *Savera* (The Morning), a stark portrayal of life under the indenture system, and was awarded an honorary degree from the UNIVERSITY OF THE SOUTH PACIFIC for his contributions to Hindi literature. C P Shiriwastav's poems were published and Raymond PILLAI's play in Fiji Hindi was staged in Wellington. Author SUBRAMANI commented in his essay collection *Alterning Imagination* that amid much talk of decline and decay of Hindi, recent literary works give a different impression, securing a new life and winning recognition.

It has been said that writers need to live through suffering in order to produce enduring literature that mirrors society's trials and tribulations and provides insights into humanity. Fiji has gone through two military coups and a change of government six times within nine months in 1987–88. The population has witnessed significant constitutional change. Throughout this period, people have been forced to confront their racial stereotypes. They have learnt to live with each other in harmony, which may well produce a flowering of indigenous literature as writers probe the meaning of humanity within a multicultural society. This will mean Fijian writers moving away from mainly didactic writings and Indo-Fijians from mainly indenture themes to more ambitious works showing insights into the reinvented post-modern Fiji.—JV

Further reading

Atherton, S S and Nandan, S P, 1985. *Creative Writing from Fiji*, Fiji Writers' Association.

'Local' writing from Hawai'i

The Hawaiian Islands have been widely celebrated and traduced in texts of all kinds, but mostly, until recent times, by outsiders. As a crude generalization, literary production from the mid 1800s through to the 1970s was determined by white writers, who, even when long resident, had their mind on 'the mainland'—physically, the United States; culturally, Europe. After the strongly assimilationist culture of the 1950s, a generation of 'local' Hawaiians emerged for whom the 'mainland' was either an irrelevance or an intrusive and oppressive cultural force. These folk had their roots in immigrant plantation labour (predominantly from China, Japan and the Philippines) with frequent family ties to indigenous Hawaiians. For them, Hawai'i was their mainland, and they sought to express local experience in a blend of cultural attitudes and expressive terms.

Steven Sumida, in his study, *And the View from the Shore* (1991), has traced the origins of this 'local motion' (to use a surfing logo) to century-old letters, stories and poems by migrants, but as a visible literary production, 'local' literature has its signposts in Milton Murayama's novel, *All I Asking for Is My Body* (1975), and in a 'talk story' conference in 1978, when people met to swap oral traditions, family histories, ghost stories and explore the written possibilities of localized English, generally disparaged as 'pidgin'. From this conference the still-running and important showcase journal *Bamboo Ridge* emerged, headed by Eric Chock and Darrell Lum. Other literary groups and journals centred around community colleges and universities: *Hawaii Review, Chaminade Review, Hapa, Ramrod, Seaweeds and Constructions*, and the Hawai'i Literary Arts Council. Amongst others,

Frank Stewart and Pat Matsueda have long been active supporters of these and are currently leading production of the island-based journal of international writing, *Manoa*.

To single out names is always difficult, but consistent producers include Marjorie Sinclair (novels), Cathy Song (a prize-winning poet), Darrell Lum (stories in local English, plays), Susan Nunes (short fiction), Juliet S Kono (poetry), Wing Tek Lum (poetry), Rodney Morales (short fiction), Joseph Stanton (poetry). Another significant contributor to the formation of a local literary scene has been the theatre group Kumu Kahua, whose selected early plays are published (1983), edited by long-time director Dennis Carroll.

The field of 'local writing' has included work by people identifying as Native Hawaiian, though in recent years this has been distinguished as a separate though related constituency (see CONTEMPORARY HAWAIIAN LITERATURE). 'Local' work crosses and conflicts with it, and increasingly, with the 'Asian-American' phenomenon, driven mostly by 'mainland' interest groups.—PS3

Contemporary Hawaiian literature

In the 1990s, Hawai'i has witnessed a flourishing of contemporary literature produced by Native Hawaiian composers, chanters, poets, short story authors, novelists, playwrights and screenwriters, including indigenous poet/rap artists. While there exists an extensive traditional, written literature closely linked to the Hawaiian language and ancient Hawaiian and Polynesian oral tradition, contemporary Native Hawaiian authors continue to write creatively and publish in standard English, Pidgin (Hawaiian Creole English), and the Hawaiian language, occasionally employing all three languages in one literary piece. Hawaiian authors use a variety of literary genres, and their works include both indigenous and non-indigenous literary models.

Neither the large US publishing houses nor the university presses have nurtured or published contemporary Native Hawaiian writers—unlike some of the major publishers of indigenous authors in Aotearoa New Zealand. Small press publishing in Hawai'i continues to play a most significant role. However, creative literature published by Native Hawaiians goes out of print quickly; often appears only in a few limited-edition literary magazines, family-run presses, or individually funded, non-commercially-oriented publications; or is available only in select archives. Problems also abound concerning book distribution for small press publishers in Hawai'i, although a recent commercial cooperative, Native Books, is marketing indigenous authors both locally and abroad. Publishing and distribution inequities for most indigenous as well as non-indigenous authors mean that readers and scholars alike must be willing to do much sleuthing.

Native Hawaiian literature needs to be understood in the context of the Hawaiian music industry which is, unlike literary publishing, a growing, multimillion-dollar business. One can visit any number of local libraries, music stores, retail outlets and web-sites, and find recordings on cassette and compact disc. Accompanying literature with these recordings occasionally contains valuable information and literary texts. Most importantly, one can simply turn on the radio to selected stations including publicly funded stations, such as Hawai'i's public radio stations and the University of Hawai'i's KTUH-FM, as well as commercial stations, and listen to yet another dimension of Hawaiian literature manifested in songs, chants, stories and poetry.

The contemporary recording industry has not only popularized Hawaiian songs and music so often associated with the omnipresent tourist industry, but has also documented chants, poetry, GENEALOGIES and other compositions, including spoken word pieces, such as short stories, legends, myths, fiction, non-fiction, comedy and satire. Author George Hu'eu Sanford Kanahele, in his book *Hawaiian Music and Musicians* (1979), documents the Hawaiian music movement from the earliest days. As interest in the Hawaiian music recording industry burgeoned, especially in the early 1970s, this in turn mirrored and helped stimulate interest, consciousness and growth in the many genres of Hawaiian literature, both contemporary and traditional. The art of HULA melds the essences and essentials of the spoken and chanted word with indigenous dance forms and skills such as featherwork and refined lei and musical instrument handicrafts. During the 1960s and 1970s, hula began its resurgence within Hawaiian communities, along with the revival of long-distance Polynesian voyages, resulting in unprecedented collaborations and exchanges between Native Hawaiians and other Pacific islanders. (See HŌKŪLE'A.)

Each year sees a growing number of recordings which reflect collaborations between musicians, composers, poets, and chanters. Works by Native Hawaiian poets, scholars, and translators include Haunani Bernadino, Manu Boyd, Kīhei de Silva, Larry Lindsey Kimura, Mary Kawena Pūku'i and Ka'upena Wong, whose compositions are performed by both indigenous and non-indigenous musicians. Hawaiian music comprises both traditional and contemporary influences. Prominent Hawaiian musicians Peter Apo, the Brothers Cazimero, the Kahauanu Lake Trio, the late Israel Kamakawiwoʻole, Kekuni Kanahele, the late Edith Kanakaʻole, Keliʻi Tauʻā, Palani Vaughn, and others, have released compositions including integrated elements of spoken word, singing, chanting and music. Recordings by Sudden Rush, a group of Native Hawaiian rappers and poets, include contemporary poetry, music, singing and Hawaiian chant in their performances. Their compositions most often relate to sovereignty, ethnic respect, and the resurgence of Hawaiian consciousness, history, culture and language.

As with the music industry, contemporary poetry in the Hawaiian language, Pidgin and standard English is flourishing, despite lack of support from university presses or national publishing houses. Contemporary Hawaiian poetry is best studied in the context of traditional Hawaiian oral literature and chant composition, and also assessed in contrast with the literature produced by non-indigenous poets. Native Hawaiian poets are numerous, eclectic and stylistically diverse, and there is an abundance of independent single-ethnic publishing efforts, multi-ethnic collaborations, as well as examples of cultural, philosophical and even ethnic factionalism. Also, since the 1970s, more Hawaiians are publishing poetry written exclusively in Pidgin, thanks largely to the local recording industry, increased public readings, stage and video productions, and small press literary magazines. Scholarly research and documentation of contemporary Hawaiian writers have increased, particularly in degree programs in ethnic, Hawaiian, and Pacific islands studies as well as in a few university English courses.

Like contemporary indigenous literary movements elsewhere in the Pacific, significant creative writing in English by Native Hawaiians emerged in the late 1960s and the early 1970s. Acclaimed poet Dana Naone Hall's first notable work was published in English in the early 1970s. A former *Hawaii Review* editor and poet-in-the-schools instructor, Naone Hall's poetry continues to be widely anthologized and her poetry is assigned in English classes throughout the state. Her Hawaiian contemporary, the late Wayne Westlake, was very much involved in the editing and publishing of both indigenous and non-indigenous literature through the late 1970s and early 1980s. Joe Balaz, Michael McPherson and Leialoha Apo Perkins followed suit in the early 1980s. Balaz and McPherson not only published poetry but also edited and published literary magazines. By the late 1970s, poets in English addressed a wide range of concerns, from local politics to land struggles, from the bombing of the Kahoʻolawe island to the eviction of Native Hawaiians. Poet and visual artist ʻImaikalani Kalāhele wrote many of his poems in all three languages mentioned. In the 1980s, several anthologies were published which included a wide variety of contemporary Hawaiian poets. In 1994 Haunani-Kay TRASK's *Light in the Crevice Never Seen* was the first Native Hawaiian collection of poetry in English to be released by a major publisher.

A variety of poetic genres are employed, revealing Hawaiian, Polynesian, Western, Asian and 'third and fourth world' influences. One important example is the impact of the international concrete poetry movement on several Native Hawaiian writers. Poets Wayne Westlake, Joe Balaz, ʻImaikalani Kalāhele, and Hawaiian photographer and collage-artist, Kapulani Landgraf, have published their graphically-oriented poetic works locally, nationally and internationally. Landgraf's concrete poetry is on permanent display at the CENTER FOR HAWAIIAN STUDIES.

To date, the late Native Hawaiian writer, poet and publisher John Dominis Holt is the most notable author of Hawaiian fiction in English. Holt established two presses, Topgallant Publishing in 1974 and Kū Paʻa Press in the 1990s. For nearly 30 years, Holt published an array of authors of many ethnicities, including his own collection of short fiction, *Princess of the Night Rides and Other Stories* (1977), as well as his acclaimed yet controversial novel, *Waimea Summer* (1976). In 1986, Leialoha Apo Perkins, through her family imprint, Kamaluʻuluolele Press, published a collection of fiction, *The Firemakers and Other Short Stories of Hawaiʻi, the Samoas, and Tonga*. Hawaiian poet Michael McPherson also published short fiction in literary magazines in the 1980s. More recently, university-related outlets have been publishing a growing number of indigenous fiction writers. Recently English professor Miyoko Sugano compiled a manuscript titled 'Hoʻokupu: an offering of literature by Native Hawaiian women' (1997, unpublished). This collection included fiction by Hawaiian playwright Victoria Nalani Kneubuhl and an excerpt of Pualani Kanakaʻole Kanahele's novel-in-progress. Novelists of Hawaiian ancestry whose work has been recently published include Leialoha Apo Perkins, Carolyn Lei-lanilau, Kiana Davenport, and Mamo Clark Rawley. Publishers of this fiction include university and small presses.

Published work by playwrights, especially Native Hawaiians, is rare but growing. In 1971 John Dominis Holt published an historical drama of the overthrow of the Hawaiian monarchy and subsequent demise of the Hawaiian nation, titled *Kaulana Na Pua, Famous are the Children*. In the late 1980s and early 1990s playwright Victoria Nalani Kneubuhl wrote and directed several plays with Hawaiian themes and characters. In the 1990s, while a handful of new Hawaiian playwrights emerged, few have found publishers for their works. Recently, Hawaiian scholar, teacher, *kumu hula* (hula master), and author Pualani Kanakaʻole Kanahele and her equally accomplished sister, *kumu hula* and poet, Nālani Kanakaʻole produced 'Holo Mai Pele', recounting, through chant, dance, oral traditions and history, the travels of Hawaiian volcano goddess Pele, from Kahiki to Hawaiʻi. This dramatic and brilliantly executed production included traditional dance, chant, music and dialogue, performed in the Hawaiian language, with occasional English narrative. Their critically acclaimed production toured the United States as well as Hawaiʻi.

As with poetry and fiction, the history of contemporary drama written and produced by Native Hawaiians is best examined in relation to the development of Hawaiian theatre, from the pageants of the early 20th century to the emergence of 'pidgin theatre' and the 'theatre of protest' when public skits were staged, mostly during land demonstrations held from the 1960s to the 1990s. The role of local drama organizations, as well as the activities of playwrights, producers, directors and actors of both Hawaiian and non-Hawaiian ancestries, should also be examined. Non-indigenous playwright, director and drama professor Dennis Carroll has written an engaging and enlightening introduction to the history of drama in Hawaiʻi in a collection which he edited, *Kumu Kahua Plays* (1983). Before the mid 1980s, published contemporary Hawaiian playwrights were few, and Carroll's essay documents very little Native Hawaiian activity in this field.

For nearly 20 years, Nā Maka o ka ʻĀina's video collaborations were the sole 'eyes' for Native Hawaiians and others interested in indigenous social struggle as well as cultural and political reclamation. Nā Maka o ka ʻĀina is a video team comprised of Hawaiian co-producer and writer Puhipau and non-Hawaiian co-producer and videographer Joan Lander. In contrast, the 1990s have given rise to Native Hawaiian filmmakers such as Edgy Lee, Eddie Kamae, and the recently founded non-profit organization, Pacific Islanders in Communications, in Honolulu, which offers information about indigenous regional filmmakers and their work, much of which is now available worldwide.—RH

Indigenous literature: Micronesia

Micronesian written literature—with particular reference to the Federated States of Micronesia (FSM), the Republic of the Marshall Islands (RMI) and the freely associated political entity of Palau—cannot be separated from the oral foundations of the Micronesian societies. Oral methods of communication have played an essential role in socio-political and cultural dynamics within Micronesia, and continue to exist alongside, against and within written literature. But the 'development' of writing, which has its basis in 19th century efforts to Christianize islanders, and in the educational systems of four colonial powers since the 1600s, has not produced a collection of published Micronesian literature. It is indeed the expectation that Micronesia should have its own creatively written literature (that is published and made available to a public) which brings these foreign influences and their relationships and disassociations with indigenous communal features to the surface. Many contemporary scholars of language and literature have ignored the oral basis for such literature, and even the construction of the term 'oral literature' is based upon the assumption that an oral verbalization of stories is or was but an unwritten text. Therefore the written form completed what would otherwise be an incomplete process; and the idea of studying orality itself has been seen as an extraordinary academic endeavour, instead of an acknowledgment of its fundamental role in the creation of many kinds of written literatures.

The American presence in Micronesia has impoverished the discussion of oral realities and foundations of Micronesian communal systems in 'literature'. This is not to suggest that acculturation has been a simple process of destructive outsider influences acting upon more virtuous forms of values and knowledge. Micronesians themselves reap benefits from the financial and educational systems that followed World War II, and acculturation has taken various forms and proceeded at different rates. Today in the FSM, the RMI and Palau, oral traditions are being reworked into forms expressing cultural identities in the contexts of traditional values and modern globalized statehood.

How useful is it to discuss Micronesian literature within the historical dynamics of foreign presences and intentions, and indigenous responses? In Australia Aboriginal playwrights, poets, and novelists such as Oodgeroo (Kath Walker), Mudrooroo (Colin Johnston), Jack Davis and Lionel Fogarty have attempted to bring vernacular oral diction to 'literature' in order to express and assert indigenous values and perceptions without the restrictions of

'Western' literary paradigms. Indigenous writers in Oceania—John KASAIPWALOVA in Papua New Guinea, Samoan Albert WENDT, Maori Keri HULME and others—have also at times given priority to the assertion of identity and values ahead of (European) literary forms and standards. Although creative literature published by PNG writers, for example, evolved initially from anti-colonial sentiments, the Micronesian response has been different.

The small amounts of poetry and short stories published so far attempt primarily to express and preserve 'culture' through standard literary genres. Between the end of World War II and 1986 when the Trust Territory of the Pacific Islands became the FSM, and Marshall Islands gained its independence, this oral mythology was condensed and popularly published while anthropologically based studies used various fragments for contextual enrichment. The secrecy and respect that confined traditional knowledge to elders and adepts on the one hand limited its transmission into general print publication and on the other, was given lip-service in prefaces to translations turning it into folkloric 'legends'. Histories of Pohnpei by Luelen Bernart written between 1932 and 1946 and Pohnpeian scholar Rufino Mauricio's use of oral histories to construct the early settlement of Pohnpei become important sources for understanding how these bridges between the foundations of orality and indigenous 'literature' could be drawn. But work remains to be done comparing the differences in colonial dynamics between the North and South Pacific and their effects on literary activity.

The scarcity of an indigenous Micronesian written literature may indeed be a matter of preserving culturally preferred means of transmitting and accepting valued knowledge. Contributions toward encouraging creative, written Micronesian literature through publishing sources such as the University of Guam's literary magazine *Storyboard* will occur within the conflicts of an 'American' education, newer 'national' cultural identities, and a deeper context of oral tradition.—NJG

Further reading

Bernart, L, 1977. *The Book of Luelen*, J L Fischer, S H Riesenberg and M G Whiting (tr and eds), Australian National University Press and University Press of Hawai'i.

Goetzfridt, N J, 1995. *Indigenous Literature of Oceania: a survey of criticism and interpretation*, Greenwood Press.

Hanlon, D, 1989. 'Micronesia: writing and rewriting the histories of a nonentity', *Pacific Studies*, 12(2).

Mauricio, R, 1987. 'Peopling of Pohnpei Island: migration, dispersal, and settlement themes in clan narratives', *Man and Culture in Oceania*, 3.

Skinner, M, 1989. Contemporary Micronesian literature: a preliminary bibliography, cyclostyled monograph, University of Hawai'i.

Samoan written and oral literature

Writing in Samoa began with the arrival of missionaries in the early 1800s who devised a Samoan orthography so that the Bible and other religious tracts could be translated and disseminated. Although early literacy was primarily for religious purposes, it also provided social and cultural knowledge necessary to participate in an emerging, Western-style economy and other secular activities which involved communal or individual writing. Samoan writing in the indigenous language therefore extended from Bible translations and other religious literature to the recording of family-oriented information and knowledge. The functions of literacy multiplied as Samoans adapted not only to the new religious environment but also an economic and literary one. Schooling and education became important because of the perceived advantages of reading and writing.

The growth of personal writing by Samoans (strongly akin to journal writing) has not been widely acknowledged, probably because it was not intended for public scrutiny or publication. Such writings are often in exercise books, chronicling personal life histories and recording family, church, village and national events. Some of these span almost an entire lifetime, from adolescence to late adulthood or death. Such private writings were much more individualistic and personal in nature than the noting of important events—which was undertaken for the purpose of holding a written record to complement oral ones.

Hence recording of family genealogies and other useful information for current and future reference by the family and community was popular and also largely undertaken by individuals: often prominent and elderly members of families who were literate and also well versed in oral traditions. References to the old man's or lady's *api* or exercise book is not uncommon in many families. Such writings are highly valued personally by family members as historical records which could also be referred to when needed in situations such as Land and Titles Court cases.

Similar writing can be seen in Church records. '*Le api o le galuega*' is a daily record of church activities and is the responsibility of the minister and his wife. Such writings can be quite literary in style and presentation, although they are not written for publication. (*Api* means a book to write in, like an exercise book, and *tusi* is a published book or letter.)

In the early 1900s Samoans who had mastered English began to translate popular literary works of European origin (such as Shakespeare, Dumas and Robert Louis STEVENSON) as well as Bible stories, folk and fairy tales. The main reason for these translations was for the entertainment of a local audience, via the newspapers and especially over the national radio station. Translations broadcast by radio were particularly appealing and seemed very closely modelled on *fagogo* or traditional story-telling. The desire to write creatively in Samoan for literary purposes spread also to highlight and accommodate the need for Samoan reading material in schools, as the curriculum became more Samoan.

The 1960s were a high point in the development of this creative writing process. Young writers emerged in the post-independence period, although many were writing in English, not in Samoan. Having learnt at school how to write creatively in English, they found it easier to continue in the more familiar language, developing the skills they had acquired. Some writers also wrote in Samoan, but the publishing outlets for these were limited to school journals and magazines, newspapers, or collections sponsored by institutions such as the UNIVERSITY OF THE SOUTH PACIFIC.

The oral medium of radio, however, provided an avenue for Samoan writing. A national radio program, 'Palolomua', popularized and developed interest in modern stories rather than translations and *fagogo*-type tales. Short stories were topical and illuminated everyday life and events. Serialized Samoan soap operas also emerged, including one unabashedly titled *'O Aso lo Tatou Olaga'*—Days of Our Lives.

Meagre financial support hampers publishing. Educational publications in Samoan provide the most effective way for writers to get their work printed and distributed at a national level. Apart from short story collections, poems and short novellas, a few prominent politicians have recently published collections of their speeches. Most publications sponsored by government continue to be traditional and conservative, such as the recording of genealogies and oral stories of old Samoa. More modern and controversial publications in Samoan are funded through grants and scholarships from various aid agencies, and so a growing number of men and women are now writing in Samoan, including many who first wrote in English. Although such writing could be labelled modern, much of it is inspired and interwoven with traditional concerns and structural forms in a contemporary context.

An important impetus for indigenous Samoan writing has come from New Zealand, which has promoted the value of indigenous languages, helping to produce Samoan books for NZ schools and communities. Many Samoan writers have published their work with Learning Media—the publishing arm of the NZ Ministry of Education. Their call for Samoan materials also allowed Samoan stories written originally in English to be translated and published in Samoan. This bulk of Samoan publications for schools undoubtedly has a spin-off effect for the schools in Samoa where there is still a dearth of interesting, lively, well-produced Samoan language material.

Samoan indigenous writing has also emerged in song compositions. Lyrics are often sung to a traditional tune and relate a contemporary event or occasion. Writing songs to tell Samoan stories has been much more popular than literary genres. There are many traditional categories of song writing: *pese aualofa*, songs of love; *pese faamatala*, songs to tell stories; songs for a special event such as *pese ole Mau*, the songs of the MAU movement; *pese lotu*, hymns; *pese autu*, didactic songs; and *pese faaneionapo*, songs of today. The lyrics of songs for special occasions are specially composed but often sung to a traditional tune well-known for telling a story. Songs are very popular with migrants, who write about their life in a new country, often comparing it with Samoa. Local songs are also composed in reply or giving the viewpoint of the non-migrant, the one who stayed behind. At times, depending on the composer, there is an overlap of style and purpose. But certainly writing is an important component of composition whether it is done solely by one person or by a group. As well, there is a healthy continuation of traditional *solo* compositions. *Solo* are traditional chants which are sung and recited by a single performer, positioned to one side during traditional rituals such as bestowing a title, a presentation at a funeral, or some similar important occasion. Sometimes these traditional chants are interspersed with modern references.

Another flourishing contemporary, semi-literary activity is Samoan drama, such as the comedy performance known as *faleaitu*. Employed in recent times by government workers for didactic purposes, *faleaitu* permits considerable poetic licence and has been an accepted form of social criticism—of government and other established institutions such as the church. *Faleaitu* remains an oral performance, not keeping to a set playscript and subject to variations depending on the occasion. Play writing in Samoan is used in schools as well, with scripts by individuals or groups. Modern plays often mix Samoan and English; and contemporary bilingual audiences certainly appreciate oral presentations which move between Samoan and English. Sometimes a play may be initially written in English, but the performance will incorporate use of Samoan language. Often a script may be prepared as a guide to a plot and basic structure only, and then set aside, permitting actors to improvise. It is in such ways that Samoan writing may be seen as part of the process of continuing adaptation to change, a response to introduced and pre-existing cultural activities. Writing in Samoan, representing a consistent set of sociolinguistic uses, has been valued for a wide range of reasons since its introduction, to the extent that the relatively small quantity of published creative 'literature' is not a useful indicator of its vitality.—EKV

Solomon Islands literature

When he opened a writers' workshop for high-school students in mid 1995, Sam Alasia, President of the Solomon Islands Creative Writers Association, told the participants that although writing was not part of their culture, he encouraged them to practise it because it was a tool for introducing new concepts and a new light for the country's progress.

Solomon Islanders, like their regional neighbours, have strong oral traditions. Histories, rituals, genealogies, incantations and customs are handed down by word of mouth. Stories, music and dance are very much influenced by the environment. The squeaking of two branches rubbing together when the wind blows, the rattle of leaves or the cries of a bird—all can be sources of inspiration. Dances are dreamed by specially appointed community members selected by departed ancestral spirits. These special people see dance movements, hear the words in their dreams and then wake up the next day to teach them to their community. Such are the different ways in which creativity and the imaginative arts come to the Solomon Islander.

When the missionaries came, they not only tried to convince people to turn to the new God but also set up schools where young people could learn to read and write. In the 1900s when the Anglicans and Catholics—and other colleagues much later—set up missions, they printed prayer-books in some of the more common local languages for general use by all churchgoers, regardless of how many different languages there were.

The old man sitting by a fire in the evening or on a beach in the moonlight and telling a story about a boy being attacked by a giant or a shark would create very vivid pictures. But the shape and size of the shark or giant would remain abstract. The pictures found in schoolbooks and religious material became a wonder, a dream come true. Exposure to education brought into reality vivid images of things not found in the traditional oral environment.

Doctor George Bogese of Santa Isabel is recorded as the first local writer in the 1950s. Sadly, however, there is no trace of his writings. Serious creative writing efforts began in the late 1960s when a handful of university-educated locals began to experiment. The first film was based on a play by the late Francis Bugotu and friends such as Tony Hughes, Solomon MAMALONI and others. Mamaloni, much later in the 1970s, wrote a hilarious radio serial called *Aedo* which was soon banned from broadcast by the then KENILOREA government. Mamaloni also wrote another play called *The Census Day* which was published in *Mana* (4/1).

At first, the most popular literary form was poetry. John Saunana published three collections in the 1970s while he was a lecturer at the University of Papua New Guinea in Port Moresby: *Cruising Through the Reverie*, *Dragon Tree: Arosi incantations and songs* and *She* (Papua Pocket Poets series, Port Moresby). In Solomon Islands the first collection was *Some Modern Poetry from Solomon Islands by Young Solomon Islands Poets*, published by the Institute of Pacific Studies (IPS) of the UNIVERSITY OF THE SOUTH PACIFIC (USP), in Suva. Another collection was published in 1977, also by a number of poets—the first work to be published in Solomon Islands by the local USP Centre.

In the early 1980s, Jo Nacola, a writer and lecturer at the USP, conducted a weekend writers' workshop in which several up-and-coming writers participated. The USP also organized television satellite sessions, providing opportunities for writers such as Albert WENDT (Samoa) and SUBRAMANI (Fiji) to share personal writing experiences with local writers. This led to a publishing 'boom' in the 1980s. The first Solomon Islands novel, *The Alternative* by John Saunana, was published in 1980. This was followed by another first, an autobiography, *Zoloveke: a man from Choiseul*, by Dr Gideon Zoloveke, published by the IPS in 1980. After this came the autobiography of Sir Frederick Osifelo, *Kanaka Boy.* Commonly known as Sir Fred, he was the first local person to be appointed district commissioner during the colonial period.

A collection of poems called *Arenga*, written and illustrated by young Solomon Islanders, was published in April 1980. Then in 1981, Leonard Maenu'u published his own collection *Who Am I?* In 1981 too, a first collection by a Solomon Islands woman poet, Jully Sipolo (now Jully MAKINI), was published (*Civilised Girl*). The IPS also published *Where Leaves Had Fallen* by Celo KULAGOE in 1981.

Sam Alasia's first collection of poems called *Hostage* was published by the USP Centre in 1988. The success of USP's promotional work can be largely attributed to a New Zealand volunteer, Stephen Oxenham, who became the editorial assistant of the Extension Centre in Solomon Islands. Apart from poetry collections, the first collection of Solomon Islands lullabies called *Poru Poru* and a book of 10 traditional dances of Solomon Islands was published in 1981. In the same year, the first collection of short stories, *Houra'a*, by Johnson Villia and others, was published. Another booster was the centre's bimonthly magazine called *Waswe?*, which regularly published short stories and poems by local writers.

Mi Mere, poems by Jully Sipolo and 10 other Solomon Islands women, was published in 1983, and the first collection of short stories by a single writer was published in 1985, *The Confession and Other Stories* by Julian MAKA'A.

In 1985 New Zealand's *Pacific Moana Quarterly* published a special issue, *Solomons: a portrait of traditional and contemporary culture in Solomon Islands*, which included a literary analysis of poems, short stories and drama, alongside articles in English and vernacular. In 1986, Jully Makini published another poetry collection, *Praying Parents*. Rexford Orotaloa's second novel, *Suremada*, was published in 1989, following his semi-autobiographical *Two Times Resurrection* (1985).

More recent works of Solomon Islands fiction include *Raetemaot* (1997), the latest collection of stories and poems by high school students around Honiara. Still to appear is Sam Alasia's first novel, *Fata'abu*. It traces the way that chiefs have been exposed by the spirits, showing the changes that have occurred from missionary arrivals, blackbirding, working in the cane-fields of Queensland, and then culminating in the Second World War and its aftermath. Also expected is a collection of poems by Celo Kulagoe, his last before becoming blind in 1994.

Books published in indigenous languages have also emerged in recent years. One popular category draws on traditional literature: *Custom Stories from Hoava* (1991); *11 Stories from Ranongga* (1991); *Historical Tales of Ranongga* (1991); *Custom Stories of Vangunu*, *Custom Stories of Choiseul*, *More Stories from Ranongga*, and *More Custom Stories from Choiseul* (all 1995). All these books are in English and vernacular, published by the IPS, and have been accompanied by an increasing number of historical and sociological works.

An interesting development in creative writing is a new literary magazine being spearheaded by the Solomon Islands Writers Association in association with the Curriculum Development Centre (CDC) of the Ministry of Education and Human Resources Development. To be called *Rorongo*, the magazine will be published free by the CDC and distributed to all secondary schools in Solomon Islands.—JM

Further reading

Maka'a, J and Oxenham, S, 1985. 'Writing in Solomon Islands: the voice in the shadow', in *Pacific Moana Quarterly* special issue, *Solomons: a portrait of traditional and contemporary culture in Solomon Islands*.

Sharrad, P, 1993. *Readings in Pacific Literature*, New Literatures Research Centre, University of Wollongong.

Indigenous writing in French Polynesia

It has often been advanced that Maohi (indigenous inhabitants of French Polynesia) have been happy to coexist with the French colonial administration in a harmonious multicultural melting pot. This is a part of the romantic image that is sold in tourist brochures and circulates around the world. However, by contrast, indigenous Maohi literature is characterized by its resistance to such stereotypical views and its opposition to the French colonial presence. Several indigenous artists, writers, critics, linguists, historians and other intellectuals have been examining the nature of the marginalization that connects Maohi and have been producing works which they hope will lead to the empowerment of their people.

It has sometimes been argued that writing is a culturally inappropriate medium to express Pacific identity and that writing reduces orality. However, written texts are playing an important role in the struggle for liberation from colonialism, as Maohi writers reconstruct the indigenous past in a different way. Written texts are increasingly understood to have the potential to effect restitution and transformation. The decision to write also acknowledges that, given the French military presence, the barrel of the pen may yet be more effective than that of the gun.

As elsewhere in the Pacific, the avant-garde of the written phase of the francophone indigenous literary movement occurred in the late 1960s and early 1970s. In Tahiti, it was led by Henri Hiro, Turo Raapoto, Vaitiare, Hubert Brémond and Charles Manutahi. Characteristically, this literature attempts to establish an initial dialogue not with the colonizer but with fellow Maohi. Reaching back to significant meanings and values of the past allows a 'revalorization' and rehabilitation of the indigenous self that gives a sense of history (however reconstructed) hitherto denied by the dominant French culture. The initial concern of these poets is to safeguard, enrich and transmit the greatness of their cultural heritage. Hiro and Raapoto have also been actively engaged in the revival and promotion of the Maohi language and in the development of programs that would lead to an interrogation about who Maohi are, where they come from, and where they ought to be going. Raapoto explains it thus

> We are not preaching a return to the past; there are always retrograde minds eager to accuse. If the imagination can be defined as the faculty to create something new from something old, then it is our duty to understand, to become impregnated with our past, our culture, our language, to create a new world in our image and in our dimension.

The 1990s has produced a new wave of writers in Tahiti, the most prominent of whom are four women: Vaitiare (who has made a transition from her earlier writing), Michou Chaze (a short-story writer), Chantal Spitz (author of the first Maohi novel) and Louise Peltzer (a poet). The first is interesting for her conciliatory approach, the second suggests discursive alternatives to cultural nationalism, and the third is interesting for her confrontational approach. Peltzer is the most recently published, and has produced a novel, *Lettres à Poutaveri.*

Vaitiare denies substantial difference between people of different cultures and offers a simple claim to equality. Her later writing is an important departure from earlier claims of ethnic difference. Her concerns include universal themes in human experience such as love, birth, death, companionship, loneliness and marriage. She assumes the responsibility of ensuring that the new generation living in French Polynesia will gain strength from cultural diversity rather than be divided by it. Resisting the nationalists' tendency to make 'difference' both the starting and end point of analysis, she demands a new way of life in Tahiti, one that would encompass both the old and the new.

Michou Chaze's position is interesting in that she is the spokesperson for a growing number of people who reject colonial rule, but who also feel alienated by the exigencies of cultural nationalism. To solve this problem, Chaze adopts a richly hybridized 'Tahitian-French'. The French language is thus adapted and transformed in such a way that it can no longer be called French. Chaze's chosen form underlines her recognition that Tahiti is a melting pot and that there is no pure language or 'race' through which everything should be done or said. This option has allowed her to create new words, new images, new meanings, new poems, new practices: a new Maohi reality.

European colonialism regularly changed local habitats to transform new territories into versions of the home country. Indigenous outrage at being thus displaced, dispossessed, and made strangers on their ancestral land is the central theme of *L'Île des Rêves Ecrasés* (The Island of Crushed Dreams), the country's first indigenous novel, written by Chantal Spitz. *L'Île des Rêves Ecrasés* traces three generations (from World War I to the present time) of a family living on the fictional island of Ruahine who endure the violation of their land by the construction of a nuclear missiles testing base. Spitz turns the idyllic image of palms, hibiscus, beaches and women into a war zone with destroyers, missile bases and troop garrisons all in service to the race for global supremacy. The change brought about by the new lifestyle in Ruahine is highly symbolic of what happened to Tahiti following the beginning of NUCLEAR TESTING in the 1960s. This novel is characterized by direct didactic authorial interventions through which all facets of Western intrusion (education, religion, etc) are scrutinized.

The playwright and poet John Mairai chose theatre as his genre. Mairai has already directed several adaptations of Shakespearean and other plays but prefers his own *Opuhara,* a play about a great Tahitian warrior who fought and died for the Maohi heritage in the infamous battle of Fei Pi (early 1800s), when King POMARE I joined forces with the missionaries to defeat anti-Christian resistance forces. Mairai also digs in the past for pride, beauty, wisdom and poetry. Mairai uses theatre, a potentially powerful medium, to raise the political consciousness of his fellow Maohi. He is aware of the need for more Maohi to publish, and he is actively involved in supporting a growing number of young Maohi writers and artists.

Maohi, like other Pacific islanders, have inherited a large reservoir of oral traditions. This rich cultural archive was embodied in the Arioi society, a large group of visiting dancers, singers, poets and historians. Together they composed and performed a rich amalgam of the social experiences of the people of Maohi Nui. They celebrated the creation of the Maohi universe, the marvels of nature, the great deeds of the various gods and other heroes, the victorious battles, and the successful voyages. This celebration of Maohi life was performed in front of huge crowds and persists to the present day in the form of the *Tiurai.*

Maohi are very keen dancers, singers and musicians. The *Tiurai* is an annual cultural festival that brings together thousands of (young and old) Maohi dancers, singers, story-tellers, poets, canoeists, traditional sportsmen and women, and throngs of spectators for a month (in July) of continuous celebrations of the Maohi culture. This annual reinvigoration of Maohi culture breathes new voices, new chants, new movements, new ideas, and new hopes on the written and literary landscape of French Polynesia.—RN

Some Pacific writers

■ *Apelu Aiavao*—born Samoa. In recent times, editor of the government paper *Savali*, Aiavao has worked in teaching, journalism and broadcasting. Literary works in Samoan included short stories and tales for children such as *O Malaga a Ulisese* (1971).

■ *Arapera Hineira Kaa Blank*—born Rangitukia, New Zealand, 1932. Has written stories since the 1950s and combined teaching with leadership in organizing Maori cultural festivals in Auckland. Her poetry, *Nga Kokako Huataratara: the notched plumes of the Kokako* (1986), is being followed with a collection of her stories and a novel. She is a founding member of the Waiata Koa poetry collective.

■ *Nora Vagi Brash*—born Dagoda, Kilakila, Central Province, Papua New Guinea, 1944. As a student at the University of Papua New Guinea (diploma in journalism, arts degree in literature and creative writing), Vagi became involved in theatre, and while actress and artistic director with the National Theatre Company, wrote her first play, *The High Cost of Living Differently* (1975). This and many of her works satirically question the 'rat race' of Papua New Guinea's modernizing middle classes and the marginalizing of village life by an urbanized élite. Her work uses a lively range of expression from TOK PISIN (Pidgin) through to 'Queen's English', and *Taurama* (1985), a dramatization of legends from the village of that name, incorporates the Motu language. This work won her the Independence Medal in 1985. Vagi also writes poetry, was associated with the production of the film documentary *Angels of War* and has travelled to international arts events in Hawai'i, Nigeria, Tahiti and Singapore. Vagi lived in Canberra for many years, having married Elton Brash, former vice-chancellor of UPNG and senior member of Australia's development programs administration, who died in 1998. She worked with overseas students at Canberra University and is currently lecturing in theatre arts at the University of Papua New Guinea. Her work is collected in *Which Way Big Man? and five other plays* (1996).

■ *Alistair Te Ariki Campbell*—born Rarotonga, 1925, of Penrhyn Island (Tongareva) descent through his mother. Long regarded as a New Zealand writer, Campbell also draws on his Tongarevan origins. He attended school in Dunedin, and later Victoria University of Wellington, trained as a teacher and edited the *School Journal* for 17 years (also writing *The Happy Summer* (1961), for children). During this time he moved in literary circles and gained a reputation as one of the country's leading poets, starting with his collection *Mine Eyes Dazzle* (1950). He worked at the New Zealand Council for Educational Research until ready for writing retirement opposite the island of Kapiti, the setting for his imaginative retelling of the battles of Chief Rauparaha in *Kapiti: selected poems 1947–1971* (1972). Other poetry: *Collected Works* (1981, won the 1982 New Zealand Book Award for poetry), *Sanctuary of Spirits* (1963), *Wild Honey* (1964), *Blue Rain* (1967), *Drinking Horn* (1970), *Walk the Black Path* (1971), *Dreams, Yellow Lions* (1975), *The Dark Lord of Savaiki* (1980) and *Soul Traps* (1985). He has written plays, notably *When the Bough Breaks* (1974), and has collaborated in film, TV and musical productions. In a quest to deal with the lasting traumas of his being orphaned and uprooted as a child, Campbell went back to Cook Islands, his story recorded in *Island to Island* (1984). The last two volumes of verse reflect his reconnection with family and island culture and led to the 'Polynesian strain' of his selected poetry collection *Stone Rain* (1992), and to the tragi-comic, sentimental farce novel trilogy, *The Frigate Bird* (1989), *Sidewinder* (1991) and *Tia* (1993).

■ *Marjorie Tuainekore Crocombe*—born Rarotonga, 1930. Teacher, educationalist, historian, writer. Began writing career in Cook Islands Education Department in the 1950s after graduation as a teacher in New Zealand, contributing to primary school readers in Maori. From 1960s, translated and published writings of early Cook Islands missionaries including Maretu and Ta'unga (jointly with Ron Crocombe), and also retold selected excerpts as simple English readers. *The Works of Ta'unga: records of a Polynesian traveller in the South Seas 1838–1896* (1968); and children's story: *If I Live: the story of Ta'unga* (1972); *Cannibals and Converts: radical change in the Cook Islands* (1983), and children's story: *They Came for Sandalwood* (1974). Primary school readers: *Te Au*

Tamariki Mearikiriki (1959), *Tamariki Mataora* (1960). History of the Cook Islands: *Two Hundred Changing Years* (1962), and *Ka E\Ua E Teau Tau Hikihikifano* (1965, Niuean language version). Several short stories. Social science readers: *The Journey of Eki* (1965), *The Cook Islanders* (1968). In the 1970s at the UNIVERSITY OF THE SOUTH PACIFIC, with writers like Albert WENDT, and staff and students, she established the South Pacific Creative Arts Society to promote the development of CREATIVE LITERATURE BY PACIFIC ISLANDERS. Editor of *Mana: A South Pacific Journal of Language and Literature* and president of SPCAS for some years. Since 1997 she has reduced her editorial work to concentrate on writing.

■ ***Sir Thomas (Tom) Davis*** (Pa Tu Terangi Ariki)—born Rarotonga, 1918. Doctor, scientist, writer and politician; master designer and builder of Polynesian voyaging canoes. Novel: *Makutu* (1960)—with his first wife Lydia Davis, *Island Boy: an autobiography* (1961), *Vaka* (1992). (See biographical entry, Sir Thomas Davis, in POLITICS chapter.)

■ ***Alan Duff***—born Rotorua, New Zealand, 1950, of Ngati Rangitihi and Tuwharetoa descent. Writer, newspaper columnist. The urban setting of his powerful first novel, *Once Were Warriors*, emerged in sharp contrast to previous work by Maori authors exploring traditional and rural themes. It was an immediate bestseller, bringing Duff into prominence, and was made into a hugely popular film by Maori director Lee Tamahori. Fiction: *Once Were Warriors* (1990), *One Night Out Stealing* (1992), *State Ward* (novella, 1994), *What Becomes of the Broken-Hearted* (1996), *Both Sides of the Moon* (1998). Non-fiction: *Maori: the crisis and the challenge* (1994).

■ ***Vincent Serei Eri***—(1936–93), born Moveave, Papua New Guinea. Famous as the first published novelist of his country, Eri also had an extensive and influential career as teacher, educational administrator and public servant, awarded a knighthood and reaching the position of governor general before retirement. Eri left school at 14 to train in store management but returned to complete an administrative course at Sogeri High School. He rose to District Inspector after some years teaching and joined Port Moresby Teachers' College in 1965. In 1967 he entered the University of Papua New Guinea and took creative writing classes under Ulli Beier, who supervised and assisted the publication of his novel, *The Crocodile* (1970). The novel was also serialized on ABC radio.

The Crocodile tells the story of Hoiri Sevese, born in the 1930s to a London Missionary Society family but schooled as a Catholic after his mother's death, who still holds the traditional beliefs of his people. The book depicts his mental struggle with the contradictions of his transitional world. Hoiri goes on a HIRI TRADING VOYAGE to Port Moresby and sees some of the goods and mysteries of white society. Proud of his English, he is recruited as carrier by a patrol officer soon after his marriage, but when his wife is taken by a crocodile, he goes to seek out the supposed sorcerer who caused the tragedy. He is then taken on as a carrier during World War II, experiencing the brutal shocks of battle and a new protonational camaraderie across tribal bounds. He meets Black American soldiers and friendly Australian troops, who contrast with the bullying colonial kiaps and ANGAU officers who strip him of his money when he is demobbed. Hoiri ends by being arrested but hoping that his son will acquire the knowledge necessary to make sense of modernity. The novel is partly autobiographical in its depiction of village childhood, and partly based on his father's wartime experiences. It was at first criticized by Australian reviewers for its satiric stereotyping of white characters, but praised for its lively mix of local colour and fictionalized social history.

■ ***Sia Figiel***—born Matautu Tai, Samoa, 1967. Performance poet and novelist, now living in New Zealand. Her novel *Where We Once Belonged* (1996) was a regional winner of the Commonwealth Writers Best First Book Award in 1997.

■ ***Florence (Johnny) Frisbie***—born Pape'ete, 1932. Dancer and writer. Eldest daughter of American author, Robert Dean Frisbie and his wife, Ngatokorua of Pukapuka, Cook Islands. Lived in Hawai'i and New Zealand for some years then returned to live in Rarotonga in 1990. Novel: *Miss Ulysses of Pukapuka* (1948). Biographical work: *Frisbies of the South Seas* (1959). Children's stories published by Learning Media (NZ Ministry of Education). Short story: 'The Bed', in *Nuanua: Pacific writing in English since 1980*, ed. Albert WENDT (1995). She plans to have her two books reprinted.

■ ***Patricia Grace***—born Wellington, New Zealand, 1937, of Ngati Raukawa, Ngati Toa and Te Ati Awa descent. Short-story writer and novelist, living near Wellington, she is a former teacher. Short fiction: *Waiariki* (1975), *The Dream Sleepers* (1980), *Electric City & Other Stories* (1987), *Selected Stories* (1991), *The Sky People* (1994).

Novels: *Mutuwhenua, The Moon Sleeps* (1978), *Potiki* (1986, won the New Zealand Book Award for fiction in 1987), *Cousins* (1992), *Baby No-Eyes* (1998). Children's books: *The Kuia and the Spider* (1981), *Watercress Tuna and the Children of Champion Street* (1985)—both books illustrated by Robyn Kahukiwa; *The Trolley* (1993), *Areta and the Kahawai* (1994). Non-fiction: *Wahine Toa* (1984)—illustrated by Robyn Kahukiwa.

■ ***Rowley Habib*** (Rore Hapipi)—born Oruanui, Taupo, New Zealand, 1933. One of the pioneers of modern literary expression by Maori, Habib published stories, poems and articles in magazines through the 1960s and has been much anthologized. Habib was an active member of the land rights movement Te Matakite o Aotearoa and co-founder of Te Ika a Maui Players. For them he wrote *The Death of the Land*, later televised as *The Gathering*. His stories have been broadcast as a series, *Tamariki*.

■ ***Epeli Hau'ofa***—born 1939, Papua New Guinea. Professor and director of the Oceania Centre at the UNIVERSITY OF THE SOUTH PACIFIC. Hau'ofa was the son of Tongan missionaries in Papua New Guinea. He built on his early years with a doctorate (Australian National University) published as *Mekeo: inequality and ambivalence in a village society* (1981), also producing a study of Pacific island demography, *Our Crowded Islands* (1977). During several years in Tonga as private secretary to the king and then director of the Rural Development Centre, Hau'ofa published *Corned Beef and Tapioca: a report on the food distribution system in Tonga* (1979) and he and his wife Barbara produced a bilingual literary magazine, *Faikara*. Hau'ofa then collected his burlesque stories of the fictional island of Tiko as *Tales of the Tikongs* (1983). These were followed by the more trenchant and scatological novel, *Kisses in the Nederends* (1987). Hau'ofa has also written poetry. After his irreverent but ultimately bleak Swiftian denunciations of both traditional abuse of religion and rank and modern development programs, Hau'ofa produced a positive reconceptualization of Oceania as a sea of migratory contributors to the world. His views are debated in *A New Oceania: rediscovering our sea of islands* (1993).

■ ***Vilsoni Hereniko***—born Rotuma, 1954. Teacher of literature and theatre, stage director, Associate Professor in Pacific Literature at the Center for Pacific Island Studies, University of Hawai'i. Hereniko was educated in Rotuma, Fiji and England, and taught high school in Suva where he produced his first play, *Don't Cry Mama* (1977). The title work in *The Monster and Other Plays* (1989) is an allegorical piece reflecting concerns over the FIJI COUPS and social prejudice. *A Child for Iva* (1980) and *Sera's Choice* (1987) (published as *Two Plays*, 1987) are realistic 'problem plays' with comic touches, also about class, cultural and ethnic conflict. Hereniko joined the UNIVERSITY OF THE SOUTH PACIFIC as a teacher of literature and theatre arts, and has also written stories and poems. His doctoral work on traditions of clowning in the Pacific is published as *Woven Gods: female clowns and power in Rotuma* (1995) and he has incorporated comic-satiric techniques into *Last Virgin in Paradise* (1993), co-written with Teresia TEAIWA.

■ ***Keri Ann Ruhi Hulme***—born New Zealand, 1947, of Kai Tahu descent. Poet, short-story writer and novelist, who lives as a reclusive whitebaiter in the remote South Island settlement of Okarito, where she built her own house. She has served as a member of the Indecent Publications Tribunal and as an adviser to government on literary grants. Fiction: *the bone people* (1983; Booker Prize-winner 1985), *Lost Possessions* (1985), *Te Kaihau/The Windeater* (short stories, 1986). Poetry: *The Silences Between: Moeraki conversations* (1982), *Strands* (1992). Non-fiction: *Homeplaces* (with Robin Morrison, 1989).

■ ***Witi Ihimaera***—born Gisborne, New Zealand, 1944, of Te Aitanga-a-Mahaki, Rongowhakaata and Ngati Porou descent. Novelist and short-story writer, he now lives in Auckland and lectures in English literature. A former New Zealand diplomat who served in Canberra, New York and Washington, he was educated at Victoria (Wellington) and Auckland universities. Awarded a Scholarship in Letters (1991) and the Katherine Mansfield Fellowship (1993), many of his books have been prize-winners in New Zealand. Short fiction: *Pounamu, Pounamu* (1972), *The New Net Goes Fishing* (1977), *Dear Miss Mansfield* (1989). Novels: *Tangi* (1973), *Whanau* (1974), *The Matriarch* (1986), *The Whale Rider* (1987), *Bulibasha, King of the Gypsies* (1994), *Nights in the Gardens of Spain* (1995). Opera libretto: *Waituhi* (premiere 1984). Non-fiction: *The Legendary Land; Land, Sea, Sky; Masks and Mirror; Maori*. Editor: *Into the World of Light* (anthology, 1982)—co-edited D S Long, *Te Ao Marama* (vols 1–4), *Vision Aotearoa* (1990).

■ ***Arthur Jawodimbari***—born Beporo, Popondetta, Papua New Guinea, 1949. Graduated from University of Papua New Guinea, where he wrote *The Sun*, an allegorized version of a Binandere legend. Other plays include *Cargo* and *The Old Man's Reward*.

Jawodimbari undertook studies in drama at Ife in Nigeria and returned to become director of the National Theatre Company, Papua New Guinea. He has many short stories in small magazines and a book of poems, *Return to my Land* (1974), plus *Wicked Eye* with Dus Mapun (1973). Jawodimbari also served in government as Director of Cultural Affairs and has returned to Oro Province to work in local government.

■ ***Jon Jonassen***—born Rarotonga, 1949. Diplomat, choreographer, composer, drummer, poet, writer. Educated in Cook Islands and New Zealand, toured with Betela Dance Troupe, a professional group. Has written over 100 musical pieces ranging from drum solos to traditional chants. Has published poetry and articles, and his books include *Cook Islands Legends* (1981, reprinted six times), *Early Immigrants to the Cook Islands: Henry Nicholas* (1986), *Cook Islands Drums* (1991), *The Ghost at Tokatarava and Other Stories from the Cook Islands* (1992).

■ ***Lilikala Kame'eleihiwa***—born Hawai'i. Associate professor at University of Hawai'i. Her publications on Hawaiian history and literature include *Native Land and Foreign Desires*, a history of changes in Hawaiian land tenure; and *A Legendary Tradition of Kamapua'a the Hawaiian Pig-God*, an annotated translation of an early Hawaiian epic.

■ ***John Kasaipwalova***—born Yalumgwa, Trobriand Islands. After high school in Australia, Kasaipwalova gained a reputation as a student radical at the University of Papua New Guinea during the anti-colonial push towards independence. His story 'Betel nut is bad magic for aeroplanes' (one of the most linguistically lively and adept PNG stories) reflects his anti-racist views, as does the long 'Ginsberg'-type fulminatory poem *Reluctant Flame* (1971) that draws on US Black Power literature. Pride in indigenist cultural renewal gave way to a bleaker social vision in *Hanuabada* (1972). Kasaipwalova wrote several satirical-comic plays (*Kanaka's Dream, The Rooster in the Confessional, The Naked Jazz, My Brother, My Enemy*) before developing the Kabisawali grass-roots co-operative and cultural movement in Trobriands Islands. Adapting traditional art forms to modern techniques, he also elaborated the aesthetic of 'Sopi', one of the few artistic theorizings of 'The Melanesian way'. Kasaipwalova was jailed briefly over alleged mishandling of government funding and during this time wrote a dance-drama *Sail the Midnight Sun* (1980). This uses the Trobriands KULA EXCHANGE trading circuit as an allegorical figure for a national quest for modern identity. It was performed at the FESTIVAL OF PACIFIC ARTS by Raun Raun Theatre Company. The Department of Education published his *Niugini, Niugini: a trilogy of folk operas* (1985). Kasaipwalova went into business and now lives on his traditional land in Trobriand Islands.

■ ***Kauraka Kauraka***—(1951–97), born Rarotonga. Poet, musician and language teacher, as well as chief anthropologist for the Ministry of Cultural Development, Cook Islands. Attended university in Suva (BA in Education, University of the South Pacific) and in Honolulu (MA in Anthropology, University of Hawai'i), Kauraka worked in the Cook Islands Education Department, and with local writing groups, and published eight collections of poetry and folk traditions, including *Tales of Manihiki* (1982) and *Legends from the Atolls* (1983). He was notable for his bilingual poetry texts that parallel his own translations between Cook Islands Maori and English. These include *Return to Hawaiki* (1985), *Dreams of a Rainbow* (1987), *Manakonako: reflections* (1992).

■ ***Celo Kulagoe***—born Reko, Guadalcanal, Solomon Islands. Educated in Catholic schools in Guadalcanal and Kieta (Bougainville), Kulagoe completed his degree in education at the University of the South Pacific. He joined the Marist Brothers teaching order from 1969 to 1974. He has published widely in magazines, and has a collection of poetry, *Where Leaves had Fallen* (1980), where he demonstrates a reflective tone and formal structure rare in Melanesian poetry in English. He has begun to work in prose, having issued *Uvipira (Roots in a Season): three short stories* (1991). Since 1985 he has worked for the Solomon Islands public service, and is now a composer of guitar songs.

■ ***Julian Maka'a***—born Tawani, Makira Province, Solomon Islands, 1957. He wrote *The Confession and Other Stories* (1985) and edited *Solomons* (a special issue of *Pacific Moana Quarterly*, 9(1) 1985). He belongs to the dance/drama group Lukluk Wantok and is active in the Solomon Islands Writers Association. Maka'a worked in civil aviation and at the USP Solomon Islands Centre, and is currently in the programs section of the Solomon Islands Broadcasting Corporation.

■ ***Jully Makini*** (formerly Jully Sipolo)—born Gizo, Western Province, Solomon Islands, 1953. Began writing after a women's conference in 1980, co-editing *Mi Mere: poetry and prose by Solomon Islands women writers* (1983). Her own verse focuses on social inequalities for women in Melanesia and development issues: *Civilized Girl* (1981), *Praying*

Parents (1991). As Jully Makini, she has contributed to *Raetemaot: creative writing from Solomon Islands* (1996). Works with the western provincial government's Department of Culture, Tourism, Environment and Women.

■ *Sano Malifa*—born Afega, Samoa. Educated in Samoa and New Zealand, Malifa's work and travel in the United States is reflected in his first book of verse, *Looking Down at Waves* (1975). Owns and edits *The Observer.* Author of a satirical play, and poems: *Song and Return* (1992), and a novel, *Alms for Oblivion* (1993).

■ *Sir Paulias Matane*—born near Tauran, New Britain, Papua New Guinea, 1930. Matane came into literary prominence with his autobiography, *My Childhood in New Guinea* (1972), which dramatizes his move from pre-war traditional New Britain culture into colonial schooling and from Kerevat High to Sogeri Teacher Training school, to teaching in New Britain and the Highlands. Matane travelled in Africa on a Churchill Scholarship in 1966, then moving to the top of Educational Administration and onto the Public Service Board. He has been Permanent Secretary of several departments and a diplomat with the United Nations in the United States. Matane has never lost sight of the need for a locally relevant education and wrote a series of instructive novels for young people: *Aimbe the Challenger* (1974), *Aimbe the School Dropout* (1977), *Aimbe the Magician* (1978), *Aimbe the Pastor* (1979). Matane has published many papers on social and political affairs and has also, while running businesses, kept up newspaper columns and educative radio programs (reflected in *Chitchat*, 1992). A later biographical work, *To Serve with Love*, appeared in 1992.

■ *Sudesh Mishra*—born Suva, 1962. Teacher of literature and language. Mishra grew up in the Hindu sugar-farming world of Nadi and encountered Eliot, Yeats and modern poetry at the UNIVERSITY OF THE SOUTH PACIFIC (USP), Suva and Wollongong University. He completed his doctorate on contemporary Indian English poetry at Flinders University of South Australia (published as *Preparing Faces: modernism in Indian poetry in English*, 1995) and made a name as a new poet with the collection *Rahu* (1987). He returned to the Literature staff at USP soon after the first of the FIJI COUPS and wrote a Beckett-like allegorical play *Ferringhi*, anti-coup poems (appearing in the collection *Tandava*, 1992), and edited with Seona Smiles *Trapped: a collection of writing from Fiji* (1992). *Memoirs of a Reluctant Traveller* (1994) reflect a journey through India. Mishra has taken up a lectureship at Stirling University where he continues to work on another book of verse and a novel about the period of the military coups.

■ *Grace Mera Molisa*—born Ambae, 1946. An active member of the Anglican church as a result of her mission education, Molisa went to high school in New Zealand and gained her degree in 1977. She helped organize the first South Pacific Women's Conference in Suva and has been an outspoken advocate of improved social conditions for women in Vanuatu. Molisa was head of a senior primary school and served on the National Constitution Committee in 1979, moving into a senior government post as secretary to the prime minister. Her work on social policy finds expression in polemical and satiric poems, collected as *Black Stone* (1983), *Colonised People* (1987) and *Black Stone II* (1989). She has also written government reports and journalistic pieces, being an advocate of an independent 'third world' information network.

■ *Satendra Pratap Nandan*—born Votualevu, Nadi, 1939. Educated in Fiji, Delhi, Leeds and London, with a doctorate in literature from the Australian National University, Nandan taught at the UNIVERSITY OF THE SOUTH PACIFIC (1969–87), and published *Faces in a Village* (1976), a book of verse about family and Indo-Fijian life notable for its formally polished technique and reissued in the expanded collection *Voices in the River* (1985). Nandan was one of the founding editors of *New Literature Review* and edited a collection of conference papers, *Language and Literature in Multicultural Contexts* (1983). He entered parliament in 1982 and was appointed to a ministerial post in 1987 by Dr BAVADRA, moving to Australia after the military coup in 1987, which he has fictionalized in *The Wounded Sea* (1991). Nandan is now Associate Professor of English and Commonwealth Studies at the University of Canberra and has recently published another collection of poetry (*Lines across Black Waters*, 1997).

■ *Sampson Ngwele*—born Ambae, Vanuatu. Senior civil servant, and Governor of the Reserve Bank of Vanuatu. Educated in Vanuatu and at the University of Papua New Guinea, where he graduated in law and economics. His poetry collection, *Bamboo Leaves*, appeared in 1990.

■ *Rexford Orotaloa*—born Malaita, Solomon Islands, 1956. Entered primary school at 12 and graduated from King George VI High in Honiara. His grandfather had taught him traditional lore and he worked as secretary to the Malaita Local Courts, using his knowledge of genealogy. Now works as a teacher. He has written poems, playscripts and articles but his published fiction, *Two Times Resurrection* (1985) and *Suremada: faces from a Solomon Islands village* (1989), is his forte. The episodic semi-autobiography and loosely connected stories centred on colourful characters from a village can be ungainly at times, but are always lively, and of particular interest for their creolized English, their generic hybridizing of oral folk-tale and written short story and their sense of a fluid interchange of modern and traditional consciousness.

■ *Ruperake Petaia*—born Samoa, 1951. Director of Post and Telecommunications, Samoa. Collections of poetry: *Blue Rain* (1980), *Patches of the Rainbow* (1992).

■ *Raymond Pillai*—born Ba, Fiji. High school teacher and writer. Has a master's degree from the University of Southern Illinois. Collection of short stories: *The Celebration* (1980).

■ *Roma Potiki*—born New Zealand, 1958, of Te Aupouri, Te Rarawa, Ngati Rangitihi descent. Poet, visual artist and dramatist who has been involved in the development of Maori theatre in New Zealand for many years. Poetry: *Stones in her Mouth* (1992); *NZpoetcardz* (1996); *Shaking the Tree* (1998). Play: *Going Home*, performed at Pacific Wave Festival, Sydney, 1997.

■ *John Pule*—born Liku, Niue, 1962. Artist and author. Novel: *The Shark that Ate the Sun* (1992). (See also ARTS TODAY: RECENT AND CONTEMPORARY).

■ *John Selwyn Saunana*—born Arosi, Makira District, Solomon Islands, 1945. Broadcaster and teacher, elected to the legislative assembly 1977 and served later as Minister of Education, also working in Foreign Affairs and Trade. While completing his BA at the University of Papua New Guinea, he produced a collection of Arosi incantations and songs, *Dragon Tree* (1972), and two booklets of poems, *Cruising through the Reverie* (1972) and *She* (1973). He co-edited *Twenty-four Poems of the Solomon Islands* (1977) and wrote a novel, *The Alternative* (1980).

■ *Russell Soaba*—born Tototo, Milne Bay, Papua New Guinea, 1950. Soaba is one of the few Pacific islanders who have continued to write as the major part of their life. As a student at the UNIVERSITY OF PAPUA NEW GUINEA (where he now lectures) he formed part of Ulli Beier's creative writing circle and went on to publish poetry (*Naked Thoughts*, 1978) and many individual pieces in journals, plays (*Scattered by the Wind*, *Wilma Wait*, *Mass Mania*), many stories and two novels. He has edited literary magazines, worked as a researcher of folklore (publishing a collection *How* with Apisai Enos, 1978) and as a teacher, currently heading the literature department at UPNG. Soaba comes from the small Anuki language group and has experimented with prose in English reflecting its syntax ('Ripples') and carried into his work the sense of being an uprooted remnant adrift in modern urban life. The visionary solitude of an artist ('Wanpis') in a materialist world becomes his dramatization of existentialist meaning-making as a hedge against absurdity and alienation (the 'lusman' drifter). These themes are developed clearly in his semi-autobiographical 'getting of wisdom' novel, *Wanpis* (1976). After a creative writing MA at Brown University, Soaba published another novel, *Maiba* (1985), a post-independence fable about power and corruption drawing on Anuki traditions and featuring women characters as a shift from the usual male-centred PNG texts.

■ *Subramani*—born Labasa, Fiji, 1943. Short-story writer and teacher of English literature at the UNIVERSITY OF THE SOUTH PACIFIC (USP), Subramani is noted for providing the first critical overview of indigenous writing, *South Pacific Literature: from myth to fabulation* (1985). He worked with the creative writing groups centred at USP and on the journal *Mana* in the mid 1970s, and his selected stories with more recent additions appeared as *The Fantasy Eaters* (1988). His stories create an atmosphere of quiet tension underlying the existentialist despair of uprooted Indo-Fijian labourers and their offspring. Subramani has served as pro-chancellor of his university, has edited studies of the indenture phenomenon, *The Indo-Fijian Experience* (1979), and its literature: *After Narrative* (1990). He worked for the maintenance of the Indian community in Fiji during the coup years and his speeches and essays are published in *Altering Imagination* (1995).

■ *Robert Sullivan*—born New Zealand, 1967. A leading contemporary voice in Maori literature. As the title of his first poetry collection (*Jazz Waiata*, 1990) suggests, he blends urban and traditional elements of culture. He has written a play, *Sale of the Treaty*, another collection of poems, *Piki Ake!* (1993) and, with Chris Sloane, a novel, *Maui: legends of the outcast* (1995).

■ *Kumalau Tawali*—born Tawi, Manus Island, Papua New Guinea, 1946. Graduated in arts from the UNIVERSITY OF PAPUA NEW GUINEA after being the first Papua New Guinean to publish a collection of poems, *Signs in the Sky* (1970), which featured the 'classic' anti-colonial piece 'The bush kanaka speaks'. His play *Manki Masta* appeared in

Five New Guinea Plays (1971) and was staged in Canberra. Tawali joined Moral Re-Armament in Europe and then returned to the Christian Leadership Training Centre in Mount Hagen. He has taught literature at UPNG and edited *The Floating Coconut: a collection of poems from the Pacific region*, 1977.

■ *Apirana Taylor*—born Wellington, 1955. One of the generation after IHIMAERA and GRACE, Taylor gained an early reputation for powerful poems of social protest. Collections of poetry: *Eyes of the Ruru* (1979), *Three Shadows* (1981, with Lindsay Robbitt and L E Scott) and *Soft Leaf Falls of Moon* (1996). Short stories: *He Rau Aroha: a hundred leaves of love* (1986) and *Ki Te Ao: new stories* (1990). Novel: *He Tangi Aroha* (1993). His other activities have been in theatre, as an actor on street, stage and film, a deviser of performance pieces for the group Te Ohu Whakaari and writer of *Kohanga* and *Te Whanau a Tuanui Jones*.

■ *Vianney Kianteata Teabo*—born Kiribati, 1962. Journalist, broadcaster and economist. Educated in Kiribati, then attended the University of Papua New Guinea, the University of the South Pacific, and Massey University in New Zealand (MA in Business Studies). Has published several short stories.

■ *Teresia Teaiwa*—born Honolulu. Teaiwa was raised in Fiji with Banaban and African-American parents. She is completing a doctorate in the History of Consciousness program, University of California, Santa Cruz, and teaching history at the University of the South Pacific in Suva. Her collection of poems, *Searching for Nei Nim'anoa* (1995), explores being a minority in the United States and seeks out her multiple, but particularly Kiribati, identities. She co-authored the satiric drama *Last Virgin in Paradise* (1993) with Vilsoni HERENIKO.

■ *Francis Tekonnang*—born Kiribati, died 1994. Teacher and poet. Educated in Kiribati, then attended the University of the South Pacific, graduating in education. Taught high school in Kiribati for many years. Published several poems and short stories, including 'Beia and Ioane', in *Nuanua: Pacific writing in English since 1980*, ed. Albert WENDT (1995).

■ *Makiuti Tongia*—born Rarotonga, 1953. Teacher, museum curator, university lecturer, writer. Educated in Cook Islands and then at the University of the South Pacific, where he was involved with the students' publication, *Unispac*, and became a founding member of the South Pacific Creative Arts Society. He published and edited poems, producing his first collection of poetry in English, *Korero* (1977), and later writing in Maori, and has published a textbook, *Learning Rarotongan Maori Language* (1991).

■ *Konaiholeva Helu Thaman*—born Nuku'alofa, 1946. Schooled in Tonga and New Zealand, Konai Helu trained as a teacher, with a degree in geography. After teaching in Tonga, 1969–72, she went to the University of California, Santa Barbara, to complete an MA in International Education. She and her husband, Randy Thaman, moved to the University of the South Pacific, Suva in 1974, where she has become head of the School of Education and served as Pro-Vice Chancellor and Director of the Institute of Education. She completed a PhD on the interaction of Tongan cultural values with education, and her poetry, for which she is most well known across the Pacific, increasingly works with traditional Tongan song forms and flower motifs. Konai has visited numerous classrooms in many countries and led creative writing workshops (she was President of the South Pacific Creative Arts Society for some time) and her personal, lyrical poems and short, pointed social critiques make her one of the most popular literary figures in the Pacific. Apart from her academic publications, she has produced *You the Choice of my Parents* (1974), *Langakali* (1981), *Inselfeuer* (1986), *Hingano* (1987) and *Kakala* (1993).

■ *Haunani-Kay Trask*—born Hawai'i. Teacher, writer, poet and film producer, and Professor, Center for Hawaiian Studies at the University of Hawai'i. Completed postgraduate studies at the University of Wisconsin–Madison with a PhD in 1981, and has written numerous articles, and a book of political analysis, *Eros and Power: the promise of feminist theory* (1986). Published *From a Native Daughter: colonialism and sovereignty in Hawai'i* in 1993, and a book of poetry, *Light in the Crevice Never Seen*, in 1994. Her poetry and creative prose have appeared in several anthologies.

■ *Hone Tuwhare*—born Kaikohe, New Zealand, 1922, of Ngapuhi descent (Ngati Korokoro, Ngati Tautahi, Te Popoto, Uri-O-Hau). The best known Maori poet, his first collection, *No Ordinary Sun*, has remained in print for more than 30 years. Spent many years in Dunedin, where he was formerly a Burns Scholar at the University of Otago. His poems have appeared in numerous anthologies and have also been translated internationally, especially in Germany.

Collections of verse: *No Ordinary Sun* (1964), *Come Rain Hail* (1970), *Sapwood & Milk* (1972), *Something Nothing* (1974), *Making a Fist of It* (1978),

Selected Poems (1980), *Year of the Dog: poems new and old* (1982), *Mihi: collected poems* (1987), *Deep River Talk* (1993).

■ ***Joseph C Veramu***—born Fiji, school teacher, now lecturer at the University of the South Pacific. Veramu has edited collections of myths and legends (*The Two Turtles and the Ungrateful Snake* and *The Snake Prince*), written a story for children (*The Shark*) and books on child rearing and education in social development (*Growing up in Fiji* and *Let's do it Our Way*). He has published poems in *Sinnet* and *Mana* and worked traditional material into playscripts. His major work in adult fiction reflects his interest in education and youth social work, and the retention of indigenous Fijian culture. *Black Messiah* (1989) contains stories and a novella, the former linked by a journalist's investigation of a syncretic cult leader's commune and the latter showing in the life of a young teacher the problems of providing relevant schooling in poor villages. *Moving through the Streets* (1994) is a naturalistic depiction of urban slum gang life, indicating education and small-scale development projects as ways out of hopeless destitution.

■ ***Momoe Malietoa Von Reiche***—born Samoa. Educated in Samoa and New Zealand, where she has taught and exhibited as a visual artist. She is known for her lyrical verse and trenchant poems on sexist abuse of power. Her writing is collected in *Solaua, a Secret Embryo* (1979), *Pao Alimago on Wet Days* (1979), *Alaoa, above the Gully of Your Childhood* (1986) and *Tai, Heart of a Tree* (1989).

■ ***Albert Wendt***—born Tauese, Apia, 1939. Educator, social activist, poet and novelist, Albert Wendt is the pre-eminent figure of modern Pacific literature. He grew up around Apia amongst the stories (traditional ones, and Samoan versions of Western tales and Bible stories) of his grandmother, Mele. When he went on a scholarship to New Plymouth Boys High School (New Zealand), he was introduced to world literature, notably George Orwell, and began writing himself. Studying history at Victoria University, Wellington (on indigenous resistance movements including Samoa's MAU), he mixed with poet-prophet James K Baxter, Hone TUWHARE and Alistair CAMPBELL and began publishing poems and short stories. He returned to Samoa to teach, becoming head of Samoa College and extending the curriculum to include creative arts drawing on local traditions. While teaching he wrote *Sons for the Return Home* (1973), a cross-racial romance that critiques both white New Zealand prejudice against Maori and islanders, and Samoan myths of perfect traditions and superior morality. The unnamed male protagonist adopts an existential isolation, caught between the two worlds. The novel (made into a feature film in 1979) was followed by short stories, *Flying Fox in a Freedom Tree* (1974), creating a lively world of street Samoan English and colourful if unscrupulous characters. *Inside us the Dead* (1976) was Wendt's first collection of verse, light lyrics, social satire of 'vampire' local élites, and self-examination as someone with a mixed ancestry implicated in the colonial process he works to reject. The novella *Pouliuli* (1977), regarded by many as his best work, creates a symbolically powerful image of an old Lear-like chieftain, sickened by the materialist grasping and power-mongering of his society and haunted by his past, attempting to opt out but tragically having to manipulate those around him until he is destroyed by madness.

Wendt left Samoa in 1974 to become a lecturer at the UNIVERSITY OF THE SOUTH PACIFIC (USP), where he coordinated distance education, taught writing classes and literature, and collected material for the journal of Pacific writing *Mana* as well as editing booklet anthologies of verse. In 1980 he followed up with the first book anthology of Pacific writing in English, *Lali*. In this period Wendt also began to articulate his view of his own role as writer and of the project of Pacific literature in essays such as 'Towards a new Oceania' and 'In a stone castle in the South Seas'. He moved back to Apia as director of the new Samoa campus of the USP and began to be involved in local politics, writing a column in one of the main newspapers. He had also edited down a mammoth saga of social change in Samoa into a novel, *Leaves of the Banyan Tree* (1979). It traces the rise of a Samoan capitalist exploiting traditional churchly and chiefly power; the rebellion of his son, who tries to bring together pre-Christian mythology and modern existentialism; and the arrival of a new, ruthless generation of power-mongers. The middle section of this, an expanded form of the title story in *Flying Fox in a Freedom Tree*, was edited into a feature film (1989).

Shaman of Visions (1984), the second volume of poetry, was followed by another collection of stories, *The Birth and Death of the Miracle Man* (1986). Wendt returned to USP, Suva, to take up the first chair in Pacific literature. Since 1988 he has lived in Auckland, where he is Professor of New Zealand and Pacific Literature. He continues to articulate the role of the Pacific writer as asserting a dynamic cultural identity against colonizing white myths about the Pacific, to work for relevant schooling and access to education for Pacific islanders and Maori, and to oppose racism and colonialist practices. His latest novels are a playfully mocking political fable, the first Pacific sci-fi detective story (*Black Rainbow*, 1992), based on a motif of French nuclear testing at Moruroa, and *Ola* (1991), featuring a woman protagonist, and moving considerations of Samoan cultural identity into a wider global arena. He has also produced a second anthology of Pacific writing, *Nuanua* (1995), and a book of verse, *Photographs* (1995).—PS3 & MTC

FIVE PACIFIC ARTS

Arts today: recent and contemporary art

'Contemporary art' is now widely used to describe the outcome of innovative developments in the visual arts of indigenous cultures in the Pacific region. It is a term that has only recently become associated with some movements and individual artists in Pacific countries, and there are few references to it in the literature on Oceanic art which has tended to focus on 'primitive art'. In art historical terms, contemporary art emerged circa 1970s, and refers to radical and innovative art in all media or technology, produced in any national or international context.

In general, contemporary refers to artworks in non-traditional media, new or recent art forms which have made a break from tradition in style, media and technique. Such art forms explore new areas of creativity and personal expression, including all forms of literature, theatre productions, band music, as well as new visual art forms—film and photography, painting in acrylics or oils, printmaking, metal sculpture and textile design. These types of art productions are found in the urban centres because people living there have greater access to contemporary art of all kinds as well as access to instruction, necessary materials and systems of marketing and promotion.

Pacific art is often encountered in galleries and exhibitions, away from its local contexts. For some, contemporary art describes new kinds of paintings and objects, generally destined for museums and private collections, collected and described for the international art market by astute curators of contemporary art. For others, contemporary works by Pacific artists are also widely accepted and integrated into their own community, reflecting their self-image. Contemporary art is also widely used by islanders to make statements about their cultural identity. For example, Ellen José assembled her 1996 installation *RIP Terra Nullius 26 January 1788–3 June 1992*, 'to remind all Australians that the Torres Strait

John Pule's *Pulenoa*—detail from triptych, 1995

people (significantly Eddie MABO from Murray Island) were instrumental in bringing native title to both the Torres Strait Islanders and Aboriginal people of this land'.

Many Pacific artists are professional by choice, producing non-traditional works for sale to an unrestricted market. The concept of a professional artist is recognized and accepted among communities; several Papua New Guinean artists now describe themselves as 'contemporary artists' and the word *artis* has entered the lingua franca, Tok Pisin. Kauage Mathias, acknowledged as one of Papua New Guinea's first and most eminent contemporary artists, signs his paintings 'Kauage Mathias, artis bilong PNG'.

The words 'art' and 'artist', and the role and vision of artists, are now well-established and recognized, but these words also reflect specific characteristics of particular societies. Similarly, systems of art training and production, and the marketing and distribution of artworks have been transformed in Pacific societies by indigenous systems and concepts. Visual cultures have other local and specific histories and art emerges out of completely different cultural institutions and practices—such as exchange and GIFT-GIVING. Art objects and events may not be found in the same locations as in Western societies. Once every four years, at the FESTIVAL OF PACIFIC ARTS, the ingeniousness of indigenous artists' interpretations of their world is apparent in both their works and the manner of presenting them at the festival.

Contemporary art should refer to the types of creative expression currently practised within the region. This art is often the expression of significant change, manifested in art objects by way of the technology used for its production, the use of imported materials, experiments with style. Contemporary art also approaches new subjects, whether social, political, religious or secular, and expresses ideas in non-traditional ways. Contemporary art also recognizes new roles for artists in Pacific societies.

While Pacific artists may be inspired by the art of their ancestors, they are not constrained by the conventions of traditions and traditional forms because they are not making their art for the distinctly local purposes of a particular community. They each find their own way of using art to express new ideas without transgressing cultural boundaries. Kanak artists Micheline Neporon and Paula Boi have revitalized the tradition of engraving bamboo, imbuing it with new meanings and using it in contexts appropriate to urbanized Kanaks in New Caledonian society.

Artists living in clan groups in remote Pacific villages also have opportunities to incorporate change and vitality in expressing developments in their local culture. Artists act as the interpreters of change in any society and assist with the acceptance into their community of new ideas and ways of doing things. For example, there are few, if any, West Papuan or Solomon Islands artists with exposure to and experience in the types of contemporary art favoured in international exhibitions. However, there are artists who are aware of the art market and other external interests in their art (to the extent that it has developed in their locality), who make innovations incorporating new ideas, new subjects and new materials into their art. Sometimes, in remote areas, something new becomes immensely popular and stimulates creative expression in different directions: a recent example of this is the depiction of comic-book heroes, slogans and logos of beer, cigarettes and football teams now appearing on the fighting shields of Wahgi Valley warriors in Papua New Guinea. (See BODY DECORATION (BILAS) IN PAPUA NEW GUINEA.)

However remote village communities may be from Pacific Rim cities where the international contemporary art scene is flourishing, and however different an island artist's knowledge and skills may be from contemporary (Western-style) arts practice, what the islander produces has validity, integrity and sophistication within their own culture. Artists are recognized first by their own community; exceptional vision and skill rapidly gains renown further afield. Those whose works reach an international sphere are generally well-established within their own domain. Confident in their culture, it suits their self-esteem as artists to venture further and explore new opportunities for their art.

Over the last 200 years or so, the network of voyages and settlements across the Pacific has become increasingly complex, constantly testing and determining the expression of cultural parameters. It is now presumptuous to think that Western art is dominant in the Pacific region. Since the 1970s the strong presence of contemporary Aboriginal and Maori art has extended well beyond the boundaries of the artists' clans and countries, reaffirming the indigenous people's cultural identity and their will for autonomy and self-expression.

Current realities and tensions in the Pacific make oppositional terminologies such as traditional/contemporary, Western/indigenous somewhat irrelevant. It may be more fruitful to consider how artworks suggest visual or conceptual relationships,

Ellen Jose: 1996 installation *RIP Terra Nullius 26 January 1788–3 June 1992*

transcend national boundaries, or reflect an individual artist's heightened response to local, national or international issues. Certain convergences may be revealing of the overlapping issues and underlying problems of ethnic, social and linguistic commonalities and differences. The common experience of colonial regimes stimulates artistic questioning on the effects of economic inequity, religious influence and the desire for political independence. The images of identity which have proliferated in emergent Pacific nations may be interpreted as a phase of post-colonial experience.

Tensions between traditional forms and contemporary creativity, perceptible in the presentation of the works, were one of the principal axes of the Melanesian artists' contribution to the second *Asia Pacific Triennial* (1996) at the Queensland Art Gallery. Michael and Anna Mel and Wendi Choulai, Papua New Guineans who have completed studies for higher degrees in Australia, chose to return to the essential form of self-expression of their respective clans—self-decoration and performance—and to explore through their artistic expression some of the dichotomies between Western and indigenous concepts of art. René Boutin's work acknowledged the paradoxes in creating a balance between the diverse interests and lifestyles of the indigenous people, Caledonians of European descent and other groups of settlers making up New Caledonian society. Micheline Neporon's forest of engraved bamboos and Denise Tiavouane's plantation *Les Taros qui Pleurent (The Crying Taros)* translated indigenous materials and concepts into the international context of installation art. Eric Natuoivi's ceramics contemplated the changing status of women in Vanuatu, where male pride finds it hard to accommodate attempts to upgrade the status of women. On a more cheerful note, Tom Deko's *Scrap Metal Band* celebrated the widespread acceptance and creativity of black 'world music' in the Pacific.

Screen print by Papua New Guinean artist Akis, 1975

The vibrant art climate of the post-war Pacific has been marginalized in the international art world, since many influential scholars deemed it had been corrupted by Western influence and had degenerated to insignificant 'tourist art'. However, the adoption of Western idioms does not invariably produce clones of Western art. The individual artworks of Pacific artists contain imagery coded with cultural references and meanings and often reinterpret motifs specific to their culture or origin.

A number of artists of European, Chinese, Indian and other ethnic backgrounds, whose families may have lived for two generations or more in their Pacific communities, consider themselves to be Pacific people, making a conscious and valid contribution to the intellectual life and creative resources of their country and region. In the 1990s, the art environment in Australia, New Zealand and elsewhere in the Pacific is inclined to privilege indigenous art—quite understandably, considering the decades of indifference and suppression faced by indigenous people. Artists of other races may either feel marginalized or aggrieved by the present trend, or else collaborate in and stimulate the vigorous and challenging creative dialogue about the nature of Pacific art and address issues and preoccupations such as political, economic and social realities.

For many second-generation New Zealand-born Polynesians, often with parents from different island nations, 'Pacific identity' is their heritage—a vastly different cultural inheritance to that of their grandparents. Their expression of this identity may include such diverse elements as corned beef cans and other recycled materials, videos, photos, computer graphics, woven plastics, TAPA and sewn fabric, as well as the media more familiar in the POLYNESIAN COLLECTIONS of 'Pacific art' in museums and art galleries: wood, stone and paint. In his artist's statement (1996) for an international contemporary art event, Jim Vivieaere wrote

> Within the mainstream of New Zealand Contemporary Art I am positioned as a Polynesian multi-media Artist…It is in this genre of Public Art, working in Public Spaces…that interests me. I have access to fibre-optic technology and an interest in creating Art on the Web-Site, and establishing Dialogues with other Artists of Colour with similar directions.

—SC

Further reading

Art and Asia Pacific, 1995. Pacific Art Issue, 2(4).
Artlink, 1996. Pacific Art Issue (October).
Cochrane, S, 1997. *Contemporary Art in Papua New Guinea*, Craftsman House Press.
Thomas, N, 1995. *Oceanic Art*, Thames & Hudson.

Documentary (non-fiction) film in the Pacific

Interest in the Pacific islands as a subject for film-making began shortly after the birth of cinema. As early as 1898 films were shot in Hawai'i and Torres Strait Islands, the first by employees of the Edison Company, the second by anthropologist Alfred Haddon. The first films of the islands, therefore, were of actualities and, despite the difference in purpose between Edison and Haddon, might be regarded as having pioneered the non-fiction film in the Pacific. Until quite recently, though, one can hardly speak of a documentary or ethnographic film 'movement', so sporadic and inconsistent was the activity. Indeed, when referring to films, the terms 'documentary' and 'ethnographic' should be used with considerable caution, since their application is nothing if not problematical, although the categorical nature of film discussion forces one into their use from time to time.

Some early pieces were not intended as much more than travelogues. In the 1920s the intrepid adventurers Martin and Osa Johnson made a number of short silent films, most of them one-reelers intended to illustrate their lectures, although a few of the longer items were commercially released. Of these only the 60-minute *Head Hunters of the South Seas* (1922) seems to have survived, and then only in part. But by the mid 1920s the Johnsons had abandoned the Pacific islands in favour of Africa and Borneo. Even the appearance of, and the admiration accorded to, Robert Flaherty's famous *Moana* (1925), with its idyllic, episodic treatment of Samoan life, gave something of an impetus to FICTIONAL FILMS of the South Seas, but it did not inspire a body of islands-based visual ethnography. One of *Moana*'s more oblique contributions was that it introduced the term 'documentary' into the cinematic lexicon, when British film-maker and critic John Grierson so described it in a review. The word was to become one of the most misused of cinematic terms, a fact later admitted by Grierson himself.

A contemporary of Flaherty was the Australian photographer and film-maker Frank Hurley (1885–1965). Although there is no evidence of mutual influence, they bear close comparison. Both had the instincts of the explorer combined with the enthusiasms of the showman. (So for that matter did Martin Johnson, although Johnson seems to have lacked totally the cinematic sensitivity and narrative flair of the others.) Both Hurley and Flaherty aspired to be total film-makers, combining a variety of skills, and both were cinematographers of genius, with superb eyes for composition and detail. In Hurley's case this was undoubtedly a result of his photographic training, a background Flaherty lacked, although he seems to have arrived at this skill instinctively. Richard Leacock, one of Flaherty's later associates, remarked that Flaherty was far more interested in arranging the shot in the viewfinder than in seeing the later result of it.

Hurley's best-known work, *Pearls and Savages* (1921), was filmed in Papua and contained magnificently photographed scenes of village life, ceremonies and dancing. Its initial success in Australia inspired him to add more material, tint every frame by hand and show it in other countries, although its reception in the United States disappointed him. He essayed a couple of films which contained fictional elements (*Jungle Woman*, 1926, and *Hound of the Deep*, 1926), but returned later to documentary, though not to the Pacific islands.

Belgian producer Henri Storck's *Easter Island—L'Île de Pâques* (1935) should be mentioned here if only for the fact that it represents one of the very few attempts by a European film-maker of the pre-World War II period to engage an islands subject. Though well-regarded, and even described as 'poetic', its international distribution was limited by its un-subtitled French commentary. It remains an interesting curiosity.

World War II aided the cause of actuality cinema by speeding up the technical development of lightweight 16 mm camera equipment and 16 mm film to facilitate the recording of combat footage. Films of the conflict in the Pacific were made in abundance by US, Australian and Japanese cameramen, but only a few items transcended the newsreel category to become recognized as documentaries of merit. Among them was *Kokoda Front Line* (1942) by Damien Parer, perhaps Australia's best-known cameraman of the period. Much of the newsreel footage, restructured and with the addition of different commentaries and sound-effects, was later used in compiling longer narratives of the war or in re-assessing aspects of the war's impact. Among the latter, *Angels of War* (1983), which examined the effects of the conflict on the people of Papua New Guinea, is probably the best-known work.

The heightened awareness of the Pacific created by the war did not immediately result in a profusion of ethnographic film-making in the islands once the war had ended. But the war experience in Papua New Guinea had created the myth of the 'fuzzy wuzzy angel' (to be explored in *Angels of War*) and Australia's relationship with her territory had also changed: Papua New Guinea became a United Nations Trusteeship administered by the federal government's Department of Territories. One result of this was a spate of films on Papua New Guinea for the department produced during the late 1950s and 1960s by the Commonwealth Film Unit.

Although rarely screened after Papua New Guinea received its independence in 1975, the films have considerable value as historical documents, perfectly illustrating the paternalistic attitude of the Australian administration to the trusteeship and its people. Among the representative titles are *New Worlds for Old* (1958) and *By Many Paths* (1962). The 'heroes' of these propagandist works are either the selfless representatives of the Australian administration or those indigenes who have demonstrated enlightenment by breaking away from their traditional communal backgrounds. Since feature film production in Australia during this time was at a standstill and the government had a virtual monopoly on the production of non-fiction films, these have an additional importance in that they represented a major part of Australia's total film output. Films made to illustrate aspects of the US Trusteeship in Micronesia during this period were not nearly as comprehensive in their coverage of subjects as their Australian counterparts.

The relatively sparse US interest in non-fiction films of the Pacific was much better served by the justly famous *Dead Birds* (1963), filmed in Irian Jaya by a team from Harvard's Peabody Museum and depicting the formalized warfare practised by the Dani people. American ethnological input also informed *Trobriand Cricket* (1973), an examination of the traditional values underlying the adaptation of a European sport in the Trobriand Islands, though the film's long-standing popularity probably has more to do with the intrinsically amusing behaviour of the game's participants than with any ethnographic exposition.

Whatever their shortcomings, the Australian administration's films of Papua New Guinea seem to have established an ongoing interest in that country on the part of Australian makers of non-fiction films. When the Commonwealth Film Unit was replaced by Film Australia in the early 1970s, much of the earlier conservatism was also replaced by a more flexible attitude to islands subject matter. Outstanding among the ethnographic films of this period is the nine-part series *Towards Baruya Manhood* (1972) on the Baruya people of Papua New Guinea, produced by Ian Dunlop, which, in its total screening time of almost eight hours, offers as detailed an observation of a Pacific culture as any film ever made. Film Australia was responsible for a series of sensitively produced short films on aspects of Solomon Islands culture and several longer works which celebrated the arrival of political independence in such countries as Vanuatu, Solomon Islands and Kiribati. An ambitious Pacific-wide project, *The Mask of Paradise*, conceived in the early 1980s, got no further than some preliminary location photography and was replaced by the more modest six-part series *Human Face of the Pacific* (1983), which drew on the established talents of Oliver Howes and Dennis O'Rourke, but lacked a unifying principle and was largely unsuccessful.

Title for *Pearls and Savages*, made by Frank Hurley

Dennis O'Rourke, whose name must figure strongly in any discussion of non-fiction film in the islands, had worked in Papua New Guinea since the early 1970s and had early established a camera style which owed something to *cinema vérité* and a philosophical outlook which informs all his films, from *Yumi Yet* (1976), on Papua New Guinean independence, to *Cannibal Tours* (1988), on the encounters of European tourists with people of the Sepik. In most of O'Rourke's films the apparent subject actually functions as a metaphor for a wider set of socio-cultural concerns and the ramifications of change.

Other Australian film-makers who have worked successfully in Papua New Guinea include Bob Connolly and Robin Anderson, and Les McLaren. The former team's first film on Papua New Guinea, *First Contact* (1983), which examined the long-term impacts on Highlands people of their encounter with white explorers in the 1930s, grew into a trilogy as Connolly and Anderson subsequently explored the relationship of one of the offspring of that encounter with his indigenous neighbours in *Joe Leahy's Neighbours* (1989) and *Black Harvest* (1992). Les McLaren documented the music and its social significance of Lake Chambri in the SEPIK RIVER region in *Namekas: music in Lake Chambri* (1979), and life in Port Moresby's squatter colonies in *Cowboy and Maria in Town* (1992), a film remarkable for its sensitive handling of the problems of social and cultural dislocation. McLaren's most recent work, *Taking Pictures* (1996), is a timely examination of the changes in the way film-makers in Papua New Guinea have regarded their subjects over the decades. Participants in the film include Chris Owen, long resident film-maker and instructor at Port Moresby's Institute of Papua New Guinea Studies. His works include the celebrated *Red Bowmen* (1983), which depicts the Ida fertility ritual of the Umeda people of West Sepik. Under the auspices of the institute, a number of Papua New Guineans have also made films, ranging from single-subject ethnographic works such as *Bark Belt* (1987) to *Tukana* (1984), a feature-length fictional film, but one with a strong sense of actuality.

In much of the work of these film-makers, the long-held distinction between documentary/ethnographic film and fiction or narrative film is blurred so frequently as to suggest it has little validity left. O'Rourke has referred to his recent work as 'documentary fictions' while the films of Connolly and Anderson have been called 'documentary dramas'. McLaren and O'Rourke have questioned the relationship of the film-makers to their subjects and raised questions about the nature of the medium itself. While the greater number of non-fiction films made in the islands will probably continue to resemble travelogues, the gradual emergence of works which examine both the subject and the process itself is a welcome trend.—ND2

Further reading

Aoki, D, and Douglas, N (comp.), 1994. *Moving Images of the Pacific Islands: a guide to films and videos*, Center for Pacific Islands Studies, University of Hawai'i.

Barnouw, E, 1974. *Documentary*, Oxford University Press.

Heider, K, 1976. *Ethnographic Film*, University of Texas Press.

Pike, A and Cooper, R, 1980. *Australian Film 1900–1977*, Melbourne University Press.

Roddick, N, 1986. 'O'Rourke's Drift', *Cinema Papers* (March).

Fictional films

For almost a century films of the Pacific islands have been characterized by the traditional dichotomy of the cinema: on one hand, depiction of fantasy or exotica, and on the other, representation of reality. At least up to the 1960s or so, the former tendency was paramount in films which took the Pacific as their subject.

With the United States in the forefront of commercial film-making for most of the century, it is not surprising that most fictional films of the Pacific were the product of Hollywood: even if they were not always made wholly in the studio, they displayed the well-known studio artifice in their construction. It is also significant that Hawai'i, as a venue or a subject for film-making, was early to the fore. The Edison Company was filming Kanakas diving for coins as early as 1898, and film historian Robert Schmitt has recorded details of no fewer than 120 feature-length fictional films made in or about Hawai'i up to 1959. Hawai'i served film-makers well as itself but also substituted, when required, for Tahiti, Samoa, Vanuatu and Solomon Islands among others, thereby influencing audience perceptions of the islands region. Its appeal for American film-makers was obvious: geographical convenience, an increasingly well-developed infrastructure, vegetation that was lush and scenery that was considered distinctive and dramatically appropriate—especially volcanoes which lent themselves iconographically to a number of movie adventures.

Increased film-making in Hawai'i coincided with its growing appeal for Americans as a tourist destination, and the presence—whether at work or play—of movie performers was valuable in assisting the state's efforts at self-promotion. In at least two films, the Elvis Presley vehicles *Blue Hawai'i* (1961) and *Paradise Hawaiian Style* (1965), the relationship between movies and tourism is made explicit since the narrative in both concerns Hawai'i's shift from earlier economic activities to tourism. It is still the case that almost any film-making activity in the Pacific is regarded by offices of tourism as valuable publicity for their country, regardless of the subject. The excitement that attended the filming in Vanuatu of the lamentable Australian effort *Till There Was You* (1990) illustrates the uncritical attitude of local tourist industries to film-making. The film, which was going to 'draw worldwide attention to Vanuatu' and boost tourism spectacularly, was not only offensive in the extreme in its use of native stereotypes, but was virtually disowned by its producers and recut for rental through video outlets. It never received a theatrical release.

The characteristics which identify American film genres began to emerge in the 1920s and 1930s and, superficially, fictional films of the Pacific have been regarded as comprising a genre in the way that Westerns, gangster films, back-stage musicals and romantic comedies—to name a few—do. In fact, genre elements are present in relatively few films about the South Seas, though the related themes of NOBLE SAVAGE and FATAL IMPACT run through most films of the Pacific (whether fiction or actuality) to the present day. If a South Seas genre flourished at all, its life was brief, far more so than other US film genres, many of which are still with us.

There were perhaps two dozen fiction films with island themes made before Robert Flaherty's famous *Moana* (1925), but the latter is often said to be a milestone in the treatment of Pacific subjects. Its influence, however, was quite slight and is apparent, at least briefly, only in two fictional films, *White Shadows in the South Seas* (1928) and *Tabu* (1931), in both of which Flaherty had some input, although the degree of that input and consequently his overall influence remains questionable.

It is in *White Shadows* that the first strong glimmers of what might be considered a South Seas genre begin to appear. The 'noble savage', a myth enthusiastically embraced by Flaherty in *Moana*, is here confronted with the 'fatal impact' personified by unscrupulous Western intruders (the white shadows of the title). In the film, as in many fiction films of the islands, miscegenation or some other illicit sexual activity—implied or actual—is a major dramatic component, invariably leading (since censorship was strong during this period) to tragic consequences. The companion piece to *White Shadows*, a little-seen and hence vastly underrated film, is the more frequently screened *Tabu* (1931), which also helped shape the genre and is dramatically similar in many respects, dealing as it does with ill-fated love arising from the breaking of cultural conventions. *Bird of Paradise* (1932) and *Hurricane* (1938) also deserve mention here as films of the period which embody the genre conventions to a considerable extent, although there are interesting narrative variations in all these items.

The apparent proliferation of the South Seas melodrama in the 1930s and 1940s can probably be explained as another response to the seeming need of audiences of the time for escapist material that was also met by the musical and the screwball comedy. In addition to the genre pieces where landscape is of iconographic significance to the narrative, the Pacific is an important component, scenically or dramatically, in such films as MUTINY ON THE BOUNTY (1935) and *Son of Fury* (1942). Even by the 1940s, however, elements of conscious self-parody were appearing, an indication that the conventions were becoming tiresome to film-makers and audiences alike. The South Seas films made during the war years, including *South of Pago Pago* (1940), *Aloma of the South Seas* (1941), *South of Tahiti* (1941) and *White Savage* (1943), have even fewer pretensions to realism than their predecessors, and one of the last of their line, the monumentally bizarre *Cobra Woman* (1944) contains almost every exotic cliché that Hollywood scriptwriters could find. 'It may be', wrote critic Pauline Kael in reference to one of them, 'that these semi-burlesques were more fun to make than to watch'. Many of these films, however, deserve to be taken seriously, not for their dramatic content or their fidelity to reality but because they helped to shape outsiders' perceptions of the Pacific for many years. A corrective to them has been a long time coming, indeed has only emerged in the past decade or so.

After the 1950s it appears that although the islands, especially Hawai'i, would continue to figure in American films as settings for war drama (*From Here to Eternity*, 1953), musical comedy (*South Pacific*, 1958), historical romance (*Hawai'i*, 1966 and its sequel *The Hawaiians*, 1970), Elvis Presley playground (*Blue Hawai'i* 1961, *Paradise Hawaiian Style*, 1965), or merely as background for ill-considered remakes of earlier works (*Hurricane*, 1979), American film-makers had little interest in maintaining the conventions that had helped to identify the South Seas genre.

The long-standing contribution of Australians to the visual literature of the Pacific has been recognized only relatively recently. Australia's proximity to, and historical involvement with, the islands gave film-makers an early interest in depicting subjects with a Pacific setting: the first two cinematic versions of the *Bounty* story (1916 and 1933), for instance, were made by Australian movie producers, and the work of photographer/documentarist Frank Hurley in Papua New Guinea (*Pearls and Savages*, 1921, *Jungle Woman*, 1926) is significant to the history of both actuality and fiction film in Australia. These early works were followed by a number of exotic melodramas, several of which incorporated elements of the South Seas genre film discussed above, including the search for pearls (*Lovers and Luggers*, 1937; *Typhoon Treasure*, 1938; *King of the Coral Sea*, 1954) and implied miscegenation (*Adorable Outcast*, 1928). However, the collapse of a commercial Australian film industry in the late 1950s effectively put an end to the closer involvement of Australian makers of fiction films with the Pacific. Such work as was done in the late 1950s and 1960s consisted almost entirely of actuality films (see DOCUMENTARY FILMS) produced by the Commonwealth Film Unit. By the time the industry revived in the early 1970s, the Pacific islands as setting or subject matter for theatrically released films seemed to have become passé, although a number of television-oriented feature films or mini-series have appeared since. These include the two-part *The Other Side of Paradise* (1992), the only significance of which is its clumsy attempt to resurrect some of the genre conventions of an earlier period. For the last 30 years or so the greatest contribution of Australian film-makers has been their documentary or ethnographic work.

There is irony in the fact that New Zealand, with little history of involvement in film by comparison with the United States and even Australia, now appears to be pointing the way to a new Pacific islands cinema. It says something about the curious history of film-making in New Zealand that the first films of Maori life were made in 1912 by a Frenchman—Gaston Melies, whose brother George is regarded by film historians as the symbolic parent of the film of fantasy as opposed to that of fact. A listing of feature films made in New Zealand between 1914 and 1980 makes a thin catalogue indeed: only 39, including those made on location in the country but with overseas finance. Although a number of these, especially those made by Rudall Hayward, dealt with New Zealand Maori themes, interest in the wider Pacific seems to have been absent, or perhaps simply constrained by production costs. It hardly needs to be said that for the greater part of New Zealand's film history, films involving Maori were made by, and from the perspective of, whites. The shift in attitude from early representations of Maori as quaint and colourful objects of historical or tourist interest to the vigorous, unapologetic and even deliberately provocative stance of many films since the mid 1970s may be seen as one element in the refocusing of social and cultural issues in New Zealand and a growing determination on the part of Maori to take charge of their own affairs. In cinema this has resulted in the emergence of indigenous film-makers with access to, and sometimes control of, the means of production. Films illustrating the new perspective include *Ngati* (1987), *Mauri* (1988) and the confrontational *Once Were Warriors* (1995), in all of which the lines between 'documentary' and 'fiction' are quite deliberately blurred if not entirely erased.

'How do indigenous people use the camera once we come to have some control over it?' Maori film-maker Barry Barclay asked in 1988. 'Perhaps it is on our own shoulders to redefine the rules.' Although Barclay is by no means the first to have questioned the precise relationship between medium and message or between the technology and the use to which it is put, it cannot yet be said that the rules have been redefined. However, in the work of New Zealanders and in the somewhat more modest efforts of indigenous film-makers elsewhere in the islands, a new perspective on the Pacific and new values are beginning to emerge.—ND2

Further reading

Aoki, D and Douglas, N (comp.), 1994. *Moving Images of the Pacific Islands: a guide to films and videos*, Center for Pacific Islands Studies, University of Hawai'i.

Blythe, M, 1988. *From Maoriland to Aotearoa: images of the Maori in New Zealand film and television*, University Microfilm International.

Reyes, L, with Rampell, E, 1995. *Made in Paradise: Holywood's films of Hawai'i and the South Seas*, Mutual Publishing Company.

Schmitt, R C, 1988. *Hawai'i in the Movies, 1898–1959*, Hawaiian Historical Society.

Polynesian collections

The earliest collections of artifacts from Polynesia that can be identified today are the some 2000 pieces collected during the three Pacific voyages of Captain James COOK from 1768 to 1780. The largest collections are in the Institute für Völkerkunde (Göttingen, Germany); Pitt Rivers Museum (Oxford); University Museum of Archaeology and Anthropology (Cambridge); Museum für Völkerkunde (Vienna); British Museum (London); Museum für Völkerkunde (Berlin).

Other early collections that can be documented include those from Vancouver, 1791–95 (now in the Museum of Mankind, London); Malaspina, 1793 (in the Museo de America, Madrid); BOUGAINVILLE, 1766–69, (in Musée de l'Homme, Paris); and the LONDON MISSIONARY SOCIETY, (in the Museum of Mankind). In the Museum of Ethnography (St Petersburg, Russia), are collections from von Krusenstern and Langsdorff, 1803–06, Lisiansky, 1803–06, Kotzebue, 1815–18, and Bellingshausen, 1819–21. In the Musée Nationale des Arts d'Afrique et d'Océanie (Paris), are collections from Dillon, 1827–28, FREYCINET, 1817–20, Duperrey and Collet, 1822–25, and DUMONT D'URVILLE, 1826–29, 1837–40. Collections made by Captain John Byron and others on HMS *Blonde*, 1824–26, are now in several museums including Pitt Rivers Museum, Museum of Mankind, Bishop Museum (Honolulu), Honolulu Academy of Arts, Field Museum (Chicago), and Metropolitan Museum of Art (New York). Collections made by Beechey, 1825–28, are in the Museum of Mankind, the Pitt Rivers Museum, and the Royal Scottish Museum (Edinburgh). The Thompson collection from the 1840s is now in Belfast, Northern Ireland. Early American whaling voyages starting in 1801 brought back collections that are now in the Peabody Museum (Salem, Massachusetts). The collections of the US EXPLORING EXPEDITION under Charles Wilkes, 1838–42, are now in the Smithsonian Institution, Washington DC.

The second half of the 19th century saw a whole new series of collectors—interested travellers, more missionaries, collectors for museums, and anthropologists. Many of these were from Germany. The Hamburg Godeffroy Museum obtained large collections from Fiji and Samoa, most of which are now in Leipzig. Collections made by Krämer in Samoa, Arning in Hawai'i, and others are in the Berlin Museum. The Reishek collection of Maori artifacts is in Vienna. Collections from this period in France include the Hawaiian collection of Ballieu (French consul in Honolulu), in the Musée de l'Homme. Collections in Britain include those of Anatole von Hugel, Sir Arthur GORDON, and Alfred Maudsley (from Fiji and elsewhere), now in the University Museum of Archaeology and Anthropology; Sir George Grey's New Zealand Maori collection is in the Museum of Mankind. Collections made in Easter Island on HMS *Topaze* in 1868 and by Katherine Routledge in 1914 are in the Museum of Mankind. Collections made by W J Thomson on the USS *Mohican* from Easter Island in 1889 are in the Smithsonian Institution, Washington DC. Collections made in Samoa in the 1870s by Albert Steinberger are in the Smithsonian.

Important collections were made by museums during the 20th century. BISHOP MUSEUM expeditions, notably the Bayard Dominick Expeditions to the Marquesas, Tonga, and the Austral Islands, and the Mangareva Expedition, yielded important collections. The expedition to Easter Island by Lavachery and Metraux produced collections for the Brussels Museum and the Musée de l'Homme. Other collections were made by individuals such as Eric Craig of New Zealand and J S Emerson of Hawai'i who sold them to museums in Hawai'i, New Zealand and elsewhere. Other collectors who never travelled to Polynesia, such as Ratton, Oldman, Fuller, Beasley and Hooper, collected Polynesian objects in Europe, traded and sold them, and they can now be found in museums in Britain, Europe, New Zealand, the United States and Japan.—ALK

■ ***Bishop Museum*** The Bernice P Bishop Museum in Honolulu holds a vast and comprehensive collection of Hawaiian and Polynesian material, maintaining natural history collections of more than 18 million animal and plant specimens, and displaying a wide variety of artifacts and items reflecting Hawaiian history, culture and society. The museum was set up by Charles Reed Bishop as a memorial to his wife, Princess Bernice Pauahi, who was the last direct descendant of the KAMEHAMEHA dynasty. The idea had been promoted by William T Brigham, who first visited Hawai'i on holiday in 1864, soon after graduating from Harvard College. More than 20 years later, when he had abandoned his law career, his natural history interests were revived and he began to plan a history of the Hawaiian islands. In 1889, his friend Bishop had been persuaded to establish a museum to house some of his late wife's treasures, and to appoint Brigham as its first director. The Deed of Trust (1896) proclaimed it as a scientific institution for 'collecting, preserving, storing and exhibiting' Polynesian ethnological specimens, as well as publishing the results of its scientific studies. Its first publication was a treatise by Brigham on Hawaiian featherwork in 1899, establishing a tradition of investigative research which has continued to attract Pacific scholars.—KRF

■ ***Jean-Marie Tjibaou Cultural Centre*** The Jean-Marie Tjibaou Cultural Centre in Noumea, New Caledonia, was opened in June 1998. Designed by Italian architect, Renzo Piano, it is intended to create a place for the development of Kanak culture as well as a centre for visual and performing artists indigenous to the South Pacific. Funded jointly by the French and New Caledonian governments, the centre embodies the spirit of the reconciliation process between France and the indigenous Kanak people. The inaugural cultural director is Emmanual Kaserhou, and there is a major collection devoted to contemporary art, curated by Susan Cochrane.—KRF

Barkcloth

The use of barkcloth, made of the inner bark of certain trees, is widespread in the Pacific and is also found in Japan, South America and Africa. Barkcloth reached one its high points in Polynesia where it was considered of great value. It is usually the work of women, but was often sacred to men and women as well as the gods.

Besides its use in sacred ceremonies, the most important uses of barkcloth were for bedding and clothing—often specially prepared and decorated for people of rank. Designs and technique can be distinguished between east and west Polynesia as well as from island to island. In general, barkcloth in west Polynesia was (and still is) made by a pasting technique and designs are added by rubbing over a stencil; in east Polynesia barkcloth was made by a felting technique and designs added with the aid of a stamp. The finest barkcloth is made of the inner bark of the paper mulberry (*Broussonetia papyrifera*), which is cultivated specifically for the purpose. Other plants include breadfruit (*Artocarpus*), fig (*Ficus*), and *Pipturaus*, called *mamaki* in Hawaiian.

When paper mulberry plants are about 2 m high they are cut and the entire bark stripped from the wood. The bark is then flattened by wrapping around the hand and the inner and outer bark are separated. After soaking in water, the inner bark is laid upon an anvil, cleaned, and beaten with a mallet, until it becomes shorter and wider. Anvils and mallets are usually made of wood. Dyes are made from plants—flowers, bark and roots.

In west Polynesia each piece of inner bark was beaten separately and then several pasted together with a paste made from a plant such as arrowroot. In Tonga these pieces are pasted together and dye rubbed onto the white cloth which is laid over a stencil. A group of women work together pasting, moving the cloth, and stencilling until they have a huge piece. The final stage is done by hand, and consists of painting over parts of the design that have been printed from the stencil with dark brown or black paint with a brush made of a pandanus key. In east Polynesia and in Fiji, barkcloth was considered sacred and often a marker of transition and transformation.

In Fiji a piece of barkcloth hung from the rafters of the godhouse, *bure kalou*, served as a pathway for the god to descend to the priest. Wood sculptures wear barkcloth to cover the genital area and adorn the head. In Rarotonga, huge bales of barkcloth formed the body of the god, and in Mangaia, special male priests made a heavy barkcloth for religious purposes.

Tongan barkcloth is distinguished by its large size and metaphorical designs. Large finished pieces, sometimes as large as 5 m by 50 m, are categorized by colour and design organization as *ngatu*, *ngatu uli* (black *ngatu*) and *fuatanga*. *Ngatu uli* are used primarily by chiefs, and derive their high status from the difficulty of making the black dye. A series of stencils form a set which has metaphorical meaning. Sometimes these sets are traditional chiefly designs or have local referents. They may be combined to commemorate specific occasions or make references to chiefs or their ancestral lines. For example, a stencil set with pine trees, the Tongan coat of arms, and a lion metaphorically refers to the monarch (pine trees form a road on one side of the palace, the coat of arms is the monarch's seal, and the lion as monarch is adapted from Europe). Such a *ngatu* set is quite popular and can be used for a wide variety of occasions. Sets of naturalistic stencils are completed with groupings of traditional geometric designs such as *manulua* (a series of triangles joined at their points) and *fata* (concentric squares) which are metaphorical references to chiefs and their deeds.

In Futuna, in addition to a pasted variety of barkcloth, special kilts made by a felting technique are distinctive. The kilts were measured in *sala*, and have fine geometric patterns painted in black or

Display of tapa cloth and weaving crafts, made by Tongan women living in Sydney, with a mixture of motifs from their native and adopted lands—at the Casula Powerhouse, April 1998

brown on beige with touches of red brown. The geometric designs surround a centre section of black and the whole piece sometimes has a black border.

In east Polynesia the inner bark was usually felted. The technique was described in Tahiti, during the voyages of Captain Cook. The cleaned and soaked strips of inner bark were laid out in two or three layers, with the longitudinal fibres laid lengthwise to form a collage 30 cm wide and 11 m long. After laying overnight, much of the water evaporated and the fibres began to adhere together. The collage was then beaten with a four-sided wooden beater, each face carved with straight lines or furrows of different widths. By this process the layers were felted together to form one large piece, which might then be folded several times and again beaten to make a very soft and thin cloth. Eighteenth-century cloth was usually a natural or solid colour, occasionally with stripes in red or yellow or with tiny circles, probably from dipping the end of small bamboo or other reed into the dye and printing it on the top of the cloth. Distinctive Tahitian designs developed from dipping a fern or other plant leaf into dye and transferring the dye to the barkcloth thereby transferring the shape of the leaf. This design was augmented by the introduction of short lines to form supplementary designs.

A striking contrast of black designs on a white background was characteristic of barkcloth of Cook Islands and probably the Austral Islands. Long, narrow loincloths worn by men in Cook Islands were printed with fine horizontally organized designs of tiny squares and rectangles. Cook Island ponchos

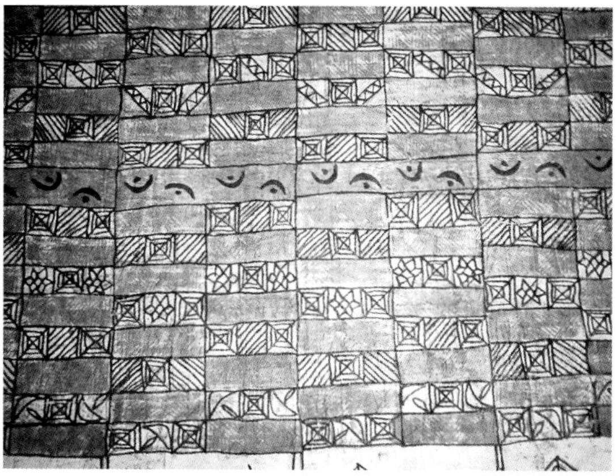

Detail of Tongan tapa cloth, presented by Leonie and Cecil Cocker to G J R Linge and P J Rimmer, in Nuku'alofa, June 1971, now displayed in Coombs Building, The Australian National University

were usually dyed red-brown and the design of tiny triangles and rectangles was made by perforating the cloth with holes.

Some of the finest barkcloth, both in quality of material and in design variation, was made in Hawai'i. The technique was a variation of felting achieved by two separate beatings. After soaking in water, the first beating produced long strips that could be dried and stored until needed. For the second beating, the dried strips were soaked, lightly beaten, placed in layers between banana leaves, and left for about ten days to mature by 'retting'. The partially rotted and layered strips were felted, by beating, into a finished rectangular piece. To make larger pieces, they were joined by sewing. Most 18th century barkcloth is relatively thick, is often ribbed

Detail of decorated barkcloth known as *ngatu* in Tonga

(on a grooving board), and has bold angular designs. Nineteenth-century barkcloth is thinner, has smaller designs organized differently, occasionally includes circular motifs, and has an elaboration of a 'watermark' derived from beating with a mallet with incised designs. This watermark impressed a design into the cloth. In pre-European times the watermarks were primarily straight lines in different widths, carved side by side on the length of the mallet, sometimes with lines in another direction. With the influx of metal nails and carving tools from Europe, more elaborate designs were carved into the mallet and impressed into the barkcloth.

A second layer of design was painted or printed on the upper surface of the cloth. In 18th century barkcloth this upper layer of design was based on creative combinations of linear elements that cross and converge to form squares, triangles, and diagonal forms, giving a feeling of boldness and directness. Nineteenth-century designs have less emphasis on linear elements, and the straight lines that do occur are more of the order of space dividers and give frames to enclosed arrangements of small motifs. Sometimes these frames are entirely filled in with one design, or the linear elements enclose or define the space for the more consciously placed motifs. These motifs were printed with stamps that were carved on the inside end section of strips of bamboo 30–45 cm in length. One end was carved with a long, narrow design (2–12 cm long, and 0.5–2 cm wide) and the non-carved section functioned as a handle. This intricate carving was made possible by imported metal tools. The tiny designs were placed in groups (by printing them end-to-end, side-to-side, or at angles) to form a larger design. Large designs, such as triangles, were filled in with small varied motifs. The top layer of design is readily apparent, but the watermark impressed from the beater is visible only when held to the light.—ALK

Further reading

Brigham, W T, 1911. *Ka Hana Kapa: the making of bark cloth in Hawai'i*, Bishop Museum Press.

Kaeppler, A L, 1975. *The Fabric of Hawaii (Bark Cloth)*, F Lewis Publishers.

——, 1995. 'Poetics and politics of Tongan barkcloth', *Pacific Material Culture: essays in honour of Dr Simon Kooijman*, Rijksmuseum voor Volkenkunde.

Neich, N and Pendergast, M, 1997. *Pacific Tapa*, David Bateman Ltd.

Mats and mat-making

In the Pacific islands, mats of various grades are used as bedding or floor coverings, or as a protective surface inside or outdoors for working or lying on. Smaller decorated mats have also traditionally been used as garments. Most commonly made from the leaves of the pandanus palm (*Pandanus tectorius*), mats can be woven or plaited in a wide variety of sizes and designs, and coloured with dyes. Melanesian mats were plaited—weaving is not a Melanesian craft. An enormous variety of mat patterns has been found throughout the islands, reflecting the creative skills of their makers. Fine mats serve a number of decorative, social and ritual purposes, but particularly in Polynesian societies, they have been used by women as items of exchange, including marriage exchanges. (See also GIFT-GIVING IN MELANESIA.)

Mats are traditionally made by women, who have their own techniques for producing the softened, bleached strips necessary for mat-weaving. In Samoa, women beat pandanus leaves into wafer-thin strips. In Vanuatu, women gather the pandanus leaves when green, hold them in the flames of a fire to soften them, and then cut them into narrow strips. The strips are soaked in water and then sun-bleached, at which point they can be stored for several months if necessary.

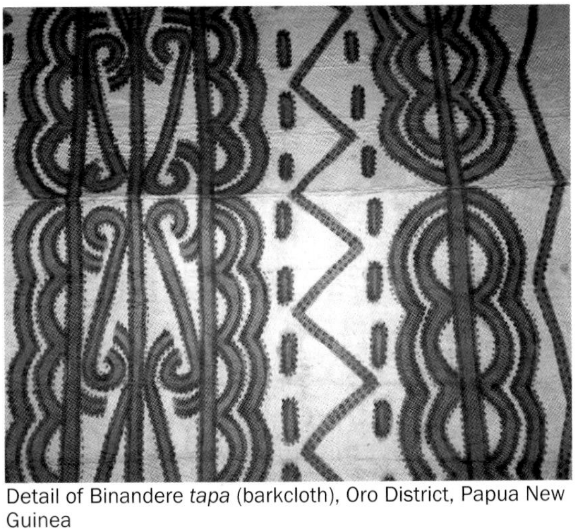

Detail of Binandere *tapa* (barkcloth), Oro District, Papua New Guinea

In traditional Samoan society, a family's most valuable possession is the fine mat known as *'ie toga*. Kept for generations, the mat's value increases with age and it would become a significant gift for the most important occasions—marriages, deaths or visits by distinguished guests. An old well-worn fine mat is given only to chiefs and very important dignitaries. Once it is presented as a gift to thank a guest for his presence, its name becomes *malo*. The quality of the *'ie toga* is judged by the fineness of the plaited work, as well as the length of time it has been kept among important families. It was the principal form of woman-generated wealth.

Large distributions of fine mats were an essential part of public ceremonies, and those who aspired to the highest SAMOAN TITLES needed to accumulate old and sacred mats that symbolized the status they sought. In discussions over the nature and quantity of mats to give at a ceremony, Samoan women were equal participants in decision-making processes.

In Tonga as well as Samoa, the primary work of women was the manufacture of mats and cloth for domestic and ceremonial use. Fine mats fringed with red feathers and sometimes honoured by personal names are exchanged on important occasions. Mats are significant family heirlooms, gaining greater value with age.

Tongan sleeping mats and floor mats known as *fala* are woven from strips of pandanus leaves and then assembled from two layers joined together for extra strength. Houses were built with raised floors of well-tamped earth, and often there was a layer of leaves or dried grass under the covering of mats. The sleeping area of the house was also enclosed with long mats, set on edge to form a low screen. Two species of pandanus were used: *fā* was used for coarse, tough sails and baskets; and *paonga* was used for finely woven sleeping mats. Fine mats were woven from a variety of materials, including the inner bark fibre of hibiscus (*Hibiscus tiliaceus*, known as *fau*). Decorative patterns were formed by dyeing certain strands in different colours. Matting for clothing was even more finely woven, made from thin strips of young leaves from both the *fā* and *paonga* species of pandanus.

In ancient Hawaiian society, women—particularly older women—made plaited mats from pandanus leaves known as *lauhala*. Fine mats, bedding and clothing were more commonly made from barkcloth called *kapa* (see BARKCLOTH). Traditionally, fine mats were part of tributary offerings to the chiefs, with varying degrees of status attached to the quality and quantity of the items. In religious rituals too, offerings and images of the gods were wrapped in fine mats. After European contact, however, cotton cloth and other foreign goods soon supplanted the traditional fine mats and barkcloth.

In Vanuatu, where exchanges of mats mark all the formal occasions of social life, mats are used only by women. On Pentecost, there are three kinds of mats: 4 m long *sese*, printed with a purple design and decorated with a long thick fringe; smaller *tsip* mats used for women's clothing, and *malmal* mats worn by men as a loincloth; and *butsuban* sleeping mats. The purple designs used on *sese* and *tsip* are made with powdered bark and involve a dyeing technique that takes a week, and occurs as an important occasion in a woman's life. The designs have special significance, for instance indicating the woman's social status. On Ambae, a new mat is valued more highly than an old one, and up to 1500

Tongan floor mat or *fala* (detail)

may be presented at a single marriage ceremony. Apart from the three types of mats used as floor mats, sleeping mats or clothing, there are additional *maraha* mats, used as ceremonial gifts and to wrap the dead. Nearly all mats are dyed—traditionally using a grated bark to produce a reddish-brown colour, but today using vivid magenta commercial dyes.

Rotuman women traditionally made four kinds of mats: *'epa* were ordinary floor mats; *apei sala* were the lowest grade of fine mats; *apei niau* were made from hibiscus bark; and the very finest mats were *armea*, made from the bark of the paper mulberry tree. Women practised a tradition known as *sa'a*, a gathering for the collective weaving of fine white mats for some important future event. Fine mats could take many weeks to produce, and the weaving process was accompanied by special rituals including CLOWNING. The completed white mats became highly valued exchange items, an essential part of wedding ceremonies, funerals, births, welcoming ceremonies, headstone unveilings and any ritual of importance.

In pre-contact Truk (Chuuk), Pohnpei and Kosrae, finely woven pandanus sleeping mats were common, but women also made narrow mats from the fibre of banana palms and hibiscus with a loom that produced a fine woven material used for clothing. A striped pattern was created by inserting vertical strips that had been dyed black. Lengths of about 120 cm, 60 cm wide, would be worn as a kind of loin cloth. Once European visitors brought cotton cloth, however, the islanders preferred to wear it. Other loosely woven mats, using fibres of the hibiscus tree, were used as mosquito nets.—LB & KRF

Quilting in Polynesia

Tivaevae, tifaifai, iripiti, kapa lau and *kapa'apana* are brightly coloured appliquéd or pieced bedcovers or 'quilts' made by women in several Polynesian islands. The tradition originated in the eastern islands of Polynesia (Hawaiian, Society, Austral, Tuamotu and Cook Islands) in the 19th century with women in western Polynesia (Tonga and the Lau Islands of Fiji) beginning quilt-making in the late 20th century. It is the eastern Polynesian core which has evolved a unique and distinctive aesthetic tradition of quilted and appliquéd bed coverlets. Like women's traditional textile production in Polynesia, quilts are created as expressions of the makers and are important items of presentation and exchange as wealth and status markers at kin and social events such as: births, deaths, marriages, first hair-cutting ceremonies, title installations and, more recently, graduations. In addition, quilts have become an important way for some of the Polynesian diaspora of some islands to fulfil kin obligations through their exchange between home and migrant communities.

Each island group which quilts or appliqués has a unique history clearly represented in the stylistic diversity of Polynesian quilts. The quilts which, today, are most readily identified as stylistically Hawaiian are known as *kapa lau* or *kapa 'apana*—a name which clearly reflects the connection with the indigenous Hawaiian barkcloth tradition. These quilts are designed with a large appliqué intricately cut from one piece of cloth which is stitched to a foundation fabric of another colour. The quilts are thus bi-coloured, with red or blue on a white backing being the most common traditional Hawaiian colours. The design is symmetrical and is achieved by folding the top cloth into eighths and cutting in layers. The overall effect is of a paper-cut snowflake

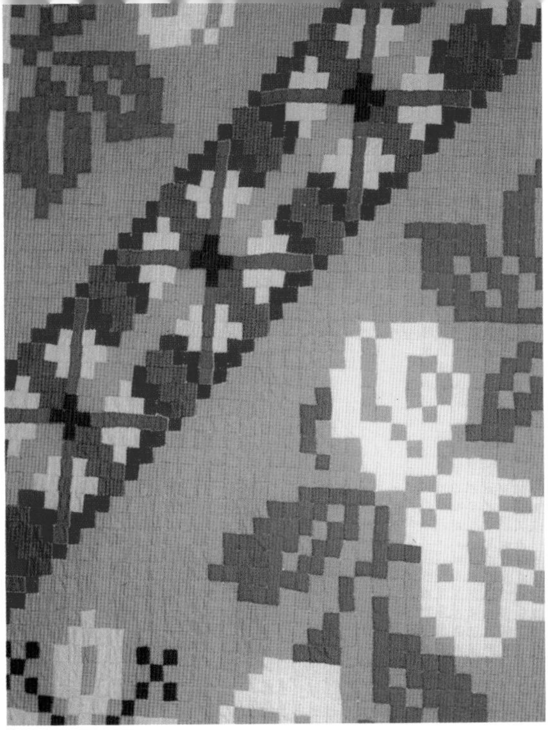

Tivaevae: quilts of the Cook Islands (detail)

or lacework. The appliqué is, then, enhanced by a distinctive quilting or stitching style, known as *luma lau*, which echoes the design and radiates out across the quilt. This technique employs a middle batting or wadding as well as a backing layer which are quilted together and requires considerable expertise and patience with some exceptional examples taking as long as two years to complete.

In the Society, Tuamotu, Austral and Cook Islands a slightly different method is employed to create one type of appliquéd bedcover. As in the Hawaiian Islands the top piece of fabric is folded, in this case in fourths, and cut to produce a symmetrical design which is then appliquéd onto a backing or foundation cloth. Unlike the Hawaiian examples, these coverlets are not batted or quilted. They are known as *tifaifai pa'oti* or *tifaifai tapiri* in Society Islands and *tivaevae manu* in Cook Islands. These coverlets are multi-coloured and bright in appearance. A second type of quilt made in the Society, Tuamotu, Austral and Cook Islands is piecework or patchwork composed of very small geometrically shaped pieces of cloth of different colours. The pieces are stitched together and then backed with a piece of fabric. The design is formed through the placement of the different coloured pieces. This type of quilt is known as *tifaifai pu* in Society Islands, *tivaevae taorei* in Cook Islands and *iripiti* in Austral Islands. Strictly speaking *tifaifai*, *tivaevae* and *iripiti* are appliquéd bed coverlets, not quilts, because they are made of only two layers—the top, appliqué design, on the foundation backing, instead of several layers of cloth and batting which are sewn or 'quilted' together. However, the coverlets are widely known as 'quilts' throughout Polynesia.

There is little direct evidence concerning the introduction of quilting to eastern Polynesia. Most scholars assume that it was the women of Christian mission groups who gave instruction upon their arrival in the islands. While it is clear that these women taught indigenous women how to sew, it is not at all certain that they taught them the craft of creating stitched bed coverlets or quilts. Indeed, the distinctive folded, intricately cut and appliquéd quilts of eastern Polynesia appear to have been influenced by Pennsylvanian German *scherenschnitte* or Victorian folded paper-cutting traditions. Multiple origins and influences thus seem likely for the eastern Polynesian quilting heritage.—PSH

Further reading

Hammond, J D, 1986. *Tifaifai and Quilts of Polynesia*, University of Hawai'i Press.

Jones, S, 1973 [1930]. *Hawaiian Quilts*, Honolulu Academy of Arts.

Rongokea, L, 1992. *Tivaevae: portraits of Cook Island quilting*, Daphne Brasell.

Shaw, R, 1996. *Hawaiian Quilt Masterpieces*, Hugh Lauter Levin & Associates.

Tivaevae: quilts of the Cook Islands (detail)

Sepik art

The masks, carvings, architecture and artifacts of the people who live in the vicinity of the SEPIK RIVER of Papua New Guinea have gained international renown since they first came to the attention of foreign explorers, traders and missionaries. Most of the art was produced for use in the elaborate ceremonies and initiations linked to men's societies. The towering *haus tambarans* (ancestral spirit houses) sometimes reached 35 m in height, with painted bark panels and carvings on the front. These were men's houses for meetings and ritual occasions, and were used to store sacred masks, musical instruments such as nose flutes, and carved artifacts such as drums and shields. Dances and dramatic performances by masked figures were used to present history, mythology, ancestral exploits and formal religious concepts to young male initiates.

Sepik sculpture includes a wide variety of figures, masks, dance shields, charms and musical instruments, usually three-dimensional and decorated with relief work. In addition to the widespread use of wood (carved exclusively by men), clay was used for roof ornaments and cooking pots, and intricately woven basketry was used for masks, costumes and small ornaments. Almost no object or implement was left undecorated: stoppers for lime containers, bowls, canoe prows and paddles, bone daggers, spears and stools. Bird feathers, cowry and nassa shells, animal fur, bones, teeth and tusks, and leaves and seeds were traditionally incorporated

Awar village on a small tributary of the Ramu River, Sepik District, New Guinea, photographed by Sarah Chinnery in 1935. Large houses with steep thatched roofs and overhanging eaves form a double line down the 'street'; decorative tassels fringe the edges. The *Haus Tambaran* (ceremonial 'spirit house' for men) had an ornately painted and decorated front wall

into fantastic designs that provided an expression of spirit content.

Masks, usually representing mythical or recently deceased ancestors, were important ceremonial objects, displayed on every ritual occasion. Throughout the Sepik they were bought and traded along with their special songs and dances. Some masks would act as guardians on the gables and doorways of the *haus tambarans;* some could be owned by family lines or significant individuals; others were secret, to be seen only by initiated men. Miniature masks were amulets, worn in the hair, on armbands, or attached to clothing. In the Maprik region, north of the Sepik River, yam masks of woven rattan were traditionally placed on the best tubers at the yam cult festival (a harvest festival to ensure the fertility of the crop) or worn by dancers.

Intricately carved wooden suspension hooks were commonly hung from the rafters of all men's and women's houses. Netted bags and baskets containing food, clothing and valuables were hung from the hooks, keeping the contents safe from rats and mice. The decorations, featuring small male or female figures and bird, animal and reptile motifs, were imbued with spiritual values for protective purposes.

Drums commonly used in dancing were formed in an hourglass shape with a snakeskin drumming surface; they could stand upright on their painted and decorated base, or be carried in the dance by their intricately carved handles. The slit-gong drum was used for sending messages, gathering people for a meeting, or delivering ancestral warnings to the uninitiated. Another kind of drum was placed beside the river, hidden in the swamp, and used to placate water spirits. The sacred flutes of the Sepik district were ornately carved and decorated objects, sometimes used in sacred ceremonies, played in pairs to impersonate spirit voices; sometimes in public ceremonies, representing bird and animal sounds; and in some areas, not played but kept—wrapped and hidden—as highly valued dowry objects. Sepik artwork is used in the architectural style and decoration of the PARLIAMENT HOUSE OF PAPUA NEW GUINEA.—KRF

Further reading

Newton, D, 1971. *Crocodile and Cassowary: religious art of the Upper Sepik River, New Guinea*, Museum of Primitive Art.

Mead, S M (ed.), 1979. *Exploring the Visual Art of Oceania*, University Press of Hawai'i.

Traditional Malanggan art

In northern New Ireland, *malanggan* is the name for the memorial ceremonial (and particularly its elaborately carved and painted wooden sculptures) that was commonly used in funeral rituals. A funeral traditionally activated a set of reciprocal obligations among the kinsmen of the dead person, and over the ensuing months the various stages of the *malanggan* ceremonial were enacted. Burials took place in the hamlet cemetery, an area of sacred ground enclosed by a low stone wall made of coral or limestone. In the adjacent yard outside the men's house—an area also enclosed by walls—the *malanggan* would be made. The *malanggan* images, carved by designated elders, were constructed in named stages, each marked by feasting, and the conclusion of the proc-

Malanggan *La Sisi* canoe, New Ireland, Papua New Guinea, photographed by Neil McLeod

ess was marked by the full display of all the completed figures to participants and visitors.—KRF

Further reading

Lewis, P, 1979. 'Art in Changing New Ireland', in S M Mead (ed.), *Exploring the Visual Art of Oceania*, University of Hawai'i Press.

Traditional island architecture

In Micronesia, traditional buildings in Yap and Palau were generally larger and more complex in architectural form than in the eastern Caroline Islands. In Yap, dwelling houses ranged from small huts to the large buildings belonging to influential men. These were oblong, generally built on stone platforms about 1 m high, and supported by poles or pillars of the breadfruit tree (*calophyllum*). Beams and crossbeams were held in place by coconut-fibre ropes. The steep roofs, thatched with nipa palm (*nipa fruticans*) or pandanus leaf, had overhanging eaves. Houses usually had windows. The outer walls were made from bamboo screens, and the stone platform extended out at the front and back. Interior bamboo screens served as partitions providing separate 'rooms', and the kitchen was a separate building.

In Palau, a stone platform about 30 cm high was built as a small family shrine in front of each house. Some houses had a number of entrances built along the longer wall, allowing more light to enter. In Truk, houses were more simply constructed rectangles with four corner poles—usually the trunks of breadfruit trees—sunk into the ground. The roof was thatched with leaves of the ivory-nut tree (*coelococcus carolinensis*), with short overhanging eaves. The walls were covered with the same leaves and there was only one room. The floor was covered with pandanus leaves. Truk villages had a communal kitchen-shed used for preparation of feasts, and a canoe-shed—a large building with a high roof—which served as a meeting place, a young men's house, and a shelter for the large canoes owned by the village or the chiefs.

Each Yap village had one or two clubhouses built in similar fashion to the stone-platform houses but much larger (10–12 m across), and usually located near the shore. The pillars were up to 7 m in height, and the gables were carved and painted. Clubhouses were communal property, used mainly by single men. The stone platform around the clubhouse served as a meeting place and a dance floor.

In Palau, the community houses or *bai* were used for ceremonies such as feasts and dancing, as well as providing lodging for visitors, a centre for men's social activities, and a council meeting-house for chiefs. Women were not usually permitted to enter them. Made entirely without nails, screws or lashings, the building was a complex construction of interlocking pieces on a heavy squared timber framework, and relied on the supervision of a master builder. The decorated clubhouses (*tetib el bai*) had pillars, beams and wooden gables all elaborately carved and coloured in ornamental patterns as well as incorporating impressions of mythological and historical events. One of the last remaining traditional *bai* in Koror is now part of the Palau Museum. There were also canoe-houses in both Yap and Palau but they were used only as boat-sheds.

Traditional Palauan decorated clubhouse (*bai*) preserved at the Palau Museum

In Polynesia, housing styles varied from group to group, but were typically constructed with posts, rafters and a ridgepole, set up in a rectangular plan. Stone bases were used in warmer climates, with closed low houses more commonly found in subtropical islands. Houses normally indicated the status of the owner by their size, height and decoration. In Tonga up until the late 1700s, most islanders lived in dispersed settlements, spread across the countryside, close to their cultivations. The only villages were settlements clustered around the great chiefs, like those of Mu'a and Kolovai, and a new one at NUKU'ALOFA. The increased insecurity during the civil wars drew people together to construct forts (*kolotau*) which they lived inside or close to. The insecurity continued so long that the habit of living together in villages became established. Most of today's villages therefore were properly established between 1800 and 1820. Any tendency to disperse in the 1830s and later was countered by the desire to live closer to their churches and schools.

Throughout Polynesia, houses were planned and situated according to their function, with a typical village containing several dwellings, cook houses,

Ni-Vanuatu children on Tanna, against a woven wall

and often a separate guest or meeting house. In Samoa the traditional dwelling house (*fale*) is a round building with a beehive-shaped roof supported by posts around the perimeter. A high-ranking chief would have a more intricate design, often with a sloping or terraced stone platform base.

In Papua New Guinea, village houses in coastal and lowland areas are often built above the ground. The floor—made of split palm wood or pandanus—is built first, and supported on piles (1–6 m high) with a central support post to hold the ridgepole and corner posts to support the walls. Some houses are open-sided, but where closed-in walls are added, they are made from sago or nipa palm leaves, pandanus leaves, bark, or wooden planks. In larger buildings, tie-beams are added, and rafters attached to intermediate wall posts. Where bamboo is available, it is used for intermediate wall posts and beams. House roofing is often sheets of atap (dried palm

Canoe-house at Fefan, Truk, photographed by Matsumura, c1915

leaves) stitched to bamboo laths. In the Highlands regions, houses are smaller and often circular. In some areas the roof is hipped to provide extra space for sleeping quarters. The walls are built first, by driving a double line of sharpened planks into the ground and completing the outer wall layer with wooden planks. The inner walls are sometimes lined with bark, grasses and plant material for warmth and the roof is usually thatched with bundles of kunai grass.

Apart from these considerable variations in family housing, there are also a number of distinctive architectural styles to be seen in men's clubhouses and community long houses (found in many areas); the highly decorated *haus tambaran* in the SEPIK RIVER region; and the yam storehouses found among societies like the Trobriand Islands which have traditional yam exchanges.

In Kiribati, traditional architecture is dominated by two building types, the tall meeting house with its huge thatched roof (*maneaba*), which was important for religious activity, and the dwelling houses (*bata*) which surround it in each village. Each residential community occupied seemingly random positions along the islets, reflecting the lack of stratification in traditional society.—KRF

Further reading

Barrow, T, 1972. *Art and Life in Polynesia*, AH & AW Reed.

Ferdon, E N, 1987. *Early Tonga 1616–1810*, University of Arizona Press.

Gilson, R P, 1970. *Samoa 1830–1900*, Oxford University Press.

Hockings, J, 1989. *Traditional Architecture in the Gilbert Islands*, University of Queensland Press.

Matsumura, A, 1918. 'Contributions to the ethnography of Micronesia', *Journal of the College of Science*, XL.

Robinson, D, 1983. 'The decorative motifs of Palauan club-houses', in S M Mead and B Kernot (eds), *Art and Artists of Oceania*, Dunmore Press.

■ ***Parliament House of Papua New Guinea*** The building of the Parliament House of Papua New Guinea at Waigani was completed in February 1984 and opened by HRH the Prince of Wales on 7 August. Combining traditional and modern design elements, its main feature is a tall facade in the *haus tambaran* style of SEPIK ART. The main building behind this facade houses the 24 m high Grand Hall, the debating chamber, and the prime minister's office suite. To one side there is a low circular building in Eastern Highlands style, with conference rooms and sports and leisure facilities for members of parliament. The design is the work of Cecil Hogan, an Australian who was principal architect for the Department of Works and Supply in the 1970s. Construction by the Fletcher company began in July 1980, with the total cost including furnishings about 27 million kina. The tile mural on the main facade displays the work of some of Papua New Guinea's best known modern artists: Akis, Jakupa, Kauage Mathias, John Man and Cecil King Wungi. Sepik and Trobriand designs feature in the speaker's chair of the debating chamber, while the ceiling uses a fabric imitating the bark paintings of spirit figures found in the court house at Ambunti.—KRF

Sepik traditional design is featured on the front of the House of Assembly, Papua New Guinea

■ ***The Center for Hawaiian Studies*** The Center for Hawaiian Studies is located just a 10-minute walk away from the middle of the Mānoa Campus of the University of Hawai'i. Designed by Kauahikaua & Chun Architects, the Center is a public academic structure that draws on pre 1778 Native Hawaiian architecture to create a unique building in Hawai'i's architectural landscape. Opened in January 1997, the Center houses the Hawaiian Studies department and functions as a locus for the Native Hawaiian community.

The Center lies between Dole Street and Mānoa stream on 2.2 acres. The architects incorporated a pre-existing taro *lo'i* (garden) into the building. A working garden, the *lo'i* accentuates the Center's connection to the *'āina* (land) and Native Hawaiian traditions. From a distance the Center appears to be a collection of tall copper-green roofs behind a wall of brown lava fieldstone. Visually the Center invokes a pre-1778 Native Hawaiian village of grass houses and sites such as *Pu'uhonua o Hōnaunau* (Place of Refuge) on the Big Island. The two-storey structure comprises a series of five connected components (student services, classrooms, resources centre, faculty offices, auditorium) linked by a *lanai* (a covered porch characteristic of 19th–20th century Hawaiian architecture). A hipped roof rises from each component. An oval hole and a series of staircases connect the Center's two levels. A skylight, the oval is referred to as the building's *piko*, 'the umbilical cord, the belly button, a connection...to space and sky'. Alternatively, the *piko*'s shape involves the Center's Hawaiian name, *Kamakakūokalani* (an 'eye perched in heaven' or 'warlike eyes of heaven'). The faculty has also dedicated the Center's rooms to male and female *akua* (deity). These dedications invest the Center with Native Hawaiian cosmology. Similarly symbolic, a burial vault containing the remains of 18 pre-1778 Native Hawaiians is set in the grass court of the Center's second level. The architects argue that the burials give the Center 'an ancestral foundation', rooting the building into the islands' long-term indigenous history. As one architect remarked on the burials, 'This was a way in which we could actually bring culture and make it a part of the physical environment. In Hawaiian culture there is nothing more sacred than the remains of your elders.'

The architects' calculated use of local material (lava fieldstone, *koa* hardwood) throughout the building furthers the Center's Native Hawaiian associations. Along with the use of Native Hawaiian architectural forms (rounded single pitched roofs, large stone wall), these materials identify the building as ethnically Native Hawaiian. The Center's almost-exclusive use of Native Hawaiian and Polynesian vegetation in the building's landscaping furthers this connection. In an environment where Hawai'i's indigenous plants have been severely depleted by introduced species, the Center's landscape adds another qualitative layer. The various practices carried out at the Center (the teaching of Hawaiian, HULA, and Hawaiian culture history, as well as political activism) also contribute to the site's symbolism as a space for the regeneration of Native Hawaiian culture in urban Hawai'i.

Center for Hawaiian Studies, 1997. Counter-clockwise from the taro *lo'i* (garden on left) is the auditorium (large hipped roof), faculty offices, the resource center (hipped roof), classrooms (indicated by two hipped roofs) and student services

The interweaving of these culturally-specific elements with other materials (concrete, glass, copper), and the building's design (which relies on a Euro-American university plan), enables the Center to transcend cultural boundaries and locate Native Hawaiians in contemporary Hawai'i. The Center relocates Native Hawaiian culture into Hawai'i's urban built environment, and challenges stereotypes that portray Native Hawaiians negatively. As expressed in the Center's design report, the building's architectural fusion demonstrates that 'traditional Hawaiian ideas have validity in the modern world'. The Center emerges as an indigenous counter to what one Native Hawaiian activist, Lydia K Aholo, decried as the 'concrete monsters' that 'ravage' the land. The Center as argued by one architect is 'the first real rendering of a building that represents Hawaiian cultural heritage'. Through its architecture, the Center combines elements of Native Hawaiian's cultural past to confront political inequalities of the present, thus helping to create a possible sovereign future for Native Hawaiians.—JAB

Further reading

Bell, J A, 1998. Negotiating space and place: an ethnography of the cultural politics of architecture in Honolulu, Hawai'i, M Phil thesis, University of Oxford, (unpublished). (Copies may be found in the Balfour Library, Oxford University; Bishop Museum, Honolulu; Hawaiian Mission Children's Society Library, Honolulu; Hamilton Library, University of Hawai'i, Mānoa Campus, Honolulu.)

Trask, H-K, 1987. 'Hawai'i: colonization and de-colonization', in A Hooper et al. (eds), *Class and Culture in the South Pacific*, Centre for Pacific Studies, University of Auckland.

eight

island profiles

Contributors

Article contributors

AAH	Antony A Hooper
AH	Alan Howard
BVL	Brij V Lal
DAB	Dirk Anthony Ballendorf
FA	Frédéric Angleviel
GMcC	Grant McCall
HRL	Helen Reeves Lawrence
JR	Jan Rensel
KEJ	Kerry James
KRF	Kate Fortune
KRH	Kerry Howe
MQ	Max Quanchi
MWW	Marion W Ward
RCK	Robert C Kiste
RJM	Ron May
RL2	Robert Langdon
SM	Steve Mullins
TCP	Thomas C Panholzer

Photo contributors

Alexander Turnbull Library (National Library of New Zealand, Wellington): Tattersall Collection: 607

Baumgart, Ian (Wellington): 575

Cunningham, Lawrence J (University of Guam, Mangilao): 577

Fortune, Kate (Wellington): 579, 595

Hendrie, Peter (Pacific Journeys, Melbourne): 557 (detail), 622

Luxton, David M (Tauranga, New Zealand): 585

Ministry of Foreign Affairs and Trade (Wellington, New Zealand): 619

PHOTOSOURCE NZ Ltd (Wellington): photograph by Fritz Prenzel: 560

VexVentures (Melbourne), flags courtesy Ralph G C Bartlett: 570–571

Maps

ANU Cartography: 559, 561, 563, 565, 567, 573, 576, 578, 582, 587, 589, 591, 593, 594, 597, 599, 601, 602, 606, 609, 611, 614, 621, 623

AMERICAN SAMOA

Constitutional status: Unincorporated territory of the United States.
Head of State: US President.
Head of Government: Governor Tauese P Sunia (1998).
Main towns: PAGO PAGO (capital, on Tutuila; population 8000).
Land area: 199 sq km (five islands): Tutuila (145 sq km), Ta'u, Ofu, Olosega, Aunu'u; and two atolls: Swains and Rose.
Sea area (EEZ): 390 000 sq km.
Population: 63 330 (1999 SPC estimate); many more Samoans live in west-coast USA and Hawai'i than in Samoa (PACIFIC ISLANDERS IN USA).
Languages: Samoan (Polynesian language closely related to Hawaiian); English.
Adult literacy: 97 per cent (1995).
Currency: US dollar.
Time: -1100 hours UTC.
National day: 17 April.
GNP per capita: US$4280 (1994).
Principal export earnings: Tourism; fishing.
Political system: American Samoa is administered by the US Department of the Interior and is represented by a non-voting delegate to the US House of Representatives—Faleomavaega Eni Hunkin in 1998. Local executive power rests with an elected governor—Hon Tauese P Sunia, with Togiola T Tulafono as lieutenant-governor in 1998. The legislature (*Fono*) has an upper senate with 18 senators elected according to Samoan custom from local chiefs or *matai* (family heads). President of the Senate was Hon Lutu Fuimaono in 1998. In the lower house of representatives, there are 20 representatives chosen by popular vote, plus one non-voting member (who represents Swains Island). Main parties: none officially, but the major factions are closely identified with the US Democratic and Republican parties.
Physical environment: Located in the central South Pacific (at latitude 14° south and longitude 168–171° west), American Samoa lies to the east of Cook Islands, and north of Niue. It has one large island, Tutuila, which occupies three-quarters of its total land area. Tutuila has been formed around five volcanic cones, now strongly eroded, and its central harbour (Pago Pago) is a collapsed caldera. The highest peak is Mt Matafao (702 m). The remaining four smaller islands also have visible volcanic features, and there are five additional islets including Swains, 350 km to the north, and Rose Island, 400 km to the east, both coral atolls, the latter comprising two uninhabited islets or *motu*. The larger islands have densely tree-covered interiors, while their coastal fringes and the atolls have coconut palms, pandanus and low scrub. Subsistence crops include bananas, taro, breadfruit, sugarcane, pineapple and kava. Livestock is grazed and there is plentiful fishing—fish processing being a major export. The climate is hot and humid, with southeast trade winds between April and November. Annual rainfall: 5000 mm, mostly occurring between November and March.

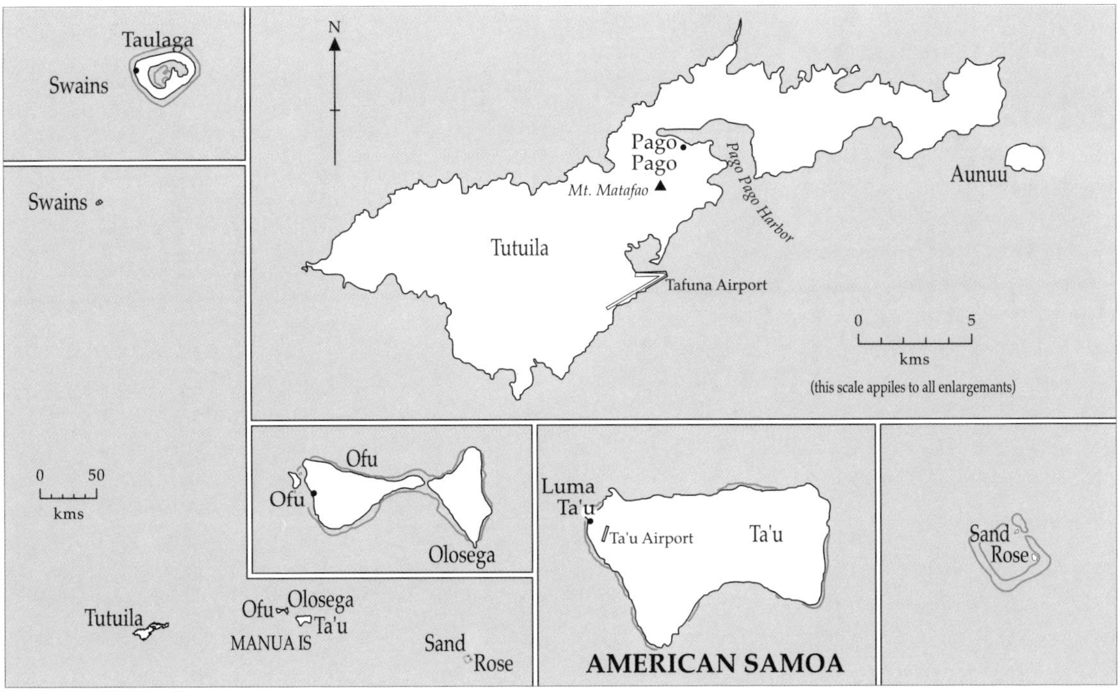

History: Archaeology has established that people were living on Tutuila almost 3000 years ago (FOOTSTEPS FROM ASIA). The Manu'a group was a probable source of stone for adze-making, and evidence of inland settlement has been found throughout the Samoan islands. West Polynesians had well-developed navigational skills and seafaring expertise, noted and admired by early European explorers from the 17th century onwards. The Manu'a islands had been first recorded by the Dutch navigator Jacob Roggeveen in June 1722, and the BOUGAINVILLE expedition of 1768 explored further and named the two groups the Navigator Islands. Aware of this earlier French exploration, Louis de FREYCINET arrived at the islands in October 1819 and named Rose Island after his wife, a name which has remained, obliterating Roggeveen's attempt to name the isolated atoll Vuyle (Bird) Island. La PÉROUSE was the next visitor, but when a dozen members of a shore party from his ships were attacked and killed on Tutuila in 1787, it was widely noted as a warning. In the early 1800s, as BEACHCOMBERS, missionaries and whalers began to arrive in increasing numbers, neighbouring Apia developed as a more popular trading port than Pago Pago.

By the 1860s Christian and trading interests were bringing Britain, the United States and Germany into administrative conflict in Western Samoa, and their rivalry was caught up in the Samoan dispute between two competing overlords. In 1872 the high chief of Tutuila offered the Americans exclusive rights to Pago Pago's land-locked harbour in return for US protection, but the offer was rejected in favour of efforts to support a formal peace settlement, achieved in April 1873. Factional fighting resumed in 1876, and a further appeal was made to the United States, which then agreed to accept the offer of a naval base. However, in 1879 Samoa offered naval stations to both Germany and Britain, and an escalating series of offensive manoeuvres and incidents over the next two decades, supported by the warships of the three nations, was finally only resolved by partition of the Samoan islands in 1889, and the introduction of colonial rule. In 1899 a commission of the three powers declared Tutuila American, its harbour at Pago Pago recognized as a valued naval base. The US Department of the Navy took up jurisdiction, and began negotiating deeds of cession with Samoans. After the Tutuila chiefs signed in 1900, the US flag was formally raised on 17 April. Manuan chiefs followed suit in 1904.

From 1905, US commanders at Tutuila Naval Station were appointed as governors of the territory, which was given the name American Samoa in 1911.

Coastal road, Alao, American Samoa

The US government formally accepted the deeds of cession in 1929, but the territory remained under naval administration until 1951. From 1 July 1951, it transferred to the jurisdiction of the US Department of the Interior, with Phelps Phelps as its first civilian governor. In 1956 Peter COLEMAN was appointed the first Samoan-born governor, and during his term of office, a constitution, containing a bill of rights and providing protection for Samoans against alienation of their lands and loss of their language and culture, was approved in 1960, and an American Samoan flag was adopted.

The pace of development was greatly accelerated during the 1960s, during Governor H Rex Lee's first term of office. The US Congress was persuaded to inject massive special funding into roads, housing, sewerage, harbour facilities, schools and hospitals, hotels, the airport, fish canneries and even educational television. Although these initiatives successfully launched tourism as a major source of revenue, the ongoing problems and costs of maintaining the new infrastructure increasingly overwhelmed the territory's resources, while US funding diminished. By the mid 1970s, the United States was eager to see Samoans accept greater autonomy, but three referenda failed to achieve this. Finally at the fourth opportunity, American Samoa voted to elect their own governors, and Peter Coleman was subsequently returned to office on 3 January 1978, this time as the country's elected head of state. He remained governor until January 1985, when A P Lutali was elected, and then served a further term from 1989 to 1993.—KRF

Further reading

Gray, J A C, 1960. *Amerika Samoa: a history of American Samoa and its US Naval Administration*, US Naval Institute.

CHATHAM ISLANDS

Constitutional status: Part of New Zealand.

Administrative centre: Waitangi (on Chatham).

Land area: 963 sq km.

Sea area: Part of New Zealand's EEZ.

Population: 760 (1995 est).

Time: +1245 hours UTC.

Political system: Chatham Islands is part of New Zealand's South Island for electoral and census administration. There is a separate Chatham Islands Territorial Council (one of 74 territorial authorities in New Zealand) with nine elected members, including a mayor, who serve a three-year term.

Physical environment: Chatham Islands (latitude 44° south and longitude 176° west) are 850 km east of Christchurch, New Zealand. There are three main islands: Chatham or Rekohu (899 sq km), Pitt (61.5 sq km) and South-East (2.4 sq km), with a number of smaller islets and rocks. Consisting of low-lying schist in the north and limestone in the centre, Chatham Island has a number of shallow lagoons occupying one-quarter of its area, the largest of them being Te Whanga. The southern plateau is formed of basalt tuffs and lava. Pitt Island is largely basalt and sandstone. The island's original forest has been replaced by fern, heath and swamp vegetation, with pasture land and some karaka and nikau palms. The coastal seas are rich in fish and crayfish (rock lobster), and there is a sizable SEA LION colony. The climate is humid and cold temperate; low cloud is common and strong southwesterly winds prevail. Annual rainfall: 900 mm; about 750 mm at Waitangi and more than 1200 mm in the higher areas of the southwest.

History: The first inhabitants of the Chathams were Polynesians: settlers from the eastern Pacific about 1000 years ago, followed by a migration of Maori from New Zealand who arrived about 800 years ago. Known as Moriori, they named the main island Rekohu, referring to the persistent mists, and lived in isolation, probably restricted in canoe-building by the shortage of trees on the islands. A peaceful people, they settled disputes with a form of ritualized warfare only, ending a battle as soon as blood was shed. They were first visited by Europeans in 1791 when Lieutenant William Broughton arrived—and named the islands after his ship, HMS *Chatham*—while on his way to Tahiti. Sporadic visits by sealers and whalers occurred after this, affecting the islanders' food supplies and introducing disease. The population is estimated to have fallen from 2000 to below 1700 by 1835.

The islanders were then overwhelmed by an invasion carried out in November 1835 by 900 members of the Ngati Mutunga and Ngati Tama people of central New Zealand, responsible for many deaths. By 1861, only 100 Moriori remained, and a ruling of the Native Land Court in 1870 allocated them only 3 per cent of the land, with 97 per cent granted to Ngati Mutunga as 'claim by conquest'. In 1910, Rangitapu Horomona Rehe had inherited almost all the shares in the largest 810-hectare Moriori reserve, and after his death, his son Tame ('Tommy Solomon') was believed to be the sole surviving full-blooded Moriori. He died in 1933, but his five children, and others of mixed Maori and European descent, have contributed to today's island residents. There are now around 2000 people on the Chathams and in New Zealand who can trace their descent from Moriori. A collection of Moriori genealogies, chants and traditions was located in 1991.

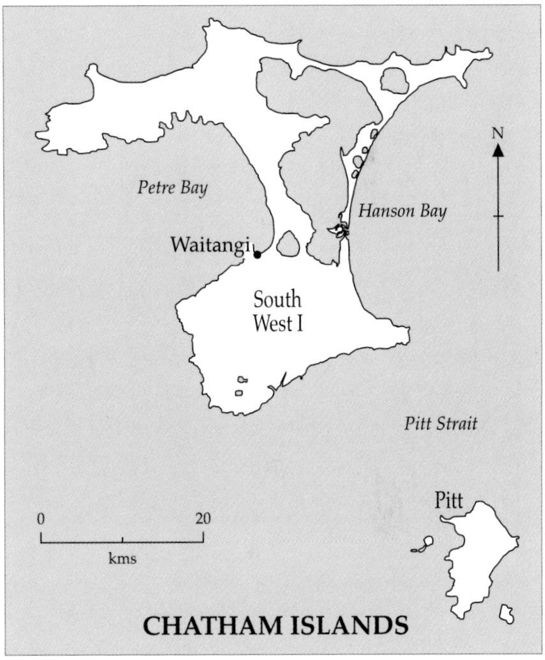

The settlement and port of Waitangi is at the southern end of Petre Bay, on the western side of Chatham. Sheep-farming and fishing, including crayfishing, are the island's main economic activities.—KRF

Further reading

King, M, 1989. *Moriori: a people rediscovered*, Viking.

'Moriori and Rekohu', *New Zealand Official Yearbook*, 1997, GP Publications.

COOK ISLANDS

Constitutional status: Self-governing in free association with New Zealand.

Head of State: Queen Elizabeth II, represented by Governor General Apenera Short.

Head of Government: Prime Minister Dr Joe Williams (July 1999).

Main town: AVARUA (capital; on Rarotonga).

Land area: 238 sq km (15 islands): Rarotonga (65 sq km), Mangaia (51 sq km), Aitutaki, Atiu, Manihiki, Manu'ae, Mauke, Mitiaro, Nassau, Palmerston, Penrhyn, Pukapuka, Rakahanga, Suwarrow, Takutea.

Sea area (EEZ): 1 830 000 sq km.

Population: 16 770 (1999 SPC estimate).

Official languages: Cook Islands Maori, English.

Adult literacy: 99 per cent (1994).

Currency: NZ dollar.

Time: -1030 hours UTC.

National day: 4 August.

GDP per capita: A$3600 (1995).

Principal export earnings: Tourism; offshore banking; black pearls; paw paw.

Political system: The Cook Islands has a 24-member parliament (one member representing Cook Islanders abroad) elected for a five-year term by universal adult suffrage, an elected prime minister and a cabinet of ministers. The upper legislative house of 21 hereditary chiefs, the House of ARIKI, has advisory functions only. Local affairs are handled by island councils and village committees in the outer islands. Many more Cook Islanders (c37 000) live in New Zealand than inhabit the islands themselves.

Political parties: Main parties include the Cook Islands Party (ruling party since 1989 elections) and Democratic Party (opposition). Each party is split into several factions.

Physical environment: Cook Islands, in the central southern Pacific (between latitude 8–23° south and longitude 156–167° west), form two distinct geographic groups. In the north, there are six coral atolls, all but Nassau having clusters of *motu* around a central lagoon. In the southern group, the islands are mostly of volcanic origin, usually with distinct central cores. Most have an elevated coral reef platform adjacent to the coast as well as recent coral reefs. Rarotonga has several sharp peaks, rising to a height of 650 m above sea level. Aitutaki has a volcanic island as well as fringing and barrier reefs which have developed into an atoll in the south. Manu'ae and Takutea are coral atolls. Natural vegetation on the nine atolls is sparse, comprising mainly coconuts and pandanus, and several coconut plantations have been established. The other islands, and especially Rarotonga, have abundant growth of coconut, breadfruit, taro and citrus fruit. Subsistence and cash crops include coconuts, bananas, citrus fruit, pineapples, taro, tapioca and kumara. The climate is warm and humid, varying from north to south and by seasons. The prevailing trade winds are from the east (in the north) and from east-southeast in the southern group. The hurricane season falls between November and March, when humidity is high, but the southern group is relatively cool during the rest of the year. Annual rainfall: 2000 mm.

History: The inhabitants are Polynesian, whose settlement dates back 2000 years. They are closely related to New Zealand Maori, and oral history indicates that Rarotonga was a departure point for early Maori immigration. In the most northwesterly island of the northern group, Pukapuka, the people are west Polynesians, closely related to Samoans and Tokelauans. Other islanders traditionally trace their descent from Tahiti and other parts of eastern Polynesia. Prior to European contact, there was considerable travel and trading between different islands: Rakahangans visited Manihiki to collect food; Aitutakians lived on Rarotonga and occupied Manu'ae (having ejected the Atiuans); and Mauke and Mitiaro suffered frequent raids from Atiu. Pukapuka was the first of all these islands to be visited by European navigators, with the arrival of the Spaniard Alvaro de Mendaña on 20 August 1595. A decade later, his compatriot Quirós made contact with the people of Rakahanga, but another 170 years passed before the next European ship—the *Dolphin*—entered these waters and confirmed the position of Pukapuka. Captain James COOK was the first European to begin charting the islands of the southern group. He reached Manu'ae on 23 September 1773, naming it Hervey's Island, in honour of one of the Lords of the Admiralty, and subsequently located Palmerston (in June 1774), and Mangaia, Atiu and Takutea in March 1777. Penrhyn was sighted and named by William Sever on 8 August 1788, when the *Lady Penrhyn* was on its way to China after delivering its load of convicts at Sydney. William Bligh called at Aitutaki in 1789, and almost certainly sighted Rarotonga also. A French ship, the *Adele*, located Nassau, and Russian expeditions reached Suwarrow (uninhabited in 1814) and Rakahanga in 1820.

A new phase in Cook Islands history began in July 1823, with the arrival of the Rev John WILLIAMS and the establishment of a mission (LONDON MISSIONARY SOCIETY) on Rarotonga. The impact of Christianity and the relative isolation of the islands helped to diminish the influence of BEACHCOMBERS, foreign traders and planters, and it was only in 1881 that the resident merchants achieved the establishment of a British consulate. At this time the southern group was known as the Hervey Islands and the islands of the northern group were named only individually. It would seem that one of the first appearances of the name Cook Islands was in Russian charts. Then official use of the name Cook Islands came with the establishment of a British protectorate in 1888; a period of British residency ensued, and then all 15 islands were annexed to New Zealand on 11 June 1901 under the name Cook Islands. Prior to 1915, when the *Cook Islands Act* was passed in the New Zealand Parliament, the Cook Islands were not one political entity but consisted of separate islands and atolls, each with its own culture, language (or dialect) and internal political structures. The nation of Cook Islands is thus a recent construct of colonialism that developed from the British protectorate established in the late 19th century.

The reins of administration were held by a resident commissioner (W E Gudgeon was the first in this position) and from 1915, the resident commissioner was responsible to the NZ Minister for the Cook Islands—later the Minister for Island Territories. In 1946 a legislative council was set up, repre-

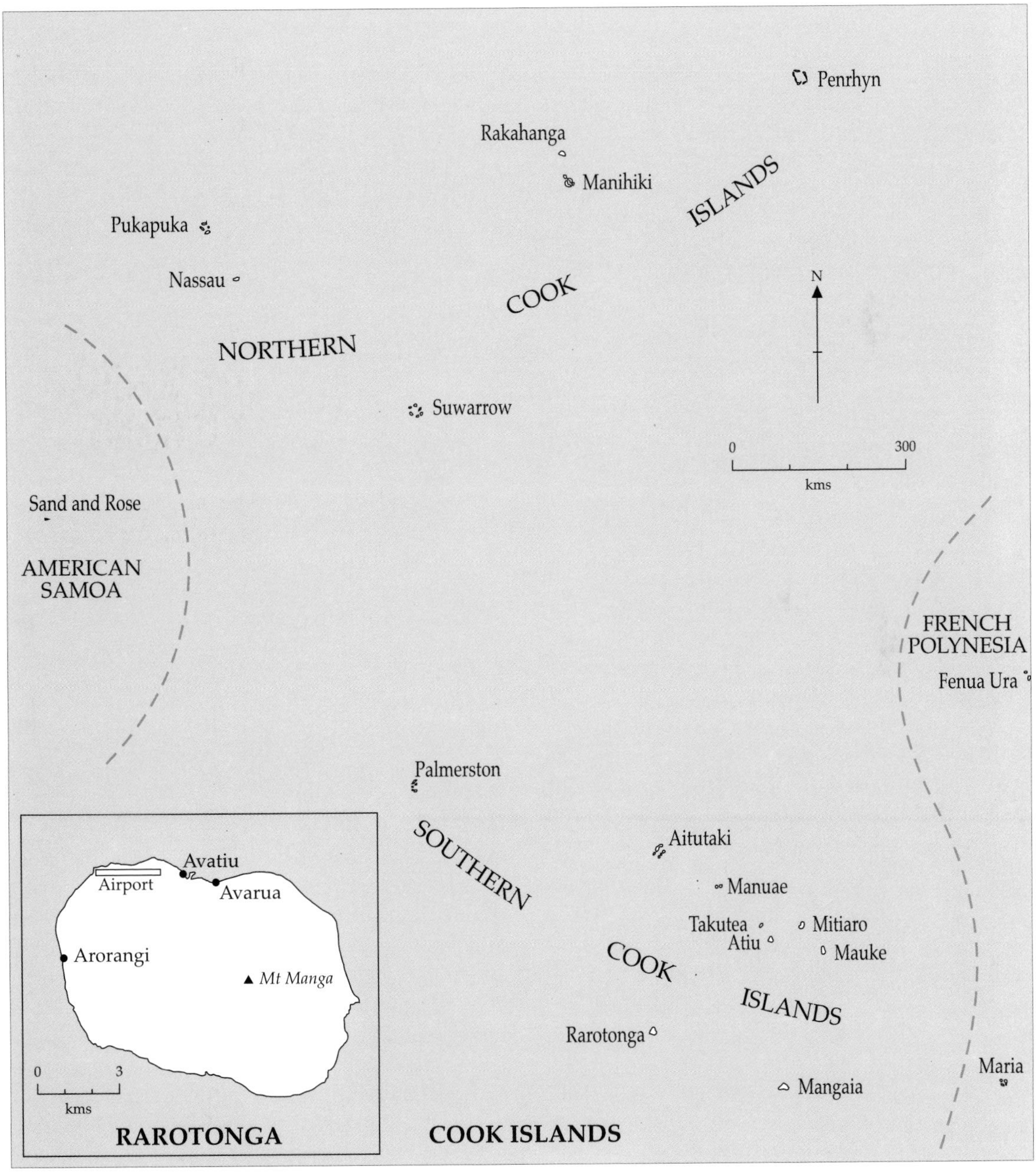

senting all the islands and government departments, and headed by the resident commissioner as president. This became a legislative assembly in 1957, with greater powers, and further supported after 1962 by an executive committee to provide policy advice and, in particular, to advise on government expenditure. In a series of preparations for self-government, the resident commissioner withdrew from the legislative assembly in 1964, and the executive committee, under a leader of government business, became a fully operating cabinet. A new constitution for the Cook Islands was passed in the NZ parliament in November 1964, and the first general election for the 22 members of the legislative assembly was held on 20 April 1965.

Constitutional amendments in 1965 provided for a House of ARIKI (*ariki* are paramount chiefs) as an advisory body; and in 1981, the assembly became 'parliament' and the premier became 'prime minister'. The term of parliament was extended from four to five years and the number of seats was increased to 24—to accommodate an additional representative for Mangaia, and to provide representation for non-resident Cook Islanders. A bill of rights was also established.

Albert HENRY, the country's first premier, led the Cook Islands Party to its fifth successive victory in March 1978, but the result was overturned by Chief Justice Gavin Donne four months later, on the grounds of electoral corruption. Dr Thomas DAVIS then took office, leading the Democratic Party, and eight members of the Cook Islands Party, including Sir Albert Henry, were charged with corruption. The March 1983 elections returned the Cook Islands Party to power with the cousin of the former leader, Geoffrey Henry, as prime minister, and also produced the first woman member of parliament, Fanaura Kingstone, who was appointed to cabinet as Minister of Internal Affairs. Once again the electoral result was overturned within months, this time with parliament being dissolved on constitutional grounds. Fresh elections in November brought Dr Davis back to power, this time in a coalition government, first with Geoffrey Henry as deputy prime minister, but a year later replaced with Dr Terepai Maote. Dr Davis (now Sir Thomas) survived the election in 1985 but lost the leadership to Dr Pupeke Robati in 1987. Sir Geoffrey Henry KBE remained prime minister for 10 years after the 1989 elections.

There are no major manufacturing industries. Tourism is the main source of foreign exchange, followed by pearl farming and offshore banking. Paw paw and taro are the main agricultural exports. Vegetables and fruit are also grown for the local market.—KRF & HRL

Further reading

Gilson, R, 1980. *The Cook Islands 1820–1950*, Victoria University Press.

Davis, T, et al., 1979. *Cook Islands Politics: the inside story*, R Crocombe (ed.), Pasifika Press.

FEDERATED STATES OF MICRONESIA

Constitutional status: Self-governing in free association with United States.

Head of State: US President.

Head of Government: President Leo Falcam (1999).

Main towns: Palikir (administrative capital; on Pohnpei); Colonia (Yap); Weno (Chuuk); KOLONIA (Pohnpei); Kosrae.

Land area: 701 sq km (600+ islands and atolls): Pohnpei (345 sq km); Chuuk (129 sq km); Kosrae (109 sq km); Yap (121 sq km).

Sea area (EEZ): 2 978 000 sq km.

Population: 116 410 (1999 SPC estimate).

Official language: English; some Carolinian languages and dialect variations exist.

Adult literacy: 81 per cent (1994).

National day: 3 November.

Currency: US dollar.

Time: +2200 hours UTC.

GDP per capita: US$1474 (1994).

Principal export earnings: Copra; commercial fishing rights.

Political system: The Federated States of Micronesia (FSM) was formerly part of the US Trust Territory of the Pacific Islands. It has four constituent states: Kosrae, Pohnpei, Chuuk and Yap. The people of the FSM are further divided among a dozen language groups and several cultural traditions. Nation building is a challenge for the new country. Today, the FSM has authority over most of its affairs, but defence and other strategic prerogative remain with the United States. In exchange, the United States provides a financial subsidy upon which the FSM is dependent. The arrangement of free association is scheduled to be renegotiated in the year 2001.—RCK

Physical environment: The Federated States of Micronesia (extending from latitude 0–14° north, and from longitude 136–166° east) comprise more than 600 tiny islands and atolls extending across 2500 km of the west central Pacific. There are mountainous islands of volcanic origin, low coral atolls and isolated reefs. In the east, Kosrae is formed of two islands linked by a causeway, and its rugged, forest-clad interior rises to Mt Finkol (630 m). Pohnpei comprises the largest single island in the group, surrounded by a barrier reef and 25 smaller islands, and another 137 widely scattered coral atolls. The densely forested island interior rises to Mt Nahnalaud (772 m); there are several streams and waterfalls and considerable coastal mangrove swamp. Chuuk in the centre of the chain consists of seven major island groups, of which Chuuk itself is made up of 15 islands surrounded by a 225 km coral reef which forms a lagoon of about 2000 sq km. Coconut, breadfruit and pandanus grow on all islands. Yap, 1440 km to the west, consists of 15 coral islands and atoll groups, including the four large islands of Yap itself, separated by narrow channels and surrounded by coral reef. Yap has low hills, forested with coconut and areca palms, bamboos and crotons, and numerous sandy beaches. The tropical oceanic climate is warm and wet with little seasonal variation, apart from a brief dry season between January and March. The prevailing southwest wind brings frequent heavy rain, particularly in the east. The western islands fall within the cyclone belt. Annual rainfall: 2500 mm for most island groups; 4500 mm for Pohnpei.

History: The Federated States of Micronesia are part of the Caroline Islands group, consisting of the entire eastern chain of the Carolines and part of the western end. Linguistic evidence points to early migrations from the Philippines and Indonesia (SETTLEMENT OF THE NORTHERN PACIFIC), and archaeology provides clues to prehistory (see POHNPEIAN CHIEFDOMS and YAP 'TRADE EMPIRE'). Each of the four states has its own language, culture, traditions and history. The first visits by Spanish explorers in 1525 and 1564 (SPAIN AND PORTUGAL IN THE PACIFIC) were followed by SPANISH EXPANSION, 1675–1899.

It was only in the mid 1800s that WHALING ships and European traders arrived, bringing diseases which ravaged the population. European colonial rivalries became intense, until GERMAN COMMERCIAL INTERESTS led to the purchase of the islands from Spain. The Germans raised their flag on 12 October 1899. They built some streets and new buildings on Pohnpei, but not a town. They had come to Micronesia to raise revenue to feed the German Empire, an empire that was beginning to carve out parts of the world and establish a powerful navy. They called the area Die Kolonie, and established a lucrative COPRA trade, setting up administrative centres at Pohnpei, Yap, Saipan and Jaluit. At first the Germans used the carrot and stick method to encourage Pohnpeians to increase copra production for the betterment of the German Empire. But after the Sokehs rebellion (1910–11) on Pohnpei, the Germans threw away the carrot. The Pohnpeians' resentment had erupted after a series of disputes over wages and compulsory labour during a road-building project. At the rebellion's end—when 17 participants had been executed—the Germans took over all land in Die Kolonie for administrative use except for lots in Pohn Rakied, Ninseitamw and the Catholic and Protestant mission areas. Their rule was short, however, for world circumstances again dictated that another ruler would make a total transformation of the island way of life.

The Japanese, in a bloodless takeover, began their period on 7 October 1914, when war began and the Japanese navy took over the Carolines. Japanese colonial rule in Micronesia (established by League of

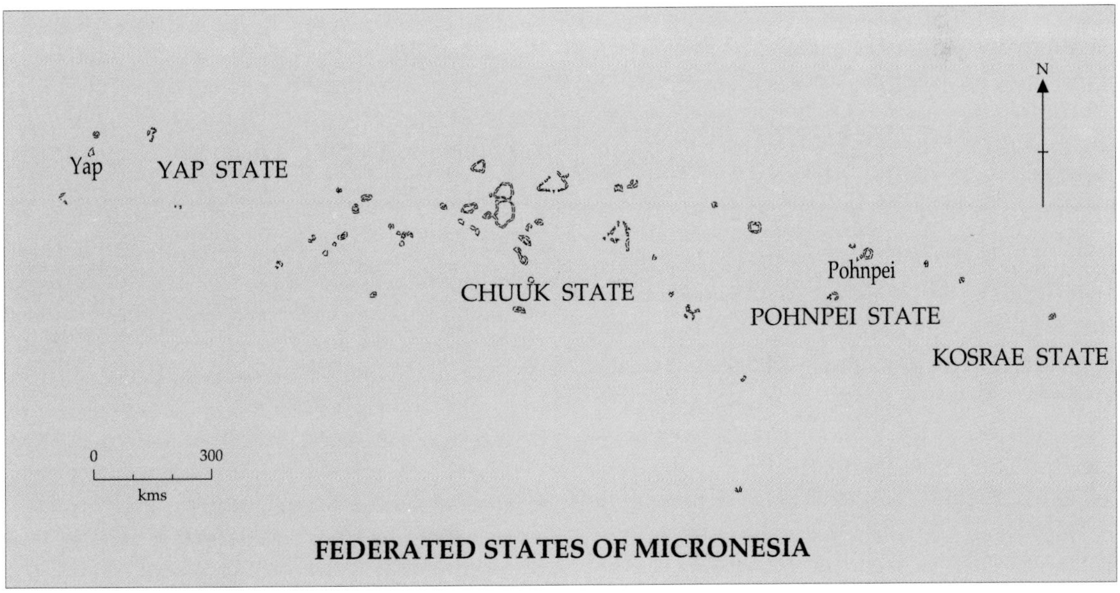

Nations Mandate on 20 December 1920) entailed extensive economic development, working from district offices at Yap, Chuuk and Pohnpei. Islanders were excluded for the most part from participation in local government, however, and the Japanese language was imposed (JAPANESE ACTIVITY IN MICRONESIA).

The Japanese began to develop Chuuk as a military base after 1935, and it played a key role in the subsequent Japanese war strategies in the South Pacific. (ISLANDER EXPERIENCES IN THE PACIFIC WAR.) By the end of the war, the economy of the Carolines, and much of their communications, had been destroyed. Micronesia became part of the US Trust Territory of the Pacific Islands (TTPI) administered first by the US Navy and later (from 1 July 1951) by the US Department of the Interior. The task of rebuilding began, and a commitment to promote the development of autonomy was made. Micronesians began to participate in their own government in 1965, when the Congress of Micronesia was set up with a house of representatives and a senate. A commission was established in 1967 to investigate options for self-government or independence, but initial attempts to reach agreement with the United States in 1969 failed to satisfy all members of the TTPI.

Negotiations continued through the 1970s and the FSM installed its first constitutional government on 10 May 1979, and reached an agreement with the United States on the compact in the following year. This draft compact was finally signed on 1 October 1982 and approved by plebiscite in 1983. In 1986 the Compact of Free Association was at last implemented, ending the status of Micronesians as citizens of the TTPI. Today the FSM has full control over its internal and external affairs. Leo Falcam, who represents Pohnpei, was elected by congress as the fifth president of the FSM, replacing Jacob Nena. Redley Killion (from Chuuk) was elected as vice-president.—KRF & TCP

FIJI ISLANDS

Constitutional status: Independent republic.

Head of State: President Ratu Sir Kamisese MARA.

Head of Government: Prime Minister Mahendra Chaudhry (May 1999).

Main centres: SUVA (capital, on Viti Levu; population 167 975 in 1996 census); Lautoka (Viti Levu; 28 728); Nadi (Viti Levu; 7709); Ba (Viti Levu; 6515); Nausori (Viti Levu; 5242); Labasa (Vanua Levu; 2179).

Land area: 18 272 sq km (about 332 islands; 110 inhabited); Viti Levu, Vanua Levu.

Sea area (EEZ): 1 290 000 sq km.

Population: 801 540 (1999 SPC estimate); Fijians 48.4 per cent, Indo-Fijians 46.4 per cent, others 5.2 per cent.

Official languages: Fijian, Hindi, English.

Adult literacy: 87 per cent (UNDP, 1994).

Currency: Fiji dollar.

Time: +1200 hours UTC.

National day: 10 October.

GDP per capita: A$2996 (1995).

Principal export earnings: Tourism; sugar and molasses; gold; fishing; lumber; garment manufacturing; ginger.

Political system: Until 1987, Fiji was an independent constitutional monarchy, recognizing the British sovereign as head of state. In the FIJI COUPS of 1987, Lieutenant-Colonel Sitiveni RABUKA overthrew the elected government, abrogated the 1970 Constitution and declared the country a republic on 7 October 1987.

On 25 July 1990, President Ratu Sir Penaia GANILAU promulgated a new constitution, creating a new bicameral legislature both racially weighted in favour of indigenous Fijians. The house of representatives had 37 Fijian members, 27 Indo-Fijian, one Rotuman and five from other communities. The senate had 24 Fijian, one Rotuman and nine members from other groups. Fijian senators are appointed by the Great Council of Chiefs which also appoints the president for a five-year term.

Rabuka was elected prime minister in May 1992 as head of a Soqosoqo ni Vakavulewa ni Taukei (SVT—Fiji Political Party) coalition. He retained the prime ministership in a snap election in February 1994, heading a coalition. In 1999 elections, Rabuka's party lost power to the People's Coalition, with Mahendra Chowdhery becoming prime minister.

Physical environment: The Fiji Islands (lying between latitude 12–22° south and longitude 177° west and 174° east, including ROTUMA) comprise more than 320 islands, islets and reefs. The two main islands, Viti Levu and Vanua Levu, and many of the others are of volcanic origin, ruggedly mountainous with limited areas of alluvial plain, and evidence of newer volcanoes, uplifted limestone and raised shorelines, and extensive coral reefs in shallow seas. Mineral deposits including gold, silver, copper, bauxite and manganese have been found (see MINING). Viti Levu has a few small hot springs and extensive river valleys, including the Sigatoka, Navua, Rewa and Ba. Nearly half of the land area (the wetter sides of the high islands) is covered with forest, with mangroves and coconut palms in coastal areas. The drier sides of the islands, where grasses and tall reeds (*gasau*) grow, are used for sugarcane cultivation. Farming includes dairying and beef cattle, and FORESTRY is becoming a significant industry. There are more than 100 species of birds, including several endemic ones. REPTILES include snakes and lizards. The generally tropical climate varies across the group, with the southeasterly trade winds prevailing between June and October. Annual rainfall: 1500–2000 mm on the leeward (northwest) coasts, ranging to 3000 mm on the windward coasts and up to 5000 mm in some inland areas.

History: The Fiji Islands were first settled about 3500 years ago, probably by people from Vanuatu and New Caledonia, which had been settled earlier by Austronesian speakers from the New Guinea region (FOOTSTEPS FROM ASIA). From Fiji, the seafaring migrants moved eastwards to Tonga and Samoa where they developed social and cultural patterns known today as Polynesian. But while the latter remained in relative isolation, Fiji continued to receive waves of migrants from western Melanesia, with the result that the physical characteristics and social organization of the indigenous Fijians exhibit Melanesian traits, particularly in the hinterlands of the two major islands, while the Polynesian traits are particularly pronounced in the eastern maritime provinces which maintained regular contact with their Polynesian neighbours.

The islands were first sighted by foreign explorers in 1643 when Dutch navigator Abel Janszoon Tasman investigated northeastern Fiji. Captain James COOK passed through the Southern Lau group in 1774. William BLIGH passed through the islands in 1789 and 1792. More intensive contacts with the outside world began early in the 19th century as BEACHCOMBERS, traders and speculators arrived, bringing with them exotic diseases, such as whooping cough, measles, influenza and dengue which took a heavy toll on the local population. Muskets, too, wreaked havoc, though perhaps not to the extent alleged in popular accounts. The trade in SANDALWOOD and BÊCHE-DE-MER introduced European tools and other goods as well as a cash economy and more intensive contact with the outside world. A new 'Lotu,' religion arrived in 1835 with the Wesleyan missionaries William Cargill and David Cross. The politics and processes of conversion had important implications for internal political struggle within Fijian society.

By the middle of the 19th century, Fiji was deeply mired in political convulsions spurred by the new forces of change. Internal struggle for political supremacy among rival kingdoms, headed by leaders such as Ma'afu and Seru CAKOBAU, was compounded by the demands made by fortune-seeking foreign nationals for stable government under European tutelage and access to land and other resources. Efforts by indigenous leaders to form Fiji-

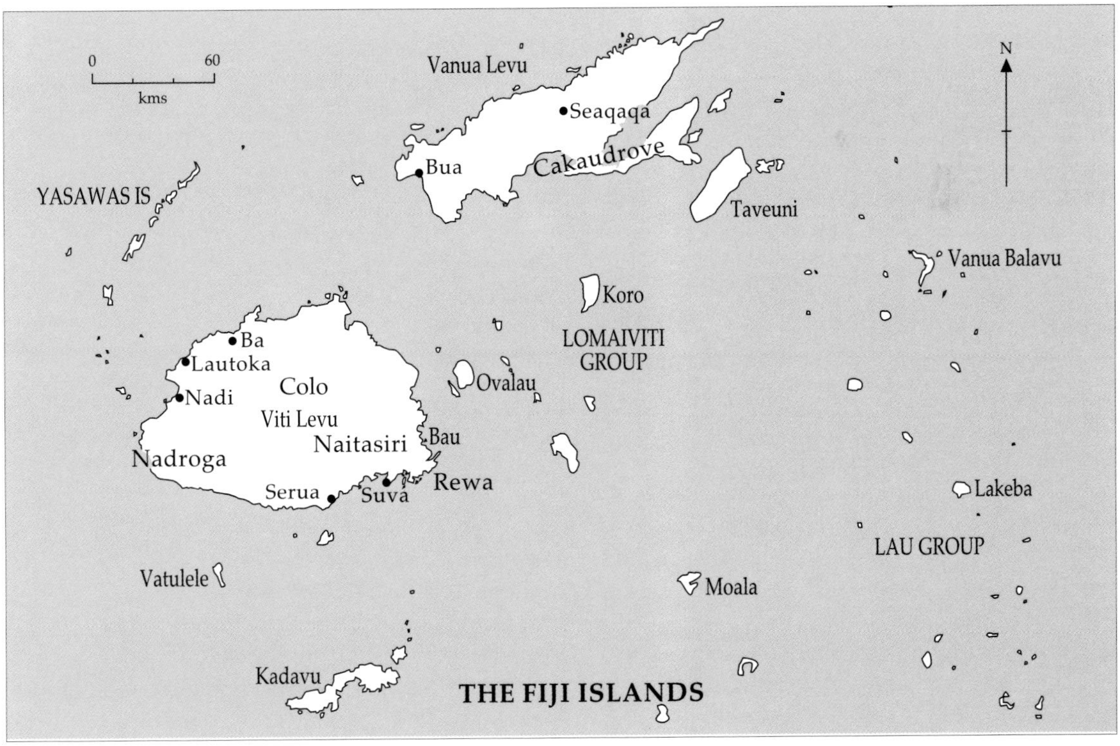

wide governments to deal with the new threats failed. Facing the prospect of continuing instability and insistent demands by outsiders, Cakobau and other leading chiefs of Fiji ceded Fiji to Great Britain on 10 October 1874 (DEED OF CESSION).

Sir Arthur GORDON was appointed the first substantive governor of the new colony. His policies and vision laid the foundations of modern Fiji. He forbade the sale of Fijian land and introduced an 'indirect system' of native administration that involved Fijians in the management of their own affairs. A chiefly council was revived to advise the government on Fijian matters. To promote economic development, he turned to the plantation system he had seen at first hand as governor of Trinidad and Mauritius. The Australian COLONIAL SUGAR REFINING COMPANY was invited to extend its operation to Fiji, which it did in 1882, remaining in the country until 1973. For cheap labour, he turned to India and to the system of indentured emigration. Begun in 1879, it brought over 60 000 Indians to the colony (GIRMITIYA). Most remained in Fiji.

In the 20th century, the three principal ethnic groups, Fijians, Indians and Europeans, remained largely separate and apart, encouraged by a colonial government intent on playing the role of an impartial mediator among them. The political system was racially based, with each ethnic group electing or nominating its own representatives in the legislative council. Demands for political change toward greater self-government were successfully resisted until the 1960s, when the winds of DECOLONIZATION reached the Pacific. A series of difficult, often contentious, constitutional negotiations in Fiji and in London paved the way for political reform, resulting in complete political independence on 10 October 1974.

Fiji's central location made it an important base for airlines, SHIPPING and telecommunications, and these advantages together with its cosmopolitan facilities attracted the headquarters of many regional and international bodies and the main campus of the regional university, the UNIVERSITY OF THE SOUTH PACIFIC. Post-colonial politics was organized essentially along racial lines, with the Fijian dominated political party, the Alliance, occupying the seat of government under the leadership of Ratu Sir Kamisese Mara. Nonetheless, social and economic changes, caused in part by external forces, including the policies of the World Bank, produced forces which challenged the race-based political order, leading to the formation of a labour party in 1985 which won the 1987 election in coalition with the Indian-based National Federation Party. On 14 May, that government was overthrown in a military coup led by Sitiveni Rabuka (FIJI COUPS). Following months of turmoil and delicate negotiations, Fiji was returned to civilian rule in December 1987. A new constitution, entrenching indigenous dominance in the political system, was decreed in 1990, which brought the chiefs-backed Fijian party to political power in 1992.

The constitution, contested by non-Fijians for its racially-discriminatory provisions, was reviewed by an independent commission in 1996 (CONSTITUTION REVIEW IN FIJI), which recommended a more open and democratic system encouraging the formation of multi-ethnic governments. A new constitution, based on the commission's recommendations, was promulgated a year later, providing for the recognition of special Fijian interests as well as a constitutionally-mandated multi-party cabinet. Within a decade, Fiji had travelled from a military coup to constitutional reconciliation, and rejoined the Commonwealth of Nations. By any measure, it was a remarkable journey.—BVL

Further reading

Lal, B V, 1992. *Broken Waves: a history of the Fiji Islands in the 20th century*, University of Hawai'i Press.

Scarr, D, 1984. *A Short History of Fiji*, Allen & Unwin.

ROTUMA

Constitutional status: Part of FIJI ISLANDS.

Population: 2500 (1998 estimate).

Physical environment: Rotuma is the northernmost island of the Fijian group, lying a little more than 500 km north of Viti Levu, on the western fringe of Polynesia. The island is of volcanic origin, comprising a land area of approximately 43 sq km, with the highest craters rising to heights of 260 m. Rotuma's geographical location (between latitude 12° south and longitude 177° east) places it very near the intersection of the conventional boundaries of Micronesia, Melanesia and Polynesia.

The vast majority of households in Rotuma maintain gardens that supply staples (taro, yams, tapioca, breadfruit and bananas). Pineapples, papaya, mangoes, watermelons and oranges are also grown in abundance to supplement the diet. While the island is exceptionally fertile, the eastern side is covered with stones and boulders, making it more difficult to work the soil. Rotation of crops is the common pattern; typically yams are planted the first season, followed by taro, then by tapioca and banana trees. Although only a few men engage in deep-sea fishing, the fringing reef surrounding the island is widely exploited for a variety of fish, octopus, crustaceans, and edible seaweed. Chicken, canned corned beef, and canned mackerel supplement the daily diet, while cattle, goats and pigs are consumed on special occasions such as weddings, funerals and welcoming ceremonies. Since the latter half of the 19th century Rotuma's main export product has been copra.

Language and population: Although Rotuma has been politically associated with FIJI ISLANDS since 1881, when the chiefs ceded the island to Great Britain, the Rotuman people are unique, forming a distinctive enclave within the Republic of Fiji. Linguistic evidence suggests that Rotuman belongs in a sub-grouping that includes Fijian and the Polynesian languages. Within this group Rotuman has a special relationship with the languages of western Fiji. The vocabulary shows a considerable degree of borrowing from Tongan and Samoan and traces of Indonesian.

The first census of Rotuma, taken in 1881, reported a population of 2452. Following a devastating measles epidemic in 1911, it declined below 2000, then gradually began to increase. As the total approached 3000, in the late 1930s, emigration to Fiji became an important means of alleviating population pressure. According to the 1936 Fiji census, 91.3 per cent of Rotumans were living on their home island. By 1956 the percentage had decreased to 67.7 per cent, and in 1986 it declined to 29.9 per cent. In recent years emigration has accelerated, not only to Fiji but to New Zealand, Australia and the United States. As a result, the population of the island has dropped to around 2500, representing less than 25 per cent of the total number of Rotumans.

History and politics: First recorded European contact was in 1791, by Captain Edwards in HMS *Pandora,* while searching for the mutineers of the BOUNTY. The first half of the 19th century was a time of increasing contact, as Rotuma became a favorite place for whalers to replenish their provisions. A substantial number of sailors jumped ship there, some marrying into the local population. Visiting vessels found Rotumans quite willing to sign on, and by the mid 19th century many Rotuman men had been abroad; some had visited centres of European civilization before returning home. In the 1860s English Wesleyan and French Roman Catholic missionaries established themselves on Rotuma, and the island was divided between them along geographical lines representing a prior factional division. Antagonisms between the two sides were exacerbated by religious rivalry, and in 1878 culminated in a war won by the numerically superior Wesleyans. The unrest that followed led the chiefs of Rotuma's seven districts to petition Queen Victoria for annexation, and in 1881 the island was officially ceded to Great Britain. Rotuma was governed as part of the Colony of Fiji until 1970, when Fiji gained independence. Since then it has been an integral part of the Fijian polity, the chiefs choosing to remain with Fiji following the FIJI COUPS of 1987.

A wharf was completed in the district of Oinafa in 1973 and an airstrip was opened in 1981, helping to alleviate Rotuma's isolation. However, shipping has remained irregular, aggravating the problem of Rotuma's distance from potential markets. This has especially inhibited the development of agricultural exports. Rotuman oranges, for example, are famous for their quality, and are extremely abundant, but as yet they have not been commercially exploited because of difficulties with storage and transportation.

Land is important to Rotumans for its symbolic significance as well as for its subsistence value. The main land-holding unit is the *kainaga*, a bilineal group based on common descent from ancestors who resided at, and held rights in, a named house-site, or *fuag ri*. Individuals have rights in the *fuag ri* of their eight great-grandparents, although claims are made selectively. Associated with each *fuag ri* are sections of bushland; membership in a *kainaga* entitles one to rights in all its land. The person who lives on the *fuag ri* normally acts as steward of the land and controls access. He or she is obligated to grant usufruct rights to *kainaga* members for any reasonable request. At times land has been sold or given for services to specific individuals, but over generations it becomes *kainaga* land again. When the population of the island approached its highest levels, during the 1950s and 1960s, land disputes intensified and access was generally restricted to close relatives. In recent years, however, emigration has relieved tensions; the main problem now is often to determine which sibling will remain behind to steward the land and care for aging parents. Household size has declined in response to emigration, from an average of 7.5 persons per household in 1960 to 4.5 in 1988.

Rotuma is divided into seven autonomous districts, each with its own headman (*gagaj 'es itu'u*). The districts are divided into sub-groupings of households, *ho'aga*, that function as work groups under the leadership of a sub-chief (*gagaj 'es ho'aga*). All district headmen, and the majority of *ho'aga* headmen, are titled. In addition, some men hold titles without headship, although they are expected to exercise leadership roles in support of the district headman. Titles, which are held for life, belong to specified house-sites (*fuag ri*). All the descendants of

Flags of the Pacific Islands

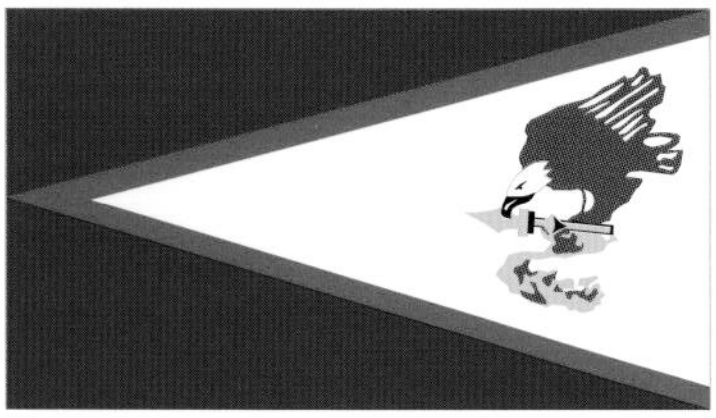

American Samoa

Cook Islands

Federated States of Micronesia

Fiji Islands

French Polynesia

Galapagos Islands

Guam

Hawai'i

Irian Jaya

Kiribati

Marshall Islands

Nauru

New Caledonia

Niue

Norfolk Island

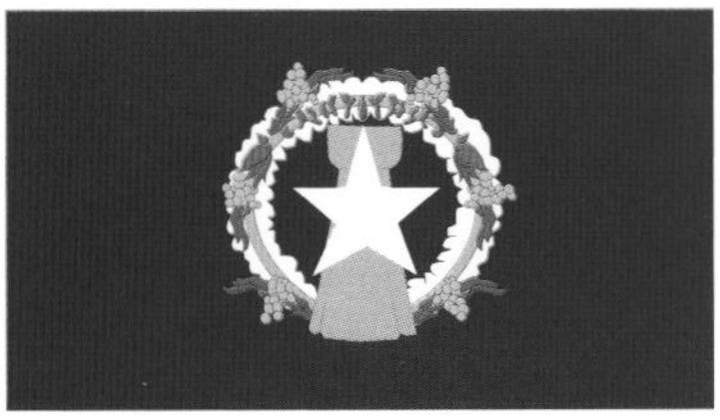

Northern Mariana Islands

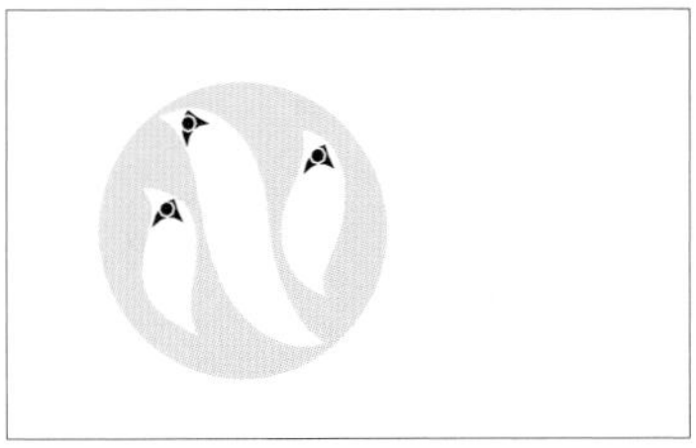

Ogasawara Islands (Bonin Islands)

Palau

Papua New Guinea

Pitcairn Islands

Ryukyu Islands

Samoa

Solomon Islands

Tokelau

Tonga

Torres Strait Islands

Tuvalu

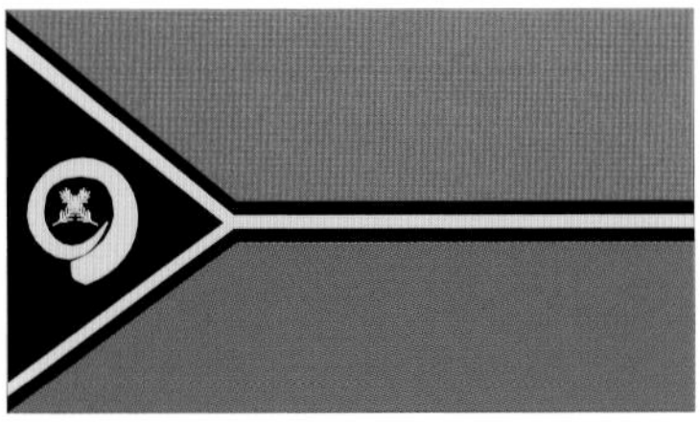

Vanuatu

Wallis and Futuna

South Pacific Forum

previous occupants of a *fuag ri* have a right to participate in the selection of successors to titles. On formal occasions titled men, and dignitaries such as ministers and priests, government officials, and distinguished visitors, occupy a place of honour. They are ceremonially served KAVA to drink, and are served food from special baskets. In the daily routine of village life, however, titled individuals are not especially privileged. As yet no significant class distinctions based on wealth or control of resources have emerged, but investments in elaborate housing and motor vehicles by a few families have led to visible differences in standard of living.

During the colonial period the Governor of Fiji appointed a resident commissioner (after 1935 a district officer) to Rotuma. He was advised by a council composed of the district headmen. In 1940 the council was expanded to include an elected representative from each district and the assistant medical practitioner. Following Fiji's independence in 1970, the council assumed responsibility for the internal governance of Rotuma, with the district officer assigned an advisory role. Until the first coup, Rotuma was represented in the Fiji legislature by a single senator. In the post-coup legislature they were given a seat in the house of representatives as well.

Prior to cession, rivalry between chiefs was intense, and warfare, though modest in scale, was endemic. During the colonial era political activity was muted, since power was concentrated in the office of resident commissioner or district officer. Following Fiji's independence, however, political rivalries emerged again. Contention over titles and competition between districts for scarce resources have resulted in numerous disputes. Following the second coup, when Fiji left the British Commonwealth, a segment of the Rotuman population rejected the council's decision to remain with the newly declared republic. Arguing that Rotuma had been ceded to Great Britain and not to Fiji, they declared Rotuma independent—and were subsequently charged with sedition. Majority opinion appears to favour remaining with Fiji, but rumblings of discontent remain.

Churches and religious activities are central to social life on Rotuma. In addition to the Wesleyan and Catholic congregations, a SEVENTH-DAY ADVENTIST church has been built serving a number of families, and a small group of Jehovah's Witnesses meet together regularly.

Rotumans today are widely scattered around the globe, forming identifiable communities in Fiji, Australia, New Zealand and the United States, as well as on Rotuma. Travel between these communities is becoming increasingly frequent, and remittances are now an important source of revenue for families on Rotuma. With a new satellite dish on the island, allowing for direct-dial telephone communication, and improved air service, Rotumans are able to maintain their links with one another more easily, forming an interactive world-wide community that is evolving in concert.—AH & JR

Further reading

Fatiaki, A et al., 1991. *Rotuma: Hanua Pumue*, Institute of Pacific Studies, University of the South Pacific.

Hereniko, V, 1995. *Woven Gods: female clowns and power in Rotuma*, University of Hawai'i Press, and Institute of Pacific Studies, University of the South Pacific.

Howard, A, 1970. *Learning to Be Rotuman*, Columbia Teachers College Press.

FRENCH POLYNESIA

Constitutional status: Overseas Territory of France.

Head of State: President of France represented by High Commissioner Jean Aribaud.

Head of Government: President Gaston FLOSSE (1998).

Main cities/towns: PAPE'ETE (capital, on Tahiti, population 25 500); Faa'a (on Tahiti, 27 000); Uturoa (Ra'iatea, 8600); Fare (Huahine, 4500).

Land area: 3521 sq km (35 islands and 83 atolls).

Sea area (EEZ): 5 030 000 sq km.

Population: 228 785 (1999 SPC estimate); 70 per cent Polynesian; others mainly European and Chinese.

Official languages: Tahitian, French.

Currency: CFP (French Pacific franc).

Time: -1000 hours UTC.

National day: 14 July.

GDP per capita: A$27 000 (1996).

Principal export earnings: Tourism; fishing; black pearls.

Political system: French Polynesia is a French Overseas Territory, operating under a statute (of September 1984) of internal autonomy which allows the territorial government to control socioeconomic policy but not defence, law and order, or foreign affairs. In addition to having its own municipal and territorial levels of government, the territory elects representatives to the French national parliament. The government is headed by a high commissioner, appointed by the French Republic.

The 1984 statute permitted the conduct of certain local affairs (local budget, health services, primary education, culture, social welfare, public works, agriculture and sports) by a 41-member territorial assembly, elected by universal adult suffrage. The assembly elects a president who appoints a council of 10 ministers. In 1998, the president of the territorial assembly was Justin Arapari. The territory is represented in the French parliament by two deputies (Michel Buillard and Émile Vernaudon) and in the senate by Gaston Flosse in 1998. The secretary-general of French Polynesia was Michel Jeanjean.

Main parties: Tahoeraa Huiraatira, Ai'a Api, Te Tiarama, Tavini Huiraatira, Te Ea no Maohi Nui, Amuitahira'a No Oteania, Te Atira a Porinetia.

Physical environment: French Polynesia (extending from latitude 7–29° south and longitude 131–156° west) is made up of a group of five archipelagos with 118 islands scattered over an area the size of Europe. The total land area of these islands and atolls amounts to only 3520 sq km, and Tahiti—lying in the centre of the Society Islands—is the largest island at 1042 sq km. The remaining archipelagos are the Austral Islands, Marquesas Islands, the Tuamotu Archipelago and the Mangareva (Gambier) Islands.

The Society group, high islands of basaltic volcanic origin, has two parts: the 'Windward Islands', (Tahiti, Moorea, Mehetia, Maiao and Tetiaora); and the 'Leeward Islands' (Huahine, Bora Bora, Ra'iatea, Tahaa and Maupiti), 200 km from Tahiti. The mountainous interior of Tahiti Nui rises to 2240 m (Mt Orohena). There are several rivers, and also a lake (Vaihiria) about 460 m above sea level. The Tuamotu Archipelago to the east of the Society Islands, which consists of 75 low-lying coral atolls enclosing a lagoon, and one raised coral island, has a land area of 726 sq km. Rangiroa (which has an airstrip) is the widest atoll of this archipelago and those of Fakarava, Anaa, Kaukura, Taaroa and Tikehau are the main ones. Moruroa, one of the most southerly atolls, was used as a NUCLEAR TESTING site and Fangataufa (also uninhabited) provided an observation post. Hao atoll was used as a military base.

The Austral Islands, the nearest of which is 500 km south of Tahiti, have five high islands with a distance of 160–230 km separating them. Each island

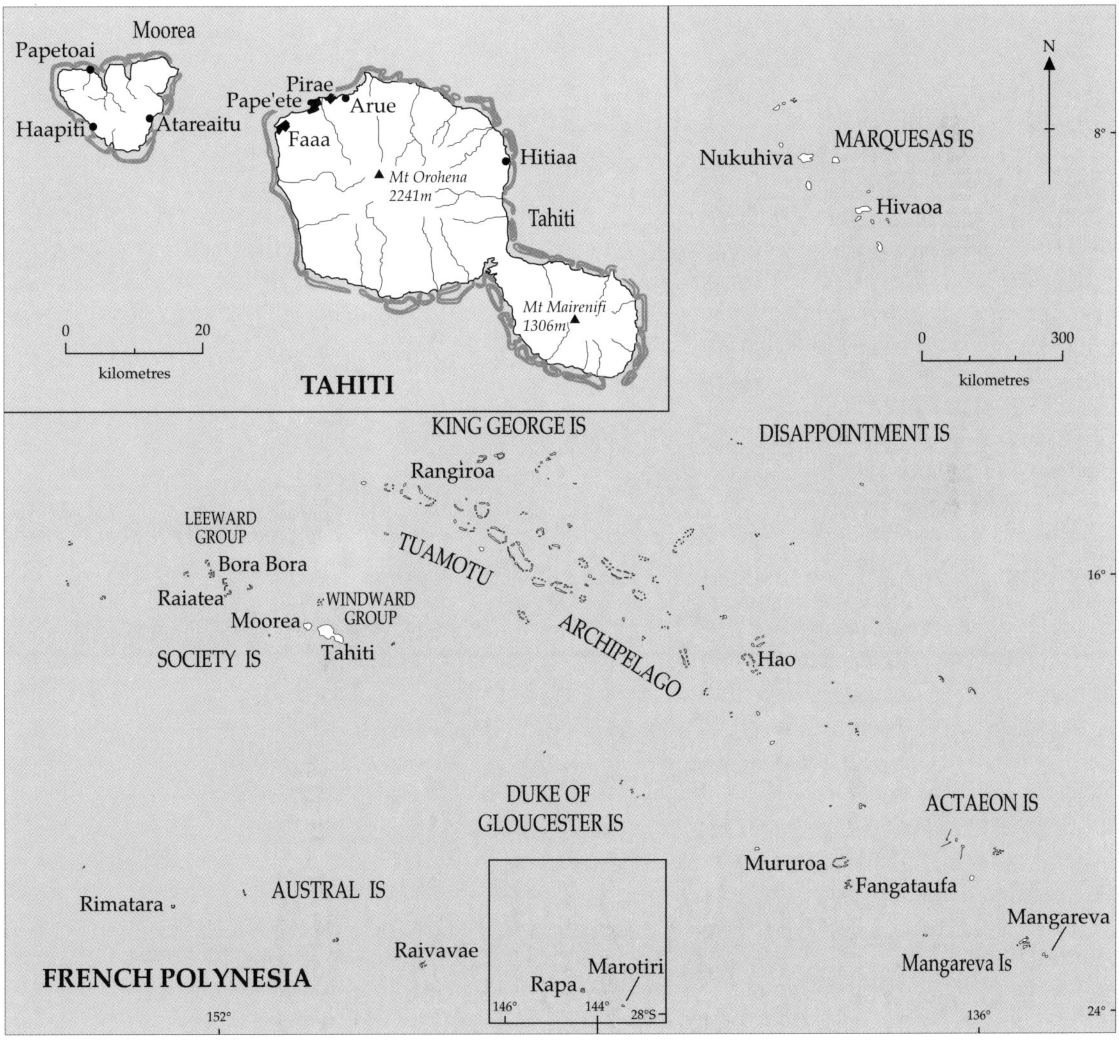

has either a fringing reef or a barrier reef, and most have mountainous interiors, ranging in elevation from Mt Perahu (600 m) on Rapa, and Mt Hiro (440 m) on Raivavae, to Rimatara which rises to 80 m above sea level. The Marquesas group is 1500 km northeast from Tahiti and consists of nine raised islands with rugged peaks and valleys, steep cliffs, and no reef. The Mangareva group extends towards the southwest of the Tuamotu Archipelago and has about 10 high volcanic islands.

Vegetation is lush on the high islands, and the island flora includes the sweet-smelling Tahitian gardenia, *tiare*, among a range of tropical flowers. The climate is tropical, with the hottest months of the year in January and February, and fairly high humidity, especially in the wet season between November and March. Annual rainfall: 1700 mm.

History: The earliest arrival of Polynesian settlers appears to have been around AD 300 in the Marquesas Islands, and in the Society group from about 800. During the period before European contact, islanders had a structured hierarchy of hereditary tribal chiefs, with no dominant tribal groups.

First visited by Europeans on 18 June 1767, the English explorer Samuel WALLIS gave Tahiti the name King George III Island and raised the British flag. Having heard but misunderstood the islanders' identification of Otahiti ('This is Tahiti'), Tahiti was referred to for many years as 'Otaheite' by visitors. In the following year, 1768, the French navigator BOUGAINVILLE arrived, and he named it La Nouvelle Cythère, and claimed it for France. James COOK reached the island in 1769, following Wallis' directions, and later explored several of the neighbouring islands which he named the Society group. It was on his second voyage that Cook brought OMAI back to England.

From the 1770s, occasional exploring vessels called from time to time, including William BLIGH in the *Bounty*, in 1788, spending five months at Matavai Bay gaining a cargo of breadfruit. The newly formed LONDON MISSIONARY SOCIETY sent a first party of evangelists on the *Duff* in 1797. They made little headway at first, but were able to establish headquarters in 1815 when POMARE II gave them his support. Their political influence grew in the 1820s, and they were able to persuade the Tahitians in 1836 to refuse permission to two French Catholic priests (see Honoré LAVAL) to extend their activities from Mangareva to Tahiti.

After the French government reacted to this affront, Queen POMARE IV was forced to yield and pay 'reparations'. She sought the protection of the British crown, but in vain. In November 1842, when Tahiti became the first island in the Pacific to come under the control of a foreign power, it was French protection—embodied in a force of 500 troops, supported by four warships—which she was obliged to accept. The French protectorate continued until 1880, when King Pomare V abdicated and a French colony was proclaimed. By 1901 it included all of the Society Islands as well as the Marquesas Islands, Austral Islands and the Tuamotu group.

Although the opening of the Panama Canal in 1914 increased the ease of access for European shipping, little development occurred in agriculture or fishing. The first sign of indigenous nationalism emerged in the early 1940s, when POUVANA'A A OOPA, from Huahine, expressed a protest strongly enough to attract official retribution. The French governor, Colonel Georges Orselli, exiled him, but he returned at the end of the war in 1945 to the enthusiastic support of 300 war veterans, who successfully promoted a claim that all Tahitians should be entitled to French citizenship. The French government also established the first territorial assembly in 1946, with 30 elected members. By 1947 Pouvana'a's supporters had formed a committee (Comité Pouvanaa) which agitated for greater political, economic and cultural freedom. The French authorities held them in custody for several months, but upon Pouvana'a's release, he had become a national hero, and was swept into public office in the 1949 elections as a representative (*deputé*) in the French parliament. The Comité Pouvanaa then developed into a political party which won a majority of seats in the 1953 and 1957 elections. In August 1957 the territory was reconstituted as French Polynesia, and Pouvana'a became vice-president. He began campaigning for independence, and the nationalist secession proposal was still being debated when Charles de Gaulle took over the French presidency and promised a referendum on independence in all French territories. It was held on 27 September 1958, with the popular majority voting to remain a French possession. Pouvana'a went to prison in exile, and the council was suspended.

The international airport at Faa'a opened in 1960, and the French government announced its proposed NUCLEAR TESTING program in the Tuamotu group in 1963. Francis SANFORD was the next major figure in the fight for Tahitian autonomy. As a *deputé* and a member of the territorial assembly, he continued to demand self-government and also strongly opposed nuclear testing. A series of aggressive and dramatic nationalist protests were staged during the 1970s, until finally the French parliament approved a new constitution (*statut*) which made the governor a high commissioner, and enabled Sanford to become vice-president of a new government council, which met for the first time on 22 July 1977.

From the early 1980s, the French administration softened its former uncompromisingly assimilationist approach; school students were permitted to speak Tahitian, and from 1982, this became the dominant language for legislative discussion also. In 1984 the French parliament passed a new French Polynesian statute which introduced a modest increase in local autonomy, with additional responsibilities able to be delegated to the territorial government. The economy, dominated by French government spending during the nuclear testing program, brought a considerable influx of people and development of infrastructure. Migration to Tahiti led to squatter settlements and high unemployment, and Pape'ete experienced riots in 1987 and 1991. Tourism and further development of island fisheries remain the best prospects for future economic growth. French nuclear testing at Moruroa and Fangataufa atolls ended in 1995, but reliance on French aid is likely to continue, and Gaston Flosse has proved to be adept at obtaining optimum levels of financial support.—RL2 & KRF

Further reading

Henningham, S, 1992. *France and the South Pacific: a contemporary history*, Allen & Unwin.

Langdon, R, 1979. *Tahiti, Island of Love*, 5th ed., Pacific Publications.

GALAPAGOS ISLANDS

Constitutional status: Province of Ecuador.

Head of State: President of Ecuador.

Head of Government: Governor.

Administrative centre: Puerto Baquerizo (on San Cristobal).

Land area: 7880 sq km (13 islands and 6 tiny islets): Isabela (4588 sq km), Fernandina (640 sq km), Santa Cruz (985 sq km), San Cristobal (560 sq km), Santiago (585 sq km), Floreana, Española, Genovesa, Marchena, Pinta, Pinzon, Baltra and Santa Fe.

Sea area: Part of Ecuador's EEZ.

Population: 4400 (1990).

Official language: Spanish.

Currency: Ecuador sucre.

National day: 10 August.

Principal export earnings: Tourism, agriculture, fishing.

Political system: The Galapagos Islands are part of the territory of Ecuador, governed as a province with three cantons, and administered by a governor who is appointed in Quito.

Physical environment: The Galapagos Islands lie across the equator (between latitude 1° 30' south and longitude 90° 30' west) in the far eastern Pacific, around 970 km off the coast of Ecuador. The largest island, Isabela, is about 100 km long by 25 km, with several high peaks rising to about 1700 m above sea level. The highest point is Mt Wolf, at 1707 m. There are 13 large islands, of volcanic origin, and many small islets and rocks. There is good fertile soil on the two largest islands, producing cash crops of coffee, citrus and tropical fruit. An extraordinarily rich variety of plant and animal life, mostly originating in South America, would have relied on birds and prevailing winds and currents to reach these isolated islands. There is a wide range of endemic species which have attracted considerable scientific interest. Nearly half the land birds, all the REPTILES and 11 species of TURTLES are unique to the Galapagos. The bird life includes finches, flamingos, pelicans and albatrosses. The giant tortoise (*Geochelone nigra*), which lives for 200 years, can weigh up to 230 kg. Humid areas have produced a tortoise with a distinctive domed shell, while drier regions have a species with a longer neck to allow it to reach its food. Lizards found in the Galapagos include the black and red marine iguana, unusual because it eats algae in the water, and several land iguanas. There are also many small lizards and various non-poisonous snakes. MARINE BIRDS and penguins are plentiful, and SEA LIONS live throughout the islands. Also adapted to the dry climate are several varieties of cactus, including one that grows up to 12 m tall and is widespread.

Kicker Rock, Galapagos Islands

In spite of its equatorial location, the island climate is moderated by the cold Humboldt Current. It is dry in the coastal regions, warmer and more humid in the interior, with a prevailing cool south-east wind from June to December which brings frequent clouds and misty conditions. This cool season often provides some light rainfall (drizzle) in the higher regions. The warm northeasterly breezes which come between January and May are accompanied by occasional heavy showers for the lowland regions, but water is scarce on all islands. DROUGHT is common, and sometimes continues for several months. Annual rainfall: about 350 mm in coastal areas, ranging to 1220–2500 mm at higher altitudes.

History: The Galapagos Islands were uninhabited when the first Europeans arrived in the 16th century, but there is evidence that Inca (American Indian) fishermen, probably from Ecuador and northern Peru, visited before the Spanish occupation. The name Galapagos, Spanish for 'tortoise', appeared on a map published in 1570, but the islands were left in isolation—apart from providing a temporary refuge for pirate ships in the late 17th century. Many of the islands were given English names by the buccaneer William Dampier who spent some time there in 1684 while engaged in sorties against Spanish traders.

Ecuador annexed the islands in 1832 and established a settlement on Floreana, using political prisoners as labour for farming and fishing, and supplying passing whalers. There was a population of about 300 by 1835 when Charles Darwin visited on the voyage of the *Beagle*. He spent 35 days making careful observations on the unique bird and animal life, and developed ideas about their adaptation to their environment which were later applied to his theory of evolution. After the first Floreana colony was abandoned in 1882, there were further attempts at settlement over the next 80 years, with varying degrees of success, mainly because of the shortage of food and fresh water. A sugarcane plantation survived on San Cristobal until the early 20th century. A penal colony was set up on Isabela in 1944, and a military base was established on Baltra during the Second World War, manned by US servicemen.

The Charles Darwin Research Station, at Academy Bay on Santa Cruz, was opened in 1964 as a centre for international scientific study and conservation of the island flora and fauna. The Galapagos National Park, declared in 1959 through the auspices of the Charles Darwin Foundation, and inaugurated in 1968, is supported by the Darwin Station. Both are funded by private sponsorship as well as by Ecuador. Galapagos became a province of Ecuador in 1973, since which time steady migration has occurred to raise the island population, especially on Santa Cruz.—KRF

Further reading

Thornton, I, 1971. *Darwin's Islands*, Natural History Press.

GUAM

Constitutional status: Unincorporated non-self-governing US territory.

Head of State: US President.

Head of Government: Governor Carl T C Gutierrez (1995–).

Administrative centre: HAGATNA (Agana), on the central northwestern coast.

Land area: 541 sq km.

Sea area (EEZ): 218 000 sq km.

Population: 149 640 (1999 SPC estimate).

Languages: English; Chamorro.

Currency: US dollar.

Time: +1200 hours UTC.

National day: 14 July.

GDP per capita: A$12 356 (1990).

Principal export earnings: Tourism, mainly, but also fisheries.

Political system: The Guam legislature consists of 21 elected members and an elected governor, for a four-year term. In 1998, the Hon Carl Gutierrez was governor, and the Hon Madeleine Z Bordallo was lieutenant-governor. The elected delegate to the US Congress was the Hon Robert A Underwood.

Physical environment: Guam (lying at latitude 13° 26' north and longitude 144° 43' east) is the largest island in Melanesia, a hilly volcanic island nearly 50 km long with fertile valleys, high plateaux and occasional steep cliffs. The highest point is Mt Humuyong Manglo (405 m above sea level). The northern part of the island is a plateau 150 m above sea level, once thickly forested but now cleared for

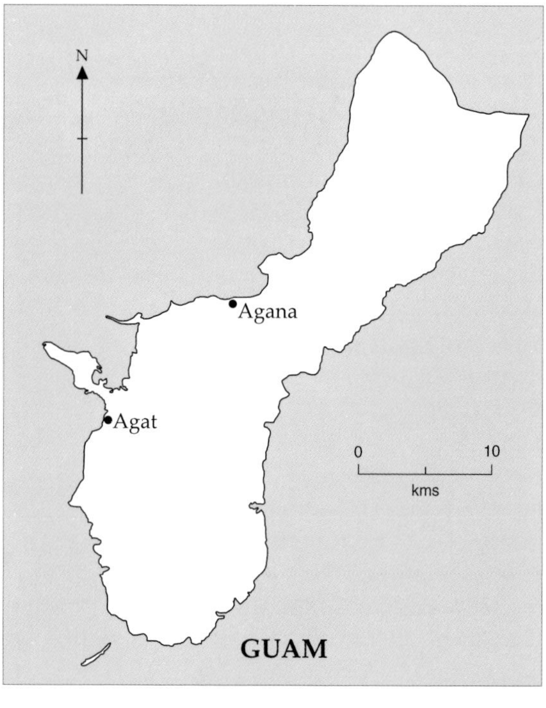

agricultural and military use, and for the airport. Hills in the south are of volcanic origin. There are coral reefs off the coast. The climate is hot and humid, with little seasonal variation and year-round trade winds. Annual rainfall: 2000 mm.

History: Archaeological evidence indicates that Guam has been inhabited for more than 3000 years, and two separate prehistoric cultures have been identified. By 1521, the inhabitants were Chamorros, of Malay-Polynesian origin, when the first European visitor, Ferdinand MAGELLAN, arrived after 3½ months at sea. Spain claimed the island in 1565 (see SPAIN AND PORTUGAL IN THE PACIFIC) but the westward-bound galleons did not begin calling at Guam until the mid 17th century. The first Jesuit missionaries arrived in 1668, but the initial warm reception from the Chamorros soon turned to mistrust and rebellion. From 1668–95, the Spanish introduced repressive, brutal measures to control the natives, and as imported diseases such as smallpox took their toll, the population of 100 000 was reduced to 5000 by 1741.

Once all resistance was crushed, Catholicism became well established, and Guam in the 18th century was known as a 'civilized' port of call for foreign traders, whalers and explorers. When Louis de FREYCINET visited in 1819, he spent three months amassing information on the history, language and culture of the people of the Marianas, greatly aided by finding a three-volume work prepared by Spanish missionaries which recorded many thousands of Chamorro words and phrases. By 1855, the Americans considered its commercial appeal warranted the establishment of a consulate. In 1898, when the Spanish-American war began, the US navy was ordered to take Guam and set up a military administration. American rule was imposed on 21 June, and Spain was obliged to accept this as part of the terms of the armistice. Captain Richard P Leary became the first American governor, and the new administration set to work on improving health, education and agricultural development on Guam. The first step towards involvement of the islanders in government was taken in 1917, with the creation of an advisory council, the first congress. This developed in the 1930s into an elected bicameral congress, of 43 members.

Then the Japanese invaded in 1941, imposing a harsh military regime that continued for almost three years. (See WORLD WAR II IN THE PACIFIC.) When the Americans recaptured Guam, the huge post-war task of reconstruction and rehabilitation lay ahead, providing plentiful employment and eventually restoring a standard of living beyond the resources of any other Pacific islanders in the late 1940s. Guam became an unincorporated territory of the United States on 1 June 1950, American citizenship now applied to all citizens, and the first civilian governor, Carlton S Skinner, was appointed. In June 1960, Joseph Flores, the first governor of Chamorro descent was appointed, and in 1971, Carlos G Camacho became Guam's first elected governor, his term ending in 1975. Later holders of the office have been Ricardo J BORDALLO (1975–79 and 1983–87), Paul M CALVO (1979–83), and Joseph F Ada (1987–95).

In 1982 Guam voted to seek a similar commonwealth status to the Northern Mariana Islands, but this developed into a requirement for greater powers in indigenous Chamorro self-determination, mutuality in defence issues and foreign relations. Through the 1990s, the continuing delay in changing the island's political status has been largely attributed to federal government intransigence, linked to the reluctance of local politicians to compromise on Chamorro self-determination.—KRF

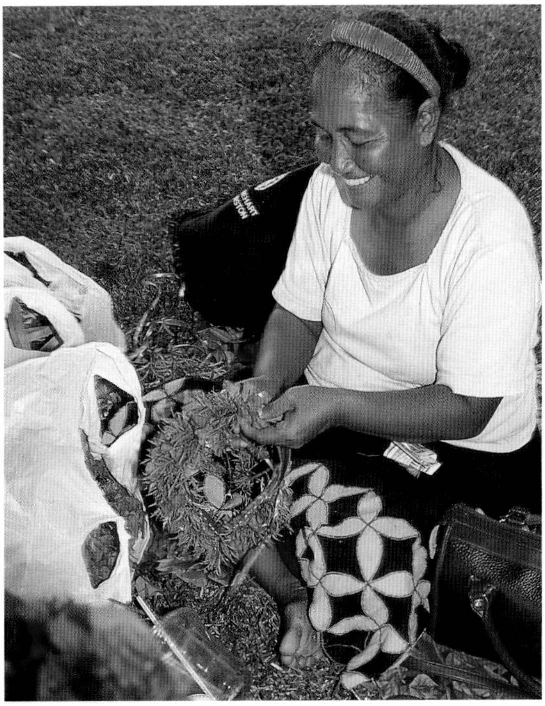

Pohnpeian woman of Guam, making floral headbands called *mwaremwar* for a cultural fair

Further reading

Carano, P and Sanchez, P C, 1964. *A Complete History of Guam*, Charles Tuttle & Co.

Rogers, R F, 1995. *Destiny's Landfall: a history of Guam*, University of Hawai'i Press.

HAWAI'I

Constitutional status: A state of United States of America.

Head of State: US President.

Head of Government: Governor Benjamin J Cayetano (1998).

Main cities/towns: Honolulu (capital, on O'ahu), Hilo (on Hawai'i).

Land area: 16 640 sq km (132 islands); Hawai'i (c11 000 sq km); O'ahu (c1500 sq km).

Sea area (EEZ): 2 157 985 sq km.

Population: 1 187 300 (1997 census): see MULTI-ETHNIC POPULATION OF HAWAI'I.

Languages: English, declared the only official language in 1896, and also Hawaiian, 'Ōlelo Hawai'i, which has undergone a revival since 1970.

Currency: US dollar.

Time: -1100 hours UTC.

National day: 4 July.

Principal export earnings: Tourism; fishing; sugar; pineapples.

Political system: The centralized political system is headed by an elected governor (since 1959, always a Democrat). In 1998 the governor is Benjamin Cayetano, and the lieutenant-governor is Mazie Hirono. There is a bicameral legislature: a senate of 25 members, elected for four years, and a house of representatives of 51 members, elected every two years. In 1997 Norman Mizuguchi was President of the Senate. The major parties, in a predominantly two-party system, are closely identified with the US Democratic and Republican parties.

Physical environment: The Hawaiian group, located in the eastern part of the north Pacific, includes seven major inhabited islands—Hawai'i, Maui, O'ahu, Kaua'i, Moloka'i, Lāna'i and Ni'ihau, and the smaller Kaho'olawe. Hawai'i Island occupies nearly two-thirds of the total land area of the group and has two active volcanoes, Mauna Loa and Kīlauea, in its mountainous interior. The highest peak is Mauna Kea (4526 m). The longest stream is on O'ahu (Kaukonahua, 53 km), and the largest lake is on Ni'ihau (Halāli'i). The islands are mountainous, of volcanic origin, with extensive coastal plains and cool plateaux. The fertile volcanic soil produces abundant vegetation, with tropical fruits and forests. Sugar and pineapple are the main trade crops. The climate is generally mild, with trade winds for most of the year producing considerable regional and seasonal variations. Annual rainfall: up to 13 000 mm on the northern island of Kaua'i, ranging to 140 mm in dry regions and 5000 mm elsewhere.

History: Probably settled from Marquesas Islands, according to the evidence of archaeologists, the vast, isolated archipelago of Hawai'i has a rich oral history tradition. (For its prehistory, see SETTLEMENT

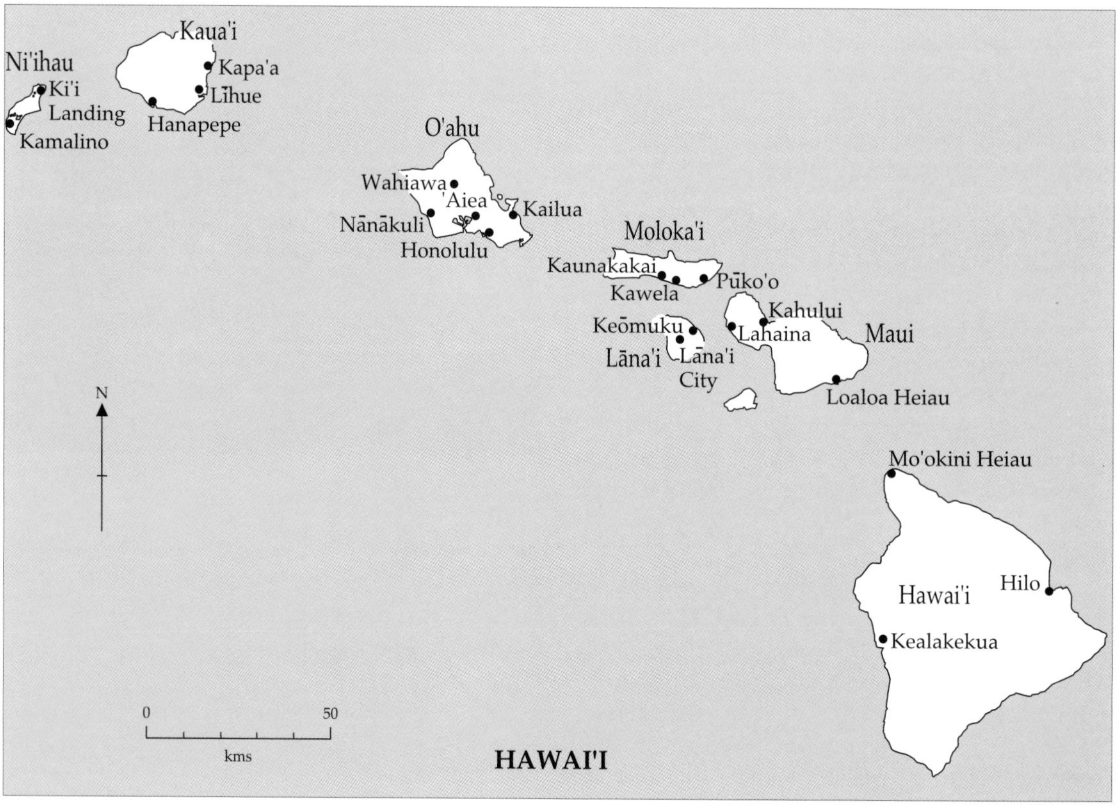

OF THE NORTHERN PACIFIC.) For many centuries, a number of high-ranking families ruled local chiefdoms, with Hawai'i originally the most densely populated and the most politically important of the islands.

It was the visit of Captain COOK in 1778 that brought the islands to the attention of the outside world. Although Cook himself was killed at Kealakekua Bay in 1779, two members of his expedition subsequently commanded the first British ships to call at Hawai'i as they crossed the Pacific in the early days of the fur trade. This era coincided with the emergence of a single powerful chief, a strong ruler who unified the islands: KAMEHAMEHA I, who became known as king. By establishing a long period of peace and prosperity, and dealing fairly with explorers and traders who came seeking provisions and sandalwood, he left Hawai'i able to maintain its independence for several decades in the face of steadily increasing European activity in the Pacific.

By the early 19th century, both LAHAINA (on Maui) and HONOLULU (on O'ahu) were receiving frequent visits from foreign ships. Honolulu had the largest harbour in the region, and its population doubled between 1820 and 1840, mainly because of its capacity to supply the WHALING industry. The first American missionaries arrived in 1820 and were aided in bringing about the conversion of Hawaiians to Christianity by the support of KA'AHUMANU. Missionary activities included the first printed work in Hawaiian, experiments with SUGAR mills and a cotton factory—together with the introduction of temperance laws, as mission influence moved into the political arena.

During the 1850s, whaling in the north Pacific began to decline and Hawaiians began to look to the country's agricultural resources, especially sugar, to provide a secure economic base. Both Kamehameha IV, and then his brother, Kamehameha V, hoped to ensure the country's independence and to end the growing interest among American residents for political union with the United States. With the development of the sugar industry, however, it was large business interests who established the plantations and—faced with a dramatic decline in the indigenous Hawaiian population through introduced diseases—began to import the necessary labour by the shipload, creating in the process the present ethnically diverse population of Hawai'i. (See COLONIAL LABOUR TRADE and MULTI-ETHNIC POPULATION OF HAWAI'I.) Shipping services made travel easier and American settlers continued to arrive. When King Lunalilo announced his cabinet in January 1873, all but one were of American origin and two were from missionary families. His successor, King Kalākaua, made a goodwill visit to the United States at the end of 1874, which was followed by the successful negotiation of a treaty of reciprocity for a seven-year term. This achieved an immediate production boom for sugar and rice, accompanied by huge investment in the large-scale sugar plantations to supply the irrigation, transportation and labour requirements.

The economic prosperity brought about by the treaty also provided an environment for political corruption and extravagance. Kalākaua went on a nine-month world tour in 1881, and entertained a huge international audience for his coronation in 1883. After a series of scandals, there was growing discontent with the monarchy both on the part of those with already existing anti-American sentiments, and among those who favoured annexation by the United States. The 'revolution' of 1887—a public mass meeting of protest—won the king's signature on a new constitution, but the reform provisions still alienated many. Queen LILI'UOKALANI, who came to the throne in 1891, was determined to regain some of the power and prestige that her brother had lost. She prepared a new constitution, but her ministers refused to sign it and were supported by a storm of protest among the pro-annexation lobby. The period of royal rule came to an end in 1893, when Lili'uokalani was forced to yield to an American military occupation in support of business interests, and a provisional government, headed by Judge Sanford B Dole, declared that the country would be incorporated into the United States. A republic was declared on 4 July 1894, followed by formal annexation as a territory, approved by the US Congress in 1898. American citizenship applied to all citizens from 1900. By 1940, sugar production had increased to more than 1 million tons per year, and the population had nearly trebled to 423 000.

'Iolani Palace, Honolulu

The Japanese attack on PEARL HARBOR on 7 December 1941 precipitated the United States into war and made O'ahu a significant strategic base. (See ISLANDER EXPERIENCES IN THE PACIFIC WAR.) Post-war development featured exceptional growth in sugar and pineapple production, and also the beginning of substantial investment in tourism. Hawai'i became the 50th state of the United States in 1959. Statehood initiated a major change in the Hawaiian economy, bringing less dependence on the cash crops of sugar and pineapple and more on tourism and land speculation. The rapid emergence of commercial and especially hotel development threatened rural Hawaiian communities, since small landowners controlled less than 10 per cent of the land. Growing urbanization (accompanied by eviction of farmers) saw the appearance of a native rights movement, seeking land restitution based on indigenous birthrights, and during the 1970s, large-scale resort and residential developments produced ongoing anti-development battles and growing concern over the military expropriation of large areas of land. By the 1980s, groups promoting trust land claims (such as the popular Ka Lāhui Hawai'i) were asserting new forms of sovereignty and it was clear that Hawaiian self-determination had become a significant issue. Ka Lāhui's supporters organised a protest march of 15 000 in 1993, and the then governor, John Waihe'e, who is of Hawaiian descent, joined the growing public calls for Hawaiian sovereignty.

The first Hawaiian Senator in the US Congress was Daniel Akaka. Today 80 per cent of the population live on O'ahu, most of them in Honolulu.—KRF

Further reading

Kuykendall, R S and Grove Day, A, 1976/1948. *Hawai'i: a history: from Polynesian kingdom to American state*, Prentice-Hall.

IRIAN JAYA

Constitutional status: A province of Indonesia.

Head of State: President of Indonesia.

Head of Government: Governor.

Main town: Jayapura (capital, population c130 000 in 1990).

Land area: 421 980 sq km.

Sea area: Part of Indonesian EEZ.

Population: 1 323 000 (1997 estimate).

Official language: Bahasa Indonesia; and about 480 Melanesian languages are spoken.

Currency: Indonesian rupiah.

Time: +0900 hours UTC.

National day: 17 August.

GDP per capita: Rp1.7 million (1992).

Principal export earnings: Oil; copper; gold; logging; copra; tuna fish; spices; cocoa; coffee; prawns; crocodile skins.

Political system: The governor is appointed by the Indonesian government. He heads a provincial council of 40 (30 elected district representatives and 10 appointed members). Irian Jaya also has 9 administrative district councils, each with 20 members.

Physical environment: Irian Jaya (between the equator and latitude 9° south, and longitude 130–141° east) forms the western half of the island of New Guinea, in the eastern South Pacific. Sharing a land border of about 725 km with Papua New Guinea, it also has a high mountainous central range, rising to 5030 m above sea level (Mt Jayawijaya). There are broad swampy lowlands in the south and some narrower coastal lowlands in the north. Animal and plant life is similar to that of Papua New Guinea, with many marsupials and a range of bird species including the BIRD OF PARADISE, the goura pigeon and the flightless cassowary. The vegetation features tropical rainforests with a wide variety of species of trees. Subsistence crops include coconuts, sago palm and pandanus. The climate is tropical (wet and humid equatorial conditions) with little seasonal variation. Annual rainfall: exceeds 2000 mm in most areas.

Economy: Irian Jaya's regional cash economy is dominated by the huge Freeport gold and copper mine at Tembagapura. Other major exports from the province include oil, nickel, timber and fisheries products. In 1992, 55.6 per cent of gross regional domestic product (GRDP) was in the mining and quarrying sector, and 16.4 per cent in agriculture. The province has recorded a relatively high rate of growth in GRDP over recent years (12.5 per cent in per capita non-oil GRDP 1990–93, compared with an all-Indonesia figure of 7.5). Most of the Melanesian population are subsistence farmers, growing mainly sweet potato, taro and bananas, and harvesting sago. Pig husbandry is also an important economic activity, especially in the highland societies where pigs play a major role in extensive cultural exchanges. In the rural areas, however, Irian Jaya ranks low on most social indicators; in 1993, 78 per cent of villages were rated 'poor' (compared with a national figure of 31 per cent). Much of the commercial activity is in the hands of merchants who have migrated from other parts of Indonesia.

History: The island of New Guinea was first settled around 50 000–40 000 years ago. The westernmost parts of New Guinea later came under the influence of the Javanese Majapahit empire and of the Sultan of Tidore. In 1545 the island was claimed for the Spanish crown, and in 1606 for the Netherlands, but the first European settlement in New Guinea was by the Dutch in 1828. Through a series of rather vague territorial claims during the 19th century West New Guinea subsequently became part of the Netherlands East Indies (NEI). Its eastern boundaries were roughly defined by agreements with Britain in 1895 and Germany in 1910 (more precise definition of the border was still in process after Papua New Guinea's independence in 1975).

During World War II West New Guinea, along with the rest of the NEI, was occupied by Japan. In 1945 Indonesian nationalists proclaimed the Republic of Indonesia 'from Ambon to Aceh', but not including West New Guinea, which was reoccupied by the Netherlands. When in 1949 the Netherlands reluctantly agreed to acknowledge the Republic of Indonesia, West New Guinea was initially not included. Its future status was set aside for negotiation between Indonesia and the Netherlands, but when talks broke down, the Netherlands consolidated its position in West New Guinea, promising to develop the territory towards self-government and eventual independence.

The pace of political development accelerated in the latter part of the 1950s, and a New Guinea Council, comprising mostly Melanesian members, was created in 1961. But the territorial dispute between the Netherlands and Indonesia intensified, with naval engagements and the landing of Indonesian paratroopers in West New Guinea in the early 1960s. In August 1962, under an agreement signed in New York, West New Guinea was transferred to a UN Temporary Executive Authority. The following year Indonesia displaced the administering authority and effectively occupied West New Guinea, pending an Act of Free Choice, to be held before 1969.

In 1969 the Act of Free Choice (Penentuan Pendapat Rakyat [Pepera], 'Declaration of the People's Opinion') was duly held. But rather than a plebiscite, the Indonesian authorities organized an assembly of 1022 appointed delegates who, predictably, expressed support for West New Guinea's incorporation into the republic. Official and unofficial observers at the time were strongly critical of the process—commonly referred to as the 'Act Free of Choice' or 'Act of No Choice'—and of the intimidation of delegates by the Indonesian military. The UN resident in West New Guinea, in his report to the UN, expressed 'reservation' about the manner in which the New York Agreement had been implemented. There were also reports, from the early 1960s, of massacres of Melanesians opposed to Indonesian rule, and large numbers of people sought refuge in the Netherlands or across the border in Papua New Guinea.

In September 1969 West New Guinea became the province of Irian Barat, renamed Irian Jaya in 1973. Since the early 1960s there has been Melanesian opposition to Indonesian rule in Irian Jaya, and sporadic armed resistance from the separatist ORGANISASI PAPUA MERDEKA (OPM, Free Papua Movement), which has called for an independent state of West Papua (WEST PAPUAN NATIONALISM). On occasion, Indonesian military operations against Melanesian nationalists have spilled across the border into Papua New Guinea, where the OPM has sometimes established camps in the dense jungle of the border area. In the 1970s and 1980s border incursions by Indonesia's armed forces, while pursuing suspected OPM sympathizers, were a recurring source of tension in relations between Indonesia and Papua New Guinea. Following the popular uprising against President Soeharto in May 1998 there have been renewed demands for self-determination in West Papua, or at least some substantial degree of autonomy.—RJM

Further reading

Crocombe, R and Ali, A (eds), 1982. *Politics in Melanesia*, University of the South Pacific.

Muller, K, 1991. *Irian Jaya*, Periplus Press.

Osborne, R, 1985. *Indonesia's Secret War: the guerilla struggle in Irian Jaya*, Allen & Unwin.

KERMADEC ISLANDS

Constitutional status: Part of New Zealand.

Land area: 33 sq km (3 islands and 10 islets); Raoul, Macauley, Curtis.

Physical environment: The Kermadec Islands (latitude 30° south and longitude 178° west) are 930 km northeast of New Zealand. The islands are the peaks of the Kermadec ridge which rises on the western side of the narrow Kermadec trench (see OCEAN TRENCHES). Raoul, the largest island in the group, is volcanically active. The islands are designated as a nature reserve, providing a habitat for MARINE BIRDS and aquatic mammals. In the past, the vast colonies of sea birds have suffered from the depredations of rats and feral cats. The subtropical climate is humid, with very warm summers, mild winters, and evenly distributed rainfall.

History: The British ship *Lady Penrhyn* brought the first European visitors in 1788, when Captain Sever named Macauley Island and Curtis. In 1793 the French explorer Bruni d'Entrecasteaux discovered and named Raoul Island, after Joseph Raoul who was quartermaster on the *Recherche*. He also named the group Kermadec Islands, after Captain Huon de Kermadec of the *Espérance*.

The islands were annexed by New Zealand in 1887. Raoul has now become the site of a meteorological station, manned from New Zealand.—KRF

KIRIBATI

Constitutional status: Independent republic.
Head of State: President.
Head of Government: President Teburoro Tito (1998).
Main town: SOUTH TARAWA (Betio, Bikenibeu and the capital—Bairiki).
Land area: 811 sq km (34 islands); SOUTH TARAWA (15.8 sq km), KIRITIMATI (Christmas Island, 388.4 sq km), Tabuaeran (Fanning, 33.7 sq km), Abemama (27.4 sq km), North Tabiteuea (25.8 sq km), Arorae (9.5 sq km), Banaba (Ocean Island, 6.3 sq km), Kanton (9.2 sq km), Makin (7.9 sq km), Tereina (Washington, 9.6 sq km); and Abaiang, Aranuka, Beru, Birnie, Butaritari, Caroline, Enderbury, Flint, Kuria, MALDEN, Orona, Maiana, Manra, Marakei, McKean, Nikumaroro, Nonouti, North Tarawa, Onotoa, Rawaki, South Tabiteuea, Starbuck, Tamana and Vostok.
Sea area (EEZ): 3 550 000 sq km.
Population: 88 550 (1999 SPC estimate). The i-Kiribati (pronounced 'ee-Kiribas') are of Micronesian stock; there is a small percentage of Tuvaluans, Europeans, and others.
Official language: English; and a Micronesian dialect is widely used.
Adult literacy: 93 per cent (1994).
Currency: Australian dollar.
Time: +1200 hours UTC. Kiribati crosses the international date line.
National day: 12 July.
GDP per capita: A$527 (1990).
Principal export earnings: Copra; tuna fish; commercial fishing rights.
Political system: Kiribati has a 41-member house of parliament (Maneaba ni Maungatabu) which elects a president (Beretitenti) for a four-year term.
Physical environment: Kiribati comprises three island groups, the Gilbert, Phoenix and Line Islands, which lie across the equator (between latitude 4° north and 11° south, and longitude 169° east and 150° west). Apart from Banaba, which rises to 80 m above sea level, the islands are all low-lying coral atolls of about 3–5 m elevation, many of them enclosing a central lagoon. The thin layer of sandy coral soil supports only sparse vegetation (predominantly COCONUT and pandanus), and there are no rivers. Breadfruit, paw paws and a kind of root crop known as *babai* (*cyrto-sperma chamissonis*) are grown on most islands. SUBSISTENCE FISHING plays a major part in the islanders' diet. The tropical climate is tempered by northeasterly trade winds from March to October, but the wet season (November–February) is hot and humid. Long periods of DROUGHT affect Banaba in particular. Annual rain-

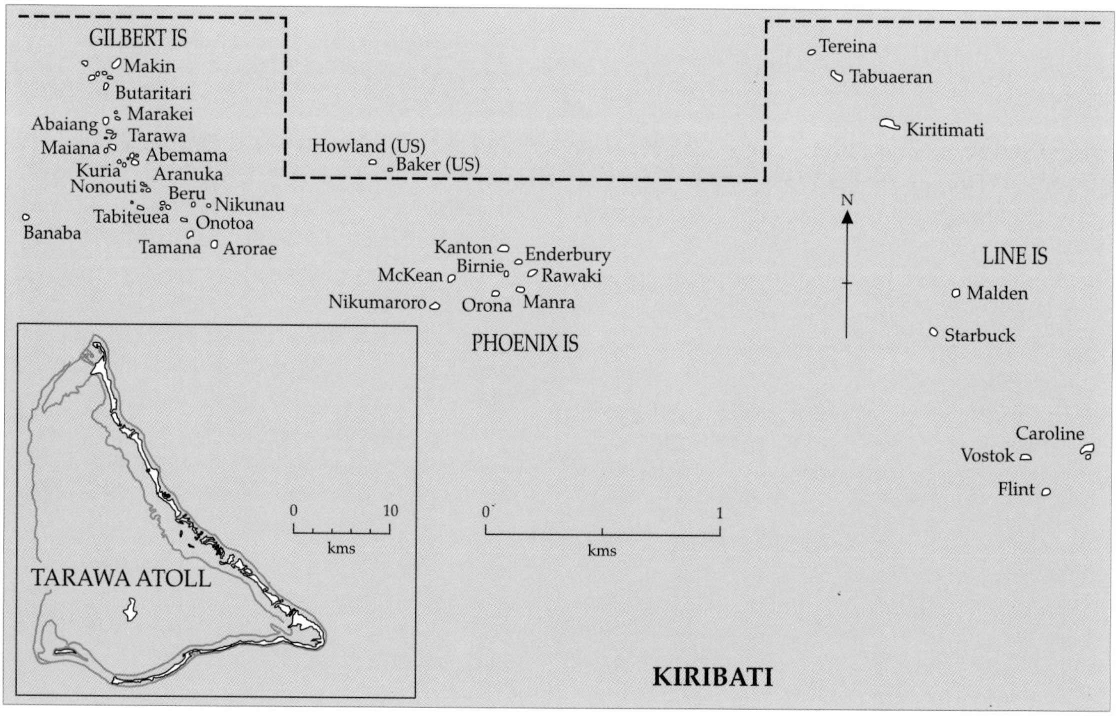

fall: varies from group to group; from 200 mm in some years for Banaba, less than 1000 mm regularly for the southern islands, about 1500 mm for South Tarawa, and up to 3000 mm for the far north islands.

History: Archaeological evidence raises the possibility that early settlement of the islands by Austronesian speaking migrants predates the arrival of Micronesian peoples about 2000 years ago (see FOOTSTEPS FROM ASIA). Gilbertese oral histories record Samoan settlement prior to their own arrival, and subsequent arrivals from Fiji and Tonga some 700 years ago. Whatever the mix and timing, the population intermarried and had merged into a unity of tradition and social order by the time that Spanish explorers first came in the 16th century. From the visit of Quirós to the northern group in 1606, there was a series of European arrivals: the British expeditions—John Byron in 1765, James COOK at Christmas Island on Christmas eve, 1777, Thomas Gilbert and John Marshall in 1788; the American, Nathaniel Fanning, in 1798; the Russian hydrographer Krusenstern in the 1820s. By 1826, all three groups of islands had been named and charted.

From this time until about 1870, WHALING ships made regular passage through the rich fishing grounds, BEACHCOMBERS came to stay in the islands, and trading vessels began calling from about 1850, in search of COPRA AND COCONUT OIL, and the copra attracted several foreign companies in the 1880s, including JALUIT GESELLSCHAFT. From the 1860s the visitors included recruiters for the PERUVIAN SLAVE TRADE, and also BLACKBIRDERS seeking labour for plantation work in Hawai'i, Fiji, Queensland and other parts of the Pacific. The American Protestant missionary Hiram BINGHAM established a mission on Abaiang in 1857, and from there, Hawaiian PASTORS spread the gospel throughout the northern islands. Samoan pastors from the LONDON MISSIONARY SOCIETY came from the Ellice Islands to Arorae, Tamana, Onotoa and Beru. In the south, Catholic priests of the Sacred Heart order established a base on Nonouti in 1888.

British jurisdiction over the Gilbert and Ellice Islands was set in train by the creation of the WESTERN PACIFIC HIGH COMMISSION in 1877. In 1892 a British protectorate was proclaimed, a move directed against US trading interests rather than German, and headquarters were established at Tarawa in 1896. Banaba (Ocean Island) was annexed to the protectorate in 1900, and within seven years, as the value of its PHOSPHATE mining escalated—Banaba also became the administrative headquarters. Its protectorate status changed to a colony in 1916, and Tabuaeran and Teraina (Fanning and Washington) were added, together with the Tokelau Islands, also a former protectorate. Kiritimati was incorporated into the colony in 1919. The Tokelau Islands were handed over to New Zealand in 1925, and the colony gained the uninhabited Phoenix Islands in 1937. Britain agreed to share jurisdiction of two of the Phoenix group, Kanton and Enderbury, with the United States in 1939 because of their strategic location for AVIATION in the Pacific.

Just two days after the attack on PEARL HARBOR, Japanese forces bombed Banaba and landed marines on Tarawa and Butaritari. Tarawa became a significant centre of fighting in the Second World War, and the interactions between American servicemen and islanders brought the beginnings of significant social change (ISLANDER EXPERIENCES IN THE PACIFIC WAR). The Japanese were driven out by American forces in November 1943, and surrendered on Banaba in 1945.

In the post-war period, the system of island COOPERATIVES was strengthened so that foreign trading companies (forced to leave the islands during the war) found it unprofitable to return. Islanders began to achieve greater participation in government, and nominated representatives attended a series of annual conferences from 1956 to 1962, to plan the colony's future directions. An executive council was set up in 1963, with an advisory council to provide islanders with an active role.

In 1972, a formal separation of the Gilbert and Ellice islands colonies from the Western Pacific High Commission occurred, and the resident commissioner, Sir John Field, became governor. Malden and the other southern Line Islands were included in the colonies in late 1972. A ministerial form of government was introduced in 1974, providing for an elected house of assembly and a chief minister. The legal separation of the Gilbert Islands from the Ellice Islands (now TUVALU) then took place on 1 October 1975. The country became fully self-governing from 1 January 1977. Kiribati became an independent republic on 12 July 1979, with Ieremia TABAI as its president and head of state.

Banabans who had left their war-ravaged island to settle in Fiji (numbering about 1000) were opposed to the idea of their incorporation in the new republic, but were unable to negotiate secession from Kiribati. Although mining on Banaba ended in 1979, most Banabans remained in Fiji, and the Kiribati constitution gives special privileges to them, ensuring them of Kiribati citizenship, and providing for representation in parliament, the return of land acquired for phosphate mining, and their right to return and live on their island.

In September 1979 Kiribati signed a treaty of friendship with the United States, which provided for joint administration of Kanton Island, together with the relinquishing of US claims (under the GUANO ACT of 1856) to 14 of the Line and Phoenix islands. This was finally ratified by the US senate on 21 June 1983. In the mid 1980s Kiribati reached an agreement with the Soviet Union on fishing rights, but this was not renewed at the end of the one-year term. However, a number of more recent fishing access agreements have been negotiated with foreign countries (see FISHERIES) and these fees now account for 45 per cent of revenue for Kiribati.—KRF

Further reading

Fairbairn, Te'o I, 1992. *The Kiribati Economy: development options and prospects for economic growth*, Australian Government Publishing Service.

KIRITIMATI (CHRISTMAS ISLAND)

Constitutional status: Part of the Republic of Kiribati.

Main settlement: London (population 1014).

Population: 2537 (1990 census).

Physical environment: Kiritimati is a slightly raised atoll in the Northern Line Islands of eastern Kiribati (between latitude 1–2° north and longitude 157° west). It is 3240 km east of Tarawa, and 2150 km south of Honolulu. Shaped like a lobster claw with the jaws opening to the northwest, it is the largest coral atoll in the world, measuring about 56 km from northwest to southeast, and 39 km from southwest to northeast. Of its total area (640 sq km), 321 sq km are land, the rest being a large semi-circular lagoon and more than 100 large and small saline lakes and interconnecting channels. EL NIÑO weather patterns are likely to result in increased rainfall. Daily temperatures range between 24–30°C, with average relative humidity of 70 per cent. Winds are more or less constantly easterly at about 14 km/hour. Annual rainfall: 873 mm, ranging from 300 to 1800 mm, with drought years expected in 5 of every 20 years.

The limited availability of fresh water restricts settlement, agriculture and development. It varies from one part of the island to another but is more abundant in the north. The land is generally flat and about 3–4 m above sea level, the highest point rising to about 12 m on the central east coast. A fringing reef up to several hundred metres wide surrounds the island. Soils, composed of fragments of shells, corals and other marine animals, contain little organic matter. They include coral sands, gravel and rubble, and lagoon mud, with many calcareous patches. The vegetation is hardy and often sparse, without much variety. Four plant associations are found: coconut plantations, high shrub, low shrub, and grass/herb. The indigenous flora consists largely of common Pacific strand and coral island species, but marine and bird life is abundant. There are large quantities of SKIPJACK TUNA, yellowfin and bigeye, billfish and pelagic SHARKS. The reefs contain deep bottom fish, shallow water reef fish, off-reef PELAGIC FISH and tropical (aquarium) species, and the lagoons have fish, lobster and BÊCHE-DE-MER. The bird life is of international significance. There are 18 species of MARINE BIRDS (including sooty terns, shearwaters, boobies and FRIGATE-BIRDS) that breed in numbers greater than six million, representing the highest species diversity of nesting seabirds and the largest number for any oceanic island in the world.

History: At some time in the past Polynesians lived on Kiritimati, leaving evidence of their occupation in the presence of coconut trees, raised rectangular platforms and curbed coral enclosures (possibly religious *maraes*), possible bases of raised graves, and tools, including a basaltic adze and shell tools. The settlements were not viable, and by the time of European contact the islands were uninhabited. In 1537 the crew of a ship of a Spanish expedition led by Hernando de Grijalva in the eastern Pacific sighted Christmas Island but did not land. Captain COOK on his third voyage was the first European to land, arriving from the southwest with the *Resolution* and *Discovery* on 24 December 1777. He stayed for nine days to observe an eclipse of the sun from the small island at the lagoon entrance now known as Cook Island. He celebrated Christmas there, and named the atoll in honour of the date. (The name is transliterated in the Kiribati language as Kiritimati.) He described the island as low, barren and waterless, but with abundant fish, TURTLES and birds.

From the 1830s to the 1860s numerous American, British, Chilean, Danish and German WHALING and trading vessels were wrecked in the broad bay on the eastern side of the island now named the Bay of Wrecks. Captains complained that the island was wrongly located on their charts. Small GUANO deposits were found in the 1850s, and in 1857 an American, Captain J L Pendleton of the *John Marshall* claimed the island under the US GUANO ACT of 1856. The deposits were worked by the American Guano Company for several years after 1858. About 1872 an American naval vessel USS *Narrangansett* visited, and formally took possession for the United

States. Pearl shell was harvested commercially from the lagoon between about 1884 and 1924.

Despite the American claim and a formal protest, Captain Sir William Wiseman of HMS *Caroline* formally annexed Christmas Island for Great Britain in 1882 (on the basis of prior discovery by Captain Cook). In 1919 it was included in the Gilbert and Ellice Islands Colony. These conflicting claims gave rise to diplomatic tensions in 1936, when the United States, looking for mid-Pacific bases for air services, challenged the British claim. In 1937 Britain sent a warship to Christmas Island, and placed an official British representative on the island to maintain a daily radio weather service.

From 1880 large coconut plantings, located on the northern and southern arms of land surrounding the main lagoon and corresponding closely with the extent of better soils and the underground fresh water table, were developed by British interests, including LEVER BROTHERS. After several ownership changes the plantation became the property of Central Pacific Cocoanut Plantations Ltd with a French Catholic priest, Father Rougier, the principal director from 1914 until his death in 1934. Although infertile sandy soil, unreliable rainfall and droughts, and labour shortage may have reduced productivity, the PLANTATIONS have been the enduring source of income for the island for over a century. Labour was originally brought from Tahiti and later from the Gilbert Islands, but the population remained very small. The settlements of London, Poland and Paris were established to serve the plantation, and temporary camps were also used for the collection and processing of COPRA. An earth road system gave internal access and linked the plantation settlements.

Annual copra production fluctuated widely, influenced by the world price of copra, and rainfall, among other factors. In the mid 1930s production was estimated to be about 500 tons per annum, and in the 1980s about 740 tonnes per annum. After Father Rougier's death his nephew took over the plantation but abandoned it during the 1930s Depression. After World War II the government of the Gilbert and Ellice Islands Colony purchased the lease and operated the plantation as Christmas Island Plantations. This was later corporatized as Atoll Plantations Ltd, but it collapsed financially in 1981. The government then established the Kiritimati Copra Scheme which licensed individuals to cut copra under specified conditions on government-owned land. The scheme was abandoned in 1991 because of substantial losses. Without regulations, there has been little organized maintenance or re-planting, and the industry is in decline.

During World War II expatriate staff were withdrawn, but the island was not occupied by the Japanese. It was garrisoned by both American and New Zealand troops (the latter leaving the legacy of an abandoned airfield on the western side of the island known as New Zealand Airfield), and provided a stopping place on the air route from Honolulu to the American base at Bora Bora. For a brief period after the war Christmas Island was a stop on a trans-Pacific service by FLYING BOATS between New Zealand and Hawai'i, resulting in the building of a protective mole on the west side of the lagoon and a hotel near Paris, but this service was short-lived, and the hotel later burnt down.

In 1957–58 the island was used as a testing ground for atmospheric H-bombs by Britain and in 1962 by the United States of America. NUCLEAR TESTING stimulated a burst of construction, resulting in two large airfields (Cassidy Airfield and an undeveloped back-up airfield in the far southeast), an extensive road network, sealed between London and Banana, and port facilities at London. In more recent years concern developed over the radioactivity that may have remained from the atmospheric tests, and a clean-up operation was undertaken. Unfortunately, although some islanders were temporarily evacuated, not all island residents nor British military personnel were adequately protected from fall-out. In recent years deaths from cancer and other health impacts attributed to radioactivity from the tests have occurred.

Port Camp, northwest coast, Kiritimati (Christmas Island), site of seaweed farming.

In the 1970s, several new enterprises were undertaken, but they include several failures: a salt processing industry based on solar evaporation that suffered from poor transport links; a brine shrimp industry; and a deep-sea game fishing operation.

More successful, as long as air transport is functioning, has been the raising of milkfish in interior lagoons for export to Hawai'i. A Japanese satellite tracking station (established in the early 1990s), the development of sport fishing in the lagoons and reefs, and the collection and export of aquarium fish from the reefs are all surviving, but dependent on air connections to Honolulu.

In the four widely separated settlements of London, Banana and Poland, housing is provided for government employees, and in Tabakea, private housing is allowed on leasehold land. This has resulted in Tabakea having higher numbers of persons per household, and more cultivation of useful trees, babai pits, and domestic livestock. It has a character of self-reliance and permanency lacking in the other settlements.

Although Kiritimati has an image of being a desirable place of retirement in Kiribati, the population is relatively youthful, with greater numbers of males between 20–29, and a relative lack of old people compared with the rest of Kiribati. Opportunities for employment are limited, not least by the isolation, and poor sea and air transport services. A comprehensive development study in 1993 suggested that the main potential for future development lies in greater use of marine resources (particularly export of tropical fish, fresh or chilled fish and/or marine products, and lagoon products); gradual increase in TOURISM (based on sports fishing, and ecotourism related to the birdlife of the island); commercial production of pig meat; handicrafts; scientific research; and service industries.—MWW

Further reading

Buck, P H, 1938. *Vikings of the Sunrise*, Frederick A Stokes Company.

Macdonald, B, 1982. *Cinderellas of the Empire*, Australian National University Press.

Ward, R G (ed.), 1967. *American Activities in the Central Pacific, 1790-1870*, vol. 2, The Gregg Press.

MALDEN ISLAND

An unoccupied, barren, raised coral island in the Line Islands (KIRIBATI), 2600 km south of Hawai'i and 3200 km east of Tarawa, Malden Island lies on a reef (6 km by 8 km) enclosing a central depression or lagoon. Ruined *marae* indicate the presence of a small community, believed to be Polynesians migrating from COOK ISLANDS. It was uninhabited when first mapped in 1825 by Commodore John Byron, captain of the HMS *Blonde*, who named it after his surveyor. Between 1860 and 1927 the low-lying central plateau was mined for GUANO using a work force of a hundred or more Cook Islanders and Niueans. In 1956–57 it was used as a support base for the British atomic test 'Operation Grapple'. (See NUCLEAR TESTING.) Plantation leases for COPRA have been short-lived and unsuccessful.—MQ

MARSHALL ISLANDS

Constitutional status: Independent republic.

Head of State: President.

Head of Government: President Imata Kabua (1998).

Main towns: MAJURO (capital; population c20 000), EBEYE (on Kwajalein), Jaluit, Wotje.

Land area: 181 sq km (29 atolls, 5 small islands, and more than 800 reefs): Majuro (9.2 sq km), Arno, Mili, Ailinglapalap, Likiep, Kwajalein, Rongelap, Bikini, Enewetak, Maloelap, Jaluit, Ebon, Roi-Namur, Taongi; islands: Jabwot, Jemo, Kili, Lib, Mejit.

Sea area (EEZ): 2 131 000 sq km.

Population: 63 225 (1999 SPC estimate). Marshallese are Micronesians, probably with distant links to Caroline Islanders.

Official language: Marshallese, but English and several local dialects are spoken.

Literacy: 91 per cent (1994).

Currency: US dollar.

Time: +1200 hours UTC.

National day: 1 May.

GDP per capita: A$1995 (1991).

Principal export earnings: Coconut oil; copra.

Political system: A legislature of 33 members, elected every four years, is known as the *Nitijela*. Members elect a president as both head of state and head of government, who appoints ministers to a cabinet. There is also an advisory Council of Chiefs (*Iroij*) of 12 members for matters relating to land and custom. There are no provinces or states, but each of the 24 inhabited atolls has a local government, including an elected mayor and council for Majuro Atoll.

Physical environment: The Marshall Islands are low-lying coral atolls (scattered between latitude 5-15° north and longitude 162–173° east over 1.2 million sq km of the central Pacific), forming the easternmost group of the Micronesian archipelagos. The 34 islands form a double chain, known as the Ratak (Sunrise) Chain and, approximately 210 km to the west, the Ralik (Sunset) Chain. Some atolls enclose very large lagoons, particularly Kwajalein, with its 90 islets and enormous lagoon covering a total surface area of 2335 sq km. Most of the five islands without lagoons are less than 1 sq km in area. The highest point in the whole archipelago is on Likiep,

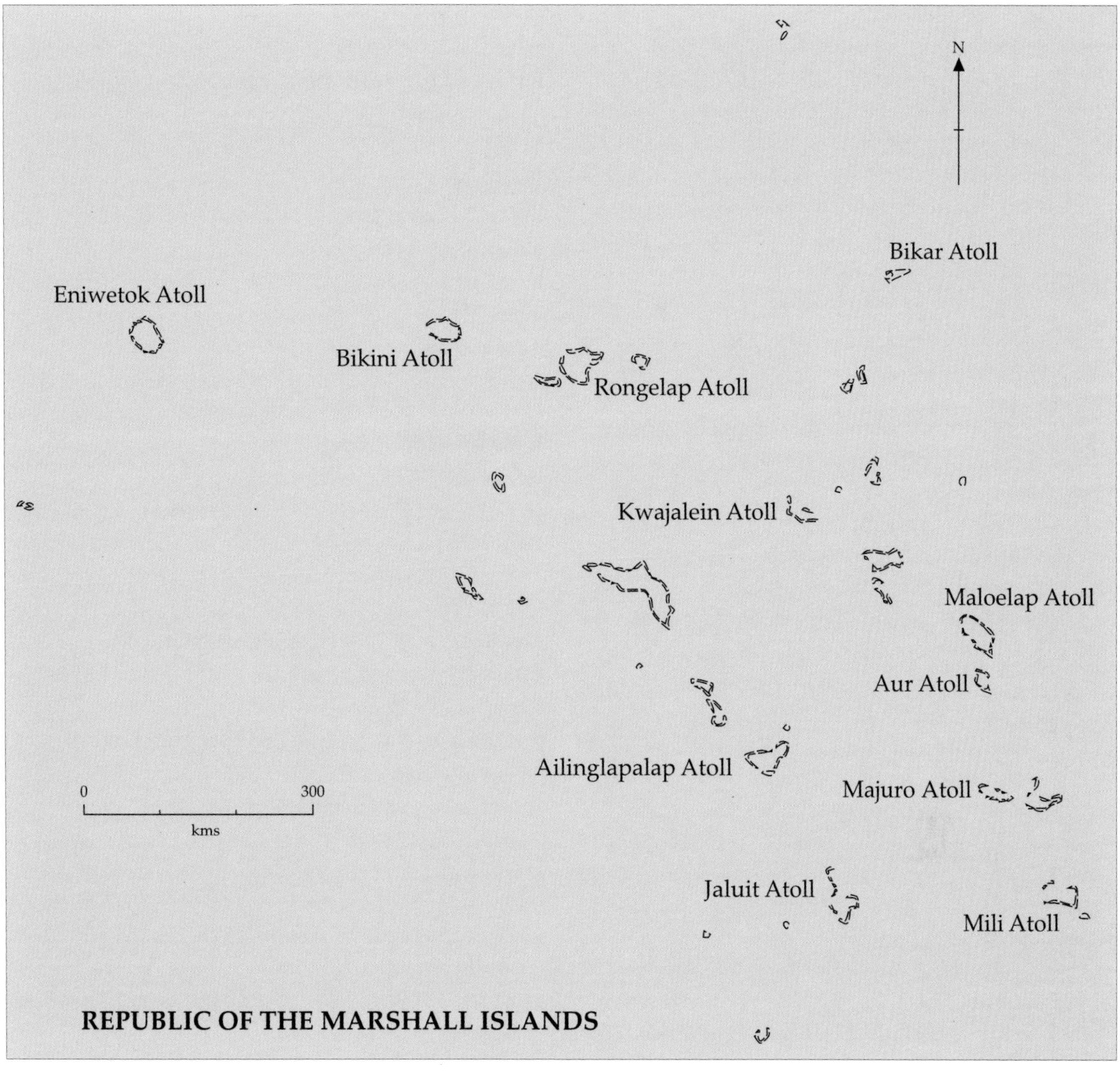

10 m above sea level. Vegetation is low and sparse, apart from coconut palms and pandanus. Breadfruit, bananas, paw paws and avocados grow widely. The seas and lagoons have abundant fish and marine life, and shore birds are common. There are several species of lizards and skinks. The climate is hot and humid, with little seasonal variation, and the prevailing trade winds are northeasterly. Annual rainfall: 2000 mm in the northern islands, ranging to 4000 mm at Jaluit in the south.

History: First settlement of the islands was probably 2000 years ago, probably from central Melanesia (see FOOTSTEPS FROM ASIA). Marshall Islanders were skilled navigators and sailors, and their ocean voyages crossed the region as far as Kosrae. Prior to European contact, traditional society was organized under chiefly rule with the two island chains each dominated by a paramount chief (see TRADITIONAL LEADERSHIP IN MICRONESIA).

Early Spanish exploration brought visitors such as Alvaro Saavedra, who visited the group in 1529, and there were several other arrivals, some of whom joined the list of LOST SHIPS, up until 1568. From this time the islands remained in virtual isolation for about 200 years until Samuel WALLIS passed by in 1767. In 1788 another British sea captain, John Marshall, undertook an exploratory voyage, giving the islands his name. Most of the mapping of the archipelago was carried out by Russian expeditions: Johann Krusenstern in 1803, and Otto von Kotzebue in 1817 and 1823. Kutzebue named the Ratak and Ralik groups, and left a comprehensive report of his voyages. From the 1820s, American WHALING vessels called in for supplies, and from the 1860s, American Protestant missionaries, sent by the AMERICAN BOARD OF COMMISSIONERS FOR FOREIGN MISSIONS, settled PASTORS in the islands.

After German companies began to establish trading operations in the region, Germany negotiated a treaty for a supply station on Jaluit, and followed up with annexation of the islands in 1884. Since then, the Marshallese population has been much influenced by successive periods of German, Japanese and American colonialism. GERMAN COLONIAL ADMINISTRATION of the protectorate was not repressive, and their headquarters were set up in Rabaul (Papua New Guinea) in 1906, ruling from a distance up until the outbreak of war in 1914. Japanese forces then seized the Marshall Islands, and their occupation continued after 1919, when they were given a League of Nations mandate to administer the group as a separate district. JAPANESE COMMERCIAL INTERESTS brought extensive economic development to Micronesia, but in the Marshall Islands this was mainly concerned with strict regulations for the pricing and exporting of COPRA. Fortification and infrastructure developments were put in place, and these military facilities were used when Japan launched an invasion of Nauru, Banaba and Kiribati at the start of the Pacific War.

During the subsequent fighting, the Allied forces gradually made headway from 1942, and were able to recapture Kwajalein after a major battle in 1943, involving massive artillery barrage. The American occupation became military administration after the war, until the Marshall Islands became part of the US Trust Territory of the Pacific Islands in July 1947. From 1946, BIKINI ATOLL had been used for atomic bomb tests, and in the 1950s American involvement in NUCLEAR TESTING included the development of both Bikini and Enewetak as testing sites. Both atolls were later extensively redeveloped and prepared for attempted resettlement, and since 1986, further spending of millions of dollars in capital improvement and infrastructure development has been provided.

Marshall Islands became a parliamentary democracy in 1979, with a ratified constitution which provides for the Council of Iroij of 12 paramount chiefs. (See MICRONESIAN LEADERSHIP AFTER WORLD WAR II.) In 1982, the Compact of Free Association between the United States and the Republic of the Marshall Islands was signed. It was finally declared operative in November 1986, following a decade of discussions and negotiations with the United States, and gives the United States long-term effective control over a range of issues such as defence and the use of the missile-testing base at Kwajalein. The founding president, Amata KABUA, brought the country into the South Pacific Commission (now PACIFIC COMMUNITY) in 1983, and membership of the SOUTH PACIFIC FORUM in the late 1980s.—KRF

Further reading

Hezel, F X, 1983. *The First Taint of Civilization: a history of the Caroline and Marshall islands in pre-colonial days, 1521–1885*, University of Hawai'i Press.

NAURU

Constitutional status: Independent republic.
Head of State: President.
Head of Government: President Rene Harris (April 1999).
Administrative centre: In Aiwo–Yaren District, on western side of Nauru (there is no designated capital).
Land area: 22 sq km.
Sea area (EEZ): 320 000 sq km.
Population: 11 360 (1999 SPC estimate).
Official languages: Nauruan (a Micronesian language) is commonly used but English is the language of government and of school instruction.
Adult literacy: 90 per cent (1994).
Currency: Australian dollar.
Time: +1200 hours UTC.
National day: 31 January (Independence Day).
GDP per capita: A$22 415 (1989).
Principal export earnings: PHOSPHATE.
Political system: A parliament of 18 members (elected from a common roll to represent Nauru's districts for a three-year term) in turn elects the president of the republic. The president chooses three or four other members to form a cabinet, which has full executive powers. The president is also head of state.

The Local Government Council, with 9 members each representing one of the districts of Nauru, elects one of its members to be head chief. Funded through phosphate royalties, the Nauru Local Government Council has a number of significant responsibilities, thus effectively creating a two-tier system of government.

Physical environment: Nauru is a single island in the southern Pacific Ocean, 306 km west of Kiribati—latitude 0.31° south and longitude 167° east. It is an uplifted coral limestone atoll, about 4 km across and 5 km in length, with a terraced rim containing caves and sinkholes. Further inland the central plateau, of phosphate-bearing rock, is about 30 m above sea level. A coral reef surrounds the coast. Soils are thin and calcareous. Coastal vegetation is low shrub, grasses, herbs and coconut palms, with pandanus on the shoreline. The barren interior plateau (which contains a single small lagoon) has extensive deposits of phosphate. The climate is warm and relatively humid. Light easterly trade

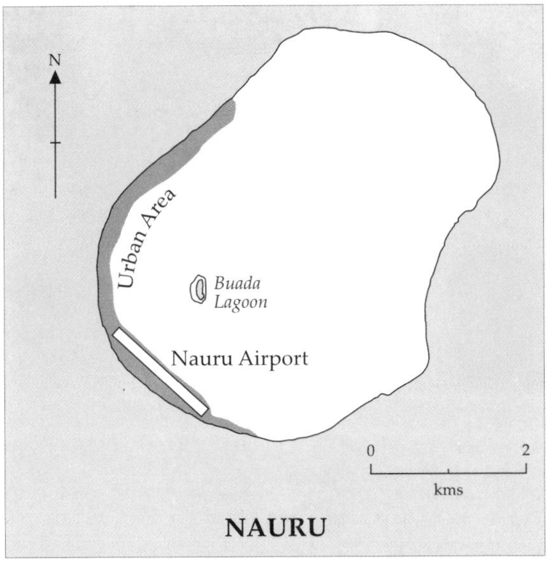

winds blow almost all year round, with occasional squalls occurring in the wet season between November and February. Annual rainfall: 1900 mm.

History: The Nauruan language, a unique Micronesian blend of elements of languages of the Gilbert, Caroline, Marshall and Solomon Islands, suggests that the original inhabitants may have come many centuries ago from various locations, possibly even as castaways. The first reported European sighting was by Captain John Fearn of the British ship *Hunter*, in 1798, who named the atoll Pleasant Island. From the 1830s there were visits from whaling ships seeking water and fresh food supplies, and a number of BEACHCOMBERS began to arrive.

German traders on the island in the mid 19th century began to agitate for the protection of the German government, and in October 1888, a German gunboat, the *Eber*, brought an imperial commissioner who raised the German flag, took formal control and immediately took steps to deal with the problem of firearms among islanders. One of the German traders was placed in charge of administration, a policy which continued until 1905.

PASTORS from the Gilbert Islands had been working in the community for some time when the first European Protestant missionary arrived in 1899, the Rev P A Delaporte, who quickly established a position of influence. He was followed in 1902 by a German Catholic missionary, Father Grundl, and both men made a substantial contribution to the work of transcribing the Nauruan language.

A representative of the Pacific Islands Company, involved in trading and plantations as well as GUANO, visited Nauru in 1898 and took back with him to Sydney some samples of what seemed to be a fossilised tree. This was subsequently identified as a rich phosphate-bearing rock, and the company launched negotiations with JALUIT GESELLSCHAFT to reach an agreement to mine Nauru's extensive deposits. The company also went to investigate the neighbouring Ocean Island (now known as Banaba) and—having found that it also offered high quality phosphatic rock—were able to persuade two chiefs to grant mining rights for a 999-year term at £50 per year.

The company—which became the Pacific Phosphate Company—began mining on Ocean Island and also reached an agreement with Jaluit Gesellschaft and the German government in 1906 to commence operations on Nauru, sending 11 630 tons of phosphate to Australia in its first year. Gilbert Islanders and Chinese were brought in as labourers and the output increased to about 100 000 tons per year. During the First World War, the Germans placed Nauru under martial law but an Australian force, sent from Rabaul, was able to take over administration in November 1914 and return the British residents who had been taken to Ocean Island. The Australian garrison remained, allowing phosphate mining to continue, until 1919 when the League of Nations placed the island under the joint mandate of Britain, Australia and New Zealand, and permitted an Australian civil administration to be installed under General T Griffiths.

From this time the British Phosphate Commission (BPC)—a board representing the three mandated governments—took over the phosphate industry on both Ocean Island and Nauru, purchasing the rights from the Pacific Phosphate Company and beginning royalty payments to Nauruans who held claims to the land being mined. The payment of royalties was soon revised and increased to cover an additional allocation for the benefit of all Nauruans and a fixed compensation rate for future land acquisitions.

In the Second World War Nauru was attacked by two German ships in 1940. They sank five phosphate-loading vessels and damaged some of the loading equipment, although mining was able to continue. At the end of 1941 Japanese planes bombed the island and most of the European residents were evacuated to safety. The Japanese took over the island in August 1942 and built an airstrip for the use of their bombers. They sent away 1200 Nauruans to work as labourers in Truk (now Chuuk), and executed the last remaining Europeans after an American bombing raid in March 1943. American raids continued over the next two years, so that the Japanese were unable to export any phosphate, and finally Australian forces recaptured

Nauru in September 1945. Those Nauruans who had survived were repatriated at the start of 1946, although the death toll in captivity—through starvation, physical abuse and disease—was about 500.

In November 1947 Nauru became a United Nations Trust Territory, officially in the joint care of Britain, Australia and New Zealand once more, but again to be administered by Australia. The BPC reestablished the phosphate industry and soon annual exports were in excess of a million tons. In the early 1950s the Nauru Local Government Council was formed, providing a base for the political aspirations of Chief Hammer DeROBURT who emerged as a voice for local autonomy. Proposals for resettlement on other islands were decisively rejected and the Nauruans then successfully negotiated substantial increases in royalty payments and the granting of a large measure of self-government through the establishment of the first legislative council in 1966. Full independence was achieved on 31 January 1968, with Hammer DeRoburt elected as president of the new republic, and in 1970 the BPC ended its control of the phosphate industry.

During the 1980s the thorny issue of the rehabilitation of mined land created considerable debate and discontent. Protracted discussions were held with the three governments behind the British Phosphate Commission, and Nauru prepared its case for the International Court of Justice. In 1993 Australia announced the outcome of a negotiated settlement—a compensation payment of A$107 million for Nauru—and in April 1994 Britain and New Zealand agreed to repay a share of this compensation, A$10 million each, to Australia.

After the death in office of Hammer DeRoburt in 1992, Bernard DOWIYOGO was elected president until 1996. Kinza Clodumar then held office from 1996 but was defeated in a no-confidence motion in June 1998. Dowiyogo, by now the longest-serving member of parliament in Nauru, served a fifth term as president, but he was replaced in April 1999 by Rene Harris, following a no-confidence vote. Clodumar remains finance minister.—KRF

Further reading

Petit-Skinner, S, 1981. *The Nauruans*, MacDuff Press.

NEW CALEDONIA

Constitutional status: Overseas Territory of France.

Head of State: President of France represented by High Commissioner, Dominique Bur.

Head of Government: Dominique Bur (1998).

Capital: NOUMEA (on southwest coast of Grande Terre; population c62 000).

Easter church service, New Caledonia, 1998

Land area: 19 103 sq km: Grande Terre (16 890 sq km), Ouvea, Mare, Lifou, Tiga, Belep islands, Isle of Pines.

Sea area (EEZ): 1 740 000 sq km.

Population: 212 800 (1999 SPC estimate); Melanesian (43 per cent); European (37 per cent); Wallisians, Tahitians, Vietnamese, Indonesians.

Official language: French, but several Melanesian languages and dialects are spoken; see KANAK LANGUAGES OF NEW CALEDONIA.

Currency: CFP (French Pacific franc).

Time: +1100 hours UTC.

National day: 14 July.

GNP per capita: cUS$4000.

Principal export earnings: NICKEL MINING; smelting; tourism.

Political system: New Caledonia is represented in France's national assembly by two elected deputies (Jacques LAFLEUR and Pierre Frogier in 1998), and a senator in the French parliament (Simon Loueckhote in 1998). A territorial assembly with 25 seats and a government council of 5 ministers, created in 1953, was then abolished in March 1962. Since then, it has been reduced to consultative status only. In 1997, the President of the Territorial Congress was Harold Martin. The provincial assemblies are headed by elected presidents: Nidoish NAISSELINE (Loyalty Islands); Jacques Lafleur (South); and Léopold Jorédié (North).

Physical environment: New Caledonia's islands, located between latitude 19–23° south and longitude 163–168° east, have a complex geological past which has produced ancient volcanic rock formations. Grande Terre is essentially a strongly eroded mountain range, with the main peaks, Mt Humboldt and Mt Panie, rising to over 1600 m. The island has a wet eastern coast (with abundant patches of rainforest) and a wide coastal plain with sparse savannah vegetation on the drier western side. The island's shallow stony soils have little ability to retain water. There is a high proportion of endemic vegetation, including mostly drought-resistant plants. Predominant trees are the Araucaria pine and the *niaouli* or cajeput tree (*Melaleuca quinquenervia*), which has silvery white foliage and thick, corky bark. The LOYALTY ISLANDS are uplifted coral atolls, mainly open forest and grassland, with coconut palms along the coasts, and there are no rivers.

Only about 10 per cent of the land area is cultivable. Bananas, pandanus, sugarcane, papaya, pines, banyans and hardwood grow inland. New Caledonia has an equable tropical climate with little seasonal variation, although extremes are experienced on exposed parts of the Loyalty Islands. Southwest trade winds prevail, and tropical CYCLONES are common. Droughts occur, especially on the west coast and in the Loyalty Islands. Annual rainfall: varies, with about 2000 mm in the east and southeast, and only about 1000 mm on the western coast. Noumea is in the dry region.

History: The first settlements of Kanaks, the indigenous Melanesian people of New Caledonia, possibly date back 6000 years, with probable migrations from New Guinea and Vanuatu. These complex patterns of settlement produced isolated communities, separated by the rugged mountain terrain, and disparate language groups, with later Polynesian migration to the Loyalty Islands adding to the linguistic and cultural diversity. Kanak traditional society was based on an agricultural economy, in which the cultivation of the yam played a significant symbolic and social function. Inter-tribal rivalries led to occasional warfare, and some groups practised cannibalism. Prior to European contact, the population is estimated at 60 000.

Captain James COOK landed in the north of Grande Terre in 1774 and named it New Caledonia, before visiting and naming the Isle of Pines. Explorers and traders became more frequent in the first part of the 19th century, in search of whales (see WHALING), SANDALWOOD and BÊCHE-DE-MER. Missionaries soon followed—Protestant PASTORS of

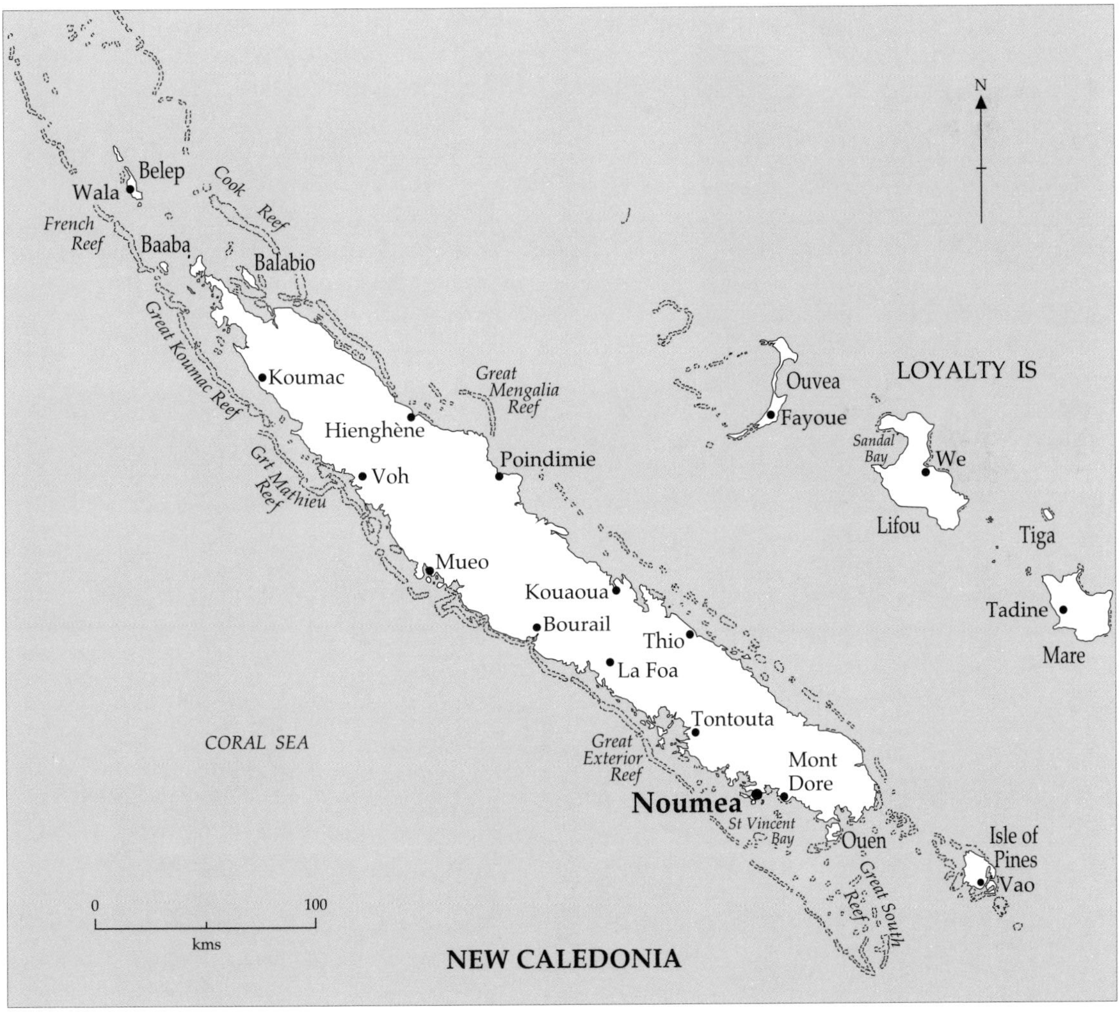

the LONDON MISSIONARY SOCIETY around 1840, and Catholic Marist priests in 1846 (see FRENCH MISSIONS IN THE PACIFIC). On 24 September 1853 New Caledonia was officially annexed by France, preempting British interest, and a military regime was established which continued until 1884. The island was designated a penal colony in 1863, and until this was abolished by the first civil governor, Feuillet, in 1896, 20 000 convicts were sent out from France. After this, settlers were encouraged and extensive cattle farming occurred. Kanaks, who by decree were not protected by French common law, were limited to three hectares of land per person (see LAND ALIENATION IN NEW CALEDONIA), and the colonial administration tended to leave their education and social welfare in the hands of the Christian missions. The French steadily appropriated the most fertile land areas, and there was a major uprising of the indigenous population (KANAK REBELLION) in 1878–79, during which whole settlements of French colonists were massacred. In the fierce reprisals which followed, Melanesian villages were destroyed and the people were confined to reserves. A second revolt occurred in 1917, protesting against harsh wartime recruitment, further land alienations, and extensive crop damage caused by roaming cattle, but it too was quickly and brutally suppressed by the colonial administration.

Gold, chrome, cobalt and nickel were discovered and mined from the 1870s, and by the 1890s, New Caledonia was the world's major supplier of nickel ore. In World War II, New Caledonia's strategic importance in the Pacific (due to its geographic location and rich mineral resources) brought thousands of US troops to build airstrips and set up their South Pacific headquarters. Soon after the war, France enacted several social and political reforms. Kanaks were allowed to leave their reserves in 1946, and in 1951 voting rights were granted and secondary education was offered for the first time.

From the 1950s Kanaks began to organize politically, first demanding land reform and local autonomy but making little headway. The referendum on independence in 1958 contained an implicit threat of withdrawal of French aid, and a large majority voted in favour of continued territorial status. During the nickel boom of the early 1970s the European population grew rapidly, and the movement for Kanak independence was launched, drawing steady support as all other Melanesian countries achieved autonomy, but continuing to face strong opposition in France and among the European community. (See NATIONALISM IN FRENCH TERRITORIES.) The escalating violence of the 1980s was finally halted by the compromise—crafted through the efforts of French Prime Minister Michel Rocard, Jean-Marie TJIBAOU, and Jacques Lafleur—achieved in the signing of the MATIGNON ACCORDS of 1988. Setting a framework for constitutional reform that has been confirmed in the 1998 NOUMEA ACCORD, the process includes provisions for education, training, business and social service projects to assist the Kanak minority, and has laid down a path towards self-determination and independence for New Caledonia in 15–20 years' time.—KRF

Further reading

Connell, J, 1987. *New Caledonia or Kanaky? The political history of a French colony*, National Centre for Development Studies, The Australian National University.

Henningham, S, 1992. *France and the South Pacific: a contemporary history*, Allen & Unwin.

Kircher, I A, 1986. *The Kanaks of New Caledonia*, Minority Rights Group Report 71.

LOYALTY ISLANDS

Constitutional status: A dependency of NEW CALEDONIA.

Physical environment: The Loyalty Islands—Maré, Lifou and Ouvea—are uplifted coral atolls which lie 100 km to the east of New Caledonia. Vegetation is open forest with patches of grassland, and coconut palms grow on the coastal areas.

History: The islands were settled by a variety of cultures out of Melanesia and had a later, small admixture from Fiji, Tonga and Samoa. Society was hierarchical and ruled by Great Chiefs, in contrast to the small-scale, 'BIG-MAN' communities of Melanesia.

Loyalty Islanders proved both resilient and adaptive in the face of European contact from the 1840s. Christianity was soon widespread, in the context of chiefs playing off English Protestant missionaries against French Catholic missionaries to further tribal enmities. Islanders became key participants in the SANDALWOOD TRADE out of Sydney and the Queensland labour trade. Although the French government annexed New Caledonia in 1853, not until the 1870s could it establish control over the Loyalty Islands and diminish English religious and commercial influences. Lacking natural resources, the islands were declared 'native reserves' in 1900, as a means of sparing inhabitants from the destructive consequences of European settlement and loss of land. Traditional lifestyles and institutions have thus remained stronger on the Loyalty Islands than neighbouring New Caledonia and some of the more powerful voices for autonomy or for independence from France now come from the citizens of the Loyalty Islands.—KRH

Further reading

Howe, K, 1977. *The Loyalty Islands: a history of culture contact, 1840–1900*, Australian National University Press.

NIUE

Constitutional status: Self-governing in free association with New Zealand.
Head of State: Queen Elizabeth II, represented by the Governor General of New Zealand.
Head of Government: Premier Sani Lakatani (1999).
Main town and administrative centre: Alofi (capital).
Land area: 259 sq km (a single raised atoll).
Sea area (EEZ): 390 000 sq km.
Population: 2040 (1999 SPC estimate). Niueans are New Zealand citizens and about 6000 Niueans live in New Zealand.
Official languages: English, Niuean (a Polynesian language closely related to Tongan and Samoan).
Adult literacy: 99 per cent (1994).
Currency: NZ dollar.
Time: –1100 hours UTC.
National day: 19 October (Peniamina Day).
GDP per capita: A$3946 (1991).
Principal export earnings: Handicrafts; agricultural products.
Political system: A legislative assembly of 20 elected members (14 from village constituencies and 6 from a common roll) elects the premier. The premier chooses three other ministers to form a cabinet, which has full legislative and executive power. The speaker of the assembly may perform some of the functions of the governor general.

Local government is the responsibility of village councils, set up in 1967. There are 14 councils with three to five councillors, elected for a three-year term of office.

Physical environment: Niue is a raised atoll (latitude 19° south and longitude 169° west) about 480 km east of Tonga and 560 km southeast of Samoa. It is 19 km long and 18 km wide, with its former reef and lagoon uplifted to about 60 m above sea level. The central plateau, with a slight depression in the middle of the island, is edged with steep slopes dropping on to a lower terrace bordered by cliffs of varying heights. A coral reef fringes parts of the coastline and there are occasional caves, chasms and blowholes. There are no rivers, but subterranean fresh water has been tapped through artesian bores. The island has fertile but not abundant soil, with areas of natural forestation which contain banyan, Tahitian chestnut and kafika trees. Thickets of secondary growth predominate with some candlenut and gardenia, and proliferating coconut trees, fan palms and pandanus flourish amid several types of fern and creeper. Subsistence food crops are grown widely, together with some export crops (limes, passionfruit, taro, yams and honey). There is limited livestock, but fish and shellfish are plentiful. There is some timber for local building. The climate is hot and humid, with east-south-east trade winds from April to December. Niue is on the edge of the hurricane belt and droughts are frequent. Annual rainfall: 2170 mm.

History: The original inhabitants, from eastern Polynesia, settled more than 1000 years ago. Oral tradition records the arrival of a second migration at the beginning of the 16th century, a Tongan war party led by a chief of Niuean ancestry who gained control of the island. Further relationships with Tonga over the next two centuries tended to involve hostilities, and it was the warlike and aggressive appearance of the islanders, noted by Captain COOK in June 1774, which led to the name he gave the atoll, Savage Island.

The Methodist missionaries, John WILLIAMS and Charles Barff, visited the island in 1830, in an unsuccessful attempt to put two Polynesian teachers ashore. Then in 1846 a Niuean called Peniamina, who had been trained at the LONDON MISSIONARY SOCIETY seminary in SAMOA, was brought back to persuade his people to accept a missionary teacher. He was able to achieve this and a Samoan pastor, Paulo, arrived to live in Niue in 1849, initiating a growing acceptance of Christianity which had about

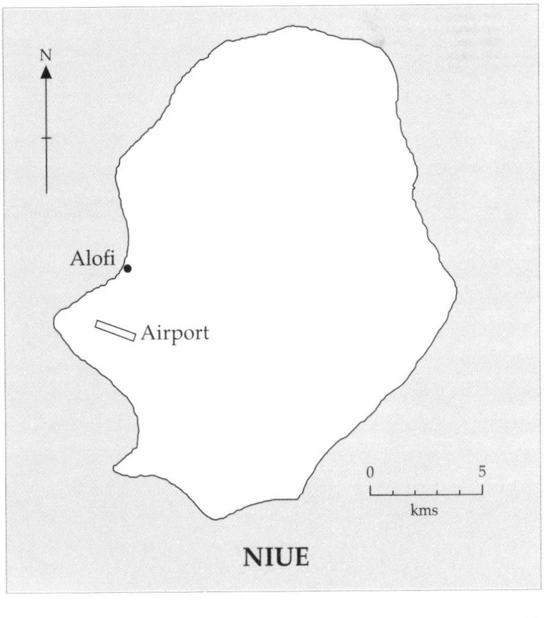

250 converts by 1852 and virtually the total population (then about 4500) by 1854.

During the later years of the 19th century, a number of Niuean men were recruited to work in other parts of the Pacific—particularly on phosphate islands in the eastern Pacific—and Peruvian 'blackbirding' slave traders raided the island in 1863. (See PERUVIAN SLAVE TRADE and COLONIAL LABOUR TRADE.) During the 1860s the two missionary Lawes brothers from England came to live on the island, and another Englishman, Henry Head, became a permanent resident, married to the daughter of a chief, after his ship was wrecked there in 1867.

In 1876 the first Niuean king was elected, Mataio Tuitoga, and a number of approaches began to be made to Queen Victoria requesting British protection for the island. The British government ignored these requests for some time, but then in 1900 it agreed to a British protectorate, which was formally declared on 10 October by the visiting Governor Ranfurly of New Zealand.

In September 1901 Niue was officially annexed to New Zealand as part of the COOK ISLANDS and Percy Smith became the first resident administrator. New Zealand then set up a separate administration in 1904, with a resident commissioner and an island council. Niue's first legislative assembly was established in 1960, with each village electing a representative. The resident commissioner remained president of the assembly but some of his powers were delegated to the assembly from 1966, and a Niuean, Robert REX, became the first 'leader of government business'.

Niue became self-governing on 19 October 1974, when the *Niue Constitution Act 1974* came into force. The first elections under the new constitution were held on 26 April 1975 and Robert Rex became the first premier. Later Sir Robert, he survived an attempt by a new opposition party, the National People's Action Party (NPAP), to persuade him to resign in 1990, and continued in office until his death in 1992. Young Vivian, the popular founder of the NPAP, had already become a member of cabinet, and was then elected premier. He was succeeded by Frank Fakaotimanava Lui in 1998, but when Lui failed to retain his parliamentary seat of Alofi North in the elections of April 1999, Sani Lakatani, a former finance minister, became premier. Niue has one of the six active financial centres (tax havens) in the Pacific islands.—KRF

Further reading

Chapman, T, et al., 1982. *Niue: a history of the island*, Institute of Pacific Studies, University of the South Pacific and Government of Niue.

Smith, S P, 1983. *Niue: the island and its people*, reprinted, University of the South Pacific.

NORFOLK ISLAND

Constitutional status: External Territory of the Commonwealth of Australia.
Head of State: Queen Elizabeth II (represented by Governor General of Australia).
Head of Government: Resident administrator.
Administrative centre: Kingston.
Land area: 34.5 sq km (main island and two uninhabited islets, Philip and Nepean).
Sea area: Part of Australian EEZ.
Population: 2000 (1996 estimate). Norfolk Islanders are citizens of Australia. About one-third are descendants of Pitcairn Islanders.
Official language: English; but 'Norfolk' is widely spoken—evolved from Pitcairnese, a combination of 18th century English and Tahitian.
Currency: Australian dollar.
Time: +1200 hours UTC.
National day: 8 June (Bounty Day).
Principal export earnings: Tourism; duty-free shopping.
Political system: The resident administrator, appointed by the governor general to represent the Australian government, acts on the advice of an executive council for municipal matters relating to Norfolk. A legislative assembly of nine members is locally elected for a three-year term. Members elect a president, deputy president, and other executive

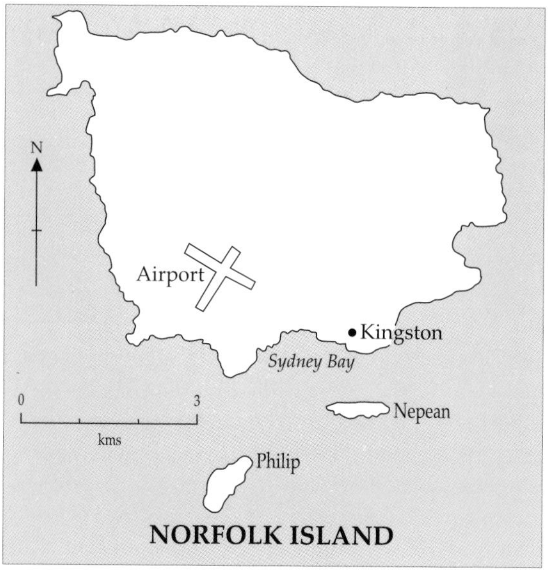

Government House at Kingston, Norfolk Island: built for the commandant of the British penal settlement c1929, and residence of the island's administrators since 1913

ministers. Australia's administrative responsibilities are held by the federal Minister for Territories.

Physical environment: Norfolk Island (latitude 29° south and longitude 168° east) is situated in the South Pacific Ocean some 1600 km northeast of Sydney and 1100 km northwest of Auckland. It is 8 km long and 5 km wide. The only inhabited island in a group of three, Norfolk is a hilly volcanic island surrounded by rugged cliffs and rising to a height of about 305 m above sea level, with several streams. There is a natural sandy beach at Kingston (on the south coast) and fair-weather jetty facilities at Cascade Bay (on the north coast), but no harbour. The striking Norfolk Island pine trees (*Araucaria heterophylla*) originally covered the island and still grow widely. There is rainforest on the slopes of Mt Pitt with palms and giant ferns. Many ornamental trees and shrubs, and the introduced kikuyu grass, thrive on Norfolk, where soil and climatic conditions are ideal for agricultural, horticultural and pastoral development. Market gardens, piggeries, cattle and fishing supply local food needs. The islet of Nepean, a limestone outcrop of about 4 hectares, lies 1 km off the southern coast. The volcanic Philip Island, almost 2 km wide, lies 6.5 km south of Norfolk. The subtropical climate is mild with low humidity. Annual rainfall: 1350 mm.

History: There is archaeological evidence of early (Polynesian) settlement, but when Captain COOK landed on the northern coast on 10 October 1774, the island was uninhabited. He named it Norfolk and recorded his opinion that the pine trees and flax bushes could be useful for ship masts and sail-making. Accordingly, Captain Arthur Phillip was instructed to occupy the island immediately after establishing a British colony at Sydney in Australia. Philip Gidley King was appointed superintendent and commandant, and despatched with a party of convicts to set up a base, arriving at Kingston on 6 March 1788. The period known as the First Settlement ended in 1814, when it was finally acknowledged that the island was not able to supply provisions to New South Wales, let alone to be self-supporting. The Second Settlement began on 6 June 1825, when Captain Turton arrived to establish a penal settlement for the extreme punishment of worst-case convicts and escapees. This brutal regime continued until the tide of public opinion turned against penal colonies in the 1850s, with the last convicts removed in 1856.

On 8 June 1856, the entire population of PITCAIRN ISLAND (194) was brought to Norfolk on the *Morayshire* and allocated land. The Governor of New South Wales became also Governor of Norfolk, although his powers were limited to acting as the link with the British Crown. Apart from two small family groups who subsequently returned to Pitcairn, the *Bounty* descendants settled permanently, enforcing the same patterns of land tenure that they had known on Pitcairn and their own community law.

The Melanesian Mission established itself on the island in October 1866, purchasing additional land over and above a free grant of 99 acres from Britain. Their mission station at St Barnabas, where a chapel was built in 1880, became a missionary training school and a base for their work in the western Pacific. It remained their headquarters until 1920, when it was moved to the SOLOMON ISLANDS.

In 1896 the islanders came into conflict with the current governor, Viscount Hampden, who believed that stricter discipline was required and therefore decided that it was time to end their right to govern themselves. In spite of their opposition, he sent a chief magistrate to Norfolk and the British government supported him. In 1897 Norfolk became a dependency of New South Wales, and although it remained legally a separate colony, its status was confirmed by a British Order in Council in 1914 as being under the authority of the Commonwealth of Australia.

Various forms of local government—with limited and essentially advisory powers—were applied over the years, none meeting with the islanders' approval, until a report was prepared by Sir John Nimmo, a judge of the Australian Industrial Court, in 1976. He recommended that Norfolk should be integrated into the Australian system of laws, social benefits and taxes, proposing that the island become politically part of the Australian Capital Territory. The Norfolk Island Council expressed its unanimous opposition to the loss of its separate political status and launched an appeal to the United Nations in February 1977, supported by some 600 residents' declarations in favour of separate status. In May 1978 the Australian Minister for Home Affairs backed down. He agreed that Norfolk Island did not need to be governed by Australian law, and indicated that some form of self-government might be developed, even while insisting that Norfolk remained part of Australia. A consensus emerged from his discussion with the council, and the new administrative arrangements were formally established by the *Norfolk Island Act 1979*. A legislative assembly, using a system of proportional representation, was created, with its decisions becoming law once they were approved by Australian authorities. Since 1985 the assembly has had a wide range of legislative and executive responsibility, including public works, civil defence, mercantile law, territory archives, control of finances and management of its own public service. In 1979 Norfolk was represented at the conference of the South Pacific Commission, but it has no right to take up membership in the (now renamed) PACIFIC COMMUNITY or the SOUTH PACIFIC FORUM.—KRF

Further reading

Treadgold, M L, 1988. *Bounteous Bestowal: the economic history of Norfolk Island*, National Centre for Development Studies, The Australian National University.

NORTHERN MARIANA ISLANDS

Constitutional status: Commonwealth in political union with United States.

Head of State: Governor.

Head of Government: Governor Froilan C Tenorio (1998).

Main town: Susupe on SAIPAN (capital).

Land area: 471 sq km (15 islands): Saipan, Tinian, Rota, Agrihan, Alamagan, Anatahan; and (uninhabited): Farallon de Pajaros, Maug, Asuncion, Pagan, Guguan, Sarigan, Farallon de Medinilla, Managaha and Aguijan.

Sea area (EEZ): 777 000

Population: 72 780 (1999 SPC estimate). The majority are Chamorro, but there are various minority groups of Carolinian, and/or Spanish, German and Japanese descent.

Languages: Chamorro, Carolinian and English.

Currency: US dollar.

Time: +1200 hours UTC.

National day: 9 January.

GDP per capita: A$12 940 (1994).

Principal export earnings: Tourism.

Political system: The legislature consists of a house of representatives (14 elected members), and a senate (9 members). The government is headed by an elected governor. In 1998 the lieutenant-governor was the Hon Jesus C Borja. The resident representative to the United States was the Hon Juan N Babauta.

Physical environment: The Northern Mariana Islands (between latitude 13–20° north and longitude 140° east) are part of the highest slopes of a massive mountain range rising out of the Mariana Trench, which creates a boundary between the Pacific and the Philippine Sea to the west (see OCEAN TRENCHES). Eight of the islands in the north—Farallon de Pajaros, Asuncion, Pagan, Agrihan, Alamagan, Guguan, Sarigan and Anatahan—are active volcanoes; Maug is a cluster of three islets. The southern islands are of limestone rock, with Saipan having a lagoon off its western coast. The mountainous islands have considerable tropical vegetation, featuring widespread COCONUTS, casuarina and pandanus, as well as bananas, breadfruit and taro on most islands, and many varieties of flowers. Archaeological evidence indicates that RICE was cultivated in the 14th century. There are several species of lizards, numerous MARINE BIRDS and shore birds, and abundant marine life. The tropical climate is hot and humid with little seasonal variation. Annual rainfall: 2030 mm.

History: There is evidence of human settlement, probably from the Philippines, on the high volcanic islands dating back to about 4000 years (SETTLEMENT OF THE NORTHERN PACIFIC). Prehistoric communities, mainly in coastal villages, ranged from 50 to 600 people. The early cultural development is described by archaeologists in relation to a period called Latte in which important houses were constructed above double rows of short stone pillars, which still survive. The preceding period, known as pre-Latte, is identified by the making of red-ware pottery.

After the arrival of MAGELLAN in 1591, the Mariana Islands (then including GUAM) became a colony of Spain (1565–1898). The islands were named in honour of Queen Mariana of Austria, mother of the Spanish king, Charles II. In the first phase of Spanish rule, the invaders encountered steady resistance from the Chamorros, and the population was moved by the Spanish to Guam and to the Caroline Islands. (See SPAIN AND PORTUGAL IN THE PACIFIC, and SPANISH EXPANSION, 1675–1899.) From about 1815, numbers of Chuuk and Yap islanders were permitted to settle on Saipan, where their descend-

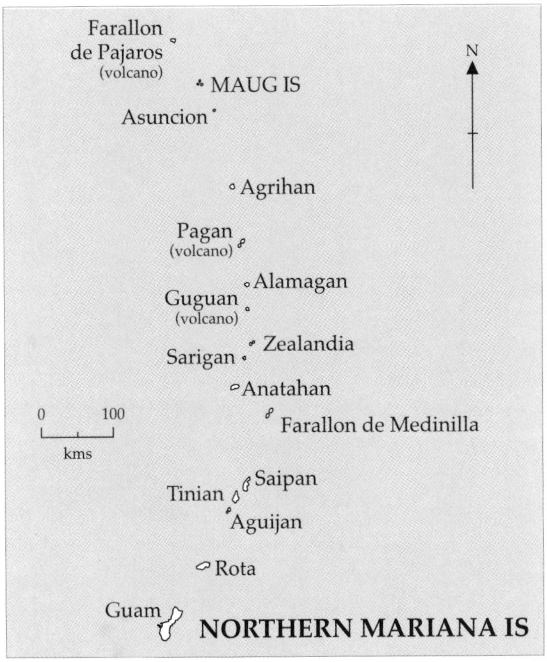

ants became a significant minority, and later in the century, some Chamorros also returned.

At the end of the Spanish-American war, the islands (excluding Guam) were purchased by Germany, and a period of improved administration followed, with greater emphasis on agricultural production (COPRA), road construction and health services. Two decades later, after Germany's defeat in World War I, the islands were placed under the League of Nations and administered by Japan. The Japanese administration, in support of JAPANESE COMMERCIAL INTERESTS, featured large-scale economic development, with SUGAR production on Saipan, Tinian and Rota substantially operated by immigrant labour. Roads, ports, electricity and water systems were developed, and elaborate fortifications were installed. The sugar industry continued for some time after the outbreak of the Pacific War, but it had come to a standstill by June 1944 when US military forces invaded Saipan. By the time the Japanese garrisons were destroyed, there were heavy casualties on both sides and widespread devastation to the island settlements and environment. In the final months of the war, American military bases were installed on Saipan and Tinian, the latter providing the launching pad for the atomic bomb strikes on Hiroshima and Nagasaki.

The US military occupation continued for three years until the islands were transferred to the administration of the United States (first under the US Navy from 1947 and then by the US Department of the Interior from 1962) as a Trust Territory of the Pacific Islands (TTPI). Saipan became the administrative centre for the Northern Mariana Islands, as well as providing the headquarters for the TTPI, in separate buildings on Capitol Hill. Amid growing concerns that the islands' political status (and relative wealth) should not be tied too closely to the future of the other districts of Micronesia, a form of internal self-government was introduced through a negotiated covenant with the United States in 1976, and implemented on 9 January 1978. The new constitution provided for a bicameral legislature, with a popularly elected governor and lieutenant-governor, similar to the status of a state of the United States. The first governor elected under the new constitution was a former doctor, Carlos Sablan CAMACHO. Full independence as the Commonwealth of the Northern Mariana Islands followed on 4 November 1986.

Tourism has been heavily promoted and by 1990 was estimated to provide 20 per cent of government revenue and half the country's GDP. A garment industry was established and has grown rapidly, employing immigrant labour from Asian and neighbouring Micronesian states and adding to the current estimate of about 40 000 contract workers in the Commonwealth. ISLAND FISHING remains undeveloped, but the sale of commercial fishing rights is a lucrative source of revenue.—KRF

Further reading

Crocombe, R, et al., 1983. *Micronesian* Politics, University of the South Pacific.

Farrell, D A, 1991. *History of the Northern Mariana Islands*, Commonwealth of the Northern Mariana Islands.

OGASAWARA ISLANDS (BONIN ISLANDS)

Constitutional status: Territory of Japan.

Physical environment: The Ogasawara group comprises 97 volcanic islands (between latitude 27° north and longitude 142° 10' east). Lying about 965 km to the southeast of Japan, they have a total area of 106 sq km and a population of less than 1000 people. The largest island in the group is Chichi Jima with an area of 39 sq km. The Kuroshio Current runs between the islands and Japan, and this renders the climate relatively mild. Cacao, cattle, sugarcane and trees are plentiful on the islands, and whaling by factory ships is also common.

History: In 1543 the islands were first visited by Ruy Lopez de Villalobos, a Spanish explorer. In 1823 the islands were claimed by the United States, and in 1825 by Great Britain, but both claims were weak and not followed up with any settlements. In 1830

some Hawaiians attempted colonization but this effort failed.

As Japan's military and industrial strength grew in the 1870s, its foreign policy became preoccupied with defence. Having already successfully claimed the RYUKYU ISLANDS in 1872, Japan reached an agreement with Great Britain and the United States in 1873, and formally annexed the islands in 1876, naming them Ogasawara-Gunto. The island population before World War II was about 6000, but after the war, the United States relocated all of the survivors, and administered the islands. In 1969 control of the islands was returned to Japan. In 1972 they were designated as a national park. Currently, over 2500 people inhabit the islands, mainly on Chichi Jima and Haha Jima.—DAB

Further reading

Craig, R and King, F (eds), 1981. *Historical Dictionary of Oceania*, Greenwood Press.

PALAU

Constitutional status: Self-governing republic in free association with the United States.

Head of State: US President.

Head of Government: President Kuniwo NAKAMURA (1998).

Main town: KOROR (capital; population c11 700).

Land area: 494 sq km (about 340 islands): Babeldaob and Koror (c400 sq km), Arakabesang, Malakal, Auluptagel, Urukthapel, Anguar, Sonsorol, Peleliu, Eli Malk, Bana (Fana), Pulo Ana, Merir, Tobi (Hatohobei), Helen Reef (Helen Island), Kayangel.

Sea area (EEZ): 629 000 sq km.

Population: 19 200 (1999 SPC estimate). Belauans are Micronesians, closely related to Caroline Islanders.

Languages: Belauan and English are the official languages in all 16 states; Sonsorolese (in state of Sonsorol); Angaur and Japanese (in Angaur); Tobi (in Tobi).

Adult literacy: 98 per cent (1994).

Currency: US dollar.

Time: +1000 hours UTC.

National day: 1 October.

GDP per capita: A$5684 (1994 est).

Principal export earnings: Fisheries; tourism.

Political system: Palau became a self-governing republic in 1994. It has authority over most of its affairs, but defence and other strategic prerogatives remain in the hands of the United States. In exchange, the United States continues to provide substantial financial subsidies for the first 15 years of the Compact of Free Association, which must be renegotiated in the year 2009. Styled on the US Congress, Palau's legislature—Olbiil Era Kelulau—comprises a senate with 18 elected members and a house of delegates (16 elected members). Elections are held every four years. The country also has 16 state governments. The vice-president and Minister of Administration (1998) is the Hon Tommy E Remengesau Jr.

Physical environment: Palau is an archipelago of about 340 islands, only nine of them inhabited, which constitutes the most western group of the Caroline Islands in the northwest Pacific. Babeldaob, Koror, Malakal and Arakabesang are volcanic islands with high centres; most of the remaining islands are raised coral atolls, and Kayangel in the north is an atoll with four small *motu*. Babeldaob, the largest island, has thick forests, a small lake and several rivers, and is linked by suspension bridge to the interconnected trio of islands, Koror, Ngerkebesand and Malakal. Many of the coral limestone islands rise to 100 or 200 m above sea level and have areas of dense forest and occasional steep coastlines. On the western side of the main islands is an extensive barrier reef, about 100 km long, creating a lagoon stretching 20 km at its widest point. Within the reef near Koror are the Rock Islands, hundreds of tiny raised coral outcrops. Palau's main reef system ends at Peleliu, once a phosphate-producing island, about 9.5 km long, with Angaur about 10 km away. More than 200 km further south is another group of small islands, including Sonsorol, Tobi, Pulo Ana, Merir and Bana, and ending in the long low reef of Helen—an atoll more than 20 km long. Varied vegetation grows on the volcanic islands, with areas of forest, scattered woodland, mangrove swamp, grasslands, palms and pandanus. There is a varied range of reptile life—lizards, skinks, snakes and crocodiles—and eels in the mangrove areas. The equatorial climate is hot and humid, with northeast trade winds prevailing from November to April, and two distinct wet seasons, in July–August and December–January. Annual rainfall: c4000 mm.

History: Caroline Islanders are thought to have originated in Southeast Asia and Malaysia (SETTLEMENT OF THE NORTHERN PACIFIC), probably first inhabiting the area in about 1000 BC. In Palau, there was ongoing political rivalry between two main village groupings (see TRADITIONAL LEADERSHIP IN MICRONESIA), and archaeological evidence confirms the existence of highly specialized shell and stone technology, and extensive agricultural terracing.

The first European visitors were Spanish, in 1710 and 1712, and they called the islands Los Palos

(SPAIN AND PORTUGAL IN THE PACIFIC). In 1783 the wreck of the *Antelope* led to the introduction of the chief's son, LEE BOO, into London society. European ships made a number of later contacts, and some mapping of the islands was conducted by the French explorer Duperrey in 1824, and a Russian expedition in 1828. Spain attempted to maintain its sovereignty over the region, but it was challenged by the Germans and the British. Finally Germany purchased the Carolines from Spain in 1899 and although its interest in Palau lay in the commercial possibilities of PLANTATIONS and PHOSPHATE, the GERMAN COLONIAL ADMINISTRATION was responsible for introducing health regulations to control epidemics of disease which had hugely ravaged the population since first European contact. At the start of the First World War, Japan took over the Carolines in October 1914. As a Japanese colony until World War II, Palau gained a modern infrastructure—harbour facilities, roads, bridges, sewerage and electricity—along with expansion of the COPRA industry and phosphate production. Japanese military authority was replaced in 1922 by the civilian South Seas Bureau, and the administrative centre of Koror had a population of 25 000 Japanese (four times the local population) in 1935. (See JAPANESE COMMERCIAL INTERESTS). Then Japan began to build up its military forces in the Pacific, setting up fortifications in the Carolines and making them a closed military area in 1938. After Japan entered the war, Palau became a base from which to attack the Philippines. (ISLANDER EXPERIENCES IN THE PACIFIC WAR.)

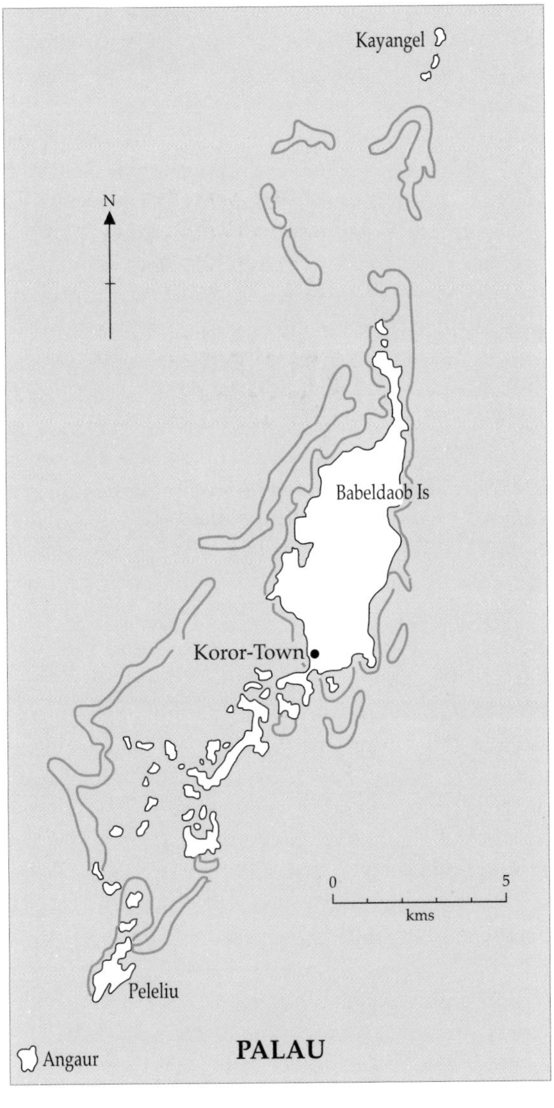

Micronesia remained under US military occupation for two years after the war ended. Palau became part of the US-administered UN Trust Territory of the Pacific Islands (TTPI) in 1947, and was the last of four political entities that emerged from the now-defunct TTPI. A nuclear-free constitution was adopted on 1 January 1981, but this long delayed a mutually acceptable Compact of Free Association, because it was seen as incompatible with American perceptions of its defence interests. The compact agreed between the United States and Palau in 1986 gave the islands independence subject to defence being the responsibility of the United States for 50 years. Successive referenda in Palau, however, failed to produce a 75 per cent majority. In 1987, Palau voted to amend the constitution to allow approval of the compact by a simple majority. In a subsequent plebiscite, 73 per cent of the votes were cast for the compact, but the Palau Supreme Court ruled this invalid in August 1988. The court also ruled there were inconsistencies between the compact and PALAU'S NUCLEAR-FREE CONSTITUTION, which was incompatible with the US defence policy, an impasse which was broken when Palau revised its constitution. Agreements with the Bush administration in 1989 provided assistance in paying off foreign debt and funds for new development. The Belau people remained citizens of TTPI. On 9 November 1993, a 68 per cent majority voted in favour of the compact. After this vote, Palau achieved self-government on 1 October 1994.

President Haruo Remeliik, who had strong anti-nuclear convictions, was assassinated in July 1985. His successor, President Lazarus SALI'I, died from gunshot wounds in mysterious circumstances although it is widely accepted that he committed suicide. Sali'i was followed in office by President Ngiratkel Etpison. The current president, Kuniwo NAKAMURA, a former teacher elected in November 1992, managed the country's change of status, achieving an agreement by the United States to pay

Palau compensation over 15 years for military and political control rights for 50 years. Palau received US$450 million for the first year.—RCK & KRF

Further reading

Ballendorf, D A and King, P (eds), 1980. *Towards New Directions and Political Self-actualization*, Micronesian Area Research Centre.

Hezel, F X, 1983. *The First Taint of Civilization: a history of the Caroline and Marshall Islands in pre-colonial days, 1521–1885*, University of Hawai'i Press.

PAPUA NEW GUINEA

Constitutional status: Independent constitutional monarchy since 1975.

Head of State: Queen Elizabeth II (represented by Governor General Sir Silas Atopare GCMG).

Head of Government: Prime Minister Sir Mekere Morauta (1999).

Main cities/towns: Port Moresby (capital; population c250 000); Lae (80 400), Madang (27 200), Wewak (26 000), Goroka (18 000), Mount Hagen (17 000)—all on mainland; Rabaul (25 000) in East New Britain.

Land area: 473 180 sq km: the mainland comprises 85 per cent of the total area; the remaining 15 per cent is represented by 600 islands, of which the Bismarck Archipelago (Manus, New Ireland and New Britain), Bougainville and Buka are the largest.

Sea area (EEZ): 3 120 000 sq km.

Population: 4 692 440 (1999 SPC estimate).

Languages: TOK PISIN (Melanesian Pidgin, widely spoken), Hiri Motu and English; also 867 local languages (see LANGUAGES OF PAPUA NEW GUINEA).

Adult literacy: 52 per cent (1994).

Currency: Kina = 100 toea.

Time: +1000 hours UTC.

National day: 16 September.

GDP per capita: A$1882 (1993).

Principal export earnings: Gold; copper; logging; coffee; palm oil; copra oil.

Political system: Papua New Guinea has a 109-member unicameral national parliament elected for five years by universal suffrage to represent the 19 provinces of Papua New Guinea. The national parliament is styled on both the Australian and British Westminster system, using a single-vote simple majority to elect members of parliament. Parliament then elects the prime minister, who therefore frequently heads a government that is an uneasy coalition of small, unstable parties and independent MPs, all prone to being split or being persuaded to defect.

For 20 years after independence, government existed at three levels: national, provincial and local. Provincial governments and legislatures were abolished in 1995 and replaced with a local government structure headed by a governor. The next general election for the national parliament, with voting by secret ballot, is due in mid 2002. Main parties: League for National Advancement, Melanesian Alliance, National Party, PANGU PATI, Papua Party, People's Action Party, People's Democratic Movement, People's Progress Party, United Party.

Physical environment: Papua New Guinea lies just below the equator in the eastern South Pacific, between latitude 0–12° south and longitude 141–160° east. It shares its main island with Indonesia, and its other close neighbours are Solomon Islands, Australia and Vanuatu to the south; Micronesia to the east; and Malaysia, Singapore and the Philippines to the north. Its 600 islands and coral atolls are mostly of younger volcanic origin, but the mainland is a massive rugged cordillera, with wide alpine valleys (almost a quarter of the country is over 1000 m above sea level) and many mountains over 4000 m. The highest point is Mt Wilhelm (4508 m). There are at least 100 volcanoes, some 14 of them still active, and a large number of geothermal springs. (VOLCANOES OF PAPUA NEW GUINEA.) South of the central mountain ranges on the main island are luxuriant lowlands, interlaced with one of the largest river systems in the world. The longest of these rivers is the FLY, some 1200 km in all, which empties into the Gulf of Papua. Tropical rainforests with a wide variety of species of trees, and over 10 000 other species of flora, cover most of the country. The lowland forests are made up of palms and vines, and strewn with ferns and orchids, and mountain forests comprise oaks, laurels and conifers. In the remainder of the country there is savannah, grassland and swamps. Subsistence crops include COCONUTS, sago palm and pandanus, while the principal cash crops are COPRA, COFFEE, COCOA, RUBBER, PALM OIL and TEA. Animal life includes many marsupials, bats and spiny anteaters, many REPTILES (snakes, lizards and crocodiles), and 1400 species of fish. There are more than 650 species of land birds, including the BIRD OF PARADISE and the cassowary, and a wide range of insects, including spectacular butterflies and moths. Situated in the wet and humid equatorial tropics, Papua New Guinea has little seasonal temperature variation, but regional variation is quite substantial, with much cooler nights in the highlands. Southeast trade winds predominate for most of the year, with the northwest monsoon occurring from December to

March. Annual rainfall: varies from 1200 mm in Port Moresby to 5000 mm at Kikori in the Gulf of Papua.

History: For details about the earliest period in Papua New Guinea's past, see SETTLEMENT OF NEW GUINEA and LAPITA CULTURE. Malay traders visited long before European exploration; Papua is a Malayan word meaning woolly-haired. The country's difficult terrain explains the isolation in which tribal groups continued to live for many centuries, and this in turn engendered a wealth of traditional cultures and rich spiritual beliefs—to become a magnet for anthropologists from the start of the 20th century. Europeans first made contact in the early 16th century, and the Dutch named the island New Guinea in the 1660s, but it was another 200 years before white colonizers made a serious effort to impose an administration. In 1884 Britain moved with some reluctance to enforce a claim first made on behalf of the Crown in 1845, to the eastern part of New Guinea. The western half (now IRIAN JAYA) had been claimed by the Dutch in 1848, and the Germans took over the northeastern quarter, naming it Kaiser-Wilhelmsland, just days ahead of the British decision in November 1884. (GERMAN COLONIAL ADMINISTRATION.) The threefold division was settled; Britain took the southeast coast and the eastern islands, and this British New Guinea became Australian Papua in 1906. German New Guinea was placed under an Australian military administration in 1914, becoming the Mandated Territory of New Guinea in 1920, entrusted to Australia by the League of Nations.

The separate Australian administrations of Papua and New Guinea came to an end with the Pacific War. A temporary union was established by Australian legislation in 1945, confirmed in 1947, and finalized in 1949. Port Moresby became the seat of government for the whole country, and a vast process of post-war change was set in train, involving considerable commercial, agricultural and educational development. Political changes to bring about increasing indigenous participation moved slowly at first, but then accelerated in the 1960s, encouraged by the persistent interest shown by the Trusteeship Council of the United Nations. Papua New Guineans first gained the right to some representation (three elected members) in the parliament in 1951. The first house of assembly was established in 1964, and by 1972, only nine Europeans held parliamentary seats. A form of self-government was officially declared on 1 December 1973, and independence followed on 16 September 1975. Sir Michael SOMARE was the first prime minister of Papua New Guinea.

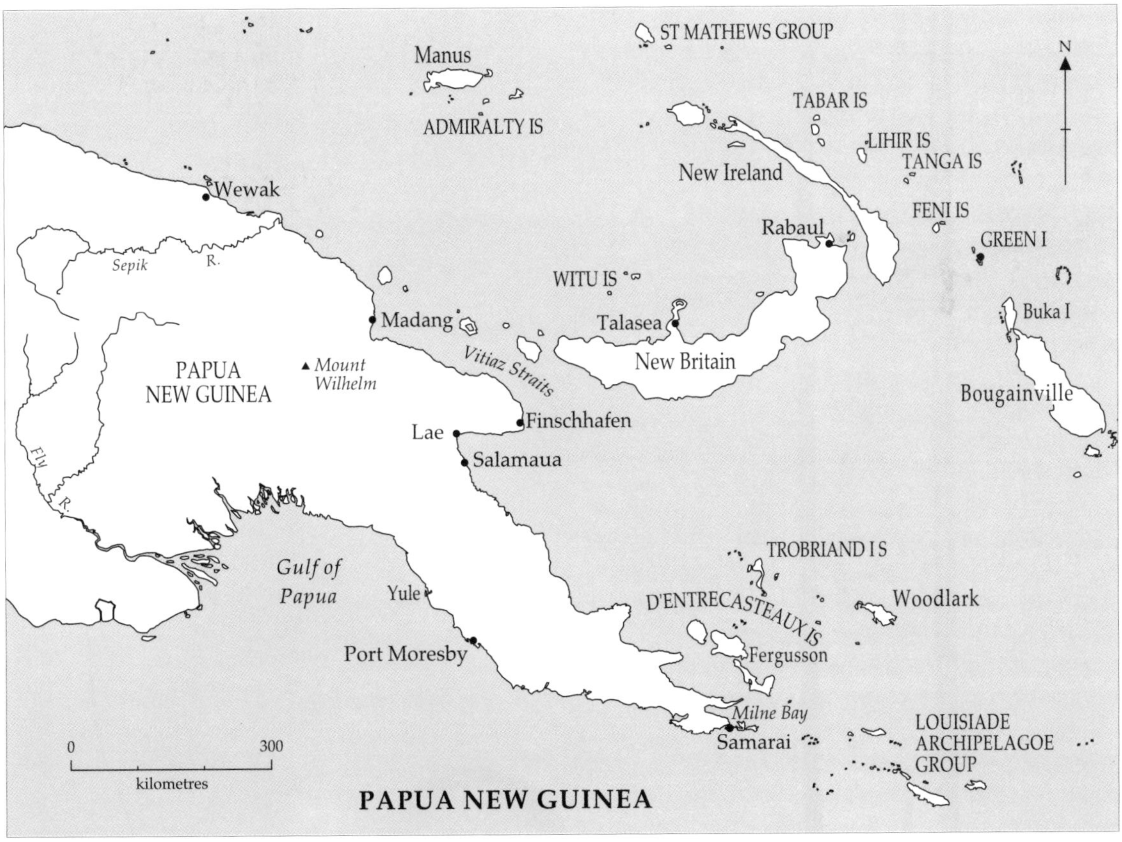

Large-scale MINING of minerals began in Bougainville in 1972, and tensions arose from the outset over land and compensation claims. The last decade has been dominated by the BOUGAINVILLE CONFLICT AND PEACE PROCESS, with three prime ministers, Sir Rabbie NAMALIU, Paias WINGTI and Sir Julius CHAN, attempting to find political or military solutions (see CHRONOLOGY OF A CRISIS). Further mining operations and oilfields have developed during the 1990s.—KRF

Further reading

Ryan, P (ed.), 1972. *Encyclopaedia of Papua and New Guinea*, 2 vols, Melbourne University Press and University of Papua New Guinea.

Griffin, J, Nelson, H and Firth, S, 1979. *Papua New Guinea: a political history*, Heinemann Educational.

Waiko, J D, 1993. *A Short History of Papua New Guinea*, Oxford University Press.

PITCAIRN ISLANDS

Constitutional status: British dependency.

Head of State: Queen Elizabeth II.

Head of Government: Governor (British high commissioner resident in New Zealand).

Administrative centre: Adamstown (on Pitcairn).

Land area: 37 sq km: Pitcairn (5 sq km), Henderson (30 sq km), Ducie, Oeno.

Sea area (EEZ): 800 000 sq km.

Population: 47 (1996 census). Only Pitcairn is inhabited.

Languages: English, and a local dialect which is a mixture of English and Tahitian.

Currency: NZ dollar.

Time: -0900 hours UTC.

National day: 23 January (Bounty Day).

Principal export earnings: Tourist artifacts; postage stamps.

Political system: The official head of government (the governor) is the British High Commissioner to New Zealand, based in Wellington. Pitcairn's local government is managed by the Island Council, with annual elections for four of its members held in December. The Island Magistrate, elected for a three-year term, is chairman of the council and the governor appoints one additional councillor and an advisory member. Another advisory member is appointed by the council and two further (ex-officio) members are the island secretary and the chairman of the internal committee, which is responsible for local works.

Physical environment: Located in the eastern Pacific, just south of the Tropic of Capricorn—latitude 25° south and longitude 130° west—Pitcairn

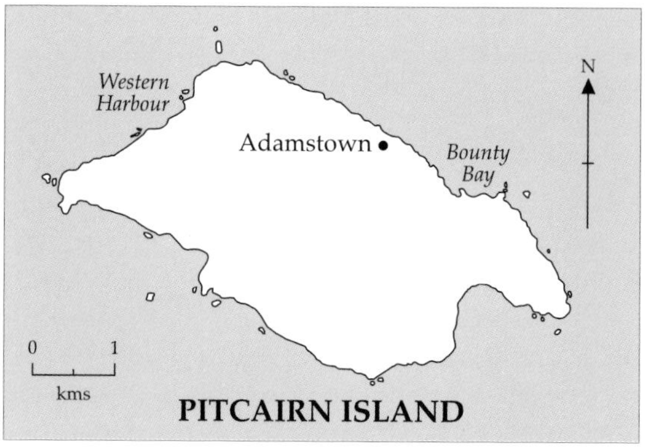

consists of deeply weathered volcanic rock, rising to a height of about 350 m above sea level. It is bounded by cliffs with no surrounding reef. Henderson, in the centre of the group, is an uplifted atoll of coral limestone, forming a broad plateau 25–30 m above sea level, edged with cliffs and a fringing reef. Ducie (500 km east of Pitcairn) and Oeno (about 120 km to the northwest) are low coral atolls. Vegetation ranges from quite thick bush and tree cover on Pitcairn and Henderson to coconut and pandanus on Oeno. On Pitcairn, the soil is of volcanic origin and very fertile. Fruit and vegetables grow readily and there are goats and poultry. Fish are plentiful. Henderson Island is a natural bird sanctuary, where at least 12 species have been observed, including two endemic land birds: a flightless rail and a green fruit pigeon. Henderson was added to UNESCO's World Heritage List in 1988. The tropical climate has seasonal variations, being cooler and wetter in May and June, and warmer and drier in February and March. Annual rainfall: 1700 mm.

History: There is archaeological evidence of early Polynesian inhabitants but the first European discovery of Pitcairn Island was in 1767, by Captain Philip CARTERET, who found it uninhabited. Twenty years later, after the MUTINY ON THE BOUNTY, mutineers led by Fletcher Christian, who had access to Carteret's charts, found their way to it after several months' searching. Having decided to make the island their home, they stripped the *Bounty* of everything that might be useful and set the ship alight on 23 January 1790. The nine mutineers, their 19 Tahitian companions and their offspring lived on in isolation, with several bouts of violence, treachery and murder, until in 1800, only one mutineer, John ADAMS (who died in 1829), nine women and 19 children remained. The island was 'rediscovered' by the American WHALING ship, *Topaz,* in 1808. The British government, recognizing some degree of responsibility for the *Bounty* descendants (a population of 87), decided that they were to be moved to Tahiti in

1831, but after several months of unhappiness and a dozen deaths from unfamiliar diseases, they were allowed to return.

In 1838 the islanders were supplied with a basic constitution and set of laws, drawn up by Captain Russell Elliott, which provided for the election of a local magistrate to hold administrative powers and also instituted compulsory schooling. Regular trade with whaling ships brought an adequate level of prosperity and the population grew to more than 190 over the next two decades. Once again the British government intervened, this time proposing to relocate the islanders on NORFOLK ISLAND, now uninhabited following the closure of the penal colony. The Pitcairners agreed to the move in 1856 and were given land. Although most settled permanently, some 16 of them returned to Pitcairn in 1858, and four more families followed in 1864, bringing the island's population to 43.

During the 1880s the island became the temporary home of John I Tay, a convert to the SEVENTH-DAY ADVENTIST (SDA) church, who persuaded the islanders to join his faith. Accordingly they adopted a formal resolution in March 1886 to make Saturday their day of worship, and to prohibit the consumption of alcohol and of pork. The SDA religion has continued to be practised on the island since that time, supported by a series of resident SDA pastors.

In the early 1890s Britain made an attempt to introduce parliamentary government in the form of a seven-member council, but this was abandoned after five years and instead administrative responsibility for Pitcairn was allocated to the HIGH COMMISSIONER FOR THE WESTERN PACIFIC in 1898. This made it possible to revert to a magisterial administration, introduced by the British consul in Tahiti, R T Simons, in 1904, and amended to its present form by H E Maude in 1940. The Governor of Fiji took over nominal responsibility for Pitcairn from the British High Commissioner for the Western Pacific in 1952. Since 1970, when Fiji became independent, the British High Commissioner in New Zealand has the title Governor of Pitcairn.

The other three (uninhabited) islands of the group had been named and charted separately from Pitcairn. Quirós sighted Ducie and Henderson in 1606, naming them Encarnion and San Juan Batista. Their present names reflect later visits from Captain Edwards of the *Pandora* in 1791 (who named Ducie); and Captain James Henderson of the *Hercules* in 1819. Oeno was sighted by Captain Henderson but named for the American whaler *Oeno* which visited in 1822. All three islands were formally annexed as dependencies of Pitcairn by Britain in 1902 when Mr Simons, the British consul, sent Captain G F Jones to visit them. In 1937 HMS *Leander* was sent to erect new signboards indicating their status and they became an official part of the Pitcairn Island colony in 1938.

A radio station was established on Pitcairn in 1938, and subsequently expanded and improved during the Pacific War when New Zealand radio operators were sent to man it. A new school was built in 1948, staffed by a New Zealand teacher, and a monthly news bulletin was established in 1959. Improved and extended roading was carried out in the 1960s, together with a number of public works projects. Tourism (and particularly the sale of artifacts) was severely set back when the CRUISE SHIPS of the Shaw Savill Line ceased to include Pitcairn as a port of call between Panama and New Zealand after 1968. Most shipping anchors off-shore at Bounty Bay (on the north coast near Adamstown), where a jetty was built in 1976. During easterly winds, Western Harbour provides an alternate open anchorage. There is no port, and no airstrip exists. Young people have tended to leave the island in search of employment and the population has suffered a steady decline in recent decades.—KRF

Further reading

Christian, G, 1982. *Fragile Paradise*, Hamish Hamilton.

RAPANUI (EASTER ISLAND)

Constitutional status: Province of Chile.

Head of State: President of Chile.

Head of Government: Governor Jacobo Hey Paoa (1997).

Administrative centre: Hangaroa.

Land area: 166 sq km.

Sea area (EEZ): 355 000 sq km.

Population: Just over 3000 (1998 estimate); most are Rapanui-born or kin to a Rapanui-born.

Languages: Spanish is the official language, but Rapanui, an Eastern Polynesian language, is known widely; English and French are also used in the tourist industry.

Currency: Chilean peso (CH$).

Time: +6 hours UTC.

National day: 18 September (Chilean national day); 9 September (celebrated officially as the day Chile annexed the island in 1888).

Principal export earnings: Tourism.

Political system: The Chilean administration of Easter Island is formally associated with the *zone* of Valparaiso, and headed by an *intendente* appointed for a fixed term, generally three years. The *intendente* recommends the appointment of the governor of the

Province of Easter Island. Under the Chilean system, the district *intendente* and the provincial governor represent the president and central government. In turn, they are expected to provide local reactions to central government policy. The municipality of Easter Island, which comprises the township of Hangaroa, has a mayor elected every four years along with five *concejal* (councillor) positions. In the October 1996 elections, the following were elected:

Mayor: Pedro Edmunds Paoa
1st Concejal: Enrique Pakarati Ika
2nd Concejal: Alberto Hotus Chávez
3rd Concejal: Marcelo Pont Hill
4th Concejal: Dr. Rodrigo Noranbueno Marchant
5th Concejal: Claudio Cristino Ferando.

Physical environment: Rapanui (Isla de Pascua in Spanish; formerly Easter Island) lies in the remote eastern Pacific (latitude 27° south and longitude 109° west), about 1500 km east of Pitcairn Island. It is a triangular shape, formed around three main volcanic cones, about 22 km across at its widest extent. The highest point is Mt Terevaka (600 m) in the north. Much of the coast is cliff-edged, 20–30 m high; there are only three or four small sandy beaches, no streams and no visible coral reefs. Natural vegetation, apart from grasses, is sparse. Pines, eucalypt and fruit trees have been introduced. Subsistence crops include corn, taro, yams, sweet potatoes, beans, squash and some fruit. The climate is semi-tropical with quite high humidity. Annual rainfall: fluctuating in cycles of abundance and drought, with an average of 1250 mm.

History: Easter Island was probably inhabited some 1600 years ago, the earliest date being the 4th century AD. The prehistoric origins of the Rapanui remain obscure (see SETTLEMENT OF THE EASTERN PACIFIC). Voyagers from Samoa and the Marquesas Islands certainly reached the island and settled, eventually producing an estimated population of about 7000. Their extraordinary achievements include the development of a genuine form of writing—ideographic and pictographic—which appears to be traceable to the Indus Valley script of the Harappans. Wooden blocks incised with script have remained undeciphered for centuries, and are still the subject of intense debate. Considerable speculation has also accompanied the discovery of about 600 huge stone images on Easter Island, extraordinary feats of stonemasonry ranging from about 1 m in height to more than 20 m. Some of these *moai* (ancestral figures) were found arranged on the huge stone *ahus* (ceremonial platforms); about 300 were set in the ground; and about 100 were still in the quarries of volcanic *tufa* or limestone where they had been carved. Many questions remain unanswered about the origins of these strange megaliths (see RAPANUI ARCHAEOLOGY, WHO CARVED THE STATUES OF EASTER ISLAND?).

The first European contact came with the arrival—at Easter, 1722—of the Dutch explorer, Jacob Roggeveen, who named the island accordingly. Then in 1770 Captain Felipe Gonzalez claimed the island for the king of Spain, obtaining what he took to be the signatures of several islanders on his document. Various other European explorers also visited during the next century: COOK (1774), La PÉROUSE (1786), Lisiansky (1804), Page (1806), Kotzebue (1816), Beechey (1825) and du Petit-Thouars (1838). Whaling ships called occasionally from the 1790s, increasing to almost annually in the first half of the 19th century. The island's population was ravaged by the blackbirding raids of the PERUVIAN SLAVE TRADE in the 1860s, and those islanders who survived and were later repatriated, suffered terribly from disease. French missonaries of the Order of Sacred Heart arrived in 1864, and over the next four years began converting to Catholicism all those who remained. When a French adventurer, Dutrou-Bornier, subsequently settled, an early accord deteriorated and the missionaries withdrew to Mangareva in 1871. Some islanders accompanied them, others were enticed to work in church plantations in Tahiti. After the departure of most of the population, Dutrou-Bornier established sheep ranching in 1872, along with a boutique agriculture catering to the Pape'ete market. By 1877, the resident population had fallen to only 110.

Chile annexed the island in 1888, confirming as its official name Isla de Pascua and commencing to use Rapa Nui as the spelling for the local place-name. On the whole, Chilean authors and those sympathetic with that country's rule of Easter Island write 'Rapa Nui' and separate the elements of many other island place-names and references. Writers who see the island as part of Polynesia and Oceania tend to use the spelling 'Rapanui' and follow a similar convention for rendering local names and references. A Chilean company with British majority holding, Compania Explotadora de la Isla de Pascua, took over the sheep-raising business, running up to 60 000 sheep (and pigs and horses) on the island, and confining the tiny population of islanders to the vicinity of Hangaroa. In the First World War, the German Pacific Squadron fleetingly established a base on the island.

Apart from a number of visits from scientific expeditions, Easter Island in the 20th century received only occasional casual sea traffic with the company's annual vessel to collect the wool clip for a British market. Also, after the First World War, there was the annual appearance of vessels of the Chilean navy, entrusted with the responsibility for administration up until 1966. The naval administration actually took over the sheep farming operations in 1953, when the foreign-dominated company felt it could no longer operate. Soil erosion owing to sheep ranching burn-off practices necessitated a reduction in the number and variety of livestock in the 1950s to about 10 000 sheep (mainly corriedales and some merino). In 1966 a civil administration was installed by Chile after extensive Rapanui protest at the increasingly harsh and restrictive military rule imposed upon the island. Since that time, Rapanui have been entitled to all the rights of Chilean citizenship. A rough airstrip was established in the 1950s and progressively upgraded. After a few charter flights in the late 1960s and more improvements, a regular jet service between Santiago and Pape'ete, with a stopover on Rapanui, commenced at the end of 1971. In 1987 the airstrip was substantially improved and extended with funding from NASA to provide emergency facilities for US space shuttles.

In 1983 Easter Islanders petitioned the United Nations, seeking support from the Committee on DECOLONIZATION on the issue of a referendum on independence, although no action of an official kind was taken either by the United Nations or the Chilean government except that the post of the appointed governor was held for the first time by a Rapanui, which remains the case today. (See also SETTLEMENT OF THE EASTERN PACIFIC; KON-TIKI EXPEDITION; SAN LESMES.)—GMcC & KRF

Further reading

Heyerdahl, T, 1989. *Easter Island: the mystery solved*, Souvenir Press.

Langdon, R and Tryon, D, 1983. *The Language of Easter Island: its development and Eastern Polynesian relationships*, University of Hawai'i Press.

McCall, G, 1994. *Rapanui: tradition and survival on Easter Island*, 2nd ed., University of Hawai'i Press.

RYUKYU ISLANDS

Constitutional status: Province of Japan.
Head of State: President of Japan.
Head of Government: Governor.
Administrative centre: Naha on Okinawa.
Land area: 3120 sq km (more than 100 islands): Okinawa (1434 sq km).
Sea area: Part of Japanese EEZ.
Population: 1 200 000 (1997 estimate).
Official language: Japanese.
Currency: Japanese yen.
National day: 23 December.
Principal export earnings: Tourism; agriculture; handicrafts.
Political system: The Ryukyu Islands are part of the territory of Japan, governed as a province, and administered by an assembly of 44 members, headed by an elected governor. Seven elected representatives have seats in the national parliament (*diet*) in Tokyo.
Physical environment: The Ryukyu Islands (between latitude 26° 30' north and longitude 128° east) form a chain of more than 100 islands reaching from Japan to Taiwan, in the northwestern Pacific Ocean. Okinawa is the largest island in the chain. The climate is subtropical, and typhoons are not uncommon. Annual rainfall: varies across the group from 1350–3050 mm; 2110 mm on Okinawa.
History: The Ryukyu or Luchu Islands (*Nansei-Shoto*) have possibly been inhabited since the Pleistocene (Ice Age) by nomadic tribes from China, Japan, Philippines and Taiwan. They were known to explorers from both China and Japan by the 7th century AD, and the ancient trading network that linked China, Japan, Korea and Southeast Asia included Okinawan traders by the 14th century.

The Ryukyu Islands became a tributary to China, but in 1872, as Japan embarked on expansion and modernization, China was unable to maintain its claim in the face of a Japanese challenge. China was obliged to relinquish the islands which then became a prefecture (district) of Japan in 1879.

When JAPANESE COMMERCIAL INTERESTS turned to the economic development of Micronesia after World War I, thousands of Okinawans were among the immigrant labour brought to the islands to engage in SUGAR production, fishing and MINING. During the first phase of the Pacific War, they continued to work the sugarcane plantations, but were placed under guard after the American occupation of Marshall Islands, Guam and Saipan. After the end of the war, the Americans repatriated the Japanese and Okinawans who had been living in Micronesia, even though some had been there for many years and had married Micronesian women.

In the final stages of the Allied forces' counter-offensive (1942–45) against Japan in the Pacific, an all-out assault was launched on Okinawa, and American troops landed on 1 April 1945. In the continuing post-war occupation of the islands, a period of intensive militarization was undertaken by the United States, after the formation of the People's Republic of China in 1949, and the outbreak of war with Korea in 1950. The US administrative control continued until 1972, when an agreement was concluded with Japan, ceding ownership to Japan but permitting the United States to retain military bases (but not nuclear weapons without Japanese consent) on Okinawa. Since the end of the Cold War, the need for forward bases in the western Pacific has been reduced, and the continuing presence of the American base has been the subject of increasing friction in Okinawan politics.—KRF

SAMOA

Constitutional status: Independent state.

Head of State: Malietoa TANUMAFILI II.

Head of Government: Prime Minister Tuilaepa Sailele Malielegaoi (November 1998).

Main town: APIA (capital, on Upolu; population c34 300 in 1994).

Land area: 2935 sq km (Savai'i, 1800 sq km; and Upolu, 1110 sq km.)

Sea area (EEZ): 120 000 sq km.

Population: 167 990 (1999 SPC estimate). Mostly of Polynesian origin, with a small percentage being of German-Samoan or Chinese-Samoan descent. Many Samoans now live overseas (see PACIFIC ISLANDERS IN NEW ZEALAND).

Official languages: Samoan, English.

Literacy: 98 per cent (1994).

Currency: Tala (WST$) = 100 sene.

Time: -1100 hours UTC.

GNP per capita: US$1140 (1995).

Principal export earnings: Coconut products; fishing; manufactured products.

Political system: The head of state (now appointed for life, but to be elected in future) appoints an executive prime minister who must have majority support of the 49-member Legislative Assembly. Executive power rests with the prime minister and his appointed cabinet of 12 members. Main parties: Human Rights Protection Party; Samoa National Development Party; also independents.

Physical environment: Samoa (latitude 14° south and longitude 170° west) lies to the west of American Samoa, east of Wallis and Futuna, and northeast of Tonga and Fiji. It has two large islands and six small islets. Upolu and Sava'i consist of volcanic domes with several peaks. Upolu's central mountain chain has deeply eroded canyons and rises to a high point of 1100 m (Mt Fito). Sava'i has a central core of mountains, of which the highest is Mt Mata'aga, 1850 m above sea level. The most recent volcanic eruption occurred in 1911.

Vegetation on both islands is dense, with tall inland forest. Coastal areas have scattered woodland with coconut palms and pandanus, and some mangrove swamp. Subsistence crops include taro, taamu and yams, and there are substantial plantations of coconut, banana and cocoa, as well as cattle grazing and forestry. The climate is hot and humid, with distinct seasonal variations. Southeast trade winds during the dry season predominate from April to October. The wet season falls between November and March, winds become northwesterlies, and hurricanes can occur. Annual rainfall: varies from

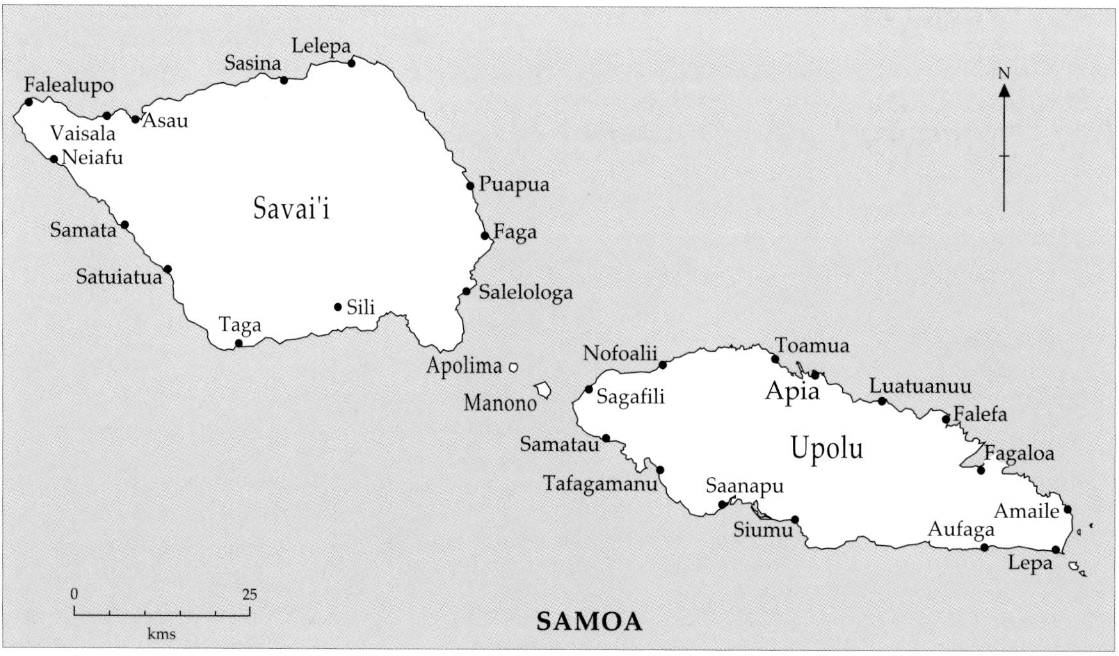

2500 mm in northwestern areas to 5000 mm in central and southeastern parts of both islands.

History: The prehistory and early post-contact history of both Samoa (formerly known as Western Samoa) and AMERICAN SAMOA is inseparable. Archaeology has established that people were living in the Samoan archipelago almost 3000 years ago (FOOTSTEPS FROM ASIA), and similar pre-contact settlement patterns have been identified. Shared oral histories of Fijian interaction and later Tongan occupation exist in the two island groups, which were first known to Europeans as the Navigators—named by BOUGAINVILLE in 1768 in honour of the seafaring skills of the Polynesian inhabitants—after being first sighted in 1722 by the Dutch explorer, Jacob Roggeveen. Missionary activity, initiated by the arrival in Apia of John WILLIAMS in 1830, produced transcribed texts in the Samoan language for the first time in 1834. A commercial treaty was negotiated in 1838 between leading chiefs and Captain Bethune of the *Conway*, to establish a system of payment of harbour dues in return for guaranteed rights, and in the following year, a similar agreement protected Commander Charles Wilkes while he carried out detailed surveys for the UNITED STATES EXPLORING EXPEDITION. By 1850 Apia was a base for Pacific traders, and had become the residence of a British consul, with the first US commercial agent being appointed in 1853. German commercial activity commenced with the arrival of August Unshelm in 1856 to set up a trading base for the Hamburg company, J C GODEFFROY & SOHN, and the subsequent appointment of a German consul in 1861.

Inter-tribal warfare occasionally erupted outside of the Apia port area. From the late 1860s there was growing rivalry between the representatives of Britain, the United States and Germany, whose competing commercial ambitions became embroiled in issues of Samoan chiefly rule. Samoa's two chiefly families had become locked in a 30-year fight between two rival 'kings' after the death of Malietoa Vaiinopu of Sava'i in 1841. The concerted efforts of the British and American representatives, aided by the involvement of another US agent, Colonel Albert B Steinberger, produced negotiations in the early 1870s resulting in a peace settlement, and Malietoa Laupepa became king in April 1873. A constitution was drafted on the European model of an independent state. Steinberger then relinquished his American interests and took up a pivotal role as premier under King Malietoa, finalizing the constitution and resolving the dispute between Malietoa and his rival, Tupua Pulepule, with a proposal for alternating four-year terms of office. Steinberger's period of influence was short-lived, ended by ignominious arrest and deportation on the instructions of the American and British consuls, who suspected him of involvement with Godeffroys. Factional fighting resumed, complicated by European efforts to purchase land for plantations, and Samoan delegations sought in vain for first British then American protection.

The Municipality of Apia was set up in 1879 by the WESTERN PACIFIC HIGH COMMISSION, with the three consuls forming a board to enforce European law on foreigners. Another temporary settlement of continued tensions was achieved with the Berlin Treaty of 1889, confirming the independent rule of King Malietoa Laupepa and the tripartite authority of the Apia Municipal Council. Within five years, however, Malietoa was under challenge and the re-ignited Samoan war was again entangled with foreign political and trading interests. This time a permanent solution was drawn up, and in a series of treaties in 1899, the Berlin Treaty was annulled, Germany annexed (Western) Samoa, US naval control was imposed on the eastern island group, and Britain renounced all claims. In return, Germany relinquished its claims to Tonga, Niue and Solomon Islands, east and southeast of Bougainville.

Mau parade on 28 December 1929, in Samoa

The GERMAN COLONIAL ADMINISTRATION from 1899 to the outbreak of the Second World War began under the governorship of Dr Wilhelm SOLF. (See GERMAN COLONIAL LAND POLICIES.) In the first 10 years, opposition to German control emerged largely in the form of the MAU A PULE, a non-violent resistance movement which was ended by the colonial government in 1909. After the declaration of World War I in 1914, New Zealand forces annexed Samoa and maintained a military administration until 30 April 1920, a period scarred by a devastating outbreak of Spanish influenza which was badly handled by the commanding officer, Colonel Robert

Logan, and which killed some 20 per cent of the population. The Treaty of Versailles then confirmed New Zealand's colonial role, with Samoa now officially its mandated territory. Opposition to New Zealand rule emerged immediately, fed by growing resentment of colonial authority in general and the particular tactlessness and condescension which marked its imposition. Events culminated in the deaths of 11 people, including Tupua Tamasese Lealofi III, when police opened fire on unarmed marchers on 28 December 1929. The marchers were members of the nation-wide opposition movement, Ole Mau A Samoa.

Samoans maintained a policy of peaceful non-cooperation and tensions began to ease only after the 1935 election of a Labour government in New Zealand—giving ministerial responsibility to Sir Maui Pomare—and the introduction of a more tolerant regime in Samoa which allowed the banned leaders to return. By the end of World War II the climate had changed, assisted by the influence of American troops stationed in Samoa, and the role of Peter Fraser, New Zealand's Prime Minister and Minister for Island Territories, in the 1945 drafting of the United Nations Charter. (Western) Samoa became a Trustee of the United Nations, administered by New Zealand, and the process of devolution leading to independence was under way. From 1947 the New Zealand High Commissioner received advice from a Council of State which included the two leading Samoan chiefs known as *Fautua*. A Legislative Assembly was formed, and a Constitutional Convention met in 1954. The *Samoa Amendment Act* of 1957 provided for appointment of a Leader of Government Business, a position which became Prime Minister in October 1959 and was held by Fiamē MATA'AFA MULINU'U II. A draft constitution, prepared in 1960 and approved by the United Nations, was endorsed by a universal plebiscite in May 1961, and independence followed on 1 January 1962.

The constitution provided for the election of the head of state by the legislative assembly for a five-year term, but it also provided that the two Fautua should become joint heads of state for their lifetimes. Tupua Tamasese held joint office until his death on 5 April 1963; Malietoa Tanumafili II has remained sole Head of State since then. Samoa joined the United Nations in 1976, using the name 'Samoa' only, and has confirmed its present name by a 1997 constitutional amendment. The issue of citizenship—and in particular, the right of Samoans to New Zealand citizenship—was tested in the courts in 1982. New Zealand's final court of appeal, the Privy Council in London, ruled that all Samoans born between 1928 and 1949, and their children, were New Zealand citizens. This was not a politically acceptable decision in New Zealand, however, and it was cancelled by New Zealand legislation, after agreement was reached between New Zealand and Samoa, negotiated by the then Prime Minister Va'ai Kolone whose Human Rights Protection Party (HRPP) had won power in February 1982. Kolone's first term of office ended in September 1982, when he lost his seat on the basis of electoral irregularities. Tupuola Efi was appointed by the Head of State to replace Va'ai, but he was unable to maintain a parliamentary majority and the new leader of the HRPP, TOFILAU Eti Alesana, became prime minister on 30 December 1982. Va'ai Kolone replaced him after the 1985 elections, won by the HRPP, having joined forces with Tupuola Efi as his deputy. The 1988 elections returned Dr Tofilau to the leadership, and he remained prime minister until ill-health forced his resignation in November 1998. He was succeeded by his deputy and Finance Minister, Tuilaepa Sailele Malielegaoi.

The *matai*-only voting system introduced at independence (restricted to chiefly titleholders; see SAMOAN MATAI TITLES) lasted nearly 30 years, surviving a legal challenge in 1982, after the Court of Appeal overturned a ruling of the Chief Justice. The general election in April 1991 was the first election in which every citizen aged over 21 years was able to vote, after universal suffrage was introduced, following a plebiscite in 1990 in which 51 per cent of voters supported change.—KRF

Further reading

Davidson, J W, 1967. *Samoa mo Samoa*, Oxford University Press.

Gilson, R P, 1970. *Samoa 1830 to 1900: the politics of a multi-cultural community*, Oxford University Press.

Meleisea, M, 1987. *The Making of Modern Samoa: traditional authority and colonial administration in the modern history of Western Samoa*, Institute of Pacific Studies, University of the South Pacific.

—— et al., 1987. *Lagaga: a short history of Western Samoa*, University of the South Pacific.

SOLOMON ISLANDS

Constitutional status: Independent constitutional monarchy.

Head of State: Queen Elizabeth II represented by Governor General, Father John Lapli.

Head of Government: Prime Minister Bartholomew ULUFA'ALU (1998).

Main town: HONIARA (capital; on Guadalcanal).

Land area: 28 370 sq km (six main islands): Guadalcanal (5650 sq km), Malaita, Choiseul, Santa Isabel, New Georgia, San Cristobal (Makira).
Sea area (EEZ): 1 340 000 sq km.
Population: 421 000 (1999 SPC estimate).
Official language: English; Pidgin is the common language, and about 40 languages and many dialects are spoken.
Literacy: 23 per cent (1994).
Currency: Solomon Islands dollar.
Time: +1100 hours UTC.
National day: 7 July.
GDP per capita: A$947 (1993).
Principal export earnings: Fishing; timber; copra; palm oil; cocoa.
Political system: Elections are held every four years by universal suffrage for the 50-seat unicameral national parliament. Main parties: Liberal Party, National Unity Party, People's Alliance Party; 1997 coalition: Alliance for Change.
Physical environment: Located just southeast of Bougainville (Papua New Guinea), and north of Vanuatu—between latitude 5–12° south and 155–170° east—Solomon Islands are a series of high, rugged islands grouped along a northwest/southeast fault system. Raised coral reefs occur in the Shortland, New Georgia and Russell Islands, around the Bougainville Strait and in the southwest. Mainly covered with dense tropical rainforest, island vegetation is plentiful in palms, tree ferns, lianas, creepers and orchids. Many river mouths are surrounded by mangrove swamps. Fertile coastal lowlands provide land for subsistence crops, coconut and palm oil plantations, cocoa and rice cultivation, and cattle grazing. The soil ranges from extremely rich volcanic to relatively infertile limestone. The climate is hot and humid, with occasional cyclones. Annual rainfall: 3000 mm on average (falling most heavily between December and March), but up to 8000 mm in some areas.
History: Solomon Islands are closely linked to Bougainville and Buka, geographically and culturally. Archaeological evidence suggests that the first inhabitants may have been non-Austronesian-speaking (Papuan) hunters and gatherers who were able to reach the archipelago during the Pleistocene (Ice Age) more than 10 000 years ago, when sea levels were lower and many of the islands were joined (SETTLEMENT OF NEW GUINEA). Later migration of Austronesian-speaking agriculturalists occurred about 4000 years ago, and the many different languages spoken are evidence of a long period of mixed settlement.

Spanish explorers, in search of the fabled riches of King Solomon, were the first Europeans to visit the islands: Alvaro de Mendaña in 1568 and 1595, and Mendaña's pilot, Quirós, in 1606. Two Dutch expeditions followed in 1616, but then it was more than 150 years later—in 1767—that CARTERET visited Santa Cruz and Malaita. Soon after, there were

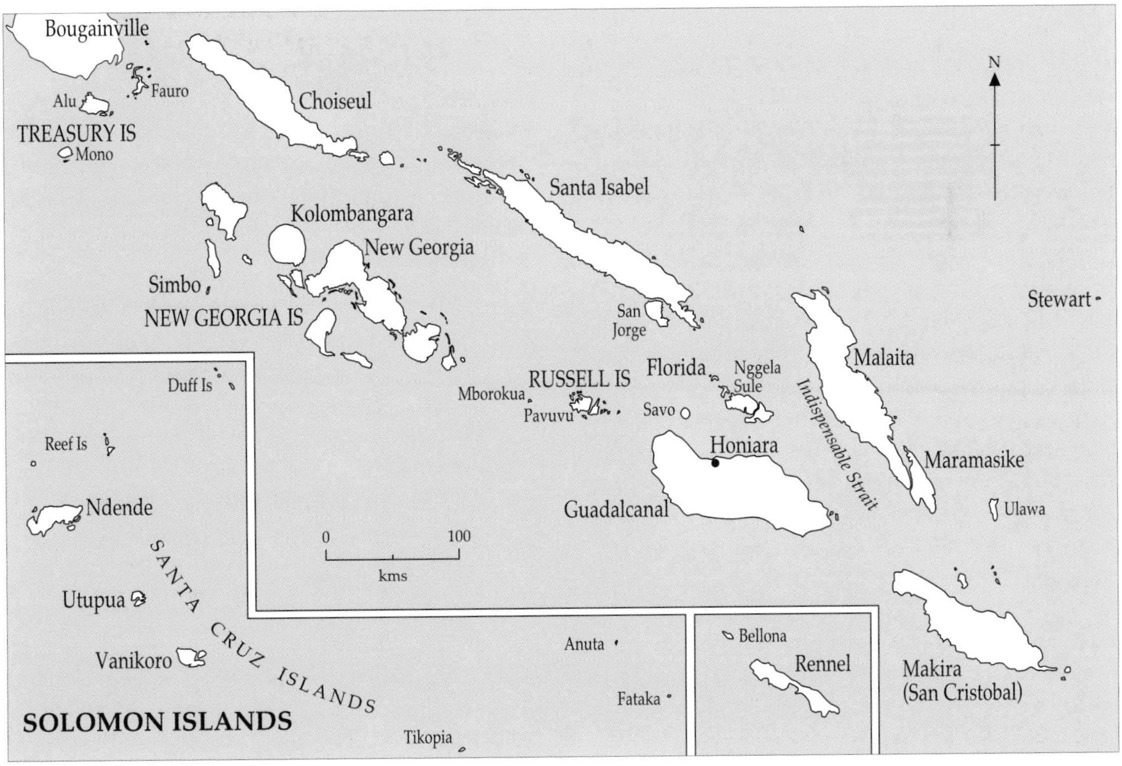

two French expeditions: BOUGAINVILLE in 1768 visited and named Choiseul and other islands to the north; and Surville in 1769 followed in the footsteps of several of his predecessors. The next French expedition in the region, two ships led by La PÉROUSE, disappeared in June 1788 and was only much later known to have foundered in a storm off the reef of Vanikolo. DUMONT D'URVILLE visited the site in 1828, and retrieved several items including anchors and cannon, and erected a monument.

From the early 1800s, Solomon Islanders came into increasingly frequent contact with WHALING vessels, followed by the traders, missionaries (ANGLICAN and Roman Catholic), and labour recruiters who roamed the Pacific. Among the encounters ending in violent deaths were the visits of Bishop ÉPALLE (1845), Ben BOYD (1851), Bishop PATTESON (1871) and Commodore J G Goodenough, of HMS *Pearl* (1875). The fate of many islanders at the hands of BLACKBIRDERS was also often brutal, although several thousand contracted workers later returned from Queensland and Fiji. (COLONIAL LABOUR TRADE; KANAKAS IN AUSTRALIA.)

Colonial rule began after Britain's declaration of the British Solomon Islands protectorate, largely in response to appeals from missionaries, over the southern islands of GUADALCANAL, Makaira, Malaita and New Georgia, in 1893. Further islands were added in 1898, 1899 and 1900, the last (northern) islands being transferred to Britain by Germany, in exchange for the right to annex Samoa. During the next decade, large commercial PLANTATIONS were established by LEVER BROTHERS, BURNS PHILP, and other European trading companies, dominating the island economy up until the 1940s. Mission influence grew, and church schools controlled the education system.

The experience of Solomon Islands in World War II was a period of almost constant warfare which left a trail of devastation. The former capital of Tulagi had been destroyed, and the British administration chose Honiara on Guadalcanal, taking advantage of some of the infrastructure of the former American base near the new site. Many roads and airstrips had been built by the Americans too. In the immediate aftermath of the war, an anti-authority movement known as MAASINA RULE emerged, causing considerable concern to the administration, and leading to the jailing of several leaders, including Jonathan FIFI'I in 1948. Other indigenous movements developed out of the Christian missions as breakaway sects, whose charismatic leadership advocated a return to *kastom* and self-reliance.

In 1960 the former advisory council (comprising a resident commissioner and four nominated members) was replaced by a legislative council, with an executive council responsible for decision-making. By the 1970s the colonial government had begun to initiate a series of changes, giving greater authority to the legislative body, and preparing the ground for greater autonomy for Solomon Islanders. A new constitution replaced the legislative council–executive council combination with a single government council, composed of 17 elected members and up to 9 public service members, and specifying certain reserve powers for the high commissioner. The new council met for the first time in July 1971, devising a system of five separate committees to prepare legislation. Then a new constitution was adopted in April 1974, creating a cabinet system under which the position of chief minister was created, and the governing council became the legislative council with 24 elected members. The high commissioner became the governor, and the chief secretary became deputy governor.

The former protectorate took the name Solomon Islands in mid 1975, gaining internal self-government on 2 January 1976, and full independence on 7 July 1978. The Westminster-style parliamentary democracy has not allowed any political figure to dominate, although general political stability has been maintained. Peter KENILOREA (now Sir Peter) became the first chief minister of Solomon Islands in 1976, then prime minister in 1978. Solomon MAMALONI, who entered politics in 1970, has held the office three times (1981–84, 1989–93, 1994–97). Bartholomew Ulufa'alu was elected in a new coalition government after the 1997 general election. In the 1980s the Solomon Islands government declared the country nuclear free, banning nuclear-armed warships and aircraft from entry.

Foreign investment has been encouraged since independence (see FISHERIES, and LOGGING IN SOLOMON ISLANDS). Borrowing has increased steadily and remains necessary to economic stability.—KRF

Further reading

Bennett, J A, 1987. *Wealth of the Solomons: a history of a Pacific archipelago, 1800–1978*, University of Hawai'i Press.

Harcombe, D, 1997. *Solomon Islands, a travel survival kit*, 3rd ed., Lonely Planet.

Economic Insights Pty Ltd, 1995. *The Solomon Islands Economy: achieving economic development*, Australian Agency for International Development.

TOKELAU

Constitutional status: Non self-governing territory under New Zealand's administration.
Head of State: Queen Elizabeth II, represented by Governor General of New Zealand.
Head of Government: Non-resident administrator: Lindsay Watt (appointed March 1993). Ulu-o-Tokelau (Tokelau): Kuresa Nasau (1998).
Administrative centre: Effectively a rotating capital, provided by atoll whose *Faipule* is serving a (one-year) term as *Ulu*. The Tokelau–Apia Liaison Office is in Samoa.
Land area: 12.2 sq km: Nukunonu (4.7 sq km), Fakaofo (4 sq km), Atafu (3.5 sq km).
Sea area (EEZ): 290 000 sq km.
Population: 1500 (1999 SPC estimate).
Languages: Tokelauan (Polynesian language similar to Samoan and Tuvaluan), and English.
Literacy: 99 per cent (1994).
Currency: NZ dollar.
Time: -1100 hours UTC.
National day: 6 February.
GDP per capita: A$478 (1990).
Principal export earnings: Postage stamps; commemorative coins; handicrafts; tuna fishing licence fees.
Physical environment: The three small atolls of Tokelau (between latitude 8–10° south and longitude 171–173° west) are spread across 150 km of ocean some 500 km north of Samoa. They are somewhat unusual among Pacific atolls in having completely enclosed central lagoons, with no deepwater passages to the open sea. There are neither harbours nor safe anchorages and all transfers between ship and shore are made by small boats. The land consists of low islets of varying size (none more than about 5 m above sea level) set along the circle of reef, mainly composed of sand and coral rubble mixed with some organic matter. There are no streams, and only a few areas where ground water can be tapped by wells. Coconuts and pandanus are grown on all islets. Fakaofo has sizeable plantations of *pulaka (Cytosperma chammisonis)* to supplement the abundant breadfruit. Marine resources are of prime importance, and are exploited by both line fishing and reef netting. Although the habitat imposes some

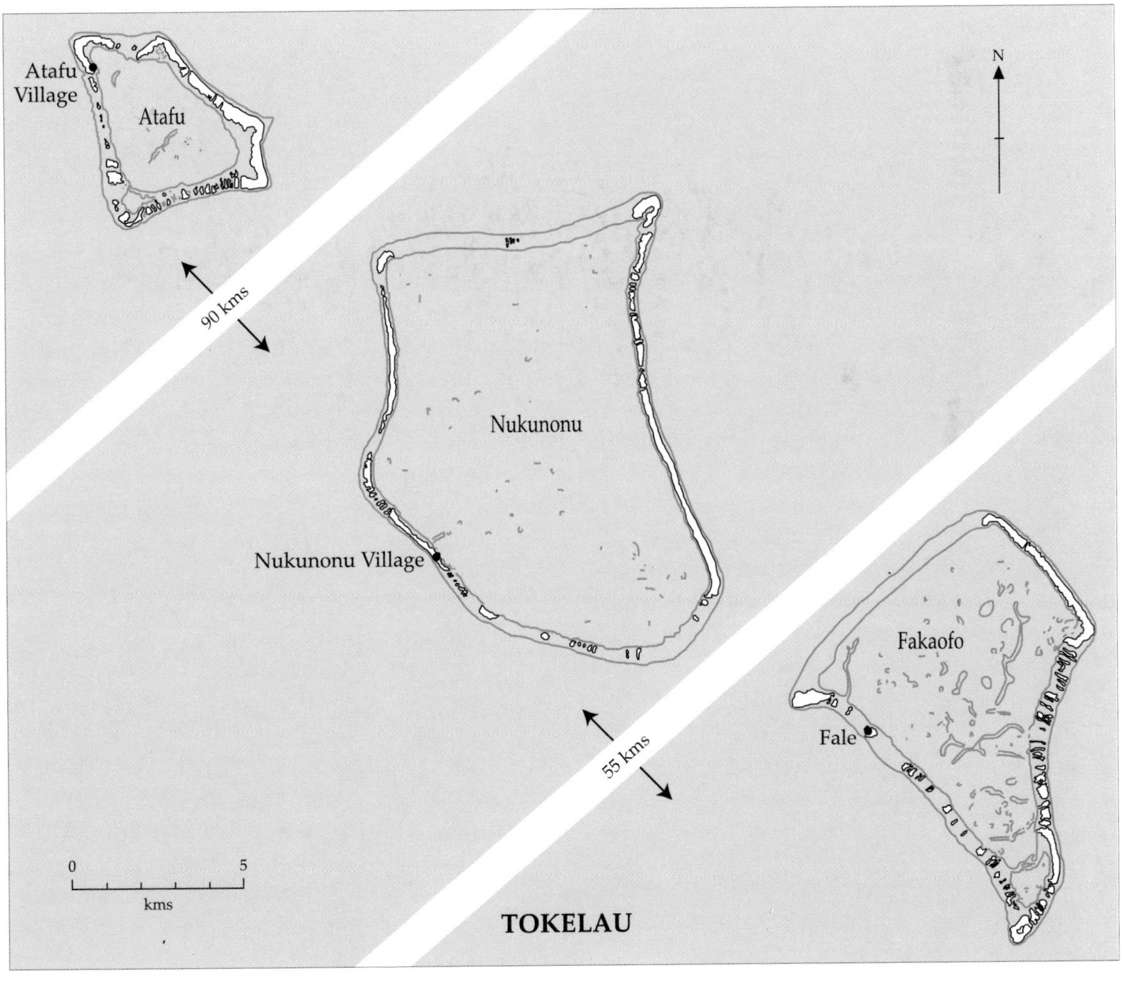

severe constraints, it has provided an abundant, if not particularly varied, subsistence. The group lies to the north of the zone of frequent CYCLONES, but severe tropical storms are not unknown. Annual rainfall: heavy rainfall can occur at any time of year but generally totals about 1600 mm.

History: Archaeological evidence shows that the atolls were settled about 1000 years ago, with some evidence of cultural remains in Fakaofo 1600 years ago. Local traditions and GENEALOGIES, however, go back only a few hundred years, telling of the origins of the social and political order that was in place by the 19th century. Tradition has it that the three atoll populations were originally separate and independent. Atafu attacked Fakaofo, killing the daughter of the local chief. In retaliation Fakaofo attacked Atafu, driving off all the inhabitants. Later, Fakaofo subjugated Nukunonu, claiming almost half the atoll, but sparing the population in order to have a source of everlasting tribute of women, mats and other valuables. Atafu was later settled by a party centred upon a Fakaofo man of chiefly descent and a Nukunonu woman. Thus a unitary political order was established under the sway of Fakaofo, 'the land of chiefs' and of the god Tui Tokelau, the controller of good fortune and productivity.

European discovery of the atolls was piecemeal and spread over some 60 years, from Commodore Byron's visit to 'Duke of York's Island' (Atafu) in 1765, through Captain Edwards' discovery of 'Duke of Clarence' (Nukunonu) in 1791, to the 1825 visit of the USS *Dolphin* to Fakaofo. There were other fleeting visits by foreign ships over the following years but there are no detailed accounts of the people before the visit of the UNITED STATES EXPLORING EXPEDITION in 1841. Atafu at that time had a population of around 120, while Fakaofo, the dominant island, had about 600; indicating that the total population of the group was somewhat under 1000.

From 1841 on, the outside world began to press more closely on Tokelau. In 1846 a drift voyage landed two canoe loads of Tokelauans on Uvea and into the care of Marist missionaries there, and in 1852 a Catholic expedition removed over 400 people from Fakaofo to Uvea. Although the ostensible motive for this was to rescue the people from 'famine', the god-house was also deliberately destroyed. During the 1850s a number of Tokelau men reached Samoa as well as Uvea, and associated themselves with the work of the Catholics and the LONDON MISSIONARY SOCIETY (LMS). These men later helped introduce Christianity to the atolls. Atafu accepted a LMS teacher in 1861, and, at about the same time, Nukunonu accepted the Catholicism brought by a local man trained in Uvea and Australia. These conversions diminished the hegemony of both Fakaofo and *Tui Tokelau*, but Fakaofo held out until 1863 when, in the aftermath of a fatal epidemic and raids by ships engaged in the PERUVIAN SLAVE TRADE, both faiths were established on the island. Missions and slavers effectively destroyed the old order. Almost half the population was taken by slave ships, leaving mostly women and children. Parish and village organizations became closely inter-twined, and the local PASTORS and catechists, mostly Samoan, came to have very considerable influence.

Declared as protectorates of Great Britain in 1889, the atolls were incorporated into the Gilbert and Ellice Islands Protectorate in 1908, and in 1916, into the Gilbert and Ellice Islands Colony. They became an administrative responsibility of New Zealand in 1925. The years between the 1860s and the 1920s saw steady population increase, and the formation of a stable neo-traditional social order. (Social organization is based on the villages—one on each atoll—and descent groups that control land rights. Local government is in the hands of village councils made up of elders, or a mixture of elders and representatives of the descent groups. Virtually all the land is held under customary title and, according to custom, both males and females inherit rights.)

The people were generally healthy, literate (in Samoan), peaceful and Christian. The British administrative presence was slight, and the separate 'Native Governments' kept order with or without recourse to the official regulations and ordinances that were promulgated. New Zealand followed very much the same administrative patterns between 1925 and World War II, leaving local government in the hands of the village councils and a few paid local officials, supplemented, when shipping allowed, by annual visits from the Administrator of Western Samoa. There was a US Loran tracking station on Atafu during 1944–45, but there were no hostilities in Tokelau waters.

The post-war administration of Tokelau was untangled from that of Western Samoa, which had begun its course toward political independence. The *Tokelau Islands Act* (of the NZ Parliament) of 1948 transferred formal sovereignty from Great Britain to New Zealand, and New Zealand citizenship was conferred on Tokelauans later that year. Education in the atolls was considerably improved, new hospitals and copra sheds were built, and radio communication with Samoa improved. By the late 1950s, the population had increased to almost 2000, with a further 500 Tokelauans established in Western Samoa. With Samoan independence in 1962, many Tokelauans there migrated to New Zealand, and New Zealand began a program of assisted migration, first of single men and women, and later of whole families. From 1963–71 there were 356 government-sponsored migrants to New Zealand. Others migrated of their own accord, resulting in an 18 per cent drop in the atoll population (from 1901 to 1558) in the decade to 1976. Migrants settled mainly in Wellington and Auckland, with smaller numbers in Taupo and Rotorua, establishing self-conscious ethnic communities based on churches and island affiliations. There are now some 5000 ethnic Tokelauans in New Zealand, and about 1500–1600 in the atolls. Given the high mobility there is a very real sense in which Tokelauans in both countries form a single community.

For 25 years, the most pressing national issues have been development and the future constitutional status of the group. In the late 1960s the Tokelau economy was dominated by subsistence production, with local products supplemented by sugar, rice and flour bought with money earned from copra exports. Housing used local materials, there was no electricity, and sailing canoes were the only transport. All this has been progressively transformed, and the economy is now predominantly an aid-driven one, dominated by an annual allocation of NZ$4.3 million of budgetary assistance from New Zealand. Other revenue is derived from New Zealand project aid, licensing fees from the EEZ, stamp and coin sales, taxes and duties, so that the total annual budget is in the region of NZ$6 million. Copra sales are now insignificant, and almost all aspects of life in the atolls have been changed by monetization. In 1991, the average annual household income was NZ$4537, with nearly 90 per cent coming from public sector payments—salaries, wages, honoraria, pensions and superannuation. Social services have been considerably upgraded. Each atoll has its hospital and primary school, staffed by qualified Tokelauans, with education to Form 5 level available to all the atolls on Nukunonu. There are no airports, but a chartered ship makes regular voyages to and from Samoa 10 times a year, carrying both cargo and passengers, and there is a small purpose-built ship based in the group for inter-atoll communications. An international telephone and fax system was installed in 1997.

In discussions with the regular visiting missions from the UN Committee on Colonialism since 1976, and in direct representations in New York, Tokelauans have taken a cautious stance on self-determination. Their priority has been development of basic infrastructure and public services, and the creation of a system of government which would be, as one Tokelau commentator put it, 'built upon local institutions rather than imposed upon them'. Since 1993, progress toward that objective has built on two long-established local institutions: the office of *faipule*, or 'village leader', filled by election every three years, and the general *fono*, a gathering of representatives from the three islands which makes all policy and budgetary decisions.

The course has been one of devolution of the executive powers of the administrator (based in Wellington) and the legislative powers of the NZ Parliament. In 1994 the powers of the administrator were delegated to the general *fono* when in session, and otherwise to the newly-formed Council of Faipule. The three *faipule* assumed 'ministerial' responsibilities for the various departments, with each becoming *Ulu o Tokelau* or 'Head of Tokelau' in rotation for a one-year term. In 1998, the *faipule* were Kuresa Nasau (Atafu); Falima Teao (Fakaofa), and Pio Tuia (Nukunonu). Like the *faipule*, the *pulenuku* (village administrative officers or mayors) are elected by universal adult suffrage for a three-year term. The public service was relocated from its base in Apia, with two departments established on each atoll, leaving only a small liaison office in Samoa. The latest development has been an amendment to the basic 1948 *Tokelau Islands Act* giving the general *fono* the power to make laws—subject to restrictions concerning treaties and to disallowance by the administrator. On this basis the outlines of a constitution are taking shape. It will be carefully adapted to local conditions and to indigenous sources of law. Tokelau has declared its intention of making an act of self determination in the near future, and has indicated a strong preference for some form of free association with New Zealand.—AAH

Further reading

Huntsman, J and Hooper, A, 1996. *Tokelau: a historical ethnography*, University of Auckland Press and University of Hawai'i Press.

TONGA

Constitutional status: Independent constitutional monarchy.

Head of State: King TĀUFA'ĀHAU TUPOU IV.

Head of Government: Prime Minister Baron Vaea (1998).

Main towns: Nuku'alofa (capital, on Tongatapu); Pangai (on Lifuka); Neiafu (on Vava'u).

Tonga

Land area: 747 sq km (169 islands; 36 inhabited): Tongatapu (260 sq km), Vava'u (114 sq km), 'Eua (88 sq km).
Sea area (EEZ): 700 000 sq km.
Population: 99 650 (1999 SPC estimate); Tongatapu: 66 915; Vava'u: 15 779; Ha'apai: 8148.
Official languages: Tongan (a Polynesian language); English used in education and administration.
Adult literacy: 99 per cent (1994).
Currency: Tongan pa'anga = 100 seniti.
Time: + 1300 hours UTC.
National day: 4 July.
GDP per capita: A$1940 (1995).
Principal export earnings: Agricultural products; live animals.
Political system: The Kingdom of Tonga is highly centralized and highly traditional. The present monarch, the fourth of the Tupou dynasty, King Taufa'ahau, personally appoints and chairs a privy council of 10 Ministers of the Crown—including an executive prime minister—and also the governors of Ha'apai and Vava'u. In 1998 the governors were the Hon Fielakepa (Ha'apai) and the Hon Ma'ulupekotofa Tuita (Vava'u). With the king at its head, the cabinet becomes the privy council, which is both the highest governing body in the land and court of appeal. The prime minister, currently the king's first cousin, Baron Vaea, does not lead cabinet so much as represent it as 'the first among equals'. A separate judiciary has a chief justice and a puisne judge both appointed for three-year terms from overseas. The unicameral legislative assembly of 28 members has 18 elected representatives. Nine are nobles' representatives elected from among their ranks, and nine are people's representatives (three from Tongatapu, two from each of Ha'apai and Vava'u, and one each from 'Eua and the Niuas) who represent more than 90 000 commoners. Crown Prince Tupouto'a is a member, and Prince Ulukalala Lavaka Ata is Minister for Foreign Affairs. Elections are held every three years and all Tongans over the age of 21 are required to vote.

There were no organized political parties until the PRO-DEMOCRACY MOVEMENT, led by 'Akilisi Pohiva, formed the Democracy Party in 1994. On 19 September 1996 Pohiva, regarded as one of the leading whistleblowers of the South Pacific, and two editors of the *Taimi 'o* Tongan newspaper were jailed for 30 days for alleged contempt of parliament. (See GOVERNMENT–MEDIA RELATIONS.)

Local government is relatively poorly developed. District and town officers elected by their constituencies every three years have limited powers devolved by central government.

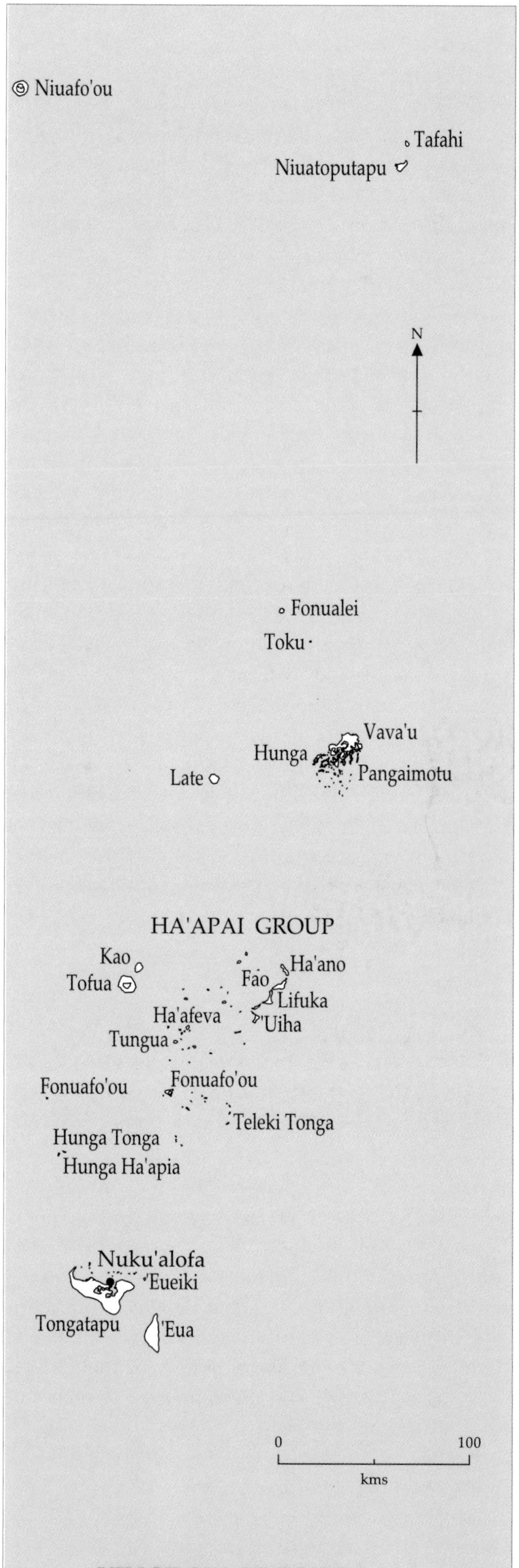

KINGDOM OF TONGA

Physical environment: The Kingdom of Tonga (stretching between latitude 15–23° south and longitude 173–177° west) comprises 169 islands in an archipelago that lies on a northeast–southwest axis 3 degrees east of the international dateline. The islands lie in two almost parallel chains. The eastern chain consists of low coral islands with a covering of volcanic ash, mostly in the Ha'apai Group, and raised coral islands such as Tongatapu and Vava'u. 'Eua has a steeper eastern coast, 300 m high, of older limestone. The western chain consists of high, recently formed volcanic islands such as Tofua (3380 m) and Kao in Ha'apai, and to the far north Niuatoputapu and Niuafo'ou, which has erupted nine times in the last century. The volcanic islands and the steep slopes of Vava'u and 'Eua are forested, while the predominant vegetation elsewhere is grassland, scrub and scattered trees. The land, only 71 per cent of which is arable, supports subsistence agriculture and cash-cropping of coconuts, bananas, root crops, and other fruit and vegetables. Vanilla and KAVA, valuable cash crops, grow well, especially in the western districts. Livestock are grazed and there is FORESTRY and SUBSISTENCE AND DOMESTIC FISHING. There are no streams or fresh water except that gathered from rain or in ground water tapped by wells. The climate has distinct seasonal variations; relatively cool and dry with southeast trade winds from May to November, but hot and humid from December to April, with sultry northerlies in February and March and occasional violent squalls from the west or northwest. Annual rainfall: usually occurring between January and April, it varies from 1700 mm in the south to 2200 mm in the north.

History: Tonga is the last remaining Polynesian kingdom, having proclaimed itself an independent constitutional monarchy in 1875. Even before it achieved that status through the legal reforms of last century, it appears to have been one of the most centralized and highly stratified societies in the Pacific. (See TONGAN CHIEFLY STATUS AND THE TU'I TONGA.) Its former chiefly system was supremely aristocratic. Religious significance was attributed to high birth rank as signifying proximity to the gods. High-ranking women were valued for the god-like qualities it was believed they imparted to their children. A graduated status system separated the high-born aristocrats and titled chiefs from their speaking chiefs (*matāpule*), skilled artisans (*mua*) and common labourers (*tu'a*). Before the 1875 Constitution dismantled the system, chiefs commanded both territories and the people on them. They provided protection and leadership in return for labour service, supplies of food, traditional wealth—the MATS and TAPA cloth made by women—and, importantly, men to help fight their wars with rival chiefs.

Internal strife had weakened the system, however, and the establishment of a Wesleyan mission in the 1820s together with the setting up of commercial trading enterprises were to weaken it further still. In addition, there was the threat of annexation by metropolitan powers as occurred in the neighbouring polities of Fiji to the northwest and Samoa to the northeast. In Tonga, a newly converted Protestant leader emerged to meet the challenges of the time and become the first modern monarch. In 1845 he was proclaimed King George TUPOU I. He defeated his rival, the semi-sacred Tu'i Tonga who was supported by the Roman Catholic missionary priests, and set about implementing a series of far-reaching changes to the institutions of his new kingdom, setting Tonga on a course quite different from that of its island neighbours. (See CONSTITUTIONAL DEVELOPMENT IN TONGA, and LAND TENURE IN TONGA.)

The boundaries of the kingdom were defined by Tupou I in the Royal Proclamation of 24 August 1887. The distances between the island groups are considerable. Niuafo'ou, known for many years as Tin Can Island because of a novel method of delivering the mail in rough seas (see PHILATELIC BUREAUX), lies 550 km directly north of Tongatapu. Air and sea transport and radio contact connect the island groups with one another and the wider world, although the outer islands still suffer many of the penalties of distance from the centre. Tonga's closest metropolitan neighbour, New Zealand, is 1720 km to the south.

Internal migration southward has brought about an increasing divergence between the distribution of population and the distribution of land, with density increasing particularly around the capital Nuku'alofa. Here, increasing URBANIZATION has resulted in extreme pressure on amenities and facilities. The 1996 census showed that the Tongatapu group which has 52 per cent of Tonga's land now has over 73 per cent of its population. Only 36 islands have settlements, although uninhabited islands are exploited for their fisheries, coconuts, and fruit trees, or used to graze livestock or to establish gardens away from the depredation of pigs that roam freely.

The church is important in Tongan life. Almost all Tongans claim at least nominal adherence to a church. The various forms of the Wesleyan church (the Free Wesleyan Church, the Church of Tonga, the Free Church of Tonga) account for well over 40 per cent of the population. While the Free Wesleyan Church is the 'state' church, the Roman Catholics claim to have 15 per cent of the population in their congregations, and others, such as the MORMONS and the SEVENTH-DAY ADVENTISTS, are growing.

Buttressed by foreign aid, mostly from Australia, New Zealand and the European Union, and remittances to the annual value of around T$40 million from migrants overseas, the government feels under no immediate pressure to alter the heavily paternalistic government-dominated political and economic systems. Tonga relies heavily on agricultural exports for revenue, having few other natural resources and largely undeveloped fishing, tourism and manufacturing industries. It is seeking entry to the World Trade Organization but may not be able to hold its own in free trade. Despite its excellent record in the provision of social services, it is not education alone but, rather, private sector policy reforms that are most likely to create new loci of power, and promote alterations in the existing entrenched hierarchies of church and state. (See also QUEEN SĀLOTE TUPOU III.)—KJ

Further reading

Ferdon, E N, 1987. *Early Tonga: as the explorers saw it 1616–1810*, University of Arizona Press.

Rutherford, N, 1977. *Friendly Islands: a history of Tonga*, Oxford University Press.

TORRES STRAIT ISLANDS

Constitutional status: Part of Australia.

Population: 5000 (1996 estimate).

Physical environment: Torres Strait was formed between 6000 and 8500 years ago when the Sahul shelf connecting the landmasses of Australia and New Guinea was flooded by post-glacial rising sea levels. At its narrowest it is about 150 km wide, bordered in the east by the northern terminus of the Great Barrier Reef and shelving off in the west to the deep waters of the Arafura Sea. Approximately 150 islands, islets, coral cays and reefs are scattered across some 30 000 sq km of shallow water, although only 16 islands are currently inhabited. Those in the southwest—Muralag, Narupay, Keriri, Moa, Badu and Mabuiag—are old volcanoes, mainly eroded carboniferous acid igneous tuffs and granites rising to nearly 400 m. The sea in this region is less than 9 m deep, broken by a profusion of reefs and sandbanks. In the west shoal water extends to the coast of Papua New Guinea, but there is less reef growth in the north because of the muddy run-off from the river sytems of the adjacent mainland. The islands close to Papua New Guinea—Boigu, Duaun and Saibai—are mainly composed of terrigenous mud, and behind their littoral belts of mangrove the soil is quite fertile. Mer, Erub and Ugar, small fertile volcanic islands, lie in deeper water in the northeast. A long broken line of platform reefs stretches from the north east to within 40 km of Cape York Peninsula, and this is dotted with islands—Massig, Sasi, Warraber, Puruma—to name a few. There are some mud and volcanic islands along this line, but most are coral cays.

History: For many centuries the vigorous Torres Strait trading network ensured constant interaction between the 4000 or so islanders and their neighbours on the adjacent mainlands of Australia and New Guinea. However, it is difficult to know when the first outsiders visited the region. Long before 1500 the people of southwest New Guinea were trading to the Indonesian archipelago, and Sulawesi fleets were collecting trepang (BÊCHE-DE-MER) on Australia's north coast by the late 1600s. Perhaps under pressure of tribute, exploratory *praus* from the peripheries of the Indonesian archipelago reached Torres Strait before European explorers, but if such was the case no memory or convincing evidence of it remains.

In contrast, the early history of contact between Torres Strait Islanders and Europeans is fairly well documented, and can conveniently be divided into four distinct yet overlapping phases. The first was that of early exploration, the second the opening of the sealane, the third scientific exploration, and the last and most significant, the colonial occupation. The earliest surviving account comes from the Spaniard de Prado who was aboard Torres's *San Pedrico* when it passed through Torres Strait in 1606. Earlier the same year Janz probed the strait from the west for the Netherlands East India Company before sailing into the Gulf of Carpentaria. Although the company continued to send vessels along the southwest coast of New Guinea until the mid 18th century, and they were expected to take prisoners for the purpose of intelligence gathering, Dutch contact with Torres Strait Islanders was minimal. Apart from de Prado, only Gonzal, who ventured into the Prince of Wales channel in 1756, reported sighting islanders.

The charting of Torres Strait by COOK in August 1770 marked the beginning of the second phase. After 1788 the strait became the shortest sailing track between Port Jackson and the ports of the Indonesian archipelago. In 1813 the British East India Company's monopoly on trade to India and the East Indies was lifted, and the incentive of commercial advantage encouraged the use of Torres Strait in preference to the long, doldrum-plagued route round the north of New Guinea. By the mid 1830s ships were passing through Torres Strait each week of the sailing season, from April to September, and however they made their way at least one night's anchorage in the lee of a Torres Strait island was normally required. Proximity lead to the development of a mutually understandable protocol of gestures and key-words which enabled barter to proceed. As shipping increased, the volume of traditional trade expanded to supply the growing market. Occasionally there were violent clashes, but Torres Strait Islanders were not subject to the reprisals inflicted by the Royal Navy on other Pacific peoples for less sanguinary offences. The attitude seems to have been that Torres Strait would always be a hazardous crossing, and it was best to try to cultivate the islanders' goodwill.

In an effort to make the strait safe for shipping a series of hydrographic surveys were commissioned. HMS *Beagle* was sent in 1837, HMS *Fly* in 1842, and HMS *Rattlesnake* in 1848. The *Fly* and the *Rattlesnake* expeditions were flotillas each manned by about 200 men. Although convoys had passed through the strait, none had experienced the continued friendly contact with Torres Strait Islanders that these Europeans enjoyed. The *Rattlesnake* sheltered for more than three months at the tip of Cape York Peninsula, which was an important meeting place for southwestern Torres Strait Islander groups, and the expedition's scientists collected fairly accurate vocabularies and ethnographic information. The goings-on at Cape York were communicated to villages throughout the strait by returning canoes, and this knowledge helped islanders cope with what was to come, the colonial occupation.

In 1864 a joint colonial-imperial 'harbour of refuge' was established at the tip of Cape York, and Charles Edwards, in association with the merchant-shipowner Robert Towns, set up the first bêche-de-mer station at Erub at the northeastern extremity of the strait. By 1868 there were about six bêche-de-mer stations in Torres Strait, most of them established by Sydney-based traders who had abandoned the declining western Pacific SANDALWOOD TRADE. In 1869 Torres Strait Islanders at William Banner's Tutu station showed the overseer the rich pearl-shell beds of Warrior Reef, and by the end of the year 50 tons had been collected. By 1872 there were 20 large pearl-shelling vessels in the strait employing some 500 Pacific islander divers, most of them Melanesian. These 'old hands' soon introduced young Torres Strait Islanders into the industry, and by the following year 200 or 300 of them were at work. Some were taken from their islands by force, though this was not usual. Others may have been intimidated into joining the boats. But the majority were lured into the fishery by what they perceived as benefits to themselves. However, despite the fact that they adapted quickly to the new way of life, the initial years of the pearl-shelling industry were violent and disruptive of village life.

In July 1871 the LONDON MISSIONARY SOCIETY (LMS), following in the wake of the trading masters, placed Loyalty Islander evangelists and their families on the islands. These Pacific islander evangelists, or teachers as they were known, were remarkably successful and by the mid 1880s most Torres Strait Islanders were at least nominally Christian. The teachers were adamant that their congregations should cast aside old customs, and on many islands new ones, brought from the Pacific and taught by Pacific islanders, were introduced. Missionaries and teachers exerted considerable control over the island communities, in effect establishing 'stern theocracies' which did not ease until the ANGLICANS took over from the LMS in 1915. Indeed, by the 1880s Torres Strait was beginning to resemble other places which had come under the sway of the Pacific maritime trades and the Christian mission.

The Torres Strait Islands were annexed to Queensland in two stages; the first in 1872 and the second in 1879. The initial extension of Queensland's maritime boundary by 95 km was more concerned with gaining control of the east coast and Gulf of Carpentaria islands. The second extension, to within sight of New Guinea, was taken for strategic reasons under imperial pressure and Queensland had little choice but to comply. It therefore attempted to govern with the least possible expense, establishing in the 1880s a system of quasi-local government on the islands, with minimal interference in the islanders' day-to-day lives. For some decades Torres Strait Islanders enjoyed a fair degree of freedom, until change was signalled by Queensland's first protection Act, *The Aboriginals Protection and Prevention of the Sale of Opium Act, 1897*. The Act was central to Queensland government control of Aborigines and Torres Strait Islanders and set them in a legislative nexus which was not broken until the late 1930s. By the mid 1920s Torres Strait Islanders were under almost complete government control and for administrative purposes were regarded as Aborigines.

The protectionist yoke did not rest easily on Torres Strait Islander shoulders, and in 1936 they staged a large-scale maritime strike, which lasted four months and involved about 70 per cent of the islander workforce. By this time a government-controlled pearl-shelling industry had been established, and only those employed on company boats, as they were called, took part: the strike was directed specifically at the government. There were a number of grievances, all of them related to the increasingly intrusive and restrictive administration of their affairs. As a result of the strike the islanders won considerable concessions. Unpopular local officials were removed, the operation of the company boats was reorganized, a system was introduced which allowed for regular consultations between administrators and Torres Strait Islander leaders, and the island councils, many of them established before the turn of the century, were given greater autonomy. The structural changes that came about as a result of the strike were enshrined in the *Torres Strait Islanders Act* of 1939, the first legislation framed to deal specifically with Torres Strait Islander issues. From that point progress was slow. Almost the entire adult male population of the strait volunteered and served 'King and country' in the Second World War, which many islanders believed entitled them to a share in the promised 'better deal' after the war. But in the 1950s and 1960s things remained much as they had been. Real change came in the early 1970s, with the establishment by Gough Whitlam of a Commonwealth Department of Aboriginal Affairs, and the commencement of negotiations between Australia, Queensland and Papua New Guinea over the new Torres Strait border. These developments provided islanders with opportunities to apply the skills honed in local island politics, and in dealing with the Queensland government. Their leaders demonstrated considerable political skill in playing off Queensland and the Commonwealth against each other, thus increasing the allocation of funds and improving services and living conditions in the strait.

However, many islanders would not wait for improved living standards. To escape poor employment opportunities and low wages brought about by the decline of the shelling industry, many left to find work on the mainland. In the late 1950s and 1960s a steadily increasing number of men found work in kin-based gangs cutting sugarcane, and later on the railways, and brought their families to settle, mainly in the coastal urban areas of Queensland. Although this pattern of migration slowed in the 1990s, it is estimated that now about 80 per cent of islanders, some 20 000, live on mainland Australia.

By the end of the 1980s Torres Strait Islanders had achieved a considerable degree of political self-management, and representatives of the peak political institution, the Islands Coordinating Council established by the Queensland government in 1984, were used to negotiating directly with Brisbane and Canberra. When the 1988 proposal for the Aboriginal and Torres Strait Islander Commission (ATSIC), which would replace the department, failed to make adequate provision for separate Torres Strait Islander representation, islander leaders refused their support until in 1989 an Office of Torres Strait Islander Affairs, and a Torres Strait Islander Advisory Board, as well as a Torres Strait Regional Council were included within ATSIC. The advisory board represents those islanders who do not reside in the strait. In 1994 a new body was established to replace the regional council, the Torres Strait Regional Authority, which provides even greater autonomy for Torres Strait within the ATSIC structure. Nevertheless, both ATSIC and the moderate Torres Strait Islander leadership regard the regional authority as transitional to a more clearly defined political autonomy, perhaps some form of free association with Australia.

There are Torres Strait Islander independence activists who are more ambitious. Dissatisfied with lagging economic development, the slow pace of indigenisation of Torres Strait service industries, the 1985 Torres Strait Border Treaty with Papua New Guinea, and inspired by the High Court of Australia's recognition of Native Title on Mer in 1992 (see MABO), they called for secession on no less than four occasions in the 1980s and 1990s. While it is unlikely the Australian government would ever allow a completely independent Torres Strait, the TORRES STRAIT INDEPENDENCE MOVEMENT has made both the Queensland and Commonwealth governments more receptive to the idea of some form of self-government.—SM

Further reading

Beckett, J, 1987. *Torres Strait Islanders: custom and colonialism*, Cambridge University Press.

Mullins, S, 1995. *Torres Strait: a history of colonial occupation and culture contact*, Central Queensland University Press.

Sharp, N, 1993. *Stars of Tagai*, Aboriginal Studies Press.

Walker, D, (ed.), 1972. *Bridge and Barrier: the natural and cultural history of Torres Strait*, The Australian National University.

TUVALU

Constitutional status: Independent constitutional monarchy.

Head of State: Queen Elizabeth II, represented by Governor General Sir Tulaga Manuella MBE.

Head of Government: Prime Minister, Ionatana Ionatana (1999).
Capital: Funafuti (government centre at Fongafale on Funafuti Atoll).
Land area: 25.9 sq km (four islands and five atolls): Vaitupu (5.6 sq km), Funafuti (2.8 sq km), Nukufetau, Nukulaelae, Nui, Nanumea, Nanumaga, Niutao, Niulakita.
Sea area (EEZ): 900 000 sq km.
Population: 9600 (1996 SPC estimate); Polynesian 96 per cent; Melanesian 2 per cent.
Official languages: Tuvaluan (Polynesian language related to Samoan), and English.
Currency: Australian dollar; also local currency.
Time: +1200 hours UTC.
National day: First Monday in October.
GDP per capita: A$1256 (1990).
Principal export earnings: Stamps; copra; handicrafts; garments.
Political system: Tuvalu has a parliament of 12 members, elected for a three-year term. The prime minister is chosen from among them, and he has a cabinet of four ministers. There are no political parties. Elected island councils provide local government on the outer islands, and Funafuti has an elected town council.
Physical environment: Tuvalu, located between latitude 5–10° south and longitude 176–179° east, is about 1100 km north of Fiji. Its islands and atolls are of coral formation, seldom rising more than 4 m above sea level. Coconut palms, pandanus, breadfruit and taro are grown. There is some mangrove swamp, and hardwood fetau trees. The climate is tropical with light (usually easterly) trade winds. Annual rainfall: 2500–3500 mm.
History: Formerly known as the Ellice Islands, and part of the Gilbert and Ellice Islands Colony until 1975 (see KIRIBATI), the name Tuvalu—adopted at independence on 1 October 1978—means 'cluster of eight', although the group comprises nine islands. The original inhabitants were Polynesian settlers, indicated by oral traditions as having come from Samoa (see also FOOTSTEPS FROM ASIA).

The first Europeans to reach Tuvalu were Spanish explorers: Alvaro Mendaña, who sighted Nui in 1568 and Niulakita on his second voyage in 1595, and Francisco Mourelle, who reached the northern atolls of Nanumaga and Nanumea in 1781. The English ship *Rebecca* visited Nukufetau and Funafuti in 1819, and its captain named Funafuti after the ship's owner, Edward Ellice. The island group then became known by English surveyors as Ellice Islands, and was charted accordingly by the UNITED STATES EXPLORING EXPEDITION which visited in 1841.

From the 1820s the islands were visited by WHALING ships and traders, and BEACHCOMBERS began to settle there. The first unofficial representatives of the LONDON MISSIONARY SOCIETY (LMS) arrived in 1861, by canoe from Manihiki (Cook Islands). From 1865 LMS PASTORS from Samoa were established throughout the islands, leading to widespread acceptance of Christianity. In the early 1860s about 450 islanders from Funafuti and Nukulaelae were rounded up by BLACKBIRDERS operating in the PERUVIAN SLAVE TRADE, and later ships came recruiting for PLANTATIONS in Fiji, Samoa and Hawai'i.

From 1877 Tuvalu's British residents were brought under the protection of the WESTERN PACIFIC HIGH COMMISSION, and in 1892 the formal status of a British protectorate (already accepted by the Gilbert Islands) was offered. The islands then became part of the Gilbert and Ellice Islands Protectorate, which became the Gilbert and Ellice Islands Colony in 1916. Tuvalu was administered as a single administrative unit from the district headquarters established at the port of Funafuti. Although the islands' direct exposure to the Pacific War was limited to isolated Japanese bombing raids in April 1943, American military bases were set up at Funafuti, Nukufetau and Nanumea in 1942. The American airstrip was used to launch raids against the Japanese in both the Gilbert and Marshall Islands, and Funafuti became the administrative centre for the colony for the period of Japanese occupation of the Gilbert Islands.

Main government building, Funafuti, Tuvalu in 1989

In the post-war years, when TARAWA resumed its role as capital of the colony, there was considerable Tuvaluan migration to Kiribati in search of better education and employment opportunities. Their growing numbers in the public service began to create tensions, and rivalries between Gilbertese and Ellice Islanders grew intense. By the 1970s, when the British were taking the first steps towards self-government for the colony, a movement towards separatism had begun to emerge. A British inquiry into Ellice Islanders' secessionist aspirations in 1973 was followed by a referendum on the issue in 1974. The vote in favour of separation was overwhelming, and Tuvalu accordingly was granted self-government on 1 October 1975, with its own constitution. Toalipi LAUTI became the first chief minister. Funafuti became the official administrative centre from 1 January 1976, and formal independence followed on 1 October 1978.

Tuvalu concluded a treaty of friendship with the United States in 1979, which formally ended the American claims (under the GUANO ACT of 1856) to Funafuti, Nukufetau, Nukulaelae and Niulakita, and provided for future consultations on security matters and marine resources.

The Tuvalu Trust Fund, created in August 1987 with grants of A$27.1 million from the governments of Australia, New Zealand and the United Kingdom, provides Tuvalu with a regular income. Overseas development assistance has been used to develop Funafuti's urban facilities: New Zealand installed street lighting in 1990, the United States provided sealed roads in 1991, the European Union sealed the airstrip in 1992, and a new airport terminal was built by Australia in 1993. The Tuvaluan government rebuilt the main hotel, the two-storeyed Vaiaku Lagi Hotel, at Funafuti in 1992.

Ionatana Ionatana was elected prime minister in April 1999, following a vote of no-confidence by the Tuvaluan parliament in his predecessor, Bikenibeu Paeniu.—KRF

VANUATU

Constitutional status: Independent republic.

Head of State: President John Bani (1999).

Head of Government: Prime Minister Donald Kalpokas (1998).

Main towns: PORT VILA (capital, on Efate; population 32 000); Luganville (on Santo; 10 000).

Land area: 12 195 sq km (12 main islands and 58 inhabited islets): Espiritu Santo, Malekula, Erromango and Efate—making up about half the total land area. Next in size are Ambrym, Tanna, Epi, Vanua Lava, Gaua (Santa Maria), Ambae, Maewo and Pentecost.

Sea area (EEZ): 680 000 sq km.

Population: 189 300 (1999 SPC estimate).

Languages: BISLAMA (Pidgin), English and French; and c100 indigenous (Austronesian) languages.

Adult literacy: 64 per cent (1994).

Currency: Vatu.

Time: +1100 hours UTC.

National day: 30 July (Independence Day).

GDP per capita: A$1678 (1993).

Principal export earnings: Copra; beef; coffee and cocoa; tourism; timber; shells.

Political system: Elections are held every four years by universal suffrage for the 52-seat unicameral assembly. The president (who is head of state) is elected by secret ballot by an electoral college of parliament and the presidents of the provincial councils, to serve a five-year term. Executive power is vested in the prime minister, elected by secret ballot by members of parliament, and the council of ministers who are selected by the prime minister.

A national council of chiefs (*malvatumauri*) is elected by district councils. The *malvatumauri* meets at least once a year, with power to discuss all matters relating to custom and tradition and to make recommendations for the preservation and promotion of ni-Vanuatu culture and languages. The *malvatumauri* elects its own president.

Local government is managed by six provincial councils, and there are municipal councils, headed by a mayor, in Port Vila and Luganville.

Physical environment: The young volcanic islands of Vanuatu—some of which are still active—form a central chain extending south from the Banks Islands, broadly located to the west of Fiji and north of New Caledonia, between latitude 12–21° south and longitude 166–171° east. While several islands (the Torres Islands, Espiritu Santo, Malekula, Maewo and Pentecost) are formed from belts of older sedimentary rock, repeatedly uplifted and tilted, the eruptions which split a large island into the present Shepherd group in the east occurred only about 600 years ago. Santo has several high peaks, rising to a height of 1875 m above sea level (Mt Tabwemasana), with Mt Lairiri at 1650 m. Yasur on Tanna is an active volcano, as are Lopevi (Ulveah) and Mt Garet, on Santa Maria and Suretimeat on Vanua Lava. The predominant vegetation is dense rainforest, broken on some of the southern islands by patches of grassland, and there is some mangrove swamp. Coconuts grow widely as do introduced flora such as flamboyants, hibiscus and frangipani. Subsistence crops include yams, taro, manioc and bananas; subsistence fishing is significant, and cattle provide local and export meat. Timber is milled on Santo, Malekula, Erromango, Efate and Aneityum. The climate is hot and wet, with southeast trade winds most of the year and occasional hurricanes from January to April. Average humidity at Vila is 83 per cent. Annual rainfall: 2330 mm (Port Vila) and 3100 mm (Luganville).

Temperatures and rainfall are lower in the southern islands.

History: The complex prehistory of Vanuatu suggests that the first Melanesian inhabitants may have settled about 4000 years ago (SETTLEMENT OF THE NORTHERN PACIFIC). Archaeological evidence indicates that LAPITA CULTURE existed on some islands between 1200 BC and the beginning of the Christian era, although there is also more pottery of a later tradition found in the central islands of the group.

First European contact came with the arrival of the Portuguese explorer, Pedro Fernández de Quirós, in 1606. He visited the largest island in the archipelago and named it Austrialia del Espiritu Santo. More than 150 years later, in 1768, Louis Antoine de BOUGAINVILLE sailed into the area and named the archipelago the Great Cyclades (*Les Grandes Cyclades*). Then Captain James COOK arrived in 1774, charted the islands and renamed them the New Hebrides, apparently because the mountains recalled to him the islands off the Scottish coast. In 1789 William BLIGH noted several islands in what he named the Banks group, during his voyage by open boat following the MUTINY ON THE BOUNTY.

In the early years of the 19th century, the New Hebrides attracted both the SANDALWOOD TRADE (with the arrival of Captain Peter Dillon in 1825) and missionary interest. The death of the Reverend John WILLIAMS of the LONDON MISSIONARY SOCIETY (LMS), who landed and was murdered on Erromango in 1839, failed to deter later proselytizing attempts. The Rev T Heath of the LMS arrived with several Samoan PASTORS in 1840, followed by two more LMS missionaries in 1841, and then two Presbyterian missionaries—John Geddie in 1848 and John Inglis in 1852. Their efforts were more successful and by 1856, the islands were well on the way towards adopting Christianity. Bishop SELWYN brought missionaries from New Zealand to the northern islands of the group in 1859, establishing a station of the Melanesian Mission at Mota. His friend John Coleridge PATTESON settled there, successfully transcribing the Mota language and using it to train native teachers.

In 1847 the islanders were raided by labour recruiters in the COLONIAL LABOUR TRADE. The first shipment—65 men from Tanna and Erromango—were taken to New South Wales to work on Ben BOYD's sheep property, although the experiment was not considered a success. From 1863 Vanuatu labour was recruited for the cotton and sugar plantations in Fiji and Queensland. The sandalwood trade ended in the mid 1860s, but BLACKBIRDING continued in Vanuatu until 1906.

European settlers began to arrive from 1865, establishing plantations on Efate in particular. The European powers negotiated an agreement in 1887 to establish a Joint Naval Commission. The Anglo–French CONDOMINIUM in 1906 gave the two countries joint administrative power, which meant the official introduction of two languages, two education systems, and two police forces. The majority of islanders who had been brought to Queensland as sugar workers were repatriated by 1906 (KANAKAS IN AUSTRALIA), but labour continued to be recruited for New Caledonia for several years. Not all migrants returned and, even among those who did, the death toll from disease was high. French settlers facing a shortage of island labour began to bring in Vietnamese workers on five-year terms of indenture from the early 1920s, although British planters were not permitted to employ Asian labour.

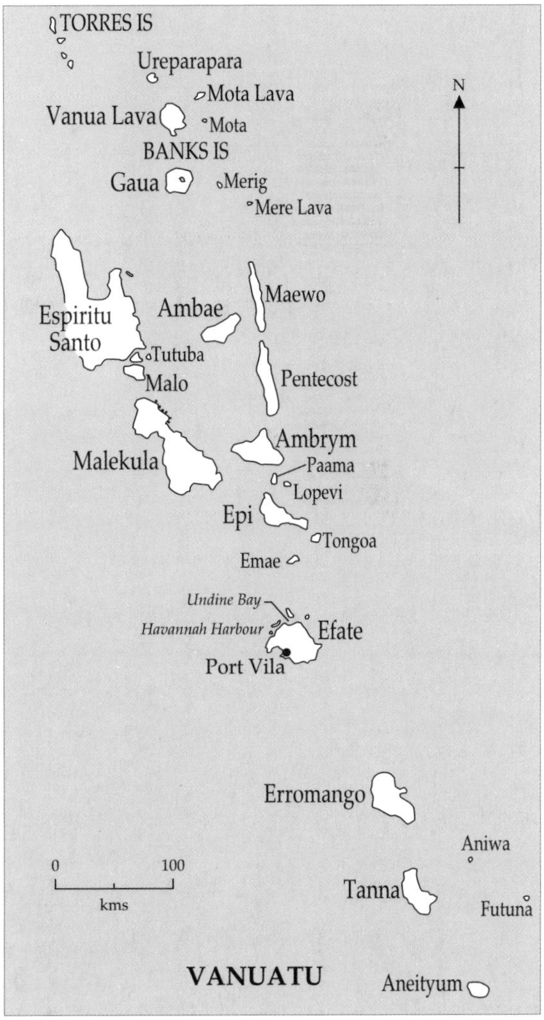

In the Second World War, the French settlers declared their support for the Free French forces of General de Gaulle, and then at the end of 1941, American troops occupied Vila and Santo, providing considerable infrastructural investment as the islands became a major base for the Pacific War. The Americans and their visible prosperity became the catalyst for the rapid blossoming of the JOHN FRUM MOVEMENT on Tanna, a semi-political kind of cargo cult that has persevered into the 1990s.

In the late 1960s, a *kastom* movement emerged near Luganville under the leadership of Jimmy Moli Stephens. Calling himself Chief President Moses, he established a movement known as NAGRIAMEL (claiming a membership of 10 000 in 1969), which called for the return of alienated land. By 1971 Nagriamel had developed political aims and petitioned the United Nations for independence for Vanuatu. In June 1971 the New Hebrides National Party (later the Vanua'aku Pati) was formed, as was a new largely francophone party, the UPNH (Union de la Population des Nouvelles Hébrides), which later became the UCNH (Union des Communautés des Nouvelles Hebrides, today the Union of Moderate Parties). As more small political parties began to be established because of increasing agitation for change, the British and French governments were persuaded to initiate some constitutional reforms. Municipal councils for Vila and Santo (initially francophone-dominated) were established, and also in 1975, elections for the first Representative Assembly were held, in which the anglophone National Party/Vanua'aku Pati (VP) performed well. In 1977 a VP boycott of the elections left the francophone-dominated assembly in an untenable position of power, and a compromise was negotiated between all parties in 1978, to arrive at a 'government of national unity', with Father Gerard Leymang as chief minister, and the VP leader, Father Walter LINI, as deputy.

The 1979 general election produced a clear majority for the VP. Lini was elected chief minister, and the country became independent as the Republic of Vanuatu on 30 July 1980. Vanuatu, meaning the 'country that stands up', was the name chosen by the indigenous population. Meanwhile, rebels on Santo and Tanna (who had opposed the 1979 result, declaring their own independence separately in February 1980) continued an escalating series of disruptive tactics. In the absence of any British or French military response to the outbreak of violence, the new government asked for assistance from Papua New Guinea, which sent troops to Santo. Jimmy Stephens, whose son was killed in the process of capturing the rebels' headquarters at Vanafo, was taken prisoner along with about 200 secessionists, and other rebels fled.

Traditional art, Vanuatu

In 1983 Vanuatu became the first island nation to declare itself nuclear free, refusing landing rights to American naval vessels and banning the dumping of nuclear waste. The 1983 and 1987 elections were again won by the VP, and Walter Lini remained in power until 1991, when he lost a no-confidence vote in parliament. In the subsequent elections, Maxime Carlot-Korman led a successful coalition group, the Union of Moderate Parties (UMP), into government and four years of unstable francophone-dominated alliances followed. The 1995 elections produced a record number of 170 candidates, with 12 political parties and 19 independents joining the contest. The internal disunity which beset the UMP centred on personal rivalry between Carlot-Korman and party president Serge Vohor Rialuth. The new assembly on 21 December elected Vohor—leader of a coalition of UMP and the National United Pati (NUP)—as prime minister. Walter Lini, now leading the NUP, agreed to become his deputy.

Their fragile partnership survived an ongoing series of crises over the next two years, with increasingly strident allegations of corruption, illegal acts and dubious investment decisions, and ending with an attempt to impeach the president, Jean-Marie Léyé. At the start of 1998 Vanuatu's court of appeal ruled that the president's decision to dissolve parliament (announced on 27 November) was 'lawful and constitutional', and new elections should be held. Public concern about political corruption erupted into a riot in Port Vila on 12 January, when members of the national superannuation scheme demanded the return of their contributions from the National Provident Fund (NPF), in the wake of a report by the OMBUDSMAN, Marie-Noëlle Ferrieux-Patterson, that NPF's coffers had been opened to provide discount loans to politicians.

Following the 1998 election, a new anti-corruption government was formed, with Donald Kalpokas (VP) elected as prime minister, supported by Walter Lini (NUP) as his deputy. After 7 months, this coalition was broken, and the government continued with the support of the UMP, with Willie Jimmy as deputy prime minister. Kalpokas, in his mid 50s, was prime minister briefly in the mid 1990s, and still retains his former portfolio of Foreign Affairs.

John Bani, elected president in May 1999, is a church minister, as was his predecessor Jean-Marie Léyé. Bani was an advocate of independence during the 1970s and he has not been involved in the political arena since 1980.—KRF

Further reading

Shineberg, D, 1967. *They Came for Sandalwood: a study of the sandalwood trade in the southwest Pacific, 1830–1865*, Melbourne University Press.

Van Trease, H N, 1987. *The Politics of Land in Vanuatu*, University of the South Pacific.

WALLIS AND FUTUNA

Constitutional status: Overseas territory of France.
Head of State: President of France represented by High Commissioner, Dominique Bur.
Head of Government: Prefect—Senior Administrator Claude Pierret (1998).
Main towns: Mata Utu (on Uvea); Sigave (on Futuna).
Land area: 145 sq km: Uvea, main island in the Wallis group, (79.5 sq km); Futuna (44 sq km); Alofi (18.5 sq km).
Sea area (EEZ): 300 000 sq km.
Population: 14 375 (1999 SPC estimate); Polynesian; Wallisians related to Tonga; Futuna islanders to Samoa.
Languages: Wallisian, Futunian (both Polynesian languages), and French.
Currency: CFP (French Pacific franc).
Time: +1200 hours UTC.
National day: 14 July.
Political system: An elected representative of Wallis and Futuna sits in France's national assembly; in 1998 this deputy (*député*) was Victor Brial, who was also president of the territorial assembly. There is a senator in the French Parliament (currently Robert Laufoaulu). Since December 1987, the former position of chief administrator, representing the French High Commissioner in New Caledonia, has been filled by a prefect. The governing council of advisers to the prefect consists of the paramount chief (*Lavelua* or king) of Wallis Island, currently Tomasi Kulimoetoke; and the two paramount chiefs of Futuna, *Tuiagaifo* or king of Alo, who is currently Tone Sagato; and *Le Kele Taona* or king of Sigave, who is M Le Keletaona. The three traditional chiefdoms became administrative districts in 1961, and the territorial assembly is elected by universal suffrage.
Physical environment: The archipelagos of Wallis and Futuna are located in central Oceania. Wallis Island (latitude 13° south and longitude 171° west) is 14 km long and 8 km wide. Its main island, called Uvea, together with the 19 islets or *motu*, was formed by two periods of volcanic activity at the end of the Tertiary and in the Pleistocene, resulting today in an underwater volcano surrounded by a ring of coral. The island is reasonably flat, with its high point (151 m) at Mt Lulufakaega. Although there are no rivers or streams, run-off has carried finer particles down on to the coastal plain, which has thus become more fertile. Uvea is surrounded by a reef and a shallow lagoon (25 m), cut off from the ocean by a barrier reef. Five passages allow entry to the lagoon.

The archipelago of Futuna is located 250 km further to the southwest. Futuna Island is no more than 15 km long and 5 km wide, and covers a surface area of 45 sq km. Without a surrounding reef, this island appears mountainous, reaching 524 m at Mt Puke. The island of Alofi, its twin sister, across a stretch of water (1800 m wide) called the Vasa, is 8 km long,

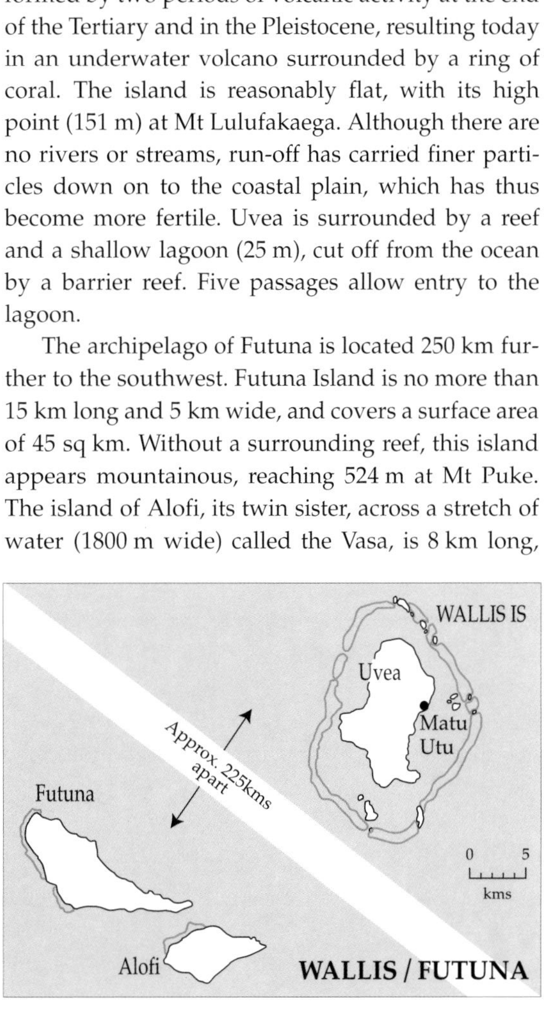

4.5 km wide, and has a surface area of 19.5 square km. Mt Kolofau, at 417 m, is Alofi's high point and its marked tiers correspond to successive phases of volcanic uplift.

Wallis and Futuna share a tropical climate. Considerable decline in the primary forest has given way to heather moorland called *Toafa*. Apart from *peka* (*Pteropus* sp), all other mammals have been introduced by man. Subsistence crops of taro, yams, manioc, kumara and coconuts are grown; there is some copra and timber production.

History: Oral traditions and linguistics link the present population of Wallis Island to Tongan settlement some time between 1450 and 1550. Steady contact was subsequently maintained with Tonga, but the next 350 years of the island's history was punctuated by warfare between rival chiefs. Futuna and Alofi appear to have been settled by Samoans, and oral traditions also refer to the successful resistance of Tongan invaders.

European navigators first arrived in the islands in 1616, when the Dutch expedition of Schouten and Lemaire visited Futuna and Alofi, naming them Hoorn Islands after the port from which they had sailed. Next was the English captain, Samuel WALLIS, who added his name to the map in 1767, and then only occasional passing ships until the arrival of Marist priests in 1837. Bishop POMPALLIER, travelling with missionaries from Tahiti to Sydney, came to Wallis on 1 November, and to Futuna a week later, leaving behind Pierre Bataillon on Wallis and Pierre CHANEL on Futuna. In spite of the efforts of Tongan Protestant missionaries, Father Bataillon succeeded in converting the island population to Catholicism, including the paramount chief, King Lavelua, who then appealed to France for protection. A French captain duly arrived in 1842 and signed an agreement with the king and two other chiefs, although the formal status of a protectorate was not ratified until 1887. Pompallier returned to Futuna in May 1842, after hearing the news that Chanel had been murdered. He brought two more missionary priests, and in November, King Nuiriki of Futuna also agreed to sign the French protectorate treaty. Many of the islanders were converted to Catholicism from this time, and the influence of the church hierarchy, backed by the French navy, helped to give greater authority to the paramount chiefs. As a French protectorate, the formerly separate islands became a group, and old tribal rivalries faded to some extent.

France granted the islands a separate administrative budget in 1909, and renegotiated the terms of the protectorate with Wallis in 1910, giving greater authority to the French Resident. On both islands, the dominance of the church remained strong, and conflict tended to occur between residents and the Catholic Mission over islander labour. Residents succeeded in diverting some of the (unpaid) labour from the church building program to roads and island development during the 1920s and 1930s, but there was little interruption to the islanders' traditional way of life. Most land remained in their possession, the expatriate community was a small minority, and there was little outside contact until the Second World War. Between 1942 and 1945, several hundred American forces came to establish a military base on Wallis, building airfields at Hihifo in the north of Uvea and at Lavegahau in the south.

Protectorate status ended in 1961, following a referendum in 1959 (which received 94 per cent support on Wallis, and 78 per cent on Futuna) for change to an overseas territory of France (see NATIONALISM IN FRENCH TERRITORIES). The 1961 statute retained the privileged position and customary authority of the three paramount chiefs, and provided protection for the role of the Catholic church. Communications improved in the late 1980s, with increased access from Fiji as well as New Caledonia and French Polynesia, but tourism is not yet well developed. Wallis and Futuna remain heavily dependent on French subsidies, although the French government has attempted to increase the islanders' economic self-sufficiency. In the 1990s, timber exports, limited agricultural expansion, and commercial deep-sea fishing have been established on a small scale. The younger generation is better educated and more likely to have contacts with the outside world, but out-migration is a growing trend in light of limited employment opportunities.—KRF & FA

Further reading

Henningham, S, 1992. *France and the South Pacific: a contemporary history*, Allen & Unwin.

SUBJECT INDEX

A

B

D

E

H

K

M

N

O

T

U

V

W

Y

Z

SECTION INDEX

D

E

F

M

N

O

P

Q

R